"In the diverse and complex field of 'bilingualism' this *Handbook* is a welcome new resource. Combining a presentation of fundamental issues with a wide sampling of offerings by major scholars actively pursuing many areas related to bilingualism, it provides the teacher, student, researcher, or lay reader with a valuable foundation in the field. The *Handbook* is especially welcome now, as the issues which underlie the collection are exceptionally current."

Barbara C. Lust, Cornell University

"From case studies of bilingualism in different parts of the globe, to socio-psychological discussions of bilinguals' language repertoires at the societal level, to psycholinguistic and neurocognitive investigations of bilingualism and biliteracy at the level of the individual, this comprehensive, multi-disciplinary compendium of state-of-the-art overviews by prominent scholars in the field, ably edited by Bhatia and Ritchie, will be an invaluable resource for students, educators, and researchers of bi- and multilingualism for years to come."

Jyotsna Vaid, Texas A&M University

Blackwell Handbooks in Linguistics

This outstanding multi-volume series covers all the major subdisciplines within linguistics today and, when complete, will offer a comprehensive survey of linguistics as a whole.

Already published:

The Handbook of Child Language
Edited by Paul Fletcher and Brian MacWhinney

The Handbook of Phonological Theory
Edited by John A. Goldsmith

The Handbook of Contemporary Semantic Theory
Edited by Shalom Lappin

The Handbook of Sociolinguistics
Edited by Florian Coulmas

The Handbook of Phonetic Sciences
Edited by William J. Hardcastle and John Laver

The Handbook of Morphology
Edited by Andrew Spencer and Arnold Zwicky

The Handbook of Japanese Linguistics
Edited by Natsuko Tsujimura

The Handbook of Linguistics
Edited by Mark Aronoff and Janie Rees-Miller

The Handbook of Contemporary Syntactic Theory
Edited by Mark Baltin and Chris Collins

The Handbook of Discourse Analysis
Edited by Deborah Schiffrin, Deborah Tannen, and Heidi E. Hamilton

The Handbook of Language Variation and Change
Edited by J. K. Chambers, Peter Trudgill, and Natalie Schilling-Estes

The Handbook of Historical Linguistics
Edited by Brian D. Joseph and Richard D. Janda

The Handbook of Language and Gender
Edited by Janet Holmes and Miriam Meyerhoff

The Handbook of Second Language Acquisition
Edited by Catherine J. Doughty and Michael H. Long

The Handbook of Bilingualism
Edited by Tej K. Bhatia and William C. Ritchie

The Handbook of Pragmatics
Edited by Laurence R. Horn and Gregory Ward

The Handbook of Applied Linguistics
Edited by Alan Davies and Catherine Elder

The Handbook of Speech Perception
Edited by David B. Pisoni and Robert E. Remez

The Blackwell Companion to Syntax, Volumes I–V
Edited by Martin Everaert and Henk van Riemsdijk

The Handbook of the History of English
Edited by Ans van Kemenade and Bettelou Los

The Handbook of English Linguistics
Edited by Bas Aarts and April McMahon

The Handbook of World Englishes
Edited by Braj B. Kachru; Yamuna Kachru, Cecil L. Nelso

The Handbook of Bilingualism

Edited by

*Tej K. Bhatia and
William C. Ritchie*

Blackwell
Publishing

© 2004, 2006 by Blackwell Publishing Ltd

BLACKWELL PUBLISHING
350 Main Street, Malden, MA 02148-5020, USA
9600 Garsington Road, Oxford OX4 2DQ, UK
550 Swanston Street, Carlton, Victoria 3053, Australia

The right of Tej K. Bhatia and William C. Ritchie to be identified as the Authors of the Editorial Material in this Work has been asserted in accordance with the UK Copyright, Designs, and Patents Act 1988.

First published 2004 by Blackwell Publishing Ltd
First published in paperback 2006 by Blackwell Publishing Ltd

1   2006

Library of Congress Cataloging-in-Publication Data

The handbook of bilingualism / edited by Tej K. Bhatia and William C. Ritchie.
       p. cm. — (Blackwell handbooks in linguistics ; 15)
    Includes bibliographical references and index.
    ISBN 0-631-22734-2 (alk. paper)
    1. Bilingualism.   I. Bhatia, Tej K.   II. Ritchie, William C.   III. Series.

P115.H365 2004
404'.2—dc22

                                                          2003023474

ISBN-13: 978-0-631-22734-2 (alk. paper)
ISBN-13: 978-0-631-22735-9 (paperback)
ISBN-10: 0-631-22735-0 (paperback)

A catalogue record for this title is available from the British Library.

Set in 10/12pt Palatino
by Graphicraft Limited, Hong Kong
Printed and bound in the United Kingdom
by TJ International, Padstow, Cornwall

The publisher's policy is to use permanent paper from mills that operate a sustainable forestry policy, and which has been manufactured from pulp processed using acid-free and elementary chlorine-free practices. Furthermore, the publisher ensures that the text paper and cover board used have met acceptable environmental accreditation standards.

For further information on
Blackwell Publishing, visit our website:
www.blackwellpublishing.com

Contents

Notes on Contributors

Jeanette Altarriba, Ph.D., is Associate Professor of Psychology and Linguistics and Cognitive Science at the University at Albany, State University of New York. She received her degree from Vanderbilt University in 1990 in the area of Cognitive Psychology. Her primary research interests are in bilingualism, second language acquisition, and language representation.

Ad Backus studied Linguistics at Tilburg University in Holland, where he received his Ph.D. in 1996. He has held research fellowships from the Netherlands Science Foundation and the Royal Netherlands Academy of Sciences and is now an Assistant Professor at Tilburg University. His work is mostly on Turkish and language contact. E-mail: A.M.Backus@uvt.nl.

Gerald P. Berent, Ph.D., is a professor in the Department of Research, National Technical Institute for the Deaf, Rochester Institute of Technology. His primary research interests concern the English language characteristics of deaf children and adults and the comparison of deaf learners' acquisition of English with hearing learners' acquisition of English as a second language.

Tej K. Bhatia is Professor of Linguistics and South Asian Languages at Syracuse University. He has published a number of books and articles in the areas of bilingualism and multiculturalism, language and cognition, media (advertising) discourse, sociolinguistics, and the structure and teaching of English and South Asian languages. He has been consultant to many academic, administrative and business organizations, including the US Department of Education. He taught by invitation in the 1999 Linguistic Society of America Summer Institute. He has been Director of the Linguistic Studies Program and Acting Director of the Cognitive Sciences Program at Syracuse University. Currently, he is Fellow at the Center for the Study of Popular Television at the S. I. Newhouse School of Public Communications.

Ellen Bialystok is Professor of Psychology at York University. Her research is in the area of language and cognitive development, literacy, and bilingualism. She has published numerous research articles and book chapters reporting this research. Her most recent book is *Bilingualism in Development: Language, Literacy, and Cognition* (Cambridge University Press).

Jeffrey M. Brown is an Assistant Professor in the Department of Psychology and Sociology, Texas A&M International University, Laredo, TX 78041. E-mail may be sent to jbrown@tamiu.edu. Most of Jeff's research concerns human memory, eyewitness memory, and tip-of-the-tongue phenomena. He has recently become interested in the nexus of mainstream cognition and bilingualism.

Yuko G. Butler is Assistant Professor of Educational Linguistics in the Graduate School of Education at the University of Pennsylvania. Her research interests include the role of metacognition in second and bilingual language learning. She may be reached at ybutler@gse.upenn.edu.

Shyamala K. Chengappa, Ph.D., is a Reader (Associate Professor), presently heading the Department of Speech Pathology at the All-India Institute of Speech and Hearing, Mysore, India. Her research work is mainly related to child and adult language disorders, including those in bi/multilinguals. She has published on these with respect to Indian languages. Her books include *Simultaneous Acquisition of Two Languages: An Overview* (1988) and *Verbal Communication in Children with Cerebral Palsy* (2001).

Albert Costa is currently a research associate at the University of Barcelona. He finished his Ph.D. degree in Psychology at that university in 1997. He has held post-doctoral fellowships at MIT, Harvard and SISSA (Italy). His research has mainly focused on psycholinguistics and especially on several aspects of monolingual and bilingual speech production.

Nancy C. Dorian is Emeritus Professor of Linguistics in German and Anthropology at Bryn Mawr College, Bryn Mawr, Pennsylvania. She has worked with minority-language communities in the Highlands of Scotland (Gaelic-English bilinguals in the former fishing villages of East Sutherland) and in Berks County, Pennsylvania (Pennsylvania German-English bilinguals). The topics of her two best-known books (*Language Death*, 1981, and *Investigating Obsolescence*, as editor, 1989) reflect the fact that East Sutherland Gaelic and Berks County Pennsylvania German are both obsolescent speech forms.

Paola E. Dussias (Ph.D. University of Arizona, 1997) is an Assistant Professor of Spanish and Applied Linguistics at the Pennsylvania State University. Her research area focuses on sentence comprehension processes in bilinguals. Her work on sentence parsing has appeared in a number of volumes and journals, such as *One Mind, Two Languages*, and *Studies in Second Language Acquisition*.

She also conducts research on the use of experimental techniques (e.g. eye-tracking data) to study psycholinguistic processes involving code-switched utterances. Some of this work is published in the *International Journal of Bilingualism*, and *Romance Phonology and Variation*.

John Edwards was born in England, educated there and in Canada, and received a Ph.D. (in Psychology) from McGill University in 1974. He is now Professor of Psychology at St Francis Xavier University. His research interests are in language, identity, and the many ramifications of their relationship. Professor Edwards is on the editorial boards of ten language journals, and is the editor of the *Journal of Multilingual and Multicultural Development*; he also edits a companion series of books. Professor Edwards's own books include *Language in Canada* (Cambridge University Press, 1998), *Multilingualism* (Penguin, 1995), *Language, Society and Identity* (Blackwell, 1985) and *The Irish Language* (Garland, 1983). He is also the author of about two hundred articles, chapters and reviews.

Anna Maria Escobar is an Associate Professor of Spanish Linguistics at the University of Illinois at Urbana-Champaign since 1989. She teaches courses in Spanish Morphology, Spanish Variation, Sociolinguistics, and Bilingualism. She has published two books and several articles on topics related to Spanish in contact with Quechua in Peru.

Joshua A. Fishman is Emeritus University Research Professor, Social Sciences, at Yeshiva University, Ferkauf Graduate School of Psychology, Albert Einstein College of Medicine Campus, Bronx, NY, and is now regularly a Visiting Professor there as well as at Stanford University (Linguistics and Education) and at New York University (Multilingual and Multicultural Education). His most recent book is *Can Threatened Languages be Saved?* (2001) while his current research (with Guadalupe Valdes) deals with Hispanic community and professional educators' views of special "Spanish courses for native speakers" offered in many high schools and colleges in California.

Fred Genesee is Professor in the Psychology Department, McGill University, Montreal. Professor Genesee has carried out extensive research on alternative forms of bilingual education for minority and majority language speakers. He has published numerous articles in scientific journals and has authored a number of professional books for educators, including *Dual Language Instruction: A Handbook for Enriched Education* with N. Cloud and E. Hamayan (Heinle & Heinle), *Beyond Bilingualism: Multilingualism and Multilingual Education* with J. Cenoz (Multilingual Matters), and *Trends in Bilingual Acquisition* with J. Cenoz (John Benjamins).

Howard Giles is a Professor in the Department of Communication at the University of California Santa Barbara, where he also holds affiliate professorial positions in the departments of both Linguistics and Psychology. He was formerly Chair in Social Psychology at the University of Bristol. He is founding editor of the *Journal of Language and Social Psychology* and the *Journal of Asian Pacific Communication*. He is a past president of the International Communication Association and the International Association of Language and Social Psychology. He was awarded the Spearman medal (1978) and the President's Award (1989) for distinguished contributions to the study of language and communication by the British Psychological Society, and elected Fellow of that society in 1982. He has published widely and cross-disciplinarily in many areas of intergroup communication including the interethnic, between-gender, and intergenerational spheres and across different cultures around the world.

Mira Goral, Ph.D., is a Research Assistant Professor of Neurology at the Boston University School of Medicine and the project manager of the Language in the Aging Brain Laboratory at the Harold Goodglass Aphasia Research Center. Her research includes work on multilingualism, aphasia, and aging.

François Grosjean received his degrees up to the Doctorat d'Etat from the University of Paris. Before his appointment at Neuchâtel University, Switzerland, where he heads the Language and Speech Processing Laboratory and is Professor of Psycholinguistics, he taught at the University of Paris VIII and at Northeastern University, Boston. In addition to his teaching and research activities that bear on language processing in monolinguals and bilinguals, he is a founding editor of *Bilingualism: Language and Cognition*.

Kenji Hakuta is Professor of Education at Stanford University, where he teaches courses on language development, bilingual education, and research methods. He may be reached at hakuta@stanford.edu.

Roberto R. Heredia is an Assistant Professor in the Department of Psychology and Sociology, Texas A&M International University, Laredo, TX 78041. Email may be sent to rheredia@tamiu.edu. Roberto's major interests are in bilingual cognition and figurative language processing. He was recently selected as the Scholar of the Year for the College of Arts and Humanities.

Elizabeth Ijalba, MA, CCC, is a Speech–Language Pathologist trained in bilingualism, whose clinical work focuses on evaluating bilingual children with language delays and academic problems as well as adult bilingual patients with aphasia. Her research in the course of her doctoral program includes projects on L2 reading acquisition and cognitive development.

Nkonko M. Kamwangamalu holds a Ph.D. in Linguistics from the University of Illinois at Urbana-Champaign. He has taught English Language and Linguistics at the University of Singapore and the University of Swaziland and is currently Professor and Director of the Linguistics Program at the University of Natal in Durban, South Africa. His main areas of research include multi-lingualism, code-switching and code-mixing, language policy and planning, new Englishes, and African linguistics.

Judith F. Kroll is Professor of Psychology and Applied Linguistics at Penn State University. Her research takes a psycholinguistic approach to the acquisition, comprehension, and production of words in two languages during second language learning and in proficient bilingual performance. She is the co-editor, with Annette De Groot, of *Tutorials in Bilingualism: Psycholinguistic Perspectives* (Erlbaum, 1997) and *Handbook of Bilingualism: Psycholinguistic Approaches* (Oxford University Press, forthcoming).

Sherman Lee is a Ph.D. student in the Department of English and Communication at the City University of Hong Kong. She received her training in Linguistics and Computer Speech at the universities of Manchester and Cambridge, UK. Subsequently, while based at the University of Newcastle-upon-Tyne, she was engaged in sociolinguistic research on the bilingual development of British-born Chinese children. Her current research interests focus on language maintenance and language shift among the Hakka population of Hong Kong.

David C. S. Li is an Associate Professor at the Department of English and Communication, City University of Hong Kong. He obtained his BA (English) in Hong Kong, MA (Linguistics and Applied Linguistics) in Besançon, France, and Ph.D. (Linguistics) in Cologne, Germany. His areas of interest include cross-linguistic influence, contrastive grammar studies, form-focused error correction, code-switching, bilingual education, world Englishes, cross-cultural pragmatics and intercultural communication. An updated list of his publications may be found at http://personal.cityu.edu.hk/~endavidl/.

William Francis Mackey, FRSC, MA (Harvard), *docteur-ès-lettres* (Geneva), is the author of twenty books and some two hundred articles on bilingualism, language education, geolinguistics and language policy. He was Senior Lecturer (1948–51) in the University of London Institute of Education and the founding director (1968–71) of the International Center for Research on Bilingualism in Laval University, where he is currently Emeritus Professor. He can be reached c/o Anne Levac at Quali-Texte@Sympatico.ca.

Jeff MacSwan is an Assistant Professor in the College of Education at Arizona State University, and a member of the ASU Interdisciplinary Committee on Linguistics. He has published several articles on bilingualism and the education of language minority students, and is the author of *A Minimalist Approach to Intrasentential Code Switching* (Garland, 1999) and editor of the forthcoming volume *Grammatical Theory and Bilingual Codeswitching* (MIT Press). His work has appeared in *Bilingualism: Language and Cognition, Bilingual Review, Bilingual*

Research Journal, *Hispanic Journal of the Behavioral Sciences*, *Southwest Journal of Linguistics*, and *Education Policy Analysis Archives*.

Jürgen M. Meisel is Professor of Linguistics in the Department of Romance Languages and Chair of the Research Center on Bilingualism at the University of Hamburg, and coordinating editor of the journal *Bilingualism: Language and Cognition*. E-mail: jmm@uni-hamburg.de.

Rachel G. Morier is a graduating senior in the Honors Program at SUNY-Albany and will be pursuing graduate training in psychology upon completion of her bachelor's degree.

Salikoko S. Mufwene is a Distinguished Service Professor of Linguistics at the University of Chicago. He is the author of *The Ecology of Language Evolution* (Cambridge University Press, 2001), co-translator and editor of *Creolization of Language and Culture* (Routledge, 2001), series editor of Cambridge Approaches to Language Contact, former columnist and associate editor of the *Journal of Pidgin and Creole Languages*, and author of over one hundred essays on language contact.

Pieter Muysken is professor of linguistics at the University of Nijmegen, having previously taught for a long time at the Universities of Amsterdam and then Leiden. His main interests lie in Andean languages, Caribbean creoles, and bilingualism and language contact. Recent publications include *One Speaker, Two Languages* (ed. with Lesley Milroy, 1996) and *Bilingual Speech: A Typology of Code-Mixing* (2000).

Loraine K. Obler, Ph.D., is a Distinguished Professor in the Programs in Speech and Hearing Sciences and Linguistics at the Graduate Center of the City University of New York. Books she has co-authored include *Language and the Brain* (1999) and *The Bilingual Brain: Neuropsychological and Neurolinguistic Aspects of Bilingualism* (1978).

Aneta Pavlenko is Assistant Professor of TESOL at the College of Education, Temple University, Philadelphia, USA. Her research examines the relationship between language and identity in bi- and multilingual individuals. She has published numerous scientific articles and co-edited three volumes, *Multilingualism, Second Language Learning, and Gender* (with Adrian Blackledge, Ingrid Piller, and Marya Teutsch-Dwyer, Mouton de Gruyter, 2001), *Negotiation Of Identities In Multilingual Contexts* (with Adrian Blackledge, Multilingual Matters, 2003) and *Gender And TESOL* (with Bonny Norton, TESOL Inc., 2003).

Ingrid Piller (Ph.D. Dresden, 1995) teaches applied linguistics, discourse analysis, and sociolinguistics in the Linguistics Department at the University of Sydney, Australia, where she is also the coordinator of the MA program in applied linguistics. She is the author of *Bilingual Couples Talk: The Discursive Construction of Hybridity* (Amsterdam, 2002), and *American Automobile Names* (Essen, 1996), and co-editor (with Aneta Pavlenko, Adrian Blackledge, and Marya Teutsch-Dwyer) of *Multilingualism, Second Language Learning and Gender* (Berlin, 2001). For further information about her teaching and research visit her website at http://www.arts.usyd.edu.au/~ingpille. Her e-mail address is ingrid.piller@linguistics.usyd.edu.au.

William C. Ritchie is Associate Professor of Linguistics at Syracuse University. His publications include an edited volume entitled *Second Language Acquisition Research: Issues and Implications* (Academic Press, 1978). His recent relevant works, co-authored with Bhatia, include two handbooks – *Handbook of Child Language Acquisition* (Academic Press, 1999) and *Handbook of Second Language Acquisition* (Academic Press, 1996). He taught courses on second language acquisition and syntactic theory by invitation in the 1976 and 1977 Linguistic Society of America Summer Institutes.

Suzanne Romaine has been Merton Professor of English Language at the University of Oxford since 1984. Her research interests lie primarily in historical linguistics and sociolinguistics, especially in problems of societal multilingualism, linguistic diversity, language change, language acquisition, and language contact. Her most recent book (with Daniel Nettle) is *Vanishing Voices: The Extinction of the World's Languages* (Oxford University Press, 2000).

Judith Rosenhouse (Ph.D. Hebrew University in Jerusalem, 1974, in Arabic Language and Literature) specializes in Arabic dialectology, but has also worked on a variety of other linguistic topics. She has published many scientific articles as well as some literary translations, and her books include *The Bedouin Arabic Dialects: General Problems and a Close Analysis of North Israel Bedouin Dialects* (Wiesbaden: Harrassowitz, 1984), textbooks (language courses) of Israeli Arabic (e.g. 1989), and a *Practical Trilingual Dictionary* (Hebrew–Colloquial Arabic–Literary Arabic; Rosh-Ha'ayin, Israel: Prolog, 2002). She co-edited (with Y. Gitay and D. Porush) *Future and Communication: The Role of Scientific and Technical Communication and Translation in Technology Development and Transfer* (San Francisco: International Scholars Publications, 1997). Associate Professor Rosenhouse has been with the Technion – Israel Institute of Technology (Haifa, Israel) – for more than 15 years now, and is currently heading the Department of Humanities and Arts for the second time.

Itesh Sachdev is a Reader in the Social Psychology of Language and Groups and the Director of the Centre for Canadian Studies at the School of Languages, Linguistics and Culture, Birkbeck College, University of London. For his work in Canadian Studies on the relationship between language and identity he was awarded the Prix du Quebec (1999) and the Seagrams International Professorship to McGill University (1998). He is the editor of the London

Journal of Canadian Studies. He has published on the social psychology of intergroup relations as well as on issues of multilingualism and multiculturalism with diverse sets of participants originating from several parts of the world including Bolivia, Canada, France, Hong Kong, India, Taiwan, Thailand, Tunisia and the UK.

Birgit N. Schlyter is Associate Professor and Head of Forum for Central Asian Studies at the University of Stockholm. She is a lecturer in Turkish, Uzbek, Central Asian Linguistics, and Central Asian Cultural History. She has published works on modern Turkish and is at present conducting research on language development and language policies in the Central Asian region. In addition to titles mentioned in the chapter included in this volume, some of her other works are *Case Marking Semantics in Turkish* (Ph.D. dissertation), Stockholm, 1985, "Turkish semantics revisited", in H. Boeschoten and L. Verhoeven (eds), *Turkish Linguistics Today* (Leiden: Brill, 1991), and an article on the language situation in Turkey and Turkish language research which is to appear in a new revised edition of *An International Handbook of the Science of Language and Society*, Berlin: Walter de Gruyter. A recent publication on Central Asia research co-edited is *Return to the Silk Routes: Current Scandinavian Research on Central Asia* (London: Kegan Paul, 1999). E-mail: Birgit.Schlyter@orient.su.se.

Andrée Tabouret-Keller is Professor Emeritus, University Louis Pasteur, Strasbourg II and Editor of *Education et sociétés plurilingues / Educazione e società plurilingue* (Aosta, Italy) and President of Centre d'information sur l'éducation bilingue et plurilingue (Aosta, Italy). In addition, she is responsible for the *Séminaire "Comment lier épistémologie et politique"*, Maison des Sciences de l'Homme, Paris and a member of *Groupe d'étude du plurilinguisme en Europe* (Strasbourg, University Marc Bloch). Her current interests are contemporary language contact phenomena, language and psychoanalysis.

Acknowledgments

We are grateful first and foremost to the contributors, whose cooperation in putting this work together was nothing short of remarkable. Our heartfelt thanks are also due to a number of people at Blackwell, including particularly Tami Kaplan, the Acquisitions Editor in Linguistics, and Sarah Coleman, our Production Editor, for their unstinting patience and encouragement.

We are also grateful to our teachers and colleagues, Yamuna and Braj Kachru, Barbara Lust, James Gair, K. Machida, Rajeshwari Pandharipande, Hans Hock, Meena and S. N. Sridhar who have deeply influenced our work. The volume also benefited immeasurably from the advice and counsel of a number of valued colleagues, Virginia Valian, Jyotsna Vaid, Loraine Obler, Judith Kroll, and John Edwards.

For Bhatia: The D.A.V. school system (India) is particularly worthy of his deepest appreciation for imparting a commendable academic training and providing much-needed global and multicultural vision during his formative years in India.

Our families – Shobha, Laurie, Jane, Peter, Kanika, and Ankit – have supported us immensely with their love and affection; no words can express our deepest appreciation to them.

Finally, we are grateful to Dr Ben Ware, Vice-President of Research and Computing, and Dean Cathryn R. Newton, College of Arts and Science at Syracuse University, for their support of this project.

In memory of my beloved sister-in-law, Mrs. Raj Kumari Bhatia.

Tej K. Bhatia

With love and affection to Marnie Ritchie, my sister, my friend, my first teacher.

William C. Ritchie

Introduction

TEJ K. BHATIA AND
WILLIAM C. RITCHIE

Bilingualism – more generally, multilingualism – is a major fact of life in the world today. To begin with, the world's estimated 5,000 languages are spoken in the world's 200 sovereign states (or 25 languages per state), so that communication among the citizens of many of the world's countries clearly requires extensive bi- (if not multi-)lingualism. In fact, David Crystal (1997) estimates that two-thirds of the world's children grow up in a bilingual environment. Considering only bilingualism involving English, the statistics that Crystal has gathered indicate that, of the approximately 570 million people world-wide who speak English, over 41 percent or 235 million are bilingual in English and some other language. The processes of globalization now in progress can only increase the extent and character of bi-/multilingualism, as people the world over continue to recognize the advantage of adding a world language to their verbal repertoires. One must conclude that, far from being exceptional, as many lay people believe, bilingualism/multilingualism – which, of course, goes hand-in-hand with multiculturalism in many cases – is currently the rule throughout the world and will become increasingly so in the future.

Perhaps not surprisingly, research on bilingualism, whether theory-driven or practically oriented, has grown dramatically in quantity, quality, and breadth in recent years. These developments have culminated in the founding of two major journals for the publication of basic research in the field – *The International Journal of Bilingualism*, which first appeared in 1997, and *Bilingualism: Language and Cognition*, which began publishing in 1998 – and the establishment of the International Symposium on Bilingualism, which held its first meeting in 1997 and has met biennially since then; the fourth meeting, held in spring 2003, attracted over 6000 abstracts.

This handbook contributes to these vital trends with 31 state-of-the-art chapters presenting developments in research areas both theoretical and practical, ranging from the bilingual brain to bilingual education and literacy to the state of bilingualism in a number of critical regions of the world. The contributors – each one a top, internationally known scholar in his or her field – have been given full rein to develop their chapters in the way that seems most fitting to their areas of expertise. Since the contributors represent fields as diverse as linguistic theory, neurolinguistics, psycholinguistics, sociolinguistics, speech and hearing, experimental psychology, developmental psychology, clinical psychology, social psychology, sociology, anthropology, language education, deaf education, and area studies, the *Handbook* is not only an exhaustive area-by-area treatment of the field, but a mosaic of different approaches to the study of bilingualism as well.

The *Handbook* is divided into four parts, each addressing one aspect of bilingualism and introduced by one of the editors. Part I provides a general orientation in the study of bilingualism; part II addresses questions concerning the bilingual individual; part III surveys the role of bilingualism in society; and part IV consists of area and case studies of bilingualism in eight different areas of the world.

We should note at this point that the choice of the title *The Handbook of Bilingualism* was not intended to exclude work on tri-, quadri-, or quinquelingualism. As we hope the phrasing adopted above in this introduction suggests, the phenomena discussed in the book include the full range of multilingualisms from knowledge and use of two languages to that of however many one can imagine.

In bringing the work of the field together in one place for the advanced student and the researcher in bilingualism as well as those who apply such research, we hope to have contributed to the deepening and broadening of our understanding not only of the many facets of bilingualism, but of the human mind/brain in general.

REFERENCE

Crystal, D. (1997). *English as a Global Language*. Cambridge, UK: Cambridge University Press.

Part I Overview and Foundations

Introduction

TEJ K. BHATIA

The investigation of bilingualism is a broad and complex field, including the study of the nature of the individual bilingual's knowledge and use of two (or more) languages as well as the broader social and cultural consequences of the widespread use of more than one language in a given society. The two chapters that make up part I provide a general orientation to this complex field.

In "Foundations of Bilingualism," John Edwards provides an insightful bird's-eye view of the field by examining a wide range of issues that are addressed in greater depth in later, more specialized chapters in the book. A matter of central importance is the very notion of a "bilingual" – who is and who is not a bilingual? Edwards addresses this question as a matter of both degree and type of mastery of the second language. The process of second language acquisition – of becoming a bilingual – also receives some attention in the chapter in terms both of observational results and of theories and models of the process. The study of the relationship between bilingualism and intelligence has a long and checkered history, which Edwards also reviews. A central and continuing question in the field concerns the interaction between the bilingual's two language systems, including the influence that each system has on the knowledge and use of the other ("interference," in a special, technical sense without negative connotations) as well as the form and motivation for using both languages in the same discourse (code switching) and the longer-term phenomenon of borrowing between languages; Edwards addresses questions concerning these effects of bilingualism. Collective bilingualism of the kind one finds in India and other highly multilingual societies raises its own range of questions, including those concerning the social identity of individuals who are members of those societies; Edwards addresses those issues as well.

François Grosjean's chapter, "Studying Bilinguals: Methodological and Conceptual Issues," discusses five issues of central importance to experimental work with bilingual individuals. First, like Edwards, he is concerned with what it means to be a bilingual – specifically, what sort of characteristics should the participants/subjects in an experiment on "bilingualism" exhibit to allow conclusions about bilinguals to be drawn from the experiment? Second is the important question – raised by several other contributors – as to what "language mode" the individual is in at the time of the experiment – that is, to what extent is the bilingual set to use either language or a mixture of the two? Third and fourth, Grosjean is concerned about problems arising from the stimuli and the tasks used in experiments with bilinguals. Finally, he addresses the complex issue of what models of the bilingual are appropriate, given what we know at this point, emphasizing – as he has in previous publications – that the bilingual is not to be regarded as simply two monolinguals in one brain but as something quite different.

1 Foundations of Bilingualism

JOHN EDWARDS

1.1 Introduction

Everyone is bilingual. That is, there is no one in the world (no adult, anyway) who does not know at least a few words in languages other than the maternal variety. If, as an English speaker, you can say *c'est la vie* or *gracias* or *guten Tag* or *tovarisch* – or even if you only understand them – you clearly have some "command" of a foreign tongue. Such competence, of course, does not lead many to think of bilingualism. If, on the other hand, you are like George Steiner (1992), who claims equal fluency in English, French, and German, and who further claims that, after rigorous self-examination – of which language emerges spontaneously in times of emergency or elevated emotion, which variety is dreamed in, which is associated with the earliest memories – no one of the three seems dominant, then bilingualism (actually trilingualism in this case) does seem a rather more apt designation. The question, of course, is one of degree, and it is a question that continues to exercise the imagination, and a matter of importance in research studies.

Competence in more than one language can be approached at both individual and social levels, and these need not be as neatly connected as might first be thought. While it is true that a country full of multilingual people is itself multilingual in an obvious sense, it may nevertheless recognize only one or two varieties and thus, in another sense, be something less than multilingual. Conversely, a country may be officially bilingual or multilingual and yet most of its citizens may have only single-language competence. Many states in Africa, for example, have two official languages – usually a strong indigenous variety and an important European one – for highly heterogeneous and multilingual populations. On the other hand, countries like Switzerland (where recognition is granted to four languages) or Canada (which officially sanctions two) hardly resemble the linguistically rich and varied settings of Africa. Both individual and social manifestations of bilingualism are of course important, but it should be noted that the emphases are quite different; a thoroughgoing discussion of individual bilingualism involves, for example, linguistic and psycholinguistic dimensions which figure much less prominently, if at all, at the social level where other dimensions – historical, educational, political, and so on – arise for consideration.

1.2 Defining and Measuring

As may be imagined, it is easy to find definitions of bilingualism that reflect widely divergent responses to the question of *degree*. In 1933, for example, Bloomfield observed that bilingualism resulted from the addition of a perfectly learned foreign language to one's own, undiminished native tongue; he did rather confuse the issue, however, by admitting that the definition of "perfection" was a relative one. With this admission, Bloomfield did not remove the question of degree, but he did imply that any division between monolingualism and bilingualism should occur nearer to the Steiner end of the continuum than to the *c'est la vie* one. Others have been purposely vaguer: Weinreich (1953) simply defined bilingualism as the alternate use of two languages; in the same year, Haugen suggested that bilingualism began with the ability to produce complete and meaningful utterances in the second language. This suggests that even members of the *c'est la vie* camp are bilingual. Generally speaking, earlier definitions tended to restrict bilingualism to equal mastery of two languages, while later ones have allowed much greater variation in competence. But since this relaxation proves in practice to be as unsatisfactory as an argument from perfection – at least for the purpose of defining bilingualism in any generally applicable fashion – most modern treatments acknowledge that any meaningful discussion must be attempted within a specific context, and for specific purposes.

Further complicating this matter of degree, this question of where bilingualism starts, is the fact that any line drawn must cross not just one general language dimension, but many more specific threads of ability. Consider, first, that there are four basic language skills: listening, speaking, reading, and writing. Consider further the possible subdivisions: speaking skill, for example, includes what may be quite divergent levels of expression in vocabulary, grammar, and accent. There is thus a substantial number of elements here, all of which figure in the assessment of bilingualism; it does not follow that strength in one means strength in another:

> a pupil may be able to understand spoken English and Welsh, speak English fluently but Welsh only haltingly, read in Welsh with a reading age of six and in English with a reading age of eight, write poorly in English and not at all in Welsh. Is that pupil bilingual?   (Baker, 1988, p. 2)

In general, given both the basic skills, and their subdivisions, there are at least twenty dimensions of language which could or should be assessed in order to determine bilingual proficiency. It may be, as Weinreich observed, that a rough gauge of relative proficiency may be easily accomplished, that in many cases we can with some certainty say which language is dominant, but these matters are not always simple, and a rough reckoning may be quite inadequate if we wish, say, to compare groups of bilingual individuals, or if we wish to study the relationship between bilingualism and other personality traits.

Many tests have been used to measure bilingualism; these include rating scales and fluency, flexibility, and dominance tests. The first of these can involve interviews, language usage measures, and self-assessment procedures. In some ways, relying upon self-ratings has a lot to recommend it, but the strengths here rest upon the capacity of an individual to self-report accurately, a roughly equivalent sense across individuals of what competence means, and a disinterested and unbiased willingness to communicate proficiency levels. None of these can be taken for granted, and the inaccuracies of census information about languages (as an illustrative example) often rest upon self-assessment difficulties. Indeed, some of the problems here can also affect the apparently more objective tests of fluency and flexibility. We might, for example, ask people to respond to instructions in two languages, measure their response times and, on this basis, try to ascertain dominance. Or we could present picture-naming or word-completion tasks, we could ask subjects to read aloud, or we might present a word which occurs in both languages (*pipe*, for example, occurs in both French and English) and see how it is pronounced. We could simply test for extent of vocabulary, or see how many synonyms for a given word a person can come up with. Yet, although the results of such tests often intercorrelate, they are clearly far from perfect.

Apart from the hazards already noted, it can easily be seen that factors such as attitude, age, sex, intelligence, memory, linguistic distance between the two languages, and context of testing are all potentially confounding. Furthermore, even if we were able to gauge with some accuracy, there would remain problems of adequate labeling; that is, it is hardly to be expected that measured individuals would neatly fall into one, or two, or four neat categories of ability, or degrees of bilingualism. There even remains confusion as to what term ought to be applied to those much sought-after individuals whose bilingual capacities are great: are they to be known as *balanced bilinguals*, or *ambilinguals*, or *equilinguals* (to cite only three such terms)? Baetens Beardsmore (1986) described the ambilingual as a person who, in all contexts, can function equally well in either language, and who shows no trace of language A when using B. Given, however, that such individuals constitute a "rare if not nonexistent species" (p. 7), the term "balanced bilingual" (or, less commonly, "equilingual") is reserved for those whose mastery of both varieties is more roughly equivalent. What we see here, in effect, is a continuation of those difficulties and hazards, of those confounding factors, to the very highest levels of ability. What is clear, however, is that the vast number of those to whom the term "bilingual" can be at all reasonably applied fall into the category of "non-fluent" bilingualism.

There are some other basic matters that cut across the larger topic of degree of fluency. For instance, a useful distinction can be made between *receptive* (or passive) bilingualism, and *productive* (or active) competence; the difference here is between those who understand a language – either spoken or written – but cannot produce it themselves, and those who can do both. A receptive competence only has been referred to as *semibilingualism*. This term should not be confused with another, *semilingualism*, which refers to a lack of complete fluency in either language. (In 1927, Bloomfield made a famous characterization of "White Thunder" as a man who "may be said to speak no language tolerably" (p. 437).) More recently, the idea of knowing neither of two languages well has been advanced in connection with ethnic minority-group speakers (for example, Hansegård's notion of the *halvspråkighet* affecting Finnish-Swedish bilinguals; see Romaine, 1995), and this has meant that semilingualism has become extended from a solely linguistic description to a catchword with political and ideological overtones relating to majorities and minorities, domination and subordination, oppression and victimization.

Added to all this is the common metaphor of some finite "containerized" competence which has bedeviled the literature for some time. At its simplest, this suggests that what you gain on the swings of one language you lose on the roundabouts of the other. But using such a container metaphor for language acquisition and skills may be quite mistaken, and it need hardly be said that naive efforts to come to grips with complexity may do more harm than good. As well, even if we were to acknowledge some finite-capacity model, all that we know of intellectual structures and functions would suggest that the capacity – for languages, among other things – is quite large enough that we need not worry about exceeding our limits. If there is any credibility at all to the idea of semilingualism, it must rest upon a rather rare complex of social deprivations and should not particularly be seen as any sort of looming danger attaching to linguistic duality – for which it represents only "a half-baked theory of communicative competence" (the title of a piece by Martin-Jones and Romaine, 1985), coupled with the view that the usual goal of the bilingual speaker is to have each language container hold not only equal but "full" amounts (see also Baetens Beardsmore, 1986). In short, semilingualism is another species of the argument from perfection. We should remember that for all "non-fluent" bilinguals (i.e. the overwhelming majority, perhaps all), the second language may be weaker than the first which, itself, will never reach perfection, and that all language matters interact strongly with demands of function and context.

Not to be confused with all of this is another distinction, that between *additive* and *subtractive* bilingualism. In some circumstances, the learning of another language represents an expansion of the linguistic repertoire; in others, it may lead to a replacement of the first. The different outcomes here reflect different social pressures and needs. Additive bilingualism generally occurs where both languages continue to be useful and valued; a classic example is found in the bilingualism of aristocracies and social elites in systems in which it was considered natural and proper that every educated person know more than one variety. Subtractive bilingualism, on the other hand, often implies a society in which one language is valued more than the other, where one dominates the other, where one is on the ascendant and the other is waning.

Yet another common distinction is between *primary* and *secondary* bilingualism, between a dual competence acquired naturally, through contextual demands, and one where systematic and formal instruction has occurred. These are not watertight compartments, of course – one might, for example, pick up a conversational (and quite fluent) grasp of a language in a relatively informal way, and then feel the need later to add some grammatical skills, for reading and writing, in a more rigorous fashion. This would, incidentally, recapture the process by which a mother tongue is developed, and it is noteworthy that more enlightened school language curricula have tried to reflect this in their second-language programs. Still, it is not difficult to appreciate that there are some interesting and broadly based differences between primary and secondary bilingualism, some of which go beyond language itself and touch upon the interweaving of language with culture. As a contemporary example, compare those English-Gaelic bilinguals, in the west of Ireland or in the Highlands and Islands of Scotland, whose fluencies result from growing up in a particular location, with those who, in Dublin, Glasgow or Edinburgh, have more self-consciously set themselves to become bilingual. Consider further the ways in which lumping these two groups together, under a single "bilingual" rubric, might give a rather inaccurate picture of the state of health of Irish and Scots Gaelic. (For further discussion of types of bilinguals, see chapters 2–5, 7–10, 22.)

1.3 Acquiring Bilingual Competence

The fact that a majority of the global population has at least some level of multilingual competence surely indicates that adding a second language is not a particularly remarkable feat. And yet, especially within powerful linguistic groups, it is common to find references to the difficulties involved or to the peculiar lack of language talents supposedly possessed. In the modern world, for example, English and American monolinguals often complain that they have no aptitude for foreign-language learning. This is usually accompanied by expressions of envy for those multilingual Europeans, and sometimes (more subtly) by a linguistic smugness reflecting a deeply held conviction that, after all, those clever "others" who don't already know English will have to accommodate in a world made increasingly safe for anglophones. All such attitudes, of course, reveal more about social dominance and convention than they do about aptitude.

Second-language acquisition has been dichotomized as *simultaneous* or *successive*. The first describes exposure to more than one variety from the onset of speech or, at least, from a very young age (some commentators have suggested age three or four as a rather arbitrary cut-off) while the second refers to the addition, at a later age, of a new variety to an existing maternal one. Simultaneous acquisition is often associated with the "one person, one language" principle – commonly found, for instance, where a child speaks different languages to each parent. There are some classic accounts of this (e.g. Ronjat, 1913; Leopold, 1939–49). Given earlier (and sometimes continuing) reservations about bilingualism – in the popular mind, to be sure, but also to be found in the writings of well-known professionals (including Firth, 1930/1970 and Jespersen, 1922, for example) – it should be noted that the literature strongly suggests that general linguistic and mental development are not adversely affected. Bringing up children bilingually need involve few risks. Furthermore, where negative consequences have been observed, these are almost always due to social, personal, cultural or other factors – and not to the bilingualism process itself. Indeed, most observers point to the advantages of an early-acquired bilingual competence; these tend to reflect, above all, the relative ease of early learning and the higher levels of fluency, vocabulary and so on. There are some controversies as to just *when* in early life bilingualism is best set in train – from birth, from the age of three? – but early childhood is generally better than anything later (particularly, perhaps, for native-like pronunciation ability). It is sometimes argued that the young brain is more "plastic" and "flexible" than the older one. On the other hand, an over-emphasis upon early acquisition and brain malleability, and the idea that there is some ethological "critical period" for adding another variety are open to criticism. Older learners have cognitive experience lacking in small children and, providing the motivation is sufficient, can often prove to be better learners. If one could combine the maturity and articulated necessity of the older with the impressionability, imitativeness, spontaneity and unselfconsciousness of the younger, we would surely have a recipe for rapid and proficient bilingual acquisition.

We have moved here, of course, from more or less simultaneous bilingualism to early successive and later successive forms. What links and fuels them all is necessity. This clearly drives the older or adult learner, but it also informs the home situation of the young "simultaneous" learner, even if the latter cannot express it. In the process of becoming bilingual, native aptitude, age and intelligence are less important than a supportive context of necessity. With the right social conditions, then, bilingualism becomes just as "natural" as monolingualism in others. There is a large literature on the specifics of second-language acquisition, both "natural" learning and that which occurs formally, at school. Given sufficient motivation and opportunity, all normally intelligent people can learn another variety; those who claim they are "no good" at foreign languages are usually lacking in one or both of these. This is not to deny that there may exist individuals who have a greater innate or acquired aptitude – a "good ear" may be helpful, as well as a good memory and a capacity for self-initiated application. Beyond these, adaptability and genuine interest in other cultures are no doubt important. It can be seen, though, that virtually all of these qualities are of general value and do not form a package specifically implicated in language learning.

There are many formal methods for teaching languages; very generally, older ones tended to emphasize the memorization of grammatical rules and lexicon in the service of literary study; little attention was given to spoken language. In more contemporary school settings this has changed, although even high-tech language laboratories sometimes merely individualize older approaches, rather than signaling a change of course towards more conversational competence. Still, while it remains difficult for the classroom to become a representation of the street, the tendency is for more and more conversation. Students are encouraged to speak before learning formal grammar, and the use of the maternal variety is often kept to a minimum; in short, second-language acquisition is meant to resemble first-language learning. (For more on bilingualism and second language acquisition, see chapters 4 and 5.)

1.4   Theoretical Perspectives

Most contemporary theories of second-language acquisition reject a simplistic behaviorist approach – which has, besides, been shown as woefully inadequate for understanding mother-tongue learning – and endorse a cognitive conception in which rules are formulated and tested. Learning occurs in a series of non-random stages, each of which is characterized by a sort of interlanguage. It can easily be seen here that the analysis of errors made at different points in the progression is very important, since they can reveal a misapplied rule. If someone says "sheeps," for example, it is clear that the "s-forms-the plural" rule has been learned but overgeneralized (this sort of error is also common, of course, in children working out the refinements of the mother tongue).

Theories within social psychology have paid particular attention to the motivational features already noted in passing, and this makes a good deal of sense. If we agree that language is a social activity, and if we accept that almost everyone is cognitively capable of learning second (and subsequent) varieties, then it follows that the force of the situation, and the attitudes it provokes in potential learners, are central. A distinction first made in the 1960s was that between *instrumental* and *integrative* motivation for second-language learning. The former refers to a desire to learn for utilitarian purposes, the latter to language learning as part of a wish to know more about, to interact with, and perhaps ultimately to immerse oneself in another culture. Perhaps, however, a well-fleshed instrumental attitude must include at least some integrative motivation, and one can also imagine a development of the former into the latter. In any event, a well-known framework for second-language learning is that of Gardner (Gardner and Lambert, 1972), who attempts to link the social context, and the cultural beliefs within it, to individual learner capacities – including, of course, motivational levels – and the formal/informal settings in which the language is to be learned. Throughout, he stresses the influence of integrative motivation upon positive outcomes. Clément's model (see Noels and Clément, 1998) aims to embed individual motivations still more deeply in the social setting. In particular, he notes that a tension exists between an integrative motivation and fear of assimilation; hence his model has particular relevance for those language learners who are also minority-group members, and whose first language is threatened by the forces of those speaking the second. Clément's emphasis upon collective forces and outcomes is carried further in the formulation of Giles and his colleagues (see Giles and Coupland, 1991). Here, language learning is seen, above all, as an intergroup process. Much more consideration is thus given to assimilative tendencies and apprehensions, to the preservation of ethnic-group boundaries and identities; this is tied closely to Giles's conception of *ethnolinguistic vitality*, in both an objective and a perceived sense, and its ramifications for language-learning motivation.

A "general theory" of second-language learning has been proposed by Spolsky (1989). It aims to synthesize earlier and more particularized efforts and, indeed, also touches in important ways upon first-language acquisition. Spolsky's approach has five pivotal features: it attempts to bring all aspects of language learning under the one roof; it aims for precision and clarity so that the broad coverage does not blur details of varying contexts, goals and outcomes; it assumes that all aspects of learning are interactive – although they need not be operative in all contexts, they all interpenetrate (on the subject of motivation, for example, Spolsky wants to detail types and strengths); it argues that all language learning must be seen within a social setting; it holds that some conditions for learning are "graded" (i.e. the more intense or favorable they are, the more likely a linguistic consequence becomes) while others are "typicality" states (i.e. they occur usually but not necessarily).

Application and prediction are the acid test in all such theoretical models – for a recent overview, see Mitchell and Myles (1998) – and some might suggest that the latter have done little more than codify and formalize what has been known for a long time. Nonetheless, they all scotch the myth that some people, or some groups, have no "head" for languages and that second-language aptitude is a rare commodity usually best seen in non-anglophones. Instead, they stress the power of the setting and, within it, the desires, needs, attitudes and motivations of ordinary people. It should be apparent that the social factors impinging upon language learning are, quite simply, the most important ones. We might also recall that, for those millions of people who pick up bilingual or multilingual competence in the informal realm of daily life, simple necessity is the great motivator and the great determiner of how far this competence develops. It can dwarf all other features and, in particular, can ride roughshod over personal attitudes and motivation. Most historical changes in language use have a bilingual component, and most owe much more to socioeconomic and political exigencies than they do to attitude. The adoption of English by the Irish population, for example, was not accompanied – for the masses – by favorable attitudes, much less integrative ones. There may have been a grudging instrumentality at work, but it certainly was not of the type which pushes students to study French or German in the hopes of joining the diplomatic service. (For more on models and theories of bilingual functioning, see chapters 2, 3, and 7–9.)

1.5   Bilingualism and Intelligence

It is one thing to say that all normal people have the basic capacity to expand their linguistic repertoires, and that doing so exacts no cognitive price. But what of the notion that bilingualism can *increase* intellectual scope? It is an historically common view that one's personality grows with extra languages – particularly among those already bilingual and, more particularly still, among the social elite for whom an additional language or two was always an integral part of civilized life. (There have also been those who demurred. In the seventeenth century, for instance, John Milton (1644/1958) and Samuel Butler (1662; see Hazlitt, 1901) argued that expanded repertoires do not, in themselves, imply intellectual breadth – the latter pointing out, in one of his "satyrs," that "the more languages a man can speak, his talent has but sprung the greater leak.")

I have already touched upon the more linguistically informed misgivings of Firth and Jespersen, and Weinreich, in his classic *Languages in Contact*, was able to cite many expressions of the problems allegedly faced by bilinguals; these included split national loyalties and problems of "marginalization" (or *anomie* – to use Durkheim's famous term), emotional difficulties, moral depravity (through receiving inadequate religious instruction in their mother tongue), stuttering, left-handedness, excessive materialism, laziness, and detrimental consequences for intelligence. All these ideas seem dated, to say the least, and Weinreich himself was generally dismissive, preferring experimental evidence – which is always, of course, in shorter supply than the speculation underpinning most of these assertions. He cites with approval, for example, a study that demonstrated that the problems of bilinguals are much more likely to stem from social factors in bilingual households than from linguistically driven "mental conflict." This is much more in line with modern thinking, although if it were true that bilingual families have a heightened level of social tension this could be taken as an indirect discouragement of bilingualism. No such evidence is available. One can imagine, of course, families applying the "one-parent-one-language" principle to children in a unduly rigid or harsh way; no doubt this occurs, and no doubt this can create problems associated with the growth and use of bilingualism. But again, there is no reason to believe that such practices are anything more than aberrations of an unsystematic kind.

Generally speaking, early studies tended to associate bilingualism with lowered intelligence, and it is unsurprising that many of them were conducted, in America, at a time of great concern with the flood of immigrants from Europe (roughly, 1900–20). The story of the intelligence-testing movement itself, which flourished at this time, is a fascinating and detailed one, as well as an example of the misuse of "science" allied to ignorance and prejudice. Suffice it to say here that the "objective" intelligence tests of the time reflected a very culture-bound ideal and, consequently, immigrants – especially those who were non-white, non-English-speaking, non-northern-European, non-educated, and so on – did not fare well. In such a climate it is easy to see that the "feeble-minded" immigrants (or hopefuls) were handicapped by their languages, and that the greater their use of English, the higher their measured intelligence. One well-known study concluded, for example, that "the use of a foreign language in the home is one of the chief factors in producing mental retardation" (Goodenough, 1926, p. 393). Incredible assertions like this are understandable only in their context but even so, even allowing for general intolerance and nativism, even understanding the feelings of those concerned to protect the *status quo* from a horde of barbarians (in the Greek sense of that word), it is still chastening to think that such comments could appear in respected academic journals.

In addition to negative associations between bilingualism and intelligence which stemmed, somewhat indirectly, from social fears of immigrants, there were more disinterested studies which pointed to problems. They are, however, flawed by inadequate controls in their experimental procedures. One typical study, for example, showed no IQ difference between urban monolinguals and bilinguals, but a substantial one for rural children – and yet it did not take into account obvious social-contact differences between the city and country dwellers, nor occupational and social-class variation among the parents (see Edwards, 1995). There is also, in all such work, a problem of statistical inference: if one observes a correlation between low intelligence and bilingualism, then has the first caused the second, or vice versa (or is there a third factor, perhaps unknown or unmeasured, which influences both and thus accounts for their relationship)? Correlation need not imply causation.

Later research tended to show essentially no relationship between intelligence and bilingualism, and this work was generally more carefully done than the earlier studies. Controlling sex, age and social-class differences became common procedure, and the lack of such control was increasingly seen to have produced the negative associations found in previous work.

What some have seen as a turning-point came in the early 1960s, when findings showing a *positive* relationship between intelligence and bilingualism began to appear. In Montreal, Peal and Lambert (1962/1972) more carefully controlled the relevant variables in an examination of ten-year-old bilingual and monolingual children. In particular, all the subjects were from middle-class backgrounds and all the bilingual youngsters had equal proficiency in French and English. The bilinguals were found to outperform their mono-lingual counterparts on both verbal and non-verbal intelligence tests and the authors concluded that the bilingual child had "mental flexibility, a superiority in concept formation, and a more diversified set of mental abilities." How-ever, they also noted that "it is not possible to state from the present study whether the more intelligent child became bilingual or whether bilingualism aided his intellectual development" (p. 277).

Following Peal and Lambert's study many others have appeared which support a positive linkage between bilingualism and intelligence. There have also been some dissenting views, as well as cogent criticism of the 1962 study itself. The latter centers upon the limitation just cited from Peal and Lambert themselves and upon the generalizability of the results. Important here are the restriction, in their study, to only "balanced" bilinguals, and questions about the representativeness of the sample of children and the difficulty of equating home backgrounds simply by holding socioeconomic status constant.

Some of the difficulties involved in attempting to show a relationship – positive or negative – between bilingualism and cognitive development, mental flexibility, intelligence, and so on involve the following questions. First, how do we adequately define bilingualism itself; do we require perfectly balanced bilinguals for the "best" contrast with monolinguals, and how do we measure bilingualism, balanced or otherwise? Second, how do we define intelligence; relatedly, how do we know that IQ tests adequately assess this quantity? Third, how do we ensure comparability between groups of bilinguals and monolinguals; controlling for age, sex and some other variables may not be difficult, but what about socioeconomic status? Most measures of this may not come to grips well enough with home differences of vital importance. Fourth, how do we interpret any relationship found between bilingualism and intelligence? Is it a causal one, and, if so, in which direction? Does bilingualism lead to increased IQ, for example, or does a higher IQ increase the likelihood of functional bilingualism?

These and other difficulties mean that strong conclusions about bilingualism and cognition are not warranted. Some feel that there may be some link between the two, but that any cognitive advantages attaching to bilingualism are rather slight. Others have been mainly concerned to show that there is not a cognitive price to be paid for bilingualism. As McLaughlin (1978, p. 206) noted: "almost no general statements are warranted by research on the effects of bilingualism . . . in almost every case, the findings of research are either contradicted by other research or can be questioned on methodological grounds." We should understand that social factors are virtually always of great importance in accounting for contradictory reports about bilingualism and cognition. Most positive findings come from studies of immersion children (where language attitudes are favorable), most negative ones from those "submersed" in second-language education (leading to subtractive bilingualism).

In essence, being bilingual (or multilingual, for that matter) is unlikely to mean any significant increase in cognitive and intellectual skills, although it is also clear that bilingualism need not lead to decreased or weakened capacities. It would be perverse, however, to deny that bilingualism can represent another dimension of one's capacities, and in that sense be a repertoire expansion. I see nothing controversial about this, just as I would see nothing controversial in the statement that a number of years' devotion to the study of great literature can lead to a heightened or, at least, altered sensitivity to the human condition. (For additional material on bilingualism and intelligence, see chapters 5, 15, 17, 22, and 23.)

1.6   Borrowing, Interference and Code Switching

Outright language choice is obviously available to bilingual individuals. It is also common to find linguistic alteration occurring within one unit of speech directed to one listener. In his classic volume, Weinreich (1953, p. 1) stated that all such "deviation from the norms of either language" may be referred to as *interference*. It seems evident, however, that not every switch from one language to another results from the unwelcome intrusion which this term suggests; speakers may often switch for emphasis, because they feel that the *mot juste* is found more readily in one of their languages than in another, or because of their perceptions of the speech situation, changes in content, the linguistic skills of their interlocutors, degrees of intimacy and so on. Some writers have thus opted for the more neutral term *transference* which implies, among other things, a greater element of volition. The most commonly investigated variety is *code switching* – "sometimes I'll start a sentence in English *y termino en español*" (as Poplack's 1980 title runs).

Different types of language transfer can be easily understood. For example, if a Brussels French speaker uses the Dutch *vogelpik* for a game of darts, rather than the standard French *fléchettes*, this is an example of lexical transfer. Further, *vogelpik* in this context constitutes a *loan word* since it is an "intrusion" regularly used in unchanged form. It may, however, be given a French pronunciation, which indicates another type of "change," an attempt to bring the foreign element into the maternal fold. Sometimes loan words become very widely used and, if we go far enough, we reach the level of permanent interlanguage borrowing (as English, for instance, has taken in Arabic words like *alcohol* and *algebra*). Not all languages can incorporate borrowed elements equally easily. Between two languages widely removed from one another typologically, for example, the grammatical constraints may be such that borrowing may be less frequent than it is between closely related varieties. More simply, borrowings from language A may not fit as easily into B as into C.

Another variety of lexical transfer occurs when loan *translation* occurs: for example, the adoption of the English *skyscraper* into Dutch (as *wolkenkrabber*), German (*wolkenkratzer*), French (*gratte-ciel*), and Spanish (*rascacielos*). Such words are called *calques* (literally, "copies"). *Morphological* transfers occur when a word in language A is more fully embraced by language B: the Dutch *kluts* (dollop) becomes, in Brussels French, *une clouche*, and *heilbot* (halibut) becomes *un elbot*. *Syntactic* transfer occurs in such examples as *"Tu prends ton plus haut chiffre"* ("You take your highest figure") – said by a native Dutch speaker, who makes his adjectives precede the noun, as they would in Dutch (*"Je neemt je hoogste cijfer"*) but not as they would in French. *Phonological* transfer is very common, of course, and is a most difficult area in which to avoid interference (think of fluent adult speakers with "horrible" accents). Equally, *prosodic* transfer – subtle differences in stress and intonation between languages, such that one's dominant variety influences the other – may also be difficult to avoid.

This discussion only scratches the surface, of course, but it does reveal something of the variety of transference and, more importantly, the variability in terms of conscious intent. That is, bilingual speakers may *choose* to use *vogelpik*, and their choice may be determined by non-linguistic, social factors; syntactic and phonological interference, on the other hand, is presumably less subject to such factors or, more accurately perhaps, is less easily or directly influenced by them, necessitating more effort to remove it. One might roughly view interference phenomena as those determined by internal factors, and code switching as more influenced by extra-linguistic constraints. This is, however, a very general statement.

However we divide the subject up, and whatever labels we apply – interference, code switching, mixing, transference, and so on – it is clear that in all cases something is "borrowed" from another language. Further, the degree to which the borrowed element is integrated (or can be integrated) into the other code may be of considerable interest for studies of group contact, of relative linguistic prestige, of the perceived or actual ease with which different languages deal with given topics. Borrowings may be on a "nonce" basis or may represent more established practice, but the latter grows from the former and presumably reflects stronger and more widespread need. However, a further subdivision has been suggested for these established borrowings; some are indeed necessary – words filling lexical gaps in the other language, for example – but some seem gratuitous, since an equivalent item already exists. The motivation here is most often perceived status and prestige, and common examples include the use of foreign words or phrases. One can observe the trendy status of English around the world, for instance, even among non-speakers. Shops in many countries often find it easier to sell their products if they are labeled in English. No English competence is implied or required in either seller or buyer; simple recognition and cachet do the trick. (For further discussion of bilingualism and borrowing, see chapters 2, 6, 28.)

It is interesting, in all of this, to recognize that attitudes towards code switching are often negative, particularly on the part of monolinguals who are sometimes inclined to dismiss it as gibberish. Terms like *Tex-Mex*, *Franglais*, *Japlish* (and many others) are often used, and often meant pejoratively. Bilinguals, too, are wont to see their behavior here as "embarrassing," "impure," "lazy," even "dangerous," but the reasons they give for the practice – fitting the word to the topic, finding a word with a nuance unavailable in the other variety, helping out a listener, strengthening intimacy, and so on – make a great deal of sense (see Myers-Scotton, 1992). If you have two languages to draw upon, why not maximize this happy circumstance as appropriate? The chimeras of impurity and laziness are exposed when we realize that, very often, switching involves the *repetition* – for emphasis, for intimacy – of the same idea in both languages. We see, then, speakers whose twin bow-strings allow them not only the style-shifting available to monolinguals but also full language-shifting. It is hard to imagine that this is anything but a valuable addition. (For more on code mixing and code switching, see chapters 2–4, 10–14, 25, 26, 28, 29, and 31; for a general proposal on the relationships between code mixing, code switching and interference, see chapter 6.)

1.7   Some Social Aspects

If we understand that bilingualism, switching and other dual-language phenomena are still seen as suspicious by some and as arcane marks of erudition by others, we should also recall their global nature. Expanded linguistic competence is usually driven by necessity but it has also historically reflected and supported upper-class boundaries. There is a distinction, in other words, between elite and folk bilingualism. In different ages, not to have known Latin or Greek or French in addition to one's mother tongue would have been simply unthinkable for educated people. At other levels and for other reasons more humble citizens have also been bilingual from earliest times: we know it was necessary under the Ptolemies to acquire Greek, even for quite minor posts, and Athenian slaves – representatives of the lowest class of all – were often bilingual as they were pressed into domestic service and teaching.

There are important differences between individual bilingualism and collective or social bilingualism, regardless of whether or not the latter is officially endorsed. Collective bilingualism in many settings, ancient and modern, is an enduring quantity, unlike the impermanent, transitional variety common in many immigrant contexts in which, in fact, bilingualism is a generational way-station on the road between two unilingualisms. The classic pattern for newcomers to the United States, for example, was bilingualism (mother tongue and English) by the second generation and English monolingualism by the third. The more permanent collective bilingualism remains, of course, largely because of a continuing necessity which is absent among most immigrant populations, and this necessity usually rests upon different social functions and different domains of use for each language. This situation is now commonly referred to as *diglossia*. This word is simply the Greek version of *bilingualism* and, on the face of it, would not seem to be a useful innovation; it doesn't, for example, logically encompass the social, collective aspect that, in practice, it refers to. However, *"la logique n'est pas maître de la terminologie"* (Mackey, 1989, p. 11). (For more on diglossia, see chapters 15, 28, 29, and 31.)

While diglossia, as collective bilingualism, is seen to be a stable condition, it should be remembered that even stability is relative. The French-English diglossia that prevailed in England after the Norman Conquest eventually broke down, for example. As well, the stability of diglossia is apt to be upset by political pressure. When the "colonels" overthrew a liberal Greek government in 1967, the previous program of extending the use of *dhimotiki* (demotic

Greek) was reversed – because of its leftist associations – and *katharévusa* (the classical "higher" form) was supported. In 1975, constitutional government returned and *dhimotiki* was declared the country's official language the following year.

The arrangement of societal bilingualism is of course variable, and the Canadian example is illustrative. Prior to the *Official Languages Act* (1969), which legally underpins French and English in Canada, a government commission on bilingualism and biculturalism was established to study and make recommendations. Paying special attention to the linguistic situations in Belgium, Finland, Switzerland and South Africa, the commissioners closely examined the so-called "personality" and "territorial" principles relating to bilingualism. In the first of these, rights are seen to inhere in *individuals*, wherever they live within a state. This operates most clearly in South Africa. According to the territorial principle, however (as in Belgium), rights vary from region to region and the linguistic arrangement is commonly some sort of "twinned" unilingualism. The distinction between these two approaches is not unlike that made by political scientists between "consociation" and "universalism"; if consociation is sometimes seen as the democratic alternative best suited to divided societies (as in Belgium and Switzerland), it is also often an elaborate and fragile system of checks and balances among ethnic groups. Universalism, with its first emphasis on individual rights, is the preferred approach in most modern democracies but it can be seen that ruling "group rights" out of court is not always possible or desirable.

The commission opted for the application of the personality principle in Canada, even though official-language minorities were small in all provinces except Québec and New Brunswick. Difficulties in following the South African example were acknowledged (66 percent of whites there claimed to be bilingual, for example, as opposed to only 12 percent in Canada; and official-language minorities in South African provinces ranged in strength from 23 percent to 39 percent, whereas they were under 15 percent in nine of the ten Canadian provinces), and the commission recognized the advantages of territorialism. However, political factors (chiefly, the "symbolic" weight of the Canadian francophone population) and a highly mobile Canadian society were seen to suggest the personality approach – this despite the fact that the commission could have considered more "mixed" possibilities (as in Switzerland, for example, where the personality principle operates only at the federal level).

The recommendation, therefore, was for federal bilingualism and the provision of bilingual services at the provincial level – but only Québec, Ontario and New Brunswick were to become "officially" bilingual. As conditions became more viable for francophones outside Québec, other provinces would adopt official bilingualism (roughly, whenever French speakers came to constitute 10 percent of the population). In fact, at the time of the commission's recommendations, Ontario was only about 7 percent francophone (and, in Québec, anglophones comprised about 13 percent). Only New Brunswick is officially bilingual today.

Now it seems as if the Canadian bilingual dream has faded, at least from the "personality" perspective. The country has moved steadily towards "twinned" unilingualisms – French in Québec and English elsewhere – with a "bilingual belt" in parts of Ontario and, especially, New Brunswick. This process has been assisted by the continuing assimilation of francophones outside Québec and the rejection, within that province, of bilingualism. "Territorialism" seems to have emerged, in other words, and some have suggested making it legal by giving only one of the two "charter" languages official status everywhere (except in New Brunswick). All of this suggests the importance of the political and social frameworks within which stable bilingualism occurs. A socially engineered policy – which is how some have described the Canadian arrangement – must ultimately, it seems, be reconciled with widespread, popular perceptions of social reality and self-interest. When perceptions differ among powerful ethnic groups – in Canada, the anglophones, francophones, aboriginals, and "allophones" (i.e. all the "others") are all central players, though no group is itself monolithic – then centrally inspired conceptions of multiculturalism, bilingualism, and diglossia are seen to be quite delicate (see Edwards, 1994, 1995).

1.8   Bilingualism and Identity

Why should bilingualism (or multilingualism) be particularly important? After all, most people in the world have some sort of facility in more than one language and, as we are regularly informed nowadays, it is monolingualism that is an aberration, an affliction of the powerful, a disease to be cured. An ability possessed by the majority of human beings – most of them relatively uneducated, many of them illiterate – and which can be almost effortlessly acquired by the youngest of them might be thought to have attracted more than its share of academic attention. Language *per se* is not, of course, a completely open book to us, and this marvelous facility – which sets us apart, in tremendous degree if not in basic principle, from even those clever apes and dolphins – is not fully transparent in either development or use. Still, within the broader study of language, what happens once could easily be seen as (*mutatis mutandis*) happening again: why should a second or subsequent language warrant more than an extending footnote to the broader linguistic enquiry? Why should bilingualism occupy its own niche in the larger enterprise?

Of course, second-language acquisition cannot, in principle, be a precise replica of mother-tongue learning, for the simple reason of being second. Heraclitus told us, a long time ago, that you can't step into the same river twice. Consequently, the complicated issues I have so briefly touched upon in the previous sections account for a great deal of what we may call the technical literature on bilingualism, a literature largely concerned with the variations among linguistic gears and axles occasioned by bilingual competence (see

Edwards, 1995). The point I wish to make here, however, is that the technicalities of this broad enterprise – vital and interesting as they are – cannot, themselves, fully explain its depth and its appeal. To understand these, we have to move beyond language itself, beyond psycholinguistics, beyond experimental studies and educational programs that illuminate and facilitate repertoire expansion. We have to go beyond instrumental matters altogether, and consider issues of psychology and sociology, of symbol and subjectivity. In a word, we must think about the relationship between language and identity, and how this relationship may alter when more than one variety is involved.

Language can certainly be considered as a marker at the individual level. The detail and nuance of psycholinguistic acquisition patterns, for instance, lead to the formation of unique *idiolects*. But, while this fine-grained individual approach has undoubted validity – notably in clinical or forensic investigations – it is generally only of anecdotal interest or concern. In fact, one could argue that even idiolectal usage is a social, or group phenomenon – on the simple grounds that all language implies someone to talk to, a communicative intent, a linking of the individual to others. Apart from this sort of argument, it is common to consider the linguistic associations with identity as group matters: the jargon of the club, the class or regional dialect, the language of the wider community. Initially, however, one or two points should be made at the personal level – or, more accurately, at the level on which the personal and the social intertwine.

Speaking a particular language means belonging to a particular speech community and this implies that part of the *social* context in which one's *individual* personality is embedded, the context which supplies the raw materials for that personality, will be linguistic. Disentangling the linguistic features from all others is not, of course, an easy task and so it has always been difficult to make a compelling case that membership in a given speech community has – in theoretical isolation, as it were, from other socializing threads – concretely specifiable consequences for personality. Whorfianism, at least in its "weaker" forms, is of course relevant here, but its implications are of more direct interest at the level of the group – the broadly stereotypic linguistic patterning of the thoughts, attitudes and habits of the collectivity. Indeed, a Whorfian perspective has been extended to cover paralinguistic features, too. Any cultural package which connects language and thought must also involve all sorts of accompanying communicative gestures (see Birdwhistell, 1970) and, by extension, virtually all aspects of the personal repertoire. In general, an influence of language upon personality may be assumed, if not easily demonstrated, but it will tend to link personalities and operate upon their socially overlapping spheres, rather than distinguishing between them or producing idiosyncratic dispositions.

One might suggest, however, that membership in more than one speech community could produce more immediately observable results at the individual level: if two or more languages are exercising some influence, then an individual could conceivably display an interesting pattern woven from several linguistic threads, a pattern which might look quite distinctive against a more unidimensional one. Arguably, any distinctiveness here would be most apparent in social settings where bilingual individuals are relatively rare, or where – if more numerous – they are at least similar amongst themselves (in terms, say, of degree or type of bilingual capacity). The fact that neither of these conditions occurs particularly frequently is a complication. And there is another important factor here, too. A line of argument which is at least implicit in the literature implies that the joint influence of more than one language upon individual psychologies is best understood as a sort of *tension* – i.e. that the individual effects will reflect one language working against the other, as it were. In any event, it is clear that this sort of tension would, indeed, produce the most observable results; after all, if the joint linguistic influences were to seamlessly merge, to pull in harness, then the results might logically be thought to be, at best, a heightening or a strengthening of influences traceable to each speech community singly. This is one way, indeed, of thinking about that alleged consequence of bilingualism to which I have already alluded: increased cognitive capabilities and intellectual sensitivities.

Much of interest rests upon the degree to which bilinguals possess either two (theoretically) separately identifiable systems of language – from each of which they can draw, as circumstances warrant – or some more intertwined linguistic and, perhaps, cognitive duality. As Hamers and Blanc (2000) point out, we are far from having compelling empirical data here. There is a difficult circularity at work, one that confounds all scientific attempts to link the observable to the intangible: the ambiguous or unclear results of the relatively few studies of the non-verbal repertoires (for example) of bilinguals do not provide clear indications of likely underlying mechanisms; on the other hand, plausible variations in rational accounts of these mechanisms make the interpretation of subtle behavioral differences hard to assess. Whether we are interested in verbal communication, its paralinguistic accompaniments or the broader reaches of personality traits generally, we find very little experimental evidence. It is interesting that, in their massive study of bilingualism, Baker and Jones (1998) give only six pages (out of more than 750) to a section on personality.

Consider, for instance, the "popular" (and, sometimes, academic) view that bilinguals must have some sort of split mentality – two individuals in one, as it were. Grosjean (1982) and others have reported that bilinguals sometimes feel, themselves, that language choice draws out, and draws upon, different personalities. But, as Baker and Jones (1998) and Hamers and Blanc (2000) note, the evidence here is anecdotal at best. Indeed, we could go a bit further, and point to the large logical and rational difficulties which some two-in-one arrangement would create. There is certainly, however, evidence that language choice may implicate different *aspects* of the personality: bilinguals responding to interviews and questionnaires are liable to give slightly different pictures of themselves, depending upon the language used. They may make different responses to objective or projective probes, responses may be more emotional through one variety (typically, but not inevitably, their maternal language), they may more strongly affirm their sense of ethnic identity in one language than in another, and so on (see, for example, studies by Ervin, Guttfreund, Bond and others, usefully summarized in Hamers and Blanc, 2000). The fact that different social settings and variations in language–affect linkages lead to different patterns of self-presentation clearly does not imply separate personalities, although it does suggest an enhanced repertoire of possibility.

Language "tensions" at the individual level have been seen to contribute to emotional strains – *anomie* and lowered self-esteem, for example. These are often most pronounced in immigrant or minority-group situations, a fact which suggests very strongly that the stresses are essentially not linguistic in origin but, rather, result from broader pressures associated with cultures in contact, with cross-group antagonism and prejudice, with poverty and disadvantage (see above). Among immigrant and minority populations, as Diebold (1968) pointed out, bilingualism is often, itself, a response to the social contact which also produces psychological stresses and strains.

We have once again, then, linked the individual to the group, and have seen how the psychological intersects with the sociological. When Baker and Jones, Grosjean, Hamers and Blanc, and other able commentators suggest that those problems which seem particularly characteristic of bilinguals are social in nature, and not linguistic *per se*, they are reminding us of a broader set of relationships which embed the individual in his or her society. So it is apposite at this point to move more directly to that wider realm, and to consider the social implications of bilingualism itself.

People belong to many groups, and all groups – all, at least, that have boundaries possessing some degree of permanence – have characteristics which mark their identity. This marking is, of course, more or less visible at the level of the individual member. The implication is that each of us may carry the tribal markings of many groups, that our "group identity" is itself a mosaic rather than a monolith. Still, it is clear that, where language issues are central, the pivotal group is the ethnocultural community: overlaps of importance may occur because of simultaneous membership in gender, socioeconomic, educational, occupational, and many other categories, but the base here is an ethnic one.

The point at issue, then, is the significance of a bilingualism which links an individual to more than one ethnocultural community. How does it feel, we might ask, to have a foot in more than one camp? Is it this that could lead to that psychological splitting which we have rejected on more purely cognitive grounds? Or is such duality the origin of the expanded acuity and awareness that some have claimed for bilinguals? The short answers to these sorts of questions are all positive, or potentially positive, in a world where complicated patterns of social relations are made more intricate still by a very wide – theoretically infinite, in fact – range of linguistic capabilities. Of course, a great deal of bilingualism has very little emotional significance: the purely instrumental fluencies needed to conduct simple business transactions do not, after all, represent much of an excursion from one's ethnic base camp. This is probably a rather larger category than is often thought. For example, breadth of multiple fluencies does not, *per se*, imply emotional or psychological depth – it may, more simply, reflect the exigencies of a complicated public life. On the other hand, it is certainly possible to hold dual (or multiple) allegiances, involving different-language groups, in the absence of personal bilingualism. The attachment felt by the English-speaking Irish or Welsh to a culture and an ancestry whose language they no longer possess is a psychologically real one, and demonstrates the continuing power of what is intangible and symbolic. Indeed, there often exists a continuing attachment to the "lost" language itself, seen as perhaps the most important specific aspect of that more general ancestry, and as the point of entry into cultural tradition. The fact that such attachments rarely lead to actual linguistic revival is regrettable in the eyes of those who feel that language is *the* pillar of culture, but this is not the place to explore the reasons why passive sympathies do not become active ones: the point is, again, that these attachments – however attenuated or residual – have a meaning, and represent a sort of symbolic bilingual connectivity. (For more on bilingualism and emotion, see chapters 9, 14, and 19.)

The argument has been made elsewhere (in Edwards, 1985, for instance) that a continuing sense of ethnic-group identity need not inevitably depend upon the continuing use of the original language in ordinary, communicative dimensions – again, this is a matter of considerable complexity which cannot be delved into here – but it can hardly be denied that linguistic continuity is a powerful cultural support. It is not the only pillar, but it is obviously an important one. There are many bilinguals whose competence is more deep-seated and whose abilities go beyond commercial instrumentality. These are the more "typical" individuals one usually has in mind when considering the relationship between bilingualism and identity. And, if we are to think about this socio-psychological relationship, it may be useful to consider the manner in which bilingualism arises. Yet again we are confronted with a topic whose complexity can only be acknowledged in passing. Still, there are two broad divisions of relevance: the first comprises those bilinguals who have a kinship attachment to each group (detouring once more around a large and often vexed literature, we can accept either real or perceived attachments for our present purposes); the second is made up of people who have, in a more formal way, acquired another linguistic citizenship, as it were (there is a redolence, here, of the *integrative* motivation once much discussed in the literature).

The latter division involves that elite bilingualism best exemplified by members of the educated classes whose formal instruction would, historically, have been seen as incomplete without the acquisition of another language or two. Typically, then, elite bilingualism involves prestigious languages – although the term could reasonably be extended to cover the competence of those whose maternal variety is of lesser-used status, as well as of those lucky, or intelligent, or industrious enough to have achieved upward mobility through education. Elite bilingualism is usually discussed in comparison with *folk* bilingualism

– where the latter signifies a necessity-induced repertoire expansion – and, indeed, the distinction seems apt, particularly when one considers that, historically, the elite variety often had as much to do with social-status marking as it did with a thirst for knowledge and cultural boundary crossing. In earlier times, as we have seen, not to have known Latin or Greek or French in addition to one's vernacular would have been unthinkable for educated people – but often unthinkable, perhaps, in the same way that it would have been unthinkable not to have had servants. Among those fortunate elite bilinguals, of course, there were – and are – many driven by purer scholastic motives. But acknowledging this also means acknowledging that elite bilingualism need not rule out motives of necessity more usually associated with the folk variety. It is just that necessity itself becomes a little more rarefied. Your intellectual pursuits and desires may demand, for example, the acquisition of other languages and the acquaintance of other cultures.

It is not difficult to see that the life's work of a sensitive scholar could depend upon or, at least, produce – as an incidental result of more specific researches – an extended allegiance or sense of belonging. Indeed, this scenario also theoretically applies to those whose excursions across boundaries are motivated by nothing more than interest. After all, given a threshold of intelligence and sensitivity, the difference between the scholar and the amateur lies in formality of focus. The general point here is that we can ally ourselves, by more or less conscious effort, with another group – and that a formally cultivated bilingualism can act as the bridge here. And it is important, I think, to acknowledge the depth that can be attained by such effort. Boundaries are really crossed, cultural and linguistic sensitivities are really enlarged, and allegiances are both refined and broadened.

What of the other broad category, those bilinguals who have some real or understood blood attachment to more than one language community? Setting aside the technicalities associated with the onset and timing of bilingual acquisition, it is surely the case that the deeper the linguistic and cultural burrowing into another community, the greater the impact upon identity. This in turn suggests that those whose bilingual competence is nurtured early will, other things being equal, have a firmer foot in the two (or more) camps. It will usually be the case, of course, that one camp will have psychological and emotional primacy. But there are some cases where home itself is difficult to establish, at least in any simple unidimensional sense. There are some cases, that is, where bilingual or multilingual capacities, linked to their several cultural bases, develop so early and so deeply that a primary allegiance is hard to discover. There are generally two ways to consider the situations of those whose bilingualism begins at the parental knees. The first is simply that two or more base camps are home simultaneously; the second is that one primary home indeed exists, but it is constructed – in a manner unique to the individual – from materials taken from the several sources. Steiner (1992), mentioned in the opening paragraph, is by his own account maternally and perfectly trilingual. Further, he has suggested that such "primary" multilingualism is an integral state of affairs in itself. There has been virtually no research on the consequences for identity of multilingual tapestries so closely woven, but one imagines that there are subtleties here that go far beyond simple additive relationships. It is difficult to define and assess perfectly and fully balanced bilingualism, and even polyglots like Steiner might fall short under the most rigorous examination; nonetheless, more attention to deep-seated multiple fluencies is indicated.

As we move towards the bilingualism of more ordinary individuals, we move more obviously towards the idea of a unitary identity – woven from several strands, to be sure, but inevitably influenced by one language and culture more than by others. But, if we move from the Steiners (and Conrads, Nabokovs, Kunderas, Stoppards and all the rest) – whose literary power, and the ability to reflect in meaningful ways upon its multifaceted origin, are simply unavailable to most people – we must not imagine that we have moved away from enlarged identities *per se*. It is both the obligation and the fulfillment of intellectual life, after all, to express what less articulate souls may somehow feel or possess. When we consider that the language competences of most bilinguals are shallower than those of the Steiners of the world – broader, sometimes, but rarely as deep – and that neither the capacity nor the inclination to think much about identity is a widely distributed quantity, we realize again what important questions remain to be asked, what research – more psychological than linguistic – still needs to be undertaken. The intellectuals can look after themselves here: Steiner (1975) has written famously about the "extraterritoriality" of multilingual writers; Ilan Stavans argues that monolingualism is a form of oppression (see Kellman, 2000); others, from Goethe to Eliot, have argued over the ability – particularly the poet's ability – to be fully expressive beyond the *muttersprache*. We need reports from more mundane quarters, too.

As it is, we rely largely upon inference to support the contention that it is the identity components, the symbols of the tribe, that energize languages beyond their instrumental existences. One large and obvious example here is the powerful association between language and nationalism. Since the latter is, among other things, a pronounced and often mobilizing sense of groupness, it follows that any language component will be carefully delineated. And so, historically, it is. The language in which you do your shopping, and which – if you thought much about it – is also the variety in which your group's tradition is inscribed, can become a symbol of your oppressed state, a rallying-point, a banner under which to assemble the troops. Would people be so ready to sacrifice for something that was of purely mundane importance? We might regret that circumstances encourage us to put aside a familiar tool, and learn to use another – but we go to war over histories, not hammers.

The important associations of a particular language with a particular base camp are made clearer – and here we move from languages in general to languages in tandem – when we think about translation. This is an exercise driven by obvious necessity and, if language were not invested with emotion and association, its operation would be unremarkable. While employing them, we might applaud those whose expertise allows them the access denied the rest of us, but we would rarely be suspicious. And yet the old proverb says *traduttori, traditori*. We would hardly equate translation with treason unless we feared that (as Steiner has put it) "hoarded dreams, patents of life are being taken across the frontier" (1992, p. 244). And what are "patents of life," if not the psychological collections of past and present that are unique – or are felt to be unique, at any rate – to ourselves? An informal Whorfianism tells us that every language interprets and presents the world in a somewhat different way, that the unique wellsprings of group consciousness, traditions, beliefs, and values are intimately related to a given variety. So, translation may mean the revealing of deep matters to others, and cannot be taken lightly. The translator, the one whose multilingual facility permits the straddling of boundaries, is a necessary quisling. But necessity is not invariably associated with comfort, and not even their employers care very much for traitors.

Both contemporary observation and the historical record suggest that language and identity can be tightly intertwined. The particular importance of this, for bilingualism, arises from the division within the former. And this, in turn, leads to a final inferential context of special relevance. For monolingual majority-group speakers in their own "mainstream" settings, the instrumentality and the symbolism of language are not split and, for most such individuals, the language–identity linkage is not problematic – indeed, it is seldom considered. Minority-group speakers, however, rarely have this luxury; for them, matters of language and culture are often more immediate. Now, while it is true that no simple equation exists between bilingualism and minority-group membership, it is also true that many bilinguals are found in the ranks of "smaller" or threatened societies. The implication is that a link will often exist between bilingualism and a heightened awareness of, and concern for, identity. Specific linguistic manifestations include attempts at language maintenance or revival, the use of language in ethnic or nationalist struggles, efforts to sustain at least some domains in the face of external influence, and so on. A more general consequence is that the position and the responses of minority groups focus attention on the possibility – and, in many instances, the inevitability – of a split between the communicative and the symbolic functions of language: you may have to live and work in a new language, a medium that is not the carrier of your culture or the vehicle of your literature. In these sorts of settings we see, in fact, an extended value to the study of bilingualism and identity. First, the attitudes and actions of bilinguals in situations of risk and transition have a special poignancy and visibility – identities, like everything else, are thrown into sharper relief when threats are perceived. Second, these same attitudes and actions can galvanize others, and can remind a larger and often unreflective society that matters of language and identity are not relevant for "ethnics" and "minorities" alone.

The importance of bilingualism, then, is of both intrinsic and generalizable value. We need to know more about it because it is an issue in its own right

– with all its many ramifications and technicalities – and, as well, because it may illuminate wider patches of ground. The importance of being bilingual is, above all, social and psychological rather than linguistic. Beyond types, categories, methods, and processes is the essential animating tension of identity. Beyond utilitarian and unemotional instrumentality, the heart of bilingualism is belonging.

REFERENCES

Baetens Beardsmore, H. (1986). *Bilingualism: Basic Principles*. Clevedon, UK: Multilingual Matters.

Baker, C. (1988). *Key Issues in Bilingualism and Bilingual Education*. Clevedon, UK: Multilingual Matters.

Baker, C. and Jones, S. (1998). *Encyclopedia of Bilingualism and Bilingual Education*. Clevedon, UK: Multilingual Matters.

Birdwhistell, R. (1970). *Kinesics and Context*. Philadelphia: University of Pennyslvania Press.

Bloomfield, L. (1927). Literate and illiterate speech. *American Speech*, 2, 432–9.

Bloomfield, L. (1933). *Language*. New York: Holt.

Diebold, A. (1968). The consequences of early bilingualism in cognitive and personality information. In E. Norbeck, D. Price-Williams, and W. McCord (eds.) *The Study of Personality*, pp. 253–63. New York: Holt, Rinehart & Winston.

Edwards, J. (1985). *Language, Society and Identity*. Oxford: Blackwell.

Edwards, J. (1994). Ethnolinguistic pluralism and its discontents. *International Journal of the Sociology of Language*, 110, 5–85.

Edwards, J. (1995). *Multilingualism*. London: Penguin.

Firth, J. (1930/1970). *The Tongues of Men and Speech*. London: Oxford University Press.

Gardner, R. and Lambert, W. (1972). *Attitudes and Motivation in Second-Language Learning*. Rowley, MA: Newbury House.

Giles, H. and Coupland, N. (1991). *Language: Contexts and Consequences*. Milton Keynes: Open University Press.

Goodenough, F. (1926). Racial differences in the intelligence of school children. *Journal of Experimental Psychology*, 9, 388–97.

Grosjean, F. (1982). *Life With Two Languages*. Cambridge, MA: Harvard University Press.

Hamers, J. and Blanc, M. (2000). *Bilinguality and Bilingualism*. Cambridge: Cambridge University Press.

Haugen, Einar (1953). *The Norwegian Language in America*. Philadelphia: University of Pennsylvania Press.

Hazlitt, W. (1901). *Table-Talk*. London: Richards.

Jespersen, O. (1922). *Language*. London: Allen & Unwin.

Kellman, S. (2000). *The Translingual Imagination*. Lincoln: University of Nebraska Press.

Leopold, W. (1939–49). *Speech Development of a Bilingual Child* (4 vols.). Evanston, IL: Northwestern University Press.

Mackey, W. (1989). La genèse d'une typologie de la diglossie. *Revue québécoise de linguistique théorique et appliquée*, 8, 11–28.

McLaughlin, B. (1978). *Second-Language Acquisition in Childhood*. Hillsdale, NJ: Erlbaum.

Martin-Jones, M. and Romaine, S. (1985). Semilingualism: A half-baked theory of communicative competence. *Applied Linguistics*, 6, 105–17.

Milton, J. (1644/1958). *Prose Writings*. London: Dent.

Mitchell, R. and Myles, F. (1998). *Second-Language Learning Theories*. London: Arnold.

Myers-Scotton, C. (1992). *Motivations for Code-Switching*. Oxford: Oxford University Press.

Noels, K. and Clément, R. (1998). Language in education. In J. Edwards (ed.) *Language in Canada*, pp. 102–24. Cambridge, UK: Cambridge University Press.

Peal, E. and Lambert, W. (1962/1972). The relation of bilingualism to intelligence. *Psychological Monographs*, 76, 1–23. (Reprinted in R. Gardner and W. Lambert, *Attitudes and Motivation in Second-Language Learning*. Rowley, MA: Newbury House.)

Poplack, S. (1980). Sometimes I'll start a sentence in English *y terminó en español*. *Linguistics*, 18, 581–616.

Romaine, S. (1995). *Bilingualism*. Oxford: Blackwell.

Ronjat, J. (1913). *Le développement du langage observé chez un enfant bilingue*. Paris: Champion.

Spolsky, B. (1989). *Conditions for Second-Language Learning*. Oxford: Oxford University Press.

Steiner, G. (1975). *Extraterritorial*. Harmondsworth, Middlesex: Penguin.

Steiner, G. (1992). *After Babel*. Oxford: Oxford University Press.

Weinreich, U. (1953). *Languages in Contact*. The Hague: Mouton.

2 Studying Bilinguals: Methodological and Conceptual Issues[1]

FRANÇOIS GROSJEAN

2.1 Introduction

Most researchers who have studied both monolinguals and bilinguals would undoubtedly agree that working with bilinguals is a more difficult and challenging enterprise. Many reasons come to mind as to why this might be so: bilingualism has been studied less extensively than monolingualism, theoretical models in areas such as bilingual competence, language development and processing are less well developed, conceptual notions and definitions show a great deal of variability, specific methodological considerations have to be taken into account, and so on. One outcome of this situation is that research dealing with bilinguals has often produced conflicting results. In the field of experimental psycholinguistics, for example, some researchers have proposed that language processing is selective (e.g. Gerard and Scarborough, 1989; Scarborough, Gerard and Cortese, 1984) while others have suggested that it is non-selective (e.g. Altenberg and Cairns, 1983; Beauvillain and Grainger, 1987); some studies have shown evidence for a language-independent lexicon (e.g. Kolers, 1966; Schwanenflugel and Rey, 1986) while others have supported language-dependent lexicons (Taylor, 1971; Tulving and Colotla, 1970); some papers propose that lexical representation is best explained by a word association model or a concept mediation model (both proposed by Potter, So, von Eckhart and Feldman, 1984) while others put forward a revised hierarchical model (Kroll and Stewart, 1994) or a conceptual feature model (de Groot, 1992); some researchers have shown that code switches in continuous text take time to produce and perceive (e.g. Macnamara, 1967; Macnamara and Kushnir, 1971) while others have shown the opposite (Chan, Chau and Hoosain, 1983;

1   This chapter was originally published as "Studying bilinguals: methodological and conceptual issues," *Bilingualism: Language and Cognition*, 1(2), 131–49 (1998). It is reprinted here by permission of Cambridge University Press.

Wakefield, Bradley, Yom and Doughtie, 1975). In the field of bilingual language development, some studies have found evidence that children who acquire two languages simultaneously go through a fusion stage (e.g. Redlinger and Park, 1980; Volterra and Taeschner, 1978) while others have questioned this stage (Meisel, 1989; Paradis and Genesee, 1996), and in the field of neurolinguistics, such questions as hemispheric lateralization and localization of language in bilinguals have been disputed (for a critical review, see Zatorre, 1989) as has the inability of some bilingual aphasics to control the production of mixed language in a monolingual environment (e.g. compare Perecman, 1984, with Grosjean, 1985b). This list is not exhaustive and other controversial findings bear on such topics as variability in code-switching patterns in various communities, perceptual boundaries in bilingual listeners, the existence or not of an input or output switch in bilinguals, the lexical routes taken when bilinguals are translating from their weaker language to their stronger language, and so on.

In what follows, it will be suggested that some of the difficulties encountered by researchers, and some of the conflicting results they have obtained, could perhaps have been lessened, if not avoided, had close attention been paid to methodological and conceptual issues. Among the issues covered are participants, language mode, stimuli, tasks and models. Concerning participants, I will review the main defining characteristics of the bilingual individual (language history, language proficiency, language use, etc.), list the problems that are encountered in choosing participants, and show that some factors that are not always taken into account in studies clearly affect the results obtained. With regard to language mode, I will describe the language modes bilinguals find themselves in, and show how this impacts on such issues as code switching patterns in bilingual speech, the independence or interdependence of language representation, language fusion in very young bilingual children, mixing in aphasics, and so on. As concerns stimuli, I will question the comparability of stimuli within and across studies and will show how some of their characteristics need to be controlled for. As for tasks, I will examine the side effects that some of them induce, what it is they are tapping into and what aspects of the results are task specific. I will end with a discussion of the advantages but also the problems of models of bilingual representation and processing such as the monolingual outlook of some, their use of discrete classifications, the absence of certain components or levels, and the scarcity of global models. (For lack of space, such issues as data collection procedures in naturalistic environments, transcription and categorization of bilingual speech, as well as the problems associated with the statistical analysis of these kinds of data, will not be addressed here.)

Each issue will be dealt with in the following way: first it is explained; then the problems it causes are discussed and, finally, tentative solutions for future research are proposed. Several points need to be made. First, a lot of what follows has been stated in one way or another over the years by researchers in the field. I will try to do justice to their comments and suggestions but I will probably not be able to refer to everyone concerned for lack of space. If this chapter can act as an echo chamber for the field and create further discussion and action around these issues, it will have served its purpose. Second, even though the discussion of each issue will end with suggestions for solutions, it is clear that these are quite tentative and that it is the field as a whole that will solve the problems that have been raised (all researchers have to struggle with these issues and finding solutions is a common challenge). Finally, even though I will mainly consider experimental studies done with adult bilinguals, I will also cover work done with speakers recorded in more natural environments, children, as well as aphasic and demented patients. Thus, of the five issues that will be discussed, three (participants, language mode and models) concern all researchers working on the bilingual individual and two (stimuli and tasks) are primarily of interest to experimentalists.

2.2   Participants

2.2.1   *Issue*

Most researchers would probably agree that bilinguals, that is those people who use two (or more) languages (or dialects) in their everyday lives, can be characterized by a number of general features. First, they are usually influenced by what has been called the complementarity principle (Grosjean, 1997b), that is, the fact that they usually acquire and use their languages for different purposes, in different domains of life, with different people. Second, and as a direct consequence of this first characteristic, bilinguals are rarely equally fluent in all language skills in all their languages. Level of fluency depends in large part on the need and use of a language (and of a particular skill). Third, some bilinguals may still be in the process of acquiring a language (or language skill) whereas others have attained a certain level of stability. Fourth, the language repertoire of bilinguals may change over time: as the environment changes and the needs for particular language skills also change, so will their competence in these skills. Finally, bilinguals interact both with monolinguals and with other bilinguals and they have to adapt their language behavior accordingly (see the section on language mode).

Even though some research questions may be able to abstract away individual differences that exist among bilinguals (e.g. theoretical questions dealing with aspects of the bilingual's grammars), many others will not be able to do so. Among these differences we find:

- Language history and language relationship: Which languages (and language skills) were acquired, when and how? Was the cultural context the same or different? What was the pattern of language use? What is the linguistic relationship between the bilingual's languages?
- Language stability: Are one or several languages still being acquired? Is the bilingual in the process of restructuring (maybe even losing) a language

or language skill because of a change of linguistic environment? Has a certain language stability been reached?

- Function of languages: Which languages (and language skills) are used currently, in what context, for what purpose and to what extent?
- Language proficiency: What is the bilingual's proficiency in each of the four skills in each language?
- Language modes: How often and for how long is the bilingual in a monolingual mode (i.e. when only one language is active) and in a bilingual mode (i.e. when both languages are active)? When in a bilingual mode, how much code switching and borrowing is taking place?
- Biographical data: What is the bilingual's age, sex, socioeconomic and educational status, etc.?

Of course, many other factors can be added to this list but these are the ones that are most often mentioned in the bilingualism literature. (For additional discussion of types of bilinguals, see chapters 1, 3–5, 7–10, 22.)

2.2.2 *Problems*

Two main problems relate to the participants issue. The first is that some researchers, admittedly only a few, do not yet fully share the field's understanding of who bilinguals really are, and the second is that the factors that have been used to choose participants are often diverse, insufficient or controversial. As concerns the first problem, some people still feel that bilinguals have or should have equal and perfect fluency in each of their languages (what has been called the two monolinguals in one person viewpoint; Grosjean, 1985a; 1989); others still see language mixing as an anomaly, be it in children acquiring their languages simultaneously or successively, or in adult bilinguals; and others still fail to remember that many bilinguals are also bicultural and that their languages will reflect this dimension. The consequences are that erroneous claims may be made about a particular bilingual behavior, inappropriate comparisons may be made with monolinguals, and exceptional cases may be taken to apply to bilinguals in general. Three examples taken from the literature will illustrate this. First, in a study pertaining to spontaneous translation and language mixing in a polyglot aphasic, Perecman (1984) finds various types of language mixing at all levels of linguistic description in the patient under study. Basing herself on earlier work by Weinreich (1966), who unfortunately did not differentiate between interferences and code switching, she states that language mixing is inappropriate switching from one language to another and that these "errors" can also be found in normal polyglots. However, language mixing in the form of code switches and borrowings in bilingual interactions has long been known to be perfectly normal behavior among bilinguals interacting with one another (Poplack, 1980; Grosjean, 1982).

A second example concerns the so-called "semilingualism" of certain bilingual children. Supposedly these children possess less than native-like skills in both languages. They show quantitative deficiencies such as smaller vocabularies when compared to monolingual children, they deviate from monolingual norms, they mix their languages a lot, and so on (see Romaine, 1995, for a survey and a critical review of the question). What proponents of "semilingualism" need to ask themselves before classifying a child in this category are the following three questions: Is the child still in the process of becoming bilingual (either learning two languages simultaneously or learning a second language and most probably restructuring the first one)? Is the child mostly in a bilingual, mixed-language mode at home and is he or she just discovering the monolingual version of one or of the other language (in the school environment, for example)? Finally, has the child been meeting his or her communicative needs up to then (before entering school, for example)? Answers to these questions will probably show that the "semilingual" child is in the process of adjusting to such things as a new social context, a new language, new language skills and language varieties, new domains of use, etc. One should also remember that the complementarity principle will explain, as it does for the bilingual adult, why the child will never become two monolinguals in one person (Grosjean, 1997b).

A third example comes from the field of psycholinguistics. In a study on speech segmentation, Cutler, Mehler, Norris and Segui (1992) used participants who they reported were as bilingual in English and French as they could find: they were accepted as native speakers of French by other speakers of French and accepted as native speakers of English by other speakers of English, they used both languages on an everyday basis, and they had been exposed to both languages simultaneously from one year of age. The authors concluded that their participants had, to all intents and purposes, equally perfect command of the two languages. The participants were tested on English and French stimuli but, in the authors' words, the results produced "a puzzling picture" as they were not really comparable to those of either monolingual group. The authors decided therefore to subdivide the participants into subgroups (we will return to how they did this below) since, they report, the overall analysis left them with no obvious point of departure for interpretation of the bilingual results. The point to make here is that bilinguals are speaker–hearers in their own right who will often not give exactly the same kinds of results as monolinguals. One should be ready to accept this and maybe not always seek alternative solutions.

The second problem that relates to participants is that the factors that have been used to choose participants are often diverse, insufficient or controversial. On the first problem, diversity, one only needs to examine the "Participants" section of most papers to realize that they are chosen very differently from one study to the next. Some researchers put the stress on fluency and use various scales or tests to evaluate their bilinguals; others stress language use (which languages are used with whom and for what); still others put the emphasis on language stability (whether their participants are still learning a language or not) and in what context they learned their two (or more) languages, and some few give their participants actual screening tests (reading aloud, counting, understanding a passage, etc.) in addition to presenting biographical data. What is clear is that because the information is so diverse, and the tools of assessment so different, we probably have very different bilinguals in the studies published. Some participants are still acquiring their second language (using language learners is a phenomenon that is on the increase), some are strongly dominant in one language, some others appear to be equally fluent in the spoken but not in the written modality, and some few appear to be quite balanced and active bilinguals. This variability is found between groups and is present within groups also.

At times the information given about participants is simply insufficient to get an idea of who they are. For example, in an often cited study by Caramazza and Brones (1980) that deals with the bilingual lexicon, we are only told that the Spanish-English bilinguals were native speakers of Spanish who ranged in their self-ratings of bilingual fluency from good to excellent (mean rating of 5.5 on a seven-point scale). No explanation is given as to what "bilingual fluency" means and none of the factors listed above (language history, language stability, function of languages, etc.) are mentioned. This problem of insufficient information is especially present in studies that deal with aphasic and demented patients. Very little information is given about the patient after the onset of the pathology and even less about him or her prior to it. For example, Perecman (1984) simply gives us the age of the patient (H. B.), where he was born, the order of acquisition of his languages and the fact that English was the language he used primarily from age eighteen on. We know nothing about the patient's proficiency in the four language skills in each language prior to his aphasia, the function of his languages, the amount of language mixing he did with other bilinguals, etc. The same problem is also present in child language studies (see, for example, Redlinger and Park, 1980; Vihman, 1985) where little is said about the children's proficiency in each language (admittedly harder to assess), the function of their languages, the amount of time they spent using the languages with monolinguals and bilinguals, and so on (see de Houwer, 1990, for a critical review).

Finally, a few studies take into account controversial factors when choosing or dividing up their participants. One approach that comes to mind is the one used by Cutler et al. (1992) to break their participants down into two groups, a French-dominant and an English-dominant group. It should be recalled that these fluent and balanced bilinguals had been chosen because they had equally perfect command of their two languages. The authors tried out several approaches to divide them up and finally found one that produced interpretable data according to them: they asked participants to indicate which language they would choose to keep if they developed a serious disease and their life could only be saved by a brain operation which would have the unfortunate side effect of removing one of their languages. One could discuss at length whether such a question is appropriate (after all, isn't a person bilingual because he or she needs two or more languages in his or her everyday life?)

but what should be stressed here is that we have no evidence concerning the validity of such a question for assessing language dominance. As a consequence, we do not really know what kinds of participants fell into each of the two groups. One unfortunate outcome is that replicating the results with similar groups of participants will be very difficult. This is exactly what Kearns (1994) found when she used the same type of highly fluent participants whom she also broke down into subgroups using the same question. Whereas her "French-dominant" participants did not show the classic crossover interaction with French stimuli (what has since been called the French syllable effect), Cutler et al.'s "French-dominant" participants did show it.[2] In addition, and surprisingly, Kearns's "English-dominant" participants showed a syllable effect with French stimuli whereas Cutler et al.'s participants did not. In sum, what is at stake here is not dividing up participants into subgroups in order to better understand the results obtained but rather the approach that is used to do so.

The problem of participant selection and description would be less crucial if we did not have evidence that the defining factors listed above (i.e. language history, language stability, function of languages, etc.) are important. In fact, this evidence does exist; concerning the language history and language relationship factor, Segalowitz (1997) shows that there is considerable variability between participants in L2 learning and that this has an impact on language knowledge and language processing; Mayo, Florentine and Buus (1997) present data showing that perception in noise is affected by age of acquisition of the second language; de Groot (1995) suggests that recent use, but also disuse, of a language affects one's lexical representations, etc. As concerns language stability, Kroll and Curley (1988) and Chen and Leung (1989) both show that the processing paths followed during simple word translation is different in language learners and bilinguals who have attained a certain stability and fluency in their languages. As for language function, it is a well-known fact that certain domains of life of bilinguals are usually covered exclusively by one language (e.g. work, religion, sports, etc.) and that many bilinguals simply do not have translation equivalents in their other language for these domains especially if they did not acquire either language in school. Regarding language proficiency, Poplack (1980) shows that one obtains different code-switching patterns depending on how fluent speakers are in their two languages (see also the four switching styles described by Bentahila and Davies, 1991, that depend in part on proficiency); Dornic (1978) shows that various linguistic tasks given to bilinguals take more time and are harder to accomplish in their

---

2   According to Frauenfelder and Kearns (1997), a syllable effect is generally characterized as a significant interaction of target type and word type. Participants are faster or more accurate to detect targets which correspond exactly to the first syllable of a word than targets which correspond to more or less than the first syllable. The authors add that according to a more stringent criterion, to be able to infer a syllable effect there must be a significant crossover interaction between target type and word type.

non-dominant language; de Groot (1995) reports that the effect found with a bilingual Stroop test depends on the participants' language proficiency; Lanza (1992) demonstrates that the type of mixing young bilingual children do depends on their language dominance; Zatorre (1989) argues that less lateral cerebral asymmetry found in some studies for a bilingual's non-dominant language could be due to comprehension problems (and not laterality reasons); Hyltenstam (1991) finds a relationship in demented patients between proficiency in a language and the ability to keep it separate from the other language, and so on. As for the language mode factor (to which we will return in the next section), Genesee (1989) makes the point that more mixing takes place in children who hear both languages used interchangeably by the same interlocutors. Finally, it is a well-known fact that certain biographical variables such as sex and handedness play an important role in language laterality studies (Vaid and Hall, 1991; Zatorre, 1989).

2.2.3 Tentative solutions

Concerning the first problem, the lack of understanding of who bilinguals really are, all that can be said is that there are a sufficient number of general introductions to the field to help researchers not to fall into this trap (see, for example, Appel and Muysken, 1987; Baetens Beardsmore, 1986; Edwards, 1995; Grosjean, 1982; Romaine, 1995). As for the second problem, factors that have to be taken into account in choosing participants, one can always make bilingual assessment measures covariate variables during the analysis of results or allow participants to be their own control when the study permits it (which is not often the case). But the main solution will no doubt be for the field to agree on the kind of information that should be reported to describe the main types of bilinguals used (adult bilinguals, second language learners, bilingual children, polyglot aphasics or demented patients, etc.). For example, papers in experimental psycholinguistics could be expected (if not required) to have an appendix containing the following information on the group(s) used: biographical data (mean age, number of males and females, educational level of participants); language history (age participants started acquiring each skill in each language; manner of acquiring the languages, etc.); language stability (skills in the languages still being actively acquired); function of languages (which languages are used and in what contexts); proficiency (proficiency ratings in the four skills in the participants' languages); language mode (amount of time spent in the monolingual and in the bilingual mode). Each of these factors may have an impact on processing and representation and should therefore be assessed. Of course, much of the information can be collected via questionnaires by means of scales and can be reported numerically (central tendencies and dispersions). Other domains may choose to add or take out factors and one could even think of adding actual performance measures. Two points need to be made. First, it is important that if self-rating scales are used, differences in the way people rate themselves be controlled for. It appears to be the case that due to various factors, some individuals, and even some groups, have no problem using endpoints of scales, and sometimes overrate themselves, while others are more conservative in their self-evaluation. Anchoring scales properly will therefore be very important for comparison across groups. For example, one could use as a yardstick native speakers of a language. Second, it appears crucial to distinguish between language learners in an academic setting who do not usually interact socially with their two languages and who therefore are not really bilingual (at least yet), and people who are acquiring a language in a natural environment and who are using both languages on a regular basis. The former should be characterized as "language learners," and maybe not as "novice" or "non-fluent" bilinguals, at least until they start using both languages on a regular basis.

2.3   Language Mode

2.3.1   *Issue*

In their everyday lives, bilinguals find themselves in various language modes that correspond to points on a monolingual-bilingual mode continuum (Grosjean, 1985a, 1994, 1997a). A mode is a state of activation of the bilingual's languages and language-processing mechanisms. This state is controlled by such variables as who the bilingual is speaking or listening to, the situation, the topic, the purpose of the interaction, and so on. At one end of the continuum, bilinguals are in a totally monolingual language mode in that they are interacting only with (or listening only to) monolinguals of one – or the other – of the languages they know. One language is active and the other is deactivated. At the other end of the continuum, bilinguals find themselves in a bilingual language mode in that they are communicating with (or listening to) bilinguals who share their two (or more) languages and where language mixing may take place (i.e. code switching and borrowing). In this case, both languages are active but the one that is used as the main language of processing (the base or matrix language) is more active than the other. These are end points but bilinguals also find themselves at intermediary points depending on the factors mentioned above.

Figure 2.1 is a visual representation of the continuum. The languages (A and B) are represented by a square located in the top and bottom parts of the figure and their level of activation is depicted by the degree of darkness of the square: black for a highly active language and white for a deactivated language. Although the figure can be used to illustrate the level of activation of the two languages during both production and perception, I will concentrate on production first and then deal with perception.

Three hypothetical positions for the same bilingual are presented in the figure (broken lines numbered from 1 to 3). In all positions, the bilingual speaker is using language A as the main language of communication (the base language) and it is therefore the most active (black square). In position 1, the

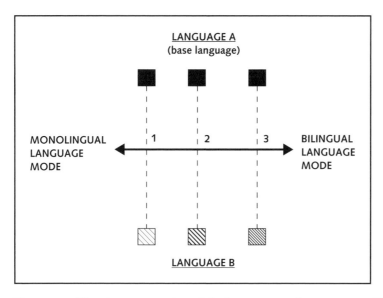

Figure 2.1 Visual representation of the language mode continuum. The bilingual's positions on the continuum are represented by the broken vertical lines and the level of language activation by the degree of darkness of the squares (black is active and white is inactive).

speaker is in a monolingual mode: language A is totally active whereas language B is deactivated (Green (1986) would even say that it is inhibited). This mode arises when the person being spoken to is monolingual (in this case, in language A), and/or the topic, the situation or the purpose of interaction require that only one language be spoken to the exclusion of the other(s). It is in this mode that interferences, that is, speaker-specific deviations from the language being spoken due to the influence of the other, deactivated language, are the most visible (they can also occur in the bilingual mode but they are difficult to separate from other forms of language mixing such as code switches and borrowings). In position 2, the speaker is in an intermediary mode. Language A is still the most active language (it is the language of communication) but language B is also partly activated. This kind of mode arises, for example, when a bilingual is speaking to another bilingual who does not wish to use the other language (in this case, language B) or when a bilingual is interacting with a person who has limited knowledge of the other language. Any number of combinations of interlocutor, topic, situation and purpose of interaction can lead to this intermediary position. In position 3, the speaker is at the bilingual end of the continuum. Both languages are active but language B is slightly less active than language A as it is not currently the language of communication. This is the kind of mode bilinguals find themselves in when they are interacting with other bilinguals who share their two (or more) languages and with whom they feel comfortable mixing languages. They usually first adopt a base language to use together (language A here, hence its greater level of activation) but the other language, often referred to as the guest language, is available in case it is needed in the form of code switches and borrowings. A code switch is a complete shift to the other language for a word, a phrase or a sentence whereas a borrowing is a word or short expression taken from the less activated language and is adapted morphosyntactically (and sometimes phonologically) into the base language. Borrowings can involve both the form and the content of a word (these are called nonce borrowings) or simply the content (called loan shifts). Of course, a change of topic or of situation may lead to a change of base language. In our example, language B would then become the most active (it would be represented by a black square) and language A would be slightly less active (the black square would contain white diagonal lines). It should be noted that bilinguals differ among themselves as to the extent they travel along the continuum; some rarely find themselves at the bilingual end whereas others rarely leave this end (for example, bilinguals who live in communities where mixed language is the norm). (For more on borrowing, see chapters 1, 6, and 28; for additional discussion of code mixing and code switching, see chapters 3, 4, 6, 10–14, 25, 26, 28, 29, and 31.)

Because figure 2.1 presents two variables (the base language on the vertical axis and the language mode on the horizontal axis), it is important that both are mentioned when describing the situation a bilingual is in. Thus, for example, a French-English bilingual speaking French to a French monolingual is in a "French monolingual mode." The same bilingual speaking English to an English monolingual is in an "English monolingual mode." If this person meets another French-English bilingual and they choose to speak French together and code switch into English from time to time, then both are in a "French bilingual mode." Of course, if for some reason the base language were to change (because of a change of topic, for example), then they would be in an "English bilingual mode," etc. It should be remembered that the base-language variable is usually independent of the language-mode variable. Hence, saying that a bilingual is in an English language mode leaves totally open whether the mode is monolingual or bilingual.

Everything that has been said about speakers also pertains to listeners or readers. For example, and whatever the base language, if listeners determine (consciously or not), or find out as they go along, that what they are listening to can contain elements from the other language, they will put themselves partly in a bilingual mode, that is, activate both their languages (with the base language being more strongly activated). This is also true of readers, whether they are reading a continuous text or looking at individual lexical items interspersed with items from the other language. Simply knowing that there is a possibility that elements from the other language will be presented (in an experiment, for example) will move the bilingual away from the monolingual endpoint of the continuum. Just one guest word in a stream of base language words can increase this displacement towards the bilingual endpoint.

Evidence for the language mode continuum concept is starting to be quite extensive. For example, in a production study, Grosjean (1997a) manipulated the language mode participants were in when retelling stories that contained code switches. He found that the three dependent measures (number of base language syllables, number of guest language syllables and number of disfluencies produced) were all affected by the language mode the speakers were in. In a developmental study, Lanza (1992) found that the same child mixed languages much more when in a bilingual context (represented by her father) than in a monolingual context (represented by her mother). As for evidence from an adult naturalistic setting, it can be found in a study by Treffers-Daller (1997) that is described below.

2.3.2 Problems

Because the mode a bilingual is in corresponds to a state of activation of the bilingual's languages and language-processing mechanisms, it has an impact both on language production (maintenance or change of the base language, amount and type of language mixing that takes place, etc.) as well as on language perception (speed of processing of a language, access to one or to both lexicons, role of the less activated language, etc.). It appears critical therefore that one control for the mode participants are in when they are being recorded or tested experimentally. This has not been the case very often as can be seen by examining examples from a number of different domains. In a first domain, research on interferences (also known by some as transfers; for a review see Odlin, 1989), the mode bilingual participants are in when interferences are observed has rarely been reported. Thus, what might appear on the surface as an interference could also be a code switch or a borrowing produced by the speaker who is aware that his or her interlocutor knows the other language (to some extent at least). For example, although "baving" (from the French verb "baver," to dribble), produced in an English monolingual mode, is probably the result of the deactivated language "intruding" onto the language being spoken (an interference, therefore), in a bilingual mode it is either an interference or, more probably, the normal access of a word in the less activated lexicon and its integration into the base language (a borrowing). It is now widely recognized that in Weinreich's (1966) classical work on bilingualism, the concept of interference covered the whole range of possible bilingual productions (true interferences in both the monolingual and the bilingual mode as well as code switches and borrowings in the bilingual mode). This is also clearly the case with the interferences discussed by Taeschner (1983) in her study of two bilingual children. In sum, to have any chance of identifying interferences correctly one needs to be sure that the data collected come from a truly monolingual mode. (See Grosjean, 1998, for further discussion of this.)

A second domain of study where it is important to know where bilinguals are positioned on the language mode continuum concerns natural interview situations. This information is not often given in the description of the interview setting and yet Treffers-Daller (1997), among others, has shown that depending on the speaker's position on the continuum (based on the interlocutor, the topic, the situation, etc.), different types of language behavior will be obtained. In her study, she placed the same speaker, a Turkish-German bilingual, in three different positions by changing the context and the interlocutors, and she found quite different code switching patterns. For example, when the participant was speaking to another bilingual he did not know well, his code switches were less numerous, more peripheral and contained various types of pauses (the latter have been called flagged switches). However, when the participant interacted with a very close bilingual friend, the code switches were more numerous, they were both intra- and intersentential and they were produced without hesitations or special highlighting (these have been termed fluent switches). Based on these results (also observed by Poplack (1981) in a different context), Treffers-Daller concludes that the language mode continuum concept may offer a new approach to study variable code switching patterns within and between communities (e.g. Bentahila and Davies, 1991; Poplack, 1985) because it can help predict the frequency and type of switching that takes place.

A third domain where the language mode needs to be controlled for is experimental psycholinguistics. Several domains of research are concerned but I will concentrate here on the language representation issue. This pertains to whether bilinguals have an integrated semantic memory for their two languages (also called a shared or a common store) or whether they have two separate, independent semantic systems. Several studies have addressed this question. For example, Schwanenflugel and Rey (1986) used a cross-language priming task in which Spanish-English bilinguals saw the prime word "body" and immediately afterwards had to say whether the following item, either "brazo" (arm) or "arm," was a word or not. The authors found that whether the prime and the following word (the target) were in the same or in different languages had no effect on the amount of priming, and they concluded that concepts in the bilingual individual are represented by a language-neutral conceptual system. In a more recent study, Fox (1996) used flanker words to prime targets and found an equal level of negative priming for monolingual and bilingual word pairs. She also concluded that mental representations of words in a bilingual's two languages are integrated within a shared representational system. Although both studies were carefully conducted and produced reliable data, it is difficult to tease apart in the results obtained what is due to the representational issue and what is caused by the language mode variable. The bilinguals were probably not in a monolingual mode when they were tested. Participants knew they were being tested as bilinguals and they saw words in the two languages. Because of this, they had probably activated both their languages (consciously or unconsciously) and were thus in a bilingual mode. (The same argument can be made about masked priming studies if considerable care is not taken to put participants in a monolingual mode.) If both languages are active, bilinguals are then in a position to react as quickly to targets in the language of the prime (or flanker word) as to targets in the other language (all other things being equal). No claim is being made here concerning the substantive issue of shared as opposed to separate semantic stores or, more concretely, which language(s) is / are primed in within- and between-language experimental studies. The only point being put forward is that the language mode variable can certainly influence, and maybe sometimes even account for, the results obtained. (The same is probably true of studies examining selective versus non-selective processing in bilinguals as will be seen later.)

Another domain of research which has not always controlled for language mode sufficiently concerns simultaneous language acquisition in bilingual children. It has been proposed by some researchers (Redlinger and Park, 1980; Volterra and Taeschner, 1978, among others) that children who acquire two languages simultaneously go through an early fusion stage in which the languages are in fact one system (one lexicon, one grammar, etc.). They then slowly differentiate their languages, first separating their lexicons and then their grammar. Evidence for this has come from the observation of language mixing in very young bilingual children and from the fact that there is a gradual reduction of mixing as the child grows older. This position has been criticized by a number of researchers (e.g. Genesee, 1989; Meisel, 1989, among others) and one of the points made each time (in addition to the fact that translation equivalents may not be known in the other language) is that the children were often in a bilingual mode, i.e. the caretakers were usually bilingual themselves and were probably overheard using both languages, separately or in a mixed form, by the children, if not actually mixing their languages with them (see Goodz, 1989). In addition, the context in which the recordings were made for the studies probably induced language mixing. If one examines the procedure followed by Redlinger and Park (1980) and Vihman (1985), for example, it is clear that the recording context was rarely (if ever) monolingual. In the first study, the investigator spoke the same languages as two of the bilingual children and, in addition, the children's parents appear to have been present, and in the second study, the person doing the taping was the mother of the child (Raivo) and she was herself bilingual. In both cases, therefore, the children were in a bilingual context which induced a bilingual mode and hence language mixing. It is interesting to note that Lanza (1992) shows clear differences in mixing behavior for the same child when interacting with two different adults, one who prefers a monolingual interaction and one who accepts language mixing. (See Genesee, Boivin and Nicoladis, 1996, for a similar type of study where the adult interlocutors were two monolinguals, one in each language, and one bilingual.)

A final domain in which language mode is a crucial variable is language pathology. For example, in the domain of bilingual aphasia, several case studies have been published of patients who appear to mix languages inappropriately. Perecman (1984), for instance, states that the language of her patient (H. B.) was strongly marked by language mixing. The author writes that H. B.

shifted from one language to another during the course of a single conversation and within the same utterance. However, we learn in the same paper that language mixing was particularly pronounced when the investigator (or investigators, it is unclear if there were one or two) shifted from one language to another within the same conversation or task, and we are actually given an extract from a dialogue in which the investigator switches languages! As was stated in a response to Perecman's paper (Grosjean, 1985b), it is interesting to speculate how much language switching H. B. would have produced had the investigator been totally monolingual. It seems only appropriate that a bilingual aphasic who is in a bilingual context, and who is faced with production problems, should use language mixing as a strategy to enhance communication (as would normal bilinguals). Another example comes from language production in bilinguals who suffer from dementia. Hyltenstam (1991), for instance, presents formally elicited data gathered from Finnish-Swedish patients recorded in what he states is a monolingual interaction, with a native speaker of each language, as well as in a bilingual interaction. The Swedish interactant was indeed monolingual but the Finnish one was also a speaker of Swedish, as we learn later in the paper. It is not surprising therefore to find in the Finnish productions language patterns ranging from monolingual Finnish utterances to mixed Finnish-Swedish utterances. It should be noted that mixing also took place in the Swedish monolingual interactions but these can clearly be attributed to the patients' dementia. One cannot say the same thing concerning mixing in the Finnish interactions.

   To conclude, failure to control for the bilingual mode factor produces at best highly variable data due to the fact that participants are probably situated at various points along the monolingual-bilingual continuum, and at worst ambiguous data given the confound between this factor and the variable under study.

2.3.3   *Tentative solutions*

Language mode is a variable to be studied independently (one will need to investigate ways of determining the bilingual's position on the continuum, among other things) but it is also a variable to control for. In what follows I will concentrate on this latter aspect as failure to control for language mode has important implications for the way in which findings are interpreted. Because of lack of space, I will only consider how bilinguals can be put either in a strict monolingual mode or in a totally bilingual mode. As concerns the monolingual mode, two inappropriate approaches have been tried. The first is to put the participants in a "language set" (also called erroneously by some a "language mode") by giving them instructions in one language, getting them to do preliminary tasks in that language, occasionally presenting reminders in that language, giving them monolingual stimuli, etc. What this does is to activate a particular base language (the variable depicted on the vertical axis in figure 2.1) but, as indicated earlier, it in no way guarantees a particular position on the monolingual-bilingual mode continuum (the variable on the horizontal axis).[3] The second approach, which has been used a lot with bilingual children, second-language learners and aphasic or demented patients, has been to hide the experimenter's or interviewer's bilingualism. This is a very dangerous strategy as subtle cues such as facial expression and body language can give away the interlocutor's comprehension of the other language. In addition, it will not prevent occasional slip-ups such as responding in the "wrong" language or showing in one's response that what has been said in that language has been understood.

The solution to the monolingual mode problem is unfortunately not quite as easy as one would like it to be. For interview situations, if the researcher is interested in observing how a bilingual can produce just one language (something a bilingual often has to do), then the interviewer must be completely monolingual in that language (and not feign to be). In addition, the situation must be monolingual and there must not be any other person present who knows the other language. For more experimental situations, the difficulty is how to prevent the bilingual from activating, to some extent at least, the other language. If interest is shown in the participant's bilingualism, if he or she is tested in a laboratory that works on bilingualism, if the experimenter is bilingual or if the participant sees or hears stimuli from both languages, then any one of these factors is sufficient to put the participant in a bilingual mode and hence activate the two languages, albeit to differing degrees. Such questions as the independence or interdependence of the bilingual's language systems or the "automatic" influence of one language on the other (selective versus non-selective processing) cannot be studied adequately if this is so, even if precautions such as masking primes are taken (e.g. Bijeljac-Babic, Biardeau and Grainger, 1997). One possibility that comes to mind appears to be to intermix bilingual participants in with monolingual participants in a monolingual experiment (for example, a study that is part of a course requirement) and once the experiment is done, and after the fact only, so as to avoid the Rosenthal effect, to go back into the list of participants and extract the bilinguals. In addition, care will have to be taken that the stimuli presented do not give the aim away. Of course, one can also make the bilingual mode an independent variable and use two or more intermediary levels of the continuum (e.g. Grosjean, 1997a) but there is no guarantee that the most monolingual level will

---

3 Interestingly, and with hindsight, the participants who were tested in Soares and Grosjean's (1984) study, "Bilinguals in a monolingual and a bilingual speech mode: The effect on lexical access," were never in a totally monolingual mode. This is because they knew the study dealt with bilingualism and they were accustomed to code-switch with one of the experimenters. Instructions in each of the two languages and practice sentences in these languages did help to establish the base language (or language set) in the "monolingual" parts of the study. This, added to the fact that the stimuli were in only one language, probably pushed the participants towards the monolingual endpoint of the continuum. Whether they actually reached that monolingual endpoint is doubtful however.

be monolingual enough to make claims about non-selective processing or interdependent representations.

As concerns the bilingual endpoint of the language mode continuum, care will have to be taken that the participants are totally comfortable producing, or listening to, mixed language. This can be done by having bilingual experimenters or interviewers who belong to the same bilingual community as the participants and, if possible, who know them well. They should interact with the participants in mixed language and the situation should be conducive to mixed language (no monolinguals present, a relaxed non-normative atmosphere, etc.).

2.4   Stimuli

2.4.1   *Issue*

Stimuli used in bilingual studies, such as syllables, words, phrases, and sentences, differ in a number of ways within and between languages. For example, words can differ on graphic form, frequency of graphic form, frequency and density of graphic form neighbors, phonetic form, frequency of phonetic form, frequency and density of phonetic form neighbors, syntactic categories and frequency of these categories, meanings of the various syntactic forms, concreteness–abstractness, animacy, etc. For instance, if one takes French "pays" (country) and English "pays," two homographs taken from a study conducted by Beauvillain and Grainger (1987), one notices that although both graphic forms are quite frequent, English "pays" probably has more graphic form neighbors than French "pays." As for the phonetic form, the two are quite different as English /peɪz/ contains a diphthong and a terminal consonant whereas French /pei/ has two vowels and no final consonant. The phonetic form frequency is probably quite similar in the two languages but the English form has more neighbors than the French form. As concerns syntactic categories, English "pays" is an inflected verb and a very rarely found noun in its plural form. As for French "pays," it is only a noun and it is far more frequent than the English noun. Moving on to meaning, the English verb form of "pays" has four meanings and the noun form has two meanings. The French noun "pays" has three meanings and they are all different from the English noun meanings. Finally, there is a certain diversity as to concreteness and animacy of the various French and English meanings. Thus, as can be seen from this apparently simple case, stimuli will differ considerably from one another.

2.4.2   *Problems*

Three problems surround stimuli in bilingual studies: differences in the stimuli used across studies, differences in stimuli used within studies, and factors that need to be controlled for in stimulus selection. As concerns differences in stimuli used across studies, what are often thought to be similar stimuli are unfortunately not always that similar. For example, much work has been done with cognates, defined by Crystal (1991) as linguistic forms that are historically derived from the same source as other language forms. When one compares how different researchers define the concept, one finds very large differences. For example, concerning the graphemic form of cognate pairs, de Groot (1995) says the members of the pair must be similar, Caramazza and Brones (1979) say they must be identical, Sánchez-Casas, Davis and García-Albea (1992) talk of a large degree of overlap, and Beauvillain and Grainger (1987) say they must be the same. As concerns meaning, the labels used respectively are: similar, same, large degree of overlap, similar. Finally, with respect to phonology, de Groot says they are similar, Caramazza and Brones state they are different (!), and the two other studies do not give any information on this factor. Because of the problem of understanding what is meant by "similar," "same," and "large degree of overlap," and based on the fact that words often have several meanings with different frequencies, among other things, it is no surprise that differences are found across studies (especially if the tasks used call on all the linguistic aspects of cognates, including phonology). In fact, Votaw (1992) shows the complexity of the issue in a six-cell table in which she presents three levels of shared form and three levels of shared meaning. Even though she does not refer to phonological form and to multi-meaning cognates, the table is useful to observe which cells are covered by the different studies that have used cognates. What has just been said about cognates also pertains to other "similar" stimuli across studies.

Concerning differences in stimuli within studies, the issue is one of variability. An example comes from the homographs used by Beauvillain and Grainger (1987). We have already seen that English "pays" and French "pays" share the noun category (although the English word is very much more frequent as a verb) and that as nouns the meanings are different in the two languages. When we compare this pair with another pair that was used in the same study, English "lame" and French "lame" (blade), we find another pattern of differences. English "lame" is an adjective and a verb (also a very rare noun) whereas French "lame" is only a noun. The cause of this variability is quite understandable (there are only a small set of homographs to choose from in the two languages), but if variability within a study is too large, it can reduce the effect that is sought or actually make it disappear.

As for factors that need to be controlled for during stimulus preparation, several have been mentioned in recent years, making studies which do not control for them somewhat problematic. For example, concreteness is an important variable both in neurolinguistics and psycholinguistics. In the former domain, Zatorre (1989) reports that concrete nouns are processed more bilaterally than abstract nouns. In psycholinguistics, de Groot (1992) has shown that concrete words are translated faster than abstract words. She also states that cognates and infrequent words are more likely to be translated by means of the word–word association route. Sholl (1995) has shown that animacy has clear effects on word translation: animate concepts are translated more rapidly then inanimate concepts. As for Grainger and Beauvillain (1987), they put forward the orthographical uniqueness of a word as a factor. In a lexical decision task, they showed a cost for language mixing in word lists; mixed lists produced longer reaction times than pure lists. The cost disappeared, however, when the words in each language were orthographically unique to that language. Finally, in research on spoken word recognition of code switches and borrowings, a number of factors have been found to play a role: phonotactics and language phonetics (Grosjean, 1988; Li, 1996), interlanguage neighbor proximity (Grosjean, 1988) and sentential context (Li, 1996). Not controlling for such factors (at least the more important ones) can lead to weak effects or no effects, to different or contradictory results across studies, and to the difficulty of replicating published studies.

2.4.3   *Tentative solutions*

At least four well-established solutions known to most researchers in psycholinguistics can be used to solve or lessen the stimuli problem. The first but also the hardest is to control for as many linguistic factors as possible when choosing stimuli. The second is to replicate the results using a new set of stimuli, and the third is to use stimuli as their own control when possible (although one must avoid repetition effects across conditions). Finally, the fourth, and probably the most appropriate for cross-study comparisons, is simply to reuse the stimuli that have appeared in an already published study so as to replicate the results or to show that some specific independent variable can modify the outcome of the experiment.

A long-term solution to the problem would be for the field to start putting together normalized stimuli for pairs of languages, such as lists of cognates and homographs controlled on a number of variables, word frequency counts and word association lists obtained from bilingual groups, etc. This kind of information already exists in monolingual research and it provides many advantages, not the least being that the experimenter can spend more time on other aspects of the study.

2.5   Tasks

2.5.1   *Issue*

Experimental tasks used to study bilinguals range from those used in production studies (reading lists or continuous text aloud, retelling stories, naming pictures under various conditions, giving word associations, etc.), to those in perception and comprehension studies (free recall, syllable identification and discrimination, Stroop tests, eye tracking, word priming, lexical decision, translation, etc.), all the way to those in hemispheric lateralization studies (dichotic listening, hemifield presentation, concurrent activity tasks, etc.).

2.5.2 *Problems*

Some problems are common to monolingual and bilingual research such as those that relate to strategic versus automatic processes involved in the task, the metalinguistic nature of the task, its processing locus, the allocation of attention during the task, etc. There is also much debate around such questions as the size of the SOA (stimulus onset asynchrony), the blocking or not of stimuli, the proportion of filler items, etc. I will concentrate however on three specific problems. The first concerns how certain tasks activate both the bilingual's languages and hence create a confound between the bilingual mode the participant is in and the variable under study. The second deals with the question of what certain tasks are tapping into, and the third concerns which aspects of the results depend on the task itself and which on the variable being studied.

As concerns the first problem, it is clear that such tasks as the bilingual Stroop test, bilingual word priming, bilingual association production, bilingual category matching, word translation, and so on, all activate both languages in the bilingual. In the bilingual Stroop test, one cannot perceive the word "red" written in green and respond "vert" (green in French) without having both languages activated. In the bilingual category matching task, one cannot see the name of a category in one language (e.g. "furniture") and then an instance of that category in another language (e.g. "silla," chair in Spanish), without activating both languages. This becomes a very real problem when the question being studied pertains to such issues as selective versus non-selective processing, the independence or the interdependence of the bilingual's language systems, or one versus two lexicons. If one is interested in these issues, one should be careful not to activate the other language by using a task that does just that. When this occurs, it becomes difficult to disentangle what is due to normal bilingual representation and processing, and what is due to the bilingual language mode induced by the task.

For example, Beauvillain and Grainger (1987) wanted to find evidence for the presence or absence of language-selective access of interlexical homographs during visual word perception. To do this, in the first experiment, they presented pairs of words in two conditions. In the related condition, the first word (the context word) was a homograph in English and French (e.g. "coin" which means corner in French) and it was followed by a test word (e.g. "money") that could be primed by its English meaning but not its French meaning. In the unrelated condition, the context word was only an English word (not a homograph) and the test word had no relationship to it. The participants were told that the first word would always be a French word and they were never informed of the presence of homographs (the pairs were mixed in with filler pairs). They were asked to do a lexical decision on the second item and were informed that it would be an English word or non-word. The authors hypothesized that selective access would be confirmed if the context word in the related condition ("coin") were found not to facilitate the test word ("money"); if there was facilitation, however, then non-selective access would be shown. The results showed that facilitation was in fact obtained, that is, that reaction times were faster in the related than in the unrelated condition. This was replicated in a second experiment and the authors concluded that lexical access in bilinguals is not initially language-selective. The problem, of course, is that despite the instructions which were meant to force participants to ignore the meaning of the homograph in the other language, the bilinguals needed their two languages to do the task, i.e. read the context word in French and then decide whether the second word was an English word or not. To do this, they had to put themselves in a bilingual language mode and activate both their lexicons. (It should be noted that as they were tested as bilinguals, they were probably already in a bilingual mode before the experiment even started.) It is no surprise therefore that a result indicating non-selective processing was obtained (the same comment can be made about another well-known study which examined the same question, that of Altenberg and Cairns, 1983). Recently, Dijkstra, van Jaarsveld and ten Brinke (1998) have shown that interlingual homographs may be recognized faster than, slower than, or as fast as monolingual control words depending on task requirements and language intermixing. Even though they did not account for their findings in terms of language mode, it is clear that both these variables affect the mode and hence the results obtained. What one can conclude from this is that, whenever possible, tasks or conditions that activate both languages should not be used to study issues such as selective versus non-selective processing, or the independence versus the interdependence of the bilingual's language systems. (For additional discussion of lexical processing, see chapters 7–9, and 28.)

The second problem that concerns tasks is that it is difficult to know what tasks are tapping into: language processing, language representation, or both? It is interesting to note that most monolingual studies that use priming tasks, lexical decision, or the Stroop test are basically aimed at understanding processing, i.e. how words are accessed in the lexicon. The findings that have come out of this research have mainly been used to build processing models and not representational models. However, probably because of an early interest in bilingual language representation, these same tasks are often used to study representation in bilinguals. Unless one espouses a view that equates processing with representation (something that becomes very difficult to defend at higher language levels), one should try to come to grips with this second, highly delicate, problem. Unfortunately, the field is hesitant about the issue and we find researchers using identical tasks to tap into representation and processing. For example, Beauvillain and Grainger (1987) used priming with lexical decision to get at the selective access issue, whereas Schwanenflugel and Rey (1986) used this same task (with minor procedural differences) to get at the representational issue. If a task is indeed reflecting representation, then we need to know which level of representation it is reflecting. For example, in lexical representation research, we have to know which of the following four levels is being tapped into: the lexeme level, the lemma level, the conceptual level or the encyclopedic level (which is outside the lexicon).

The third problem concerns which aspects of the results depend on the specific processing demands of the task itself and which on the variable being studied. Many conflicting results in the literature, in particular those concerning the one versus two lexicons issue, can be accounted for by this problem. It will be recalled that in the 1960s and 70s an extensive debate took place around whether bilinguals have one language-independent store or whether they have two language-dependent stores. Much evidence was collected for each hypothesis but little by little researchers started realizing that there was a confound between the tasks used to study the question and the question itself. Kolers and Gonzalez (1980) were among the first to state that two different issues had become confused in the study of bilingual memory, the issue of representation, its commonness across languages or its means dependency, and the way the issue is tested. They suggested that the bilingual's linguistic representations are independent or dependent to the degree that particular skills are utilized in a given context or task. Scarborough, Gerard and Cortese (1984) stated practically the same thing when they wrote that a bilingual might appear to have a separate or an integrated memory system depending upon how task demands control encoding or retrieval strategies (see also Durgunoglu and Roediger, 1987). Since then the focus has shifted away from the one versus two lexicons question to how the bilingual's lexical representation might be organized (see for example de Groot, 1992; Kroll and Stewart, 1994; Potter et al., 1984), but the problem of what the task is doing has not disappeared completely as can be seen in discussions by Fox (1996) and Kroll and de Groot (1997), among others. The task effect is also present in neurolinguistics where it has been shown that orthographic comparisons yield consistent left visual field advantages while phonological and syntactic judgments give right visual field advantages (Vaid, 1983, 1987; Zatorre, 1989).

2.5.3   *Tentative solutions*

The first problem mentioned, the fact that certain tasks activate both the bilingual's languages, is very difficult to solve if one is interested in issues such as selective processing or the independent nature of language representation in bilinguals. If that is the case, one must make sure that the task is not artefactually activating the bilingual's two languages and/or processing systems. The task must be monolingual in nature and must not involve processes such as cross-language priming, perception in one language and production in the other, etc. If the question of interest is different, such as whether distinct groups of bilinguals behave differently when perceiving or producing language, then the dual language activation nature of the task should simply be controlled for.

The other two problems (what it is that tasks are reflecting and which aspects of the results are task-specific) can be addressed by having a very good understanding of the tasks used in bilingualism research: what issues can be studied with them, which variables can be tested, what the dependent measures are, the advantages and problems of the tasks, and so on. It would be important one day to develop a guide to bilingual research paradigms along the lines of the one proposed by Grosjean and Frauenfelder (1997) for spoken word recognition paradigms. Finally, several paradigms can be used to obtain converging evidence, but one must keep in mind that similar effects, revealed by similar values of a dependent measure, may not always reflect similar processing routes and similar underlying representations.

2.6   Models

2.6.2   *Issue*

One of the main aims of research on bilingualism, whether descriptive, theoretical or experimental, is to develop models of how the bilingual's languages are acquired, represented, and processed. Since research started in the field, researchers have met this aim with proposals such as the coordinate, compound, subordinate distinction, the one versus two lexicons hypotheses, the switch or monitor proposals, various models of lexical representation, ventures to describe written and spoken word recognition in the bilingual, and the fused versus separate language development models of simultaneous language acquisition. By their very existence, these theoretical contributions have been a real asset to the field in that they attempt to step back from data to give a general description of a phenomenon. In addition, they allow other researchers to confirm or invalidate certain predictions and hence propose variants or new models. Their advantages therefore far outweigh the problems as will be seen below.

2.6.2   *Problems*

A first problem that is slowly disappearing is that some models still have a monolingual view of the bilingual individual. Instead of accepting that bilinguals are specific speaker-hearers who through the contact and interaction of two or more languages are distinct from monolinguals (Cook, 1992; Grosjean, 1985a), some researchers still use a monolingual yardstick to describe aspects of bilingual behavior and representation. Earlier work on the input and output switches (reviewed in Grosjean, 1982) was based in part on the notion that bilinguals had one language switched on, and the other switched off, but never the two switched on at the same time. And yet, it is now recognized that in a bilingual language mode, both languages are active and the bilingual can produce mixed language utterances at the same rate as monolingual utterances (and, of course, decode them at that rate). This monolingual viewpoint can still be found in certain areas where it is expected that "dominant" bilinguals will behave in large part like monolinguals in their dominant language. Of course, this might be the case in some instances but one should be ready to accept bilingual specificities when they appear.

A second problem concerns the discrete classifications that are found in the field. For example, Weinreich's (1966) coordinate, compound, subordinate trichotomy and Ervin and Osgood's (1954) coordinate, compound dichotomy, triggered much research. But contradictory findings and theoretical considerations have led various researchers to move away from these distinctions and hypothesize that within the very same bilingual, some words in the two lexicons will have a coordinate relationship, others a compound relationship and still others a subordinate relationship, especially if the languages were acquired in different cultural settings and at different times. Recent work on lexical representation in bilinguals appears to defend such a position (see various chapters in de Groot and Kroll, 1997). The same kind of discrete classification problem can be found in the long debate that has surrounded the number of lexicons the bilingual possesses (reviewed by Grosjean, 1982). Paradis's subset hypothesis (1981, 1986) was instrumental in helping researchers view this question in a different light and recent proposals of lexical organization such as the word association model and the concept mediation model (Potter et al., 1984), the revised hierarchical model (Kroll and Stewart, 1994), and the conceptual feature model (de Groot, 1992) have also contributed to an improved understanding of the organization of the bilingual's lexical representations. It should be noted though that some researchers still propose that distinct groups of bilinguals are best characterized by just one of these models (or variants of it). It is only recently that de Groot (1995), based on an extensive review of the literature, comes to the conclusion that *the* bilingual memory does not exist. The memory of every individual is likely to contain structures of various types and these structures will occur in different proportions across bilinguals. This will depend on factors such as level of proficiency of the languages known, the characteristics of the words, the strategy used to learn them, the context in which the languages are used, the age at which a language was acquired, and so on. In sum, one should be extremely wary of discrete classifications that do not do full justice to the representational and processing complexity found within the individual bilingual.

A third problem is that some models may not contain all the necessary components or levels needed. An example comes from recent work on lexical representation where most of the models proposed (see above) contain only two levels: a lexeme (or form) level and a conceptual (or meaning) level. And yet there is quite a bit of evidence in the literature that the lexicon contains a third level, the lemma level, that is situated between the lexeme and the conceptual level. Lemmas contain morphological and syntactic information about the word (Jescheniak and Levelt, 1994; Myers-Scotton and Jake, 1995). Just recently Kroll and de Groot (1997) have proposed to take this level into account and have presented the general outline of a distributed lexical/conceptual feature model of lexical representation in the bilingual that contains this level. At some point their model will probably have to take into account a fourth level (world knowledge) at least to explain the underlying operations that take place when participants are involved in paradigms that include nonlinguistic operations (such as picture naming). Paradis (1995) states, as he has done repeatedly, that one of the major problems in the field has been the failure to distinguish between the meaning of words and nonlinguistic representations. Based on research in neurolinguistics, he states that we must distinguish between the lexical meaning of words, which is a part of the speaker's linguistic competence, and conceptual representations which are outside of implicit linguistic competence. (Note here that he uses the expression "lexical meaning" for what corresponds to the conceptual level in most models and "conceptual representation" for nonlinguistic, world knowledge.) He adds that the conceptual system, where messages are elaborated before they are verbalized in the course of the encoding process, and where a mental representation is attained at the end of the decoding process, remains independent and isolable from the bilingual's language systems. It would be interesting to know whether tasks such as word repetition, word translation and picture naming, for example, require access to this nonlinguistic level. Some must (e.g. picture naming) whereas others may not have to.

A fourth problem is that the field has too few global models that give a general picture of bilingual competence, bilingual production and perception, as well as bilingual language acquisition. For example, until de Bot's (1992) attempt at adapting Levelt's (1989) 'speaking' model to the bilingual, there was no general overall view of how the bilingual speaker goes from a prelinguistic message to actual overt speech. Even though de Bot's model still needs to give a clear account of how language choice is conducted, how the language mode is chosen and the impact it has on processing, how code switches and borrowings are actually produced, how interferences occur, and so on, it has the very real quality of dealing with the complete production process and hence of encouraging debate in the field (e.g. de Bot and Schreuder, 1993; Poulisse, 1997; Poulisse and Bongaerts, 1994). This is true also of Green's (1986) resources model of production for normal and brain-damaged bilinguals. In the domain of perception and comprehension, no model as broad as Marslen-Wilson and Tyler's (1987) interactive model or Forster's (1979) modular model of language processing has been proposed. However, headway is being made by two computational models that are relatively broad: a bilingual model of visual word recognition (BIA) (Dijkstra and van Heuven, 1998; Grainger and Dijkstra, 1992), and a model of spoken word recognition in bilinguals (BIMOLA) (Grosjean, 1988; Léwy and Grosjean, in preparation).

A final problem, which is admittedly in partial contradiction with the previous one, is that models are not always detailed or explicit enough. For example, Myers-Scotton (1993) has proposed a model, the Matrix Language Frame (MLF) Model, which states that a number of hierarchies, hypotheses, and principles govern the structuring of sentences containing code switches.

The model has attracted the attention and the interest of linguists and psycholinguists but, like other important models, it has also raised many questions. For example, Bentahila (1995) states that it is not specific enough on such things as what constitutes a matrix language, the difference the model makes between an extensive embedded language (EL) island and a change of matrix language, what a system morpheme is, and so on. For Bentahila, models must be explicit and their validity depends on clear definitions which are externally verifiable without circularity.[4]

2.6.3 *Tentative solutions*

If there is one issue for which solutions can only be tentative, it is the one which deals with models. This is by far the most delicate and complex issue raised so far and what follows is only one researcher's viewpoint. First, and from what has been said, it is clear that any model will have to take into account the full complexity of the bilingual speaker–hearer as illustrated in the first two sections of this paper (participants and language mode). For example, bilinguals should not be viewed as two monolinguals in one person or be classified once and for all in discrete linguistic or psycholinguistic categories. Second, it is crucial that general models be proposed. The field is in dire need of general theories of the bilingual speaker–hearer as well as of models of bilingual language acquisition and processing. Third, models must contain all the necessary components or levels needed and they must be as explicit as possible so that they can be put to the test. Fourth, it is important that cross-fertilization takes place between the various domains of bilingualism. A theoretical linguistics of bilingualism that attempts to account for the bilingual's competence, a developmental psycholinguistics that models how children acquire their two languages simultaneously or successively, a neurolinguistics of bilingualism that accounts for normal and pathological brain behavior, and a psycholinguistics that models processing in bilinguals can each bring a lot to the other domains and receive a lot from them. Finally, bilingual models will have to use, after being adapted, the new approaches and the new theories that are constantly being developed in the various fields of cognitive science primarily to study monolinguals. In return, these fields will be enriched by what is learned about bilinguals. (For more on models and theories of the bilingual, see chapters 1, 3, and 7–9.)

2.7 Concluding remark

Dealing with the methodological and conceptual issues that have been presented in this chapter will take time, work and some inventiveness. The outcome,

---

4 It should be noted that Myers-Scotton (pc) reports that many issues raised by Bentahila are discussed and clarified in the "Afterword" of the 1997 paperback version of her book, *Duelling Languages* (Myers-Scotton, 1993).

however, will be clearer and less ambiguous results as well as models that take into account the full complexity of the bilingual individual.

ACKNOWLEDGMENTS

Some of the ideas expressed here were first proposed in a chapter that is part of de Groot and Kroll, 1997. Preparation of this paper was made possible in part by two grants from the Swiss National Science Foundation (1213-045375.95 and 3200-049106.96). The author would like to thank the paper's action editor, Judith Kroll, for her very helpful suggestions during the reviewing process. Special thanks go to the following for their comments on various aspects of the paper: Hugo Baetens Beardsmore, Dino Chincotta, Michael Clyne, Anne Cutler, Margaret Deuchar, David Green, Kees de Bot, Ton Dijkstra, James Flege, Karen Heck, Ruth Kearns, Nicolas Léwy, Ping Li, Brian MacWhinney, Lesley Milroy, Carol Myers-Scotton, Shana Poplack, Nanda Poulisse, Tove Skutnabb-Kangas, Jeanine Treffers-Daller, and Jyotsna Vaid. Additional thanks go to Marc Grosjean for stimulating discussions on experimental methodology and modeling, as well as Jacqueline Gremaud-Brandhorst, Lysiane Grosjean, Isabelle Racine, and Cornelia Tschichold for their careful reading of the manuscript.

REFERENCES

Altenberg, E. and Cairns, H. (1983). The effects of phonotactic constraints on lexical processing in bilingual and monolingual subjects. *Journal of Verbal Learning and Verbal Behavior*, 22, 174–88.

Appel, R. and Muysken, P. (1987). *Language Contact and Bilingualism.* London: Arnold.

Baetens Beardsmore, H. (1986). *Bilingualism: Basic Principles.* Clevedon: Multilingual Matters.

Beauvillain, C. and Grainger, J. (1987). Accessing interlexical homographs: Some limitations of a language-selective access. *Journal of Memory and Language*, 26, 658–72.

Bentahila, A. (1995). Review of C. Myers-Scotton: *Duelling Languages: Grammatical Structure in Codeswitching. Language*, 71, 135–40.

Bentahila, A. and Davies, E. (1991). Constraints on code-switching: A look beyond grammar. *Papers for the symposium on code-switching in bilingual studies: Theory, significance and perspectives*, pp. 369–404. Strasbourg: European Science Foundation.

Bijeljac-Babic, R., Biardeau, A., and Grainger, J. (1997). Masked orthographic priming in bilingual word recognition. *Memory and Cognition*, 25, 447–57.

Caramazza, A. and Brones, I. (1979). Lexical access in bilinguals. *Bulletin of the Psychonomic Society*, 13, 212–14.

Caramazza, A. and Brones, I. (1980). Semantic classification by bilinguals. *Canadian Journal of Psychology*, 34, 77–81.

Chan, M., Chau, H., and Hoosain, R. (1983). Input/output switch in bilingual code-switching. *Journal of Psycholinguistic Research*, 12, 407–16.

Chen, H.-C. and Leung, Y.-S. (1989). Patterns of lexical processing in a non-native language. *Journal of Experimental Psychology: Learning, Memory, and Cognition*, 15, 316–25.

Cook, V. (1992). Evidence for multicompetence. *Language Learning*, 42, 557–91.

Crystal, D. (1991). *A Dictionary of Linguistics and Phonetics*. Oxford: Blackwell.

Cutler, A., Mehler, J., Norris, D., and Segui, J. (1992). The monolingual nature of speech segmentation by bilinguals. *Cognitive Psychology*, 24, 381–410.

De Bot, K. (1992). A bilingual production model: Levelt's "speaking" model adapted. *Applied Linguistics*, 13, 1–24.

De Bot, K. and Schreuder, R. (1993). Word production and the bilingual lexicon. In R. Schreuder and B. Weltens (eds.), *The Bilingual Lexicon*, pp. 191–214. Amsterdam: John Benjamins.

De Groot, A. M. B. (1992). Bilingual lexical representation: A closer look at conceptual representations. In R. Frost and L. Katz (eds.), *Orthography, Phonology, Morphology and Meaning*, pp. 389–412. Amsterdam: Elsevier.

De Groot, A. M. B. (1995). Determinants of bilingual lexicosemantic organisation. *Computer Assisted Language Learning*, 8, 151–80.

De Groot, A. M. B. and Kroll, J. F. (eds.) (1997). *Tutorials in Bilingualism: Psycholinguistic Perspectives*. Mahwah, NJ: Lawrence Erlbaum Associates.

De Houwer, A. (1990). *The Acquisition of Two Languages from Birth: A Case Study*. Cambridge, UK: Cambridge University Press.

Dijkstra, A. and van Heuven, W. (1998). The BIA-model and bilingual word recognition. In J. Grainger and A.

Jacobs (eds.), *Localist Connectionist Approaches to Human Cognition*, pp. 189–225. Mahwah, NJ: Lawrence Erlbaum Associates.

Dijkstra, A., van Jaarsveld, H., and ten Brinke, S. (1998). Interlingual homograph recognition: Effects of task demands and language intermixing. *Bilingualism: Language and Cognition*, 1, 51–66.

Dornic, S. (1978). The bilingual's performance: Language dominance, stress and individual differences. In D. Gerver and H. Sinaiko (eds.), *Language Interpretation and Communication*, pp. 259–71. New York: Plenum.

Durgunoglu, A. and Roediger, H. (1987). Test differences in accessing bilingual memory. *Journal of Memory and Language*, 26, 377–91.

Edwards, J. (1995). *Multilingualism*. London: Routledge.

Ervin, S. and Osgood, C. (1954). Second language learning and bilingualism. *Journal of Abnormal and Social Psychology*, 49 (suppl.), 139–46.

Forster, K. (1979). Levels of processing and the structure of the language processor. In W. Cooper and E. Walker (eds.), *Sentence Processing*, pp. 27–85. Hillsdale, NJ: Lawrence Erlbaum Associates.

Fox, E. (1996). Cross-language priming from ignored words: Evidence for a common representational system in bilinguals. *Journal of Memory and Language*, 35, 353–70.

Frauenfelder, U. and Kearns, R. (1997). Sequence Monitoring. In F. Grosjean and U. Frauenfelder (eds.), *A Guide to Spoken Word Recognition Paradigms*, pp. 665–74. Hove, UK: Psychology Press.

Genesee, F. (1989). Early bilingual development: One language or two? *Journal of Child Language*, 16, 161–79.

Genesee, F., Boivin, I., and Nicoladis, E. (1996). Talking with strangers: A study of bilingual children's communicative competence. *Applied Psycholinguistics*, 17, 427–42.

Gerard, L. and Scarborough, D. (1989). Language-specific lexical access of homographs by bilinguals. *Journal of Experimental Psychology: Learning, Memory, and Cognition*, 15, 305–15.

Goodz, N. (1989). Parental language mixing in bilingual families. *Journal of Infant Mental Health*, 10, 25–44.

Grainger, J. and Beauvillain, C. (1987). Language blocking and lexical access in bilinguals. *Quarterly Journal of Experimental Psychology*, 39A, 295–319.

Grainger, J. and Dijkstra, T. (1992). On the representation and use of language information in bilinguals. In R. Harris (ed.), *Cognitive Processing in Bilinguals*, pp. 207–20. Amsterdam: Elsevier.

Green, D. (1986). Control, activation, and resource: A framework and a model for the control of speech in bilinguals. *Brain and Language*, 27, 210–23.

Grosjean, F. (1982). *Life with two languages: An introduction to bilingualism*. Cambridge, MA: Harvard University Press.

Grosjean, F. (1985a). The bilingual as a competent but specific speaker-hearer. *Journal of Multilingual and Multicultural Development*, 6, 467–77.

Grosjean, F. (1985b). Polyglot aphasics and language mixing: A comment on Perecman (1984). *Brain and Language*, 26, 349–55.

Grosjean, F. (1988). Exploring the recognition of guest words in bilingual speech. *Language and Cognitive Processes*, 3, 233–74.

Grosjean, F. (1989). Neurolinguists, beware! The bilingual is not two monolinguals in one person. *Brain and Language*, 36, 3–15.

Grosjean, F. (1994). Individual bilingualism. *The Encyclopedia of Language and Linguistics*, pp. 1656–60. Oxford: Pergamon Press.

Grosjean, F. (1997a). Processing mixed language: Issues, findings, and models. In A. M. B. de Groot and J. F. Kroll (eds.), *Tutorials in Bilingualism: Psycholinguistic Perspectives*, pp. 225–54. Mahwah, NJ: Lawrence Erlbaum Associates.

Grosjean, F. (1997b). The bilingual individual. *Interpreting: International Journal of Research and Practice in Interpreting*, 2 (1/2), 163–87.

Grosjean, F. (1998). Transfer and language mode. Commentary of N. Müller, Transfer in bilingual first language acquisition. *Bilingualism: Language and Cognition*, 1(3), 175–6.

Grosjean, F. and Frauenfelder, U. (eds.) (1997). *A Guide to Spoken Word Recognition Paradigms*. Hove, UK: Psychology Press.

Hyltenstam, K. (1991). Language mixing in Alzheimer's dementia. *Papers for the workshop on constraints, conditions and models*, pp. 221–58. Strasbourg: European Science Foundation.

Jescheniak, J. and Levelt, W. (1994). Word frequency effects in speech production: Retrieval of syntactic information and of phonological form. *Journal of Experimental Psychology: Learning, Memory, and Cognition*, 20, 824–43.

Kearns, R. (1994). *Prelexical speech processing by mono- and bilinguals*. Unpublished doctoral dissertation. Cambridge University, Cambridge.

Kolers, P. (1966). Reading and talking bilingually. *American Journal of Psychology*, 3, 357–76.

Kolers, P. and Gonzalez, E. (1980). Memory for words, synonyms, and translations. *Journal of Experimental Psychology: Human Learning and Memory*, 6, 53–65.

Kroll, J. F. and Curley, J. (1988). Lexical memory in novice bilinguals: The role of concepts in retrieving second language words. In M. Gruneberg, P. Morris and R. Sykes (eds.), *Practical*

Aspects of Memory, vol. 2, pp. 389–95. London: Wiley.

Kroll, J. F. and de Groot, A. M. B. (1997). Lexical and conceptual memory in the bilingual: Mapping form to meaning in two languages. In A. M. B. de Groot and J. F. Kroll (eds.), *Tutorials in Bilingualism: Psycholinguistic Perspectives*, pp. 169–99. Mahwah, NJ: Lawrence Erlbaum Associates.

Kroll, J. F. and Stewart, E. (1994). Category interference in translation and picture naming: Evidence for asymmetric connections between bilingual memory representations. *Journal of Memory and Language*, 33, 149–74.

Lanza, E. (1992). Can bilingual two-year-olds code-switch? *Journal of Child Language*, 19, 633–58.

Levelt, W. (1989). *Speaking: From intention to articulation*. Cambridge, MA: MIT Press.

Léwy, N. and Grosjean, F. (in preparation). The computerized version of BIMOLA: A bilingual model of lexical access.

Li, P. (1996). Spoken word recognition of code-switched words by Chinese-English bilinguals. *Journal of Memory and Language*, 35, 757–74.

Macnamara, J. (1967). The bilingual's linguistic performance: A psychological overview. *Journal of Social Issues*, 23, 59–77.

Macnamara, J. and Kushnir, S. (1971). Linguistic independence of bilinguals: The input switch. *Journal of Verbal Learning and Verbal Behavior*, 10, 480–7.

Marslen-Wilson, W. and Tyler, L. (1987). Against modularity. In J. Garfield (ed.), *Modularity in Knowledge Representation and Natural Language Understanding*, pp. 37–62. Cambridge, MA: MIT Press.

Mayo, L., Florentine, M., and Buus, S. (1997). Age of second-language acquisition and perception of speech in noise. *Journal of Speech, Language, and Hearing Research*, 40, 686–93.

Meisel, J. (1989). Early differentiation of languages in bilingual children. In K. Hyltenstam, and L. Obler (eds.), *Bilingualism Across the Lifespan: Aspects of Acquisition, Maturity and Loss*, pp. 13–40. Cambridge, UK: Cambridge University Press.

Myers-Scotton, C. (1993). *Duelling Languages: Grammatical Structure in Codeswitching*. Oxford: Clarendon Press.

Myers-Scotton, C., and Jake, J. (1995). Matching lemmas in a bilingual language competence and production model: Evidence from intrasentential codeswitching. *Linguistics*, 33, 981–1024.

Odlin, T. (1989). *Language Transfer: Cross-Linguistic Influence in Language Learning*. Cambridge, UK: Cambridge University Press.

Paradis, J. and Genesee, F. (1996). Syntactic acquisition in bilingual children: Autonomous or interdependent? *Studies in Second Language Acquisition*, 18, 1–25.

Paradis, M. (1981). Contributions of neurolinguistics to the theory of bilingualism. In R. Herbert (ed.), *Applications of Linguistic Theory in the Human Sciences*, pp. 180–211. Department of Linguistics, Michigan State University.

Paradis, M. (1986). Bilingualism. In *International Encyclopedia of Education*, pp. 489–93. Oxford: Pergamon Press.

Paradis, M. (1995). Introduction: The need for distinctions. In M. Paradis (ed.), *Aspects of Bilingual Aphasia*, pp. 1–9. Oxford: Pergamon Press.

Perecman, E. (1984). Spontaneous translation and language mixing in a polyglot aphasic. *Brain and Language*, 23, 43–63.

Poplack, S. (1980). Sometimes I'll start a sentence in Spanish Y TERMINO EN

ESPAÑOL: Towards a typology of code-switching. *Linguistics*, 18, 581–618.

Poplack, S. (1981). Syntactic structure and social function of code-switching. In R. Duran (ed.), *Latino discourse and communicative behavior*, pp. 169–84. Norwood, NJ: Ablex.

Poplack, S. (1985). Contrasting patterns of code-switching in two communities. In H. Warkentyne (ed.), *Methods V: Papers from the V International Conference on Methods in Dialectology*, pp. 363–86. Victoria, BC: University of Victoria Press.

Potter, M., So, K.-F., von Eckhardt, B., and Feldman, L. (1984). Lexical and conceptual representation in beginning and proficient bilinguals. *Journal of Verbal Learning and Verbal Behavior*, 23, 23–8.

Poulisse, N. (1997). Language production in bilinguals. In A. M. B. de Groot and J. F. Kroll (eds.), *Tutorials in Bilingualism: Psycholinguistic Perspectives*, pp. 201–24. Mahwah, NJ: Lawrence Erlbaum Associates.

Poulisse, N. and Bongaerts, T. (1994). First language use in second language production. *Applied Linguistics*, 15, 36–57.

Redlinger, W. and Park, T.-Z. (1980). Language mixing in young bilinguals. *Journal of Child Language*, 7, 337–52.

Romaine, S. (1995). *Bilingualism*. Oxford: Blackwell.

Sánchez-Casas, R., Davis, C., and García-Albea, J. (1992). Bilingual lexical processing: Exploring the cognate/non-cognate distinction. *European Journal of Cognitive Psychology*, 4, 293–310.

Scarborough, D., Gerard, L., and Cortese, C. (1984). Independence of lexical access in bilingual word recognition. *Journal of Verbal Learning and Verbal Behavior*, 23, 84–99.

Schwanenflugel, P. and Rey, M. (1986). Interlingual semantic facilitation: Evidence for a common representational system in the bilingual lexicon. *Journal of Memory and Language*, 25, 605–18.

Segalowitz, N. (1997). Individual differences in second language acquisition. In A. M. B. de Groot and J. F. Kroll (eds.) *Tutorials in Bilingualism: Psycholinguistic Perspectives*, pp. 85–112. Mahwah, NJ: Lawrence Erlbaum Associates.

Sholl, A. (1995). *Animacy effects in picture naming and bilingual translation: Perceptual and semantic contributions to concept mediation*. Unpublished doctoral dissertation, University of Massachusetts, Amherst.

Soares, C. and Grosjean, F. (1984). Bilinguals in a monolingual and a bilingual speech mode: The effect on lexical access. *Memory and Cognition*, 12, 380–6.

Taeschner, T. (1983). *The Sun is Feminine: A Study on Language Acquisition in Bilingual Children*. Berlin: Springer-Verlag.

Taylor, I. (1971). How are words from two languages organized in bilinguals' memory? *Canadian Journal of Psychology*, 25, 228–40.

Treffers-Daller, J. (1997). Variability in code-switching styles: Turkish-German code-switching patterns. In R. Jacobson (ed.), *Code-switching Worldwide*, pp. 177–97. Berlin: Mouton de Gruyter.

Tulving, E. and Colotla, V. (1970). Free recall of trilingual lists. *Cognitive Psychology*, 1, 86–98.

Vaid, J. (1983). Bilingualism and brain lateralization. In S. Segalowitz (ed.), *Language Functions and Brain Organization*, pp. 315–39. New York: Academic Press.

Vaid, J. (1987). Visual field asymmetries for rhyme and syntactic category judgments in monolinguals and fluent early and late bilinguals. *Brain and Language*, 30, 263–77.

Vaid, J. and Hall, D. (1991). Neuropsychological perspectives on bilingualism: Right, left and center. In A. Reynolds (ed.), *Bilingualism, Multiculturalism And Second Language Learning*, pp. 81–112. Hillsdale, NJ: Lawrence Erlbaum Associates.

Vihman, M. (1985). Language differentiation by the bilingual infant. *Journal of Child Language*, 12, 297–324.

Volterra, V. and Taeschner, R. (1978). The acquisition and development of language by bilingual children. *Journal of Child Language*, 5, 311–26.

Votaw, M. (1992). A functional view of bilingual lexicosemantic organization. In R. Harris (ed.), *Cognitive processing in bilinguals*, pp. 299–321. Amsterdam: Elsevier.

Wakefield, J., Bradley, P., Yom, B., and Doughtie, B. (1975). Language switching and constituent structure. *Language and Speech*, 18, 14–19.

Weinreich, U. (1966). *Language in Contact: Findings and Problems*. The Hague: Mouton.

Zatorre, R. (1989). On the representation of multiple languages in the brain: Old problems and new directions. *Brain and Language*, 36, 127–47.

Part II   Neurological and Psychological Aspects of Bilingualism

Introduction

WILLIAM C. RITCHIE

The chapters in Part II are dedicated to research on the bilingual individual – ranging from what the study of bilingual aphasia can tell us about the representation of the bilingual's two languages in the brain to the role of the bilingual's social identity in the choice of language in a given set of circumstances. Part II is divided into five sections, each devoted to an aspect of the bilingual's knowledge and use of his or her languages. The first section is concerned with the neurology of bilingualism, the second with the process of second language acquisition, and the third with the interaction of the bilingual's two languages. The fourth and fifth sections treat memory and general cognition in relation to bilingualism and the bilingual's capacity and motivation for switching from one of his or her languages to the other.

The single chapter in the first section (*Neurology*) is chapter 3 "Bilingual Aphasia," by Elizabeth Ijalba, Loraine Obler, and Shyamala Chengappa. After a historical overview and a discussion of methodological issues, the authors evaluate two models of bilingual brain functions – the Declarative/Procedural-Memory Model and the Inhibitory Control Model – with respect to the available evidence from the research literature on aphasia. The first model addresses the issue of which of the bilingual's two languages is more impaired, and in what ways, depending on the location of the lesion. The second model concerns the bilingual aphasic's ability (or inability) to switch language under appropriate circumstances.

The second section in part II, *Approaches to Bilingualism and Second Language Acquisition*, consists of two chapters that take quite different approaches to the study of language acquisition and use. In "The Bilingual Child" (chapter 4), Jürgen Meisel adopts a linguistic-theoretical position under which the object of inquiry is the learner's tacit or unconscious grammatical knowledge and its attainment whereas Yuko Butler and Kenji Hakuta (chapter 5, "Bilingualism and Second Language Acquisition") focus on the development of language proficiency – a more complex and variable notion. Both chapters address the issue of age and second language acquisition – each from its point of view

– and the consequences of age for ultimate degree of bilingualism in the individual. In addition, Meisel takes up the questions of whether bilingual children fare as well in each of their languages as monolinguals do in their one language, the outcome of both simultaneous and successive acquisition of two languages, and the problem of whether the child's two languages are autonomous from each other or interdependent. In addition to the age question, Butler and Hakuta provide a rich classification of bilinguals along a number of dimensions as well as a discussion of the interaction of the first and second languages and a review of work on socio-psychological factors in second language acquisition.

The third section of part II (*Bilingual Language Use: Knowledge, Comprehension, and Production*) treats of the interaction between the grammars of the two languages as well as the deployment of the grammar in speech comprehension and production in bilinguals. Pieter Muysken (chapter 6, "Two Linguistic Systems in Contact: Grammar, Phonology, and Lexicon") proposes that the structural influence between the two languages on one hand and the form of language alternation referred to as code switching or code mixing on the other differ only in that the latter involves the lexicon of the two languages and the former does not. He provides a thorough description of the conditions under which code mixing occurs in terms of a system of hierarchies of such conditions. Judith Kroll and Paola Dussias (chapter 7, "The Comprehension of Words and Sentences in Two Languages") review the research on bilingual comprehension, considering a number of current models of how the bilingual's two languages interact in utterance processing and how the available evidence bears on each. In Chapter 8, "Speech Production in Bilinguals", Albert Costa examines the research on the interaction of the bilingual's two languages in the production of speech, focusing in particular on lexical access and the question of whether or not the language not in use at the time of utterance plays a role in lexical selection.

Bilingualism: Memory, Cognition, and Emotion, the fourth section of part II, consists of two chapters. Chapter 9, "Bilingual Memory" by Roberto Heredia and Jeffrey Brown, reviews past attempts to model the memory of bilinguals including the distinction between compound and coordinate bilinguals, which predicts shared and separate memory systems, respectively, as well as more recent models such as the Revised Hierarchy Model and the Distributed Model. Heredia and Brown also touch on the character of autobiographical memory in bilinguals, a topic taken up in more detail in chapter 10, "Bilingualism: Language, Emotion, and Mental Health"), by Jeanette Altarriba and Rachel Morier. Altarriba and Morier examine issues of bilingualism and biculturalism in psychotherapy – how the bilingual's memories of past experiences may be more accessible in one language than in the other and the effect this may have on the success or failure of psychotherapy for bilinguals.

The final section in part II (*The Bilingual's Repertoire: Code Mixing, Code Switching, and Speech Accommodation*) is concerned with one of the more extensively researched areas in the study of bilinguals. It includes four chapters, the first of which, Jeff MacSwan's chapter 11, "Code Switching and Grammatical Theory", reviews the previous attempts to characterize restrictions on intrasentential language alternation (code switching) in terms of independently motivated theories of grammatical structure and sentence production. He then provides explanations within the Minimalist Program for several constraints on switching that have been proposed in the descriptive research literature. Gerald Berent (chapter 12, "Sign-language–Spoken-language Bilingualism: Code Mixing and Mode Mixing by ASL-English Bilinguals") examines the phenomenon of code mixing in the special case of cross-modal bilingualism and argues for the existence of a condition on such mixing that has been proposed independently for code mixing involving spoken languages.

Two chapters round out this section on code mixing and switching by looking at the social and psychological circumstances under which switching and mixing occur. Chapter 13, by William Ritchie and Tej Bhatia ("Socio-Psychological Factors in Language Mixing"), addresses the issues of whether or not language mixing is random, what motivates bilinguals to mix (assuming that mixing is not random), what the social evaluation of mixing is, and, lastly, how bilinguals themselves view mixing. Finally, Itesh Sachdev and Howard Giles (chapter 14, "Bilingual Accommodation") offer an account of mixing and switching within the Communication Accommodation Theory, an account of language choice that has been developed over a number of years within Social Identity Theory.

Neurology

3 Bilingual Aphasia

ELIZABETH IJALBA, LORAINE K. OBLER, AND SHYAMALA CHENGAPPA

3.1 Introduction

The study of aphasia – the set of language disorders that arise after brain damage – provides us with a window to understand brain organization for language functions. The study of aphasia in bilinguals or polyglots permits us to answer not only questions about bilingual aphasia (such as: Can one language evidence aphasia and another show none? Which language returns first following a lesion?), but also questions about bilingualism *per se* such as: Does our brain provide separate stores for each language we know? How are we able to switch between languages and use them appropriately and without interference?

In this chapter we describe the evolution of discussion of language break-down in polyglots that has taken place across the century-and-a-quarter of modern aphasiology. We discuss the questions that have been addressed and explore two models that focus on different but complementary aspects: one model emphasizes different memory systems that influence language processing in bilinguals, and the other model focuses on executive control of language functions. This structure permits us to discuss the literature on clinical cases of bilingual aphasics, focusing on the phenomenology of disorders seen in them, including language switching, translation disorders, and order of language return during recovery from aphasia.

3.2 Issues in the Case Literature on Bilingual or Polyglot Aphasias

The late nineteenth century marked a period of intense debate focused on answering questions of language representation in the brain. Initial findings were the result of clinical observation and pathological correlates discovered

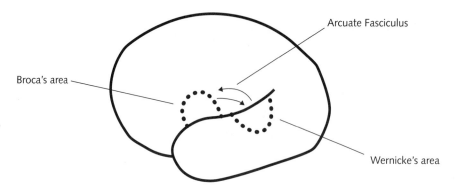

Figure 3.1 Broca's area involved in speech production and Wernicke's area involved in the comprehension of speech. The two areas are connected by the arcuate fasciculus.

in the brain during autopsy. Paul Broca (1865/1977) is credited with labeling the inferior part of the third frontal convolution in the left hemisphere as the "motor center" for spoken words (see figure 3.1). He based his conclusions on the fact that his patient, Leborgne, was unable to speak, except to say the single syllable "tan," and that an autopsy of Leborgne and then of six additional similar patients later revealed this part of the brain to be damaged. A few years later, Carl Wernicke (1874) complemented Broca's findings by revealing the posterior part of the first temporal gyrus as the area responsible for the "sensory image of words" or comprehension for language (see figure 3.1). Wernicke also created the first model drawn right onto an outline of the brain, delineating a "motor speech area" and a "sensory speech area," connected by a bundle of fibers transmitting information between the two centers. This simple model explained many of the known aphasic symptoms of the time, including the difficulties with speaking concomitant with preserved ability to understand spoken language, the preserved ability to speak concomitant with difficulties with understanding language, and the preserved ability to both speak and understand yet failure to repeat back a word or phrase.

Because these initial observations on brain function took place in Europe, where most people spoke more than one language or dialect, the debates on brain organization of language were soon enriched with the question of how multiple languages are represented in the brain. This question arose naturally as a result of counterintuitive symptoms demonstrated during recovery from aphasia by some bilingual and polyglot speakers. Neurologists began to report unusual recovery patterns in patients who had spoken two or more languages before their aphasia but showed differential recovery patterns for each language after an aphasia-producing incident. The earliest known theory from this period was that each language has separate brain representation or "language centers" and that recovery is determined in accordance with which language centers were disrupted, explaining why some languages of the polyglot were regained and others were not because of damage to their specific representation in the brain (Scoresby-Jackson, 1867). While not useful in its strongest form, a modified version of this theory has returned. Thanks to modern imaging techniques, such a theory of bilingual representation for speech/language production in normals has regained some plausibility, in modified form, in the past decade (Abutalebi, Cappa, and Perani, 2001; Illes et al., 1999; Kim et al., 1997; Klein et al., 2001; Tan et al., 2001).

Albert Pitres (1895/1953), a neurologist who was Dean of the Faculty of Medicine at Bordeaux, was first to propose a view that persists to this time. He reviewed the clinical studies of bilingual aphasics published by his contemporaries and rejected the notion of separate language representation in the brain for each language by pointing out that each language would need at least "four distinct cerebral centres: two sensory centres, for auditory and visual images, and two motor centres, for graphic and phonetic motor images" (p. 45), making it very unlikely that lesions would be distributed in such coordinated fashion. Pitres's strategy, like that of other aphasiologists at the end of the nineteenth century, was to replace the neuro-anatomical perspective with analysis of the functional quality of the disorder. He pointed out that during recovery from aphasia, patients initially go through a stage of "inertia" during which they fail to understand or use all known languages, and that this is due to disruption but not total destruction of their language centers. Gradual return of understanding the most familiar language follows, continued in turn by regaining the ability to speak the most familiar language. This same pattern is repeated for any or all of the other languages that the patient spoke prior to onset of the lesion, for each, language comprehension returns first followed by production.

Mieczyslaw Minkowski (1927/1983), a Swiss neurologist, supported Pitres's rejection of separate neuro-anatomical centers for each language in the bilingual's brain. He proposed that within a common area, active elements from known languages combine and interact at a linguistic level. Minkowski also pointed out that systems should not be viewed as destroyed but as "weakened"; therefore, aphasic symptoms are a reflection of the language system functioning at a reduced level of activation. This position had been strongly advocated by pioneers such as Hughlings Jackson (1879) and Sigmund Freud (1891/1953) in the study of monolingual aphasia. Indeed, the idea that later-learned languages are superimposed on the first-learned language, and that destruction through lesion results in greater impairment of the later-learned language, was a position advocated by Hughlings Jackson (1879) and reaffirmed by Freud (1891/1953, pp. 60, 61). The degree to which a later-learned language is used and the age of its acquisition were also considered by Freud as important factors in determining which language is preserved following a lesion.

If all the languages of a multilingual speaker have a common or shared neural representation, aphasic symptoms should be evident across languages and language recovery should also be similar among languages. However, if neural representation for each language is separate, then each language known by the speaker may show different levels of impairment and the order of return may also vary among languages. Pitres's report opened the gates to a century of research on bilingual aphasia aimed at addressing which language is first to return subsequent to a cerebral lesion. Albert and Obler (1978) pointed out that in most cases of bilingual aphasia, the two (or more) languages recover proportionally to their pre-morbid proficiency. In those instances where differential recovery was evidenced, however, the language most frequently used at the time of the patient's lesion was the most likely to be first recovered (Albert and Obler, 1978). This pattern of recovery follows the rule of Pitres rather than that of Ribot whose general theory of memory predicted that the first-learned language should return first.

Paradis (1977) pointed out that predicting recovery in the individual polyglot speaker is still not easy. He created a taxonomy of patterns of recovery influencing degree of impairment and language return in polyglots who do show differential (each language may show different impairment and recovery at the same or different rate): parallel (languages may show similar impairment and rate of recovery); antagonistic (there is regression in one language but progress in another); successive (one language is restored first followed only then by progress in the other language); selective (one or more of the languages previously known remains selectively impaired); and mixed (the speaker combines all languages to communicate). Individual cases have been reported of each of these types of recovery, with the first two being by far the most frequent.

In addition to the reports about recovery from aphasia, to which we return in section 3.4, two other issues have been discussed in a set of papers on bilingual aphasia over the past half-century. One is the question of whether crossed aphasia (lesion to the right hemisphere causing loss of language) occurs with greater frequency among bilinguals and polyglots, and the second is what we can learn from patterns of generalization across languages of aphasia therapy done in one of the languages of the bilingual.

As to crossed aphasia, it was Gloning and Gloning (1965) who raised this question, and a small series of studies since their report on four patients has argued both for and against increased incidence of crossed aphasia in bilinguals or polyglots. The question is of interest because greater incidence of crossed aphasia in bilinguals than in monolinguals would be reflective of greater right-hemisphere participation in language processing among bilinguals. At this time, however, we conclude that no convincing, methodologically sound study has supported increased incidence of crossed aphasia in bilinguals.

The small literature on therapy-aided recovery from aphasia includes articles by Fredman (1975), whose participants were speakers of many languages who were given therapy in Hebrew. Fredman reported generalization across to other languages, based on aphasics' family-members' reports. Additional literature has suggested that generalization is more likely to occur for comprehension than for production (e.g. Watamori and Sasanuma, 1978, for Japanese-English bilinguals). Faroqi and Chengappa (1998), for example, investigated trace deletion hypothesis (Grodzinsky 1986, 1995) and its implications for intervention in a multilingual agrammatic aphasic patient with knowledge of Kannada, Hindi, English and Telugu. They found that disruption of traces in D-structure representations was a reasonable explanation for the deficits in agrammatic aphasics. Generalization of the trained concepts was facilitated only when the patient was a compound bilingual and the languages were cognates (Kannada and Telugu) and when both the languages were used to an equal extent in the patient's pre-morbid environment (Hindi and English). Cross-language generalization was better for comprehension than for production. This suggests that the perceptual system of bilinguals is unified whereas production is dual. Parallel recovery was evidenced with respect to Kannada and Telugu and differential recovery for English and Hindi, which was explained on the basis of differences in language structure and of pre-morbid language use and proficiency.

Even more specific studies have been done on groups of bilingual aphasics. Bose and Chengappa (2000), for example, investigated naming deficits in three Kannada-English bilingual aphasics for three different naming tasks and compared their performance with that of age- and gender-matched controls. Parallel deficits were observed in Kannada and English for aphasics except for results on confrontation naming where differential impairment was observed. There was no statistically significant difference between L1 and L2 performance. As to comprehension disturbances, Sreedevi (2000) studied them in Tamil-English bilingual aphasics for whom Tamil was their mother tongue and English their second language. Their performance on the Revised Token Test did not reveal any significant difference between languages in normal subjects, and aphasics performed poorly on all subtests compared to normals. As expected, among different types of aphasics, anomics had better comprehension in both languages, followed by Broca's, Wernicke's and global aphasics. In sum, the recovery pattern was differential, with no consistent pattern for both naming and comprehension of better L1 or L2.

In the twentieth century, certain psychological notions contributed to our understanding of brain organization for bilingualism. Age of acquisition for each language, for example, has also been found to influence hemispheric representation, with earlier-acquired languages being more left-lateralized and later-acquired languages being more bilaterally represented (Albert and Obler, 1978; Neville et al., 1997; Vaid and Hall, 1991; Vaid and Hull, 2002). However, age of acquisition, to the extent the data were available, was not statistically linked to the patterns of recovery from aphasia (Albert and Obler, 1978).

Language models that differentiate how bilinguals acquire a first and a second language provided an early bridge between language function and neural correlates. Weinreich (1953) suggested that manner of acquisition of a second or later language would influence the functional organization of the two languages of the bilinguals. He posited that there are coordinate bilinguals, who learned different languages at the same time but in separate environments, and compound bilinguals, who learned different languages within the same context and used them concurrently, as well as sub-coordinate bilinguals who interpret words of the weaker language through words in the stronger language. Weinreich posited separate lexical stores for coordinate bilinguals, as the languages are learned in different contexts. Compound bilinguals were described as having a single lexical store common to both languages, reflecting that the languages are interdependent. Sub-coordinate bilinguals have primary representation in their native language and an additional lexical store for the other language that is dependent on the primary language. Therefore, words in the second language have to be interpreted through words in the first language. Evidence supporting this model of functional representation of bilinguals' language was found by Lambert and Fillenbaum (1959), who pointed out that coordinate bilingual aphasics tended to show damage that was more localized with respect to each language, while the disturbance in compound bilinguals was more generalized across both languages (see Romaine, 1995, and Appel and Muysken, 1997 for reviews of early literature in bilingualism). (For additional discussion of the distinction among compound, coordinate, and sub-coordinate bilinguals, see chapters 7 and 9; for more on lexical processing, see chapters 7, 8, 9, and 28.)

Cross-linguistic research has also shown that characteristics of each language may influence the way in which language is represented in the brain. Most of this work has been done on differing orthographies, rather than on structural differences in languages *per se* (see Obler, 1983). Reading and writing of ideographic scripts, one can conclude, may include more occipital areas and right-hemisphere involvement than that of alphabetic scripts more associated with temporal areas in the left hemisphere (Tan et al., 2001; Vaid and Genesee, 1980).

A body of research on non-aphasic bilinguals, however, has demonstrated the influence of differing linguistic patterns across a bilingual's two languages in influencing the performance in those languages (e.g. Bates et al., 1984). Some of those findings have been extended to the bilingual-aphasia population. Vaid and Chengappa (1988), for example, demonstrated that bilingual aphasic speakers of Kannada and English showed the same patterns of preferring animacy cues over word-order cues in comprehending ambiguous phrases, as did non-aphasic control bilinguals.

3.3   Methodological Concerns in the Bilingual Aphasia Case Literature

We must note at this point that much of the bilingual-aphasia case literature mentioned up to this point has been flawed in that methodological differences arise at all levels to further complicate matters. Many studies report the site of lesion whereas other investigations have a different focus and primarily provide clinical profiles based on symptoms. Age of acquisition in each language plays an important role when analyzing language breakdown in patients, but it is not always mentioned, nor is it easy to determine (e.g. when one has studied a language ill-taught in school and then migrates to the country in which it is spoken, which age is to be used?). It is similarly unclear which age or age-interval is the crucial one distinguishing early from late acquisition. Lenneberg (1967) would have nominated puberty, Johnson and Newport (1989) age four, and Fabbro (2001) age seven. Moreover, earlier- and later-acquired languages may be subserved by different processing mechanisms with correspondingly different neural correlates (Neville et al., 1997). Paradis (1994), for example, argued that languages learned at different times result in different types of knowledge: Those learned earlier involve implicit knowledge whereas later-acquired languages involve an explicit type of knowledge.

Additionally, attained language proficiency and language exposure as opposed to age of acquisition have been identified by many researchers as more determinant of cerebral representation in the languages of adult bilingual and polyglot speakers (Abutalebi, Cappa, and Perani, 2001; Illes et al., 1999; Perani et al., 1998). Increased language proficiency is associated with the activation of common neural networks within the language areas of bilingual and polyglot speakers. In addition to these variables, the contextual demands and actual use patterns for each language and the speaker's attitudes toward each language tend to be omitted in studies of bilingual aphasia.

Much of the early literature on aphasia relies on clinical case studies of one aphasic or a small group of aphasics. Current research, by contrast, more frequently looks at group data. Differences in design and methodology distinguish these studies. We can find experimental vs. clinical methods, differences in the type of stimuli and variables measured, variety in diagnostic instrumentation and interpretation, and differences in the time at which patients are evaluated: (i.e. at the acute stage post-lesion and onset of symptoms vs. a later stage). Even the selection of participants in studies varies in factors such as age, gender, and handedness that are not necessarily reported. For a comprehensive review of differences in methodology and the problems that this lack of uniformity presents in interpreting and applying research findings, see Vaid and Hull, 2002 and, concerning neurolinguistic studies of bilingualism more generally, Obler et al., 1982.

Summarizing thus far, left-hemisphere cortical specialization for language and localization for language functions within specific regions in frontal and temporal areas were elucidated in the nineteenth century. These findings in turn generated questions regarding the organization of language in polyglot speakers. Questions regarding bilingual language representation have pivoted on the concept of separate brain centers for each language or shared neural networks that may be variably disrupted by lesion. Current research carefully attempts to account for variables such as sequence of language acquisition, intrinsic and extrinsic characteristics influencing the speaker (e.g. individual differences and environmental factors), and even cross-linguistic differences.

Moreover, brain regions outside those identified during the nineteenth century are now being discussed, as their role in cognitive abilities underlying language behavior seems important for understanding the phenomena of bilingual aphasia. Neural support for the languages in polyglot speakers may be associated with different memory systems, a theory proposed by the Declarative/Procedural model. Effective use of the known languages by bilingual and polyglot speakers may in turn be determined by control over inhibition or activation of each language, a theory posited by the Inhibition Control model. We turn now to a discussion of these two models.

3.4   Models of Bilingual Processing that Address Bilingual Aphasia

3.4.1   *The declarative/procedural-memory model*

The learning of language seems to be mediated by two different memory mechanisms as they interact with age of acquisition (Paradis, 1994; Ullman, 2001). The procedural memory system is responsible for motor and cognitive functions acquired early in life. This system is mediated by frontal and basal ganglia structures with contributions from inferior parietal regions in the left hemisphere (see figures 3.2 and 3.3). The learning of a first language – or even of a second language that is learned early in life – relies primarily on this system for grammar computation and lexical processing. The declarative memory system mediates semantic and episodic memory and is supported by medial and temporo-parietal neural structures in both left and right

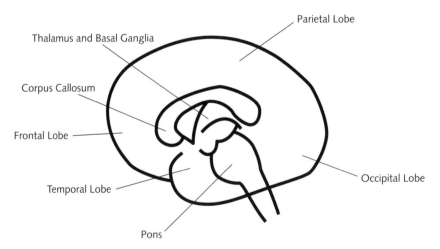

Figure 3.2   Medial view of the human brain showing basal ganglia in relation to corpus callosum and cortical lobes.

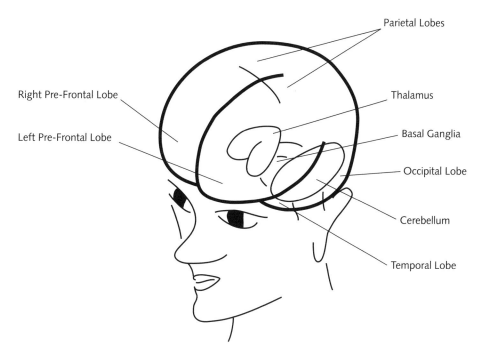

Parietal Lobes

Right Pre-Frontal Lobe

Left Pre-Frontal Lobe

Thalamus

Basal Ganglia

Occipital Lobe

Cerebellum

Temporal Lobe

Figure 3.3 Approximate structural relationship of the thalamus and basal ganglia to cortical areas within the human brain.

hemispheres. The learning of a second language later in life involves greater reliance on this system for the learning of grammar, if not lexicon. Therefore, later exposure to a second language implies a shift from procedural to declarative memory systems and increased right-hemisphere representation.

According to the exponents of this model (Fabbro, 2001; Paradis, 1994; Ullman, 2001), the study of language recovery in polyglot aphasics is closely related to the order of acquisition of the languages (simultaneous vs. sequential) and the memory systems involved in language acquisition. A first language tends to be learned informally and in natural settings, relying more on implicit/ procedural memory mechanisms and unconscious cognitive processes rooted in subcortical structures. Languages that are acquired later in life tend to rely more on declarative memory, are often learned in more structured and less natural settings, such as school, and are more exclusively represented in the cerebral cortex than the first language. The role of what neuropsychologists call "executive processes" influencing inhibition may also play a role in explaining why during the recovery process of some polyglot aphasics, fluctuation in the reappearance of languages is seen.

Many studies lend support to the declarative/procedural model and link the differential language recovery in aphasics to subcortical lesions involved in automatic language processes (Aglioti et al., 1996; Aglioti and Fabbro, 1993;

Fabbro, 2001; Moretti et al., 2001). Moretti et al. (2001) point out the role of subcortical language structures and implicit memory in explaining the recovery of a patient who developed an impairment of the mother tongue following an infarct of the caudate. The authors further describe how, during follow-up, improvement of the mother tongue was accompanied by worsening of the second language as the ischemic lesion extended to the cortex.

The declarative/procedural model posits that brain damage in left neocortical temporal and temporo-parietal regions will be associated with increased difficulty in a later-learned and less used L2 than in L1 or in an earlier-learned or well-practiced L2. Alternatively, lesions to the left-hemisphere frontal or basal ganglia would result in greater impairment to grammatical L1 structures or to an earlier-learned and well-practiced L2 than to a less used or later-learned L2. Lexical performance should be affected for all cases.

The case of a 16-year-old Chinese immigrant who learned English after the age of 10 upon his arrival in the US presents interesting evidence linking the left temporal lobe with L2 learning (Ku, Lachmann, and Nagler, 1996). This patient developed herpes simplex encephalitis evident only in the left temporal lobe, and subsequently lost the ability to speak or comprehend English but retained these abilities in his native language, Chinese. This selective impairment of the second language with relative preservation of the mother tongue effectively links left temporal structures with a later-learned language (English) that was the most impaired subsequent to the lesions that this patient presented.

Lesions that would involve the left frontal or basal ganglia structures would be associated with increased difficulty in L1, since these structures mediate implicit-memory processes. Fabbro and Paradis (1995) present four cases of bilingual and polyglot aphasics with lesions primarily circumscribed to the left basal ganglia. All four patients showed worse grammatical performance in their native or most proficient language than in their non-native or less proficient language. Cases such as these also lend support to the declarative/procedural model, which associates native language performance to the left frontal and basal ganglia. Lesions specific to these areas are mainly associated with greater impairment in the first language than in later-acquired languages.

More difficulty in using the mother tongue than in the use of a second language subsequent to a subcortical lesion was reported by Aglioti et al. (1996). Their bilingual patient, E. M., whose mother tongue was Venetian and whose second language was Italian, suffered a subcortical lesion involving the left basal ganglia and subsequently presented increased difficulty spontaneously using her mother tongue, even though this was her most frequently used language. E. M. also had increased difficulty translating into her mother tongue as compared to translating into her second language. Her deficits were stable and sustained after five years from the time of stroke. E. M.'s symptomatology supports the declarative/procedural model, in that her deficits and recovery patterns were related to lesions in the left basal ganglia with greater corresponding impairment in the first language with respect to the second language. The important role of the basal ganglia in automatized motor and cognitive performance affecting the first language was thus evident again in this case.

3.4.2 The inhibitory control model

Polyglots are able to control and determine when to use each language, or when one language should be activated and the other suppressed or inhibited. The rules determining language-choice and language-switching behaviors in normal speakers allow great flexibility, from intrasentential language switches to intersentential switches that may mark a shift in the language used. However, a general rule that is always observed by bilingual and polyglot speakers is that language switching takes place only when the listener shares the language codes being used. This ability to switch language codes only when contextually appropriate is a skill that has been reported in bilingual speakers as young as two years old (Leopold, 1949).

There are three main components in bilingual and polyglot speakers' language systems that must be accounted for in order to explain regulation in the use of two or more languages, according to Green (1986). Any language system must first address the issue of control. How are normal bilingual speakers with access to both language systems able to control which language they produce? If a bilingual speaker were not able to effectively separate language systems, code switching (alternating use between one language and the other) would violate many of the rules observed by normal bilinguals in alternating between languages. Successful control of the language systems primarily implies the avoidance of error, such as blending two words in one language or across languages. In normal speakers, failure to exercise full control over an intact language system does occur, and may be due to a variety of reasons, such as temporary distraction, stress, fatigue, or the influence of toxic substances. In the aphasic speaker, however, brain damage itself provides the "stressful" situation that may bring about failure to exercise full control over two or more language systems, even in otherwise non-stressful conditions. This lack of control by the aphasic over his or her language systems is pervasive, often interfering with functional communication.

The second component in the language system of bilingual and polyglot speakers involves the issue of activation determined by the internal representation of words from the known languages. Word frequency may be influential in determining activation or inhibition at both semantic and phonological levels of word production. More frequent words will generate larger activation patterns in lexical access than words that are less frequent or familiar. Finally, the third component described by Green involves the issue of resources linked to processes of control and regulation. Language representation systems in polyglot speakers must possess excitatory and inhibitory resources in the selection or deselection of languages when speaking.

Green (1998) explains that there are multiple levels of control in the language processing of bilingual speakers. Accordingly, he elaborated his inhibitory control (IC) model by specifying one level of control involving language task schemas that compete to control output; the locus of word selection is the lemma level and involves the use of language tags; and control at the lemma level is inhibitory and reactive. In these papers Green delineates a functional-control circuit with three basic loci of control: an executive locus that is in charge of supervisory attention and is critical in establishing and maintaining the speaker's language goals; a locus at the level of language-task schemas that the speaker selects; and a locus within the bilingual lexicosemantic system itself where lemmas are established.

The bilingual speaker possesses a conceptualizer that builds conceptual representations from long-term memory and is driven by a goal to communicate through language. The speaker's communicative and planning intention is mediated by a supervisory attentional system (SAS) and components of the language system itself, such as the lexico-semantic system and language task schemas. These language task schemas (e.g. translation or word production schemas) are in competition to control output (production) from the lexico-semantic system. The speaker's selection of a word is determined through communication between the SAS and the task schemas and between the SAS and the conceptualizer. Another important aspect of this system is that once a speaker specifies a task schema to regulate behavior, the speaker must maintain the task as a goal in order to avoid competing task schemas becoming active and producing error behavior.

The bilingual speaker must therefore first establish language task schemas to determine when to speak in one language or another or when to translate between languages. These task schemas determine access to the lexico-semantic system within each language when selecting responses in one language or another. Therefore the lexico-semantic system and a set of language task schemas (such as translation or word production) both compete to control output from the lexico-semantic system.

Language task schemas regulate responses from the lexico-semantic system by altering the activation levels of representation within the system and by inhibiting responses in the language that is not needed. In other words, when the speaker is responding in one of the languages, other languages are inhibited and cannot interfere by also introducing responses in the output. Cases of paradoxical translation in bilingual aphasics are a good example of how language task schemas can be disrupted. In cases of paradoxical translation the patient translates more efficiently from L1 to L2, whereas normal bilinguals typically translate best when going from the less proficient to the more proficient language, usually L2 to L1. Such a failure to inhibit one language over another can be explained as a breakdown in the supervisory attentional system and in the control of language task schemas.

Code switching between languages in bilingual and polyglot speakers becomes a pathological behavior when it is inappropriately used within a context where speakers do not share both language codes. The fact that this constitutes inappropriate "use" of specific language(s) suggests the specificity of a pragmatic language disorder. Fabbro (2001) points out that pathological switching between languages is associated with lesions of the frontal lobe (left and right), whereas persistent mixing of elements from languages constitutes an aphasic disorder associated with fluent aphasias and tends to be correlated with left postrolandic lesions (Fabbro, 1999, 2001; Fabbro, Skrap, and Aglioti, 2000). The problem, of course, is that symptoms are not always clear-cut in patients and that pathological language switching may coexist with language mixing, thus reflecting impairment of executive control along with true language deficits affecting grammatical constructions or lexical search.

Increased use of switching between languages by aphasics may also denote linguistic deficits in both languages and the need to rely on all available language codes to communicate more effectively. This kind of language-switching behavior should be distinguished from the subtle pragmatic deficits that can be present in bilingual aphasics. Muñoz, Marquardt, and Copeland (1999) compared discourse samples from four aphasic and four neurologically normal Hispanic bilinguals in monolingual-English, monolingual-Spanish, and bilingual contexts, finding consistent matching of the language context by both the aphasic and normal subjects. However, the aphasic subjects demonstrated increased code switching not evident in the speech samples of the normal subjects, indicating increased dependence on both languages for communication subsequent to neurological impairment. A comparison of code switching in Malayalam-English and Kannada-English bilingual aphasics with normals has also revealed that there is only increase in the quantity of code switching and no difference in type of switches (Bhat and Chengappa, 2003; Chengappa and Krupa, 2003). It seems to be the case, then, that in bilingual speakers increased code switching between languages will often take place as the result of compensatory strategies for deficits in lexical retrieval. These studies indicate the need to establish careful distinctions in discriminating between normal and pathological use of this communicative strategy.

Support for this model can be found in cases of bilingual and polyglot aphasic patients where pathological switching and language mixing are evidenced. Fabbro (1999) reports that some of the early cases describing pathological fixation on one language point to areas affecting the left supramarginal gyrus and the left temporal lobe. Cases involving pathological switching among languages involve the ventral anterior nucleus of the thalamus, the right hemisphere (reported in cases of right-temporal epilepsy), and the left prefrontal lobe. Paradis (1993) argues that language switching mechanisms are part of a general system responsible for the selection of behaviors and that even though their localization is unclear, it should involve structures of the frontal system.

Translation disorders also can be accounted for within Green's model. According to Green (1986), aphasics possess weakened language systems in which executive processes in charge of inhibiting or activating one language over the other fail to do so effectively, thus generating some of the symptoms often reported in the literature. Bilingual aphasics sometimes reveal disorders associated with translation characterized by different features. One of these is when a bilingual or polyglot aphasic patient presents with an *inability to translate*. This kind of patient may thus be able to understand and use either language, yet be unable to translate from the first to the second language or from the second to the first language. This lack of flexibility in alternating between one language and the other in spite of comprehension and use of both languages may denote the pervasiveness of the aphasic symptoms in the polyglot speaker.

Patients presenting with paradoxical translation can translate only from the more proficient language into the language that is most difficult to speak spontaneously (however, normal bilinguals have an easier time translating from the less proficient language into their mastered language). Clinical cases exhibiting this pattern of language recovery were first described by Paradis, Goldblum, and Abidi in 1982. One of these patients, A.D., communicated only in Arabic some days and was subsequently able to express herself only in French for a number of days. On one day this patient was able to comprehend both languages but paradoxically translated from Arabic into French, while the next day she was only able to translate from French into Arabic. DeVreese, Motta, and Toschi (1988), discuss paradoxical translation and spontaneous translation in a patient diagnosed with presenile dementia of the Alzheimer's type who was able to translate correctly and without hesitation from his mother tongue into French which he had difficulty speaking spontaneously. At the same time, he could not translate from French into his mother tongue. This patient also demonstrated involuntary translation of his own and others' utterances.

More curious yet is the symptomatology wherein patients are able to translate verbal information that they cannot understand. Cases involving *translation without comprehension* have been reported in patients who fail to understand commands that are given to them, but can nevertheless translate the sentences uttered by an interlocutor to express these commands (Fabbro, 2001; Fabbro and Paradis, 1996). The case of a 65-year-old woman who suffered a stroke with aphasia and right-sided hemiplegia was described by Veyrac in 1931. This patient's native language was English; she acquired French after the age of 15. Subsequent to a stroke, she spoke a few utterances in French but did not understand even simple commands in French. When her physician gave her spoken instructions in English, the patient spontaneously translated these into French but was unable to carry them out, suggesting a dissociation between comprehension and translation.

Language choice is a third area of phenomena that the IC model can account for. Cases of alternating antagonism refer to a patient's alternating ability to control which language to use. Thus, the patient may be able to communicate in one language but not in another on some days and alternate to only using another language at a different time. Nilipour and Ashayeri (1989) reported such symptoms in a patient who developed a left fronto-temporal injury as a consequence of an explosion. This patient was reportedly equally proficient in Farsi and German and with a good knowledge of English pre-morbidly. He was unable to speak during the first week post-trauma. He then only spoke limited Farsi for five days, but regained use of German for the following three weeks. The patient then switched to using only Farsi for four days until finally regaining control of all his languages, including English.

Decreased use of switching among languages may also be seen in demented bilingual patients, who, unlike aphasic polyglots, will often address interlocutors in the patient's native language despite the fact that the interlocutor speaks only the second language (DeSanti et al., 1989; Hyltenstam and Stroud, 1989). Dementias of the type in which such problems are reported (namely, Alzheimer's dementia), it should be noted, affect frontal-lobe non-language structures primarily. In sum, several of the phenomena observed in bilingual aphasia (namely, pathological switching between languages and translation disorders) are consistent with the IC model that Green has developed. (For discussion of code mixing and code switching in normals, see chapters 2, 4, 6, 10–14, 25, 26, 28, 29, and 31.)

3.5 Conclusions

Over a century and a quarter, interest in bilingual and polyglot aphasia has progressively increased. Initially, questions concerning the order of recovery of the two or more languages predominated, along with questions of what the causes of observed recovery patterns were. Questions about the incidence of crossed aphasia, with its implications for lateralized participation in language production and processing, entered in the mid-twentieth century as language lateralization became a topic of great interest in neurolinguistics generally. In the past quarter-century linguists, speech–language pathologists, and investigators within related disciplines have joined behavioral neurologists in the study of bilingual aphasia and its particular phenomenology (e.g. day-to-day fluctuations in language accessibility, disordered translation, and language-choice, code-switching and -mixing behaviors). In the past decade, psychologists have joined the discussion, contributing models of the ways in which frontal-system executive control and subcortical memory systems subserve healthy bilingual processes, and can account for deficits documented in bilingual aphasia.

REFERENCES

Abutalebi, J., Cappa, S. F., and Perani, D. (2001). The bilingual brain as revealed by functional neuroimaging. *Bilingualism: Language and Cognition*, 4, 2, 179–90.

Aglioti, S. and Fabbro, F. (1993). Paradoxical selective recovery in a bilingual aphasic following subcortical lesions. *NeuroReport*, 4, 1359–62.

Aglioti, S., Beltramello, A., Girardi, F., and Fabbro, F. (1996). Neurolinguistic and follow-up study of an unusual pattern of recovery from bilingual subcortical aphasia. *Brain*, 119, 1551–64.

Albert, M. L. and Obler, L. K. (1978). *The Bilingual Brain: Neuropsychological and Neurolinguistic Aspects of Bilingualism.* New York: Academic Press.

Appel, R. and Muysken, P. (1997). *Language Contact and Bilingualism,* pp. 117–28. New York: Arnold.

Bates, E., Friederici, A., and Wulfeck, B. (1987). Grammatical morphology in aphasia: Evidence from three languages. *Cortex*, 23, 545–74.

Bates, E., MacWhinney, B., Caselli, C., Devescovi, A., Natale, F., and Venza, V. (1984). A cross-linguistic study of the development of sentence interpretation strategies. *Child Development*, 55, 341–54.

Bhat, S. and Chengappa, S. (2003). Code switching in normal and aphasic Kannada-English bilinguals. Forthcoming.

Bose, A. and Chengappa, S. (2000). Naming deficits in bilingual aphasics. Paper presented at annual conference of CASLPA, Toronto, May.

Bose, A. and Shyamala, K. C. (1977). Naming deficits in bilingual aphasics. Unpublished master's dissertation. University of Mysore, India.

Broca, P. (1865/1977). Remarks on the seat of the faculty of articulate speech, followed by the report of a case of aphemie. Translated by C. Wasterlain and D. A. Rottenberg, in D. A. Rottenberg and F. H. Hochberg (eds.), *Neurological Classics in Modern Translation*, pp. 136–49. New York: Hafner, 1977.

Chee, M. W. L., Hon, N., Ling Lee, H., and Siong Soon, C. (2001). Relative language proficiency modulates BOLD signal change when bilinguals perform semantic judgments. Blood oxygen level dependent. *Neuroimage*, 13, 1155–63.

Chengappa, S. and Krupa (2003). Language mixing and switching in Malayalam bilingual aphasics. Forthcoming.

De Renzi, E. (1989). Apraxia. In F. Boller and J. Grafman (eds.), *Handbook of Neuropsychology, vol. II*, pp. 245–63. New York: Elsevier Science.

DeSanti, S., Obler, L. K., Sabro-Abramson, H., and Goldberger, J. (1989). Discourse abilities and deficits in multilingual dementia. In Y. Joanette and H. Brownell (eds.), *Discourse Abilities in Brain Damage: Theoretical and Empirical Perspectives.* New York: Springer-Verlag.

DeVreese, L. P., Motta, M., and Toschi, A. (1988). Compulsive and paradoxical translation behaviour in a case of presenile dementia of the Alzheimer type. *Journal of Neurolinguistics*, 3, 233–141.

Fabbro, F. (1999). *The Neurolinguistics of Bilingualism: An Introduction.* Hove, UK: Psychology Press.

Fabbro, F. (2001). The bilingual brain: Cerebral representation of languages. *Brain and Language*, 79, 211–22.

Fabbro, F. and Paradis, M. (1995). Differential impairments in four multilingual patients with subcortical lesions. In M. Paradis (ed.), *Aspects of Bilingual Aphasia*, pp. 139–76. Oxford: Pergamon Press.

Fabbro, F., Skrap, M., and Aglioti, S. (2000). Pathological switching between languages after frontal lesions in a bilingual patient. *Journal of Neurology, Neurosurgery and Psychiatry*, 68, 650–2.

Faroqi, Y. and Chengappa, S. (1998). Trace deletion and its implications for invention in a multilingual agrammatics. Osmania Papers in Linguistics, 23, 79–107.

Flege, J. E., Komshian, G. Y., and Liu, S. (1999). Age constraints on second-language acquisition. *Journal of Memory and Language*, 41, 78–104.

Fodor, J. A. (1983). The modularity of mind: An essay on faculty psychology. Cambridge, MA: MIT Press.

Fredman, M. (1975). The effect of therapy given in Hebrew or the home language of the bilingual or polyglot adult aphasic in Israel. *British Journal of Disorders of Communication*, 10, 61–9.

Freud, S. (1891/1953). *Zur Auffassung der Aphasien. Eine kritische Studie.* Leipzig and Vienna: Franz, Deutsche. Translated by E. Stengel (1953). New York: International University Press.

Gloning, I. and Gloning, K. (1965). Aphasien bei Polyglotten. *Wiener Zeitschrift für Nervenheilkunde*, 22, 362–97.

Green, D. W. (1986). Control, activation, and resource: A framework and a model for the control of speech in bilinguals. *Brain and Language*, 27, 210–23.

Green, D. W. (1998). Mental control of the bilingual lexico-semantic system. *Bilingualism: Language and Cognition*, 1, 67–81.

Grodzinsky, Y. (1986). Language deficits and the theory of syntax. *Brain and Language*, 27, 135–59.

Grodzinsky, Y. (1995). A restrictive theory of agrammatic comprehension. *Brain and Language*, 50, 27–51.

Hyltenstam, K. and Stroud, C. (1989). Bilingualism in Alzheimer's dementia: Two case studies. In K. Hyltenstam and L. K. Obler (eds.), *Bilingualism across the Lifespan: Aspects of Acquisition, Maturity, and Loss.* Cambridge: Cambridge University Press.

Illes, J., Francis, W. S., Desmond, J. E., Gabrieli, F. D. E., Glover, G. H., Poldrack, R., Lee, J. C., and Wagner, A. D. (1999). Convergent cortical representation of semantic processing in bilinguals. *Brain and Language*, 70, 347–63.

Jackson, J. H. (1879). On affections of speech from disease of the brain. *Brain*, I, 304–30.

Johnson, J. and Newport, E. (1989). Critical period effects in second language learning: the influence of maturational state on the acquisition of English as a second language. *Cognitive Psychology*, 21, 60–99.

Kandel, E. R., Schwartz, J. H., and Jessell, T. M. (2000) (eds.). *Principles of Neural Science.* New York: McGraw-Hill.

Kim, D. H., Relkin, N. R., Lee, L. M., and Hirsch, J. (1997). Distinct cortical areas associated with native and second languages. *Nature*, 10, 388, 6638, 171–4.

Klein, D., Zatorre, R. J., Milner, B., and Zhao, V. (2001). A cross-linguistic PET study of tone perception in Mandarin Chinese and English speakers. *Neuroimage*, 13, 646–53.

Ku, A., Lachmann, E. A., and Nagler, W. (1996). Selective language aphasia from herpes simplex encephalitis. *Pediatric Neurology*, 15, 2, 169–71.

Lambert, W. E. and Fillenbaum, S. (1959). A pilot study of aphasia among bilinguals. *Canadian Journal of Psychology*, 13, 28–34.

Lenneberg, E. H. (1967). *Biological Foundations of Language.* New York: Wiley.

Leopold, W. (1949). *Speech Development of a Bilingual Child*, 4 vols. Evanston, IL, Northwestern Press.

Levy, E., Goral, M., and Obler, L. K. (1999). Neurolinguistic perspectives on mother tongue: Evidence from aphasia and brain imaging. *La Langue Maternelle*, V, 27. Paris: Publications de l'Université de Paris 7, 141–57.

Lichtheim, L. (1885), On aphasia. *Brain*, 7, 433–84.

Menn, L. and Obler, L. K. (1990). Cross-language data and theories of agrammatism. In L. Menn and L. K. Obler (eds.), *Agrammatic Aphasia: a Crosslinguistic Narrative Sourcebook*, pp. 1369–89. Amsterdam: John Benjamins.

Minkowski, M. (1927/1983). A clinical contribution to the study of polyglot aphasia especially with respect to Swiss-German. In M. Paradis (ed.), *Readings on Aphasia in Bilinguals and Polyglots*, pp. 205–32. Montreal: Didier.

Moretti, R., Bava, A., Torre, P., Antonello, R. M., Zorzon, M., Zivadinov, R., and Cazzato, G. (2001). Bilingual aphasia and subcortical-cortical lesions. *Perceptual Motor Skills*, 92 (3 Pt 1), 803–14.

Muñoz, M. L., Marquardt, T. P., and Copeland, G. (1999). A comparison of the codeswitching patterns of aphasic and neurologically normal bilingual speakers of English and Spanish. *Brain and Language*, 66, 249–74.

Neville, H. J., Coffey, S. A., Lawson, D. S., Fischer, A., Emmorey, K., and Bellugi, U. (1997). Neural systems mediating American sign language: Effects of sensory experience and age of acquisition. *Brain and Language*, 57, 3, 285–308.

Nilipour, R. and Ashayeri, H. (1989). Alternating antagonism between two languages with successive recovery of a third in a trilingual aphasic patient. *Brain and Language*, 36, 1, 23–48.

Obler, L. K. (1983). Dyslexia in bilinguals. In R. N. Malatesha and H. A. Whitaker (eds.), *Dyslexia: A Global Issue*, pp. 477–96. The Hague: Martinean and Nijhoff.

Obler, L. K., Zatorre, R. J., Galloway, L., and Vaid, J. (1982). Central lateralization in bilinguals: Methodological issues. *Brain and Language*, 15, 40–54.

Paradis, M. (1977). Bilingualism and aphasia. In H. Whitaker and H. A. Whitaker (eds.), *Studies in Neurolinguistics*, vol. 3, pp. 65–121. New York: Academic Press.

Paradis, M. (1993). Linguistic, psycholinguistic, and neurolinguistic aspects of "interference" in bilingual speakers: The activation threshold hypothesis. *International Journal of Psycholinguistics*, 9, 133–45.

Paradis, M. (1994). Neurolinguistic aspects of implicit and explicit memory: implications for bilingualism and second language acquisition. In N. Ellis (ed.), *Implicit and Explicit Language Learning*. London: Academic Press.

Paradis, M. (1998). Language and communication in multilinguals. In B. Stemmer and H. Whitaker (eds.), *Handbook of Neurolinguistics*, pp. 418–31. San Diego: Academic Press.

Paradis, M. (2000). The neurolinguistics of bilingualism in the next decades. *Brain and Language*, 71, 178–80.

Paradis, M., Goldblum, M. C., and Abidi, R. (1982). Alternate antagonism with paradoxical translation behavior in two bilingual aphasic patients. *Brain and Language*, 15, 1, 55–69.

Perani, D., Paulesu, E., Sebastian Galles, N., Dupoux, E., Dehaene, S., Bettinardi, V., Cappa, S. F., Fazio, F., and Mehler, J. (1998). The bilingual brain, proficiency and age of acquisition of the second language. *Brain*, 121, 1841–52.

Pitres, A. (1895/1953). Aphasia in polyglots. In M. Paradis (ed.), *Readings on Aphasia in Bilinguals and Polyglots*, pp. 26–49. Montreal: Didier.

Price, C. J., Green, D. W., and von Studnitz, R. (1999). A functional imaging study of translation and language switching. *Brain*, 122, 12, 2221–35.

Romaine, S. (1995). *Bilingualism*. Oxford: Blackwell.

Scoresby-Jackson, R. E. (1867). Case of aphasia with right hemiplegia. *Edinburgh Medical Journal*, 12, 696–706.

Sreedevi, N. (2000). Comprehension deficits in bilingual aphasics.

Unpublished master's dissertation, University of Mysore.

Stroop, J. R. (1935). Studies of interference in serial verbal reactions. *Journal of Experimental Psychology*, 28, 643–62.

Tan, L. H., Liu, H. L, Perfetti, C. A., Spinks, J. A., Fox, P. T., and Gao, J. H. (2001). The neural system underlying Chinese logograph reading. *Neuroimage*, 13, 836–46.

Ullman, M. T. (2001). The neural basis of lexicon and grammar in first and second language: the declarative/procedural model. *Bilingualism: Language and Cognition*, 4, 1, 105–22.

Vaid, J. and Chengappa, S. (1988). Assigning linguistic rules: Sentence interpretation in normal and aphasic Kannada-English bilinguals. *Journal of Neurolinguistics*, 3(2), 161–83.

Vaid, J. and Genesee, F. (1980). Neuropsychological approaches to bilingualism: a critical review. *Canadian Journal of Psychology*, 34, 417–45.

Vaid, J. and Hall, D. G. (1991). Neuropsychological perspectives on bilingualism: Right, left, and center. In A. Reynolds (ed.), *Bilingualism, Multiculturalism, and Second Language Learning: The McGill Conference in Honour of Wallace E. Lambert*, pp. 81–112. Hillsdale, NJ: Lawrence Erlbaum.

Vaid, J. and Hull, R. (2002). Re-envisioning the bilingual brain using functional neuroimaging: Methodological and interpretive issues. In F. Fabbro (ed.), *Advances in the Neurolinguistics of Bilingualism: Essays in Honor of Michel Paradis*, pp. 315–55. Udine Forum: Udine University Press.

Veyrac, G. J. (1931). A study of aphasia in polyglot subjects. In M. Paradis (ed.), *Readings on Aphasia in Bilinguals and Polyglots*, pp. 320–38. Montreal: Didier.

Watamori, T. S. and Sasanuma, S. (1978). The recovery process of two English-Japanese bilingual aphasics. *Brain and Language*, 6, 127–40.

Weinreich, U. (1953). *Languages in Contact*. The Hague: Mouton. First edn. 1953. New York: Linguistic Circle of New York, Publication No. 2.

Wernicke, C. (1874). The symptom complex of aphasia. *Boston Studies in the Philosophy of Science*, IV, 34–97.

Approaches to
Bilingualism and
Language Acquisition

4 The Bilingual Child

JÜRGEN M. MEISEL

4.1 Introduction

This chapter deals with the development of child bilingualism, more specifically with children growing up with two or more languages from birth or soon afterwards. This focus on developmental aspects of early bilingualism constitutes, in more than one way, a rather special research topic. Not only has the number of research studies dedicated to this subject increased dramatically over the past two decades, it also attracts considerable attention among a wider audience, and research studying the bilingual child may therefore count on a stronger public resonance than is normally the case for linguistic or psycholinguistic publications. The reason why this fact, in principle gratifying, is mentioned here is that the discussion frequently reflects strong emotional involvement on the part of all participants, sometimes tainted by ideological biases, resulting in campaigns *pro* or *contra* child bilingualism. This situation not only influences the public debate; reflections can also be found in research reports where comparable findings may lead to contradictory assessments of the children's bilingualism. It is quite possible that in many cases these reactions can be traced back to a well-intentioned desire to protect the defenseless child from potentially harmful influences. In combination with the belief that monolingualism represents the natural or normal case of language development, this attitude may lead to the assumption that deviating from this norm implies risks which had better be avoided. The most frequently articulated concern is that the child exposed to more than one language during early developmental phases might be confused linguistically, cognitively, emotionally, and possibly even morally. Confronted with concerns and prejudices of this sort, parents, educators and law makers find themselves in a situation of serious doubts about the feasibility of bilingual education. In cases where raising children bilingually is not a social necessity but one of several options, e.g. family bilingualism in a predominantly monolingual environment (immigrants, bilingual couples, etc.), they may therefore opt for what appears to be the more prudent choice, namely monolingualism. (For more on bilingual education, see chapters 15, 23–5, 27, and 28.)

Research on child bilingualism must not simply ignore this situation, whether researchers believe that such worries are well-founded or not. In fact, enthusiastic support of bilingual education can equally be motivated by ideological biases. Research therefore needs to take seriously the fears of those directly concerned and try to establish to what extent alleged risks and advantages of early bilingualism are justified. In this sense, research on linguistic development in a multilingual setting is indeed of immediate practical relevance. At the same time, it deals with matters of deep philosophical and epistemological concern if it can indeed be shown that the human language faculty has an endowment for multilingualism. Assuming that this can be confirmed, the view of child bilingualism as a potential source of possible disturbances must be abandoned. Instead, monolingualism can be regarded as resulting from an impoverished environment where an opportunity to exhaust the potential of the language faculty is not fully developed.

Systematic investigations of child bilingualism began approximately one hundred years ago with the careful study by Ronjat (1913), culminating, during the early history of this type of research, in the monumental work by Leopold (1939–49). Many of the earlier studies were carried out by laymen, frequently reporting on observations with their own children, e.g. missionaries whose children grew up in an environment where they acquired the local language in addition to the language which the parents spoke at home, or linguists or psychologists normally not specializing in language development, but whose children grew up bilingually because the parents worked in a foreign country or because their spouses came from a different language background. Although these studies represent a rich source of observations, their analyses of bilingual language development are not always reliable. Moreover, some of these works are strongly influenced by the aforementioned prejudices. This is one reason why research results obtained subsequently frequently arrive at rather different conclusions. In fact, the first surge of publications on language acquisition by psychologists and linguists investigating bilingual children happened during the 1960s and brought along a professionalization and a further increase of research activities from the 1980s on, contributing to the establishment of bilingual studies as an autonomous discipline with its own textbooks and journals. It is this research of the past 25 years which the following discussion will focus on.

4.2   Contrasting Bilingualism with Monolingualism

The problem area which has attracted by far the largest number of studies over the past years relates to the question of whether bi- or multilingual children fare as well, in each of their languages, as do the respective monolinguals. Quite obviously, this reflects a perspective strongly biased toward monolingualism in that it implicitly assumes that monolingual acquisition is the norm. Indirectly, at least, such an approach conveys the view that multilingualism deviates from what may be regarded as normal. From there, it is not a big step to judging multilingualism as some kind of freak condition. But in view of what has been said in the introductory remarks, it is precisely because of possible misrepresentations of this sort that a monolingual perspective must temporarily be adopted. If, then, it can be demonstrated that the simultaneous acquisition of bilingualism is indeed an instance of "normal" first language development (see the following section), two objectives are accomplished. On the one hand, claims concerning alleged problems of bilingual children are refuted, thus also eliminating causes of parental and educator worry about a possible confusion on the part of the children. At the same time, such a result has important implications for theories of language and of grammar which then need to be conceptualized in a way allowing for an explanation of this capacity for multilingualism.

To avoid misunderstandings, in contrasting bilingual with monolingual first language acquisition, the goal is not to promote an idealized concept of the bilingual person as an individual whose linguistic knowledge consists of two perfectly equal parts and who is able to behave in every respect and in each situation precisely like the respective monolinguals. Grosjean (1989) insists that "the bilingual is not two monolinguals in one person." He argues correctly that bilinguals rarely use their languages equally frequently in every domain of their social environment. Rather, they use each of them for different purposes, in different contexts, and in communicating with different partners. Consequently, their abilities and skills in using each of these languages reflect their preferences and needs in the multifaceted social contexts in which they interact with others. And since demands and purposes of interactions vary, bilinguals are able to shift on a continuum which ranges from a more monolingual to a truly bilingual mode; in other words, their knowledge of each of their languages is activated more or less strongly (Grosjean, chapter 2 of the present volume). Such a holistic view of bilingualism takes into account the fact that a person who uses two languages regularly is not necessarily equally at ease in each of them in all communicative contexts and does not even have to be able to use them equally well. On the other hand, by choosing between their languages and by switching between them, bilinguals have available additional communicative means which monolingual speakers lack. Comparisons between the language use of monolinguals and of bilinguals must take these considerations into account. One specific speech sample can, in fact, hardly do justice either to one or to the other. (For further discussion of the notion of language mode, see chapters 2, 3, 6, and 8.)

This is not to say that contrasting bilingualism with monolingualism could not lead to important insights, but the point is not to demonstrate that bilinguals behave in every respect and in each situation like monolinguals. Rather, comparisons of this sort are likely to yield significant results only if the underlying knowledge of the two types of speakers are targeted. More precisely, it is the investigation of the less variable aspects of grammatical knowledge which should prove to be most promising. Although the competence of individual speakers will necessarily exhibit a certain amount of variation as compared to that of other individuals, monolinguals as well as multilinguals, a core part of their grammars ought to be invariant across individuals if the generation of structures shared by the speech community and underlying comprehension and production of utterances is to be possible. From a psycholinguistic perspective, one can describe the object of comparison as the mental representation of grammatical knowledge; with respect to children, the focus will be on invariant properties of the development of this knowledge. One example concerns invariant developmental sequences of grammatical structures which have been established for monolingual development in many languages, following the example of Brown (1973). If bilingual children exhibit the same developmental sequences as the respective monolinguals acquiring the same languages, this may be interpreted as strong evidence in support of the claim that the two types of acquisition are not qualitatively different. This leaves open the question of whether there exist quantitative differences of various sorts, e.g. the average rate at which individuals proceed through these sequences, the relative frequency of use of particular constructions, and so forth.

The preceding remarks on the comparison between monolinguals and bilinguals apply in much the same way to possible contrasts opposing the two languages of the bilingual. The question of whether a bilingual person can achieve what has been referred to as "balanced bilingualism" has led to controversy, and it has, indeed, been argued repeatedly that such balanced bilingualism might not be possible. However, the notion clearly refers to language proficiency and to performance in both languages. Understood in this way, it is indeed not implausible in view of what has been mentioned above concerning the domain-specific distribution of languages in the communicative environment of multilinguals, preferred choice, ease of access, etc. Mainly because most bilinguals do not use both languages equally frequently in all domains, they tend not to be "balanced" in their proficiency for each of the languages. But "dominance" of one language, defined as the one in which a person is more proficient, can shift repeatedly, not only during childhood but over the entire life span, depending on a person's communicative needs. Neither balance nor dominance, understood in this fashion, is of particular interest in the present context, however, since this chapter is mainly concerned with the type of grammatical knowledge available to a bilingual child. And with respect to the child's competence, it can and will be argued that it is not only possible but, indeed, normal for bilingual children to develop grammatical knowledge, in each of their languages, not qualitatively different from that of the respective monolingual children. (For additional discussion of types of bilinguals, see chapters 1–3, 5, 7–10, and 22.)

4.3   Simultaneous Acquisition of Bilingualism as First Language Development

The most important insight gained from studies on child bilingualism over the past 25 years is perhaps that simultaneous acquisition of two or more languages can indeed be qualified as an instance of multiple first language acquisition. In phrasing it in this way, the claim is that the development of each of the bilingual's languages proceeds in the same way and leads to the same kind of grammatical competence as in the respective monolingual children. In order to corroborate this claim, it is necessary to demonstrate that bilingual development is not qualitatively different from what is known about monolingual acquisition. As mentioned in the preceding section, "qualitative" similarities and differences refer to the invariant aspects of grammatical development. Accordingly, the main concerns which emanate from the literature on bilingual children, as well as from the worries articulated by parents and educators, relate to the children's ability to differentiate the linguistic systems, the possibility of significant delays in the rate of acquisition, and possible deviations from developmental paths observed in monolingual acquisition. In this section, rate of acquisition will be briefly discussed; the focus, however, will be on the issue of grammatical differentiation; the latter point will then be taken up in the following section.

The question of whether bilingual acquisition tends to happen at a significantly slower rate, when compared to monolinguals, is not a crucial one in the present context, since if this was indeed the case, it would really represent a quantitative rather than a qualitative property of development. It should, nevertheless, be addressed here briefly because quantitative differences of this sort could, in fact, become qualitative ones if linguistic development were delayed beyond the range of what can be considered normal in non-pathological cases. A potential risk of this type can, however, clearly be discarded. Although some researchers report that bilinguals tend to begin to speak late, i.e. after age 2;0 (= two years, zero months), the observed delays are well within the range of what counts as a normal rate of language development for monolingual children. As for the more principled question of whether bilingual acquisition does indeed progress at a slower rate than monolingual acquisition, a conclusive answer cannot be given. This is mainly due to the fact that a reliable yardstick against which to measure the pace of linguistic development is difficult to find. Among the criteria used in child language research are the mean length of utterances (MLU) at a given age, the emergence of specific structures at a given age or, more reliably, simultaneously with a certain MLU value, and the number of words produced at a given age. Irrespective of which of these criteria is applied, one finds a considerable amount of variation across individuals, among monolinguals as well as bilinguals. Looking, for example, at the emergence of a grammatical phenomenon like subject–verb agreement, one finds variation in age of up to nine months. Similarly, up to 20 percent of monolingual children have been qualified as late talkers, based on the criterion number of words (= less than 50) produced at age 2;0. These as well as similar findings thus lead to the conclusion that, although there may be an overall tendency for a slower acquisitional rate in bilingual acquisition, there is no indication that bilinguals fall outside the norms established for monolingual acquisition.

A more serious concern about potential qualitative differences between bilingual and monolingual acquisition relates to the problem of differentiation of grammatical systems. If it should be the case that bilinguals initially develop a single mental system for the two or more languages they acquire, such a *fusion* of grammatical systems might be difficult to disentangle. Moreover, it could have long-lasting effects on later phases if the learner then follows a developmental path different from the one characteristic of monolingual acquisition. The topic of differentiation of language systems has therefore been the crucial issue of research on bilingual acquisition.

The crucial fact which has led numerous authors to speculate that bilinguals might encounter difficulties, at least initially, in separating the lexicons and the grammatical systems of the languages which they are learning is that their language use normally exhibits a certain amount of mixing; i.e. bilinguals tend to mix languages within a conversation, a turn, or an utterance. From a monolingual perspective, this appears to indicate an inability to keep the languages apart. However, as early as the 1970s, researchers agreed that children growing up with more than one language eventually succeed in separating their languages, without much effort or specific pedagogical support. The possibility of an early developmental phase characterized by a fusion of lexical and grammatical systems has, nevertheless, been regarded as a potentially serious problem, especially by parents and educators fearing that such a phase of undifferentiated linguistic knowledge might continue to last through age periods during which it could prejudice the intellectual development of the child or that it might lead to deficiencies in subparts of the competence of one or both languages. The essential question to be answered, thus, is whether language mixing by children represents a particular kind of language use in multilingual settings or whether it reflects properties of the underlying linguistic competence, i.e. the children's ability to comprehend and produce well-formed sentences, and to judge their grammaticality (or rather their acceptability) in much the same way as do monolinguals.

A tentative first answer to this question can be found by looking at the language use of adult bilinguals. As is well known, language mixing is a common feature of communication among bilinguals, and it is frequently the result of code switching, a form of language use determined by a complex network of sociolinguistic variables and constrained by grammatical properties of the utterances. In fact, it has even been suggested that code switching is used more frequently by those who are most at ease and competent in both languages (Poplack, 1980). One may therefore plausibly assume that children also code-switch, in other words, that their mixes are at least in part a testimony to their ability to use their linguistic knowledge in much the same way as adults do in multilingual interactions. However, in order to be able to do so, they need to acquire both the grammatical knowledge and the social skills required for adult-like code switching. It follows that if children mix languages at a point of development when they have not yet acquired this kind of know-ledge and these skills, their early mixes might not yet be instances of code switching. What, then, do we know about the acquisition of code switching? (For more on code mixing and code switching in adults, see chapters 1–3, 6, 10–14, 25, 26, 28, 29, 31.)

A review of the literature on early code switching (Köppe and Meisel, 1995) shows that bilingual children acquire the necessary knowledge very early. Already by age 2;0, they choose the language according to the addressee, and soon afterwards they begin to adapt to other sociolinguistic requirements. Structural constraints impose restrictions on where a switch can happen intrasententially. Consequently, their role in children's language use can only be studied once multi-word utterances are used productively. The fact that, during the first half of the third year, these children violate such grammatical constraints only rarely, suggests that they have access to separate grammatical systems at this point of development, for these structural constraints rely on properties of both grammars. Importantly, constraints on code switching do not constitute a separate acquisitional task. Rather, this kind of implicit know-ledge appears to become accessible automatically once the relevant grammat-ical knowledge is available. As for the latter, functional categories (INFL, COMP, etc.) seem to play a crucial role. In sum, language mixing around or soon after age 2;0 can be explained, for the most part, as code switching.

Note that these and similar findings demonstrate, contrary to what some authors had suspected, that it is not generally the case that frequency of mixing decreases with increasing competence. In fact, not all children mix frequently during early phases, and others tend to increase the frequency of code switching over time. Nevertheless, what remains to be discussed are the earliest instances of mixing, prior to the phase of grammatical development which enables bilingual children to code-switch. Their structural properties are difficult to assess since they consist almost exclusively of single-word mixes. The function of these mixes is not transparent either, since they consist, for the most part, of lexical items which are undoubtedly known in both languages (e.g. the equivalents of *yes, no, this, that*); consequently, they are not likely to fill gaps in the lexical knowledge of either language. At any rate, although these early mixes are probably not instances of code switching as we under-stand them from adult bilingual language use, they also cannot be interpreted as evidence in support of the claim of early grammatical fusion, since they do not involve combinations of structural properties of the two languages, and they occur during an age span when the children's behavior with respect to language choice indicates that they do separate their languages. This observa-tion is supported by the fact that awareness of bilingualism begins to develop during the second half of the children's second year of life, possibly as early as

1;7, certainly around age 2;0, as is shown by the first metalinguistic utterances referring to their bilingualism.

To conclude, one can say that the earliest mixes of some bilingual children may not yet represent instances of code switching, but they do not support the fusion hypothesis either. Moreover, adult-like code switching emerges early during the third year, and the kind of knowledge underlying this type of language use supports indeed the hypothesis of early grammatical differentiation. The fact, then, that young bilinguals mix languages is, more than anything else, a sign of increasing sensitivity to the linguistic behavior of their environment. It certainly does not conflict with the assumption of language separation.

The hypothesis of early grammatical differentiation, frequently also referred to as to the "dual system hypothesis," is not only based on careful observations of children's linguistic behavior in bilingual settings but, importantly, also on analyses of early morphosyntactic development. The most elaborate version of the previously defended single-system hypothesis has been proposed by Volterra and Taeschner (1978). The basic idea is that bilingual acquisition is characterized by an initial period during which children develop only one system before they succeed in differentiating the lexical and grammatical systems of their languages.

The three-stage model of bilingual language development (Volterra and Taeschner, 1978)
I   The child has only one lexical system comprising words from both languages.
II   Distinct lexical systems develop, but children still rely on one syntax for both languages.
III Distinct grammatical systems develop, resulting in differentiation of two linguistic systems.

This scenario, however, turned out not to capture the typical developmental pattern of bilingual children; see De Houwer (1990), Genesee (1989), Meisel (1989). More sophisticated analyses of the emergence of lexical knowledge and of grammatical structures underlying child utterances in various longitudinal corpora revealed that the early separation of systems is not the exception but the rule in the simultaneous acquisition of various languages. Already during the holophrastic phase when children typically use one-word utterances, one finds unambiguous evidence indicating that two distinct lexicons are acquired by these children, thus contradicting the claim of an initial stage with only one lexical system; see for example Quay (1995).

In order to decide on the point when grammatical systems are differentiated, one obviously has to rely on data from developmental phases during which multi-word utterances and productively used inflectional morphology emerge in the speech of the children. Moreover, one needs to focus on grammatical phenomena which are functionally equivalent but formally different in the target languages investigated. With respect to inflectional morphology, this is normally not difficult to achieve, and there seems to be general consensus that bilingual children combine grammatical morphemes of one language with lexical morphemes of the same language as soon as they are able to use grammatical morphology productively. In other words, they do not randomly attach inflectional morphemes from both languages to lexical material from each of the languages they are acquiring. Note that this seems to be acknowledged by the three-stage model, too, since stage II only refers to syntax. It is here that the abovementioned formal distinctions between the target systems become relevant. If, for example, the placement of adjectives with respect to nouns is studied in the simultaneous acquisition of a Romance and a Germanic language, one needs to take into account the fact that Romance adjectives can appear in pre-nominal as well as in post-nominal position, even though pre-nominal placement is restricted to certain adjectives or to specific contexts in the adult language. How, then, can one interpret the finding that some French-German children temporarily use only pre-nominal adjective placement in both languages? In view of the fact that adult French allows for this word order with the adjectives appearing in these data and German also requires pre-nominal position of adjectives anyhow, this is not sufficient evidence in favor of the single system hypothesis.

The kind of evidence needed in order to decide between these competing hypotheses is provided by the so-called verb-second (V2) effect, characteristic of Germanic languages (except for English), and it clearly speaks in favor of the dual-system hypothesis. In V2 languages, the finite verb is placed in the second structural position of the sentence, i.e. if some constituent other than the subject is placed in initial position, the subject follows the finite verb. Given that young children frequently use constructions beginning with a deictic expression like "there" or with some other type of adverbial, examples of this sort are likely to appear in the recordings of young children. A number of studies investigated this phenomenon in different corpora where German is acquired simultaneously with a non-V2 language like French, Italian, Portuguese, or English. The results unambiguously show that in such constructions children place the finite verb in second position when using German main clauses and in third position in the respective other languages. Moreover, during the earliest period of multi-word utterances, one already finds that, in German as an OV language (placing non-finite verbs in final position of main clauses and both, finite as well as non-finite, verbs in final position of subordinate clauses), bilingual children use clause-final position of verbs, but not in VO languages like French and Portuguese. In addition, it has been shown that word order patterns which are specific to these Romance languages and which are commonly attested in monolingual corpora, are never used in German, e.g. VOS order appears in French utterances of French-German bilinguals, but not in their use of German, neither during this early period nor later. What matters here, and what is essential for the single-system versus dual-system controversy, is the finding that the differences in word order patterns used in the two languages of bilingual children begin to appear as soon as they start using multi-word utterances, usually around age 1;10 when their MLU attains a value of approximately 1.75. In other words, the average utterance, at this point of development, contains less than two words. For obvious reasons, it is not possible to establish an earlier moment in linguistic development at which any reasonable generalizations could be made concerning the acquisition of syntax. One may thus conclude that the differentiation of grammatical systems happens very early and apparently with ease. Analyses of the acquisition of other grammatical phenomena confirm this conclusion, e.g. negative constructions in Basque-Spanish and in German-French children or the omission of subjects in cases where only one of the languages is a null subject-language (Italian-German, Portuguese-German). In each of these cases, bilingual children behave like their monolingual counterparts in each of their languages.

In summary, then, the available evidence favors very strongly the dual-system hypothesis. Morphosyntactic systems can be shown to be differentiated by children acquiring two languages simultaneously as soon as the earliest pieces of empirical evidence for a productive use of syntax and morphology become available. Note that most of the studies dealing with these questions are based on data from the production of spontaneous speech. It is very likely that more extensive research on language comprehension will be able to show that differentiation of grammatical systems occurs even earlier than toward the end of the second year. Moreover, although more research is still needed, analyses of phonological development in bilinguals suggest that differentiation of phonological systems happens with similar ease and that it precedes chronologically the separation of syntactic systems. In fact, it is not implausible to assume that language differentiation is initiated and enhanced by phonological bootstrapping into two distinct systems.

4.4   Autonomous or Interdependent Development

Recall that it has been claimed that the simultaneous acquisition of two or more languages can be qualified as first language development in more than one language. This claim is based on the assumption that the course of development in each of the languages of bilingual children does not differ qualitatively from the acquisition of the respective languages by monolinguals. So far, in view of what has been discussed in the previous section, one can conclude that this claim has been corroborated – neither the rate of acquisition nor the kind of language mixing observed in bilingual language use constitute serious evidence against it. Most importantly, there is broad consensus on the issue of early grammatical differentiation, and this is a necessary prerequisite for qualifying bilingual acquisition as first language development.

The fact, however, that the initial phases of bilingual development are qualitatively not distinct from what is observed in monolingual first language acquisition, is not sufficient to conclude that the course of development is essentially the same in monolingual and multilingual acquisition. If it can be shown that during later developmental phases bilingual acquisition is characterized by cross-linguistic influence, it cannot be excluded, *a priori*, that such interactions will result in qualitative differences, as compared to monolinguals. Importantly, possible influence of this sort is not restricted to transfer or interference, as discussed in research on L2 acquisition. Rather, as Paradis and Genesee (1996) have pointed out, grammatical interdependence in acquisition might lead to acceleration or delay of development as well as to transfer. This, however, could indeed result in qualitative differences, as compared to monolingual development, after all. Take the example of developmental sequences again, introduced above as characterizing qualitative similarities and differences between various types of acquisition. If certain grammatical devices are acquired earlier in some languages than in others, the availability of such grammatical means in one language might trigger in bilingual children the acquisition of corresponding ones in the other language. In other words, interdependent developments need not have negative effects, as is sometimes conveyed by notions like transfer or interference; rather, both acceleration and delay are imaginable as well. Most importantly, however, both might cause alterations in developmental sequences. Since, by definition, such sequences specify strictly ordered and irreversible successions of phases, each defined by the emergence of grammatical phenomena previously not used productively by the child, earlier as well as later emergence of one of the defining phenomena, resulting from the influence of the other language of a bilingual person, could have the effect of reordering a sequence and thus of qualitative change in bilingual as opposed to monolingual first language acquisition.

In view of these potentially important consequences, interdependence constitutes one of the major topics of current research on bilingual acquisition. Interestingly, some of the results obtained so far confirm that the three types of cross-linguistic development do occur, but qualitative alterations of the sort mentioned have not been found to date. In fact, rather than attesting to differences in the development of grammatical knowledge, these research results suggest that cross-linguistic influence causes it to be used more or less frequently during a given developmental phase. Another possibility is what has been referred to as a "temporary pooling of resources," as suggested by the Bilingual Bootstrapping Hypothesis proposed by Gawlitzek-Maiwald and Tracy (1996). The idea here is that if each language develops at a different pace, the more advanced system will boost the development of the less advanced. Thus, although the two grammars are seen as developing independently, the child is said to occasionally use sentences consisting of grammatical constructions imported into the use of the language which lags behind in development. This hypothesis remains controversial. Note, however, that independently of whether one agrees with this concept of bilingual bootstrapping, it refers to a phenomenon which surfaces only in specific contexts. This reveals the importance of defining those factors which favor cross-linguistic influence. One crucial variable appears to be the fact that the two languages do not develop at the same pace. Other relevant factors suggested in the literature are consistency of parental input, language dominance, and structural properties of the languages involved. What transpires quite clearly from this discussion is that none of these factors can explain the observed types of language use in a satisfactory fashion; see also the comments on dominance, above. A major problem for all these approaches is that only some of the children who can be characterized by one or more of these factors actually do show signs which might support the idea of interdependence. This suggests that they capture, at best, necessary but not sufficient requirements for cross-linguistic interaction to happen, and also that, in all likelihood, additional factors favoring interdependence still remain undiscovered.

Some of the most promising results in this debate have been obtained by focusing on structural properties of the two languages which are claimed to exhibit signs of interdependent developments. The basic idea behind these investigations is that there exist structural domains which are particularly prone to cross-linguistic influence. Several authors have explored the possibility, for example, that structural areas in which the two languages overlap are the ones where interdependence is most likely to be observed. Moreover, it has been argued that it is structural ambiguity in one of the bilingual's languages what makes such areas vulnerable for cross-linguistic interaction. The term "ambiguity," as it is used here, refers to constructions which, analyzed by means of developing grammars, appear to allow for more than one grammatical interpretation. If, then, the other language overlaps in surface constructions with the one exhibiting ambiguity and the unambiguous one provides strong positive evidence in favor of one of these options, bilingual learners are predicted to carry over the unambiguous solution to the other language. Müller and Hulk (2001), who develop this approach, interpret this as a case of unidirectional influence, independent of dominance and other more general properties attributed to one of the languages. They view this as a kind of "indirect" influence of one language on the other, as opposed to transfer which represents direct influence. As an illustration, they discuss the omission of objects in child language. In Germanic languages like German and Dutch, target deviant omission of objects is not uncommon among monolingual children; in Romance languages like French and Italian, on the other hand, this happens much less frequently. A possible explanation refers to the fact that the Germanic languages allow for topic drop in adult language use, i.e. elements placed in initial position can be omitted if they are identified by the context; in Romance languages, this phenomenon is restricted to a small set of verbs. This may lead children, during early phases of acquisition, to employ a pragmatic strategy by which empty elements are licensed via discourse. The use of this strategy fades out as syntactic knowledge develops which ultimately excludes this option. In the Germanic languages this happens later than in Romance because topic drop in adult language use offers apparent support for discourse licensing of empty categories. Bilingual learners are said to transfer this phenomenon from the language offering unambiguous input into the one with apparently ambiguous constructions. Hypotheses like this one, about direct and indirect cross-linguistic influence in bilingual children, offer sophisticated accounts of interdependent developments. Müller and Hulk (2001) propose, in fact, a generalization which, if correct, promises to lead to a deeper understanding of the mechanisms underlying these observations. They suggest that ambiguity of overlapping constructions alone will not suffice for the triggering of cross-linguistic interaction. Rather, only very specific structural domains are vulnerable in this sense, namely the interface levels where, according to grammatical theory, syntax interacts with other cognitive systems. In syntactic terms, the most likely candidate is the so-called C-domain, i.e. the structural level of the CP.

In conclusion, one can say that the issue as to how cross-linguistic influence might determine the course of acquisition in the two languages of bilingual children remains open to explanation. Three possibilities are suggested in this debate, namely transfer, delay and acceleration of the pace of development. In addition, such influences may also affect the frequency of use of specific structures. Importantly, the evidence currently available suggests that bilingual first language acquisition is not characterized by interdependent development of a type which would alter developmental sequences. Consequently, even if cross-linguistic interaction is confirmed as a phenomenon habitually found in the acquisition of bilingualism, it appears to refer to quantitative rather than qualitative properties of this type of language development. In other words, it does not constitute evidence against the claim that the simultaneous acquisition of two languages should be qualified as first language development in each of the languages acquired.

4.5 Successive Acquisition of Bilingualism: Maturation and Age

It has been argued above that one of the major findings of the research on child bilingualism is that the simultaneous acquisition of two or more languages can be characterized as an instance of first language development in each of the child's languages. This by now largely uncontroversial statement is mainly based on the study of bilingual development in children who are exposed to both languages from birth. The question, however, as to whether the same is also true for children acquiring their two or more languages successively is more controversial. The problem addressed here relates to the role of age and maturation in language development. The crucial issue on which this controversy hinges is whether the human language faculty or, more precisely, the "language-making capacity" is available indefinitely or whether it becomes accessible as a result of neuronal maturation and remains accessible only during a limited age period. If the latter view is correct, it follows that, if the onset of acquisition of another language occurs after such a *critical period*, the prediction is that there will be qualitative differences in the course of acquisition as well as in the grammatical knowledge ultimately attained, as compared to simultaneously acquired languages or monolingual first language acquisition. Importantly, the existence of a critical period for language development has significant implications not only for the acquisition of bilingualism but also for situations in which children do not have full access to the appropriate linguistic environment from birth onwards. The most dramatic cases are undoubtedly those where monolingual development is significantly delayed or interrupted, e.g. when children grow up in isolation. But this issue also becomes relevant, for instance, when children are deprived, in part or totally, of normal exposure to language, e.g. deaf children who are not exposed to sign language. Although important questions still remain unanswered, the evidence gathered so far suggests strongly that the human language-making capacity is, indeed, subject to maturational changes resulting in a critical period for language development. It is therefore necessary to explore the consequences of the critical period hypothesis (CPH) for the acquisition of bilingualism.

In its classical version developed by Lenneberg (1967), the critical period hypothesis claimed that native competence cannot be attained by mere exposure if the onset of acquisition happens after a certain age. Although it had to be modified in some respects, e.g. the claimed causal relationship between lateralization and the critical period is wrong, this hypothesis has proven to be correct; see Hyltenstam and Abrahamsson (2003) for a summary of the state of the art on this issue. An important modification of the original hypothesis concerns the age period, i.e. what may count as "a certain age," as mentioned above. This is still a particularly controversial issue, but it is obvious that the initial suggestion of a critical period ending approximately during puberty has to be abandoned. Note that the CPH does not specify a point of development at which the optimal age for language acquisition ends. Rather, it is generally understood as referring to an extended period, characterized by an abrupt onset, followed by a period which can be qualified as the optimal age (peak), and subsequently by a period of gradual offset. The issue is further complicated by the fact that the various components of grammar are affected by these changes during different age spans, e.g. phonological knowledge appears to become inaccessible before syntactic knowledge – in fact, subcomponents of phonology seem to fade out at different points of development. Allowing for a certain amount of individual variation, one can tentatively suggest that the peak begins shortly before the age of two years, and the gradual decline sets in before the age of five; the critical period then ends during an age span ranging approximately from age seven through ten years. (For a different approach to the study of the putative critical period, see chapter 5.)

More linguistic and neuropsychological research is needed in order to verify whether the age periods given here are indeed correct. But independently of whether the proposed age limits need to be modified or not, it can be deduced from the critical period hypothesis that one should distinguish between three types of bilingual acquisition: (1) simultaneous acquisition of bilingualism (2L1), if the child begins to acquire two or more languages during the first three or four years of life; (2) child second language (L2) acquisition, if the onset of acquisition of the second or further language happens between ages five and ten; (3) adult L2 acquisition, after the age of ten. Note that this classification of three acquisitional types hypothesizes qualitative differences with respect to the course of acquisition and the ultimate attainment by the three types of bilinguals. Whether this is indeed the case needs to be decided in the light of empirical research investigating linguistic and neuropsychological aspects of bilingualism acquired during different age ranges. Let us briefly look at what is reported from this type of research, in order to be able to assess the well-foundedness of these claims.

In the section on simultaneous acquisition of bilingualism above, it has been argued that this type of acquisition represents a case of multiple first language development; however, these children had been exposed to more than one language from birth. According to the typology of bilingualism based on the critical period hypothesis, successive acquisition of bilingualism during early childhood, i.e. when a child is exposed to one or more additional languages within the critical period, should be qualified in the same way. In other words, multiple first language competence should be attainable if the child is exposed to more than one language before the beginning of the offset phase of the critical period. Some authors, however, have claimed, in contradiction to this prediction, that successive acquisition of bilingualism will necessarily result in substantial competence differences, as compared to those cases in which children are exposed to their languages from birth. Our discussion of this controversy can be brief since the available empirical evidence is so scarce that it is impossible to draw serious conclusions. The little we know about this issue is sufficient to allow us to speculate that exposure to two or more languages during the optimal age for language development is a necessary but not sufficient condition for acquiring a native (L1) competence. This speculation is motivated by the fact that some studies report that severely limited intake during the first two years of life, e.g. due to temporary hearing impairment, may result in certain deficiencies of grammatical knowledge which, during later childhood years, can still be detected in tests although they are not apparent in ordinary language use. If it can indeed be corroborated that seriously reduced access to the input offered in the child's linguistic environment can have negative consequences for grammatical development, the question should be asked whether this might also happen in the acquisition of the second or third language in situations of successively acquired languages in early childhood. In fact, a similar problem could arise when one of the bilingual's languages is much "weaker" than the other one(s). It is well known that bilingual children sometimes use one of their languages more reluctantly or that they avoid using it altogether during several months although they interact normally in response to that language. Limited production need not, of course, indicate a lack of knowledge, but the possibility cannot be excluded that this is the case. Some authors have even suggested that a "weak" language in 2L1 acquisition might be acquired like an L2. Unfortunately, this issue is far from being settled, but, based on the limited evidence available, it is indeed imaginable that the development of grammatical knowledge might not lead to full native competence if, during the optimal age period, certain triggering data are not accessible at the critical moment, either because of delayed onset of acquisition or as a result of limited intake. For the time being, these speculative remarks must suffice; more research is needed on these issues.

Similar considerations apply in characterizing the second type of bilingualism, child second language acquisition, i.e. when the onset of the acquisition of another language falls within a period when the optimal age is past, but the learner still remains in the offset phase of the critical period. The onset for the acquisition of bilingualism thus falls within the range from five through ten years of age. The decision of whether child L2 acquisition must indeed be viewed as a distinct type of bilingual acquisition hinges on the question of whether it shares crucial properties with bilingual L1 development or rather with adult L2 acquisition. According to the critical period hypothesis outlined above, one should expect to find substantial differences between it and bilingual L1 development, but also some properties in which they resemble one another and differ crucially from adult L2. In order to be able to address this problem in a meaningful fashion, it is necessary to briefly comment on the latter, although this chapter is dedicated to the bilingual child.

Following the critical period hypothesis, the addition of one language or more after the optimal age, as in adult second language acquisition, implies that the human language-making faculty is no longer available to the learner, at least not in the same way as during early childhood. This does not mean, of course, that language acquisition is not possible any more. Rather, it suggests that learners have to resort to other cognitive capacities in order to develop a knowledge system about that language. Moreover, given that, in cases of successive acquisition of bilingualism, the language-making capacity of an individual has already been activated at least once, subsequent language acquisition might, in principle, draw on this previously acquired knowledge and could thus proceed as in those instances which happen during the critical age period. Assuming this perspective, one can predict that L2 learners' knowledge about the target grammar constitutes a hybrid system, partly made up of an L1-type competence and partly consisting of generalizations about surface properties of L2 utterances directly observable in the primary linguistic data.

In the literature on second language acquisition, one finds, in fact, a fairly broad consensus that adult L2 acquisition differs in a number of ways from (monolingual) L1 development. The two types of acquisition differ in, among other things, the following properties: (1) The initial state and very early phases are clearly different, presumably because, in L2 acquisition, previously acquired linguistic knowledge can be activated, possibly as a result of transfer of grammatical knowledge, and certainly in terms of language-processing mechanisms (parser, formulator) which are shaped by previous linguistic experience. (2) In both types of language acquisition one finds strictly ordered acquisitional sequences. These are not, however, identical in L1 and L2 acquisition. (3) As opposed to the relative uniformity of L1 developmental patterns, the course of L2 acquisition is characterized by a considerable amount of variability across learner types as well as across individual learners. (4) Leaving pathological cases aside, in monolingual as well as in bilingual first language development, all children attain complete competence in the target grammar. In L2 acquisition, it is only exceptionally the case that learners reach a level of L2 knowledge allowing them to behave linguistically in such a way as not to be distinguishable from native speakers.

Whereas many L2 researchers will probably not object to the points listed here, there is no consensus as to the explanations of such differences in terms of the underlying knowledge available to learners. The main point of disagreement concerns the question of whether L2 learners continue to have access to the language-making capacity of the child, as mentioned above. Much of this discussion over the past years has been couched in the framework of the theory of Universal Grammar (UG), assuming that UG accounts for the innate "knowledge" of L1 learners at the initial state of L1 development, i.e. the core of grammatical principles attributed to the language-making capacity. If this extensive debate on the accessibility of UG in L2 acquisition has not led to consensual solutions, it is partly because there is little agreement on what counts as empirical evidence in favor of or against UG accessibility. Still, some progress has been made in this debate, in that "all or nothing" claims tend to be abandoned in favor of more sophisticated approaches inquiring into which aspects of grammar are most likely to become inaccessible. Note that UG is conceived as comprising invariant principles which apply uniformly to all grammars of human languages, whenever the phenomena to which the principles apply exist in the grammar of a given language, as opposed to parameterized principles which are underspecified by UG, in the sense that they offer two (or possibly more) options, e.g. whether the subject of a sentence may be omitted or whether it must be phonetically realized. Thus, grammatical acquisition requires fixation of parameterized principles to one of the parametric options (setting the parameter to one of its values). In addition, the appropriate invariant principles need to be instantiated in the developing grammar, and language-specific properties of the target grammar need to be learned inductively. Arguably, it is the parameterized principles of UG which represent the type of grammatical knowledge that is subject to maturational change, since they define those aspects of grammar which are situated at the interface level where genetically transmitted information interacts with knowledge based on experience. It has been argued, on the other hand, that invariant principles remain available permanently; according to this view, they are triggered infallibly if a structure of the target grammar falls into the scope of their applicability. Language-specific properties, finally, must be learned by experience, independently of the innate linguistic knowledge specified by UG principles, and this is obviously possible during the critical period as well as afterwards.

On the basis of these ideas, one can sketch a scenario for L2 acquisition which allows one to formulate a number of empirically testable hypotheses about underlying similarities and differences between successive development of bilingualism and L2 acquisition. UG accessibility during the critical period for language acquisition implies that parameterized principles continue to be accessible and parameter values not instantiated in the previously acquired grammar can still be set on the value required by the target system. In L2 acquisition past the optimal age period, invariant principles of UG may still be expected to guide the acquisitional process, since these principles are not subject to maturational change. With respect to the acquisition of language-specific features, not constrained by UG, no significant differences between 2L1 and L2 are predicted to show up in the course of acquisition, either. Qualitative difference between the two types of language acquisition should become apparent, however, when it comes to the instantiation of parameterized principles in the developing grammars. Since this kind of information is claimed to become inaccessible, parameter values not activated during L1 acquisition cannot be retrieved anymore. This applies to parameters not instantiated at all in the previously acquired language as well as to parametric options not activated in the L1 grammar. Only the value to which a parameter has been set in the L1 is still available in L2 acquisition and might be transferred to the L2 system, but it cannot be "reset," in case L1 and L2 differ with respect to the appropriate parameter value. Note that this does not mean that the phenomenon in question cannot be acquired anymore. Rather, it follows that L2 learners need to learn the respective target properties in the usual sense of the term, i.e. inductively and by trial and error, whereas, in L1 development, knowledge is available prior to experience and must be triggered by exposure to the data. Thus, given that, according to this scenario, L2 knowledge is in part constrained by UG principles and in part the result of learning surface properties of the target language, it may indeed by characterized as a hybrid system, as suggested above.

In sum, following this approach, the essential difference between L1 and L2 acquisition is that parameterized grammatical knowledge is acquired, in part, by triggering the setting of parameters to specific values in L1, whereas in L2 only learning of the corresponding surface phenomena is possible. Interestingly, these two acquisitional mechanisms are empirically distinguishable. One of the differentiating properties is that the L1 development of grammatical structures is guided by task-specific principles provided by UG. This not only accounts for the fact that there exist developmental sequences, but also that they are uniform across learners and that they lead to full grammatical competence. Moreover, parameters refer to abstract grammatical features, each motivating the presence of a number of apparently unrelated surface phenomena; the setting to a specific value therefore leads to the chronologically simultaneous emergence of a cluster of constructions in the language use of the child. L2 learners, on the other hand, acquire these structures individually, if at all. These and a number of further empirically detectable characteristics make it possible to distinguish the different types of acquisition.

Let us, then, return to child L2 acquisition. It has been suggested, above, that, following the critical period hypothesis, one should expect to find substantial differences, as compared to monolingual as well as bilingual L1 development, since the onset of acquisition happens after the optimal age. In the light of what has been said about the role of triggering the setting of grammatical parameters for language acquisition, one can now ask whether the kind of empirical evidence alluded to before makes child L2 acquisition look more like L1 or like L2. Again, the available results from research studying children during the crucial age range between five and ten years are not conclusive, especially since some of the crucial pieces of empirical evidence mentioned above can only be obtained in longitudinal studies. Moreover, very few studies contrast child L2 with bilingual L1 acquisition; but it is this sort of contrast which is most telling, for in comparisons of L2 with monolingual acquisition, observed differences could be due to the presence of another language. By comparing simultaneous with successive acquisition of bilingualism, i.e. 2L1 with L2, this difference is minimized, and it becomes plausible that such differences are caused by factors related to the age of the learners. With this *caveat* in mind, one can nevertheless formulate a preliminary hypothesis. The available evidence suggests, in fact, fairly strongly that child L2 acquisition shares most properties with adult L2 acquisition. This is true for the widely acknowledged differences between L1 and L2 acquisition, mentioned earlier, i.e. concerning the initial state and early phases of acquisition, the kinds of acquisitional sequences found in longitudinal studies, the variability in the course of acquisition across L2 learners, and, less clearly, the incomplete ultimate attainment of grammatical competence. The strong resemblance between child and adult L2 is also confirmed by the lack of properties indicating parameter setting rather than ordinary learning, e.g. structures related to a specific setting of a parameter do not appear during one and the same acquisitional phase but are learned individually with varying success.

The tentative conclusion which may thus be suggested here claims that successive acquisition of bilingualism results in qualitative differences, as compared to monolingual as well as bilingual first language development, if the onset of acquisition falls into an age period after the optimal age for language learning. As for successive acquisition of bilingualism in childhood, exposure to another language during later childhood, i.e. approximately between ages five and ten, can indeed be considered as child L2, resembling more adult L2 than bilingual L1 development. If, however, bilingual acquisition begins during early childhood, e.g. before the age of five, it seems to be essentially identical to simultaneous acquisition of two first languages since birth.

It should be emphasized, again, that part of the findings reported here must be considered as preliminary, particularly the ones referring to successive acquisition of bilingualism during childhood. It is therefore important to note that some of these results gained by analyses of bilingual language use seem to be corroborated by evidence from neurophysiological and neuropsychological studies. The basic idea is that processing of grammatical structures activates certain task-specific processes in the brain and that L1 processing relies on a dedicated left-hemispheric cerebral network, if language acquisition happens during the optimal age. In L2 acquisition, on the other hand, different and/or additional processes are triggered, and processing of this information involves different and/or additional areas of the brain, left- and right-hemispheric, and highly variable across individuals. The question then is what happens in the case of simultaneous and of successive child bilingualism. Results of studies using hemodynamic (measuring blood flow) as well as electrophysiological (measuring neuronal activity) methods confirm the importance of age of acquisition for the functional specialization of language in the brain. Functional neuronal imaging experiments, e.g. functional magnetic resonance imaging (fMRI), suggest a common anatomical substrate and common pattern of activation for both languages acquired during early infancy; late bilinguals, on the other hand, exhibit spatial separation of the languages in the brain. Interestingly, it has been suggested that an increasing activation of the right hemisphere can be observed if the onset of acquisition of a language happens after the age of four. In sum, although much more research is needed, especially with bilinguals who acquired their languages simultaneously since birth or successively during early childhood, evidence compiled by behavioral as well as by neurophysiological investigations emphasizes the role of maturation and age for the successive acquisition of bilingualism. Only if the second language is acquired during early infancy is it likely to result in a native-like competence, much as in the simultaneous acquisition of bilingualism since birth. (For additional discussion of types of bilinguals, see chapters 1–3, 5, 7–10, and 22; for a different approach to problems in the study of second language acquisition and bilingualism, see chapter 5.)

4.6 Summary and Conclusions

The bilingual child has attracted the attention of a rapidly increasing number of research studies, especially over the last 25 years. One important result of these investigations is that they have established, beyond reasonable doubt, that children acquiring two or more languages from birth are able to differentiate the grammatical systems of their languages from very early on and without apparent effort. The subsequent course of acquisition proceeds through the same developmental phases as those observed in the respective monolingual children. The overall rate of acquisition in each of these languages is also comparable to that of monolinguals, i.e. it falls within the range of what is generally regarded as normal. One can thus conclude that bilingual acquisition is not different qualitatively from monolingual first language development and leads to the same kind of grammatical competence. This does not mean, however, that the bilingual child is "two monolinguals in one person." Rather, bilinguals acquire abilities and skills in using each of their languages which reflect specific needs and preferences; this includes the capability of switching between languages in a systematic fashion, constrained by social requirements as well as by grammatical restrictions.

But although bilingual development has been shown not to be qualitatively distinct from monolingual acquisition, the question of whether bilingual acquisition is typically characterized by cross-linguistic influences, or whether it proceeds in an autonomous fashion in each of the languages being acquired, is still open for discussion. A preliminary summary of this debate indicates that possible interdependent developments may result in an acceleration or delay in the acquisition of specific constructions, or in an increase or decrease in the frequency of use of particular structures. This does not, however, seem to result in qualitative changes of either the course or the ultimate success of grammatical acquisition. In fact, even among researchers who emphasize the importance of cross-linguistic interactions, there appears to be a general consensus that the effects are, at most, temporary and do not affect the nature of the ultimately attained competence.

What has been said so far refers to the simultaneous acquisition of bilingualism from birth. With respect to the successive acquisition of bilingualism, the picture is much less clear. There is good evidence speaking in favor of the critical period hypothesis according to which the acquisition of a further language beyond the optimal age range will lead to substantial differences in the course of acquisition as well as in the grammatical knowledge ultimately attained. This hypothesis is, however, not generally accepted with respect to adult second language acquisition, and it is even more controversial when it comes to contrasting child L2 acquisition with monolingual or bilingual first language development. The preliminary conclusion which has been drawn in this chapter states that due to brain maturation, significant changes happen around the age of five; consequently, both child and adult second language acquisition differ in important respects from those cases where the onset of acquisition occurs during the earlier age ranges. Admittedly, however, much more research is needed on this issue. As for successive acquisition of bilingualism during the first three or four years of life, we know even less. It appears that onset of acquisition during the optimal age is a necessary but not sufficient condition for the development of a native L1 competence. But due to the limitations of our current knowledge, this is a rather speculative conclusion.

The research summarized in this chapter has, nevertheless, attained a number of important goals, notwithstanding the gaps of knowledge about some important issues. Most importantly, it has demonstrated that the simultaneous acquisition of two or more languages from birth qualifies as an instance of multiple first language acquisition in that the bilingual child attains the same type of grammatical knowledge as the respective monolinguals. Native competence seems attainable in successive acquisition of bilingualism, too, if it happens during early childhood, although this issue still requires more thorough investigation. These research results have significant implications beyond the immediate concern of gaining a better understanding of language acquisition in the bilingual child. On the one hand, concerns about possible problems of bilingual children have been shown to be unwarranted, thus eliminating reasons for concerns by parents and educators. On the other hand, these results have implications for linguistic theories which need to account for this capacity for multilingualism. Clearly, the human language faculty has an endowment for multilingualism.

REFERENCES

Brown, R. (1973). *A first language.* Cambridge, MA: Harvard University Press.

De Houwer, A. (1990). *The acquisition of two languages from birth: A case study.* Cambridge, UK: Cambridge University Press.

Gawlitzek-Maiwald, I. and Tracy, R. (1996). Bilingual bootstrapping. *Linguistics*, 34, 901–26.

Genesee, F. (1989). Early bilingual development, one language or two? *Journal of Child Language*, 16, 161–79.

Grosjean, F. (1989). Neurolinguists, beware! The bilingual is not two monolinguals in one person. *Brain and Language*, 36, 3–15.

Grosjean, F. (1999). The bilingual's language modes. In J. L. Nicol (ed.), *One Mind, Two Languages: Bilingual Language Processing*, pp. 1–25. Oxford: Blackwell.

Hyltenstam, K. and Abrahamsson, N. (2003). Maturational constraints in second language acquisition. In C. Doughty and M. Long (eds.), *Handbook of Second Language Acquisition*. Oxford: Blackwell.

Köppe, R. and Meisel, J. M. (1995). Code-switching in bilingual first language acquisition. In L. Milroy and P. Muysken (eds.), *One Speaker – Two Languages: Cross-Disciplinary Perspectives on Code-Switching*,

pp. 276–301. Cambridge, UK: Cambridge University Press.

Lenneberg, E. (1967). *Biological foundations of language.* New York: Wiley & Sons.

Leopold, W. F. (1939–49). *Speech Development of a Bilingual Child: A Linguist's Record*, 4 vols. Evanston, IL: Northwestern University Press. (New York: AMS Press, 1970.)

Meisel, J. M. (1989). Early differentiation of languages in bilingual children. In K. Hyltenstam and L. Obler (eds.). *Bilingualism Across the Lifespan: Aspects of Acquisition, Maturity, and Loss*, pp. 13–40. Cambridge, UK: Cambridge University Press.

Müller, N. and Hulk, A. (2001). Crosslinguistic influence in bilingual acquisition: Italian and French as recipient languages. *Bilingualism: Language and Cognition*, 4, 1–21.

Paradis, J. and Genesee, F. (1996). Syntactic acquisition in bilingual children: Autonomous or independent? *Studies in Second Language Acquisition*, 18, 1–15.

Poplack, S. (1980). Sometimes I'll start a sentence in English Y TERMINO EN ESPAÑOL: Toward a typology of code-switching. *Linguistics*, 18, 581–618.

Quay, S. (1995). The bilingual lexicon: Implications for studies of language choice. *Journal of Child Language*, 22, 369–387.

Ronjat, J. (1913). *Le Développement du langage observé chez un enfant bilingue*. [The development of language in a bilingual child.]

Paris: Librairie Ancienne H. Champion.

Volterra, V. and Taeschner, T. (1978). The acquisition and development of language by bilingual children. *Journal of Child Language*, 5, 311–26.

FURTHER READING

Deuchar, M. and Quay, S. (2000). *Bilingual Acquisition: Theoretical Implications of a Case Study*. Oxford: Oxford University Press.

Döpke, S. (1992). *One Parent – One Language: An Interactional Approach*. Amsterdam: John Benjamins.

Köppe, R. (1996). Language differentiation in bilingual children: The development of grammatical and pragmatic competence. *Linguistics*, 34, 927–54.

Lanza, E. (1997). *Language Mixing in Infant Bilingualism: A Sociolinguistic Perspective*. Oxford: Clarendon Press.

Meisel, J. M. (ed.) (1990). *Two First Languages: Early Grammatical Development in Bilingual Children*. Dordrecht: Foris.

Meisel, J. M. (ed.) (1994). *Bilingual First Language Acquisition: French and German Grammatical Development*. Amsterdam: John Benjamins.

Schlyter, S. (1993). The weaker language in bilingual Swedish-French children. In K. Hyltenstam and A. Viberg (eds.). *Progression and Regression In Language: Sociocultural, Neuropsychological and Linguistic Perspectives*, pp. 289–308. Cambridge, UK: Cambridge University Press.

5 Bilingualism and Second Language Acquisition

YUKO G. BUTLER AND KENJI HAKUTA

5.1 Introduction

In this chapter, we focus on key issues at the intersection of bilingualism and second language acquisition that have proven to have longevity and have become some of the core issues in the field. First, we introduce definitions and major typologies for classifying bilingual individuals. We then discuss the related theoretical, methodological, and applied issues that influence such typologies. Topics covered include the construct of language proficiency, the effect of age of exposure in second language (L2) acquisition, the interaction between L1 and L2, and the socio-psychological aspects of L2 acquisition.

5.2 Definitions of Bilingualism

Bilinguals are often broadly defined as individuals or groups of people who obtain the knowledge and use of more than one language. However, bilingualism is a complex psychological and socio-cultural linguistic behavior and has multi-dimensional aspects. There is no agreed-upon definition of bilingualism among researchers. How much does one need to "know" of more than one language in order to be qualified as "a bilingual individual"? What do we mean by "knowing" two languages?

As is often believed, bilinguals could be defined as individuals who have "native-like control of two languages" (Bloomfield, 1933, p. 56). However, this strict view of bilingualism limits the number of individuals and groups that could be classified as bilingual, not to mention the fact that such a definition makes it difficult to operationalize "native-like fluencies."

On the other hand, Haugen (1953) defined bilinguals as individuals who are fluent in one language but who "can produce complete meaningful utterances in the other language" (p. 7). This definition allows even early-stage L2 learners to be classified as bilinguals. Many researchers employ this broader view of bilinguals and include in their definition of bilinguals those individuals who have various degrees of proficiency in both languages (e.g. Hakuta, 1986; Macnamara, 1967; Mohanty and Perregaux, 1997; Valdés and Figueroa, 1994). Broader definitions of bilingualism have an advantage in that they incorporate the developmental processes of second language acquisition into the scope of studies of bilingualism (Hakuta, 1986). Grosjean (1999), for instance, focuses on the daily use of two languages among bilinguals, and distinguishes bilinguals who use more than two languages in daily life from "dormant bilinguals" who retain knowledge of different languages but no longer use them in daily life.

In this chapter, we adopt a broader notion of bilinguals which corresponds to the recent shift of focus among bilingual researchers away from the acquisition of formal rules of language and onto communicative skills (Mohanty and Perregaux, 1997). The present authors define bilinguals as individuals or groups of people who obtain communicative skills, with various degrees of proficiency, in oral and/or written forms, in order to interact with speakers of one or more languages in a given society. Accordingly, bilingualism can be defined as psychological and social states of individuals or groups of people that result from interactions via language in which two or more linguistic codes (including dialects) are used for communication. Hamers and Blanc (2000) called individual bilingualism "bilinguality" and distinguish it from societal bilingualism. In this chapter, we focus on individual bilingualism or "bilinguality."

5.2.1 Classifications of individual bilinguals

A favorite activity for the field is attempting to classify bilinguals into different categories depending on linguistic, cognitive, developmental, and social dimensions. Some of the major typologies that often appear in the bilingual literature are summarized in table 5.1. There are a number of elements that account for the complexity of understanding bilingualism.

First, one should note that bilingualism has multiple dimensions. Reflecting the multi-dimensionality of bilingualism, researchers have proposed different classifications depending on which dimensions of bilingualism they focus on. For example, the distinction between *balanced* and *dominant* (or *unbalanced*) bilinguals (Peal and Lambert, 1962) is based on the relationship between the proficiencies of the respective languages that bilinguals master. Balanced bilinguals are those who acquire similar degrees of proficiency in both languages, whereas dominant (or unbalanced) bilinguals are individuals whose proficiency in one language is higher than that in the other language(s).

Compound, *coordinate*, and *subordinate* distinctions (Weinreich, 1953) focus on the dimensions of how two (or more) linguistic codes are organized by individuals. In compound bilinguals, two sets of linguistic codes (e.g. 'dog' and 'perro') are stored in one meaning unit, whereas in coordinate bilinguals, each linguistic code is presumed to be organized separately into two sets of

Table 5.1 Typology of bilingualism.

Typology	Point of focus (Dimension)	Characteristics of SLA	Possible outcomes	Related issues and educational implications
Balanced Dominant (Peal & Lambert, 1962)	Relationship between proficiencies in two languages	Functional differences; related to age factor (?)	Differences in proficiencies in L1 and L2: achieving equal level of proficiency in L2 with L1 (balanced); L2 proficiency varies but not the same as L1 (dominant)	Conceptualizing and assessing one's language proficiency; Cummins's threshold hypothesis and interdependent hypothesis; semilingualism
Compound Coordinate Subordinate (Weinreich, 1953)	Organization of linguistic codes and meaning unit(s)	Functional differences; differences in form–meaning mapping	Differences in semantic representation and information processing for L1 and L2	Difficulties with operationalizing distinctions and testing differences
Early Simultaneous Sequential Late (Genesee et al., 1978)	Age of acquisition	Maturational differences; schooling differences	Attainment of L2 proficiency varies by age of acquisition; L1 proficiency is not addressed	Neurolinguistic differences (?); critical period hypothesis

Incipient Receptive Productive	Functional ability	Functional and motivational differences	Different proficiencies in L1 and L2 in different domains	
Additive Subtractive (Lambert, 1974; 75)	Effect of L2 learning on the retention of L1	L2 as enrichment with or without loss of L1; status of a language in a given context	L2 as enrichment without loss of L1 (additive); L1 is replaced by L2 (subtractive)	Social status of individual groups and the social value of their L1 greatly influences the retention of L1; support for literacy in L1 and L2 literacy development
Elite Folk (Fishman, 1977); Circumstantial Elective (Valdés & Figueroa, 1994)	Language status and learning environment; literacy support of L1	Differences in language status and value of bilingualism	No or little additive value of L1 as a language minority status (folk); additive value of L2 (elite)	Support for literacy in L1 and L2 literacy development
Bicultural L1 monocultural L2 acultural Deculturated (Hamers & Blanc, 2000)	Cultural identity	Differences in acculturation process	Cultural identity shaped by two cultures (bicultural); identity in one culture; loss of L1 culture	High bilingual competence does not necessarily coincide with dual identity

meaning units. In subordinate bilinguals, linguistic codes in their L2 are presumed to be interpreted through their L1. Namely, they are thought to have
two sets of linguistic codes but only one meaning unit, which is accessible
only through their L1. Bilinguals also can be classified into *early* and *late
bilinguals* depending on the age of exposure to two (or more) languages. Various other classifications are possible depending on variables such as language
usage and cultural identity.

In addition to these individual variables, bilinguals can be classified based
on various social variables. Focusing on the social status of language, Fishman
(1977) distinguished *folk bilinguals* from *elite bilinguals*. Folk bilinguals are language minority groups whose own language does not have a high status in the
dominant language society in which they reside, whereas elite bilinguals are
those who speak a dominant language in a given society and who also speak
another language which gives them additional value within the society. Valdés
and Figueroa's (1994) classification between *circumstantial* and *elective bilinguals*
is also based on dimensions similar to those proposed by Fishman (1977).

Lambert (1974) focused on how one's L2 affected the retention of one's L1.
Bilinguals who can enhance their L2 without losing L1 proficiency have been
referred to as *additive bilinguals*, whereas those whose L2 was acquired or
learned at the expense of losing their L1 have been referred to in the literature
as *subtractive bilinguals*. To be additive bilinguals, both of the languages learned
by bilingual individuals must be valued in the society in which they reside. It
is important to note that these dimensions are often interrelated. One may
argue that those who are exposed to two languages from birth (*simultaneous
bilinguals*) have a better chance to be balanced bilingual individuals. In sum,
bilingual individuals can be classified on the basis of different dimensions
both at the individual and social levels, and thus can be classified into different types of bilinguals depending on which dimensions of their bilingual characteristics are the focus of attention.

A second element of complexity comes from the fact that these dimensions
of bilingualism are continuous and not simply categorical constructs. One
cannot draw clear boundaries between different types of bilinguals within a
given dimension. Take, for instance, the dimension of proficiency. There could
be a wide range of combinations of proficiencies in two languages, as indicated schematically in figure 5.1.

Moreover, such combinations can be independently considered for different
aspects of language. For example, one can follow the traditional four skill
domains (listening, speaking, reading, and writing), or use other ways to characterize domains of language proficiency (e.g. Bachman and Palmer's (1996)
distinction of *real-life domains* and *language instructional domains*, or Cummins's
(1979) *basic interpersonal communicative skills* and *cognitive/academic language skills*).
As has been frequently documented among the second and third genera-
tions of immigrant families, for example, individuals may obtain very high
oral skills in both languages, but have limited literacy skills in one of the
languages.

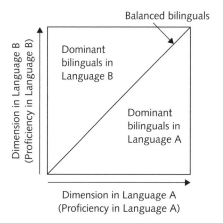

Figure 5.1   The relationship between two languages and the degree of bilingualism: the case of proficiency.

Conceptually, balanced bilinguals can be located on the diagonal line in figure 5.1, whereas dominant (or unbalanced) bilinguals can be located anywhere else. Conventionally, however, the term "balanced bilingual" is often used to refer only to those bilinguals who have equally high proficiencies in both languages. However, this terminology does not specify the level of proficiency; the term "high proficiency" itself is frequently ill-defined. There are many issues to consider in determining balanced and dominant bilinguals both conceptually and methodologically. These issues, including the notion of semilingualism, are discussed in more detail in later sections of this chapter. (For additional discussion of types of bilinguals, see chapters 1–4, 7–10, and 22.)

The context in which a language is used often adds further complexity to understanding bilingualism: bilinguals' language use is deeply embedded in context. For example, consider a situation in which a bilingual individual is participating in a discussion in a statistics class at college in the US. She may use only the language of instruction (English in this case) during the discussion. This may be because English is the only language that is common to all of the participants, or she may simply have a vocabulary that is sizeable enough to carry out an academic discussion in English. In this latter case, she may have very limited linguistic resources in her alternate language(s) in the given academic context. On another occasion, the same individual may code-switch between the two languages or use one of the languages exclusively when she talks about a popular movie with her sister who is also a bilingual. Once the sisters' mother (who may have limited oral skills in English) joins their conversation, the sisters may exclusively use the language that their mother understands. In each of these contexts, the individual can alternate between the two languages depending on the topic of discussion, interlocutors, formality/ informality of the conversational setting, psychological and physical conditions (e.g. under stress or anxiety), and so on. In other words, contexts define not only one's proficiency levels in the two languages of each skill domain, but they also determine the extent to which bilinguals can alternate between the two languages and the extent to which they can manage to or fail to use the two languages separately. Mackey (1967) labeled these factors "alternation" and "interference" respectively, and suggested that they are important enough to be included along with "degree" and "function" in describing bilingualism.

Grosjean's notion of language mode, which he defined as "a state of activation of the bilingual's language and language processing mechanism" (1999, p. 136; see also Grosjean, 2001), is similarly controlled by various contextual factors. According to Grosjean, language mode is also a continuum, ranging from monolingual mode to bilingual mode, and there are individual differences in ability among bilinguals when it comes to changing their mode along this spectrum.

Finally, it is also important to note that one's bilingual profile may change over time: bilingualism is not static but dynamic. An individual may lose oral proficiency in her primary language once she starts engaging in more activities in her second language. The profile of a bilingual individual is therefore constantly changing.

One can clearly see by now that bilingualism is a very complex and multi-dimensional linguistic behavior. Having acknowledged this complexity, we would like to focus on some of the major issues of bilingualism and second language acquisition that have emerged from these typologies. First, issues in conceptualizing and assessing bilingual individuals' language proficiencies will be discussed. Next, we address some of the primary factors that uniquely contribute to individual differences in attaining proficiency among L2 learners including: (1) influences stemming from the age of acquisition of L2; (2) the effect of L1 on L2 learning; and (3) socio-psychological factors that influence L2 learning.

5.3   The Construct of Language Proficiency

Until the early 1960s, psychometric studies tended to show negative associations between bilingualism and intelligence (Hakuta, 1986). A landmark study, Peal and Lambert (1962), pointed out a number of methodological problems in previous studies, including selection bias for bilingual participants and the language used for testing. After making adjustments for these methodological problems, they found a positive relationship between intelligence and bilingualism. Since then, various studies have reported the positive effects of bilingualism on one's cognition and metacognition in both verbal and non-verbal domains (Hamers and Blanc, 2000). (Studies conducted after 1962 are still not free from methodological problems, however. Reynolds (1991) provides a good discussion of some of the problems with study design and measurements that have surfaced in studies conducted after 1962.) (For more discussion of bilingualism and intelligence, see chapters 1, 15, 17, 22, and 23.)

One of the key factors in studies that have shown positive effects of bilingualism on cognition seems to have been the selection of balanced bilinguals. As long as one can become a balanced bilingual, one can benefit from more positive effects than one's monolingual counterparts, and the more balanced one's proficiency becomes, the higher cognitive advantage one can enjoy (Hakuta and Diaz, 1984). As mentioned already, balanced and dominant bilinguals are determined on the basis of the relationship between the bilingual individual's proficiency in both languages. However, determining a person's proficiency in two languages is much more complicated than it looks at first glance. How can we measure someone's proficiency in two languages? What is one's proficiency in a given language from the beginning?

Proficiency can be conceptualized and measured in various ways, reflecting the different views that exist towards what the term "language" itself designates. In SLA research, which is widely influenced by the theories and methodology used in L1 acquisition research, one can summarize the major views of language into three groups: (1) the formal linguistic view; (2) the cognitive and functionalist view; and (3) the socio-cultural view (Hakuta and McLaughlin, 1996). This grouping itself may be rather oversimplified; there are approaches that integrate parts of each view. However, this classification scheme gives a convenient overview of how "language" is conceptualized in different schools of thought.

The formal linguistic view defines language in the narrowest sense and primarily focuses on the syntax of languages. The formal linguistic view is heavily influenced by the theoretical framework originally developed by Chomsky (1965). In answering the "logical problem" of why children can acquire (not simply imitate) languages despite insufficient input, Chomsky proposed that human beings are equipped with an innate ability to access an unconscious knowledge of grammar called *universal grammar (UG)*. In his Principles and Parameters theory (Chomsky, 1981), UG involves a set of principles, some of which are universal and some of which are parameterized (that is, variable). Depending on the child's exposure to a particular linguistic environment, different values are set for a given parameter. This system of principles and parameters is considered to be the basis for language acquisition. That is to say, from this viewpoint, language acquisition is considered to be a process of developing the grammar of a particular language by exposure to an immediate environment consisting of speech in the language being acquired.

There are several points worth highlighting here in order to clarify the differences that exist between this view of language and the other two views. First is Chomsky's distinction between competence and performance. Competence was originally defined as "the speaker-hearer's knowledge of language," and performance as "the actual use of language in concrete situations" (Chomsky, 1965, p. 4). Importantly, what he focused on investigating was speakers' knowledge of abstract rules of grammar (namely, grammatical competence).

Second, what Chomsky postulated was the "ideal" speaker's (intuition) of syntax of his or her first language "in a completely homogeneous speech-community" (1965, p. 3). Variation of language use within and across individuals did not fall within his scope of interest.

Third, UG was considered to be specific to language, or what Chomsky refers to as "task-specificity"; this was not a general cognitive system. Language primarily functions as "the vehicle of cognitive growth" (Brown, 1996, p. 3), but it is not part of general cognition. Although Chomsky did not directly mention the mechanism of second language acquisition (SLA), his theory of language has been extended to serve as a base for SLA research by many formal linguists (for detailed reviews that have recently been published, see Hawkins, 2001; Herschensohn, 2000; White, 1989, 1996). The central issue for many of these SLA researchers has been whether or not L2 learners can access the principles of UG. How do L2 learners set and/or reset parameters through exposure to L2 based on the parameters that have already been set in their L1? Some researchers have argued that L2 learners can fully access their UG (e.g. Flynn, 1991, 1996). Others have argued that while L2 acquisition is constrained by UG, the types of competence attained by L2 learners differ from those of native speakers (e.g. White, 1989, 1996). And yet others claim that L2 learners do not have direct access to UG (Clahsen and Muysken, 1986), or have access only through their L1 (Bley-Vroman, 1990; Schachter, 1996). In his "Fundamental Difference Hypothesis" Bley-Vroman argues (1990) that there is a fundamental difference between L1 and L2 acquisition. According to him, adult L2 learners do not access UG; however, using the knowledge of their L1 as well as other general cognitive abilities, adult L2 learners can handle abstract rules in their L2.

While the formal linguistic view focuses on the linguistic aspects of competence, other researchers have taken a broader view of language and have included the communicative aspects in their research. *Communicative competence* was proposed by Hymes (1967, 1972); the term refers to both the *knowledge* and the ability to use language that is socially acceptable in a given context (*ability for use*). Such knowledge and ability are considered to be part of native speakers' overall competence in their L1. In other words, Hymes's notion of communicative competence concerns both psycholinguistic and sociolinguistic knowledge of language and the ability to use knowledge that is considered to be part of *performance* in Chomsky's theory. Canale and Swain (1980) identify three components of communicative competence (grammatical competence, sociolinguistic competence, and strategic competence). Discourse competence was later added as a fourth component in the model later proposed by Canale (1983). Canale and Swain's notion of communicative competence is different from that of Hymes in that they cover only the knowledge aspect of Hymes's communicative competence, not the ability for use (McNamara, 1996). Despite criticisms of this framework, Canale and Swain's model has widely influenced both cognitive/functionalist approaches and sociocultural approaches to the study of SLA (Shohamy, 1996).

Whereas the formal linguistic view sees language acquisition as innate and as a specialized operation that is distinct from general cognition, the cognitive/ functionalist view considers language acquisition to be data-driven and a part of general cognition. Drawing from cognitive and learning theories such as information-processing models (e.g. Anderson, 1983; Gagné, 1985; Shiffrin and Schneider, 1977), schema theory (e.g. Gagné, 1985; Rumelhart and Ortony, 1977), research on experts versus novices (e.g. Chi, Glaser, and Farr, 1988; de Groot, 1965; Simon and Chase, 1973), and connectionist modeling (Rumelhart and McClelland, 1986), researchers who take this approach see L2 acquisition as a case of cognitive problem solving.

The aspects of language investigated under this perspective are not limited to rule-governed structures of language (primarily syntax) but extend to such areas as vocabulary, comprehension and production of oral and written languages, strategies, attention, metacognition, and translation (Bialystok, 1991a, 2001; de Groot and Kroll, 1997; Juffs, 2001; Nicol, 2001). Proponents of this perspective have been interested in: learners' linguistic information, such as how their lexicons are organized and stored in memory (e.g. de Groot, 1992; Kroll and Stewart, 1994; Pavlenko, 1999; Potter et al., 1984; see also chapter 9 of the present volume); how learners utilize knowledge-based and control-based skills, and the role of metacognition (e.g. Bialystok, 1991b; Bialystok and Ryan, 1985; chapters 7 and 8 of the present volume); the mechanism by which cognitively demanding control processes eventually become automatic processes (e.g. McLaughlin, Rossman, and McLeod, 1983); in the restructuring of internal representations (e.g. McLaughlin, 1987, 1990); in the mechanisms of form–meaning mapping processes (Bates and MacWhinney, 1982; MacWhinney, 1997); in how the focus of attention shifts (e.g. Segalowitz, 2000); and in translation ability (e.g. Malakoff and Hakuta, 1991); and so on.

A third view, the socio-cultural view, provides a broader definition of language than the other two approaches. This view stresses the social and interpersonal communicative aspects of language. Socio-cultural approaches to SLA are concerned with both the variation of language and the sociological and socio-psychological aspects of language (Preston, 1996).

It has been claimed that socio-cultural variables constrain SLA in both systematic and non-systematic ways (Ellis, 1985). Inspired by William Labov's series of pioneering works on speech variation (1972), researchers have demonstrated how L2 learners show contextual variability depending on variables such as the linguistic environment (Dickerson, 1975), social norms of L1 variation (Schmidt, 1977), interaction partners (Beebe and Zuengler, 1983), the function of interaction (Tarone, 1983, 1985), and discourse topics (Eisenstein and Starbuck, 1989; Zuengler, 1989). Although there is no dispute over the existence of variation, there is some concern with regard to how such variation can be accounted for in theories of SLA (Gregg, 1990; Schachter, 1986). Some sociolinguists have taken the position that all variation is systematic. To support this claim, they have attempted to develop models that incorporate probabilistic values for influences on various forms in the language produced by L2 learners (Preston, 1993, 1996).

Socio-cultural approaches to L2 acquisition also cover a wide range of social and cultural aspects of language that are related to the learner's acquisition of communicative competence. As mentioned before, communicative competence is not limited to knowing linguistic codes or referential meanings, but also involves the ability to use language appropriate to a given socio-cultural context, employing various interaction strategies, and understanding the various functions of language as used in speech acts defined by a given speech community. A substantial amount of sociolinguistic research has been conducted using both micro- and macro-level analyses (e.g. Goffman, 1981; Gumperz, 1982; Kramsch, 1993; McKay and Hornberger, 1996; Wolfson, 1989). This research has provided a wealth of information with regards to the sociolinguistic and pragmatic aspects of communicative competence. The assessments of a person's language proficiency should include sociolinguistic and pragmatic knowledge as well as the ability to use such knowledge. Thus, the importance of employing communicative and pragmatic assessments using authentic material is stressed.

Reflected in these different views of "language," there is no simple answer to how to conceptualize language proficiency and how to measure it. Does proficiency refer to the mastery of one's knowledge of language or does it include the ability to use such knowledge? Is knowledge of language limited to knowledge of grammar, or does it include other psycholinguistic and socio-cultural aspects of language? Which components of communicative competence should be considered as the subjects of proficiency? To what extent should non-linguistic cognitive factors and non-cognitive factors (e.g. "motivation" and other affective factors) be included in measuring proficiency? How are all these different aspects of language related? How do different domains and contexts relate to proficiency?

Various "language proficiency" tests have been developed, but they measure different aspects of language. Hernandez-Chavez, Burt, and Dulay (1978) proposed a model of language proficiency that has 64 separate components. In stark contrast, Oller (1979) suggested that there is only one factor, "global language proficiency," that underlies language proficiency. Others have seen more than one factor in language proficiency data. Snow (1987a, 1990, also Snow et al., 1991) found that bilingual children's performance in a conversational task had little correlation, in either language, with their performance in a definition task that was highly decontextualized.

Cummins (1979, 1980) introduced a similar task analysis using two dimensions, "range of contextual support" and "degree of cognitive involvement," and proposed two types of proficiencies. *Basic interpersonal communicative skills* (those required in context-rich and less cognitively demanding tasks) are easily acquired, while *cognitive/academic language proficiency* (required in context-reduced and cognitively demanding tasks) takes longer to acquire. Researchers such as Cummins stressed the importance of considering the contexts in which tasks are conducted in order to fully understand someone's proficiency, arguing that "[t]here is no universal structure of proficiency that can be defined outside of particular contexts" (Cummins, 2000, p. 136).

Assessing an individual's relative proficiency between two languages in a given context is very complicated. In determining whether an individual is a balanced or dominant bilingual individual, there are two factors one needs to consider: (1) how to determine such a person's proficiency in each of his or her two (or more) languages; and (2) how to compare the individual's proficiencies in each language. The first question deals with how to locate someone's proficiency in the continuum ranging from monolingual individuals in Language A to monolingual individuals in Language B in figure 5.1 above. The second question deals with how to adequately determine proficiency measurements compatible with both languages in order to compare the proficiencies across languages.

There are several challenges in completing this task. First of all, it is not clear how we can determine the norm for a monolingual *native speaker*. At least at the performance level, one can observe variations among native speakers in any given language. Some native speakers have more vocabulary than other native speakers. Some can make jokes much better, read faster, or write better than other native speakers. It has been reported that there are ranges of abilities even among "educated native speakers," and it is still controversial as to what monolingual native speakers can or cannot do with respect to language and how "accurately" they can use their language (Valdés and Figueroa, 1994).

A second problem is the validity of locating monolingual native speakers and bilinguals on the same spectrum: one cannot determine bilinguals' proficiencies in relation to monolingual native speakers' proficiencies if linguistic abilities between these two groups are qualitatively different. Grosjean (1982, 1998, 1999, 2001) has criticized a monolingual view of bilinguals, that is, the view that bilinguals are essentially two monolinguals coexisting in one individual. He argues that bilinguals are not simply juxtapositions of two monolinguals and should be qualitatively distinguished from monolingual speakers. Under this "holistic" view of bilingualism, it does not make sense to use the monolingual norm as the guideline for bilingual proficiency. Similar points have been made by other researchers (e.g. Cook, 1992, 1996; Herdina and Jessner, 2000).

A third problem stems from the limitations of existing measurements. In order to compare someone's proficiency in each of two languages, we need to develop a set of proficiency assessments in two languages that are "equivalent" in terms of both validity and reliability. Moreover, as we have already seen, bilingual individuals' knowledge and their use of language vary from domain to domain and from context to context in each language. Since it is impossible to cover all the areas that a bilingual individual possibly experiences in both languages, limited domains and contexts have been chosen for assessment. Existing measurements for language proficiency tests for bilingual children vary greatly in terms of the aspects and constructs that they attempt to measure (Zehler et al., 1994).

In sum, different ways to conceptualize someone's "proficiency" have been proposed in the L1 and L2 acquisition literature, and accordingly there are a number of challenges in accurately assessing a bilingual individual's "proficiency" in his or her two languages.

5.3.1   The age factor in L2 acquisition

We now turn to efforts to explain the substantial variability in attainment of L2 among learners and the factors that underlie this variability, the first of which is the age of the learner. It is often believed that in order to acquire high proficiencies in both languages, or to be balanced bilinguals, one has to start being exposed to L2 at a young age. The age factor is one of the most frequently discussed variables for explaining individual differences in L2 acquisition. While L1 acquisition usually starts at the same time for all L1 learners (i.e. birth), there is tremendous variation as to when individuals start learning a second language. Does research support the assumption that children are more efficient L2 learners than adults? Does one need to start learning L2 before reaching a certain age in order to attain native-like proficiency in L2?

In examining the effects of age on L2 acquisition, we need to separately consider its effect on the route of acquisition, the rate of acquisition, and the ultimate attainment of L2 proficiency. Regarding the route of acquisition, the age factor does not seem to have much effect. Bailey, Madden, and Krashen (1974), using the Bilingual Syntax Measure, showed that their adult L2 learners (regardless of their L1 backgrounds) acquired grammatical morphemes in an order similar to the L2-learning children who were reported in Dulay and Burt (1974). Fathman (1975) reported a similar result for 20 grammaticality items. However, these studies are not without problems with their methodology and measurements, and their results should be interpreted with caution. Because of a lack of carefully designed longitudinal studies, the effect of age on the route of L2 acquisition is inconclusive at this point.

Regarding the rate of acquisition, there is some evidence that adults outperform children when the amount of their exposure to L2 is controlled (e.g. Lowenthal and Bull, 1984; Olson and Samuels, 1973). However, Snow and Hoefnagal-Hohle (1978) found that in a typical, unstructured exposure to L2 (Dutch) for three months, their teenage group (consisting of 12- to 15-year-olds) showed the most rapid progress, followed by their adult group (15 years and older), and finally by their group of children (ages 3 to 10). Moreover, the advantage of older learners seemed to be only in the short term. After a 10-month exposure to L2, the children caught up with the adult group on most measures. In some specific domains, advantages for child learners were reported (e.g. Cochrane, 1980; Tahta, Wood, and Lowenthal, 1981), while others have not found any differences in the rate of acquisition between children and adult L2 learners (e.g. Slavoff and Johnson, 1995).

Researchers have been focused on the effect of age on second language acquisition, and the question of whether or not there is a critical period for language acquisition and how such a period might affect SLA has been a matter of heated debate. The notion of a critical period for language acquisition was first proposed by Penfield and Roberts (1959). Lenneberg (1967) later elaborated on this concept. On the basis of clinical data on patients with brain injuries and children with Down's syndrome, Lenneberg proposed that the critical period starts at around one year of age and ends at puberty, by which time the brain loses its plasticity (the critical period hypothesis). Although subsequent neurological research does not support his explanation, the notion of the critical period has inspired much research.

There is some evidence implying the existence of a critical period in L1 acquisition from data among deprived children (e.g. Curtiss, 1977), and deaf children who started being exposed to American Sign Language (ASL) at different ages (Newport, 1990). A few interesting points are worth noting in Newport's data. First, differences were found between native signers and those who were exposed to ASL at 4–6 years of age as well as those who were exposed to ASL after 12 years of age. Second, there were certain morphosyntactic domains (e.g. word order) which did not show any differences in performance among groups. In other words, age of first exposure seemed to constrain the mastery of certain domains but not others, and the age effects seem to start much earlier than "puberty."

There is substantial disagreement over whether or not the ultimate attainment of L2 is constrained by a critical period. Various empirical studies show that there is a decline in performance in different domains among older acquirers of a given L2. This trend is particularly evident in the domain of phonology acquisition. This general tendency of decline in performance itself is not a matter of dispute. What is controversial, however, is (1) whether or not this decline can be attributed to biological and neurological factors, namely, the existence of a critical period, and (2) whether or not it is actually possible for older learners to attain native-like proficiency in their L2. The disagreements are partially due to differences in the definition and interpretation of what constitutes the critical period.

In order to substantiate the existence of a critical period, Hakuta (2001) proposed that the following characteristics must be observed: "(1) there should be clearly specified beginning and end points for the period; (2) there should be a well-defined decline in L2 acquisition at the end of the period; (3) there should be evidence of qualitative differences in learning between acquisition within and outside the critical period; and (4) there should be a robustness to environmental variation inside the critical period" (pp. 195–6). According to Hakuta, to meet the conditions for (2), a linear decline in performance is not sufficient to be considered evidence for the critical period.

In the literature, there is no consensus as to when the onset and closure of the critical period take place. Researchers have suggested different times for closure, such as: at 5 years old (Krashen, 1973); 6 years old (Pinker, 1994); 12 years old or "puberty" (Lenneberg, 1967), and 15 years old (Johnson and Newport, 1989). Moreover, no clear explanations have been offered as to the reasons for the specific timing of the closure of the period.

Researchers who support the existence of a critical period in L2 acquisition have shown a significant negative correlation between the age of arrival in the country where the target language is spoken and the performance in chosen domains. At the same time they have argued that other factors such as length of residence in the country where the target language is spoken, affective factors (e.g. motivation and attitude), and years of studying L2 before arrival did not account for the decline (DeKeyser, 2000; Johnson and Newport, 1989; Oyama, 1976; Patkowski, 1980). Johnson and Newport (1989), for example, gave a grammaticality judgment test to English learners who arrived in the US between the ages of three and 39 years as well as to native English speakers. The results indicate that there is an age-related decline in performance at around seven years old and that this shows a gradual decline until 15 years of age. Performance was negatively correlated with the age of immigration among those who arrived in the US before the age of 15. However, no correlation was observed among those who arrived in the US after 17 years of age; large individual differences were observed. While these studies have been considered as yielding strong supporting evidence for the existence of the critical period in L2 acquisition, limitations with sampling, methods, instruments, and statistical analyses in existing studies have also been noted (e.g. Bialystok and Hakuta, 1994; Juffs and Harrington, 1995; Kellerman, 1995; Snow, 1987b).

Other researchers suggested that factors other than age might also be responsible for the ultimate attainment of L2. These researchers pointed to cases of adult groups and individuals who were able to successfully attain native-like proficiencies in a given L2 (e.g. Birdsong, 1992; Bongaerts, Mennen, and van der Slik, 2000; Coppieters, 1987; Ioup et al., 1994). These successful individuals received intensive instruction, showed very high motivation, and received continuous and massive L2 input (Bongaerts, 1999). Aptitude may be an important factor in the ultimate acquisition of an L2 for later starters (DeKeyser, 2000). It is important to note, however, that while the performance of such highly successful L2 learners may indeed be "native-like," some studies have still been able to locate subtle differences in performance in certain aspects between these successful L2 learners and "native speakers" (Coppieters, 1987; Ioup et al., 1994; Moyer, 1999).

Other opponents have attempted to provide evidence that there are no discrete changes in learning outcomes after the critical period (e.g. Bialystok and Hakuta, 1999; Birdsong and Molis, 2001; Butler, 2000; Flege, 1995, 1999; Flege, Munro, and MacKay, 1995; Hakuta, Bialystok, and Wiley, 2003). Flege, Munro, and MacKay (1995) examined the relationship between the degree of foreign accentuation (rated by native speakers of English) among Italian-speaking English-learners and their age of arrival in Canada. The results showed a linear decline: no discontinuity was observed. Flege (1999) proposed that L2 learners' pronunciation deviates not because they lose the ability to pronounce L2 sounds well, but because of their L1 sounds. According to Flege, interactions between L1 and L2 sounds among bilingual individuals "constrain" their accuracy of pronunciation in both languages. Similar evidence has been presented in other studies showing that those who started being exposed to an L2 at a very young age still show some deviations from monolingual native speakers (Hyltenstam, 1992).

Hakuta, Bialystok, and Wiley (2003) modeled a large sample of immigrants taken from the US census to specifically test for changes in slope and mean at certain putative critical ages. Although they demonstrated decline in self-reported English proficiency as a function of age of immigration, there was no evidence of a change in slope or any categorical shifts. They concluded that the key hallmark of the critical period could not be found in their large and representative sample. In short, the question of whether or not a "critical period" exists in L2 acquisition has yet to be definitively answered.

So far, the domains of investigation have been limited; a number of studies have focused on learners' morphosyntactic knowledge and pronunciation, but other aspects of language have not been studied (Hyltenstam and Abrahamsson, forthcoming). What makes it challenging to attribute age differences in performance to biological factors is that there are other non-biological factors (e.g. socio-cultural factors) that are closely interrelated to age. One can easily imagine that older learners and younger learners have different types of socio-cultural experiences when L2 learning takes place. Recently, some studies have even suggested that non-biological variables may be better predictors than the age of immigration, with one such variable being the learner's years of education (Flege and Liu, 2001). Flege, Yeni-Komshian and Liu (1999) demonstrated that age effects over performance disappeared if learners' educational backgrounds were controlled for.

Educational factors appear to have the most direct effect on language domains that are related to academic settings. Nakajima (1998) compared English reading performance among Japanese children who arrived in Canada at different ages (before 3, 3–6, 7–9, and 10–12), and examined how long they took to reach the norm among monolingual English-speaking children who were in equivalent age groups. Note that what Nakajima focused on was the domain of *cognitive academic language proficiency* (Cummins, 1979, 1980, 2000). She found that Japanese children who arrived in Canada between the ages of seven and nine years (and not the youngest group) took the shortest time to catch up with their native counterparts. It was also found that children's reading performance in their L1 (Japanese) was a good predictor for their performance in L2 reading (English). To what extent, then, is L1 involved in L2 acquisition? (For a different approach to the question of the existence of a critical period, see chapter 4.)

5.4 The Interaction Between L1 and L2

Another unique factor to consider in SLA is the influence of learners' first languages. How do learners' L1s influence their L2 acquisition processes? In the last 50 years, researchers have taken different views of the role of L1 in SLA. In the 1960s, employing contrastive analysis, it was believed that L1 had primary influence over L2 acquisition. During the heyday of behaviorism, language acquisition was considered to be a form of habit formation, and it was assumed that the learners' L1 habits interfered with their L2 habits

(Lado, 1957). It was claimed that learners' errors reflected the structure of their L1.

In the 1970s, however, researchers took a totally opposite view of the role of L1: the role of L1 in L2 acquisition was considered to be minimal. Error analysis revealed that, in fact, many of the errors made by learners could not be explained by L1 transfer. The errors could not be predicted by contrastive analysis. Studies of the order of acquisition of grammatical morphemes, such as Dulay and Burt (1974), also indicated that the acquisition order between L1 and L2 were strikingly similar, regardless of learners' L1 backgrounds. Learners' *interlanguage* (Selinker, 1972) was considered to be a unique intermediate system that emerged during the process of L2 acquisition and that differed from their L1.

Since then, the notion of transfer has been extended, and researchers have taken different approaches to transfer. Linguists who take the UG approach have been interested in investigating whether or not UG is accessible by L2 learners as well as what the role of L1 is in interacting with input from the L2 (White, 1996). Others have been interested in the cognitive mechanisms through which transfer occurs. For example, in the Competition Model, researchers investigated how L2 learners' information-processing mechanisms that function as part of their L1 can be "adjusted" to L2 sentence interpretation (Bates and MacWhinney, 1981; MacWhinney and Bates, 1989). The domains of investigation have not been limited to the structure of languages (e.g. syntax, phonology, and lexicon), but have been expanded to other complex cognitive and psychological domains such as reading, writing, communicative and metacognitive strategies, and pragmatics. Recently, it has been suggested that learners' first languages not only influence their acquisition of second languages *per se* but also affect the cognitive procedures that are employed in processing second languages (Koda, 1997).

Transfer has been found to occur in both formal and informal contexts, and among both children and adults, although the exact age and nature of transfer are still unclear (Odlin, 1989). Interestingly, it has been suggested that language distance influences the rate of L2 acquisition rather than the types of transfer; evidence of this can be seen, it is argued, in the patterns of errors that L2 learners produce (Odlin, 1989). In other words, if one learns a language that is typologically very different from one's L1, it may take longer to acquire the L2 compared with a language that is similar to one's L1. There is evidence from a simulation study using a neural-network model that indicates that language distance affects the rate of learning: the greater the distance between two languages, the longer it takes to learn. The model also showed an interaction between the language distance and the type of learning (i.e. simultaneous versus sequential types) (Inoue, 1996).

Schachter (1983) broadened the notion of transfer to include any prior knowledge that L2 learners have, including L2 learners' "imperfect" knowledge of L2. Transfer refers not only to the negative influences on L2 learning (interference) but also to the positive influences (facilitation). Transfer was observed not only from L1 to L2, but also from L2 to L1 (e.g. Verhoeven, 1991, 1994). Zobl (1992) also observed that multilinguals were more open when it came to judging ungrammatical sentences than monolinguals. Learners' L1 and L2 interact with each other. As a result, transfer is no longer considered to be either uni-directional or uni-dimensional, and some authors prefer to describe such interaction as "cross-linguistic influence" rather than transfer (e.g. Kellerman and Sharwood-Smith, 1986; Zobl, 1984). It has also been noted that socio-cultural contexts greatly influence the way in which transfer occurs (Odlin, 1989).

The influence of transfer on various aspects of language proficiency in academic contexts has gained substantial attention in the literature, reflecting a growing concern about educational achievement among language-minority students in a variety of countries. Numerous studies have reported that academic-related skills developed in L1 are related to those in L2. Recently, in particular, a growing number of studies on early literacy acquisition among bilinguals have indicated that there are relationships between various literacy subskills in L1 and L2. For example, relationships between L1 and L2 were found in receptive vocabulary knowledge (Umbel and Oller, 1995), cognates and morphological knowledge (Hancin-Bhatt and Nagy, 1994; Nagy et al., 1993), word recognition (Durgunoğlu, 1998; Durgunoğlu, Nagy, and Hacin-Bhatt, 1993), word recognition and reading comprehension (Verhoeven, 1994), and reading strategies used in L1 and L2 (e.g. Calero-Breckheimer and Goetz, 1993; García, 1998; Jimenez, García, and Pearson, 1994; Langer et al., 1990).

Cummins's interdependence hypothesis, stating that academic proficiency in L1 and L2 are interdependent, provided a theoretical framework for understanding the mechanism of bilingual proficiency in academic contexts. This "common underlying proficiency," composed of both conceptual and procedural knowledge and skills, enables bilinguals to transfer academic skills from one language to another. This transferability may be influenced by differences in language structures and orthographic systems (e.g. Verhoeven, 1994; also see Koda, 1994, 1997, for a review of transfer among adult L2 readers).

Cummins's (1976, 1979) threshold hypothesis attempted to describe the underlying mechanisms leading to individual differences in terms of positive and negative cognitive consequences among bilinguals. His original proposal stated that bilingual individuals can enjoy cognitive advantages if they attain "native-speaker competence" in both languages. However, if they have not attained such competence in either of the languages, they may fall into a state of "semilingualism" and may not be able to avoid negative consequences in their cognitive and academic development. The use of the label semilingualism, which was first introduced by Hansegard (1972) and its interpretation led to a heated debate (e.g. MacSwan, 2000; Martin-Jones and Romaine, 1986; Paulston, 1982). As Cummins admitted, "the term has no explanatory or predictive value but is rather a restatement of the equally ill-defined notion of 'limited proficiency in two languages'" (2000, p. 104). Whatever term is used and whatever "semilingualism" refers to, there are indeed individual differences in academic performance among L2 learners as well as monolingual students. The key questions seem to be (1) to what extent such individual differences in academic performance among L2 learners can be attributed to their "language proficiency" as opposed to their ability to master academic content knowledge and skills ("achievement"); and/or (2) whether or not individual variations in academic performance are better explained by qualitatively different constructs (i.e. separately for monolingual students and L2 learners).

5.4.1   Socio-psychological factors: identity and attitude

Another set of important factors influencing outcomes in L2 acquisition is the cluster of socio-psychological factors such as identity and motivation that are developed in a given socio-cultural learning context. Language acquisition is embedded in societies and cultures, and language development can be considered as an *acculturation* process. By encountering multiple cultural and ethnic groups and values, bilingual individuals can develop unique cultural and ethnolinguistic identities, separate from those of monolinguals (Hamers and Blanc, 2000).

In one of the earliest attempts in this area, Lambert (1974) conceptualized socio-psychological variables that underlie the mechanism for bringing about the various consequences of bilingualism. In his model, learners' attitudes and motivations (along with aptitude) influence the degree of language attainment. One's language attainment in turn influences one's identity. Additive bilingualism is possible if the learning environment values both the learners' L1 and L2 and allows them to develop a positive identity with both cultural/ ethnolinguistic groups and values. In contrast to this, if the society does not value the learners' L1, the result would be a subtractive bilingualism. While Schumann (1978) (in his "Acculturation Model") stressed that the actual "social distance" between the learner and the target language and culture influences the acculturation process, Giles and his colleagues argue that the "perceived social distance" is important for L2 acquisition (e.g. Giles and Byrne, 1982).

Much effort has been made to uncover the socio-psychological mechanisms that underlie language acquisition and to identify influential variables for successful L2 acquisition. A number of models have been proposed, including the "Socioeducational Model" (Gardner, 1979, 1983, 1985), the "Social Contextual Model" (Clément, 1980, 1987; Clément and Kruidenier, 1985), the "Self Determination Model" (Noels, Clément, and Pelletier, 1999), and various empirical studies have been reported in this regard. Positive attitudes are generally found to be related to higher degrees of L2 performance. Except for this general finding, the results of these studies are mixed.

Such mixed results can be attributed to (1) inconsistent definitions and conceptualizations of attitudes and other related variables, such as motivation, and (2) contextual variations under which these studies were conducted. The construct of "attitude" itself varies from model to model, and even within the same model in some cases. For example, Gardner (1985) distinguished motivation from attitude where motivation is composed of *instrumental* and *integrative* motivation. Instrumental motivation is based on functional goals, such as getting a good job by learning L2, whereas integrative motivation is based on a desire to integrate into the target language group and culture. However, in Tremblay and Gardner (1995), the authors included both integrative and instrumental motivation in attitude, and in Gardner, Tremblay, and Masgoret, (1997), the authors included only integrative motivation as an aspect of attitude.

The distinction between integrative and instrumental motivation is likewise not particularly straightforward (Au, 1988; Oller, Hudson, and Liu, 1977). Yet there is a strident debate over which types of motivation are strongly related to L2 performance. While some researchers claim that integrative motivation is more positively correlated to L2 performance (e.g. Gardner and Lambert, 1959; Gardner, Tremblay, and Masgoret, 1997; Lalonde and Gardner, 1985), others argue for a larger effect for instrumental motivation (e.g. Hinkel, 1996; Lukmani, 1972; LoCastro, 2001). The results seem to be greatly affected by the contextual variations where learning takes place.

One of the major limitations of this line of research is its limited ability to explain the causal relationship among variables. Many studies have demonstrated correlations among variables, but the causal relations among variables have not been fully understood. This has been the case even with recent efforts to introduce Causal Modeling by Gardner and his colleagues, as the researchers themselves have pointed out (Clément and Gardner, 2001; Gardner, 2000). Perhaps, as McLaughlin (1987) suggests, the relationship between attitude and L2 performance is bi-directional: those who have positive attitudes may attain higher achievement, and higher achievement also contributes to a more positive attitude.

In addition, a developmental perspective needs to be more fully incorporated into such theories. To date mixed results have been reported regarding the relationship between age and attitude (namely, whether attitudes are positively or negatively correlated with age). We know little about the mechanism of how learners form attitudes, how their attitudes may change over time, and how such attitudes may affect L2 acquisition in various socio-cultural contexts.

Crookes and Schmidt (1991), in their influential paper, pointed out that previous models of motivation in SLA have been limited to attitudes and other social and psychological aspects of language learning. They further argued that such approaches failed to adequately capture the concept of motivation as commonly used by L2 teachers. More recently, various motivation models have been proposed based on classroom perspectives (Dörnyei, 1994; Williams and Burden, 1997). Dörnyei further attempted to incorporate a developmental perspective in his model (a process-oriented approach) (Dörnyei, 2000, 2001). Efforts also have been made to explain the mechanisms of acquiring L2 as well as L1 in larger, dynamic socio-cultural contexts, as one can see in the model proposed by Landry and Allard (1992). Alternative methodological approaches have been suggested as well; incorporating behavioral observation in classrooms and other learning settings into survey methodology may be very informative (e.g. Baker, 1992; Crookes and Schmidt, 1991; McLaughlin, 1987). In short, the effect of socio-psychological factors on L2 outcomes and its mechanisms has not yet been fully understood. The results of various studies performed to date seem to largely depend on the conceptualization of attitudes and motivation and the socio-cultural contexts wherein learning takes place. More empirical evidence from different socio-cultural contexts is necessary in order to suitably attest to the validity of such models.

In places such as the US where there is a strong demand for assimilating into an English-speaking mainstream society, attitudinal differences towards L2 (English) among L2 learning children may not have much effect on the overall success of mastering the L2, while attitudes towards their L1 and their own culture may have a stronger effect on their use of L1 (Hakuta and D'Andrea, 1992). Butler and Gutiérrez (2003) found that fourth-grade bilingual students in California who had high reading performance in their L2 (English) tended to believe that other monolingual English-speaking friends had positive attitudes towards their L1 and their bilingual abilities (e.g. their code-switching and biliteracy skills). Butler and Gutiérrez argued that such learners' perceptions about other people's beliefs, as well as their own abilities and behaviors, which the authors labeled "learning climates" are related to a given learner's use of both languages and his or her proficiency in certain contexts.

5.5   Conclusion

In the present chapter, we have tried to give some flavor of the complex nature of bilingualism, and a select group of issues that influence individual variations in acquiring bilingual proficiency were discussed in relation to SLA. Individual bilinguals can be classified differently according to different dimensions, such as the relative relationships between L1 proficiency and L2 proficiency, the age of exposure to a given language, and the status of a particular language in a given society. However, such typologies can capture only a small subset of the many aspects of bilingualism. Bilingualism is indeed very dynamic and entails multi-dimensional, continuous variables.

There are a number of difficulties in accurately measuring bilingual individuals' proficiencies in both languages. Proficiency can be conceptualized differently depending on how one approaches "what accounts for language." Accordingly, current "proficiency" assessments measure different aspects of language. Comparing a bilingual individual's proficiency with that of monolingual native speakers and across languages introduces numerous challenges. It is crucially important to understand what constitutes proficiency and how languages interact with each other. Such identification has to be conducted in context. In particular, there is growing concern among educators with regard to how best to measure language minority students' language proficiencies in academic contexts. Without proper identification of constructs for language proficiency in a given context, we cannot develop contextually and culturally appropriate measurements.

It is also very important to identify factors that contribute to individual variation in language learning. The present chapter focused on three of the major factors that uniquely influence L2 attainment, namely, age, the role of L1, and socio-psychological factors. It is evident that each factor is influenced by socio-cultural contextual conditions. There also is certainly a maturational effect in L2 learning. However, it is not clear whether or not such differences in performance are limited to biological factors, given that the age factor is closely related to other psychological and socio-cultural factors such as schooling. One's L1 and L2 also influence each other, and the conditions for cross-linguistic influence depend on the context. How a given society values a bilingual individual's L1 and L2, for instance, influences his or her attainment and maintenance of both languages. Since language acquisition itself is deeply embedded in social contexts, how we account for context in understanding variations in L2 acquisition and bilingualism is extremely important. In doing so, we should keep in mind that learning another language is not simply adding additional knowledge and socio-cultural experiences. Each bilingual individual will develop a unique linguistic, cognitive, and socio-cultural profile that is distinct from that of monolingual individuals.

REFERENCES

Anderson, J. R. (1983). *The Architecture of Cognition*. Cambridge, MA: Harvard University Press.

Au, S. (1988). A critical appraisal of Gardner's socio-psychological theory of second language learning. *Language Learning*, 38, 75–100.

Bachman, L. F. and Palmer, A. S. (1996). *Language Testing in Practice*. Oxford: Oxford University Press.

Bailey, N., Madden, C., and Krashen, S. (1974). Is there a "natural sequence" in adult language learning? *Language Learning*, 24, 235–43.

Baker, C. (1992). *Attitudes and Language*. Clevedon, UK: Multilingual Matters.

Bates, E. and MacWhinney, B. (1981). Functionalism and the competition model. In B. MacWhinney and E. Bates (eds.), *The Crosslinguistic Study of Sentence Processing*, pp. 3–73. New York: Cambridge University Press.

Bates, E. and MacWhinney, B. (1982). Functional approaches to grammar. In E. Wanner and L. Gleitman (eds.), *Language Acquisition: The State Of The Art*. New York: Cambridge University Press.

Beebe, L. and Zuengler, J. (1983). Accommodation theory: An explanation for style shifting in second language dialects. In N. Wolfson and E. Judd (eds.), *Sociolinguistics and Second Language Acquisition*, pp. 195–213. Rowley, MA: Newbury House.

Bialystok, E. (ed.) (1991a). *Language Processing in Bilingual Children*.

Cambridge, UK: Cambridge University Press.

Bialystok, E. (1991b). Metalinguistic dimensions of bilingual language proficiency. In E. Bialystok (ed.), *Language Processing in Bilingual Children*, pp. 113–40. Cambridge, UK: Cambridge University Press.

Bialystok, E. (2001). Bilingualism in Development: *Language, Literacy, and Cognition*. Cambridge: Cambridge University Press.

Bialystok, E. and Hakuta, K. (1994). *In Other Words: The Science and Psychology of Second-Language Acquisition*. New York: Basic Books.

Bialystok, E. and Hakuta, K. (1999). Confounded age: Linguistic and cognitive factors in age differences for second language acquisition. In D. Birdsong (ed.), *Second Language Acquisition and the Critical Period Hypothesis*, pp. 161–81. Mahwah, NJ: Lawrence Erlbaum.

Bialystok, E. and Ryan E. B. (1985). A metalinguistic framework for the development of first and second language skills. In D. L. Forrest Pressley, G. E. Mackinnon and T. G. Waller (eds.), *Metacognition, Cognition, and Human Performance. Vol. 1: Theoretical Perspectives*, pp. 207–52. Orlando, FL: Academic Press.

Birdsong, D. (1992). Ultimate attainment in second language acquisition. *Language*, 68, 706–55.

Birdsong, D. and Molis, M. (2001). On the evidence for maturational constraints in second-language acquisition. *Journal of Memory and Language*, 44, 235–49.

Bley-Vroman, R. (1990). The logical problem of foreign language learning. *Linguistic Analysis*, 20, 3–49.

Bloomfield, L. (1933). *Language*. London: Allen and Unwin.

Bongaerts, T. (1999). Ultimate attainment in L2 pronunciation: The case of very advanced late L2 learners. In D. Birdsong (ed.), *Second Language*

Acquisition and the Critical Period Hypothesis. Mahwah, NJ: Lawrence Erlbaum.

Bongaerts, T., Mennen, S., and van der Slik (2000). Authenticity of pronunciation in naturalistic second language acquisition: The case of very advanced late learners of Dutch as a second language. *Studia Linguistica*, 54, 298–308.

Brown, G. (1996). Introduction. In G. Brown, K. Malmkjær, and J. Williams (eds.), *Performance and Competence in Second Language Acquisition*, pp. 1–8. Cambridge, UK: Cambridge University Press.

Butler, Y. G. (2000). The age effect in second language acquisition: Is it too late to acquire native level competence in a second language after the age of seven? In Y. Oshima-Takane, Y. Shirai, and H. Shirai (eds.), *Studies in Language Sciences*, 1, pp. 159–69. Tokyo: The Japanese Society for Language Sciences.

Butler, Y. G. and Gutiérrez, M. B. (2003). Learning climates for English language learners: A case of – students in California. *Bilingual Research Journal*, 27(2), 207–240.

Calero-Breckheimer, A. and Goetz, E. T. (1993). Reading strategies of biliterate children for English and Spanish texts. *Reading Psychology: An International Quarterly*, 14, 177–204.

Canale, M. (1983). From communicative competence to communicative language pedagogy. In J. C. Richards and R. W. Schmidt (eds.), *Language and Communication*, pp. 2–27. London: Longman.

Canale, M. and Swain, M (1980). Theoretical bases of communicative approaches to second language teaching and testing. *Applied Linguistics*, 1, 1–47.

Chi, M. T. H., Glaser, R. and Farr, M. J. (eds.) (1988). *The Nature of Expertise*. Hillsdale, NJ: Erlbaum Associates.

Chomsky, N. (1965). *Aspects of the Theory of Syntax*. Cambridge, MA: MIT Press.

Chomsky, N. (1981). Principles and parameters in syntactic theory. In N. Hornstein and D. Lightfoot (eds.), *Explanations in Linguistics*. London: Longman.

Clahsen, H. and Muysken, P. (1986). The availability of universal grammar to adult and child learners: A study of the acquisition of German word order. *Second Language Research*, 2, 93–110.

Clément, R. (1980). Ethnicity, contact and communicative competence in second language. In H. Giles, W. P. Robinson and P. M. Smith (eds.), *Language: Social Psychological Perspectives*, pp. 147–59. Oxford: Pergamon Press.

Clément, R. (1987). Second language proficiency and acculturation: An investigation of the effects of language status and individual characteristics. *Journal of Language and Social Psychology*, 5(4), 21–37.

Clément, R. and Gardner, R. C. (2001). Second language mastery. In W. P. Robinson and H. Giles (eds.), *The new handbook of language and social psychology*, pp. 439–504. Chichester, UK: J. Wiley.

Clément, R. and Kruidenier, B. G. (1985). Aptitude, attitude, and motivation in second language proficiency: A test of Clément's model. *Journal of Language and Social Psychology*, 4(1), 21–37.

Cochrane, R. (1980). The acquisition of /r/ and /l/ by Japanese children and adults learning English as a second language. *Journal of Multilingual and Multicultural Development*, 1, 331–60.

Cook, V. (1992). Evidence for multicompetence. *Language Learning*, 42(4), 557–91.

Cook, V. (1996). Competence and multi-competence. In G. Brown, K. Malmkjær and J. Williams (eds.), *Performance and Competence in Second Language Acquisition*, pp. 57–69. Cambridge, UK: Cambridge University Press.

Coppieters, R. (1987). Competence differences between natives and near-native speakers. *Language*, 63, 544–73.

Crookes, G. and Schmidt, R. W. (1991). Motivation: Reopening the research agenda. *Language Learning*, 41(4), 469–512.

Cummins, J. (1976). The influence of bilingualism on cognitive growth: A synthesis of research findings and explanatory hypotheses. *Working Papers on Bilingualism*, 9, 1–43.

Cummins, J. (1979). Linguistic interdependence and the educational development of bilingual children. *Review of Educational Research*, 49, 222–51.

Cummins, J. (1980). The exit and entry fallacy of bilingual education. *NABE Journal*, 4(3), 25–59.

Cummins, J. (2000). *Language, Power and Pedagogy: Bilingual Children in the Crossfire*. Clevedon, UK: Multilingual Matters.

Curtiss, S. (1977). *Genie: A psycholinguistic study a modern-day "wild child."* New York: Academic Press.

de Groot, A. D. (1965). *Thought and Choice in Chess*. The Hague: Mouton.

de Groot, A. M. B. (1992). Bilingual lexical representation: A closer look at conceptual representations. In R. Frost and L. Datz (eds.), *Orthography, phonology, morphology and meaning*, pp. 389–412. Amsterdam: Elsevier.

de Groot, A. M. B. and Kroll, J. F. (eds.) (1997). *Tutorials in Bilingualism: Psycholinguistic Perspectives*. Mahwah, NJ: Lawrence Erlbaum.

DeKeyser, R. M. (2000). The robustness of critical period in second language acquisition. *Studies in Second Language Acquisition*, 22, 499–533.

Dickerson, L. (1975). Interlanguage as a system of variable rules. *TESOL Quarterly*, 9, 401–7.

Dörnyei, Z. (1994). Motivation and motivating in the foreign language classroom. *Modern Language Journal*, 78, 273–84.

Dörnyei, Z. (2000). Motivation in action: Towards a process-oriented conceptualization of student motivation. *British Journal of Educational Psychology*, 70, 519–38.

Dörnyei, Z. (2001). *Motivational Strategies in the Language Classroom*. Cambridge, UK: Cambridge University Press.

Dulay, H. and Burt, M. (1974). Natural sequences in child second language acquisition. *Language Learning*, 24, 37–53.

Durgunoğlu, A. Y. (1998). Acquiring literacy in English and Spanish in the United States. In A. Y. Durgunoğlu and L. Verhoeven (eds.), *Literacy Development in a Multilingual Context: Cross-Cultural Perspectives*, pp. 135–45. Mahwah, NJ: Lawrence Erlbaum Associates.

Durgunoğlu, A. Y., Nagy, W. E., and Hancin-Bhatt, B. J. (1993). Cross-language transfer of phonological awareness. *Journal of Educational Psychology*, 85(3), 453–65.

Eisenstein, M. and Starbuck, R. (1989). The effect of emotional investment on L2 production. In S. Gass, C. Madden, D. Preston, and L. Selinker (eds.), *Variation in Second Language Acquisition: Psycholinguistic Issues*, pp. 125–37. Clevedon, UK: Multilingual Matters.

Ellis, R. (1985). *Understanding Second Language Acquisition*. Oxford: Oxford University Press.

Fathman, A. (1975). The relationship between age and second language productive ability. *Language Learning*, 25, 245–53.

Fishman, J. A. (1977). The social science perspective. In *Bilingual Education: Current Perspectives. Social Science* pp. 1–49. Arlington, VA: Center for Applied Linguistics.

Flege, J. E. (1995). Second-language speech learning: Findings, and problems. In W. Strange (ed.), *Speech Perception and Linguistic Experience: Theoretical and Methodological Issues*, pp. 233–73. Timonium, MD: York Press.

Flege, J. E. (1999). Age of learning and second language speech. In D. Birdsong (ed.), *Second Language Acquisition and the Critical Period Hypothesis*, pp. 101–31. Mahwah, NJ: Lawrence Erlbaum.

Flege, J. E. and Liu, S. (2001). The effect of experience on adults' acquisition of a second language. *Studies in Second Language Acquisition*, 23(4), 527–52.

Flege, J. E., Munro, M., and MacKay, I. (1995). Factors affecting degree of perceived foreign accent in a second language. *Journal of the Acoustical Society of America*, 97, 3125–34.

Flege, J. E., Yeni-Komshian, G., and Liu, S. (1999). Age constraints on second language learning. *Journal of Memory and Language*, 41, 78–104.

Flynn, S. (1991). Government-binding: Parameter setting in second language acquisition. In C. Ferguson and T. Heubner (eds.), *Crosscurrents in Second Language Acquisition and Linguistic Theories*, pp. 143–67. Amsterdam: John Benjamins.

Flynn, S. (1996). A parameter-setting approach to second language acquisition. In W. C. Ritchie and T. K. Bhatia (eds.), *Handbook of Second Language Acquisition*, pp. 121–58. San Diego, CA: Academic Press.

Gagné, E. D. (1985). *The Cognitive Psychology of School Learning*. Boston, MA: Little, Brown and Company.

García, G. E. (1998). Mexican-American bilingual students' metacognitive reading strategies: What's transferred, unique, problematic? *National Reading Conference Yearbook*, 47, 253–63.

Gardner, R. C. (1979). Social psychological aspects of second language acquisition. In H. Giles and R. St Clair (eds.), *Language and Social Psychology*, pp. 193–220. Oxford: Blackwell.

Gardner, R. C. (1983). Learning another language: A true social psychological experiment. *Journal of Language and Social Psychology*, 2, 219–39.

Gardner, R. C. (1985). *Social Psychology and Second Language Learning: The Role of Attitudes and Motivation*. London: Edward Arnold.

Gardner, R. C. (2000). Correlation, causation, motivation, and second language acquisition. *Canadian Psychology*, 41(1), 10–24.

Gardner, R. C. and Lambert, W. E. (1959). Motivational variables in second language acquisition. *Canadian Journal of Psychology*, 13, 266–72.

Gardner, R. C., Tremblay, P. F., and Masgoret, A. M. (1997). Towards a full model of second language acquisition. *The Modern Language Journal*, 81, 344–62.

Genesee, F., Hamers, J., Lambert, W. E., Mononen, L., Seitz, M., and Starck, R. (1978). Language processing in bilinguals. *Brain and Language*, 5, 1–12.

Giles, H. and Byrne, J. (1982). An intergroup approach to second language acquisition. *Journal of Multilingual and Multicultural Development*, 3, 17–40.

Goffman, E. (1981). *Forms of Talk*. Philadelphia: University of Pennsylvania.

Gregg, K. (1990). The variable competence model of second language acquisition and why it isn't. *Applied Linguistics*, 11, 364–83.

Grosjean, F. (1982). *Life with Two Languages: An Introduction to Bilingualism*. Cambridge, MA: Harvard University Press.

Grosjean, F. (1998). Studying bilinguals: methodological and conceptual issues. *Bilingualism: Language and Cognition*, 1(2), 131–49.

Grosjean, F. (1999). Individual bilingualism. In B. Spolsky (ed.), *Concise Encyclopedia of Educational Linguistics*, pp. 284–90. London: Elsevier.

Grosjean, F. (2001). The bilingual's language modes. In J. L. Nicol (ed.), *One Mind, Two Languages: Bilingual Language Processing*, pp. 284–90. Oxford: Blackwell.

Gumperz, J. J. (1982). *Discourse Strategies*. Cambridge, UK: Cambridge University Press.

Hakuta, K. (1986). *Mirror of Language: The Debate on Bilingualism*. New York: Basic Books.

Hakuta, K. (2001). A critical period for second language acquisition? In D. Bailey, J. Bruer, F. Symons, and J. Lichtman (eds.), *Critical Thinking About Critical Periods*, pp. 193–205. Baltimore, MD: Paul H. Brookes.

Hakuta, K., Bialystok, E., and Wiley, E. (2003). Critical evidence: A test of the critical period hypothesis for second language acquisition. *Psychological Science*, 14(1), 31–8.

Hakuta, K. and D'Andrea, D. (1992). Some properties of bilingual maintenance and loss in Mexican background high-school students. *Applied Linguistics*, 13(1), 72–99.

Hakuta, K. and Diaz, R. (1984). The relationship between bilingualism and cognitive ability: A critical discussion and some new longitudinal data. In K. E. Nelson (ed.), *Children's Language*, vol. V, pp. 319–45. Hillsdale, NJ: Lawrence Erlbaum Associates.

Hakuta, K. and McLaughlin, B. (1996). Bilingualism and second language learning: seven tensions that define the research. In D. C. Berliner and R. C. Calfee (eds.), *Handbook of Educational Psychology*, pp. 603–21. New York: Simon and Schuster/Macmillan.

Hamers, J. F. and Blanc, M. H. (2000). *Bilinguality and Bilingualism*, 2nd edn. Cambridge, UK: Cambridge University Press.

Hancin-Bhatt, B. and Nagy, W. E. (1994).
Lexical transfer and second language
morphological development. *Applied
Psycholinguistics*, 15, 289–310.

Hansegard, N. E. (1972). *Tvasprakighet
Eller Halvsprakighet?* Stockholm: Aldus
Series, 253.

Haugen, E. (1953). *The Norwegian
Language in America*. Philadelphia:
University of Pennsylvania Press.

Hawkins, R. (2001). *Second Language
Syntax: A Generative Introduction*.
Oxford: Blackwell.

Herdina, P. and Jessner, U. (2000). *A
Dynamic Model Of Multilingualism:
Changing The Psycholinguistic
Perspective*. Clevedon, UK: Multilingual
Matters.

Hernandez-Chavez, E., Burt, M.,
and Dulay, H. (1978). Language
dominance and proficiency testing:
Some general considerations. *NABE
Journal*, 3, 41–5.

Herschensohn, J. (2000). *The Second
Time Around: Minimalism and Second
Language Acquisition*. Amsterdam: John
Benjamins.

Hinkel, E. (1996). When in Rome:
Evaluation of L2 pragmalinguistic
behaviors. *Journal of Pragmatics*, 26,
51–70.

Hyltenstam., K. (1992). Non-native
features of near-native speakers: On
the ultimate attainment of childhood
L2 learners. In R. J. Harris (ed.),
Cognitive Processing In Bilinguals,
pp. 351–68. Amsterdam: Elsevier
Science Publishers.

Hyltenstam, K. and Abrahamsson,
N. (forthcoming). Maturational
constraints in second language
acquisition. In C. Doughty and
M. Long (eds.), *Handbook of Second
Language Acquisition*. Oxford:
Blackwell.

Hymes, D. H. (1967). Models of the
interaction of language and social
setting. *Journal of Social Issues*, 23(2),
8–38.

Hymes, D. H. (1972). On communicative
competence. In J. B. Pride and
J. Holmes (eds.), *Sociolinguistics:
Selected Readings*, pp. 269–93.
Harmondsworth, UK: Penguin.

Inoue, M. (1996). *Kaosu to fukuzastukei
no kagaku* [Science of chaos and
complexity]. Tokyo: Nihon Jistugyo.

Ioup, G., Boustagui, E., El Tigi, M., and
Moselle, M. (1994). Reexamining the
critical period hypothesis: A case
study in a naturalistic environment.
Studies in Second Language Acquisition,
16, 73–98.

Jimenez, R. T., García, G. E., and
Pearson, P. D. (1994). Three children,
two languages, and strategic reading:
Case studies in bilingual/monolingual
reading. *American Educational Research
Journal*, 32, 67–98.

Johnson, J. S. and Newport, E. L.
(1989). Critical period effects in
second-language learning: The
influence of maturational state on
the acquisition of English as a second
language. *Cognitive Psychology*, 21,
60–99.

Juffs, A. (2001). Psycholinguistically
oriented second language research.
Annual Review of Applied Linguistics, 21,
207–20.

Juffs, A. and Harrington, M. (1995).
Parsing effects in second language
sentence processing: Subject and object
asymmetries in wh-extraction. *Studies
in Second Language Acquisition*, 17,
483–516.

Kellerman, E. (1995). Age before beauty:
Johnson and Newport revisited. In L.
Eubank, L. Selinker, and M.
Sharwood-Smith (eds.), *The Current
State of Interlanguage*, pp. 219–31.
Amsterdam: John Benjamins.

Kellerman, E. and Sharwood-Smith, M.
(eds.) (1986). *Crosslinguistic Influence in
Second Language Acquisition*. New York:
Pergamon Press.

Koda, K. (1994). Second language
reading research: Problems and

possibilities. *Applied Psycholinguistics*, 15, 1–28.

Koda, K. (1997). Orthographic knowledge in L2 lexical processing: A cross-linguistic perspective. In J. Coady and T. Huckin (eds.), *Second Language Vocabulary Acquisition*, 35–52. Cambridge, UK: Cambridge University Press.

Kramsch, C. (1993). *Context and culture in language teaching*. Oxford: Oxford University Press.

Krashen, S. (1973). Lateralization, language learning, and the critical period: Some new evidence. *Language Learning*, 23, 63–74.

Kroll, J. F. and Stewart, E. (1994). Category interference in translation in picture naming: Evidence for asymmetric connection between bilingual memory representations. *Journal of Memory and Language*, 33, 149–74.

Labov, W. (1972). *Sociolinguistic Patterns*. Philadelphia: University of Pennsylvania Press.

Lado, R. (1957). *Linguistics across Cultures*. Ann Arbor: University of Michigan Press.

Lalonde, R. N. and Gardner, R. C. (1985). On the predictive validity of the attitude/motivation test battery. *Journal of Multilingual and Multicultural Development*, 6(5), 403–12.

Lambert, W. E. (1974). Culture and language as factors in learning and education. In F. F. Aboud and R. D. Meade (eds.), *Cultural Factors in Learning and Education*. Bellingham, WA: Western Washington State University.

Landry, R. and Allard, R. (1992). Ethnolinguistic vitality and the bilingual development of minority and majority group students. In W. Fase, K. Jaspaert, and S. Kroon (eds.), *Maintenance and Loss of Minority Languages*, pp. 223–51. Amsterdam: John Benjamins.

Langer, J. A., Bartolome, L., Vasquez, O., and Lucas, T. (1990). Meaning construction in school literacy tasks: A study of bilingual students. *American Educational Research Journal*, 27, 427–72.

Lenneberg, E. (1967). *Biological Foundation of Language*. New York: Wiley & Sons.

LoCastro, V. (2001). Individual differences in second language acquisition: Attitudes, learner's subjectivity and L2 pragmatics norms. *System*, 29, 69–89.

Lowenthal, K. and Bull, D. (1984). Imitation of foreign sounds: What is the effect of age? *Language and Speech*, 27, 95–7.

Lukmani, Y. (1972). Motivation to learn and language proficiency. *Language Learning*, 22, 261–73.

McKay, S. L. and Hornberger, N. H. (eds.) (1996). *Sociolinguistics and Language Teaching*. Cambridge, UK: Cambridge University Press.

Mackey, W. (1967). *Bilingualism as a World Problem*. Montreal: Harvest House.

McLaughlin, B. (1987). *Theories of Second Language Learning*. London: Edward Arnold.

McLaughlin, B. (1990). Restructuring. *Applied Linguistics*, 11, 1–16.

McLaughlin, B., Rossman, T., and McLeod, B. (1983). Second-language learning: An information-processing perspective. *Language Learning*, 33, 135–58.

Macnamara, J. (1967). The bilingual's linguistic performance: a psychological overview. *Journal of Social Issues*, 23, 59–77.

McNamara, T. (1996). *Measuring Second Language Performance*. London: Longman.

MacSwan, J. (2000). The threshold hypothesis, semilingualism, and other contributions to a deficit view of linguistic minorities. *Hispanic Journal of Behavioral Sciences*, 22(1), 3–45.

MacWhinney, B. (1997). Second language acquisition and the competition model. In A. M. B. deGroot and J. F. Kroll (eds.), *Tutorials in Bilingualism: Psycholinguistic Perspectives*, pp. 113–42. Mahwah, NJ: Lawrence Erlbaum.

MacWhinney, B. and Bates, E. (eds.) (1989). *The Cross-Linguistic Study of Sentence Processing*. Cambridge, UK: Cambridge University Press.

Malakoff, M. and Hakuta, K. (1991). Translation skill and metalinguistic awareness in bilinguals. In E. Bialystok (ed.), *Language Processing in Bilingual Children*, pp. 141–66. Cambridge, UK: Cambridge University Press.

Martin-Jones, M. and Romaine, S. (1986). Semilingualism: A half-baked theory of communicative competence. *Applied Linguistics*, 7, 26–38.

Mohanty, A. K. and Perregaux, C. (1997). Language acquisition and bilingualism. In J. W. Berry, P. R. Dasen, and T. S. Saraswathi (eds.), *Handbook of Cross-Cultural Psychology. Vol. 2: Basic Processes and Human Development*, pp. 217–53. Boston, MA: Allyn and Bacon.

Moyer, A. (1999). Ultimate attainment in L2 phonology: The critical factors of age, motivation, and instruction. *Studies in Second Language Acquisition*, 21, 81–108.

Nagy, W. E., García, G. E., Durgunoğlu, A. Y., and Hancin-Bhatt, B. (1993). Spanish-English bilingual students' use of cognates in English reading. *Journal of Reading Behavior*, 25(3), 241–55.

Nakajima, K. (1998). *Bailingaru kyoiku no hoho* [Methods of bilingual education]. Tokyo: Alc.

Newport, E. L. (1990). Maturational constraints on language learning. *Cognitive Science*, 14, 11–28.

Nicol, J. L. (ed.) (2001). *One Mind, Two Languages: Bilingual Language Processing*. Malden, MA: Blackwell.

Noels, K. A., Clément, R., and Pelletier, L. G. (1999). Perceptions of teachers' communicative style and students' intrinsic and extrinsic motivation. *The Modern Language Journal*, 83, 23–34.

Odlin, T. (1989). *Language Transfer: Cross Linguistic Influence in Language Learning*. Cambridge, UK: Cambridge University Press.

Oller, J. W. (1979). *Language Test at School*. London: Longman.

Oller, J. W., Hudson, A., and Liu, P. (1977). Attitudes and attained proficiency in ESL: A sociolinguistic study of native speakers of Chinese in the United States. *Language Learning*, 27, 1–27.

Olson, L. and Samuels, S. J. (1973). The relationship between age and accuracy of foreign language pronunciation. *Journal of Educational Research*, 66, 263–7.

Oyama, S. (1976). A sensitive period for the acquisition of a nonnative phonological system. *Psycholinguistic Research*, 5, 261–85.

Patkowski, M. S. (1980). The sensitive period for the acquisition of syntax in a second language. *Language Learning*, 30, 449–72.

Paulston, C. B. (1982). *Swedish Research and Debate about Bilingualism*. Stockholm: Swedish National Board of Education.

Pavlenko, A. (1999). New approaches to concepts in bilingual memory. *Bilingualism: Language and Cognition*, 2(3), 209–30.

Peal, E. and Lambert, W. E. (1962). The relation of bilingualism to intelligence. *Psychological Monographs*, 76, 1–23.

Penfield, W. and Roberts, L. (1959). *Speech and Brain Mechanisms*. New York: Athenaeum.

Pinker, S. (1994). *The Language Instinct*. New York: Morrow.

Potter, M., So, K.-F., von Eckhardt, B., and Feldman, L. (1984). Lexical and conceptual representation in beginning and proficient bilinguals. *Journal of*

Verbal Learning and Verbal Behavior, 23, 22–8.

Preston, D. (1993). Variation linguistics and SLA. *Second Language Research*, 9, 153–72.

Preston, D. (1996). Variationist linguistics and second language acquisition. In W. C. Ritchie and T. K. Bhatia (eds.), *Handbook of Second Language Acquisition*, 229–65. San Diego, CA: Academic Press.

Reynolds, A. G. (1991). The cognitive consequences of bilingualism. In A. G. Reynolds (ed.), *Bilingualism, Multiculturalism, and Second Language Learning: The McGill Conference in Honour of Wallace E. Lambert*, pp. 145–82. Hillsdale, NJ: Erlbaum.

Rumelhart, D. E. and McClelland, J. L. (1986). On learning the past tense of English verbs. In D. E. Rumelhart and J. L. McClelland (eds.), *Parallel Distributed Processing: Explorations in the Microstructure of Cognition. Vol. 2: Psychological and Biological Models*, pp. 216–71. Cambridge, MA: MIT Press.

Rumelhart, D. E. and Ortony, A. (1977). The representation of knowledge in memory. In R. Anderson, R. Spiro, and W. Montague (eds.), *Schooling and the Acquisition of Knowledge*, pp. 99–135. Hillsdale, NJ: Erlbaum.

Schachter, J. (1983). A new account of language transfer. In S. Gass and J. Selinker (eds.), *Language Transfer in Language Learning*, pp. 98–111. Rowley, MA: Newbury House.

Schachter, J. (1986). In search of systematicity in interlanguage production. *Studies in Second Language Acquisition*, 8, 119–34.

Schachter, J. (1996). Maturation and the issue of Universal Grammar in second language acquisition. In W. C. Ritchie and T. K. Bhatia (eds.), *Handbook of Second Language Acquisition*, pp. 159–93. San Diego, CA: Academic Press.

Schmidt, R. (1977). Sociolinguistic variation and language transfer in phonology. *Working Papers on Bilingualism*, 12, 79–95.

Schumann, J. (1978). *The Pidginization Process: A Model for Second Language Acquisition*. Rowley, MA: Newbury House.

Segalowitz, N. (2000). Automaticity and attentional skill in fluent performance. In H. Riggenbach (ed.), *Perspectives on Fluency*, 200–19. Ann Arbor: University of Michigan Press.

Selinker, L. (1972). Interlanguage. *International Review of Applied Linguistics*, 10, 209–30.

Shiffrin, R. M. and Schneider, W. (1977). Controlled and automatic human information processing: II. Perceptual learning, automatic attending, and a general theory. *Psychological Review*, 84, 127–90.

Shohamy, E. (1996). Competence and performance in language testing. In G. Brown, K. Malmkjær, and J. Williams (eds.), *Performance and Competence in Second Language Acquisition*, pp. 138–51. Cambridge, UK: Cambridge University Press.

Slavoff, G. R. and Johnson, J. S. (1995). The effect of age on the rate of learning a second language. *Studies in Second Language Acquisition*, 17, 1–16.

Simon, D. P. and Chase, W. G. (1973). Skill in chess. *American Scientist*, 61, 394–403.

Snow, C. E. (1987a). Beyond conversation: Second language learners' acquisition of description and explanation. In J. Lantolf and A. Labarca (eds.), *Research in Second Language Learning: Focus on the Classroom*, pp. 3–16. Norwood, NJ: Ablex.

Snow, C. E. (1987b). Relevance of the notion of a critical period to language acquisition. In M. Bornstein (ed.), *Sensitive Periods in Development*, pp. 183–209. Hillsdale, NJ: Erlbaum.

Snow, C. E. (1990). The development of definition skill. *Journal of Child Language*, 17, 697–710.

Snow, C. E., Cancino, H., de Temple, J., and Schley, S. (1991). Giving formal definitions: A linguistic or metalinguistic skill? In E. Bialystok (ed.), *Language Processing in Bilingual Children*, pp. 90–112. Cambridge, UK: Cambridge University Press.

Snow, C. E. and Hoefnagal-Hohle, M. (1978). The critical period for language acquisition: Evidence from second language learning. *Child Development*, 49, 1114–28.

Tahta, S., Wood, M., and Lowenthal, K. (1981). Age changes in the ability to replicate foreign pronunciation and intonation. *Language and Speech*, 24, 363–72.

Tarone, E. (1983). On the variability of interlanguage systems. *Applied Linguistics*, 4, 143–63.

Tarone, E. (1985). Variability in interlanguage use: A study of style-shifting morphology and syntax. *Language Learning*, 35, 373–95.

Tremblay, P. F. and Gardner, R. C. (1995). Expanding the motivation construct in language learning. *The Modern Language Journal*, 79, 505–20.

Umbel, V. M. and Oller, D. K. (1995). Development changes in receptive vocabulary in Hispanic bilingual school children. In B. Harley (ed.), *Lexical Issues in Language Learning*, pp. 59–80. Ann Arbor, MI: Research Club in Language Learning.

Valdés, G. and Figueroa, R. A. (1994). *Bilingualism and Testing: A Special Case of Bias*. Norwood, NJ: Ablex Publishing.

Verhoeven, L. T. (1991). Acquisition of biliteracy. In J. H. Hulsijn and J. F. Matter (eds.), *Reading in Two Languages*, pp. 61–74. Amsterdam: AILA.

Verhoeven, L. T. (1994). Transfer in bilingual development: The linguistic interdependent hypothesis revisited. *Language Learning*, 44, 381–415.

Weinreich, U. (1953). *Languages in Contact*. The Hague: Mouton.

White, L. (1989). *Universal Grammar and Second Language Acquisition*. Amsterdam: John Benjamins.

White, L. (1996). Universal grammar and second language acquisition: Current trends and new directions. In W. C. Ritchie and T. K. Bhatia (eds.), *Handbook of Second Language Acquisition*, pp. 85–120. San Diego, CA: Academic Press.

Williams, M. and Burden, R. (1997). *Psychology for Language Teachers*. Cambridge, UK: Cambridge University Press.

Wolfson, N. (1989). *Perspectives: Sociolinguistics and TESOL*. Cambridge, UK: Newbury House/HarperCollins.

Zehler, A. M., Hopstock, P. J., Fleischman, H. L., and Greniuk, C. (1994). *An Examination of Assessment of Limited English Proficiency Students*. Arlington, VA: Development Associates.

Zobl, H. (1984). Aspects of reference and the pronominal syntax preference in the speech of young child L2 learners. In R. Andersen (ed.), *Second Languages: A Cross-Linguistic Perspective*, 375–91. Rowley, MA: Newbury House.

Zobl, H. (1992). Prior linguistic knowledge and the conservation of the learning procedure: Grammaticality judgments of unilingual and multilingual learners. In S. Gass and L. Selinker (eds.), *Language Transfer in Language Learning*, pp. 176–96. Amsterdam: John Benjamins.

Zuengler, J. (1989). Performance variation in NS-NNS interactions: Ethnolinguistic difference, or discourse domain? In S. Gass, C. Madden, D. Preston, and Selinger (eds.), *Variation in Second Language Acquisition: Discourse and Pragmatics*, pp. 228–44. Clevedon, UK: Multilingual Matters.

Bilingual Language Use: Knowledge, Comprehension, and Production

6 Two Linguistic Systems in Contact: Grammar, Phonology and Lexicon

PIETER MUYSKEN

6.1 Introduction

This chapter outlines some of the recent findings in the domain of language contact, focusing on three sub-domains of the language system: morpho-syntax, phonology, and lexicon. I will treat these in two clusters. The problem one is faced with is that there are findings in individual areas in sub-domains, but that so far these have not been integrated into a single perspective, let alone a single model encompassing these three sub-domains.

I will first discuss the sub-domains of morpho-syntax (section 6.2), and then phonology and lexicon together (section 6.3). In section 6.4 I turn to what I think is a crucial question at the present state of the game, namely research methodology.

6.2 Morpho-syntax

At present the fields of code switching and morpho-syntactic interference are organized as separate domains of enquiry. The difference between them is simple: in the case of *code switching* or *code mixing*, there is lexical material from two languages present in the clause, in addition to morpho-syntactic structure from both languages. Interference – in Weinreich's (1953) sense of mutual influence between a bilingual's two languages – involves morpho-syntactic structure from two languages, but lexical material from only one of them.

This difference can be illustrated with a few examples. A first example of code mixing is:

(1) *A ver*, q'aya suya-wa-nki *las cuatro*-ta.
     let's see, tomorrow wait-1ob-2 four o'clock-AC.
     'Let's see, tomorrow you wait for me at four.'

(Quechua/Spanish; Urioste, 1964)
(1ob = 1st person object; 2 = second person; AC = Accusative)

Here the basic utterance is Quechua, and is preceded by a Spanish expression, *a ver* 'let's see'; in addition there is a Spanish temporal expression *las cuatro* 'at four' embedded in it, with Quechua accusative marking.

The next example involves two closely related languages:

(2)   Weet je *what she is doing*?
       'Do you know . . .'
       (English/Dutch; Crama and van Gelderen, 1984)

Here the sentence starts out in Dutch and at the point of *what*, which is very similar in pronunciation to the equivalent Dutch *wat*, switches to English.

In the case of *interference*, there is only morpho-syntactic material from both languages, but no lexicon. A typical example of interference again is taken from Quechua and Andean Spanish:

(3)   a.   De mi mamá en su casa estoy ye-ndo.
             GE 1sg.POSS mother LO 3sg.POSS house be.1sg go-ing
             'I go to my mother's house.'
             (GE = Genitive; 1sg = 1st person singular; POSS = Possessive;
             LO = Locative; 3sg = 3rd person singular)
       b.   Voy a la casa de mi mamá.
       c.   mama-:-pa wasi-n-ta-n li-ya-:
             mother-1sg.POSS-GE house-3sg.POSS-DI-AF go-PR-1sg
             (Quechua/Spanish; Cerrón-Palomino, 1972, 155–6)
             (DI = Directional; AF = Affirmative)

Here (3a) represents the Andean Spanish example, which follows the Quechua word order, double possessor marking (*de mi mama en su casa*), and generalized locative (*en*) illustrated in the Quechua example (3c), rather than the standard Spanish word order of (3b). However, no Quechua lexicon or morphology is present in (3a).

The next example presents Dutch as spoken by a native English learner of the language:

(4)   a.   Morgen **ik zal gaan** boodschappen doen **in** de markt.
             tomorrow I shall go shopping do in the market
       b.   Tomorrow **I'll go** shopping **in** the market.
       c.   Morgen **ga ik** boodschappen doen **op** de markt.
             tomorrow go I shopping do on the market
             (English/Dutch; constructed examples)

In (4a) the speaker does not invert subject and inflected verb after a clause-initial adverb (the Dutch pattern illustrated in (4c)), there is future tense rather than the present tense form (as in the English example in (4b)), and the wrong preposition is used. Again, however, no lexicon or morphology is present from the interfering language.

Before going on to discuss the differences between code mixing and interference and characterizing the two processes in more detail, I should make a few methodological and terminological points. First, I will be using the term "code mixing" instead of "code switching" here for all cases of code switching within the clause, contrary to much usage in the literature, since it is more neutral, making no claims about the actual mechanism involved. The term "switching" is more specific about what is involved, and was introduced to deal with alternation between clauses, sentences, or utterances.

Second, neither the term "code mixing" nor the term "interference" necessarily implies that it is a result of momentary, spontaneous production. Both may be stable patterns in bilingual communities. In Muysken (2002) I have argued that there are well-known patterns of code mixing that involve some measure of stabilization – are in fact learned. For "interference" there is a much longer tradition, dating back at least to Weinreich's metaphor of sediment at the bottom of a stream (1953). Thus, the boundary between interference and contact-induced morpho-syntactic change is hard to draw.

Third, the shift in recent usage from "syntax" to "morpho-syntax" is an appropriate one, given the growing recognition that many syntactic processes are intricately linked to morphological distinctions. However, it is an awkward term, and I will use the traditional cover term "grammar" for "morpho-syntax".

6.2.1   Interference

The field of code mixing research is one of the most active and interesting domains in the area of language contact studies. The reason for this is that three approaches are combined in it in essential ways: contrastive linguistics, sociolinguistics, and psycholinguistics. Indeed, as Tabouret-Keller noted in her postscript to the volume on code switching edited by Milroy and Muysken (1995), the proper study of code mixing presupposes the joint contribution of all three disciplines in a kind of Borromean knot.

The phenomenon of interference is much less studied, and it is intriguing to consider why this is. One simple reason may be that it is much more difficult to study. If one is considering, say, Finnish/English language contact using naturalistic data, it is much easier to spot lexical borrowing and code mixing than patterns of grammatical interference, just by searching for English and Finnish morphemes. Thus grammatical interference in bilingual speech is surely understudied at present. I will tentatively suggest, and this hypothesis is very difficult to confirm or disconfirm, that it may also be less frequent than code mixing in bilingual speech. The reason for this is that it often will go unnoticed, since many cases of interference will be momentary and will not acquire sociolinguistic meaning, in the way that code mixing carries meaning

Table 6.1   The components of language arranged
from immediately perceived outer form to
relatively unnoticeable inner form.

outer form	pronunciation
	vocabulary
	morphology
	surface syntax
	deep syntax
inner form	semantics

in different communities. The reason for that, again, is that the different components of language can be arranged on the Humboldtian scale from *innere Form* (inner form) to *äussere Form* (outer form), as in table 6.1 (1836).

Since code mixing involves vocabulary, it is much more likely to be noticeable, and hence carry sociolinguistic meaning, than interference. Phenomena imbued with sociolinguistic meaning, in turn, are much more likely to be picked up by speakers from others, and hence become frequent in a bilingual corpus, than those which are mere flukes of misfired processing operations.

In spite of these possible differences in frequency and sociolinguistic meaning, interference and code mixing have two things in common. First, they both occur in those phases in a bilingual interaction when the speakers are in a bilingual mode (Grosjean, 1995, 2001, chapter 2 of the present volume), since both rely on immediate access to the two languages involved. Second, they often co-occur in the same utterances. As stressed particularly by Gardner-Chloros (1995), many code-mixed sentences evidence grammatical interference phenomena as well. Some of these may actually facilitate code mixing.

Of course there are many different instances of grammatical interference, but I will single out three recurrent patterns: null pronouns, non-focalized fronted elements, and overextensions of a correlative pattern.

First, the degree to which non-topical pronominal elements may be null, or put differently, the frequency with which they are null in actual speech, can covary between neighboring languages. In Florida, varieties of Spanish show a higher percentage of subject pronouns under the influence of English (Lipski, 1996) than other varieties of Caribbean Spanish. In contrast, varieties of English Creole in Nicaragua show null subjects, under the influence of Spanish (Holm, 1978; O'Neil, 1993), while other English Creoles lack these. Similarly, some varieties of Turkish in Germany and the Netherlands show a higher percentage of subject pronouns than Anatolian Turkish (Pfaff, 1993; Schaufeli, 1991). In contrast, some varieties of German and Dutch spoken by Turks show a greater range of null subject constructions than native German and Dutch.

A second type of interference is the *pragmatic bleaching* of fronted constituents, under the influence of another language, where a superficially similar grammatical pattern does not carry a particular pragmatic weight. Thus in Andean Ecuadorian Spanish, complements and adverbs frequently occur in pre-posed position (a), while the (b) equivalents in Standard Latin American Spanish do not show such fronting in ordinary circumstances:

(5) a. Bien has hecho.
         Well you.have done
         'You have done well.'
     b. (Lo) has hecho bien.
         (It) you.have done well.
         'You have done (it) well.'

(6) a. La casa estaba barriendo.
         the house he.was sweeping
         'He was sweeping the house.'
     b. Estaba barriendo la casa.
         he.was sweeping the house
         'He was sweeping the house.'

These (a) sentences with a fronted constituent are not impossible at all in standard varieties. However, there they are pragmatically marked, indicating special contrastive focus on the fronted constituent, and hence not particularly frequent. However, in the Andean varieties, they have no special pragmatic status, and are quite frequent, particularly among Quechua-Spanish bilinguals. We are dealing here with a case of interference since in Quechua the unmarked position of the object and the adverb is preverbal. However, the structures in the (a) sentences are not directly modeled upon Quechua grammar, since the presence of a lexical subject seriously constrains, if it does not impede, adverb and object fronting (Muysken, 1982). In Quechua there is no such constraint; the canonical sentence order is SXV. Similar patterns of pragmatic bleaching have been reported in Yiddish-influenced American English (Prince, 2001); here it is not interference from a Yiddish OV pattern, but rather from the possibility in the West Germanic languages of having non-focused elements in the preverbal position.

   Third, there is the overextension of correlative patterns, to form new relative clause structures (Appel and Muysken, 1987). The earliest published sources for sixteenth-century Quechua already provide correlative structures of the type: "**How** you live, **that way** you will die." In some dialects, like Bolivian Quechua, at present this pattern is overextended to all relative clauses, presumably under the influence of Spanish. In the same vein, we find the reinterpretation of question words as conjunctions. While in monolingual Turkish, clausal subordination is accomplished through verbal suffixes; in bilingual Turkish (influenced by German) in Germany, however, question words in embedded questions also function as pivots linking the main clause to the embedded question clause (Herkenrath, Karakoç, and Rehbein 2002). Typically, it is only in an analysis involving the discourse context that this shift becomes apparent.

These three types of interference have in common that stylistic options already present in the language are overexploited, in ways that remain relatively imperceptible until they become new fixed patterns.

In the absence of a more elaborate typology of interference phenomena, an urgent task for future research, I offer this preliminary overview of three types of interference which have actually led to differences on the level of the linguistic variety. Much ongoing research considers subtle differences in individual bilingual processing (to name but two recent studies, Dussias, 2001; Sanz and Bever, 2001), but many of the individual patterns never crystallize into patterns in actual language use on the group level. (For additional discussion of the relationship between the two languages in the mind of the bilingual, see particularly chapters 1–5, 7–10, 18, 22, and 30.)

6.2.2   Code mixing

I now turn to the much better-explored terrain of code mixing. Rather than giving a complete overview of code mixing studies, I will sketch some of the recent developments in the field. In this sketch the focus will be on grammatical aspects of code mixing, although some attention will be paid to sociolinguistic and psycholinguistic considerations as well. The first question must be: where do we stand in present-day code mixing research? What do we know? From a comparative meta-analysis of findings in different bilingual settings a number of empirical generalizations can be drawn about code mixing.

First, in all bilingual communities, some speakers can *alternate* between stretches of speech in different languages, subject to specific pragmatic conditions (Muysken, 2000). The complexity of and the relation between these stretches of speech are subject to what appears to be a hierarchy:

(7)   separate sentences < coordinate clauses < adverbial clauses < adverbial phrases < dislocated arguments < . . .

What this hierarchy implies is that whenever in a bilingual community speakers switch between two coordinate clauses or between an adverbial clause and a main clause (as frequently happens), there will also be cases of true intersentential (between sentence) switching. However, alternation between smaller units, such as dislocated elements, will be less frequent.

A hierarchy such as the one in (7) can be interpreted as a claim involving either distribution across languages, or frequency within a given language:

distribution
For any language, if a borrowed category high in the hierarchy (i.e. to the right in (7)) is found, categories lower in the hierarchy will also be found;

frequency
For any language, categories low in the hierarchy (i.e. to the left in (7)) will occur more frequently than categories higher in the hierarchy.

Furthermore, in all bilingual communities, some speakers can *insert* elements from language A into utterances in language B, subject to considerations of normativity and style, and three grammatically defined (but possibly processing-based) hierarchies (Muysken, 2000). Normatively governed speech generally involves a relatively purist stance, leading to fewer insertions. Stylistic considerations may lead to greater amounts of insertion in formal styles, e.g. from prestige languages, or in informal styles, where non-prestige languages are involved. Three relevant grammatical hierarchies governing insertability are (with elements to the right on the scale being less easily insertable):

(8)   a.   **category**: nouns < adjectives < adverbs < verbs < adpositions < conjunctions < ...
      b.   **complexity**: stems < compounds < fixed phrases < modifier + head combinations < discontinuous idioms < ...
      c.   **morphology**: nominal plural < participle ending < derivational morphology < ...

Thus bilingual speakers who insert adjectives will generally also insert nouns; a corpus containing inserted modifier + head combinations (Sankoff, Poplack, and Vanniarajan, 1990) will also contain inserted stems and compounds; when morphologically inflected items are inserted, the most common case involves nominal plural elements. A caveat is in order regarding elements marking discourse cohesion in a broad sense (e.g. de Rooij, 1996), such as discourse markers, conjunctions, and other linkers. These can be inserted rather easily and escape the insertability hierarchy.

Third, mixing of closely related codes (dialects, styles) appears to follow rather different rules, or rather, virtually no clear grammatically definable rules or tendencies. This type of mixing was termed *congruent lexicalization* in Muysken (2000). It has received little systematic attention in the research literature, since it could not be systematically distinguished from Labovian variation (Labov, 1972). If we can speak of hierarchies, here, the dominant one involves *relatedness*:

(9)   different styles or registers of the same variety < closely related varieties or dialects < closely related separate languages < highly converged varieties of related languages < highly converged varieties of unrelated languages

Thus congruent lexicalization is almost unavoidable when different styles of the same variety are involved, but not as frequent when converged varieties of unrelated languages are involved.

Most recorded samples of bilingual speech can be characterized in terms of these three main types of code mixing, with phenomena low in the hierarchies in (7), (8), and (9) being most frequent. However, in some cases, *complex mixing* occurs, which involves phenomena high in the three hierarchies listed:

(10) a. **alternation**: small constituents switched
      b. **insertion**: diverse categories, including function words, inserted; complex, sometimes discontinuous constituents inserted; morphologically complex elements inserted
      c. **congruent lexicalization**: irregular patterns involving unrelated languages

Upon reflection, these three hierarchies converge in their upper end, as indicated in (10). Thus there are a few bilingual data sets that show highly complex mixing:

(11) Spanish/English in New York (Poplack, 1980, 2001)
      Chinese/Malay/English in Singapore (Loke Kit-Ken, 1991)
      Moluccan Malay/Dutch in the Netherlands (Huwaë, 1992)
      Sranan/Dutch in the Netherlands (Bolle, 1994)
      English/German/Dutch in Australia (Clyne, 1987)

Several linguistic factors may further this type of complex mixing, as listed in (12):

(12) a. linear equivalence of the languages involved
      b. categorial equivalence of the languages involved
      c. simple or absent inflectional morphology
      d. lexical similarity or cognate status

In table 6.2 it is indicated whether these factors are characteristic for the situations of complex code mixing listed in (10).

Table 6.2 Situations of complex code mixing analyzed in terms of the factors favoring complexity.

	Linear	Categorial	Morphology	Lexicon
Spanish/English	+	+	±	±
Chinese/Malay/English	+	±	+	−
Moluccan Malay/Dutch	±	±	±	−
Sranan/Dutch	±	±	±	±
English/German/Dutch	±	+	−	+

Structural factors provide the conditions under which complex mixing becomes an option, but it is not an exaggeration to state that various non-linguistic factors are equally essential to the occurrence of complex mixing:

(13)   *Competence*: Complex mixing involves high bilingual competence.

Several studies (Nortier, 1990; Poplack, 1980) have shown that different types of bilinguals engage in code mixing, but complex mixing is mostly character-istic of speakers with high competence in both languages.

(14)   *Language mode* (Grosjean, 2001, chapter 2 of this volume): In the data sets analyzed with respect to this (Backus, 1996), complex mixing is not evenly spread through the bilingual conversation but clustered in sections of bilingual interchanges.

This result needs more study, on the basis of the distribution of switches throughout a bilingual corpus. This information is not available for most reported studies.

(15)   *Normativity*: Complex mixing is particularly frequent when monolingual norms have been relaxed and convergent patterns emerge.

In some bilingual communities, the languages involved are constantly under the influence of norms imposed by monolingual communities where these same languages are spoken. This is particularly the case in non-migrant set-tings where the bilingual regions are adjacent to monolingual regions. It also holds in migrant settings where there is continuous contact with the country of origin and in this country strong norms are imposed. However, sometimes links with the country of origin are weak. Thus, the Moluccan community in the Netherlands was cut off from Indonesia, and new varieties of Malay emerged. In the case of speakers of Sranan in the Netherlands, the problem was not so much the absence of a link with the country of origin, Surinam, but rather the absence of clear norms for Sranan anywhere. Both Sranan and Moluccan Malay have undergone considerable changes in the Netherlands in bilingual settings, greatly facilitating complex mixing.

(16)   *Attitudes*: When there is strong competition or political conflict between two language communities, non-complex mixing between their respect-ive languages is prevalent.

This can be seen from the cases of Barcelona, Ottawa, and Brussels. In Brussels, competition and conflicts between French- and Dutch-speaking communities have contributed to the relative absence of complex mixing in that bilingual city (Treffers-Daller, 1999). Similarly, Poplack and associates found relatively little complex mixing in Ottawa, where French and English have been in competition since the 1970s (Poplack, 1985). Finally, various researchers have commented on the relative absence of complex code mixing in Barcelona, a city with a large Catalan-Spanish bilingual population but intense competition between the languages. In none of these cases would dissimilarities between the languages involved be able to explain the absence of complex mixing.

Attitudinal and socio-political factors influence the views people have of code mixing as a stylistic option. These, in turn, influence the rate, density, and ultimately, complexity of code mixing.

(17)   *Age*: The most complex types of code mixing have been documented with adolescents and young adults.

Although no systematic study of the relation between age and code mixing has been done, it is clear from the data in most studies that we find a strong concentration of younger speakers in the group that engages in complex mixing.

(18)   *Style*: Most, and certainly all complex, code mixing has been recorded in informal in-group conversations.

Complex code mixing is notorious for its sensitivity to contextual effects. The presence of outsiders and more formal styles constitute a clear blocking effect on complex code mixing.

(19)   *Generation*: Most cases of complex code mixing have been recorded with second generation speakers in immigrant communities.

In a number of studies, most clearly perhaps in Backus (1992, 1996, chapter 26 of the present volume), the importance of generation (and, it should be added, peer group as part of a generation) is stressed. Members of intermediate generations show most evidence of complex mixing. It should be added that Backus presents a more complex picture, in that the most complex switching in his material comes from speakers half-way between the first and the second generations, i.e. Turkish migrants who have arrived in the Netherlands at a young age.

Before concluding, perhaps a few other rather disparate issues need to be briefly discussed: directionality of switching, code mixing and language change, and code mixing in child language.

When we consider directionality of mixing (Does the switching "go from language A to B"?), we must distinguish right away between *insertion* and *alternation*. In addition, some studies also recognize the type of intensive bi-directional mixing found for example in the corpus described in Poplack (1980) and which later has been claimed to be characteristic of matrix language reversal (Myers-Scotton, 2002), "deep" code mixing, and *congruent lexicalization* (Muysken, 2000). In the Matrix Language framework-model, directionality is explicitly encoded as a central notion in the switching process, in the distinction between the matrix language and the embedded language. This does not hold for the Equivalence Constraint and the Free Morpheme Constraint formulated by Poplack, where directionality is an epiphenomenon at best.

As to the relation between code mixing and language change, this topic can be viewed from two perspectives: the possible *consequences* of code mixing for language change and code mixing *as* language change. An interesting observation stems in this respect from Hudson (1996, p. 44):

> Features presumably spread across language boundaries as the result of bilin-
> gualism, and the preference of syntactic features among areal features may
> be due to a tendency among bilingual individuals to mix languages in mid-
> sentence. The more similar the sentence-structures are in the two languages, the
> easier this is; so language-mixing may encourage the suppression of syntactic
> differences. The areal diffusion of syntactic features is otherwise hard to under-
> stand, since syntax generally seems relatively impervious to historical change.

A very productive area of research has been in recent years the study of code mixing in child language development in bilingual families. Work in this area has progressed along two dimensions: the issue of separation versus fusion in bilingual language development (notably Genesee, 1989 and Meisel, 1989), and the issue of the interactional basis of bilingual development (Deuchar and Quay, 2000; and Lanza, 1997).

6.2.3   Code mixing and interference

The study of code mixing and that of interference have so far proceeded along separate lines. For one reason, they look like rather different phenomena. How-ever, more importantly, there has been an ideological bias in the code mixing research tradition, holding that the two languages involved in the mixing are relatively pure (Gardner-Chloros, 1995). This was to counter the view preval-ent in many bilingual speech communities that code mixing is a sign of lin-guistic degeneration and loss of competence. In the previous subsection I ar-gued that this is not correct; indeed, fluent code mixers are often fluent speakers of the different languages involved. However, this does not mean that code mixing and interference do not co-occur in bilingual corpora. They do, and an integrative framework for both phenomena is urgently needed. Closest to such a framework so far is the work of Myers-Scotton (2002), which does not treat the phenomenon of grammatical interference systematically, however, since its starting point is the lexicon. In recent models, interference will necessarily be closely linked to functional categories, and a definition of interference is given in Sanchez (in preparation), where two hypotheses are proposed:

(20)   *The Functional Interference Hypothesis*
       Interference in lexical entries (n-insertion, v-insertion) does not trigger
       syntactic changes in the bilingual grammar. Only interference in func-
       tional features triggers syntactic changes in the bilingual grammar.

Table 6.3 Interference and (insertional) code-mixing analyzed in a single framework.

	Mixed-in lexical category	*Mixed-in functional category*
Phonetically realized as matrix category	Lexical interference	Syntactic interference
Phonetically realized as embedded category	Insertional code-mixing	Code-mixing involving functional elements and restructuring

(21) *The Functional Convergence Hypothesis*
Convergence, the specification of a common set of features shared by the equivalent functional categories in the two languages spoken by a bilingual individual, takes place in a contact situation when a set of features is unstable or a new functional category emerges due to input in one of the languages that is compatible with input from the other language.

Exploring the definitions in these hypotheses, we can tentatively analyze syntactic interference as invisible code mixing, or as mixing in functional categories without their lexical content. This in turn would lead to a four-way categorization, as represented in table 6.3.

Viewed in this way, insertion of lexical elements or phrases closely resembles lexical interference on one dimension, while the two types of interference, syntactic and lexical, can be contrasted on the other dimension. Interference could be viewed as a sub-case of code mixing, namely that type of mixing not involving lexical material. (For further on code mixing and code switching, see chapters 1–4, 10–14, 25, 26, 28, 29, and 31.)

Lexical interference has often been noted, but is rarely systematically studied. A few examples of Dutch interference into Turkish lexical expressions in the migrant population in the Netherlands are given below (Dorleijn, 2002, p. 225):

(22) a. suçu bana veriyor
          the.guilt to.me he.gives
          'He blames me.' (cf. Du *de schuld geven*)
      b. ileriye gitmek
          forward go
          'to progress' (cf. Du *vooruit gaan*)
      c. piyano oynamak
          piano play
          'to play the piano' (cf. Du *piano spelen*)

This brings us to the lexicon rather naturally, discussed in the next section.

6.3   Phonology and Lexicon

The study of phonology in language contact remains underrepresented, not just on the empirical, but certainly also on the conceptual level. There have been some phonological studies of intonation in language contact, both with respect to ethnolectal variation (Carlock and Wölck, 1981), and with respect to the transfer of intonational patterns in L2 development (Wennerstrom, 1997). However, most phonological work has been done on the level of the lexicon, and therefore I will discuss phonology and lexicon together here. With respect to the lexicon, two issues have been dominant: (a) Are different kinds of categories treated differently in language contact processes? and (b) Does L1 or L2 provide the primary material? I will begin by discussing the second question.

6.3.1   L1-oriented or L2-oriented

Research on the lexicon in language contact has centered around the two processes isolated in the work of Thomason and Kaufmann (1988): L1-oriented borrowing and L2-oriented shift. I propose to treat these two not so much as separate processes but as part of a single continuum. Given the various facets of a lexical item, we must distinguish at least four dimensions in its adaptation: phonological, morphological, syntactic, and semantic (see also the distinction between *importation* and *substitution* in Haugen, 1950). This is systematically represented in table 6.4.

Table 6.4   Dimensions of retention vs. adoption in lexical contact.

	L1-oriented	*<< degree of adaptation >>*	*L2-oriented*
Phonology	adaptation to L1-phonology	. . . .	adoption L2-phonology
Morphology	adding L1-morphology	. . . .	adoption L2-morphology
Syntax	adaptation to L1 syntax	. . . .	adoption L2-syntax
Semantics	retention L1-meanings	. . . .	adoption L2-meanings

With respect to the first dimension, much remains to be systematically investigated. Here are a few preliminary observations:

(a)   It has been clear at least since Van Coetsem's (1988) study of contact phonology that we should clearly distinguish between loan phonology and L2 phonology. Even though, in borrowed words and in words acquired in L2 learning, both L1 and L2 phonological systems play a role, they carry a different weight. In the adaptation of borrowed items, the role of the native L1 phonological system is much more important.

Table 6.5   Prosodic hierarchy of Media Lengua.

Domain	Expected rule-supplying language
Phonological utterance	Quechua
Intonational phrase	Quechua
Phonological phrase	Quechua
Prosodic word	Quechua (and Spanish?)
Foot	Quechua (and Spanish)
Syllable	Spanish (stems) and Quechua (affixes)

(b)   In the so-called intertwined or mixed languages, both the lexifier language and the language providing the grammatical skeleton contribute aspects of the phonological system. However, the division of labor is not arbitrary here (van Gijn, 2001, p. 140). "Some parts of phonology are less likely to be adapted to the phonology of the grammar language than other parts of phonology (like certain voicing rules, intonation, allophony)." More specifically, the contributions of the two languages involved follow the prosodic hierarchy adopted in much recent work. The lower the phonological domain on this hierarchy, the more likely that phonological aspects of the intruding language play a role. This is illustrated by van Gijn (2001, p. 146) for Media Lengua, as in table 6.5. The Spanish stems inserted in Media Lengua retain some of their features on the lower levels, but not on the higher levels of prosodic structure (Muysken, 1996). It remains to be investigated whether the prosodic hierarchy is a useful notion in all domains of contact phonology, and how it interacts with the distinction between lexical and post-lexical processes in level-ordered phonology.

(c)   Bilinguals are capable of matching the phonemes of one language to those of another, establishing interlingual identifications, even where the phonetic substance of the sounds involved may differ somewhat (Flege, 1987).

With regard to the retention of L1 morphology or the adoption of L2 morphology, several conclusions can be drawn from the research literature:

(a)   In L2 learning, there is no transfer of L1 morphology. L1 affixes never appear on L2 lexical items in interlanguage, and a rare L1 lexical item may carry L1 affixes, but then they form part of an unanalyzed whole.

(b)   In code mixing, L2 affixes never enter the matrix language as separate units. Embedded items may carry L2 morphology that is either derivational or part of a very limited set of inflectional categories, such as nominal plural and past or present participle.

(c) Typological considerations are crucial in determining the degree to which borrowed elements can be marked with native morphology. At the one extreme, a language like Quechua adopts elements of any category and freely adds affixes to it, while, in other languages, borrowings are very constrained in terms of the native affixes they receive. Thus, in Moroccan Arabic, very few verbs are borrowed from Dutch, because of incompatibilities of the two morphological systems.

As to syntax, there is quite a range in the degree to which L1 and L2 syntactic properties are linked to individual lexical items, and this is a domain where there is substantial disagreement. A few of the main conclusions are as follows:

(a) In classical relexification, as found for example in Media Lengua (Muysken, 1981, 1996), grammatical patterns are very much tied to specific affixes. However, in the case of Michif (Bakker, 1997), full French noun phrases are imported, with their integral grammatical pattern, into Cree.

(b) In L2 learning, we find that specific grammatical domains, such as possession, are linked to L1 functional categories, even if these categories are not specifically tied to L1 lexical items (van de Craats, van Hout, and Corver, 2002). These we rarely if ever find in the L2 spoken output of ordinary L2 learners.

(c) In lexical borrowing the matrix language patterns tend to be preserved, almost by definition.

Finally, the domain of lexical semantics in language contact remains to be fully explored, as noted in the discussion above about lexical interference. It may be possible to hierarchically organize aspects of lexical semantics.

6.3.2 *Categorial distinctions*

A further issue is the rate at which different words are borrowed. Universally, certain types of words are borrowed with much greater frequency than others. Thus, the chance of finding a borrowed noun or adjective is much greater than that of finding a borrowed article or conjunction. The question is how we can represent this information. One possibility is to directly model the observation in terms of an *implicational hierarchy*, of the type already encountered above in the discussion of insertability:

(23)   noun < adjective < . . . < verb < . . . < conjunction < article

The position of other categories, such as adpositions, in this hierarchy is less certain. In addition to the distribution and frequency claims which may hold for any hierarchy as suggested above, in the case of borrowing there is a third possible claim:

(24) *Diachrony*: For any language, categories low in the hierarchy (i.e. to the left in (22)) will be borrowed earlier in the course of language contact than categories higher in the hierarchy.

The three claims (distribution, frequency, diachrony) are of course rather different, although they may have parallel effects in concrete cases. Only claim (b) has been studied in some detail in Nortier and Schatz (1992), Poplack, Sankoff, and Miller (1988), and van Hout and Muysken (1994). The noun < verb hierarchy has been studied cross-linguistically in Moravcsik (1978). As far as I know, the diachronic claim has not been studied systematically.

In van Hout and Muysken (1994) an attempt is made to decompose the categorial hierarchies in language contact in terms of general features, such as [paradigmatic structuring], [closed class membership], [abstract meaning], [transitivity], [inflection], etc. Thus the linear hierarchies of insertability and borrowability are potentially replaced by multi-factorial models, in which a number of factors conjointly determine the behavior of words in language contact situations. Up to now, mostly structural considerations have been taken into account, but it is possible that factors could be lexical semantic properties, the sound shape of an element, frequency, cross-linguistic similarity, etc.

An approach related to, but somewhat separate from, the one in terms of categorial hierarchies is in terms of function words, closed-class items, or system morphemes (Myers-Scotton, 1993). The basic insight here is that the different status of function words in language processing leads to their participation in syntactic patterning rather than lexical conceptual planning, and hence their role in language-contact processes is different from that of content words. This insight was further elaborated in a more detailed typology of function morphemes in Myers-Scotton (2002) in terms of the 4-M model. However, even the more refined typology of functional morphemes does not account for the fact that overall there are many differences between different lexical categories in language contact.

6.4   New Research Methodologies

At this point in the development of the field, research methodology has become an increasingly important concern. In my opinion it is high time for innovations in this area. The reason for this is that we start having a much clearer notion of the role of language processing in code mixing and other contact processes, and thus of the relation between competence and performance.

Actual bilingual speech behavior involves not only our knowledge of the languages concerned, but also a number of processing considerations. Thus it makes sense theoretically to separate competence from performance. However, it is not so clear what belongs where. To give just one example, a literature survey suggests that the following language-related factors play a role in furthering or constraining code mixing (Muysken: 2000):

- selection and subcategorization restrictions of individual elements impose coherence on the sentence, which block easy mixing at the core, and facilitate mixing in the periphery of the clause;
- matching word orders in the languages involved facilitate code mixing;
- the status of an element as functional blocks its insertion by itself and a switch in its immediate context;
- when an element to be inserted is perceived by the speaker as being equivalent or congruent with an element in the base or matrix language, this will facilitate its being mixed in.

Assuming for the moment that these factors are indeed the correct ones, the question may be raised whether they should be grouped under *competence* or *performance*. If we take the orthodox position that grammatical theory describes competence, and that selection is a key element in grammatical theory, then that is competence. However, for the other three factors, this is less clear. The word order matching could well be a processing consideration, as could be the status of an element as functional or not. Similarly, metalinguistic intuitions about equivalence or congruence of a certain element may also well belong to performance rather than competence.

In earlier studies on code mixing and other language-contact research several methodologies were used:

Incidental observations of spontaneously produced switches. This is of course the same technique used in much earlier speech-error research, and is meant to recover online behavior. The problem in the case of code mixing research is that code-mixed sentences are often quite complex, and it is easy to remember them incorrectly. Also, this method is not accountable, and the types of switches one notes are of course only a small subset of the ones one might be interested in.

Introspection. Introspection by a bilingual researcher has the great advantage that in principle any kind of phenomenon is at the finger tips of the researcher, since he or she is the direct source of data. However, introspection data have problems as well. In bilingual communities code mixing is often highly stigmatized and intuitions about mixing may only reflect part of the mixing behavior. (I would venture the hypothesis that intuitions about insertions are clearest (cf. Halmari, 1997), while intuitions about alternations and congruent lexicalization are often unreliable.) The fact that code mixing is most frequent in informal, non-monitored speech lower considerably the chance that reliable grammaticality judgments can be given for it.

The study of historical and literary texts. In various domains of language-contact studies historical texts have been used. Most obviously, of course, this is the case for the analysis of loan words in historical linguistics, which had to be kept apart in the reconstruction of proto-languages and in the formulation of sound laws. In addition, there are a number of studies of code mixing in medieval texts. Famous are the xarja's, multilingual Arabic/Hebrew/Old Spanish poems from Andalusia (Zwartjes, 1993/4), but other examples from Provençal, Low German, etc. abound.

Table 6.6 Criteria for evaluating methodologies of language contact research.

	Accountable	*Online*	*Coverage*
Incidental observations	−	+	−
Introspection	−	−	+
Grammaticality judgments	−	+	+
Historical and literary texts	+	?	−
Recorded spontaneous speech	+	+	−
Semi-structured tasks	+	−	±
Experiments	+	±	+

Recorded spontaneous speech. This is by far the most common technique in code mixing research, and it is also quite frequent in other areas of language contact. Given the great sensitivity of bilingual speech to contextual factors, it is clear that this way of gathering data is very valuable. However, particularly in the domain of grammar, it is clear that many structures will not appear in a natural corpus of reasonable size, or will not be frequent enough to permit any firm conclusions to be drawn about them. Also, recording and transcribing large samples of natural speech is very time-consuming and expensive.

Semi-structured tasks. Several researchers have experimented with semi-structured tasks (a recent example is Toribio, 2001), in which subjects had to combine languages in various ways. The main advantage of this method is that bilingual behavior can be triggered fairly easily in this way and the subjects can be guided in a certain direction. Disadvantages are that often the tasks involved do not necessarily reflect only on-line bilingual speech processing, and that the direction of the construction triggered remains a bit vague.

Experiments. Only a few successful experiments have been carried out to date, and there is no validation of experimental results so far with recorded spontaneous speech.

We can apply three criteria to evaluate these different techniques, as summarized in table 6.6. Here **+/− Accountable** refers to the possibility of accounting for the accuracy of the data found to another researcher; **+/− Online** refers to the question of whether code mixing is studied as an online process or not; **+/− Coverage** refers to the possibility of studying exactly the feature or construction that the researcher is interested in with this method. The three criteria may not all have equal weight. Coverage is a desideratum, while Accountable and Online are absolute requirements for a successful methodology.

Taking these criteria seriously, it is clear that recorded spontaneous speech and good experimental results are probably the most desirable techniques. Most serious studies of language contact have so far relied on recorded spontaneous speech. It is a challenge for the future to see whether experimental paradigms can bring us further.

6.5   Concluding Remarks

The necessarily superficial and selective (some may say eclectic) survey given above suggests that the field of language contact is very much alive. While partial results have been achieved in specific domains, and an impression of stasis may reign in some of these, much remains to be accomplished. Progress will come from two main trends, I think:

(a)   The further integration of the different subfields: code mixing, interference, borrowing, and bilingual acquisition both conceptually and in specific empirical domains;
(b)   The combination of different research methodologies, some of which still need to be further developed, from comparative linguistics, historical linguistics, field linguistics, sociolinguistics, and psycholinguistics.

A more specific point is that the phonological dimensions of the study of language contact require further elaboration, first of all conceptually. Once contact phonology is studied as a whole and brought onto a solid conceptual foundation, empirical work in this area will receive a new impetus.

REFERENCES

Appel, R. and Muysken, P. (1987). *Language Contact and Bilingualism.* London: Edward Arnold.

Backus, A. (1992). *Patterns of Language Mixing: A Study in Turkish-Dutch Bilingualism.* Wiesbaden: Otto Harassowitz.

Backus, A. (1996). *Two in One: Bilingual Speech of Turkish Immigrants in the Netherlands.* Ph.D. dissertation, Katholieke Universiteit Brabant, Tilburg, Studies in Multilingualism 1, Tilburg University Press.

Bakker, P. (1997). *A Language of our Own: The Genesis of Michif, the Mixed Cree-French Language of the Canadian Métis.* Oxford: Oxford University Press.

Bolle, J. (1994). Sranan Tongo-Nederlands, codewisseling en ontlening. Unpublished MA thesis, University of Amsterdam.

Carlock, E. and Wölck, W. (1981). A method for isolating diagnostic linguistic variables: The Buffalo ethnolect experiment. In D. Sankoff and H. Cedergren (eds.), pp. 17–24. *Variation Omnibus.* Edmonton: Linguistic Research.

Cerrón-Palomino, R. (1972). Enseñanza del castellano: deslindes y perspectivas. In Alberto Escobar (ed.), *El reto del multilingüismo en el Perú,* pp. 143–66. Lima: Instituto de Estudios Peruanos.

Clyne, M. (1987). Constraints on code-switching: how universal are they? *Linguistics,* 25, 739–64.

Crama, R. and van Gelderen, H. (1984). Structural constraints on code-mixing. MA thesis, University of Amsterdam.

de Rooij, Vincent (1996). Cohesion through contrast: French-Swahili code-switching and Swahili style shifting in Shaba Swahili. Ph.D. dissertation, University of Amsterdam/IFOTT.

Deuchar, M. and Quay, S. (2000). *Bilingual Acquisition: Theoretical Implications of a Case Study*. Oxford: Oxford University Press.

Dorleijn, M. (2002). "Ik leg mijn schoen met Sinterklaas." Leenvertalingen in het Turks en Nederlands. In H. Bennis, G. Extra, P. Muysken, J. Nortier (eds.), *Een buurt in beweging. Talen en culturen in het Utrechtse Lombok en Transvaal*, pp. 217–34. Amsterdam: Aksant.

Dussias, P. (2001). Sentence-parsing in fluent Spanish-English bilinguals. In J. L. Nicol (ed.), pp. 159–76.

Flege, J. (1987). The production of "new" and "similar" phones in a foreign language: Evidence for the effect of equivalence classification. *Journal of Phonetics*, 15, 47–65.

Gardner-Chloros, P. (1995). Code-switching in community, regional and national repertoires: the myth of the discreteness of linguistic systems. In Milroy and Muysken, pp. 68–89.

Genesee, Fred (1989). Early bilingual development: one language or two? *Journal of Child Language*, 16, 161–79.

Grosjean, F. (1995). A psycholinguistic approach to code-switching. In Milroy and Muysken, pp. 259–75.

Grosjean, F. (2001). The bilingual's language modes. In J. L. Nicol (ed.), pp. 1–22.

Halmari, H. (1997). *Government and Code-switching: Explaining American Finnish*. Amsterdam: Benjamins.

Haugen, E. (1950). The analysis of linguistic borrowing. *Language*, 26, 210–31.

Herkenrath, A., Karakoç, B., and Rehbein, J. (2002). Interrogative elements as subordinators in Turkish: Aspects of Turkish-German bilingual children's usage. University of Hamburg: *Working Papers in Multilingualism* 44.

Holm, J. (1978). The Creole English of Nicaragua's Miskito Coast: Its sociolinguistic history and a comparative study of its lexicon and syntax. Unpublished Ph.D. dissertation, University College, University of London.

Hudson, R. A. (1996). *Sociolinguistics*, 2nd edn. Cambridge: Cambridge University Press.

Huwaë, R. (1992). Tweetaligheid in Wierden: het taalgebruik van jongeren uit een Molukse gemeenschap. MA thesis in linguistics, University of Amsterdam.

Labov, W. (1972). *Sociolinguistic Patterns*. Philadelphia: University of Pennsylvania Press.

Lanza, E. (1997). Language mixing in infant bilingualism: A sociolinguistic perspective. Oxford: Clarendon Press.

Lipski, J. M. (1996). Patterns of pronominal evolution in Cuban-American bilinguals. In A. Roca and J. B. Jensen (eds.), *Spanish in Contact: Issues in Bilingualism*. Cascadilla Press: Somerville, MA.

Loke Kit-Ken (1991). Code-switching in children's play. *Papers from the Symposium on Code-Switching in Bilingual Studies: Theory, Significance and Perspectives*. Barcelona, 21–23 March 1991. European Science Foundation.

Meisel, J. (1989). Early differentiation of languages in bilingual children. In K. Hyltenstam and L. Obler (eds.), *Bilingualism across a Lifespan*, pp. 13–40. Cambridge, UK: Cambridge University Press.

Milroy, L. and Muysken, P. (eds.) (1995). *One Speaker, Two Languages*. Cambridge, UK: Cambridge University Press.

Moravcsik, E. (1978). Language contact. In J. E. Greenberg (ed.), *Universals of*

Human Language I, pp. 95–122. Stanford: Stanford University Press.

Muysken, P. (1981). Half-way between Quechua and Spanish: The case for relexification. In A. Highfield and A. Valdman (eds.), *Historicity and Variation in Creole Studies*, pp. 52–78. Ann Arbor, MI: Karoma.

Muysken, P. (1982). The Spanish that Quechua speakers learn. In R. W. Andersen (ed.), *Second Languages*, pp. 101–24. Rowley, MA: Newbury House.

Muysken, P. (1996). Media Lengua. In S. G. Thomason (ed.), *Contact Languages. A Wider Perspective*, pp. 365–426. Amsterdam: Benjamins.

Muysken, P. (2000). *Bilingual Speech: A Typology of Code-Mixing*. Cambridge, UK: Cambridge University Press.

Muysken, P. (2002). Storage and computation in language contact. In S. Nooteboom, F. Weerman, and F. Wijnen (eds.), *Computation and Storage in Language*, pp. 157–79. Dordrecht: Kluwer Academic.

Myers-Scotton, C. (1993). *Duelling Languages: Grammatical Structure in Codeswitching*, Oxford: Clarendon Press.

Myers-Scotton, C. (2002). *Contact Linguistics: Bilingual Encounters and Grammatical Outcomes*. Oxford: Oxford University Press.

Nicol, J. L. (ed.) (2001). *One Mind, Two languages: Bilingual Language Processing*. Oxford: Blackwell.

Nortier, J. (1990). *Dutch-Moroccan Arabic Code-switching among Young Moroccans in the Netherlands*. Dordrecht: Foris.

Nortier, J. and Schatz, H. (1992). From one-word switch to loan: A comparison of between-language pairs. *Multilingua*, 11, 173–94.

O'Neil, W. (1993). Nicaraguan English in history. In C. Jones (ed.), *Historical Linguistics: Problems and Perspectives*, pp. 279–318. London: Longman.

Pfaff, C. (1993). Turkish language development in Germany. In G. Extra and L. Verhoeven (eds.), *Immigrant Languages in Europe*, pp. 119–46. Clevedon, UK: Multilingual Matters.

Poplack, S. (1980). Sometimes I'll start a sentence in Spanish Y TERMINO EN ESPAÑOL, *Linguistics*, 18, 581–618.

Poplack, S. (1985). Contrasting patterns of code-switching in two communities. In H. J. Warkentyne (ed.), *Methods V. Papers from the Fifth International Conference on Methods in Dialectology*, pp. 363–86. Victoria, B.C.: University of Victoria Press.

Poplack, S. (2001). Postscript to Poplack (1980). In Li Wei (ed.), *The Bilingualism Reader*, pp. 221–3. London: Routledge.

Poplack, S., Sankoff, D., and Miller, C. (1988). The social correlates and linguistic processes of lexical borrowing and assimilation. *Linguistics*, 26, 47–104.

Prince, E. (2001). Yiddish as a contact language. In N. S. H. Smith and T. Veenstra (eds.), *Creolization and Contact*, pp. 263–90. Amsterdam: Benjamins.

Sanchez, L. (in preparation). Interference and convergence in functional categories: A study on Quechua-Spanish child bilingualism at the Steady State. MS, Rutgers University.

Sankoff, D., Poplack, S., and Vanniarajan, S. (1990). The case of the nonce loan in Tamil, *Language Variation and Change*, 2, 71–101.

Sanz, M. and Bever, T. G. (2001). A theory of syntactic interference in the bilingual. In J. L. Nicol (ed.), pp. 134–58.

Schaufeli, A. (1991). Turkish in an immigrant setting: A comparative study of the first language of monolingual and bilingual Turkish children. Unpublished Ph.D. dissertation, University of Amsterdam.

Tabouret-Keller, A. (1995). Conclusion: Code-switching research as a theoretical challenge. In Milroy and Muysken, pp. 344–55.

Thomason, S. G. (ed.) (1996). *Contact Languages: A Wider Perspective.* Amsterdam: Benjamins.

Thomason, S. G. and Kaufmann, T. (1988). *Language Contact, Creolization, and Genetic Linguistics,* Berkeley: University of California Press.

Toribio, J. (2001). Accessing bilingual code-switching competence. *International Journal of Bilingualism,* 5, 403–36.

Treffers-Daller, J. (1999). Borrowing and shift-induced interference: Contrasting patterns in French-Germanic contact in Brussels and Strasbourg. *Bilingualism: Language and Cognition,* 2, 1–22.

Urioste, J. L. (1964). *Transcripciones Quechuas.* Cochabamba, Bolivia: Instituto de Cultura Indígena.

Van Coetsem, F. (1988). *Loan Phonology and the Two Transfer Types in Language Contact.* Dordrecht: Foris.

Van Coetsem, F. (2000). *A General and Unified Theory of the Transmission Process in Language Contact.* Heidelberg: C. Winter Verlag.

van de Craats, Ineke, van Hout, R., and Corver, N. (2002). The acquisition of possessive HAVE-clauses by Turkish and Moroccan learners of Dutch. *Bilingualism: Language and Cognition,* 5, 147–74.

van Gijn, Rik (2001). The syllable in mixed languages. Unpublished MA thesis, University of Amsterdam.

van Hout, R. and Muysken, P. (1994). Modelling lexical borrowability. *Language Variation and Change,* 6, 39–62.

von Humboldt, Wilhelm (1836). *Über die Verscheidenheit des menschlichen Sprachbaues und ihren Einflusz auf die geistlichen Entwicklung des Menschengeschlechts.* In Wilhelm von Humboldts gesammelte Werke, vol. 6. Berlin: G. Reimer, 1848.

Weinreich, U. (1953). *Languages in Contact.* The Hague: Mouton.

Wennerstrom, A. (1997). Intonation and Second Language Acquisition. Unpublished Ph.D. dissertation, University of Washington.

Zwartjes, O. (1993/4). La alternancia de código como recurso estilístico en las *xarja-s* andalusíes. *La Corónica,* 22, 1–5.

7   The Comprehension of Words and Sentences in Two Languages

JUDITH F. KROLL AND PAOLA E. DUSSIAS

7.1   Introduction

Psycholinguists have only recently taken seriously the idea that bilinguals are more representative language users than their monolingual counterparts. The consequence has been a dramatic increase in research on language processing in bilinguals and second language learners. In part, this recent research focuses on how individuals who understand and speak more than a single language negotiate the boundaries of two language systems that may or may not share common features. However, another equally important focus is to use bilingualism as a tool to address questions about the nature of mental representations and processes and the learning mechanisms that support them. In this chapter we review evidence on the perception and comprehension of words and sentences in bilinguals. At each level of analysis we attempt to address issues that arise from each of these foci. We will consider research on the perception and comprehension of words and sentences when bilinguals are reading or listening in one language only and also when they find themselves in a mixed-language context in which the two languages may be used interchangeably.

For the purpose of our review, we assume a broad definition of bilingualism. We take anyone who actively uses two languages at some level of proficiency to be bilingual. Because few bilinguals are genuinely balanced in their use of two languages, we assume that for most bilinguals there will be one dominant language, although it need not necessarily be the native language. In reporting the results of different studies, the specific characteristics of the participants' language experience will be described to enable cross-study comparisons. Most of the research that we review examines language processing in late bilinguals who acquired their second language (L2) sometime after early childhood, although there are a few exceptions. Among the factors that distinguish different bilingual groups, the age at which the L2 was acquired and the relative dominance of the two languages will be important considerations.

The two main sections of the chapter, one on words and the other on sentences, are organized around a set of critical issues. First, we review the evidence and models within each of these aspects of language processing and address the relation of this evidence to claims about monolingual performance. An important aspect of the comparison of bilingual and monolingual performance is to consider how independently the bilingual's two languages are processed. As we will see in the sections that follow, the recent evidence suggests a great deal of permeability across language boundaries. One consequence of cross-language interaction is that the bilingual will potentially encounter competition from the presence of alternative lexical candidates in the case of word recognition and alternative parsing preferences in the case of sentence processing. Second, we consider how cross-language competition may be resolved. The solution to this problem has implications not only for our understanding of how bilinguals manage to negotiate their two languages, but also for fundamental assumptions about the relation between language and cognition.

7.2   Understanding Words

How do bilinguals understand words in each of their languages? Models of the bilingual lexicon make different assumptions about the relation of words in bilinguals' two languages. For the purpose of the present discussion, we review three models that focus on different aspects of lexical processing and consider the evidence that supports them. Because much more research has been performed on comprehension of the written word in comparison to the spoken word, these models were specifically proposed to characterize bilingual performance during reading and other tasks initiated by visual input (e.g. translation), but we also consider extensions to the case of spoken word recognition.

7.2.1   *Models of the bilingual lexicon*

The models of the bilingual lexicon can each be viewed as a different answer to the question of what is shared across words in the bilingual's two languages. We describe three models, one of which explores the way in which the orthography of the written languages may be shared, another which considers the implications of shared semantics, and a third which examines the implications of the way in which aspects of lexical form may be linked to semantics for each of the bilingual's two languages.

7.2.1.1   *The Bilingual Interaction Activation model (BIA)*
The BIA model (Dijkstra and Van Heuven, 1998; Dijkstra, Van Jaarsveld, and Ten Brinke, 1998; Van Heuven, Dijkstra, and Grainger, 1998) is a connectionist

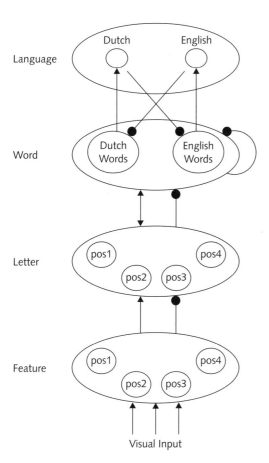

Figure 7.1   The bilingual interaction activation model (adapted from Dijkstra, Van Heuven, and Grainger, 1998).

model that extends the McClelland and Rumelhart (1981) Interactive Activation (IA) model to the bilingual case. The architecture of the model, shown in figure 7.1, assumes the same basic architecture as the IA model, namely letter features, letters, and words. Like monolingual word recognition, processing is hypothesized to be initiated bottom-up upon presentation of visual input and nonselectively so that all information similar to the input is activated. Unlike the monolingual case, the BIA model assumes that nonselectivity extends to orthographically similar letter strings in any of the languages the bilingual reads. Thus words sharing overlapping or identical orthography in the bilingual's two languages will all receive some activation. Inhibitory connections then modulate competition among both same- and other-language alternatives. The BIA model includes an additional layer of language nodes, one for each language, to allow top-down inhibition of the nontarget language.

A critical feature of the BIA model is the assumption that when words are read in one language, lexical form relatives of those words are activated in both the target and nontarget languages. Thus, when a Dutch-English bilingual reads the word *room* in English, not only do similar-looking English words become active (e.g. *roof, boom*) but similar-looking Dutch words also become active, including the word *room* itself, which happens to be an interlexical homograph which means 'cream' in Dutch. Bilingual word recognition is therefore thought to reflect the process of sorting out the activation and resulting competition among lexical alternatives in both of the bilingual's languages.

A key source of evidence for the BIA model has come from studies in which aspects of word type have been experimentally manipulated. For example, if a Dutch-English bilingual is asked to decide whether the word *room* is a valid letter string in English (i.e. to perform language-specific lexical decision), will he or she perform any differently than when asked to decide whether an unambiguously English word is a valid letter string? If access to the lexicon is language-specific, then bilinguals should perform no differently on words that share properties across their two languages than on those that do not. A large number of recent studies taking this approach have provided support for the claim that lexical access is nonselective and that bilinguals cannot help but respond as if information in both languages was active. These studies include the use of interlingual homographs, words that share lexical form but not meaning (e.g. De Groot, Delmaar, and Lupker, 2000; Dijkstra, Van Jaarsveld, and Ten Brinke, 1998; Dijkstra, Timmermans, and Schriefers, 2000; Jared and Szucs, 2002; Von Studnitz and Green, 2002), cognates, words that share both lexical form and meaning (e.g. Dijkstra, Van Jaarsveld, and Ten Brinke, 1998; Van Hell and Dijkstra, 2002), and cross-language neighbors, words belonging to a cohort of words that resemble the target word but in the nontarget language (e.g. Jared and Kroll, 2001; Van Heuven, Dijkstra, and Grainger, 1998). In general, bilingual performance on word recognition tasks, even when focused on one language only, appears to reflect the activation of information in the other language. A number of recent papers and chapters provide detailed reviews of this evidence (e.g. Brysbaert, 1998; Dijkstra and Van Heuven, 2002; Kroll and Dijkstra, 2002; Kroll and Sunderman, 2003). We therefore only briefly illustrate the nature of the empirical results for the purpose of the present discussion.

Dijkstra, Van Jaarsveld, and Ten Brinke (1998) examined the lexical decision performance of highly proficient Dutch-English bilinguals on English and Dutch words that were unambiguous within each language or interlingual homographs (e.g. *room*). When the task was simply to decide whether the letter string was a real word in English, and to say "no" to pseudowords (i.e. letter strings that are legal in English but not real words), the Dutch-English bilinguals were as fast to judge the homographs as the unambiguous English control words, as if they were able to selectively access English and switch off their Dutch. However, a second condition in that experiment suggested otherwise. When the English words were cognates, words with similar form and the same meaning in both English and Dutch, they were significantly faster to judge them as words than the controls. In a second experiment, Dijkstra et al. increased the difficulty of the task by including real Dutch words among the pseudowords. The task was still English lexical decision, but now the task was to respond "yes" if the letter string was a real English word and "no" otherwise (i.e. to both pseudo-words and real Dutch words). With this change in the composition of the materials, bilinguals were now slower to accept letter strings as English words when they were interlingual homographs, suggesting that it was difficult to ignore the irrelevant sense of the word. In a final experiment, Dutch-English bilinguals were asked to perform a generalized lexical decision task which required them to respond "yes" to any real word in either language. Under these conditions, the bilinguals were faster to judge homographs than controls, again suggesting that both readings of the word were available. Dijkstra et al. argued that the results supported the predictions of the BIA model in that shared orthographic properties of words in both languages affected performance regardless of whether the task required attention to one language only.

The fact that the BIA model restricts cross-language interaction to shared orthographic information might be taken as a criticism of its generality because many languages are not alphabetic, or use different alphabets, or differ on other dimensions of the written form. However, recent work has shown that the same general principles that apply to orthography also appear to extend to phonology and to the recognition of spoken words (e.g. Brysbaert, Van Dyck, and Van de Poel, 1999; Dijkstra, Grainger, and Van Heuven, 1999; Jared and Kroll, 2001; Marian and Spivey, 1999; Schulpen, Dijkstra, Schriefers, and Hasper, 2003; Schwartz, Kroll, and Diaz, in preparation).

Notably absent in the BIA model is the representation of semantics. The assumption at this level of analysis is that lexical form properties of words in the bilingual's languages are activated in a bottom-up fashion and only later in processing does the output of the lexical identification system interact with semantics and higher-level context. The questions of how the phonology and semantics are represented, how interactions across these levels eventually take place, and how deeply the system can be affected by contextual factors and task goals are topics of current research activity and theorizing (e.g. Altarriba, Kroll, Sholl, and Rayner, 1996; Dijkstra and Van Heuven, 2002; Elston-Güttler, 2000; Van Heuven, 2000; Von Studnitz and Green, 2002a; Von Studnitz and Green, 2002b). We will return to this issue when we consider the question of negotiating cross-language competition.

7.2.1.2   The distributed feature model

In the past literature, there are two different research traditions that have given rise to alternative accounts of bilingual semantics. One line of research, investigating the representations of words and concepts in two languages, assumes that in most essential respects the same semantics support meaning representations in the bilingual's two languages (Kroll, 1993; Kroll and De Groot, 1997). For example, research on picture naming and translation, Stroop-type interference tasks, semantic priming, and semantic categorization all suggest that words in each language access conceptual representations that are common to both languages (e.g. Altarriba, 1990; Caramazza and Brones, 1980; Chen and Ng, 1989; Costa, Miozzo, and Caramazza, 1999; Dufour and Kroll, 1995; Hermans, Bongaerts, de Bot and Schreuder, 1998; La Heij, Kerling, and Van der Velden, 1996; La Heij et al., 1990; Potter, So, von Eckardt, and Feldman, 1984; Schwanenflugel and Rey, 1986; Tzelgov and Eben-Ezra, 1992). Moreover, recent neuroimaging studies have shown that the same neural tissue appears to support semantic processing in each of the bilingual's two languages, suggesting a common representation (Illes et al., 1999). Bilinguals may take longer to understand the meaning of words in the L2 than in the L1, and they may have more extensive knowledge of the meanings of L1 than L2 words, but the same underlying representations and processes are assumed (see Francis, 1999 for a general review of the literature on bilingual semantics). A criticism of much of this work is that its scope is necessarily restricted by the focus on pictured objects and their names, thereby excluding many concepts and grammatical categories other than nouns that are also representative of bilinguals' vocabulary.

An alternative view is that the larger cultural and linguistic context in which the bilingual's two languages are used have profound consequences for the understanding of even common words. Research on linguistic relativity reflects this assumption (see Green, 1998, and Pavlenko, 1999, for recent discussions of this issue). Observations of language use both within and outside the laboratory make it clear that not all words in one language possess direct, single-word translation equivalents in another language, and that sometimes translation equivalents are only approximate. Within the literature on bilingual psycholinguistics, these ideas have been developed most extensively by the work of De Groot and her colleagues (De Groot, 1992, 1993, 1995; De Groot, Dannenburg, and Van Hell, 1994; Van Hell, 1998; Van Hell and De Groot, 1998). The distributed feature model, shown in figure 7.2, represents the relation between translation equivalents in terms of the overlap of a set of semantic features. As in other recent proposals in the domain of semantics and computational modeling (e.g. McRae, de Sa, and Seidenberg, 1997; Vigliocco, Vinson, Damian, and Levelt, 2002), the notion is that the similarity of word meanings is graded and that the resulting representations account for many of the emergent properties of category structure and word type. In the case of bilinguals, the similarity of the meaning representation that is retrieved for translation equivalents will be a function of how much the concepts that are activated by words in the two languages overlap. The claim is that some words, notably concrete nouns and cognates, are more likely to map onto virtually the same pool of semantic features across languages than abstract nouns and noncognates. The more overlap between semantic features, the more quickly the translation will be retrieved and the more likely bilinguals will be to consistently produce the same response.

The evidence for the distributed feature model comes primarily from studies of translation by proficient bilinguals (e.g. De Groot, 1992, 1993, 1995; De

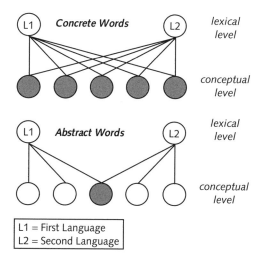

Figure 7.2   The distributed feature model (adapted from Van Hell and De Groot, 1998).

Groot, Dannenburg, and Van Hell, 1994; Van Hell, 1998; Van Hell and De Groot, 1998). As the model predicts, performance is faster and more accurate for concrete than for abstract words and for cognate than for noncognate translations (see Van Hell, 1998 for converging support from word association and lexical decision tasks). Critical questions for the distributed feature model are whether there is any consequence of which particular features are shared across languages and whether the number of features required to identify a particular concept is an important factor in determining cross-language similarity. The model as it stands makes predictions that are primarily quantitative so that response time will be fastest when the highest proportion of features overlap, regardless of their status.

Another issue that requires examination is whether a special similarity mechanism is required in the bilingual case. It is possible that any factor that affects the ease of concept retrieval will also influence cross-language performance in tasks in which semantics is engaged. For example, the concreteness of words within a single language has been shown to affect performance in a variety of tasks (e.g. Kroll and Merves, 1986; Paivio, 1971; Schwanenflugel, Harnishfeger, and Stowe, 1988; Schwanenflugel and Shoben, 1983). It is possible that the observed cross-language effects are only a reflection of more general aspects of semantic and conceptual representation. One recent set of studies suggests that this may be the case for words that have more than a single translation equivalent in one or the other of the bilingual's two languages (Kroll and Tokowicz, 2001; Schönpflug, 1997; Tokowicz and Kroll, in preparation; Tokowicz, Kroll, De Groot, and Van Hell, 2002). These studies show that the time to translate is a function of the number of translation equivalents, with

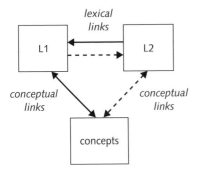

Figure 7.3   The revised hierarchical model (adapted from Kroll and Stewart, 1994).

longer latencies when words in one language map to more than one alternative in the other language. These effects are even more robust than the concreteness effects previously reviewed and provide support for the hypothesis that the ambiguity of the lexical and/or semantic representation will have consequences for understanding and speaking words across languages.

Just as the BIA model does not include or make a commitment about the nature of semantics, the distributed feature model does not make any claims about the representation of the lexical form itself nor how lexical form and meaning might interact during word recognition. Indeed, one might consider a model in which both lexical form and semantic aspects of the lexicon are represented as distributed features (see Kroll and De Groot, 1997, for an illustration of this approach, Dijkstra and Van Heuven, 2002, for an extension of the BIA model, and Van Hell, 1998, for an example of a distributed model at both levels). The final model at the lexical level that we consider addresses the nature of the interconnection between lexical forms and meaning.

7.2.1.3   *The revised hierarchical model (RHM)*
The models described thus far examine aspects of the bilingual lexicon for individuals who have achieved a relatively high level of proficiency in their second language. However, as we noted at the outset of the chapter, few bilinguals are balanced across the two languages; typically one language, often the native language, is more dominant than the other. The revised hierarchical model (RHM) was proposed by Kroll and Stewart (1994) to characterize the consequences of differential expertise in the two languages for the connections between words and concepts. The model, shown in figure 7.3, includes independent lexical representations for each language, with L1 assumed to be larger than L2, and a shared conceptual representation. Unlike the BIA and distributed feature models, the RHM does not make a detailed commitment to the structure of the lexical and conceptual information, but rather focuses on the connections between them. The model assumes that words in the L1 can more readily access their respective meanings than words

in L2. This asymmetry in the strength of connections between words in the two languages and meaning is a feature of the model that is implicitly, if not explicitly, shared with other research on this topic. The unusual claim of the model, and the one that has received the most scrutiny, is that lexical representations in L2 are strongly associated to their translations in L1. In this respect, the model represents the consequences of the learning history of the late second language learner for whom lexical and conceptual representations are already in place for L1 when L2 learning begins. The hypothesis is that L2 words take advantage of the existing lexical-to-meaning connections by accessing the L1 translation. This process will be most salient for learners but still evident even for relatively proficient bilinguals. The model thus assumes asymmetric connections in two ways. At the lexical level, L2 words are more strongly associated to their L1 translations than the reverse. At the level of accessing concepts, L1 words have stronger connections to meaning than their L2 counterparts.

Extensive reviews of the evidence supporting and failing to support the RHM are available in recent chapters (e.g. Gollan and Kroll, 2001; Kroll and De Groot, 1997; Kroll, Michael, and Sankaranarayanan, 1998; Kroll and Sunderman, 2003; Kroll and Tokowicz, 2001). For present purposes we describe the major results.

The empirical observation that led to the RHM initially was the finding that translation from L1 to L2, the forward direction, is typically slower and more error-prone than translation from L2 to L1, the backward direction. According to the model, the asymmetry in performance in the two directions of translation can be understood as a consequence of the asymmetric connections between words and concepts in the two languages. In the L2 to L1 direction, the strongly associated translation equivalents will be accessed directly. In the L1 to L2 direction, the bias to activate the meaning of the L1 word will encourage reliance on a translation route that engages semantics. The latter process will require additional processing and also the potential negotiation of lexical competition prior to selecting an L2 response. The L1 to L2 direction is hypothesized to be particularly difficult for less proficient bilinguals for whom the concept to L2 links are relatively weak. Experiments on translation generally support these predictions, with a larger translation asymmetry at lower levels of L2 proficiency and L1 to L2 translation changing most dramatically with increasing L2 skill (e.g. Kroll, Michael, Tokowicz, and Dufour, 2002, but see De Groot and Poot, 1997 for evidence to the contrary).

If the claims of the RHM about the two directions of translation are correct, then concepts are accessed in only one of the two translation directions, from L1 to L2. Kroll and Stewart (1994) tested this prediction by examining the effect of a semantic variable, the presence of a list context that was semantically categorized or not, on the two translation tasks. The experiment, performed with highly proficient Dutch-English bilinguals, provided clear support for the predictions. In the L1 to L2 direction, bilinguals suffered interference when translating in the context of categorized lists. In the L2 to L1 direction,

hypothesized to be accomplished directly via access to lexical-level translations, there was no effect of the semantic manipulation. The results thus supported the main features of the RHM (see Sholl, Sankaranarayanan, and Kroll,
1995; Sunderman, 2002; and Talamas, Kroll, and Dufour, 1999, for other tests
of the model including an examination of the implications for development of
L2 proficiency, and La Heij, Kerling, and Van der Velden, 1996, for evidence
that both directions of translation may be semantically processed).

As we noted earlier, the RHM does not make a precise commitment to the
structure of lexical and conceptual representations. Although it might be possible to incorporate aspects of the BIA and distributed feature models while,
at the same time, maintaining the differential asymmetries proposed by the
RHM (see Kroll and De Groot, 1997, for a specific proposal along these lines),
the models were proposed to answer different questions about bilingual lexical representation. In particular, the claim of the BIA model that lexical form
relatives are active during word recognition is quite distinct from the claim
of the RHM that translation equivalents are accessed by L2 words. These
differences may be understood if one remembers that the RHM is fundamentally a model of the development of L2 proficiency and that the BIA model is
a model of the state of the lexicon in the proficient bilingual. It is possible that
translation equivalents play a critical role during early stages of development,
but by the time a bilingual is reasonably proficient in L2, representations for
L2 words are established and function like L1 words (see Frenck-Mestre and
Pynte, 1997, for evidence that L2 words are processed autonomously even
early in L2 acquisition). An alternative way to understand these different claims
about lexical activation is to consider that the RHM may be more likely to
capture the processes engaged in production tasks that require the top-down
lexicalization of concepts to words, whereas the BIA model may better account for the bottom-up aspects of processing during the earliest stages of
word recognition. (For a discussion of bilingual production models, see Costa,
chapter 8 in this volume, and La Heij, 2005.) Although perception and production may contact the same lexical representations, the manner in which the
output of the lexical system is used may differ depending on the nature
of the task that is performed (see Kroll and Dijkstra, 2002, for a comparison of
lexical processing in perception and production). (For additional discussion of
the RHM, see chapter 9.)

7.2.2   *Negotiating cross-language competition*

If words in both of the bilingual's languages are active at some level, even
when the bilingual reads or hears spoken language in only one of his or her
two languages, then some mechanism must be in place to allow effective
negotiation of the potential cross-language competition. Because there does
not appear to be a simple language switch that enables language selection
based on the intention of the reader or speaker or on the language-specific
properties of the input (e.g. Thomas and Allport, 2000), the problem of how

cross-language competition is resolved requires additional assumptions about the architecture of the recognition system.

One solution to the control problem, illustrated by the BIA model discussed earlier, is to assume that there is a level of representation within the lexicon, the language nodes, that accumulates information about the intended language and serves to inhibit the unintended language (e.g. Dijkstra, Van Jaarsveld, and Ten Brinke, 1998; Van Heuven, Dijkstra, and Grainger, 1998). If the internal properties of the lexical system are sensitive to factors that signal language membership, then differential levels of information might be needed to recognize a word as belonging to one language rather than the other. For example, an early study by Grainger and Beauvillain (1987) showed that there was a cost to switching between the bilingual's two languages in lexical decision that appeared to be overcome when words possessed language-specific orthography. However, a more recent study by Thomas and Allport (2000) revealed a confounding in the Grainger and Beauvillain study such that only the real words in lexical decision contained language-specific sequences. When the confounding was removed, the effect of language-specific cues was independent of switch costs, suggesting that the switch costs themselves arise outside of the lexicon. The result is surprising in some ways, because one might expect, especially when the cues to language membership are salient (e.g. in bilinguals for whom one language is alphabetic and the other is not, or where one language utilizes diacritical markings and the other does not), that selection would be possible on the basis of the input alone. To the contrary, the observation of cross-language effects based on phonology alone, even in the absence of common orthography, suggests that early selection may not be possible, at least in comprehension (e.g. Gollan, Forster, and Frost, 1997; Jiang, 1999; but see Vaid and Frenck-Mestre, 2002 for an illustration of how orthographic cues may be used to decide language membership).

A number of recent papers have argued that there are processes outside the lexicon that serve to modulate and influence the output of the lexical system (e.g. Dijkstra and Van Heuven, 2002; Green, 1998). On this account, the degree of cross-language activity within the lexicon is determined by a bottom-up process engaged by the similarity of the input to lexical and sub-lexical features in each of the bilingual's two languages. However, because the configuration of different tasks will make distinct demands on the way the lexical output is used and require different decision criteria to be adopted (see Green, 1998, for a discussion of the notion of task schemas), a variety of cross-language patterns will be observed (e.g. Dijkstra, De Bruijn, Schriefers, and Ten Brinke, 2000; Michael, Dijkstra, and Kroll, 2002; Von Studnitz and Green, 2002a, 2002b).

How can these alternatives be distinguished? One empirical approach has been to determine whether the homograph interference effect in lexical decision (De Groot et al., 2000;), taken to reflect the presence of nonselective activation of information in both of the bilingual's languages, can be modulated. Dijkstra et al. (2000) reported that advance knowledge that words in the nontarget language would be present did not affect the presence of the homograph interference effect; only the actual presentation of those words appeared to induce the effect. This result suggests that the observed cross-language effects were the outcome of a bottom-up process that proceeded independently of task instructions. Using a related but slightly different manipulation, Von Studnitz and Green (2002) demonstrated that informing participants about the presence of interlingual homographs did modulate the magnitude of the effects; they also argued that the observed modulation was primarily due to mechanisms likely to fall outside the lexicon itself. Furthermore, Michael, Dijkstra, and Kroll (2002) showed that individual differences in working memory capacity, a factor that is related to performance on a range of language-processing tasks including translation, did not affect the magnitude of homograph interference in lexical decision. To the extent that differences in working memory capacity reflect differences in the ability to select among multiply active alternatives, then the result suggests that at least in the case of homograph interference, the enhanced ability to juggle alternatives does not eliminate the apparently bottom-up contribution of cross-language activation.

7.2.3 *Summary on understanding words*

The picture that emerges from the research we have reviewed is one of permeable lexical systems in which sources of shared information interact. The question of how the resulting activation and competition across languages is resolved is an active area of research that will require that additional evidence from a variety of tasks and approaches be considered before a clear conclusion can be reached. For example, a very recent neuroimaging study by Rodriquez-Fornells et al.. (2002) examined brain activity while Spanish-Catalan bilinguals read words in one language and ignored the other language. Contrary to the claims of most of the behavioral studies cited above, they argue that phonological information can be used during lexical access to block the nontarget language. It will remain to be seen whether different approaches to this question produce converging evidence.

A further critical issue for the models we have discussed is how context modulates cross-language activation. Although many previous bilingual studies have examined the effects of single word semantic and/or translation context on lexical access (e.g. Altarriba, 1990; Chen and Ng, 1989; Gollan, Forster, and Frost, 1997; Jiang, 1999; Keatley, Spinks, and De Gelder, 1994; Meyer and Ruddy, 1974; Schwanenflugel and Rey, 1986; Tzelgov and Eben-Ezra, 1992), only a few studies have examined the consequences of sentence context for lexical access (e.g. Altarriba, Kroll, Sholl, and Rayner, 1996; Elston-Güttler, 2000). The findings of the semantic priming studies are mostly consistent with the claim that semantics is generally shared across the bilingual's two languages, regardless of whether the two languages also share lexical form. Consistently with the claims of the revised hierarchical model, these effects are typically larger from the L1 to L2 than the reverse, which is consistent with the notion that semantic representations for L1 words are accessed more rapidly than those for L2 words. The findings of the few sentence priming studies are also consistent with the claim that semantics may be shared across languages, but are less clear about the conditions under which the language nonselectivity that is such a compelling feature of out-of-context word recognition performance is maintained or eliminated in context. At a theoretical level, Dijkstra and Van Heuven (2002) argue that sentence context effects should reflect linguistic interactions that would be permissible within an encapsulated lexical system, and thus distinct from the apparent insensitivity of the system to task-level expectations described earlier. However, virtually all of the research on bilingual word recognition has been conducted in a framework that is independent of sentence-level considerations. We turn now to the question of how bilinguals process sentences in one or both of their languages. At the end of the chapter we discuss briefly the connections and future directions that emerge from considering these two levels of processing together. (For additional discussion of bilingual lexical processing, see chapters 2, 9, and 28.)

7.3 Understanding Sentences

Sentence comprehension is a highly complicated process. Within the span of a few thousand milliseconds, the average reader or listener is able to identify the players in a sentence, the roles that these players fulfill, the events and states being described, and the meaning of the sentence as a whole. Given the speed with which this process takes place, it is quite remarkable that people are rarely unsuccessful at understanding sentences. Few other human tasks are accomplished so quickly, efficiently, and successfully by so many. What is even more surprising is that we are able to arrive at the intended interpretation of sentences that we have never encountered before. So how do we accomplish this? Much of the research on sentence processing has been directed precisely at answering this question. A number of accounts have emerged which make different claims about how the sentence parser computes the initial syntactic structure of sentences. Distinguishing among these accounts is beyond the scope of this paper. However, we will outline the assumptions made by two different types of accounts: restricted and unrestricted (for a detailed discussion, see Pickering, 1999).

Restricted accounts claim that during initial sentence processing (i.e. the stage at which a first analysis is formed), the parser can only employ a limited number of all the relevant existing sources of information. Perhaps the most well-developed instantiation of a restricted account is Frazier's *Garden-Path* model (1978; see also Frazier and Rayner, 1982; Rayner, Carlson and Frazier, 1983). The model, which is principle-based, assumes that the sentence processor is faced with computational limitations that require it to ignore potentially useful information during initial parsing decisions. Confronted with the task of assigning a structural analysis to a sentence, the parser initially consults only limited grammatical information; discourse context and semantic information play a role only during subsequent stages, when late-arriving grammatical information or extra-grammatical information, i.e. pragmatic context or plausibility, indicate that some other legitimate interpretation is preferred to the first analysis. To explain how the parser assigns a single immediate analysis to a sentence fragment, Frazier and her colleagues postulated the existence of a small set of universal parsing principles, the most important of which are *Minimal Attachment* and *Late Closure*. For illustrative purposes, we will describe the latter principle.

(1)   Late Closure: "If grammatically permissible, attach new items into the clause or phrase currently being processed." (Frazier, 1987, p. 562)

To show how Late Closure works, consider (2):

(2)   Peter fell in love with the daughter of the architect who studied in Spain.

Example (2) is structurally ambiguous in that the relative clause *who studied in Spain* can modify the first or the second noun in the complex noun phrase *daughter of the architect*. *Late Closure* predicts attachment of the relative clause to *the architect*, since the phrase containing this noun phrase is also the phrase more recently postulated.

Although both Minimal Attachment and Late Closure receive empirical support from a number of studies involving a variety of languages (e.g. Carreiras, 1992; Cuetos and Mitchell, 1988; Ferreira and Henderson, 1990; Frazier and Clifton, 1996; Frazier and Rayner, 1982; Igoa, Carreiras, and Meseguer, 1998; Mitchell and Cuetos, 1991), the Garden-Path model has undergone considerable revision because of the existence of cross-linguistic evidence that challenges the universality of Late Closure as a parsing principle (see Frazier and Clifton, 1996).

In marked contrast with restricted accounts of parsing, unrestricted accounts put forward the claim that all sources of information can be employed during initial parsing decisions. This is the position adopted in *Constraint-based Satisfaction* models of sentence parsing (e.g. MacDonald, 1994; MacDonald, Pearlmutter and Seidenberg, 1994; Trueswell, Tanenhaus and Kello, 1993), which assume that multiple alternative analyses are available during initial sentence parsing, but that their availability undergoes continuous changes caused by the strength of probabilistic syntactic and non-syntactic cues (or constraints) and by the availability of alternative analyses. For example, MacDonald, Pearlmutter and Seidenberg (1994) postulate that the semantic, phonological, orthographical and morphological (e.g. past tense vs. past participle) information of words, as well as information about their alternative argument structure and frequencies of occurrence is encoded in the lexicon and is activated to differing degrees during sentence parsing.

The different models outlined above raise interesting questions regarding sentence processing in bilinguals. Given the existence of cross-linguistic variation in argument structure, for example, how do bilinguals use information about the two languages in assigning initial structure to a sentence? And how do bilinguals' different language histories influence the strategies employed during real-time sentence parsing? Does language comprehension in bilinguals differ qualitatively from that of native readers (or listeners) when faced with phrase structure violations, or is there only a quantitative difference between the two? The fundamental goal of this line of inquiry is not only to arrive at an understanding of the precise nature of bilingual sentence processing, but also to contribute to the understanding of the fundamental properties of the human sentence-processing mechanism.

7.3.1 Sentence processing in bilinguals

Although syntactic parsing has been the object of much investigation and heated debate in the monolingual literature, few studies have examined sentence parsing from a second language (L2) perspective. Harrington (2001) offers a number of explanations for the limited attention that sentence processing has received in the SLA literature. Mainstream sentence-processing research is largely interested in the process of structure building by mature speakers, and is less preoccupied with issues related to learning and individual differences. SLA research, on the other hand, being primarily concerned with explaining how individuals acquire proficiency in an L2, focuses both on the learning process and on individual outcomes. The divergent goals in the two fields, coupled with the lack of technical resources and methodological expertise among SLA researchers, have kept L2 sentence processing research in a peripheral setting. However, as Gregg (2001) rightly points out, a theory of second language acquisition needs both a property theory – a specific theory of linguistic knowledge, *and* a transition theory – a theory that accounts for the cognitive mechanisms responsible for explaining changes of state within the L2 learner's linguistic system. It is in the latter that parsing research is relevant to SLA acquisition. A second language learner's encounter with input from the second language is filtered through the parser, a device whose role is to apply the facts of a grammar it has available to an input word string. The parser acts as a mediator between word strings and the grammatical representation that such strings are assigned during real-time sentence processing. If second language learners use the available processing strategies from their L1 to process L2 input, and if these processing strategies are not suited for parsing the incoming L2 string – for example, if they are different from those employed by monolingual speakers of the target language – L2 learners may be drawing incorrect conclusions about the target language grammar and about its properties, with the result that the interlanguage grammar is not restructured in ways that approximate the target linguistic system. The empirical question that stems from this line of reasoning, then, is whether what may be preventing learners from acquiring the L2 grammar is the set of processing strategies that are used during syntactic parsing (see Fernández, 1999; Van Patten, 1996).

L2 sentence processing research is useful in another respect. It is a well-known fact that languages vary cross-linguistically with regard to verb-argument structure. Given the assumptions that (1) comprehension processes are guided by rule-based representations which are used by the parser (Frazier and De Villiers, 1990), and (2) that verb-subcategorization and verb-thematic information affect parsing decisions (Gorrell, 1995; Pritchett, 1992; Trueswell, Tanenhaus and Garnsey, 1994), it follows that sentence parsing research can be used as an indirect measure for investigating differences in semantics–syntax representations between monolingual and second language speakers, in cases where the L1 and the L2 differ with respect to the way in which concepts in verb roots are lexicalized. In other words, sentence parsing research can be used to make claims about the competence that learners have at any particular point during the process of second language acquisition (see, e.g. Juffs, 1998b).

Finally, L2 parsing research complements L2 research devoted to the investigation of how language is understood and used in communicative contexts. To best illustrate this, consider the case of understanding written sentences. To understand written text, L2 speakers must, among other things, identify individual words and compute the structural relationships among them. Comprehending written sentences can be particularly challenging for L2 learners, since printed text lacks the prosodic information that presumably helps listeners to make decisions about phrasal groupings during spoken language comprehension. Now, if one of the goals of communication is to arrive at a common interpretation of the written text, readers must, minimally, parse sentences in ways that are consistent with the intentions of the interlocutor. In other words, L2 learners must be able to parse sentences in the L2 in a manner *similar* to that of native speakers of the target language. Although this task may turn out to be successful when the processing routines that are used to parse the L1 and the L2 converge, when a particular reading of a sentence is linked to the application of language-specific parsing strategies, one expects to find differences in sentence interpretation in cases where the L1 parsing routines are not adequate for parsing L2 input.

7.3.1.1 *L2 comprehenders: How different are they from monolinguals?*

One obvious fact about language comprehension is that L2 speakers approach the task of L2 sentence comprehension with a fully developed processing system from their L1. One natural question that follows, then, is whether the specific semantic and syntactic subprocesses engaged during L2 language comprehension are different for second language speakers as compared to native speakers. As we will show, L2 speakers resemble their monolingual counterparts in the semantic domain of sentence comprehension; however, when syntactic processes are involved, differences arise.

The most compelling type of evidence in support of this claim comes from studies that have used event-related brain potentials (ERPs) while L2 speakers are exposed to sentences that vary systematically with respect to particular linguistic characteristics. (ERPs are recordings of brain electrical activity, measured at the scalp, that are used to obtain temporal information regarding different subprocesses during language comprehension.) Weber-Fox and Neville (1996) investigated semantic and syntactic processing during reading in proficient Chinese-English bilinguals who had learned the L2 at the ages of 1–3, 4–6, 7–10, 11–13, and after 16 years. Participants read semantically anomalous sentences in their L2 (e.g. *The scientist criticized Max's event of the theorem.*), as well as sentences containing phrase structure rules violations (e.g. *The scientist criticized Max's of proof the theorem.*), and specificity-constraint violations (e.g. *What did the scientist criticize Max's proof of?*). The results indicated that, in response to semantic anomalies, the learners who were exposed to the L2 before age 11 were remarkably similar to the monolingual speakers. Moreover, the differences observed between the participants who acquired the second language after age 11 and the monolinguals were only quantitative in nature. That is, whereas the two groups of participants displayed the expected (*N400*) brain activity typically associated with the processing of semantic anomaly, the peak latency for the participants who acquired the L2 after age 11 was delayed. With respect to syntactic processing, marked qualitative differences in the responses were noted, with learners exposed to English after age 16 consistently displaying the greatest differences in ERP patterns compared with those observed in monolinguals (for similar findings regarding semantic aspects of language processing in bilinguals, see Ardal et al., 1990; Kutas and Kluender, 1991).

In a more recent study using the same methodological tool, Hahne (2001; see also Hahne and Friederici, 2001) compared semantic and syntactic processing in proficient second language learners of German who are native Russian speakers. ERP responses to auditory stimuli containing semantic and syntactic anomalies were recorded. Similarly to Weber-Fox and Neville (1996), they found that the differences in processing semantic incongruities between native and L2 speakers were quantitative only, but there were qualitative differences with regard to syntactic processing between the two groups, suggesting that the second language learners did not process or integrate syntactic information into the existing phrase structure in the same way that native listeners did.

These studies indicate that semantic processing in bilinguals parallels that of monolingual speakers and that the differences observed between the two groups arise because these processes are slowed down in L2 speakers. On the other hand, when syntactic processes are involved, the differences between the two groups are both quantitative and qualitative in nature. One question that arises from this observation is whether during the process of assigning structure to an incoming string of words (i.e. sentence parsing), bilinguals are less like monolingual speakers where syntactically based information plays a role in biasing readers toward a particular parse vis-à-vis some alternative competitor.

To address the question at hand, we examine studies that investigate how thematic role assignment proceeds during sentence processing when the bilingual's two languages rely on different sources of information to arrive at a decision. We also review research on influence of verb argument structure during L2 parsing, and then follow with a discussion of parsing adjunct phrases and modifiers by second language speakers, as this topic is revealing of the parsing processes that L2 readers follow in the absence of lexical information carried by the verb.

7.3.1.2   The assignment of theta roles during L2 sentence processing

Early work on theta-role assignment in bilingual sentence processing is grounded in the *Competition Model* (Bates and MacWhinney, 1982; MacWhinney, 1987). The model aims to explain how speakers determine semantic relationships (e.g. agent, patient, goal, etc.) among elements in a sentence. To capture particular relations between surface forms and associated functions, the notion of cue is brought into play. Sentence processing is seen as convergence of or competition among various cues, each contributing to a different resolution in sentence interpretation. Cues are said to converge when they concomitantly designate the same thematic relation, and to compete when they point to different relations. For example, in the English sentence *The girl sees the plant*, three cues converge to assign *the girl* the function of agent: word order, subject agreement on the verb, and animacy. However, in *The pencil kicks the donkey*, word order and agreement enter into competition with animacy.

Studies involving a variety of typologically different languages have shown the existence of cross-linguistic variation in the way forms map onto semantic functions, as well as in the weights associated with different form–function mappings. Given this, researchers of this persuasion ask whether second language learners are able to learn the mappings and weights that are specific to the second language. Although this issue has been investigated extensively in the past fifteen years, the overall picture is somewhat unclear. Gass (1987, for L1 Italian speakers learning English) and Harrington (1987, for L1 Japanese speakers learning English) found evidence that learners who favored semantically based cues (e.g. noun animacy) as the primary source of information in their L1, were strongly dependent on these cues when assigning thematic roles in English, a language in which word order provides the strongest cue (for additional results see Liu, Bates and Li, 1992, and Su, 2001 for Chinese; McDonald, 1987 for Dutch; Heilenman and McDonald, 1993, and McDonald and Heilenman, 1991 for French; Sasaki, 1994 for Japanese; and Hernandez, Bates and Ávila, 1994 and Wulfeck, Juárez, Bates and Kilborn, 1986, for Spanish). On the other hand, Gass (1987) and Sasaki (1991) found that L1 English learners of Italian and Japanese were able to abandon their reliance on word order and to employ animacy as the primary cue in interpreting Japanese and Italian sentences. This directional asymmetry may indicate that semantic cues occupy a position of universal importance relative to grammatical cues (Gass, 1987).

However, subsequent studies have not supported this proposal. A recent study examining whether transfer patterns change as a function of proficiency (Su, 2001) found differences between Chinese adult learners of English and English adult learners of Chinese. Overall, the English learners used English word-order strategies most of the time in processing Chinese sentences. At the same time, there was evidence that as proficiency increased, the learners became more aware of the important role of animacy in Chinese processing. For the Chinese learners of English, the pattern was quite different. Beginning learners used their L1 animacy cue as their strongest cue when reading English and Chinese, and intermediate learners used both animacy and word order at about the same rate in both of their languages. Advanced learners more closely resembled the English native speakers in employing the word-order cue when reading English. These findings indicate that language proficiency is an important factor, and hint at the preponderance of syntactic cues over semantic cues.

Recent work by Juffs and Harrington (1995, 1996) examines theta-role assignment under a framework that attributes parsing preferences to argument preference principles. Following Pritchett (1992), these authors assume that the parser attempts to arrive at a complete syntactic analysis of a sentence, with principles of grammar such as Case and Theta Attachment satisfied as soon as possible. In a series of experiments, the authors examined how Chinese learners of English processed sentences such as *Who did Ann believe _____ likes her friend?* and *Who did Ann believe her friends like ___?*. The sentences differ in that the first one is assumed to require extraction of the *wh* element from a subject site (indicated by the _____), whereas the second requires extraction from an object site. Juffs and Harrington (1995) predicted that subject extraction sentences ought to present more difficulty for the parser than object extraction sentences, because the former would force the parser to reanalyze the wh-gap several times before finally arriving at a complete analysis of the sentence. Data collected using a moving-window technique confirmed the predictions, but also revealed that L2 learners parsed the structures in question qualitatively and quantitatively differently from native English monolingual speakers. By and large, these studies suggest that L2 speakers exhibit non-native-like processing patterns during the assignment of thematic roles to noun phrases in their second language.

7.3.1.3 *The influence of lexical information during L2 parsing*

A common assumption in the L2 parsing literature is that when verb meaning and argument structure in the L1 and L2 match, speakers are not expected to show L2 parsing difficulties whose source is argument structure. This is because the transfer of L1 information onto the L2 will result in a structure that conforms to the L2 grammar. Conversely, differences between the two languages are expected to cause differences in parsing decisions.

There are only a handful of studies on the influence of verb subcategorization information during L2 language processing. Contrary to what we reported in the previous section, these studies find that the bilinguals are guided by L2 argument structure information during processing, and indeed parse sentences in the second language in accordance with the lexical constraints of that language.

In one such study, Frenck-Mestre and Pynte (1997, Experiment 2) recorded the eye movements of French-dominant and English-dominant bilinguals while reading sentences that contained temporary subject/object ambiguities, as in *Every time the dog obeyed the pretty girl showed her approval.* The critical difference between French and English is that in English, the noun phrase *the pretty girl* can be interpreted as the object of the verb *obeyed* in the subordinate clause, or as the subject of the forthcoming clause. In other words, it is the optional transitivity of the verb that gives rise to the ambiguity. In French, the ambiguity does not exist because the verb is used with an intransitive reading. The results failed to show any qualitative differences between the native and second language speakers.

Additional support for the claim that L2 speakers make use of lexical-semantic information from the L2 during sentence comprehension comes from a study conducted by Juffs (1998a). Using a word-by-word reading task, Juffs examined how L2 learners from different language backgrounds processed sentences containing reduced relative clause ambiguities such as *The bad boys criticized almost every day were playing in the park.* He found that the advanced L2 learners were slower than native speaker controls, but processed the experimental sentences in a way similar to that of native speakers. As in Frenck-Mestre and Pynte (1997), the results suggested that L2 learners were guided by information about the L2 argument structure during sentence parsing.

In a related experiment, Hoover and Dwivedi (1998) investigated syntactic processing in highly fluent L2 French learners while they were reading sentences containing constructions that do not exist in their L1 (English). The construction under investigation involved pre-verbal pronominalization in French causative and non-causative constructions. The findings revealed similar patterns of reading times for French second language learners and French L1 speakers, indicating, once again, that L2 readers exhibit L2-like syntactic processing during the on-line analysis of L2 constructions not found in their L1 (but see Juffs, 1998b).

7.3.1.4   The processing of adjunct phrases

In the previous section we saw that processing L2 sentences where the argument structures of the L1 and the L2 differ sometimes results in L2 parsing patterns that are like those of native speakers. An interesting question that has been raised in the L2 sentence parsing literature regards the issues of how the L2 parser proceeds in the absence of lexical constraints, as in the cases of adjunct phrases or modifier phrases. Although several studies exist that have examined the way L2 learners process adjunct phrases in real time, the results obtained are far from conclusive.

The first study to explicitly investigate the processing strategies used by L2 learners during the parsing of modifier phrases was Fernández (1995) (see also Fernández, 1998, 1999; Juffs and Harrington, 1995, 1996). Fernández examined the intuitions of early and late learners of English about the preferred reading of temporarily ambiguous sentences like *Roxanne read the review of the play that was written by Dianne's friend*. In sentences of this type, the ambiguity arises because the relative clause ('that was written . . .') can be attached high to 'the review' or low to 'the play.' Fernández found that the strongest preference for low attachment was displayed by the English monolinguals, followed by the early bilingual group and then by the late bilingual group. She also reported that language proficiency seemed to be the best predictor of attachment preferences. That is, subjects who rated their Spanish proficiency higher than their English proficiency favored high attachment, and subjects who rated English as their dominant language tended to show a preference for low attachment.

Somewhat different results were obtained by Dussias (1998a,1998b), see also Dussias, 2001; Dussias and Sagarra, 2001) in a self-paced reading task with Spanish-English and English-Spanish bilinguals. The study investigated the attachment preferences with the structure NP1-of-NP2-RC (e.g. *El perro mordió al cuñado de la maestra que vivió en Chile con su esposo*/ 'The dog bit the brother-in-law of the teacher (fem.) who lived in Chile with her husband.') She found that the control groups (i.e. Spanish and English monolinguals) showed the conventional bias for high attachment and low attachment, respectively, that has been reported in the literature for Spanish and English. The English-Spanish bilinguals did not exhibit any preference for high or low attachment when processing the ambiguous sentences. This result adds to the evidence indicating that L2 speakers are not like monolinguals when they parse structures in the L2. Strikingly, the Spanish-English speakers showed a consistent preference for low attachment when reading sentences in both their first and second languages, suggesting that the parsing routines used to process the second language had an impact on the processing of the first language as well.

In a more recent study, Papadopoulou and Clahsen (2001) compared relative clause attachment preferences of Spanish, Russian and German L2 speakers of Greek with those of native Greek speakers. The materials were similar in structure to the ones described in previous studies, where a relative clause is preceded by a complex noun phrase. In one condition, the second noun in the complex NP carried genitive case (. . . *of the teacher*), and in another condition the second noun was the complement of the preposition *with* (. . . *with the teacher*). The findings showed that monolingual Greek speakers and second language learners of Greek performed similarly (i.e. preferred low attachment) in cases where the second noun phrase was the complement of *with*. However, for cases with the genitive construction, the Greek monolingual speakers preferred high attachment, but the learners did not show any preference for one attachment site over the other. Given that the native languages involved have all been shown to exhibit a high attachment preference with the genitive construction, these findings argue against an L1 transfer explanation (for similar findings, see also Felser, Roberts, Gross, and Marinis, 2003).

7.3.2   *Summary on understanding sentences*

To examine the question of whether bilingual speakers resemble monolingual speakers in the domain of sentence comprehension, we reviewed a number of studies that looked at sentence processing by bilingual speakers of different language backgrounds and language proficiencies. We also examined studies that investigated parsing processes in languages whose structures reflect different syntactic properties. As the studies reviewed suggest, the picture that emerges is a complex one. Sometimes, bilinguals behave like monolingual speakers; at other times, they transfer L1 information when processing the L2; at still other times they don't resemble monolingual speakers of either of their languages.

Admittedly, this apparent complexity in the research findings may arise because the theoretical underpinnings that motivate the study of L2 sentence parsing are vastly different. In addition, researchers employ a variety of psycholinguistic techniques, from untimed intuitions about the preferred interpretation of a sentence, to self-paced reading tasks and eye-tracking data (which are presumed to reflect more directly the initial decisions), to the analysis of brain activity. In our discussion, we have abstracted away from the differences across these studies to explore L2 sentence processing as broadly as possible with the intention of opening up this area of study.

We saw that research on sentence processing by bilinguals has been primarily concerned with investigating whether second language speakers use the same syntactic and semantic information as monolingual speakers do during sentence processing. Although this question is still at the core of L2 sentence processing studies, much impetus is being directed at the study of sentence parsing by second language learners, with the goal of explaining (1) whether incomplete second language attainment may come about when learners use L1 parsing strategies that are not suitable for the development of the underlying grammar of the target language, and (2) the effects of second language learning on first language sentence parsing.

Clearly, there is much ground yet to be covered. Few studies have examined in detail the variables that may affect parsing in a second language. These factors include, but are not restricted to, language proficiency and exposure, age of acquisition, and working memory capacity. This direction of research will contribute not only by deepening our knowledge of the processes that govern sentence understanding in speakers of two languages, but, most importantly, it will also allow us to examine under different perspectives and using different sets of data, the validity and generality of current monolingual language processing theories, with the purpose of formulating models capable of accounting for bilingual as well as monolingual behavior.

7.4 Conclusions: Comparing Words and Sentences

The research reviewed in this chapter examines the way in which bilinguals understand words and sentences. Although the frameworks that guide research on each of these topics owe their intellectual commitments to different theoretical traditions in psychology, linguistics, and cognitive science, a number of common themes emerge. In this final section we identify some of these issues and the ways in which examining these two levels of language processing together might inform research in the future.

If there is a single conclusion that can be drawn from both the bilingual word and sentence processing literatures, it is that the language systems of the bilingual are permeable in the sense that processing in both languages is affected by the acquisition and use of more than a single language. We note three implications of this observation. First, the availability of alternative parsing preferences in sentence comprehension and/or additional lexical candidates in word recognition, requires that we formulate a theory of control. The fact that proficient bilinguals are able to code switch in a systematic manner but at the same time understand and speak in each language with few errors, suggests that they possess highly developed skills for negotiating cross-language competition (see also Costa, chapter 8 in this volume, for a discussion of this issue with respect to language production). In word recognition, it appears that even when lexical forms differ across languages, by virtue of the nature of the written code or by differences in the regularity of spelling-to-sound correspondences, there are still cross-language interactions that suggest that even in the presence of distinctive cues and with the intention to use one language alone, there is still activity in the nontarget language. Identifying the locus of control in recognition will require that we better understand how these effects occur in and out of context and for bilinguals whose language experiences differ in terms of how independently the two languages are used in everyday life. In the context of sentence comprehension, it may be that control is modulated by the presence or absence of particular types of structural information in the input. We saw, for example, that when structural information guided parsing decisions, bilinguals behaved much like monolingual speakers; in the absence of such information, they generally failed to show a parsing preference. It could be, then, that structural cues are more salient than non-structural ones, and that this saliency favors the selection of a particular type of parse, with the result that alternative competitors are suppressed. Clearly, it remains to be seen whether all types of structural information have the same effect on bilingual sentence parsing. This is also an area in which there may be important theoretical connections between word and sentence processing, in considering, for example, whether the conditions which give rise to language-specific parsing preferences also give rise to language-selective lexical access when words are processed in these sentence contexts.

Second, for words and sentences alike, there is evidence showing not only that L1 affects L2, but that L1 is itself also affected by L2. Although the direction of these effects is typically stronger from the more dominant to the less dominant language, the observation that L1 changes at all in the face of proficiency in L2 has profound implications for our efforts to model language processing. For word recognition, this observation has important consequences for understanding the consequence of age of acquisition and for theories of automaticity (e.g. Segalowitz and Segalowitz, 1993). At the sentence level, we noted that learning a second language can sometimes result in the convergence of parsing routines, so that one particular parse, typically one that is available in the bilingual's two languages, is used to process not only the L2, but also the L1. Why this should be the case is, at this point, a matter of speculation, although one possible explanation may have to do with bilingual sentence comprehension and workload (see, for example, Hasegawa, Carpenter, and Just, 2002).

Finally, research in both areas suggests that those aspects of the linguistic representation that are critical for computing meaning may be shared across languages. At the level of word recognition and lexical access, it is possible that much of the functioning semantic representation for the L2 is borrowed directly from the L1 (see Jiang, 2000, for a model of how the L2 lexical representation develops). Although meanings for words in the two languages may be computed to form distinct concepts, the pool of features on which these computations are based appears to be accessed in a manner that is blind to language. In future research it will again be important to understand how the semantic interface is established across languages and how second language learners come to understand the subtle senses of meaning that differ in their two languages. The most convincing type of evidence on this issue at the sentence level comes from ERP studies which provide incontrovertible evidence that in the semantic domain of sentence processing, bilinguals are much like their monolingual counterparts. We anticipate that our research agenda will be increasingly sensitive to each of these concerns as we seek to develop models of word and sentence processing and their relation. (For more on models and theories, see chapters 1–3, 8, and 9.)

ACKNOWLEDGMENT

The writing of this chapter was supported in part by NSF Grant BCS-0111734 and NIMH Grant RO1MH62479 to Judith F. Kroll, and by a Research and Graduate Studies Office Grant from the College of the Liberal Arts, Penn State University, to Paola E. Dussias.

REFERENCES

Altarriba, J. (1990). Constraints on interlingual facilitation effects in priming in Spanish-English bilinguals. Unpublished dissertation, Vanderbilt University, Nashville, TN.

Altarriba, J., Kroll, J. F., Sholl, A., and Rayner, K. (1996). The influence of lexical and conceptual constraints on reading mixed-language sentences: Evidence from eye-fixation and naming times. *Memory & Cognition*, 24, 477–92.

Ardal, S., Donald, M. W., Meuter, R., Muldrew, S., and Luce, M. (1990). Brain responses to semantic incongruity in bilinguals. *Brain and Language*, 39, 187–205.

Bates, E. and MacWhinney, B. (1982). Functionalist approaches to grammar. In E. Wanner and L. Gleitman (eds.), *Language Acquisition: The State of the Art*, pp. 173–218. New York: Cambridge University Press.

Brysbaert, M. (1998). Word recognition in bilinguals: Evidence against the existence of two separate lexicons. *Psychologica Belgica*, 38, 163–75.

Brysbaert, M., Van Dyck, G., and Van de Poel, M. (1999). Visual word recognition in bilinguals: Evidence from masked phonological priming. *Journal of Experimental Psychology: Human Perception and Performance*, 25, 137–48.

Caramazza, A. and Brones, I. (1980). Semantic classification by bilinguals. *Canadian Journal of Psychology*, 34, 77–81.

Carreiras, M. (1992). Estrategias de análisis sintáctico en el procesamiento de frases: Cierre temprano versus cierre tardío. *Cognitiva*, 4, 3–27.

Chen, H-C. and Ng, M.-L. (1989). Semantic facilitation and translation priming effects in Chinese-English bilinguals. *Memory & Cognition*, 17, 454–62.

Costa, A., Miozzo, M., and Caramazza, A. (1999). Lexical selection in bilinguals: Do words in the bilingual's two lexicons compete for selection? *Journal of Memory and Language*, 41, 365–97.

Cuetos, F. and Mitchell, D. C. (1988). Cross-linguistic differences in parsing: Restrictions on the use of the Late Closure strategy in Spanish. *Cognition*, 30, 73–105.

Daneman, M. and Green, I. (1986). Individual differences in comprehending and producing words in context. *Journal of Memory and Language*, 25, 1–18.

De Groot, A. M. B. (1992). Determinants of word translation. *Journal of Experimental Psychology: Learning, Memory, and Cognition*, 18, 1001–18.

De Groot, A. M. B. (1993). Word-type effects in bilingual processing tasks: Support for a mixed representational system. In R. Schreuder and B. Weltens (eds.), *The Bilingual Lexicon*, pp. 27–51. Amsterdam: John Benjamins.

De Groot, A. M. B. (1995). Determinants of bilingual lexicosemantic organization. *Computer Assisted Language Learning*, 8, 151–80.

De Groot, A. M. B., Dannenburg, L., and Van Hell, J. G. (1994). Forward and backward word translation by bilinguals. *Journal of Memory and Language*, 33, 600–29.

De Groot, A. M. B., Delmaar, P., and Lupker, S. J. (2000). The processing of interlexical homographs in a bilingual and a monolingual task: Support for nonselective access to bilingual memory. *Quarterly Journal of Experimental Psychology*, 53A, 397–428.

De Groot, A. M. B. and Poot, R. (1997). Word translation at three levels of proficiency in a second language: The ubiquitous involvement of conceptual memory. *Language Learning*, 47, 215–64.

Dijkstra, A., De Bruijn, E., Schriefers, H., and Ten Brinke, S. (2000). More on interlingual homograph recognition: Language intermixing versus explicitness of instruction. *Bilingualism: Language and Cognition*, 3, 69–78.

Dijkstra, A., Grainger, J., and Van Heuven, W. J. B. (1999). Recognizing cognates and interlingual homographs: The neglected role of phonology. *Journal of Memory and Language*, 41, 496–518.

Dijkstra, A., Timmermans, M., and Schriefers, H. (2000). On being blinded by your other language: Effects of task demands on interlingual homograph recognition. *Journal of Memory and Language*, 42, 445–64.

Dijkstra, A. and Van Heuven, W. J. B. (1998). The BIA model and bilingual word recognition. In J. Grainger and A. Jacobs (eds.), *Localist Connectionist Approaches to Human Cognition*, pp. 189–225). Hillsdale, NJ: Lawrence Erlbaum Associates.

Dijkstra, A. and Van Heuven, W. J. B. (2002). The architecture of the bilingual word recognition system: From identification to decision. *Bilingualism: Language and Cognition*, 5, 175–97.

Dijkstra, A., Van Jaarsveld, H., and Ten Brinke, S. (1998). Interlingual homograph recognition: Effects of task demands and language intermixing. *Bilingualism: Language and Cognition*, 1, 51–66.

Dufour, R. and Kroll, J. F. (1995). Matching words to concepts in two languages: A test of the concept mediation model of bilingual representation. *Memory & Cognition*, 23, 166–80.

Dussias, P. E. (1998a). Late Closure in Spanish/English Bilinguals. Invited paper presented at the *Linguistics Colloquium Series on Language Processing in the Bilingual*. University of Arizona, Tucson, AZ.

Dussias, P. E. (1998b). Parsing in two languages: Some on-line results. Paper presented at the *23rd Annual Boston University Conference on Language Development*. Boston, MA, November, 1998.

Dussias, P. E. (2001). Bilingual sentence parsing. In J. L. Nicol (ed.), *One Mind, Two Languages: Bilingual Language Processing*, pp. 159–76. Malden, MA: Blackwell.

Dussias, P. E. and Sagarra, N. (2001). The loss of parsing strategies by native Spanish speakers: Evidence from eye-movements. Paper presented at the 3rd International Symposium on Bilingualism, Bristol, UK.

Elston-Güttler, K. E. (2000). An inquiry into cross-language differences in lexical-conceptual relationships and their effect on L2 lexical processing. Unpublished Ph.D. dissertation, University of Cambridge.

Felser, C., Roberts, L., Gross, R., and Marinis, T. (2003). The processing of ambiguous sentences by first and second language learners of English. *Applied Psycholinguistics*, 24, 453–89.

Fernández, E. M. (1995). Processing strategies in second language acquisition: Some preliminary results. Paper presented at the 3rd GASLA, CUNY, New York.

Fernández, E. M. (1998). Language dependency in parsing: Evidence from monolingual and bilingual processing. *Psychologica Belgica*, 38,197–230.

Fernández, E. M. (1999). Processing strategies in second language acquisition: Some preliminary results. In E. C. Klein and G. Martohardjono (eds.), *The Development of Second Language Grammars: A Generative*

Approach, pp. 217–39. Amsterdam: John Benjamins.

Ferreira, F. and Henderson, J. M. (1990). The use of verb information in syntactic parsing: A comparisons of evidence from eye movements and word-by-word self-paced reading. *Journal of Experimental Psychology: Learning, Memory and Cognition*, 16, 555–68.

Francis, W. (1999). Cognitive integration of language and memory in bilinguals: Semantic representation. *Psychological Bulletin, 125*, 193–222.

Frazier, L. (1978). On comprehending sentences: Syntactic parsing strategies. Ph.D. dissertation, University of Connecticut. Distributed by Indiana University Linguistics Club.

Frazier, L. (1987). Sentence processing: A tutorial overview. In M. Coltheart (ed.), *Attention and Performance XII*, pp. 559–86. Hillsdale, NJ: Lawrence Erlbaum Associates.

Frazier, L. and Clifton, C. (1996). *Construal*. Cambridge, MA: MIT Press.

Frazier, L. and De Villiers, J. (1990). *Language Processing and Language Acquisition*. Dordecht: Kluwer.

Frazier, L. and Rayner, K. (1982). Making and correcting errors during sentence comprehension: Eye movements in the analysis of structurally ambiguous sentences. *Cognitive Psychology*, 14, 178–210.

Frenck-Mestre, C. and Pynte, J. (1997). Syntactic ambiguity resolution while reading in second and native languages. *Quarterly Journal of Experimental Psychology*, 50, 119–48.

Gass, S. (1987). The resolution of conflicts among competing systems: A bidirectional perspective. *Applied Psycholinguistics*, 8, 329–50.

Gollan, T., Forster, K. I., and Frost, R. (1997). Translation priming with different scripts: Masked priming with cognates and noncognates in Hebrew-English bilinguals. *Journal of Experimental Psychology: Learning, Memory, and Cognition*, 23, 1122–39.

Gollan, T. and Kroll, J. F. (2001). Bilingual lexical access. In B. Rapp (ed.), *The Handbook of Cognitive Neuropsychology: What Deficits Reveal about the Human Mind*, pp. 321–45). Philadelphia, PA: Psychology Press.

Gorrell, P. (1995). *Syntax and Parsing*. Cambridge, UK: Cambridge University Press.

Grainger, J. and Beauvillain, C. (1987). Language blocking and lexical access in bilinguals. *Quarterly Journal of Experimental Psychology*, 39A, 295–319.

Gregg, K. R. (2001). Learnability and second language acquisition theory. In P. Robinson (ed.), *Cognition and Second Language Instruction*, pp. 152–80. Cambridge, UK: Cambridge University Press.

Green, D. W. (1998). Mental control of the bilingual lexico-semantic system. *Bilingualism: Language and Cognition*, 1, 67–81.

Hahne, A. (2001). What's the difference in second-language processing? Evidence from event-related brain potentials. *Journal of Psycholinguistic Research*, 30, 251–66.

Hahne, A. and Friederici, A. (2001). Processing a second language: Late learners' comprehension mechanisms as revealed by event-related brain potentials. *Bilingualism, Language and Cognition*, 4, 123–41.

Harrington, M. (1987). Processing transfer: Language-specific processing strategies as a source of interlanguage variation. *Applied Psycholinguistics*, 8, 351–77.

Harrington, M. (2001). Sentence processing. In P. Robinson (ed.), *Cognition and Second Language Instruction*, pp. 91–124. Cambridge, UK: Cambridge University Press.

Hasegawa, M., Carpenter, P. A., and Just, M. A. (2002). An fMRI study of bilingual sentence comprehension and workload. *Neuroimage*, 15, 647–60.

Heilenman, L. and McDonald, J. (1993). Processing strategies in L2 learners of French: The role of transfer. *Language Learning*, 43, 507–57.

Hermans, D. (2000). Word production in a foreign language. Unpublished Ph.D. dissertation, University of Nijmegen, The Netherlands.

Hermans, D., Bongaerts, T., De Bot, K., and Schreuder, R. (1998). Producing words in a foreign language: Can speakers prevent interference from their first language? *Bilingualism: Language and Cognition*, 1, 213–29.

Hernandez, A., Bates, E., and Ávila, L. (1994). On-line sentence interpretation in Spanish-English bilinguals: What does it mean to be "in between"? *Applied Psycholinguistics*, 15, 417–46.

Hoover, M. and Dwivedi, V. (1998). Syntactic processing by skilled bilinguals. *Language Learning*, 48, 1–29.

Igoa, J. M., Carreiras, M., and Meseguer, E. (1998). A study on late closure in Spanish: Principle-grounded vs. frequency based accounts of attachment preferences. *Quarterly Journal of Experimental Psychology*, 5A, 676–703.

Illes, J., Francis, W. S., Desmond, J. E., Gabrieli, J. D. E., Glover, G. H., Poldrack, R., Lee, C. J., and Wagner, A. D. (1999). Convergent cortical representation of semantic processing in bilinguals. *Brain and Language*, 70, 347–63.

Jared, D. and Kroll, J. F. (2001). Do bilinguals activate phonological representations in one or both of their languages when naming words? *Journal of Memory and Language*, 44, 2–31.

Jared, D. and Szucs, C. (2002). Phonological activation in bilinguals: Evidence from interlingual homograph naming. *Bilingualism, Language and Cognition*, 5, 225–39.

Jiang, N. (1999). Testing processing explanations for the asymmetry in masked cross-language priming. *Bilingualism: Language and Cognition*, 2, 59–75.

Jiang, N. (2000). Lexical representation and development in a second language. *Applied Linguistics*, 21, 47–77.

Juffs, A. (1998a). Main verb vs. reduced relative clause ambiguity resolution in second language sentence processing. *Language Learning*, 48, 107–47.

Juffs, A. (1998b). Some effects of first language argument structure and morphosyntax on second language sentence processing. *Second Language Research*, 14, 406–24.

Juffs, A. and Harrington, M. (1995). Parsing effects in second language processing: Subject and object asymmetries in wh-extractions. *Studies in Second Language Acquisition*, 17(4), 483–516.

Juffs, A. and Harrington, M. (1996). Garden Path sentences and error data in second language sentence processing research. *Language Learning*, 46, 286–324.

Keatley, C., Spinks, J., and De Gelder, B. (1994). Asymmetrical semantic facilitation between languages. *Memory & Cognition*, 22, 70–84.

Kroll, J. F. (1993). Accessing conceptual representation for words in a second language. In R. Schreuder and B. Weltens (eds.), *The Bilingual Lexicon*, pp. 53–81. Amsterdam: John Benjamins.

Kroll, J. F. and De Groot, A. M. B. (1997). Lexical and conceptual memory in the bilingual: Mapping form to meaning in two languages. In A. M. B. De Groot and J. F. Kroll (eds.), *Tutorials in Bilingualism: Psycholinguistic Perspectives*, pp. 169–99. Mahwah, NJ: Lawrence Erlbaum.

Kroll, J. F. and Dijkstra, A. (2002). The bilingual lexicon. In R. Kaplan (ed.),

Handbook of Applied Linguistics, pp. 301–21. Oxford: Oxford University Press.

Kroll, J. F., Dijkstra, A., Janssen, N., and Schriefers, H. (2000). Selecting the language in which to speak: Experiments on lexical access in bilingual production. Paper presented at the 41st Annual Meeting of the Psychonomic Society, New Orleans, LA.

Kroll, J. F. and Merves, J. S. (1986). Lexical access for concrete and abstract words. *Journal of Experimental Psychology: Learning, Memory, and Cognition*, 12, 92–107.

Kroll, J. F., Michael, E., and Sankaranarayanan, A. (1998). A model of bilingual representation and its implications for second language acquisition. In A. F. Healy and L. E. Bourne (eds.), *Foreign Language Learning: Psycholinguistic Experiments on Training and Retention*, pp. 365–95). Mahwah, NJ: Lawrence Erlbaum.

Kroll, J. F., Michael, E., Tokowicz, N., and Dufour, R. (2002). The development of lexical fluency in a second language. *Second Language Research*, 18, 137–71.

Kroll, J. F. and Stewart, E. (1994). Category interference in translation and picture naming: Evidence for asymmetric connections between bilingual memory representations. *Journal of Memory and Language*, 33, 149–74.

Kroll, J. F. and Sunderman, G. (2003). Cognitive processes in second language acquisition: The development of lexical and conceptual representations. In C. Doughty and M. Long (eds.), *Handbook of Second Language Acquisition*, pp. 104–29. Malden, MA: Blackwell.

Kroll, J. F. and Tokowicz, N. (2001). The development of conceptual representation for words in a second language. In J. L. Nicol (ed.), *One Mind, Two Languages: Bilingual Language Processing*, pp. 49–71. Malden, MA: Blackwell.

Kutas, M. and Kluender, R. (1991). What is who violating? A reconsideration of linguistic violations in light of event-related brain potentials. In H. J. Heinze, T. F. Münte, and G. R. Mangun (eds.), *Cognitive Electrophysiology*, pp. 183–210. Boston, MA: Birkhäuser.

La Heij, W. (2005). Selection processes in monolingual and bilingual lexical access. In J. F. Kroll and A. M. B. De Groot (eds.), *Handbook of Bilingualism: Psycholinguistic Approaches*, pp. 289–307. New York: Oxford University Press.

La Heij, W., De Bruyn, E., Elens, E., Hartsuiker, R., Helaha, D., and Van Schelven, L. (1990). Orthographic facilitation and categorical interference in a word-translation variant of the Stroop task. *Canadian Journal of Psychology*, 44, 76–83.

La Heij, W., Kerling, R., and Van der Velden, E. (1996). Nonverbal context effects in forward and backward translation: Evidence for concept mediation. *Journal of Memory and Language*, 35, 648–65.

Liu, H., Bates, E., and Li, P. (1992). Sentence interpretation in bilingual speakers of English and Chinese. *Applied Psycholinguistics*, 13, 451–84.

McClelland, J. L., and Rumelhart, D. E. (1981). An interactive activation model of context effects in letter perception. Part 1: An account of basic findings. *Psychological Review*, 88, 375–405.

McDonald, J. (1987). Sentence interpretation in bilingual speakers of English and Dutch. *Applied Psycholinguistics*, 8, 379–413.

McDonald, J. and Heilenman, K. (1991). Determinants of cue strength in adult first and second language speakers of French. *Applied Psycholinguistics*, 12, 313–48.

MacDonald, M. C. (1994). Probabilistic constraints and syntactic ambiguity. *Language and Cognitive Processes*, 9, pp. 157–201.

MacDonald, M. C., Pearlmutter, N. J. and Seidenberg, M. S. (1994). Syntactic ambiguity resolution as lexical ambiguity resolution. In C. Clifton, L. Frazier and K. Rayner (eds.), *Perspectives on Sentence Processing*, pp. 123–53. Hillsdale: Lawrence Erlbaum Associates.

McRae, J., de Sa, V. R., and Seidenberg, M. S. (1997). On the nature and scope of featural representations of word meaning. *Journal of Experimental Psychology: General*, 126, 99–130.

MacWhinney, B. (1987). Applying the Competition Model to Bilingualism. *Applied Psycholinguistics*, 8, 315–27.

Marian, V. and Spivey, M. (1999). Activation of Russian and English cohorts during bilingual spoken word recognition. In M. Hahn and S. C. Stoness (eds.), *Proceedings of the Twenty-first Annual Conference of the Cognitive Science Society*, pp. 349–54. Mahwah, NJ: Lawrence Erlbaum.

Meyer, D. E. and Ruddy, M. G. (1974). Bilingual word recognition: Organization and retrieval of alternative lexical codes. Paper presented at the Eastern Psychological Association Meeting, Philadelphia, PA.

Michael, E., Dijkstra, T., and Kroll, J. F. (2002). Individual differences in the degree of language nonselectivity in fluent bilinguals. Paper presented at the meeting of the International Linguistic Association, Toronto.

Mitchell, D. C. and Cuetos, F. (1991). Restrictions on late closure: The computational underpinnings of parsing strategies in Spanish and English. Unpublished MS, University of Exeter, UK.

Paivio, A. (1971). *Imagery and verbal processes*. New York: Holt, Rinehart and Winston.

Papadopoulou, D. and Clahsen, H. (2001). Parsing strategies in L1 and L2 sentence processing: A study of relative clause attachment in Greek. Unpublished MS, University of Essex, UK.

Pavlenko, A. (1999). New approaches to concepts in bilingual memory. *Bilingualism: Language and Cognition*, 2, 209–30.

Pickering, M. J. (1999). Sentence comprehension. In S. C. Garrod and M. J. Pickering (eds.), *Language Processing*, pp. 123–53. Hove, UK: Psychology Press.

Potter, M. C., So, K.-F., Von Eckardt, B., and Feldman, L. B. (1984). Lexical and conceptual representation in beginning and more proficient bilinguals. *Journal of Verbal Learning and Verbal Behavior*, 23, 23–38.

Pritchett, B. L. (1992). *Grammatical Competence and Parsing Performance*. Chicago: University of Chicago Press.

Rayner, K., Carlson, M., and Frazier, L. (1983). The interaction of syntax and semantics during sentence processing: Eye-movements in the analysis of semantically biased sentences. *Journal of Verbal Learning and Verbal Behavior*, 22, 358–74.

Rodriquez-Fornells, A., Rotte, M., Heinze, H.-J., Nösselt, T., and Münte, T. (2002). Brain potential and functional MRI evidence for how to handle two languages with one brain. *Nature*, 415, 1026–9.

Sasaki, Y. (1991). English and Japanese interlanguage comprehension strategies: An analysis based on the Competition Model. *Applied Psycholinguistics*, 12, 47–73.

Sasaki, Y. (1994). Paths of processing strategy transfers in learning Japanese and English as foreign languages: A Competition Model approach. *Studies in Second Language Acquisition*, 16, 43–72.

Schachter, J. and Yip, V. (1990). Why does anyone object to subject extraction? *Studies in Second Language Acquisition*, 12, 379–92.

Schönpflug, U. (1997). *Bilingualism and memory*. Paper presented at the International Symposium on Bilingualism, Newcastle-upon-Tyne, UK.

Schulpen, B., Dijkstra, A., Schriefers, H. J., and Hasper, M. (2003). Recognition of interlingual homophones in bilingual auditory word recognition. *Journal of Experimental Psychology: Human Perception and Performance*, 29, 1155–78.

Schwanenflugel, P. J., Harnishfeger, K. K., and Stowe, R. W. (1988). Context availability and lexical decisions for abstract and concrete words. *Journal of Memory and Language*, 27, 499–520.

Schwanenflugel, P. J. and Rey, M. (1986). Interlingual semantic facilitation: Evidence for a common representational system in the bilingual. *Journal of Memory and Language*, 25, 605–18.

Schwanenflugel, P. J. and Shoben, E. J. (1983). Differential context effects in the comprehension of abstract and concrete verbal materials. *Journal of Experimental Psychology: Learning, Memory, and Cognition*, 9, 82–102.

Schwartz, A., Kroll, J. F., and Diaz, M. (in preparation). Mapping spelling-to-sound correspondences in two languages: Evidence from word naming and bilingual translation.

Segalowitz, N. S. and Segalowitz, S. J. (1993). Skilled performance, practice, and the differentiation of speed-up from automatization effects: Evidence from second language word recognition. *Applied Psycholinguistics*, 14, 369–85.

Sholl, A., Sankaranarayanan, A., and Kroll, J. F. (1995). Transfer between picture naming and translation: A test of asymmetries in bilingual memory. *Psychological Science*, 6, 45–9.

Smith, M. C. (1997). How do bilinguals access lexical information? In A. M. B. De Groot and J. F. Kroll (eds.), *Tutorials in Bilingualism: Psycholinguistic Perspectives*, pp. 145–68. Mahwah, NJ: Lawrence Erlbaum.

Su, I. (2001). Transfer of sentence processing strategies: A comparison of L2 learners of Chinese and English. *Applied Psycholinguistics*, 22, 83–112.

Sunderman, G. (2002). *Lexical Development in a Second Language: Can the First Language be Suppressed?* Unpublished Ph.D. dissertation, Pennsylvania State University, University Park, PA.

Talamas, A., Kroll, J. F., and Dufour, R. (1999). From form to meaning: stages in the acquisition of second language vocabulary. *Bilingualism: Language and Cognition*, 2, 45–58.

Thomas, M. S. C., Allport, A. (2000). Language switching costs in bilingual visual word recognition. *Journal of Memory and Language*, 43, 44–66.

Tokowicz, N. and Kroll, J. F. (in preparation). Accessing meaning for words in two languages: The effects of concreteness and multiple translations in production.

Tokowicz, N., Kroll, J. F., De Groot, A. M. B., and Van Hell, J. G. (2002). Number of translation norms for Dutch-English translation pairs: A new tool for examining language production. *Behavior Research Methods, Instruments, and Computers*, 34, 435–51.

Trueswell, J. C., Tanenhaus, M. K. and Garnsey, S. (1994). Semantic influences of parsing: Use of thematic role information in syntactic ambiguity resolution. *Journal of Memory and Language*, 33, 285–318.

Trueswell, J. C., Tanenhaus, M. K., and Kello, C. (1993). Verb-specific constraints in sentence processing: Separating effects of lexical preference from garden-path. *Journal of Experimental Psychology: Learning, Memory, and Cognition*, 19(3), 528–53.

Tzelgov, J. and Eben-Ezra, S. (1992). Components of the between-language semantic priming effect. *European Journal of Cognitive Psychology*, 4, 253–72.

Vaid, J. and Frenck-Mestre, C. (2002). Do orthographic cues aid language recognition? A laterality study with French-English bilinguals. *Brain and Language*, 82, 47–53.

Van Hell, J. G. (1998). Cross-language processing and bilingual memory organization. Unpublished Ph.D. dissertation, University of Amsterdam.

Van Hell, J. G. and De Groot, A. M. B. (1998). Conceptual representation in bilingual memory: Effects of concreteness and cognate status in word association. *Bilingualism: Language and Cognition*, 1, 193–211.

Van Hell, J. and Dijkstra, T. (2002). Foreign language knowledge can influence native language performance: Evidence from trilinguals. *Psychonomic Bulletin and Review*, 9, 780–9.

Van Heuven, W. J. B. (2000). Visual word recognition in monolingual and bilingual readers: Experiments and computational modeling. Ph.D. thesis, University of Nijmegen, The Netherlands. NICI Technical Report 20–01.

Van Heuven, W. J. B., Dijkstra, A., and Grainger, J. (1998). Orthographic neighborhood effects in bilingual word recognition. *Journal of Memory and Language*, 39, 458–83.

Van Patten, B. (1996). *Input Processing and Grammar Instruction*. Norwood, NJ: Ablex.

Vigliocco, G., Vinson, D. P., Damian, M., and Levelt, W. J. M. (2002). Semantic distance effects on object and action naming. *Cognition*, 85, B61–9.

Von Studnitz, R. and Green, D. W. (2002a). Interlingual homograph interference in German-English bilinguals: Its modulation and locus of control. *Bilingualism: Language and Cognition*, 5, 1–23.

Von Studnitz, R. and Green, D. W. (2002b). The cost of switching language in a semantic categorization task. *Bilingualism: Language and Cognition*, 5, 241–51.

Weber-Fox, C. and Neville, H. J. (1996). Maturational constraints on functional specialization for language processing: ERP and behavioral evidence in bilingual speakers. *Journal of Cognitive Neuroscience*, 8, 231–56.

Wulfeck, B., Juárez, L., Bates, E., and Kilborn, K. (1986). Sentence interpretation strategies in healthy and aphasic bilingual adults. In J. Vaid (ed.), *Language Processing in Bilinguals: Psycholinguistic and Neuropsychological Perspectives*, pp. 199–219. Hillsdale, NJ: Erlbaum.

8 Speech Production in Bilinguals

ALBERT COSTA

8.1 Introduction

Speaking is one of the most useful skills that a human being acquires. This skill is acquired seemingly effortlessly, and young children at the age of five are already able to produce complex sentences to express their thoughts. As adults, we produce language on a regular basis and we experience such behavior as quite automatic and not very demanding (we produce an average of about three words per second). Despite the ease with which we produce speech, the mechanisms and representations involved are large in number and complex. The aim of this chapter is to discuss some issues related to speech production in the context of bilingual speakers. I will focus on the processing mechanisms involved in the production of speech in the context of psycho-linguistic models that try to account for or describe the cognitive processes involved in such a skill.

The main issue that will be addressed in the chapter refers to the role of the language-not-in-use[1] during speech production. I will discuss the extent to which the linguistic properties (lexical, grammatical, and phonological) of the words of the non-response language are activated during speech production, and whether their activation affects processing in the response language. In some cases, I will discuss experimental results that provide evidence in favor of or against an effect of the non-response language on the processing mechanisms in the response language. In other cases, I will just discuss some hypotheses about how the two languages of a bilingual might interact during speech production. As a general guide, one can approach the issues discussed in the chapter by comparing two different views of lexical access in bilingual

1 Throughout the chapter I make use of the terms "language-not-in-use" and "non-response language" interchangeably. These terms refer to the language in which the speaker is not performing the naming task or, more generally, the language in which she is not speaking.

speech production: the target-language specific view, under which access is largely limited to the lexicon of the language-in-use, and the target-language non-specific view, under which the language-not-in-use is also accessed. The chapter focuses on the role of the non-response language in the communicative situation in which the speaker is producing speech in only one of her languages (when the speaker is in the so-called monolingual mode; see Grosjean, 1997, 1998, 2000, chapter 2 of this volume). Thus, issues related to code switching will not be discussed here.

The rest of the chapter is divided into four sections. In section 8.2 I will briefly describe some of the main proposals related to lexical access in speech production in the context of monolingual speakers. These proposals will be used, in section 8.3, as a general framework in which to discuss specific claims about language production in bilingual speakers. In section 8.4, some experimental evidence relevant to the issues described above will be discussed. Finally, section 8.5 summarizes and discusses what conclusions can be drawn from the available experimental evidence regarding whether activation flow and selection processes in bilingual speech production are target-language specific or target-language non-specific.

8.2   Lexical Access in Speech Production: General Issues

Language production starts with the selection of the conceptual message the speaker wants to convey. The structure of the conceptual system as well as other conceptual information, such as knowledge about the communicative situation in which the speaker is placed, have an impact in the format of the so-called preverbal message (e.g. Levelt, 1989). However, the issue of the structure of the preverbal message falls outside of the scope of the present chapter. Once the preverbal message is delivered to the linguistic system, two main processes start. The speaker needs to "translate" the conceptual representations into the lexical nodes (or words) that correspond to the intended meaning. This translation process entails what has been called, in the context of psycholinguistic models of speech production, lexical selection. Simultaneously the speaker must also perform another type of "translation," that by which the syntactic structure of the message is built.

Because models of speech production have been developed in the context of single-word production, they have paid more attention to the issue of lexical selection and less to the issue of how the syntactic structure is generated (but see Bock and Levelt, 1994; Bock, Loebell, and Morey, 1992; Garrett, 1976, 1980, 1988; Pickering et al., 2000). The main question that has been addressed refers to the processes by which the speaker selects the word that corresponds to the intended concept and that will eventually be produced (e.g. Caramazza and Costa, 2000, 2001; Dell, 1986; Dell et al., 1997; Levelt, 1989; Levelt, Roelofs and

Meyer, 1999; Roelofs, 1992; Ruml, Caramazza, Shelton, and Chialant, 2000; Starreveld and La Heij, 1995, 1996). Lexical selection is needed because the conceptual system does not activate just the target lexical node but instead it activates several lexical nodes that are potential candidates for production, and therefore a decision must be made about which lexical node corresponds to the intended meaning. The coactivation of several words comes about because it is assumed that the conceptual system spreads activation to words that fully or partially match the target concept. For example, if the speaker wants to convey the meaning of "dog," the conceptual system activates, to a different degree, the lexical nodes corresponding to related concepts "dog," "cat," "bark," etc. The word that is finally produced is determined by the lexical selection mechanism. In our example, if this mechanism picks out the word "dog," the speaker's final production will match her intention. However, if by mistake the selection mechanism picks out the word "cat," a spontaneous speech error occurs. It is, then, a central issue for models of lexical access to explain the processes that govern this crucial stage in speech production. In other words, the issue here is to specify the parameters involved in lexical selection. Most of the proposals regarding this issue have assumed that the selection mechanism is sensitive to the word's activation levels (e.g. Caramazza, 1997; Dell, 1986; Levelt, 1989; Roelofs, 1992). That is, the selection mechanism inspects at a given moment in time which lexical node (or word) has the highest level of activation and selects it for further processing. There is also a wide agreement in assuming that the selection mechanism is not only sensitive to the activation level of the target lexical node, but also to that of other lexical items. In this view, the ease with which lexical selection takes place depends, among other things, on the level of activation of the to-be-selected lexical node in relation to the level of activation of other lexical nodes that act as competitors (e.g. Roelofs, 1992). And, the smaller the difference in activation levels between the target lexical node and other lexical nodes, the more difficult successful lexical selection is.

In the example presented above, lexical selection is mostly driven by the activation that a lexical node receives from the conceptual system. However, not all the lexical nodes are selected on the basis of only conceptual information. Consider the case of some function words such as determiners in languages where these words are gender-marked. In these cases, the selection of the determiner depends not only on conceptual information (such as definiteness), but also on grammatical information, such as whether the noun that is modified by the determiner is feminine or masculine (see Alario and Caramazza, 2002 for a model of determiner selection). For example, when a Catalan speaker wants to produce the phrase *El cotxe blanc* [literally, 'the car white'], she needs to retrieve the grammatical gender of the noun *cotxe* 'car', in order to select the determiner *el*. This is because if the noun is masculine the determiner should be *el*, but if it were feminine the determiner would be *la*. Therefore, a complete description of how lexical selection proceeds requires an understanding of how the grammatical properties of the lexical nodes are accessed. Furthermore, the words' grammatical properties not only have an impact on the selection of other lexical nodes, as in the case of determiner (and/or inflections), but will also govern the type of relationships that words can take in the utterance. Two proposals have been put forward regarding the retrieval of grammatical features during speech production.[2] According to one proposal, access to the grammatical properties of words is a direct consequence of lexical selection (Caramazza et al., 2001; Schiller and Caramazza, 2003). That is, once a lexical node is selected its grammatical properties will become automatically available for further processing. The other view assumes that the selection of a lexical node does not necessarily entail the availability of its grammatical properties, but rather a subsequent selection process is engaged in order to retrieve them (Levelt, 2001; Schriefers, 1993; Schriefers and Teruel, 2000). Furthermore, this selection process is supposed to be sensitive to the level of activation of the to-be-selected grammatical value.

The second main step during the production of speech is that in which the phonological properties of the words are retrieved, the process of phonological encoding. The models here diverge considerably regarding the timing between lexical selection and phonological encoding. Although all the models assume that the activation of lexical nodes precedes the activation of phonological segments, they diverge in the extent to which the latter information affects the processes involved in lexical selection. The so-called feed-forward models assume that the activation of the phonological properties of the words does not affect the processes involved in the selection of the lexical nodes. There are two versions of this view. The first corresponds to the so-called discrete models of lexical access (e.g. Levelt et al., 1991; Levelt, Roelofs, and Meyer, 1999; Schriefers, Meyer and Levelt, 1990) which assume that phonological activation is only present after the process of lexical selection has been finished and that the only phonological activation present in the system corresponds to that of the selected lexical node. The second version corresponds to the so-called cascaded models (Caramazza, 1997; Costa, Caramazza and Sebastian-Galles, 2000; Harley, 1993; Humphreys and Riddoch, 1988; Peterson and Savoy, 1998; Starreveld and La Heij, 1995) in which phonological activation is not restricted to the selected lexical node. Instead, it is assumed that the activation of any given lexical node spreads to its phonological properties. In this view, phonological activation of the to-be-selected lexical node and of other lexical nodes is present in the system even before lexical selection has been achieved. That is, when a speaker wants to produce the word *dog*, the discrete models of lexical access posit that the only phonological representations that will be activated are those corresponding to *dog*, while the cascaded models posit that phonological activation of other activated lexical nodes (such as *cat*, *bark*, etc.) will also be present.

---

2   Actually these proposals have dealt more specifically with the topic of the retrieval of grammatical gender during speech production.

The interactive models assume that the activation of phonological properties may affect the processes involved in lexical selection (e.g. Dell, 1986; Dell et al., 1997; Dell and O'Seaghdha, 1991, 1992; Rapp and Goldrick, 2000; Stemberger, 1985). Accordingly, the activation of the phonological properties of both target and non-target words would feed back to any of the words to which they are linked. For example, when producing the word *dog*, and before the selection of the corresponding lexical node, the phonological properties of *dog* would become activated, and they would send activation back to any lexical node containing them, such as *doll* or *dot*. These lexical nodes that are activated not from the conceptual system but rather from the phonological system would then behave as potential candidates for selection.

Regardless of the specific timing between lexical selection and phonological encoding, the processes involved in the latter have the goal of selecting the phonological segments of the words that will finally be produced. In fact, the retrieval of the phonological segments of the words is not enough, since they also need to be adjusted to the phonological context in which they appear. For example, when a noun phrase of the type "indefinite determiner + noun" is produced, the form of the determiner depends on the phonological properties of the noun – you say "an apple" and "a pear." The specific processes and representations involved in this stage fall outside the scope of this chapter. What is important for our purposes is the notion that according to several models of speech production, the retrieval of the phonological segments of the target word is also governed by activation levels; that is, the higher the activation-level of a given phonological segment the easier its selection (e.g. Costa and Sebastián-Gallés, 1998; Meyer and Schriefers, 1991; Roelofs, 1999, 2000).

8.3 Lexical Access in Bilingual Speech Production

In this section, I will discuss the implications of the proposals described above for cases of bilingualism. The main issue addressed here is the role of the language-not-in-use during speech production. I entertain two hypotheses about speech production in bilinguals – the target-language specific and the target-language non-specific. It is important to keep in mind that these proposals refer not only to the processes involved in lexical selection but also to the extent to which activation flows through the linguistic system in a target-language specific or non-specific manner.

8.3.1 Selecting words from only one out of two lexicons

A major question that psycholinguistic models of speech production in bilinguals try to answer is: How does the bilingual speaker manage to select words in only one of her languages, and what is the effect of having a very close semantic neighbor (a translation) for virtually each word that is produced. In other words, how is it possible for a bilingual to keep her two languages separate during language production, and therefore to "translate" the preverbal message into words of only one lexicon? This is an important issue, because a failure to achieve lexical selection in the desired language may have disastrous consequences for communication. Although code switching is a valid communicative strategy in some contexts, in many others the recipient of the message may not know the other language of a bilingual. Thus, for a bilingual speaker, it is crucial to be able to place herself in the so-called monolingual mode (see the discussion about language modes by Grosjean, 2000, and chapter 2 of this volume) and to be able to ignore the existence of the language not-in-use. Certainly, the information of the language in which the speaker wants to produce the message has to be included in some way in the preverbal message; that is, the decision of which language to use depends on conceptual variables (e.g. who is/are the interlocutor/s, what is the topic of the discussion, etc.). Therefore, the language in which the message needs to be produced must be set prior to lexical access. How is this information used in order to select the appropriate lexical item and not its translation, and what is the effect of the existence of such translation?

As described above, it is generally assumed that the conceptual system activates several lexical nodes that act as competitors during lexical selection. Here we assume that, to a large degree, the conceptual system is shared by the two languages of a bilingual (see also de Groot, 1992; Gollan and Kroll, 2001; Kroll and Stewart, 1994; La Heij et al., 1996; Van Hell and de Groot, 1998). One possible way to ensure that only words from the target language are selected is to channel the flow of activation from the conceptual system into the specific lexical system. This view corresponds to the most extreme target-language specific hypothesis. According to this view, the activation coming from the conceptual system, and by means of the language specification in the preverbal message, would spread only to the words of the target language, therefore ensuring that lexical selection will eventually pick out the target lexical node in the intended language. However, this radical target-language specific view, in which the linguistic system of the non-response language is not even activated, has not received much support (but see McNamara, Krauthammer, and Bolgar, 1968; Penfield and Roberts, 1959). Instead, current models of speech production and bilingualism assume that the flow of activation from the conceptual system to the linguistic systems is target-language non-specific (e.g. Costa and Caramazza, 1999; de Bot, 1992; Green, 1986, 1998; Hermans, 2000; Hermans, Bongaerts, de Bot and Schreuder, 1998; Kroll et al., 2000; Poulisse, 1997; Poulisse and Bongaerts, 1994). That is, the conceptual system spreads activation to the words of the two languages of a bilingual regardless of the language in which the task is being performed.

The assumption that the conceptual system activates words belonging to the two lexicons of a bilingual speaker not only leaves open the question of how the speaker avoids selecting the words of the non-response language, but also raises the question of what the effects are of having lexical nodes of a non-target language activated. As we have described above, the lexical selection mechanism is supposed to be sensitive to the level of activation of the target lexical node in relation to that of other lexical nodes that act as competitors – the larger the difference between the activation level of the target word and that of other lexical nodes, the easier it is to achieve lexical selection. The question then is the extent to which the activated lexical nodes of the non-response language also act as competitors during lexical access. Is the activation of the words in the non-response language interfering with the selection of words in the response language? An affirmative answer to this question would mean that, to some extent, lexical selection is somewhat less demanding for monolingual speakers than for bilingual speakers.

Regardless of whether the words of the non-response language enter into competition or not, the question still remains of how the lexical selection mechanism ends up selecting the intended word instead of its translation. Two different mechanisms have been advanced to account for such a remarkable skill. The first mechanism assumes the existence of inhibitory processes in charge of suppressing or inhibiting the activation of the words that belong to the non-target language (Green, 1998; Hermans et al., 1998; Lee and Williams, 2001; Schreuder and Hermans, 1998). Thus, although the conceptual system would activate lexical nodes of the non-response language, a subsequent mechanism will suppress their activation to allow the lexical selection mechanism to pick out the target word in the response language. In this view, lexical selection is target-language non-specific in the sense that any lexical node can be a potential candidate for selection, and in principle interference across languages is possible.

The second solution assumes the existence of a selection mechanism that considers only the level of activation of the lexical nodes belonging to the response language, neglecting any activation of the words belonging to the non-response language (Colomé, 2001; Costa and Caramazza, 1999; Costa, Caramazza, and Sebastian-Galles, 2000; Costa, Miozzo, and Caramazza, 1999; Roelofs, 1998). Accordingly, no interference from the non-response language is expected in this case. This proposal embraces the notion that lexical selection is target-language specific. Notice that both types of models assume the existence of an external conceptual mechanism that determines either which lexicon needs to be inhibited (as in the former proposal) or which lexicon needs to be neglected (as in the latter proposal).

To summarize, models of lexical access in speech production postulate that the activation that flows from the conceptual system into the lexical representations is target-language non-specific, namely that the two lexicons of a bilingual are activated. However, different views are held regarding the way lexical selection is achieved, and also regarding the extent to which the words from the non-response language may affect the processes of lexical selection in the language-in-use.

8.3.2   *The interaction between the grammar of the two lexicons*

Crucial information that needs to be retrieved in order to construct well-formed utterances is the words' grammatical properties. The issue of the relationship between the grammatical properties of two languages has captured the attention of researchers mostly in the context of code-switching situations (e.g. Fuller and Lehnert, 2000; Karousou-Fokas and Garman, 2001; Myers-Scotton, 2000, Myers-Scotton and Jake, 1997, 2001. Also, researchers in second language acquisition have paid attention to whether the acquisition of the L2 grammar is in any way affected by the already existing L1 grammar (e.g. Bates and MacWhinney, 1989; Döpke, 2000, 2001; Müller and Hulk, 2001). However, much less attention has been devoted to the effects of grammatical properties of the non-response language during speech production in the response language, at least from the psycholinguistic point of view. Here we discuss some points regarding this issue with the main goal of reflecting on the relationship between the two grammatical systems of the bilingual speaker. As in the case of activation of lexical nodes, the first question that needs to be addressed is whether the grammatical properties of the language-not-in-use are activated during lexical access. A negative answer to this question would suggest that grammatical encoding for bilingual and monolingual speakers functions similarly. However, if the grammatical properties of the language-not-in-use are activated then we could ask the question of how much this activation affects processing of the response language. There are different domains for which one could ask that question. Here we discuss two examples in relation to two of these domains.

The first example refers to grammatical gender. Consider the case of a bilingual who speaks two languages in which the grammatical gender of the noun is needed in order to retrieve other lexical nodes or to inflect gender-marked words, such as Spanish and Italian. A given word in one of these languages (e.g. Italian) may or may not have the same gender as in its Spanish translation. For example, the Italian word meaning 'knife' and its translation in Spanish have the same gender value (*coltello* masc, *cuchillo* masc), while the Italian word meaning 'fork' and its corresponding Spanish translation have different genders (*forchetta* fem, *tenedor* masc). Assuming that the bilingual speaker has successfully acquired the gender value of words in the two languages, the question is whether the gender value of the translation word in the non-response language is activated during speech production, and if it is, whether it affects the retrieval of the noun's gender value in the response language.[3] Answers to these questions require making hypotheses regarding

---

3   The issue of how gender in L2 is acquired has been the focus of several studies (e.g. Bartning, 2000; Carroll, 1999; Dewaele & Veronique, 2001; Mohring, 2001; Oliphant, 1998).

how the grammatical properties of words are retrieved and also about the organization of the grammatical gender system across languages. For example, one may postulate that once the gender values of the words in the L2 are properly learned, the gender systems of the two languages become separated or autonomous (see Dewaele and Veronique, 2001, for a proposal of this sort). In this scenario, it is reasonable to assume that the two gender systems of a bilingual do not interact during gender retrieval; therefore, the selection of the noun's gender value in the response language should be independent of the gender value of its translation. This view is in line with a target-language specific access to grammatical properties.

Alternatively, it is possible that when the two languages have similar gender systems, both are integrated in one single system. In this view, when a word and its translation have the same gender value, the two lexical nodes will share the same gender feature. When the two words have different genders they will be linked to two different gender features. In such a scenario, and assuming that the selection of the noun's gender value is sensitive to activation levels, the retrieval of the gender feature for the target word would be easier when its translation has the same gender than when it has a different gender. In other words, in this framework, the gender values of the words in the non-response language may affect the retrieval of the noun's gender value in the response language. This hypothesis is more in line with a target-language non-specific access view.

A second example of the hypothetical effect that the grammatical properties of the non-response language may exert on the response language refers to word order. Consider the case of word order of relatively simple Noun Phrases such as determiner + adjective + noun (*the red car*). The order of the lexical items in a phrase of this type varies from language to language. For example, in English the adjective occupies a prenominal position (*the red car*). In Spanish, it usually occupies a postnominal position (*el coche rojo*, literally 'the car red'). Now consider a Spanish-English bilingual who is asked to produce the NP in English (*the red car*). How much will the specific order of the lexical items in the non-response language (Spanish) affect the word-ordering processes in the response language? Notice that the order of the words in these types of NPs is relatively easy to acquire and that relatively fluent Spanish-English bilinguals do not usually make mistakes of the type *the car red*. Despite the fact that these errors are infrequent, it is still possible that the specific word order of the non-response language affects to some extent the construction of the NP frame in the response language.

An interesting issue that psycholinguistic models of lexical access in bilingual speech production need to address is what type of grammatical information is more likely to interact across languages when speaking. Notice that the examples presented above represent two different types of grammatical information. While grammatical gender is an intrinsic feature of the lexical items corresponding to nouns, word order is a relational property among lexical items. Thus, the issue here is not simply one of studying which specific grammatical properties of a language behave with relative autonomy with respect to the other language, but rather to explore what *types* of grammatical properties are more likely to be autonomous or shared across languages.

8.3.3   *Activating phonological representations*

That the conceptual system activates multiple lexical nodes (that of the target word and those of other semantically related words) is an assumption widely shared by monolingual models of language production (e.g. Dell, 1986; Levelt, Roelofs, and Meyer, 1999). However, the extent to which all activated lexical items send activation to their phonological segments is controversial. According to the so-called cascaded models of lexical access, any activated lexical node would spread some proportional activation to their phonological segments. In contrast, the so-called discrete models assume that the only lexical node that activates its phonological segments is the selected one (e.g. Roelofs, 1992). What are the implications of these two views for the case of bilingualism? Recall that models of bilingual speech production also assume that the conceptual system activates lexical nodes that match conceptual information regardless of the language they belong to; therefore, words in the response language as well as in the non-response language are activated (when an English-Spanish bilingual wants to say *dog*, both the lexical nodes corresponding to that concept in the two languages are activated – *dog* and *perro*). Thus, the question becomes one of identifying whether the phonological properties of the words in the non-response language are also activated. That is, do activated lexical nodes corresponding to the non-response language activate their phonological segments? If one applies the cascade processing to any lexical item regardless of the language it belongs to, then we should expect lexical items of the non-response language to send activation to their phonological segments.[4] Thus, according to this view the activation of phonological representations is target-language non-specific. If one extends the discrete view of lexical access to any non-selected lexical node irrespective of the language it belongs to, then we should not expect any activation of the phonological properties of the words belonging to the non-response language, since they are not selected. Therefore, a discrete model of lexical access predicts that the activation of phonological representations is target-language specific.[5] The issue of whether the phonological properties of words that belong to the non-response language are nevertheless activated is important, because it may

4   However, this hypothesis only holds if the lexical nodes of the non-response language are not inhibited. If they are, then the activation that they could spread to their phonological properties should be negligible.
5   A hybrid model is conceivable in which a discrete processing is applied to the words in the response language, while at the same time allowing cascade processing for the words in the non-response language. However, the motivation for postulating such an unparsimonious system is unclear.

help us to better understand the interaction between the two phonological systems of a bilingual speaker.

It is important to stress that the hypothesis described above refers to the on-line interaction of the two language systems of a bilingual when producing speech. This is a different issue than whether the two languages of a bilingual interact when the speaker acquires their respective phonological repertoires. As mentioned above for the case of grammatical properties, there are a large number of studies that have addressed whether it is possible for a bilingual to develop a phonological system of their L2 independent from the L1 phono-logical system – also whether the acquisition of a new phonological inventory affects that which has already been acquired (e.g. Bosch, Costa and Sebastián-Gallés, 2000; Caramazza et al., 1973; Cutler et al., 1992; Flege, 1995, 1999; Pallier, Bosch, and Sebastián-Gallés, 1997; Yeni-Komshian, Flege, and Liu, 2000). Here we do not deal with the issue of how the phonological systems are acquired. Rather, we asked a relatively independent question, namely, the extent to which the phonological properties of the words of the non-response language are activated and affect the performance when producing speech in the response language.

As in the case of lexical selection, if the phonological properties of the words in the non-response language are not activated, phonological encoding in the response language can proceed in the same way in bilinguals and monolinguals. However, if the phonological properties of the lexical items of the non-response language are activated, the issue becomes one of identifying whether their activation affects the retrieval of the phonological properties of the target word in the response language. That is, would the activation of the segmental information of a translation word affect the retrieval of the phonological segments of the target word in the response language?[6]

8.4 Target-Language Specific vs. Target-Language Non-specific Processing: Empirical Evidence

In this section I will review various studies that have addressed some of the issues described above. This review is not intended to be exhaustive, but rather the goal is to exemplify some of the experimental strategies followed by

---

6 This hypothesis is based on the assumption that there may be cross-language competi-tion at the level of the two phonological systems (that of the response language and that of the non-response language). However, if this latter assumption were to be wrong, and the bilingual speaker has two completely autonomous phonological repertoires and can also ignore the phonological activation of the phonological system not-in-use, then the activation of the phonological properties of the words belonging to the non-response language would be irrelevant during speech production in the response language (but see the following section).

researchers to answer the questions presented above. I will focus on two issues: (a) whether lexical activation of the non-response language affects lexical
selection, and (b) the extent to which there is phonological activation of words
that belong to the language-not-in-use.

8.4.1   Does lexical activation in the non-response language affect lexical selection?

The parallel activation of the two lexicons of a bilingual leads to the question
of whether the activation levels of the lexical nodes that belong to the non-
response language interfere with the selection of the target lexical node.

Two studies have addressed this issue directly by means of the contextual
effects observed in the picture–word interference paradigm. In this task, participants are asked to name pictures (the most used speech production task),
while ignoring the presentation of distractor words (see McLeod, 1991 for a
review of Stroop-like tasks). The ease with which the picture-naming task is
carried out depends on the relationship between the target picture and the
distractor word, and that ease is revealed by the speed and accuracy with
which the naming task is performed. For example, picture-naming latencies
are slower when the two stimuli belong to the same semantic category (picture: *dog*, distractor: *horse*) than when they do not (picture: *dog*, distractor: *pen*)
(e.g. Lupker, 1979; Rosinski, 1977). Importantly, these effects are supposed to
reveal the processes involved in lexical access, and specifically the ease with
which lexical selection is achieved (see Caramazza and Costa, 2000, 2001;
Roelofs, 1992, 2001; Schriefers, Meyer, and Levelt, 1990; Starreveld and La
Heij, 1995). The logic behind the paradigm is that the larger the activation
of the lexical node corresponding to the distractor word in relation to that
corresponding to the target lexical node, the more difficult lexical selection is.
In this context, it is assumed that the larger the semantic overlap between the
concepts corresponding to a distractor and a picture the larger the interference.

Following this logic Hermans et al. (1998) hypothesized that a modulation
of the level of activation of the target's translation word would result in a
modulation of its interference during lexical selection in the response language (see also Ehri and Ryan, 1980). Hermans et al. asked Dutch-English
participants to name pictures in their L2 (English) while ignoring distractors
presented in their L1 (Dutch). The crucial condition included in this study is
that in which the distractor word was phonologically related to the translation
of the target word (the phonologically-related-to-translation condition). For
example, when naming the picture of a mountain in English, the distractor
word corresponding to the phonologically-related-to-translation condition was
berm 'verge,' which is phonologically similar to the Dutch translation (*berg*) of
the target word. The authors used this condition in order to modulate the level
of activation of the target's translation word (*berg*). They hypothesized that the
level of activation of the lexical node *berg* would be higher when presented

with the distractor *berm* than with an unrelated distractor *kaars* 'candle.' Therefore, if the words in the non-response language enter into competition during
lexical selection, then selecting the target word *mountain* should be more difficult in the context of *berm* than in the context of *kaars*. In fact, picture-naming
latencies were slower for the picture–word pair "mountain/*berm*" than for the
pair "mountain/*kaars*." This result was given the following interpretation. During the process of naming the picture of a mountain in English, its Dutch translation (*berg*) is activated. However, when the distractor word *berm* is presented
the lexical node *berg* receives activation from two sources (the conceptual system, and the presentation of the distractor word *berm*), while in the unrelated
condition it only receives activation from one source (the conceptual system).
The authors conclude that the words in the non-response language are activated and that they interfere with the selection of the target lexical node in the
response language, therefore supporting a model of lexical access in which both
activation flow and selection mechanism are target-language non-specific.

The second set of studies that have addressed the extent to which words
from the language-not-in-use enter into competition during lexical access
have explored the so-called between-languages identity facilitation effect (Costa
and Caramazza, 1999; Costa, Miozzo, and Caramazza, 1999; Goodman et al.,
1985; Hermans, 2000). For example, Costa and Caramazza (1999) asked English-Spanish bilinguals to name a set of pictures in their L2, while ignoring
the presentation of various types of distractor words. The most interesting
condition was that in which the distractor word corresponded to the target's
translation, the identity across-languages condition. For example, if the participant was asked to name the picture of a bed in Spanish (*cama*), the distractor
for the between-language identity conditions was the English word corresponding to the target's translation (*bed*), while for the unrelated condition
it was *stone*. Following the same logic as before, a model in which lexical
selection considers the activation levels of the words irrespective of the language they belong to (the target-language non-specific view) would predict
slower naming for the related than for the unrelated condition. This is because
in the former case the lexical node corresponding to the target's translation
would receive activation from two sources (the distractor word and the conceptual system), while in the latter case that node will be activated only from
the conceptual system. However, the results did not support such a prediction, instead naming latencies were *faster* when the distractor word was the
target's translation (the *cama/bed* pair) than when it was an unrelated word
(the *cama/stone* pair) – the so-called between-language identity facilitation
effect. These results have been replicated with bilinguals of different languages
and different proficiencies (Costa, Miozzo, and Caramazza, 1999; Hermans,
2000), and support a model of lexical access in which lexical selection does
not consider the activation of the words that do not belong to the response
language. That is, identity facilitation across languages supports a target-
language specific lexical selection mechanism.

Thus, we have two sets of seemingly contradictory results supporting the target-language specific selection and the target-language non-specific selection mechanism. Therefore, the issue of whether lexical nodes that belong to the non-response language compete during lexical selection is far from resolved. New experimental data is needed to adjudicate between the target-language specific and the target-language non-specific selection processes. Furthermore, this issue needs to be addressed considering other factors that may have an impact on the extent to which bilinguals can ignore the activation levels of the words that do not belong to the response language, such as age of acquisition of the second language and L2 proficiency. (For more on lexical processing, see chapters 2, 7, 9, and 28.)

8.4.2   Is there phonological activation of the words belonging to the language-not-in-use?

Given the assumption that the two lexicons of a bilingual are activated, the next question is, to what extent are the phonological segments of the words that do not belong to the response language also activated? The target-language specific view could be considered as an extension of discrete models of lexical access. Accordingly, activation of the non-response language is restricted to lexical levels, and the phonological representations of the words in the non-response language are not activated. Alternatively, the target-language non-specific view holds that the flow of activation is not restricted to the language of the response; therefore, the activation of a lexical node would spread to its phonological properties, regardless of the language to which the word belongs.

There are two sets of studies that have produced results relevant to this issue. In the first set, the effects of the cognate status of words in a picture-naming task and in tip-of-the-tongue states have been explored (Costa, Caramazza, and Sebastián-Gallés, 2000; Gollan, Acenas, and Smith, 2001; Kroll et al., 2000). Cognates are words whose translations are formally similar (Spanish: *pera*, English: *pear*), while non-cognates are words whose translations are dissimilar (Spanish *manzana*, English: *apple*). In the Costa, Caramazza, and Sebastián-Gallés (2000) and Kroll et al. (2000) studies, naming latencies for pictures with cognate names were compared to those with non-cognate names. Two predictions about the effect of the cognate status of words in picture-naming latencies were derived from the target-language specific and non-specific views. First, if phonological activation is target-language non-specific, then the lexical node corresponding to the translation of the target word would spread some activation to its phonological properties, resulting in faster naming latencies for pictures with cognate than with non-cognate names. This is because the phonological overlap for cognate words is much larger than for non-cognate words. Therefore, in the case of cognate words, the phonological segments (or features) of the target word would be receiving activation from two sources (the target lexical node in the response language and its translation). In the case of non-cognate words, the target's phonological segments would receive activation only from one source. In contrast, if phonological activation is target-language specific, and therefore words that do not belong to the response language do not activate their phonological segments, then naming latencies should be independent of the cognate status of the picture's name. The results of these studies revealed faster naming latencies for pictures with cognate names than with non-cognate names – the so-called cognate facilitation effect (for Spanish-Catalan bilinguals in the case of Costa, Caramazza, and Sebastián-Gallés, 2000, and for Dutch-English bilinguals in the case of Kroll et al., 2000). Furthermore, the difference between the two sets of pictures was present only for bilingual speakers, not for monolingual speakers, suggesting that cognate facilitation is related to the effects of the non-response language on the response language. Thus, the cognate facilitation effect was interpreted as supporting a model of lexical access in which the flow of activation is target-language non-specific. That is, activation flows from the conceptual system to the various levels of linguistic representation independent of the language in which the response has to be given.[7]

Gollan, Acenas, and Smith (2001) reached a similar conclusion in their analysis of the effect of cognate status in the probability of having a tip-of-the-tongue state (TOT). TOT states refer to the situation in which the speaker cannot retrieve the word she wants to produce, despite having an intense feeling of knowing the word and in some cases, partial information about it. In this study, Spanish-English and Tagalog-English bilinguals were shown to be more prone to TOT states in picture naming than monolingual speakers (see also Gollan and Silverberg, 2001). However, this difference disappeared when cognate words were used to elicit TOT states. That is, when a word and its translation are phonologically similar, a bilingual speaker is as prone to fall into a TOT state as a monolingual speaker. The authors attribute this cognate facilitation effect to the fact that the phonological properties of the language-not-in-use help the retrieval of the phonological properties of the target word in the response language, making them more likely to be retrieved.

Further evidence supporting the notion of target-language non-specific activation at the level of phonological information comes from two phoneme-monitoring experiments, Colomé, 2001 and Hermans, 2000. Colomé asked Spanish-Catalan bilinguals to decide whether a target phoneme was present in the Catalan name of a given picture. Some of the trials required a positive answer (e.g. *t* is in the Catalan word meaning 'table' – *taula*), while other trials required a negative answer (e.g. *n* is not in the Catalan word for 'table'

---

7   However, the extent to which the language-not-in-use affects the processing of the language-in-use may be modulated by whether participants perform the task in L1 or L2. Indeed, the magnitude of the cognate facilitation effect in Costa, Caramazza, and Sebastián-Gallés's (2000) study was modulated by this factor, the cognate effect being larger when participants were producing the words in their L2. In the same way, in Kroll's study the cognate effect (in the block naming task) was only present when the naming task was performed in L2.

– taula). Two different negative trials were included: (a) trials in which the target phoneme was present in the Spanish translation of the Catalan name of the picture, and (b) trials in which the target phoneme was not present in the Spanish translation of the Catalan name of the picture. For example, participants would be presented with the target phonemes *m* or *n* and subsequently with the picture of a table. In both cases, participants had to give a negative response, since neither *m* nor *n* is present in the Catalan name of the picture (*taula*). However, while one of the target phonemes, *m*, is present in the Spanish translation of the picture name (*mesa*, 'table' in Spanish), the other one (*n*) is not. Participants were faster in rejecting a target phoneme that was not present in the Spanish translation (e.g. *n*) than a target phoneme that was part of the translation (*m*). Colomé interpreted this result as reflecting that the phoneme *m* but not the phoneme *n* was activated during the retrieval of the Catalan target word. This is because during the process of retrieving the phonological properties of the Catalan name of the picture (e.g. *taula*), the phonological segments of its Spanish translation (e.g. *mesa*) are also activated. These results suggest that the phonological properties of the words of the language-not-in-use are activated during speech production. These results have been replicated by Hermans (2000) with another population of bilingual speakers (Dutch-English).

Thus, there appears to be enough experimental evidence to suggest that the activation of linguistic representations belonging to the non-response language reaches even the phonological level.

8.5   The Role of the Language-not-in-Use during Speech Production: Concluding Remarks

In this chapter, I have reviewed some issues related to speech production and bilingualism. I have focused primarily on the role of the language-not-in-use during speech production by bilingual speakers in their other language. Two different views have been contrasted – the target-language specific and the target-language non-specific views. I have also considered the claims and predictions made by these two views at different levels of linguistic representation. In the following, I summarize the issues presented above and also the extent to which we have enough experimental evidence to adjudicate between the different hypotheses made by the two views. The following discussion is structured considering two different issues, activation flow and effects of the language-not-in-use.

The first issue refers to the extent to which activation flows through the lexical system in a target-language specific or non-specific way. There are two sources of evidence that indicate that activation for representations belonging to the non-response language is present at different levels of processing. Regarding the activation flow from the conceptual system to the linguistic system, the results reported by Hermans et al. (1998) support the target-language non-specific view; that is, they support the parallel activation of the words belonging to the two languages. Regarding the phonological level, the cognate facilitation effect (both in picture naming and TOT states), along with the data reported by Colomé (2001), suggests that segmental information of lexical items belonging to the non-response language is activated during speech production. Furthermore, these last two results also provide indirect evidence of the existence of target-language non-specific activation from the conceptual system to the lexical system, since (at least in feed-forward models) a necessary requirement for the activation of phonological properties of a given lexical node is its previous activation from the conceptual system. In other words, if the sounds of the word *perro* and the sounds of its English translation (*d, o, g*) are activated, then it follows that their corresponding lexical nodes have been previously activated from the conceptual system.

The question of whether or not there is target-language specificity in the activation of the grammatical properties of the lexical items has not been deeply explored; therefore it is one of the issues that requires not only more experimental studies but also an important development of theoretical frameworks. Furthermore, it is entirely possible that both the target-language specific and non-specific hypotheses apply to different types of grammatical information.

At any rate, the present experimental evidence seems to support the claim that activation flows freely from the conceptual system into the linguistic systems of the speaker irrespective of the language being used at a given moment in time. That is, regarding the flow of activation, the bilingual system seems to be target-language non-specific.

Given this scenario, the question is: To what extent does the activation of the representations of the non-response language affect the processing of the response language? We have reported some experimental evidence regarding the effects of the non-response language on the response language at two different levels of representation, the lexical level and the phonological level. Regarding the first level, the effects reported by Costa, Miozzo, and Caramazza, 1999, and Hermans, 2000 support the target-language specific lexical selection mechanism, while the results reported by Hermans et al., 1998, support the target-language non-specific selection hypothesis. At this point, the extent to which the words that belong to the non-response language also enter into competition during lexical access is still unresolved. One of the issues that future research has to focus on is whether competition across languages is restricted to L2 speech production for non-proficient bilinguals. Concerning whether the phonological activation of the words that belong to the non-response language affect performance in the response language, I think the experimental evidence supports the target-language non-specific view. That is, the activation of the phonological segments of the words belonging to the non-response language affects the retrieval of the target's phonological composition. This conclusion is supported by the results of Costa, Caramazza, and Sebastián-Gallés, 2000, and Kroll et al., 2000. This certainly raises the question of the extent to which the phonological representations of the two languages of a bilingual overlap and also whether they are integrated into one common system. This is an important issue that needs to be addressed by trying to replicate the cognate effects with bilinguals of languages with very different phonological systems. In the same way, it will be interesting to assess whether the mastery of the phonological repertoires of the two languages of a bilingual affects the magnitude of the cognate effect.

To conclude, the processing mechanisms involved in the production of speech in bilingual speakers entail the activation of both the language-in-use and the language-not-in-use even when the communicative context entails only one language (the so-called monolingual mode). Furthermore, the activation of the language-not-in-use expands the lexical level and reaches the phonological level. The effects of the activation of the representations of the language-not-in-use in the processing of the language-in-use may be different for lexical and sublexical levels. At the phonological or sublexical level, the activation of the phonological properties of the language-not-in-use has an impact on the retrieval of the phonological properties of the language-in-use. However, the extent to which the activation of the lexical nodes of the language-not-in-use (or of its grammatical properties) affects lexical selection in the response language is still unclear. (For additional discussion of models and theories of bilingual processing, see chapters 1–3, 7, and 9.)

ACKNOWLEDGMENTS

This research was supported in part by NIH grant DC 04542. Also, the author was supported by a post-doctoral fellowship from SISSA, and by a research contract at the Universitat de Barcelona. The author is grateful to Mohinish Shukla and Pam Miller for their helpful suggestions on this work.

REFERENCES

Alario, F. X. and Caramazza, A. (2002). The production of determiners: Evidence from French. *Cognition*, 82, 179–223.

Bartning, I. (2000). Gender agreement in L2 French: Pre-advanced vs. advanced learners. *Studia Linguistica*, 54, 225–37.

Bates, E. and McWhinney, B. (1989). Functionalism and the Competition Model, in B. McWhinney and E. Bates (eds.), *The Cross-Linguistic Study of Sentence Processing*. Cambridge: Cambridge University Press, 1989.

Bock, J. K. and Levelt, W. J. M. (1994). Language production: Grammatical encoding. In M. A. Gernsbacher (ed.), *Handbook of Psycholinguistics*. San Diego, CA: Academic Press.

Bock, J. K., Loebell, H., and Morey, R. (1992). From conceptual roles to structural relations: Bridging the syntactic cleft. *Psychological Review, 99,* 150–71.

Bosch, L., Costa, A., and Sebastian-Galles, N. (2000). First and second language vowel perception in early bilinguals. *European Journal of Cognitive Psychology, 12,* 189–221.

Caramazza, A. (1997). How many levels of processing are there in lexical access? *Cognitive Neuropsychology, 14,* 177–208.

Caramazza, A. and Costa, A. (2000). The semantic interference effect in the picture-word interference paradigm: Does the response set matter? *Cognition, 75,* B51–B64.

Caramazza, A. and Costa, A. (2001). Set size and repetitions are not at the base of the differential effects of semantically related distractors: Implications for models of lexical access. *Cognition, 80,* 291–8.

Caramazza, A., Miozzo, M., Costa, A., Schiller, N., and Alario, F. X. (2001). A crosslinguistic investigation of determiner production. In E. Dupoux (ed.), *Language, Brain, and Cognitive Development: Essays in honor of Jacques Mehler,* pp. 209–26. Cambridge, MA: MIT Press.

Caramazza, A., Yeni-Komshian, G., Zurif, E., and Carbone, E. (1973). The acquisition of a new phonological contrast: The case of stop consonants in French-English bilinguals. *Journal of the Acoustical Society of America, 54,* 421–8.

Carroll, S. (1999). Input and SLA: adults' sensitivity to different sorts of cues to French gender. *Language Learning, 39,* 535–94.

Colomé, A. (2001). Lexical activation in bilinguals' speech production: Language-specific or language-independent? *Journal of Memory and Language, 45(4),* 721–36.

Costa, A. and Caramazza, A. (1999). Is lexical selection language specific? Further evidence from Spanish-English bilinguals. *Bilingualism: Language and Cognition, 2,* 231–44.

Costa, A., Caramazza, A., and Sebastián-Gallés, N. (2000). The cognate facilitation effect: Implications for models of lexical access. *Journal of Experimental Psychology: Learning, Memory and Cognition, 26,* 1283–96.

Costa, A., Miozzo, M., and Caramazza, A. (1999). Lexical selection in bilinguals: Do words in the bilingual's two lexicons compete for selection? *Journal of Memory and Language, 41(3),* 365–97.

Costa, A. and Sebastián-Gallés, N. (1998). Abstract syllabic structure in language production: Evidence from Spanish. *Journal of Experimental Psychology: Learning, Memory and Cognition, 24(4),* 886–903.

Cutler, A., Mehler, J., Norris, D., and Segui, J. (1992). The monolingual nature of speech segmentation by bilinguals. *Cognitive Psychology, 24,* 381–410.

Cutting, J. C. and Ferreira, V. S. (1999). Semantic and phonological information flow in the production lexicon. *Journal of Experimental Psychology: Learning, Memory and Cognition, 25(2),* 318–44.

De Bot, K. (1992). A bilingual production model: Levelt's speaking model adapted. *Applied Linguistics, 13,* 1–24.

De Groot, A. M. (1992). Determinants of word translation. *Journal of Experimental Psychology: Learning, Memory and Cognition, 18(5),* 1001–18.

Dell, G. S. (1986). A spreading activation theory of retrieval in sentence production. *Psychological Review, 93,* 283–321.

Dell, G. S. and O'Seaghdha, P. G. (1991). Mediated and convergent lexical priming in language production: A comment on Levelt et al. (1991). *Psychological Review, 98,* 604–14.

Dell, G. S. and O'Seaghdha, P. G. (1992). Stages of lexical access in language production. *Cognition*, 42, 287–314.

Dell, G. S., Schwartz, M. F., Martin, N. M., Saffran, E. M., and Gagnon, D. A. (1997). Lexical access in aphasic and nonaphasic speakers. *Psychological Review*, 104, 801–38.

Dewaele, J. M. and Veronique, D. (2001). Gender assignment and gender agreement in advanced French interlanguage: a cross-sectional study. *Bilingualism: Language and Cognition*, 275–97.

Döpke, S. (2000). Generation of and retraction from cross-linguistically motivated structures in bilingual first language acquisition. *Bilingualism: Language and Cognition*, 3, 209–26.

Döpke, S. (2001). *Cross-Linguistic Structures in Simultaneous Bilingualism*. Amsterdam: John Benjamins.

Ehri, L. C. and Ryan, E. B. (1980). Performance of bilinguals in a picture-word interference task. *Journal of Psycholinguistic Research*, 9(3), 285–302.

Flege, J. E. (1995). Second language speech learning: theory, findings, and problems. In W. Strange (ed.), *Speech Perception and Linguistic Experience: Issues in Cross-Language Research*, pp. 233–77. Baltimore, MD: York.

Flege, J. E. (1999). Age of learning and second language speech. In D. Birdsong (ed.), *Second Language Acquisition and the Critical Period Hypothesis: Second Language Acquisition Research*, pp. 101–31. Mahwah, NJ: Lawrence Erlbaum Associates.

Fuller, J. M. and Lehnert, H. (2000). Noun phrase structure in German-English codeswitching: Variation in gender assignment and article use. *International Journal of Bilingualism*, 3, 399–420.

Garrett, M. F. (1976). Syntactic processes in sentence production. In R. Wales and E. Walker (eds.), *New Approaches to Language Mechanisms*. Amsterdam: North Holland Press.

Garrett, M. F. (1980). Levels of processing in sentence production. In B. Butterworth (ed.), *Language Production. Vol. 1: Speech and Talk*. London: Academic Press.

Garrett, M. (1988). Processes in language production. In F. Newmeyer (ed.), *Language: Psychological and Biological Aspects. Linguistics: The Cambridge Survey III*. Cambridge, UK: Cambridge University Press.

Gollan, T., Acenas, L. A., and Smith, E. (2001). Tip-of-the-tongue incidence in Spanish-English and Tagalog-English Bilinguals. Third International Symposium on Bilingualism, Bristol.

Gollan, T. H and Kroll, J. F. (2001). Bilingual lexical access. In Rapp, B. (ed.), *The Handbook of Cognitive Neuropsychology: What Deficits Reveal about the Human Mind*. Philadelphia, PA: Psychology Press.

Gollan, T. H. and Silverberg, N. B. (2001). Tip-of-the-tongue states in Hebrew-English bilinguals. *Bilingualism: Language and Cognition*, 4(1), 63–83.

Goodman, G. S., Haith, M. M., Guttentag, R. E., and Rao, S. (1985). Automatic processing of word meaning: Intralingual and interlingual interference. *Child Development*, 56, 103–18.

Green, D. W. (1986). Control, activation and resource: A framework and a model for the control of speech in bilinguals. *Brain and Language*, 27, 210–23.

Green, D. W. (1998). Mental control of the bilingual lexico-semantic system. *Bilingualism: Language and Cognition*, 1, 67–81.

Grosjean, F. (1997). Processing mixed language: Issues, findings and models. In A. M. B. de Groot and J. F. Kroll (eds.), *Tutorials in Bilingualism: Psycholinguistic*

Perspectives. Mahwah, NJ: Lawrence Erlbaum Associates.

Grosjean, F. (1998). Transfer and language mode. *Bilingualism: Language and Cognition*, 1, 175–6.

Grosjean, F. (2000). The bilingual's language modes. In Nicol, J. (ed.), *One Mind, Two Languages: Bilingual Language Processing*. Oxford: Blackwell.

Harley, T. A. (1993). Phonological activation of semantic competitors during lexical access in speech production. *Language and Cognitive Processes*, 8, 291–309.

Hermans, D. (2000). Word production in a foreign language. Unpublished thesis. Katholieke Universiteit Nijmegen, The Netherlands.

Hermans, D., Bongaerts, T., de Bot, K., Schreuder, R. (1998). Producing words in a foreign language: Can speakers prevent interference from their first language? *Bilingualism: Language and Cognition*, 1(3), 213–30.

Humphreys, G. W. and Riddoch, M. J. (1988). Cascade processes in picture identification. *Cognitive Neuropsychology*, 5(1), 67–104.

Jescheniak, J. and Schriefers, H. (1998). Discrete serial versus cascaded processing in lexical access in speech production: Further evidence from the coactivation of near-synonyms. *Journal of Experimental Psychology: Learning, Memory and Cognition*, 24, 1256–74.

Karousou-Fokas, R. and Garman, M. (2001). Psycholinguistic interpretation of codeswitching: Evidence from fluent Greek-English bilingual adults. *International Journal of Bilingualism*, 1, 39–69.

Kroll, J. F., Dijkstra, A., Janssen, N., and Schriefers, H. (2000). Selecting the language in which to speak: Experiments on lexical access in bilingual production. Paper presented at the 41st annual meeting of the Psychonomic Society, New Orleans, LA.

Kroll, J. F. and Stewart, E. (1994). Category interference in translation and picture naming: Evidence for asymmetric connection between bilingual memory representations. *Journal of Memory and Language*, 33(2), 149–74.

La Heij, W., Hooglander, A., Kerling, R., and van der Valden, E. (1996). Nonverbal context effects in forward and backward translation: Evidence for concept mediation. *Journal of Memory and Language*, 35, 648–65.

Lee, M. W. and Williams, J. (2001). Lexical access in spoken word production by bilinguals: Evidence from a semantic priming paradigm. *Bilingualism: Language and Cognition*, 4, 233–48.

Levelt, W. J. M. (1989). *Speaking: From Intention to Articulation*. Cambridge, MA: MIT Press.

Levelt, W. J. M. (2001). Spoken word production: A theory of lexical access. *Proceedings of the. National. Academy of Sciences*, 98, 13464–71.

Levelt, W. J. M., Roelofs, A., and Meyer, A. S. (1999). A theory of lexical access in speech production. *Behavioural and Brain Sciences*, 22, 1–75.

Levelt, W. J. M., Schriefers, H., Vorberg, D., Meyer, A. S., Pechmann, T., and Havinga, J. (1991). The time course of lexical access in speech production: A study of picture naming. *Psychological Review*, 98, 122–42.

Lupker, S. J. (1979). The semantic nature of response competition in the picture-word interference task. *Memory and Cognition*, 7, 485–95.

McLeod, C. M. (1991). Half a century of research on the Stroop effect: An integrative review. *Psychological Bulletin*, 109, 163–203.

McNamara, J., Krauthammer, M., Bolgar, M. (1968). Language switching in bilinguals as a function of stimulus and response uncertainty. *Journal of*

Experimental Psychology, 78(2, Pt 1), 208–15.

Meyer, A. S. and Schriefers, H. (1991). Phonological facilitation in picture-word interference experiments: Effects of stimulus onset asynchrony and types of interfering stimuli. *Journal of Experimental Psychology: Learning, Memory and Cognition*, 17, 1146–60.

Mohring, A. (2001). The acquisition of French by German children of pre-school age: An empirical investigation of gender assignment and gender agreement. In S. Foster-Cohen and A. Nizegorodcew (eds.), *EUROSLA Yearbook 2001*, 1, 171–94. John Benjamins.

Müller, N. and Hulk, A. (2001). Crosslinguistic influence in bilingual language acquisition: Italian and French as recipient languages. *Bilingualism: Language and Cognition*, 1, 1–21.

Myers-Scotton, C. (2000). What matters: The out of sight in mixed languages. *Bilingualism: Language and Cognition*, 3, 119–21.

Myers-Scotton, C. and Jake, J. L. (1997). Codeswitching and compromise strategies: Implications for lexical structure. *International Journal of Bilingualism*, 1, 25–39.

Myers-Scotton, C. and Jake, J. L. (2001). Explaining aspects of codeswitching and their implications. In Janet Nicol (ed.), *One Mind, Two Languages: Bilingual Language Processing*, pp. 91–125. Oxford: Blackwell.

Oliphant, K. (1998). Acquisition of grammatical gender in Italian as a foreign language. *The Canadian Modern Language Review*, 54, 239–61.

Pallier, C., Bosch, L., and Sebastian-Galles, N. (1997). A limit on behavioral plasticity in speech perception. *Cognition*, 64, B9–B17.

Penfield, W. and Roberts, L. (1959). *Speech and Brain Mechanisms*. Princeton, NJ: Princeton University Press.

Peterson, R. R. and Savoy, P. (1998). Lexical selection and phonological encoding during language production: Evidence for cascaded processing. *Journal of Experimental Psychology: Learning, Memory and Cognition*, 24, 539–57.

Pickering, M. J, Branigan, H. P, Cleland, A. A., and Stewart, A. J. (2000). Activation of syntactic information during language production. *Journal of Psycholinguistic Research*, 29(2), 205–16.

Poulisse, N. (1997). Language production in bilinguals. In A. M. B. de Groot and J. F. Kroll (eds.), *Tutorials in Bilingualism: Psycholinguistic Perspectives*, pp. 201–24. Mahwah, NJ: Lawrence Erlbaum Associates.

Poulisse, N. and Bongaerts, T. (1994). First language use in second language production. *Applied Linguistics*, 15, 36–57.

Rapp, B. and Goldrick, M. (2000). Discreteness and interactivity in spoken word production. *Psychological Review*, 107, 460–99.

Roelofs, A. (1992). A spreading-activation theory of lemma retrieval in speaking. *Cognition*, 42, 107–42.

Roelofs, A. (1998). Lemma selection without inhibition of languages in bilingual speakers. *Bilingualism: Language and Cognition*, 1, 94–5.

Roelofs, A. (1999). Phonological segments and features as planning units in speech production. *Language and Cognitive Processes*, 14, 173–200.

Roelofs, A. (2000). WEAVER++ and other computational models of lemma retrieval and word-form encoding. In Linda Wheeldon (ed.), *Aspects of Language Production*, pp. 71–114. Studies in Cognition Series. Philadelphia, PA: Psychology Press.

Roelofs, A. (2001). Set size and repetition matter: Comment on Caramazza and Costa (2000). *Cognition*, 80(3), 283–90.

Rosinski, R. R. (1977). Picture-word interference is semantically based. *Child Development*, 48, 643–47.

Ruml, W., Caramazza, A., Shelton, J. R., and Chialant, D. (2000). Testing assumptions in computational theories of aphasia. *Journal of Memory and Language*, 43, 217–48.

Schiller, N. O. and Caramazza, A. (2003). Grammatical feature selection in noun phrase production: Evidence from German and Dutch. *Journal of Memory and Language*, 48, 169–94.

Schreuder, R. and Hermans, D. (1998). Mental control and language selection. *Bilingualism: Language and Cognition*, 1(2), 96–7.

Schriefers, H. (1993). Syntactic processes in the production of noun phrases. *Journal of Experimental Psychology: Learning, Memory and Cognition*, 19, 841–50.

Schriefers, H., Meyer, A. S., and Levelt, W. J. M. (1990). Exploring the time course of lexical access in production: Picture-word interference studies. *Journal of Memory and Language*, 29, 86–102.

Schriefers, H. and Teruel, E. (2000). Grammatical gender in noun phrase production: The gender interference effect in German. *Journal of Experimental Psychology: Learning, Memory and Cognition*, 1368–77.

Starreveld, P. A. and La Heij, W. (1995). Semantic interference, orthographic facilitation and their interaction in naming tasks. *Journal of Experimental Psychology: Learning, Memory and Cognition*, 21, 686–98.

Starreveld, P. A. and La Heij, W. (1996). Time-course analysis of semantic and orthographic context effects in picture naming. *Journal of Experimental Psychology: Learning, Memory and Cognition*, 22, 896–918.

Stemberger, J. P. (1985). An interactive activation model of language production. In W. Ellis (ed.), *Progress in the Psychology of Language*, vol. 1, pp, 143–86. Hillsdale, NJ: Lawrence Erlbaum.

Van Hell, J. G. and de Groot, A. M. B. (1998). Conceptual representation in bilinguals' memory: Effects of concreteness and cognate status in word association. *Bilingualism: Language and Cognition*, 1(3), 193–211.

Yeni-Komshian, G. H., Flege, J. E., and Liu, S. (2000). Pronunciation proficiency in the first and second languages of Korean-English bilinguals. *Bilingualism: Language and Cognition*, 3, 131–49.

Bilingualism:
Memory, Cognition,
and Emotion

9 Bilingual Memory

ROBERTO R. HEREDIA AND JEFFREY M. BROWN

9.1 Introduction

How do bilinguals represent their languages in memory? Do bilinguals organize their languages in separate or in shared memory stores? In this chapter, we review some of the major theories of how bilinguals organize their two languages in memory. We start by reviewing early theoretical formulations, and then we go on to evaluate current hierarchical models that assume a memory architecture composed of language-specific mental lexicons and a shared conceptual system. Next, we critically evaluate the distributed model of bilingual memory that poses a bilingual memory structure based on word type. We conclude by evaluating current work on bilingual lexical ambiguity that attempts to determine the extent to which bilinguals activate their two languages simultaneously during language retrieval. Our purpose in this chapter is to be critical and provide, where appropriate, both theoretical and methodological alternatives, as well as suggestions to extend bilingual research to other memory and language processing domains. We begin by discussing and evaluating the formulations of Weinreich (1953) and Ervin and Osgood (1954).

9.2 Early Theoretical Formulations

Weinreich (1953) makes an important theoretical distinction between two levels of representing information in bilingual memory. The signifier or the mode of expression corresponds to the word level or what we presently refer to as the lexical level (e.g. Potter, So, Eckardt and Feldman, 1984). The signified or semanteme corresponds to the meaning or semantic-conceptual representation of the concept represented by a word.

Three types of possible bilingual representations are posed. The coordinate system (figure 9.1) assumes a cognitive configuration that is independent at both the signifier (word) and signified (meaning representation, labeled "A" and "B") levels. This organization suggests that the definitions of *libro* and *book*

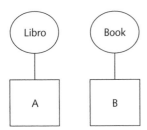

Figure 9.1   Coordinate (Model adapted from Woutersen, Cox, Weltens, and De Bot, 1994; printed with the permission of Cambridge University Press).

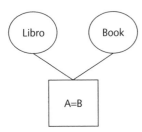

Figure 9.2   Compound (Model adapted from Woutersen, Cox, Weltens, and De Bot, 1994; printed with the permission of Cambridge University Press).

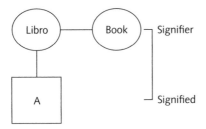

Figure 9.3   Subordinate (Model adapted from Woutersen, Cox, Weltens, and De Bot, 1994; printed with the permission of Cambridge University Press).

are different and represent meanings that may be unique to each language (cf. De Groot, 1993). Thus, for a coordinate Spanish-English bilingual, the meaning of the Spanish word *libro* and its translation (*book*) are different, and both meanings are associated with information that is language-specific.

In the compound system (see figure 9.2), bilinguals possess a single or a fused signified (depicted by A=B) and two signifiers. Thus, for the Spanish-English bilingual the concept of *libro* and *book* is represented by two different words, whereas the underlying meaning is the same across languages. The subordinate system (figure 9.3), on the other hand, views the bilingual as containing one meaning-based representational system in which the second-language (L2) word is simply a translation equivalent of the first-language (L1) word. This architecture suggests that during early stages of L2 learning, bilinguals link every L2 word with the L1 translation equivalent (Kroll and Sholl, 1992; Kroll and Stewart, 1994), and access to the meaning-based representational system must necessarily go through L1 (cf. Kroll and Sholl, 1992; Potter et al., 1984).

Although it is not clear if Weinreich proposed a general model of bilingual memory, or a bilingual memory organization based on word type (cf. De Groot, 1993), Weinreich was the first one to make the theoretical distinction between what present hierarchical models refer to as the lexical (i.e. word) and the conceptual levels (e.g. Kroll and Sholl, 1992; Kroll and Stewart, 1994; Potter et al., 1984). Moreover, Weinreich underscores a memory structure in which L2 learners must go through a series of stages to become fully functional in their two languages. On their way to becoming fully functional bilinguals, L2 learners must first link every L2 word to the L1 equivalent (subordinate), establish relationships between concepts (compound), and, finally, differentiate between the two languages in the appropriate settings. Note, however, that "coordinate bilingual" is not synonymous with "ideal bilingualism" because it would be difficult to argue for a complete separation at the signified level. In other words, there will always be some overlap between the meanings of concepts across languages. Here we are thinking about cognates (words that have similar spelling and meaning across languages) such as *hospital* in English and *hospital* in Spanish, and coordinate concepts such as abstract words (e.g. *temor* vs. *fear*) whose meanings are somewhat constrained to their specific language, but nonetheless they share certain meaning features with the other language. We return to this issue in section 9.3.

9.3 The Bilingual Coordinate–Compound Distinction

The intuitive appeal of Ervin and Osgood's (1954) reformulation of Weinreich's (1953) compound–coordinate representational systems is that it proposes a bilingual memory structure that is based on how or where the L1 and L2 are learned. Whether the bilingual possesses a coordinate or a compound system would depend on the acquisition context. Thus, a person learning the L1 in Mexico and the L2 in the United States would be likely to develop a coordinate representational system. Moreover, this configuration may also arise in an environment in which the L1 is learned at home and the L2 is learned at school or at work. The basic idea here is that each language is learned in different places, taught by different people and in different situations, and these differences are the basis of the somewhat distinct meaning-based representations.

In contrast, the individual learning the two languages in a situation in which both languages are spoken simultaneously by the same people and in the same context would develop a compound structure. Learning an L2 through direct association or by associating every L2 item to its L1 equivalent would give rise to this bilingual mental configuration as well.

Is the compound–coordinate distinction theoretically useful? First, as a general model of bilingual memory, this theory implies that during language learning, bilinguals code linguistic information in a context-specific manner and, moreover, that this information remains somewhat stored and unaltered according to how it was learned. According to this theory, in learning a word such as *padre* in Mexico, one would specifically store an "episodic trace" in LTM of the specific associations surrounding the acquisition of that concept, and likewise in learning the English counterpart *father*. Even if we were to accept "culture-context-specific" associations to this word, these associations would be short-lived and would not play a role in the overall meaning of the concept, especially when using on-line experimental techniques that measure the manner in which bilinguals retrieve information as it occurs in real-time. Any differences that may exist during the learning processes may be due to the nature of the concepts themselves. For example, abstract words and other concepts that are more likely to exhibit language-specific characteristics, in relationship to their usage and overall meanings, will be encoded in a coordinate fashion. Other words such as cognates which share orthographic and meaning representations across languages (cf. De Groot, 1992; De Groot, Dannenburg, and Van Hell, 1994; see also Heredia, 1995, 1997) will be coded in semantic memory in a compound fashion regardless of when or where the learning process took place. What we are suggesting here is that the compound vs. coordinate distinction could be useful when applied to bilingual models describing a bilingual memory configuration based on the degree of semantic overlap between words across languages (cf. De Groot, 1993). However, as a general model of bilingualism, and a model of how L2 is learned and organized, it is difficult to defend, especially if bilinguals achieve higher proficiency levels in their L2 and their L2 becomes the dominant language (Heredia, 1997).

Second, studies supporting the compound-coordinate distinction (e.g. Jakobovitz and Lambert, 1961; Lambert, Havelka, and Crosby, 1958), and those failing to support such a distinction (e.g. Gekoski, Jacobson and Frazao-Brown, 1982; Kolers, 1963; Lambert, Havelka, and Crosby, 1958), may represent underlying differences in the level of bilingual representation. That is, it is not clear whether the research methodology used in this domain was actually measuring the signified or the signifier level as described by Weinreich (1953). Differences in the results may simply reflect the findings that different tasks measure different levels of representation (e.g. Durgunoğlu and Roediger, 1987; Heredia and McLaughlin, 1992; Smith, 1991).

Third, while Ervin and Osgood's proposition may not correspond to a general model of bilingual memory, the compound–coordinate distinction may be useful in the study of bilingual autobiographical memory and bilingual long-term memory. Indeed, Ervin and Osgood's formulation is reminiscent of

Tulving's encoding specificity principle (Tulving and Thompson, 1973), which suggests that contextual factors play an important role in learning and that what is stored in memory represents a combination of the to-be-remembered material and the context. In addition, the to-be-remembered item is encoded in relation to the context in which the learning took place, and as a consequence, it produces a memory trace that contains information from the item and context. Coordinate bilingualism involves learning the two languages in different physical or geographical locations thus leading to two distinct memory traces for the languages. Since encoding specificity entails encoding additional information (e.g. environmental context, mood, etc.), when an item is encoded, it could be argued that learning two languages in two distinct locations would lead to the encoding of two distinct (and different) memory traces (e.g. Schrauf, 2000). In short, what we are proposing here is that autobiographical memories could be classified as coordinate (language-specific) where certain information is only accessible through one language or compounded in the sense that they can be stored and accessed by both languages. The issue here is probably purely methodological and getting to these personal autobiographical memories would require specific studies utilizing appropriate stimuli that are relevant to the particular population in question. We return to the issue of bilingual autobiographical memory later in our discussion. (For additional discussion of the compound–coordinate distinction, see chapters 3 and 7; for more on types of bilinguals, see chapters 1–5, 7, 8, 10, and 22.)

9.4   One Versus Two Memory Systems

The *shared and the separate memory hypotheses* are perhaps the most influential views of bilingual memory representation. According to this proposal, bilinguals either organize their two languages into one shared memory store or into two separate memory systems, where each language is organized independently.

Briefly, the basic methodology in this approach involved having participants learn bilingual (e.g. *house–casa*) and monolingual (e.g. *house–home*) word pairs followed by either a free recall or a recognition task (e.g. Durgunoğlu and Roediger, 1987) or having bilinguals generate word associations in both languages (e.g. Kolers, 1963). Experiments revealing language differences in retrieval were taken as supporting the two memory systems view, whereas failure to obtain language effects was taken as supporting the one memory system approach. Again, the empirical data supported both models (e.g. Keatley, 1992). These mixed results led researchers to conclude that even if experimental findings supported both hypotheses, the shared memory model explained some aspects of language, while the separate model was more appropriate for other aspects. Moreover, it was suggested that bilinguals had neither separate nor shared memories, because some information was restricted to the language of encoding, while some was accessible to both linguistic systems (Durgunoğlu and Roediger, 1987; Kolers and González, 1980).

9.5   The Processes View of Bilingual Memory

One theoretical approach that attempted to clarify the nature of these conflict-ing results emphasized processes rather than mental representations (Durgunoğlu and Roediger, 1987; Heredia and McLaughlin, 1992; Smith, 1991). According to this view, the mixed results in the bilingual literature were due primarily to the fact that previous research failed to consider task demands (e.g. Morris, Bransford, and Franks, 1977). The general argument was that the evidence for the one- or two-memory hypotheses depended upon the processing demands of the retrieval tasks used. Recall tasks that were sensit-ive to semantic and conceptual processes yielded results consistent with the shared memory model (see Paivio, Clark, and Lambert, 1988). On the other hand, tasks that were sensitive to perceptual or lexical processes (i.e. the sim-ilarity between the surface features of the study and test stimulus) generally produced results that showed language-specific features, thus supporting the two-memory model (Durgunoğlu and Roediger, 1987; Kirsner, Smith, Lockhart, King, and Jain, 1984; Scarborough, Gerard, and Cortese, 1984; but see Caramazza and Brones, 1980; Schwanenflugel and Rey, 1986).

Overall, the general conclusion of the processes view was that in studying bilingual memory, task requirements should be considered. Conceptually driven tasks such as free recall measure the bilingual's semantic and conceptual word representations, thus supporting a one memory system view. Moreover, these tasks can be seen as measuring the processes required to access the overall general knowledge store of the two languages, or the general conceptual system. In contrast, data-driven tasks (e.g. lexical decision, word-fragment completion, and naming) that involve perceptual processing support the two memory hypo-thesis. As such, these tasks can be seen as measuring the processes required to access the bilingual lexical system (Smith, 1991).

If bilingual memory representation is a function of how it is measured, what is the current status of bilingual memory research? At the present time, bilin-gual research is more concerned with developing specific memory models to determine how the bilingual's two languages are related in real time and what mechanism and processes are involved during word retrieval and language processing. However, before discussing these models, let us discuss some exciting new developments in bilingual autobiographical memory. (For more on bilingual lexical processing, see chapters 2, 7, 8, and 28.)

9.6   Bilingual Autobiographical Memory

Although theoretical work on bilingual memory, using the traditional learning and memory approach, has diminished in recent years, there remains the vir-tually untouched realm of research on the testing and application of these findings in a practical world setting. Recent work in autobiographical memory seems to be making a mark in the bilingual memory literature by investigating very long-term memory (e.g. Bahrick, Hall, Goggin, Bahrick, and Berger, 1994). This approach is important not only because of its use of applied/naturalistic methods to provide convergent evidence to existing mainstream theoretical formulations from the monolingual literature (see for example, Schrauf and Rubin, 2000), but also for its contribution to the ongoing debate concerning the manner in which bilinguals organize their two languages in memory (e.g. Schrauf, 2000). Likewise, it is interested in determining the extent to which bilingual autobiographical information is stored in a language-specific manner, or in a mode in which information is encoded in both languages and, during retrieval, both languages have equal access to the particular episodic memory trace.

Most notable in this domain is the research by Schrauf and Rubin (e.g. Schrauf, 2000; Schrauf and Rubin, 1998, 2000), which concerns testing the autobiographical memory of Spanish-English bilingual adult immigrants in either Spanish or English. In one study, bilinguals were given a series of cue words used to elicit memories for events in their personal past. Bilinguals were immigrants from various countries in Latin America and all of them immigrated to the United States between the ages of 20 and 35 years. All participants had lived in the United States for 30 years or more. One of the two experimental sessions was performed entirely in Spanish, with Spanish cue words, whereas the other session was done in English, with English cue words. Schrauf and Rubin's (2000) goal was to determine the extent to which autobiographical memories are encoded in a language-specific manner, and whether access to such memories is achieved only through the language in which the experience originally took place. Notice that the encoding specificity principle (see discussion on the coordinate–compound distinction for further details) would predict that earlier memories (i.e. pre-immigration) would be remembered better in Spanish, whereas later memories (i.e. post-immigration) would be remembered better in English. Thus, the bilingual's memories for their personal past would be directly tied to the original language of encoding. Note that in this experiment participants were given the language cues on different days. On one day, participants used the Spanish language cues to try to remember their experiences in Spanish, and on a different day, they were given the English cues to remember their English memories.

The results revealed that when memories were analyzed by language cue, no differences were found in the number of memories accessed between Spanish and English. That is, when bilinguals were asked to produce memories in the Spanish cue word condition, the memories produced were not significantly different from the memories produced in the English cued condition (cf. Marian and Neisser, 2000). However, a major drawback of this methodology is the lack of control over the language of retrieval. In other words, even though the experimental session may have been performed in English, with English cue words that elicited a memory from the bilingual's pre-immigrant past, the participant could have actually recalled the event in Spanish (as the encoding specificity principle would predict), yet reported the event in English, simply because they were required to remember the information in English. In other words, autobiographical memories (as reported by the subjects) may not have appeared to be language-specific, when in actuality they were. Therefore, when participants were asked to say whether the internal language of memories differed from the language cue (i.e. to report the language in which they retrieved the personal memory), the results showed that Spanish memories represented events that occurred earlier in life prior to migration. Likewise, English memories represented events that had occurred after migrating to the United States (see also Schrauf and Rubin, 2000). In short, with this methodological modification, Schrauf and Rubin (2000) demonstrated that autobiographical memories appeared to be encoded in a language-specific manner, as predicted by the encoding specificity principle. That is, pre-immigration autobiographical memories, which were encoded in Spanish, tended to be recalled in Spanish more often than in English. Again, this trend was also evident in the English-only session, in that pre-immigration memories that were communicated in English (as the procedure required) were also reported as being internally retrieved in Spanish. In other words, personal memories that were encoded in Spanish were remembered in Spanish, but reported to the experimenter in English. (For more on bilingual memory and emotion, see chapters 10, 14, and 19.)

Overall, Schrauf and colleagues (see also Marian and Neisser, 2000) provide an important approach to the study of bilingual autobiographical memory. However, one shortcoming of this research is the lack of a theory. At the present time, the usefulness of the shared vs. the separate memory hypotheses is not clear, simply because this view, as we have been arguing, has failed to distinguish between the different possible levels (i.e. lexical vs. conceptual representations) of bilingual memory organization and, undoubtedly, these bilingual memories are encoded beyond the lexical level. Now, the question of interest that remains is how exactly bilinguals encode a particular episode, and how that episode is later retrieved. Is the autobiographical episode recorded as a function of language, or as a function of the event itself (i.e. event-specific)? So far, the evidence suggests that bilingual autobiographical memory retrieval is language-specific.

To conclude this section, we would like to comment on a methodological issue that needs to be addressed. As I (the first author) reminisce about my own memories, at times it is somewhat difficult to assert the extent to which a particular memory has occurred in Spanish or English. However, I may be able to rate (e.g. through a self-rating scale) the extent to which a memory experience has occurred in one language or the other. For example, on a 1 to 7 scale (where 1 = memory all in Spanish and 7 = memory all in English), I might rate a memory episode as a 7 if I am certain that it occurred in Spanish, and perhaps as a 3 if I am not at all sure of the language. What we are suggesting here is that in addition to using frequency or percentages as the dependent variable in the retrieval of autobiographical memories, researchers in this area might wish to consider other measurements such as rating scales. Moreover, as a general issue, the view that bilingual autobiographical memory research may be taken to support the shared or the separate memory hypotheses is reminiscent of some of the original findings using association tasks to measure bilingual capacity (cf. Kolers, 1963; Lambert et al., 1958). Differences in associations generated by bilinguals between their two languages were interpreted as supporting the separate store hypothesis, whereas a lack of differences between languages was seen as supporting the shared memory view. Notice that it would be possible to argue that rate of association generation is a function of language dominance. Simply put, the language that is used more frequently will be more readily accessible, thus generating a higher percentage of associations. Similarly, the frequency or percentage of remembered memories in one particular language could be due to other psycholinguistic mechanisms such as language dominance.

9.7   Bilingual Eyewitness Memory

Another avenue of research that has received virtually no attention is bilingual eyewitness memory. This is surprising given the breadth of research on eyewitness memory and the increasing number of bilinguals in modern society. One exception to this is research by Shaw, García, and Robles (1997), which demonstrated that cross-language misinformation effects are comparable to same-language misinformation effects. This finding suggests that misinformation presented in one language can contaminate the other language. Although this is an interesting finding, further bilingual research is also needed in the areas of eyewitness confidence and the amount and veracity of information elicited from questioning of the witness. These related topics lend themselves to answering various important applied and theoretical questions. For example, does the language of questioning affect the number, quality, and veracity of the bilingual's responses? Schrauf's research would lead us to predict that events that were encoded and later recalled in the bilingual's mother tongue would be more numerous, more emotional, more detailed, and more truthful. Similarly, we argue that a bilingual's confidence and accuracy-confidence correlations (i.e. calibration) could also be moderated by language. If witnesses use ease of retrieval and amount recalled (e.g. Koriat and Sadot, 2001) as subjective measures of confidence, we would predict that questions in the bilingual's L1 (or most proficient language) would elicit more confidence. Moreover, we would also predict higher accuracy-confidence correlations. Clearly, answers to these questions can have profound implications for the legal system while adding to the growing theoretical literature in eyewitness memory.

9.8   Hierarchical Models of Bilingual Memory

9.8.1   *Word association and concept mediation models*

The present view of bilingual memory starts with the assumption that bilinguals organize their two languages into two separate lexicons (Gerard and Scarborough, 1989; Kirsner et al., 1984; Scarborough, Gerard, and Cortese, 1984), and one conceptual system subserving both languages (e.g. Altarriba, 1992; Chen, 1990; Kroll and Sholl, 1992; Kroll and Stewart, 1994; Potter et al., 1984; see also Caramazza and Brones, 1980; Schwanenflugel and Rey, 1986). At the lexical level, bilinguals represent their two languages in separate lexicons, with information specific to each language. The shared conceptual system, on the other hand, is said to contain general abstract information that is language-free.

Early hierarchical models proposed two bilingual memory structures (e.g. Potter et al., 1984; see also Chen, 1990). The *word association model* (figure 9.4) proposes a bilingual memory architecture in which the bilingual's two

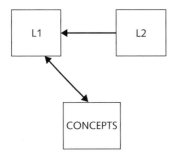

Figure 9.4   Word association model. (Adapted from Kroll and Stewart, 1994; by permission of Academic Press.)

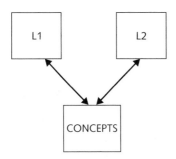

Figure 9.5   Concept mediation model. (Adapted from Kroll and Stewart, 1994; by permission of Academic Press.)

languages interact at the lexical level, based on translation equivalents (Potter et al., 1984). According to this model, the bilingual's L2 is subordinated to the L1. Access to the general conceptual system via the L2 is not possible, unless the L2 word is translated into L1 (cf. Weinreich's (1953) subordinate system). In contrast, the *concept mediation model* (figure 9.5) assumes that the bilingual's two languages operate independently of each other. More important, both lexicons are connected directly (independently) to the conceptual memory store common to both languages. In other words, a bilingual can activate the meaning of a particular concept, regardless of the language or whether the word is translated. Thus, according to Potter et al. (1984), the native and non-native languages of a bilingual operate independently so that words are not associated interlingually, but instead they are associated with the nonlinguistic conceptual system common to both languages. That is, the only connection between the bilingual's two languages is via an underlying amodal conceptual system. An important aspect of these hierarchical models is the assumption that the L2 lexicon is smaller than the L1 lexicon. This difference in lexicon size, it is argued, reflects the notion that bilinguals know more words in their L1 than their L2 (Kroll and Stewart, 1994).

Are these two models describing two different bilingual structures? According to Potter et al.'s original findings, the results supported the concept mediation model, regardless of the participant's second-language proficiency. Potter et al. suggested that words of a second language were associated with corresponding words in the L1 via a common conceptual store, and not by direct associations between vocabulary items, as predicted by the word association model, even for nonfluent bilinguals (Potter et al., 1984). However, other evidence (see for example, Kroll and Sholl, 1992; Kroll and Stewart, 1994) suggested that the word association model described a bilingual structure corresponding to bilinguals at early stages of L2 learning, associating every new L2 word learned with the L1 translation equivalent. In contrast, the concept mediation model described a bilingual structure corresponding to bilinguals with high proficiency levels in their L2. More important were the findings showing that bilinguals translated faster from their L2 to their L1 than from their L1 to their L2. This translation asymmetry held for early and advanced bilinguals (Kroll and Sholl, 1992). Neither the word association model nor the concept mediation model taken alone could account for this pattern of results.

9.8.2 The Revised Hierarchical Model (RHM)

To account for the possibility that bilingual memory may be a function of L2 proficiency and translation direction, Kroll and Sholl (1992) and Kroll and Stewart (1994) (see also Kroll and Tocowicz, 2001) incorporated both the association and the concept mediation models into the RHM (figure 9.6). According to the RHM, the bilingual lexicons are bi-directionally interconnected. The lexical link (represented by a solid line) from the L2 lexicon to the L1

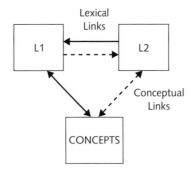

Figure 9.6   Revised Hierarchical Model. (Model adapted from Kroll and Stewart, 1994; by permission of Academic Press.)

lexicon is stronger than the L1 to L2 link, to reflect the way the L2 was learned. Accordingly, during L2 acquisition, bilinguals learn to associate every L2 word with its L1 equivalent (e.g. they learn *house* and associate it with *casa*), thus forming a lexical-level association that remains active and strong (Kroll and Stewart, 1994). Furthermore, this link is assumed to be sensitive to processes that require physical or perceptual characteristics of word translation equivalents. Stronger lexical links from L2 to L1 than in the reverse direction reflect the bilingual's ease of translation. Thus, for a native Spanish speaker, it would be easier to translate *house* to *casa* than *casa* to *house* because every L2 word is mapped onto its L1 equivalent, but not every L1 word is mapped onto its L2 equivalent (Kroll and Stewart, 1994). Moreover, the connection from the L1 to L2 language lexicon (depicted by a broken line) is assumed to be weaker because of a lack of translation practice. However, this link is hypothesized to be sensitive to semantic factors.

At the conceptual level, the conceptual link from the L1 (depicted by a solid line) is stronger than the link from the L2 (represented by a broken line). This difference in strength reflects the fact that L1 is the native language, and bilinguals are more familiar with word meanings in their L1 (Kroll and Sholl, 1992; Kroll and Stewart, 1994). Although it is theoretically possible that the link from L2 to the conceptual store may develop strong connections, Kroll and Stewart argue that this link remains weaker, even for bilinguals with high L2 proficiency levels.

Evidence for the RHM comes from experiments in which bilinguals are asked to translate words from L1 to L2 and vice versa. The general finding, as predicted by the RHM, was the translation asymmetry where translation is faster from L2 to L1 than from L1 to L2. Other evidence supports the assumption that the bilingual's two lexicons are susceptible to differential processing. For example, Kroll and Stewart (1994) utilized a translation task and manipulated the semantic context in which translations were performed.

Participants in this task translated randomized or categorized (e.g. *dress*, *suit*, and *pants* belong to the category 'clothes') lists of words from L1 to L2 or from L2 to L1. The question of interest was whether L1 to L2 translations would be affected more by the change of semantic context (i.e. categorized vs. randomized lists) than L2 to L1 translations, which were assumed to be lexically mediated. Because of the finding that L1 picture naming – which presumably requires conceptual-semantic processing – produced category interference with categorized lists and not randomized lists (experiments 1 and 2) and that translations are similar to L1 picture naming (Potter et al., 1984), Kroll and Stewart (1994) predicted that if L1 to L2 translations were indeed conceptually mediated, L1 to L2 translation would also exhibit category interference.

The results supported the predictions that L1 to L2 translation would be influenced by the change in semantic context of the lists. It took 120 ms more to translate categorized lists from L1 to L2 words than to translate randomized lists from L1 to L2. In contrast, semantic context did not affect L2 to L1 translations. More interestingly, L2 to L1 translations behaved similarly in both the naming and translation tasks (see also Cheung and Chen, 1998). Additional support for this model comes from experiments reporting asymmetrical cross-language priming effects. Briefly, priming is the phenomenon in which a word (e.g. *war*) is responded to faster when preceded by a related word (e.g. *peace*) than when preceded by a nonrelated word (e.g. *cat*). In the bilingual version, participants are presented with a bilingual word pair that is either related (*peace–guerra: war*) or unrelated (*peace–gato: cat*). In one language condition, the prime may be in L1 (*paz*) and the target in L2 (*war*) or vice versa. In general, cross-language priming is obtained, but only if an L2 target is preceded by a related rather than an unrelated L1 prime (but see Fox, 1996; Keatley and De Gelder, 1992). In contrast, regardless of the relatedness between the target and prime, no cross-language priming is obtained if the critical prime is in the L2 (e.g. Fox, 1996; Keatley, Spinks, and De Gelder, 1994). That is, cross-language facilitation is obtained only if the prime is in L1 and the target is in L2. Consistently with the revised hierarchical model, the results suggest that accessing L2 from L1 is conceptual because it is achieved via the conceptual store that is the locus of the semantic priming effect (Keatley, Spinks, and De Gelder, 1994, p. 77). On the other hand, accessing L1 from L2 takes place only at the lexical level, thus producing no semantic priming.

However, experimental findings are beginning to call into question some of the RHM's main assumptions. Recent studies have suggested that both translation directions may be sensitive to meaning-based processing (e.g. De Groot, Dannenburg, and Van Hell, 1994; Heredia, 1995, 1997; La Heij, Hooglander, Kerling, and Van der Velder, 1996; see also Altarriba and Mathis, 1997). For example, Heredia (1995, 1996) had Spanish-English bilinguals translate concrete and abstract words in both language directions. Heredia's results revealed no translation time differences for concrete words in either language direction, suggesting that both translation directions were sensitive to the semantic factors provided by the concrete words (cf. De Groot, 1992; De Groot, Dannenburg, and Van Hell, 1994). More inconsistent with the predictions of the RHM was the finding that in the abstract condition, translating from L1 to L2 was actually faster than translating from L2 to L1. At least in the abstract condition, it appeared that the bilingual's L1 had actually become the L2 (see also Altarriba, 1992, 2001; cf. Jiang and Forster, 2001). These findings were replicated using a translation task (e.g. translate *house* to Spanish *casa*) and a translation recognition task (e.g. see *house–casa* and decide if the word pairs are translation equivalents) (De Groot, 1992), in both the visual (Heredia, 1995) and the auditory modalities (Heredia, 1996, 1997).

Is the RHM able to explain the language translation reversal reported by Heredia (1995, 1996) and others (e.g. Altarriba, 1992)? At the present time, the RHM does not allow for the possibility that effects of translation direction and strength of word translations, and to some extent priming, are not fixed characteristics in bilingualism. Thus unlike the predictions of the RHM, the L1 can fall in strength while L2 can become the dominant language. In other words, bilingual memory representation is not a static representational system but a dynamic system that can be influenced by language usage (Heredia, 1997; Heredia and Altarriba, 2001).

To account for this bilingual translation reversal, Heredia (1996, 1997) proposed a *re-revised hierarchical model* (R2-HM) (see figure 9.7). As can be seen, the main difference between this model and the RHM in figure 9.6 is that R2-HM avoids the terms "L1" and "L2." This is done to avoid the misconception that the L1 or native language has special status and that the L2 is subordinated to the L1. For this reason, R2-HM depicts the bilingual lexicons in terms of the "most dominant language" (MDL) and the "least dominant language" (LDL) lexicons. Our definition of language dominance is similar to the word-frequency effect in which commonly used or high-frequency words are retrieved more quickly than low-frequency or less commonly used words (e.g.

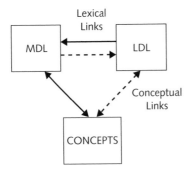

Figure 9.7   Re-revised Hierarchical Model. (Model based on Kroll and Stewart, 1994; by permission of Academic Press.)

Whaley, 1978). The idea here is that words in the language that is used more frequently will be responded to more quickly. By the same token, words in the language that is used less frequently will be responded to more slowly. Thus, according to the R2-HM, regardless of which language is learned first, the more active (dominant) language would determine which lexicon would be accessed faster. According to this model, Heredia's Spanish-English bilinguals were faster in accessing their L2 lexicon simply because it was the language they used more frequently or their most dominant language. Thus, it is theoretically possible for the bilingual's L2 to become the dominant language and the L1 to become the less dominant language. As argued by Heredia (1997), regardless of which language is learned first, the more frequently used language will subordinate the other. In other words, bilingual lexical memory is not a function of lexical capacity, but of which language the bilingual uses more often (Heredia, 1997, p. 38; see also Heredia and Altarriba, 2001). (For additional discussion of the RHM, see chapter 7.)

9.9 Bilingual Memory Representations at the Word Type Level

9.9.1 The distributed model of bilingual memory representations

Next, we briefly discuss a model that, unlike hierarchical models, allows for the possibility that bilingual memory may be represented at the word level (e.g. De Groot, 1992, 1993; De Groot, Dannenburg, and Van Hell, 1994; Van Hell and De Groot, 1998). As can be seen from figure 9.8A–C, the *distributed model of bilingual memory*, henceforth "the distributed model," like hierarchical models, distinguishes between the lexical and conceptual levels. However, the distributed model further elaborates on how the conceptual store may be represented at the word level for different word types. As can be seen in figure 9.8, this model postulates connections from the bilingual lexicons to the conceptual nodes or features, which represent each word meaning. The number

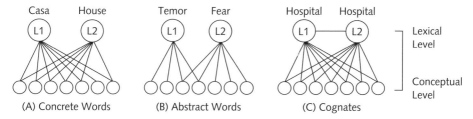

Figure 9.8A–C The distributed model of bilingual memory representations for different word types. (Models adapted from De Groot, 1992.)

of conceptual elements in these memory structures may determine their activation or translation performance. The more similar two concepts are, the more nodes (meaning elements) they will have in common. For example, it has been argued that concrete words (figure 9.8A) are more likely than abstract words (figure 9.8B) to share a number of semantic features across languages. Notice in figure 9.8A that the links from the lexical level to the conceptual level for Spanish *casa* and its English equivalent *house* overlap completely. The same argument applies to cognate words shown in figure 9.8C. In contrast, for abstract words in figure 9.8B the overlap is greatly diminished. Therefore, concrete and cognate words are more likely to be *very similar* in meaning across languages, and abstract words are more likely to exhibit language-specific information (e.g. De Groot, 1992, 1993; De Groot, Dannenburg, and Van Hell, 1994; Van Hell and De Groot, 1998).

Evidence for this model comes from experiments revealing the concreteness effect, in which concrete words are recognized and translated faster than abstract words (De Groot, 1992; Heredia, 1995; Van Hell and De Groot, 1998). In general, concrete words provide more imagery (e.g. Paivio, Clark, and Lambert, 1988), are used more frequently and acquired earlier than abstract words (Schwanenflugel, Akin, and Luh, 1992), are easier to retrieve, and are more accessible. Other recent studies (e.g. Van Hell and De Groot, 1998) suggest a distinction between words of different grammatical status; nouns are more likely to behave similarly to concrete words, and verbs are more likely to behave similarly to abstract words (see also Altarriba, in press).

The usefulness of the distributed model is its explanatory power to describe and capture our intuitions about similarities and differences between words across languages. Figure 9.9 shows a schematic description of the emotion word "love" and its Spanish equivalent "amor" (e.g. Altarriba, in press). Figure 9.9 shows that the English "love" can be used equally for animate (living things) and inanimate (nonliving things). Note that the English concept is polysemous in which some of its meanings can differ substantially from others (e.g. Matlock and Heredia, 2002). In contrast, the hierarchy for Spanish is more complex. "Amor" cannot be used with inanimate things (depicted by a rectangle)

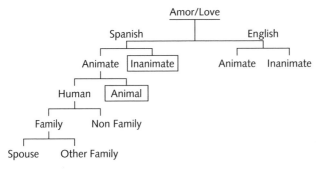

Figure 9.9   A schematic description of *amor* and *love*.

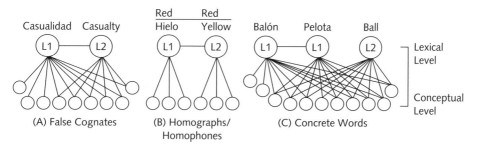

Figure 9.10A–C Possible distributed memory representations for different word types.

and, at the animate level, animals are also excluded. At the human level, the term could be used with non-family members such as "boyfriend" or "girl-friend," whereas at the family level, it is exclusive to husband and wife. However, it would be permissible to describe a "type of love" such as "fatherly love," but not to describe a strong affection towards one's father (e.g. *amo a mi padre*). Again, the distributed model does a very good job in capturing these intuitions.

Similarly, this model does an excellent job in explaining the relationship between false cognates (words that sound or are spelled similarly across languages, but whose meanings are different) across languages (cf. Lalor and Kirsner, 2001). Figure 9.10A depicts a bilingual structure for an "advanced" bilingual that has fused the meanings of *casualidad* and *casualty*, in which the related Spanish meaning ("coincidence") has been replaced/influenced by the English meaning connoting "death" or "injury." The model predicts a configuration with a high degree of semantic overlap between the two concepts, both at the lexical and conceptual levels. However, the Spanish concept may or may not maintain a certain degree of language specificity. Figure 9.10B shows the predicted configuration between homographs (words that are spelled identically but have different meanings) and homophones (words that sound similar, but have different meanings). According to the model, these words may only be related at the lexical level.

Figure 9.10C presents an interesting situation in which an L2 word (*ball*) exhibits a high degree of overlap with one of its Spanish translation equivalents (*pelota*), and less overlap with an alternative translation (*balón*). For example, all *balls* are *pelotas*, but not all balls can be translated to *balones*. The Spanish concept of *balón* describes a large heavy ball that is usually a specialized sports ball, the exception being that a *baseball*, which is small, cannot be called a *balón*. What we are arguing here is that even at the concrete level, words across languages can share some overlapping features, while other features may or may not overlap. In other words, it is possible for concrete words to exhibit both compound and coordinate representations across languages.

In general, the distributed model does an excellent job of describing why certain concepts are similar or different across languages, though, as a general bilingual model, it is limited because it is unable to generate specific testable hypotheses. At least, it is not clear how we can objectively operationalize "degree of word overlap." However, an important aspect of this model is that its claims in terms of degrees of overlapping could easily be implemented into bilingual connectionist models that rely on computer simulations to explain bilingual memory representations (e.g. Li and Farkas, 2002; Léwy and Grosjean, 2001; Van Heuven, Dijkstra, and Grainger, 1998).

9.10   Bilingual Lexical Access

The last issue we address is whether bilinguals retrieve information in a language-selective or nonselective fashion. That is, during lexical access, do bilinguals retrieve information in such a way that only the language that is being used is activated (i.e. *language-selective access*)? Alternatively, during language processing, are the bilingual's two languages activated simultaneously (i.e. *nonselective access*)? Although this important issue has been addressed using such paradigms as speech production and picture processing (e.g. Colomé, 2001; see also Costa, Miozzo, and Caramazza, 1999, and Costa, chapter 8 in this volume), and other traditional word-recognition techniques (e.g. Scarborough, Gerard, and Cortese, 1984), we focus our discussion on cross-language homographs. Cross-linguistic homographs are words such as "pan" whose spellings are identical across languages, but whose meanings are different. The term "pan" in Spanish is associated with "pastries" whereas in English it is related to "cooking utensils." Unlike other word types, cross-language homographs provide a unique opportunity to investigate how bilinguals organize and retrieve these words. Can these words be accessed independently from their respective lexicons without the interference of the other language? Although our purpose in this brief discussion is not to review the monolingual literature (for a review see Simpson, 1994; see Altarriba and Gianico, 2002 for a more recent review of both monolingual and bilingual findings), let us relate the language-selective and nonselective access hypotheses to the monolingual literature. Simpson (1994) discusses three important models of ambiguous word processing that could easily be applied to how bilinguals process and access information. First, the *context-dependent model* states that when ambiguous words (e.g. "bug" as in spy device or as in insect) occurs in a context, the preceding context or the contextually appropriate meaning determines which meaning will be activated in memory. Thus, if the word "bug" is preceded by a context relevant to "James Bond and spy agents" only the meaning appropriate to this context would be activated (but see Swinney, 1979). Notice that this model is similar to the bilingual language-selective access hypothesis. In the bilingual case, language provides the contextual information.

Second, the *context-independent model* holds that during language processing, previous context does not influence the activation of word meanings.

According to this model, the meaning that is more frequent or "dominant" will be retrieved (Simpson, 1994). This model corresponds to the bilingual "nonselective access" hypothesis. Third, the *exhaustive or multiple access model* assumes that during language processing all meanings of an ambiguous word are activated, and that this activation is not influenced by frequency or prior context. Accordingly, selection of the proper meaning occurs only after all possible meanings have undergone initial processing (Simpson, 1994, p. 360).

To summarize, the bilingual literature on homograph processing supports the context-independent model. For example, in a now classic study, Beauvillain and Grainger (1987) had English-French and French-English bilinguals perform lexical decisions on homographs (*pain*) followed by their related English meaning (*ache*) or unrelated English meaning. Participants were told that the first word (the homograph) would always be a French word and that the second word would always be a related or unrelated English word. In this experiment, the target homograph was never followed by its French related meaning. The results revealed that at short stimulus onset asynchrony (SOA) durations (150 ms), significant priming was obtained for the French reading of the homograph and the English related meaning. However, no priming or lexical activation was found when longer SOAs (750 ms) were used. English related words were no different than unrelated words. This finding suggests that during initial processing of homographs, bilingual lexical access is indeed nonselective. In an additional experiment that manipulated language mode (whether presentation was in English or French) and relative frequency (whether the homograph was high or low frequency in English and French), Beauvillain and Grainger found no effects of language mode, and greater lexical activation for high-frequency words only (cf. Gerard and Scarborough, 1989). These results suggest that bilingual lexical activation is a function of the homograph's relative frequency, as predicted by the context-independent model (see also De Groot, Delmaar, and Lupker, 2000; Jared and Kroll, 2001; cf. Colomé, 2001; Costa, Miozzo, and Caramazza, 1999).

Overall, the idea that bilingual lexical access is independent of language mode is an exciting possibility that needs further research and clarification. However, this issue is perhaps best addressed with studies using the sentence as the experimental unit (e.g. Hernández, Bates, and Ávila, 1996; see also Heredia and Altarriba, 2002; Heredia and Stewart, 2002). Simply put, to assess whether or not language mode is playing a role in bilingual lexical access, Beavillain and Grainger's results need to be replicated at the sentential level. Moreover, another factor that needs further examination is the influence of contextual information on both language mode and bilingual lexical access. That is, to what extent is contextual information influencing both language mode and lexical access? As an example, consider sentence (1a). The English term *YELLOW* and the Spanish word *Hielo* are English-Spanish homophones. Upon listening to this sentence, are bilinguals more likely to activate the English-related meaning (e.g. 'color') than the Spanish related meaning (e.g. 'ice')? Now consider sentence (1b). In this sentence, prior context is biased toward the English meaning of the homophone.

(1a)   She liked *YELLOW* because it was a pleasant color

(1b)   She liked [**blue more than**] *YELLOW* because it was a pleasant color

Notice that with this kind of design it would be possible to address the *exhaustive or multiple access model* that assumes lexical access is not influenced by word frequency or prior context (cf. Li and Yip, 1998). How can we best address these issues methodologically? What we are suggesting here is the use of such tasks as the cross-modal lexical priming technique or the phoneme-triggered lexical decision task, which use spoken sentences and rely on priming as an index of lexical activation (e.g. Heredia and Stewart, 2002; see also Altarriba and Gianico, 2002; Hernández, Bates, and Ávila, 1996). For example, in sentences (1a,b), activation of the English meaning of the homophone would lead to a statistically significant priming effect, where bilinguals respond faster to a related word, than an unrelated word. In contrast, lack of lexical activation for the Spanish meaning of the homophone would be revealed by the absence of the priming effect. Clearly, more research in this area is needed to determine the extent to which bilingual lexical access is context-independent or exhaustive in nature (see for example, Hernández et al., 1996).

9.11   Conclusions

In this chapter, we have reviewed what we believe are the most influential theories and research topics in the study of bilingual memory. Another topic that we did not cover, but which deserves further examination is the tip-of-the-tongue phenomenon (TOT). TOTs are examples of temporary retrieval failures in which people are unable to recall a specific word, yet they have strong subjective feelings that given enough time they would eventually recall the desired word. Although this phenomenon has received a lot of attention in the monolingual literature, to the best of our knowledge, there is only one study in the bilingual literature (Askari, 1999). Researchers investigating issues related to code switching or language mixing would benefit from using TOTs to understand retrieval failures and the processes associated with code switching. Overall, most of the studies that we covered in this review have utilized the isolated word as the experimental unit. However, recent developments in the field suggest that bilingual research is beginning to move away from the isolated-word level and to address other general language-processing issues such as bilingual sentence processing and figurative language processing (e.g. Heredia and Altarriba, 2002).

ACKNOWLEDGMENT

We would like to thank our students in the Psychology of Bilingualism class (Spring 2002) for their insightful comments and suggestions in the preparation of this manuscript.

REFERENCES

Altarriba, J. (1992). The representation of translation equivalents in bilingual memory. In R. J. Harris (ed.), *Cognitive Processing in Bilinguals*, pp. 157–74). Amsterdam: Elsevier Science.

Altarriba, J. (2001). Language processing and memory retrieval in Spanish-English bilinguals. *Spanish Applied Linguistics*, 4, 215–45.

Altarriba, J. (in press). Does "cariño" equal "liking"? A theoretical approach to conceptual nonequivalence between languages. *International Journal of Bilingualism*.

Altarriba, J. and Gianico, J. L. (2002). The use of sentence contexts in reading, memory and semantic disambiguation. In R. R. Heredia and J. Altarriba (eds.), *Bilingual Sentence Processing*, pp. 111–35. Amsterdam: Elsevier Science.

Altarriba, J. and Mathis, K. M. (1997). Conceptual and lexical development in second language acquisition. *Journal of Memory and Language*, 36, 550–68.

Askari, N. (1999). Priming effects on the tip-of-the-tongue states in Farsi-English bilinguals. *Journal of Psycholinguistic Research*, 28, 197–212.

Bahrick, H. P., Hall, L. K., Goggin, J. P., Bahrick, L. E., and Berger, S. A. (1994). Fifty years of language maintenance and language dominance in bilingual Hispanic immigrants. *Journal of Experimental Psychology: General*, 123, 264–83.

Beauvillain, C. and Grainger, J. (1987). Accessing interlexical homographs: Some limitations of a language-selective access. *Journal of Memory and Language*, 26, 658–72.

Caramazza, A. and Brones, I. (1980). Semantic classification by bilinguals. *Canadian Journal of Psychology*, 34, 77–81.

Chen, H.-C. (1990). Lexical processing in a non-native language: Effects of language proficiency and learning strategy. *Memory and Cognition*, 18, 279–88.

Cheung, H. and Chen, H.-C. (1998). Lexical and conceptual processing in Chinese-English bilinguals: Further evidence for asymmetry. *Memory and Cognition*, 26, 1002–13.

Colomé, A. (2001). Lexical activation in bilinguals' speech production: Language-specific or language-independent? *Journal of Memory and Language*, 45, 721–36.

Costa, A., Miozzo, M., and Caramazza, A. (1999). Lexical selection in bilinguals: Do words in the bilinguals' two lexicons compete for selection? *Journal of Memory and Language*, 41, 365–97.

De Groot, A. M. B. (1992). Determinants of word translation. *Journal of Experimental Psychology: Learning, Memory and Cognition*, 18, 1001–18.

De Groot, A. M. B. (1993). Word-type effects in bilingual processing tasks:

Support for a mixed-representational system. In R. Schreuder and B. Weltens (eds.), *The Bilingual Lexicon*, pp. 27–51. Amsterdam: John Benjamins.

De Groot, A. M. B., Dannenburg, L., and Van Hell, J. G. (1994). Forward and backward word translation by bilinguals. *Journal of Memory and Language*, 33, 600–29.

De Groot, A. M. B., Delmaar, P., and Lupker, S. J. (2000). The process of interlexical homographs in translation recognition and lexical decision: Support for non-selective access to bilingual memory. *Quarterly Journal of Experimental Psychology: Human Experimental Psychology*, 53, 397–428.

Durgunoğlu, A. Y. and Roediger, H. L. (1987). Test differences in accessing bilingual memory. *Journal of Memory and Language*, 26, 377–91.

Ervin, S. and Osgood, C. (1954). Psycholinguistics: A survey of theory and research problems. In C. Osgood and T. Sebeok (eds.), *Psycholinguistics*, pp. 139–46. Baltimore, MD: Waverly Press.

Fox, E. (1996). Cross-language priming from ignored words: Evidence for a common representational system in bilinguals. *Journal of Memory and Language*, 35, 353–70.

Gekoski, W. L., Jacobson, Z. J., and Frazao-Brown, A. P. (1982). Visual masking and linguistic independence in bilinguals. *Canadian Journal of Psychology*, 36, 108–16.

Gerald, L. D. and Scarborough, D. L. (1989). Language-specific lexical access of homographs by bilinguals. *Journal of Experimental Psychology: Learning, Memory and Cognition*, 15, 305–15.

Heredia, R. R. (1995). Concreteness effects in high frequency words: A test of the revised hierarchical and the mixed models of bilingual memory representations. Unpublished Ph.D.

dissertation, University of California, Santa Cruz.

Heredia, R. R. (1996). Bilingual memory: A re-revised version of the hierarchical model of bilingual memory. *The Newsletter of the Center For Research in Language*, 10 (Winter), 3–6. University of California, San Diego.

Heredia, R. R. (1997). Bilingual memory and hierarchical models: A case for language dominance. *Current Directions in Psychological Science*, 6, 34–9.

Heredia, R. R. and Altarriba, J. (2001). Bilingual language mixing: Why do bilinguals code-switch? *Current Directions in Psychological Science*, 10, 164–8.

Heredia, R. R. and Altarriba, J. (eds.). (2002). *Bilingual sentence processing*. Amsterdam: Elsevier Science.

Heredia, R. R. and. McLaughlin, B. (1992). Bilingual memory revisited. In R. J. Harris (ed.), *Cognitive Processing in Bilinguals*, pp. 91–103. Amsterdam: Elsevier Science.

Heredia, R. R. and Stewart, M. T. (2002). On-line methods in spoken language research. In R. R. Heredia and J. Altarriba (eds.), *Bilingual Sentence Processing*, pp. 7–28. Amsterdam: Elsevier Science.

Hernández, A. E., Bates, E., and Ávila, L. X. (1996). Processing across the language boundary: A cross-modal priming study of Spanish-English bilinguals. *Journal of Experimental Psychology: Learning, Memory and Cognition*, 22, 846–64.

Jakobovitz, L. A. and Lambert, W. E. (1961). Semantic satiation among bilinguals. *Journal of Experimental Psychology*, 62, 576–82.

Jared, D. and Kroll, J. F. (2001). Do bilinguals activate phonological representations in one or both of their languages when naming words? *Journal of Memory and Language*, 44, 2–31.

Jiang, N. and Forster, K. I. (2001). Cross-language priming asymmetries in lexical decision and episodic recognition. *Journal of Memory and Language*, 44, 32–51.

Keatley, C. W. (1992). History of bilingualism research in cognitive psychology. In R. Harris (ed.), *Cognitive Processing in Bilinguals*, pp. 157–74. Amsterdam: Elsevier Science.

Keatley, C. and De Gelder, B. (1992). The bilingual primed lexical decision task: Cross-language priming disappears with speeded responses. *European Journal of Cognitive Psychology*, 4, 273–92.

Keatley, C. W., Spinks, J. A., and De Gelder, B. (1994). Asymmetrical cross-language priming effects. *Memory and Cognition*, 22, 70–84.

Kirsner, K., Smith, M. C., Lockhart, R. S., King, M., and Jain, M. (1984). The bilingual lexicon: Language-specific units in an integrated network. *Journal of Verbal Learning and Verbal Behavior*, 23, 519–39.

Kolers, P. A. (1963). Interlingual associations. *Journal of Verbal Learning and Verbal Behavior*, 2, 291–300.

Kolers, P. A. and González, E. (1980). Memory for words, synonyms, and translations. *Journal of Experimental Psychology: Human Learning and Memory*, 6, 53–65.

Koriat, A. and Sadot, R. (2001). The combined contributions of cue-familiarity and accessibility heuristics to feeling of knowing. *Journal of Experimental Psychology: Learning, Memory and Cognition*, 27, 34–53.

Kroll, J. F. and Sholl, A. (1992). Lexical and conceptual memory in fluent and nonfluent bilinguals. In R. J. Harris (ed.), *Cognitive Processing in Bilinguals*, pp. 191–206. Amsterdam: Elsevier Science.

Kroll, J. F. and Stewart, E. (1994). Category interference in translation and picture naming: Evidence for asymmetric connections between bilingual memory representations. *Journal of Memory and Language*, 33, 149–74.

Kroll, J. F. and Tokowicz, N. (2001). The development of conceptual representation for words in a second language. In J. Nicol (ed.), *One Mind, Two Languages: Bilingual Language Processing*. Malden, MA: Blackwell.

La Heij, W., Hooglander, A., Kerling, R., and Van der Velder, E. (1996). Nonverbal context effects in forward and backward word translation: Evidence for conceptual mediation. *Journal of Memory and Language*, 35, 648–65.

Lalor, E. and Kirsner, K. (2001). The representation of "false" cognates in the bilingual lexicon. *Psychonomic Bulletin and Review*, 8, 552–9.

Lambert, W. E., Havelka, J., and Crosby, C. (1958). The influence of language-acquisition contexts on bilingualism. *Journal of Abnormal Social Psychology*, 56, 239–44.

Lévy, N. and Grosjean, F. (2001). The computerized version of BIMOLA: A bilingual model of lexical access. MS in preparation, University of Neuchâtel, Switzerland.

Li, P. and Farkas, I. (2002). A self-organizing connectionist model of bilingual processing. In R. R. Heredia and J. Altarriba (eds.), *Bilingual Sentence Processing*, pp. 59–85. Amsterdam: Elsevier Science.

Li, P. and Yip, M. C. (1998). Context effects and the processing of spoken homophones. *Reading and Writing: An Interdisciplinary Journal*, 10, 223–43.

Marian, V. and Neisser, U. (2000). Language-dependent recall of autobiographical memories. *Journal of Experimental Psychology: General*, 129, 361–8.

Matlock, T. and Heredia, R. R. (2002). Lexical access of phrasal verbs and verb-prepositions by monolinguals and bilinguals. In R. R. Heredia and J. Altarriba (eds.), *Bilingual Sentence Processing*, pp. 251–03). Amsterdam: Elsevier Science.

Morris, C. D., Bransford, J. D., and Franks, J. J. (1977). Levels of processing versus transfer appropriate processing. *Journal of Verbal Learning and Verbal Behavior*, 16, 519–33.

Paivio, P., Clark, J. M., and Lambert, W. E. (1988). Bilingual dual-coding theory and semantic-repetition effects. *Journal of Experimental Psychology: Learning, Memory and Cognition*, 14, 163–72.

Potter, M. C., So, K., Eckardt, V., and Feldman, L. (1984). Lexical and conceptual representation in beginning and proficient bilinguals. *Journal of Verbal Learning and Verbal Behavior*, 23, 23–38.

Scarborough, D. L., Gerard, L., and Cortese, C. (1984). Independence of lexical access in bilingual word recognition. *Journal of Verbal Learning and Verbal Behavior*, 23, 84–99.

Schrauf, R. W. (2000). Bilingual autobiographical memory: Experimental studies and clinical cases. *Culture and Psychology*, 6, 387–417.

Schrauf, R. W. and Rubin, D. C. (1998). Bilingual autobiographical memory in older adult immigrants: A test of cognitive explanations of the reminiscence bump and the linguistic encoding of memories. *Journal of Memory and Language*, 39, 437–57.

Schrauf, R. W. and Rubin, D. C. (2000). Internal languages of retrieval: The bilingual encoding of memories for the personal past. *Memory and Cognition*, 28, 616–23.

Schwanenflugel, P. J., Akin, C., and Luh, W.-M. (1992). Context availability and the recall of abstract and concrete words. *Memory and Cognition*, 20, 96–104.

Schwanenflugel, P. J. and Rey, M. (1986). Interlingual semantic facilitation: Evidence for a common representational system in the bilingual lexicon. *Journal of Memory and Language*, 25, 605–18.

Shaw, J. S., III, García, L. A., and Robles, B. E. (1997). Cross-language postevent misinformation in Spanish-English bilingual witnesses. *Journal of Applied Psychology*, 82, 889–99.

Simpson, G. B. (1994). Context and the processing of ambiguous words. In M. A. Gernsbacher (ed.), *Handbook of Psycholinguistics*, pp. 33–56. San Diego, CA: Academic Press.

Smith, M. C. (1991). On the recruitment of semantic information for word fragment completion evidence from bilingual priming. *Journal of Experimental Psychology: Learning, Memory and Cognition*, 17, 234–44.

Swinney, D. A. (1979). Lexical access during sentence comprehension: (Re)consideration of context effects. *Journal of Verbal Learning and Verbal Behaviour*, 18, 645–59.

Tulving, E. and Thompson, D. M. (1973). Encoding specificity and retrieval processing in episodic memory. *Psychological Review*, 80, 352–73.

Van Hell, J. G. and De Groot, A. M. B. (1998). Conceptual representation in bilingual memory: Effects of concreteness and cognate status in word association. *Bilingualism: Language and Cognition*, 1, 193–211.

Van Heuven, W. J. B., Dijkstra, T., and Grainger, J. (1998). Orthographical neighborhood effects in bilingual work recognition. *Journal of Memory and Language*, 39, 458–83.

Weinreich, U. (1953). *Languages in Contact*. New York: The Linguistic Circle of New York.

Whaley, C. P. (1978). Word-nonword classification time. *Journal of Verbal Learning and Verbal Behavior*, 17, 143–54.

Woutersen, M., Cox, A., Weltens, B., and de Bot, K. (1994). Lexical aspects of standard dialect bilingualism. *Applied Psycholinguistics*, 15, 447–73.

FURTHER READING

De Groot, A. M. B. and Nas, G. L. J. (1991). Lexical representation of cognates and noncognates in compound bilinguals. *Journal of Memory and Language*, 30, 90–123.

Francis, W. S. (1999). Cognitive integration of language memory in bilinguals: Semanttc Representation. *Psychological Bulletin*, 125, 193–222.

Javier, R. A., Barroso, F., and Muñoz, M. A. (1993). Autobiographical memory in bilinguals. *Journal of Psycholinguistic Research*, 22, 319–38.

Macnamara, J. and Kushnir, S. L. (1971). Linguistic independence of bilinguals: The input switch. *Journal of Verbal Learning and Verbal Behavior*, 10, 480–7.

Nicol, J. (ed.) (2001). *One Mind, Two Languages: Bilingual Language Processing*. Malden, MA: Blackwell.

Sholl, A., Sankaranarayanan, A., and Kroll, J. F. (1995). Transfer between picture naming and translation: A test of asymmetries in bilingual memory. *Psychological Science*, 6, 45–9.

10 Bilingualism: Language, Emotion, and Mental Health

JEANETTE ALTARRIBA AND
RACHEL G. MORIER

10.1 Introduction

Most researchers in the field of bilingualism would agree that there are likely more people in the world who consider themselves bilingual or multilingual than monolingual (cf. Bialystok, 2001; Schreuder and Weltens, 1993). The complexity, however, with defining oneself as bilingual comes from the fact that language proficiency might range from having some conversational fluency and no reading ability in a second language to being fully versed in reading, writing and speaking in two languages. There may be different degrees of bilingualism depending upon the language modality one considers. Researchers have sometimes described bilinguals in terms of the degree of knowledge they possess in a given language. The term *functional* might be used to describe a bilingual's language abilities in one or the other language if they have enough proficiency within a specific knowledge domain such as their job or career (Baetens-Beardsmore, 1986). Some researchers consider the age at which an individual acquires each language or the context within which the languages are acquired (e.g. structured training and instruction vs. informal instruction at home) as the primary determinants of the definition of bilingualism (Hamers and Blanc, 2000; Hoffmann, 1991). Other definitions exist that focus on *how* a bilingual's languages were acquired. Individuals who learn one language exclusively for the first part of their life and later learn a second language, typically in a different context or location than the first, are often called *coordinate* bilinguals (Ervin, 1961; Ervin and Osgood, 1954; Grosjean, 1982). In other instances, bilinguals may learn both of their languages simultaneously within the same context and timeframe. These individuals are often referred to as *compound* bilinguals. In this case, individuals are often more likely to code experiences in two languages and learn to label their thoughts and emotions by the use of two language systems at the same time. For compound bilinguals, it is possible that certain past experiences can be revealed easily in two languages. However, interestingly, for coordinate bilinguals, it might be the case that certain experiences, such as the first time certain emotions are experienced and labeled, occur only in one language – the native language. The idea then that emotions might be coded differently in two languages emerges as a function of when an individual learns emotion concepts and which language is used when they are first expressed (Altarriba, 2003).

Language is a primary means through which emotions are labeled and later expressed (Altarriba, Bauer, and Benvenuto, 1999). In the case of bilinguals, more than one language is involved in coding emotional events in the past and learning how to label those emotional experiences. It has often been noted (e.g. Goleman, 1995) that the ability to correctly label one's emotions and to describe appropriately emotions in others is directly related to overall mental health and well-being. The ability to express one's own emotions and describe them in detail is often one of the primary steps towards positive therapeutic outcomes with clients who seek mental health services. The primary purpose of the present work is to describe how bilingual speakers use their languages to express emotion, how language is used to code past experiences and personal events differentially across languages, and how language-specific and culture-specific techniques and procedures can be applied to a mental health setting involving bilingual speakers. Cultural issues in treatment that relate to bilingualism such as difficulties in assessment and evaluation and issues regarding the use of language interpreters will also be discussed. In addition, considerations for the training and education of mental health workers will be described as culturally sensitive treatment modalities are being developed that address the specific issues facing bilinguals and their mental health (Santiago-Rivera, 1995).

10.2 Bilingualism and Emotion: How Bilinguals Use Language to Express their Emotions

Researchers have noted that emotions are often shaped by the social or cultural context in which they are experienced rather than being the result solely of biological determinants (see e.g. Campos, Campos, and Barrett, 1989; Lutz, 1988). Kitayama and Markus (1994) noted that cultural processes work to organize and structure emotional experiences and that descriptions of emotions may vary cross-culturally. In fact, anthropologists have identified a category of emotion called indigenous emotions – those that are non-Western and have no clear counterparts in the West (Doi, 1986, 1990). In the therapeutic setting, emotions are most commonly expressed using language and language labels. Therefore, emotion and culture are closely intertwined and can likely best be examined through the use of the language in which they are expressed. The current section reviews the literature on how emotion is coded and used in therapeutic sessions, how descriptions of emotions are tied to the language in which they were experienced, and the implications of switching between languages when discussing emotionally charged experiences.

10.2.1 Emotional expression in the mother tongue vs. a second language

Researchers have examined the role of language and the order in which languages are acquired when investigating the origin of emotion word vocabulary (e.g. Guttfreund, 1990; Schrauf, 1999). A native or mother tongue will likely be used to code very early experiences during childhood, and those language codes will be associated to thoughts and feelings driven by the context of acquisition (Silva, 2000). The way in which these emotion word labels are represented in memory is likely different than the ways in which words learned later, in a second language, are stored. Bond and Lai (1986) have claimed that one's second language is typically acquired in a more emotionally neutral setting than one's first language.

However, not all researchers have reported this mother-tongue benefit for emotion word representation. Guttfreund (1990) investigated the effects of language usage on the reported emotional experiences of Spanish-English and English-Spanish bilinguals. Participants were randomly assigned to either a mother-tongue condition or a second-language condition. They were asked to complete several measures aimed at assessing their mood state and trait anxiety. The results indicated that all participants answered with significantly greater affect in *Spanish* whether or not it was the mother tongue or the second language learned. Moreover, different levels of anxiety and depression were reported depending upon which particular language the participant used to respond. These findings are important as they contradict earlier work by Marcos (1976) and Rozensky and Gomez (1983) who reported a bias towards responding in the mother tongue on emotionally related topics. The present findings indicate that not only might context of acquisition play a significant role in how emotion is encoded, but the nature of the specific language might also influence emotion word representation (Altarriba, 2003). Language-specific nuances should play a role in the usage of emotion word terms in a given language. In conclusion, it is clear that in cases of psychological assessment and diagnosis, a bilingual may appear to present him- or herself in different ways depending on the language used. Guttfreund further concluded, "for the Hispanic population the therapeutic process may be far more meaningful in Spanish, because members of this population are likely to feel more comfortable expressing their feelings in Spanish" (p. 606).

10.2.2 Bilingual autobiographical memory

An area of current research interest in both the monolingual and bilingual literature is the area of autobiographical memory – memory for events in one's own past (Hunt and Ellis, 1999). It appears from the literature cited earlier that individuals code emotion differently in different languages and that those representations may depend on the events that occurred when the emotion was acquired. The relationship between the context of acquisition of an emotion word label and its subsequent use and recollection from memory appears to moderate the use of emotion in the therapeutic setting. The current section provides a critical review of the extant literature on bilingual autobiographical memory.

How are past events linguistically coded for bilingual speakers? Javier, Barroso, and Muñoz (1993) investigated memory for personal events in a group of Spanish-English bilingual speakers. They claimed that prior bilingual memory research reflected the encoding, storage and retrieval of information of a non-personal nature and therefore the results could not be transferred to memory for autobiographical events. Javier and colleagues noted that language can serve as a powerful retrieval function, a cue, to the events that were experienced in the past. Language serves as a feature with which to organize events that have been stored in memory. They noted, "Thus, a word, for instance, may function as a schema of experience which includes symbolic representation as well as the more sensory and perceptual components of the experience under consideration" (p. 321).

Javier et al. (1993) had bilingual participants describe an event in their personal histories for approximately five minutes. Individuals were asked to select an interesting or dramatic personal life experience. These same participants were later asked to discuss the same experience, but in the alternate language. The experimenters analyzed their recall protocols in terms of numbers of ideas or idea units expressed and the organizational structure of the ideas that were recalled. Across languages, differences were observed in the quantity and quality (affectively) of the idea units that were expressed. As predicted, the nature and quality of the reports given in the language in which the experience occurred was richer than in the second language of report. There was evidence of language-specific information as individuals who recalled life experiences that were coded in a particular language produced more elaborate recall of that information when probed in the corresponding language. It appears that each language of a bilingual may serve to represent experiences in slightly different ways. If the corresponding language is accessed as a cue to memory retrieval, the resulting account may prove richer and more elaborate. Experiences appeared to be related more vividly when recounted in the language in which they had been experienced.

While the work of Javier et al. (1993) was important in many ways, not the least of which was to serve as a beginning to this area of investigation, their work is not without concerns. Perhaps including controls in which more neutral experiences were also discussed would aid in discerning whether non-emotion experiences would also benefit from dominant language recall. In addition, it is clear that there would be variation in terms of the event that is selected by individuals. Perhaps having individuals describe an equally emotional event that was more public or known, such as the death of a president or a major news item, would aid in equating the types of experience that are described. The use of "flashbulb memory" (e.g. Brown and Kulik, 1977) experiences such as these are yet to be explored among bilingual speakers.

Javier (1995) continued along similar lines and investigated the area of repressed memories with reference to the language in which they were originally experienced. He contended that certain memories might be more accessible in one language (perhaps the language in which they were encoded) than in another language for a bilingual speaker. Repression, therefore, may be a function of the accessibility of a memory, in a particular language. In a psychoanalytic approach to therapy, it is clear that one goal leading to positive outcomes might be to recover memories and anxiety-provoking thoughts from the unconscious and bring them into conscious awareness. However, with bilingual patients it is important to note that those memories might be coded in a specific language and might only be revealed by processing the events in that language in therapy (see also Aragno and Schlachet, 1996; Buxbaum, 1949; Greenson, 1950; Javier, 1989; and Pérez-Foster, 1992). Javier (1995) reported in one case study that a female patient was only able to access her repressed memories by discussing them in a language other than the one in which their initiating events occurred. That is, in this Spanish-English bilingual, English was used to assist in distancing the individual from the pain associated with the repressed memories and allowed the individual to discuss those events in a productive fashion. Later, once the events had been verbalized, Spanish became possible as a language that could be used in therapy, revealing the actual events that had occurred. In this way, it appears that the least dominant language, the one in which the traumatic events had not been encoded, served as a stepping-stone allowing for the release of the repressed memory into conscious awareness. Clearly, the analysis of a variety of case studies dealing with repressed memories in bilinguals may provide a clearer picture of how language can be used strategically to produce positive outcomes in therapy. Further analysis of a full array of experiences is warranted for further verification of Javier's (1995) suggestions.

Additional experimental research on the issue of autobiographical memory retrieval in bilinguals comes from work by Schrauf and Rubin (1998). They asked ten elderly participants who were Spanish-English bilinguals and had lived in the United States for at least 30 years to associate specific word cues (e.g. dream, love, dog) to memories from their past. Individuals wrote brief descriptions of these personal events in either English or Spanish on alternate days. Certain memories that had been recalled specifically in Spanish related to earlier experiences that pre-dated the participants' emigration. Likewise, memories that had been recalled in English represented a greater proportion of more recent events – those following immigration. However, when the data are viewed in terms of the nature of the events reported to a word in a specific language prompt, first-language prompts did not seem to elicit more early memories than second-language prompts. It is possible that these individuals, who had been in the United States for over 30 years, had used both languages sufficiently to be able to exhibit a certain degree of language independence when performing the current task.

In a more recent investigation, Marian and Neisser (2000) examined bilingual autobiographical memory from the perspective of encoding specificity theory (e.g. Tulving and Thompson, 1973). This theory notes that a cue that was present when information was encoded will be successful at retrieval in helping to recollect the original event. One can consider a specific *language* as an effective retrieval cue if it matches the language in which the original event or experience was encoded. In their first experiment, Marian and Neisser predicted that Russian-English participants would produce a greater number of memories of events that occurred in their first language if they were interviewed in that same language. If interviewed in the second language, the authors hypothesized that a greater number of memories would emerge for events that occurred when the second language was in use. Participants did indeed retrieve more experiences in Russian from the Russian-speaking periods within their lifetimes and more English-speaking memories from those epochs in their lifetimes. Thus, their initial hypotheses regarding encoding specificity were confirmed. However, unlike the work of Schrauf and Rubin (1998), participants in the current study also produced more language-specific memories to specific language prompts. Language prompts (e.g. birthday) served as specific retrieval cues leading individuals to respond with memories that matched the language of the prompts, at interview. The authors suggest that these individuals were still processing information in both of their languages sufficiently to have a more balanced set of memories coded in each language – some of which were actually coded in *both* languages. Therefore, in contrast to Schrauf and Rubin, word prompts here acted to cue specific episodic memories that could be relatively accessed and retrieved within the course of the experimental session. One comment that would apply to both of the aforementioned studies is that participants had to respond under the pressure of time, leading to the activation of memories that was likely more automatic than strategic. It would be interesting to investigate the processing of language-specific memories without the constraint of time to assess the differential patterns of language access. It is possible that given enough time, individuals would be able to report similar experiences in both languages, depending on the specific memory, rather than in just one, primary language.

Many of the events that are recounted in the process of therapy or counseling are emotion-laden or emotion-related. One question that arises is whether or not the notion of language-specificity in autobiographical memory relates specifically to memories of emotional events. Schrauf (2000) notes that memories from childhood and adolescence that were experienced in the mother tongue or native language are typically richer in terms of emotional significance when recounted in that specific language. One might consider this an example of *state-dependent* learning where the state is, in fact, the language context in which the event was originally experienced. According to the Mother Tongue Hypothesis, an individual should retrieve memories from their childhood in greater detail and with a richer emotional vocabulary in the language that was spoken during childhood. Schrauf suggests that these states are also self-representations and are mired in culture and socialization practices that involve linguistic coding. As a bilingual speaker's languages are a tool for representing the self in therapy, the implications are clear – the use of one language to the exclusion of the other may present a representation of an individual that is lacking or not wholly accurate. The use of both languages is therefore recommended when probing issues regarding the personal past (see also Altarriba and Santiago-Rivera, 1994).

In a related article, Schrauf and Rubin (2000) noted that language of encoding for events in one's life becomes a stable characteristic or property of a memory. Just as one might encode physical context, feelings, information, etc., the language in which that episode takes place becomes an entry in the representation of the totality of the event. Schrauf and Rubin examined autobiographical memory recall for individuals whose average age was 66 years. These were Spanish-English bilinguals who had lived in the United States for an average of approximately 38 years. All were competent in both Spanish and English. Participants were presented with a series of cue words (e.g. party, money, doctor) and were asked to write down a related memory that came to mind. Cues were presented in either English or Spanish on two separate days. The results indicated that participants retrieved memories in Spanish for those events that occurred in the country of origin; memories retrieved in English were those that had been created in the United States. This occurred despite the fact that participants were not given instructions as to whether or not the memories should be recent or from some prior point in the past. Participants selectively reported information that was consistent with the language in which the event was encoded, as it related to a particular cue. The authors concluded, "The internal language of retrieval points to an underlying, specifically linguistic, memory that is stable over time and that reflects the language used at the time of encoding" (p. 622).

10.2.3 Code/language switching and emotion

Finally, not only is it the case that certain memories appear to be coded with specific *language tags* (Altarriba and Soltano, 1996), bilinguals often take advantage of the ability to switch between languages in order to capture the concepts that they are trying to communicate. In this section, an attempt will be made to define code switching and provide examples of how this might occur. Further, some possible explanations for this phenomenon will be explored in preparation for a discussion of the use of this skill in the therapeutic setting.

In code switching or language mixing, an individual substitutes a word or phrase in a given language with a counterpart in another language. This can occur within phrases or across sentences (see Heredia and Altarriba, 2001, and Bhatia and Ritchie, 1996, for reviews). For example, an individual might say, "*Yo quiero un glass of water.*" Representing the entire sentence in English would yield, "*I want a glass of water.*" In the first instance, the early part of the sentence context has been expressed in Spanish while the second part is expressed in English. It is interesting to note that the act of language mixing is actually rule-governed and happens in such a way as to preserve grammatical structure within languages. Little is known about why individuals choose to code-switch, especially since it has been noted that there may be a time cost associated with switching (see e.g. Kolers, 1966). While it has been suggested that code switching occurs because of a knowledge deficit in one or the other language (cf. Grosjean, 1982), it is likely that part of the problem resides in the inability to access the appropriate word in the base language one is speaking in, in a timely fashion. This *tip-of-the-tongue phenomenon* may explain why individuals switch languages thus providing an easier route to the access of a particular concept (see A. S. Brown, 1991, for a review of the monolingual literature). A final possible explanation is that bilingual speakers choose to code-switch in a strategic manner in order to be better understood. It has been noted that words often do not have direct word-to-word translations across languages (Altarriba, 2003). Therefore, certain language-specific words can best be expressed in a given language and cannot be captured by any single word or perhaps group of words in another language. This nonequivalence between language concepts may be a major motivating factor behind code-switching behavior (see also Wierzbicka, 1997). As described in the next section, this latter explanation underlies the use of language mixing and language switching in therapeutic settings with bilingual populations.

10.3   Therapy with Bilinguals: How Differences in Language Expression Affect Therapy

Effective therapy requires that an understanding between the client and the counselor be reached. The counselor must understand the presenting issues of the client as well as the goals that the client may wish to reach through therapy. The client must trust the counselor and feel they are being understood. In this section we will explore the unique position of the bilingual client. We will consider the effects and possible benefits of language switching, cultural implications, strategies when dealing with bilinguals, benefits and pitfalls when using interpreters, and how education of counselors has been adapted to treat the ever-growing bilingual population, and discuss the imperative considerations that one must examine when working with bilinguals. Lastly, we will demonstrate how educational programs must grow with the better understanding of bilinguals and therapeutic interventions that are to be gained from documented research.

10.3.1   *Implications of code/language switching*

As we have seen, the access that bilinguals have to two languages has benefits. For instance, they can be more expressive since they are not limited to just one language. Clients have a choice as to what language to use and thereby have the ability to select the word that most clearly captures the essence of what they are trying to communicate. Bilinguals can also use their second language to serve a distancing function when discussing troubling events (Pérez-Foster, 1998; Pitta, Marcos, and Alpert, 1978). Likewise, studies have shown that words themselves elicit different emotions when spoken in one's native language as opposed to the second language.

Gonzalez-Reigosa (1976) found taboo words to be associated with higher anxiety when presented in the native language rather than the second language. Bond and Lai's (1986) study took this idea a step further by looking at how easily embarrassing topics were discussed in a native language (Cantonese) and a second language (English). A group of female undergraduate students from the University of Hong Kong conducted interviews with one another in both the first and second languages. The topics of the interviews were either neutral or embarrassing. The two embarrassing topics called for a description of a recently experienced embarrassing event that they had personally experienced, as well as a discussion of sexual attitudes prevalent in Chinese and Western culture. Based on the length of time that the interviewee spoke on the topics, this study appears to show that code switching into one's second language made it easier for the interviewee to speak about the embarrassing topic for a greater length of time. This finding seems to suggest a distancing function inherent in a bilingual's second language.

Marcos (1976) named the emotional detachment that bilinguals often have in their second language as the *detachment effect*. In his theory, he described the second language as serving an intellectual function and being devoid of emotion; whereas the native language expressed the emotional content. Marcos believed that this split could be maximized or minimized depending upon what the goals of the therapy were. For instance, if the patient were describing a particularly upsetting event to the therapist, the second language could be used to prevent the client from becoming too overcome with grief to continue. The therapist could serve as a guide to the patient with regard to what language is used. If patients seemed ready to deal with the emotions, the therapist could encourage patients to use their native language. Depending on whether or not the therapist was also bilingual, patients would then be asked to fully translate what they had said, or a trained interpreter would be asked to translate. Ideally, the therapist would be able to understand the native tongue and continue the conversation in the language that the patient wished to continue speaking in (Altarriba and Santiago-Rivera, 1994; Santiago-Rivera and Altarriba, 2002).

Rozensky and Gomez (1983) take Marcos's (1976) ideas involving emotion and language a step further by looking at them in light of a psycholinguistic model, and a psychodynamic model. Thass-Thienemann (1973) introduced the idea that the context through which the mother tongue and second language are acquired affects the ways in which the languages are expressed. Since the learning of a second language is often formalized, rationalized, and "founded upon the conflict-free sphere of the ego" (p. 131), it is often not involved in the emotional conflicts in the way that the mother tongue is. Therefore, feelings, repressed emotions, and emotional awareness are more likely to reside in the mother tongue and are best expressed in that language.

Based on the perspective of a psycholinguistic model, communication is seen as a two-step process, constructed first from the way we ourselves see the world, then from how we express our representation of the world to others (Bandler and Grinder, 1975). Mixing psychotherapeutic principles with this psycholinguistic idea in the case of bilinguals, experiences undergo a double linguistic distortion when discussed in therapy (Grinder and Bandler, 1976). First, the client must remember the event or emotion in the native tongue and then structurally translate the memory into the foreign language. In therapy, the client would hopefully be able to use the two languages to gain a fuller understanding of the situation, utilizing language switching as a way to move closer to or to create distance from the emotional conflict.

In light of a psychodynamic model, the mother tongue is seen as useful in recognizing unconscious thoughts, desires, and affect, as well as early emotions and memories. However, a return to the mother tongue may also be used to regress to a childlike state or even repress material further (Rozensky and Gomez, 1983). Rozensky and Gomez believed that repressed material may be accessed through the first or second language; however, the mother tongue would reflect the event most accurately. The therapist could gain the clearest understanding of these emotions through the controlled use of language switching in therapy. The authors provided four case examples of how the language switching technique is used as a powerful tool in therapy.

In the first case, a 47-year-old Hispanic woman was experiencing a reactive depression due to marital conflicts. She was feeling lonely and "out of touch" with her husband and had begun an affair with a 20-year-old Hispanic man. Throughout the affair she and the man spoke to each other in Spanish, and she felt being with him filled part of her emptiness. In her relationship with her husband, and also with her bilingual therapist she predominantly spoke English. The relationship with her lover and her confusion over what to do in the situation prompted her to begin therapy, but the focus soon shifted to her hurt and anger over her lover's decision to leave first and go back to his native land. Language switching was used to help her describe the emotions she was feeling. In English the anger, hurt, and sadness she was describing did not match her affect; instead, she appeared detached and described it in a very intellectualized manner.

The mother tongue once again brought forth the appropriate affect and opened up the emotionality of the patient in the second case. In this case a 57-year-old woman with a history of stressful conflicts and both physical and sexual abuse throughout her life was referred to a therapist because of numerous physical and psychological ailments. She suffered from depression, anxiety, and memory problems. Physically she was obese, in large part due to an ever present nervous hunger. Her obesity contributed to heart palpitations, ulcers, headaches, and swollen extremities. Her home life was extremely stressful and her abusive children had all turned to drugs, crime, and prostitution. Her feelings of self-worth were being explored through therapy and she was expressing her strong objections to her own possible hospitalization. As the therapist probed her to explain her trepidation she could not provide an explanation. The therapist then asked her to try in Spanish. At this point she began to cry stating she couldn't because she was too afraid. She was too afraid that if she opened up in Spanish that she would "never come out." This clearly illustrates the distancing function of the second language. The hurt and conflict that appeared to be stored in her mother tongue was able to hide behind the less emotional and more intellectualized second language.

In cases three and four it is shown how switching into the mother tongue can allow for earlier memories which explain present emotions to be accessed and uncovered. Case three was that of a 40-year-old German woman who had lived in the United States for 15 years. She was a widow and had a difficult time in relationships with men, often feeling as though she was being controlled. In a discussion with the therapist on how she felt about herself, she described herself as "marked" and "evil." When asked to describe herself in German she stated her mother used to call her the "*unbestandig*," the German word for unpredictable. This unpredictability also caused her father not to trust her around boys. Although this seems to suggest nonequivalence between languages, in the ensuing conversation, by uncovering her reasons for linking these two words, we are able to infer that the cause of the apparent nonequivalence may be that her memories have been coded in two separate languages. Her mother's early description of her as unpredictable and lacking impulse control appeared to carry over into her later feelings of sexuality and natural impulses toward men. These feelings seemed to be translated into evil as she began relationships with men. Without the early memory of her mother speaking to her in German, her understanding of her difficulty in relationships with men could not have transpired.

The last case was that of a 42-year-old Hispanic woman who was seeking treatment to alleviate her feelings of depression and anxiety. She felt unsupported and ineffectual within her family and had a deep fear of rejection and loss of love. As she tried to explain her past family life in an effort to understand her current emotions, she struggled to articulate her memories. As she switched over into her native language of Spanish her memory of being taken out of the home of her beloved grandmother to move back in with her mother became all the more clear. At this moment she began to understand how it felt to be taken away from the person she felt closest to and whom she felt the most love from and for. She also remembered how helpless she was in this situation. Recalling this situation in Spanish brought up all of the emotions she had not been in touch with. She began to cry and remember once again the tremendous loss she had felt as a child.

These case examples demonstrate clearly how language switching can be so useful in therapy. The skilled therapist is able to assess the situation and lead the patient to switch languages in a way that allows for memories and emotions to be accessed (Santiago-Rivera and Altarriba, 2002). In addition, patients are allowed the freedom to use the languages they have stored to understand their own feelings and past memories. This benefit to the patient can be maximized as the therapist learns to understand the role of language switching in therapy with bilinguals.

Rozensky and Gomez (1983) added several other factors that are important for the therapist to be aware of when working with a bilingual patient. For one, the therapist should be aware of what language is predominantly used in the patient's life as well as in which situation each language is used. Secondly, the age at which the patient acquired the second language as well as the circumstances through which they learned it is an important variable to consider. Lastly, the affective level of the languages should be assessed. If the language is considered highly emotionally expressive, then it can be assumed that more affective material would be stored in that particular language. Grinder and Bandler (1976) felt that it was of the utmost importance that the therapist had a full understanding of how clients organize their experience and what language system is the most valued in their understanding of the world. This then could allow the therapist to proceed in therapy to expand the client's understanding of the world in a way that is most beneficial to the client.

10.3.2   The transference and countertransference phenomena

Clauss (1998) describes the process through which clients verbalize their understanding of the world to the therapist, and the extent to which the therapist clearly understands the clients' perceptions. This process added to the bicultural experience of bilingual patients is central to the psychodynamic transference –countertransference phenomenon. Clauss presents a case showing how the transferential phenomenon serves an object relational function through its association with language switching for the bilingual. Clauss also introduces information on countertransferential processes and how they affect the clinician's language experience.

These phenomena take into account the way language alters how clients view themselves, and how this in turn affects the therapist. A classic example was presented by Greenson (1950): a bilingual woman revealed herself as an anxious woman in English, and as a dirty child in her native language of German. This difference in her self-representation had to do with her memories and experiences in each language. This occurrence provides more evidence for what Javier (1989) termed *language independence*. Language independence refers to the bilingual's ability to acquire and maintain two separate languages, complete with their own lexical, syntactic, semantic, phonetic, and ideational aspects. The languages each house separate cognitive and emotional components for the individual. Therefore, simply speaking in one language as opposed to another can change the client's self-concept.

10.3.3   Cultural implications of language structure

Language structure itself can explain a lot regarding the values of the culture itself. Understanding the values of the culture is important in realizing what therapeutic interventions will be most helpful to the patient. For instance, in the English language the pronoun *I* is always capitalized, exhibiting the emphasis on the individual that is inherent in American culture. In Spanish *yo* is used to express the individual. The *y* is not capitalized, implying that the focus is less on the individual and more on the family or group. The contrast between the two cultures is important in explaining the research finding that group psychotherapy is a successful method of intervention for Spanish-speaking cultures (J. A. Brown, 1981; Clauss, 1998; Delgado, 1981, 1983; Maduro, 1976; Tylim, 1982). In individual-centered cultures, in contrast, therapy often involves just the individual and the therapist. To conclude, the cultural values of the patient should be fully understood and assessed by the clinician so that a course of treatment can be designed to fully maximize benefits to the patient.

Altarriba (2002) has discussed the semantic or conceptual nonequivalence between many words across languages. This phenomenon greatly impacts the therapeutic process between bilinguals and the clinician. Whereas there are benefits to having knowledge of two languages, it has been shown time and time again that the nonequivalence can greatly complicate therapeutic matters. It has been pointed out that although some concrete, abstract, and emotion words are similarly represented across certain languages with regard to their concreteness and imageability, emotion words are more easily contextualized in Spanish (Altarriba, 2002). These findings present issues that should be taken into account in therapy with bilinguals. In particular, miscommunication may be present when a monolingual clinician is trying to fully understand what the bilingual patient is trying to express. When the parties have different ideas of what has and has not been expressed, then the therapy session is jeopardized.

10.4   Culture-specific Strategies in Therapy

Since the early 1960s, public criticism of the ethnocentric and culturally encapsulated traditions of the mental health field has persisted (Pedersen, Draguns, Lonner, and Trimble, 1981; D. W. Sue, 1981; Wrenn, 1962, 1985). Research has shown the negative effects of culturally insensitive services, citing findings that have shown that Asian Americans, blacks, Latinos, and Native Americans often fail to use traditional mental health services, or choose to terminate therapy after only one session (Special Populations Task Force of the President's

Commission on Mental Health, 1978; D. W. Sue, 1977; S. Sue, 1977). The following sections outline some of the cultural values and beliefs that affect the outcome of mental health treatments in specific populations. The idea is that cross-cultural differences in both verbal and nonverbal communication should be considered in mental health care settings.

10.4.1   Cultural differences and norms

Hall (1969) identified the amount of space that is typical in United States culture in different levels of interpersonal communication. He found that when the communication was of an intimate nature, distance ranged from contact to 1.5 feet. Personal communication ranged from 1.5 to 4 feet. For social communication the distance ranged from 4 to 12 feet, and public settings such as lectures or speeches typically had a distance of 12 or more feet. Reactions to an invasion of space were found to be anywhere from withdrawal to anger or conflict (Baron and Needel, 1980; Pearson, 1985).

There is a marked difference between the amount of space many Americans prefer and that preferred by other cultures. This type of research is called *proxemics*. Proxemics is the study of how one perceives and uses both personal and interpersonal space (Sue and Sue 1990). This area has yielded many interesting findings within and between different cultures. Jensen (1985) found that Arabs, South Americans, French, Africans, and Indonesians liked a much closer stance than Northwest Europeans. Jensen also found a cultural difference among Americans. He found that black and Hispanic Americans stood closer during interactions than Caucasian populations. This illustrates that even within one's own country (particularly a diverse country like the United States) differences must be acknowledged so that groups of people are not alienated or misunderstood. In a counseling setting it is imperative that these differences are acknowledged so that seating as well as other arrangements are made that will ensure the greatest amount of comfort for the client, as well as for the counselor.

Kinesics and *paralanguage* are other areas of research that could become very useful in helping to understand the less obvious parts of the communication process. Kinesics includes body movements such as posture, facial expression, eye contact, and other gestures, which are often dependent upon culture. In some east Asian cultures such as Chinese and Japanese, restraint from all emotion ranging from anger and sadness to happiness and love is considered a sign of strength, maturity, and wisdom. This has led to stereotypes of some Asian peoples as inscrutable, sneaky, or deceptive, and in the case of therapy can cause them to be seen as out of touch with their emotions. In the reverse, this can also cause stereotypes to arise about less restrained cultures.

Among many Americans, handshaking is a common type of greeting. This seemingly simple act varies quite a bit depending on the culture and the situation. For example, Latin Americans have been shown to shake hands more often and vigorously, and for longer periods of time (Eakins and Eakins, 1985; Jensen, 1985). Eye contact is another example of a nonverbal behavior that can be considered a sign of respect in some cultures, while in other cultures it can be seen as a sign of disobedience and outward hostility. Traditional Navajos rely mostly on peripheral vision when speaking to others and consider direct stares to be hostile and are most often used to direct or punish children (Knapp, 1972). Direct eye contact is also avoided by some Mexican Americans and Japanese, and is seen as a sign of disrespect. Eye contact appears to be more valued by whites than blacks as a sign of attention to the conversation (Smith, 1981). Another notable difference between black and white Americans was the lack among the former of minor vocal cues such as "uh-huhs" and of head nods as a sign of active listening (Hall, 1976; Kochman, 1981; Smith, 1981). It seemed to be superfluous to many blacks as it was already expected that one was listening.

Differences between cultures must be understood by therapists to avoid alienating patients who may be from particular cultural backgrounds. Learning about the culture of the patient one is treating is important, as it is the only way to put their issues into proper perspective. The importance of culture is also central to therapeutic treatments, as we will demonstrate in the next section in a discussion on specific therapies and techniques.

10.4.2 *Culturally specific techniques for therapy*

A useful tool in clinical therapy is the metaphor. The ability of the metaphor to "apply a word or phrase to an object or concept it does not literally denote, in order to suggest comparison with another object or concept" (Urdang and Flexner, 1968, p. 840) allows for a better understanding of a situation through comparison with something similar. Looking at situations peripherally as opposed to straight on may allow a clearer view, since it moves it out of the original realm so it can be broken down and defined. Barker (1985) noted that clients often resist points that are made directly. As Littleman (1985) suggested, metaphors have the ability to reach an affective aspect of an individual's personality that often is too strongly defended to be accessible.

Ingrained in metaphors is the power to motivate people and springboard new insights and ideas. Metaphors facilitate an openness of the mind that is very beneficial in therapy. Metaphors exhibit cultural beliefs and ideas that can and should be used in therapy. In Latino culture, *dichos* (folk sayings) may be used to promote a culturally appropriate ambience for the patient. Establishing a relationship with clients, particularly through *platicando*, which is casual, leisurely chatting, has been documented as extremely important when working with Latinos (Gomez and Cook, 1977). This type of chatting creates a warm atmosphere conducive to conversation.

Zuñiga (1992) explains how *dichos* express the heritage and cultural values of Mexican and Spanish heritage, and aid in therapy with Latino clients. In Spanish culture these sayings are used to develop and demonstrate moral values, attitudes and appropriate social behaviors. Through *dichos*, the world view and psychology of the people can be understood. Zuñiga offers ways in which *dichos* can be implemented in therapy. For one, clinicians should become aware of the different kinds of *dichos* so that they can be used in appropriate situations. For instance, a client coming in feeling dispirited or hopeless may like to hear something comforting, such as *"No hay mal que por bien no venga,"* which translates into "there is nothing bad from which good does not come." This phrase is much like the common phrase in English, "it's a blessing in disguise" (Galvan and Teschner, 1989, p. 132). Other important messages that *dichos* may include center around principles such as self-responsibility, taking risks, hard work, patience, forgiveness, and dealing with novel situations (Zuñiga, 1992).

It is sometimes difficult for patients to accept changes during therapy, because of fear related to being stripped of their cultural values. Zuñiga (1992) explains this tendency by providing a case example of a 23-year-old Chicana college student. This young woman came from a dysfunctional family. She was under tremendous pressure from an overabundance of familial responsibilities that were having a negative effect on her academic performance. In therapy, she was working through issues resulting from being the child of an alcoholic mother and father. This situation in her family caused her to lose her role as a child, and instead become the "parentified child." In addition, she was made to feel guilty for having college and career aspirations. The social worker used a *dicho* that dealt with a person's own individuality and uniqueness as a way to help her understand her role, in a culturally sensitive way. This *dicho*, "Cada cabeza es un mundo", existed in the client's own culture and enabled her to embrace the idea that "you have a right to seek something, even if it is different from those around you" (Zuñiga, 1992).

Another case of a young woman feeling pressure to fulfill a cultural script of becoming a wife and mother led to therapy when she found herself in an abusive relationship. This 21-year-old Chicana college student was feeling family pressure to get married. The man she was expected to marry was unfaithful to her, and had begun beating her as she became more assertive in the relationship. Confused, and afraid to disappoint her family, she was afraid to leave the relationship. The therapist recited a *dicho* for her and asked her to explain what she felt it meant. The *dicho*, *"Mejor sola que mal acompañada,"* stated that it was better to be alone than to be in an unhealthy relationship. The young woman immediately recognized this point and now felt assured that her own culture would support her decision not to marry her abusive boyfriend. Through therapy, she eventually worked up the courage to apply to graduate school and reach for the goals she wished to accomplish before starting a family.

Using *dichos* or other culturally specific proverbs with bilingual clients can be very successful in therapy. However, there are proper ways in which they should be used in order to provide the maximum benefit. Naturally, bilingual clinicians familiar with the particular culture of a client have an advantage in that they are more aware of useful metaphors for various situations. Clinicians who do not have a lot of familiarity with the client's culture can still make use of such metaphors by familiarizing themselves with some of the cultural values of the client and the culture, as well as through research on various cultural metaphors. The sole fact that the clinician recognized the culture of the client and would make an effort to become familiar with it would surely help foster the relationship with the client. The client may also provide assistance to the clinician with pronunciation or further share their culture. This type of respectful, considerate, and reciprocal relationship is conducive to very valuable therapy sessions for both the client and the clinician.

10.5   Use of Interpreters

One of the more controversial solutions in helping bilinguals communicate with mental health professionals is the use of interpreters. While this is often the most realistic and easiest way for a counselor who doesn't speak the patient's native language to converse with the bilingual patient, there are many concerns and problems with this method, some of which are described below.

10.5.1   *Problems and issues when using interpreters in therapy*

Marcos (1979) and Vasquez and Javier (1991) acknowledged several common errors that less trained interpreters make when included in therapy sessions. These errors include omission of valuable information or emotional expression, addition, substitution, and misinterpretation of the patient's communications, as well as condensation of the patient's thoughts. Interpreters have been found in some cases to paraphrase or try to "make sense" of the patient's cognitions and phrases. When there is a relationship between the patient and the interpreter, familial or otherwise, the interpreter may try to answer for the patient. The interpreter may also try to protect the client by maximizing or minimizing the emotions of the patient.

Vasquez and Javier (1991) explained the process of role exchange between the interpreter and clinician and its implications. The sense of power that interpreters feel in their role has a tendency to get out of hand in some cases and the interpreter attempts to take on the role of the therapist. Interpreters may interject their own opinions as to the diagnosis or treatment methods, and not ask or explain pertinent questions that the clinician is trying to discuss with the patient. Errors such as these can have very negative effects on the therapeutic process and, most importantly, the overall outcome for the patient. In two case examples from Vasquez and Javier's study, the use of an untrained interpreter caused suicidal tendencies to be enhanced and exaggerated in one patient, and downplayed and ignored in another.

In the first case, a Spanish-speaking woman was brought into the ER (Emergency Room) after swallowing a number of pills. The woman was interviewed by an English-speaking doctor and had her 15-year-old nephew acting as her interpreter. The woman had been suffering from depression and other problems in large part due to the recent death of her mother, financial difficulties, and other problems due to her recent immigration. Fearing what would happen if she were to be hospitalized she had the boy tell the doctor it was a mistake and nothing was ever mentioned with regard to her depression and the voices she was hearing of her dead mother. A week later the woman was admitted again after attempting to jump out of a fifth-floor window. This case exhibits the dangers of using both untrained interpreters and family members. It is not difficult to imagine the awkward position of the young boy who not only didn't completely understand the situation, but also did not want to go against the wishes of his aunt. If the person interpreting is a family member, then the objectivity that is necessary when interpreting is lacking and makes it difficult for the therapist to do their job.

In the second case, a 40-year-old woman came to seek advice from the therapist on how to deal with her 14-year-old mildly retarded son who had just been hospitalized with an acute psychotic condition. The therapist's aide acted as an interpreter. Throughout the conversation with the client, the interpreter paraphrased what both the therapist and the client expressed. The interpreter was also treated as the middle-man with the clinician directing questions and comments toward the interpreter. This caused the interpreter to change the question when asking the client. The interpreter also focused on certain parts of what the client said and repeated them back to the clinician out of context, often not using the same words. In this case, the feelings of frustration that the woman was experiencing because of the situation with her son were presented by the interpreter as hopelessness and helplessness in her life as a result in part of the problems with her son. She was made to look as though she was having suicidal thoughts and was ready to kill herself. The focus was taken away from her son and was put onto her and her own difficulties. The distortion caused by the interpreter caused the woman to be misunderstood and as a result not to receive the treatment that she was seeking. Had the therapist had a clear view of what was actually occurring in the patient's mind through what they were expressing, the patient could have been treated properly.

The necessity of the therapist to provide appropriate empathetic responses in the therapeutic process may also be jeopardized by unskilled interpreters. In some cases the subtle expressions of empathy are completely ignored by the interpreter and not expressed to the patient. Empathy is extremely useful in helping the client to feel comfortable and, in turn, serves as a guide encouraging the client to further express their emotions. Also, the subtle utterances of the patient often speak volumes to the skilled therapist; unless these subtleties are picked up by the interpreter, they are lost. If an interpreter is being used in therapy they need to be aware of such subtleties and be trained to be sensitive to how even slight changes to what the client communicates can greatly impact the therapeutic process. It is very easy for language to be changed and put into a different context.

Due to the likelihood of such errors, Vasquez and Javier (1991) suggest that untrained interpreters not be used in therapy. However, if they are used it is strongly advised that the counselor carefully observe the patient's nonverbal cues and responses, as well as be aware of the interpreter's behavior. In doing so, the counselor can notice and hopefully cut down on role exchange, omission, addition, condensation, and substitution.

10.5.2   Benefits to having interpreters in therapy sessions

Despite the aforementioned concerns, the interpreter has a very interesting and valuable role. The understanding of the client's culture, and familiarity with the culture of the therapist can help bridge the gap between the two different cultures. The interpreter can aid in an understanding between the therapist and the patient that goes beyond the level of just language. Unique cultural traditions exist in all cultures, and recognition of them allows for better communication and understanding all round.

In addition, the interpreter would be responsible for putting at ease the client who may be uncomfortable with the idea of receiving mental health services. Many cultures have preconceived notions regarding mental health services. In some Asian cultures, it is seen as a pitiable profession. In Hispanic cultures it is often considered unnecessary, because it is expected that problems will be discussed within the family or with a member of the clergy (Altarriba and Bauer, 1998a, b). The trained bilingual, bicultural person would act as an outreach worker serving to inform the other members of the community and break through some of the cultural barriers.

However, interpreters themselves may share some difficult memories with those they are helping, and recognition of this possibility should be addressed. Since many immigrants come to the United States, for example, to seek refuge from devastating circumstances in their homelands, with them may come disturbing memories or traumas from their past. Such is the case with refugees from the Middle East, Bosnia, and other countries facing hardship. If the person interpreting such atrocities has had similar trauma, then it is possible that taking an active role in such a discussion could bring forth upsetting memories and force them to relive such traumas. This is another reason why training interpreters is so important. Training interpreters to be aware of possible situations, as well as to find their own boundaries in what they feel comfortable being exposed to, is necessary, and only fair to the interpreter.

10.5.3   Training and education for interpreters

A full understanding of the possible pitfalls that can occur with the presence of interpreters in therapy aids in the development of educational programs that can prevent such problems. It has been concluded repeatedly that untrained interpreters should be eliminated from therapy. Education for bilingual and bicultural persons wishing to act as interpreters should cover many areas. Musser-Granski and Carillo (1997) suggest that in the USA coursework should include topics such as English language and American culture, mental health terminology, concepts and interventions, interpretation of words and affect, medications, crisis intervention, case management, beginning counseling skills, interviewing techniques, and many others. The bilingual, bicultural trainee would have a better understanding of the therapeutic process and be able to assist the therapist in an informed and professional manner.

10.6 Cultural Issues in the Treatment of Bilinguals

As was discussed in the previous section, when treating bilingual individuals the therapist must be aware of particular matters involving language and culture. Minding these factors in therapy with bilinguals and bicultural populations is most important in increasing the quality of mental health services and also in decreasing the overall dropout rate (Flaskerud, 1986). It has been reported that minority populations, in comparison to whites, have been under-represented in the case loads of mental health agencies considering the break-down of the population (Snowden and Cheung, 1990, cited in Sue, 1991; Sue, 1977). In this section, we will further examine the actual utilization of mental health services by various minority populations, as well as some of the cultural barriers that prevent them from seeking out and maintaining therapy.

10.6.1 Utilization of mental health services by minority populations

Several factors have been cited as contributing to the underutilization of mental health services by ethnic minorities. In an investigation of mental health services received by thousands of outpatients in Los Angeles, Sue (1991) noted many differences among races and ethnic groups. The population studied consisted of many thousands of Asian American, Mexican American, African American, and white clients over a five-year period. The study was specifically designed to examine the length of treatment, the kind of services received, and the overall outcome of the clients. The authors hypothesized that an ethnic match between client and therapist would be beneficial to the client. This study yielded many interesting findings. It was found that African Americans tended to overutilize mental health services, whereas Asian and Mexican Americans underutilized them. However, dropout rates were highest in African Americans then, in descending order, whites, Mexican Americans, and Asian Americans. Although Asian Americans were least likely to go into treatment, once they entered they typically stayed longer and had significantly better outcomes than African Americans. Ethnic match proved to have an effect on the length of treatment, but not on the outcomes except in the case of Mexican

Americans. Perhaps most important to this particular topic was the finding that among clients who spoke a dominant language that wasn't English, an ethnicity and language match between client and therapist was a predictor of both the length of treatment and the overall outcome. This seems to suggest that a certain rapport and understanding is evoked by the similar ethnic characteristics between the therapist and client. Other reasons may include language and cultural understanding of the therapist. This is not to say that a therapist must be of the same ethnicity as the client, but it does make a case for the importance of culturally sensitive services.

Ethnicity-specific mental health programs have been shown to help alleviate the problem of high dropout rates among minority groups (Takeuchi, Sue, and Yeh, 1995). Wu and Windle (1980) also reported a direct relationship between utilization of mental health services by African and Asian Americans, and an increase in the hiring of diverse groups by these services. In a study similar to that by Sue (1991) previously discussed, Takeuchi and colleagues (1995) conducted a study over a six-year period comparing return rates, length of treatment program, and the overall outcome as a function of either an ethnicity-specific or mainstream therapeutic program. Ethnicity-specific programs provide more culturally appropriate services through ethnically similar staff and modified treatment (Sue, 1977). The purpose of the authors' research was to test whether these programs are effective, and the research showed that they were actually quite effective. The return rate for ethnicity-specific programs was higher than that of mainstream programs in African Americans, Asian Americans, and Mexican Americans, although the overall treatment outcome wasn't very clear from the data. Also unclear was what specific aspects made ethnicity-specific programs more beneficial in terms of rate of return. This is an area that future research may need to examine further. It also should be noted that the study conducted by Takeuchi and colleagues primarily looked at culture and did not address language. Nevertheless, due to the cultural diversity of bilinguals, these findings are important to their position as consumers of mental health services.

10.6.2   *Cultural barriers in treatment with bilinguals*

An explanation for the underutilization of mental health services appears to be that in many family-centered cultures it is expected that mental health problems should not be discussed outside of the family. Relatives, elders, clergy, and/or family doctors are typically the people that they are expected to turn to when having difficulties. Aside from relying on family to help solve emotional problems and mental health issues, many cultures rely on religion, faith, and spirituality to get through difficult times. Traditional healers such as acupuncturists, root doctors, herbalists, *curanderos*, and voodoo practitioners, in addition to family doctors, are some of the resources that are used to treat mental problems (Flaskerud, 1986; Lin, 1983; Keefe, Padilla, and Carlos, 1979; Maduro, 1983; Snow, 1983).

Family cohesiveness is particularly strong among Cuban, Puerto Rican, and Mexican Americans (Altarriba and Bauer, 1998a, b; Boswell and Curtis, 1983; Comas-Diaz, 1993). Asian Americans and Pacific Islanders also prefer to deal with problems within the family or with the help of a family doctor and not seek out psychiatric interventions (Yu and Cypress, 1982). Snowden and Cheung (1990) point out the lack of research on help-seeking behaviors by Native Americans and Alaskans.

Level of acculturation also appears to be an important factor in predicting those who seek therapy and those who do not. Wells, Hough, Golding, Burnam, and Karno (1987) examined the utilization of mental health services by Mexican Americans as a function of their level of acculturation. They discovered that the less acculturated Mexican Americans used services the least, highly acculturated Mexican Americans used services at an intermediate level, and non-Hispanic, white Americans used mental health services to the greatest degree.

Language is certainly a barrier for many bilinguals having little proficiency in the language spoken by the therapist. In addition to language, there are negative attitudes and stereotypes regarding mental health services and the mentally ill that are common in many cultures, but are found to be particularly prevalent among ethnic-minority populations. Shame and negative stigmas attached to the mentally ill have been shown to be ubiquitous among ethnic minorities. Negative stigma and shame often results from the association of emotional problems and mental illness with immoral thoughts and behaviors; and issues of familial inheritance make it shameful for the entire family as a unit (Anderson, 1983; Muecke, 1983; Powell, 1983; Skolnick, 1978; Sue and Morishima, 1982).

Economic barriers plague a number of ethnic minorities wishing to receive mental health care, as well. Minority groups are disproportionately represented among poor and near-poor economic groups. This finding appears to affect their usage of mental health services. Often, recently immigrated ethnic minorities are forced to deal with difficulties such as language barriers, acculturation issues, and poverty. Discrimination and segregation are also common stressors that they face which contribute to unemployment. Due to these difficulties, minority clients often have higher rates of mental illness than do other clients (Anderson, 1983; Maduro, 1983; Muecke, 1983; Sue and Morishima, 1982). However, this is in part because these groups typically do not seek services until their symptoms and illnesses become severe.

10.7 Developing Multicultural Counseling Competencies: Implications for Training and Education

The changing demographics within the United States and other nations has prompted an interest in training and educational programs for the development of multicultural competencies in counselors and mental health workers (e.g. Javier, 1989; Ponterotto, 1987; Sciarra and Ponterotto, 1991). Sue, Arredondo, and McDavis (1992) described a number of multicultural standards and competencies that should form part of the training leading to the development of culturally competent counselors. It can be argued that these competencies should include linguistic and psycholinguistic training, in light of the research reported here. The following section will review specific recommendations for training counselors and clinicians who assist in the development of treatment plans for bilingual-bicultural clients.

10.7.1   *Training multicultural counselors*

Mio and Morris (1990) have indicated that the American Psychological Association (APA) has endorsed the inclusion of cross-cultural issues in the training of mental health specialists since approximately 1973. This was the result of a conference held by the National Institute of Health on the development of professional training measures that included some aspect of cultural sensitivity. These discussions later led to the formal organization of ethical guidelines by the APA and the American Association for Counseling and Development (AACD) in the early 1980s. Despite the awareness that was generated by the creation of these guidelines, Mio and Morris noted that resistance to the incorporation of these treatment modalities into programs in professional and practical training continued into the 1990s. The authors noted that there were likely some misperceptions regarding the inclusion of culturally sensitive approaches in standard curricula that slowed the incorporation of these ideas into programs in training and education for counselors. Mio and Morris further discuss a model program developed at Washington State University that can perhaps be adapted to other similar courses at other institutions. To summarize their recommendations, students should be introduced to general issues in cross-cultural psychology such as an attempt at defining culture and the influence of culture on human behavior, issues regarding worldviews across cultures and the etic-emic distinction, issues regarding psychopathology, assessment and diagnosis from an intercultural perspective, and issues regarding psychotherapeutic approaches that are culture-specific. Clearly, with advance knowledge of how cultural variables can interact with positive outcomes in mental health care settings, therapists would be better equipped for working with bicultural and bilingual populations.

Das (1995) broadens the perspective that can be taken when training counselors and mental health care workers to include additional knowledge on the historical, societal, political and demographic context within which a client has developed and within which the therapy is actually taking place. An application of multicultural theory can add to the development of training programs by introducing to students various aspects of cultural development, how culture shapes behavior, how values and beliefs guide mental health development, and how those beliefs also affect an individual's willingness to engage in mental health treatment. Most importantly, Das aptly recognizes that in training individuals in aspects of culture, their awareness of their *own* cultural biases and perceptions can be raised, leading to a questioning of values and beliefs. "Education of multicultural counselors should make them aware of their own cultural assumptions and skillful and sympathetic in working with individuals whose cultural assumptions and experiences might be different from their own" (p. 50). Curiously, researchers or practitioners rarely mention a specific need to incorporate *language* and language-related issues into multicultural training paradigms. More will be said about this issue, in the concluding section.

10.7.2 *The development of specific competencies*

Sue (1990) underscores the need to develop culture-specific strategies in the development of counseling skills. He notes that the development of these techniques or competencies should derive from a *conceptual framework* rather than from a simple attempt at applying cultural factors or cultural knowledge to the treatment plan for a given client. Sue cautions that the application of culture-specific techniques should be well grounded in conceptual and theoretical thinking and research involving an examination of communication styles, nonverbal communication, paralanguage or vocal cues and their social and political connotations both within and across cultures. Sue warns that no one approach is going to be appropriate for working with individuals across all cultures. However, within any theoretical orientation that one might adopt, there is likely room for the application of culturally and ethnically based strategies that can improve counselor effectiveness. Finally, Sue asks that individuals question how specific cultural groups addressed their mental health needs before there was a Western approach to mental health practices. This question will likely elicit some of the core beliefs and rituals followed by a specific group and enhance the ability of the therapist or counselor to embed those beliefs into a treatment plan that might prove beneficial for the client.

Sue, Arredondo, and McDavis (1992) outlined a number of specific competencies that mental health professionals should develop in order to provide treatment that encompasses cultural and cross-cultural information. In addition to those mentioned earlier, counselors who are interested in becoming culturally skilled should obtain the following: awareness of their own stereotypes and those of other cultural, racial, and ethnic groups, the latest research knowledge and skills related to ethnic and cultural groups, a knowledge of the religious and spiritual beliefs held by groups under consideration, knowledge of minority family structures and values, training in traditional assessment techniques, and finally, knowledge of the sociopolitical structures and institutions surrounding a given client. Most importantly, Sue et al. clearly state that language should be assessed and a language match should be made feasible whenever possible. If translators are not available for working with bilingual clients, then the therapist or counselor should seek a competent bilingual therapist for referral. These same sentiments are echoed by Santiago-Rivera (1995), along with the recommendation that language dominance and language preferences should be assessed prior to engaging in treatment with a bilingual client. These later works are among the first to note the importance of language variables in the counseling domain when working with bilingual clients (see also Altarriba and Santiago-Rivera, 1994; Santiago-Rivera and Altarriba, 2002).

10.8 Conclusions and Directions for Further Research

The study of language and language processing goes hand in hand with research on mental health issues. Individuals have long examined the role of verbal behavior in the therapeutic setting and its influence on every facet of counseling and mental health treatment. What has not received much attention is the role of multilingualism or the use of more than one language in therapy and its relation to positive outcomes in mental health treatment. The current review suggests that verbal labels that indicate emotion are often a primary means of communication within a therapeutic setting and that for a bilingual individual, those emotion word labels may be represented differently in each language. The current work argues that there is a need to understand the development and representation of emotion word knowledge in bilingual speakers so that this information might be used as a tool when working with bilingual and bicultural individuals in mental health settings. It appears that past experiences are often coded in the language in which they occurred and that the appropriate language can be used successfully as a retrieval cue when engaging in dialogue with a bilingual client. The use of linguistic devices that are culturally specific and rich (e.g. *dichos* or proverbs) can be useful in connecting with clients and forming a bond within mental health settings that can contribute to an atmosphere of trust and confidence between the therapist and the client. It is argued here, therefore, that linguistic and cultural factors should be incorporated into treatment plans and treatment modalities when working with bilingual clients. Moreover, training and education for potential counselors and mental health care specialists should incorporate an approach that covers societal, political, historical and cultural issues that are relevant to clients as well as training that addresses tools for the assessment of language use and language dominance. Indeed, the ability to code-switch between languages can be seen as a valuable technique to gain further insight into problematic issues and psychological issues facing a bilingual client.

Future research and investigation should focus on a broader range of cultures and languages than those that have been examined thus far. The bulk of the information regarding language switching and language mixing in therapy has addressed issues regarding emotion word knowledge for bilinguals who are knowledgeable regarding English and Spanish, while other languages have largely been ignored. Also, there is a greater need for investigations on cross-cultural representations of emotion and emotion word concepts. While information is beginning to emerge on the emotionality that is embedded in specific language cultures, this work is in its infancy. It is likely, as noted previously, that emotion itself is coded differently in different languages regardless of the order in which they might be acquired by a multilingual speaker. Could Spanish simply be a richer, deeper language in terms of emotion than, say, English? Little is known regarding this area of inquiry. Further, more research is needed on the language nuances such as idiomatic expressions and metaphors that are commonly used in many languages to express morals, beliefs, and values. While this has been explored in one or two languages in the mental health literature, there remains much to be gained by spanning a broader range of languages in this domain. Yet another area of inquiry that has not been tapped is the use of language switching with children or adolescents who might engage in mental health treatment. Almost all of the work that can be gathered to date on the above topic examines language processing in adult speakers. A lot is yet to be gained from the investigation of emotion word knowledge in bilingual children and its application to mental health and well-being. Future research should examine these areas of inquiry with an eye to incorporating the findings and results into training and educational programs for those dealing with children in counseling and clinical settings.

REFERENCES

Altarriba, J. (2003). Does *cariño* equal "liking"? A theoretical approach to conceptual nonequivalence between languages. *International Journal of Bilingualism*, 7, 305–22.

Altarriba, J. and Bauer, L. M. (1998a). Counseling Cuban Americans. In D. R. Atkinson, G. Morten, and D. W. Sue (eds.), *Counseling American Minorities: A Cross-Cultural Perspective*, 5th edn, pp. 280–96. New York: McGraw-Hill.

Altarriba, J. and Bauer, L. M. (1998b). Counseling the Hispanic-American client: Cuban Americans, Mexican Americans, and Puerto Ricans. *Journal of Counseling and Development*, 76, 389–96.

Altarriba, J., Bauer, L. M., and Benvenuto, C. (1999). Concreteness, context availability, and imageability ratings and word associations for abstract, concrete, and emotion words. *Behavior Research Methods, Instruments, and Computers*, 31, 578–602.

Altarriba, J. and Santiago-Rivera, A. L. (1994). Current perspectives on using linguistic and cultural factors in counseling the Hispanic client. *Professional Psychology: Research and Practice*, 25, 388–97.

Altarriba, J. and Soltano, E. G. (1996). Repetition blindness and bilingual memory: Token individuation for translation equivalents. *Memory and Cognition*, 24, 700–11.

Anderson, J. N. (1983). Health and illness in Philipino immigrants. *Western Journal of Medicine*, 139, 811–19.

Aragno, A. and Schlachet, P. J. (1996). Accessibility of early experience through the language of origin: A theoretical integration. *Psychoanalytic Psychology*, 13, 23–34.

Baetens-Beardsmore, H. (1986). *Bilingualism: Basic Principles* (2nd edn.). San Diego, CA: College-Hill Press.

Bandler, R. and Grinder, J. (1975). *The Structure of Magic*. Palo Alto, CA: Science and Behavior Books.

Barker, P. (ed.) (1985). *Using Metaphors in Psychotherapy*. New York: Brunner/ Mazel.

Baron, R. M. and Needel, S. P. (1980). Toward an understanding of the differences in the responses of humans and other animals to density. *Psychological Review*, 87, 320–6.

Bhatia, T. K. and Ritchie, W. C. (1996). Bilingual language mixing, universal grammar, and second language acquisition. In W. C. Ritchie and T. K. Bhatia (eds.), *Handbook of Second Language Acquisition*, pp. 627–88. San Diego, CA: Academic Press.

Bialystok, E. (2001). *Bilingualism in Development: Language, Literacy, and Cognition*. Cambridge, UK: Cambridge University Press.

Bond, M. H. and Lai, T. M. (1986). Embarrassment and code-switching into a second language. *Journal of Social Psychology*, 126, 179–86.

Boswell, T. D. and Curtis, J. R. (1983). *The Cuban American experience*. Totowa, NJ: Rowman and Allanheld.

Brown, A. S. (1991). A review of the tip-of-the-tongue experience. *Psychological Bulletin*, 109, 204–33.

Brown, J. A. (1981). Parent education groups for Mexican Americans. *Social Work in Education*, 3, 22–31.

Brown, R. and Kulik, J. (1977). Flashbulb memories. *Cognition*, 5, 73–99.

Buxbaum, E. (1949). The role of second language in the formation of ego and superego. *Psychoanalytic Quarterly*, 18, 279–89.

Campos, J. J., Campos, R. G., and Barrett, K. C. (1989). Emergent themes in the study of emotional development and emotion regulation. *Developmental Psychology*, 25, 394–402.

Clauss, C. S. (1998). Language: The unspoken variable in psychotherapy practice. *Psychotherapy*, 35, 188–96.

Comas-Díaz, L. (1993). Hispanic/Latino communities: Psychological implications. In D. R. Atkinson, G. Morten, and D. W. Sue (eds.), *Counseling American Minorities: A Cross-cultural Perspective*, 4th edn., pp. 241–96. Madison, WI: Brown and Benchmark.

Das, A. K. (1995). Rethinking multicultural counseling: Implications for counselor education. *Journal of Counseling and Development*, 74, 45–52.

Delgado, M. (1981). Hispanic cultural values: Implications for groups. *Small Group Behavior*, 12, 69–80.

Delgado, M. (1983). Activities and Hispanic groups: Issues and recommendations. *Social Work with Groups*, 6, 85–96.

Doi, T. (1986). *The Anatomy of Self: The Individual Versus Society*. Tokyo: Kodansha.

Doi, T. (1990). The cultural assumptions of psychoanalysis. In J. W. Stigler, R. A. Shweder, and G. Herdt (eds.), *Cultural Psychology: The Chicago Symposia on Culture and Human Development*, pp. 446–53. Cambridge, UK: Cambridge University Press.

Eakins, B. W. and Eakins, R. G. (1985). Sex differences in nonverbal communication. In L. A. Samovar and R. E. Porter (eds.), *Intercultural Communication: A Reader*. Belmont, CA: Wadsworth.

Ervin, S. M. (1961). Semantic shifts in bilingualism. *American Journal of Psychology*, 74, 233–41.

Ervin, S. M. and Osgood, C. E. (1954). Second language learning and bilingualism. *Journal of Personality and Social Psychology*, 58, 139–45.

Flaskerud, J. H. (1986). The effects of culture-compatible intervention on the utilization of mental health services by minority clients. *Community Mental Health Journal*, 22, 127–41.

Galvan, R. and Teschner, R. (1989). *El Diccionario del Español Chicano: The Dictionary of Chicano Spanish*. Lincolnwood, IL: National Textbook Co.

Goleman, D. (1995). *Emotional Intelligence*. New York: Bantam.

Gomez, E. and Cook, K. (1977). *Chicano Culture and Mental Health*. Monograph I, Centro del Barrio, Worden School of Social Services, San Antonio, TX.

Gonzalez-Reigosa, F. (1976). The anxiety-arousing effect of taboo words in bilinguals. In C. D. Spielberger and R. Diaz-Guerrero (eds.), *Cross-cultural Anxiety*, pp. 89–105. Washington, D.C.: Hemisphere.

Greenson, R. R. (1950). The mother tongue and the mother. *The International Journal of Psychoanalysis*, 31, 18–23.

Grinder, J. and Bandler, R. (1976). *The Structure of Magic II*. Palo Alto, CA: Science and Behavior Books.

Grosjean, F. (1982). *Life with Two Languages: An Introduction to Bilingualism*. Cambridge, MA: Harvard University Press.

Guttfreund, D. C. (1990). Effects of language usage on the emotional experience of Spanish-English and English-Spanish bilinguals. *Journal of Consulting and Clinical Psychology*, 58, 604–7.

Hall, E. T. (1969). *The Hidden Dimension*. Garden City, NY: Doubleday.

Hall, E. T. (1976). *Beyond Culture*. New York: Anchor Press.

Hamers, J. F. and Blanc, M. H. A. (2000). *Bilinguality and Bilingualism* (2nd edn.). Cambridge, UK: Cambridge University Press.

Heredia, R. R. and Altarriba, J. (2001). Bilingual language mixing: Why do bilinguals code-switch? *Current Directions in Psychological Science*, 10, 164–8.

Hoffmann, C. (1991). *An Introduction to Bilingualism*. London: Longman.

Hunt, R. R. and Ellis, H. C. (1999). *Fundamentals of Cognitive Psychology* (6th edn.). Boston, MA: McGraw-Hill.

Javier, R. A. (1989). Linguistic considerations in the treatment of bilinguals. *Psychoanalytic Psychology*, 6, 87–96.

Javier, R. A. (1995). Vicissitudes of autobiographical memories in a bilingual analysis. *Psychoanalytic Psychology*, 12, 429–38.

Javier, R. A., Barroso, F., and Muñoz, M. A. (1993). Autobiographical memory in bilinguals. *Journal of Psycholinguistic Research*, 22, 319–38.

Jensen, J. V. (1985). Perspective on nonverbal intercultural communication. In L. A. Samovar and R. E. Porter (eds.), *Intercultural Communication: A Reader*. Belmont, CA: Wadsworth.

Keefe, S. E., Padilla, A. M., and Carlos, M. L. (1979). The Mexican-American extended family as an emotional support system. *Human Organization*, 38, 144–52.

Kitayama, S. and Markus, H. R. (eds.). (1994). *Emotion and Culture: Empirical Studies of Mutual Influence*. Washington, D.C.: American Psychological Association.

Knapp, M. I. (1972). *Nonverbal Communication in Human Interaction*. New York: Holt, Reinhart, and Winston.

Kochman, T. (1981). *Black and White Styles in Conflict*. Chicago: University of Chicago Press.

Kolers, P. (1966). Reading and talking bilingually. *American Journal of Psychology*, 3, 357–76.

Lin, T. (1983). Psychiatry and Chinese culture. *Western Journal of Medicine*, 139, 868–74.

Littleman, S. K. (1985). Foreword. In P. Barker (ed.), *Using Metaphors in Psychotherapy*, pp. vii–viii. New York: Brunner/Mazel.

Lutz, C. (1988). *Unnatural emotions: Everyday Sentiments on a Micronesian Atoll and their Challenge to Western Theory*. Chicago: University of Chicago Press.

Maduro, R. (1976). Journey dreams in Latino group psychotherapy. *Psychotherapy: Theory, Research, and Practice*, 13, 148–55.

Maduro, R. (1983). Curanderismo and Latino views of disease and curing. *Western Journal of Medicine*, 139, 868–74.

Marcos, L. R. (1976). Linguistic dimensions in the bilingual patient. *American Journal of Psychoanalysis*, 36, 347–54.

Marcos, L. R. (1979). Effects of interpreters on the evaluation of psychopathology in non-English speaking patients. *American Journal of Psychiatry*, 136, 171–4.

Marian, V. and Neisser, U. (2000). Language-dependent recall of autobiographical memories. *Journal of Experimental Psychology: General*, 129, 361–8.

Mio, J. S. and Morris, D. R. (1990). Cross-cultural issues in psychology training programs: An invitation for discussion. *Professional Psychology: Research and Practice*, 21, 434–41.

Muecke, M. A. (1983). In search of healers – Southeast Asian refugees in the American health care system.

Western Journal of Medicine, 139, 835–40.

Musser-Granski, J. and Carrillo, D. F. (1997). The use of bilingual, bicultural paraprofessionals in mental health services: Issues for hiring, training, and supervision. *Community Mental Health Journal*, 33, 51–60.

Pearson, J. C. (1985). *Gender and Communication*. Dubuque, IA: Brown.

Pedersen, P. B., Draguns, J. G., Lonner, W. J., and Trimble, J. E. (eds.) (1981). *Counseling across Cultures*. Honolulu, HI: University of Hawaii Press.

Pérez-Foster, R. (1992). Psychoanalysis and the bilingual patient: Some observations on the influence of language choice on the transference. *Psychoanalytic Psychology*, 9, 61–76.

Pérez-Foster, R. (1998). *The Power of Language in the Clinical Process*. Northvale, NJ: Jason Aronson.

Pitta, P., Marcos, L. R., and Alpert, M. (1978). Language switching as a treatment strategy with bilingual patients. *American Journal of Psychoanalysis*, 38, 255–8.

Ponterotto, J. G. (1987). Counseling Mexican Americans: A multimodal approach. *Journal of Counseling and Development*, 65, 308–12.

Powell, G. J. (1983). *The Psychosocial Development of Minority Group Children*. New York: Brunner/Mazel.

Rozensky, R. H. and Gomez, M. Y. (1983). Language switching in psychotherapy with bilinguals: Two problems, two models, and case examples. *Psychotherapy*, 20, 152–260.

Santiago-Rivera, A. L. (1995). Developing a culturally sensitive treatment modality for bilingual Spanish-speaking clients: Incorporating language and culture in counseling. *Journal of Counseling and Development*, 74, 12–17.

Santiago-Rivera, A. L. and Altarriba, J. (2002). The role of language in therapy with the Spanish-English bilingual client. *Professional Psychology: Research and Practice*, 33, 30–8.

Schrauf, R. W. (1999). Mother tongue maintenance among North American ethnic groups. *Cross-Cultural Resarch*, 33, 175–92.

Schrauf, R. W. (2000). Bilingual autobiographical memory: Experimental studies and clinical cases. *Culture and Psychology*, 6, 387–417.

Schrauf, R. W. and Rubin, D. C. (1998). Bilingual autobiographical memory in older adult immigrants: A test of cognitive explanations of the reminiscence bump and the linguistic encoding of memories. *Journal of Memory and Language*, 39, 437–57.

Schrauf, R. W. and Rubin, D. C. (2000). Internal languages of retrieval: The bilingual encoding of memories for the personal past. *Memory and Cognition*, 28, 616–23.

Schreuder, R. and Weltens, B. (eds.) (1993). *The Bilingual Lexicon*. Philadelphia: John Benjamins.

Sciarra, D. and Ponterotto, J. G. (1991). Counseling the Hispanic bilingual family: Challenges to the therapeutic process. *Psychotherapy*, 28, 473–9.

Silva, R. S. (2000). Pragmatics, bilingualism, and the native speaker. *Language and Communication*, 20, 161–78.

Skolnick, A. (1978). The myth of the vulnerable child. *Psychology Today*, 11, 56–60.

Smith, E. J. (1981). Cultural and historical perspectives in counseling Blacks. In D. W. Sue (ed.), *Counseling the Culturally Different: Theory and Practice*. New York: Wiley & Sons.

Snow, L. (1983). Traditional health beliefs and practices among lower class Black Americans. *Western Journal of Medicine*, 139, 820–8.

Snowden, L. R. and Cheung, F. K. (1990). Use of inpatient mental health services by members of ethnic minority groups. *American Psychologist*, 45, 347–55.

Special Populations Task Force of the President's Commission on Mental Health (1978). *Task panel reports submitted to the President's Commission on Mental Health*, vol. 3. Washington, D.C.: US Government Printing Office.

Sue, D. W. (1977). Counseling the culturally different: A conceptual analysis. *Personnel and Guidance Journal*, 55, 422–4.

Sue, D. W. (1990). Culture-specific strategies in counseling: A conceptual framework. *Professional Psychology: Research and Practice*, 21, 424–33.

Sue, D. W. (1991). A conceptual model for cultural diversity training. *Journal of Counseling and Development*, 70, 99–105.

Sue, D. W. (1999). *Counseling the Culturally Different: Theory and Practice*, 3rd edn. New York: Wiley & Sons.

Sue, D. W., Arredondo, P., and McDavis, R. J. (1992). Multicultural counseling competencies and standards: A call to the profession. *Journal of Multicultural Counseling and Development*, 20, 64–88.

Sue, D. W. and Sue, D. (1990). *Counseling the Culturally Different: Theory and Practice*, 2nd edn.). New York: Wiley & Sons.

Sue, S. (1977). Community mental health services to minority groups: Some optimism, some pessimism. *American Psychologist*, 32, 616–24.

Sue, S. and Morishima, J. K. (1982). *The Mental Health of Asian Americans*. San Francisco: Jossey-Bass.

Takeuchi, D. T., Sue, S., and Yeh, M. (1995). Return rates and outcomes from ethnicity-specific mental health programs in Los Angeles. *American Journal of Public Health*, 85, 638–43.

Thass-Thienemann, T. (1973). *The Interpretation of Language. Volume I: Understanding the Symbolic Meaning of Language*. New York: Jason Aronson.

Tulving, E. and Thompson, D. (1973). Encoding specificity and retrieval processes in episodic memory. *Psychological Review*, 80, 352–73.

Tylim, I. (1982). Group psychotherapy with Hispanic patients: The psychodynamics of idealization. *International Journal of Group Psychotherapy*, 32, 339–50.

Urdang, L. and Flexner, S. B. (1968). *Random House Dictionary of the English Language*. New York: Random House.

Vasquez, C. and Javier, R. A. (1991). The problem with interpreters: Communicating with Spanish-speaking patients. *Hospital and Community Psychiatry*, 42, 163–5.

Wells, K. B., Hough, R. L., Golding, J. M., Burnam, A., and Karno, M. (1987). Which Mexican-Americans underutilize health services? *American Journal of Psychiatry*, 144, 918–22.

Wierzbicka, A. (1997). *Understanding Cultures Through their Key Words*. New York: Oxford University Press.

Wrenn, C. G. (1962). The culturally-encapsulated counselor. *Harvard Educational Review*, 32, 444–9.

Wrenn, C. G. (1985). Afterword: The culturally-encapsulated counselor revisited. In P. Pedersen (ed.), *Handbook of Cross-cultural Counseling and Therapy*. Westport, CT: Greenwood Press.

Wu, I. H. and Windle, C. (1980). Ethnic specificity in the relative minority use and staffing of community mental health centers. *Community Mental Health Journal*, 16, 156–68.

Yu, E. S. and Cypress, B. K. (1982). Visits to physicians by Asian/Pacific Americans. *Medical Care*, 20, 809–20.

Zuñiga, M. (1992). Using metaphors in therapy: *Dichos* and Latino clients. *Social Work*, 37, 55–9.

The Bilingual's Repertoire: Code Mixing, Code Switching, and Speech Accommodation

11 Code Switching and Grammatical Theory

JEFF MACSWAN

11.1 Introduction

Code switching is the alternate use of two (or more) languages within the same utterance, as illustrated in (1) (Belazi, Rubin, and Toribio, 1994).

(1a) This morning *mi hermano y yo fuimos a comprar* some milk[1]
This morning my brother and I went to buy some milk

(1b) The student brought the homework *para la profesora*
The student brought the homework for the teacher

Code switching of the sort shown in (1), in which an alternation occurs below sentential boundaries, is known as *intrasentential code switching*, whereas switching between sentences is known as *intersentential code switching*. Because grammatical theory is primarily focused on relations below the sentence level, research on grammatical aspects of code switching has focused almost exclusively on intrasentential code switching.

The chapter begins with a discussion of early research on code switching, and the emergence of code switching as a field of linguistic research. We then review a number of theoretical approaches to code switching, focusing on a discussion of the implications of current research in syntactic theory for the analysis of code switching data. We end with some comments regarding directions for future research in code switching.

First, however, a brief word on appropriate data in code switching research is in order. A recurring controversy in the code switching literature regards whether naturalistic data or experimental data (sentence judgments, in particular) are more appropriate sources for theorizing about bilingual language

---

1 As is conventional in the literature, I will signal code switching by a change from regular to *italicized* text.

mixing. While some researchers have strongly rejected all experimental data (e.g. Mahootian and Santorini, 1996), others have voiced a strong preference for experimental data (e.g. Toribio, 2001). While naturalistic data collection has the advantage of placing code switching in a more realistic context, it has a great disadvantage as well: It does not provide instances of starred or ill-formed sentences – or if it does, they are not labeled as such. This is a significant problem if one is interested in constructing an explicit theory of a bilingual's linguistic competence, because such a theory must generate all of the well-formed utterances in a bilingual's repertoire and none of the ill-formed ones. Without examples of utterances inconsistent with a bilingual's linguistic intuitions, it is not possible to construct such a theory. Hence, a balanced perspective is preferred, one which advocates careful consideration of all linguistic data, along with its inherent messiness and unique limitations.

11.2 Early Research

Myers-Scotton (1993a) credits Blom and Gumperz (1972) with sparking interest in the study of code switching in the late 1960s and early 1970s. Blom and Gumperz had studied code switching between dialects in Hemnesberget, a Norwegian fishing village, and outlined the formal and informal functions dialect switching played in various social settings and events. Although the topic had been discussed before, Blom and Gumperz's chapter received considerably more exposure because it was included in Gumperz and Hymes's (1972) edited collection, which became a standard textbook in the many new sociolinguistics courses created in universities in the 1970s. Earlier, Gumperz and co-author Eduardo Hernandez-Chavez (Gumperz, 1970; Gumperz and Hernandez-Chavez, 1970) had discussed code switching between English and Spanish in the US.

Gumperz's code switching research was primarily concerned with the analysis of conversational events, foregrounding, and the role of switching in the composition of a speech event or situation. However, it was not long before researchers began to take an interest in the grammatical properties of code switching, a matter Gumperz (1976) also addressed in later work. For some of these researchers, inspired by Walt Wolfram's (1969) and William Labov's (1970) work on African-American vernacular, the search for an underlying structure of code switching was guided by a desire to inform political and social discussions regarding bilingual/bidialectal communities.

11.3 Constraints on Code Switching, Constraints on Syntax

The earliest studies on the grammatical properties of code switching were naturally highly language-specific, and focused on characterizing the licit structural boundaries of code-switched speech. For instance, Timm (1975) identified five constraints on Spanish-English code switching, arguing that switching does not occur within NPs containing nouns and modifying adjectives, between negation and the verb, between a verb and its auxiliary, between finite verbs and their infinitival complements, and between pronominal subjects and their verbs. Wentz and McClure (1976) and Pfaff (1979) attempted to refine Timm's proposed constraints. An important finding of this early descriptive literature was the observation that code switching behavior, like other linguistic behavior, was rule-governed and not haphazard. This important finding set the stage for a program of linguistic analysis which would aim to account for the full range of observed language-specific "constraints."

Note that the term "constraint" is used in two very different senses in the code switching literature, one descriptive and the other theoretical. In the descriptive sense, when we speak of constraints on code switching, we mean only that some code-switched constructions are well-formed and others are ill-formed, as shown in (2) (Belazi, Rubin and Toribio, 1994; cf. Timm, 1975).

(2a)   The students *habían visto la película italiana*
       The students had seen the Italian movie

(2b)   *The student had *visto la película italiana*
       The student had seen the Italian movie

Although the word order is the same in both instances, the switch in (2b) is judged to be ill-formed. This fact shows that code switching behavior, like other linguistic behavior, is constrained or rule-governed, but does not in itself tell us what the nature of the underlying rule system is.

However, the literature on code switching soon began to move from constraints in the descriptive sense to constraints in the theoretical sense, as syntacticians working independently within the so-called "Extended Standard Theory" of the 1970s enumerated constraints on transformations, constraints on phrase structure, and constraints on surface structure (Newmeyer, 1986). A constraint in this sense applies to a system of linguistic rules or to the form of a representation, and attempts to capture a range of linguistic facts. It is by definition part of our linguistic competence, a statement within the grammatical system itself. This is a much stronger claim than is made in the descriptive literature just discussed, and Poplack was among the first to articulate constraints on code switching in this sense.

11.4   The Emergence of Theoretical Approaches to Code Switching

Poplack (1980, 1981) proposed the Equivalence Constraint and the Free Morpheme Constraint, defined in (3) and (4).

(3)   The Equivalence Constraint
      Codes will tend to be switched at points where the surface structures of
      the languages map onto each other.

(4)   The Free Morpheme Constraint (Sankoff and Poplack, 1981, p. 5)
      A switch may not occur between a bound morpheme and a lexical item
      unless the latter has been phonologically integrated into the language of
      the bound morpheme.

The idea in (3), given Poplack's examples, is that code switches are allowed
within constituents so long as the word order requirements of both languages
are met at S-structure; (4) tells us that a bound morpheme cannot affix to a
lexical item unless it has been phonologically integrated into the language
of the bound morpheme. To illustrate, (3) correctly predicts that the switch in
(5) is disallowed, and (4) correctly disallows (6).

(5)   *told *le*, le *told*, him *dije*, dije *him*   [Poplack, 1981, p. 176]
      told *to-him*, to-him *I-told*, him *I-told*, I-told *him*
      '(I) told him'

(6)   **estoy* eat-*iendo*   [Poplack, 1980, p. 586]
      I-am eat-ing

   The Free Morpheme Constraint has been somewhat controversial. While
it is attested in numerous corpora (Bentahila and Davies, 1983; Berk-Seligson,
1986; Clyne, 1987; MacSwan, 1999), others claim to have identified counter-
examples (Bokamba, 1989; Chan, 1999; Jake, Myers-Scotton and Gross, 2002;
Myers-Scotton, 1993b; Nartey, 1982). However, in presenting counter-examples, researchers have often given too little attention to the specific syntactic
and phonological characteristics of the examples cited, making it difficult to
determine whether they are in fact violations of (4) or instances of *nonce borrowing* (see Meechan and Poplack, 1995; Poplack, Wheeler and Westwood,
1989; Sankoff, Poplack and Vanniarajan, 1990).
   Poplack's Equivalence Constraint, on the other hand, has had few supporters in recent years. The example in (2b), for instance, is ill-formed, contrary
to the prediction of (3), even though the surface word orders of Spanish and
English are identical. Also consider the examples in (7) and (8), where code
switches occur between a subject pronoun and a verb, both in their correct
surface structure positions for Spanish or Nahuatl, yet one example is ill-
formed and the other well-formed (MacSwan, 1999).

(7)   *Tú *tikoas tlakemetl*
      tú ti-k-koa-s tlake-me-tl
      you/SING 2S-3Os-buy-FUT garment-PL-NSF
      'You will buy clothes'

(8)   Él *kikoas tlakemetl*
      él 0-ki-koa-s tlak-eme-tl
      he 3S-3Os-buy-FUT garment-PL-NSF
      'He will buy clothes'

For additional examples, see studies of code switching corpora involving language pairs with different basic word orders, in which we observe great variation in word order within mixed-language constructions (Chan, 1999; Lee, 1991; Mahootian, 1993; Stenson, 1990).

However, Poplack's constraints are not intended as simple surface-level descriptions of code switching, but as actual linguistic principles which are part of a bilingual's linguistic competence. While this is a theoretically rich goal, the particular formulation is problematic. Linguists take particular grammars to be derivative in nature, not primitive constructs, since primitives are by definition part of universal grammar. A particular language is a set of parameter values over the range of variation permitted by universal grammar, and code switching involves the mixing of discrete languages. Hence, positing a constraint or other principle which explicitly refers to code switching suggests that particular languages are primitives in syntactic theory, leading to an ordering paradox. Thus, principles or "constraints" on code switching should not refer to the phenomenon of code switching itself, but should rather appeal to independently motivated principles of linguistic theory. In other words, for theory-internal reasons, we do not expect the language faculty to use code switching-specific rules, but rather expect the observed constraints on code switching to follow from other factors.

Woolford (1983) was perhaps the first to recognize that a theory of code switching consistent with leading assumptions in linguistic theory would include no code switching-specific rules. As she put it,

> The problem, from the point of view of theoretical linguistics, is to look beyond these surface strings to determine how one can switch grammars in mid-tree and still end up with a coherent and interpretable sentence. How can two separate grammars team up to generate a hybrid phrase structure tree, insert lexical items into its terminal nodes, and perform all the other syntactic and semantic tasks that sentences require?   (p. 522)

Woolford proposed a model of code switching in which language-specific lexicons projected phrase structures, which could be connected under the condition that the subset of phrase structure rules shared by the two languages permitted it. This model allowed Woolford to derive Poplack's Equivalence Constraint in a theoretically rich framework which made no mention of rules or constraints specific to code switching. (Other researchers who emphasized this important requirement in code switching include Mahootian, 1993, and MacSwan, 1999, 2000.)

Although Woolford's model was theoretically sophisticated for its time, subsequent empirical findings revealed that its predictions were incorrect. Like

Poplack's Equivalence Constraint, Woolford's model predicts that switching between languages where common phrase structure exists should uniformly result in well-formed sentences. However, (2b), (7), and numerous other published counter-examples show that this is not so. Taking Woolford (1983) as a point of departure, Bhatia (1989) argued that under specific conditions of language contact involving non-native Englishes, code switching may have the effect of yielding hybrid rules. As we shall see below – with respect to switches between languages with different basic word orders, for instance – the kind of hybrid-rule phenomena left unexplained by Woolford's highly phrase structure-oriented approach can be accommodated more readily by broadening the scope of relevant linguistic principles and operations.

In another influential proposal, Di Sciullo, Muysken and Singh (1986) argued that there is an anti-government requirement on code switching boundaries, an approach recently defended in Halmari (1997). Their constraint is given in (9).

(9)   Government Constraint
    a. If L_q carrier has index q, then Y_q^{max}.
    b. In a maximal projection Y^{max}, the L_q carrier is the lexical element that asymmetrically c-commands the other lexical elements or terminal phrase nodes dominated by Y^{max}.

The proposed constraint in (9) has the virtue that it refers to an independently motivated principle of grammar (government). However, because government holds between a verb and its object and between a preposition and its object, (9) predicts that a verb or preposition must be in the language of its complement. This is shown to be incorrect by examples in (10), where switches occur in case-marked positions.

(10a)   This morning *mi hermano y yo fuimos a comprar* some milk
        This morning *my brother and I went to buy* some milk

(10b)   J'ai joué avec *il-ku:ra*
        I have played with the-ball
        'I have played with the ball'

(10c)   Mi hermana *kitlasojtla in Juan*
        mi hermana 0-ki-tlasojtla in Juan
        my sister 3S-3Os-love in Juan
        'My sister loves Juan'

Furthermore, recent work in syntactic theory has moved away from the notion of government as a syntactic relation (Chomsky, 1995). Thus, besides its empirical challenges, the Government Constraint additionally requires independent justification for the existence of the government constraint if it is to avoid becoming a code switching-specific constraint.

Another recent proposal, due to Mahootian (1993) and Santorini and Mahootian (1995), offers an account focusing on the complement relation in phrase structure (see also Pandit, 1990, and Nishimura, 1997, where similar proposals are made); Mahootian argued that (11) defines syntactic code switching boundaries.

(11)   The language of a head determines the phrase structure position of its complements in code switching just as in monolingual contexts.

Mahootian's "null theory of code switching" emphasized that there should be no code switching-specific constraints on language mixture, just as Woolford had done before her.

Mahootian (1993) used a corpus of Farsi-English code switching data which she collected in naturalistic observations. In Farsi, objects occur before the verb, contrasting with basic word order in English. Mahootian observed that in code switching contexts the language of the verb determines the placement of the object, as (12) illustrates.

(12)   You'll buy *xune-ye jaedid*
       you'll buy house-POSS new
       'You'll buy a new house'

Mahootian used a tree-adjoining grammar (TAG) formalism which she stressed is an implementation of general work in the generative tradition. However, note that (12) is predicted by (11) only if the *branching direction* of the complement is encoded in the head. TAG formalisms encode branching direction by positing the existence of "auxiliary trees," partial structures which represent a complement on the left or right of its head, as appropriate to the language under consideration. However, classic work in the generative tradition has long argued against encoding branching directionality (Chomsky, 1981; Stowell, 1981), and current work in this tradition posits a universal base in which all complements branch to the right (Chomsky, 1995; Kayne, 1995). Thus, for the approach to work outside the TAG framework, some elaboration would be needed.

In addition, there are some well-known counter-examples to (11) which are troublespots for this approach. For instance, in both English and Spanish, it is generally assumed that Neg(ation) selects a tensed verb to its right. Despite the adherence to (11), the code switches in (13) are strongly deviant.

(13a)   *El no *wants to go*
        he not want to go
        'He doesn't want to go'

(13b)   *He doesn't *quiere ir*
        He doesn't want/3Ss go/INF
        'He doesn't want to go'

Mahootian and Santorini (1996) discuss a number of counter-examples to Mahootian's model, rejecting them as spurious because they do not come from naturalistic corpora. The basic argument for rejecting them relies upon the assumption that code switching is a socially stigmatized behavior, so code switchers may be influenced by this stigma in rendering judgments on sentences (Mahootian, 1993). However, the basic premise here seems incorrect. Code switching is not universally stigmatized; indeed, in many settings it is regarded as a prestigious display of linguistic talent. Moreover, there are individual languages which are extremely stigmatized in some places (indigenous languages in the US and Mexico, for instance), but linguists have fruitfully studied them using traditional elicitation methods for many years. As suggested earlier, it seems that both elicitation data and naturalistic data should be examined with the usual caution in the study of both monolingual and bilingual language.

Concurrent with the appearance of Mahootian (1993), Belazi, Rubin and Toribio (1994) proposed a rather different model of code switching, known as the Functional Head Constraint (FHC). The FHC, recently defended in Toribio (2001), is argued to emerge from principles independently motivated in the theory of grammar. According to these researchers, the descriptive facts are these:

(14)   A code switch may not occur between a functional head and its complement.

To explain the observation in (14), Belazi, Rubin and Toribio (1994) appeal to "feature checking," independently motivated to be at work in numerous other phenomena. However, these authors also add an additional item to the feature stack. According to them, a *language feature*, such as [+Spanish] or [+English], is checked along with other features such as case and agreement. If the features do not agree (a Spanish functional head with an English complement, or vice versa), then the code switch is blocked. They formulate their constraint as in (15).

(15)   The Functional Head Constraint
       The language feature of the complement f-selected by a functional head, like all other relevant features, must match the corresponding feature of that functional head.

Since (15) applies only to f-selected configurations (a complement selected by a functional head, as in Abney, 1987), switches between lexical heads and their complements are not constrained.

Note that the operation of (15) requires a language feature such as [+Spanish] or [+Greek]. Since this proposed "language feature" is not independently motivated for any other linguistic phenomenon, it serves only to relabel the descriptive facts, and is therefore tautological. Also, note that features generally have a relatively small set of discrete values, such as [±past] or [±finite]. By contrast, there are many, many particular languages, quite possibly infinitely many, as Keenan and Stabler (1994) have argued, and the dividing lines between them are often quite obscure. Thus, a language feature set to [−Greek] introduces extreme, possibly unresolvable computational complexity. Furthermore, the feature [+Chinese] would presumably include all the mutually unintelligible languages of China, and [+Norwegian] would exclude Swedish even though Swedish and Norwegian speakers generally understand each other. Indeed, as Chomsky (1995, p. 11, n6) has noted in another connection,

> what we call "English," "French," "Spanish," and so on, even under idealizations to idiolects in homogeneous speech communities, reflect the Norman Conquest, proximity to Germanic areas, a Basque substratum, and other factors that cannot seriously be regarded as properties of the language faculty.

However, the analysis is greatly improved if we regard [+English] to be a collection of formal features which define "English," as Jacqueline Toribio (personal communication) has suggested. On this view, names for particular languages act as variables for bundles of features which formally characterize them. The ordering paradox disappears, because language features like [+English] or [+Spanish] are no longer taken to be primitives in the theory of grammar. This now gives the Functional Head Constraint (FHC) in (15) new empirical content. In particular, to evaluate the FHC, particular hypotheses are needed regarding which features of English, being distinct from features of Spanish, result in a conflict. Unfortunately, no such hypotheses are developed.

In addition, the idea that head-complement configurations are checking domains must also be independently motivated. If current approaches are correct in assuming that only head-head and head-spec configurations are checking domains (Chomsky, 1995; Sportiche, 1995), then the FHC could not be correct, even if "the language feature" were given the empirical content it now lacks. For empirical counter-examples to the FHC, see Dussias (1997); MacSwan (1999); Mahootian and Santorini (1996); Nishimura (1997); for a defense, see Toribio (2001).

Finally, the Matrix Language Frame (MLF) Model of Myers-Scotton and colleagues deserves some discussion. Like Joshi (1985) and others, Azuma (1991, 1993) and Myers-Scotton (1993b) differentiate the languages involved in code switching; one language is known as the *matrix language* (ML), the other as the *embedded language* (EL). According to this approach, the matrix language defines the surface structure positions for content words and functional elements. Azuma (1993) offers, among other data, the examples in (16) as support for this theory. In this framework, we expect (16a) to be well-formed but not (16b) since in (16b) the determiner *the* is not in the surface position of the ML.

(16a)   Uchi wa *whole chicken* o kau noyo
         we TOPIC *whole chicken* ACC. buy TAG
         'We buy a whole chicken'

(16b)   *Watashi ga katta *the* hon wa takai
         I NOM. bought *the* book TOPIC expensive
         'The book I bought is expensive'

Myers-Scotton (1993b) articulates these requirements in terms of the Morpheme Order Principle, which requires that morphemes within a bilingual constituent follow the order prescribed by the ML, and the System Morpheme Principle, which states that all "system morphemes" – defined as morphemes which have grammatical relations with other constituents – come from the ML in any mixed-language utterance.

The definition of the ML is crucially important. In earlier work, Myers-Scotton (1993b) proposed a "frequency-based criterion," claiming that the ML was the language which contributed the greater number of morphemes to the discourse, excluding cultural borrowings from the EL for new objects and concepts (p. 68), and that "the ML may change across time, and even within a conversation" (p. 69). This way of casting the ML made it difficult to know, for any given utterance, which language functioned as the ML and which as the EL. Concern over the vagueness of the definition of the ML has been voiced in Bentahila (1995), MacSwan (1999, 2000), Muysken (2000), and Muysken and de Rooij (1995).

In more recent work, this issue has been addressed. Jake, Myers-Scotton, and Gross (2002) resolve these ambiguities by providing a structural definition of the ML as part of their Uniform Structure Principle: "The ML may change within successive CPs, even within a multi-clausal sentence, but we stress that the ML does not change within a single bilingual CP" (p. 73). The MLF Model now makes clear empirical predictions that can be verified by inspecting the structure of code-switched utterances. Put simply, below the CP, the MLF Model predicts that all grammatical morphemes will be from one language only (System Morpheme Principle), and will be in the surface order required by the ML (Morpheme Order Principle).

As an additional nuance, Myers-Scotton and colleagues stipulate that an "EL island" may occur below the CP: "[A]s well-formed maximal constituents in the EL, [EL islands] are not inflected with ML system morphemes, although they occur in positions projected by the ML, following the Morpheme Order Principle" (Jake, Myers-Scotton, and Gross, 2002, p. 77). Hence, EL islands are essentially lawful violations of the System Morpheme Principle because they contain grammatical morphemes that are not in the ML, but an EL island must be a maximal projection and must remain true to the Morpheme Order Principle (that is, its position within the utterance must be dictated by the ML).

Let us consider some empirical evidence bearing on these predictions, focusing on the System Morpheme Principle. The French-Italian data in (17) are reported in Di Sciullo, Muysken and Singh (1986).

(17a)   No, *parce que* hanno *donné des cours*
        no, because have given of the lectures
        'No, because they have given the lectures'

(17b)   Oui, alors j'ai dit quie *si potev* aller comme ça
        yes so I have said that REF could walk like that
        'Yes, so I said that we could go like that'

Note that in both cases we observe a switch between an auxiliary or modal and its complement. Because these forms have grammatical relations with other lexical heads within the structure, they meet the MLF Model's definition of a system morpheme. Yet, contrary to the requirements of the System Morpheme Principle, each utterance involves system morphemes from different languages below the CP.

To rescue the MLF Model, one might argue that [*donné des cours*] in (17a) is an EL island, projected as a VP complement of the auxiliary verb, and that (17b) similarly involves an EL island [*aller comme ça*], an IP complement of the modal. However, note that the examples in (17) contrast with Spanish-English data in (2), repeated below as (18), where a switch between an auxiliary and a participle is ill-formed. The construction in (18b) is eligible for the same structural analysis as (17a), in which an EL island is hypothesized, yet it is ill-formed, contrary to the predictions of the MLF Model.

(18a)   The students *habían visto la película italiana*
        The students had seen the Italian movie

(18b)   *The student had *visto la película italiana*
        The student had seen the Italian movie

The contrast in (19), French-Italian examples reported in MacSwan (1999), is also problematic for the MLF Model. Here, acceptability judgments differ depending on whether the subject of the embedded clause has been promoted to the main clause or not, although the verbal complex is identical in both cases: [è *donné*]. In both instances, grammatical morphemes are mixed below the CP, and any plausible analysis of an EL island should apply in the same way in both instances. Yet the examples contrast, once again contrary to the predictions of the MLF Model.

(19a)   Si è *donné un cadeau*
        si essere given a gift
        'A gift is given'

(19b)   **Un cadeau* si è *donné*
        a gift *si* essere given
        'A gift is given'

As an additional example, consider the Spanish-Nahuatl examples in (20), reported in MacSwan (1999, 2000). Notice that Spanish negation (*no*) does not tolerate a Nahuatl complement, while Nahuatl negation (*amo*) permits a Spanish complement. Both the agreement morphology on the verbs and negation count as system morphemes since they enter into grammatical relations with other morphemes (in the less obvious case of negation, it c-commands a negative polarity item and may form a syntactic clitic with its verb). Hence, according to the System Morpheme Hypothesis, both (20a) and (20b) should be ill-formed because system morphemes are mixed below the CP, yet this is not so. Remarkably, the constructions contrast in acceptability, even though they appear to have identical underlying structures.

(20a)   *No *nitekititoc*
         no ni-tekiti-toc
         not 1S-work-DUR
         'I'm not working'

(20b)   Amo *estoy trabajando*
         amo estoy trabaja-ndo
         not be/3Ss work-DUR
         'I'm not working'

As a final example, consider the Spanish-English code switches reported in (21), provided by Spanish-English bilinguals in central Arizona.

(21a)   ¿Funciona *the computer* de tu hermano en la oficina?
         function-3perSg   of your brother in the office
         'Does your brother's computer function in the office work?'

(21b)   ¿Quiere *the boy* del pueblo algo de comer?
         want-3perSg   from the town something to eat
         'Does the boy from the town want something to eat?'

Note that [*the computer*] in (21a) and [*the boy*] in (21b) cannot count as EL islands because they each contain a prepositional phrase within the maximal projection. Here again, then, we see violations of the System Morpheme Principle, involving a system morpheme of the "embedded language" mixed in with system morphemes of the "matrix language" (*the*, in both cases).

The evidence considered thus far appears to strongly disfavor the Matrix Language Frame Model, particularly with respect to the System Morpheme Principle. Counter-examples to the Morpheme Order Principle are much more difficult to come by, primarily due to the peculiar set of candidate counter-examples defined by the system. Because the Morpheme Order Principle dictates that the sequence of morphemes in an utterance be ordered according to the requirements of the ML, and because the ML is by definition the language which contributes the system morphemes within the CP, there would seem to be only two broad categories of possible counter-examples which could involve language mixing in this case:

(22a) expressions in which morphemes with lexical content as well as system morphemes are contributed by one language, but in which word order is prescribed by another; or

(22b) expressions in which system morphemes are contributed by one language, but morphemes with lexical content *and* word order are prescribed by another.

Expressions of the type (22a) are referred to as *calques* or *loan translations* in the language contact literature; to the extent that one wishes to view these as part of the corpus of mixed-language data, numerous examples are available for review which might be considered counter-examples to the Morpheme Order Principle (Hakuta, 1986; Hill and Hill, 1986). Expressions of type (22b) involve word-internal switching at the level of inflectional morphology. Because clear cases involving switches of this type are rare and controversial (Bentahila and Davies, 1983; Berk-Seligson, 1986; Clyne, 1987; MacSwan, 1999; Poplack and Meechan, 1995; Sankoff and Poplack, 1981), and likely to be ruled out for reasons related to the phonological component, as discussed below, counter-examples of this type will be unavailable due to the nature of the system of word formation, a factor completely unrelated to the Morpheme Order Principle. These factors lead to the expectation, then, that while we will discover many violations of the System Morpheme Principle, very few counter-examples of the Morpheme Order Principle are likely to surface, due to its overlap with well-attested restrictions on mixing languages at the level of inflectional morphology.

Finally, as suggested by comments made in the discussion of other models, the MLF Model has the added weakness, noted in connection with other proposals, that it brings along principles and hypotheses, presumed to be part of the theory of linguistic competence, which have no known justification in the theory of grammar. Although there is indeed evidence from speech error research that monolingual sentence production involves the construction of something like a "language frame," as Jake, Myers-Scotton and Gross (2002) point out, such evidence does not suffice to make the point that the MLF Model has independent justification. Garrett (1988) and numerous others, for instance, report speech errors such as "Make it so the *apple* has more *trees*," in which the grammatical morphemes associated with the speaker's intended expression ("Make it so the tree has more apples") remain in place even though the lexical content words have been inverted. We might readily assume that bilingual language production similarly involves such mechanisms. This would lead us to expect code-switched speech errors in parallel to this, in which inflectional morphemes do not get inverted with lexical content words, as in, "Make it so the apple has *más árboles*." However, note that there is no concurrent implication that a ML/EL contrast is operative in the linguistic system of bilinguals, or that all system morphemes should come from only one language in the course of sentence production, or even that only one language should be activated in generating the bilingual "language frame." These provisions are strictly stipulations of the MLF Model. (For some additional discussion of the MLF Model, see Muysken and de Rooij, 1995; Bentahila, 1995; Ritchie and Bhatia, 1995; Bhatia and Ritchie, 1996; Muysken, 2000; and MacSwan, 2005).

Despite the controversies, considerable progress has been made in our understanding of the nature of bilingual code switching. Various proposals have been made, some quite different from others, some similar. As in many other domains of empirical inquiry, we might prefer proposals which are simplest and most elegant, and which share an analytical framework common to the broadest possible domain. In the case of code switching research, this approach involves the use of well-known and independently justified principles of linguistic theory. In the next section, an approach which takes up precisely these aims within the context of current syntactic theory is outlined.

11.5   A Minimalist Approach to Code Switching

Chomsky (1991) commented on the promise of a syntactic theory in which parameters, which define cross-linguistic variation, are restricted to the lexicon rather than operating on syntactic rules:

> If there were only one human language, the story would essentially end there. But we know that this is false, a rather surprising fact. The general principles of the initial state evidently allow a range of variation. Associated with many principles there are parameters with a few – perhaps just two – values. Possibly, as proposed by Hagit Borer, the parameters are actually restricted to the lexicon, which would mean that the rest of the I-language is fixed and invariant, a far-reaching idea that has proven quite productive.   (p. 23)

Restricting parameters to the lexicon means that linguistic variation falls out of just the morphological properties (abstract and concrete) of the lexicon (Borer, 1984). Essentially, the pursuit of this research objective led to the development of the Minimalist Program (MP).

In the MP, there are two central components of the syntax: C_{HL}, a computational system for human language, which is presumed to be invariant across languages, and a lexicon, to which the idiosyncratic differences observed across languages are attributed. In addition, note that the suggestion that the I-language is fixed and invariant in this way introduces a version of the Universal Base Hypothesis, the idea that phrase structure does not vary across languages; surface differences in word order relate only to the rearrangement of elements in the syntactic tree as the result of movement operations, triggered by lexically encoded morphological features.

Even phrase structure is derived from the lexicon in the minimalist program. An operation, which syntacticians call *Select*, picks lexical items from the lexicon and introduces them into the *numeration*, an assembled subset of the lexicon used to construct a derivation. Another operation, *Merge*, takes items from the numeration and forms new, hierarchically arranged syntactic objects. The operation *Move* applies to syntactic objects formed by Merge to build new structures. Hence, in the MP, phrase structure trees are built derivationally by the application of the three operations Select, Merge, and Move, constrained only by the condition that lexically encoded features match in the course of a derivation.

Movements within the structure are driven by *feature checking*, and may be of two types: A head may undergo *head movement* and adjoin to another head (forming a complex head), or a maximal projection may move to the specific position of a head (*XP movement*); in either case, the element moves for the purpose of checking morphological features of case, number, person, and gender. In addition, its movement may be *overt* or *covert*. Overt movements are driven by strong features and are visible at PF (phonetic form, formerly known as "the surface structure") and LF (logical form, the interpretive level). Covert movements, driven by weak features, are visible only at LF.

Principles of Economy form an important aspect of the MP. One such principle, Full Interpretation (FI), requires that no symbol lacking a sensorimotor interpretation be admitted at PF; applied at LF, FI entails that "every element of the representation have a (language-independent) interpretation" (Chomsky, 1995, p. 27). Thus, uninterpretable features must be checked and deleted by LF. The uninterpretable features are *case, person, number* and *gender*.

As mentioned, *derivations* are built by the application of Merge and Move to the set of lexical items within the numeration (placed there by Select). A derivation is said to *converge* at an interface level (PF or LF) if it satisfies FI at that level; it converges if FI is satisfied at both levels. A derivation that does not converge is also referred to as one that *crashes*. If features are not checked, the derivation crashes. Derivations that crash are ill-formed constructions.

At some point in the derivation, an operation *Spell-Out* applies to strip away from the derivation those elements relevant only to PF; what remains is mapped to LF by a subsystem of C_{HL} called the *covert component*. The elements relevant only to PF are mapped to PF by operations unlike the covert component, operations which comprise the *phonological component*. The phonological component is also regarded as a subsystem of C_{HL}. The subsystem of C_{HL} which maps the lexicon to Spell-Out is the *overt component*. Note that the various components (overt, covert, phonological) are all part of C_{HL}, the computational system for human language. The syntactic model might be represented graphically as in figure 11.1.

11.5.1 Code switching on Minimalist assumptions

The leading aim of the MP is the elimination of all mechanisms that are not necessary and essential on conceptual grounds alone; thus, only the *minimal*

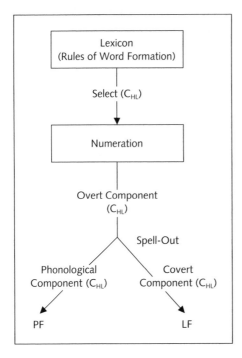

Figure 11.1   The Minimalist framework.

theoretical assumptions may be made to account for linguistic data, privileging more simplistic and elegant accounts over complex and cumbersome ones. These assumptions would naturally favor accounts of code switching which make use of independently motivated principles of grammar over those which posit rules, principles or other constructs specific to it. In general terms, this research program may be stated as in (23), where the minimal code switching-specific apparatus is assumed:

(23)   Nothing constrains code switching apart from the requirements of the mixed grammars.

Notice that (23), an articulation of a particular research program, does not imply that there are no unacceptable code-switched sentences. In (23), *constrain* is used in the technical or theoretical sense described above, and as such it implies that there are no statements, rules or principles of grammar which refer to code switching. Put differently, (23) posits that all of the facts of code switching may be explained just in terms of principles and requirements of the specific grammars used in each specific utterance.

Thus, a Minimalist approach to code switching which adheres to the agenda in (23) might posit that lexical items may be drawn from the lexicon of either language to introduce features into the numeration, which must then be checked for convergence in just the same way as monolingual features must be checked, with no special mechanisms permitted. In this lexicalist approach, no "control structure" or code switching-specific rules are required to mediate contradictory requirements of the mixed systems. The requirements are simply carried along with the lexical items of the respective systems. Thus, it makes sense to formalize the grammar used for code switching as the union of the two lexicons, with no mediating mechanisms.

As indicated in figure 11.1, at Spell-Out a derivation is split, with features relevant only to PF sent to the phonological component where it is mapped to π (or PF), and interpretable material treated by further application of the syntactic component in the mapping to λ (or LF). The specific differences between the syntactic and phonological components of the grammar become particularly relevant to the analysis of code switching data, and therefore require some additional elaboration. As Chomsky proposes,

> at the point of Spell-Out, the computation splits into two parts, one forming π and the other forming λ. The simplest assumptions are (1) that there is no further interaction between computations and (2) that computational procedures are uniform throughout: any operation can apply at any point. We adopt (1), and assume (2) for the computation from N to λ, though not for the computation from N to π; the latter modifies structures (including the internal structure of lexical entries) by processes very different from those that take place in the N $\rightarrow$ λ computation. (1995, p. 229)

A salient difference, then, between syntax and phonology is that phonological rules are ordered with respect to one another and vary cross-linguistically, as also noted by Bromberger and Halle (1989). (In Optimality Theoretic terms, "constraints" are "ranked," or ordered in relative importance, and these rankings vary cross-linguistically.)

There are other differences between syntax and phonology, of course, but this particular difference is one which might be easily exploited to rule out code switching within the PF component. We have been assuming that code switching is formally the *union* of two (lexically encoded) grammars, where the numeration may draw elements from the union of two (or more) lexicons. Each lexical item imposes certain requirements on the derivation in terms of the encoded features, and syntactic operations need take no notice of what particular language a lexical item is associated with.

However, suppose that a PF component PF_x contains rules ordered such that R1 > R2 and R3 > R4, and suppose that in PF_y rules are ordered such that R1 < R2 and R3 < R4. Then the union of PF_x and PF_y will have no ordering relations for Rn. In other words, under union (code switching), the PF components cannot meet their requirement that they have (partially) ordered rules or constraints, ruling out language mixing within the phonological component. I will take this formal property, then, to bar code switching at PF, stated succinctly in (24) as the PF Disjunction Theorem.

(24)   *PF Disjunction Theorem*
    (i)   The PF component consists of rules/constraints which must be (partially) ordered/ranked with respect to each other, and these orders vary cross-linguistically.
    (ii)   Code switching entails the union of at least two (lexically-encoded) grammars.
    (iii) Ordering relations are not preserved under union.
    (iv) Therefore, code switching within a PF component is not possible.

We might think of (24) as an instantiation of the Principle of Full Interpretation (FI), the requirement that every object have a sensorimotor interpretation to qualify as a legitimate representation, a kind of "interface condition" (Chomsky, 1995). Since phonological systems cannot be mixed, code switching at PF generates "unpronounceable" elements which violate FI. Because (24) may be deduced from more elementary considerations, it is termed a "theorem" rather than a "principle."

Let us now consider some implications of (24) for the data of code switching. Recall Poplack's Free Morpheme Constraint in (4), which stipulated that a switch may not occur between a bound morpheme and a lexical item unless the latter has been phonologically integrated into the language of the bound morpheme, as illustrated in the sharply ungrammatical constructions in (25).

(25a)   *Juan está *eat*-iendo
       Juan be/1Ss eat-DUR
       'Juan is eating.'

(25b)   *Juan *eat*-ió
       Juan eat-PAST/3Ss
       'Juan ate.'

(25c)   *Juan *com*-ed
       Juan eat-PAST
       'Juan ate.'

(25d)   *Juan eat-*ará*
       Juan be/1Ss eat-FUT/3Ss
       'Juan will eat.'

When the stem is phonologically integrated into the language of the inflectional morpheme, as in (26), no ill-formedness results.

(26a)   Juan está parqueando su coche
       Juan be/1Ss park-DUR his car
       'Juan is parking his car.'

(26b) Juan parqueó su coche
       Juan park-PAST/3Ss his car
       'Juan parked his car.'

(26c) Juan parqueará su coche
       Juan be/1Ss park-FUT/3Ss
       'Juan will park his car.'

The PF Disjunction Theorem captures the facts which the Free Morpheme Constraint intended to capture, but has a critical advantage: Unlike the Free Morpheme Constraint, the PF Disjunction Theorem is not taken to be a principle of grammar, but is a deduction from elementary facts regarding the nature of rule ordering in phonology and syntax.

An additional assumption we have made regarding the organization of the bilingual language faculty regards the lexicon. Chomsky (1995, p. 20) takes rules of word formation to be internal to the lexicon. Because of the evidence that the phonological components must be separate and discrete, and because affixation is a phonological operation, we assume that the language-particular nature of morphosyntax has the effect of isolating a bilingual's repertoire of words into separate and discrete lexicons, each accessible to the syntactic component. In parallel to the diagram in figure 11.1, figure 11.2 presents an

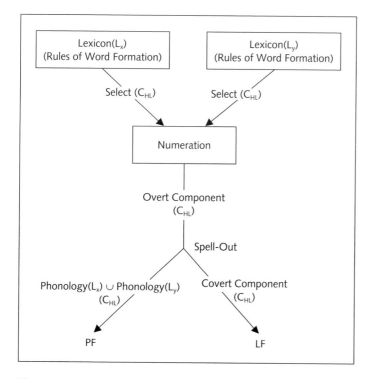

Figure 11.2 Organization of the bilingual language faculty.

illustration of the organization of the bilingual's language faculty (a theory of linguistic competence, not of production).

Now let us return to some more specifically syntactic phenomenon. Chomsky (1995, p. 319) suggests that heads – or X^0s, more generally – are inputs to phonology. Complex X^0s are formed by head movement, and take the form $[_{X^0} X^0 X^0]$. In addition, Chomsky (2001) has recently assigned a wide range of head-raising processes to the phonological component, concluding that head movement is a phonological operation. If correct, the PF Disjunction Theorem in (24) takes on the additional implication that code switching cannot occur in the context of head movement, where the phonological component is implicated.[2] In the next section, we return to examples (17)–(19), presented earlier as counter-examples to the MLF Model.

11.5.2   Code switching in restructuring contexts

Rizzi (1982) analyzed Italian modals,[3] aspectuals and motion verbs as "restructuring" verbs as a way of accounting for (among some other peculiarities) the contrasts in (27)–(28).

(27a)   Finalmente si comincerà a costruire le nuove case popolari
        Finally *si* begin/FUT to build the new houses people/GEN
        'Finally we'll begin to build the new houses for the poor.'

(27b)   Finalmente le nuove case popolari si cominceranno a costruire
        (Same as (27a).)

(28a)   Finalmente si otterrà di costruire le nuove case popolari
        Finally *si* get.permission/FUT to build the new houses people/GEN
        'Finally we'll get permission to build the new houses for the poor.'

(28b)   *Finalmente le nuove case popolari si otterranno di costruire
        (Same as (28a).)

2   Jake, Myers-Scotton and Gross (2002) misinterpret the PF Disjunction Theorem as prohibiting code switching in the context of singly occurring items, an "apparent position" they ascribe to MacSwan (1999, 2000). I am at a complete loss as to how this misconception came about; however, nothing about the PF Disjunction Theorem makes this implication, and MacSwan (1999, 2000) discusses numerous examples of singly occurring code switches, never once suggesting that such cases are uniformly "banned" or are examples of some other kind of language contact phenomenon. For additional comment, see MacSwan (2003).
3   Rizzi (1983, p. 41, n5) uses the term *modal* "as a simple mnemonic label for a homogeneous, small class of main verbs," regarding them to be of the same lexical category as other Vs for Italian.

In Rizzi's (1982) analysis, *comincerà* 'will begin,' but not *otterrà* 'will get permission,' triggers an optional reanalysis of the form Vx (P) $V_2 \Rightarrow V$, where Vx is a verb of the restructuring class, (P) an optional intervening preposition, and V_2 is the verb of the embedded sentence. This restructuring process is essentially a type of compounding. In (27) a reanalysis of the constituents allows the object of the embedded clause in an impersonal *si* construction to move to the subject position of the matrix clause; in (28) this promotion is barred because reanalysis cannot apply for *otterrà*. Importantly, reanalysis is *optional* in Italian; it has applied in (27b), allowing the promotion of the embedded object to subject position, but it has not applied in (27a) where the object of the embedded clause remains in situ.

Aspectual *essere* is used with a past participle in Italian passive impersonal *si* constructions. In constructions such as (29a), *essere* too may be viewed as a restructuring verb, allowing promotion of the embedded object to subject position, shown in (29b).

(29a)　Si è dato un regalo
　　　　si essere given a gift
　　　　'A gift is given.'

(29b)　Un regalo si è dato
　　　　a gift *si* essere given
　　　　'A gift is given.'

On Rizzi's (1982) analysis, restructuring has applied to (29b) but not to (29a), forcing the promotion of [$_{NP}$ *un regalo*] in the former example.

However, note that a very different pattern of judgments emerges when code switching is involved in constructions like (19), repeated here. Consider the French-Italian facts in (19).

(19a)　Si è *donné un cadeau*
　　　　si essere given a gift

(19b)　*Un cadeau* si è *donné*
　　　　a gift *si* essere given

The movement of [$_{NP}$ *un cadeau*] indicates that reanalysis has occurred in (19b), just as it did in (29b). The verbal complexes are identical in both cases: A mixture of the Italian aspectual auxiliary *è* immediately adjacent to the French past participle *donné*. Thus, the unacceptability of (19b) indicates that code switching in restructuring configurations is prohibited.

The question of interest, of course, is why. Since Rizzi's (1982) original observations regarding restructuring, a variety of proposals have appeared (in particular, see Haegeman and van Riemsdijk, 1986; Roberts, 1997; and Wurmbrand, 1997). Like Rizzi (1982), these newer proposals assume that a sort of compounding takes place in the two verbs, forming a structure of the form [$_{V^0}$ V^0 V^0]. Because (24) rules out code switching in the environment of complex heads such as [$_{V^0}$ V^0 V^0], the pattern in (29) is predicted to have the judgments rendered; and examples in (17), repeated as (30), are predicted to be well-formed, as attested.

(30a)   No, *parce que* hanno *donné des cours*
            no, because have given of the lectures
            'No, because they have given the lectures.'

(30b)   Oui, alors j'ai dit que *si potev* aller comme ça
            yes so I have said that REF could walk like that
            'Yes, so I said that we could go like that.'

An analysis of (18), repeated below as (31), similarly follows: In (31b), the aspectual *had* triggers restructuring with *visto* 'seen,' creating the structure [$_{V^0}$ V^0 V^0]. Because languages cannot be switched in such structures due to (24), (31b) crashes at PF.

(31a)   The students *habían visto la película italiana*
            The students had seen the Italian movie

(31b)   *The student had *visto la película italiana*
            The student had seen the Italian movie

Let us consider, as a final example, the analysis of data involving code switching between languages with different basic word orders.

11.5.3 Word order

A striking result of the MP is the account of differences in basic word order in terms of movement requirements associated with feature strength. The universal base structure is assumed to be underlyingly SVO with a VP-internal subject. V^0 raises to T^0 (=I^0) to check φ-features. If the subject overtly checks its case feature in the specifier position of T^0, then an SVO order results. If it checks its case feature covertly, however, then the resulting word order will be VSO. Thus, the typological distinction between SVO and VSO languages is captured in terms of the strength of the case feature in T^0.

Recall that the formation of mixed-language heads is ruled out by the PF Disjunction Theorem in (24). Therefore, if V^0 raises to T^0 to check φ-features, both elements must be of the same language. As a result, the language of the verb will determine the language of T^0, hence the value of its case feature. In this way the system developed here predicts that the language of the verb will determine the position of the subject – if the verb is from an SVO language, the subject should occur preverbally, whether it is from an SVO language or not; if the verb is from a VSO language, the subject should occur postverbally, regardless of the requirements of the language of the subject. These facts are attested in a wide range of corpora, as shown in (32).[4]

(32a) VS verb (Irish), SV subject (English) (Stenson, 1990, p. 180)
Beidh *jet lag* an tógáil a pháirt ann
be-FUT   taking   its part in-it
'Jet lag will be playing its part in it'

(32b) VS verb (Irish), SV subject (English) (Stenson, 1990, p. 180)
Fuair sé *thousand pounds*
get-PA he
'He got a thousand pounds'

(32c) VS verb (Breton), SV subject (French) (Pensel, 1979, p. 68)
Oa   ket *des armes*
be-3S IMP NEG of-the arms
'There were no arms'

(32d) VS verb (Breton), SV subject (French) (Troadec, 1983, p. 35)
Setu oa   *l'état-major*   du-se barzh ti Lanserot
There be-imp the military-staff down-there in house Lanserot
'There was the military staff down there in Lanserot's house'

(32e) VS verb (SLQ Zapotec), SV subject (Spanish) (MacSwan, 2003, p. 12)
S-to'oh *mi esposa* el coche
DEF-sell my wife the car
'My wife will definitely sell the car'

Now consider the placement of objects in code switching contexts. If an object moves covertly out of the VP-shell to the specifier position of *v* (a preverbal position), then the elements remain in the order SVO for purposes of PF. If the object moves overtly, however, an SOV word order is derived at

4 Stenson (1990, p. 174) reports the following example which is not consistent with the generalization just made:

(i) SV verb (English), VS subject (Irish)
Decided *Aer Lingus go raibh sé ro-chancy*
decided Aer Lingus that be-PA it too-chancy
'Aer Lingus decided that it was too chancy.'

It is difficult to know how to reconcile this datum with others considered. Stenson reports that the Irish-English bilinguals used in her studies all had "at least a working knowledge of English" (p. 575), so it is possible that the speaker here had only "a working knowledge" that was not sufficient to derive the expected construction. Other analyses are possible.

PF. The parameter responsible for this difference is associated with v. If the case feature of v is weak, SVO is formed; if it is strong, SOV results. It is natural to assume that the verb undergoes a checking relation with v by head movement, guaranteeing that the language of the verb will determine the position of the object at PF, just as in the case of subjects. The expected results are attested:

(33a)   VO (English) verb, OV object (Farsi) (Mahootian, 1993, p. 152)
    Tell them you'll buy *xune-ye jaedid* when you sell your own house
    Tell them you'll buy house-POSS new when you sell your own house
    'Tell them you'll buy a new house when you sell your own house.'

(33b)   OV verb (Farsi), VO object (English) (Mahootian, 1993, p. 150)
    Ten dollars *dad-e*
    ten dollars give-PERF
    'She gave ten dollars.'

(33c)   VO verb (English), OV object (Japanese) (Nishimura, 1985, p. 76)
    . . . we never knew *anna koto nanka*
    . . . we never knew such thing sarcasm
    '. . . we never knew such a thing as sarcasm.'

(33d)   OV verb (Japanese), VO object (English) (Nishimura, 1985, p. 129)
    In addition, his wife *ni yattara*
    in addition, his wife DAT give-COND
    'In addition, if we give it to his wife.'

(33e)   VO verb (English), OV object (Korean) (Lee, 1991, p. 130)
    I ate *ceonyek* quickly
    'I ate dinner quickly.'

(33f)   OV verb (Korean), VO object (English) (Lee, 1991, p. 129)
    Na-nun *dinner*-lul pali meokeotta
    I-SM dinner-OM quickly ate
    'I ate dinner quickly.'

Analyses of other data presented in this chapter may be reviewed in other work. The agreement asymmetry in (7)–(8) and Poplack's Spanish-English clitic data in (5) are discussed in MacSwan (1999), and the negation data presented in (13) and (20) are discussed in MacSwan (1999, 2000). For extensive comments on the "modified minimalist" approach of Jake, Myers-Scotton, and Gross (2002), see MacSwan (2003). In the final section, we present a perspective on the history of research in bilingual code switching, and present some thoughts on directions for future research.

11.6 Conclusions

Efforts to construct formal theories of grammar have a long history in linguistics and are rooted in general principles of science developed during the Enlightenment. As Chomsky pointed out in the Preface to *Syntactic Structures* (1957, p. 5), the use of formalism in linguistics has a number of concrete advantages:

> The search for rigorous formulation in linguistics has a much more serious motivation than mere concern for logical niceties or the desire to purify well-established methods of linguistic analysis. Precisely constructed models for linguistic structure can play an important role, both negative and positive, in the process of discovery itself. By pushing a precise but inadequate formulation to an unacceptable conclusion, we can often expose the exact source of this inadequacy and, consequently, gain a deeper understanding of the linguistic data. More positively, a formalized theory may automatically provide solutions for many problems other than those for which it was explicitly designed.

In addition, theories which lack the precision possible through formalism may be too vague to properly evaluate. In *Discourse on Bodies of Water* (1612), for instance, Galileo refuted an anonymous Jesuit opponent in a discussion of the nature of sunspots by pointing out that his arguments were so vague as to be true in all conceivable situations (tautological), hence not falsifiable. Galileo turned to the formal language of mathematics in order to express his claims in explicit terms, thus establishing an account of physical phenomena in a precisely formulated way. In linguistics too, "obscure and intuition-bound notions can neither lead to absurd conclusions nor provide new and correct ones, and hence they fail to be useful in two important respects" (Chomsky, 1957, p. 5).

The historic tendency within the field of code switching to posit all-inclusive constraints or principles which define the totality of language mixing has turned the attention of researchers away from fine-grained linguistic analysis which might take advantage of advances in the core domains of the linguistic sciences. As Santorini and Mahootian (1995) have noted, such broad and sweeping constraints, posed as principles of linguistic competence, have met with demise. As the review discussed here suggests, for each proposed constraint, there are multiple counter-examples and objections to be made.

It has been the primary goal of this chapter to demonstrate that this approach can be successful, and may reveal interesting and extremely subtle properties of the languages under analysis. Since it has been shown that code switching-specific constraints cannot account for the data under analysis, and since the data under analysis may be explained without reference to such constraints, we may assume that such mechanisms do not exist by general principles of scientific parsimony, and in the interest of making use of minimal theoretical apparatus. This was the aim articulated in (23), repeated here:

(34)   Nothing constrains code switching apart from the requirements of the mixed grammars.

Rather than continuing to propose broad and sweeping constraints on code switching, the field should embark upon a program of research which evaluates precisely formulated proposals and hypotheses in terms of well-known categories and independently motivated principles of linguistic theory, taking advantage of ongoing basic research in core areas of linguistics. As Chomsky suggests, evaluating such precisely formulated theories will play an important role in the process of discovery itself, perhaps leading, in the case of code switching research, to significant insight into the nature of bilingual linguistic competence.

The linguistic study of code switching is still very much in its infancy, but is an exciting and intriguing field. We hope that continued research will lead to refinements, new insights, and expanded inquiry.

REFERENCES

Abney, S. P. (1987). The English noun phrase in its sentential aspect. Ph.D. dissertation, MIT.

Azuma, S. (1991). Processing and intrasentential code-switching. Ph.D. dissertation. University of Texas, Austin.

Azuma, S. (1993). The frame-content hypothesis in speech production: Evidence from intrasentential code switching. *Linguistics*, 31, pp. 1071–93.

Belazi, H. M., Rubin, E. J., and Toribio, A. J. (1994). Code switching and X-bar theory: The functional head constraint. *Linguistic Inquiry*, 25(2), pp. 221–37.

Bentahila, A. (1995). Review of *Duelling Languages: Grammatical Structure in Codeswitching*. *Language*, 71(1), 135–140.

Bentahila, A. and E. E. Davies (1983). The syntax of Arabic-French code-switching. *Lingua*, 59, pp. 301–30.

Berk-Seligson, S. (1986). Linguistic constraints on intrasentential code-switching: A study of Spanish-Hebrew bilingualism. *Language in Society*, 15, 313–48.

Bhatia, T. K. (1989). Bilinguals' creativity and syntactic theory: Evidence for emerging grammar. *World Englishes*, 8(3), 265–76.

Bhatia, T. K. and Ritchie, W. C. (1996). Light verbs in code-switched utterances: Derivational economy in I-Language or incongruence in production? *Proceedings of the Annual Boston University Conference on Language Development*, 20(1), 52–62. Somerville, MA: Cascadilla Press.

Blom, J. P. and Gumperz, J. J. (1972). Social meaning and structure: Code-switching in Norway. In J. Gumperz, and D. Hymes (eds.), *Directions in Sociolinguistics*. New York: Holt, Reinhart, Winston.

Bokamba, E. G. (1989). Are there syntactic constraints on code-mixing? *World Englishes*, 8, 277–92.

Borer, H. (1984). *Parametric Syntax: Case Studies in Semitic and Romance Languages*. Dordrecht: Foris.

Bromberger, S. and M. Halle. (1989). Why phonology is different. *Linguistic*

Inquiry, 20, pp. 51–70. Also in A. Kasher (ed.) (1991), *The Chomskyan Turn*.

Chan, B. H.-S. (1999). Aspects of the syntax, production and pragmatics of code-switching with special reference to Cantonese-English. Ph.D. dissertation, University College, London.

Chomsky, N. (1957). *Syntactic Structures*. The Hague: Mouton.

Chomsky, N. (1981). *Lectures on Government and Binding*. New York: Mouton de Gruyter.

Chomsky, N. (1991). Linguistics and cognitive science: Problems and mysteries. In Kasher (ed.) (1991), *The Chomskyan Turn*.

Chomsky, N. (1995). *The Minimalist Program*. Cambridge, MA: MIT Press.

Chomsky, N. (2001). Derivation by phase. In M. Kenstowics (ed.), *Ken Hale: A Life in Language*, pp. 1–51. Cambridge, MA: MIT Press.

Clyne, M. (1987). Constraints on code switching: How universal are they? *Linguistics*, 25, 739–64.

Di Sciullo, A.-M., Muysken, P., and Singh, R. (1986). Government and code-switching. *Journal of Linguistics*, 22, pp. 1–24.

Dussias, P. E. (1997). Switching at no cost: Exploring Spanish-English codeswitching using the response-contingent sentence matching task. Ph.D. dissertation, University of Arizona

Galileo, G. (1960) [1612]. *Discourse on Bodies in Water*. Trans. T. Salisbury. Urbana: University of Illinois Press.

Garrett, M. F. (1988). Process in sentence production. In F. Newmeyer (ed.), *The Cambridge Language Survey*, vol. 3, pp. 69–96. Cambridge, UK: Cambridge University Press.

Gumperz, J. (1970). Verbal strategies and multilingual communication. In J. E. Alatis (ed.), *Georgetown Round Table on Language and Linguistics*. Washington, D.C.: Georgetown University Press.

Gumperz, J. (1976). The sociolinguistic significance of conversational code-switching. *Papers on Language and Context: Working Papers*, 46, 1–46.

Gumperz, J. and D. Hymes (eds.) (1972). *Directions in Sociolinguistics*. New York: Holt, Reinhart, Winston.

Gumperz, J. and Hernandez-Chavez, E. (1970). Cognitive aspects of bilingual communication. In W. H. Whitely (ed.), *Language and Social Change*. Oxford: Oxford University Press.

Haegeman, L. and van Riemsdijk (1986). Verb projection raising, scope, and the typology of rules affecting verbs. *Linguistic Inquiry*, 17(3), 417–66.

Hakuta, K. (1986). *Mirror of Language: The debate on Bilingualism*. New York: Basic Books.

Halmari, H. (1997). *Government and Code Switching: Explaining American Finnish*. New York: J. Benjamins.

Hill, J. H. and Hill, K. C. (1986). *Speaking Mexicano: Dynamics of Syncretic Language in Central Mexico*. Tucson: University of Arizona Press.

Jake, J., Myers-Scotton, C., and Gross, S. (2002). Making a minimalist approach to codeswitching work: Adding the Matrix Language. *Bilingualism: Language and Cognition*, 5(1), 69–91.

Joshi, A. (1985). Processing of sentences with intrasential code switching. In D. R. Dowty, L. Kattunen, and A. M. Zwicky (eds.), *Natural Language Parsing: Psychological, Computational and Theoretical Perspectives*. Cambridge, UK: Cambridge University Press.

Kasher, A. (ed.) (1991). *The Chomskyan Turn*. Cambridge, UK: Blackwell.

Kayne, R. S. (1995). *The Antisymmetry of Syntax*. Cambridge, MA: MIT Press.

Keenan, E. L. and Stabler, E. P. (1994). There is more than one language. *Proceedings of Langues et Grammaire-I*, Université Paris-8.

Labov, W. (1970). The logic of non-standard English. In F. Williams (ed.), *Language and Poverty*. Chicago: Rand McNally.

Lee, M.-H. (1991). A parametric approach to code-switching. Ph.D. dissertation, State University of New York at Stonybrook.

MacSwan, J. (1999). *A minimalist approach to intrasentential code switching*. New York: Garland Press.

MacSwan, J. (2000). The architecture of the bilingual language faculty: Evidence from codeswitching. *Bilingualism: Language and Cognition*, 3(1), 37–54.

MacSwan, J. (2003). The derivation of basic word orders in code switching. Paper presented at the 4th International Symposium on Bilingualism, Arizona State University, April 30–May 3.

MacSwan, J. (2003). Codeswitching and generative grammar: A critique of the MLF Model and some remarks on "modified minimalism." *Bilingualism: Language and Cognition*, 8(1), 1–22.

Mahootian, S. (1993). A null theory of code switching. Ph.D. dissertation, Northwestern University.

Mahootian, S. and Santorini, B. (1996). Code switching and the complement / adjunct distinction: A reply to Belazi, Rubin and Toribio. *Linguistic Inquiry*, 27(3), pp. 464–79.

Meechan, M. and Poplack, S. (1995). Orphan categories in bilingual discourse: Adjectivization strategies in Wolof-French and Fongbe-French. *Language Variation and Change*, 7(2), 169–94.

Muysken, P. (2000). *Bilingual Speech: A Typology of Code-mixing*. Cambridge, UK: Cambridge University Press.

Muysken, P. and de Rooij, V. (1995). Review of *Social Motivations for Code-switching: Evidence from Africa* and *Duelling Languages: Grammatical Structure in Codeswitching*. *Linguistics*, 33, 1043–66.

Myers-Scotton, C. (1993a). *Social Motivations for Codeswitching: Evidence from Africa*. Oxford: Clarendon Press.

Myers-Scotton, C. (1993b). *Duelling Languages: Grammatical Structure in Codeswitching*. Oxford: Clarendon Press.

Nartey, J. S. (1982). Code-switching, interference or faddism? Language use among educated Ghanaians. *Anthropological Linguistics*, 24, 183–92.

Newmeyer, F. J. (1986). *The Politics of Linguistics*. Chicago: The University of Chicago Press.

Nishimura, M. (1985). Intrasentential code-switching in Japanese and English. Ph.D. dissertation, University of Pennsylvania.

Nishimura, M. (1997). *Japanese/English Code-switching: Syntax and Pragmatics*. Vol. 24 of *Berkeley Insights in Linguistics and Semiotics*, ed. I. Rauch. New York: Peter Lang.

Pandit, I. (1990). Grammaticality in code switching. In R. Jacobson (ed.), *Code Switching as a Worldwide Phenomenon*. New York: Peter Lang.

Pensel, I. (1979). Testeni. *Hor Yezh*, 126, 47–73.

Pfaff, C. (1979). Constraints on language mixing: Intrasentential code-switching and borrowing in Spanish/English. *Language*, 55, 291–318.

Poplack, S. (1980). "Sometimes I'll start a sentence in Spanish y termino en Español": Toward a typology of code-switching. *Linguistics*, 18, pp. 581–618.

Poplack, S. (1981). The syntactic structure and social function of code-switching. In R. Durán (ed.), 1981. *Latino Language and Communicative Behavior*. Norwood, NJ: Ablex.

Poplack, S. and Meechan, M. (1995). Patterns of language mixture: Nominal structure in Wolof-French and Fongbe-French bilingual discourse. In L. Milroy and P. Muysken (eds.), *One*

Speaker, Two Languages: Cross-Disciplinary Perspectives on Code-Switching. Cambridge: Cambridge University Press.

Poplack, S., Wheeler, S., and Westwood, A. (1989). Distinguishing language contact phenomena: Evidence from Finnish-English bilingualism. *World Englishes*, 8, 389–406.

Ritchie, W. C. and Bhatia, T. K. (1995). Codeswitching, grammar, and sentence production: The problem of dummy verbs. In Charlotte Koster and Frank Wijnen (eds.), *Proceedings of the Groningen Assembly on Language Acquisition*. Groningen, The Netherlands: Centre Language and Cognition.

Rizzi, L. (1982). *Issues in Italian Syntax*. Dordrecht: Foris.

Roberts, I. (1997). Restructuring, head movement, and locality. *Linguistic Inquiry*, 28(3), pp. 423–60.

Sankoff, D. and Poplack, S. (1981). A formal grammar for code-switching. *Papers in Linguistics*, 14, 3–45.

Sankoff, D., Poplack, S., and Vanniarajan, S. (1990). The case of the nonce loan in Tamil. *Language Variation and Change*, 2, 71–101.

Santorini, B. and Mahootian, S. (1995). Code switching and the syntactic status of adnominal adjectives. *Lingua*, 96, pp. 1–27.

Sportiche, D. (1995). Sketch of a reductionist approach to syntactic variation and dependencies. In H.

Campos and P. Kempchinsky (eds.), *Evolution and Revolution in Linguistic Theory: Essays in Honor of Carlos Otero*. Washington, D.C.: Georgetown University Press.

Stenson, N. (1990). Phrase structure congruence, government, and Irish-English code switching. *Syntax and Semantics*, 23, 169–99.

Stowell, T. (1981). Origins of Phrase Structure. Ph.D. dissertation, Massachusetts Institute of Technology.

Timm, L. A. (1975). Spanish-English code-switching: El porqué and how-not-to. *Romance Philology*, 28, pp. 473–82.

Toribio, A. J. (2001). On the emergence of bilingual code-switching competence. *Bilingualism: Language and Cognition*, 4(3), 202–31.

Troadec, B. (1983). Tri fennad-kaoz gant an Itron Bernadette Troadec. *Hor Yezh*, 71–127.

Wentz, J. and McClure, E. (1976). Ellipsis in bilingual discourse. *Papers from the regional meeting of the Chicago Linguistics Society*, pp. 656–65. Chicago: Chicago Linguistics Society.

Wolfram, W. (1969). *Detroit Negro Speech*. Washington, D.C.: Center for Applied Linguistics.

Woolford, E. (1983). Bilingual code-switching and syntactic theory. *Linguistic Inquiry*, 14(5), pp. 520–36.

Wurmbrand, S. (1997). Deconstructing restructuring. Paper presented at the III Langues et Grammaire, Paris.

12 Sign Language–Spoken Language Bilingualism: Code Mixing and Mode Mixing by ASL-English Bilinguals

GERALD P. BERENT

12.1 Introduction

The study of sign language–spoken language (SL-SpL) bilingualism addresses the same kinds of linguistic, psychological, social, political, and educational issues that the broader field of bilingualism does. Indeed, a solid understanding of SL-SpL bilingualism requires familiarity with the relevant issues in each of these domains of SL-SpL bilingual studies. However, this chapter focuses on a largely unexplored area of SL-SpL bilingualism that relates to the unique variable – *modality* – that distinguishes sign languages from spoken languages. Whereas spoken languages are communicated through the *auditory-vocal* (AV) modality, sign languages are communicated through the *visual-spatial* (VS) modality. When a sign language and a spoken language are in contact, the two distinct modalities allow extraordinary options for language mixing. Specifically, SL-SpL contact allows the combining of elements from the two languages not only *sequentially*, as in SpL-SpL mixing, but both sequentially and *simultaneously*.

Studies of SL-SpL mixing have generally been descriptive studies that attempt to characterize the features and diversity of the communication that emerges from SL-SpL contact (e.g. Lucas and Valli, 1992). In the broader field of spoken language bilingualism, there has been an attempt not only to describe but to explain language mixing phenomena observed among spoken language bilinguals by identifying universal linguistic principles that constrain this language mixing (see Bhatia and Ritchie, 1996). Such explanatory studies within the field of SL-SpL bilingualism are virtually non-existent. Therefore, the purpose of this chapter is to propose a theory-based approach to the study of SL-SpL bilingualism with suggestions for identifying the universal linguistic principles that constrain the unique language mixing phenomena that emerge from SL-SpL contact.

Users of sign languages around the world interact with the spoken languages of their respective hearing communities. Accordingly, there are many instances of SL-SpL bilingualism that could be explored. However, American Sign Language (ASL), used by many deaf persons in the United States and Canada, has been the target of the largest body of research during the relatively short history of contemporary sign language studies (30 to 40 years). Therefore, ASL-English bilingualism will be the target of discussion in this chapter as an exemplar of SL-SpL bilingualism.

In this chapter, the spelling "Deaf" with a capital D is used by convention to refer to the Deaf community and its members viewed as a distinct cultural group with its own social conventions and identity and its own language. The spelling "deaf" is used in a neutral sense to refer to persons with significant hearing losses without any assumption about an individual's affiliation or identification with the Deaf community.

12.2   American Sign Language

To understand ASL-English bilingualism, one needs to understand the grammatical devices that ASL employs as well as the typological differences between ASL and English. Over the past 30 years or so, linguistic research on ASL has led to a more thorough understanding of the linguistic properties of ASL, and these properties appear to be associated with the same universal linguistic principles that apply to spoken languages (Lillo-Martin, 1991). With respect to specific properties of ASL, Newport and Supalla (2000, pp. 107–8) succinctly summarized the central findings in ASL research that have emerged:

> [ASL] is a language with a quite different type of structure than that of English, but one that is found among spoken languages (e.g. it shares certain typological similarities with Navajo). Word structure in ASL is quite complex, particularly in verbs. Typical verbs are marked morphologically for agreement in person and number with both subject and object, and for temporal aspect and other grammatical features common to verbs in other languages. . . . Verbs of motion are particularly complex, with stems involving morphemes for path, manner of motion, orientation, and classifier morphemes marking the semantic category or size and shape of both the moving object and a secondary object with respect to which the movement path occurs. . . . Word order in ASL is relatively free, with an unmarked SVO order but a number of order-changing syntactic structures commonly used (e.g. topicalization of the object, subject, or VP). Moved constituents are obligatorily marked by grammaticized facial expressions, which are produced throughout the signing of the words of that constituent. . . . When verbs are marked for agreement and/or when discussing subjects and objects

that have already been mentioned, the subject and object NPs may be omitted from the sentence – that is, the language permits null arguments. . . . In short, the grammatical properties of ASL are unlike those of English but are quite familiar to students of other languages of the world. This body of findings thus suggests that principles of word and sentence structure are, at least to some degree, common to both signed and spoken languages and are not inherently connected to the auditory-vocal mode.

This summary reveals that ASL and English are quite different typologically: ASL verbs exhibit verb agreement with objects and often subjects; English exhibits verb agreement only with subjects. ASL has a rich system of classifier morphemes; English does not. ASL deviates frequently from SVO word order; English rarely does. ASL permits null arguments; English does not.

With respect to "phonological" structure, an ASL sign consists of phonemes that utilize handshapes, orientation of the hand(s), location of the hands within a constrained physical space, and movement of the hands within the signing space. Fischer and van der Hulst (2003) provide an overview of the structure of ASL and other sign languages, including their phonological, morphological, and syntactic properties, along with comparisons with analogous spoken language properties. For example, while English marks tense with an inflectional affix (e.g. -ed), ASL has no mechanism for marking tense but instead marks *time* through the use of adverbials (e.g. the sign LONG-AGO to indicate past time). By convention ASL signs are glossed using all capitals, and hyphens between words in an English gloss indicate that one sign is glossed by two English words.

With respect to agreement, unlike English, which signals subject–verb agreement through word order and with the inflectional suffix -s (e.g. *brings*), ASL sets up points in space toward which or away from which a verb moves or faces. Fischer and van der Hulst (2003) provide a sentence containing the ASL agreement verb KICK as illustrated in (1a) (= their example (12)).

(1) a.   COW INDEX$_a$ HORSE INDEX$_b$ $_a$KICK$_b$
          'The cow kicked the horse.'
     b.   COW$_a$ HORSE$_b$ $_a$KICK$_b$
     c.   COW$_a$ HORSE$_b$ $_b$KICK$_a$
          'The horse kicked the cow.'

The subscripts *a* and *b* in (1) represent two points within the signing space. In (1a), COW is signed followed by INDEX$_a$, which indicates a finger point toward a point in the signing space, for example, toward the space at a 45-degree angle to the signer's left. HORSE is then signed followed by a finger point (INDEX$_b$) toward a different point in the signing space, for example, toward the space at a 45-degree angle to the signer's right. Then the agreement verb KICK is signed in the direction from point *a* toward point *b*, as indicated by the ordering of the subscripts in the gloss $_a$KICK$_b$.

ASL agreement can also be expressed without the use of the INDEX to set up reference points. In (1b), the signs COW$_a$ and HORSE$_b$ must each be accompanied by an eye gaze toward distinct spaces *a* and *b* where the two nouns are set up. The agreement verb KICK is signed in the direction from point *a* toward point *b*, as in (1a), and (1b) therefore has the same meaning as (1a). However, despite the same word order, if the verb KICK is signed in the direction from point *b* toward point *a*, as indicated by $_b$KICK$_a$ in (1c), then the agreement pattern changes the meaning of the sentence as indicated in (1c).

In the quotation above, Newport and Supalla (2000) referred to "grammaticized facial expressions" in ASL. This term refers to *nonmanual* grammatical processes that are characteristic of sign languages. As discussed in Wilbur (2000), these nonmanuals include head position, body position, eyebrow and forehead position, eye gaze, nose position, and the mouth, tongue, and cheek. In a process called *layering*, nonmanuals can co-occur with signs and sign sequences and can even be layered on top of other nonmanuals. The result of layering is that "morphosyntactic information is layered on top of the lexical sign, conveying a bigger bundle of information in a complex sign in less time than would be required if each piece of information had to be signed in separate signs" (Wilbur, p. 219). A clear example of layering in ASL is provided in the following sentence from Wilbur (p. 226):

(2)
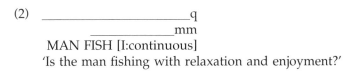

MAN FISH [I:continuous]
'Is the man fishing with relaxation and enjoyment?'

The notational representation used in (2) is interpreted as follows: The sentence consists of two signs, MAN and FISH. The bracketed information after the verb FISH indicates that there is a layered inflectional modification on FISH, such that the sign is articulated with repetition, in this case indicating continuous aspect. The line ending with "q" above the sign sequence indicates that the nonmanual question marker spans the sign sequence and is articulated by the signer leaning forward, with the head forward, and with the eyebrows raised. This is the obligatory grammatical marker of a yes–no question. The line ending with "mm" begins with the signing of FISH and spans the duration of the repeated articulation of that sign. This separate nonmanual marker is an adverbial modification of the verb FISH using the mouth with the lips pressed together. This articulation indicates that the action of the verb is done with relaxation and enjoyment, as reflected in the English translation of the sentence. As will be seen below, layering plays an important role in ASL-English language mixing.

12.3 Manually Coded English

In contrast to the natural sign language ASL, several artificial systems of *Manually Coded English* (MCE) were devised in the 1970s to represent English in the VS modality. The assumption was that deaf children who learned a signed version of English would develop English skills naturally and at a pace equivalent to that of hearing children learning English. MCE uses a large base of ASL signs along with a sizable inventory of invented signs for English bound inflectional morphemes such as -*ed* and -*ing* and derivational morphemes such as *pre-* and -*tion*. Thus, in order to express the English form *playing*, MCE uses the ASL sign PLAY followed by the invented sign -ING.

Since ASL and English employ distinct, modality-dependent morphological mechanisms, Supalla (1991) argued that, on theoretical grounds, MCE systems should be unlearnable. He found evidence that children using MCE would modify their signed English verbs in a way that approximated the manner in which a sign language might employ space morphologically and that the children were not consistent in their use of English word order and other aspects of English. Supalla concluded that there are serious learnability problems for artificial MCE sign systems.

However, Schick and Moeller (1992) found that deaf children using MCE exhibited good skills in the use of English word order, embedding, argument structure, prepositions, and pronouns but weak skills in the use of auxiliaries, copulas, and inflectional morphemes. They concluded that, rather than being completely unlearnable, certain aspects of MCE, such as English morphology, are indeed difficult to learn. (See Schick, 2003, for a detailed comparison of the acquisition of ASL and the acquisition of MCE.)

12.4   ASL and English as L1 or L2

A significant factor in the discussion of ASL-English bilingualism, as in any discussion of bilingualism, is bilinguals' levels of competency in each of their languages. As with the study of SpL-SpL bilingualism, critical period effects for language acquisition influence the determination of which language is the SL-SpL bilingual's first language (L1) and which is the second language (L2). However, along with the modality variable discussed above, there is another exceptional variable that is relevant to the study of SL-SpL bilingualism and that also significantly distinguishes SL-SpL bilingualism from SpL-SpL bilingualism. *Hearing status* determines which modality is the most natural modality for language acquisition and interacts with critical period effects in determining L1 and L2.

Because of hearing loss, deaf persons generally have severely restricted access to spoken language input in the AV modality, although they have full access to sign language input in the VS modality. Thus, unlike hearing bilinguals, deaf bilinguals are challenged in their attainment of competency in the spoken language to which they are exposed on the basis of hearing status. In contrast, hearing persons have access to both modalities and are not disadvantaged on the basis of hearing status. However, as with SpL-SpL bilinguals, the bilingual competencies of both deaf and hearing SL-SpL bilinguals are influenced by critical period effects.

With respect to the acquisition of ASL as an L1, Lillo-Martin (1999) summarized the existing body of research on the acquisition of ASL by Deaf children of Deaf parents who use ASL (only 5 to 10 percent of deaf children). From this body of research, Lillo-Martin concluded that deaf children acquire ASL in much the same way that hearing children acquire spoken languages. Deaf children follow the same acquisitional sequences at roughly the same ages as hearing children.

However, the vast majority of deaf children do not learn ASL as an L1, and therefore critical period effects yield differences in the sign language knowledge of these L2 ASL learners (see Fischer, 1998). L2 ASL is sometimes difficult to define because non-native but early learners (ages 5 to 10) of ASL often attain native-like knowledge of ASL, as compared to late learners, who learn ASL after puberty. Despite these differences, the accessibility of the VS modality establishes ASL as the *primary* language of many deaf persons. (For further discussion of age, language acquisition, and bilingualism, see chapters 4, 5, and 21.)

With respect to deaf children's acquisition of English, restricted access to the AV modality has major consequences for the attainment of English knowledge. Quigley and King (1980) reported that, on average, the English knowledge of 18-year-old deaf students is less developed than the English knowledge of 8-year-old hearing students. What often happens is that, even if English is the first or only language to which a deaf child is exposed, the restricted access to the AV modality results in English knowledge that simulates L2 knowledge (Berent, 1988, 1996a, characterized this situation as "L1.5 acquisition"). Therefore, the L1/L2 labels are often difficult to apply. On modality grounds alone, ASL is sometimes regarded by members of the Deaf community and proponents of bilingual/bicultural models of deaf education as the L1 and English as the L2 of deaf persons, despite age of exposure or levels of competency in the two languages.

Whatever label is used, the fact is that learning English is a life-long struggle for many deaf persons. The variable English language knowledge exhibited by deaf children and adults has been described from several different perspectives. Bochner and Albertini (1988) compared deaf children's acquisition of English to stages observed along continua associated with pidginization and creolization processes. Berent (1988) explained deaf students' relative mastery of specific English structures in terms of the degree to which structures explicitly represent grammatical relations. Berent and Samar (1990) and Berent (1996b) explained aspects of deaf students' English knowledge in terms of default settings of parameters of universal grammar (Chomsky, 1981) and the learning of "smaller languages" (Berent, 1996a). And de Villiers, de Villiers, and Hoban (1994) explained deaf children's English competency in terms of underdeveloped knowledge of "functional categories." Collectively, these and other studies have contributed significantly to our understanding of the acquisition of English by deaf persons. Whatever the explanation, the L1.5- or L2-type knowledge of English exhibited by many deaf persons is a common characteristic of the bilingual knowledge of many deaf ASL-English bilinguals.

Despite this fact, many other deaf persons do indeed attain high levels of English competency. Toscano, McKee, and Lepoutre (2002) found that profoundly deaf college students whose reading and writing skills did not differ from the skills of their hearing peers all reported a sustained heavy bombardment of English language input and communicative interactions within their families as they were growing up, independently of modality. Some parents signed; some signed using English word order; some did not sign at all. The key appears to be early and intense English input through any available channel. Clearly, early intervention is a critical factor in a deaf person's attainment of high English competency (see Marschark, Lang, and Albertini, 2002).

12.5 ASL-English Bilinguals

Given the numerous variables influencing the acquisition of ASL and English, who is an ASL-English bilingual? Table 12.1 provides a list of categories according to which an ASL-English bilingual can be classified. With respect to hearing status, knowledge of ASL, and knowledge of English, a given bilingual would be associated with one letter category from each of the three columns. For example, an ACF bilingual would be a deaf person for whom both ASL and English are L1s. Such an individual would be a native ASL signer who had internalized English language input sufficiently early to possess native(-like) English competence. The ASL column distinguishes early (D) from late (E) L2 learners because ASL research has identified distinct ASL features and levels of attainment between these two L2 groups. For example, it was noted above that early learners easily develop native-like ASL competence. An ACH bilingual would be a native ASL signer for whom English is truly the L2. Category G, L1.5 (Berent, 1988), is included in the English column simply because, as noted above, under conditions of restricted input, many deaf persons develop L2-like competence in English even if they were exposed to English in an L1 environment. Thus, many deaf persons would fall into the bilingual categories ADG or AEG.

With respect to deaf bilinguals, it is important to note that the expression of their English competence, whether L1, L1.5, or L2, may or may not involve the use of speech. Learning and using speech depends on whether a deaf person receives speech training as part of their education and also on whether they prefer to use or not to use speech for personal or cultural reasons. Therefore, many deaf persons' English competence is demonstrated through reading and writing or in the VS modality through the use of some form of MCE.

As for hearing bilinguals, a BCF bilingual would be a child of deaf adults (CODA), who grew up in a home with Deaf parents who use ASL. Sign language interpreters and hearing educators of deaf students would likely be BEF bilinguals or, if English is their spoken language L2, BEH bilinguals. Under normal circumstances, English category G would not be relevant to describing a hearing ASL-English bilingual.

Table 12.1   Categories defining ASL-English bilinguals.

Hearing status	Language	
	ASL	English
(A) Deaf	(C) L1	(F) L1
(B) Hearing	(D) L2: Early	(G) L1.5
	(E) L2: Late	(H) L2

The term ASL in table 12.1 is used broadly. As discussed below, many ASL-English bilinguals produce a type of signing, with influences from both ASL and English, that is referred to as "contact signing" (Lucas and Valli, 1992). Section 12.6 explores the nature of contact signing.

12.6   Contact Signing

Lucas and Valli (1992) analyzed ASL-English contact signing in elicited interview data from deaf signers who had acquired ASL under a variety of conditions. Some were native signers and some late learners. Some came from Deaf families, some from hearing families. Some had attended residential schools for the deaf, some deaf day schools, and some had been mainstreamed in public schools. The authors' goal was to describe the kind of signing that emerges naturally from ASL-English interactions among signers exhibiting a broad range of background characteristics.

For years it has been assumed that the product of ASL-English interactions yielded a type of signing known as *Pidgin Sign English*, or PSE (see Woodward, 1973), which has the characteristics of an English pidgin. For example, PSE was described as using English word order and lacking articles, among other characteristics of pidgins. Lucas and Valli (1992) rejected the characterization of this product of ASL-English interaction as a pidgin by arguing that PSE has characteristics not typically found in pidgins, such as embedded clauses. Rather than a pidgin, they described the system that emerges from ASL-English interaction as contact signing. Through extensive analysis of their videotaped interview data, Lucas and Valli (p. 76) isolated what they consider the linguistic characteristics of contact signing, which are listed in table 12.2.

Lucas and Valli (1992) claimed that contact signing is "a third system" that consists of features of both languages, as well as some idiosyncratic features. It is neither a variety of ASL nor a variety of English. They assigned contact signing the status of a third system primarily on the basis of two criteria. First, they isolated features of ASL and English that consistently showed up in their

Table 12.2 Linguistic characteristics of contact signing (based on Lucas and Valli, 1992).

A	ASL and ASL-like lexical items (signs)
B	mouthing of English words during signing
C	single isolated spoken English words
D	whispering of English words during signing
E	ASL, English, and idiosyncratic lexical meanings and functions
F	reduced ASL and English morphology
G	some inflected ASL verbs
H	some signs for English inflections
I	ASL nonmanual markers
J	reduced English syntax
K	embedding
L	constructions with prepositions
M	ASL use of space (for establishing a referent)
N	ASL use of eye gaze
O	ASL pronouns and determiners
P	classifier predicates
Q	discourse markers

data, indicating "a predictable and consistent system" (p. 104). Second, there was mutual intelligibility among their participants and never a communication breakdown.

At the same time that the authors argued that contact signing is a third system, they recognized that there is great variation in contact signing and that the linguistic backgrounds of the individuals using it will determine which features of contact signing show up. For example, the contact signing of a Deaf native user of ASL will differ from the contact signing of a late learner of ASL, which will differ from the contact signing of a hearing English speaker competent in ASL. Despite this wide variation, Lucas and Valli asserted that contact signing is not the product of traditional bilingual behaviors such as code mixing or code switching. Their view is summarized in the following quotation (p. 108):

> As concerns unequivocally assigning a base language to a stretch of bilingual discourse, it seems that it is hard enough to do when the features of the two languages occur *sequentially* in various combinations. In our contact signing data, where the . . . features of two different languages are most often produced *simultaneously*, assigning stretches of discourse to ASL or to English seems like a fruitless exercise and also misses the point. The point *is* a third system which combines elements of both languages and may also have some idiosyncratic features.

Lucas and Valli's (1992) criteria for defining a third system are not convincing. The fact that features of English and ASL consistently show up in their data would be expected in any language contact situation. For example, see Haugen's (1977) principled account of the features of Norwegian and English that show up in the bilingual behaviors of Norwegian-English communities in America. Haugen noted particular "norms" (constraints) and wide variation but found no basis on which to describe these bilinguals' behaviors as a third system. Bilingual behaviors would be expected to be driven by grammatical and discourse factors that constrain the products of language contact in principled ways. However, those products would not be characterized as a third system unique to a particular group.

Furthermore, mutual intelligibility is not a reliable criterion to establish a third system. All of the participants in Lucas and Valli's study were competent signers. Despite the variability of their signing, their fluency as signers and an assumption that their communication was constrained by universal linguistic principles would more likely result in mutual intelligibility than not.

Finally, the rejection of an explanation of contact signing in terms of traditional bilingual behaviors because the task of identifying features of the two languages would be difficult is no argument for discarding the search for traditional bilingual behaviors. The complexity introduced by the additional variable of modality simply makes the explanation of ASL-English discourse more of a challenge. A better theory-based understanding of ASL-English contact is a necessity for understanding the principles guiding SL-SpL bilingualism and for bringing more objectivity to issues affecting deaf education.

12.7 Code Mixing by ASL-English Bilinguals

Some researchers *have* examined ASL-English contact by looking for traditional bilingual behaviors. For example, Hoffmeister and Moores (1987) compared the code-switching behaviors of native ASL signers and non-native later ASL learners. By code switching they meant the variation between more ASL-like signing and more English-like signing, emphasizing that such code switching is part of the everyday communication of deaf persons. The results of their study revealed that, in addressing a hearing audience, the native signers represented English more effectively than the non-native signers did. Paradoxically, because the signing of the non-native signers was more ASL-like, they were judged by raters to be earlier learners of ASL than the native signers. The results of the study suggest that native ASL signers are more effective code-switchers.

Kuntze (2000) studied ASL-English code mixing (CM). His study is unique in that he proposed a methodology for measuring CM in ASL sentences. His methodology involved focusing on the degree to which English elements appear in ASL sentences by recording signed sentences in naturalistic settings and then providing hypothetical ASL translations against which to compare potentially code-mixed sentences. Kuntze videotaped a native ASL signer communicating with students in a residential school for deaf students in which ASL is promoted as the language of instruction.

Kuntze noted that, although fingerspelling is an integral component of ASL, sentences containing fingerspelled words are good candidates for the investigation of CM. One of the sentences he recorded (p. 296) is shown in (3a), followed by the ASL translation in (3b) and the English translation in (3c). The elements in bold are identified in the process as the code-mixed English elements.

(3) a. ${}_T$*GREAT fs-WALL*${}_T$, **fs-WHEN fs-WAS fs-IT** FIRST BUILD fs-WHEN?
     b. ${}_T$*GREAT fs-WALL*${}_T$, WHEN FIRST BUILD WHEN?
     c. When was the Great Wall first built?

In Kuntze's notation, "fs" before an item indicates that the item is fingerspelled. An underlined sequence bordered by subscripted "T's" indicates that the sequence is a topic that is accompanied by the ASL nonmanual topic marker of eyebrow raising. Thus, both (3a) and the ASL translation (3b) begin with a clearly marked ASL topic. (3a) continues with the fingerspelled English words *when was it* and then resumes with the ASL signs FIRST BUILD WHEN. Though not indicated, in both (3a) and (3b) the sequences after the topic must be accompanied by eyebrow lowering, the nonmanual grammatical marker of a *wh*-question. ASL *wh*-questions have the option of beginning with the *wh*-word and ending with the *wh*-word repeated (Petronio and Lillo-Martin, 1997). Note that there is an ASL sign for *when* as well as a fingerspelled loan sign. Thus, fs-WHEN at the end of (3a) is a legitimate ASL sign articulated differently from the fingerspelling of the English word *when* (i.e. **fs-WHEN**).

With respect to the bold sequence in (3a), Kuntze (2000) noted that it represents an English passive formation, a construction that ASL lacks. (Despite the absence of a morphological passive, ASL word order and agreement can serve the same functions as a morphological passive.) The switch back to ASL in (3a) is verified by the fact that the sign BUILD cannot be part of the English passive construction because a fingerspelled past participle **fs-BUILT** would be required in that case. So the code-mixed sentence (3a) contains both ASL and English grammatical features. Kuntze's methodology thus provides a comparison of a signed ASL sentence suspected of containing a code-switch to English (in the signed mode) against a hypothetical ASL translation of that sentence.

12.8 Linguistic Constraints on Code Mixing

In attempting to identify universal linguistic constraints on bilingual CM, Belazi, Rubin, and Toribio (1994, p. 228) proposed the *Functional Head Constraint* (FHC) defined in (4).

(4)   The language feature of the complement f-selected by a functional head, like other relevant features, must match the corresponding feature of that functional head.

In the linguistic framework of Chomsky (1986), syntactic categories are either *lexical* or *functional*. Lexical categories include categories such as Noun, Verb, Adjective, and Preposition, and functional categories include categories like Complementizer, Inflection, and Determiner. All of these categories are considered *heads*, which are associated with particular structures that serve as their *complements*. Heads and complements have abstract features that must match in order for a sentence to be grammatical. There is a special relationship between a functional head and its complement known as *f-selection* (Abney, 1987), alluded to in (4).

Belazi et al. (1994) extended f-selection to the analysis of language mixing in bilingualism. The FHC stipulates that, in addition to the matching of other relevant features, the *language feature* of a functional head must match the language feature of its complement in order to yield a grammatical code-mixed sentence. An example of Spanish-English CM is provided in (5), based on Belazi et al.'s (p. 224) example (10).

(5)   a.   The professor said *que el estudiante había recibido una A.*
      b.   *The professor said that *el estudiante había recibido una A.*
           'The professor said that the student had received an A.'

The grammaticality of (5a) and the ungrammaticality of (5b) are explained by the FHC as follows: The Spanish complementizer *que* and the English complementizer *that* are functional heads; each has a finite clause (*el estudiante había recibido una A*) as its complement. In (5a), the functional head *que* has the same language feature, [+Spanish], as its complement, *el estudiante había recibido una A*. Therefore, the FHC is satisfied and (5a) is a grammatical code-mixed sentence. In (5b), the complementizer *that* is [+English] while its complement is [+Spanish]. Therefore, (5b) is an ungrammatical code-mixed sentence.

The FHC does not restrict CM between a *lexical* head and its complement. There is no prohibition against CM between the English lexical head *publisher*, a noun, and its Spanish complement *para el libro* in (6a) or between the Spanish noun head *título* and its English complement *for the manuscript* in (6b) (example (25) in Toribio, 2001, p. 209):

(6)   a.   a new publisher *para el libro*
           'a new publisher for the book'
      b.   *un nuevo título* for the manuscript
           'a new title for the manuscript'

Based on Toribio's (2001) discussion of the application of the FHC in constraining CM, (7) below summarizes the environments in which CM is grammatical (in conventional grammatical terms), and (8) summarizes the environments in which CM is ungrammatical.

(7) Permissible code mixing
    a. between a main verb and its object or complement clause
    b. between a preposition and its object noun phrase
    c. between a noun and its prepositional phrase complement (as in (6))
    d. between an adjective and its prepositional phrase complement
    e. between a subject and its predicate phrase
    f. between a noun phrase and a modifying relative clause
    g. between an adverbial clause and a main clause
    h. between a topic phrase and the main clause

(8) Impermissible code mixing
    a. between a modal or auxiliary verb and the rest of the verb phrase
    b. between a negative marker and the rest of the verb phrase
    c. between a complementizer and the rest of the embedded clause (as in (5))
    d. between a number or a quantifier and the rest of the noun phrase
    e. between a coordinating conjunction and the conjoined phrase or clause

Although the FHC has been proposed as a universal constraint on bilingual CM, which adequately explains a wide range of CM behaviors across languages, Toribio (2001) demonstrated that conformity to the FHC correlates with the level of a speaker's bilingual competence. Specifically, as a bilingual's competence in the two languages becomes more balanced, that bilingual will exhibit a greater sensitivity to the FHC.

To date, no one has attempted to test data on ASL-English CM against the predictions of constraints like the FHC. The following section explores possible applications of the FHC to ASL-English bilingual behaviors.

12.9   Constraints on ASL-English Code Mixing

Given the modality factor in SL-SpL bilingualism, can a universal principle such as the FHC adequately explain ASL-English CM? This is an empirical question, but the kind of question that must be explored in a theory-based approach to SL-SpL contact phenomena. A preliminary examination of available examples of ASL-English CM can set the stage for exploring such a question.

Regarding Kuntze's (2000) sentence (3a) above, the switch from the ASL topic $_T GREAT$ *fs-WALL*$_T$ to the English sequence is not blocked by the FHC, as indicated in (7h) above. However, the switch from English **fs-WHEN fs-WAS fs-IT** to ASL FIRST BUILD fs-WHEN does appear to violate the FHC. In the derivation of a sentence like (3a), the auxiliary verb (**fs-WAS**) moves through the functional category INFL (Inflection) up to COMP, the Complementizer position (Chomsky, 1986). In order to pass through INFL, **fs-WAS** must match all the features of INFL, including the language feature. Therefore, INFL in (3a) has the feature [+English] because [+English] **fs-WAS** of the fingerspelled English sequence has to have passed through INFL in the derivation of the sentence. As noted, the verb phrase (VP) FIRST BUILD has the [+ASL] feature. VP is the complement of INFL, which is the functional head of the Inflectional Phrase (IP). Because VP and INFL differ in their language feature, CM between the fingerspelled English sequence and the ASL sequence in the VP is prohibited by the FHC, defined above in (4).

Notwithstanding the violation of the FHC, the switch back to ASL in (3a) prevents the completion of the passive, at least in terms of English morphology, because ASL BUILD lacks the required past participle marking as in *built*. Although (3a), as described by Kuntze, is an ASL sentence containing English elements, contact signing (Lucas and Valli, 1992) includes signed sequences parallel to the English passive formation without any inflection on the sign that appears in the position that the English past participle would assume (see Lucas and Valli, p. 137, segment #15).

Accordingly, despite the switch back to ASL in (3a), the word order from **fs-WHEN** through BUILD parallels the English word order of a *wh*-question containing a passive verb formation. In addition, the ASL word order expressed in FIRST BUILD fs-WHEN provides redundancy to the entire sequence already marked nonmanually by the *wh*-question feature. Moreover, along with the topic phrase at the beginning of (3a), the ASL sequence FIRST BUILD fs-WHEN is itself the functional equivalent of a passive. A reasonable question, then, is whether these kinds of redundancies conspire to offset violations of the FHC or whether ASL BUILD sufficiently simulates the English past participle *built* and somehow sustains the [+English] feature into the [+ASL] segment. Principled approaches to ASL-English CM need to explore such questions and to determine what principle(s) license such CM.

With regard to options for CM across modalities, ASL-English CM involves the sequential alternation of elements from the two languages as well as the simultaneous articulation of elements. We can call CM that operates bimodally *mode mixing* to distinguish it from sequential CM. Another question, then, is whether one principle constrains both CM and mode mixing or whether more than one principle is involved.

Lucas and Valli (1992) noted that a common feature of contact signing is the mouthing of English words (table 12.2). Mouthing during a signed sequence involves mode mixing because speaking, whispering, or mouthing are all considered manifestations of speech. If mouthing is not constant across a signed sequence, another empirical question is whether a principle like the FHC can account for mouthing patterns in contact signing. An example of mode-mixed mouthing is shown in (9), adapted from Lucas and Valli's clip #7 (p. 134). In their notation, +M marks the beginning of mouthing, and the point of the arrow indicates the spot at which mouthing ceases.

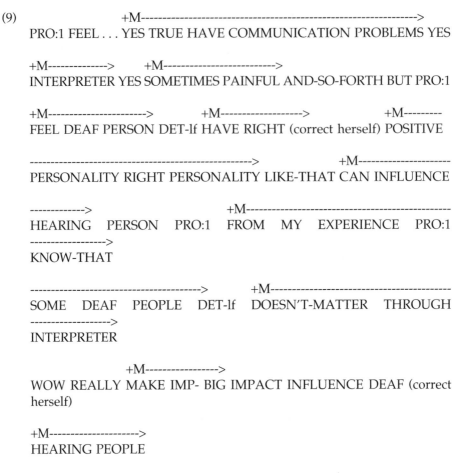

(9)

```
                        +M---------------------------------------------------------->
      PRO:1 FEEL . . . YES TRUE HAVE COMMUNICATION PROBLEMS YES

      +M-------------->      +M------------------------->
      INTERPRETER YES SOMETIMES PAINFUL AND-SO-FORTH BUT PRO:1

      +M----------------------->          +M-------------------->          +M---------
      FEEL DEAF PERSON DET-lf HAVE RIGHT (correct herself) POSITIVE

      ------------------------------------------------------->          +M---------------------
      PERSONALITY RIGHT PERSONALITY LIKE-THAT CAN INFLUENCE

      ------------->                      +M------------------------------------------------
      HEARING    PERSON   PRO:1   FROM    MY    EXPERIENCE   PRO:1
      ------------------>
      KNOW-THAT

      ----------------------------------------->          +M------------------------------------------
      SOME    DEAF   PEOPLE   DET-lf   DOESN'T-MATTER    THROUGH
      -------------------->
      INTERPRETER

                        +M----------------->
      WOW REALLY MAKE IMP- BIG IMPACT INFLUENCE DEAF (correct
      herself)

      +M-------------------->
      HEARING PEOPLE
```

'I feel . . . yes, true, there are communication problems and yes, some-times it's painful with the interpreter and so forth, but I feel that if the deaf person has the right . . . a positive personality, they can influence the hearing person. I know from my experience that some deaf people really make a big impact on deaf . . . I mean hearing people, even if they're using an interpreter.'

PRO:1 in (9) represents the ASL first person pronoun, and DET-lf indicates the use of the ASL determiner involving pointing toward the left signing space where the referent has been set up.

   The mouthing spans in (9) are remarkable in the extent to which they appear to follow the FHC. The switch to mouthing between FEEL and YES at the beginning of the segment reflects permissible CM (mode mixing) as de-scribed above in (7a). The switches between PRO:1 and FEEL DEAF PERSON and between PRO:1 and FROM MY EXPERIENCE conform to (7e). In addition to these FHC-constrained switches between mouthing and non-mouthing, other switches in (9) are permitted through other factors. Mouthing ceases between

HEARING and PERSON in the sequence CAN INFLUENCE HEARING PERSON. Where two languages are parallel in nominal phrase structure, a switch can occur between the adjective and noun positions (Bhatia and Ritchie, 1996, p. 641). Because both ASL and English permit the order ADJECTIVE + NOUN within noun phrases, the switch from mouthing to non-mouthing between HEARING and PERSON is permitted. Other switches in (9) are instances of "tag switching," in which sentence fillers such as interjections occur at phrase or clause boundaries (Bhatia and Ritchie, 1996, pp. 635–6). Thus mouthing is interrupted during the signs YES, AND-SO-FORTH, LIKE-THAT, and WOW REALLY in (9).

Other instances of mode mixing in (9) seem to be motivated by grammatical distinctions between ASL and English. For instance, mouthing ceases during the articulation of the ASL determiners DET-lf. In this case, the determiner occurs at the end of the noun phrase, creating an incompatibility between the signed mode and the mouthed mode, which follows English word order. Another switch to non-mouthing might be tied to the use of ASL signs in ways that deviate from ASL grammar. In discussing the last portion of their clip #7, REALLY MAKE . . . HEARING PEOPLE, Lucas and Valli (1992, p. 83) commented that the signs IMPACT and INFLUENCE are agreement verbs in ASL but are used as nouns in (9). Interestingly, mouthing ceases with their articulation. Although all the phenomena discussed above in connection with (9) need to be explored in depth, mode mixing in ASL-English contact signing appears to be constrained in principled ways.

12.10 Constraints on Manually Coded English

Despite the argument that MCE may be an unlearnable system because of morphological incompatibility between the VS and the AV modalities (Supalla, 1991), MCE does incorporate elements of two natural languages, ASL and English. What if we view MCE, despite its "artificiality," not as a system grappling with cross-modality incompatibility but simply as a code-mixed linguistic system? Under this view, MCE can be evaluated with respect to the extent to which it conforms to universal linguistic principles like the FHC.

The fact that children exposed to MCE exhibited relatively good skills in the use of English word order, embedding, argument structure, prepositions, and pronouns (Schick and Moeller, 1992) might be attributable to the fact that these aspects of MCE do not violate any universal principles. However, the reportedly unlearnable morphological aspects of MCE might indeed violate universal principles. Marking a verb for past tense in MCE requires two free morphemes: the lexical sign for the verb followed by the sign PAST. For example, *went* is rendered as GO + PAST. Supalla's (1991) argument was that this kind of morphological process is incompatible with the VS modality.

From the CM perspective, GO + PAST could be interpreted, on typological grounds, as a switch from a [+English] element GO to a [–English] element PAST. If MCE incorporates aspects of English that are learnable because they maintain, among other characteristics, the natural typology of English, an MCE learner who has internalized the system may perceive the distinction between typologically compatible [+English] elements and typologically incompatible [–English] elements. Specifically, morphological processes that involve a sequence of equally stressed free morphemes are at odds with the English system of suffixing a phonologically reduced bound morpheme to a free morpheme.

With respect to the FHC, as noted earlier, INFL is the functional head of IP, which contains VP; therefore, INFL takes VP as its complement and contains the tense feature associated with the verb within VP. The FHC thus requires that INFL match the language feature of that verb. An MCE "inflected" verb consists of a [+English] stem (GO) but a [–English] tense marker (PAST) in the form of a free morpheme. This switch occurs between the head of the functional category and its complement VP and therefore violates the FHC.

Under this analysis, morphological aspects of MCE should be difficult to learn on principled grounds associated with constraints on CM, irrespective of modality. Of course, the details and tenability of such a proposal need to be explored further.

12.11   Simultaneous Communication

The most extreme manifestation of ASL-English mode mixing occurs during *simultaneous communication* (SC), the simultaneous production of English in the AV modality and contact signing or MCE in the VS modality. SC is used both educationally and in communication between deaf and hearing persons. During SC, English is spoken (or mouthed or whispered) and is accompanied by ASL signs or some form of MCE along with fingerspelling. In most cases, SC is "speech-driven," although SC used by deaf signers can sometimes be "sign-driven" (Stewart, Akamatsu, and Bonkowski, 1990).

There is great variation in the nature of SC and in the extent to which SC successfully represents the message in both modalities. Fischer, Metz, Brown, and Caccamise (1991) found that deaf adults who were highly skilled in speech, sign, and English reading and writing produced SC in which there was no significant decrement or improvement in speech or sign intelligibility. However, these individuals were essentially balanced bilinguals, who are more successful in their implementation of CM competence than nonbalanced bilinguals (Toribio, 2001).

CM success by balanced bilinguals is supported by the results of Wilbur and Petersen (1998), who studied the SC produced by two groups of hearing persons – CODAs who were native ASL signers and fluent MCE users who did not know ASL. In using speech combined with MCE (i.e. SC), both groups omitted more function signs (e.g. inflectional markers) than content signs (e.g. main verbs). However, overall, the CODAs omitted fewer signs than the MCE users and omitted fewer signs that are considered "impermissible deletions" in SC (Mallery-Ruganis and Fischer, 1991). Most significantly, the CODAs used compensatory nonmanual ASL mechanisms for their deleted signs. Thus, knowledge of ASL, which in this case indicates the CODAs' balanced ASL-English bilingual competence, results in more successful SC in terms of the accurate and equivalent production of both sign and speech.

Maxwell, Bernstein, and Mear (1991) conducted a study of the SC produced by both deaf and hearing individuals. Despite the presence of a variety of types of semantic and structural mismatches, Maxwell et al. observed a very high level of compatibility between their participants' sign and speech and noted that their participants did not seem to be saying one thing and signing another. However, they determined that their participants' SC was largely English-driven: The speech mode (whether spoken or mouthed) presented English with complete morphology, whereas the signed mode was an altered version of the message containing systematic omissions or substitutes for the English morphemes.

In terms of the types of morphemes omitted from the signed mode, copulas and auxiliary verbs were the most frequent omissions. Maxwell et al. (1991) stated that these omissions had very little effect on message equivalence between modes because these morphemes are often not obligatory across languages, including in ASL. Also omitted from the sign mode were the English morphemes expressing tense, aspect, and plurality. Again, these omissions did not affect message equivalence because the signers used redundancy mechanisms to allow recoverability of information contained in the rest of the utterance. An example of the recoverability of tense through redundancy is provided in (10) (Maxwell et al.'s (9.9), p. 185):

(10)   I think   maybe she's ready   now   because   last   August
     THINK MAYBE   READY NOW BECAUSE LAST AUGUST
     for   her   birthday   we thought about   it . . .
     FOR HER BIRTHDAY WE THINK ABOUT IT . . .

In (10), the time expression *last August*/LAST AUGUST clearly establishes that the event took place in the past. Therefore, despite the speaking of *thought* during the signing of THINK, the past context is recoverable from the redundancy provided by the time expression. Other omissions to note in (10) are the omission of a sign for the first person pronoun *I* as well as the sign for *she* and the copula -'s. Maxwell et al. attributed the omission of *I* to the fact that in ASL the omission of the subject is interpreted to be the signer. Regarding the omission of SHE, such referents are generally recoverable from the context in which the sentence is produced. With respect to the omission of the copula, in ASL the copula is typically omitted. Like Fischer et al. (1991), Maxwell et al. described the synergy that exists in SC between the signed and spoken modes that preserves the integrity of the total message.

It may be that CM constraints such as the FHC might also explain mode mixing in successful SC and account for the observed synergy that exists between the two modalities. For example, the pronoun omissions in the sign mode in (10) occur in a CM environment permitted by the FHC, specifically (7e) above. As with other products of ASL-English contact, approaching SC from the perspective of universal constraints on CM may prove fruitful.

12.12   Theoretical Conclusions

Bhatia and Ritchie (1996, p. 645) stated that "the real challenge is not whether or not CM is subject to constraints but how best to capture those constraints and how to make deeper claims about human language in general and bilinguals' mixing competence and their language acquisition in particular." This chapter has emphasized that the study of SL-SpL bilingualism is not exempt from the challenge of discovering the universal linguistic principles that constrain ASL-English contact in any of its manifestations. To date, CM in ASL, contact signing, MCE, and SC have not been studied from the perspective of universal linguistic constraints. Doing so should result in a more principled and objective understanding of SL-SpL contact phenomena and also contribute to a deeper understanding of human language in general.

In this regard, the arguments provided above against the claim by Lucas and Valli (1992) that contact signing represents "a third system" are further supported by principles of theory building, including the criterion of parsimony. In evaluating several proposed linguistic constraints on CM, Toribio (2001, p. 207) rejected the notion that the interaction of two grammars in CM results in "a third grammar." She argued that "code-switching-specific notions diminish the strength of the theory of grammar that includes them. It would be preferable for code-switching to be restated in syntactic-theoretical terms by independently motivated universal principles of grammar." Rather than building a theory of contact signing by declaring it a third system, contact signing must be explained by principles of grammar independent of the phenomenon itself. Ultimately, contact signing will undoubtedly be shown to be the product of a very broad range of principled CM and mode-mixing behaviors in the natural communication that emerges from ASL-English contact.

Several of the studies cited in this chapter indicated that native knowledge of ASL and more balanced ASL-English bilingual knowledge contributed to more successful and more principled ASL-English CM. These observations are supported by the results of Toribio (2001), who confirmed that bilingual speakers with lower proficiency in the L2 had less of an awareness of the universal principles that constrain CM and that the ability to apply constraints on CM emerged with increasing L2 proficiency. In view of this competency factor and diversity of bilingual knowledge apparent from table 12.1, the products of ASL-English contact in the larger population of ASL-English bilinguals will not necessarily be driven by the universal constraints that come with higher and more balanced competencies. The identification of principles constraining ASL-English CM will certainly need to take this confound into consideration. (For additional discussion of code mixing and code switching, see chapters 1–4, 6, 10, 11, 13, 14, 25, 26, 29, and 31.)

12.13   Final Remarks

This chapter has touched on one domain of SL-SpL bilingualism, specifically, ASL-English CM and mode mixing, and has proposed a theory-based approach to exploring these phenomena. Even within this one domain, there are many other phenomena that could have been explored had space permitted it. For example, fingerspelling in ASL, contact signing, SC, etc., is one such contact phenomenon in need of more theory-based research. Fingerspelling was illustrated in (3) above and discussed in this chapter (and in Kuntze, 2000) as CM between ASL and English. There is some debate over what kind of phenomenon fingerspelling actually is, because it is an "alphabetic" rather than a "spoken" representation of English (Padden, 1996). As a bilingual phenomenon, fingerspelling needs to be better characterized in terms of borrowing and CM, and constraints on fingerspelling need to be better understood theoretically.

It was noted in the introduction that a solid understanding of SL-SpL bilingualism requires familiarity with issues in all the relevant domains of bilingual studies. Addressing the psychological, social, political, and educational aspects of ASL-English bilingualism is clearly beyond the scope of this chapter. However, there are critical issues and heated controversies that have persisted for many years that readers should be aware of. One issue concerns bilingual-bicultural models of education for deaf children (Strong, 1988), including the assumption that the development of L2 (English) literacy can best be achieved through the instructional medium of ASL as the L1 (see Mayer and Akamatsu, 2003, for discussion of the major issues). Another critical issue concerns the sign language competencies of many educators of deaf students (mostly BEF bilinguals, table 12.1), whose use of SC with deaf students contains impermissible deletions of signs and other inaccuracies that drastically distort the intended message (Johnson, Liddell, and Erting, 1989). Accurate signing and principled CM are vital to the education of deaf students. The reader is referred to works referenced in this chapter and to the list of suggested further reading to gain familiarity with these and other critical issues related to ASL-English bilingualism.

One final point to re-emphasize is that the components and products of SL-SpL bilingualism exhibit tremendous complexity resulting from the exceptional variables of modality and hearing status. Because the majority of deaf children are born to two hearing parents, these children often receive minimal linguistic input in either the VS or the AV modality for several years. The consequence of this diminished input is that many deaf persons truly have no L1 in the conventional sense. Many of them are ADG or AEG bilinguals (table 12.1). Accordingly, it is all the more essential that SL-SpL bilingualism be explored through rigorous, theory-based research so that major decisions affecting the lives of deaf persons are based on principled information and are not driven by opinions, false assumptions, or partial information.

ACKNOWLEDGMENTS

I am indebted to Susan Fischer, Ila Parasnis, and John Albertini for their valuable feedback during the development of this chapter and to Robert Whitehead, Frank Caccamise, and Sara Schley for conversations related to some of the topics covered here.

REFERENCES

Abney, S. P. (1987). The English noun phrase in its sentential aspect. Unpublished Ph.D. dissertation, Massachusetts Institute of Technology.

Belazi, H. M., Rubin, E. J., and Toribio, A. J. (1994). Code-switching and X-bar theory: The functional head constraint. *Linguistic Inquiry*, 25, 221–37.

Berent, G. P. (1988). An assessment of syntactic capabilities. In M. Strong (ed.), *Language Learning and Deafness*, pp. 133–61. Cambridge, UK: Cambridge University Press.

Berent, G. P. (1996a). The acquisition of English syntax by deaf learners. In W. Ritchie and T. Bhatia (eds.), *Handbook of Second Language Acquisition*, pp. 469–506. San Diego, CA: Academic Press.

Berent, G. P. (1996b). Learnability constraints on deaf learners' acquisition of English wh-questions. *Journal of Speech and Hearing Research*, 39, 625–42.

Berent, G. P. and Samar, V. J. (1990). The psychological reality of the subset principle: Evidence from the governing categories of prelingually deaf adults. *Language*, 66, 714–41.

Bhatia, T. K. and Ritchie, W. C. (1996). Bilingual language mixing, universal grammar, and second language acquisition. In W. C. Ritchie and T. K. Bhatia (eds.), *Handbook of Second Language Acquisition*, pp. 627–88. San Diego, CA: Academic Press.

Bochner, J. H. and Albertini, J. A. (1988). Language varieties in the deaf population and their acquisition by children and adults. In M. Strong (ed.), *Language Learning and Deafness*, pp. 3–48. Cambridge, UK: Cambridge University Press.

Chomsky, N. (1981). *Lectures on Government and Binding*. Dordrecht: Foris.

Chomsky, N. (1986). *Barriers*. Cambridge, MA: MIT Press.

de Villiers, J., deVilliers, P., and Hoban, E. (1994). The central problem of functional categories in the English syntax of oral deaf children. In H. Tager-Flusberg (ed.), *Constraints on Language Acquisition: Studies of Atypical Children*, pp. 9–47. Hillsdale, NJ: Lawrence Erlbaum Associates.

Fischer, S. D. (1998). Critical periods for language acquisition: Consequences for deaf education. In A. Weisel (ed.), *Issues Unresolved: New Perspectives on Language and Deaf Education*, pp. 9–26.

Washington, D.C.: Gallaudet University Press.

Fischer, S. D., Metz, D. E., Brown, P. M., and Caccamise, F. (1991). The effects of bimodal communication on the intelligibility of sign and speech. In P. Siple and S. D. Fischer (eds.), *Theoretical Issues in Sign Language Research. Volume 2: Psychology*, pp. 135–47. Chicago: Chicago University Press.

Fischer, S. D. and van der Hulst, H. (2003). Sign language structures. In M. Marschark and P. E. Spencer (eds.), *The Handbook of Deaf Studies, Language, and Education*, pp. 319–31. New York: Oxford University Press.

Haugen, E. (1977). Norm and deviation in bilingual communities. In P. A. Hornby (ed.), *Bilingualism: Psychological, Social, and Educational Implications*. New York: Academic Press.

Hoffmeister, R. and Moores, D. F. (1987). Code switching in deaf adults. *American Annals of the Deaf*, 132, 31–4.

Johnson, R. E., Liddell, S. K., and Erting, C. J. (1989). *Unlocking the Curriculum: Principles for Achieving Success in Deaf Education*. Washington, D.C.: Gallaudet University, Gallaudet Research Institute.

Kuntze, M. (2000). Codeswitching in ASL and written English language contact. In K. Emmorey and H. Lane (eds.), *The Signs of Language Revisited: An Anthology to Honor Ursula Bellugi and Edward Klima*, pp. 287–302. Mahwah, NJ: Lawrence Erlbaum Associates.

Lillo-Martin, D. (1991). *Universal Grammar and American Sign Language*. Dordrecht: Kluwer Academic Publishers.

Lillo-Martin, D. (1999). Modality effects and modularity in language acquisition: The acquisition of American Sign Language. In T. K. Bhatia and W. C. Ritchie (eds.), *Handbook of Child Language Acquisition*,

pp. 531–67. San Diego, CA: Academic Press.

Lucas, C. and Valli, C. (1992). *Language Contact in the American Deaf Community*. San Diego, CA: Academic Press.

Mallery-Ruganis, D. and Fischer, S. (1991). Characteristics that contribute to effective simultaneous communication. *American Annals of the Deaf*, 136, 401–8.

Marschark, M., Lang, H. G., and Albertini, J. A. (2002). *Educating Deaf Students: From Research to Practice*. New York: Oxford University Press.

Maxwell, M., Bernstein, M. E., and Mear, K. M. (1991). Bimodal language production. In P. Siple and S. D. Fischer (eds.), *Theoretical Issues in Sign Language Research. Volume 2: Psychology*, pp. 171–90. Chicago, IL: University of Chicago Press.

Mayer, C. and Akamatsu, C. T. (2003). Bilingualism and literacy. In M. Marschark and P. E. Spencer (eds.), *The Handbook of Deaf Studies, Language, and Education*, 136–49. New York: Oxford University Press.

Newport, E. L. and Supalla, T. (2000). Sign language research at the millennium. In K. Emmorey and H. Lane (eds.), *The Signs of Language Revisited: An Anthology to Honor Ursula Bellugi and Edward Klima*, pp. 103–14. Mahwah, NJ: Lawrence Erlbaum Associates.

Padden, C. A. (1996). Early bilingual lives of Deaf children. In I. Parasnis (ed.), *Cultural and Language Diversity and the Deaf Experience*, pp. 99–116. New York: Cambridge University Press.

Petronio, K. and Lillo-Martin, D. (1997). WH-movement and the position of Spec-CP: Evidence from American Sign Language. *Language*, 73, 18–57.

Quigley, S. P. and King, C. M. (1980). Syntactic performance of hearing impaired and normal hearing individuals. *Applied Psycholinguistics*, 1, 329–56.

Schick, B. (2003). The development of American Sign Language and Manually-Coded English systems. In M. Marschark and P. E. Spencer (eds.), *The Handbook of Deaf Studies, Language, and Education*, pp. 219–31. New York: Oxford University Press.

Schick, B. and Moeller, M. P. (1992). What is learnable in manually coded English sign systems? *Applied Psycholinguistics*, 13, 313–40.

Stewart, D. A., Akamatsu, C. T., and Bonkowski, N. (1990). Synergy effect: Sign driven and speech driven simultaneous communication. In W. Edmondson and F. Karlsson (eds.), *SLR 87: Papers from the Fourth International Symposium on Sign Language Research*, pp. 235–42. Hamburg: Signum Press.

Strong, M. (ed.) (1988). *Language Learning and Deafness*. Cambridge, UK: Cambridge University Press.

Supalla, S. J. (1991). Manually Coded English: The modality question in signed language development. In P. Siple and S. D. Fischer (eds.), *Theoretical Issues in Sign Language*

Research. Volume 2: Psychology*, pp. 85–109. Chicago: University of Chicago Press.

Toribio, A. J. (2001). On the emergence of bilingual code-switching competence. *Bilingualism: Language and Cognition*, 4(3), 203–31.

Toscano, R. M., McKee, B., and Lepoutre, D. (2002). Success with academic English: Reflections of deaf college students. *American Annals of the Deaf*, 147, 5–23.

Wilbur, R. B. (2000). Phonological and prosodic layering of nonmanuals in American Sign Language. In K. Emmorey and H. Lane (eds.), *The Signs of Language Revisited: An Anthology to Honor Ursula Bellugi and Edward Klima*, pp. 215–44. Mahwah, NJ: Lawrence Erlbaum Associates.

Wilbur, R. B. and Petersen, L. (1998). Modality interactions of speech and signing in simultaneous communication. *Journal of Speech, Language, and Hearing Research*, 41, 200–12.

Woodward, J. C. (1973). Some characteristics of Pidgin Sign English. *Sign Language Studies*, 3, 39–46.

FURTHER READING

Easterbrooks, S. R. and Baker, S. (2002). *Language Learning in Children who are Deaf and Hard of Hearing: Multiple Pathways*. Boston, MA: Allyn and Bacon.

Lane, H. (1992). *The Mask of Benevolence: Disabling the Deaf Community*. New York: Alfred A. Knopf.

Lucas, C. (ed.) (1989). *The Sociolinguistics of the Deaf Community*. San Diego, CA: Academic Press.

Lucas, C. (ed.). (1996). *Multicultural Aspects of Sociolinguistics in Deaf

Communities*. Washington, D.C.: Gallaudet University Press.

Lucas, C. (ed.). (2001). *The Sociolinguistics of Sign Languages*. Cambridge, UK: Cambridge University Press.

Maxwell, M. M. (1990). Simultaneous communication: The state of the art and proposals for change. *Sign Language Studies*, 69, 333–90.

Metzger, M. (ed.) (2000). *Bilingualism and Identity in Deaf Communities*. Washington, D.C.: Gallaudet University Press.

Parasnis, I. (1996). *Cultural and Language Diversity and the Deaf Experience*. New York: Cambridge University Press.

Paul, P. V. (2001). *Language and Deafness*, 3rd edn. San Diego, CA: Singular Publishing Group.

Whitehead, R. L., Schiavetti, N., Whitehead, B. H., and Metz, D. E. (1995). Temporal characteristics of speech in simultaneous communication. *Journal of Speech and Hearing Research*, 38, 1014–24.

Wilbur, R. B. (1987). *American Sign Language: Linguistics and Applied Dimensions*, 2nd edn. Boston, MA: Little Brown.

13 Social and Psychological Factors in Language Mixing

WILLIAM C. RITCHIE AND TEJ K. BHATIA

13.1 Introduction

13.1.1 Preliminary remarks

Any unified treatment of the bilingual's capacity for language use has to account for two fundamental aspects of bilingual linguistic competency: language separation and language integration. It is often observed that bilinguals can switch from one language to another with as much ease and competence as a driver of a stick-shift car changes gear under appropriate conditions. Although this bilingual behavior has been the subject of linguistic investigation for quite some time, general attitudes toward language mixing have often been based on fundamental misconceptions about these two aspects of bilingual linguistic competency. This chapter focuses on the following four questions concerning bilingual verbal behavior:

- Is language mixing or switching a random phenomenon?
- If it is not, what motivates bilinguals to mix and alternate two languages?
- What is the social evaluation of this mixing and alternation?
- What is the perception of bilinguals themselves about their language mixing?

(The question of the grammar of mixing and switching, as opposed to its motivation, is addressed in chapter 11.)

13.1.2 Definitions of code mixing and code switching, borrowing, and other related phenomena

A distinction has often been made in the research literature between code switching and code mixing. We will use these terms as follows.

We use the term *code switching* (CS) to refer to the use of various linguistic units (words, phrases, clauses, and sentences) primarily from two participating grammatical systems across sentence boundaries within a speech event. In other words, CS is intersentential and may be subject to discourse principles. It is motivated by social and psychological factors.

We use the term *code mixing* (CM) to refer to the mixing of various linguistic units (morphemes, words, modifiers, phrases, clauses and sentences) primarily from two participating grammatical systems within a sentence. In other words, CM is intrasentential and is constrained by grammatical principles and may also be motivated by social-psychological factors.

The distinction between CS and CM as described above is controversial with some scholars doubting the usefulness of the distinction (Hatch, 1976, p. 202). Hatch maintains that there is no sharp distinction between intersentential CS and intra-sentential CM and other scholars reject the distinction on functional grounds and treat them both as "situational shifting" (Gumperz, 1982, p. 70; Pakir, 1989; Tay, 1989). Others find it important and useful (Bokamba, 1988; Kachru, 1978; McLaughlin, 1984; and many others), particularly if the goal is to develop a grammar of language mixing.

Other differences among researchers appear to be purely terminological. For instance, Pfaff (1979, p. 295) employs the term "mixing" as a neutral cover term for both CM and borrowing while Beardsome (1991, p. 49) rejects the use of the term code mixing "since it appears to be the least-favored designation and the most unclear for referring to any form of non-monoglot norm-based speech patterns." Yet others use the term "code mixing" to refer to other related phenomena such as borrowing, interference, transfer, or switching (McLaughlin, 1984, pp. 96–7).

This chapter does not make a distinction between CM/CS on one hand and other related phenomena – borrowing, etc. – on the other, for the reason that the grammar of code mixing is beyond the scope of this chapter. Instead, we use "language mixing/switching" (LM/S) as a cover term for both code mixing and code switching (see Bhatia and Ritchie, 1996 for more discussion of the grammar of CM and its distinction from other mixed language systems such as pidgin and creole languages and linguistic borrowing; see also Weinreich, 1953, and Romaine, 1989).

13.1.3   The structure of the rest of the chapter

The rest of the chapter deals with the four questions concerning LM/S formulated above – whether it is random or systematic, what its motivations are, what societal attitudes are toward it, and, finally, what the attitudes of bilinguals themselves toward the phenomenon are.

13.2   The Systematicity of LM/S

The depth, strength, and tacitness of the pragmatic conventions that determine language choice (thereby making it systematic) are well illustrated by the following account of an incident concerning a sting operation planned by a US intelligence agency.

A few years ago, an officer in the US intelligence community approached the second author of this chapter. The intelligence officer was quite distressed about the trustworthiness of one of the agency's moles. The intelligence agency had made a good decision by hiring a bilingual mole who spoke the language of the target community in addition to English. However, since the agency and its members could not speak the ethnic language of the mole, they felt totally in the dark and were hopelessly dependent on the mole and began to doubt his/her intentions.

At one point the decision was made that during a major upcoming interaction between the mole and a suspect, the mole would use English so that an officer of the agency could determine his/her loyalty. Eager to prove his/her sincerity to the agency, the mole agreed to such a language negotiation. The day came when the mole telephoned the suspect in the presence of the officer, (s)he started the conversation with the suspect in their shared ethnic language. However, something remarkable then happened: because of the tacit pragmatic conventions of LM/S, the violation of which would have tipped the suspect off (with possible dire consequences for the mole), (s)he could not switch to English in spite of his/her explicit assurance to the agency in general and the officer in particular that (s)he would do so. Feeling betrayed, the agency lost its faith in the mole and sought expert advice from the second author. After playing a couple of tape recordings between the mole and the suspect in their native language, the officer asked: Is the mole trustworthy? Is (s)he trying to hide something from the agency? Why didn't (s)he switch to English in accordance with the agency's explicit directive and the mutual agreement?

This incident does not represent an isolated case of an encounter between monolinguals and bilinguals. On the contrary this incident and particularly the agency's questions underscore the fundamental misconception that monolinguals often have about the bilingual verbal behavior and the tacit pragmatic conventions that guide it. Even more interesting was the bilingual's apparent lack of awareness of these conventions (perhaps even of their existence) until (s)he was actually in the situation of having to put them to use.

The mixing of a wide array of linguistic elements of different types on the part of bilinguals led some earlier researchers to conclude/speculate that LM/S either is not subject to constraints (Lance, 1975, p. 143) or, equivalently, exhibits only "irregular mixture" (Labov, 1971, p. 457). Labov went on to claim that the mixing of Spanish and English on the part of the bilingual New York Puerto Rican bilingual speaker is a "strange mixture of the two languages."

He argued that "no one has been able to show that such rapid alternation is governed by any systematic rules or constraints." Needless to say, there is now a unanimous consensus among linguists and other scholars that language mixing/switching behavior of bilingual is systematic but complex.

13.3 Motivations for Language Choice and Mixing

Unlike the monolingual, who has access to only one set of mutually intelligible styles, the bi-/multilingual may exercise a range of styles in two or more varieties that are not mutually intelligible. The bilingual's pragmatic competence enables him or her to determine the choice of one language over the other in a particular interaction. On the basis of a number of factors such as *with whom* (participants: their backgrounds and relationships), *about what* (topic, content), and *when* and *where* a speech act occurs, bilinguals make their language choice. For most bilinguals, overt or explicit language negotiation is rather unnatural and counterproductive and can yield communication mishaps and sometimes alarming results as exemplified by the sting operation instance described above where a switch from the ethnic language to English would have been a deadly mistake. Obviously overt negotiations in formal and professional settings such as conferences do in fact take place; however, such negotiations are not representative of most day-to-day interpersonal verbal interaction among bilinguals. In most cases, the unmarked choice is made almost instantaneously and smoothly, which in turn results in language matching by participating bilinguals.

The rule of thumb is that LM/S marks a socio-psychological change of some kind. This change could be prompted by the presence of an out-group member, by constantly changing social relations or identities or by the need to create a special effect (in terms of socio-psychological, stylistic effects) within the sentence or beyond the sentence, i.e. within a discourse unit. In short, the following four factors determine language choice and mixing on the part of bilinguals: (1) the social roles and relationships of the participants; (2) situational factors: discourse topic and language allocation; (3) message-intrinsic considerations, and (4) language attitudes including social dominance and security. These four factors are interrelated in a speech event; they do not represent watertight compartments. We will now address each of these factors.

13.3.1 Participant roles and relationships

Participants' roles and the dynamics of their relationships play a crucial role in bilinguals' unconscious agreement or disagreement on language choice. Based on a mutual understanding of the obligations and rights of participants (see Myers-Scotton, 1993, p. 84, and 2002, pp. 43–6), agreement leads to language matching, which in turn reflects the nature of their perceived social relationship.

13.3.1.1   Language mismatching and repair

There are instances, though, when the unconscious process of language negotiation does not work smoothly. This results in language mismatching which is, interestingly enough, still subject to systematic considerations. Such mismatching occurs primarily under two conditions: (1) bilinguals are uncertain of each other's language identity/backgrounds and are thus still in an exploratory mode, or (2) their preference for mutual identity through language shows a differing preference for identities, or degree of formality and power relations, among other possibilities. For instance, in a South Asian restaurant, a bilingual waiter might choose to speak in English in spite of the fact that the customer has already made a move by choosing a shared South Asian language. The waiter might show preference for English rather than matching the customer's language. This linguistic mismatch is the result of failure of the waiter and the customer to negotiate a preferred identity. The waiter's choice of English shows his or her preference for educated identity and other perks (dominance, image of the restaurant, etc.) as opposed to seeking ethnic and regional solidarity. What is important is that the waiter's choice is not a marked choice; it exhibits a difference in personal choice like that of choosing coffee over tea on a particular occasion or as an attempt to calibrate the dominance relation between the two participants. If the process of repair is not carried out quickly by arriving at a mutually agreeable code, the consequence is likely to be a widening distance between the two participants which can ultimately lead to deteriorating relations or even hostility, if each of the two participants sticks to his or her own choice.

13.3.1.2   Dual/multiple identities, social distancing, and speech accommodation

Language mismatching does not necessarily reflect a failure of language negotiation. On the contrary, it may exemplify an accommodation to circumstances. Consider the following situation. Suppose two bilinguals, one Telugu-English and the other Hindi-English bilingual, are conversing with each other. The language of the conversation must naturally be English, the shared language of the participants. A third bilingual, a mutual friend of the two participants, joins them by greeting the Telugu-English bilingual in Telugu. The greeted bilingual does not greet back in Telugu, but chooses to respond in English instead. This situation is different from the one described above in a South Asian restaurant. The language mismatch signals the intention on the part of the greeted bilingual to stick to the code already agreed upon between the Telugu-English and Hindi-English bilingual. The choice of English in this instance is viewed as a "neutral" strategy and reflects speech accommodation on the part of the greeted bilingual, unlike the case of speech divergence in the restaurant example. Since the three participants are mutual friends, the phenomenon of language mismatching does not result in any ill-feeling toward the greeter. The mismatch is the result of an optimization process: while ethnic identity is already achieved through Telugu, the switch to English on the part of the greeted is an invitation to join in the formation of the mutually beneficial collective identity among all three participants. The greeter accepts this by responding in English. This shows how effectively and efficiently bilinguals can modulate between two identities, with the result that social distance is narrowed as desired by the participants. The language mismatch in such instances occurs in a group of diverse participants and usually it takes place at either the beginning or the closure phase of the interaction.

Consider now the exchange among four graduate students in Singapore given in (1) below. The background of the participants is as follows: A is a computer science graduate who has just found a job and a speaker of Teochew, one of the seven mutually unintelligible "dialects" of Chinese spoken in Singapore; B is an accountancy graduate who is looking for a job and speaks Hokkien, another of the Chinese varieties of Singapore; and D is an arts graduate and speaks Teochew and Hokkien. Also present but not included at this point in the conversation is C, an accountancy graduate, who has been working for a week and speaks Cantonese, another of the varieties of Chinese spoken in Singapore. All four participants speak English in addition to one or more varieties of Chinese. Now observe the following piece of conversation among them.

(1) English-*Hokkien*-Teochew (Tay, 1989, p. 416)
     D to B: Every day, you know *kào taim*
     'Every day, you know at nine o'clock'
     D to A: lì khi á
             'You go.'

In the above conversation, D addresses B in Hokkien but speaks to A in Teochew. In other words, the function of switching is to direct the message to one of the several possible addressees.

Consider now the exchange in (2), in which language mismatching occurs in the middle of an interaction and conflict resolution takes place afterwards. Four young office workers in the same government ministry in Nairobi are chatting. Interestingly, the languages mismatch in the middle of the interaction.

(2) Kikuyu-*Swahili*-English (Myers-Scotton, 1989, p. 338)
     (The conversation up to this point has been in English and Swahili – the expected choices under the circumstances.)
     Kikuyu II: Andu amwe nimendaga kwaria maundu maria matari na ma namo.
                  'Some people like talking about what they're not sure of.'

Kikuyu I:	Wira wa muigi wa kigina ni kuiga mbeca. No tigucaria mbeca. 'The work of the treasurer is only to keep money, not to hunt for money.'
Kisii:	*Ubaya wenu ya kikuyu ni ku-<u>assume</u> kila mtu anaelewa kikuyu.* 'The bad thing about Kikuyus is assuming that every one understands Kikuyu.'
Kalenjin:	*Si mtumie lugha ambayo kila mtu hapa atasikia?* . . . <u>We are supposed to solve this issue.</u> 'Shouldn't we use the language which everyone here understands?' (said with some force): 'We are supposed to solve this issue.'

Two are Kikuyu, one is Kisii, and one is a Kalenjin. As noted, Swahili and English have been the unmarked choice up to the switch to Kikuyu. The conversation about setting up a group 'emergency fund' has been proceeding, when the two Kikuyus switch to Kikuyu to make a negative comment on what has been said, a marked choice communicating solidarity between the two Kikuyus, but distancing them from the others. At this point, the Kisii complains in Swahili and English and the Kalenjin makes a switch from Swahili to a sentence entirely in English, a marked choice, to return the discussion to a more business-like plane, and thus conflict resolution takes place.

Of course, in those societies in which language identity ranks highest in the range of identities accessible to bilinguals (e.g. among Bengali-speakers in South Asia, French-speakers or Japanese-speakers), in a diverse group setting, linguistic accommodation may not take place, thus diminishing the incidence of language switching.

13.3.2 Situational factors

In bi-/multilingual societies, languages generally do not overlap each other's discourse domain. The pie of discourse domains is cut up by the various languages used in such societies into mutually exclusive pieces. Consequently, some languages are viewed as more suited to particular participant/social groups, settings or topics than others. For instance, very often bilinguals organize their two languages according to their public vs. their private world. The public language often serves as the "they" code and the private language as the "we" code. The "they" code can be used to perform a range of functions, from creating distance, asserting authority, and expressing objectivity, to suppressing the tabooness of an interaction. The "we" code conveys a range from in-group membership, informality, and intimacy, to emotions. Richard Rodriguez (1982) notes that Spanish was the language of his private world. His Spanish voice insisted, "We are family members. Related. Special to one another," whereas English sounded loud, booming with confidence. The day the family decided to use English at home, family intimacy was not the same. In professional domains such as advertising, different languages carve their topical and social-psychological domains. (For more details, see the discussion of advertising in chapter 20, particularly table 20.3.)

13.3.2.1 Social variables

Social variables such as class, religion, gender, and age can influence the pattern of LM/S both qualitatively and quantitatively. The social cueing of mixing is exemplified in (3) and (4).

(3) Hindi-<u>Persian</u>-*English*

    (a) **A.** are <u>cacaa</u> <u>jaan.</u> <u>aadaab.</u>, sab <u>xairiyat</u> hai, na?
           hey uncle HON hello   all OK   is, Q
           'Hey uncle. Hello. All is OK, isn't it?'
           (HON = Honorific; Q = Tag question marker)

    (b) **B.** <u>xush</u>   raho,   sab <u>xairiyat</u> hai aur tumahaara
           happy remain all OK   is   and your
           kyaa   haalcaal   hai?
           what   condition is
           'Be happy. All is fine. And how are you?'

    (c) **A.** aapkii <u>duaa</u>   hai
           your   kindness is
           'It is your kindness.'

    (d) **B.** kidhar jaa rahe   ho?
           Where go PROG are
           'Where are you going?'
           (PROG = Progressive)

    (e) **A.** bhaaii <u>jaan</u>   ne bulaayaa thaa. unke <u>daftar</u>
           brother HON AG called   was his   office
           jaa rahaa huun.
           Go PROG am
           'My brother called me. (I) am going to his office.'
           (AG = Agent marker)

(4) (a) **A.** are *ankal* jii   namaste, sab Thiik hai, na?
           Hey uncle HON hello   all OK is, Q
           'Hey uncle. Hello. All is OK, isn't it?

    (b) **B.** <u>xush</u>   raho,   sab <u>Thiik</u> hai aur tumahaaraa
           happy remain all OK is and your
           kyaa   haalcaal   hai?
           what   condition is
           'Be happy. All is fine. And how are you?'

    (c) **A.** aapkii kripaa   hai
           your   kindness is
           'It is your kindness.'

    (d) **B.** kidhar jaa rahe   ho?
           Where go PROG are
           'Where are you going?'

Table 13.1 Markers of Hindi-Persian and Hindi-English mixing.

Line	Gloss	(3) Hindi-Persian mixing (all forms Persian)	(4) Hindi-English mixing
a	'uncle'	*cacaa*	*ankal* (English)
	honorific	*jaan*	*jii* (Hindi)
	'hello'	*aadaab*	*namaste* (Hindi)
	'OK'	*xairiyat*	*Thiik* (Hindi)
c	'kindness'	*duaa*	*kripaa* (Hindi)
e	'office'	*daftar*	*aafis* (English)

Table 13.2 Functions of code mixing.

Functions	Persian-Hindi LM/S	English-Hindi LM/S
Role identification	Muslim participants	Educated Hindu/other religions
Socio-psychological	Romantic, centered	Elitist, modern, western
Stylistic	Legal, business	Scientific, technological, etc.

(e) **A.** bhaiyaa ne bulaayaa thaa. unke *aafis*
   brother AG called   was his   office
   jaa rahaa huun.
   go PROG am
   'My brother called me. (I) am going to his office.'

The exchanges in (3) and (4) mark LM/S with Persian and English, respectively. The lexical markers of the two styles are given in table 13.1. The two styles in (3) and (4) are in general not compatible. For example, though one might say *cacaa jaan* (with the Persian-Arabic honorific *jaan*) or *cacaa jii* (Hindi honorific *jii*) or *ankal jii*, the form **ankal jaan* is not possible.

Even if the identity of the participants (A and B) is not given explicitly in (3) and (4), the pattern of LM/S provides sufficient indexical cues about the participants and their roles. The conversational roles played by participants are given in table 13.2 together with other roles played by the two aspects of mixing.

In many traditional societies, where gender roles are clearly demarcated, i.e. men work outside the home and women are engaged in domestic activities, LM/S in women is qualitatively different from that in men (e.g. lack of LM/S with English among women; see chapter 19). Similarly, age plays an important role in determining the nature of LM/S; see, for example, the case of second-generation Turkish immigrants (chapters 6, 19, and 26).

Consideration of situational factors such as shifting personality, thoughts, audience and topic can further promote language alternation. This behavior can be well exemplified here by Kipling's portrayal of a Tibetan Lama in his novel *Kim*, which is renowned for the author's mastery of insights into the verbal repertoire of multilingual India.

> He [the Lama] began in Urdu the tale of Lord Buddha, but borne by his own thoughts, slid into Tibetan, and a long-drawn-out text from a Chinese book of the Buddha's life. The gentle, tolerant folk looked on reverently. All India is full of holy men stammering gospel in strange tongues. . . . The Lama fell back on Urdu, remembering he was in a strange land.

13.3.3   Message-intrinsic factors

LM/S is also a function of additional linguistic and pragmatic considerations such as those outlined below.

13.3.3.1   Quotations

Direct quotation or reported speech triggers LM/S among bilinguals cross-linguistically. This function has been attested by a wide variety of empirical studies. The following example illustrates this function.

(5)   *Spanish*-English (Gumperz, 1982, p. 76)
      From a conversation between two Chicano professionals. While referring to her babysitter, the speaker says the following:
      She doesn't speak English, so, *dice que la reganan*: *"Si se les va olvidar el idioma a las criaturas."*
      'She does not speak English. So, she says they would scold her: "the children are surely going to forget their language."'

13.3.3.2   Reiteration

Reiteration or paraphrasing marks another function of mixing. The message expressed in one language is either repeated in the other language literally or with some modification to signify emphasis or clarification. The following examples illustrate the emphatic and clarificatory role of mixing, respectively.

(6)   English-*Spanish*: Chicano professionals (Gumperz 1982, p. 78)
      A: The three old ones spoke nothing but Spanish. *No hablaban ingles*.
      '. . .   They didn't speak English.'

(7)   English-*Chinese* (Mah, 1997, p. 104)
      The moment my aunt saw the jacket, she knew that Miss Chen was dishonest and had *fu zhong lin jia* (scale and shell in her belly).

13.3.3.3 *Message qualification*

Frequently, mixing takes the form of a qualifying complement or argument as exemplified by the disjunctive argument and the adverbial phrase respectively in the following sentences.

(8) Slovenian-*German* (Gumperz, 1982, p. 60)
     Uzeymas ti kafe? *Oder te?*
     'Will you take coffee? or tea?'

13.3.3.4 *Topic–Comment/relative clauses*

Related to the function of message qualification is yet another function – the Topic–Comment function. Nishimura's (1989) study devoted to Japanese-English LM/S revealed that the topic is introduced in Japanese (formally marked with *wa*) and the comment is given in English, as shown in the following example:

(9) Japanese-English (Nishimura 1989, p. 370)
     Kore wa   she is at home
     this topic
     'As for this (person – referring to a photograph of her daughter), she is at home.'

A similar situation can be witnessed with respect to English-Hindi relative clauses. Hindi has three different types of relative clauses (see Bhatia 1974; Lust et al., 1988). The English relativized head NP can be mixed with Hindi as in (10).

(10) English-Hindi
      The boy who is going meraa dost   hai.
                           my   friend is
          '...   is my friend.'

In English-Hindi LM/S, the English sequence *the boy* is understood to be a Topicalized NP with two associated Comments – the English *who is going* and the Hindi *meraa dost hai*.

13.3.3.5 *Hedging*

LM/S serves an important function in hedging (e.g. taboo suppression, de-intensification, or a vague "sort of" expression). Although the formal and functional range of hedging is quite wide and both languages of a bilingual can contribute, the language which is allocated as the "they" code is often used for this purpose, particularly when hedging performs the function of taboo suppression. This aspect of LM/S is often deliberate and is by and large a conscious process. The passage in (11) concerns a veterinarian doctor's attempt to explain to villagers in rural India the process of artificial insemination. When the listeners fail to understand the English term, the doctor attempts to explain the concept by paraphrasing it figuratively into Hindi. The dilemma regarding how to suppress the tabooness via Hindi is clear from his hesitation and halting speech.

(11)   Doctor to villagers (Hindi-<u>English</u>)
       "<u>artificial insemination</u>." Dekho ise kyaa kahte hain hindi men . . . barii aasaan ciiz hai . . . jab bhains garam ho rahii ho . . . to use <u>AI Center</u> le jaaiyee aur uskaa AI karva Daaliye
       "Artificial insemination." Look, what do people call it in Hindi . . . It is very easy (to explain). When a buffalo is in heat, take her to the AI Center and have her artificially inseminated." (Literally: have AI done on her)

13.3.3.6   Interjections
Another function of LM/S is to mark an interjection or sentence filler. Bilinguals in Singapore are well known to exploit this function by mixing a number of particles, as in (12). Interlocutors A, C, and D are as described for (2) above.

(12)   English-*Hokkien* (Tay 1989, p. 416)
       D: Do what?
       A: System analyst *la*
          'System analyst, what else?'
       C: *hà*
          'Is that so?'
       A: Programmer *la*.

13.3.3.7   Idioms and deep-rooted cultural wisdom

(13)   English-*Chinese* (Mah, 1997, p. 238)
       The solution is simple – *yi dao liang duan*
       'The solution is simple – let's sever this kinship with one whack of the knife.'

The determinants of LM/S are summarized in table 13.3.

Table 13.3 Motivation for language mixing.

Participants	Situational factors	Socio-psychological factors	Linguistic/pragmatic considerations
Indexical (speaker/ addressee's social class, gender, age, etc.)	Formality, settings, private vs. public world, etc.	Dominance, group membership, neutrality, speech accommodation	Repetition, clarification, contrast, quotation, paraphrase, message qualification, deep-rooted cultural knowledge, topic–comment, hedging, language trigger

Table 13.4   Attitudes and the pattern of language mixing.

Speech community	Covert attitude (unconscious)	Overt attitude (conscious)	Pattern of mixing
Arabic-French-English community in Lebanon	+	+	Very high
Puerto Rican community in New York	+	–	High
Punjabi-English community in UK	+	–	High
Hindi-English community in India	+	–	High
English-French community in Ottawa-Hull	–	+	Middle
Flemish-French bilinguals in Brussels	–	–	Low

13.3.4   *Language attitudes, dominance, and security*

Other factors such as individual and social attitudes, language dominance, and linguistic security determine the qualitative and quantitative properties of language mixing. The positive attitudes in table 13.4 are indicated by the plus symbol [+], while the negative attitude is signified by the minus symbol [–].

On the basis of differences in language attitudes, one can postulate primarily four types of language-mixing communities. For instance, Puerto Rican bilinguals in New York City unconsciously have positive attitudes toward bilingualism and LM/S; consequently, they tend to code-mix/switch 97 percent of the time and this mixing/switching is smooth, as observed by Poplack (1987). English-Hindi mixing in India and Punjabi-English mixing in Great Britain follow this pattern. When such mixing becomes the mark of cultural or social identity, the speech community begins to view mixing positively at both the unconscious and the conscious levels. This may further promote the incidence of LM/S both quantitatively and qualitatively. As a case in point, extensive Arabic-French-English LM/S occurs in Lebanon, where trilingual mixing is viewed as a distinctive feature of Lebanese culture (see Grosjean, 1982, p. 149).

The third type of attitude toward mixing can be exemplified by the Ottawa-Hull speech community (Poplack, Wheeler, and Westwood, 1989). In Hull the English-French mixing is one-third to one-fourth as frequent as in Ottawa. The metalinguistic commentary offered by bilinguals and accompanied by flagged mixing provides evidence that bilinguals view mixing covertly in negative terms although consideration of linguistic accommodation at the conscious level leads to flagged mixing.

The last type of bilingual, who considers bilingualism negatively on both conscious and unconscious grounds, is exemplified in the speech patterns of Flemish and French bilinguals in Brussels. Because of the long history of linguistic rivalry and conflict in Belgium, one witnesses Flemish-speakers and French-speakers entrenched in their own language while talking with each other and no attempt is made to switch or mix the two linguistic systems (see Grosjean, 1982).

Within each community, variables such as gender and topic add further intricacy to language mixing. In India, male and female attitudes toward mixing are quite divergent. Males prefer mixing with English whereas women do not. Women's role in the preservation of Indian culture goes largely uncontested by men. Therefore, the incidence of language mixing with English is much lower in women than in men. Unlike the Western English-speaking speech community, where men's speech is regarded as standard, in South Asia, women's speech is considered more standard than men's. However, in the discussion of certain topics such as children's education, one can witness the phenomenon of over-compensation of mixing with English among women. That is why female Indian writers often poke fun at excessive or odd mixing on the part of middle-class women. A case in point is women's use of phrases such as *childrens kii education* 'the education of children,' and *childrenon kii education* 'the education of children.' In the first form, the speaker effectively reduplicates the English plural marker; in the second example, the speaker adds *-on-*, the Hindi oblique marker, to English *children*. Men will tend either to use *children kii education* or to prefer not to use English in the modifier position.

The speaker's language proficiency and language dominance also determine the incidence and nature of LM/S. For instance, in South Asia English educators tend to code-switch with English more than balanced Hindi-English bilinguals.

13.4   Societal Evaluation of Language Mixing

From the above discussion, it is evident that creativity and complexity are the two salient features of code mixing and code switching. The innovative multifunctions performed by LM/S in bilingual communication lead one to assume, on a common sense basis, that LM/S will be valued and admired immensely by the society. Ironically, just the reverse turns out to be true. The misconception widely held by prescriptivists and language puritans is that bilinguals have "trouble expressing themselves in either language" because of (1) their asymmetrical language proficiency or language deficiency and/or (2) their memory recall limitations. In this view, language switching is primarily a strategy for masking linguistic deficiency. However, neither of the two reasons actually explains the normal verbal behavior of bilinguals. It is shown in a number of studies that bilinguals often employ strategies such as paraphrasing and elaboration either to show speech accommodation or to provide comprehensible input to bilingual children (e.g. Spanish mothers). These strategies enable them to retrieve words from both languages almost instantaneously. Zentella (1997) shows that even non-fluent bilingual children, let alone balanced bilinguals, rarely use language switching for masking purposes. On the contrary, language switching and mixing is used by balanced bilinguals to meet their creative needs which cannot be met by sticking to just one language.

LM/S invites, at least overtly, a near-universal negative evaluation among lay people. Grosjean (1982, pp. 146–8) provides a cross-linguistic array of such attitudes. A cursory examination of these attitudes reveals that LM/S is considered a linguistic phenomenon which lacks "grammar/rules." Puritans and self-appointed guardians of language decry LM/S as a sign of the linguistic death of one of the two participating languages and call for action to maintain the "purity" of the linguistic systems in question. The following remarks of Haugen's (1969) are instructive in this regard. Commenting on the linguistic behavior and reporting of Norwegian-American prescriptivists, he notes, "Reports are sometimes heard of individuals who 'speak no language whatever' and confuse the two to such an extent that it is impossible to tell which language they speak. No such cases have occurred in the writer's experience, in spite of the many years of listening to American-Norwegian speech" (p. 70).

13.5 Bilinguals' Perception of Language Mixing

Turning to the last question, what is even more remarkable is that with the exception of highly linguistically aware bilinguals, the vast majority of bilinguals themselves hold a negative view of code-mixed speech. They consider LM/S to be a sign of "laziness," an "inadvertent" speech act, an "impurity," an instance of linguistic decadence and a potential danger to their own linguistic performance. Usually, they apologize for their "inappropriate" verbal behavior. Gumperz notes that when bilinguals are made aware of their mixed speech, they blame a "lapse of attention" for their "poor" linguistic performance and promise improvement by eliminating LM/S. So natural is LM/S among bilinguals that one witnesses the return of the mixed system either immediately or very shortly after such expressions of guilt. No hesitation or pauses in sentence rhythm or pitch level are witnessed and the speakers maintain an even and fluent mode of communication.

The above discussion provides evidence for a discrepancy between overt (conscious) and covert (unconscious) attitudes towards LM/S. If Hindi-English bilinguals do not report having positive attitudes towards LM/S, then how can one explain such speakers' return to LM/S in spite of the pledge to avoid it altogether? They must find this form of language use appropriate for their communicative needs at the unconscious level; otherwise they would avoid it.

13.6 Conclusions

Language mixing reflects a natural and universal aspect of bilingual verbal behavior. Although remarkable progress has been registered in our understanding of bilinguals' language mixing over the past two decades, many challenges still need to be met. The long history of prescriptivism and foreign language teaching has resulted in the severe negative societal evaluation of this speech form, which is ironically capable of unlocking new dimensions of human linguistic creativity; therefore, its value in the study of language – ranging from theoretical linguistics to neuro- and educational linguistics – can hardly be overestimated. Furthermore, a phenomenon which was and in some circles still is seen as ad hoc, random, and inconsequential seems to have a natural and central role in studies of language contact in general and language mixing in particular.

REFERENCES

Beardsome, H. B. (1991). *Bilingualism: Basic Principles*, 2nd edn. Philadelphia: Multilingual Matters Ltd.

Bhatia, T. K. (1974). Testing four hypotheses about relative clause formation and the applicability of Ross's constraints in Hindi. MS, University of Illinois, Urbana.

Bhatia, T. K. and Ritchie, W. C. (1996). Bilingual language mixing, universal grammar, and second language acquisition. In W. C. Ritchie and T. K. Bhatia (eds.), *Handbook of Second Language Acquisition*, pp. 627–88. San Diego: Academic Press.

Bokamba, E. (1988). Code-mixing, language variation and linguistic theory: Evidence from Bantu languages. *Lingua*, 76, 21–62.

Grosjean, F. (1982). *Life with Two Languages*. Cambridge, MA: Harvard University Press.

Grosjean, F. (1989). Neurolinguists, beware! The bilingual is not two monolinguals in one person. *Brain and Language*, 36, 3–15.

Gumperz, J. J. (1982). Conversational code-switching. *Discourse Strategies*, ch. 4, pp. 233–74. Cambridge, UK: Cambridge University Press.

Hatch, E. (1976). Studies in language switching and mixing. In W. C. McCormack and S. A. Wurm (eds.), *Language and Man: Anthropological Issues*, pp. 201–14. The Hague: Mouton.

Haugen, E. (1969). *The Norwegian Language in America*. Cambridge, MA: Harvard University Press.

Kachru, B. B. (1978). Toward structuring code-mixing: An Indian perspective. *International Journal of the Sociology of Language*, 16, 28–46.

Kachru, B. B. (1982). The bilingual's linguistic repertoire. In B. Harford and A. Valdman (eds.), *Issues in International Bilingual Education: The Role of the Vernacular*, pp. 25–52. New York: Plenum.

Kipling, R. (1901). *Kim*. London: Macmillan.

Labov, W. (1971). The notion of "system" in creole languages. In D. Hymes (ed.), *Pidginization and creolization of languages*, pp. 447–72. Cambridge, UK: Cambridge University Press.

Lance, D. (1975). Spanish-English code-switching. In E. Hernández-Chavez, A. D. Cohen, A. F. Beltramo (eds.), *El lenguaje de los Chicanos: Regional and Social Characteristics used by Mexican Americans*, pp. 138–53. Arlington, VA: Center for Applied Linguistics.

Lust, B., Bhatia, T., Gair, J., Sharma, V., and Khare, J. (1988). A parameter setting paradox: Children's acquisition of Hindi anaphora. Cornell Working Papers in Linguistics, 8, 107–12.

Mah, R. Y. (1997). *Falling Leaves*. New York: Broadway Books.

McLaughlin, B. (1984). *Second-language Acquisition in Childhood. Volume 1: Preschool Children*. Hillsdale, NJ: Lawrence Erlbaum.

Myers-Scotton, C. M. (1989). Code-switching with English: Types of switching, types of communities. *World Englishes*, 8(3), 333–46.

Myers-Scotton, C. M. (1993). *Social Motivations for Codeswitching: Evidence from Africa*. Oxford: Clarendon Press.

Myers-Scotton, C. M. (2002). *Contact Linguistics: Bilingual Encounters and Grammatical Outcomes*. Oxford: Oxford University Press.

Nishimura, M. (1989). The topic-comment structure in Japanese-English code-switching. *World Englishes*, 8(3), 365–77.

Pakir, A. (1989). Linguistic alternants and code selection in Baba Malay. *World Englishes*, 8(3), 379–88.

Pfaff, C. (1979). Constraints on language mixing: Intrasentential code-switching and borrowing in Spanish/English. *Language*, 55, 291–318.

Poplack, S. (1987). Contrasting patterns of code-switching in two communities. In Erling Wande et al. (eds.), *Aspects of Multilingualism*, pp. 51–77. Uppsala: Borgström.

Poplack, S., Wheeler, S., and Westwood, A. (1989). Distinguishing language contact phenomena: Evidence from Finnish-English bilingualism. *World Englishes*, 8(3), 389–406.

Rodriguez, R. (1982). *Hunger of Memory*. New York: Bantam Books.

Romaine, S. (1989). *Bilingualism*. Oxford: Basil Blackwell.

Tay, M. W. J. (1989). Code switching and code mixing as a communicative strategy in multilingual discourse. *World Englishes*, 8(3), 407–17.

Weinreich, U. (1953). *Languages in Contact*. (Reprinted 1979.) The Hague: Mouton.

Zentella, A. (1997). *Growing up Bilingual: Puerto Rican Children in New York*. Oxford: Basil Blackwell.

14 Bilingual Accommodation

ITESH SACHDEV AND HOWARD GILES

14.1 Introduction

A variety of interdependent processes associated with globalization, including greater geographical, demographic, social and information exchange and mobility, have enabled contacts and communication between cultures and languages to grow almost exponentially. Being bilingual is "a normal and unremarkable necessity for the majority of the world today" (Edwards, 1994, p. 1) and researchers have increasingly focused on the complexities underlying bilingualism in individual, communicational, developmental, and societal perspectives (e.g. Grosjean, 1982; Hamers and Blanc, 2000; Romaine, 1995; this volume). The aim of this chapter is to provide a general overview of a social psychological approach to bilingual communication that springboards from notions of bilingual accommodation.

Consider what happens when a bilingual makes a request (or greeting, etc.) in one language. At least three classes of replies may be observed, those in: (1) the same language as the request; (2) a different language from the request; and (3) a combination of languages. Within and between these three possible general options, there is a complex number of variations. For instance, although interactants may use the same language, they may vary their communication on other linguistic (e.g. accent, lexis), discoursal, and non-verbal features. When interactants use combinations of languages, there may be variation in terms of employing two languages in the same sentence, or different languages between sentences, or different languages between speaker turns (see Sachdev and Bourhis, 2001 for examples). In order to understand and model the vast array of acts of multilingual communication, this chapter invokes Communication Accommodation Theory (CAT), a view that Giles and his colleagues have been developing over the last thirty years (e.g. Coupland and Giles, 1988; Giles, 1984; Giles, Coupland, and Coupland, 1991; Niedzielsky and Giles, 1996). CAT has been revised many times over the years and has, on occasion, been presented in ever more refined propositional formats (e.g.

Gallois, Giles, Jones, Cargile, and Ota, 1995; Giles, Mulac, Bradac, and Johnson, 1987). In this context, we will resist that kind of approach and present the essence of CAT by purely textual means. The review presented herein is necessarily selective: it focuses specifically on bilingual and multilingual accommodation – and not on other types of accommodation (accent, speech rate, etc.). For the remainder of this chapter, the term "bilingual" includes "multilingual", unless specifically indicated. After we have provided readers with a flavor of CAT, we shall introduce the components of a modestly revised social psychological model of bilingualism (Sachdev and Bourhis, 2001) which derives, in no small part, from these theoretical beginnings.

14.2   CAT: A Brief Overview of Some Basic Concepts and Processes

There is a substantial body of literature showing that languages and language choices are not just "neutral" means of communication (e.g. Giles and Johnson, 1981; Gumperz and Hymes, 1972; Sachdev and Bourhis, 1990). Which language(s) is or are used, when, why, and by whom, are important questions given the crucial role that language plays as "the recorder of paternity, the expressor of patrimony and the carrier of phenomenology" (Fishman, 1977, p. 25). CAT is presented as a social psychological approach employed to integrate micro-individual aspects with the macro-collective levels of bilingual communication (Bourhis, 1979; Clément and Bourhis, 1996; Giles, Bourhis, and Taylor, 1977). Before we engage the basic strategies and ideas inherent in CAT, let us outline four major assumptions of the theory:

- Bilingual communication is influenced not only by features of the immediate situation and participants' initial orientations to it, but also by the socio-historical context in which the interaction is embedded (see also Johnson, 2000). For example, language choices occurring in a chance, one-off encounter between a police officer and an immigrant could be influenced (and even marred) by alleged and past hostile relations between other members of these two groups in the neighborhood and/or on the media. Indeed, this facet of CAT is so important that we shall devote a significant proportion of our chapter to such issues in due course.
- Bilingual communication is not *only* a matter of exchanging referential information, but salient social category memberships are often negotiated during an interaction through the processes of accommodation. An example of this has been noted in bilingual Montreal (Canada) where anglophones perceive francophones more favorably when the latter converge toward English rather than continuing in French, and also vice versa. Bourhis (1984a, p. 34), in discussing this situation, notes that "since both . . . interlocutors communicated in each other's weaker language, this study showed that

mutual language convergence could be used as a strategy to promote ethnic harmony, even at the potential cost of communicative effectiveness."

- Interactants have expectations regarding *optimal* levels of bilingual accommodation. These anticipations can be based on stereotypes about outgroup members, ways of conducting appropriate intergroup business, and the prevailing social and situational norms. Giles, Taylor, and Bourhis (1973) reflected an example provided them by Dell Hymes in which a westerner accommodated to a Tanzanian official (thinking he was being socially sensitive and bilingually competent). However, the official construed this as an (over-accommodating) insult to the extent that it implied the Tanzanian could not speak good English; it was, in contrast, perceived as patronizing and over-ingratiating. In another part of the world, Ross and Shortreed (1990) found that some Japanese were extremely uncomfortable with westerners who were proficient in Japanese. In response, they might intentionally switch to English or adopt a foreigner talk register in Japanese. Calibrating the amount of perceived non-, under-, and even overaccommodating language that one receives can be an important ingredient in withdrawing from an interaction, or continuing with it in a particular way.

There are, of course, an array of reasons why bilinguals switch their languages, including not finding the right word at that moment, allowing others to have practice at one's language, the desire to impart a cosmopolitan identity or a community identity through humor, and so on and so forth (see, for example, Burt, 1994, 1998; O'Driscoll, 2001). CAT attempts to model the motives and evaluations of switching in terms of a balance of social psychological processes focusing on social integration and differentiation.

14.3   Strategies of Convergence and Divergence: Motives and Evaluations

As described above, CAT suggests that individuals use communication, in part, to indicate their attitudes toward each other and, as such, communication is a barometer of the level of social distance between them. This constant movement toward and away from others, by changing one's communicative behavior, is called *accommodation*. Among the different accommodative strategies that speakers use to achieve these goals, *convergence* has been the most extensively studied – and can be considered the historical core of CAT (Giles, 1973; see also Bell, 1984). It has been defined as a strategy whereby individuals adapt their communicative behaviors in terms of a wide range of linguistic (e.g. speech rate, accents), paralinguistic (e.g. pauses, utterance length), and nonverbal features (e.g. smiling, gazing) in such a way that they become more similar to their interlocutor's behavior. It is noteworthy that even in the apparently socially sterile laboratory setting of Giles, Taylor, and Bourhis's (1973) study, at least 14 different types of bilingual convergence were observed.

For our purposes here, convergence is not only confined to situations where a bilingual objectively moves toward the language preference of another but, importantly, when they *believe* they have accomplished this fact (Thakerar, Giles, and Cheshire, 1982). An undergraduate of one of us resides in a basically anglophone city where a significant proportion of the population is Hispanic. It is not uncommon for her, given her physiognomy, to be addressed immediately in Spanish; an approach that sometimes incurs her consternation. She is actually Russian-American in origin and has no Latina ancestry whatsoever yet, as it happens, is very proficient in Spanish. On occasion, her conversants will never be made aware by her that they were guilty of ethnic miscategorization and that their convergent moves miscarried (see Platt and Weber, 1984).

Conversely, the strategy of *divergence* leads to an accentuation of language (and cultural) differences. Again one of us (an English-only monolingual) recalls many years ago walking into a North Welsh pub to be greeted by the whole clientele switching from English into Welsh as he opened the door. Finally, the strategy of *maintenance* is, as the term implies, an act of not converging (or actively diverging) from another but, instead, sustaining (somewhat purposively) one's own native language usage (see Bourhis, 1979). A classic instance of this was in the 1970s when an Arab diplomat issued a global media communiqué about the Middle East oil situation in Arabic rather than in English, as had traditionally been the case; a forerunner to this event was that the Arab nations cognized their economic muscle in this business domain.

Another important conceptual distinction is whether the convergence or divergence is "upward" or "downward" in terms of its societal valence (Giles and Powesland, 1975). Upward convergence would be illustrated by a French Canadian worker's adoption of the prestige language patterns of an English-speaking (albeit bilingual) manager (see Barkhuizen and de Klerk, 2000; Bourhis, 1991). Upward divergence would be indicated by the latter commencing that interaction in French and then suddenly shifting to English. Downward divergence would be illustrated by one of us shifting to Gujarati in a London store where the English-speaking shop assistant evinced indications of anti-Asian prejudice (see also Nair-Venugopal, 2001).

We will now examine some of the principal motives that lie behind the strategies of convergence and divergence, considering their evaluative demeanor as well as the importance of stereotypes and social norms in defining participants' expectations about how much convergence or divergence a speaker should display. As mentioned above, an important *cause* for convergence, for us, is the desire to gain approval from a recipient (and hence, perhaps, access to the social networks to which the recipient is believed to belong). The premise is that of similarity attraction (Byrne, 1969): the more similar we are to our interlocutor, the more he or she will like or respect us, and the more social rewards we can expect. Converging to a common linguistic style also improves the effectiveness of communication: this has been associated with increased predictability of the other and hence a lowering of uncertainty and interpersonal anxiety, and gains in mutual understanding (see Gudykunst, 1995).

Convergence by immigrants (and especially with an accommodated accent as well) to the host culture's language is not only expected by many members of mainstream society, but is also regarded as a vivid indication that they have acculturated to the host culture's values (see Kim, 2001). Thus, it would be expected that Latino migrants converge to English-speakers in the United States, and Turkish gastarbeiter and their families converge to their hosts in German. Members of the German *dialect*-speaking majority converge to the French-speaking minority in Switzerland. (For a discussion of social normative parameters of CAT, see Gallois and Callan, 1991.) In this sense, accommodation is unidirectional, termed "asymmetric," rather than "symmetrical" or reciprocal (see Gallois and Giles, 1998).

But convergence is not always rewarding (as we have noted above), it may well entail some costs, such as the possible loss of personal or social identity. If a Chinese student – in the days before Hong Kong was handed back to the People's Republic of China (PRC) – converged towards a bilingual western professor's English, the student might be rewarded by the professor, who could perceive him as particularly communicatively competent, but the student might also, nonetheless, feel deprived of his social identity. Members of his ingroup (i.e. other students) who happened to hear him might also perceive him as a "traitor" and label him derogatorily (Hogg, D'Agata, and Abrams, 1989). Accommodative moves are also diversely appreciated by ingroup members, depending on the strength of their attachment to the group. In a study conducted in Hong Kong one year before its handover to the PRC, respondents with a strong identification to Hong Kong evaluated more favorably their ingroup members who, by using Cantonese, diverged more from Mandarin-speaking Chinese people than did respondents who identified themselves with mainland China (Tong, Hong, Lee, and Chiu, 1999).

This is where divergence comes in: the motive lying behind this strategy is precisely the desire to emphasize distinctiveness from one's interlocutor, usually on the basis of group membership. Following the premises of Social Identity Theory (e.g. Tajfel and Turner, 1986), this will likely occur when interactants define a situation more in "intergroup" than "interindividual" terms; the former activates one's shared social identity, the latter a personal identity. Put another way, intergroup communication occurs where individuals treat each other entirely in terms of their social category memberships, whereas interindividual communication takes place when they communicate with each other *entirely* on the basis of their individual differences in temperament and personality – and where their ethnicity, gender, age, and so forth are not at a premium.

Intergroup theorists would contend that intergroup encounters are actually far more common than is usually realized, and that their interindividual counterparts are much less frequent than they are given credit for in the study of so-called interpersonal communication. Given that ingroup language is often a core dimension of what it is to be a member of an ethnic group (e.g. Fishman, 1977), divergence can be regarded as a very important tactic of intergroup distinctiveness for bilinguals wishing to feel good about their ethnicity, and thereby about themselves. As we belong to many different social groups, we have, thus, multiple social identities that are more or less salient in any interaction. The dynamics of communication are made even more complex by the fact that some of these social identities are shared between the interactants, and some are not. In this vein, Jones, Gallois, Barker, and Callan (1994) showed that the visible, vocal (and potentially potent) intercultural dimension of whether an individual was Anglo- or Chinese-Australian was quite *non*-predictive of their communicative behavior; what was predictive, however, was their occupational group memberships as professors or students.

However, divergence can also be adopted in order to shape receivers' attributions and feelings (Simard, Taylor, and Giles, 1976). For example, a French-speaking student in a tutorial at an English university could purposely say a string of words in French during the conversation in order to remind her peers that she does not belong to the same ethnolinguistic group. By so doing, she signals that her (possibly unsubtle) discourse should be attributed to her linguistic (in)competence rather than to deficient intellectual capacities.

Attempts at social integration, linguistic acculturation or identification by means of convergence have been *generally* accorded positive evaluation by their receivers (Giles, Taylor, and Bourhis, 1973; Bourhis, Giles, and Lambert, 1975). In this sense, it validates the recipients' own ways of expressing themselves. Increasing similarity in communicative behavior can increase both a speaker's perceived attractiveness and their ability to gain addressees' compliance (see also Buller, Le Poire, Aune, and Eloy, 1992). Not only are bilingually converging speakers perceived as communicatively more efficient and as more cooperative, they are also generally viewed more favorably than diverging and maintaining speakers. As a case in point, white English-speaking South African students judged an audiotaped Cape Colored Afrikaans-speaking criminal suspect as being less guilty when he converged in English to his white interrogator than when he either partially or fully diverged away in Afrikaans (Dixon, Tredoux, Durrheim, and Foster, 1994). Being even the receiver of *non*-accommodation tells you that the speaker overtly dares not to value your approval – a stance we, as personal recipients of it, have difficulty applauding! However, there can also be negative outcomes for convergence too (as indicated above). Preston (1981) found that full convergence, in the case of foreign language learning, is not always desired by either the speaker or the addressee. He states that full convergence, or native-speaker-like fluency, is often considered with distrust and seen as controlling by the addressee.

The power variable should not be left aside either: it is generally expected, as we have illustrated above, that people in subordinate positions would converge to those in superordinate positions (*upward convergence*). In a study of K'iche' speakers in Guatemala using ethnolinguistic vitality (see below), Lewis (2001) observed what he called the "ladino effect" where K'iche' speakers would adopt Spanish when talking to ladinos ("ladino" includes people of European or mixed blood in Guatemala). He noted that "in some communities, this effect was so strong that language use patterns of Mayans were indistinguishable from those of ladinos if *a* ladino was present as one of the participants" (p. 231, our italics; for a discussion of accommodative behaviors in group settings, see Ros and Giles, 1979).

Bilingual behavior as objectively measured, the intent of the initiator of it, and how the addressee perceives the behavior can mean three different things. The latter two of these three levels have been termed *psychological* and *subjective accommodation*, respectively (see Thakerar et al., 1982). Speakers may converge to their listener objectively (as assessed through direct observation of communication behavior), but the intent behind this convergence may not be to show intimacy but, on the contrary, be crafted to indicate social distance. Woolard (1989) reported on a language norm in Spain at that time stating that Catalan should only be spoken between Catalans. Hence, Castilian speakers who attempted to speak Catalan often received a reply back in Castilian. At one level, they were recipients of objective convergence, but the psychological intent here was to keep Castilians in their own social-linguistic space and hence the act was perceived and felt as decisively divergent. Likewise, subjective accommodation does not necessarily correspond with the objective behavior nor with the intent that was behind it (see Thakerar et al., 1982).

As alluded to above, accommodation can vary (e.g. as "full" or "partial") to the extent that speakers approximate the communicative patterns of their receivers (Bradac, Mulac, and House, 1988; Dixon et al., 1994; Street, 1982). A strategy that is neither full convergence nor divergence – yet could be regarded in accommodative terms as "partial accommodation" – involves "the alternate use of two or more languages in the same utterance or conversation," what has been referred to as *code switching* (Gardner-Chloros, 1991; Grosjean, 1982; Milroy and Muysken, 1995; also see Bhatia and Ritchie, 1996). That said, it is noteworthy that code switching, regarded by many researchers as the most common form of bilingual and multilingual communication, has many variants (Hamers and Blanc, 2000; Sachdev and Bourhis, 2001), and its definition is a topic of considerable debate amongst linguists and sociolinguists (e.g. Blommaert, 1992; Eastman, 1992; Myers-Scotton, 1997; Poplack, 1980; Romaine, 1995). Bilingual code switching has often evoked unfavorable evaluations from observers (and even speakers) of it. For instance, many students in Hong Kong claim Chinese-English mixing is "irritating" (Gibbons, 1987), some Moroccans construe French-Arabic code switching to be indicative of "still [being] colonized," and Nigerians regard this phenomenon as a "verbal salad" (Lawson and Sachdev, 2000, p. 1345). Participants in these, and other, studies consider code switching to be an unneeded and disturbing mixture of languages and yet, interestingly, their reports of using code switching are often discrepant from their attitudes. For instance, in a diary phase of their study, Lawson and Sachdev (2000) found that students reported using this language style pervasively, despite the fact that they had evaluated it as being low in status and solidarity in a matched-guise study; clearly it has some "covert prestige" (Trudgill, 1974). In this sense, and despite the reluctance of users of it to label it so, code switching appears to be a satisfying form of communication because it engages a delicate balance between convergence – to demonstrate willingness to communicate – and divergence – to incur a healthy sense of group identity (see Cargile, Giles, and Clément, 1996). (For further discussion of code mixing and code switching, see chapters 1–4, 6, 10–13, 25, 26, 28, 29, and 31.)

Having outlined some important premises, concepts, and processes associated with CAT, we now move to our larger theoretical schema.

14.4   A Social-Psychologically Oriented Model of Bilingual Accommodation

Based on CAT and Sachdev and Bourhis (2001), figure 14.1 presents a schematic overview of three classes of variables that may be expected to affect bilingual communication: (1) societal intergroup context variables; (2) sociolinguistic setting variables; and (3) social psychological processes. Intergroup context variables are discussed first and include the objective "ethnolinguistic vitality" of groups (Giles, Bourhis, and Taylor, 1977; Harwood, Giles, and Bourhis, 1994; Landry and Allard, 1994a; Sachdev and Bourhis, 1993), state language policies (Bourhis, 1984a, b, 2001), and the stability, legitimacy, and permeability of intergroup stratification (Tajfel and Turner, 1986). Such macro-level intergroup context factors greatly affect variables associated with the sociolinguistic setting.

Sociolinguistic setting variables, considered next, include normative factors governing language use (Gumperz, 1982; Myers-Scotton, 1993, 1998; Scotton, 1983), and the networks of linguistic contacts within and between language groups (e.g. Landry and Allard, 1994b; Milroy, 1980). The next section considers a large variety of social psychological processes as mediators, with the individual as the unit of analysis, while also incorporating the influence of the broader intergroup context and the sociolinguistic setting. Mediating processes explaining and predicting bilingual accommodation include those at the interpersonal level (e.g. similarity attraction, Byrne, 1969) and the intergroup level (e.g. social categorization, Tajfel, 1978).

Various proximal and distal outcomes are presented in figure 14.1. In this chapter, our concerns are restricted to bilingual accommodation as exemplified by convergence, divergence, maintenance, and code switching. Considerations of space preclude discussion of discoursal attuning and non-verbal accommodation (but see Giles and Coupland, 1991; Giles, Mulac, Bradac, and Johnson, 1987; Giles and Noels, 1998; Giles and Wadleigh, 1999; Shepard, Giles, and Le Poire, 2001). Our proximal concerns are expected to contribute to patterns of

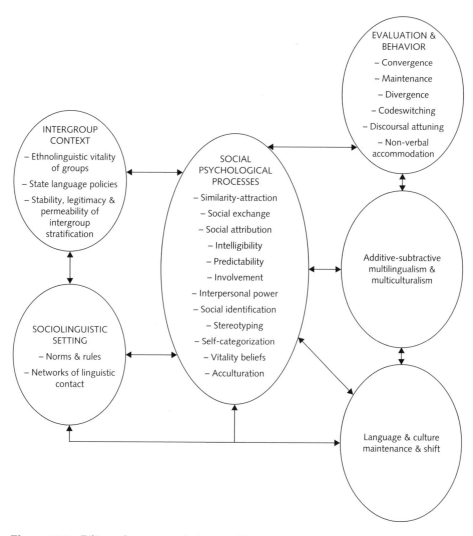

Figure 14.1   Bilingual accommodation model.

additive/subtractive bilingualism (Lambert, 1980) and multiculturalism which, in turn, contribute to the longer-term maintenance and loss of languages and cultures (see Giles, Leets, and Coupland, 1990; Leets and Giles, 1995). This schematic model is considerably broader than the focus of this chapter. It is meant to account for the macro-level language shift across generations, shifts which lead to language loss or "reversing language shift" (Fishman, 1991) in which a minority reclaims its language loss through a language shift towards language maintenance and language revival (see Bourhis, 2000, 2001). In terms of our focus on bilingual accommodation, new patterns of language use towards first language maintenance rather than convergence to a high-status second language can signal the beginning of a language shift and revival. It is important to note that our model is a dynamic one, with all classes of language outcomes affecting social psychological processes, intergroup context variables, and the sociolinguistic setting (as indicated by feedback arrows in figure 14.1). (For more discussion of language maintenance and shift, see chapters 15, 16, 18, 25, 26, and 28.)

14.4.1   *Intergroup context*

Bilingual communication generally involves members of different ethnolinguistic groups of unequal power and status within majority/minority settings (Hamers and Blanc, 2000; Johnson, 2000; Sachdev and Bourhis, 2001). The construct of *ethnolinguistic vitality*, introduced by Giles, Bourhis, and Taylor (1977) serves as an important heuristic for assessing the impact of sociostructural factors in bilingual communication (see reviews by Bourhis, 2000; Harwood et al., 1994; Sachdev and Bourhis, 1993; see also Kindell and Lewis, 2000). Defining the vitality of ethnolinguistic groups as the ability of groups to behave and survive as distinctive and active collective entities in multi-group settings, Giles, Bourhis, and Taylor (1977) examine it using three main sets of variables: demographic strength, group status, and institutional support.

Demographic variables relate to the sheer number of ethnolinguistic group members and their distribution through urban, regional, and national territories. Demographic variables also include the rates of immigration, emigration, and endogamy, and the birth rates of groups. Status variables pertain to the socio-historical prestige and social and economic status of language groups as well as the status of the languages used by speakers locally and internationally. Institutional support variables refer to the representation and control that language groups have in formal and informal institutions in the spheres of education, politics, religion, economy, culture and mass media. Groups' strengths and weaknesses on each of these dimensions, gathered from available sociological, economic, and demographic information, may be combined to provide an overall classification of ethnolinguistic groups as having low, medium, or high *objective* vitality. This can then be linked to bilingual accommodation and other outcome measures shown in figure 14.1. For instance, it might be expected that people would converge (and have more positive attitudes about converging) to the languages of objectively high-vitality groups than to the languages of objectively low-vitality groups.

Bourhis, Giles, and Rosenthal (1981) and Allard and Landry (1986, 1994) argued for the mediating effect of perceptions and beliefs about vitality in predicting bilingual behavior (see also Bourhis and Sachdev, 1984; Sachdev, Bourhis, Phang and D'Eye, 1987). Studies on the evaluation of bilingual communication in two different vitality contexts (Montreal and Quebec City, Canada) between anglophone and francophone clerks and clients conducted by Genesee and Bourhis (1982, 1988) demonstrate the import of objective vitality while reinforcing the mediating role of perceptions and beliefs. Specifically, in Quebec City (overwhelmingly francophone), evaluations by high-vitality (francophone) and low-vitality (anglophone) listeners were consensual in evaluating the client's switches to French more positively than switches to English. In Montreal, where anglophones had traditionally enjoyed relatively high vitality and were threatened by language legislation favoring French (Bourhis, 1984b), the findings revealed strong ingroup-favoring evaluations by all groups of anglophone listeners.

In an impressive program of bilingual research across Canada, Allard and Landry gathered evidence from several studies confirming that *egocentric* (self) and *exocentric* (non-self) beliefs about vitality variables are better predictors of bilingual attitudes and behavior than simple general vitality perceptions (Landry and Allard, 1984, 1990, 1994b; Landry and Bourhis, 1997). Perceptions and beliefs about vitality are important components of social psychological processes in the model of bilingual accommodation outlined in figure 14.1.

In their model of multilingual communication, Sachdev and Bourhis (2001) outline how dominant ideologies, in the form of official language policies, influence the conduct of bilingual communication. Language policies may be situated along an ideological continuum ranging from "pluralism" at one pole, through "civic and assimilation" in the middle, to "ethnist" at the opposite pole (Bourhis, 2001). Given our prior discussion of social power, groups in society are expected to adopt the *public* values of the dominant groups under all these clusters of ideologies. Public values include founding principles enshrined in constitutions and codes of "rights and freedoms," and include basic civil and criminal codes of the state.

However, the *private* values of different groups are expected to fare differently under these ideologies. Whereas there may be both official and financial support for minority languages and cultures in states which endorse the *pluralism* ideology (e.g. Canada), states which endorse the *civic* ideology avoid outright official support and provide little or no financial support for the maintenance of minority languages and cultures (e.g. the UK until devolution). Those which endorse the *assimilationist* ideology usually impose conformity to the dominant ethnolinguistic group in the name of a unitary founding myth advocating the equality of all citizens regardless of ethnocultural background (e.g. France, USA). States which endorse the *ethnist* ideology tend to repress linguistic minorities as a way of enforcing assimilation to the dominant language while they may exclude from citizenship targeted minorities deemed undesirable or "incapable" of ever assimilating to the ethnolinguistic "mainstream" (e.g. Germany, Israel). Contrasting language policies situated along this ideological continuum may be adopted at the national, regional, and local levels and, together, contribute to the climate of tolerance or intolerance toward the use of different languages (and varieties), not only in public settings, but also in private settings such as the home and friendship networks.

Official language policies and the permeability of ethnolinguistic group boundaries (allowing "passing" via bilingualism or linguistic assimilation) are affected by the stability (actual and perceived, e.g. demographic, economic) and the legitimacy (e.g. political power) of the position of ethnolinguistic groups (Giles and Johnson, 1981, 1987; see also Tajfel and Turner, 1986). For instance, demographic changes may lead to changes in language policies from civic to pluralist (e.g. local Education Boards in Vancouver and Toronto, Canada). Equally, active minority agitation may force the dominant language group to change the oppressive assimilationist language policies to more tolerant civic language policies (e.g. UK). However, as in the rise of right-wing lobbies such as the English-Only Movement in the USA, language policies and the general social mood may reverse a civic trend back towards a more assimilationist climate (see Barker et al., 2001; Crawford, 2000; also, Bourhis and Marshall, 1999, for a comparison of USA and Canadian language policies).

Taken together, the intergroup context variables create communication climates that influence the sociolinguistic setting, social psychological factors, and the various outcomes of bilingual communication. For instance, in an unstable intergroup hierarchy under an assimilationist state language policy, divergence by low-vitality linguistic minorities from the dominant language to the minority language in public situations may become more frequent, giving rise to unfavorable discourse content, dissociative non-verbal communication, and reactive divergent language switching by dominant language interlocutors. Based on CAT, Sachdev and Bourhis (2001) suggest that social psychological processes would mediate such dominant group reactions, which are most likely to be voiced by those who wish to exclude and segregate ethnolinguistic minorities. This illustrates how variables of the intergroup context (state-level language policies, intergroup vitalities, and the stability/legitimacy of intergroup situations) combine with social psychological factors (including acculturation orientations (Bourhis, 2001) to predict bilingual behavior. Macro-level factors associated with the intergroup context also affect the normative framework of communication and the networks of linguistic contacts in the sociolinguistic setting (figure 14.1).

14.4.2 Sociolinguistic setting

Sociolinguists have traditionally developed taxonomies of situational norms affecting bilingual communication in terms of variation as a function of the topic of communication, the social setting in which it occurs, the purpose of the communication and the characteristics of the interlocutors (e.g. Fishman, 1972; Gumperz and Hymes, 1972; Hymes, 1972; Trudgill, 1974). For example, early research in Israel (Herman, 1961), Tanzania (Beardsley and Eastman, 1971), and Japan (Ervin-Tripp, 1964) showed that bilinguals revert to their native dialect or language when discussing emotional issues or when talking about topics relevant to the cultural contexts in which they live. (For additional discussion of bilingualism and emotion, see chapters 9, 10, and 19.) Similarly, in the Philippines and Paraguay, the use of English and Spanish, respectively, was normative amongst courting couples who, once wedded, would switch to Tagalog and Guarani respectively (Rubin, 1962; Sechrest, Flores, and Arellano, 1968). In all of these (and numerous other) cultural contexts, the local vernacular is restricted to the role of informal communication in private settings, while the more prestigious cosmopolitan language is considered the voice of intellect and of public formal communication. Similar situational determinants of language choice have been observed in Morocco (Bentahila, 1983), Hong Kong (Gibbons, 1987), Kenya (Myers-Scotton, 1993; Scotton, 1983), India (Pandit, 1979), Singapore (Platt, 1980), and many other settings across the world (see Eastman, 1992; Hamers and Blanc, 2000; Milroy and Muysken, 1995; Romaine, 1995). A variety of bilingual settings mentioned above may be termed diglossic (Ferguson, 1959; Fishman, 1967) or polyglossic (Platt, 1977) in the sense that certain codes are specifically reserved for high-status formal functions, while others serve as modes of communication in private and informal situations. Extensive discussions of the relationships between diglossia and bilingualism may be found in Fasold (1984), Romaine (1995), and Hamers and Blanc (2000); space precludes discussion of these relationships here.

The normative and situationally determined approach to language behavior proposed by traditional sociolinguists led to several critiques (e.g. Sachdev and Bourhis, 2001; Scotton, 1983). Specifically, it was argued that (1) people are not "situational automatons," and languages are often used either in the absence, or in spite, of a normative framework (Bourhis, 1979; Giles, 1977); (2) the existence of multiple and competing situational norms makes interpretation and prediction of language behaviors difficult; (3) normative analyses are often post hoc and potentially tautological; (4) even within normatively constrained settings there may be a wide latitude of acceptable language behaviors; (5) language use may be negotiated creatively to dynamically define and redefine social norms (Giles and Hewstone, 1982; Myers-Scotton, 1993). The normative bias in traditional sociolinguistics was an important impetus for the development of CAT which sought to account for language use in terms of interlocutors' motives, attitudes, perceptions, and group loyalties (Giles and Powesland, 1975).

Patterns of language use are deeply embedded in the social networks of interlocutors, and networks play an important role in reinforcing normative behavior (Milroy, 1980). In their macroscopic model of bilingual behavior, Landry and Allard (1990, 1994b) propose the notion of *individual networks of linguistic contact* (INLC) as a "bridge between the sociological and psychological levels" (Allard and Landry, 1994, p. 121). According to them, the INLC represents the level where the "individual lives the totality of his ethnolinguistic experiences" (Allard and Landry, 1994, p. 121). It consists of all occasions in which individuals have the opportunity to use their own languages when interacting with family members, friends, neighbors, school peers, co-workers, and others. The INLC also includes occasions to use the ingroup language when consuming services from private- and public-sector bodies including education, culture, municipal and state governments, shops, businesses, financial establishments, and electronic and printed mass media. In bilingual contexts, the INLC incorporates contact with both ingroup and outgroup language users. High "objective" ethnolinguistic vitality of the ingroup allows wider and stronger ingroup INLC, leading to greater opportunities for speaking the ingroup language (Bourhis, 1991). Conversely, low "objective" ingroup vitality leads to smaller ingroup INLC, and fewer occasions for speaking the ingroup language. The mediating role of INLC, between a group's "objective" vitality, perceptions of group vitality, and patterns of language use by individuals, has received good support in a sustained program of research across Canada (Landry and Allard, 1994b; Landry and Bourhis, 1997).

The INLC notion was adapted by Bourhis (1994a) to study English-French accommodation amongst employees of the Canadian Federal Administration in the officially bilingual province of New Brunswick, where anglophones constitute a two-thirds majority relative to francophones. His findings revealed that the intensity of francophone presence in work contexts was related to bilingual civil servants' self-reports of their use of French and English at work. As expected, environments with a higher intensity of francophone presence were associated with greater use of French than those with low intensities of francophone presence, especially for francophone respondents. Interestingly, differences in accommodation between anglophones and francophones were also observed: convergence to francophones by anglophones (by using French) was significantly lower than convergence to anglophones by francophones (by using English). The high vitality of English as the language of work was thought to underlie this pattern of results, reinforcing the importance of macro-level intergroup context variables in explaining patterns of language choice.

Even in a non-status-stressing setting, such as casual encounters between francophone and anglophone pedestrians in downtown Montreal, Moise and Bourhis (1994) found that while 90 to 100 percent of francophones made the effort to converge to English while giving directions to an anglophone, only 60 to 70 percent of anglophones made the effort to switch to French when giving directions to a francophone. These results were obtained in studies conducted from 1977 to 1991, representing fifteen years of language planning effort designed to increase the status of French in relation to English in Quebec (Bourhis, 1994b; 81 percent of the Quebec population have French as a mother tongue).

Such findings confirm the importance of considering the interactive effects of the intergroup context and the sociolinguistic setting in multilingual communication. Additionally, from a social psychological perspective, it is important to consider how individuals' perceptions and beliefs about the intergroup context and the sociolinguistic setting mediate the impact of the "objective" intergroup context and the sociolinguistic setting.

14.4.3   *Social psychological processes*

Central to CAT is the notion that interlocutors' communications are not only designed to satisfy a variety of motivations, but that accommodative behaviors have specific evaluative connotations (see above). Motivations and evaluations were discussed above in terms of various social psychological processes thought to be responsible for communication accommodation. Convergence was discussed in terms of processes of social integration, language maintenance and divergence are explained in terms of speakers' desires for differentiation from their interlocutors. Thus, bilingual convergence would be expected to facilitate interpersonal and intergroup interaction where linguistic dissimilarities may otherwise be a barrier to communication (Bourhis, 1979; Giles, Bourhis, and Taylor, 1973; Giles, Mulac, Bradac, and Johnson, 1987). Linguistic convergence is also likely to increase interlocutors' intelligibility (Triandis, 1960), predictability (Berger and Bradac, 1982), and interpersonal involvement (LaFrance, 1979). Clearly, interlocutors are more likely to converge (or diverge) when rewards (e.g. material rewards, social approval) outweigh the potential costs (e.g. linguistic effort, group identity loss) of converging (Homans, 1961; van den Berg, 1986). Moreover, evaluative and behavioral reactions to bilingual accommodation may depend significantly on the attributions of interlocutors (e.g. Hewstone, 1989; Simard, Taylor, and Giles, 1976).

When language becomes the most salient dimension of group identity, language divergence may be used to assert ingroup identification and accentuate intergroup boundaries (Giles and Johnson, 1981; Sachdev and Bourhis, 1990; see also, Le Page and Tabouret-Keller, 1985; Tabouret-Keller, 1997). Divergence to identity threat has been observed in a variety of other bilingual settings including Belgium, Quebec, Wales, and Hong Kong (e.g. Bourhis, 1984a; Bourhis and Giles, 1977; Bourhis, Giles, and Lambert, 1975; Bourhis, Giles, Leyens, and Tajfel, 1979; Giles and Johnson, 1986; Taylor and Royer, 1980; Tong, Hong, Lee, and Chiu, 1999). There is also evidence for divergence in interethnic communication without any apparent threat. For instance, Lawson-Sako and Sachdev (1996) reported that requests (in either Arabic or French) made by an African researcher to Arab pedestrians in Tunisia resulted in greater linguistic divergence (e.g. responding in French to a request in Arabic, and in Arabic to a request in French) than requests made by a European or an Arab confederate (cf. Moise and Bourhis, 1994). Clearly, group identification is an important mediator in bilingual accommodation. However, this study also underlines the importance of stereotyping in communication (Giles and Coupland, 1991; Hewstone and Giles, 1986). The presence of ingroup or outgroup interviewers "switches on" the ethnic identities of participants, leading them to either converge to, or diverge from, the linguistic stereotypes of ingroups and outgroups (Beebe, 1981; also see Clément and Noels, 1992). Accommodation to stereotypes may be conceived in terms of Self-Categorization Theory (Turner, Hogg, Oakes, Reicher, and Wetherell, 1987). Since groups primarily exist cognitively in the minds of individuals as social identifications (see also Tajfel and Turner, 1986; Turner, 1982), Turner, Hogg, Oakes, Reicher, and Wetherell (1987) describe the process of self-categorization as "the formation and internalization of a social categorization . . . to include the self – and function as a social identification producing group behavior. . . . Thus self-categorization leads to stereotypical self-perception and depersonalization, and adherence to and expression of ingroup normative behavior" (pp. 101–2). Bilingual convergence and divergence could therefore be conceptualized as individual conformity to language norms through self-categorization and self-stereotyping (Hogg and Abrams, 1988).

The bidirectional transformation that takes place in language groups in contact may be considered under the general rubric referred to as "acculturation." The Interactive Acculturation Model (IAM) (Bourhis, 2001; Bourhis, Moise, Perrault, and Senecal, 1997) categorized different types of acculturation orientations that members of dominant and subordinate groups have about responding to the ethnolinguistic and cultural diversity exemplifying societies today. Acculturation orientations are concerned with the sharing and exchange of ingroup/outgroup cultures, values, resources and identities. Integrationists value a plurality and sharing of languages and cultures, while assimilationists expect conformity to dominant values (assimilation). Separatists/segregationists may value plurality, but only if it *does not* involve the sharing of cultural identities between groups. Exclusionist individuals would have orientations that are not only intolerant of other languages and cultures but may also believe that such outgroups can never be incorporated culturally as rightful members of their society. Other acculturation orientations have also been identified in the IAM and include those characterized either by the denial of (and/or by) ingroup and outgroup cultures (marginalization) or by the rejection of group ascriptions *per se* (individualism).

Sachdev and Bourhis (2001) provided some illustrative hypotheses of how acculturation orientations may affect bilingual accommodation. Assimilationist individuals may be expected to use language in line with prevailing language norms and emphasize dominant languages in all aspects of bilingual accommodation (i.e. upwardly converge), while separatists and segregationists may be expected to diverge in *inter*group yet converge in *intra*group communication encounters. Segregationists and exclusionists would be expected to diverge in encounters with members of linguistic minorities, be least likely to abide by sociolinguistic norms of intercultural politeness, and be unlikely to converge to minority language greeting or leave-taking expressions. Since individualist orientations involve interaction with others as individuals rather than as members of contrasting social categories, individualists are likely to be linguistic chameleons, ready to accommodate to suit their own motives, agendas, dictates of sociolinguistic norms and/or the linguistic and psychological needs of their interlocutor. It is important to note that the acculturation orientations described above are not reductionistic personality differences but, rather, orientations likely to manifest themselves in person-by-situation circumstances.

Sachdev and Bourhis (2001) also argued that the basic CAT processes governing bilingual behavior are likely to prevail in interaction, though acculturation orientations are likely to interact with social psychological processes postulated within CAT. Taken together, social psychological processes are likely to be important mediators for the outcomes shown in figure 14.1. Convergence, divergence, and code switching (as well as discourse structures and non-verbal behaviors) are manifest within the immediacy of intercultural encounters at the interpersonal level and affect the climate of communication (Giles and Noels, 1998). Additive-subtractive multilingualism and multiculturalism are developmental outcomes affected by the combined effects of the predictor (and mediator) variables and bilingual accommodation over time, within an individual and across linguistic communities. Perhaps the most distal long-term outcomes of the cumulative effects of all the variables discussed thus far are language maintenance and language shift (loss or reversal). This is measured by examining patterns of bilingual knowledge and use across decades in official census data and also in terms of the inter-generational transmission of languages (Bourhis, 2000, 2001; Fishman, 1991; Sachdev, 1998).

14.5 Conclusion

The focus of this overview and model of bilingual accommodation has been on how social psychological processes provide an understanding of bilingual behavior. In this chapter, previously neglected variables such as state language policies have been included explicitly as macro-level variables, whilst mediator variables such as acculturation orientations have been conceptually integrated with other social psychological processes in a broader model of bilingual accommodation. In addition to the empirical elaboration of aspects of the model on factors that have received little attention in the past (e.g. state language policies, acculturation orientations, vitality; also see Bissoonauth and Offord, 2001, for interesting data on accommodation in Mauritius), further conceptual refinement in terms of the multi-factorial complexities underlying bilingual accommodation is needed.

Much of the previous research presented in this chapter has adopted synchronic methodologies. However, bilingual behavior is not only multi-factorial but also dynamically evolving throughout the course of communication. Future studies adopting a more sequential approach to bilingual communication (see Bourhis, 1985; Lawson-Sako and Sachdev, 1996) and a broader diachronic perspective will be invaluable. For instance, systematic research between 1977 and 1999 allowed Bourhis and colleagues to conclude that it took 20 years of intensive French-language planning in Quebec to raise the status and use of French amongst Quebec anglophones (Bourhis, 1994b, 2000). Moreover, their most recent studies also showed that both anglophones and francophones overwhelmingly converged to each other's languages. Bilingual exchanges in Quebec seem to be losing the intergroup tension that has characterized such intercultural interactions in the past, at least as regards language choices in private face-to-face encounters between anonymous French and English Quebeckers (Amiot and Bourhis, 1999; Moise and Bourhis, 1994).

A focus on bilingual (as opposed to monolingual) contexts has contributed significantly to the development of accommodation theory from the very beginning (e.g. Giles et al., 1973). Surprisingly, code switching, "a quite normal and widespread form of bilingual interaction" (Muysken, 1995, p. 177), has not been frequently investigated within the framework of accommodation. Although code switching may be conceptualized as partial accommodation, it may be worth exploring further the importance of code switching as a distinct linguistic and autonomous code having its own special social, psychological and cultural significance, particularly for intragroup communication (Bentahila, 1983; Gibbons, 1987; Lawson and Sachdev, 2000). Relatedly, evaluative aspects of code switching need to be investigated in a systematic manner (see Lawson and Sachdev, 2000; Romaine, 1995). The social psychological approach underpinning accommodation theory is particularly well suited to exploring attitudes to code switching including aspects of ambivalence about code switching and discrepancies between evaluation and actual frequency of code switching (Agnihotri, 1998; Bentahila, 1983; Gibbons, 1987; Lawson and Sachdev, 2000). Furthermore, it would be important to place on the agenda the role of cognitive awareness in evaluations of bilingual accommodation (see Burt, 1998). This issue has been relatively neglected and models of strategic planning in communication (Berger, 1997) on the one hand and information-processing of language attitudes on the other (Cargile and Bradac, 2001) might yield valuable theoretical as well as pragmatic payoffs (see Leets and Giles, 1993).

CAT, with its relatively humble origins in monolingual accent evaluation nearly three decades ago (Giles, 1973), has expanded into an "interdisciplinary model of relational and identity processes in communicative interaction" (Coupland and Jaworski, 1997, pp. 241–2). Research on bilingual communication has been very important for the development of accommodation theory and this chapter presents a revised model of bilingual accommodation. While this conceptualization was never intended to be hegemonic in its invocation of a finite set of (constrained) social motives for bilingual accommodation, it has, nonetheless, focused attention on bilinguals' use of specific communication strategies (in particular, convergence, divergence, code switching) to signal their attitudes toward each other and each other's social groups. In this way, bilingual accommodation is a subtle balance between needs for social inclusiveness on the one hand and differentiation on the other.

REFERENCES

Agnihotri, R. (1998). Mixed codes and their acceptability. In R. K. Agnihotri, A. L. Khanna, and I. Sachdev (eds.), *Social Psychological Perspectives on*

Second Language Learning, pp. 215–30. New Delhi: Sage.

Allard, R. and Landry, R. (1986). Subjective ethnolinguistic vitality viewed as a belief system, *Journal of Multilingual and Multicultural Development*, 7, 1–12.

Allard, R. and Landry, R. (1994). Subjective ethnolinguistic vitality: A comparison of two measures. *International Journal of the Sociology of Language*, 108, 117–44.

Amiot, C. and Bourhis, R. Y. (1999). Ethnicity and French-English communication in Montréal. Poster presented at the 60th convention of the Canadian Psychological Association, Halifax, NS, June.

Barker, V., Giles, H., Noels, K. A., Duck, J., Hecht, M., and Clément, R. (2001). The English-only movement: A communication analysis of changing perceptions of language vitality. *Journal of Communication*, 51, 3–37.

Barkhuizen, G. and de Klerk, V. (2000). Language contact and ethnolinguistic identity in an Eastern Cape army camp. *International Journal of the Sociology of Language*, 144, 95–118.

Beardsley, R. B. and Eastman, C. M. (1971). Markers, pauses, and code-switching in bilingual Tanzanian speech. *General Linguistics*, 11, 17–27.

Beebe, L. (1981). Social and situational factors affecting the strategy of dialect code-switching. *International Journal of the Sociology of Language*, 32, 139–49.

Bell, A. (1984). Language style as audience design. *Language in Society*, 13, 145–204.

Bentahila, A. (1983). *Language Attitudes among Arabic-French bilinguals in Morocco*. Clevedon, UK: Multilingual Matters.

Berger, C. R. (1997). *Planning Strategic Interaction*. Mahwah, NJ: Erlbaum.

Berger, C. R. and Bradac, J. J. (1982). *Language and Social Knowledge*. London: Edward Arnold.

Bhatia, T. and Ritchie, W. (1996). Bilingual language mixing, universal grammar and second language acquisition. In W. Ritchie and T. Bhatia (eds.), *Handbook of Second Language*

Acquisition, pp. 627–88. New York: Academic Press.

Bissoonauth, A. and Offord, M. (2001). Language use of Mauritian adolescents in education. *Journal of Multilingual and Multicultural Development*, 22, 381–400.

Blommaert, J. (1992). Codeswitching and the exclusivity of social identities: Some data from Campus Kiswahili. *Journal of Multilingual and Multicultural Development*, 13, 57–70.

Bourhis, R. Y. (1979). Language in ethnic interaction: A social psychological approach. In H. Giles and B. Saint-Jacques (eds.), *Language and Ethnic Relations*, pp. 117–42. Oxford: Pergamon Press.

Bourhis, R. Y. (1984a). Cross-cultural communication in Montreal: Two field studies since Bill 101. *International Journal of the Sociology of Language*, 46, 33–47.

Bourhis, R. Y. (ed.) (1984b). *Conflict and Language Planning in Quebec*. Clevedon, UK: Multilingual Matters.

Bourhis, R. Y. (1985). The sequential nature of language choice in cross-cultural communication. In R. L. Street, Jr. and J. N. Cappella (eds.), *Sequence and Pattern in Communicative Behavior*, pp. 120–41. London: Edward Arnold.

Bourhis, R. Y. (1991). Organizational communication and accommodation: Towards some conceptual and empirical links. In H. Giles, J. Coupland, and N. Coupland (eds.), *Contexts of Accommodation: Developments in Applied Sociolinguistics*, pp. 270–303. Cambridge, UK: Cambridge University Press.

Bourhis, R. Y. (1994a). Bilingualism and the language of work: The linguistic work-environment survey. *International Journal of the Sociology of Language*, 105–6, 217–66.

Bourhis, R. Y. (1994b). Ethnic and language attitudes in Quebec. In J. Berry and J. Laponce (eds.), *Ethnicity and Culture in Canada: The Research*

Landscape, pp. 322–60. Toronto: Toronto University Press.

Bourhis, R. Y. (2000). Reversing language shift in Quebec. In J. Fishman (ed.), *Reversing Language Shift: Can Threatened Languages be Saved?*, pp. 5–38. Oxford: Blackwell.

Bourhis, R. Y. (2001). Acculturation, language maintenance and language loss. In J. Klatter-Folmer and P. Van Avermaet (eds.), *Language Maintenance and Language Loss*, pp. 5–37. Tilburg, The Netherlands: Tilburg University Press.

Bourhis, R. Y. and Giles, H. (1977). The language of intergroup distinctiveness. In H. Giles (ed.), *Language, Ethnicity and Intergroup Relations*. pp. 119–35. London: Academic Press.

Bourhis, R. Y., Giles, H., and Lambert, W. E. (1975). Social consequences of accommodating one's style of speech: a cross-national investigation. *International Journal of the Sociology of Language*, 6, 55–72.

Bourhis, R. Y., Giles, H., Leyens, J.-P., and Tajfel, H. (1979). Psycholinguistic distinctiveness: Language divergence in Belgium. In H. Giles and R. N. St. Clair (eds.), *Language and Social Psychology*, pp. 158–85. Oxford: Basil Blackwell.

Bourhis, R. Y., Giles, H., and Rosenthal, D. (1981). Notes on the construction of a "Subjective Vitality Questionnaire" for ethnolinguistic groups. *Journal of Multilingual and Multicultural Development*, 2, 144–55.

Bourhis, R. Y. and Marshall, D. E. (1999). The United States and Canada. In J. A. Fishman (ed.), *Handbook of Language and Ethnic Identity*, pp. 244–64. New York: Oxford University Press.

Bourhis, R. Y., Moise, L. C., Perrault, S., and Senecal, S. (1997). Towards an interactive acculturation model: A social psychological approach. *International Journal of Psychology*, 32, 369–86.

Bourhis, R. Y. and Sachdev, I. (1984). Vitality perceptions and language attitudes: some Canadian data. *Journal of Language and Social Psychology*, 3, 97–126.

Bradac, J. J., Mulac, A., and House, A. (1988). Lexical diversity and magnitude of convergent versus divergent style-shifting: Perceptual and evaluative consequences. *Language and Communication*, 8, 213–28.

Buller, D. B., Le Poire, B. A., Aune, R. K., and Eloy, S. V. (1992). Social perceptions as mediators of the effect of speech rate similarity on compliance. *Human Communication Research*, 19, 286–311.

Burt, S. M. (1994). Code choice in intercultural conversation: Speech accommodation theory and pragmatics. *Pragmatics*, 4, 535–59.

Burt, S. M. (1998). Monolingual children in a bilingual situation: Protest, accommodation, and linguistic creativity. *Multilingua*, 17, 361–78.

Byrne, D. (1969). Attitudes and attraction. *Advances in Experimental Social Psychology*, 4, 35–89.

Cargile, A. C. and Bradac, J. J. (2001). Attitudes toward language: A review of speaker-evaluation research and a general process model. *Communication Yearbook*, 25, 347–82.

Cargile, A. C., Giles, H., and Clément, R. (1996). The role of language in ethnic conflict. In J. Gittler (ed.), *Racial and Ethnic Conflict: Perspectives from the Social Disciplines*, pp. 189–208. Greenwich, CT: PAI Press.

Clément, R. and Bourhis, R. Y. (1996). Bilingualism and intergroup communication. *International Journal of Psycholinguistics*, 12, 171–91.

Clément, R. and Noels, K. (1992). Towards a situated approach to ethnolinguistic identity: The effects of status on individuals and groups.

Journal of Language and Social Psychology, 11, 203–32.

Coupland, N. and Giles, H. (eds.) (1988). Communicative accommodation: Recent developments. *Language and Communication*, 8 (double special issue), 175–327.

Coupland, N. and Jaworski, A. (1997). Relevance, accommodation, and conversation: Modeling the social dimension of communication. *Multilingua*, 16, 235–58.

Crawford, J. (2000). *At War with Diversity: US Language Policy in an Age of Anxiety*. Clevedon, UK: Multilingual Matters.

Dixon, J. A., Tredoux, C. G., Durrheim, K., and Foster, D. H. (1994). The role of speech accommodation and crime type in attribution of guilt. *Journal of Social Psychology*, 134, 465–73.

Eastman, C. M. (1992). Codeswitching as an urban language-contact phenomenon. *Journal of Multilingual and Multicultural Development*, 13, 1–17.

Edwards, J. (1994). *Multilingualism*. London: Routledge.

Ervin-Tripp, S. M. (1964). An analysis of the interaction of language, topic and listener. In J. A. Fishman (ed.), *Readings in the Sociology of Language*, pp. 192–211. The Hague: Mouton.

Fasold, R. (1984). *The Sociolinguistics of Society*. Oxford: Blackwell.

Ferguson, C. A. (1959). Diglossia. *Word*, 15, 325–40.

Fishman, J. A. (1967). Bilingualism with and without diglossia; diglossia with and without bilingualism. *Journal of Social Issues*, 32, 29–38.

Fishman, J. A. (1972). Domains and the relationship between micro- and macro-sociolinguistics. In J. J. Gumperz and D. Hymes (eds.), *Directions in Sociolinguistics: The Ethnography of Communication*, pp. 435–53. New York: Holt, Rinehart and Winston.

Fishman, J. A. (1977). Language and ethnicity. In H. Giles (ed.), *Language, Ethnicity and Intergroup relations*, pp. 15–57. London: Academic Press.

Fishman, J. A. (1991). *Reversing Language Shift*. Clevedon, UK: Multilingual Matters.

Gallois, C. and Callan, V. J. (1991). Interethnic accommodation: the role of norms. In H. Giles, J. Coupland, and N. Coupland (eds.), *Contexts of Accommodation: Developments in Applied Sociolinguistics*, pp. 245–69. Cambridge, UK: Cambridge University Press.

Gallois, C. and Giles, H. (1998). Accommodating mutual influence. In M. Palmer (ed.), *Mutual Influence in Interpersonal Communication: Theory and Research in Cognition, Affect, and Behavior*, pp. 135–62. New York: Ablex.

Gallois, C., Giles, H., Jones, E., Cargile, A. C. and Ota, H. (1995). Accommodating intercultural encounters: Elaborations and extensions. In R. Wiseman (ed.), *Theories of Intercultural Communication*, 19th International and Intercultural Communication Annual, pp. 115–47. Thousand Oaks, CA: Sage.

Gardner-Chloros, P. (1991). *Language Selection and Switching in Strasbourg*. Oxford: Clarendon Press.

Genesee, F. and Bourhis, R. Y. (1982). The social psychological significance of code-switching in cross-cultural communication. *Journal of Language and Social Psychology*, 1, 1–28.

Genesee, F. and Bourhis, R. Y. (1988). Evaluative reactions to language choice strategies: The role of sociostructural factors. *Language and Communication*, 8, 229–50.

Gibbons, J. (1987). *Code-mixing and Code Choice: A Hong Kong Case Study*. Clevedon, UK: Multilingual Matters.

Giles, H. (1973). Accent mobility: A model and some data. *Anthropological Linguistics*, 15, 87–109.

Giles, H. (1977). Social psychology and applied linguistics: Towards an integrative approach. *ITL: Review of Applied Linguistics*, 33, 27–42.

Giles, H. (1984). The dynamics of speech accommodation. *International Journal of the Sociology of Language*, 46, 1–155.

Giles, H., Bourhis, R. Y., and Taylor, D. (1977). Towards a theory of language in ethnic group relations. In H. Giles (ed.), *Language, Ethnicity and Intergroup Relations*, pp. 307–48. London: Academic Press.

Giles, H., Coupland, J., and Coupland, N. (eds.) (1991). *Contexts of Accommodation: Developments in Applied Sociolinguistics*. Cambridge, UK: Cambridge University Press.

Giles, H. and Coupland, N. (1991). *Language: Contexts and Consequences*. Milton Keynes, UK: Open University Press.

Giles, H. and Hewstone, M. (1982). Cognitive structures, speech and social situations: Two integrative models. *Language Sciences*, 4, 187–219.

Giles, H. and Johnson, P. (1981). The role of language in ethnic group relations. In J. C. Turner and H. Giles (eds.), *Intergroup Behavior*, pp. 199–243. Oxford: Blackwell.

Giles, H. and Johnson, P. (1986). Perceived threat, ethnic commitment, and inter-ethnic language behavior. In Y. Kim (ed.), *Interethnic Communication: Recent Research*, pp. 91–116. Newbury Park, CA: Sage.

Giles, H. and Johnson, P. (1987). Ethnolinguistic identity theory: A social psychological approach to language maintenance. *International Journal of the Sociology of Language*, 68, 69–99.

Giles, H., Leets, L., and Coupland, N. (1990). Minority language group status: A theoretical conspexus. *Journal of Multilingual and Multicultural Development*, 11, 37–55.

Giles, H., Mulac, A., Bradac, J. J., and Johnson, P. (1987). Speech accommodation theory: The first decade and beyond. In M. L. Mclaughlin (ed.), *Communication Yearbook 10*, pp. 13–48. Beverly Hills, CA: Sage.

Giles, H. and Noels, K. (1998). Communication accommodation in intercultural encounters. In J. Martin, T. Nakayama, and L. Flores (eds.), *Readings in Cultural Contexts*, pp. 139–49. Mountain View, CA: Mayfield.

Giles, H. and Powesland, P. F. (1975). *Speech Style and Social Evaluation*. London: Academic Press.

Giles, H., Taylor, D. M., and Bourhis, R. Y. (1973). Toward a theory of interpersonal accommodation through speech: Some Canadian data. *Language in Society*, 2, 177–92.

Giles, H. and Wadleigh, P. M. (1999). Accommodating nonverbally. In L. K. Guerrero, J. A. DeVito, and M. L. Hecht (eds.), *The Nonverbal Communication Reader: Classic and Contemporary Readings*, 2nd edn., pp. 425–36. Prospect Heights, IL: Waveland Press.

Grosjean, F. (1982). *Life with Two Languages: An Introduction to Bilingualism*. Cambridge, MA: Harvard University Press.

Gudykunst, W. (ed.) (1986). *Intergroup Communication*. London: Edward Arnold.

Gudykunst, W. B. (1995). Anxiety/uncertainty management (AUM) theory: Current status. In R. L. Wiseman (ed.), *Intercultural Communication Theory*, pp. 8–58. Thousand Oaks, CA: Sage.

Gumperz, J. J. (1982). *Discourse Strategies*. Cambridge, UK: Cambridge University Press.

Gumperz, J. J. and Hymes, D. (eds) (1972). *Directions in Sociolinguistics*. New York: Holt, Rinehart and Winston.

Hamers, J. F. and Blanc, M. H. A. (2000).
Bilinguality and Bilingualism.
Cambridge, UK: Cambridge University
Press.

Harwood, J., Giles, H., and Bourhis,
R. Y. (1994). The genesis of vitality
theory: Historical patterns and
discoursal dimensions. *International
Journal of the Sociology of Language,*
108, 167–206.

Herman, S. (1961). Explorations in the
social psychology of language choice.
Human Relations, 14, 149–64.

Hewstone, M. (1989). *Attribution Theory.*
Blackwell: Oxford.

Hewstone, M. and Giles, H. (1986).
Social groups and social stereotypes
in intergroup communication: A
review and a model of intergroup
communication breakdown. In W.
Gudykunst (ed.), *Intergroup
Communication,* pp. 10–26. London:
Edward Arnold.

Hogg, M. A. and Abrams, D. (1988).
Social Identifications. London: Methuen.

Hogg, M. A., D'Agata, P., and Abrams,
D. (1989). Ethnolinguistic betrayal and
speaker evaluations across Italian
Australians. *Genetic, Social, and General
Psychology Monographs,* 115, 155–81.

Homans, G. C. (1961). *Social Behavior.*
New York: Harcourt, Brace and
World.

Hymes, D. (1972). Models of the
interaction of language and social life.
In J. J. Gumperz and D. Hymes (eds.),
Directions in Sociolinguistics, pp. 35–71.
New York: Holt, Rinehart and
Winston.

Johnson, F. (2000). *Speaking Culturally:
Language Diversity in the United States.*
Thousand Oaks, CA: Sage.

Jones, E., Gallois, C., Barker, M., and
Callan, V. J. (1994). Evaluations of
interactions between students and
academic staff: Influence of
communication accommodation, ethnic
group, and status. *Journal of Language
and Social Psychology,* 13, 158–91.

Kim, Y. Y. (2001). *Becoming Intercultural:
An Integrative Theory of Communication
and Cross-cultural Adaptation.* Thousand
Oaks, CA: Sage.

Kindell, G. and Lewis, M. P. (eds.)
(2000). *Assessing Ethnolinguistic Vitality:
Theory and Practice.* Dallas, TX: SIL
International.

LaFrance, M. (1979). Nonverbal
synchrony and rapport: Analysis by
the cross-lag panel technique. *Social
Psychology Quarterly,* 42, 66–70.

Lambert, W. E. (1980). The social
psychology of language: A perspective
for the 1980s. In H. Giles, W. P.
Robinson, and P. M. Smith (eds.),
*Language: Social Psychological
Perspectives,* pp. 415–24. Oxford:
Pergamon.

Landry, R. and Allard, R. (1984).
Bilinguisme additif, bilinguisme
soustractif et identité
ethnolinguistique. *Recherches
Sociologiques,* 15, 337–58.

Landry, R. and Allard, R. (1990). Contact
des langues et développement
bilingue: un modèle macroscopique.
*Revue Canadienne des Langues Vivantes/
Canadian Modern Language Review,* 46,
527–53.

Landry, R. and Allard, R. (1994a).
Ethnolinguistic vitality: a viable
construct? *International Journal of the
Sociology of Language,* 108, 5–14.

Landry, R. and Allard, R. (1994b).
Diglossia, ethnolinguistic vitality and
language behavior. *International Journal
of the Sociology of Language,* 108, 15–42.

Landry, R. and Bourhis, R. Y. (1997).
Linguistic landscape and
ethnolinguistic vitality: An empirical
study. *Journal of Language and Social
Psychology,* 16, 23–49.

Lawson, S. and Sachdev, I. (2000).
Codeswitching in Tunisia: Attitudinal
and behavioral dimensions. *Journal of
Pragmatics,* 32, 1343–61.

Lawson-Sako, S. and Sachdev, I. (1996).
Ethnolinguistic communication in

Tunisian streets. In Y. Suleiman (ed.), *Language and Ethnic Identity in the Middle East and North Africa*, pp. 61–79. Richmond, Surrey: Curzon Press.

Leets, L. and Giles, H. (1993). Does language awareness foster social tolerance? *Language Awareness*, 2, 159–68.

Leets, L. and Giles, H. (1995). Intergroup cognitions and communication climates: New dimensions of minority language maintenance. In W. Fase, K. Jaspaert, and S. Kroon (eds.), *The State of Minority Languages: International Perspectives on Survival and Decline*, pp. 37–74. Lisse, The Netherlands: Swets and Zeitlinger.

Le Page, R. B. and Tabouret-Keller, A. (1985). *Acts of Identity: Creole-based approaches in Language and Ethnicity*. Cambridge, UK: Cambridge University Press.

Lewis, M. P. (2001). *K'iche': A Study in the Sociology of Language*. Dallas, TX: SIL International.

Milroy, L. (1980) *Language and Social Networks*. Oxford: Blackwell.

Milroy, L. and Muysken, P. (1995). Introduction: Code-switching and bilingualism research. In L. Milroy and P. Muysken (eds.), *One Speaker, Two Languages: Cross-disciplinary Perspectives on Code-switching*, pp. 1–14. Cambridge, UK: Cambridge University Press.

Moise, L. C., and Bourhis, R. Y. (1994). Langage et ethnicité: Communication interculturelle à Montréal, 1977–1991. *Canadian Ethnic Studies*, 26, 86–107.

Muysken, P. (1995). Code-switching and grammatical theory. In L. Milroy and P. Muysken (eds.), *One Speaker, Two Languages: Cross-disciplinary Perspectives on Code-switching*, pp. 177–98. Cambridge, UK: Cambridge University Press.

Myers-Scotton, C. (1993). *Social Motivations for Codeswitching: Evidence from Africa*. Oxford: Clarendon Press.

Myers-Scotton, C. (1997). Code-switching. In F. Coulmas (ed.), *The Handbook of Sociolinguistics*, pp. 217–37. Oxford: Blackwell.

Myers-Scotton, C. (1998). *Codes and Consequences: Choosing Linguistic Varieties*. New York: Oxford University Press.

Nair-Venugopal, S. (2001). The sociolinguistics of choice in Malaysian business settings. *International Journal of the Sociology of Language*, 152, 21–52.

Niedzielski, N. and Giles, H. (1996). Linguistic accommodation. In H. Goebl and P. Nelde, H. and S. Zdenek, and W. Wölck (eds.), *Contact Linguistics: An International Handbook of Contemporary Research*, pp. 332–42. Berlin and New York: Walter de Gruyter.

O'Driscoll, J. (2001). A face model of language choice. *Multilingua*, 20, 245–68.

Pandit, P. B. (1979). Perspectives on sociolinguistics in India. In W. C. McCormack and S. A. Wurm (eds.), *Language and Society*, pp. 171–82. The Hague: Mouton.

Platt, J. (1977). A model for polyglossia and multilingualism with special reference to Singapore and Malaysia. *Language in Society*, 6, 361–78.

Platt, J. (1980). The lingua franca of Singapore: An investigation into strategies of interethnic communication. In H. Giles, W. P. Robinson, and P. M. Smith (eds.), *Language: Social Psychological Perspectives*, pp. 171–7. Oxford: Pergamon.

Platt, J. and Weber, H. (1984). Speech convergence miscarried: An investigation into inappropriate accommodation strategies. *International Journal of the Sociology of Language*, 46, 131–46.

Poplack, S. (1980). "Sometimes I'll start a sentence in Spanish Y TERMINO EN ESPAÑOL": Toward a typology of code-switching. *Linguistics*, 18, 581–618.

Preston, D. R. (1981). The ethnography of TESOL. *TESOL Quarterly*, 15, 105–16.

Romaine, S. (1995). *Bilingualism*. Oxford: Blackwell.

Ros, M. and Giles, H. (1979). The language situation in Valencia: An accommodation framework. *ITL: Review of Applied Linguistics*, 44, 3–24.

Ross, S. and Shortreed, I. M. (1990). Japanese foreigner talk: Convergence or divergence? *Journal of Asian Pacific Communication*, 1, 135–45.

Rubin, J. (1962). Bilingualism in Paraguay. *Anthropological Linguistics*, 4, 52–8.

Sachdev, I. (1998). Language use and attitudes amongst the Fisher River Cree in Manitoba. *Canadian Journal of Native Education*, 22, 108–19.

Sachdev, I. and Bourhis, R. Y. (1990). Language and social identification. In D. Abrams and M. Hogg (eds.), *Social Identity Theory: Constructive and Critical Advances*, pp. 33–51). Hemel Hempstead, UK: Harvester Wheatsheaf.

Sachdev, I. and Bourhis, R. Y. (1993). Ethnolinguistic vitality: Some motivational and cognitive considerations. In M. Hogg and D. Abrams (eds.), *Group Motivation: Social Psychological Perspectives*, pp. 33–51. New York and London: Harvester-Wheatsheaf.

Sachdev, I. and Bourhis, R. Y. (2001). Multilingual communication. In W. P. Robinson and H. Giles (eds.), *The New Handbook of Language and Social Psychology*, pp. 407–28. Chichester: Wiley.

Sachdev, I., Bourhis, R. Y., Phang, S.-W., and D'Eye, J. (1987). Language attitudes and vitality perceptions: Intergenerational effects amongst Chinese Canadian communities. *Journal of Language and Social Psychology*, 6, 287–307.

Scotton, C. M. (1983). The negotiation of identities in conversation: A theory of markedness and code-choice. *International Journal of the Sociology of Language*, 44, 115–36.

Sechrest, L., Flores, L., and Arellano, L. (1968). Language and social interaction in a bilingual culture. *Journal of Social Psychology*, 76, 155–61.

Shepard, C. A., Giles, H., and Le Poire, B. A. (2001). Communication accommodation theory. In W. P. Robinson and H. Giles (eds.), *The New Handbook of Language and Social Psychology*, pp. 33–56. New York: Wiley.

Simard, L., Taylor, D. M., and Giles, H. (1976). Attribution processes and interpersonal accommodation in a bilingual setting. *Language and Speech*, 19, 374–87.

Street, R. L., Jr. (1982). Evaluation of noncontent speech accommodation. *Language and Communication*, 2, 13–31.

Tabouret-Keller, A. (1997). Language and identity. In F. Coulmas (ed.), *The Handbook of Sociolinguistics*, pp. 315–26. Oxford: Blackwell.

Tajfel, H. (ed.) (1978). *Differentiation Between Social Groups: Studies in the Social Psychology of Intergroup Relations*. London: Academic Press.

Tajfel, H. and Turner, J. C. (1986). An integrative theory of intergroup conflict. In W. G. Austin and S. Worchel (eds.), *Psychology of Intergroup Relations*, 2nd edn., pp. 7–17. Chicago: Nelson Hall.

Taylor, D. M. and Royer, E. (1980). Group processes affecting anticipated language choice in intergroup relations. In H. Giles, W. P. Robinson, and P. M. Smith (eds.), *Language: Social Psychological Perspectives*, pp. 185–92. Oxford, Pergamon.

Thakerar, J. N., Giles, H., and Cheshire, J. (1982). Psychological and linguistic parameters of speech accommodation theory. In C. Fraser and K. R. Scherer (eds.), *Advances in the Social Psychology of Language*, pp. 205–55. Cambridge, UK: Cambridge University Press.

Tong, Y.-Y., Hong, Y.-Y., Lee, S.-L., and Chiu, C.-Y. (1999). Language use as a carrier of social identity. *International Journal of Intercultural Relations*, 23, 281–96.

Triandis, H. C. (1960). Cognitive similarity and communication in a dyad. *Human Relations*, 13, 175–83.

Trudgill, P. (1974). *The Social Differentiation of English in Norwich*. Cambridge, UK: Cambridge University Press.

Turner, J. C., Hogg, M., Oakes, P., Reicher, S., and Wetherell, M. (1987). *Rediscovering the Social Group: A Self-categorization Theory*. Oxford: Basil Blackwell.

van den Berg, M. E. (1986). Language planning and language use in Taiwan: Social identity, language accommodation and language choice behavior. *International Journal of the Sociology of Language*, 59, 97–115.

Woolard, K. A. (1989). *Double Talk: Bilingualism and the Politics of Ethnicity in Catalonia*. Stanford, CA: Stanford University Press.

Part III   Societal Bilingualism and its Effects

Introduction

TEJ K. BHATIA

The existence of widespread bilingualism in a given society raises many issues about language use in that society, ranging from the role of each of the languages in the life of the community, to the maintenance of the languages in question over time and the process of shift from one language to the other to the endangerment (and, in the extreme case, the death) of some of these languages, to the long-term effects of bilingualism on each of the languages involved, the allocation of linguistic resources in terms of social categories such as gender, and the places of the languages in education and public communication. These issues are addressed in part III.

Part III is divided into two sub-parts: *Language Contact, Maintenance, and Endangerment* and *Bilingualism: The Media, Educaton, and Literacy*. The first sub-part consists of five chapters. Chapter 15 by Suzanne Romaine, "The bilingual and multilingual community," provides an overview of types of bilingual communities and their composition, including discussions of diglossia and public policy issues in bilingual societies. Joshua Fishman (chapter 16, "Language maintenance, language shift, and reversing language shift") presents a blueprint for the restoration of endangered languages, an issue of major concern to many members of linguistic minorities. Nancy Dorian's chapter 17, "Minority and endangered languages," provides an in-depth review of a wide variety of issues concerning the process of language endangerment, focusing on the role of various ideologies of shift and maintenance. Salikoko Mufwene (chapter 18, "Multilingualism in linguistic history: Creolization and indigenization") argues against the traditional view that special processes of creolization and indigenization occur in multilingual societies and in favor of the notion that the processes that have been called creolization and indigenization are processes that occur in any case of language change determined – at least in part – by language contact. Finally, Ingrid Piller and Aneta Pavlenko (chapter 19, "Bilingualism and gender") review a number of approaches to the issue of gender and language in general and then treat issues surrounding gender and bilingualism in the bilingual marketplace, in intimate relationships, in parent–child relationships, in friendship networks, and in education.

The first of the three chapters in the second sub-part of part III examines advertising in bilingual societies (chapter 20 by Tej Bhatia and William Ritchie, "Bilingualism in the global media and advertising"). The chapter is a review of work on the place of the languages in a bi-/multilingual society in the media in general and in advertising in particular. It addresses the question of why more than one language might be used in the advertiser's effort to attract buyers for products and services. Reference is also made in the chapter to Mobile and Distance Learning. Chapters 21 and 22 address issues concerning bilingualism and education. Fred Genesee's chapter 21 ("What do we know about bilingual education for majority students?") reviews in depth the research on one case of bilingual education where the results seem quite clearly positive – that in which majority-language students acquire the language of the linguistic minority in their communities. Finally, chapter 22 by Ellen Bialystok ("The impact of bilingualism on language and literacy development") discusses the wide range of factors that contribute to (or detract from) success in the attainment of literacy in bilinguals.

Language Contact, Maintenance, and Endangerment

15 The Bilingual and Multilingual Community

SUZANNE ROMAINE

15.1 Introduction

Bilingualism and multilingualism are a normal and unremarkable necessity of everyday life for the majority of the world's population. In this chapter I use the terms "bilingualism" and "multilingualism" interchangeably to refer to the routine use of two or more languages in a community. Although there are no precise statistics on the number or distribution of speakers of two or more languages, Grosjean (1982, p. vii) estimates that probably about half the world's population is bilingual. Multilinguals can be found in all walks of life, among ordinary people such as rural villagers in Kupwar, India (see Gumperz and Wilson, 1971), and Indagen, Papua New Guinea (see Romaine, 1992), as well as among famous historical persons like Jesus and Gandhi and contemporary individuals such as Pope John Paul II and Canadian singer Céline Dion. However, this chapter will be concerned primarily with multilingualism as a societal rather than an individual phenomenon.

15.2 Types of Bilingual and Multilingual Speech Communities

Although linguists usually draw a distinction between individual and societal multilingualism, it is not always possible to maintain a strict boundary between the two. Part of the problem lies in the difficulty in defining bilingualism as a phenomenon (see for example chapters 1 and 5 of the present volume and Romaine, 1995), as well as the varying ways in which one can define the notion of "community" (see the papers in Romaine, 1982).

15.2.1 Defining communities

We all belong to many communities and sub-communities, based on characteristics such as social class, ethnicity, nationality, religion, etc. Language is not by itself usually the sole determiner of social groupings. In many cases, however, language becomes intertwined in complex ways with these various other indicators of group membership. In New York City, for example, the retention of Yiddish is a marker of membership in the Ultra-Orthodox Jewish community, while in the secular Jewish community Yiddish is declining and survives primarily among the few remaining elderly speakers.

Bilingual individuals may belong to communities of various sizes and types, and they interact in many kinds of networks within communities, not all of which may function bilingually. Baker and Prys Jones (1998, p. 96), for instance, speak of a "language community" formed by those who use a given language for part, most, or all of their daily existence. Such communities may range in size from a few individuals to many thousands of individuals in a region of a country or part of a large city. The bilingual neighborhoods of most large cities such as Little Havana in Miami, Little Italy in New York City, and the so-called China Towns of San Francisco, London, and other cities around the world are bilingual communities. The individuals living in these communities are also part of larger language communities in which they may participate to varying degrees.

Thus, the Haitian Creole-speaking family members who run a small store in Miami's Little Haiti are also members of the larger English-language community in Miami, as well as the United States, and beyond, even if all the family members do not possess equal degrees of English proficiency. The 1,700 or so children being educated in various Hawaiian-medium immersion schools in different locations around the state of Hawaii form a language community of sorts too, even though most of them come from homes where English (or Hawaii Creole English) is the first (and sometimes only) language spoken, and do not use the Hawaiian they have learned in the classroom outside school or school-organized functions. Like the Haitian Creole family, they too are also members of the larger English-speaking community in the state where they live, as well as of the United States.

Most definitions of communities are not concerned about the size of the unit (which may be as few as two people, or involve millions), or even its geographical cohesiveness. Although a circumscribed geographic location such as a neighborhood, restaurant or school provides a context for interaction among members of a language community, a language community need not have an absolute geographic reference or boundaries. Ultra-Orthodox Jews in New York City share the use of Yiddish as their language of everyday interaction with their Ultra-Orthodox counterparts in Israel, while the larger communities in which they reside use another language, English and Modern Hebrew respectively. For both communities, however, Yiddish is the language which represents the continuity of the Jewish experience. In the Israeli Orthodox community the modern revived Hebrew has less status than Yiddish and it is not identified with Biblical Hebrew (Loshen Koydesh), the language of holy studies. Modern Hebrew is learned only because it is the language of the state, just as Ultra-Orthodox New Yorkers learn English. Participation in

Hebrew-language networks may also be a marker of gender differences. Israeli-born Orthodox women usually know more Hebrew than Yiddish because they are more engaged with the modern world than men and they have been educated in Hebrew-medium schools. Outside Orthodox communities women still tend to know Yiddish more than men (see Harshav, 1993).

What is crucial, then, to most definitions of community is the sense of perceived solidarity and interaction based on reference to a particular language and the relationships among people who identify themselves as members of that community. In this sense, they constitute what Wenger (1998) calls "communities of practice," rather than simply a group of people who happen to speak the same language and live in the same neighborhood, but never interact. Communities of practice are often informal groups who interact and communicate regularly, and most people belong to a number of them. Each community of practice has a shared repertoire of communal resources that binds its members together in mutual engagement. Among those communal practices will be shared ways of communicating, including possibly the use of two or more languages. The linguistic choices made by members play an important role in constructing meaning and social identity.

In some cases, membership in bilingual communities of practice may be defined not so much by active use of two or more languages, but primarily in terms of passive competence and shared norms of understanding. In her work in Gaelic-English bilingual communities along the east coast of Sutherland in Scotland, Dorian (1982) found some speakers who had minimal control of Scottish Gaelic, but whose receptive competence was outstanding. It included a knowledge of the sociolinguistic norms which operated within the community, as evidenced by their ability to understand everything, appreciate jokes, or interject a proverb or other piece of formulaic speech at the appropriate place in a conversation. Their weak productive skills often went unnoticed by more proficient speakers in the community because they were able to behave as if they were ordinary members of the bilingual speech community by participating so fully in its interactional norms.

Baker and Prys Jones (1998, p. 99) conclude that "there is no preferred term that is capable of summing up all the complexity, dynamism and color of bilinguals existing in groups. Simple labels hide complex realities. The way forward is to recognize the limitations of our terminology and to acknowledge the many dimensions underlying them." Or to put it another way, as Sharp (1973, p. 11) has, "each bilingual community is unique."

15.2.2 The nation-state as a multilingual speech community

Perhaps the most common vantage point from which to discuss societal bilingualism has been to look at it within countries. Viewing countries as communities, however, relies on a considerable level of abstraction of the kind suggested by Anderson (1991), who discusses the way in which nation-states are "imagined communities" which have come into being at least partly through the spread of national languages and print literacy. Hence, these are communities which do not rely primarily on everyday face-to-face interaction for their cohesion, and of course, such a large community consists of many sub-communities, whose linguistic practices may be quite varied.

Linguists estimate that there are roughly 6,700 languages in the world, but only about 200 nation-states. This means that there are over 30 times as many languages as there are countries, or in other words, that bilingualism or multilingualism is present in practically every country in the world, whether it is officially recognized or not. Australia, Britain, and the United States, for example, see themselves as largely monolingual English countries, despite the presence of a considerable number of indigenous and (im)migrant communities using languages other than English. The United States is now the fifth-largest Hispanic country in the world. Miami is now predominantly hispanophone. As many as 50 different languages may be spoken in parts of London. Similarly, Melbourne, once primarily a monolingual town, now has the largest concentration of Greek-speakers in the world.

Despite the near universal presence of more than one language in every country, the distribution of linguistic diversity is strikingly uneven. Over 70 percent of all languages in the world are found in just 20 nation-states, among them some of the poorest countries in the world. They include Papua New Guinea (860), Indonesia (670), Nigeria (427), India (380), Cameroon (270), Australia (250), Mexico (240), Zaire (210), Brazil (210), the Philippines (160), Malaysia (137), Tanzania (131), Vanuatu (105), Laos (92), Vietnam (86), Ivory Coast (73), Ghana (72), Solomon Islands (66), Benin (51), and Togo (43). These data come from Nettle and Romaine (2000, p. 32), who compiled them from statistics in the Ethnologue (Grimes, 1996).

As many as 83 percent of the world's languages are spoken only in one country. Moreover, most languages do not even claim a territory as large as a country. Fewer than 4 percent of the world's languages have any kind of official status in the countries where they are spoken. The fact that most languages are unwritten, not recognized officially, restricted to local community and home functions, and spoken by very small groups of people reflects the balance of power in the global linguistic market place.

Papua New Guinea alone contains 13.2 percent of the world's languages, but only 0.1 percent of the world's population and 0.4 percent of the world's land area. The overall ratio of languages to people is only about 1 to 5,000. If this ratio were repeated in the United States, there would be 50,000 languages spoken there. Even within Papua New Guinea, a small country, however, there is an uneven distribution of languages to people. The ten largest indigenous languages belong to the large groups of the interior Highlands; they have from 30,000 to 100,000 speakers, and between them they account for nearly one-third of the population. Perhaps 80 percent of the languages have fewer than 5,000 speakers, and as many as one-third have fewer than 500. This distribution does not appear to be a recent development, resulting from a depopulation of small groups. On the contrary, the evidence suggests that the extremely small scale of language groups has been a stable phenomenon for some time.

The relevance of the nation-state with respect to the connection between individual and societal bilingualism is immediately apparent when we consider some of the reasons why certain individuals are or become bilingual. Usually the more powerful groups in any society are able to force their language upon the less powerful. Although most nation-states incorporate a number of groups with distinct languages, usually only one or a few languages will be recognized for use within the education system and for other societal institutions. Hence, the language(s) a person learns at school and is educated in are determined by the policies of individual governments which favor the dominant state language(s).

For example, in Papua New Guinea, almost all children will be educated in English, particularly at secondary level, because this language policy is a legacy of the country's colonial heritage. English now shares official status with two other languages, Hiri Motu, an indigenous pidgin, and Tok Pisin, an English-based pidgin. Indeed, many children will already know a local language and Tok Pisin before they enter English-medium education, so they are usually multilingual on leaving school, if they are not already so when entering.

15.2.3 The composition of multilingual nation-states

Despite its arbitrariness, most studies of societal bilingualism have taken the nation-state as their reference point, and have relied on census data and various typologies to determine the linguistic composition of these units. Although there is no generally accepted typology of bilingual communities (see Lewis, 1978), there have been a number of attempts to classify minority language communities or linguistic minorities, as they are sometimes called. The term "minority" is often ambiguous because it may have both numerical and so-cial/political dimensions. Catalan, for instance, is spoken by a minority of people within Spain, but by a majority in Catalonia, where it has official recognition (see Strubell, 1999). The label "minority" is often simply a euphemism for non-elite or subordinate groups, whether they constitute a numerical majority or minority in relation to some other group that is politically and socially dominant. What is common to most minority languages from a socio-political perspective is the fact that their status is defined in relation to some administrative unit, which in the modern world is generally the nation-state. Thus, speakers of Basque, Catalan, and Welsh, for example, are of a different ethnic origin than the group in control of the countries where they reside. They have suffered from the in-migration of politically more powerful speakers from the majority, and are themselves a minority in the nation-states into which they are incorporated.

The legacy of Sweden's 650-year colonization of Finland is an ongoing tension between the two languages and peoples. As long as Finland was part of Sweden, Finnish was a minority language both demographically and functionally. Within Greater Sweden, the Finns were a minority and any Finn who wished to get ahead had to learn Swedish. The linguistic fate of Finnish changed dramatically, however, when Finland became a grand duchy within Russia in 1809. Finns had considerable autonomy and the Fennoman movement arose which, among other things, worked to raise the status of Finnish. With the publication in 1835 of the *Kalevala*, the Finnish national epic, the language became a symbol of nationality. After independence, Finnish was no longer a minority language, but for Swedish in Finland, the result was demotion to minority status. In the Tornedal valley, however, which was retained by Sweden, the Tornedalers ended up on the wrong side of the border (as did many Mexicans when the United States annexed Texas in 1846) and now have to fight the Swedish state to guarantee the right to their own language.

15.2.3.1   *Borders*

Because the heterogeneity of some countries reflects the linguistic arbitrariness of shifting political boundaries and the encapsulation of distinct ethnic groups or nationalities with their own languages, it follows that the borders of most countries are often linguistically diverse areas. Due to a variety of political and historical factors, bilinguals may be concentrated in particular geographic areas constituting regions where the use of a language other than the state language is normal. The northeastern corner of Italy shares a border with Slovenia to the east and Austria to the north, and contains a substantial population speaking either Slovenian or German as well as Friulian, the largest minority language of Italy (more closely related to Provençal than to standard Italian), and standard Italian as well (see Denison's 1972 description of Sauris as a German linguistic island severed from the Austrian empire and incorporated into the Italian state). In the south and on the east coast, Greek and Albanian are spoken in some communities by descendants of refugees and mercenaries.

In Oberwart, an Austrian village near the present-day border of Austria and Hungary, Hungarian speakers have been surrounded by German-speaking villages for at least 400 years, so that all are now bilingual in Hungarian and German. However, it was only during the last century that Hungarian speakers became a minority there. In 1920 Hungarian was spoken by three-fourths of the population, but by 1971 only one-fourth of the population could speak it. Today, the use of Hungarian is largely confined to networks containing older people and those engaged in traditional peasant agriculture. Young people in general use more German than older people, and young women use more German than men. The women's choice of German can be seen as a linguistic expression of their rejection of peasant life. Because a woman's possibilities are largely determined by whom she marries, women increasingly were choosing non-peasant husbands, who tended to use German more (Gal, 1979).

Alsace is another interesting border region whose linguistic heterogeneity reflects its shifting political affiliation, at times attached to Germany, and presently to France. The local Germanic dialect, Alsatian, has thus been in contact with French and German not only as a result of geographic proximity, but as a consequence of the language policies promoting either standard French or German imposed on the population by various regimes at different stages.

Gardner-Chloros (1991) shows how language use can often be the product of necessity rather than choice. After the Second World War when Alsace was returned to France following a five-year period of annexation to the Third Reich, some people felt they had to speak French to their children as a matter of principle. One elderly couple interviewed by Gardner-Chloros (1991, p. 29) told her their daughter was overwhelmingly francophone. Subsequently, however, that daughter told Gardner-Chloros she spoke mainly Alsatian dialect, but she made sure her own children's first language was French. However, upon interviewing a schoolteacher who had those children in class, it was evident that the teacher viewed the children as examples of young Alsatians who could not speak French properly because Alsatian dialect was the language of the home! Her study underlines the mismatches between actual linguistic competence and the competence people wish others to believe they possess.

Along another kind of border in quite a different part of the world, Gumperz and Wilson (1971) describe multilingualism in Kupwar, a village of about 3,000 people in the Indian state of Maharashtra, about seven miles north of the Mysore border. Four languages are spoken, Marathi, Urdu, Telegu, and Kannada; the first two belong to the Indo-European language family, while the latter two are members of the genetically distinct Dravidian family. Due to centuries-long contact among the four languages, however, the varieties spoken in Kupwar have become more similar to one another and are distinct from varieties of these languages spoken in other parts of India.

15.2.3.2 Indigenous vs. immigrant minorities

Terms such as "community language" or "less used language" have become popular in referring to certain kinds of language minorities in certain countries. In the UK, for example, the term is used to designate the newer non-indigenous minorities found in most large cities, e.g. Panjabi, Bengali. Similarly in Australia, Clyne (1991) has popularized the term CLOTE (community language other than English) to refer to communities using immigrant languages such as Greek, Italian, etc.

The labels are important, as will become evident in 15.5, when we see some of their ramifications in the area of policy and planning. The language politics of the European Union, for instance, are oriented towards national languages which are automatically accorded special protected status. Most nation-states apply one set of rules to the national language and another to minority languages within their boundaries, and often, in addition, apply differing standards to indigenous and non-indigenous minorities. Bilingualism and bilingual education have been differently conceived of in reference to majority and minority populations. The designation of "community" language may be politically significant to immigrant groups who cannot claim an association between their languages and distinct territories as can many minorities who are deemed indigenous.

Most scholars distinguish at least two basic types of minorities: indigenous (or autochthonous) and non-indigenous (or immigrant/migrant). The distinction is often contentious due to the issue of how long a group has to have resided in a place before it is deemed indigenous. The United Nations and various other bodies such as the International Labor Organization have legal definitions for recognizing the status of indigenous persons, groups and minorities. When in 1991 the Japanese government finally admitted the existence of 100,000 some Ainu people as an ethnic minority as defined by the Covenants, it still refused to acknowledge that the Ainu are indigenous. Turkey is a country which has no officially recognized minorities, despite the existence of a large population of Kurds.

Edwards (1994) proposes a three-way typology of languages: those that are unique to a state, languages not unique to a state which are nevertheless still minority languages, and minority languages that are local only. Minorities can be adjoining or non-adjoining, and cohesive or non-cohesive. Using these parameters along with the distinction between indigenous and immigrant, we can contrast the following bilingual communities based on the nature of the minority language. Friulian, Sardinian, and Welsh are examples of unique and cohesive indigenous minority language communities. Pennsylvania Dutch represents a case of a unique and cohesive immigrant language community. The Basques in Spain and France, and the Catalans in Spain, France, Italy and Andorra are non-unique, adjoining and cohesive indigenous language minorities. The Romanies of Europe are an example of a non-unique, non-adjoining and non-cohesive minority.

Ogbu (1978) has also attempted to distinguish significant differences among indigenous and immigrant minorities, as well as within different immigrant minorities. He recognizes caste-like, immigrant, and autonomous minorities. Autonomous minorities, such as the Ultra-Orthodox Jewish community in New York City, have distinct separate identities and are not subordinate, either politically or economically, to the dominant group. Caste-like minorities, on the other hand, such as Mexicans, Native Americans, and African Americans in the United States, or Aboriginal people in Australia, tend to be subordinate to the dominant group and are often regarded as inferior by them. These two groups are generally quite distinct in terms of their levels of educational achievement, with caste-like minorities showing disproportionately high levels of educational failure.

The minorities whom Ogbu classifies as immigrants often show more motivation to succeed and assimilate to the dominant society, e.g. Italians in the United States, particularly when immigration has been voluntary rather than forced. Although they too may lack power, they tend to perform better at school and to be able to use opportunities offered by schooling to improve their social and economic status. This typology too has its limitations in trying to generalize across groups which are quite variable. As Hoffmann (1991,

p. 233) points out, "Minorities may vary in size, geographical situation, social composition and economic strength, and the political status that they enjoy may range from almost full autonomy to total suppression."

15.3 Diglossia and Domains of Language Use in Bilingual Communities

The way in which language resources are organized and allocated in bilingual societies and language communities has implications for a wide range of activities. In each domain there may be pressures of various kinds, e.g. economic, administrative, cultural, political, religious, which influence the bilingual towards use of one language rather than the other. Often knowledge and use of one language is an economic necessity. Such is the case for many speakers of a minority language, like Gujarati in Britain, or French in provinces of Canada where francophones are in a minority. The administrative policies of some countries may require civil servants to have knowledge of a second language. For example, in Ireland, knowledge of Irish is required. In some countries it is expected that educated persons will have knowledge of another language. This is probably true for most of the European countries, and was even more dramatically so earlier in countries like pre-Revolutionary Russia, where French was the language of polite, cultured individuals. Languages like Greek and Latin have also had great prestige as second languages of the educated. As is the case with accent, the prestige of one language over another is a function of the perceived power of those who speak it. A bilingual may also learn one of the languages for religious reasons. Many minority children in Britain receive religious training in Arabic at mosques or in Panjabi at Sikh temples, just as Jewish children in the US may study Hebrew at synagogues.

The choices made by individuals in a variety of situations may become institutionalized at the societal level in communities where bilingualism is widespread. Often each language or variety in a multilingual community serves a specialized function and is used for particular purposes. Many bilingual communities are characterized by diglossia, a term used to refer to a kind of functional specialization between languages (referred to as High and Low) so that the language used within the home and in other personal domains of interaction between community members is different from the one used in higher functions such as government, media, education (see Ferguson, 1959; Fishman, 1967). In Paraguay, for instance, Spanish is the High variety, the official language of government and education, while Guaraní, spoken by 90 percent of the population, is the Low variety, the language of most homes and everyday informal interaction. Table 15.1 shows a typical, though not universal, distribution for High and Low varieties in diglossia. (For additional discussion of diglossia, see chapters 28, 29, and 31.)

Due to competing pressures, it is not possible to predict with absolute certainty which language an individual will use in a particular situation. Variable

Table 15.1   Some situations for High and Low varieties in diglossia.

	High	*Low*
Religious service	+	
Instruction to a servants, waiter, etc.		+
Personal letter	+	
Speech in parliament, political speech	+	
University lecture	+	
Conversation with family, friends, colleagues		+
News broadcast	+	
Radio soap opera		+
Newspaper editorial, news story	+	
Comedy		+
Poetry	+	
Folk literature		+

language use can arise when domains become unclear, and setting and role relationships do not combine in the expected way. In cases such as these, either the setting takes precedence over role relationship and the speaker chooses the language associated with that setting, or the role relationship takes precedence and the speaker uses the language associated with it. In Quechua-speaking parts of Peru, for instance, the indigenous language, Quechua, is identified with the physical territory of rural communities, while the colonial language, Spanish, is linked with the cities, mines and coastal areas. Quechua-speakers perceive Quechua to be the language for community/family/home (*ayllu*), and Spanish the language for everything outside those domains. Although in the past probably most, if not all, language interactions in the *ayllu* domains were in Quechua, and all interactions outside it were in Spanish, that is not true today. Spanish has gradually encroached on traditionally mono-lingual Quechua-speaking communities so that some Spanish is used within the confines of the communities.

Not surprisingly, the school is the setting where mismatches often occur and speakers are presented with a choice. This is because the school, although physically located within the community, is not considered part of it. For instance, school pupils who would ordinarily address one another in Quechua as peers outside schools, often do so inside the school, although they continue to address the teachers in Spanish. Here the role relationship takes precedence over the setting. In other cases the setting takes precedence over role relation-ship; for example, a mother sitting in front of her home addresses the school director in Quechua as he approaches. Moreover, female community members may make different choices from males in the same setting, as for example in a women's association meeting where the women talk to each other in Quechua and a group of visiting men vaccinating the children give all their information in Spanish (Hornberger, 1988).

Choices made by individuals on an everyday basis in such bilingual communities have an effect on the long-term situation of the languages concerned. Language shift generally involves bilingualism (often with diglossia) as a stage on the way to eventual monolingualism in a new language. Typically a community which was once monolingual becomes bilingual as a result of contact with another (usually socially more powerful) group and becomes transitionally bilingual in the new language until their own language is given up altogether (see chapter 17 of the present volume).

15.4 The Changing Face of Multilingualism in the Modern World and the Decline of Small Speech Communities

The changing character of multilingualism in the world today can be seen in several patterns. The first is that over the last few centuries in particular, some languages have shown an awesome propensity to spread. Speakers of the ten largest languages make up about half the world's population, and this figure is increasing. The hundred largest languages account for 90 percent of all people, with the remaining 6,000 some confined to 10 percent of the world's most marginalized peoples, who have generally been on the retreat for several hundred years. European colonization of the New World created many such language spreads, and most of the largest European languages are also widely spoken outside Europe. Today an Indo-European language, either English, Spanish or Portuguese, is the dominant language and culture in every country in North, Central, and South America.

A second noteworthy trend is increasing bilingualism in a metropolitan language, particularly English. Two thousand years ago there were about 250 million people in the whole world; now more than that number speak English alone. Indeed, there are more speakers of English as a second language (350 million, according to one estimate) than there are native English speakers.

The Industrial Revolution, which began in eighteenth-century England, and today globalization, have spread English and a few other international languages on a scale never before possible. Improved means of travel and communication brought about by the steam engine, the telegraph, telephone, radio, and television increased contacts between speakers. Internet traffic is increasing every year with more and more users being linked, and air travel makes it possible to circumnavigate the globe in a matter of hours rather than months. The corporations and financial institutions of the English-speaking countries have dominated world trade and made English the international language of business and publishing. English has become the lingua franca of the internet because the technology facilitating these developments in mass communications originated largely in the English-speaking world.

Globalization has increasingly led to layers of diglossia on an international scale. Within Sweden, for instance, Swedish is in a diglossic relationship with a number of other languages such as Finnish, Saami, and the newer migrant communities, such as Greek. While it is usually sufficient for a Swede to know Swedish and English, the Saami cannot afford the luxury of monolingualism, or even bilingualism in Saami and an international language. The Saami need to know the dominant language of the state in which they live, either Swedish, Norwegian, or Finnish, as well as some language which allows them to communicate beyond national borders. Within Scandinavia, Sweden has a diglossic relationship with other Scandinavian languages, with Swedish more often learned by others than Swedes learn other Scandinavian languages. Within the larger context of Europe and beyond, however, Swedish is on a par with other Scandinavian languages and continental European languages such as Dutch in relation to other European languages of wider currency such as English, French, and German.

A third trend is the extinction of many smaller languages due to the spread of a few world languages such as English, French, Spanish, and Chinese (see, in particular, chapter 17 of this volume). In this respect, the majority of the world's languages are minority languages with respect to large languages like English and Chinese. Nettle and Romaine (2000) estimate that about half the known languages of the world have vanished in the last five hundred years, and that at least half, if not more, of the 6,700 languages spoken today will become extinct over the next century. (For more discussion of language maintenance and shift in general, see chapters 14, 16, 18, 25, 26, and 28; on language endangerment and extinction, see chapters 16–18, 25, 27, and 28.)

Another major force is migration, with continuing and new waves of immigration leading to increased linguistic and cultural diversity in parts of Europe and the US. In the European Union, for instance, already, 10 percent of the school-age population have a culture and language different from that of the majority of the country in which they reside. This figure naturally obscures wide variation among member states. In the Netherlands, for instance, Extra and Verhoeven (1993, p. 72) say that the influx of ethnic-minority children in elementary schools in the four largest cities increased to more than 50 percent in the year 2000. As far as the future demography of the European Union as a whole is concerned, Extra and Verhoeven (1998) stated that in the year 2000 one-third of the urban population under the age of 35 would be composed of ethnic minorities. In the US the projections for increasing diversity in the twenty-first century indicate that Hispanics alone may comprise over 30 percent of the total population.

These trends represent a struggle between, on the one hand, increasing internationalization and cultural and linguistic homogenization (Coca-Colonization, as it has sometimes been called) and, on the other, diversification. In most parts of the world, however, there is little enthusiasm for the languages of immigrant minorities, even when the language concerned is a world language such as Spanish (as is the case in the US) or Arabic (as in France and the Netherlands). This is due to status differences between the majority and minority populations. Distinctive food, dress, song, etc. are often accepted and allowed to be part of the mainstream, but language seldom is. Another irony in the resistance to providing support in the form of home language instruction to immigrant pupils is that opposition to it in the US has occurred side by side with increasing concern over the lack of competence in foreign languages. Thus, while foreign-language instruction in the world's major languages in mainstream schools has been seen as valuable, both economically and culturally, bilingual education for minority students has been equated with poverty, and loyalties to non-mainstream culture which threaten the cohesiveness of the state. (For additional discussion of bilingual education, see chapters 23–5, 27, and 28.)

15.5 Public Policy Issues: Language Planning for Bilingual Speech Communities

The widespread existence of multilingual communities of various kinds raises questions about some of the consequences of linguistic heterogeneity as a societal phenomenon. Basic questions about the relationship between bilingualism and cognitive and social development, whether certain types of bilingualism are good or bad, and the circumstances under which they arise, impinge on educational policy. Likewise, the issue of equal access to governmental institutions in multilingual societies is a major concern in democratic societies. (For additional discussion of bilingualism and intelligence, see chapters 1, 5, 17, 22, and 23.)

15.5.1 The regulation of bilingualism within multilingual nation-states

Humans had been managing or mismanaging multilingualism for centuries well before modern notions such as "language policy" or "language planning" came onto the scene. What is new, however, is the attempt to manage such linguistic and cultural contacts and potential conflicts resulting from them within the framework of agencies of the modern nation-state. The boundaries of modern nation-states in Africa and parts of the New World have been arbitrarily drawn, with many of them created by the political and economic interests of Western colonial powers. With the formation of these new nation-states, the question of which language (or which version of a particular one) will become the official language arises and has often led to bitter controversy.

The new democratic regime in South Africa has recognized the linguistic reality of multilingualism that had been ignored under apartheid. The new constitution of 1994 stipulated 11 official languages, and that the state must take practical and positive measures to elevate their status and advance their use. More specifically, the national government and provincial governments must use at least two official languages. However, in practice, the public life of the country has become more monolingual (Webb, 1998). Afrikaans, which no longer enjoys legal and political protection as a language co-official with English, has experienced dramatic losses, one of the most visible being in the area of television, where it formerly shared equal time with English. The new broadcasting time is now more than 50 percent for English, while Afrikaans, Zulu and Xhosa get just over 5 percent each. Although greater emphasis is to be given to languages hitherto marginalized, and more than 20 percent of broadcasting time is supposed to be multilingual, in practice this time has been taken up mostly by English. Similarly, the South African National Defence Force, which formerly used Afrikaans, declared in 1996 that English would be the only official language for all training and daily communication. The demand for English among pupils and parents also works against implementing multilingualism in education (Kamwangamalu, 1998, and chapter 27 of the present volume).

15.5.2 De jure *vs.* de facto *bilingualism*

Mackey (1967, p. 12) and others have distinguished between *de facto* ("by fact") and *de jure* ("by law") bilingualism. However, he points out that "there are fewer bilingual people in the bilingual countries than there are in the so-called unilingual countries. For it is not always realized that bilingual countries were created not to promote bilingualism, but to guarantee the maintenance and use of two or more languages in the same nation."

A good example is Switzerland, where territorial unilingualism exists under federal multilingualism. Although Switzerland is widely cited as a successful example of multilingualism, only about 6 percent of Swiss citizens can be considered multilingual in the country's four official languages: German, French, Italian, and Romansch. English is much preferred over the other official languages as a second language. Of the 26 cantons, 22 are officially monolingual. Similarly, Canada recognizes both French and English at the federal level and certain provinces are officially declared bilingual, while others, like Ontario (where the national capital lies) are not. The incidence of individual bilingualism in the official languages varies greatly among the provinces, and is typically asymmetrical, reflecting the balance of power between speakers of the official languages. Francophones are more likely to be bilingual in English than anglophones bilingual in French. In addition, there are a large number of indigenous First Nations languages like Cree and Inuktitut and languages of immigrant minorities such as Ukrainian which receive no official recognition.

In Europe and many other parts of the world, it has generally been the case that language differences have been associated with distinguishable territories, and subsequently, the nation-states occupying those territories. Thus, the majority of European countries are officially monolingual, even though virtually all contain indigenous and non-indigenous language minorities, who are usually bilingual in a non-recognized community language as well as the official state language, usually the principal language of the state education system.

Within the European Union many languages, like Catalan, have larger numbers of speakers than do the officially recognized national languages. Catalan with its roughly 6 million speakers, despite having more speakers than Danish, is not an official language because the country in which it is officially recognized, Andorra, is not a member of the European Union. In the member states where it is spoken, France, Spain, and Italy, it does not have official status. While denying official status to some languages like Catalan, the regulations of the European Union have continually been expanded to accommodate the entrance of new member states with their national languages.

Tensions between individual and societal multilingualism underlie the official recognition of languages according to territorial principles. As Wright (1999, p. 1) points out, the fundamental conflict between individual freedoms and groups is nowhere more evident than in language. Do languages belong to speakers or groups of speakers wherever they may be found, or to regions and territories? Welsh speakers are granted certain language rights by the Welsh Language Act of 1993, such as using Welsh in courts of law in Wales, but they have no such rights in England. Thus, rights are not portable or personal; they are territorial and pertain to a specific region or domain of use within a region. The Government of Wales Act of 1998 made Welsh and English official languages of the newly formed National Assembly of Wales.

Magga and Skutnabb-Kangas (2001, p. 26) underline difficulties in implementing the provisions of the Saami Language Act passed in 1992 in Norway which designated certain areas as Saami administrative districts. Many of the municipalities outside these districts withdrew services in Saami, claiming that the law did not require them. Even in traditional Saami areas, where there is one Norwegian speaker in a class, it is assumed that all teaching must be done in Norwegian. When teachers have used Saami in such contexts, allegations of discrimination against Norwegians ensued. Magga and Skutnabb-Kangas attribute such actions to a culture clash between the Saami community's collective right to develop their language and the right of individual Norwegian speakers. The choice to use Saami is thus politicized and restricted territorially. The legal approach to reconciling status differences in languages with equality in a world where majority rights are implicit, and minority rights are seen as "special" and in need of justification, is fraught with difficulty.

Additional conflicts between individual and societal multilingualism arise over the issue of who is counted as bilingual or not. This often depends on the purpose of the investigation, and in some cases, is regulated by law. In some countries which are officially bilingual such as Finland, individuals cannot count themselves as "officially bilingual." This means that individuals with a bilingual background have difficulty in deciding which language they should choose "officially." The official language reported by an individual does not necessarily reflect the language most used or best known, or even the group the individual thinks he or she belongs to most (see Tandefelt, 1992, p. 166).

In Singapore, simultaneously a nation-state and a city, four languages, English, Tamil, Mandarin Chinese, and Malay, are officially recognized, and virtually all are multilingual to varying degrees, with two languages (English plus mother tongue) required at school. However, a person's mother tongue is automatically defined as identical with the person's race (Chinese, Malay, or Indian), regardless of the language actually spoken. A Chinese family, for instance, may actually speak Hakka, Cantonese, or Hokkien, all distinct languages which differ from the Mandarin Chinese taught at school. A child's mother tongue is automatically determined by the father's race. Hence, a child born to a Hokkien-speaking father and a Malay-speaking mother will be classified officially as Chinese and as having Mandarin Chinese as its mother tongue (see Gupta, 1993). In practice, a high degree of individual multilingualism exists, although this is changing due to language planning carried out within the Ministry of Education.

The government claims bilingualism is actually increasing but in reality multilingualism is declining. What they mean is that bilingualism in "official" languages (i.e. English and one of the other three official languages, Tamil, Malay, and Mandarin) is increasing. The government's very peculiar definitions of terms such as "first language," "mother tongue," and "second language" aid in this public obfuscation. What is actually happening is an increase in Mandarin-English bilingualism.

The success of the government's promotion of Mandarin at the expense of Malay and Tamil owes much to fact that the architect of modern Singapore, Lee Kwan Yew, recognized the need for identity planning. His "Speak Mandarin" campaign was largely a counter-measure aimed at preventing English from becoming too dominant in a context where it is the most widely used language of interethnic contact. The campaign forced those of Chinese ethnic origin, who constitute three-fourths of the population, to speak Mandarin as their second language, and has triggered a shift away from other Chinese languages such as Hakka and Hokkien at the same time as it has tried to provide the younger generation with an identity rooted in Asian rather than Western values. The co-official status that Singapore attaches to Tamil and Malay (also designated the national language) is not matched by supportive language policies that guarantee their transmission. School outcomes clearly reflect the advantages being given to the Chinese majority (see Gupta, 1993).

These few examples show that surveys and official census statistics on the composition of multilingual nation-states will yield quite a different perspective on questions of language use than detailed ethnographic case studies. The kinds of questions that can be asked about bilingualism are usually restricted by a variety of constraints (see Lieberson, 1969, p. 286, and de Vries, 1985 for discussion of some of the problems in doing research on multilingualism using census statistics). A census is usually tightly constrained by limitations of time and money, and thus many facets of bilingualism, such as extent of interference and code switching, cannot be investigated in any detail. A respondent and census taker may not share the same ideas about what terms like "mother tongue," "home language," "first language," etc., mean. On the other hand, census statistics can yield data on bilingualism for a population of much larger size than any individual linguist or team could hope to survey in a lifetime. This is the main reason why they have been so widely used by sociolinguists.

In cases of *de jure* bilingualism, knowledge about the demographic concentration of particular ethnic minorities defined in terms of language is necessary for the implementation of language legislation. In Canada, for instance, it is required in order that so-called bilingual districts may be provided with services of the federal government in both French and English. Hence, the claims made by individuals about their language knowledge and use of languages on census forms have important ramifications.

According to Finnish law, Swedish-speakers in Finland are entitled to have mother-tongue instruction in Swedish. Moreover, there has to be a Swedish-medium school in grades 1 through 9 in any municipality where there are 18 Swedish-speaking children. In Sweden, however, Finnish-speaking parents had to organize an 8-week strike in 1984 to ensure that their children received adequate teaching in Finnish (see Honkala, Leporanta-Morley, Pirkko and Rougle, 1988).

When policy statements rely on notions like "mother tongue," "home language," "native language," etc., the issue of who has a mother tongue or home language is fraught with political problems. As Gardner-Chloros and Gardner (1986) have observed, in Europe, it is the country and not the children which is deemed to have a mother tongue. The 1977 Directive of the Council of the European Community on the education of the children of migrant workers (Brussels 77/486/EEC) instructed member states to "take appropriate measures to promote the teaching of the mother tongue and of the culture of the country of origin of the children of migrant workers, and also as part of compulsory free education to teach one or more of the official languages of the host state." This means that for Italian children who may speak a regional dialect quite divergent from standard Italian, mother-tongue teaching will be in standard Italian rather than in the variety used at home.

In the US at least one state (Massachusetts) has had to develop programs of bilingual instruction for creole-speaking children, whose "home language," Cape Verdean Creole, is not recognized in their country of origin. In the Cape Verde Islands the official language of education is Portuguese.

Language planning on a supranational regional basis would clearly make better sense for languages such as Saami, Basque, Catalan, and other languages cutting across national boundaries. The contradictions between respecting national interests and defending minority interests often create a complex juggling act. The European Union, for instance, has generally avoided taking any action which would interfere with national laws or policies concerning linguistic minorities, or for that matter with laws concerning its national languages. Paradoxically, it is the commitment to monolingualism in national languages, multiplied by the number of member states, which leads the union to support multilingualism, at least in principle, and to some extent in practice.

The 1992 European Charter on Regional or Minority Languages provides a legal instrument for the protection of languages, but the only institutions with authority to regulate language politics exist within the political bodies of individual states. Although it specifies no list of actual languages, the languages concerned must belong to the European cultural tradition, have a territorial base and be separate languages identifiable as such. The terms of reference are deliberately vague in order to leave open to each member state how to define cultural heritage and territory. Thus, each state is free to name the languages which it accepts as being within the scope of the charter.

Most European nation states apply one set of rules to the national language and another to minority languages within their boundaries, and often in addition, apply differing standards to indigenous and non-indigenous minorities (see chapter 25). Many minority languages have more status outside their territories than within them, as is evidenced by the fact that Quechua is taught in universities in the United States and elsewhere, while it struggles for survival in many parts of South America.

Many developing countries opted to use the language of their former colonizers rather than try to develop their own language(s). Using English or French in Africa seems to be cheaper than multilingualism. Such utilitarian methods of accounting do not, of course, factor in the social cost of effectively disenfranchising the majority of citizens who do not know English or French in many Third World nations where these are the official languages. Such policies lead to cultural poverty when linguistic diversity is lost. When large portions of the population are denied forms of self-expression, the nation's political and social foundations are weakened. A nation that incorporates cultural and linguistic diversity is also richer than one which denies their existence.

15.6   Conclusion

Despite the high incidence of multilingualism in the world, monolingualism has been assumed to be the norm, and many cultures have stories to account for the rise of different languages. In what is perhaps one of the most familiar stories, linguistic diversity is the curse of Babel. In this account, related in *Genesis*, people all spoke the same language in a primordial time. God, however, decided to punish them for their presumptuousness in erecting the tower by making them speak different languages. According to this scenario, multilingualism became an obstacle to further cooperation and placed limits on human worldly achievements, a view still common among both lay people and a variety of professionals in many parts of the world.

In a less familiar story of the origins of linguistic diversity, the Maidu people of what is now California explain it this way. California Indians came to speak many different languages because they did not all receive an equal share of fire. Coyote, a trickster, interrupted Mouse as he sat on top of the assembly house, playing his flutes and dropping coals through the smokehole. The people who sat around the edge of the room did not get any fire and now when they speak, their teeth chatter with the cold. And thus began linguistic diversity (Gifford and Block [1930] 1990, p. 136).

In both these stories the consequences of linguistic diversity are negative. There is, however, no reason to believe that bilingualism is an inherently problematic mode of organization, either for a society, or for an individual, or for human cognitive systems. The co-existence of more than one language is not in itself a cause of inter-group conflict. While the media often suggest otherwise, conflicts involving language are not really about language, but about fundamental inequalities between groups who happen to speak different languages (see chapter 17 in this volume). In 1951 Frisian language activists were involved in a street riot in the Dutch town of Leeuwarden protesting the inadmissibility in Dutch courts of the Frisian language spoken by many of the members of the major indigenous minority group. Many of the world's political hot spots involve instances in which linguistic differences become intertwined with other indicators of group membership in rather complex ways.

REFERENCES

Anderson, Benedict (1991). *Imagined Communities: Reflections on the Origin and Spread of Nationalism.* London: Verso.

Baker, Colin and Prys Jones, Sylvia (1998). *Encyclopedia of Bilingualism and Bilingual Education.* Clevedon, UK: Multilingual Matters.

Clyne, Michael (1991). *Community Languages: The Australian Experience.* Cambridge, UK: Cambridge University Press.

de Vries, J. (1985). Some methodological aspects of self-report questions on language and ethnicity. *Journal of Multilingual and Multicultural Development*, 6, 347–69.

Denison, Norman (1972). Some observations on language variety and plurilingualism. In John Pride and Janet Holmes (eds.), *Sociolinguistics*, pp. 65–77. Harmondsworth: Penguin.

Dorian, Nancy C. (1982). Defining the speech community to include its working margins. In S. Romaine (ed.), (1982). *Sociolinguistic Variation in Speech Communities*, pp. 25–35.

Edwards, John R. (1994). *Multilingualism.* London: Routledge.

Extra, Guus and Verhoeven, Ludo (1993). A bilingual perspective on Turkish and Moroccan children and adults in the Netherlands. In Guus Extra and Ludo Verhoeven (eds.), *Immigrant Languages in Europe*, pp. 67–100. Clevedon, UK: Multilingual Matters.

Extra, Guus and Verhoeven, Ludo (1998). Immigrant minority groups and immigrant minority languages in

Europe. In Guus Extra and Ludo Verhoeven (eds.), *Bilingualism and Migration*, pp. 3–28. Berlin: Mouton de Gruyter.

Ferguson, Charles A. (1959). Diglossia. *Word*, 15, 325–40.

Fishman, Joshua A. (1967). Bilingualism with and without diglossia; diglossia with and without bilingualism. *Journal of Social Issues*, 23, 29–38.

Gal, Susan (1979). *Language Shift: Social Determinants of Linguistic Change in Bilingual Austria.* New York: Academic Press.

Gardner-Chloros, Penelope (1991). *Language Selection and Switching in Strasbourg.* Oxford: Oxford University Press.

Gardner-Chloros, Penelope H. and Gardner, James P. (1986). The legal protection of linguistic rights and of the mother tongue by the European institutions. *Grazer Linguistische Studien*, 27, 45–66.

Gifford, Edward Winslow and Block, Gwendolin Harris ([1930] 1990). *Californian Indian Nights.* Reprint. Lincoln, NE and London: University of Nebraska Press.

Grimes, Barbara (1996). *The Ethnologue.* Dallas, TX: Summer Institute of Linguistics.

Grosjean, François (1982). *Life with Two Languages: An Introduction to Bilingualism.* Cambridge, MA: Harvard University Press.

Gumperz, John J. and Wilson, R. D. (1971). Convergence and creolization: a case from the Indo-Aryan-Dravidian border. In Dell Hymes (ed.), *Pidginization and Creolization of Languages*, pp. 151–69. Cambridge, UK: Cambridge University Press.

Gupta, Anthea Fraser (1993). *The Step-Tongue: Children's English in Singapore.* Clevedon, UK: Multilingual Matters.

Harshav, Benjamin (1993). *Language in the Time of Revolution.* Berkeley: University of California Press.

Hoffmann, Charlotte (1991). *An Introduction to Bilingualism.* London: Longman.

Honkala, Tuula, Leporanta-Morley, Pirkko, Liukka, and Rougle, Eija (1988). Finnish children in Sweden strike for better education. In Tove Skutnabb-Kangas and Jim Cummins (eds.), *Minority Education: From Shame to Struggle*, pp. 239–51. Clevedon, UK: Multilingual Matters.

Hornberger, Nancy H. (1988). *Bilingual Education and Language Maintenance: A Southern Peruvian Quechua Case.* Dordrecht: Foris.

Kamwangamalu, Nkonko M. (1998). Preface: Multilingualism in South Africa. *Multilingua*, 17(2/3): 119–25. Special issue: Aspects of Multilingualism in Post-apartheid South Africa.

Lewis, E. Glyn (1978). Types of bilingual communities. In James E. Alatis (ed.), *International Dimensions of Bilingual Education*, pp. 19–35. Washington, D.C.: Georgetown University Press.

Lieberson, Stanley (1969). How can we describe and measure the incidence and distribution of bilingualism. In Louis G. Kelly (ed.), *Description and Measurement of Bilingualism*, pp. 286–95. Toronto: University of Toronto Press.

Mackey, William F. (1967). *Bilingualism as a World Problem/Le Bilinguïsme: phénomène mondial.* Montreal: Harvest House.

Magga, Ole Henrik and Skutnabb-Kangas, Tove (2001). The Saami languages: The present and the future. *Cultural Survival Quarterly*, 25(2), 26–31; 51.

Nettle, Daniel and Romaine, Suzanne (2000). *Vanishing Voices: The Extinction of the World's Languages.* Oxford: Oxford University Press.

Ogbu, John (1978). *Minority Education and Caste: The American System in*

Cross-Cultural Perspective. New York: Academic Press.

Romaine, Suzanne (ed.) (1982). *Sociolinguistic Variation in Speech Communities*. London: Edward Arnold.

Romaine, Suzanne (1992). *Language, Education and Development: Urban and Rural Tok Pisin in Papua New Guinea*. Oxford: Oxford University Press.

Romaine, Suzanne (1995). *Bilingualism*. 2nd edn. Oxford: Blackwell.

Sharp, Derrick (1973). *Language in Bilingual Communities*. London: Edward Arnold.

Strubell, Miquel (1999). Language, Democracy and Devolution in Catalonia, pp. 4–39. In Sue Wright (ed.), *Language, Democracy and Devolution in Catalonia*, pp. 4–39. Clevedon: Multilingual Matters.

Tandefelt, Marike (1992). The shift from Swedish to Finnish in Finland. In W. Fase, K. Jaspaert, and S. Kroon (eds.), *Maintenance and Loss of Minority Languages*, pp. 150–68. Amsterdam: John Benjamins.

Webb, Vic (1998). Multilingualism as a developmental resource: Framework for a research program. *Multilingua* 17(2/3): 125–54. Special issue: Aspects of Multilingualism in Post-apartheid South Africa.

Wenger, Etienne (1998). *Communities of Practice: Learning as a Social System*. Cambridge, UK: Cambridge University Press.

Wright, Sue (1999). Foreword. In Sue Wright (ed.), *Language, Democracy and Devolution in Catalonia*, pp. 1–3. Clevedon: Multilingual Matters.

16 Language Maintenance, Language Shift, and Reversing Language Shift

JOSHUA A. FISHMAN

16.1 Introduction: Perspective: American and International

Discussions of societal phenomena more generally and sociolinguistic processes quite specifically tend to be highly perspectival and contextual. Thus, in writing about such phenomena, it seems best to admit one's perspective from the very outset. Mine will be American and programmatic, to begin with, and then international and theoretical toward the end, thereby combining the points of view of the activist and the scholar, i.e. one who not only seeks objective understanding but pluralistic societal impact as well. These perspectives, like all perspectives, bring with them both advantages and disadvantages. Among the advantages is the fact that the American sociolinguistic scene has been widely researched and its findings are easily searchable in terms of library and archival retrievability and linguistic accessibility. The major disadvantage of starting from an American perspective is that the immigrant case is overly represented while the indigenous case is severely underrepresented. Therefore, it is fitting that we will end with an international perspective so that the initial America-based conclusions can be immediately confronted and tested from a totally different point of departure.

16.2 Language Shift as the Societal Norm

The sociolinguistic profile of speakers of non-English languages in the USA is a direct reflection of the country's constantly ongoing history as a nation of immigrants. Such speakers are overwhelmingly either immigrants themselves or the children of immigrants. This is an important point at which to begin the examination of our tripartite topic, because, unlike most other countries in which societal multilingualism exists, there are relatively few speakers of sidestream languages in the USA who are more than two generations removed from their family's immigrant origins. This is tantamount to saying three things: (1) the grandchildren and great-grandchildren of immigrants have overwhelmingly become English monolinguals, having lost direct and socially patterned contact with speakers of the language brought to this country by their grandparents and great-grandparents; (2) there also remain very few "linguistically different" indigenous (or "Native") Americans ("Amerindians") who still speak their traditionally associated aboriginal languages (and those who remain are becoming fewer and fewer, even though the Amerindian population itself continues to grow); and (3) neither travel, work experience, nor education succeeds in imparting daily speaking facility in any non-English language to any but a very small number of Americans.

The USA is a country largely established and built by voluntary and involuntary immigrants and its social dynamics have been such that to this very day any multilingualism present among its inhabitants generally remains a marker of fairly recent immigrant status. Since during the course of the past three centuries millions upon millions of immigrants have arrived on American shores, whereas the total number of monolingual Non-English speakers (NES) is now only approximately 2–5 million and the total number of NEMT (Non-English Mother Tongue, i.e. non-school-based) multilinguals in the USA is only about 25–30 million, it becomes inescapably self-evident that the process of language shift (or non-English mother tongue loss) has been a dominant (and perhaps even *the* dominant) "American experience" almost since the very beginning of the founding of the country. Thus, if we persist in examining non-English language maintenance in the USA today, as we intend to do in this chapter, we are clearly examining an interesting but somewhat "exotic" phenomenon as soon as we leave the immigrant generations themselves behind (and, indeed, even before we leave them behind).

Of course, "leaving the immigrant generations behind," once and for all, is easier said than done in the USA. During the past 220 years or so, there has never been more than a two-generational hiatus between the impact of one mass-immigrational period and the impact of the next such period. Beginning with the relatively large French and German "presences" at the end of the eighteenth century (starting even before our nation was created) along our border with Canada, on the one hand (giving rise to hundreds of Franco-American churches, parochial schools, fraternal organizations and periodical publications), and the concentrated German settlements in Pennsylvania and Ohio (with their hundreds of churches and closed communities) on the other, the story has gone on and on for over 200 years. Soon after the Revolution there came the Irish mass-immigration of the early 1800s (when most of these newcomers were still Irish-speakers and Boston and New York became the capitals of a vibrant and extensive Irish press, church and book-publication culture). Then came the second German mass-immigration of the mid-1800s (when thousands of German schools, churches, newspapers, books, and even several colleges and theological seminaries were omnipresent in the American mid-West). No sooner were the former beginning to be anglified and mainstreamed than the arrival of the millions of Southern and Eastern Europeans began. It continued from the 1880s to the early 1920s (bringing Italians, Russian, Polish, Romanian and Austro-Hungarian Jews, Poles, Ukrainians and Southern Slavs more generally). Less than 50 years later the Hispanic and Asian/Pacific immigrations began (and have continued apace). *There has never been much time to fully cultivate and clinch the illusion of an indigenous monolingual, monocultural, monoethnic mainstream* American society, even though every mass-immigration was followed by its own nativistic backlash. However, no fully stable and legitimated multilingual/multiethnic society has ever developed either. Seemingly, two generations are time enough to wipe out non-English language proficiency, but by no means time enough to wipe out the cultural memories and part-identities, nor to counteract the grievances derived from discrimination, marginalization and denials of cultural democracy aspirations, upon which both ethnic identities and revernacularization movements can be based.

And yet, the newest linguistic resources (actual and potential) of this country have always been so monstrously squandered and destroyed (at worst) or neglected and ignored (at best) that – except for the very most recent immigrants, some of their atypical children, and some rare and very "exotic" other exceptions – the USA has become an overwhelmingly monolingual English-speaking country. Why has this happened and is this past history destined to repeat itself ad infinitum (and not only in the USA)? During the entire twentieth century several world languages were caused or allowed to atrophy in the USA. The "big six" throughout that entire century were German (about half of its speakers having been Protestant and the rest Catholic), Italian, French, Spanish, Polish (all overwhelmingly Catholic) and Yiddish (all Eastern European Jews, Ashkenazim). Nevertheless, neither the prestige of most of these tongues, their numbers of speakers (in the many millions), nor their worldwide utility in commerce, travel, contact with "the old country," industry, academic research, and governmentally conducted international relations has spared them from the very same fate as that which has overtaken their much smaller, culturally more distant from the Western experience, and far less practically useful counterparts on the world scene. That being the case, even the future of Spanish, the "macho" language on the American non-English language scene for the past two decades, must also be contemplated with concern and even with alarm.

16.2.1   Local and periodic ups and downs vs. straight line trends

If we consider mother-tongue transmission as being socio-culturally constructed, i.e. as being the result of certain social, economic and political experiences throughout history, we must conclude that the unrelenting monolingualization of a nation of millions of immigrants was not an automatic or inevitable outcome. Each one of the non-mainstream languages mentioned in the previous paragraph can point to other places in the world where their resettled immigrant speakers have successfully pursued and attained a far greater measure of intergenerational mother-tongue transmission. Contrasts with Canada (for French), Australia (for Macedonian and Arabic), Latin America (for German and Yiddish), and Israel (for English, Yiddish and, perhaps, Russian) could be particularly instructive. *Why did the American soil prove to be so inhospitable by contrast?* "Der shteynerner amerikaner bodn!" ("the stone-hard American soil"), my father would whisper under his breath, when faced with yet another reversal in connection with his constant Yiddish language maintenance efforts in the USA.

The first thing that must be realized in this connection is that the attrition of American multilingualism has not proceeded at a monotonic downward rate throughout the past two centuries, i.e. it cannot be represented by a single, unrelenting downward line. The recurring rise-and-fall manifestations of non-English languages in the USA reveal substantial variation over time, as to both degree and rate. There are often years (even decades) of upswing (when the arrival of young immigrants of a particular mother tongue continues for a long time and they settle in close proximity to one another, so that they are both absolutely and relatively concentrated with respect to other (and, particularly, to English-speaking) residents. Even some relatively small language groups such as the Pennsylvania Dutch (all of whom are also English-speakers and readers, as well as being speakers of Pensilfawnish and knowledgeable listeners to sermons in "Luther German") have succeeded relatively well in both multiplying and in retaining their mother tongues via establishing themselves in rural areas "of their own," wherein they can distance themselves from most kinds of social interaction with those who are "outsiders" to their own sheltered communities. The same is true for Yiddish-speaking Ultra-Orthodox Jews, although they are overwhelmingly urban in their residential pattern. French-speakers in northern Vermont, New Hampshire and Maine (close to the border with Quebec) have been much more language-retentive than their counterparts in inland Massachusetts and Rhode Island (more distant from the border and closer to various English-dominated urban centers).

Spanish-speakers in long-established, small-scale, rural Texas, New Mexico, and Arizona communities have been notably successful in maintaining their mother tongue over 6 to 8 generations, in comparison with Hispanic newcomers to secondary settlement areas in the mid-West. Hamtramck is an example of a Polish town, in Michigan, that has steadfastly retained its Polish character, in language, religion, and culture, while participating substantially in American life as well. Amerindian groups that are sufficiently independent economically and sufficiently isolated spatially (e.g. various parts of the Navajo Nation) have succeeded in bilingualizing most of their young during some recent periods of their punishing exposure to mainstream America.

There are other similar examples scattered throughout the length and breadth of America.

All of the above examples of language maintenance, short-lived though some of them may have been from a fully intergenerational perspective, lead us to appreciate the demographic, geographic, economic, and cultural bases of influencing and self-regulating the social interaction boundaries that are a prerequisite for providing non-English languages with functions and statuses that can compete longer and more successfully with those of the mainstream. In addition to the above objective factors, there are undeniably subjective ones as well, e.g. when generalized anti-multilingualism or pro-multilingualism attitudes become important operative considerations as well. Anti-German legislation and popular sentiment during and after the First World War finally resulted in the 1923 Meyer vs. Nebraska ruling by the Supreme Court (prohibiting states from usurping parental authority to decide which languages their children should learn and in which languages they should be taught). But much damage to German (and a variety of other immigrant languages concentrated in particular areas) had already been done by then, followed by similar damage during the Second World War, only a generation or so later.

An upturn in non-English language attitudes and language transmission efforts occurred during the "ethnic revival" of the mid-1960s to the mid-1970s in the USA (see tables 16.1 and 16.2). At that time a large-scale youth-involving anti-mainstream upsurge occurred, in part merely co-occurring with and in part directly related to the war in Vietnam. It resulted in a more visible display of ethnic pride and in elevated non-English mother-tongue claiming (NEMTC) on the 1970 census. This was *particularly so among so-called "third generation" individuals*, and is clearly revealed through comparisons with the claims made in 1940 or 1960, even among those NEMT groups that had experienced no (or next to no) immigration in the interim and were, on the average, already far beyond child-bearing age. These increases might easily be pooh-poohed as merely artifacts resulting from slight inconsistencies in the wording of the mother-tongue questions *per se* in 1960 and 1970. However, other related increases also cropped up in 1970, increases that were unclouded by any wording changes. Thus, ethnic community broadcasts (radio and TV), periodicals offering all or part of their contents in languages other than English, community schools and local religious units that included traditional non-English language efforts in their programming, also multiplied precipitously during this short 1960–70 period. Furthermore, when examined on a state-by-state basis, the correlation between the abovementioned 1970 ethnic-community institutional resources and the incidence of 1970 NEMTC was very high (e.g. .90 between non-English broadcasting time for a particular language and "native of native" non-English mother tongue claiming of that language).

However, after 1979, when concerns grew about America's slower economic growth in relation to South-East Asia and when the "English-Only" movement found it easy to exploit these concerns (focused on "illegal" Hispanics "flooding" into the USA to escape poverty and US-financed (Iran–Contra)

Table 16.1 Mother tongue of the native of Native parentage for 25 languages (1940–1970), with percent increase (decrease) 1940–1970 and 1960–1970[a]. Originally published in the author's *Rise and Fall of the Ethnic Revival* (Mouton de Gruyter, 1985, pp. 139–140); reprinted by permission of the publisher.

Mother tongue	1940	(Estim) 1960	1970	Change 1940–1970	1940–1970 % increase (decrease)	Change 1960–1970	1960–1970 % increase (decrease)
Total	84,124,840	145,275,265	169,634,926	85,510,086	101.65	24,359,661	16.77
English	78,352,180	—	149,312,435	70,960,255	90.57	—	—
Norwegian	81,160	40,000	204,822	123,662	152.37	164,822	412.06
Swedish	33,660	17,000	113,119	79,459	236.06	96,119	565.41
Danish	9,100	6,000	29,089	19,989	219.66	23,089	384.82
Dutch	65,800	74,000	102,777	36,977	56.20	28,777	38.89
French	518,780	383,000	1,460,130	941,350	181.45	1,077,130	281.23
German	925,040	588,000	2,488,394	1,563,354	169.00	1,900,394	323.70
Polish	185,820	87,000	670,335	484,515	260.74	583,335	670.50
Czech	81,760	34,000	148,944	67,184	82.18	114,944	338.07
Slovak	29,260	10,000	86,950	57,690	197.16	76,950	769.50
Magyar (Hungarian)	13,180	16,000	52,156	38,976	295.72	36,156	225.98

Table 16.1 (cont'd)

Mother tongue	1940	(Estim) 1960	1970	Change 1940–1970	1940–1970 % increase (decrease)	Change 1960–1970	1960–1970 % increase (decrease)
Serbo-Croatian	5,200	7,000	24,095	18,895	363.37	17,095	244.21
Slovenian	5,780	3,000	9,040	3,260	56.40	6,040	201.33
Russian	13,980	18,000	30,665	16,685	119.35	12,665	70.36
Ukrainian	2,780	10,000	22,662	19,882	715.18	12,662	126.62
Armenian	1,880	—	13,785	11,905	633.24	—	—
Lithuanian	9,400	8,000	34,744	25,344	269.62	26,744	334.30
Finnish	14,880	4,000	58,124	43,244	290.62	54,124	1353.10
Rumanian	2,060	2,000	5,166	3,106	150.78	3,166	158.30
Yiddish	52,980	39,000	170,174	117,194	221.20	131,174	336.34
Greek	6,160	12,000	56,839	50,679	822.71	44,839	373.66
Italian	125,040	147,000	605,625	480,585	384.35	458,625	311.99
Spanish	718,980	1,291,000	4,171,050	3,452,070	480.13	2,880,050	233.09
Portuguese	11,380	7,000	62,252	50,872	447.03	55,252	789.31
Arabic	3,720	4,000	25,765	22,045	592.61	21,765	544.13
Total non-English	2,917,780	2,807,000	10,646,702	7,728,922	264.89	7,826,017	278.80
Total non-English minus Spanish	2,198,800	1,516,000	6,475,652	4,276,852	194.51	4,945,867	328.41

[a] Sources: 1940 and 1960 data from Language Loyalty in the United States, J. A. Fishman et al., 1966. 1970 data from PC(2)-1A, 1973.

Table 16.2 Correlations between institutional frequencies and demographic characteristics of their ethnic mother-tongue claimants. Originally published in the author's *Rise and Fall of the Ethnic Revival* (Mouton de Gruyter, 1985, p. 203); reprinted by permission of the publisher.

	(5) Total MT claim 1970	(6) NN MT claim 1970	(7) % NN MT claim 1970	(8) Total MT claim 1979
(1) Broadcasting	.84	.90	.27	.94
(2) LRUs	.43	.47	.24	.50
(3) Publications	.82	.83	.13	.89
(4) Schools	.18	.20	.03	.23
(5) Total MT claim 1970	—	.94	.25	.97
(6) NN MT claim 1970		—	.34	.96
(7) % NN MT claim 1970			—	.29
(8) Total MT claim 1979				—
(9) % change Total MT claim '70–'79				
(10) MT claim '60–'70				
Number of languages	41	41	41	39

Variation in n from one column to the other is due to the variable availability of United States Census data for particular languages in particular years.

warfare in their homelands "south of the border"), new laws and state constitutional amendments were enacted against use of languages other than English. It should be noted that in every case the prohibitions passed apply only to the state governments themselves (and many of the more egregious among these prohibitions have been found by the courts to be unconstitutional). In most cases, these laws and ordinances are purely symbolic and annoying by design and are, in reality, unenforced and unenforceable. Nevertheless, such English-Only laws foster suspicions, divisiveness, and recriminations that discourage individuals and businesses from public use of languages other than English and, doubtlessly, have again helped undercut non-English mother-tongue transmission in the country as a whole.

No *federal* law or constitutional amendment along the above "English-Only" lines has thus far succeeded in being passed (not for want of trying, however), but should such a dark-dark day ever arrive (and should such legislation or amendments be upheld subsequently, on appeal, by the Supreme Court), it would amount to yet another ideological/attitudinal blow to the language resources of the USA. Given the well-nigh complete absence of language-*supportive* legislation of the "English Plus" variety, as opposed to the purely *permissive* stance of the 1923 Meyer vs. Nebraska ruling (which, while outlawing the essentially anti-German legislation of the Nebraska legislature, stopped well short of requiring or even suggesting authoritative assistance to the maintenance of instruction in languages other than English in the USA) the negative impact and tone of restrictive NEMT legislation easily carries the day as a sociolinguistic mood-setter in many corners of American life. The objective demographic, interactive and economic factors, which have been mentioned above and which in modern urban settings overwhelmingly favor language shift, then rule doubly supreme. Under such circumstances parents and communities must constantly justify themselves, in the face of a wall of doubt and disbelief, for simply doing what is normal all over the world, namely, making sure that their children are following in the ethnolinguistic and ethnocultural footsteps of their parents and grandparents. Still, as we have learned from the 1970 census data, the process of language retention is not simply a monotonically downward one and periods of upswing, as well as localities that are well above the general curve of language maintenance, will certainly continue to occur. They should remind us all that those who advocate multilingualism as a general resource for their communities and for the country as a whole are not sentenced to inevitable failure and that local circumstances and efforts are frequently the ultimate determiners of local success or failure.

16.2.2   *Intergenerational NEMT transmission*

Among the success stories of immigrational non-English mother-tongue retention in the USA, as mentioned above, are the rural Pennsylvania German Old Order Amish and Mennonites, as well as the urban Khasidic Yiddish-speaking

Jews. Their successes hinge primarily on their non-participation in either American secular or religious life and their limited interaction with English-speaking Americans outside of the economic realm. This particular "Old Order" pattern has nevertheless not kept either group from acquiring English both early and well. However, their self-isolating rejection of modernization does not represent a pattern that is either acceptable or available to most other Americans of non-English background. Thus, while self-isolation needs to be understood and some of the lessons to be derived from it need to be tailored for local use in other ethnolinguistic settings, there is neither any chance nor any danger that it will be adopted en masse. Perhaps the main generally applicable lesson from such isolation is that of maintaining residential concentration in urban neighborhoods (Khasidim) or in rural settlement areas (Old Order Amish and Mennonites). Such residential concentration would seem to be a necessary (although, ultimately, not in itself a fully sufficient) prerequisite for the intergenerational transmission of non-English mother tongues, whether immigrant or indigenous. It provides for at least *internal* concentration, so that the bulk of the informal and intimate interactions that children and young folk will encounter in the home-family-neighborhood-community domain will be in the traditional ethnic mother tongue.

But this obvious initial desideratum is not enough. The rationale for an "own language" (a "lengua propia," as the Catalans are accustomed to say about Catalan in Catalunya, in contrast to Castilian throughout all of Spain) must be fully developed. It need not necessarily be anchored in non-participationism, as is the case among the Khasidim and the Old Order Amish and Mennonites. It may be anchored in religion alone, or in ethnocultural affiliation, or in the expectation of ethnocognitive enrichment, or even in the conviction that via multilingualism one is contributing a special service on behalf of the nation (sharing the "wealth" derived via multilingualism with the nation as a whole). Whatever the rationales for multilingualism in the midst of an English-speaking sea may be, they must be fully and consensually verbalized, strikingly ideologized, organizationally implemented and frequently reiterated, so that most Americans will support them and be readier than hitherto to bear both their costs and their benefits.

Both the Khasidim and the Old Order Amish and Mennonites support their own institutions (schools, local religious units, and neighborhood organizations), receiving only a modicum of support, at best, from either "outsider" agencies or "outsider" individuals for doing so. These groups have obviously learned a lesson which only some of the Amerindian groups have learned, namely, that unless a culture supports its own major institutions it becomes dependent upon "outsiders" (the federal government, the city council, the state legislature, foundations and other "foreign" charities) for the continuation, stabilization and growth of its own ethnolinguistic lifelines. That in turn fosters interactive dependencies of other kinds; all in all, *not an enviable position for a culture to be in and not one well calculated to guarantee intergenerational continuity of the culture's most valued customs, traditions and outlooks.* Of course, there is a world of difference between accepting or even competing for outside support and being dependent upon such support. The latter is contra-indicated for any self-respecting culture concerned with its own cultural reproduction in a context of globalization and modernization.

Perhaps "local religious units" (the term "churches" is not appropriate for other than Christian cultures) are the best examples of what is involved. We Americans do not depend on others – and particularly not on the government – to basically support our places of worship; yet we are a highly religious nation and, due to our predominant Protestant sectarianism, an unusually diversified one as well. True to its Protestant mainstream nature, the overall number of religious bodies (often called "sects" by the mainstream) continues to expand decade by decade, both by "fission" and by "spontaneous generation," far outstripping any smaller unificatory or amalgamating tendencies that also obtain. Nevertheless, notwithstanding the "wall of separation between church and state", religious bodies in the USA do accept tax-exempt status for their real estate, for their charitable receipts, for that portion of their clergy's salary that is expended for parsonage purposes, and, in addition, their schools receive lunch funds, book funds, student health care and health examination funds, and busing funds or services. This same general principle of "primarily self-supporting operation" is fully applicable to ethnic community-based schools and neighborhood institutions whether or not they are also religiously affiliated. These too, like the Navajo Contract Schools (and Charter Schools more generally), must place the main onus of support on the community itself rather than on public or other outside sources. A culture and its language cannot live on an externally dependent life-support system and there is nothing that promotes good cultural health more than collective efforts to stay alive and to remain healthy on one's own.

Without such self-supported, self-protected and self-initiated islands of demographically concentrated local non-English language-and-culture transmission, particularly given the social mobility, modernization, and urban interaction so typical of American life, non-English mother tongues lack "safe houses" or "safe harbors" wherein the young can be socialized according to the languages, values, and traditions of sidestream cultures. They also increasingly lack a protected intimate space for adults and old folks during their after-work and out-of-work lives. The work sphere, the mass media and the common political system will all guarantee that cultural "safe harbors" do not become foreign, isolated, or hostile enclaves. Indeed, the brunt of American historical experience as a whole has provided ample evidence – even among avowedly separatist language-and-culture groups – that the major language maintenance problem faced is one of engulfment by the mainstream rather than one of excessive separation from it. The "state into nationality" process continues along in its own inexorable way and, thereby, "Americans" continue to slowly become a "state nationality," just as have so many others in the past whenever the stability of polity fosters a shared culture and where cultural stability fosters a corresponding ethnicity.

16.2.3   *Minority languages in the national interest*

A dispassionate analysis of the goal of fostering multilingualism in the United States must lead to the conclusion that although the immigrant and cultural-enclave derived sectors have a powerful contribution to make toward this goal, these sectors are too weak and too situationally disadvantaged to attain this goal by themselves. Nor is there any rational need for them to do so, if one seriously evaluates the benefits to be gained by the USA via greater non-English language resources. There are other contributory streams that are already involved in contributing toward these resources, albeit not necessarily on an intergenerational basis. Federal (and, to a lesser extent, also state) agencies are *manifoldly involved in funding the preparation and utilizing the talents of advanced non-English-speaking expertise,* doing so for the better pursuit of their own normal activities. Whether for the innumerable purposes of *internal* services (in such areas as health, education, welfare, civil rights, voter registration, job training and retraining, immigration and naturalization services, flood relief, other disaster relief, social security advisement, etc.), or for the equally ubiquitous purposes of *external* services (on behalf of fostering military security, foreign policy goals, commercial advancement, scientific progress, consular presence, United States Information Agency services, etc.), there is a huge governmental reliance upon and involvement in the fostering of functional and high level multilingualism in the USA. Obviously, it is both reprehensibly wasteful and utterly self-defeating of many of our most important national/ local goals and processes to (with one hand, so to speak) vitiate and plow under our immigrant-based language resources while (with the other hand) attempting to foster very similar resources on the basis of governmentally initiated language (re)training programs, language crash-courses, language fellowships, and even language schools. Some coordination is urgently required here (as I have been arguing in print for the past 35 years; see Fishman, 1967). It is just as scandalous and injurious to waste "native" language resources as to waste our air, water, mineral, animal, and various non-linguistic human resources. How long must languages and cultures be trivialized if they are learned at home, in infancy and childhood, and only respected if they are acquired later, during adulthood, when they are usually learned less well and at much greater cost in competence, time and money?

Another major intrapunitive partner-and-culprit, in connection with respecting, utilizing and fostering our natural non-English mother tongue resources, is the world of American industry and commerce. Once again we note a frenzied, "off again, on again" scramble for intensive (and expensive) adult courses, on the one hand, and, on the other hand, a deaf ear to the native language resources that, were they recognized and cultivated on a stable basis, would be of greater benefit to all concerned. Nor, finally, can the world of American higher education be pardoned for its largely continuing deafness, blindness and general ineptness relative to the languages which are in its own backyard, not to mention its front yard as well. Our universities not only do not adequately recognize, utilize, or reward the non-English multilingual talents that they possess on their faculties and among their students, but they commonly and regularly denigrate and plow under these talents as well. Of course, it will require special methods, special texts, and special classes (with a judicious and selective use of the materials that our ethnolinguistic minorities themselves have created for educational purposes) if these largely unused and unrecognized language resources within the world of American higher education are to be constructively tapped and cultivated. This is now finally beginning to be done in a very few places, for a very few languages and by a very few sensitively skilled academics and pedagogues (note, for example, the "Secular Yiddish Schools of America Collection" at Special Collections, Stanford University Libraries, and the "Spanish for Native Speakers" efforts at Stanford University's School of Education), but, on the whole, this arena is just another example of waste, ignorance and hostility toward our own natural multilingual resources.

16.3   Making the World Safe (or at least Safer) for Cultural Democracy

The attrition visited by the American mainstream upon home-grown multilingualism has come full circle to bite the very hands of the mainstream-dominated governmental, industrial, educational, and recreational establishments that have so studiously abetted and ignored this attrition for most of America's still-brief history. Can our miserable record thus far be improved? Unfortunately, a country as rich and as powerful as our own, smugly speaking "the language that rules the world," can long afford to continue to disregard the problem. But a problem that is disregarded does not therefore cease to be a problem and simply go away.

Instead of quick fixes, a program of "cultural democracy" (affirmative ethnolinguistic pluralism) is needed in order to "make our country safe for home-grown multilingualism." It is a misperception to claim that in our Anglo-Saxon legal tradition we only recognize individual rights and turn a deaf ear to group rights. The old are recognized as a group that requires special financial and physical support. Women are acknowledged, as a group, to require special health and welfare provisions and "gender"-abuse protection. Children are recognized separately under the law. Handicapped groups are specially recognized by specific laws and literally billions have been expended on making our sidewalks, public buildings and even public buses "user friendly" for them via the Americans with Disabilities Act. These are all groups that have been recognized (and in large part, have been self-organized) for particularistic treatment, because it is their due from the point of view of both justice and equity. Furthermore, the distinction between individual rights and group rights is not a hard and fast or clear-cut one (Kymlicka, 1995). Furthermore, even group rights, as such, have also been recognized in the "affirmative action" cases of African-Americans, Hispanics, Pacific Islanders and American Indians, as well as in cases pertaining to the health, education, and welfare of Old Order Amish and Mennonites. Some laws have been repealed and other laws have been passed so that Khasidim would not suffer from disadvantages as Saturday Sabbath observers or as requiring (as do the Old Order folk) quite different schools for their young (and particularly for their learning-disabled young). The overriding American constitutional need for separation between church and state has been modified in these instances by the recognition that entire religious groups (rather than merely an unrelated class of individuals) would be severely injured unless they were separately recognized in constructive ways. Has not the entire affirmative action effort been one on behalf of group rights where widespread injustice to a group is recognized as having taken place? Why should group rights be extended only reluctantly and in confrontational contexts, rather than willingly and creatively, in a constructive context of maximizing human resources? And what is the moral distinction between such rights and the rights already granted to selected ethnic and religious minorities?

Are not our internal language resources demonstrably and primarily preserved and fostered by separate cultural groups? Must America again merely anglicize the Hispanics, the Orientals, the Pacific Islanders, the Alaskan natives, the Amerindians (from both south and north of the Rio Grande, because we conveniently forget or overlook the fact that many of those whom we prefer to view as Hispanics – a designation foreign even to Spanish-speaking newcomers – are, in their own innermost hearts and minds, primarily speakers of Mayan languages, Nauwatl-speakers, Quechua-speakers, Aymara-speakers, etc.), the Africans, the Asia-Indians, the Chinese, the Russians, the Ukrainians, the Iranians, the Iraqis (all of the seven last-mentioned group-names also being catch-all designations that reveal our ignorance of ethnolinguistic identities), as we have done throughout our history, only to find that we lack speakers of these languages when "national interest needs" arise? Would group rights on behalf of fostering their languages for the national good be inherently balkanizing and conducive to civil strife? Certainly not, if their speakers' material progress and political participation in the national arena were also forthcoming, as they have been for most Americans since the disadvantages once suffered by women, blacks and Catholics (all of whom have benefited from group rights) have been increasingly overcome. Yes, we need group rights along language lines in order to foster "more stable multilingualism for the general good" in the USA. This has long been recognized by such pioneers of the evolving American dream as Horace Kallen, Michael Waltzer and Loni Guinier. If we are serious about making America safe for home-grown multilingualism as a national and natural resource, we must become serious about real cultural democracy and group rights for this purpose. Doing so hasn't harmed Switzerland any, nor Finland, nor post-Franco Spain, nor even such whipping boys (in the American press) as Belgium, India, or Canada.

Indeed, there is ample empirical evidence that multilingualism does not lead to increased social strife nor to lowered per-capita gross national product, as shown by the European Union's increased protection of "less used languages" in the course of (and in pursuit of) its unparalleled economic progress of the past two decades. How odd that Europe, the continent that has suffered longest from linguistic repression and linguistic violence in the past, is most willing to forgive and forget such past violence in the hope of future benefits from supportive policies on behalf of more and more state and non-state languages. On the other hand, the USA – where no language wars have ever been waged – is still excessively timid and even paranoid about utilizing more productively the enviable language resources that it still possesses.

Can the Monolingual Mainstream be persuaded that it REALLY needs languages other than its own? That's the rub! If its government, commerce and industry, and academic "forces" can ever really be persuaded of this need, they will have to act more inventively and forcefully on behalf of the speakers of those overlooked languages that are already in their own midst. If they can't, then most Americans will be consigned to being "linguistically retarded" (or, in currently more fashionably euphemistic terms, to being "linguistically challenged") in an increasingly multilingual world. Particularly in the USA, one cannot just platonically proclaim one's love for "multilingualism" while neglecting to provide all that multilingualism needs in order to exist and prosper. "Language defense" is a possible focus within both the status-planning (or sociofunctional planning) and the corpus-planning (or "language *per se*" planning) halves of any successful language-planning enterprise that genuinely aims at assisting contextually weaker or threatened languages. In line with Skutnabb-Kangas and Phillipson (1995), I will largely restrict myself here to status-planning types of language defenses (although I have no doubt whatsoever that in most cases linguistic standardization, elaboration, and cultivation efforts too would turn out to be necessary). Various types of language-defense activities have been reported in the status-planning literature by a large number of investigators. Along more global lines, two of my own recent works (1991, 1997) have sought to derive more general principles of language defense from a multitude of cases throughout the world and even throughout history. Additional individual country or regional cases of language defense have recently been provided by Hamel (1997, re Latin America), Schiffman (1996, particularly re France and re India), and Topolinska (1998, re Macedonia). A careful review of the cited publications and of a veritable multitude of other studies (which space limitations do not permit me to cite here) discloses that although they all devote attention to one type or another of language status defense, these types differ quite substantially from each other and should not be lumped together. A systematization of the types of language status defenses might serve to bring greater order into the frequent bewilderment of scholars, students and policy makers alike as to what could possibly be done to foster that multilingualism that recurringly and currently functions on a communal basis both in the USA and in other mainstream blocks (e.g. France, much of Latin America, and much of the Muslim belt in the Near East and Central Asia).

16.3.1   Permissive language defense

The most modest and elementary type of language defense is to seek or foster a "permissive" stance on the part of the majority authorities. Such a stance does not obligate the authorities to overtly or constructively do anything on behalf of disadvantaged languages, but rather to abstain from oppositional or deleterious actions with respect to these (or any other) languages. The "freedom of speech" provision in the Bill of Rights amendments to the American Constitution does not itself directly assist those who would like to foster non-English language use in the USA, in addition to English, but, on the other hand, if enforced, it does prohibit the most obvious legislation against such use. Permissive language defense legislation would not render the English-Only movement inoperative in the USA, nor would it necessarily prohibit declaring English to be the only language of government. It might merely be a statement of good wishes toward languages other than English in their home-family-neighborhood-community realms.

Note, however, that even the previously mentioned Meyer vs. Nebraska decision of the US Supreme Court (1923), which invalidated Nebraska's prohibition of using any modern foreign language as a medium for teaching children below the age of 12 (this invalidation subsequently being designated the "Magna Carta of language freedom in the USA" (Kloss, 1977)), neither led to any *requirement* nor even to any explicit *encouragement* vis-à-vis government *support* for any such efforts, even along strictly instructional lines. Actually, such permissiveness is merely a "hands off" decision and, therefore, it leaves functionally and contextually disadvantaged languages just as disadvantaged as they were before. These languages remain exposed to the Darwinian law of the linguistic jungle: the strong survive and, in competition with the strong, the weak die off.

Basically, permissive rulings and legislation are largely decorative or "purely symbolic" gestures. They imply more than they deliver. At best, they may prepare the ground for future meaningful support but, in and of themselves, they do not provide any such support. Non-English languages in the United States have been trifled with via what amounts to no more than Fourth of July oratory for far too long. When they are more than a generation away from their immigrational origins they are usually not sufficiently robust to be trifled with further, particularly because time is then of the essence insofar as their intergenerational continuity is concerned. Most serious non-linguistic matters that are assumed to require immediate attention are not merely given permissive nods. If education is assumed to be important, laws are passed requiring it, supporting it, fostering it. If language defenses (and, therefore, better safeguarded multilingual/multicultural societies within monolingual establishments) are really considered to be in the public interest (rather than merely a private hobby or even a private passion), then such societies too cannot merely be permissively tolerated. A permissive policy alone even falls short of a symbolic treatment (see below) and, therefore, it does not even begin to rise to the level of either active or preventive language defense on behalf of multilingualism and the non-mainstream mother tongue societies currently held captive (at worst) or considered expendable (at best) in many of the world's largest monolingual blocs, including the USA.

16.3.2   *Active language defenses*

Active language defenses attempt to be therapeutic vis-à-vis disadvantaged languages. They are undertaken when danger is not only *recognized* but when ameliorative steps are *implemented* in order to counteract language endangerment. If we were to follow a medical metaphor, we might say that active language defenses treat the patient in order to overcome whatever illness has been ascertained. But therapy – no matter how restorative it may be – is never as good a defense as the prevention of illness to begin with. To make matters even worse, most of the active language defense on record is more symbolic than substantive. Aggrieved language communities are mollified by having their languages declared "co-official": Hawaiian in the Hawaiian Islands, and Navajo on the ballots in New Mexico. Activists for endangered languages are often mollified by having their languages utilized on official letterheads or by having a song of theirs sung on an important festive occasion (such as on "Norwegian Language Day" at some Lutheran churches in Minnesota). Even if such commemorative occasions are frequent (like the formal opening exercises of the school day), such remedial steps are not only frequently too late but also commonly too little (as in the case of transitional bilingual education involving recessive languages). Effective language defenses require more than window-dressing. Symbolic decorations are not what either daily life or language life is all about, not even for the healthy, let alone for those who are in ill-health. In the absence of serious empirical supervision, experimentation, evaluation, and follow-up relative to defined criterial achievements (such as "overt language use in function X, Y or Z"), it is very likely that even so-called "action research" will be only small-scale and symbolic rather than curative. Research may be informative, but by itself it is not curative. Many a sick language has been (and is still being) researched to death. An honorable and informed burial is not an effective language defense. An effective theory of remedial language defense requires a theory that fits all ameliorations to the nature and degree of the illness. Subsidizing the televised viewing of adult films that are available in a particular threatened language (for example, National Public Television programming of more foreign-language films selected for linguistic rather than purely artistic reasons) will very probably be totally ineffective in terms of assistance to languages with inadequate and increasingly diminishing rates of intergenerational transmission from Xish-speaking child-bearing adults to Xish-speaking offspring (where Xish is any particular language undergoing shift) who would, in turn, become Xish-speaking child-bearing adults themselves. For such intergenerational transmission processes really to be institutionally reinforced, assistance is needed much closer to the juncture of transmission, for example in connection with language-infused nursery centers, childcare centers, parenting courses, grandparenting courses, joint parent–child play-groups, etc.

16.3.3 *Preventive (proactive) defenses of threatened multilingualism in the USA*

The most effective assurance of continued physical health is *preventive* medicine. Similarly, demographically, economically, symbolically, and functionally minoritized languages – which is what minoritized languages everywhere really are – require preventive defenses before they reach stages of advanced difficulty. This view is recognized constitutionally in Belgium, where, in small pockets assigned to one or another of the two stronger languages (Walloon/French and Flemish/Dutch), yet another language (e.g. German) is nevertheless recognized as meriting particular facilitation. Proactive language defense requires constant evaluation to catch possible difficulties before they reach the galloping contagion or language-threatening stage. The "sign inspectors" of the Office de la Langue Française in Quebec might, most charitably, be said to be engaged in proactive francophone language defense efforts in a province in which 90-some percent of the population is of francophone origin. In fact, the entire francophone movement in Quebec is proactive in the sense of being on behalf of a locally dominant but nationally (and, in historical perspective, even internationally) minoritized language. A similar type of assistance in the USA would foster a more frequent use of Spanish at the ballot box, at city council meetings, in the local courthouse, post office and fire station in many election districts, and would actively foster Navajo or Yakima in others. Most of those who shed crocodile tears on discovering the sad conditions within the USA of our own outposts of such world community languages as French, German, Russian, Chinese, Persian, Swahili, Hindi, Urdu, and Arabic are protesting their alarmed ignorance too vehemently. Can it be that they preferred not to know about the "language killing fields" in their own backyards? Of course, the rights of English speakers, as individuals or as groups, must not be harmed in any way by any co-recognition and co-validation of other locally appropriate languages. In addition, such languages will be, all the more readily and realistically, available languages from then on, for the cultural enrichment and for the greater functional versatility of Anglo children as well. Let us learn from world experience that proactive efforts undertaken in the context of and on behalf of local multilingualism, via expanding cultural democracy and multiplying positive intergroup contacts, is not the "beginning of the end" for the mainstream but the beginning of new advantages for all (definitely including the mainstream). Multilingualism is a valid and, indeed, even an urgent goal for multicultural citizenship in the modern, globalized world, a goal that must not elude the ongoing modernization and globalization of the American experience. Social and personal identity are and will remain complex and multifaceted and very much in need of languages and cultures of daily intimate identity and continuity. Any attempts to subvert this complexity and to replace it by English-language uniformation will only elicit opposition and acrimony both within and across borders all over the world.

As I write these words, the Palo Alto School District, near Stanford University, has renewed its long-term support for two-way bilingual education (Spanish-English) in two of its elementary schools and approved the opening of a new elementary bilingual school in Mandarin-English. Of course, this is a relatively affluent school district and one in which the high standard of living effectively limits the numbers of resident and incoming minorities speaking languages other than English. All of the children involved in these two-way programs have learned, early and clearly, to simultaneously achieve very high levels of English competence and Spanish competence, and now more and more of them will be able to do so in another language as well. This is the same school district that also enables two other languages (Korean and Japanese) to be taught in its school buildings on weekends, as well as during weekday after-school hours, in order that any interested students can retain or attain fluency in these languages, thereby (1) getting high-school foreign-language credit for studying them, (2) offering test scores in these languages among their College Entrance Examination Board credentials, and (3) obtaining advanced placement in these languages at the college level upon graduating from high school. All in all, this promises to be a very successful proactive way of rewarding and fostering childhood and adolescent societal multilinguals in the USA.

I am proud of "my" school district's efforts to foster native and early childhood multilingualism and, at the same time, to disprove "gloom and doom" prognostications in that connection. It is only a drop in the bucket relative to what the USA needs, but it may also be a straw in the wind, indicating that perhaps the tide of fear and suspicion may be turning once again and that many Americans now feel sufficiently secure to at least foster multilingualism among those who are already among our more fortunate sons and daughters of elementary-school age. It is a beginning. Multilingualism cannot be intergenerationally maintained by proactive schools alone, however. Other forces in society must contribute as well: the family-home-neighborhood-community, first and foremost among them, but also the mass media, the work sphere, the higher education sphere and the major agencies of government as well. Hopefully, there will be no turning back! Hopefully, a true language-fostering alliance between governmental programs, ethnic community programs, industrial/commercial sector programs and higher educational programs will come into being at last, in place of the traditional wasteful and morally sad American approach of "too little and too late" on the societal multilingualism front.

16.4   Can Language Shift be Reversed?

Obviously, great damage has already been done to hundreds and even thousands of indigenous and immigrant languages in the USA and all over the globe. Helping them recover so that they can comfort their own speakers as well as enrich all who would learn them, will take much determination and intelligence, even more than funds and activists.

Before the advent of sociologically informed sociolinguistic theory it was not uncommon to attempt to explain the waning of languages via recourse to such intuitively popular factors as "proximity to a more powerful language" (often referred to cryptically as "geography"); "conviction that the language be retained" (often referred to as "positive language attitudes" or "motivation"), and absolute number of speakers (often referred to as "speech-community size"). The problem with such theoretically innocent explanatory attempts is that they do not spell out or relate to societal processes, whether of intragroup interaction or intergroup interaction, that is, they are basically neither sociological (and, therefore, not sociolinguistic) nor related to any body of disciplined inquiry or application. It is my conviction that "geography," "motivation," and "size" are all folk concepts that need to be sociologically reinterpreted and operationalized into their manipulable societal counterparts. Reversing language shift efforts are particularly in need of both conceptually integrated social theory and a structured set of priorities for application that derives from such theory. What follows is a brief attempt along such lines.

16.4.1   *What is Reversing Language Shift (RLS)?*

RLS constitutes that corner of the total field of language status planning that is devoted to improving the sociolinguistic circumstances of languages that suffer from a prolonged negative balance of users and uses. It is not necessarily entirely an applied field of endeavor, since any hope for successful application – here as well as elsewhere – depends on the prior development of conceptually integrated diagnostic and corrective theory. When I initially laid out the field of "language maintenance and language shift" (Fishman, 1964), it was my intention that the referents on both sides of the conjunction receive equal attention. Unfortunately, that has not proven to be the case and the negative process has received far more attention than has the positive one. Perhaps that is the result of a general bias, common to modern humanistic and social science scholarship and to various ideologies of the left, center and right alike, toward assuming (and, at times, even preferring) the uniformation and massification of culture, based upon the massification and unification of the market and of modern technology across cultural boundaries, i.e. to focus upon social class and prefer it to ethnic stratification as the major societal accompaniment to globalization.

As a result, "the other side (or the plus side) of the ethnolinguistic ledger" has tended to be neglected, if not ideologically stigmatized. The study of RLS represents an attempt to redress the perspectival balance and to direct attention to the fact that not only are millions upon millions of speakers of small languages on all continents convinced of the creative and continuative contributions of their languages (usually their mother tongues but sometimes their historically associated religious/classical languages) to their personal and collective lives, but also many millions are engaged in individual and collective efforts to assist their mother tongues to reverse the language shift processes that threaten or have engulfed them.

Language shift can impinge on various societal communicative functions and, accordingly, the study of RLS must be concerned with the entire sociofunctional profile of language use in any particular community under study. However, sociofunctional features of language use are neither universal nor fixed and they must, in all honesty, be established anew empirically whenever a hitherto unstudied (or not recently studied) ethnolinguistic collectivity is (re-)examined. Nevertheless, due to the worldwide encroachment of Western-derived modernization, it is possible to make heuristic use of a parsimonious subset of functions that tend to be rather generally encountered (except where undislocated non-western cultures still hold sway; Fishman, 2001). In our discussion below, these sociofunctions will be discussed from the point of view of RLS-efforts for the purpose of attaining and augmenting intergenerational mother-tongue transmission. The intergenerational transmission of regional languages (lingua francas), of languages of wider econotechnical communication, or of religious classicals (in general, the intergenerational transmission of additional languages for special purposes) has been discussed elsewhere (Fishman, 1991, chapter 12), although it should be stressed that the theoretical underpinnings of that discussion are the same as those which follow here.

16.4.2 A conceptually parsimonious approach to describing and prescribing: The Graded Intergenerational Dislocation Scale (GIDS)

It would be conceptually parsimonious to adopt an approach to analyzing RLS situations such that it would simultaneously (1) lend itself to comparative (that is, to between-language) description or analysis; and (2) indicate the nature (location) and intensity (seriousness) of the sociofunctional disarray impacting any particular cases under discussion. Simply put, RLS is in need of an approach to sociofunctional analysis which will both describe the situation and prescribe the necessary ameliorative steps, at one and the same time, insofar as the needs of threatened languages are concerned after an intergenerational period of Western-impacted dislocation. Table 16.3 represents an effort along those very lines. Note that the stages for RLS in table 16.3 are

Table 16.3 Toward a theory of reversing language shift: Stages of reversing language shift and severity of intergenerational dislocation (read from the bottom up).

1   Educational, work sphere, mass media and (quasi-)governmental operations in Xish at the highest (nationwide) levels
2   Local/regional mass media and (quasi-)governmental services in Xish
3   The local/regional (i.e. supra-neighborhood) work sphere, both among Xmen and among Ymen
4b Public schools for Xish children, offering some instruction via Xish, but substantially under Yish curricular and staffing control
4a Schools in lieu of compulsory education and substantially under Xish curricular and staffing control

B. RLS-efforts to transcend diglossia, subsequent to its attainment?

5   Schools for Xish literacy acquisition, for the old and/or for the young, and not in lieu of compulsory education
6   The organization of intergenerational and demographically concentrated home-family-neighborhood efforts: the basis of Xish mother-tongue transmission
7   Cultural interaction in Xish primarily involving the community-based older generation (beyond the age of giving birth)
8   Reconstructing Xish and adult acquisition of XSL

A. RLS to attain diglossia (assuming prior ideological clarification)?

ordered with the highest degree of modern reward-power (the last stage in RLS) listed at the top of the table as '1' and the lowest degree of modern reward-power (the first stage in RLS) at the bottom of the table under '8'. Hence the recommended temporal order of RLS reads from the bottom of the table to the top to stress that fundamental lower-order and intergenerational functions must be secured before higher-order ones can be pursued.

Stage 8 indicates the greatest dislocation of all (from the point of view of achieving intergenerational mother-tongue continuity), namely, a language which lapsed into general disuse sufficiently long ago that it is now in need of reconstruction from shreds of evidence that can be provided by its last speakers and other incomplete and even vestigial sources. In order to reduce the number of steps in the table (the number can be greatly increased if finer functional distinctions are desired), stage 8 also includes those languages for which ample written evidence is available but which have lost their native speakers to such a degree that these languages must first be learned as second languages before further sociofunctional repertoire expansion can be envisioned for them. All in all, stage 8 represents maximal dislocation precisely because it constitutes Xish language use outside of natural society, that is, outside of daily, effortless societal interaction among individuals actually implementing Xish in their normal, ongoing, community-based ethnocultural lives.

Note, however, that no evolutionary or implicational (required) progression is suggested. Even the attainment (or implementation) of vernacular cultural interaction on a community basis is insufficient for intergenerational mother-tongue continuity if the community of speakers consists of individuals who are primarily past childbearing age (stage 7). Indeed, it is precisely the fashioning (attainment or retention) of Xish-implementing intergenerational and demographically concentrated home-family-community life, and the diglossic sheltering of such life from the inroads upon Xish intimacy that can stem from Yish ("wye-ish", our abbreviation for the competitively stronger language surrounding Xish), that is the *sine qua non* of mother-tongue transmission (stage 6). All efforts that come later *may* (and should optimally be so regulated that they *will*) help shelter stage 6, but cannot substitute for it, nor, as we will see, can they directly help stage 6 insofar as its creation or attainment is concerned. In addition certain stages (e.g. stage 5) may be totally unnecessary given certain contextual circumstances. Other characteristics of table 16.3, and the underlying theory that it represents, will become clear from the ensuing discussion of ambivalences that often enfeeble RLS-efforts on behalf of intergenerational mother-tongue continuity.

In general terms, stage 6 may be viewed as the dynamic fulcrum of a field of forces. If stage 6 is not attained and vigorously retained, the RLS efforts concentrated at other stages will be less contributory to the intergenerational continuity of Xish. Efforts closer to stage 6 are more nearly under Xish community control and, therefore, do not depend crucially on Yish support, funding, cooperation, or permission. Although the approach sketched here assumes that *something* can always be done on behalf of threatened languages (even those at stage 8), it clearly implies that not everything that is done will contribute with equal ease and directness to intergenerational mother-tongue continuity. This conclusion (often a contra-intuitive one for RLS workers, resulting in their ambivalence toward the process of RLS) is spelled out below.

16.4.2.1   *Ambivalence 1: The premature attraction and distraction of pursuing high status/power functions*

The striving toward Xish implementation in and control of econotechnical modernity, a striving which is so typical of the modern situation which we have assumed generally to be part of the total language shift process impinging upon Xish, leads to an overly early concentration on stages 4 through 1 among those working on behalf of RLS. Such premature efforts to cross the continental divide between *attaining diglossic L(ow) protection* for Xish, on the one hand, and *dismantling diglossic L status for Xish in favor of diglossic H(igh) status* (or even monolingual Xish self-sufficiency), on the other hand, are evidenced by rushing into efforts on behalf of Xish schooling-in-lieu-of-compulsory-education and even by a stress on Xish use in the non-neighborhood work sphere, media and governmental operations. RLS efforts which pursue such goals prematurely are inevitably faced by several problems. On the one hand, these goals engender intergroup conflict precisely with respect to functions in which Xmen are weakest relative to Ymen and where they will most often initially require the greatest amount of Yish support and cooperation, even if only a nominal Xish presence is to be approved and funded.

Unfortunately, any nominal Xish presence in upper status and power functions will more often than not be completely overshadowed (if not totally eclipsed) by the vastly more frequent and often far superior Yish presence in those very same functions. The unequal struggle for "recognition" in these high-status and -power functions frequently renders RLS efforts completely hopeless, disillusioned, and innocent of concrete results. What is worse, *the overly early concentration on high-status and -power goals not only does not feed back directly to stage 6 but often postpones the tackling of stage 6 until it is too late from the point of view of capitalizing on still available Xish demographic concentrations and on Xish speakers who are still of childbearing age.* Trickle-down theories that claim that power functions imply and guarantee intimate mother-tongue acquisition and use are seriously mistaken, unless the former are specifically controlled and oriented via feedback systems so as to constantly keep the latter at the forefront of attention and concern. It is ever thus for non-dominant X's, where social dynamics flow effortlessly from Y to displace X but never in the reverse direction.

While the attainment of type 4a schools (primarily Xish-staffed and -regulated) or even 4b schools (primarily Yish-staffed and -regulated but intended for Xish children) certainly constitutes a worthwhile RLS goal, nevertheless, many Yish-dominated years must pass before the graduates of such schools can found new Xish-speaking families of their own. Of course, such schools can serve to further motivate and protect stage 6, but stage 6 must be alive and well for such motivation and protection to emerge. Finally, and specifically in relation to schools, various postmodernization processes have served to render the school–home continuity relationship more tenuous than ever before (Fishman, 1991, chapter 13), even for Yish, thereby rendering schools above the optional type 5 quite questionable investments of time and effort for RLS movements that are still weak and without stage 6 foundations securely under their control. Successful and constant feedback from stage 4 to stage 6 requires ongoing out-of-school and after-school involvement of school staff in most home, neighborhood and community efforts from the earliest toddler years onward. The Maori Kohanga-Reo nursery schools did just that, with some success for Maori revernacularization.

The Irish RLS case was long a prime example of the inadvisability of disproportionate concentration on stage 4 in relation to stage 6, and of the resulting *institutionalization of Irish as an occasional, formal second language among the*

school-focused middle class (each successive generation of which has nevertheless started out, and generally still starts out, even after three-quarters of a
century of governmentally sponsored RLS-efforts, totally without Irish when
it arrives in school), *rather than as a mother tongue and informal medium among
members of Irish society more generally.* The current case of battle-fatigue among
Irish RLSers, and the substantial peripheralization of their struggle vis-à-vis
the interests of society more generally, can be attributed to their precipitous
over-concentration on advanced GIDS stages. *The latter do not spontaneously
feed back to intergenerational mother-tongue continuity and require substantial inge-
nuity* (as persuading water to flow uphill always does) *if they are to do so even
when linkages for that purpose are kept prominently in mind.*

16.4.2.2   Ambivalence 2: First attaining and then overcoming diglossia, and doing each at an appropriate time

If the headlong rush into highly improbable (if not totally impossible) serious
competition with Yish represents a distinct danger for the success of RLS
efforts on behalf of intergenerational mother tongue continuity, then the
insufficient pursuit of substantially self-regulated modern status and power
functions, even when such can be erected upon a strong stage 6 base, constitutes an equally great (although far less common) danger to such efforts.
A disproportional stress on traditionalism, revivalism or other expressions
of "anthropological revitalization" exposes RLS efforts to the risk of being
rejected by Xmen who seek a path marked by both modernity and Xishness. In
the absence of sufficient RLS interest in rationally defining the priorities to be
followed in beating such a path, RLS may come to be viewed as anachronistic
or backward-looking and more symbiotic alternatives to it (combining Xishness
and Yish in some fashion) may come into being (e.g. movements on behalf of
"Xmen-via-Yish" as rivals and competitors with the RLS movement *per se*
among Xmen). Some of the Ultra-Orthodox Yiddish-speaking communities in
New York are exposed to this very dilemma today as young people protest
against their community's overly slow progression from stage 4 to stage 3. The
insufficient availability of stage 3 functions under Ultra-Orthodox sponsorship
is leading more and more young people into the Yish controlled work sphere
(and into social mobility via that work sphere), with evident effect on their
own intragroup use of Yiddish. Community leaders, however, are concerned
about young folks entering stage 3 wholeheartedly, because of its manifold
links with the Yish world. The dilemma here needs to be recognized because
of its "damned if you do, damned if you don't" potential. It is a very resource-
demanding stage and one that few minority communities can really control
and link back to stage 6.

Given that both the premature abandonment of the diglossic protection of
stage 6 and the overly prolonged inability to transcend the encapsulation of
stage 6 are clearly problematic vis-à-vis RLS success, it is, nevertheless, clear
that the attainment of diglossic protection for Xish by weak RLS movements

lacking in stage 6 is infinitely more common and difficult (and less glamorous) than is its subsequent gradual transcendence by an RLS movement with a secure basis in everyday intergenerational life. RLS movements are ethnicity-linked and they must build upon the putative kinship claim of all ethnicity movements in order to counteract the blandishments of greater (and often even purportedly unlimited) individual social mobility via Yish and through Yish institutions, blandishments which render Xmen less ideologically disposed toward the behavioral and motivational prerequisites of RLS-movements on behalf of the "Xmen-via-Xish" model. The Irish and Frisian movements are good examples of the difficulties encountered in this very diglossia-attaining connection. Stage 6 never having been reconstituted on a sufficiently ample base (a base which many Ultra-Orthodox Yiddish speakers *have* secured), there is no widely available safe harbor in daily life against the influences of the upper Yish-controlled stages.

Furthermore, the transcendence of diglossic bilingualism into a virtually monolingual Xish *de facto* control of everyday public and intergroup life, is often considered by Ymen to be unattainable without civil strife. However, the actual incidence of civil strife is more genuinely related to the removal of authoritarian control after periods of both long-term and short-term depriva-tion (Fishman and Solano, 1990) than to RLS processes or other ethnolinguistic processes themselves. The Franco-Canadian and the Catalan RLS cases are both examples of relatively successful negotiations of this difficult passage, the latter being almost entirely without serious intergroup recriminations between indigenous Catalans and immigrant Castilian speakers thus far. Note, how-ever, that without the successful attainment and maintenance of stage 6, no sustained transcendence of that stage is possible. There is a dilemma here of no mean proportions.

16.4.2.3 *Ambivalence 3: The difficulty of planning spontaneity and intimacy*

The basic problem of weak RLS movements is whether the attainment and maintenance of stage 6 is at all susceptible to planning. Given that inter-generational mother tongue transmission is a function of the childhood intim-acy and spontaneity that characterizes home-family-neighborhood life, this problem boils down to whether this complex of culturally infused interper-sonal processes can only be informally cultivated "en flagrante," so to speak, or whether it can be fostered by rational planning. The evidence supporting the latter alternative is, quite frankly, sparse indeed. The major RLS success cases of the twentieth century generally entered the fray while their stage 6 processes were still (or already) rather intact at least in some language islands. Attempts to build stage 6 directly (e.g. the community and housing schemes of Irish RLS efforts in the mid- to late 1980s) have demonstrated how elusive the informal interaction processes really are and how difficult it is to really plan them or to do so without smothering (i.e. formalizing) them. Yet the revernacularization of Hebrew in Palestine on the part of secular (indeed, anti-clerical) Zionists was accomplished precisely along the lines of giving priority to self-regulatory home-family-community building for the attainment of intergenerational mother tongue transmission and reached its goal during the decades immediately before and after the First World War, long before any power and status functions (beyond the settlements and their community-controlled fields, chicken-coops, nursery-kindergartens and elementary schools) were widely attained on a broader societal base. Years of child-rearing by specially trained caregivers were passed in a quite separate children's home, with only very occasional visits on the part of the children to their parents, until *the children had taught the parents* the revived vernacular. Such back-linkages between higher stages and stage 6 require careful and constant attention, so that neither insufficiency nor top-to-bottom formalization occurs.

Obviously there is also considerable need for ideological clarification (more about this below) and for neighborhood organization expertise and organization theory expertise in general (on the latter, see, Hart 2001) within the total RLS enterprise. Nevertheless, the dilemma which underlies this third area of ambivalence must be recognized as such. Intergenerational mother tongue transmission depends on processes which have for too long remained overlooked by RLS movements but, to make matters worse, even when squarely acknowledged, these processes are difficult to plan because they require the establishment and fostering of interactional contexts and relationships which are inherently difficult to plan and to cultivate, doubly so as long as Xish-imbeddedness in Yish-dominated everyday sociocultural processes remains uninterrupted. It was the very ability of the new Zionist settlements to break away from their dependence on all other Jewish and non-Jewish norms and associations, both in the diaspora and in Palestine itself, that made it possible for them to create home-family-neighborhood (= settlement) contexts in which their preferred Xish was protected and could finally attain intergenerational roots. It was only thereafter that efforts to hebraize others and higher sociocultural processes were successfully focused upon. On the other hand, Eliezer ben Yehuda, who had focused upon such higher-order processes from the very outset (c.1890) was distinctly unsuccessful in vernacularizing Hebrew, regardless of the subsequent symbolic mythologization of ben Yehuda in that very connection.

16.4.3   A glance at a few selected cases

Table 16.4 presents data on the standing of a baker's dozen of RLS cases with respect to their present GIDS status. These cases are drawn from three continents (North America, Europe and Asia/Pacific; for Latin American and African cases see Fishman, 2001) and include both indigenous and immigrant groups. Both the right- and the leftmost columns of Part A of the table consist primarily of the GIDS stages that were presented in table 16.3 above, and that have provided the basis of most of the foregoing discussion. The only addition to the table proper is the notation IC (ideological clarification), which has been

Table 16.4 Graded Intergenerational Dislocation Stages (GIDS) in thirteen monitored RLS settings.

Abbreviations: AA = Australian Aborigines (selected cases), AIR = Australian Immigrant (post WW2), B = Basque, C = Catalan, FQ = Francophone Quebec, F = Frisian, H = Hebrew, I = Irish, M = Maori, NR = Navajo (selected reservation community 1), S = Spanish: New York City Puerto Ricans, YO = Yiddish Ultra-Orthodox (NYC), YS = Yiddish Secular (NYC); IC = Ideological clarification; Numbers = GIDS stages (X = stage[s] currently receiving most attention in RLS-efforts); Ts = Total dislocation score.

#	AA	AIR	B	C	FQ	F	H	I	M	NR	S	YO	YS	#
1			X	X	X		X							1
2		X	X	X		X		X						2
3			X	X								X		3
4b						X			X		X			4b
4a	X	X	X					X		X		X		4a
5									X				X	5
6*	+–	–	–	+	+	–	+	–	–	+–	+–	+	–	6*
7	X	X				X		X	X	X	X		X	7
8	X		X					X	X				X	8
IC*	+–	+	+	+	+	+	+–	+–	+–	+–	+–	+–	+–	IC*
Ts**	19	13	18	6	1	13	1	21	24	11	11	7	20	Ts**
	AA	AIR	B	C	FQ	F	H	I	M	NR	S	YO	YS	

* Average Ts for – or +– at stage 6: 15.75; at IC: 14.13
Average Ts for + at stage 6: 3.75; at IC: 10.20

** Languages ranked by the *sum* of their GIDS scores (Ts):

	+ on 6		+ on IC
1 = FQ, H	X	X	X
6 = C	X		X
7 = YO (NYC)	X		
10 = S (NYCPR)			
11 = NR			
13 = AIR, F			X X
18 = B			X
19 = AA			
20 = YS (NYC)			
21 = 1			
24 = M			

scored on a three-point scale (+, +−, −) reflecting the availability of positive ideological consensuality within the 13 studied RLS circles today. The total GIDS score (referred to as Ts) for each case consists of the grand total of all of the numbers representing stages at which major RLS efforts are concentrated today on behalf of that case. Higher total scores indicate efforts that are still focused on societally more basic dislocated stages. The highest (most dislocated) scores are obtained for Maori, Irish, Yiddish in secularist circles in New York City, and selected Australian Aboriginal "outstation" cases. The lowest (least dislocated) scores are obtained for Hebrew in Israel, French in Quebec, Catalan in the Autonomous Catalan Community (Catalunya), and Yiddish in Ultra-Orthodox circles in New York. Another way of estimating the current relative positions of these 13 communities is by examining their mean GIDS scores. The correlation between the total GIDS score and the mean GIDS score is .79, confirming that the Ts is not merely an artifact of the number and variety of efforts involved.

It is quite clear from Part A of table 16.4 (5–IC) that there are some cases significantly involved in efforts above the "continental divide" that are, nevertheless, still in a poor state of health with respect to their overall RLS status, e.g. Irish and Basque. There are also (and even more obviously) a few cases where there is little if any ideological focus (IC) on RLS which are doing relatively well with respect to their overall RLS standing, e.g. Navaho (selected reservation) and Ultra-Orthodox Yiddish in New York. Part B of table 16.4 (I–4a) reveals that the consideration that really seems to distinguish between cases doing well and cases doing less well or poorly, as far as RLS is concerned, is whether stage 6 (home-neighborhood-community) is substantially under self-regulatory RLS auspices.

The average total GIDS score for the four cases in which this is so is 3.75, whereas the average total GIDS score for the nine cases in which it is not so is 15.75. The difference in total GIDS scores between cases with and without positive ideological consensuality is less impressive (10.20 vs. 14.13), although it too is clearly in the right direction (detailed information concerning all 13 cases in the early 1990s can be found in Fishman, 1991 and, for the early 2000s, in Fishman, 2001). Current ambivalence regarding the importance of Hebrew in Israel (particularly in comparison with the nearly universal rejection of any corresponding "Xmen-via-Xish" position among francophones in Quebec or among Catalans in the Autonomous Catalan Community) is attributable to a growing philosophical pluralism on this issue, a pluralism which can be attributed to the post-struggle phase which Xish has now achieved there. The IC analysis clearly implies that even an RLS-engineered ideological consensus (by no means the same as spontaneous "positive attitudes" or "positive motivation" relative to Xish) is of clearly lesser RLS importance than establishing Xish supremacy vis-à-vis the societal processes of everyday home-family-community life.

Obviously, table 16.4 does not try to show the historical development that has occurred with respect to the RLS statuses of the speech communities involved. Clearly, it deals only with the reasonably current situations in each case. A series of such tables, decade by decade from the beginning of the twentieth century, would unambiguously reveal which cases have advanced, which have regressed, and which have remained stationary with respect to their RLS statuses. I have attempted to present the relevant information precisely for one such analysis and to do so in a less compressed non-tabular (that is, in narrative) form in Fishman, 1991.

16.5   Concluding and Summary Observations

Our discussion has tried to help clarify why "geographic" considerations, "absolute size" considerations, and attitudinal/motivational considerations cannot be considered to be either conceptually or analytically fruitful, or, indeed, manipulably rewarding, dimensions in connection with understanding RLS differentials. Letzeburgisch, the vernacular of Luxembourg, is "next door" to (indeed, surrounded by) two world languages, French and German, both of which are even part of the very Xish identity-and-behavior pattern that Letzeburgisch itself serves to clinch. Furthermore, Letzeburgisch mother-tongue speakers constitute a rather small speech community and one which gives its mother tongue rather little explicit ideological attention. Rather than fixating on the former non-manipulable intragroup considerations we have tended to emphasize intergroup processes and a search for manipulable "planning" considerations. Nevertheless, a number of ambiguities and dilemmas must be recognized as plaguing or rendering extremely difficult the pursuit of RLS. Even ameliorative efforts that are well understood, correctly sequenced and interrelated via feedback efforts are not thereby necessarily successful, but the pursuit of folk notions, the lack of strong linkages to the crucial stage 6 and the childish belief that "doing anything" (or "a little bit of everything," even if in random order) is necessarily better for RLS than "doing nothing" are all definitely contraindicated. They only serve to squander time, resources and trust, commodities that are in short supply and that need to be wisely used and husbanded.

Intergenerational RLS may safely focus on the school, on the place of worship or on the workplace if specific non-mother-tongue functions are being aimed at. However, if intergenerational mother-tongue transmission is being aimed at, there is no parsimonious substitute for focusing on the home-family-neighborhood-community processes which bind together adults and children (most frequently, but not only, grandparents and grandchildren and parents and children) in early bonds of intergenerational and spontaneous affect, intimacy, identity, and loyalty. This is not to say that this arena is itself sufficient to guarantee that mother-tongue-oriented RLS efforts focused upon it will succeed, but it is to say that RLS control of this arena is necessary, a *sine qua non* for such success. Subsequent stages can provide RLS with additional latitude and instrumental feedback reinforcement. Long before diglossic arrangements are fully transcended there are types of schooling (particularly types 5 and 4a) that can support this arena materially and with only meager dependence on Yish regulation, approval, or support. Thereafter, Xish with a firm, demographically concentrated community base can increasingly pursue economic and even political co-regulatory power. As one would have hoped, a proper theory of RLS is also a useful theory of language maintenance and, in this way, our analysis has now come full circle. (For additional discussion of language maintenance and shift, see chapters 14, 15, 18, 25, 26, and 28; for more on language endangerment, see chapters 15, 17, 18, 25, 27, and 28.)

REFERENCES

Fishman, Joshua A. (1964). Language maintenance and language shift as a field of inquiry. *Linguistics*, 9, 32–70.

Fishman, Joshua A. (1967). *Language Loyalty in the United States*. The Hague: Mouton.

Fishman, Joshua A. (1990). What is Reversing Language Shift and how can it succeed? *Journal of Multilingual and Multicultural Development*, 11, 5–36.

Fishman, Joshua A. (1991). *Reversing Language Shift: Theory and Practice of Assistance to Threatened Languages*. Clevedon, UK: Multilingual Matters. (See chapter 12, "The intergenerational transmission of 'additional' languages for special purposes," for an analysis of the intergenerational transmission of non-mother tongues; chapter 13 "Limitations on school-effectiveness in connection with mother tongue transmission" for a discussion of the societal prerequisites for school effectiveness in the RLS process.)

Fishman, Joshua A. (1997). *In Praise of the Beloved Language: A Comparative View of Positive Ethnolinguistic Consciousness*. Berlin: Mouton de Gruyter.

Fishman, Joshua A. (ed.) (2001). *Can Threatened Languages be Saved?* Clevedon, UK: Multilingual Matters.

Fishman, Joshua A. and Solano, Frank R. (1990). Civil strife and linguistic heterogeneity/homogeneity: An empirical examination. *Canadian Review of Studies in Nationalism*, 17, 131–46.

Hamel, Ranier Enrique (ed.) (1997). Linguistic human rights from a sociolinguistic perspective. *International Journal of the Sociology of Language*, no. 127, entire issue.

Hart, Stephen (2001). *Cultural Dilemmas of Progressive Politics: Styles of Engagement Among Grassroots Activists*. Chicago: University of Chicago Press.

Kloss, Heinz (1977). *The American Bilingual Tradition*. Rowley, MA: Newbury House.

Kymlicka, Will (1995). *Multicultural Citizenship: A Liberal Theory of Minority Rights*. Oxford: Clarendon Press.

Schiffman, Harold F. (1996). *Linguistic Culture and Language Policy*. New York: Routledge.

Skutnabb-Kangas, Tove and Phillipson, Robert (eds.) (1995). *Linguistic Human Rights: Overcoming Linguistic Discrimination*. Berlin: Mouton de Gruyter.

Topolinska, Elizaveta (ed.) (1998). Sociolinguistics in the Republic of Macedonia. *International Journal of the Sociology of Language*, no. 131, entire issue.

17 Minority and Endangered Languages

NANCY C. DORIAN

17.1 Introduction

Languages regarded as endangered are in most cases the languages of minority peoples within the state where the population in question lives. While the languages of some minority peoples have official status of some kind in the state or in a particular region of the state, as do French in Canada, Catalan in Spain, and Assamese in India, far more of the world's minority languages have no official standing of any kind. The consequences, for speakers of languages without official status, amount to a sharp power differential, both linguistic and social. Government, the legal system, education, print media and broadcasting are conducted largely or wholly in other languages. Insofar as mother-tongue speakers of a minority language without official status hope to be served by those activities or to participate in them, they must either speak an additional language or have the assistance of bilingual intermediaries.

   How a minority population and its language stand in relation to the official language(s) varies greatly from region to region, reflecting a particular local history of contact and of national policy. Many groups become minorities through migration into an area where another group and their language are dominant. If enough people make the migration and they are able to achieve some settlement density, they may be able to maintain their original language in the new location for a shorter or longer time. Some minority peoples represent an established population which was always small and localized, around which a modern nation-state came into being without much direct contact being effected between state institutions and the original inhabitants, as in the Amazon basin, say, or in parts of Papua New Guinea. But a great many present-day minority peoples have had higher populations, a wider territorial base, and/or more autonomy at some previous time and have become minorities through a process of subordination involving conquest or political reorganization. Movement in the opposite direction also occurs, of course, even when, as in the present day, the ideological climate deeply favors the nation-state and its officially promoted language(s): some peoples long relegated to minority-group status achieve more autonomy or even full independence, with a corresponding rise in the status of their language, as has happened in recent times with the people of Greenland (greater autonomy) and their language and with the people of Slovenia (independence) and their language. With only something over two hundred nations presently in existence, however, and with most of them intent on maintaining the territorial and political status quo, it seems clear that most of the world's 6,000 or so languages, insofar as they survive at all, will remain the languages of peoples who are minorities within a relatively small number of nation-states.

Under conditions of steadily expanding communication and transport networks and of ongoing economic and cultural globalization, genuine geographic and social isolation can only grow rarer in coming decades. The outlook for endangered minority languages is linked to the willingness of minority peoples to sustain the bi- or multilingualism that characterizes many of them now or to cultivate it deliberately in those cases where the ancestral language has become the valued possession only of the elderly. Such willingness is as much a matter of ideology and cultural values as of objective factors like population size, a viable economy, or political autonomy. Because minority peoples are subordinate peoples, furthermore, the ideologies of the dominant group are fully as important to the outcome as those of the minorities themselves.

17.2   Monolingualism vs. Bi- or Multilingualism in the Absence of a Nation-state

Monolingualism, now usually considered the unmarked condition by members of the dominant linguistic group in modern nation-states, was in all likelihood less prevalent before the rise of the nation-state gave special sanction to it (see section 17.3). But it was not unknown in pre-state settings where, for example, geographical isolation and/or a reasonably large population buffered a group from frequent contact with other peoples. Such groups would typically have had some members, even in the most demographically central areas, who became bilingual or multilingual for the purpose of representing the group in contacts with other populations as negotiators of some kind (in trade, in alliance building, in assertion of political claims, and so forth), while other group members residing in demographically central areas might well have remained monolingual. At the borders of a large-group territory, however, where members came into more frequent contact with populations speaking other languages, the number of bilinguals and multilinguals would increase. Population size typically had an effect on which group had the greater number of border-area bilinguals. If one of two neighboring peoples was smaller in size, members of the smaller population were more likely to acquire the large-group language than vice versa, though each group would have included bilingual members. This is the general linguistic situation reconstructed, for example, for the larger and smaller peoples of the Papua New Guinea Highlands in contact with each other in the period before contact with people of European descent (Sankoff, 1980, pp. 108–9). Where interaction among a variety of peoples was very frequent, bi- or multilingualism was also more widespread. This seems to have been the norm, for example, in much of Aboriginal Australia and in parts of sub-Saharan Africa, and it is still the prevailing condition among some groups in both settings.

Where a number of languages coexisted interactively within a particular region, hierarchies of power and prestige often existed among the languages, reflecting hierarchies of power and prestige among the various groups who spoke them. One factor in the establishment of such hierarchies was demography, as the Highland Papua New Guinea instance suggests: larger peoples had an obvious advantage, since they were better able to assert their control via warfare or political domination. Abundance of natural resources could also play a role. In one interconnected island complex in Micronesia, the resource-rich high-volcanic island of Yap constituted the center of a tribute system that involved a great many outlying island groups made up of coral atolls. Distance from Yap corresponded to place in the social and political hierarchy of islands, so that the most outlying atoll groups ranked lowest while those closest to Yap ranked highest. The origins of Yap dominance are not now entirely certain, but access to resources available only on Yap (e.g. timber, certain spices and foods) and fear of Yapese sorcery seem to have sustained the system, remembered and resented even now by islanders from the outlying atoll groups, despite the fact that it ceased to operate more than a hundred years ago (Flinn, 1992, pp. 21–3).

17.3 Bilingualism and Multilingualism Within Nation-state Settings

The establishment of a nation-state typically confers distinct advantages on a select language or set of languages, namely any language(s) adopted as official by the state or acknowledged as the official language(s) of a particular province within the state. Until quite recent years (and indeed in a good many areas still) the best that speakers of other languages could hope for was a benign neglect of their language, while non-benign treatment ran the gamut from denial of the existence of a particular language and its speakers, through the labeling of a particular language as inferior and of its speakers as socially or intellectually limited, to the active suppression – including killing, in the worst cases – of speakers of some minority languages.

Disparities in factors such as population size, access to resources, and control of trade are fully as important in nation-state settings as in non-state settings, since advantages in these spheres are often important to establishing a viable state in the first place. A uniquely significant disparity in the nation-state context, however, is precisely that primary institutional and social status is reserved exclusively for whatever language(s) the state espouses officially. Where the state promotes a particular language as the sole legitimate linguistic medium of national identity and state authority, that language typically moves to an unchallenged place at the pinnacle of a hierarchy of utility and prestige among all the languages that may be spoken within the state boundaries.

In most cases this concentration on a single favored language works to the disadvantage of all other languages, for which neither comparably high regard nor institutional support will be available. If minority populations in such settings either find by experience or come to believe that the official state language confers major advantages in terms of access to schooling, employment, political participation, and state services, the psychological ground for a language shift may be prepared. Parents who suffered social penalties or educational and occupational disadvantage through limited knowledge of the official language during their own youth may reach a decision not to transmit the ancestral language to their children. Reports of conscious blocking of home-language transmission are commonplace in the literature of language endangerment and shift, e.g. for Scottish Gaelic, for Pennsylvania German, and for Tlingit (Dorian, 1981, pp. 104–5; Huffines, 1989, p. 225; and Dauenhauer and Dauenhauer, 1998, pp. 64–66, respectively). Unconscious blocking also occurs. Parents in one Papua New Guinea language community, for example, expressed disappointment that their children were not speaking Taiap, the traditional language. But when the parents' actual speech behavior with their young children was closely observed, they turned out to be switching to Tok Pisin, a creole increasingly used as a lingua franca in Papua New Guinea, when they addressed their children, even though they generally used Taiap when speaking to one another (Kulick, 1992). Blocked minority-language transmission can produce majority-language monolingualism within as little as two generations, though three is the commoner pattern. In the latter case, the first of the three generations is either monolingual in the ancestral language or ancestral-language dominant, the second is highly bilingual but more likely to be majority-language dominant, and the third is monolingual in the majority-group language (with or without purely passive bilingualism in the ancestral language).

Because shift away from a limited-currency minority language to a wider-currency state-promoted language occurs with considerable frequency, it is sometimes asserted that bilingualism is essentially a practical matter, governed by social or economic necessity. On a very elemental level there is a good deal of truth to this. Acquisition and maintenance of more than one language arises from a contact between peoples that is frequent enough to make it useful for members of at least one group to speak the language of the other group(s). But stronger positions, such as the assertion that people "will not indefinitely maintain two languages when one will serve across all domains" (Edwards, 1994, p. 110), are too extreme, since this would suggest that bilingualism is not long sustained in settings where a lingua franca is in wide use, or in settings where all or very nearly all members of a community are fully bilingual in the language of some other group. Sustained bilingualism can be found in both types of setting, but – tellingly – relatively seldom among people of European origin.

17.4   The Nation-state and European Language Ideologies

Embrace of the nation-state in the modern era has gone hand-in-hand with embrace of a one-language, one-nation ideology. This ideological construct is generally associated with French and German philosophers of the eighteenth century and linked with policies that took shape in France during the closing decade of the eighteenth century, after the Revolution of 1789 (Grillo, 1989, pp. 22–42; Woolard, 1998, pp. 16–17). At that time the longstanding and previously unremarkable existence within the French polity of substantial subcommunities who neither spoke nor understood French came to be viewed as unacceptable. The unity of the new revolutionary state was henceforth to be expressed via a common language, replacing the linguistic heterogeneity that in the revolutionary view had served the purposes of a discredited monarchy by preventing various segments of the country's population from making common cause with one another. The Alsatians, the Basques, the Bretons, and the Occitanians would come to feel their national unity and would express it, according to revolutionary tenets, by adopting the use of the French language. Certain characteristically European ideological positions were given expression in the implementation of this policy. A single language variety associated with people of high social position (the king and his court, in this case) was accorded fixed form and unique authority through standardization, and a monopoly of legitimacy and prestige was conferred on that single form. In the resultant linguistic hierarchy, the unstandardized language varieties of politically and socially subordinate peoples within the state underwent a parallel attitudinal subordination and were subjected to what has been termed an "ideology of contempt" (Grillo, 1989, pp. 173–4).

A small but highly suggestive study has found an ideological position that similarly favors linguistic homogeneity still prevailing in the expression of European nationalism at the present day (Blommaert and Verschueren, 1998). Coverage of the perceived role of language in nationalist ideologies, as reflected in editorials and news stories that appeared in mainstream Western European newspapers and magazines published in Germany, France, the Netherlands, and England (with the International Herald Tribune also included, representing the USA) was closely monitored during the first weeks of November 1990, a time when ethnic/nationalist conflicts were particularly prominent and were much discussed, as were associated questions of asylum and immigration. The media data revealed a very considerable degree of popular consensus on the desirability of homogeneity, with the ideal model of society taken to be not only monolingual but also monoethnic, monoreligious, and monoideological.

This European ideological bias in favor of monolingualism has been detected not only in popular opinion but even within the canonical texts of sociolinguistics and the sociology of language. Sociologist Glyn Williams (himself a Welsh-English bilingual) identifies a none-too-subtle evolutionary viewpoint in these texts, according to which traditional societies are characterized by linguistic diversity and multilingualism, while modern societies move steadily ("progress," in the terms of this viewpoint) toward a single official language and monolingualism. Within this framework, Williams points out, "the elimination of minority languages is a natural, evolutionary process" (1992, p. 100). Williams objects to what he considers an identification of monolingualism with rationality, as in Edwards's notion that it is in effect irrational to maintain two languages when one will serve for all purposes ("across all domains"). Edwards's position represents what has generally been the mainstream European viewpoint,[1] however, and it is useful when assessing accounts of minority peoples' multilingualism to recall that nearly all such accounts have been produced by Europeans (or by their heritors in settings colonized by Europeans), most of them speakers of highly standardized national languages of European origin.

While the study of minority peoples and their language choices has made the pattern of shift from a minority language to a majority-group language familiar, this pattern is more likely to occur under some circumstances than others. Paulston notes, for example, that the opposite pattern, sustained group-wide bilingualism, is unusual only under particular conditions, namely when the modern nation-state is the setting and when both socioeconomic incentives and access to the dominant language are present:

> Maintained group bilingualism is unusual, *if* opportunity of access to the dominant language is present and incentives, especially socioeconomic, motivate a shift to the dominant language. If not, as with India's former caste system and ascribed status, the result is language maintenance. But given access and incentive, the norm for groups in prolonged contact within a modern nation-state is for the subordinate group to shift to the language of the dominant group, either over several hundred years as with Gaelic in Great Britain or over the span of three generations as has been the case of the European immigrants to Australia and the United States in a very rapid shift. (Paulston, 1994, pp. 12–13; emphasis in original)

---

1   In the same chapter, expanding on his claim that bilingualism is sustained only so long as it has practical – chiefly economic – value, Edwards quotes directly from my work (Dorian, 1982, p. 47) in a way that makes it appear as though I were in agreement with his position (Edwards, 1994, p. 116). It is the unfortunate omission of a lead-in sentence and a following sentence, both strongly qualifying the quoted material, that gives rise to that misleading impression.

Within nation-states the frequency of shift to an official national language when access and socioeconomic incentives are present is undeniable and underlies what many see as a language-endangerment crisis. Furthermore, this shift pattern appears to be growing in geographical distribution as well as in frequency, lending a sense of urgency to discussions about threats to linguistic diversity world-wide.

In spite of the frequency and seeming ubiquity of shift from a minority-group language to an official majority language, however, it should not be considered an inevitable or "natural" pattern. The conditions and ideologies which give rise to it do not universally hold sway, as recurrent reports by fieldworkers in various parts of the world demonstrate.

17.5 Environments Favorable to Bi- and Multilingualism

Environments that favor the maintenance of multiple languages are not difficult to find, but they are reported largely from non-European cultural contexts where quite different language ideologies prevail. Since as noted the reporters are in most cases members of Western societies, there is sometimes a striking contrast between the expectations of the Western investigator and the linguistic situation encountered and described. This is the case, for example, with a 1998 field report by English researcher Roger Blench on two languages that he searched out during a field trip in Plateau State, northern Nigeria. He found the Niger-Kordofanian language Horom spoken in one main village by a maximum of perhaps 1,500 people, while the inhabitants of nearly all the other villages in the area spoke varieties of a Chadic language called Kulere. He described the Horom people as "extremely multilingual," since they reported themselves to be fluent in Kulere as well as Horom and also in Rindre, another Niger-Kordofanian language, and still more significantly in Hausa, an important and very widely spoken Chadic language of northern Nigeria and the Niger Republic. Kulere and Rindre are both spoken by larger populations than is Horom (Rindre by a considerably larger population), while Hausa has many millions of first-language speakers in Nigeria and the Niger Republic and also increasingly serves as a lingua franca in West Africa. Blench was surprised, by his own account, to find that Horom did not appear to be an endangered language: children present during his language elicitation session "were able to produce the required lexical items simultaneously with the adults" (Blench, 1998, p. 10). He suggested that remoteness might have acted as a buffer in the maintenance of Horom, though he acknowledged that remoteness had not sufficed to keep Chadic languages in the Bauchi area of Nigeria from disappearing. He remarked, too, on the cultural vitality of the Horom people, whose traditional religion, pottery, weaving, and music he found likewise to persist strongly.

The linguistic tenacity of another small and isolated Niger-Kordofanian-speaking people in Plateau State, the residents of Tapshin village, struck Blench still more strongly. He gives the following account of their vigorous Nsur language:

> On the face of it, Nsur should be a prime candidate for language loss. All adults appear to be fluent in Ngas and Hausa and Tapshin is an enclave within the Ngas, a numerous population speaking a Chadic language, by whom they are culturally dominated. The number of speakers [of Nsur] cannot be more than 3–4,000. . . . However it was apparent during the interviews that even young children are learning the language and there is no evidence of a decline in competence. Even more surprisingly, but no doubt related, the language is by no means full of loanwords from Hausa and Ngas.   (1998, p. 11)

The explicit surprise expressed by Blench on encountering this situation can serve as a reflection of the Western ideological perspective on what might be called "unnecessary" multilingualism, or, following Lewis, "irrational" multilingualism.

The matter-of-factly maintained multilingualism of these two small peoples is not unduly exceptional, however, in that general part of the world. Routine multilingualism is reported also among the peoples of the Mandara Mountains at the border between northeastern Nigeria and Cameroon, for example (MacEachern, forthcoming). Men belonging to one or another montagnard group typically speak three or four different languages, including their own and that of the closest neighboring group, plus at least one language spoken on the plains below the mountains; women usually speak almost as many. MacEachern traces the ethnic and linguistic complexity of the Mandara Mountains peoples to an uncoordinated but steady movement, over the past five centuries, of various smaller peoples from the plains into the mountains as they attempted to avoid conquest by larger peoples and to escape capture by slave-traders. He notes that multilingualism has been a factor in negotiating temporary alliances that made it possible for montagnard communities to take military action against plains-dwelling peoples, and that as recently as the late 1980s fluent bilingualism in a neighboring language made it feasible for one montagnard people to avoid coming under the political control of the Wandala, the locally dominant plains-dwelling people, by claiming close affiliation with another montagnard group that was successfully contesting a Wandala claim to hegemony in a Cameroon court case. MacEachern makes the point that a people's use of a particular language is not necessarily a given – that is, a purely passive matter of the group one is born into. Rather, in areas of ethnic complexity and multilingualism linguistic relationships and the identities that they signal can be consciously manipulated to particular sociopolitical effect. In response to centuries of attempts at controlling them, "montagnards have used their language abilities and the cultural complexity that goes along with those abilities to erect alliances and maintain their own independence in a dangerous political environment" (MacEachern, 2002). Occasions for deploying multilingualism as a social and political resource have appeared with enough frequency in the Mandara Mountains setting to sustain a pattern of acquisition and maintenance of multiple languages over a period of five hundred years.

Africa, of course, is a part of the world where the territories which later became nations were brought into being by European colonial powers concerned with establishing the geographical bounds of their own control. No consideration was given to ethnolinguistic distributions within or across the boundaries created, and in consequence most African states south of the Sahara were multilingual and multicultural at their creation. In the absence of any single language community with numerical or social dominance great enough to support a claim to official-language status, many remain so today. Continuing use of the former colonial language, often as a lingua franca for urban populations or the educated elite, then adds another layer to the multilingualism.

17.6 Obligatory Exogamy and Multilingualism

Extreme multilingualism is a well-recognized phenomenon where obligatory exogamous marriage practices prevail: members of any one of a number of language communities in a particular region can contract marriages only with members of a different language community. Among the Hua, a people of the Eastern Highlands of Papua New Guinea, Haiman reported for example that the immemorial practice of women going to live in the village of a husband who must come from a group speaking a different language

> has made the community phenomenally multilingual. In a survey of 359 adult speakers in 1974, it was found that [in addition to speaking Hua] 305 were fluent in Gimi, 287 in Siane, and 103 in Chimbu. A smaller number of people spoke at least half a dozen other languages. Only two respondents claimed to be totally monolingual, and only eleven knew only one other language besides Hua. All the others spoke at least two, and many were fluent and at ease in four or five. (Haiman, 1987, p. 36)

The differences among the languages in question are not by any means minor dialectal features. According to Haiman, Gimi, Siane, and Chimbu are impressionistically as different from Hua as French, German, and Russian are from English.

Similar patterns of exogamous marriage and resultant multilingualism among all or nearly all group members have been reported from the Vaupés region of the Amazon basin and from Burma. A linguist working in Burma tells of meeting exogamous Kachin in Burma "who can converse happily in at least half a dozen languages, with native knowledge of three or more," though he relates their profound multilingualism more particularly to a low place in the regional linguistic hierarchy, noting that speakers of another low-position language (Lisu) can be equally multilingual (Bradley, 2001, p. 155).

17.7   Profound Multilingualism and the Native-Speaker Concept

Among males in the Mandara Moutains, MacEachern speaks of "variable command" of three or four languages. But another account of routine multi-lingualism from West Africa indicates that the multilingualism in question can be profound indeed, even to the point of making the concept "native language" moot. In an unusual dual presentation of the fieldwork experience, linguist Fiona Mc Laughlin offers her own account of work on noun classes in three Niger-Congo languages of Senegal – Wolof, Pulaar, and Seereer – side by side with a parallel account from her principal Pulaar teacher, Thierno Seydou Sall (Mc Laughlin and Sall, 2001). At one point Mc Laughlin declined an offer from Sall, whom she had found to be a natural linguist with remark-able ability to analyze the structure of Pulaar, to work on the noun classes of Wolof with her, in addition to their work on the Pulaar noun classes, because she categorized him as a native speaker of Pulaar. Sall gives this account of the interaction:

> I grew up in a Seereer village in a Haalpulaar family, so when I was a small child I spoke Pulaar and Seereer better than Wolof, but even then I cannot remember ever not having known Wolof. When I was fourteen I went to Dakar where my Wolof improved, and then I spent five years in Kayor, the heart of Wolof coun-try, where pure Wolof is spoken. By pure Wolof I mean Wolof with very little French in it. Fiona thought that I could not give her the noun classes in Wolof, but for me, it would be the same thing as giving them to her in Pulaar.   (2001, p. 207)

Sall notes that because he speaks the "deep Wolof" of the heartland he knows the noun classes of Wolof better than a good many Wolofs who live in towns and cities, where they mix with non-Wolofs a great deal, and that he therefore sometimes corrects Wolof people's Wolof, including their noun classes.

Mc Laughlin, reflecting on her experience with multilingual Senegalese like Sall in the Sahelian town of Fatick, where she lived and worked for a year and where Sall lived as part of a large traditional family, revised her notion of what it meant to be a native speaker of a language:

> [G]iven my experience with native Pulaar and Seereer speakers who spoke fluent Wolof, and learning that many of them could not remember a time when they did not speak Wolof, the very notion of a 'native speaker of Wolof' was thrown into question. I had rejected grammatical judgments on Wolof from Thierno because he was a native Pulaar speaker, but could not he, or others like him, also

be native speakers of Wolof? In this context, could it not be possible to have more than one native language? Although at the time I did not hold these views, I now think that the urban-rural distinction in Wolof is a much more salient variable in distinguishing between varieties of the language than whether the Wolof speaker has another mother tongue, such as Seereer or Pulaar.   (2001, p. 202)

Mc Laughlin is not the only linguist of European descent to have allowed fieldwork practices to be constrained by the notion that an individual has one, and only one, native language. A similar case is reported from Australia, where a researcher realized belatedly that he had probably let precious chances to gather data on an endangered Aboriginal language slip away because he did not take the opportunity to work with profoundly fluent speakers who were officially native speakers of some other Aboriginal language (cited in Evans, 2001, pp. 255–6). The passage from Bradley quoted above is notable in attributing "native knowledge" of three or more languages to multilingual Kachin speakers. Bradley does not say whether he did or would accept such speakers as full-fledged data sources for more than one language, but just such work needs to be done by way of plumbing the full capacities of profoundly multilingual individuals.

17.8   Ideological Aspects of Sustained Bi- and Multilingualism

Apart from the considerable practical benefits bi- or multilingualism may confer (with exogamous marriages and manipulable identities included among such practical benefits), additional benefits that qualify at least in part as ideological are recognized among peoples who have traditionally cultivated knowledge of more than one language. Among some such peoples, multilingual skills are regarded as a sign of intellectual or cultural superiority. In the same general area of the New Guinea Highlands where Hua is spoken, a variety of Siane known as Komunku was spoken by people whose neighbors spoke a variety of Dene. While members of the Emenyo tribe spoke Komunku and often spoke Dene as well, Dene speakers less frequently spoke Komunku. An anthropologist who worked with Emenyo in the 1950s and 1960s summed up Emenyo attitudes as follows (Salisbury, 1972 [1962], p. 56):

> The fact that there are more Emenyo bilingual in Dene, than Dene-speakers who are bilingual in Komunku is not associated with any feeling among the Emenyo that they are politically less important or that their language is inferior to Dene. Bilingualism is treated as a desirable accomplishment and their command of Dene makes them, if anything, superior to the Dene.

Salisbury reported that Emenyo "actively cultivate bilingualism," noting that when a group of laborers who had acquired pidgin during indentured service at the coast returned to Emenyo village, they immediately began giving the rest of the village males pidgin lessons. Pidgin was of course already a language of potentially unique utility, in the 1960s, because of its role as a lingua franca; but Salisbury reported further that two Emenyo youths took advantage of the availability of a Gahuku speaker who had come to the village in Salisbury's employ to set about learning some of this more easterly language from the same family as Komunku. The presence of a catechist who came from a different language group was similarly used as an occasion for acquiring knowledge of religious materials in the catechist's language, and songs seemed almost universally to be learned and publicly sung in a variety of foreign languages (1972, pp. 56–7). Prestige attached to knowledge of other languages generally.

A well-informed account of Arizona Tewa attitudes toward the acquisition of other languages indicates that they held views similar to those of the Emenyo. The small Arizona Tewa population "enjoyed a reputation for commanding multiple languages" and attained fluency in English earlier than did the Hopi, among whom the Arizona Tewa have been enclaved since finding refuge there following their flight from the Pueblo area of present-day New Mexico after the second Pueblo revolt against the Spanish in 1696 (Kroskrity, 1993, pp. 23, 8–9). Kroskrity's extensive ethnographic work persuaded him that the Arizona Tewa viewed a knowledge of Hopi and Navajo as instrumentally valuable (Hopi as the language of the society within which they were enclaved, and Navajo as a trade language), and of course knowledge of English (and formerly Spanish) had obvious instrumental value as well. But he noted that there was in addition a notion of cultural superiority involved, especially with regard to the Hopi, most of whom did not acquire Arizona Tewa despite several centuries of immediate proximity: "In the Arizona Tewa case . . . the Tewa view the fact that they speak Hopi but few Hopi speak Tewa as a cultural victory on their part" (Kroskrity, 1993, p. 218).

The conservative and puristic model of speech associated with religious practice in Arizona Tewa life also acts to support language maintenance and supports linguistic compartmentalization as well. Ceremonial "kiva talk" is a variety strictly reserved for religious practice. Its norms are zealously upheld, with any introduction of foreign terms during ceremonials physically punished. Kroskrity sees in the near-total absence, even in ordinary non-ceremonial Arizona Tewa, of lexical borrowings from Spanish, English, and especially Hopi the effect of a general linguistic conservatism rooted in native cultural ideals (1993, pp. 38, 220).

Where the exogamous multilingual Indians of the Vaupés region are concerned, one observer (Sorensen, 1972) described them as having an "instrumental and practical" orientation to multilingualism. But he noted at the same time that multilingualism was actively cultivated, as with the Emenyo, and cultivated furthermore across an entire lifetime despite universal command of a regional lingua franca. Children, typically fluent speakers from their early years of both their mothers' and their fathers' languages and also of Tukano, the regional lingua franca, not only acquired during their adolescence several other languages spoken in the community's longhouse, but might go on to acquire still more in adulthood. Nor did the learning process stop there: "as he [a longhouse resident] approaches old age, field observation indicates, he will go on to perfect his knowledge of all the languages at his disposal" (Sorensen, 1972, p. 86). The degree to which expert knowledge of additional languages was actively pursued indicates an ideological orientation to multilingualism that ultimately transcends the strictly practical level of which Sorensen spoke.

17.9   Receding Multilingualism

Bi- and multilingualism are familiar phenomena in a number of settings around the world. Attitudes toward bi- and multilingual peoples have been various, but they have often been considerably more favorable than has been typical in Western Europe since the eighteenth century (and since then also in parts of the world heavily settled by people of European descent). Over the course of the twentieth century, however, conditions conducive to language shift on the part of minority peoples became more widespread. Many features associated with modernization and national development contributed to this process, such as the improvements in transport and communications that reduced isolation. With reduced isolation came stronger links between a central government and outlying regions. Schools that used a colonial language or an official national language could be more widely introduced; police and army presences could be established in far-flung areas, reducing local autonomy. Traditional lifeways followed by minority peoples were often disrupted, not only by these developments but also by the movement (sometimes government-sponsored) of expanding populations from more developed regions into less crowded rural areas, in a search for new agricultural land or pasturage. Food resources essential to minority peoples' traditional subsistence modes were often reduced or lost by such intrusions, and this was even more true wherever major extractive industries moved into previously isolated regions to exploit such resources as timber, ores, gemstones, or oil. Involuntary relocations of minority peoples (already widely perpetrated in earlier centuries) became easier than ever to carry out. Under all these pressures the ancestral languages of many small peoples either passed out of use altogether or came to be spoken by so few people that they appear likely to pass out of use in the near future.

In some cases linguists or anthropologists working with a people living in one of the multilingual settings described above can shed light on the process by which traditional multilingualism has receded or been lost. In the Vaupés region of Brazil, where multilingualism was associated with exogamous marriage practices, Aikhenvald worked with the last generation to be fluent in Tariana, an Arawakan language spoken where most of the many other languages in use belong to the Tukano language family. She links the beginnings of a breakdown in traditional cultural and linguistic patterns to the coming of Salesian missionaries to the area in the early 1920s. The Salesians considered the traditional multilingualism of the region a pagan practice, according to Aikhenvald, and in their effort to make the local Indians monolingual "('like other civilized people in the world')"[2] they chose to employ only Tukano, the language spoken by the largest number of people. They also relocated Indian settlements closer to mission centers and substituted structures housing nuclear-family units for the traditional longhouses. Participation in the routine multi-lingualism of the longhouses was eliminated by these changes, and because able-bodied Indian men also began to go off to take up paid employment in Brazilian rubber plantations or mining operations, children's exposure to their father's language in particular was reduced. The children of absent fathers might speak other languages more often than Tariana, especially Tukano; fur-thermore, some Portuguese began to enter the mix via men returning from jobs. Within a few generations Tukano and a regional form of Portuguese predominated, with only some elderly people retaining a good knowledge of Tariana (Aikhenvald, 2002).

Among the Arizona Tewa, too, Kroskrity found that the way in which edu-cation was being delivered favored the official language and disfavored the minority language. Many of the young people got their secondary education at boarding schools in which English was not only the sole medium of instruc-tion but also the only common language among Native American young people who came from a variety of southwestern tribes. Socialization of young people by older kinsfolk and other community members was curtailed by this educa-tional experience, and in addition an influential new reference group was formed for the young people, one that consisted of English-speaking age-mates with off-reservation experience. Kroskrity found young people signaling their allegiance to this new reference group by replying in English when their elders spoke to them in Arizona Tewa. The young people had become aware of the economic disadvantages of reservation life and of the possibilities of material advantage elsewhere, through exposure to mass media and also through their time in urban boarding schools. In Kroskrity's view socio-economic factors were primary in motivating young people's increased use of English, but because the actual economic possibilities for young Arizona Tewa in off-reservation settings are extremely limited, he considered it possible that an unrewarding venture into off-reservation employment might ultimately provide an incentive for return to a more traditional reservation life. The future for Arizona Tewa – maintenance or loss – could depend, consequently, on whether the preference for English among young people proved to be a life-cycle phase, with a later reaffirmation of Arizona Tewa traditional values

---

2   Aikhenvald (personal communication, 7 February 2002) heard older Salesian missionar-ies make remarks to this effect in conversation. She notes that a younger generation of Salesians is now active in promoting indigenous languages, but for small language groups such as the Tariana the change in attitude and policy most likely comes too late.

(including the language), or whether it proved to be permanent (Kroskrity, 1993, pp. 103–5).

Post-adolescent decisions to stay in the home area after all, and therefore also to maintain the ancestral language, have in fact been known to change the apparent outlook for a small group and their language. In the 1970s a linguist working in an enclaved village in southern Italy, where a Francoprovençal language had been spoken for more than 500 years, predicted on the basis of his census of bilingual speakers of various ages and also by his observations of language use that Faetar, the local Francoprovençal language, would be dead by the year 2000. The villagers themselves expressed the same opinion. Another linguist, arriving to work in the same village in the 1990s, found the Faeto villagers as bilingual as ever, but she heard them give much the same prediction: Faetar would be dead in twenty years. Because the earlier linguist had done his census by age groups, the second linguist was able to establish that adolescents who were using Italian almost to the exclusion of Faetar in the 1970s were adults using Faetar among themselves and with their children in the 1990s. The adolescents of the 1990s, however, were again using mostly Italian by preference, and their language preference was again giving rise to fears that the language would soon cease to be spoken (Nagy, 2000, pp. 128–9). The most serious threat to Faetar appeared to lie in a gradual shrinkage of village population as more people left in pursuit of greater economic opportunity, a depopulation common to agricultural regions of Italy. Lack of sufficient population to keep the village viable remains a future possibility, therefore, but lack of adolescent speakers as such is to some extent an age-graded phenomenon in Faeto. Awareness of such temporary age-related shift patterns explains Kroskrity's reluctance to predict the future for Arizona Tewa.

17.10   Shift as the Norm, Maintenance as the Exception

In cases such as those of Tariana and Arizona Tewa, in competition with Tukano and Portuguese and with English respectively, major disparities in the currency of competing languages are evident. Tariana had currency only in the traditional longhouses of Indians in the Vaupés area where some individuals had fathers with a Tariana identity; both Tukano and Portuguese by contrast are used by larger numbers of people and across a wider range of geographical and social settings. Arizona Tewa, too, has obviously limited currency by comparison with English. Yet previous generations of Indians in the Vaupés region spoke the lingua franca Tukano without relinquishing their local-currency languages, and the Arizona Tewa were competent speakers of Spanish and of English relatively early, without the much wider currency of those languages estranging them from Arizona Tewa. The new and unfavorable development in such settings is not the acquisition of other languages, including languages of wider currency, but the abandonment of an ancestral language in the process. That is, at the present day extended encounters between minority peoples and dominant-group members are more likely than not to produce subtractive bilingualism, whereas in the past there was more chance that additive bilingualism would be the result.

It is not difficult to understand why members of groups speaking smaller local-currency languages would wish to acquire the wider-currency language of a larger, more prosperous, and relatively dominant people. But a fundamental question that is frequently left unasked is this: why, in view of both the contemporary frequency and the historical frequency of bi- and multilingualism, should speakers of smaller local-currency languages stop speaking their own ancestral languages when they acquire a wider-currency language?

Giving up a limited-currency minority language altogether when taking up a wider-currency language may seem so ordinary a phenomenon as to be unremarkable, but this is in all likelihood an ahistorical notion. Even in Europe it was not expected before the end of the eighteenth century, and outside the European sphere of influence dominant groups were known to tolerate the maintenance of subordinate peoples' languages readily. The Ottoman Turks made no attempt to turn the diverse peoples whom they ruled into Ottoman Turkish speakers, and the Thai kingdom is said to have been equally tolerant of nearly all the many minority languages spoken under its rule (Smalley, 1999, pp. 341–9).

Acquisition of a second (or third or fourth) language need not imply loss of a first language. The ideologies and behaviors of *two* populations are relevant in this matter. Not only do the villagers of Tapshin continue to speak Nsur, even though they also speak Ngas and Hausa, but the numerically and culturally dominant Ngas speakers who surround them apparently have no objection to the continuing use of Nsur in their midst. The relevance of dominant-group attitudes becomes more obvious, perhaps, when the Arizona Tewa case is considered. The Hopi, a somewhat larger population and a well-established one by comparison with the Tewa who took refuge among them, found it acceptable for the Tewa not only to learn Hopi but also to continue to use their original language during the roughly 300 years of their residence on the Hopis' First Mesa. Paradoxically, anglophone America, with an overwhelming numerical dominance and a uniquely secure majority language, exerts serious pressure on the Arizona Tewa (as on all other minority groups) for an assimilation that includes abandonment of the ancestral language as well as adoption of the majority language. Hundreds of years of enclavement among a numerically superior group, and even a degree of Tewa-Hopi intermarriage, did not threaten the survival of the Tewa language during its earlier history in Arizona; yet it is possible that boarding-school education in English is now doing just that.

Greatly increased pressure for a shift to dominant-language monolingualism in many parts of the contemporary world seems likely to rest in part on continuing dissemination, despite the decline of colonialism, of European language ideologies: above all the one-language, one-nation ideology associated with nationalism and the "ideology of contempt" for subordinate peoples, but also European notions that the languages of peoples who exhibit low technological development must necessarily be equally limited, while the languages of peoples who have achieved politically and technologically dominant positions must necessarily be superior linguistic instruments (Dorian, 1998). This self-serving view justifies the established ascendancy of a few "superior" European languages in a post-colonial world still linguistically shaped by European colonialism, while simultaneously rendering the displacement of innumerable "lesser" languages unimportant. Still other elements of European linguistic ideology have been identified in the pressure for monolingualism, for example the notion that acquisition and use of an ancestral minority language early in life is deleterious to full competence in the state-promoted language. As one researcher memorably put it, in connection with the pressure exerted on children from minority groups in far northern Norway, Sweden, and Finland to make as rapid a shift to the national language as possible, "it was believed that a child's head (especially a minority child's head) would not have space for two languages" (Huss, 1999, p. 129). Huss follows other scholars in tracing such attitudes to the influence of seriously flawed bilingualism research that supposedly detected lower intelligence and inferior linguistic and cognitive development among bilingual children, especially the children of late nineteenth-century and early twentieth-century immigrants to the US.[3] Certainly such notions have been communicated to minority-group parents, both among immigrant populations and among indigenous peoples, with some of those who have gone over to raising their children with the majority language explaining their decision in such terms. (For more on the issue of bilingualism and intelligence, see chapters 1, 5, 15, 22, and 23.)

17.11   Ethnolinguistic Vitality Assessment

Since the 1970s ethnolinguistic vitality studies have attempted to account for observed cases of shift or maintenance and to predict how likely a minority population will be to maintain its language or to give it up. Three sets of objective factors were originally the chief focus of evaluative efforts: status factors (economic, social, and sociohistorical factors, and status within and without the group), demographic factors (proportion of the overall population, concentration of the minority population, birthrate, etc.), and institutional support and control factors (use in mass media, education, government services, industry, religion, culture, politics (Allard and Landry, 1994)). If the "surprisingly" vigorous Nsur language is taken as a test case, these factors are clearly

3   Huss (1999, p. 129) cites Peal and Lambert, 1962, pp. 1–2 and Skutnabb-Kangas, 1981, p. 222 in this connection.

inadequate for predictive purposes. The Ngas language was said to be spoken by many more people than Nsur and the Ngas were also described as culturally dominant. Whether Ngas had any institutional support is not evident in Blench's report, but Nsur almost certainly did not. By these measures Nsur speakers ought to be in the process of shift to Ngas, just as Blench expected them to be.

Among the various efforts to refine ethnolinguistic vitality assessment, the approach with perhaps the greatest potential for uncovering the roots of maintenance or shift in a non-Western setting like Tapshin village is the development of a Beliefs on Ethnolinguistic Vitality Questionnaire (Allard and Landry, 1986). This is not to say that an oral version of the questionnaire as such would be a suitable instrument for research in Tapshin and its neighboring villages (an unlikely prospect, since questionnairing is a research procedure that does not always travel well, culturally speaking), but rather that examination of beliefs as a fundamental part of the environment that produces language behaviors might best be able to tap into the underpinnings of Nsur linguistic persistence and of Ngas linguistic tolerance.

17.12   Reactive Language Maintenance and Assertive Language Maintenance

Despite the weight of the many factors that favor language shift, some countercurrents are observable. One pattern of maintenance involves early shift with later reversion to traditional cultural and linguistic behaviors, in the reactive pattern that Kroskrity considered a possibility for Arizona Tewa young people. Initially, contact with the dominant society, especially educational contact, appears to open a route to economic advance. But where minority peoples are visibly distinguishable from members of the dominant group (and have often acquired a distinctive local version of the dominant language besides), job scarcity combined with a lingering racism can limit advancement and assimilation. This is said to have happened already among the Kwak'wala Indians of Vancouver Island: the Kwak'wala young people have shifted entirely to English, but without reaping the material benefits that the shift seemed to promise (Anonby, 1999, p. 35). In a study of the outlook for the survival of New Caledonian vernaculars, Schooling found that Melanesian New Caledonians educated in French with an expectation of job opportunities that did not materialize settled back into traditional life patterns in their villages of origin, where kin networks remained strong and they had kin-based claims on land. Schooling reported disillusionment among young New Caledonians whose parents had emphasized the acquisition of French more than that of the local vernacular, to the point where some young adults were reversing the pattern and consciously speaking the vernacular with their own children even though husband and wife might frequently use French between themselves (Schooling, 1990, pp. 51–2).

Another pattern favoring maintenance can appear when a group succeeds in achieving some measure of hoped-for economic advance, whether through education or through development of resources (e.g. scenic resources for tourism or sport), before shift to a dominant language is complete. Economic success can produce enough psychosocial confidence among still-bilingual speakers to encourage assertion of their ethnolinguistic identity and of the right to use their heritage language more widely, including in education, as has happened in Wales, for example.

Also favorable to ethnic self-assertion are wider recognition of linguistic human rights in some parts of the world and increased communication (especially electronic communication) among widely separated small peoples. Local, regional, or national governments inclined to ignore or mistreat an indigenous group find themselves in the glare of unwelcome publicity when small and seemingly isolated indigenous peoples succeed in attracting support from human rights observers or from a vocal coalition of indigenous peoples.

17.13 Revitalization Efforts on Behalf of Endangered Languages

Languages are sometimes viewed as endangered even when nearly all group members are still speakers. If dominant-group assimilative pressures are seen to be rising while resistance on the part of a minority group would seem to require resources that are not in evidence (such as a large population, a strong ethnolinguistic identity, a viable and locally based means of subsistence), long-term survival of the minority-group language cannot be taken for granted. If a shift has already begun – if young children prefer to use a school-acquired dominant language with one another, for example – the future of the language begins to look questionable. If lack of ancestral-language knowledge reaches into the ranks of young parents who are raising children, the outlook becomes a little darker still.

In a number of shift-prone settings some young parents can be found going against the tide and taking pains to raise their children in and with the minority-group language, as has occurred for example in Scotland and Nova Scotia (Scottish Gaelic), in Finland (Sami), and in Hawaii (Hawaiian). Among these parents accomplished learners are often to be found, either individuals of the relevant ethnic group who were not raised with the ancestral language themselves or outsiders who have married into the ethnic group and learned the traditional ethnic language. Speakers of both sorts value the ethnic language the more for having had to acquire it effortfully, and with infants of their own they progress from being dedicated learners to being dedicated transmitters.

It would take a good many fluent parents deeply devoted to home transmission to produce a numerically significant number of fluent new minority-language speakers, however, and many endangered-language communities turn to schooling, in particular to immersion schooling, for the relatively rapid multiplicative effect it can produce: a handful of dedicated and well-trained teachers, using only the minority-group language in the classroom, can produce scores of new minority-language speakers over a period of several years. Such immersion programs have by now amply demonstrated their success, especially in the cases where primary immersion schooling is followed by secondary immersion schooling.

There are nonetheless limitations to the effectiveness of immersion schooling. Unless there is a good sprinkling of native-speaking home-transmission children in the immersion classroom, the pupils have only one fluent-speaker model available, namely the teacher. They must begin to use the target language themselves before they have had enough exposure to it to acquire its grammatical and phonological structure fully, and before very long their teacher's well-formed utterances make up only a small part of the classroom language model, since they are providing many imperfect models for each other. The resulting school-based version of the minority-group language often differs quite noticeably from the original native-speaker model, partly by showing a good deal of influence from the majority-group language that most of the children speak at home and partly also by the introduction of many newly coined school-register words. Communities differ about the acceptability of this outcome. For some, a reconfigured version of the group's language is preferable to no version at all. For others, a version of the language that the children's grandparents can barely recognize as their own tongue is a very dubious "success."

Few minority-language groups expect or even wish to replace the majority language with their ancestral language. Their goal is rather well-developed dual or multiple language capacities which in the one case offer access to the heritage that is available in and through the ancestral language and in the other case offer participation in at least one broader language community besides. Clearly there is nothing inherent in bi- or multilingualism as cognitive or social phenomena that poses an obstacle to such an outcome. The ideological and political obstacles can be considerable, however, as the issues discussed here indicate. (For more discussion of language maintenance and shift, see chapters 14–16, 18, 25, 26, and 28; for more on reversing language shift, see chapter 16; for more on language endangerment, see chapters 15, 16, 18, 25, 27, and 28.)

REFERENCES

Aikhenvald, Alexandra Y. (2002). Traditional multilingualism and language endangerment. In David Bradley and Maya Bradley (eds.), *Language Maintenance for Endangered* *Languages: An Active Approach*, pp. 24–33. London: Curzon Press.

Allard, Réal, and Landry, Rodrigue. (1986). Subjective ethnolinguistic vitality viewed as a belief system.

Journal of Multilingual and Multicultural Development, 7, 1–12.

Allard, Réal and Landry, Rodrigue (1994). Subjective ethnolinguistic vitality: A comparison of two measures. *International Journal of the Sociology of Language*, 108, 117–44.

Anonby, Stan J. (1999). Reversing language shift: Can Kwak'wala be revived? In Jon Reyhner, Gina Cantoni, Robert N. St. Clair, and Evangeline Parsons Yazzie (eds.), *Revitalizing Indigenous Languages*, pp. 33–52. Flagstaff, AZ: Northern Arizona University.

Blench, Roger (1998). Recent fieldwork in Nigeria: Report on Horom and Tapshin. *Ogmios*, 9, 10–11.

Blommaert, Jan and Verschueren, Jef (1998). The role of language in European nationalist ideologies. In Bambi B. Schieffelin, Kathryn A. Woolard, and Paul V. Kroskrity (eds.), *Language Ideologies: Practice and Theory*, pp. 189–210. New York and Oxford: Oxford University Press.

Bradley, David (2001). Language attitudes: The key factor in language maintenance. In Osamu Sakiyama and Fubito Endo (eds.), *Lectures on Endangered Languages: 2*, pp. 151–60. Kyoto: Endangered Languages of the Pacific Rim.

Dauenhauer, Richard and Dauenhauer, Nora Marks (1998). Technical, emotional, and ideological issues in reversing language shift: Examples from Southeast Alaska. In Lenore A. Grenoble and Lindsay J. Whaley (eds.), *Endangered Languages: Current Issues and Future Prospects*, pp. 57–98. Cambridge, UK: Cambridge University Press.

Dorian, Nancy C. (1981). *Language Death: The Life Cycle of a Scottish Gaelic Dialect*. Philadelphia: University of Pennsylvania Press.

Dorian, Nancy C. (1982). Language loss and maintenance in language contact situations. In Richard D. Lambert and Barbara F. Freed (eds.), *The Loss of Language Skills*, pp. 158–67. Rowley, MA: Newbury House.

Dorian, Nancy C. (1998). Western language ideologies and small-language prospects. In Lenore A. Grenoble and Lindsay J. Whaley (eds.), *Endangered Languages: Current Issues and Future Prospects*, pp. 3–21. Cambridge, UK: Cambridge University Press.

Edwards, John (1994). *Multilingualism*. London and New York: Routledge.

Evans, Nicholas (2001). The last speaker is dead – long live the last speaker! In Paul Newman and Martha Ratliff (eds.), *Linguistic Fieldwork*, pp. 250–81. Cambridge, UK: Cambridge University Press.

Flinn, Juliana (1992). *Diplomas and Thatch Houses: Asserting Tradition in a Changing Micronesia*. Ann Arbor: University of Michigan Press.

Grillo, R. D. (1989). *Dominant Languages: Language and Hierarchy in Britain and France*. Cambridge, UK: Cambridge University Press.

Haiman, John (1987). Hua: A Papuan language of New Guinea. In Timothy Shopen (ed.), *Languages and their Status*, pp. 35–89. Philadelphia: University of Pennsylvania Press, for the Center for Applied Linguistics.

Huffines, Marion Lois (1989). Case usage among the Pennsylvania German sectarians and nonsectarians. In Nancy C. Dorian (ed.), *Investigating Obsolescence: Studies in Language Contraction and Death*, pp. 211–26. Cambridge, UK: Cambridge University Press.

Huss, Leena (1999). *Reversing Language Shift in the Far North: Linguistic Revitalization in Northern Scandinavia and Finland*. Uppsala: University of Uppsala.

Kroskrity, Paul V. (1993). *Language, History, and Identity: Ethnolinguistic*

458   *Nancy C. Dorian*

Studies of the Arizona Tewa. Tucson: University of Arizona Press.

Kulick, Don (1992). *Language Shift and Cultural Reproduction: Socialization, Self, and Syncretism in a Papua New Guinean Village.* Cambridge, UK: Cambridge University Press.

MacEachern, Scott (2002). Residuals and resistance: Languages and history in the Mandara Mountains. In Brian D. Joseph, Johanna Destefano, Neil Jacobs, and Ilse Lehiste (eds.), *When Languages Collide: Perspectives on Language Conflict, Language Competition, and Language Coexistence,* 21–44. Columbus: The Ohio State University Press.

McLaughlin, Fiona and Sall, Thierno Seydou (2001). The give and take of fieldwork: Noun classes and other concerns in Fatick, Senegal. In Paul A. Newman and Martha Ratliff (eds.), *Linguistic Fieldwork,* pp. 189–210. Cambridge, UK: Cambridge University Press.

Nagy, Naomi (2000). Fieldwork for the new century: Working in Faeto, an endangered language community. *Southern Journal of Linguistics,* 24, 121–36.

Paulston, Christina Bratt (1994). *Linguistic Minorities in Multilingual Settings: Implications for Language Policies.* Amsterdam and Philadelphia: John Benjamins.

Peal, Elisabeth and Lambert, Wallace (1962). The relation of bilingualism to intelligence. *Psychological Monographs,* 76, no. 546.

Salisbury, R. F. (1972). Notes on bilingualism and linguistic change in New Guinea. In J. B. Pride and Janet Holmes (eds.), *Sociolinguistics: Selected Readings,* pp. 52–64. Harmondsworth: Penguin. Reprint of *Anthropological Linguistics,* 4 (1962), 1–13.

Sankoff, Gillian (1980). Multilingualism in Papua New Guinea. *The Social Life of Language,* pp. 95–132. Philadelphia: University of Pennsylvania Press.

Schooling, Stephen J. (1990). *Language Maintenance in Melanesia: Sociolinguistics and Social Networks in New Caledonia.* Arlington: The Summer Institute of Linguistics and the University of Texas at Arlington.

Skutnabb-Kangas, Tove (1981). *Tvåspråkighet.* Lund: Liber Läromedel.

Smalley, William A. (1999). *Linguistic Diversity and National Unity: Language Ecology in Thailand.* Chicago and London: University of Chicago Press.

Sorensen, A. P., Jr. (1972). Multilingualism in the northwest Amazon. In J. B. Pride and Janet Holmes (eds.), *Sociolinguistics: Selected Readings,* pp. 78–93. Harmondsworth: Penguin.

Williams, Glyn (1992). *Sociolinguistics: A Sociological Critique.* London and New York: Routledge.

Woolard, Kathryn A. (1998). Language ideology as a field of inquiry. In Bambi B. Schieffelin, Kathryn A. Woolard, and Paul V. Kroskrity (eds.), *Language Ideologies: Practice and Theory,* pp. 3–47. New York and Oxford: Oxford University Press.

FURTHER READING

Edwards, John (ed.) (1984). *Linguistic Minorities, Policies and Pluralism.* London: Academic Press.

Fase, Willem, Kaspaert, Koen, and Kroon, Sjaak (eds.) (1992). *Maintenance and Loss of Minority Languages.* Amsterdam

and Philadelphia: John
Benjamins.

Fishman, Joshua A. (1991). *Reversing Language Shift*. Clevedon, UK: Multilingual Matters.

Fishman, Joshua A. (ed.) (2001). *Can Threatened Languages be Saved?* Clevedon, UK: Multilingual Matters.

Grenoble, Lenore A. and Whaley, Lindsay J. (eds.). (1998). *Endangered Languages: Current Issues and Future Prospects*. Cambridge, UK: Cambridge University Press.

Jones, Mari C. (1998). *Language Obsolescence and Language Revitalization: Linguistic Change in Two Sociolinguistically Contrasting Welsh Communities*. Oxford: Oxford University Press.

Joseph, John Earl. (1987). *Eloquence and Power: The Rise of Language Standards and Standard Languages*. New York: Basil Blackwell.

King, Kendall A. (2001). *Language Revitalization Processes and Prospects: Quichua in the Ecuadorian Andes*. Clevedon, UK: Multilingual Matters.

Nettle, Daniel and Romaine, Suzanne. (2000). *Vanishing Voices: The Extinction of the World's Languages*. Oxford: Oxford University Press.

Robins, Robert H. and Uhlenbeck, Eugenius M. (eds.) (1992). *Endangered Languages*. Oxford and New York: Berg.

18 Multilingualism in Linguistic History: Creolization and Indigenization

SALIKOKO MUFWENE

18.1 Introduction

My primary goal in this chapter is to dispel some myths about the development of varieties identified as *creolized* and *indigenized*. I start by questioning notions such as "creolization" and "indigenization," which have been invoked to account for their development. I argue that the terms and notions are misnomers that reflect negative colonial biases toward non-European populations and their ways of speaking languages whose genetic classification should for all intents and purposes be Germanic or Romance. The notions have no solid grounding in how languages evolve and speciate. We should dispense with these biases if we care to learn from the development of these particular varieties some important lessons about language evolution in general. For instance, we must realize that contact has always played a central role in all cases of language change, diversification, and shift, as well as its consequences identified as "endangerment" or "death." I subsume all these phenomena under *language evolution* in Mufwene (2001), where I also argue that speakers, native and non-native alike, are the unwitting agents of this process, through selections they make consciously or unconsciously during their communicative acts.

As in Mufwene (2001), I maintain that there are no particular restructuring processes that can be identified as *creolization* or *indigenization* in the sense of speakers applying any special combination of evolutionary processes that transform a language into a creole or an indigenized variety. Both creole and indigenized varieties have developed by the same restructuring processes that have produced other languages, be they in terms of particular changes in the production of phonological, morphosyntactic, or semantic units, or in terms of selecting particular phonological, morphosyntactic, or semantic-interpretation rules. The varieties are reminders of how languages have changed and speciated several times throughout the history of mankind.

Usage of the terms *creolization* and *indigenization* to identify their divergence from the European languages from which they developed reflects both a colonial disfranchising attitude toward the populations speaking them and ignorance among linguists of the role that contact has always played in language diversification. These factors have also biased part of the scholarship on language evolution, for instance in suggesting or claiming, without support from the socioeconomic histories of the relevant territories, that creoles have evolved from anteceded pidgins (e.g. Bickerton, 1981 and subsequent publications) and only they are byproducts of imperfect language learning (e.g. Holm, 1988; Thomason and Kaufman, 1988). Some of the same literature has also claimed or suggested that "indigenized Englishes" (spoken in former European exploitation colonies) differ from "native Englishes" (spoken in the United States or Australia, for example) in being alone byproducts of second-language acquisition.

I submit that second-language acquisition has had a role to play in the development of all ex-colonial (and other) language varieties, although there are differences in the structures of the ensuing systems. Such variation can be correlated with differences between using the new language variety as a lingua franca and using it as a vernacular, as well as with whether or not the population of non-native speakers has or has not been integrated within that of native speakers. These factors have to do with the ecology of language spread (especially regarding dynamics of competition among variants in the feature pool), not with particular mechanisms of language change. I also argue below that part of the problem follows from the typical misconception of 'acquisition' itself as appropriation of a ready-made language rather than as a reconstruction process, especially when native speakers are concerned. Moreover, the literature has unfortunately also discussed the spread of the relevant colonial European languages (Dutch, English, French, Portuguese, and Spanish in particular) as if the same varieties were involved in all the relevant contact settings.

I focus below on societal multilingualism and say very little of substance, if anything, about individual multilingualism. (See, e.g. Romaine, 2000 and chapter 15 of the present volume on the distinction.) Nonetheless, individual multilingualism will always be assumed, because, as explained in Mufwene (2001), the real loci of language contact are individual speakers (Weinreich, 1953), the makers and hosts of a communal language qua species. The main reason for this focus on societal multilingualism is simply the fact that histories of languages as accounts of their evolutions have focused on communal languages. They have disregarded I-languages (or idiolects), although the immediate causes of changes that accumulate to produce evolution (at the communal level) lie nowhere but in the communicative acts of individual speakers. These behave linguistically not as members of an organized team with a common goal of winning a game but rather as interconnected individuals focused on solving their respective instantaneous communicative problems in particular communicative acts of the moment, without any specific plans for future communicative acts. (This observation does not discount the fact that their memories help them draw from past solutions to solve new instantaneous challenges.)

Interconnectedness is indeed what has made speakers produce similar systems that non-linguists have typically characterized as the particular way a given population speaks. (This can be inferred from names of languages in, or associated with, particular communities, e.g. *Kiswahili* as the language of *Waswahili* 'Swahili people' and *Japanese* as the language of the Japanese people.) It is only by extrapolation that linguists have inferred communal systems from idiolects that they have analyzed, thus often overlooking idiolectal variation, for the convenience of their complex and difficult analytical challenges. Through mutual accommodations, speakers who interact regularly with each other end up speaking alike, though not necessarily in identical ways (see below). It is also from the same communal perspective that diachronic processes discussed as *creolization* and *indigenization* have been identified as evolutionary. For convenience' sake, I will still do the same, hoping that more interested readers will read Mufwene (2001) to realize how complex evolutionary processes really are and how much more work it will take before we understand what Weinreich, Labov, and Herzog (1968), McMahon (1994), and a few other historical linguists have characterized as "the actuation problem/question" and Keller (1994) as the "invisible hand" of linguistic change.

Consequently, I discuss multilingualism here from the point of view of the coexistence of more than one language within the same community in which members of the relevant ethnolinguistic groups interact with each other (as individuals rather than as "team members") and resolve their instantaneous communicative challenges by using one language or another, even if they alternate between the codes during (parts of) individual communicative acts. Within Mufwene's (2001) approach to language evolution, multilingualism is part of the external ecology of a language to the extent that its structures and vitality are affected by other languages spoken in the community in which it is used. In the particular context of "creolization" and "indigenization" (not as development toward a well-defined state but rather as divergence from a Western-based yardstick), the affected language is the one that was once targeted by speakers of other languages, which influenced how they spoke it and therefore partly determined the direction of its divergence from what they were exposed to.

I use the term ecology as articulated in Mufwene (2001). As in macroecology, what it denotes breaks down into *internal* and *external* ecology. The former subsumes things internal to the relevant language itself qua species, such as what kind of variation obtains within its system and whether it is its standard or nonstandard variety (or varieties) to which the other population is/was exposed. External ecology includes a wide range of ethnographic and other factors that bear on language evolution, such as what particular languages are spoken by those targeting a specific language, whether the language is being appropriated in a naturalistic or scholastic setting, and whether it is appropriated as a vernacular or as a lingua franca.

18.2 Language Transmission and Acquisition

The processes of language "transmission" and "acquisition" are central to language evolution. Quite fundamental in this case are the questions of whether any speaker or group of speakers ever passes on an integrated system of units and rules to any learner, and whether such a transmission process is conceivable even in a classroom setting where learners are drilled in several grammatical rules and the constraints over them to apply in their interpretation and/or production of discourse. What kind of understanding must we develop of the concepts "transmission" and "acquisition" in order to figure out whether multilingualism makes second-language "acquisition" (by adult speakers) fundamentally different from first-language "acquisition" (by children), and, if it does, how?

   Both the reality of interidiolectal variation (well underscored in Chomsky, 2000, Mufwene, 2001, and Weinreich et al., 1968) and the fact that a speaker develops competence in a language (first or second) only gradually suggest that no language is ever transmitted wholesale from one group to another. No group of speakers passes on a ready-made grammar to a new group of speakers, no individual speaker does to any other speaker. As pointed out by DeGraff (1999a, b), Hagège (1993), Meillet (1929), and Mufwene (2001), language is a reconstructive process, which indeed proceeds piecemeal. As with the development of any social competence, this reconstruction process – actually the development of one's I-language or idiolect – depends both on the learner's individual skills and on the particular network that he or she has participated in. The network has consequently determined the particular E-language qua collection of utterances to which they have been exposed and from which they could infer the grammar that they put into use. For someone who subscribes to a distinction between the structural peculiarities of internally and externally motivated change, it would be difficult to explain why internally motivated change occurred in the first place if language transmission proceeded wholesale among native speakers and there were no room for imperfect replication.

   The acquisition-qua-gradual-reconstruction conception of the development of linguistic competence makes it easier to understand Lass's (1997) observation that there is no perfect replication in language "transmission"/"acquisition." It also makes it easier to understand where the partial causes of internally motivated change lie. The distinction between internally and externally motivated changes becomes especially difficult to sustain once one acknowledges the role of mutual accommodation in the way every speaker uses their language and develops their own idiolectal system. Accommodations reflect influences that speakers exert on each other's idiolect. They are conceivably small changes that can eventually accumulate, through little-understood dynamics of group selection, into changes in the communal language (what Weinreich et al., 1968 translate from Paul, 1880 as "Language Custom"). They instantiate the level at which language contact really operates, namely, that of idiolects (Mufwene, 2001; Paul, 1880).

Recall that I have in mind interactions of individuals who are just interconnected by their social practices but are not organized as members of a sport team playing for a common goal. It really makes little difference whether the idiolects in contact are native and xenolectal, because the whole game of influences is grounded in efforts that speakers make to communicate successfully. How individual speakers' selections may translate into their community's overall selections (i.e. spread and stabilize within the community) is a function of still obscure dynamics of the interaction of various internal and external ecological factors that bear on competition and selection in the community's feature pool (Mufwene 2001). Only future research will shed light on this aspect of the competition and selection aspect of language evolution. (For more on this subject matter, see Milroy, 1996, 1997; Mufwene, 2001; and Pargman 2002.)

The dynamics of group selection amount to the "invisible hand" invoked by Keller (1994). Our challenge is to identify specific ecological factors that determine whose innovations or deviations and which particular accommodations spread to become (parts of) communal norms, and which particular ones do not survive. The same challenge is as critical of monolingual as of multilingual communities. An important difference to remember in multilingual communities is that xenolectal deviations or innovations are added to the range of variants that already obtain in the monolingual feature pool produced by native speakers only. However, this difference is merely quantitative, not qualitative, and the particular ethnographic ecology in which speakers interact determines whether xenolectal deviations or innovations stand a chance of prevailing in a multilingual community. The challenge for the linguist interested in language evolution in such settings is to figure out what particular principles regulate competition and selection during language use, "transmission," and "acquisition," and therefore affect language evolution. The proposed approach dispels the myth that only creoles (and pidgins), and apparently also indigenized varieties, owe their development to imperfect learning. The reality remains that imperfect replication in language appropriation is the norm and accounts for all cases of language evolution.

One thing that the proposed approach makes more obvious is the need to better understand how languages coexist in the individual speaker's mind, how competition and selection operate among languages and among their respective structural features. *Competition* is nothing more than the unequal relations that hold between languages and among their features (not always in tandem) when they coexist in the speaker's mind and in a speech community (hence in the feature pool they generate), such that one feels compelled to speak a particular language rather than an alternative or prefers particular features over others. *Selection* amounts to no more than the cumulation of such choices into a preferred language form that is marked by a specific combination of features which at a particular point in time make it different from how it was spoken at a preceding time. Understanding how competition and selection work thus amounts to finding out under what specific conditions particular features of languages already known by a learner influence the appropriation of structures of the language being targeted, a phenomenon that is facilitated by the fact that linguistic systems are naturally osmotic. It also entails examining under what particular conditions the accumulation of such restructuring processes (natural even in cases where dialects of the same language are in contact) lead to the development of new systems (idiolectal or communal) and thus produce evolutions of all kinds (structural and pragmatic).

We can thus recast the difference between first- and second-language acquisition in terms of whether or not there is another language, previously known by the learner, whose features come to compete with those of the target language. Since there are individuals who grow up bilingual, perhaps it is too biased to present things this way. An interesting question is therefore also the following: If two languages are appropriated concurrently as native systems, to what extent do their respective systems influence each other? In the context of the present chapter, this question is secondary, because it is not clear how extensive child bilingualism was in the communities where creoles developed, nor that children had a particular role to play in the introduction of xenolectal features (i.e. other than in selecting some of them in their idiolects from the environment in which they "acquired" the emergent creole language, as suggested by DeGraff 1999a, b). (For more on transfer and interference, see chapters 4–6 and 30.)

If the development of creoles is correctly associated with an ethnographic process of language shift, the primary agents of their divergence from the European colonial koinés from which they emerged are the adults who participated in the shifts and introduced xenolectal features – misidentified as "substrate" features – into their idiolects of the emergent vernaculars. (See also the next section. I say "misidentified" because, as pointed out by Goodman (1993), the relevant non-European languages did not precede the European languages in the territories where the new vernaculars developed. At best they were brought at the same time as the rulers arrived in the colonies which Chaudenson (1992, 2001) characterizes as "exogenous" – because both the rulers and the relevant dominated groups were foreign to them.) On the other hand, indigenized varieties are byproducts of alternations between the indigenous vernaculars of the colonized populations and the European lingua francas they learned in school. No shift has been involved in this case. Nonetheless, both creoles and indigenized varieties can help us better understand linguistic osmosis and the ways in which xenolectal influence works.

18.3 The Development of Creole and Indigenized Varieties

In the context of this handbook, creoles and indigenized varieties are definitely interesting to investigate because they are largely byproducts of second-language appropriation by adults, *pace* Bickerton's various versions of the language bioprogram hypothesis (1981, 1984, 1989, 1999). Nonetheless, one must remember that the ecological specifics involved in the case of individual creoles or indigenized varieties are not the same, and there are also kinds of ecological factors that distinguish the former from the latter. For instance, in plantation settlement colonies, where creoles developed, children appear to have "acquired" language in the same way as in any other community with speakers around them providing the E-language from which they selectively worked out their I-languages. They reconstructed the vernaculars of their plantations with fewer deviations than the adult bozal (new, unseasoned) slaves around them. On the other hand, the adult learners produced (additional) xenolectal features, some of which found their ways into the new communal systems targeted by the children (DeGraff, 1999a, b). Creoles' structures would have diverged more significantly from the relevant European languages if it had not been for the role of children as a stabilizing factor. They helped balance adults' higher rates of deviations and innovations with their own higher rates of closer approximations of the local vernaculars (Mufwene, 1996, 2001). Part of the variation in creole continua is a consequence of this coexistence of (largely) overlapping individual speakers' systems produced by the different language "acquisition" outcomes of children and adults.

In this particular case, we cannot miss an important lesson from indigenized varieties, whose norms are set by the older speakers. Rather than metropolitan native speakers, teachers and parents have functioned as model speakers to the younger learners. These circumstances of language appropriation are somewhat reminiscent of the racially segregated plantations on which children targeted the local colonial vernacular as their native language. Their models were mostly older creole or seasoned slaves and the target was literally what these adults spoke, notwithstanding influence from bozal slaves around them. This was a continuum of approximations of, and divergences from, the original homestead koiné vernacular, which never fully disappeared in the first place (Chaudenson, 1992, 2001). What children recreated relatively more faithfully was simply what they were exposed to, depending on who they interacted with, as in any social setting. They were not in any privileged position to develop a creole for the growing slave community. They never had parents who were deprived of a vernacular or who relied exclusively on some pidgin qua reduced language of minimal communication in a setting of sporadic contact (*pace* Bickerton, 1981 and subsequent publications). What we cannot overlook, however, is the high degree of xenolectal features to which the children must have been exposed, which, as explained above, made more complex (than in "non-contact" communities) the way in which competition and selection proceeded in the development of creoles as communal systems.

It is also noteworthy that creoles developed through naturalistic language appropriation, with no formal language classes involved in the process (despite frequent invocations of the "seasoning" of bozal slaves by creole and "seasoned," or more experienced, slaves in the process). Given the multitude of idiolectal, native and xenolectal, varieties of the local colonial vernacular involved, there could not be a more propitious setting for testing competition and selection in the development of idiolectal competence and of a new communal system.

Unlike "creolization," "indigenization" starts with relatively controlled "transmission" of a preselected, scholastic variety of the European language, although the involvement of non-native speakers as its "transmitters" affects the interpretation of the system itself. However, as in the development of creoles, restructuring away from the original model is accelerated by uses to which (imperfect) internalizations of the scholastic model are put when the learners interact not only with more experienced speakers but also among themselves. In the same vein another important difference between "creolization" and "indigenization" must be articulated, namely that, in the case of indigenized varieties, speakers are putting into use a model that was acquired primarily from a written medium. The process amounts to naturalizing an artificial means of communication.

We may also want to think over the question of whether the fact that indigenized varieties typically function as lingua francas bears on how they have been restructured away from the original scholastic models. In any case, from the point of view of language evolution, hence of speciation, creole and indigenized varieties had different starting points. In measuring the extent of their divergence from the relevant European language, we must remember to compare them each with the right starting point, unlike the poor job done in the literature that has compared creoles typically with the standard varieties of the corresponding European languages instead of with the nonstandard colonial koinés from which they have diverged gradually toward their basilects – a process identified as *basilectalization* by Chaudenson (1992, 2001) and Mufwene (1996, 2001).

Why did I state above that creoles did *not* develop from erstwhile pidgins, *nor* abruptly? Focusing, as in Mufwene (2001), on varieties that developed from European languages, some of which have served as our heuristic prototypes (simply because we happen to know most about them), a close look at the world map shows a complementary distribution between pidgins and creoles that is correlated with differences in colonization styles. Creoles are concentrated in Cape Verde, on the Gulf of Guinea islands (such as Principe and São Tomé), in the Caribbean and surrounding mainland (including Suriname and Guyana), on the southeastern coast of the United States, and in the Indian Ocean. They have been identified precisely where during the seventeenth and eighteenth centuries Europeans developed settlement colonies that thrived primarily on sugar cane or rice cultivation, which required intensive slave labor.

Curiously, there is no evidence that a creole ever developed on Barbados or Martinique during the earlier colonial period when their colonists cultivated tobacco rather than sugar cane. Likewise, the Virginia colony, which chose to grow tobacco (rather than rice, as in South Carolina, or sugar cane), developed

African-American vernacular English, not considered to be a creole, rather than a Gullah-like variety. Likewise, no comparable creoles nor pidgins based on European languages have been identified in Brazil (*pace* Holm's 1988 notion of "semi-creole"), where industrial sugar cane cultivation started, at least outside the African coastal islands. (As argued in Mufwene, 1997, 2000, identifying particular colonial vernaculars as creoles has had nothing to do with the presence or absence of particular structural features, *pace* McWhorter, 1998. See also DeGraff, 2001a. Social bias in favor of disfranchising vernaculars associated primarily with descendants of non-Europeans has been the primary criterion uncritically espoused by linguists.)

In the case of Brazil, the main reason seems to lie in a different pattern of colonization and its pace of population growth. Its homestead phase (see below) lasted long, and sugar cane cultivation did not boom until the early seventeenth century, almost 100 years after the colony was founded in 1500 and a little over half a century after the first slaves were imported in 1538. Although by the eighteenth century populations of (partial) African descent constituted close to two-thirds of the overall population – with 80 percent of them in the northeastern region – the gradual pattern of population growth and freer miscegenation between populations of European and non-European descents (compared to Dutch, English, and French colonies) did not favor the development of varieties that are particularly Africanized. The admitted social and regional variation in Brazilian Portuguese (Naro and Scherer, 1994) has to do more with the time of settlement and origins of the European immigrants than with the presence of Africans. More or less the same explanation holds for the scarcity of Spanish creoles in the Americas and the rest of the world (Chaudenson, 1992, 2001; *pace* McWhorter, 2000).

However, the question arises now of why Portuguese creoles *did* emerge on Cape Verde, in Casamance (southern Senegal) and Guinea-Bissau, and on the Gulf of Guinea islands. What particular colonization differences obtained between them and the American territories? These are questions worth exploring in the future. For instance, although we know that in the seventeenth century the Gulf of Guinea islands turned largely into slave depots (Le Page, 1960; like the Netherlands Antilles in the eighteenth century, where Papiamentu developed), it is not clear how quickly they shifted from the homestead to the plantation phase, nor whether miscegenation was less tolerated there. (Lorenzino (1998) reports that Portugal encouraged race-mixing during the early, pre-seventeenth-century period.) Did São Tomense, Angolar, Principense, and Fa d'Ambu (also known as Annobonese) develop after the abolition of the slave trade in the nineteenth century, under conditions similar to those of Suriname in the seventeenth century, or (much) earlier, as claimed by Ferraz (1979, p. 19) and Post (1995, p. 191)? Ferraz also points out that in the sixteenth century at least the free Africans spoke Portuguese rather than anything identifiable as pidgin or creole (p. 17). Lorenzino (1998) observes that the departure of Portuguese planters for Brazil during the seventeenth century and the relative isolation of the islands from Portugal fostered a contact more favorable to the development of these creoles. The post-Emancipation recruitment of indentured laborers from Angola and Cape Verde during the second half of the nineteenth century and the first half of the twentieth (about 100 years) adds more to the complex history of the islands.

Suriname is an interesting comparison case because in the second half of the seventeenth century local colonial English, from which its creoles largely developed (see below), was retained as the vernacular among the non-Europeans and as the lingua franca between them and the Europeans during the Dutch rule, after the English colonists had left. The linguistic evidence suggests that some local colonial form of Portuguese remained the vernacular among the Africans on the Gulf of Guinea islands even after the Portuguese developed more interest in Brazil and neglected or abandoned their central African plantations. (The islands *did* remain their colonies.) Does this explanation also apply to Cape Verde, which also played the role of slave depot during the slave trade of the seventeenth and eighteenth centuries? I have no answers to this question at the moment.

In any case, pidgins based on European languages are concentrated on the Pacific islands and on the coast of West Africa – where the most common one until the early nineteenth century was Portuguese-based, according to Huber (1999). During that time period the Europeans developed no more than trade colonies in both regions and originally communicated with the Natives through interpreters and middlemen (*grumettes*) who had been trained in a European language. It is only during the nineteenth century that the Europeans would transform them into exploitation colonies. While Portuguese Pidgin has vanished, English pidgins became expanded pidgins, corresponding to the progression of interactions from sporadic to more regular ones and to the evolution of their functions from lingua francas to urban vernaculars. This coevolution of structure and function occurred in the urban centers of the exploitation colonies of Africa and in the Pacific sugar cane plantations to which large numbers of indentured laborers were imported from neighboring Pacific islands.

Whether or not a trade colony developed into a European exploitation colony in the nineteenth century may explain why Chinese Pidgin English, which developed in Canton in the late eighteenth and early nineteenth centuries and bequeathed us the term *pidgin* itself, has not survived. (In addition to the hitherto plausible etymology provided by Baker and Mühlhäusler (1990), deriving *pidgin English* from *business English*, Smith and Matthews (1996, p. 146) have observed that "a more likely origin might be the common expression [*bei chin*] which means 'give money' or 'pay' in Cantonese." Congruence of forms, in a context of undoubtedly societal variable pronunciation, would have contributed to the emergence of the term *pidgin*, which is no closer phonological match to English *business*.)

Expanded pidgins are recognized to be structurally as complex as creole vernaculars (de Féral, 1991; Jourdan 1985, 1991). Because adult second-language learners are more likely than children to introduce xenolectal features into a target language, the massive incontrovertible evidence of "substrate" influence in Melanesian pidgins discussed by Keesing (1988), Sankoff (1984, 1993), and Sankoff and Brown (1976) supports the hypothesis submitted earlier by Sankoff (1979) for the significant agency of adults rather than children in their developments. Rather than nativization (as acquisition of native speakers), vernacularization (as usage of a language variety as a vernacular) is the explanation for the structural expansion of these pidgins into stable and more complex systems identified as *expanded pidgins*.

We learn from their case that the agency of creole populations (to which I return below) was not critical to the development of creole vernaculars (*pace* Bickerton's 1981 and subsequent publications overemphasis on the innovative agency of children). As explained below, the story is not quite the same for creoles, since they developed by divergence in the direction of their present basilects, away from earlier and closer approximations of the relevant European languages during the homestead phase, contrary to claims of decreolization. See Chaudenson 1992, 2001; Mufwene 2001. However, Hawaii, on which both a pidgin and a creole are said to have developed (Bickerton 1981, 1984; though Hawaiians themselves refer to the continuum of their varieties as *Pidgin*) deserves some discussion.

Hawaii was not a typical plantation settlement colony. It did not develop on the model of the Caribbean and Indian Ocean settlement colonies presented below. Colonized in the nineteenth century by Americans, rather than by the English, it was developed partly on the model of plantation exploitation colonies of the Pacific, with an abrupt transition from a whaling and trade colony into a plantation alternative, without an initial homestead phase during which proletarian European and non-European populations would have been integrated (see below). According to Masuda (1995, pp. 276–7), the first non-European laborers, the Chinese, were not brought to the islands until 1853. The Japanese arrived apparently after 1878 (over 25 years later, during what Roberts (1998, p. 6) identifies as a "major plantation expansion" phase), and the Koreans and Filipinos apparently after 1900 (a period during which the labor population also increased by birth).

One factor is especially significant in this case: Although the plantation laborers came from different parts of Asia, they do not seem to have been ethnically mixed, at least not in the overwhelming, if not Babelic, way that the African slaves from more diverse linguistic backgrounds were in the plantation settlement colonies that developed a century or two earlier around the Atlantic and in the Indian Ocean. Aside from the fact that the different ethnic groups were not brought in during the same period, Asian laborers lived in separate quarters, consistent with their waves of immigration. This was more or less in the same way that Singapore (and perhaps other Straits of Malacca colonies) was peopled, with the different ethnic groups kept in their quarters and their members interacting more among themselves than with outsiders. Overall, pressure to socialize (on a regular basis) with speakers of other languages was less intense on Hawaiian islands than in the New World and

Indian Ocean plantations. Thus, at least before 1900 (see below), most Asian laborers in Hawaii did not have to use English as a vernacular, only as a lingua franca, more or less as in Pacific exploitation colonies. An important difference is that Hawaii was also a settlement colony and English quickly became the vernacular needed by those who crossed ethnic boundaries.

Interestingly, Roberts (1998) reports that the structural features associated with Hawaiian Creole (henceforth "creole features") do not seem to have developed until the early twentieth century and apparently off the plantations, where "the majority of foreign-born individuals were [then] living" and "where English speakers were more common" (p. 34). She credits nativization for the development of Hawaiian Creole (p. 35), but she also reports that the relevant "creole features" occurred in the speech of immigrant adults (p. 19). Although the features became much more common in the speech of the locally born, it is debatable whether their role really extended beyond what Mufwene (1996, 2001) characterizes as slowing down the basilectalization process. In any case, Roberts also observes that one of the "creole features" she discusses is attested in the pidgin spoken earlier on the plantations, that "what Hawaiians spoke early on was a second-language register of English" (p. 14), and that her early texts "exhibit more stylistic sophistication and structure than" his pidgin texts (p. 33). The historical scenario suggests that Hawaiian Pidgin English and Hawaiian Creole English developed under different ecological conditions of contact and at different times, regardless of whether or not their developments were influenced by Pacific pidgin and Atlantic and creole varieties that had developed earlier.

The socioeconomic histories of the Atlantic and Indian Ocean plantation settlement colonies suggests that their creoles developed neither from pidgin ancestors, nor concurrently with any pidgins spoken by some Africans in the same settings. I am deliberately overlooking pidgins (such as Delaware Pidgin, Chinook Jargon, Mobilian, and Lingua Geral) which developed from the concurrent trade interactions of Europeans and Native Americans, and which are based on indigenous languages and had no significant bearing on the development of New World creoles. The same is also true of the varieties that the French colonists in the Caribbean identified as *baragouins* (Chaudenson, 1992, 2001; Prudent, 1980; Wylie, 1995) which seem to be based on French (and other European languages) but did not survive the expansion of settlement colonization in the Americas. The Africans of the initial, homestead phase of these colonies interacted more regularly with the European colonists than with Native Americans outside the settlements. (The fact that there is hardly any mention of the contribution of Native American languages to the structures of New World creoles shows that: 1) non-European languages did not contribute significantly to the divergence of varieties appropriated by the non-European populations until the plantation phase of colonization; and 2) the enslavement of Native Americans was avoided during that period.) African slaves in the Atlantic and Indian Ocean settlement colonies are not reported to have spoken Pidgin (under the name of either *jargon* or *baragouin*), though they had to go through interlanguages while developing competence in the local colonial vernaculars of the time of their arrival. There are also several reports of these earlier slaves becoming fluent in the European colonial koinés of the homestead phase. We can safely conclude, along with Alleyne (1971) and Chaudenson (1979, 1992, 2001), that African slaves did not develop their creoles from antecedent pidgins of any kind.

What the socioeconomic histories of the former plantation settlement colonies suggest about the evolution of European languages from the sixteenth to the nineteenth centuries is particularly relevant to the hypotheses submitted in this chapter, namely that creoles developed according to the same restructuring processes as other languages, diverging from their *termini a quo*. One must remember that colonization was an economic venture involving cautious investments of large amounts of capital that were not always easily available. The colonies developed only gradually into large plantation settlement economies, starting on average with a 15- to 50-year homestead phase during which the main industry consisted of farming and trade with the neighboring indigenous populations. (Exceptions to this generalization include Mauritius, Réunion, Cape Verde, and the Gulf of Guinea islands, which had been uninhabited before the Europeans arrived.) Interaction with the indigenous populations was reserved to trade and wars, so that concessions which functioned as homesteads experienced socioeconomic developments of their own, which were more or less independent from the non-coastal lands where the Natives continued their traditional economies or adjusted to the threat of the invaders.

On the homesteads, the Europeans were numerically either superior or equal to the non-Europeans. The small demographic size of the colonies and the greater familiarity of the non-Europeans with these mostly tropical physical ecologies produced societies that were generally integrated and in which captive and free residents interacted regularly with each other and even had and raised children, identified in the literature as creoles, together. Regardless of their status and ethnic affiliations (or political classification of their race), these children all spoke the same vernaculars. While the economy was still too weak to shift to the plantation phase, the population grew more by birth than by importation, providing the local European colonial koiné some stability and making non-European creole populations an important proportion of the future "transmitters" of the European language during the plantation phase. There was thus never a period of "break in the transmission" of the European language, as its "transmission" no longer depended on contact with Europeans, even after race segregation had become the norm, especially in Dutch, French, and English colonies, when the non-Europeans became the overwhelming majority.

In respect to language evolution, there has all along been something to learn from the ongoing "indigenization" of European languages in former exploitation colonies, especially the fact that those who spread the former colonial language, even more fervently after their independence, were themselves members of the indigenous populations. The divergence from the original scholastic, or standard, model of the European language has also intensified during that time, as more and more non-Europeans have used it to communicate more among themselves than with the Europeans, notwithstanding the fact that some of the Europeans with whom they have communicated have not been native speakers anyway.

Keeping in mind that creoles actually developed from nonstandard varieties of European languages, the evolutionary paths of both creole and indigenized varieties were quite similar. In the case of creoles, as the relevant settlement colonies shifted from the homestead to the plantation phase and these estates grew in ways that produced overwhelming non-European majorities without a non-European language of their own in common, these majorities were driven by the circumstances of power and adaptation to the local socioeconomic ecologies to adopt the relevant European colonial language as their vernacular. Its "transmitters" were either the creole slaves or the seasoned ones, who had come a few years earlier. As the proportion of non-native speakers grew, sometimes to the majority within the non-European population, there was room for more and more xenolectal influence on the structure of the evolving vernacular and for divergence from the European varieties. Thus developed creoles, by gradual restructuring away from the original colonial European koiné, without any evidence of break in the transmission of the European language, contrary to the myth fostered in much of the literature on the development of creoles.

Even in places like Suriname, where the English left about fifteen years after founding their colony and took most, but not all, of their slaves with them (Richard Price, personal communication, November 2001), there was always a cohort of non-Europeans who knew the local colonial English vernacular and transmitted it to the slaves brought later on by the Dutch. The evidence of post-English European influence on that vernacular lies in the extensive Dutch influence on Sranan and Portuguese influence on Saramaccan. Sranan developed on the coast, where the Dutch were the most heavily represented, whereas Saramaccan developed in the interior, where the planters were predominantly Sephardic Jews who had been expelled from Brazil.

These evolutions suggest that accounts of the development of creoles must always factor in the varieties spoken by the Europeans. A critical factor in the particular case of Surinamese creoles is that the Dutch let a language variety that they found in place remain the vernacular of the non-Europeans in their colony. Otherwise, no English pidgin seems to have developed there either, because Suriname was still in its homestead phase, without any plantations, when the English traded it against the Dutch North American colony of New Netherland, and the conditions of sporadic contact associated with pidgins never obtained. Hard to discount in this particular case is the possibility that, aside from the Africans as the central agents of change, the Europeans themselves influenced the restructuring of the vernacular left by the English colonists into Surinamese creoles.

It is helpful to distinguish pidgins as stable communal varieties associated with minimal and irregular contacts from interlanguages, which are individual and transitional stages during the development of competence in a new language. Vernacular usage of interlanguages among non-native speakers definitely had a lot to do with the restructuring of European languages into the divergent vernaculars called creoles. However, nothing in this evolutionary pattern makes them different from the contact-induced divergence of European languages into the new varieties now spoken by European-majority populations in former settlement colonies such as Canada, the United States, Argentina, and Australia. Nor are their evolutionary patterns different from what produced, say, the diversification of Vulgar Latin into the Romance languages. In both cases, history suggests that second-language acquisition in settings where more and more non-native speakers became models for new learners was critical to the speciation process. Thus, rather than being an exception to the rule, creoles, like indigenized varieties, illustrate how language diversification has proceeded in the history of mankind, as languages were taken to different places and were appropriated by new speakers. Differences in the extents of divergence from the earlier and congener kin varieties can be attributed to variation in external ecological factors.

18.4   Language Shift, Socioeconomic Status, and Language Diversification

I have deliberately avoided unnecessarily using the terms *slave* and *slavery* above, because I assume that slavery was one of the many factors in the history of mankind that have brought populations into contact and have created particular socioeconomic conditions under which speakers of different languages have come to interact with each other. The development of creole vernaculars and other varieties to which the term *creole* has been extended was not exclusively associated with slavery. In places such as Sri Lanka and Macau, there emerged, without the involvement of slavery and out of the seemingly intimate coexistence of Portuguese and Asian populations, some colonial Portuguese vernaculars that have also been called creoles (Holm, 1988; Smith, 1995). The same may be said of English vernaculars that developed in Queensland and in the Torres Straits (north of Australia) among non-Europeans who have shifted to English.

To be sure, even to those like me who believe that "creolization" is the social act of disfranchising a divergent European colonial language variety appropriated primarily by a non-European population, it is not clear that these particular vernaculars should be called creoles. (Note that many of these varieties have been branded with this label by linguists, not by their speakers, to whom the term *creole* itself is often unknown. This is especially true of Gullah, for which no particular local name is recorded in its history, and of Caribbean English creoles, which the locals identify as *Patwa*, from the French derogatory term *patois* for a nonstandard language variety.) Nonetheless, the varieties illustrate particular conditions of language shift concurrent with the divergence of structures of the adopted vernacular, under xenolectal influence, away from its European ancestor or congeners.

Other developments around the world have also shown that the language shift and appropriation of a new vernacular with modification in the way that has been associated with creole vernaculars of the Atlantic and the Indian Ocean (our heuristic prototypes) are not limited to cases where the relevant populations were underprivileged. Being underprivileged or enslaved had nothing to do with the development of Baba Malay by the Peranakans of the Straits of Malacca. Biologically, the Peranakans are partly descendants of the Chinese merchants who developed trade colonies in the Malay Southeast Asia (particularly Penang, Melaka, and Java). They came as single males, married low-class Malay-speaking women, and developed a Chinese-influenced culture (especially in religion) in which the male children could marry in the Malay population but the female children had to marry Chinese men, until the sexes were more or less equal and then they became a closed community.

The Peranakans are, like the creole populations of the Atlantic and Indian Ocean, locally born Chinese, many of them of mixed ethnic/racial ancestry. They all speak Malay as their vernacular, and until recently those who spoke Chinese (primarily Hokkien) had to learn it as a second language. What is more relevant to this chapter is of course the fact that they developed a particular Malay variety called *Baba Malay*, after the local name for the male Peranakans, *Baba*. The variety was predetermined by the conditions under which the men came in contact with the more indigenous populations, namely the market (and trade), also identified as *bazaar*, hence its common confusion with Bazaar Malay. It is closer to nonstandard Malay spoken by the commoners in the Malay population and diverges from it by xenolectal influence from primarily Hokkien Chinese (Ansaldo and Matthews, 1999; Collins, 1984; Pakir, 1986). The lesson is quite consistent with that from the socioeconomic histories of the territories where creoles have developed; that is, the particular kinds of contacts maintained with speakers of a language and the particular variety spoken by that population have largely determined the kind of variety developed from the contacts. The status of the learner may *not* be a primary factor in language shift and diversification, whereas the need to communicate with the population within which one evolves is.

Language shift had indeed a significant role to play in the development of creoles, unlike in the case of "indigenization." In Atlantic and Indian Ocean plantation settlement colonies, the shift was accelerated by both the heterogeneity of the places where the Africans were captured and the size of the homesteads, in which integrated Africans, isolated from each other, could hardly speak their native languages. Even if two or more slaves found themselves in the same homestead, the chances that they spoke the same language were very much reduced, in part because they may not have arrived at the same time or from the same place. Even if two or more slaves living in neighboring homesteads (often miles apart) spoke the same language, they did not socialize often enough to maintain it.

As in today's sub-Saharan African cities, where children have preferred the urban vernaculars to the ethnic vernaculars of their (grand)parents, creole children may have found it more advantageous to speak the European colonial vernacular than their parents' languages, to the extent that these could be regularly "transmitted" to them. As discussed in section 18.5, the same socio-economic history suggests that African languages could have been spoken more easily under the segregated conditions of the late plantation phase and during the post-Abolition indentured-labor period than during the earlier stages of colonization. Africans were then brought from more linguistically homogeneous areas, as in the case of the Yorubas in Trinidad, who maintained their language until the first half of the twentieth century (Warner-Lewis, 1996). Moreover, the fact that nineteenth-century African indentured laborers were not immediately absorbed by the former slaves favored the longer maintenance of the African languages.

More or less the same thing happened to the languages of indentured Indian laborers (identified as "East Indians" in the Caribbean) in all former plantation colonies in the Indian Ocean, South Africa, the Atlantic, and the Pacific. They too went through a similar gradual assimilation or integration process, although things have been more complex in the latter case. In places like Jamaica, where the proportion of Indians has been very small (about 1.3 percent, Jamaican 1991 census) and the original indentured laborers had few women among them, the integration with the overall non-European and creole-speaking population proceeded fairly rapidly. In places like Trinidad and Guyana, where their numbers came to equal or surpass those of the creole populations of African descent who preceded them (40 percent East Indians vs. 41 percent Africans in Trinidad; over 50 percent East Indians vs. 43 percent blacks or mixed in Guyana), the pressure to mix with other ethnic groups was not greater than in places like Singapore, where most of the immigrants have resided in their respective quarters and only a few have chosen to mix. While the late-comers have adopted the local creole as their language of wider communication, they have not necessarily had to give up their ethnic Indian languages, at least not until a little over a decade ago. Yet the attrition of the Indian languages under the influence of the local creole cannot be ignored (Bhatia 1988; Mohan and Zador 1986).

As in South Africa, the gradual loss of (East) Indian languages in the Caribbean has largely depended on factors having to do with multilingualism among themselves and what the larger population had to offer as a linguistic advantage. More specifically, according to Mohan and Zador (1986), the majority of the earliest indentured laborers came from East India, where Bhojpuri was a major vernacular. The next numerically important group consisted of Hindi-speakers. Structural similarities between Hindi and Bhojpuri, compounded with the sentiment that Bhojpuri is one of the nonstandard varieties of Hindi, led to the prevalence of Bhojpuri in a koinéized form as the East Indian vernacular in Trinidad and of standard Hindi as their language of literacy.

Pressures from the larger community led Hindi to lose its acrolectal function among East Indians to the local English acrolect and Bhojpuri to Creole (to the extent that the acrolect and Creole are truly separate languages). The agency of this demise of Indian languages is primarily that of children, or the younger generation, who found it less and less useful to use their ancestral languages and to speak like the descendants of Africans who preceded them.

Mesthrie (1991, 1992) gives an elaborate account of this process in South Africa, which first also favored a koinéized Bhojpuri and then South African Indian English. In Mauritius, which is closer to the motherland and where the Indians have become the majority (two-thirds of the population according to Chaudenson (2001, p. 31), Bhojpuri and perhaps some ethnic Indian languages have survived, although Creole has been also claimed as the common national language, in opposition to attempts by creole populations (largely of African and Malagasy descent) to claim it as their own group language (Chaudenson, 2001). It is equally important to highlight the fact that the situation of Indians in South Africa is not the same as in the other former British colonies, because South African Indians have really been the counterparts of Africans in bondage in plantation settlement colonies or of other Asian indentured laborers in the Pacific. (Black South Africans are the counterparts of Native Americans, especially in having been dispossessed of their lands and having long been marginalized from the economic developments of the new nations.)

One must remember that in former plantation settlement colonies, the newly arriving slaves of the plantation phase were being integrated into the local non-European populations, which had already been subjugated to the local colonial system partly inherited from the homestead phase. The new slaves followed these local creole and seasoned slaves as their models, adopting their language too. The particular status and privileges that creole populations (as opposed to the bozal slaves) acquired during slavery must have contributed to attrition of non-European languages if they did not totally die (see section 18.5). The survival, or slower decline, of (East) Indian languages is largely due to their critical mass relative to, and slow integration in, the creole-speaking populations that preceded them. It seems that an understanding of the conditions of language attrition and loss during the development or appropriation of creoles in former plantation settlement colonies should contribute to a better understanding of the subject matter of language endangerment and extinction in general. (For additional discussion of language maintenance and shift, see chapters 14–16, 25, 26, and 28; for more on language endangerment, see chapters 15–17, 25, 27, and 28.)

18.5 Language Shift and Loss in Creole-speaking Communities and Elsewhere

In Mufwene (2001, chapter 6), I submit that language shift is inversely correlated with socioeconomic integration. I could not then explain to my own satisfaction why (descendants of) Africans in European settlement colonies were among the first to lose their languages while they have been the most conspicuously segregated against, especially during the later stages of those colonies. Segregation, with the smaller number of interactions with the socioeconomically privileged group(s) that it entails, favors the maintenance of the languages of the underprivileged groups! This is a plausible explanation for the post-Abolition maintenance of African American English, despite the fact that it is highly stigmatized.

A simple explanation for the loss of African languages in European settlement colonies is that the Africans of the homestead phase were under more pressure to suddenly give up their languages, regardless of whether or not they were prohibited from speaking them. They hardly formed critical masses that would help them continue to speak them, certainly not at the ratio of one or two domestic slaves per homestead (in which they were socially integrated though discriminated against). As noted above, even if by accident they knew another African speaking the same language in a neighboring homestead, a few miles away, they would not have interacted regularly enough (as opposed to with Europeans of their respective homesteads) to maintain (fluent command of) their languages. For those who produced creole offspring, the conditions were not favorable to the acquisition of these African languages as vernaculars, although some offspring undoubtedly learned something of their parents' languages.

As noted above, the conditions for societal multilingualism must have been different during the plantation phase. Sheer numbers alone increased the probability that some slaves found themselves together with some others who spoke the same African language natively or as a second language. The preference expressed by some planters for slaves from particular African regions must have made it more likely for several slaves in (the second half of) the eighteenth century to have found cohorts speaking the same African language, especially those that had also served as lingua francas on the continent. This would explain why, as reported by Manessy (1996) and d'Ans (1996), leaders of the Haitian Revolutionary War were able to use African languages as secret codes. Thus, although slaves are reported to have typically been forbidden to speak African languages, it is not obvious how rigorously such a law would have been followed or enforced, especially during activities that Chaudenson (2001) identifies as "communal" (i.e. restricted to the slave population) as opposed to those interactions that he characterizes as "transcommunal" (i.e. involving both Europeans and non-Europeans).

Here, one is again easily reminded of colonial and post-colonial sub-Saharan African cities, where, although most of the different ethnic groups have had enough critical mass to maintain their languages – especially when most of them have lived in their own ethnic neighborhoods – they have still generally and gradually lost their languages to the non-European urban vernacular. The relevant groups have owed the loss of their languages to the agency of children who have generally found it more beneficial to communicate either exclusively or mostly in the urban vernacular. Interethnic marriages and the integration of some neighborhoods have also precipitated the process, typically favoring the urban vernacular over the ethnic languages. Newcomers to the city have done their best to speak the urban vernacular, at least as a lingua franca outside the home and with relatives who are ignorant of their ethnic languages. Their children have typically selected their vernaculars in the same ways as those born in the city.

One can imagine Africans of the plantation phase to have experienced similar pressures for abrupt language shift. The pressures must have been intensified by being mixed with speakers of other African languages that were not intelligible to them. The pressure to shift vernaculars was thus universally experienced, regardless of opportunities many must have had to meet somebody who knew their language, especially during the (late) eighteenth century, when some plantation owners expressed preference for slaves from particular parts of Africa. As in sub-Saharan African cities, it was pressure to assimilate to, or be integrated in, slave communities (in which the creoles and seasoned slaves set the standards of their norms of conduct) that led to the loss of African languages. The pressure then came more from within the slave community itself than from the European master. And this pressure was undoubtedly stronger in Atlantic and Indian Ocean settlement colonies than in Hawaii, where the non-European indentured laborers came from only four major linguistic groups and lived in quarters that were ethnically segregated. These conditions left room for the development of a pidgin, whereas the former Atlantic and Indian Ocean plantation settlement colonies did not.

This particular history also sheds more light on the spread of indigenized varieties of European languages, even if language shift (in the sense of giving up one's vernacular in favor of another) played no particular role in the process. Before independence, indigenized varieties of European languages were regularly used, especially in written form, primarily by handfuls of colonial auxiliaries, who had been taught these varieties for the specific purpose of serving the local colonial administration. (As accurately noted by Brutt-Griffler (2002), the exploitation colonial intention was less to educate the colonized populations in general as bilinguals in the European languages than to reduce the cost of administering the colonies by using some Natives in the local administration.) The indigenous colonial auxiliaries served as interpreters between minorities of European administrators and the masses of the colonized populations. Although they represented some intermediate colonial authority, the socioeconomic status and power of this elite increased after independence, as they ascended to positions vacated by the European colonizers and to new ones, using the same colonial language to rule and administer their countries. The new political states also prescribed a universal teaching of the European official language in all schools, while more and more educated Natives adopted it as a lingua franca and as an emblem distinguishing them from the less educated masses. Competition for higher social status and better positions in the economic system increased the desire by many more non-Europeans to learn these otherwise colonial languages. More extensive usage of them by and among non-native speakers whose xenolectal features reinforced each other produced more extensive divergence from the original scholastic model. Eventually, the scholastic system itself would be indigenized, as it has been taught more and more by non-native speakers (Bamgbose, 1992).

"Indigenization" and "creolization" undoubtedly differ from each other as regards whether the nature of the European language to which the non-Europeans were exposed was or was not standard, and whether it was primarily spoken or written, as well as whether the setting of language appropriation was naturalistic or scholastic. Creoles and indigenized varieties are, none-theless, similar outcomes of the non-native appropriation of a language by populations which have influenced it with features from languages they spoke previously.

"Creolization" on the plantations of the Atlantic and Indian Ocean can very well be characterized as Africanization of the European languages appropriated by the African slaves. We must bear in mind that in places like Mauritius, Trinidad, and Guyana the Indian indentured laborers learned and shifted to a local creole that they found in place, although they have also minimally modified it with their own later contributions, at least by way of new structural variants and, more obviously, lexico-semantic additions. The fact that today's Indian members of these communities have the same phonological peculiarities as the descendants of Africans is consistent with the following observation: As in any other established community (European countries or today's North American polities), adult immigrants have died away with their xenolectal features while their children have "acquired" the local vernacular relatively faithfully, regardless of where they were born. Overall, the more extensively a language has been used almost exclusively by and among non-native speakers, the more xenolectal elements have influenced the structural direction of its "indigenization." Otherwise, divergence is less extensive.

18.6   Some Clarifications

Some clarifications are in order now. My position that creoles of the Atlantic and Indian Ocean can be considered as Africanized varieties of the European languages from which they developed does not presuppose some of the myths propounded in the literature on the development of these vernaculars. For instance, I do not at all assume that creoles are varieties with vocabularies inherited overwhelmingly from a language called the *lexifier* (a misnomer, considering my discussion below) and their grammars from languages previously spoken by the populations that targeted the "lexifiers." Even extremist accounts such as the relexification hypothesis (e.g. Lefebvre, 1998) have not been able to explain mismatches between creoles' structures and the alleged models in the relevant non-European languages. Nor could they account for the fact that critical masses of other non-European populations speaking different languages would have equally contributed to the development of the same creoles, because they were in the same plantation settings during the same critical periods of the developments of these new vernaculars. Overall, hypotheses advocating such unnatural macaronic mixing have partly invoked the absence of a target language, because the "lexifier" was heterogeneous (e.g. Baker, 1990, 1997; Thomason, 1997). They have generally ignored the fact that in any setting of naturalistic language acquisition the target has been heterogeneous (since, as explained above, idiolects are not identical) and acquisition itself is a selective constructive process. (See also Mufwene (2000) for an elaborate discussion on this issue.)

Thomason and Kaufman (1988) have also claimed that creoles cannot be genetically classed. None of those subscribing to this view has ever applied systematic comparisons of structural features of creoles with those of the nonstandard varieties of European languages that were targeted by the slave populations. Sylvain (1936), who has often been mistakenly associated with the relexification hypothesis, actually reveals many plausible sources of Haitian Creole's structural peculiarities in nonstandard French varieties, though she invokes African corroborative or determinative influence. Unfortunately she did not address competition and selection in a heterogeneous feature pool as a critical factor in the development of new varieties. However, more and more recent comparisons (especially by Chaudenson (1992, 2001), Chaudenson, Mougeon, and Beniak, 1993, and DeGraff 2001a, b for French creoles; Pargman, 2002 for Gullah) have revealed similarities between structural features of these "lexifiers" and those of creoles, though the systems that resulted from the appropriation processes are not identical.

This is precisely the context in which "substrate" influence becomes a critical explanation. As argued in Mufwene (1991, 1996, 2001), it determined which of the particular options already available in the competing models of the "lexifier" were, by the principle of least effort, more consistent with structural features already familiar to adult learners and could have been preferred. They also determined the likely direction of divergence in cases of partial similarity. Chaudenson (1992, 2001) correctly observes that without substrate influence, creoles' systems would be more similar to those of other nonstandard varieties of European languages spoken in former European settlement colonies, bearing in mind that these varieties are themselves restructured varieties.

I argue in Mufwene (2001) that more or less similar things occurred in the development of these other vernaculars spoken primarily by descendants of Europeans, as more and more Europeans speaking diverse languages joined colonists from the ruling nation whose language was prevailing as the vernacular, say, English in the United States. Aside from the original restructuring that was induced by new patterns of contacts among native dialects, contacts with other European languages influenced the way selection operated over the variants in competition in the contact feature pool. White American English varieties are different from each other not only because of new contacts among British English dialects and because of isolation from the British Isles (Algeo, 1991), but also because of the contacts of native English dialects with xenolectal varieties spoken by other European immigrants. The possibility of the latter's influence on colonial English increased as the European populations became more and more integrated. The divergence of American and British varieties of English cannot be fully understood without an understanding of the way in which such xenolectal varieties, therefore second-language "acquisition," affected the evolution of English in North America.

Going farther back in time, the same approach to appropriation with modification of European languages under xenolectal influence, especially in former exploitation colonies, sheds more light, for instance, on how Vulgar Latin speciated into the Romance languages. Although Latin functioned as the colonial language in the relevant Romance European countries, it was originally used only by the local elite who interfaced with the Roman administration and militia, and by a few other locals who married some of the colonizers. (It is less clear that usage of Latin as a scholarly language, everywhere in Western Europe till the eighteenth century, had a particular impact on the development of Romance languages. I will ignore this aspect in this discussion.)

After the Romans withdrew in the fifth century, it was the locals who remained behind and whose status had been enhanced by their association with the former colonizers who strengthened the superior ethnographic position of Latin. (Language speciation in former European exploitation colonies is thus somewhat a repetition of history, subject to ecological variation.) It actually took about three centuries for varieties of Old Romance (Old French, Old Iberian) to develop, not much longer than it took creoles to emerge, or be identified, as separate languages. The rest of their evolution has been a history of gradual shift from Celtic languages to Old Romance, therefore its appropriation with modification under xenolectal influence, with the consequential divergence of the old colonial language into modern Romance languages.

Posner (1996) was quite justified in characterizing Romance creoles and other colonial offspring of Romance languages as neo-Romance languages, recognizing in their evolution similar kinds of contact situations and restructuring processes that had produced the European Romance languages. (As I note below, the distinction between sameness and similarity of contact settings is a critical one in the ecological approach to language evolution articulated in Mufwene (2001). No two settings are ever identical in their evolutions and linguistic consequences.) As argued in Mufwene (1994, 2000, 2001), the difference between indigenized and native new varieties of European languages in their former colonies of the sixteenth to twentieth centuries is primarily an ideological one. It has nothing to do with the specific processes that produced them, although ecological differences account for differences among all national and/or regional varieties.

18.7   Conclusions

In this chapter, I have chosen to use my understanding of the development of creoles and indigenized varieties of European languages in a provocative way, to invite scholars to re-examine some misguided positions on language speciation. The development of creoles has usually been treated as not following the normal course of language evolution. As pointed out in Mufwene (2001), nothing much has changed in the general assumptions that can be recognized in any hypothesis about their development since Hugo Schuchardt (1884) spoke against their dismissal as aberrations. Thomason and Kaufman (1988) argue that they cannot be classed genetically, because they are mixed and therefore have more than one ancestor. In a recent column in the *Journal of Pidgin and Creole Languages*, Thomason (2002) reiterates that they have their vocabularies from one language but their grammars from many sources, especially from the "substrate" languages. Hock and Joseph (1996, p. 444) argue that they are not ordinary dialects of their "lexifiers" because of their "special historical origins [in language contact] and [their] formidable structural differences" from other varieties that can be related genetically to the same "lexifiers." Yet no evidence has been adduced to back any of these assertions.

I know of no creolist or historical linguist who has adduced arguments based on the comparative method to verify Thomason and Kaufman's conclusion. They just reiterate their foregone conclusion that the comparative method is not applicable in the case of creoles. This may have to do with a number of unjustified positions about the "lexifier" and linguistic homogeneity in traditional approaches to language speciation. Reversing the tables, I have discussed bilingualism-related topics in this chapter to show that a better understanding of the many evolutionary processes involved in the development of creoles and indigenized varieties can shed light on certain ecological factors that have influenced the evolution of other languages. Comparisons of language evolutionary processes in various colonial contexts, including those of language "indigenization" and urban multilingualism in sub-Saharan Africa appear to be particularly informative, especially about the concurrence of language shift and language loss.

I cannot help reiterating that "creolization" and "indigenization" are not structural evolutionary processes. There is no particular restructuring equation that converts a language into a creole or indigenized one. Therefore, it would be absurd to conclude that all languages have evolved by "creolization" and or "indigenization." My conclusion is the same as in Mufwene (2001), namely, that more or less the same structural processes and ecological factors have been involved in all cases of language evolution, except that they have not combined nor been weighted in identical ways from one evolutionary case to another. The better we understand the development of creole and indigenized varieties, the more compelling it becomes to reopen the books on the evolution of other languages. More needs to be learned about the ecologies of the evolution of languages as species, including both speciation and their sustained, increasing, or decreasing vitality.

ACKNOWLEDGMENT

This chapter has benefited from discussions with Michel DeGraff and Alison Irvine, to whom I am very grateful. I am alone responsible for the remaining shortcomings.

REFERENCES

Algeo, John (1991). Language. In Eric Foner and John A. Garraty (eds.), *The Reader's Companion to American History*, pp. 637–40. Boston: Houghton Mifflin.

Alleyne, Mervyn C. (1971). Acculturation and the cultural matrix of creolization. In Dell Hymes (ed.), *Pidginization and Creolization of Languages*, pp. 169–86. Cambridge, UK: Cambridge University Press.

Ansaldo, Umberto and Matthews, Stephen (1999). The Minnan substrate and creolization of Baba Malay. *Journal of Chinese Linguistics*, 27, 38–68.

Baker, Philip (1990). Off target? Column, *Journal of Pidgin and Creole Languages*, 5, 107–19.

Baker, Philip (1997). Directionality in pidginization and creolization. In Arthur K. Spears and Donald Winford (eds.), *The Structure and Status of Pidgins and Creoles*, pp. 91–109. Amsterdam: John Benjamins.

Baker, Philip and Mühlhäusler, Peter (1990). From business to pidgin. *Journal of Asian Pacific Communication*, 1, 87–115.

Bamgbose, Ayo (1992). Standard Nigerian English: Issues of identification. In Braj Kachru (ed.), *The Other Tongue: English across Cultures*, pp. 148–61. Urbana: University of Illinois Press.

Bhatia, Tej K. (1988). Trinidad Hindi: Its genesis and generational profile. In Richard K. Barz and Jeff Siegel (eds.), *Language Transplanted: The Development of Overseas Hindi*, pp. 179–96. Wiesbaden: Otto Harrassowitz.

Bickerton, Derek (1981). *Roots of Language*. Ann Arbor, MI: Karoma.

Bickerton, Derek (1984). The Language Bioprogram Hypothesis. *Behavioral and Brain Sciences*, 7, 173–221.

Bickerton, Derek (1989). The lexical learning hypothesis and the pidgin-creole cycle. In Martin Pütz and René Dirven (eds.), *Wheels within Wheels: Papers of the Duisburg Symposium on Pidgin and Creole Languages*, pp. 11–31. Frankfurt am Main: Verlag Peter Lang.

Bickerton, Derek (1999). How to acquire language without positive evidence: What acquisitionists can learn from creoles. In Michel DeGraff (ed.), *Language Creation and Language Change: Creolization, Diachrony, and Development*, pp. 49–74.

Brutt-Griffler, Janina (2002). *World English: A Study of its Development*. Clevedon, UK: Multilingual Matters.

Chaudenson, Robert (1979). *Les créoles français*. Paris: Fernand Nathan.

Chaudenson, Robert (1992). *Des îles, des hommes, des langues: essais sur la créolisation linguistique et culturelle.* Paris: L'Harmattan.

Chaudenson, Robert (2001). *Creolization of Language and Culture.* London: Routledge.

Chaudenson, Robert, Mougeon, Raymond, and Beniak, Edouard (1993). *Vers une approche panlectale de la variation du français.* Aix-en-Provence: Institut d'Etudes Créoles et Francophones.

Chomsky, Noam (2000). *New Horizons in the Study of Language and Mind.* Cambridge, UK: Cambridge University Press.

Collins, James (1984). Malaysian and Bazaar Malay: Polarity, continuity and communication. In Asmah Hj. Omar (ed.), *National Language and Communication in Multilingual societies*, pp. 151–74. Kuala Lumpur: Dewan Bahasa dan Pustaka.

d'Ans, André-Marcel (1996). Essai de socio-linguistique historique à partir d'un témoignage inédit sur l'emploi des langues, notamment africaines, en Haïti, au cours de la guerre de libération et des premières années de l'indépendance. *Etudes Créoles*, 19, 110–22.

de Féral, Carole (1989). *Pidgin-English du Cameroun.* Paris: Peters/SELAF.

DeGraff, Michel (ed.). 1999. *Language Creation and Language Change: Creolization, Diachrony, and Development.* Cambridge, MA: MIT Press.

DeGraff, Michel (1999a). Creolization, language change, and language acquisition: A prolegomenon. In Michel DeGraff (ed.), *Language Creation and Language Change: Creolization, Diachrony, and Development*, pp. 1–46.

DeGraff, Michel (1999b). Creolization, language change, and language acquisition: An epilogue. In Michel DeGraff (ed.), *Language Creation and Language Change: Creolization, Diachrony, and Development*, pp. 473–543.

DeGraff, Michel (2001a). On the origin of creoles: A Cartesian critique of neo-Darwinian linguistics. *Linguistic Typology*, 5, 213–310.

DeGraff, Michel (2001b). Morphology in creole genesis: Linguistics and ideology. In Michael Kenstowicicz (ed.), *Ken Hale: A Life in Language*, pp. 53–121. Cambridge, MA: MIT Press.

Ferraz, L. Ivens (1979). *The Creole of São Tomé.* Johannesburg: Witwatersrand University Press.

Goodman, Morris (1993). African substratum: Some cautionary words. In Salikoko S. Mufwene (ed.), *Africanisms in Afro-American Language Varieties*, pp. 64–73. Athens: University of Georgia Press.

Hagège, Claude (1993). *The Language Builder: An Essay on the Human Signature in Linguistic Morphogenesis.* Amsterdam: John Benjamins.

Hock, Hans Henrich and Joseph, Brian D. (1996). *Language History, Language Change, and Language Relationship.* Berlin: Mouton de Gruyter.

Holm, John (1988). *Pidgins and Creoles. Volume 1: Theory and Structure.* Cambridge, UK: Cambridge University Press.

Huber, Magnus (1999). Atlantic creoles and the Lower Guinea Coast: A case against Afrogenesis. In Magnus Huber and Mikael Parkvall (eds.), *Spreading the Word: The Issue of Diffusion among the Atlantic Creoles*, pp. 81–110. London: University of Westminster Press.

Jourdan, Christine (1985). Creolisation, nativisation or substrate influences: What is happening in *bae* in Solomon Islands Pidgin. *Papers in Pidgin and Creole Linguistics*, 4, 67–96.

Jourdan, Christine (1991). Pidgins and creoles: The blurring of categories. *Annual Review of Anthropology*, 20, 187–209.

Keesing, Roger M. (1988). *Melanesian Pidgin and the Oceanic Substrate*. Stanford, CA: Stanford University Press.

Keller, Rudi (1994). *On Language Change: The Invisible Hand in Language*. London: Routledge.

Lass, Roger (1997). *Historical Linguistics and Language Change*. Cambridge, UK: Cambridge University Press.

Lefebvre, Claire (1998). *Creole Genesis and the Acquisition of Grammar: The Case of Haitian Creole*. Cambridge, UK: Cambridge University Press.

Le Page, R. B. (1960). An historical introduction to Jamaican Creole. In R. B. Le Page and David De Camp, *Jamaican Creole*, pp. 1–124. Cambridge, UK: Cambridge University Press.

Lorenzino, Geraldo A. (1998). The Angolar creole Portuguese of São Tomé: Its grammar and sociolinguistic history. Ph.D. dissertation, City University of New York.

Manessy, Gabriel (1996). Réflexions sur les contraintes anthropologiques de la créolisation: de l'improbabilité du métissage linguistique dans les créoles atlantiques exogènes. *Etudes Créoles*, 19, 61–71.

Masuda, Hirokuni (1995). TSR formation as a discourse substratum in Hawaii. *Journal of Pidgin and Creole Languages*, 10, 253–88.

McMahon, April (1994). *Understanding Language Change*. Cambridge, UK: Cambridge University Press.

McWhorter, John H. (1998). Identifying the creole prototype: Vindicating a typological class. *Language*, 74, 788–818.

McWhorter, John H. (2000). *The Missing Spanish Creoles: Recovering the Birth of Plantation Contact Languages*. Berkeley: University of California Press.

Meillet, Antoine (1929). Le développement des langues. In *Continu et discontinu*, pp. 119ff. Paris:

Bloud and Gay. Reprinted in Antoine Meillet, 1951, pp. 71–83.

Meillet, Antoine (1951). *Linguistique historique et linguistique générale*, volume 2. Paris: Klincksieck.

Mesthrie, Rajend (1991). *Language in Indenture: A Sociolinguistic History of Bhojpuri-Hindi in South Africa*. Johannesburg: Witwatersrand University Press.

Mesthrie, Rajend (1992). *English in Language Shift: The History, Structure and Sociolinguistics of South African Indian English*. Cambridge, UK: Cambridge University Press.

Milroy, James (1996). Linguistic ideology and the Anglo-Saxon lineage of English. In J. Klemola, M. Kytö, and M. Rissanen (eds.), *Speech Past and Present: Studies in English Dialectology in Memory of Ossi Ihalainen*, pp. 169–86. Frankfurt am Main: Peter Lang.

Milroy, James (1997). Internal vs external motivations for linguistic change. *Multilingua*, 16, 311–23.

Mohan, Peggy (1990). The rise and fall of Trinidadian Bhojpuri. *International Journal of the Sociology of Language*, 85, 21–30.

Mohan, Peggy and Zador, Paul (1986). Discontinuity in a life cycle: The death of Trinidad Bhojpuri. *Language*, 62, 291–320.

Mufwene, Salikoko S. (1991). Pidgins, creoles, typology, and markedness. In Francis Byrne and Thomas Huebner (eds.), *Development and Structures of Creole Languages: Essays in Honor of Derek Bickerton*, pp. 123–43. Amsterdam: John Benjamins.

Mufwene, Salikoko S. (1994). New Englishes and criteria for naming them. *World Englishes*, 13, 21–31.

Mufwene, Salikoko S. (1996). The Founder Principle in creole genesis. *Diachronica*, 13, 83–134.

Mufwene, Salikoko S. (1997). Jargons, pidgins, creoles, and koinés: What are they? In Arthur K. Spears and Donald

Winford (eds.), *The Structure and Status of Pidgins and Creoles*, pp. 35–70. Amsterdam: John Benjamins.

Mufwene, Salikoko S. (2000). Creolization is a social, not a structural, process. In Ingrid Neumann-Holzschuh and Edgar Schneider (eds.), *Degrees of Restructuring in Creole Languages*, pp. 65–84. Amsterdam: John Benjamins.

Mufwene, Salikoko S. (2001). *The Ecology of Language Evolution*. Cambridge, UK: Cambridge University Press.

Naro, Anthony and Scherer, Maria Marta (1994). Sobre as origens do português popular do Brasil. *DELTA*, 9, 437–54.

Pakir, Anne Geok-In Sim (1986). A linguistic investigation of Baba Malay. Ph.D. dissertation, University of Hawaii.

Pargman, Sheri (2002). Internal and external factors in language change. Ph.D. dissertation, University of Chicago.

Paul, Herman (1880). *Prinzipien der Sprachgeschichte*. Halle: Niemeyer.

Posner, Rebecca (1996). *The Romance Languages*. Cambridge, UK: Cambridge University Press.

Post, Marike (1995). Fa d'Ambu. In Jacques Arends, Pieter Muysken, and Norval Smith (eds.), *Pidgins and Creoles: An Introduction*, pp. 191–204. Amsterdam: John Benjamins.

Prudent, Lambert-Félix (1980). *Des baragouins à la langue antillaise: Analyse historique et sociolinguistique du discours sur le créole*. Paris: Editions Caribéennes.

Roberts. Sarah Julianne (1998). The role of diffusion in the genesis of Hawaiian Creole. *Language*, 74, 1–39.

Romaine, Suzanne (2000). Multilingualism. In Mark Aronoff and Janie Rees-Miller (eds.), *Handbook of Linguistics*, pp. 512–32. Malden, MA: Blackwell.

Sankoff, Gillian (1979). The genesis of a language. In Kenneth Hill (ed.), *The Genesis of Language*, pp. 23–47. Ann Arbor, MI: Karoma.

Sankoff, Gillian (1984). Substrate and universals in the Tok Pisin verb phrase. In Deborah Schiffrin (ed.), *Meaning, Form, and Use in Context: Linguistic Applications*, pp. 104–19. Washington, D.C.: Georgetown University Press.

Sankoff, Gillian (1993). Focus in Tok Pisin. In Francis Byrne and Donald Winford (eds.), *Focus and Grammatical Relations in Creole Languages*, pp. 117–40. Amsterdam: John Benjamins.

Sankoff, Gillian, and Brown, Penelope (1976). The origins of syntax in discourse: A case study of Tok Pisin relatives. *Language*, 52, 631–66.

Schuchardt, Hugo (1884). *Slavo-deutsches und Slavo-italienisches*. Graz: Leuschner and Lubensky.

Smith, Geoff and Matthews, Stephen (1996). Pidgins and creoles. In Bernard Comrie, Stephen Matthews, and Maria Polinsky (eds.), *The Atlas of Languages: The Origin and Development of Languages Throughout the World*, pp. 144–61. New York: Facts on File.

Smith, Norval (1995). An annotated list of pidgins, creoles, and mixed languages. In Jacques Arends, Pieter Muysken, and Norval Smith (eds.), *Pidgins and Creoles: An Introduction* (pp. 331–374). Amsterdam: John Benjamins.

Sylvain, Suzanne (1936). *Le créole haitien: morphologie et syntaxe*. Wettern, Belgium: Imprimerie De Meester.

Thomason, Sarah G. (1997). A typology of contact languages. In Arthur K. Spears and Donald Winford (eds.), *The Structure and Status of Pidgins and Creoles*, pp. 71–88. Amsterdam: John Benjamins.

Thomason, Sarah G. (2002). Creoles and genetic relationship. Column, *Journal of Pidgin and Creole Languages*, 17, 101–09.

Thomason, Sarah G. and Kaufman, Terrence (1988). *Language Contact, Creolization, and Genetic Linguistics.* Berkeley: University of California Press.

Warner-Lewis, Maureen (1996). *Trinidad Yoruba: From Mother Tongue to Memory.* Tuscaloosa: University of Alabama Press.

Weinreich, Uriel (1953). *Languages in Contact: Findings and Problems.* New York: Linguistic Circle of New York.

Weinreich, Uriel, Labov, William, and Herzog, Marvin I. (1968). Empirical foundations for a theory of language change. In W. P. Lehman and Yakov Malkiel (eds.), *Directions for Historical Linguistics: A Symposium,* pp. 97–195. Austin: University of Texas Press.

Wylie, Jonathan (1995). The origins of Lesser Antillean French Creole: Some literary and lexical evidence. *Journal of Pidgin and Creole Languages,* 10, 77–127.

19   Bilingualism and Gender

INGRID PILLER AND ANETA PAVLENKO

19.1   Introduction

The field of language and gender research has "exploded" (Kendall and Tannen, 2001) since 1990. One of the directions in which the field has expanded is away from its former monolingual bias towards research into the ways in which gender is played out in multilingual contexts. This increase in research activity is apparent from a number of recent review articles (Ehrlich, 1997; Pavlenko, 2001a; Pavlenko and Piller, 2001; Sunderland, 2000; Winter and Pauwels, 2000) and edited volumes (Burton, Dyson, and Ardener, 1994; Pavlenko, Blackledge, Piller, and Teutsch-Dwyer, 2001). The expansion of language and gender research into multilingual contexts was made possible by a paradigm shift in the field which entailed a reorientation away from an early focus on "women's language" towards an understanding of gender as a system of social relations. Gender is now seen as structuring social contexts and, by implication, language use in a given context. We will start out by reviewing this paradigm shift (section 19.2), and then we will go on to provide an overview of the interplay between bilingualism and gender in five social contexts, which tend to be heavily gendered in many societies. These five contexts are the marketplace (section 19.3), intimate relationships (section 19.4), parent–child relationships (section 19.5), friendship networks (section 19.6) and education (section 19.7). In the concluding section we will discuss three factors that mediate the relationship between bilingualism and gender in all these contexts, namely ideology, access, and motivation. Throughout, our definition of bilingualism is an inclusive one, and we consider the use of two or more languages on a regular basis, irrespective of proficiency and age of acquisition as a bilingual practice (cf. Grosjean, 1982).

19.2   Approaches to Language and Gender

The expansion of the field of language and gender in the early 1990s was made possible by a theoretical reorientation of the field towards poststructuralist approaches. Prior to that, language and gender research had mainly been concerned with "women's language" and how it differed from "men's language." At the time of the inception of the field in the 1970s, bilingualism and gender was immediately put on the table as a promising area of inquiry (Gal, 1978; Schlieben-Lange, 1977; Solé, 1978). However, this early work in bilingual contexts found only few followers. Until the publication of Burton et al. (1994), language and gender researchers steered as clear of bilingualism as bilingualism researchers did of gender issues. The rather limited number of bilingualism and gender studies published during that early period adopted one of three frameworks, which also dominated the more general field of language and gender at that time: deficit, difference, or dominance.

In the deficit framework women are seen as a "muted group" (Ardener, 1975) of inferior language users, who speak a "powerless language": uncertain, weak, excessively polite, full of hedges, tag questions, emphatic stresses, and hypercorrect grammar (Lakoff, 1975). In the study of bilingualism, this approach translated into the "linguistic lag hypothesis," which suggests that minority women are less bilingual than men, and, thus, lagging linguistically behind them (Stevens, 1986). The deficit framework has been criticized because it treats men's linguistic practices as the norm, renders women's linguistic practices as problematic, treats women as an undifferentiated group, and postulates a one-to-one mapping between linguistic phenomena and their meaning (see Talbot (1998) for an overview). With regard to bilingual women, Gal (1991) and Spedding (1994) argued that women might be rendered mute and monolingual by the research context itself. They suggested that some of the earlier studies might have misrepresented the extent of women's bilingualism because it would not have become apparent in the "unequal encounters" with white middle-class male anthropologists, linguists, and ethnographers.

The dominance framework is similar to the deficit framework in that it is also centrally concerned with women's vs. men's language. However, it explains the speech differences between the two groups differently, preferring to theorize them as a result of male dominance and female oppression. Key studies in this framework showed that men dominate conversations by interrupting women (e.g. West and Zimmerman, 1983) or by failing to listen and to uphold their end of the conversational bargain (e.g. Fishman, 1983). In the study of bilingualism, the dominance approach offered an alternative interpretation of the presumed fact that women were less proficient bilinguals than men by portraying them as linguistically oppressed (Burton, 1994). Despite the fact that this framework explicitly acknowledges the importance of power relations, criticism of the dominance model has centered around the fact that it fails to recognize the social, historical, and political situatedness of power, the effects of which are mediated not only by gender, but also by class, race, ethnicity, and sexuality (Cameron, 1992; Eckert and McConnell-Ginet, 1992). Therefore, the dominance approach oversimplifies gender relations by portraying "women-as-a-group" as dominated by "men-as-a-group," and by overlooking the fact that ethnic or sexual minority men may be equally oppressed, and that women themselves may be part of the dominant group in a society (e.g. white middle-class women). This matters even more in bilingual than in monolingual contexts as bilingual contexts are often characterized by long-standing status differences between majority and minority language groups. In addition, it was also shown that the presumed fact that women are less bilingual than men simply did not stand up to closer scrutiny in a range of contexts. On the contrary, not only did women in some contexts turn out to be more bilingual than the men in their community, but it was also shown that it often was the women who initiated language shift in their community (Constantinidou, 1994; Gal, 1978; Holmes, 1993; McDonald, 1994; Schlieben-Lange, 1977; Solé, 1978).

Finally, the difference framework shares the basic research question "how do women and men use language differently?" with the deficit and the dominance framework. However, in contrast to both, it does not seek to explain these differences, but rather argues that sex or gender constitute the explanation in themselves. That is, women and men talk differently because they belong to two different sex categories (as, for instance, Chambers (1995) has argued) or because they belong to two different gender categories (as most famously espoused in the work of Tannen (1986, 1990, 1994)). This approach was most readily transferred to bilingual contexts by researchers in second language acquisition, who often posit that female learners generally do better than males (see Ellis (1994) for an overview). This claim, of course, does not sit easily with the assumption that women are less bilingual than men, which was embraced by the deficit and dominance frameworks, as we have shown. And, not surprisingly, there is indeed evidence to the contrary as well: sometimes female learners of a second language do worse than male learners (Hill, 1987; Holmes, 1993; Polanyi, 1995).

All three frameworks – deficit, dominance, and difference – reached an impasse in the late 1980s and early 1990s when more and more contradictory findings appeared. Conflicting evidence produced by researchers pursuing the same basic question "how do women and men speak differently?" – or, in the more specific form relevant to this chapter, "are women more or less bilingual than men?" – made the question itself seem fundamentally misguided. It became apparent that the question betrayed an unjustifiable universalizing assumption, which obscures heterogeneity across and within cultures (e.g. Bergvall, Bing, and Freed, 1996; Bucholtz, Liang, and Sutton, 1999; Cameron, 1992, 1998; Crawford, 1995; Hall and Bucholtz, 1995; Talbot, 1998). On the basis of this assumption, findings that are true for, say, the English-speaking monolingual white middle class of urban America had all too easily been transferred to other contexts. Consequently, the static opposition between "women's language" and "men's language" was reappraised in a paradigm shift towards a variety of feminist poststructuralist approaches.

Feminist poststructuralist approaches, as applied to linguistics by Cameron (1992, 1997, 1998), cease to view language as a set of disembodied structures. Instead, language becomes the locus of social organization, power, individual consciousness, and a form of symbolic capital (Bourdieu, 1991). Language use, in turn, is considered a situated process of participation in multiple and over-lapping communities of practice, which may entail the negotiation of ways of being a person in that context (Eckert and McConnell-Ginet, 1992; Holmes and Meyerhoff, 1999). Furthermore, gender cannot be fully understood as an individual attribute: femininities relate to masculinities and all are connected to other social categories. Gender is thus no longer seen as a set of traits, a variable or a role, but as a product of social doings, "a system of culturally constructed relations of power, produced and reproduced in interaction between and among men and women" (Gal, 1991, p. 176). Thus, the production of gender, ideologies of gender, and beliefs and ideas about relations between the sexes vary over time and across cultures (Bonvillain, 1995). With language seen as a collection of heterogeneous discourses, individual linguistic strat-egies are no longer directly linked to gender and cease to be the main focus of research. Instead, the locus of study shifts to ideologies of language and gender, which embody speakers' normative conceptions of gender identities, gender relations and gender-appropriate uses of language, and are produced, reproduced, challenged and negotiated in talk, and other forms of discourse (Bergvall, 1999). Similarly, with gender seen as a system of social relations and discursive practices, the goal of the study of language and gender becomes twofold: on the one hand, to study ways in which gender is constructed and negotiated in multiple discourses, and, on the other, to investigate the effects of gender on individuals' access to linguistic resources and possibilities of expression.

Feminist poststructuralism also allows us to view the relationship between bilingualism and gender in a new light (Pavlenko, 2001a; Pavlenko and Piller, 2001). Instead of asking whether it is women or men who are more or less bilingual, research interest shifts towards the linguistic practices of particular women and particular men living in specific communities at a specific point in history. In turn, their linguistic practices are interpreted in terms of access to linguistic resources, agency, and gender performance. As noted above, in the following, we will exemplify this approach, as well as its findings, with case studies from the bilingual marketplace, intimate relationships, parent–child relationships, friendship networks, and classrooms.

19.3 Gender in the Bilingual Marketplace

The job market and workplaces constitute prime discursive spaces where access to linguistic resources may be gendered. These are major sites where the symbolic capital of linguistic practices is transformed into economic and social capital. In bilingual contexts this means that knowledge of or proficiency in the majority language or the more highly valued language (or languages) will allow speakers to compete for more prestigious, better-paid or physically less strenuous jobs and to pursue career paths that will advance them socially and economically. By contrast, not knowing the "right" language/s often renders other forms of symbolic capital (e.g. professional expertise) worthless or diminishes their value, as is seen, for instance, in the numerous cases of highly qualified immigrant professionals who are finding it difficult to restart their careers in a new country.

Gendered economic prospects can explain why minority women are often found to be less proficient in the majority language than a community's men. If a society assigns the role of breadwinner to men and unpaid domestic work to women – as many societies do – men may encounter more opportunities to become bilingual, since more chances for interactions in the majority language exist outside the home. This pattern has been reported for many indigenous communities in Latin America (e.g. Hill, 1987; Spedding, 1994). There, men are likely to be more proficient in Spanish than women because they are more likely to engage in paid work. By contrast, women are more likely to be restricted to non-paid domestic and agricultural work. For instance, Hill (1987) studied the use of Spanish and Mexicano, or Nahuatl, in rural communities in the region of the Malinche Volcano in Mexico. Women in this community had less access to education than men and spoke less Spanish. As a result, it was difficult for them to join the paid labor force, for which the use of Spanish was crucial, and they had limited opportunities to practice whatever Spanish they knew. Often, a vicious circle emerges in which limited proficiency in the majority language limits access to paid employment, which, in turn, limits interactional opportunities in the majority language.

It comes as no surprise that women in such contexts often relate their bleak social and economic situation to their use of the minority language. Consequently, they may be ready to spearhead language shift to the majority language if they have the opportunity. This pattern was first demonstrated by Gal (1978) in her work on the bilingual town of Oberwart in Austria. In the minority Hungarian community there, young women led the shift towards German. They were motivated by a symbolic link between German and industrial work that was becoming available at the time. For these peasant women, (German-speaking) factory work represented a significant improvement over the drudgery of (Hungarian-speaking) peasant life. McDonald (1994) reports similar findings for Breton peasant women for whom language shift from Breton to French represented a symbolic journey "from cow-shit to finery" (McDonald, 1994, p. 91). At the time of the research, young women moved away from rural Brittany in droves, in search of a better life in the urban centers. Of course, the move entailed a language shift away from Breton towards French. The gendered migration pattern was so pronounced that Breton-speaking men could not find local wives, just like the Hungarian peasant men in Oberwart. As a result, a new New Year greeting emerged in Breton: "I wish you a Happy New Year and a lady wife before it's out." (McDonald, 1994, p. 100). Even those women who stayed on and married local men spoke French to their children instead of Breton, in the hope that this would afford their children better social and economic opportunities than they themselves had had. In Constantinidou's (1994) work in Scotland, old Scottish Gaelic-speaking women reported that they had had similar hopes when they started to transmit English, rather than Gaelic, to their children early in the twentieth century.

However, while many researchers attribute minority and immigrant men's greater bilingualism to their role as breadwinners, Goldstein (1996, 2001) and Holmes (1993) show that participation in the workforce alone does not guarantee access to the majority language for women. Even when they are in paid employment, minority women are more often employed in workplaces where only the minority language is used. In her review of language maintenance and shift among immigrant communities in Australia and New Zealand, Holmes (1993) found that immigrant men were more often employed in workplaces where English was required than immigrant women, who often worked in places where they used their native language. Similarly, Goldstein (1996, 2001) found in her ethnographic work with immigrant Portuguese women in a Canadian factory that the unspoken rules of that workplace prevented the women from using English. Portuguese was considered as the solidarity code by all the workers, who were either native speakers of Portuguese or proficient second language users of Portuguese (as was the case for some Spanish- and Italian-speaking women in that factory). Consequently, this Toronto workplace afforded no opportunities to interact in English, and many of the women assembly-line workers did not speak or understand it well. Goldstein (1996, 2001) points out that while this practice ensured solidarity and cooperation on the factory floor, it also kept the women in question from the social and economic advancement that their English-speaking compatriots enjoyed. Furthermore, the researcher also points out that gender relations in the immigrant Portuguese community further limited the women's access to educational opportunities. It was, for instance, considered unacceptable for women to be in a classroom with male strangers, thereby preventing them from attending ESL classes.

Indeed it is often the case that communities have gatekeeping practices in place that restrict access to the most valued forms of linguistic capital. Ehrlich (2001), for instance, describes how sexual harassment or the fear of sexual harassment is a powerful deterrent that keeps women language learners – be they from minority and immigrant backgrounds or exchange students and sojourners in a foreign country – from seeking out interactions in the target language. In this view, sexual harassment is a form of social and economic, as well as sexual coercion. The same goes for less tangible gatekeeping practices such as ridicule and reprimands, which are most often expressions of ideologies about interpersonal relationships – intimate, parenting or friendship relationships – and we will investigate how such ideologies structure bilingualism in the following sections.

In sum, linguistic capital can be transformed into social and economic capital in the bilingual marketplace. Societal groups vie for access to symbolic capital just as they vie for access to social and economic capital. Given that many societies are structured hierarchically along gender lines it is not surprising that women's access to the most valued forms of linguistic capital – the first of which, in bilingual contexts, is most often proficiency in the majority or dominant language – is often limited, as is their access to social and economic capital. At the same time, access to the most valued forms of linguistic capital may hold out greater promise for women than for men and they may seek to obtain it more actively than men. Of course, economic considerations are just one of many that motivate human practices, including bilingualism. In the following we will turn to gender and bilingualism in the family, a context where actions are more typically motivated by love and affection and the need for affiliation and group membership. For the sake of textual organization, we break the family context up into one of intimate relationships (section 19.4) and one of parent–child relationships (section 19.5).

19.4   Gender in Bilingual Intimate Relationships

Another important discursive space for the construction of gender is the context of romantic love and intimate relationships. Comparatively few cultures explicitly sanction exogamy and treat bilingual intimate relationships as the norm. Such groups include the Tucanoan in the Vaupés region of Brazil and Colombia (Gomez-Imbert, 1986; Grimes, 1985; Jackson, 1983), as well as some groups on the Solomon Islands (Lincoln, 1979) and in New Guinea (Salisbury, 1962). All the members of these communities are multilingual, and the rule of exogamy requires that marriage partners must be sought from another language group. Residence is patrilocal, but both husband and wife continue to use their native language actively and receive the other's language in return. In these communities the gender identity of a person is clearly marked by the language he or she speaks. Evidence from exogamous cultures such as these suggests that multilingual groups in which each member uses mainly one language actively and understands many others passively are much better equipped to deal with the threat that globalization poses to minority-language maintenance than are traditionally monolingual minority groups (Holmes, 1992).

By contrast, the vast majority of cultures consider linguistic outmarriage as a deviation from endogamous norms. Minority groups that do not sanction exogamy but are characterized by high levels of exogamy (because of their proximity to another group or the effects of internationalization and globalization), often express concern that exogamy will lead to language shift and language loss. In the Canadian context, for instance, talk about the "threat" of exogamy to francophone language maintenance (Bernard, 1994) is common. Exogamy takes on even more sinister connotations when it is described as a "Trojan horse" type of threat (Mougeon, Savard, and Carroll, 1978). It is most often women who are faced with such negative perceptions of their exogamous relationships because women are also often seen as the "guardians of the minority language" who, as mothers, socialize the next generation into the community (see section 19.5 for details). Heller and Lévy (1992a, b, 1994), for instance, describe the sense of guilt that an ideology of treason – to their native language and culture – engenders in francophone Canadian women married to anglophone men. Similarly, many of the female partners in the Afrikaans-English marriages studied by De Klerk (2001) report initial negative reactions to their exogamous choice by their families and friends, as do female partners in Castellano-Catalan marriages (Boix, 1997). In Mexican culture there is even the archetype of La Malinche, whose story warns of the dangers of seeking out a partner from another culture (Lenchek, 1997). La Malinche, an Aztec woman who was given to Cortes as a slave and who became his interpreter and lover, is said to be responsible for the success of the conquest (conveniently ignoring the Spaniards' superior firepower, the diseases they brought, and the internal weakness of the Aztec empire). The moral of the La Malinche story thus equates female bilingualism with treason and loose sexual morals. Immigrant communities that are strongly preoccupied with maintaining their native language, culture and traditions often attempt to do so by sexual coercion of their daughters. In her interviews with Filipina Americans, Espiritu (2001) learned that immigrant families from the Philippines tend to restrict the autonomy, mobility, and personal decision making of their daughters more than those of their sons in an effort to maintain the daughters' sexual virtue and, thereby, their virtue as potential transmitters of the home language and culture. If daughters make independent choices, their behavior is described as cultural ignorance and betrayal – an accusation which hurt even the more "rebellious" daughters deeply. Attempts to maintain the minority language and culture are thus part and parcel of a patriarchal discourse of "cultural 'authenticity' that locates family honor and national integrity in the group's female members" (Espiritu, 2001, p. 435).

However, despite the fact that exogamy is often met with disapproval in the culture of origin, bilingual relationships are on the rise internationally, as chances for people from different backgrounds to meet have been increasing dramatically. Often, the desire to learn another language goes hand in hand with a sexual desire for a partner from another culture. This was already evident in the work of Gal (1978) and McDonald (1994) (see section 19.3). Furthermore, many of the participants in Piller's (2002) study of English-German couples reported a long-standing desire for the other language and culture that for some culminated in their choice of a partner from that background. A German woman, for instance, describes how she spent her adolescence listening to the British Forces Radio, imagining herself as English and dreaming of English men. At the same time, her future husband, a Briton, read

German literature and watched German movies of the 1970s and imagined himself leading the life of an intellectual Bohemian in continental Europe. Similarly, Espín (1999) found in her interviews with migrant women to the USA that many considered that becoming bilingual and becoming romantically involved with a partner from the target culture somehow belonged together. Like some of the Filipinas interviewed by Espiritu (2001), they saw a love affair with a partner from another culture as the only way to break free from the sexual restrictions imposed on them by their native families. This connection between language desire and sexual desire is most apparent in Takahashi's (2001) exploration of the English-learning journeys of young Japanese students in Australia. This researcher finds that many of the women tell stories of "akogare," 'desire' for the English language and for Western men that motivate them in their pursuit of an overseas education at an Australian university. Some of them take finding an Australian boyfriend as an important measure of their success in learning English. By contrast, the male students in the sample do not have discourses of "akogare" at their disposal and romantic relationships are not an avenue into the target language and culture that they imagine for themselves. The gendered desires of the learners are matched by those of their host society, which also portrays Asian women as desirable partners for Western men, but does not view Asian men as desirable partners for Western women.

Once a bilingual intimate relationship has been established, the question of language choice arises. It is often assumed that this is a gendered choice in which the male partner's language prevails because women are "more likely to adapt their language use than men in cross-language relationships" (Lyon, 1996, p. 188; quoted in De Klerk, 2001, p. 209). Piller (2002) shows that bilingual couples do not necessarily choose between the two languages but often engage in a range of bilingual practices which allow them to use and maintain both languages. Thus, the question whether "her" or "his" language is chosen by bilingual couples is misguided in itself. Furthermore, the evidence that suggests that it is the male partner's language that is preferably chosen needs to be re-evaluated in the light of residence and proficiency. To begin with residence, Piller (2001b) shows that migration patterns are a prime factor which genders a couple's language choice. International couples from developed countries are more likely to choose the male partner's native country as their place of residence than the female's. This preference is due to economic reasons: migration often involves downward occupational mobility, and on average women continue to earn less than men. Therefore, migration of the male partner would be more disadvantageous for the couple as an economic unit than migration of the female partner tends to be. Secondly, proficiency overrides gender factors and it is gendered research, with its traditional focus on women's – rather than everyone's – practices, which may have produced the impression that women are more likely to adapt to their partner's language than vice versa. For instance, the work of Heller and Lévy (1992a, b, 1994) shows indeed that the couple language for the anglophone and francophone Canadian couples they studied was the husband's language in the overwhelming majority of cases. However, the explanation for that pattern is a proficiency issue rather than a gender issue. All the wives in the sample were francophone and all the husbands were anglophone. While all the wives could speak at least some English when they met their partner, few of the husbands could speak any French at the time. Further evidence for the crucial importance of proficiency comes from De Klerk's (2001) study where the gender-nexus does not hold. Most of the Afrikaans- and English-speaking couples in South Africa whom this researcher interviewed had chosen English over Afrikaans as their couple language irrespective of whether it was the female or the male partner who had Afrikaans or English as their first language. The couples explained that in most cases the English-speaking partner had had little or no Afrikaans at the time they met while the Afrikaans-speaking partners in all cases knew at least some English. In yet another context, it is the female partner's language that is chosen in most cases. In his interviews with Anglophone wives married to Tunisian husbands in Tunisia, Walters (1996) found that most of them used English together, and some French, the colonial lingua franca. However, no couple used Tunisian Arabic with each other and very few of the women were actually proficient in it. Indeed, this study shows that the partner whose language is chosen is not necessarily at an advantage – an assumption that, explicitly or implicitly, often pervades work on linguistic intermarriage. By contrast, Walters (1996) found that the women would have loved to learn more Arabic but found that their husbands did not necessarily support their endeavors. As reasons the researcher cites the fact that the men felt that Tunisian Arabic-speaking Western wives would sound stupid and would lose their status as "trophy wives." For the women, their limited proficiency in Arabic resulted in exclusion from or restricted access to female family and friendship networks and limited control over their children's education (see section 19.5). Evidence that linguistic accommodation in an intimate relationship is not necessarily beneficial to the speaker who is accommodated to also comes from the work of Teutsch-Dwyer (2001). This longitudinal study of the naturalistic acquisition of English in the USA by a Polish man in his thirties found that the man's English fossilized at a very early stage. It emerged that one of the reasons for his lack of bilingual development was the fact that his American girlfriend accommodated to his limited proficiency: she only used basic grammatical structures and only lexical items which she knew he could understand. These accommodations, as well as those of other female members of his circle of friends and acquaintances, hampered his acquisition of English considerably.

In sum, the gendered nature of intimate relationships also genders bilingualism. In exogamous cultures, gender may be indexed by the language a person uses. In endogamous societies, some people may be motivated to imagine new and different identities for themselves which they aim to attain through becoming bilingual and engaging in intimate relationships with a partner from the target group. To date, female attempts to transcend the confines of their native language and culture have been more often recorded than those of men. However, as argued in Pavlenko's (2001b) study of immigrant narratives and language learning memoirs, rather than reflecting "reality," this disparity suggests that in some cases women may be more willing than men to discuss intimate relationships.

19.5 Gender in Bilingual Parent–Child Relationships

As we showed in the previous section, female exogamy is considered problematic in many cultures. This is so because images of ideal femininity place women firmly inside the community, making them the transmitters of the home language, and of cultural, ethnic, and religious traditions. Consequently, language maintenance efforts in immigrant and minority communities are often seen to stand and fall with the community's women. In many cultures, parenting practices are strongly gendered and mothers spend significantly more time socializing their children than fathers do. If that is the case, it is not surprising to find that minority languages are better maintained if the mothers are the minority speakers or choose to transmit the minority language. An example comes from Boyd's (1998) study of the maintenance of English in the children of US-Americans married to Danes, Finns, or Swedes in Scandinavia. The children of these couples were more fluent in English – in addition to the local Scandinavian language – if the mother was the English speaker. The researcher explains this pattern as a result of gendered family roles: a breadwinner father who uses English "virtually all the time" with his child, will expose the child far less to English than a homemaker mother who uses English to the same degree.

However, as we demonstrated in section 19.3, the role of guardians of the minority language is not always accepted by mothers. For instance, Constantinidou (1994) and McDonald (1994) show that Scottish Gaelic- and Breton-speaking mothers chose to educate their children in English and French respectively because they felt that would open opportunities to their children they themselves had been denied. Indeed, mothers often seem rather reluctant "guardians" of the minority language and culture. Language transmission is often forced upon them by ideologies of femininity and motherhood which obfuscate the fact that the "guardian" role is not highly valued and comes at a significant price for their own bilingualism. In the contexts of indigenous Latin America (Hill, 1987; Spedding, 1994; see section 19.3 for details), for instance, local ideologies construct indigenous women as more Indian than men, both in their looks and in their speech. This Indianness, in turn, positions women simultaneously as guardians of the home language and as backward members of the community. Another example comes from Kouritzin's (2000) interviews with immigrant mothers in Canada. One woman, an immigrant from India, could not attend ESL classes despite the provision of government-funded childcare because her husband was adamant that only family – which, in the absence of an extended family in the migration context, meant the mother – should care for the children. In an attempt to explain the origins of bilingual mothers' frequent linguistic oppression, Cameron (1992) points to the paradoxical situation in which many immigrant and minority men find themselves with regard to assimilation: while beneficial socially and economically, it may also undermine their way of life, their values, their beliefs, and ultimately their ethnic and cultural identity. Positioning women-as-mothers in charge of language maintenance may become a way out: "In a male-dominated society, men can resolve this problem by taking the rewards of cultural change for themselves while requiring the community's women to be living symbols of tradition" (Cameron, 1992, p. 202). (For an additional case in which women are seen as carriers of the traditional culture, see chapter 29.)

Furthermore, ideologies of motherhood do not only emanate from the minority community and place language maintenance in the mothers' hands. Because of their roles as prime caregivers and socializers of the next generation, immigrant and minority mothers may also become the target of assimilatory efforts on the part of the majority culture. An example comes from the "Americanization" movement at the beginning of the twentieth century. Then, immigrant women were seen as the main reason for the insufficient assimilation of immigrants and thus became the key locus of educational efforts. The Association of Collegiate Alumnae in Milwaukee, for instance, argued that "one of the gravest problems that our harassed government has to face at the present moment is the Americanization of emigrant women, the mothers of the citizens of the future" (1916–17; as cited in Schlossman, 1983, p. 177). Similarly, McClymer (1982, p. 98) demonstrates that the General Federation of Women's Clubs viewed immigrant mothers as a "reactionary force" and became determined to "carry the English language and American ways of caring for babies, ventilating the house, preparing American vegetables, instead of the inevitable cabbage, right into the new houses." Not all assimilatory approaches are necessarily as forceful as the early Americanization movement was, but oppressive ideologies of motherhood may also inform approaches from the majority to the minority in the more benign context of contemporary social work with its "benevolent racism" (Villenas, 2001). Blackledge (2000, 2001), for instance, describes how British primary school teachers talk about the mothers of their Bangladeshi pupils. They imagine those mothers to be the primary caregivers while fathers are imagined to be largely absent from the household. At the same time, those mothers were perceived as incompetent caregivers who had nothing to contribute to their children's education, particularly their literacy in English. As the researcher convincingly argues, less stereotypical views of Bangladeshi women, and Muslim women more generally, might have opened avenues to bilingual education in which the parents could have supported their children's education in English and Bengali.

These findings are echoed by Villenas (2001) in her ethnographic work with Latina mothers in a small town in North Carolina. Public discourses in that town are pervaded by a perception of Latin immigrants as a problem. As such they are at the receiving end of all kinds of "helping" responses from welfare agents, who unwittingly strengthen this perception. Latina women are portrayed as a particular problem because they are seen as victims of the Latino men's machismo, and as lacking English, culture, and, particularly, parenting skills. Thus, Villenas's (2001) discussion offers convincing evidence that the use of English and white middle-class parenting practices are normalized while Spanish and Hispanic cultural practices, including parenting, are pathologized. The women Blackledge (2000, 2001) and Villenas (2001) spoke to affirmed the value of their own linguistic and parenting practices in the face of racist attitudes – whether benevolent or not – on the part of the majority society. Their insistence on maintaining their traditional culture, which they saw as one of the few avenues they had in the face of poverty in their native countries and discrimination in their new ones, was interpreted by the majority society as mindless submission to Muslim or Latino patriarchy.

In sum, in the eyes of minority communities, women-as-mothers may become the main "culprits" for initiating language change. At the same time, the dominant society may blame these same women for being a reactionary force that resists and subverts assimilation efforts. Thus, in a classical double-bind situation, bilingual mothers carry the double burden of guarding the minority language and culture and facilitating their children's entry into the majority language and culture.

19.6 Gender in Bilingual Friendship Networks

While most of the work on gender in bilingual contexts centers on women, there is some work in the context of bilingual friendship networks that centers around boys' and men's practices. Woolard's (1997) ethnographic case study of high school students in the Barcelona area was one of the first to indicate that gender differences in the ways in which friendship networks are structured can affect the use of the bilingual repertoire. In that context, the girls' friendship circles were more solidary and cohesive than the boys' groups. Therefore the girls' groups favored ethnic and linguistic homogeneity and set stronger constraints on linguistic behavior. In contrast, the boys' peer groups often were ethnically mixed and linguistically diverse, with Catalan and Castilian boys mixing more freely than Catalan and Castilian girls. As a result, the girls were more monolingual in either Catalan or Castilian while the boys tended to be more bilingual.

However, it is not only between girls and boys that differences in bilingual friendship practices emerge. Different boys' friendship groups also value different forms of masculinity and use their two languages differently, as

Pujolar (1997, 2001) shows. This researcher also worked in Barcelona, and the participants in his ethnographic study were two groups of adolescents, the Rambleros and the Trepas. The Rambleros were a tight-knit friendship group of working-class adolescents of Castilian descent. They usually spoke Castilian with each other although they had grown up in Barcelona, had learnt Catalan in school, and some of them had to use it at work. By contrast, the members of the Trepas group, who were also children of Castilian-speaking immigrants, made significant efforts to use Catalan in their group. In contrast to the Rambleros, the Trepas saw themselves as drop-outs whose use of Catalan was motivated by their desire to challenge the predominant conventions of language choice. Pujolar (1997, 2001) demonstrates that ideologies of language, ethnicity, sexuality, gender, and class shaped the groups' linguistic practices and forms of self-expression, but they did so in different ways for the two groups. The Rambleros used Castilian to construct and evoke working-class masculinities, and they strongly resisted the use of Catalan, which they found ingenuous, posh, and unmasculine. By contrast, the Trepas used Catalan for its political dimensions. To them, it implied a rejection of Spanish chauvinistic attitudes, and the use of a code-switched variety seemed to them to be as transgressive of traditional gender arrangements as it was linguistically transgressive with regard to the pervasive assumption that conversations should be monolingual.

It is particularly in adolescent peer networks that the importance of the feminine or masculine connotations of languages emerges. Labov (1966) was the first to distinguish between overt and covert prestige in language choice in monolingual contexts (where the choice is between standard and non-standard varieties). Standard varieties carry overt prestige, which means that they are sanctioned by the educational system. While the standard has officially recognized prestige, it also often carries connotations of femininity or effeminacy. By contrast, non-standard varieties often have "street cred" – their prestige is licensed by their associations with authenticity and transgressions against authority (therefore "covert"). Varieties with covert prestige often carry associations of tough, rugged working-class masculinity. The importance of such gendered connotations of languages to language maintenance efforts has so far received little attention, but the work of Pujolar (1997, 2001) clearly indicates that Catalan has little appeal to the Rambleros boys because they find it to sound feminine and effeminate – "unmasculine." Similarly, Pavlenko (2001b) describes an instance where an American man failed in his efforts to learn French because he found the language to sound effeminate. The learner, the philosopher Richard Watson, traced his negative attitude to ideologies of masculinity internalized in early childhood, in particular, the deep-seated belief that "real men don't speak French." Not surprisingly, he could not bring himself to speak French although he reads it well. The desire of some young men to sound hyper-masculine as a crucial factor in their linguistic choices also emerges from the work of Bucholtz (1999) and Cutler (1999). These researchers describe how white US-American boys of highly privileged backgrounds use code switching into African American Vernacular English in order to perform a stylized tough hyper-masculinity. Like the discourse of benevolent racism exposed by Blackledge (2000, 2001) and Villenas (2001) (see section 19.5), these appropriations of a language construct not only gender but also race. By seeking identification with African-American masculinity, the boys whose code-switching practices are described by Bucholtz (1999) and Cutler (1999) also "reproduce the 'racialization' of African-American men as violent and dangerous" (Hill, 1999, p. 547). Indeed, a gendering of languages very often goes hand in hand with racist stereotyping of their speakers. Hill's (1995, 1998) work on "Mock Spanish" – the use of Spanish or pseudo-Spanish expressions by speakers of American English – for instance, shows that code switching into Mock Spanish constructs the speaker as colloquial, relaxed, capable of humor, streetwise and masculine. However, by iconic extension, Spanish and the "real" speakers of that language are constructed as disorderly and given to obscenity. By contrast, languages that carry connotations of femininity are often used to construct them and their speakers as weak, inferior and affected. Hutton (1999, p. 222), for instance shows that European anti-Semitic writing from the pre-Holocaust period regularly included comments about the feminine nature of Yiddish.

In sum, bilingual friendship networks are further discursive spaces where bilingualism may be gendered. Like all the other contexts discussed so far there is no simple mapping between gender and bilingual practice. Rather, linguistic practices do not only construct gender but they simultaneously construct other aspects of social identity, such as class, race, or political stance. Furthermore, the relationship between gender and bilingualism is mediated by ideologies of femininity and masculinity and the gendered connotations that languages carry in the attitudes of users.

19.7   Gender and Bilingualism in Education

None of the contexts we have discussed so far is strictly separable from education in bilingual settings. To begin with, access to languages that carry symbolic value is first and foremost access to education in that language. Second, desire for a second language may make some people seek out education in that language while ideologies of feminine virtue may restrict access to the classroom for others. Third, the obligations of motherhood may keep some women out of the classroom while they and their children may be the target of educational efforts that do nothing to alleviate their poverty and disadvantage. Fourth, peer networks are often constituted in and around educational practices, and gendered connotations of languages may make them desirable or undesirable to learn. Sunderland (2000), for instance, argues that boys do not choose foreign language subjects at school, do not like them, and are likely to fail in them because they see foreign language learning as a "girls' thing," an unmanly activity. While none of the contexts we are discussing here is thus strictly separable from issues of access to the classroom, this section focuses on gendered classroom interactions (see also Corson, 2001; Pavlenko, forthcoming; Sunderland, 2000).

Even when students have access to formal education and do access the classroom, interaction patterns – teacher talk, student talk to the teacher and with each other during pair- and group-work – may be gendered, and favor some groups more than others. In the 1970s and 1980s there was a lot of concern that boys dominate classroom talk and get the lion's share of the teacher's attention (see Pavlenko (forthcoming) and Sunderland (2000) for overviews of this research tradition and Chavez (2000) and Shehadeh (1999) for recent examples). As Pavlenko (forthcoming) explains, these studies are flawed for a number of reasons, including, most crucially, the assumption of a simple dual gender dichotomy within which they operate. As a result, they fail to take into account linguistic, ethnic, cultural and socioeconomic diversity in the classroom. It is not girls or boys who are advantaged or disadvantaged, but certain groups of girls or certain groups of boys. In particular, it appears that immigrant and minority girls are the least visible and most disempowered in majority schools. Losey (1995), for instance, studied the classroom participation patterns of American and Mexican-American students in a community college classroom. Mexican-American women participated less than Anglo women and men, and also less than Mexican-American men. The Mexican-American women were thus doubly marginalized in the class, both as women and as ethnic-minority members. Thus, it is not surprising that the school drop-out rates of Latina girls in the USA continue to increase and have reached the alarming rate of 30 percent (American Association of University Women, 1999) and that immigrant girls exhibit lower self-esteem and higher depression rates the longer they are in the USA (Olsen, 1997). In short, educational systems oftentimes fail minority and immigrant girls and women.

However, it is not only minority and immigrant girls and women who may be disadvantaged by classroom interaction patterns. In some cases, stereotypes about immigrant and minority boys may actually contribute to their failure in the classroom, as Willett (1995) demonstrates. This study of four 7-year-old ESL children within a mainstream US classroom shows that the combined effects of differences in gendered peer cultures and the seating arrangements – which were designed to keep the boys apart but allowed the girls to sit together – favored the three female learners. The friendship between these three ESL girls allowed them to collaborate and support each other, thus earning them a high status in the girls' subculture and the status of "good learners" in the eyes of the teacher. In contrast, the boy, who was of working class Mexican-American background, did not get any help from his female seatmates and was not allowed to get out of his seat to get help from his male bilingual friends. As a result, he had to rely on adults for help, thus acquiring the status of a needy child, unable to work independently. This view became so entrenched that, when all four children scored the same on the Bilingual Syntax Measure test, the three girls were allowed to exit the ESL class while the boy had to stay on. These findings are echoed by McKay and Wong (1996) whose ethnographic study of four Chinese ESL students in California found that the student who got least attention, was judged the most harshly, and was the least successful – he ultimately dropped out of school – was a boy from mainland China, whose parents had experienced considerable downward economic mobility since their immigration to the USA. This boy neither fit the nerdy stereotype of the "model minority" that applied well to two other ESL students from Taiwan (a boy and a girl), nor did he excel in sports, which was another "boys' identity" that made sense to the majority teachers and students. Similarly, Heller (1999, 2001) found that one of the most alienated student groups in the French-medium Toronto high school she observed consisted of working-class boys. These monolingual speakers of vernacular Canadian French were marginalized by the valorization of Standard French referenced to France norms as well as by their peers' preference for English in peer interactions. They often stopped speaking French at school altogether, dropped out, or dreamt of the day when they and their families would move back to Quebec.

In sum, research into classroom interaction in bilingual contexts shows that there are not two undifferentiated groups of "girls" and "boys" or "women" and "men." Rather, ideologies of gender and gendered friendship groups marginalize specific learners and/or groups of learners, be they immigrant women or working-class boys. Furthermore, once a student or student group has been stereotyped as poor learners, the perception is likely to become a self-fulfilling prophecy, which may permanently alienate such students or groups from mainstream formal education.

19.8   Conclusion

Increased attention to gender and power relations provides exciting new perspectives on the sociolinguistics of bilingualism. To begin with, gender structures access to linguistic resources as symbolic capital that can, in turn, be converted into social and economic resources. In the context of the bilingual marketplace, studies in a diversity of contexts have to date found that access to highly valued linguistic practices is most restricted for minority and immigrant women. At the same time, these women often stand to gain more from actively pursuing those resources than men do, and therefore women actively pursue language shift in a number of contexts. In the bilingual marketplace, women are more likely to face gatekeeping practices that make access to valued linguistic resources more difficult for them. Even in communities that have espoused gender equality as a common value and where hierarchical differences between women and men are minimal, valued linguistic practices continue to be iconically linked to masculinity as Heller (2000) and Piller (2001a) demonstrate for the bilingual business elites of the European Union and Germany.

Second, research in the contexts of bilingual intimate, parent–child, and friendship relationships shows that gender relations cannot be reduced to questions of economic and social power. People also become bilingual or give up their first languages for reasons rooted in their personal desires and dreams, in love, affection, and affiliation. These factors are as potent in bilingual language choices, code-switching practices and learning outcomes as economic and social factors are. Furthermore, there is significant interplay between the two areas, as ideologies of romantic love, parenthood, and friendship often constrain people as rational economic actors. As regards romantic love, ideologies of feminine virtue often associate bilingualism with loose sexual morals and treason against one's native community. Ideologies of motherhood are also frequently designed to keep minority and immigrant women from transgressing linguistic and social boundaries. Finally, friendship networks can serve to create connotations between a language and femininity or masculinity. Depending which ideal of femininity or masculinity a person or peer group aspires to they may engage in linguistic practices that iconically associate them with the language(s) with the "right" connotations.

Third, gender ideologies and the gendering of friendship and peer groups, with their particular developmental importance to adolescents, also have a crucial role to play in the ways in which discursive interactions in the classroom are structured. While negative stereotypes of immigrant women may keep them silent in the classroom, negative stereotypes of working-class boys may leave them disaffected. In each context discussed in this chapter, it has become obvious that the relationship between gender and bilingualism is not a straightforward one. Rather, it is mediated by speaker status (as based on ethnicity, race, class, sexuality etc.) and language status in local contexts.

REFERENCES

American Association of University Women. (1999). *Gender Gaps: Where Schools Still Fail our Children*. New York: Marlowe.

Ardener, E. (1975). The "problem" [of women] revisited. In S. Ardener (ed.), *Perceiving Women*, pp. 19–27. London: J. M. Dent.

Bergvall, V. L. (1999). Toward a comprehensive theory of language and gender. *Language in Society*, 28, 273–93.

Bergvall, V. L., Bing, J. M., and Freed, A. F. (eds.) (1996). *Rethinking Language and Gender Research: Theory and Practice*. London: Longman.

Bernard, R. (1994). Les enjeux de l'exogamie [The threats of exogamy].

Langue et Société [Language and Society], 46, 38–9.

Blackledge, A. (2000). *Literacy, Power and Social Justice*. Stoke-on-Trent, UK: Trentham Books.

Blackledge, A. (2001). Complex positionings: Women negotiating identity and power in a minority urban setting. In A. Pavlenko, A. Blackledge, I. Piller, and M. Teutsch-Dwyer (eds.), *Multilingualism, Second Language Learning and Gender*, pp. 53–75. Berlin and New York: Mouton de Gruyter.

Boix, E. (1997). Ideologías lingüísticas en familias lingüísticamente mixtas (catalán-castellano) en la región metropolitana de Barcelona [Linguistic ideologies in linguistically mixed families (Catalan-Castilian) in the Barcelona metropolitan region]. In K. Zimmermann and C. Bierbach (eds.), *Lenguaje y comunicación intercultural en el mundo hispánico* [Language and intercultural communication in the Spanish-speaking world], pp. 169–90. Frankfurt am Main: Vervuert.

Bonvillain, N. (1995). *Women and Men: Cultural Constructs of Gender*. Englewood Cliffs, NJ: Prentice-Hall.

Bourdieu, P. (1991). *Language and Symbolic Power*. Cambridge, UK: Polity.

Boyd, S. (1998). North Americans in the Nordic region: Elite bilinguals. *International Journal of the Sociology of Language*, 133, 31–50.

Bucholtz, M. (1999). You da man: Narrating the racial other in the production of white masculinity. *Journal of Sociolinguistics*, 3, 443–60.

Bucholtz, M., Liang, A. C., and Sutton, L. A. (eds.) (1999). *Reinventing Identities: The Gendered Self in Discourse*. New York and Oxford: Oxford University Press.

Burton, P. (1994). Women and second-language use: An introduction. In P. Burton, K. K. Dyson, and S. Ardener (eds.), *Bilingual Women: Anthropological Approaches to Second-language Use*, pp. 1–29. Oxford and Providence, RI: Berg.

Burton, P., Dyson, K. K., and Ardener, S. (eds.) (1994). *Bilingual Women: Anthropological Aapproaches to Second-language Use*. Oxford and Providence, RI: Berg.

Cameron, D. (1992). *Feminism and Linguistic Theory*. London: Macmillan.

Cameron, D. (1997). Theoretical debates in feminist linguistics: Questions of sex and gender. In R. Wodak (ed.), *Gender and Discourse*, pp. 21–36. London: Sage.

Cameron, D. (1998). Gender, language, and discourse: A review essay. *Signs:*

Journal of Women in Culture and Society, 23, 945–73.

Chambers, J. K. (1995). *Sociolinguistic Theory*. Oxford: Blackwell.

Chavez, M. (2000). *Gender in the Language Classroom*. Boston, MA: McGraw Hill.

Constantinidou, E. (1994). The "death" of East Sutherland Gaelic: Death by women? In P. Burton, K. K. Dyson, and S. Ardener (eds.), *Bilingual Women: Anthropological Approaches to Second-language Use*, pp. 111–27. Oxford and Providence, RI: Berg.

Corson, D. (2001). *Language, Diversity, and Education*. Mahwah, NJ: Lawrence Erlbaum Associates.

Crawford, M. (1995). *Talking Difference: On Gender and Language*. London: Sage.

Cutler, C. A. (1999). Yorkville crossing: White teens, hip hop and African American English. *Journal of Sociolinguistics*, 3, 428–42.

De Klerk, V. (2001). The cross-marriage language dilemma: His language or hers? *International Journal of Bilingual Education and Bilingualism*, 4, 197–216.

Eckert, P. and McConnell-Ginet, S. (1992). Think practically and look locally: Language and gender as community-based practice. *Annual Review of Anthropology*, 21, 461–90.

Ehrlich, S. (1997). Gender as social practice: Implications for second language acquisition. *Studies in Second Language Acquisition*, 19, 421–46.

Ehrlich, S. (2001). Gendering the "learner": Sexual harassment and second language acquisition. In A. Pavlenko, A. Blackledge, I. Piller, and M. Teutsch-Dwyer (eds.), *Multilingualism, Second Language Learning and Gender*, pp. 103–29. Berlin and New York: Mouton de Gruyter.

Ellis, R. (1994). *The Study of Second Language Acquisition*. Oxford: Oxford University Press.

Espín, O. M. (1999). *Women Crossing Boundaries: A Psychology of Immigration and Transformations of Sexuality.* New York and London: Routledge.

Espiritu, Y. L. (2001). "We don't sleep around like white girls do": Family, culture, and gender in Filipina American lives. *Signs: Journal of Women in Culture and Society,* 26, 415–40.

Fishman, P. (1983). Interaction: The work women do. In B. Thorne, C. Kramarae, and N. Henley (eds.), *Language, Gender and Society,* pp. 89–101. Cambridge, MA: Newbury House.

Gal, S. (1978). Peasant men don't get wives: Language and sex roles in a bilingual community. *Language in Society,* 7, 1–17.

Gal, S. (1991). Between speech and silence: The problematics of research on language and gender. In M. Di Leonardo (ed.), *Gender at the Crossroads of Knowledge,* pp. 175–203. Berkeley: University of California Press.

Goldstein, T. (1996). *Two Languages at Work: Bilingual Life on the Production Floor.* Berlin and New York: Mouton de Gruyter.

Goldstein, T. (2001). Researching women's language practices in multilingual workplaces. In A. Pavlenko, A. Blackledge, I. Piller, and M. Teutsch-Dwyer (eds.), *Multilingualism, Second Language Learning and Gender,* pp. 103–29. Berlin and New York: Mouton de Gruyter.

Gomez-Imbert, E. (1986). Puesto que hablamos distinto, quiere Ud. casarse conmigo? [Given that we speak differently, would you like to marry me?] *Glotta,* 1, 18–22.

Grimes, B. F. (1985). Language attitudes: Identity, distinctiveness, survival in the Vaupés. *Journal of Multilingual and Multicultural Development,* 6, 389–401.

Grosjean, F. (1982). *Life with Two Languages: An Introduction to Bilingualism.* Cambridge, MA: Harvard University Press.

Hall, K. and Bucholtz, M. (eds.) (1995). *Gender Articulated: Language and the*

Socially Constructed Self. New York and London: Routledge.

Heller, M. (1999). *Linguistic Minorities and Modernity: A Sociolinguistic Ethnography.* London: Longman.

Heller, M. (2000). Bilingualism and identity in the post-modern world. *Estudios de Sociolingüística,* 1, 9–24.

Heller, M. (2001). Gender and public space in a bilingual school. In A. Pavlenko, A. Blackledge, I. Piller, and M. Teutsch-Dwyer (eds.), *Multilingualism, Second Language Learning and Gender,* pp. 257–82. Berlin and New York: Mouton de Gruyter.

Heller, M. and Lévy, L. (1992a). La femme francophone en situation de mariage mixte [The Francophone woman in a mixed marriage]. *Recherches féministes* [Feminist Studies], 5, 59–82.

Heller, M. and Lévy, L. (1992b). Mixed marriages: Life on the linguistic frontier. *Multilingua,* 11, 11–43.

Heller, M. and Lévy, L. (1994). Les contradictions des mariages linguistiquement mixtes: Stratégies des femmes Franco-Ontariennes [The contradictions of linguistically mixed marriages: strategies of Franco-Ontario women]. *Langue et Société* [Language and Society], 53–88.

Hill, J. H. (1987). Women's speech in modern Mexicano. In S. Philips, S. Steele and C. Tanz (eds.), *Language, Gender, and Sex in Comparative Perspective,* pp. 121–60. Cambridge, UK: Cambridge University Press.

Hill, J. H. (1995). Junk spanish, covert racism, and the (leaky) boundary between public and private spheres. *Pragmatics,* 5, 197–212.

Hill, J. H. (1998). Language, race, and white public space. *American Anthropologist,* 100, 680–9.

Hill, J. H. (1999). Styling locally, styling globally: What does it mean? *Journal of Sociolinguistics,* 3, 542–56.

Holmes, J. (1992). *An Introduction to Sociolinguistics*. London and New York: Longman.

Holmes, J. (1993). Immigrant women and language maintenance in Australia and New Zealand. *International Journal of Applied Linguistics*, 3, 159–79.

Holmes, J. and Meyerhoff, M. (1999). The community of practice: Theories and methodologies in language and gender research. *Language in Society*, 28, 173–83.

Hutton, C. M. (1999). *Linguistics and the Third Reich: Mother-tongue Fascism, Race and the Science of Language*. London and New York: Routledge.

Jackson, J. (1983). *The Fish People: Linguistic Exogamy and Tukanoan Identity in Northwest Amazonia*. Cambridge, UK: Cambridge University Press.

Kendall, S. and Tannen, D. (2001). Discourse and gender. In D. Schiffrin, D. Tannen, and H. E. Hamilton (eds.), *The Handbook of Discourse Analysis*, pp. 548–67. Malden, MA, and Oxford: Blackwell.

Kouritzin, S. G. (2000). Immigrant mothers redefine access to ESL classes: Contradiction and ambivalence. *Journal of Multilingual and Multicultural Development*, 21, 14–32.

Labov, W. (1966). *The Social Stratification of English in New York City*. Washington, D.C.: Center for Applied Linguistics.

Lakoff, R. (1975). *Language and Woman's Place*. New York: Harper & Row.

Lenchek, S. (1997). "La Malinche" – harlot or heroine? *El ojo del lago* [Eye of the lake], 14, http://www.mexconnect.com/mex_/history/malinche.html.

Lincoln, P. C. (1979). Dual-lingualism: Passive bilingualism in action. *Te Reo*, 22, 65–72.

Losey, K. (1995). Gender and ethnicity as factors in the development of verbal skills in bilingual Mexican American women. *TESOL Quarterly*, 29, 635–61.

Lyon, J. (1996). *Becoming Bilingual*. Clevedon, UK: Multilingual Matters.

McClymer, J. (1982). The Americanization movement and the education of the foreign-born adult, 1914–25. In B. Weiss (ed.), *American Education and the European Immigrant: 1840–1940*, pp. 96–116. Urbana: University of Illinois Press.

McDonald, M. (1994). Women and linguistic innovation in Brittany. In P. Burton, K. K. Dyson, and S. Ardener (eds.), *Bilingual Women: Anthropological Approaches to Second-language Use*, pp. 85–110. Oxford and Providence, RI: Berg.

McKay, S. L. and Wong, S.-L. C. (1996). Multiple discourses, multiple identities: Investment and agency in second-language learning among Chinese adolescent immigrant students. *Harvard Educational Review*, 66, 577–608.

Mougeon, R., Savard, H., and Carroll, S. (1978). Les mariages mixtes: Le cheval de Troie de l'assimilation à Welland? [Mixed marriages: The Trojan horse of Welland assimilation?]. *L'Express de Toronto*, 3, 42.

Olsen, L. (1997). *Made in America: Immigrant Students in our Public Schools*. New York: New Press.

Pavlenko, A. (2001a). Bilingualism, gender, and ideology. *International Journal of Bilingualism*, 5, 117–51.

Pavlenko, A. (2001b). Language learning memoirs as a gendered genre. *Applied Linguistics*, 22, 213–40.

Pavlenko, A. (forthcoming). Gender in foreign/second language education: Critical and feminist approaches to research and pedagogy. In B. P. Norton and K. Toohey (eds.), *Critical Pedagogy in Language Education*. Cambridge, UK: Cambridge University Press.

Pavlenko, A., Blackledge, A., Piller, I., and Teutsch-Dwyer, M. (eds.) (2001).

Multilingualism, Second Language Learning and Gender. Berlin and New York: Mouton de Gruyter.

Pavlenko, A. and Piller, I. (2001). New directions in the study of multilingualism, second language learning, and gender. In A. Pavlenko, A. Blackledge, I. Piller, and M. Teutsch-Dwyer (eds.), *Multilingualism, Second Language Learning and Gender*, pp. 17–52. Berlin and New York: Mouton de Gruyter.

Piller, I. (2001a). Identity constructions in multilingual advertising. *Language in Society*, 30, 153–86.

Piller, I. (2001b). Linguistic intermarriage: Language choice and negotiation of identity. In A. Pavlenko, A. Blackledge, I. Piller, and M. Teutsch-Dwyer (eds.), *Multilingualism, Second Language Learning and Gender*, pp. 199–230. Berlin and New York: Mouton de Gruyter.

Piller, I. (2002). *Bilingual Couples Talk: The Discursive Construction of Hybridity*. Amsterdam: John Benjamins.

Polanyi, L. (1995). Language learning and living abroad: Stories from the field. In B. F. Freed (ed.), *Second Language Acquisition in a Study Abroad Context*, pp. 271–91. Amsterdam: John Benjamins.

Pujolar, J. (1997). Masculinities in a multilingual setting. In S. Johnson and U. H. Meinhof (eds.), *Language and Masculinity*, pp. 86–106. Oxford: Blackwell.

Pujolar, J. (2001). *Gender, Heteroglossia, and Power: A Sociolinguistic Study of Youth Culture*. Berlin and New York: Mouton de Gruyter.

Salisbury, R. E. (1962). Notes on bilingualism and linguistic change in New Guinea. *Anthropological Linguistics*, 4, 1–13.

Schlieben-Lange, B. (1977). The language situation in Southern France. *Linguistics*, 19, 101–8.

Schlossman, S. (1983). Is there an American tradition of bilingual education? German in the public elementary schools, 1840–1919. *American Journal of Education*, 91, 139–86.

Shehadeh, A. (1999). Gender differences and equal opportunities in the ESL classroom. *ELT Journal*, 53, 256–61.

Solé, Y. (1978). Sociocultural and sociopsychological factors in differential language retentiveness by sex. *International Journal of the Sociology of Language*, 17, 29–44.

Spedding, A. (1994). Open Castilian, closed Aymara? Bilingual women in the Yungas of La Paz (Bolivia). In P. Burton, K. K. Dyson, and S. Ardener (eds.), *Bilingual Women: Anthropological Approaches to Second-language Use*, pp. 30–43. Oxford and Providence, RI: Berg.

Stevens, G. (1986). Sex differences in language shift in the United States. *Sociology and Social Research*, 71, 31–4.

Sunderland, J. (2000). Issues of language and gender in second and foreign language education. *Language Teaching*, 33, 203–23.

Takahashi, K. (2001). An ethnographic study of the second language learning of Japanese ELICOS students in Australia. Unpublished manuscript, University of Sydney.

Talbot, M. M. (1998). *Language and Gender: An Introduction*. Cambridge, UK: Polity.

Tannen, D. (1986). *That's Not What I Meant! How Conversational Style Makes or Breaks Relationships*. New York: Ballantine Books.

Tannen, D. (1990). *You Just Don't Understand: Women and Men in Conversation*. New York: Ballantine Books.

Tannen, D. (1994). *Gender and Discourse*. Oxford: Oxford University Press.

Teutsch-Dwyer, M. (2001). (Re)constructing masculinity in a new linguistic reality. In A. Pavlenko, A. Blackledge, I. Piller, and M. Teutsch-Dwyer (eds.), *Multilingualism, Second Language Learning and Gender*, pp. 175–98. Berlin and New York: Mouton de Gruyter.

Villenas, S. (2001). Latina mothers and small-town racisms: Creating narratives of dignity and moral education in North Carolina. *Anthropology and Education Quarterly*, 32, 3–28.

Walters, K. (1996). Gender, identity, and the political economy of language: Anglophone wives in Tunisia. *Language in Society*, 25, 515–55.

West, C. and Zimmerman, D. H. (1983). Small insults: A study of interruptions in cross-sex conversations between unacquainted persons. In B. Thorne, C. Kramarae, and N. Henley (eds.), *Language, Gender, and Society*, pp. 102–17. Rowley, MA: Newbury House.

Willett, J. (1995). Becoming first graders in an L2: An ethnographic study of L2 socialization. *TESOL Quarterly*, 29, 473–503.

Winter, J. and Pauwels, A. (2000). Gender and language contact research in the Australian context. *Journal of Multilingual and Multicultural Development*, 21, 508–22.

Woolard, K. A. (1997). Between friends: Gender, peer group structure, and bilingualism in urban Catalonia. *Language in Society*, 26, 533–60.

Bilingualism: The Media, Education, and Literacy

20 Bilingualism in the Global Media and Advertising

TEJ K. BHATIA AND
WILLIAM C. RITCHIE

20.1 Introduction

The economic forces of globalization together with the rise of global media have set the stage for a dramatic, exponential rise in global bilingualism. Even now, worldwide language contact prompted by global advertising, internet communication, and other electronic media forms (e.g. DVD and entertainment technology) is unprecedented in the history of human communication. Not only is the degree, scope and magnitude of language contact increasing at an astonishing pace, but the processes and the impact of such contact on global bilingualism call for a new examination and new approaches to the study of bilingualism. This chapter focuses on the pattern of English-based bilingualism as reflected primarily in global print and television advertising. Not only will the chapter discuss the role of English as a global language and the changes it is undergoing in this role, but it will also posit a long-neglected bilingual approach to advertising media discourse which in turn sheds light on the processes and underlying reasons for the spread of English in global media.

The main reasons for the choice of advertising to illustrate the spread of bilingualism worldwide are as follows: (1) advertisers consciously or unconsciously favor bilingualism; (2) advertising is an integral part of modern-day communication; and (3) language use in advertising has profound implications for communication generally. While print and television advertising provide a picture of bilingualism as a result of globalization from the top down (multinational to national; primarily urban), an attempt is also made here to touch on advertising which is rarely acknowledged in the Western world and is a byproduct of globalization from the bottom up (e.g. from rural to urban).

Finally, the Further Reading section deals with new horizons in language learning resulting from the emergence of the DVD, internet and mobile learning technology.

20.2   Globalization and International Advertising: Key Issues

Globalization is defined as the integration of finance, markets, technologies, and information systems in a way that is tying the world together so as to enable each of us to reach around the world faster, more cheaply, and more deeply than ever before (Friedman, 2000).

One of the central concerns of globalization for international advertisers is how to resolve the paradox of globalization and localization (national and regional interests, appeals, affiliations, etc.) in terms of formal and functional linguistic manifestations. This concern has manifested itself in the form of the "standardization" vs. "adaptation" debate in international advertising, media, and marketing. (See e.g. Heileman, 1997; Hite and Fraser, 1988; Kanso, 1991; Kujala and Lehtinen, 1989; Mueller, 1992; Onkvisit and Shaw, 1987; Ryans and Ratz, 1987.) In 1983 Theodore Levitt declared in an article in *Harvard Business Review* that with the dawn of globalization, the era of multinational companies customizing their products and advertising in numerous ways to meet the individual tastes and choices of different markets is over. However, if the market research on this topic is any indicator, the dilemma of "to customize or not to customize" is currently far from resolved.

What is the most suitable linguistic vehicle for globalization and customization? There is no doubt that the question of language choice is practically resolved. English is the choice of global advertisers and marketers. English has effectively dethroned its competitor languages, such as French and Russian, in this arena and continues to do so with more vigor and dynamics, thus becoming the single most important language of globalization.

Although the language choice is settled, the question of which variety of English is appropriate is still very much alive. English is undergoing dynamic changes in the process of engendering and shaping global market discourse; this has important ramifications for international advertising media and marketing on one hand and bilingualism on the other. Consider, for example, the reach of media in figure 20.1. Japan has the highest number of vending machines of any country in the world. This photograph was taken in a village in the Gunma region, about 120 miles from Tokyo. In this village there is no high school or any other provision to learn English, yet advertisers are there, interestingly, with messages in English.

The customization debate has ramifications for bilingualism and for the theory of linguistic accommodation. Although a cursory view of the debate seems to show an advantage for monolingualism and monolingual texting in advertising, even in its narrowest view advertising actually promotes bilingualism based in English. This chapter will argue that, in practice, international advertisers can use – and, in fact, do use – an approach that goes beyond monolingual texting. By doing so, they solve the paradox of "globalization"

Figure 20.1   Media reach: English in rural Japan (Gunma).

and "localization" in an optimal fashion by following an innovative approach grounded in bilingualism. This creates communicative accommodation, which is a key ingredient for gaining maximum appeal for the product in terms of creating favorable affective consequences. (For more on linguistic accommodation, see chapter 14.)

In addition to exploring the issues of globalization and international advertising, linguistic creativity and language change, the chapter will attempt to answer the following specific questions:

1   Is English mixing a random phenomenon in global advertising?
2   What are the factors which favor mixing with English?
3   What kind of linguistic elements can be mixed? Where and how?
4   Why do advertisers mix languages – particularly local languages with English?
5   How is mixing in advertising qualitatively and quantitatively different from normal language mixing by bilinguals?
6   What is the social evaluation of English mixing in advertising? How do advertisers overcome the negative social evaluations often created by language mixing?

20.3   Approaches to Advertising Discourse

The language of advertising has been studied from a wide variety of approaches; these can broadly be grouped into three categories: (1) linguistic, (2) literary, and (3) semiotic. The linguistic approaches to the language of advertising can be grouped into the following four categories: (a) linguistic/structural, (b) semantic, (c) pragmatic, and (d) psycholinguistic and information processing. For more information on these approaches, see Bhatia, 2000, pp. 108–17. What is common to these approaches is that they view ads primarily from the angle of monolingualism. Topics such as deception, media literacy, the Gricean notion of conversational maxims and preferred structural choices all play a central role in such analysis.

20.3.1   *A bilingual view: Conceptual framework*

This chapter attempts to fill this gap by positing a bilingual approach to advertising discourse which is grounded in research on bilingual verbal behavior. The three salient features of the approach are as follows:

1   Advertising is essentially a mixed system – a system of verbal and non-verbal components (picture, music, etc; for a parallelism with sign and spoken language, see chapter 12). The two components exhibit a complex pattern of information sharing which can form a continuum. At one end of the continuum are ads in which one component – either verbal nor non-verbal – is essentially redundant or irrelevant, and at the other end lie ads in which each component complements the other in the transmission of meaning. In the absence of either one, there is a significant loss of meaning. In other words, the task of information sharing is critical to both verbal and non-verbal components.
2   The verbal component of an ad mirrors the two critical complementary aspects of bilingual verbal behavior – (1) ability to keep two linguistic systems separate, and (2) ability to integrate and mix the two systems.
3   Although language mixing is an integral aspect of bilingual verbal behavior, society often views it negatively and regards it as a sign of linguistic deficiency. That is why bilinguals are sometimes regarded as having trouble expressing thoughts and why their language usage is regarded as lacking grammar or system. In short, their language is regarded as – bad language. What is interesting is that bilinguals themselves consider language mixing to be "bad language" as well.

Bhatia (2001) postulated three attitudes toward language mixing in advertising. Before we describe these attitudes in detail, let us indulge ourselves in the narration of an incident which took place in Mexico City a couple of years ago. This incident is instructive and will shed light on the relevance and validity of the attitudes described below.

While strolling in Mexico City with several friends who were scholars of Spanish literature, the first author came across an advertisement on a billboard that read *Este colchó box spring* ('this box spring mattress'). The Anglicism in the ad prompted one scholar to comment that, "Mexicans are basically lazy people. They do not even want to translate English words into Spanish in their own country." This evaluation won approval from a majority of the group, though a minority (including the first author) dissented strongly. One individual became so concerned with the mixed nature of the ad that he could not resist asking the salesperson in English, "Why do you advertise the product half in Spanish and half in English?" The immediate response of the salesman was, "I would sell only half, if I did not use English." This exchange is quite revealing about the underlying reason(s) why mixing with English is so widely favored in global advertising, and at the same time it also cautions advertisers about the potential backlash that English can induce if a delicate balance of language mixing is disturbed.

Incidents such as this are, in fact, quite common. A case in point is a recent article by Tan (2002) reporting that the government of Singapore has banned the movie *Talk Cock*. The main reason given for the banning of the movie is that it uses a mixed variety of English, called "Singlish". Linguistic prescriptivism clearly played a key role in the decision. Not only societies at large but governments feel compelled to regulate language varieties and particularly mixed varieties in media and entertainment to wipe out the perceived negative effects of "bad language." These two types of incident (one involving a government and one involving society at large) have led us to recognize the following three attitudes toward language mixing in global advertising: the negative attitude, the neutral attitude, and the positive or systematic view.

20.3.2 *Negative view*

The negative attitude – found almost universally among the population at large – is based on the view that language mixing is an unsystematic form of behavior. Due to the long history of linguistic prescriptivism and puritanism worldwide, the language-mixing behavior of bilinguals is generally regarded as a "linguistic deficiency" of some kind. Not only do monolingual societies view language mixing as a sign of bad linguistic behavior, but, as noted above, even bilinguals themselves often do. Gumperz (1982) and others have pointed out that if one makes bilinguals consciously aware of their language mixing, they tend to apologize for their "bad" verbal behavior.

If it is true that language mixing is negatively evaluated, then, given the fact that the failure of any advertisement is economically taxing, advertisers should distance themselves from language mixing. However, even a cursory analysis of any large sample of advertisements readily discredits the role of this attitude in determining the design of advertising worldwide: not only do advertisers find language mixing to be natural, they also find language mixing and even multiple language mixing, together with the mixing of various scripts, worthy of inclusion in their advertisements.

20.3.3   *Neutral view*

The neutral attitude consists in the assumption that language mixing accomplishes low-level cosmetic effects, such as ad hoc attention getting. Therefore, language mixing is employed as a transient fad or as a one-time charm that is always short-lived. The evidence for this attitude lies in the fact that advertisers occasionally use foreign language material just to get the attention of the potential customer. In the process, advertisers often disregard even the expression of meaning. However, this use of language mixing is globally rare (except in Japan); it does not come close to accounting for even the tip of the iceberg of the actual incidence of language mixing in advertising. Furthermore, it misses the underlying reasons for the widespread language mixing actually found in advertising. Recall the discussion on figure 20.1 above.

20.3.4   *Positive view*

The positive or systematic view is compatible with the current position on language mixing adopted by most sociolinguists. It views language mixing as a systematic and rule-governed phenomenon which satisfies the creative needs of bilinguals, especially those needs which can be met neither effectively nor efficiently by means of the single, separate linguistic systems which are at the disposal of bilinguals. (For a recent state-of-the-art treatment of language mixing in the research literature, see Bhatia and Ritchie (1996); see also chapter 13 of the present volume.) This view recognizes that language mixing in advertising can satisfy the deeper innovative and creative needs of advertisement writers to create the desired effects of persuasion, naturalness, and other socio-psychological effects in their language. Our analysis of English mixing in global advertising lends support to this view by making correct predictions about the qualitative and quantitative pattern of language mixing with English in global advertising. The discussion of global advertising which follows will reveal not only that the incidence of language mixing with English is on the increase but also that socio-psychological functions and domains allocated to English cannot be easily and naturally duplicated by other languages in the production of advertising discourse.

   In short, advertisers in general appear, perhaps not surprisingly, to adopt the view of language mixing expressed by the salesman in Mexico City (who would prefer to sell *all* of his merchandise rather than just half of it) as opposed to that of the literary scholars, who clearly had other priorities.

20.4 Typology of the Global Spread of English and Language Mixing

English is perhaps the single most important linguistic source for the promotion of global bilingualism and for linguistic creativity. English has official or special status in at least 75 countries with a total population of over 2 billion (Crystal, 1997, p. 90). It is spoken as a first language by around 300 million and as a second or official language along with one or more other languages by around 375 million speakers in the world. Speakers of English as a second language will soon outnumber those who speak it as a first language. Around 800 million people are believed to speak English as a foreign language. One out of four of the world's population speaks English to some level of competence.

According to the British Council website, English is the main language of books, newspapers, airports and air-traffic control, international business and academic conferences, science, technology, diplomacy, sport, international competitions, pop music, and advertising. Over two-thirds of the world's scientists read in English, three-quarters of the world's mail is written in English, 80 percent of the world's electronically stored information is in English. Of the estimated forty million users of the internet, some eighty percent communicate in English. Although the global dominance of English is self-evident, and is growing rapidly, it is premature to claim that other major languages of the world are dying and English is the killer language. In fact, the ten most widely spoken languages of the world are rapidly catching up with English in the arena of global electronic communication and media. Furthermore, English in itself is changing due to its contact with other languages and its use in advertising and other forms of communication. Not only this, but English cooperates and coexists with other languages from which it derives its mixed character.

Research on the global spread of English-speaking communities has led to the development of various typologies and models based on the users and uses of language. One such typology is characterized as "three concentric circles of English." It was originally proposed by Kachru (1985) and has, subsequently, been updated to account for the dynamic and demographic spread of English, notably in Kachru (1992, 1994). The three circles are characterized as the inner circle, the outer circle, and the extending or expanding circle. The inner circle represents those countries or societies where English is spoken as a native language. The outer circle refers to the spread of English in its nonnative context in which English came into contact with genetically and culturally unrelated languages (e.g. in Asia and Africa). All the countries in the outer circle are multilingual and multicultural. Furthermore, in most of these countries English has official status in the government's language policies. For instance, the Indian constitution recognizes English as an "associate" official language. Similarly, in Singapore English is recognized as an official language.

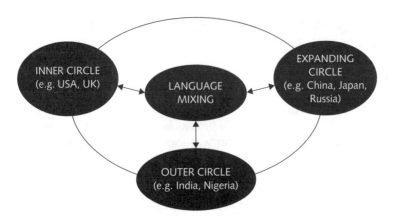

Figure 20.2   Global English typology: Mutually feeding relationship.

In Nigeria and Zambia, English is one of the state languages. In these regions, English plays an important role in day-to-day social interaction.

The expanding circle includes those countries which recognize the importance of English as an international language (e.g. China, Greece, Israel, Poland) and teach English as a foreign language. English has no official status, but is valued for international business and scientific, technological and academic discourse. Needless to say, the three-circle typology is not watertight. Although Japan belongs to the expanding circle, the new teaching guidelines of the government of Japan call for the introduction of English at primary and middle schools in fiscal 2002 and at high schools in fiscal 2003. For the purpose of this chapter, countries such as Germany, France, and Spain are grouped into the outer circle because of a long but unofficial association with English, whereas Russia is grouped in the expanding circle. In figure 20.2, these three circles are joined by a line to show the pattern of global communication through world Englishes. Language mixing represents one important parameter which contributes to the divergence and convergence of the use of Englishes in the three circles. Although language mixing with English particularly in the outer and expanding circles exhibits some distinctive properties such as the adaptation of English phonology and syntax in Japanese, Spanish, and Indian advertising (see Bhatia, 1987, 1992 for details), this chapter will focus on those shared aspects of English mixing which are donated by the inner circle to the outer and extended circles of English and which are the typical ingredients of the formation and the marketization of global advertising discourse. Product names such as Walkman are the contribution of the expanding circle to the inner and outer circles of English.

With regard to the phenomenon of mixing of other languages in the inner circle of English advertising, such mixing with French, Spanish, German and other languages is quite well known, and therefore will not be considered here. Also outside the scope of this chapter is the discussion of the status of mixing which blurs the distinction between borrowing and code mixing/code switching. (For more details see Bhatia and Ritchie (1996) and chapters 6 and 26 of this volume.)

20.5 Bilingualism Through Non-Roman Scripts

A cursory examination of English in advertising in the outer-circle and extending-circle countries might lead one to conclude that the incidence of English mixing is not very significant. However, such a conclusion would be a premature one. If one takes into account the use of English wrapped in non-Roman scripts, one would arrive at a totally different conclusion about the use of English in global advertising. Consider, for example, the Hindi advertisement from India in figure 20.3 below. This advertisement is deceptive in the sense that it gives the appearance of a totally monolingual Hindi text.

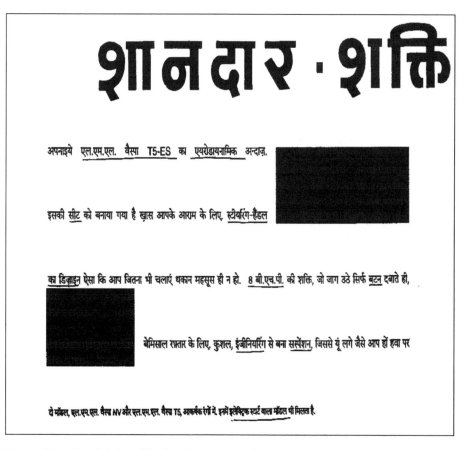

Figure 20.3   English in a Hindi advertisement (in Devangari script).

The same is true of the Korean advertisement in figure 20.4 below. The two ads subscribe to two distinct processes of introducing bilingualism. The Hindi ad from outer-circle India capitalizes on the relatively high incidence of bilingualism with English and makes no attempt to reinforce English either by means of paraphrasing the English terms in Hindi or writing them in Roman script, the creators of the ad assume that their readers will be bilinguals. If they are not they are being initiated to bilingualism via Devanagari script. In contrast the process of inducing bilingualism in the Korean ad is different. The Korean ad does not expect the same degree of bilingual competency on the part of its readers as does the Hindi ad. The ad is built primarily on a paraphrasing strategy. The readers are initiated into bilingualism by the inclusion in the ads of both script-based transliterations of the English word and paraphrasing of English into Korean.

In the Hindi ad the only overt sign of English presence is in the model number which is given in Roman script. The seemingly monolingual character of the text is further reinforced by the fact that the attention-getter employs a monolingual text drawn from Hindi (*shandar shakti* 'superb power'). However, an analysis of the body of the advertisement reveals that the Hindi text is interwoven with italicized English text written in the Devanagari script.

(1)   Line   Mixed structure (*English* + Hindi)

1   *L.M.L. Vespa* T5-ES kaa *aerodynamic* andaaz
                 of   style
       'The aerodynamic style of the L.M.L. Vespa T5-ES.'

2   iskii   *seat*   'its seat'

2–3   *steering handle*   kaa *design*
                       of
       'The design of the steering handle.'

3   *8 BHP* kii shakti
           of power
       'The power of 8BHP.'
       button dabaate hii
           press   as soon as
       'As soon as (one) presses the button'

4   kushal *engineering* se   banaa *suspension*
       skillful   with made
       'suspension made with skilled engineering'

5   *electric start* vaalaa *model*
                 one
       'the electric start model'

English lexical items outnumber Hindi items. Not only is the use of English quite extensive, but the ad also demonstrates the feature of complex inter-sentential mixing with Hindi.

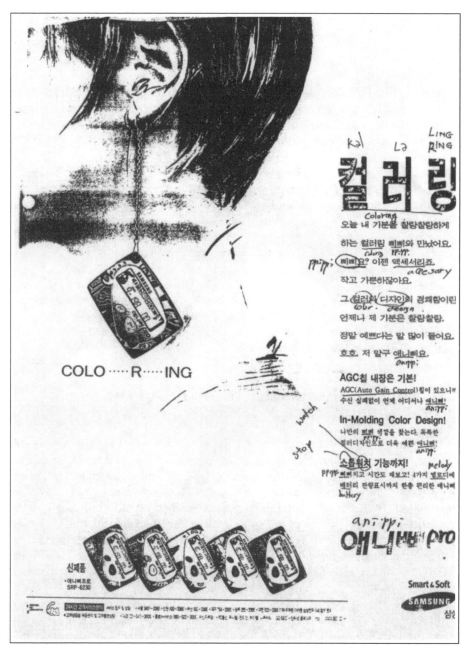

Figure 20.4 English in Han'gul (Korea).

This use of English in non-Roman scripts is not an exception, but quite a widespread tendency in global advertising. As pointed out earlier, the Korean advertisement in figure 20.4 exhibits the use of English in a more elaborate way. Although Roman script is obvious in the acronym AGC, and the expressions *In-Molding Color Design!* and *COLO . . . R . . . ING*, more words appeared in the Korean script called Han'gul than in Roman. Words such as *coloring, color design, stop watch,* and *battery* appear in the main body of the advertisement in Han'gul. Even the Korean attention-getter at the beginning of the advertisement belongs to English, i.e. *coloring,* which is written in Han'gul.

In Japanese advertising, English carves out a place by means of Katakana script, the script in which foreign words are usually written. Some expressions or words of English are assimilated to the extent that they are written in Hiragana script, the script used for ordinary Japanese words.

Infiltration of English into ads by means of non-Roman scripts can also be attested to in Chinese and Russian advertising. The unmarked pattern is similar to that of Korean. However, Chinese advertising in Taiwan and Singapore exhibits some parallelism with Indian advertising. In addition to promoting bilingualism with English, the non-Roman scripts provide an important manipulative threshold for the penetration of English into those structural domains which are usually difficult to access. The following discussion will further clarify this point.

20.6   Bilingualism and Structural Domains

Viewing an ad as a discourse unit, one sees the following eight parts to its structure: (1) product name, (2) company name or logo, (3) labels, (4) pricing, (5) availability, (6) slogans, (7) main body, and (8) headlines and subheaders. Although properties such as pricing and availability are primarily content-based and thus more semantic than structural in nature, they are treated as a distinct structural domain since print ads impose a visual structure on them, thus separating them like other structural parts. Not all ads show all eight parts. The structural domains are not mutually exclusive either. It is not uncommon to find a product name or a slogan as a headline, thus neutralizing the distinction between the headline and slogan parts of an ad.

Similarly, the properties vary according to medium (television, wall advertising, internet, etc.). Wall advertising (see subsection 20.8.1, "Globalization from the bottom up") often does not incorporate the body of the ad, while print ads show a counter-tendency in this regard. Furthermore, some structural parts might be incorporated into others.

Consider the Tirupati spices ad in figure 20.5 below. With the exception of pricing, all other structural properties are present in the ad, as described below:

Figure 20.5 Structural domains of an advertisement.

Headlines: jale   par namak zaruur   chiRkiye.
             burnt on salt   definitely sprinkle
             'Certainly rub salt in the wound.'
Body of ad: Three-paragraphs-long body appears to the right of the product
             label display.
Slogan: bhojan kii shaan   baRhaaiye
             Food of grandeur increase
             grihiNii   kii shaan baRhaaiye
             housewife of dignity increase
             'Add grandeur to [your] food [and] add to the dignity of the
             lady of the house.'
Product name: *tirupati* (in Hindi).
Company's name or logo: *daadhiich* industries.
Wrappers or labels: Given in English to the left of the body text.

The ad uses the rule-violation strategy to get attention. Common sense dictates
that one not rub salt in a wound. Nevertheless, the attention-getter encourages
us to violate traditional wisdom by doing so. The body of the ad then reveals
that the wound in question is that of a neighbor who would be jealous of the
great taste and smell of your cooking with the Tirupati spices. The body of the
ad goes on to advise not giving away the secret of your great cooking to your
neighbor. The third paragraph stresses the purity and the natural ingredients
of the product. Packaging information is also provided, and the seal of approval of the government of India is emphasized. The body of the ad goes on
to provide a list of the spices produced by the company. The product name is
given in Hindi at the end of the body of the ad and is reinforced by the
package display, but this time in English. The company name and address are
separated from the rest of the ad by a line and so is the slogan. The address of
the company together with contact information connotes product availability
and corporate reliability.

The ad also reflects changing societal values. The notion of making one's
neighbor jealous by one's possessions runs counter to the traditional Indian
value system, which values neighbors as a part of one's extended family and
discourages the unnecessary display of valued objects.

20.6.1   English and structural domain dependency

Viewing the eight structural parts as domains of an advertisement, it is
important to observe that English is assigned these structural domains neither
randomly nor symmetrically. As the following discussion will reveal, some
structural domains admit English more freely than other.

20.6.1.1   Product naming

The most favored and most easily accessible domains to English are *product naming* and *company naming*. Bhatia (1987) analyzed more than 1,200

advertisements primarily in Hindi that were printed between 1975 and 1985. The study revealed that more than 90 percent of the 1,200 advertisements analyzed carried a product name in English, for example, *Sanforized*, *Supertax*, *Trigger*, *Signal-2*, *Mustang*, *Click-IV*, *Freedom Mealmaker*, *VIP*, *Travel-light*, *Fair and Lovely*, *Protein Conditioner Shampoo*, *Clinical Special*, *High Power Surf*, and *Oriental Stereo Recorded Cassettes*. According to the Hobson-Jobson dictionary, the English word *shampoo* is borrowed from the Hindi word *champii*; however, it is the English reincarnation of the word *shampoo* which is prevalent in Indian advertising and the *shampoo* product names. Even with the culturally sensitive Indian product names, English does not hesitate to take a share of the pie (e.g. *Morarjii Fabrics*, *Ambiprincess*). Not only this, but common products produced by indigenous companies and aimed at indigenous populations are named in English (e.g. *Mohan's Gold Coin Apple Juice*). In Japan, English product names qualified with English first person possessive pronouns (e.g. *my juice*, *my car*) are quite frequent. The possessive pronoun can be further subjected to the process of reduplication. Meraj (1993, p. 224) shows a similar trend in Urdu advertising in Pakistan. Her sample reveals that English product names account for 70 percent of the ads while only 9 percent of product names were drawn from Urdu. The remaining 21 percent were mixed product names (English + Urdu) such as *Chanda Battery Cell*, *Good Luck Haleem*, and *National Kheer*. The same trend is widely attested in Russia and other European countries.

It should be noted that inner-circle English is in turn being enriched by product names drawn from other languages: *Nike* (Greek), *Volvo* (Latin), *Samsaar* (Sanskrit), and *Nokia* (Finnish).

20.6.1.2   Company's name or logo
Next to product names, company names show the most use of English among parts of ads. Globalization of business has given further impetus to English in this domain. Even the names which are not English are given an English look either by means of linguistic adaptation or by writing in Roman. Sony is known worldwide through Roman lettering. Abbreviations and acronyms heavily favor the employment of English on a near-universal basis.

20.6.1.3   Labeling and packaging
Like many product names, the labels of products shown in an advertisement overwhelmingly favor not only English but also the Roman script. Numerical information (e.g. in graphs; and telephone numbers) is another site for the selection of English in an advertisement. Packing information such as *family pack*, *set* is provided in English.

20.6.1.4   Pricing
The language of pricing is as sensitive to local constraints as culturally sensitive products. However, one can witness a trend towards English or US currency, e.g. in Spanish advertising in Latin America. Discount information (e.g. 40 percent off) in non-English Japanese ads is invariably given in English.

20.6.1.5   Slogans

English is witnessed less often in slogans than in the product or company name domains. However, when English is utilized in slogans, it is usually wrapped in a sentence-like (or phrasal) structure rather than the nominal or one-word structure preferred by product or company naming. Another feature of English in slogans is that English is only rarely represented in non-Roman scripts. Usually no attempt is made to either paraphrase or translate English slogans into native languages. Whether it is Chinese, Japanese, Russian, or Hindi advertising, the slogans can be expressed in full-length English sentences and Roman script. Slogans such as *freedom is my birth right* (India), *We grow quality* (Japan), *Digital PC – Beyond the Box* (Hong Kong), *Smart & Soft – Samsung* (Korea), and *Let's make things better* (Germany) can be witnessed throughout the world.

20.6.1.6   Main body

The employment of English in the main body of an advertisement or in the language of pricing constitute the last and the most difficult barrier for English. Since the product description and explanations about the utility of the product are given in the main body of an advertisement, it is not surprising that this structural domain departs from the other domains in terms of its preference for a sentence-like structure. Hence, in this domain, native languages usually override English. On the other hand, English is conquering this last barrier by way of capitalizing on those domains which are within its easy reach such as product names and lexicon associated with product types such as computer, technological, fashion, etc. New technologies such as internet and multimedia have provided a special boost to English usage. The discussion of futuristic themes and developments is often carried out by means of key words which are drawn from English. Numbers, graphs, and figures are presented in English.

20.6.1.7   Headers and subheaders

As is the case with English in the body of the advertisement, English takes a back seat in headers. This domain is occupied by other languages in advertising. The English-only Roman text as a header usually appears in the form of a product name as in example (3) below. The English-only structures are often nominal or phrasal as in examples (2) and (3) below. If a header goes beyond the phrasal level (i.e. either a sentence or conjunct sentence), the use of English is discouraged. Nevertheless, like slogans, this domain is gradually surrendering to English as in example (6), a header drawn from a Hong Kong advertisement. With the emergence of multimedia and internet technologies, the language of the header is becoming more and more bold even in the expanding countries (see, for example, headers from Japanese advertising in example (7)). The use of English in headers is expanding to subheaders. In a mixed structure, English forms either a subject or a predicate argument of the sentence as exemplified in (5), or occurs in a topic–comment structure as in example (4). The following attention-getters illustrate the generalizations drawn here.

(2) *Phrasal*
   a feast of elegance
   Expanding frontiers of Telecommunication

(3) *Nominal*
   Golden moments. McDowell moments.
   The cotton collection
   Cooking

(4) *Mixed: topic–comment*
   Kancan, mixer grinders aur non-stick cookwares
   Kancan,   and

(5) *Mixed: object argument*
   super champion baniye.
                          become
   'Be a super champion.'

(6) *Full sentence*
   What is girdle?

(7) *Full sentence: futuristic themes*
   See what tomorrow will bring (Japan)
   Multimedia: A world where all communications are one.

On the basis of the generalizations drawn about the pattern of English use in outer and expanding circles, the structural hierarchy in figure 20.6 can be postulated.

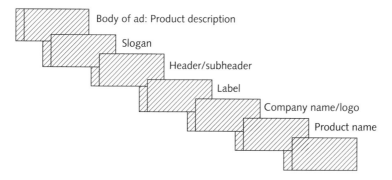

Figure 20.6   English – The structural dependency hierarchy.

The hierarchy, represented in a staircase fashion, claims that in order to reach the highest step of the staircase, English must pass through all those steps which precede it (from right to left in the figure). When English manages to reach the step of product naming, then other, more difficult steps, such as company name, become available to English. However, if the use of English is restricted to product naming, the probability of its being used in the body of the advertisement is not high. If one finds the incidence of English in the main body of an ad, one can predict that all the domains of advertisement for that product are within the reach of English. The real test of the presence of English in the body of an advertisement is when English, as in slogans, begins to appear with verbs coded with English tense-aspectual information. This hierarchy does not include pricing because of its very restricted currency in advertising. In addition to predicting structural dependencies, this hierarchy also predicts the process by which English gains currency in global advertising. The onset of English penetration begins with naming, and then spreads to other domains. The reversal of this process appears not to occur.

20.7   Globalization and Marketization of English

Globalization is a consumer culture of the twentieth century in which "writers of the advertising copy offer themselves as poet laureates of the global village" (Barnet and Cavanagh, 1994, p. 14). The new world economy rests largely on Global Bazaars, the Global Shopping Mall, the Global Workplace, and the Global Financial Network (Barnet and Cavanagh, 1994, p. 15). In these four aspects of the new economic order, English is the leading linguistic vehicle for the homogenization of global advertising discourse. The following sections present a partial list of some terms and expressions which are common to global advertising. For lack of space, a large number of names of American and British musicians, Hollywood movies, bands, musicals, actors, actresses, directors, international companies, and product names, etc. are excluded from this list. The examples below constitute just the tip of the iceberg in global advertising discourse.

Fashion:
Cream, design, eye-liner, lotion, mascara, makeup, model, moisturizing cream, perfume, top model.

Entertainment: Food, drinks, and restaurants
Action-packed, album, art show, artist, bar, beef, burger, cafe, cappuccino, cast, cheese, chicken, classical music, Coca-Cola, coffee house, coffee shop, cold coffee, director, espresso, film, guitar, ham, hamburger, happy hour, host, hot coffee, ice jazz, junk food, liqueur, lunch, lunch-special, menu, mineral water, music, office, Pepsi, piano, pizza, production, punk rock, restaurant, rock, rum, salad bar, scotch, sidewalk cafe, stand-up comedy, steak, talent, tea, thriller, taste bud, *tiffin carrier*, vodka, whisky, wine.

Sports:
Baseball, blazer collection, cap, casual, classic, design, dress code, dress up, fashion line, hand-made, jacket, label, made in USA, model, see-through, sport wear, sweater, trend.

English is the single most important transmitter of global cultural discourse manifesting itself largely in American films, television, music, magazines, fashion, sports, and Disney theme parks. As a result, advertising worldwide is unified by vocabulary drawn from the inner circle of English.

Here is a partial list of the words and expressions used in the global workplace and financial network:

Advertisement, agency, appointment, backup system, bytes, bits, bond, CD-ROM, contact, demo, download executive, easy control, fax, fax modem, file, floppy, format, graphics, growth, hard disk, information highway, input, junk, manager, megabyte, memo, multimedia, on-site installation, on-site training, power book, program, promotion, sale, salesman, scanner, strategy, tape recorder, TQ (total quality), tour, training, user-friendly, visibility, Windows, word processing, work, workstation, upgrade.

When these words and expressions participate in the process of language mixing and formation of new linguistic categories (e.g. the light verb formation including a verb translatable as *do* in Indian and Japanese advertising: *down load karnaa, suttato botan o kuirkku suru* 'to download'; literally 'down load do,' 'start button click do', respectively) and discussions of new themes (e.g. futuristic multimedia, internet, etc., yuppie culture in Asia and America), they lend further productivity and marketization to English in global advertising. Advertising even from the expanding countries carry headers and attention-getters such as *cutting edge, core value, on demand, details, open systems, open solution, networking, personal products, software and services, ATM,* in English only and only in the Roman script, often with no translation, but perhaps followed by an explanation in the body of the advertisement. The same is true with adjectives and qualifiers such as *new improved,* and *maximum strength.*

Structures such as a string of noun phrases (*Oak Wood Furniture Express*), negative structures (*no hassle, no payment,* etc.), and discourse styles (e.g. informationalization, promotional discourse, "cold call" scripting; see Goodman and Graddol, 1996, pp. 141–57) reflect the two important ways in which the qualitative aspect of global bilingualism is undergoing homogenization. The homogenization impact of advertising discourse in English worldwide on other languages is so profound that it is affecting the general rules of information structuring. For instance, a simple inquiry "Where are you from?" might evoke the answer "By Unilever, the makers of Colgate, I have been sent from Delhi." Notice that where in traditional discourse the information sequencing will be: (1) location disclosure, (2) company name, (3) product name, the order is changed to (1) company's name, (2) product name and (3) location disclosure. For more details see Bhatia, 2000, pp. 93–4.

20.8   Quantitative Aspects of English

Let us now turn to the question of quantitative aspects of English usage in global advertising. Is the incidence of mixing with English in global advertising increasing? To answer this question, a raw analysis of advertising from the outer circle (India, and European countries such as Germany, Spain, Italy, and France), and the expanding circle (China, Japan, Korea, Russia) shows that use of English is increasing in quantitative terms. A quantitative and qualitative analysis of a cream (*Fair and Lovely*) aimed at lower-middle-class women in India in the 1980s (see plate 1 in Bhatia, 1987) and 1990s (see figure 20.7) reveals a surge in the use of English. These advertisements are representative of Indian advertising. They are not rare or special cases. One advertisement from the 1990s employs 122 words in the body and 20 words in the header. The advertisement from the 1980s has 19 words in the header and 448 words in the body. Although the number of words used in the body is reduced in the 1990s to one-third of that used in the 1980s, the incidence of the use of English has increased. The new advertisement carries the following six English expressions which are displayed in the Devanagari script only: *winter special, formula, double sun screen, moisturizing, lotion,* and *cream.* The corresponding version of the 1980s uses only four English expressions: *sun screen, bleach, pigment, ultraviolet.* The last three words are a natural consequence of the themes which are absent in the 1990s advertisement. The 1990s advertisement does not address the ill-effects of ultraviolet rays on human skin, particularly on the skin pigment, which are elaborated in the opening paragraph of the body of the 1980s advertisement. The second paragraph in the old advertisement is devoted to ingredients such as *bleach,* which are found in other creams but are absent in the cream in question. This theme is also excluded from the 1990s advertisement.

The theme which is shared by both advertisements is a more reliable indicator of the increase of English usage. In this context, the 1990s advertisement uses six expressions (ten words), whereas the 1980s advertisement contains only one word which is common to both advertisements (*sunscreen*). Notice that the increase in English in the 1990s advertisement is not due to the use of technical terms; rather these words are predominantly drawn from an area in which Hindi words are/were easily accessible. Even if one does not take into account the factor of shared theme, the increment of English is up by approximately 50 percent in raw word count (33 percent in terms of expressions).

In the domain of header and subheader, although the word count is essentially the same (19 words in the 1980s and 20 words in the 1990s), the advertisement of the 1990s carries an additional English expression, *winter lotion* which is written in the Devanagari script only. The labels of both advertisements are only in English and the Roman script, which displays the product name "Fair & Lovely." The only change is that in the 1990s, the English expression "with

Figure 20.7 Cosmetic advertisement: Fair and Lovely cream.

special winter cure" is added together with "new" in small print. The display
is in English and in Roman script in both advertisements. The Hindi slogan
from the 1980s *gorepan kii sukomal tarkiib* 'the delicate way of lightening (the
skin)' is eliminated from the advertisement of the 1990s. This illustrates not
only the growing use of English in general, but also the increasing penetration
of English into the structural domains. In short, the use of English is increasing
in both quantitative and qualitative terms.

Another example of the increasing use of English is in cosmetic and beauty
product advertising in France. Given the international status of French, the
linguistic rivalry between French and English, together with the linguistic
attitudes of French-speakers and the French Academy, it is particularly surprising to find English in a domain in which French has asserted its supremacy,
authority, and international status for centuries. Bhatia (1992) presents an analysis of French fashion and cosmetic advertisement which reveals a pattern
similar to the one found in other countries discussed so far. (See also Martin,
1998.) Product names and attention-getters favor the use of English over French.
Expressions such as *advanced cream*, *extra help makeup*, *multi-protection* are being
steadily used in the body of French advertisements in the context of offering
explanations for the merits of the product in question.

What is the proportion of English in a non-English ad? According to a
Dutch study of television commercials, one-third of the commercials on Dutch
television contain English words (Gerritsen et al., 2000). Although research
on mixing with English is gaining momentum, the distributive language load
in quantitative terms is rarely addressed. Martin (2001) attempts to answer
this question by proposing the cline of code-mixing advertising shown in
figure 20.8.

If one attempts to integrate the continuum within the framework of models
of globalization (table 20.1), the competitive model endorses the end points of
the continuum, while the cooperative model falls in between the two end
points.

20.8.1 Globalization from the bottom up

Although in the Western world, wall advertising is associated with graffiti, it
represents a vibrant economic life in Asia and Africa. Furthermore, this form
of advertising reflects a pattern of globalization from the bottom up (from
rural to urban). Wall advertising comes close to the banner type of advertising
witnessed in sports arenas in the West and internet advertising generally,
rather than the elaborate print advertising found in magazines. The only difference is that wall advertising contains an invitational closing structure that
often gives information about the availability of the product and its distri-
butor. While such structural units are invariably absent from the banner ads,
they are present in print ads.

Color schemes and the physical properties of a wall are usually exploited
(un)consciously and systematically to impose a structure on an ad and at the

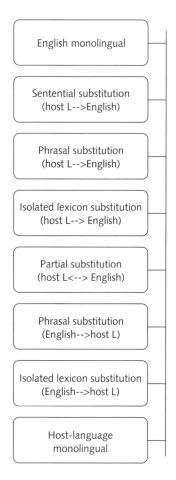

Figure 20.8   Cline of code-mixed advertising (Martin, 2002, p. 385).

same time distinguish its different structural properties (for more details on the structural properties of print advertising, see Bhatia, 2000, pp. 132–5 and, on wall advertising, Bhatia, 2000, pp. 142–3). Consider, for example, the tea ad for *Taaza* in figure 20.9. The ad carries a Hindi-Urdu attention-getter in Roman script. The attention-getter turns out to be the product name (*Lipton taaza*), which is prominently displayed on the package. A subheader, *daane daar caay* 'the grainy tea' is from Hindi and is written in the Devanagari script. The third structural property, the slogan (*taazaa kii taazgii* 'the freshness of Taazaa'; *lipTan caay* 'Lipton Tea'), is written in Urdu with Perso-Arabic script. This demonstrates yet another facet of promoting bilingualism/mulitilingualism through the multiple mixing of scripts and languages, particularly in those

Table 20.1   Models of globalization: Competitive and cooperative.

Model	Approach	Language/script	Text
Competitive	either/or	one	monolingual
Cooperative	mixed	two or more	bilingual or multilingual

Figure 20.9   Wall advertising.

parts of the world where the incidence of bilingualism with English is very great.

20.9   English and the Mystique Factor

Now let us return to the answer of the Mexican businessman in section 20.3 on the use of English. The quantitative and qualitative pattern of use of English worldwide has added yet another, but invisible, dimension to English which we will term the "mystique factor." Although it is possible to make use of an existing translational equivalent of English in other languages or to coin a new corresponding native term, this strategy does not yield the desired socio-psychological effects which only English is capable of transmitting. After all, is there a language in the world which lacks an English equivalent of words such as *new*, *design*, or *juice*? This is the underlying reason that motivated the salesperson in Mexico to make the profound observation that English sells. The suggestion of the Spanish literature scholar missed this potential of English because of the centuries-old Western tradition of linguistic prescriptivism that would have excluded language mixing and therefore been counterproductive in the context of marketization and advertising.

Our analysis of the invisible socio-psychological features which English has acquired in the process of being used in global advertising shows that English is often called into service to achieve certain positive and exclusive effects. Rather than treating them as free, unstructured, and mutually exclusive features, an attempt is made here to classify these features into the threshold (seed-like) socio-psychological features which can best be characterized as general, but core, features. Once these threshold features are acquired, like an entry to a house, the access to proximity zones (different rooms) becomes opened, which leads to a domino effect. Proximity zones can be characterized as subsets of threshold features. The threshold features and the proximity zones posited here are presented in table 20.2. An analogy will further clarify the point we are making here. Just as a door threshold gives access to different zones in a house or building, threshold categories provide access to proximate zones which in turn can lead the way to other related zones. How these thresholds are created and contrasted in their interaction with the structural properties of an advertisement is the subject of an independent investigation; therefore, we will not go into it here. Instead, we will attempt to account for the threshold phenomenon and its relatedness to the zones described in table 20.2.

Table 20.2   English: Socio-psychological features.

Threshold trigger	Proximity zones
Future and innovation	vision, foresightedness, advancement, betterment
American or English culture	limited Westernization, Christianity, values such as independence, freedom, modernization
Internationalism and standardization	certification, standards of measure, authenticity
Rationality and objectivity	scientific appeal, problem solving
Competence	efficiency, organization, quality, safety, protection, functionality, pragmatism
Sophistication	elegance, style, rarity
Physical fitness	self-improvement

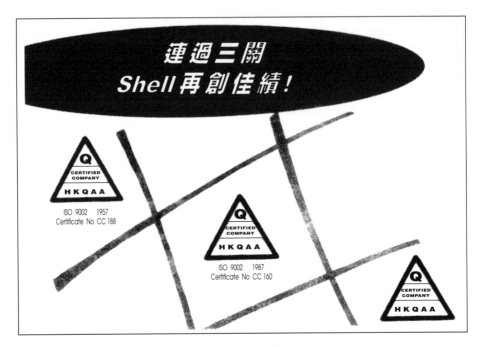

Figure 20.10   Social-psychological function: Certification and trustworthiness.

As we have already discussed, English is considered a natural candidate for transmitting themes of futuristic global communication in Japanese advertising. Japanese is not viewed as equally equipped to carry out this task. Perhaps that is the reason that attention-catching headlines are given in English rather than in Japanese, even in corporate documents. Naturally, English is also best suited to convey American or British culture. Sports images and physical fitness themes dominate the globe to market products, such as Nike shoes, through English. To best convey standardization, technical information is provided in the form of abbreviations, graphs, tables, and acronyms rendered in English. Companies such as Shell convey their competence, reliability, and supremacy by presenting certificate numbers only in English. A case in point is the Chinese advertisement from Hong Kong (see figure 20.10). Not even once is the actual seal and evidence of a certified company expressed in Chinese.

Bhatia (1987) points out that the Indian fabric industry in the 1980s maintained a delicate balance between modernization and Westernization. The themes of modernization were conveyed non-linguistically by means of visual images. The use of English was discouraged, for example, in saree advertising. However, in the 1990s, a shift was noticeable. Today, it is common to find an English attention-getter such as "a feast of elegance" to mark the sophistication and style of a saree.

Even the Italian leather and fashion industry, which is known the world over for its style, prefers to express its uniqueness of style by employing an English attention-getting headline, *Style*. Similarly, the English word *design* surfaces in German advertising as a part of the phrase *Funktionales Design*. The sense of quality is better conveyed by means of English, than by German.

The socio-psychological features listed in table 20.2 are multiplying like a splicing and copying gene, leading to a domino effect. The new features are being added to the already large inventory of the socio-psychological features of English. Threshold features such as American culture are opening the way to a proximate zone of other related features. For example, the association of English with American culture places it within easy reach of other zones of proximity such as individuality, independence, and self-help – "do it your-self" themes.

20.9.1 Literary and psycholinguistic determinants

In addition to rendering the socio-psychological features, mixing with English performs other literary and psycholinguistic functions such as rhyming (*Trentenaire On Air* – a French radio station ad), Reduplication (*MyMy Work-man* in the Korean ad), puns (*must* with two meanings: English *must* and Hindi *must* 'crazy'); humor, slogans (changing value system: slogan such as 'Free-dom is my birthright' aimed at gender equality and empowerment). These functions have immense psycholinguistic power since they play important roles in product recall and information primacy effects.

These are special effects and creative meanings which advertisers strive for. The creativity through English enables them to conquer the negative social evaluation of mixing.

20.10 Language Change: The Interaction of Outer and Expanding Circles

Let us briefly discuss some of those formal features which give inner-circle English a distinct flavor in the outer and expanding circles. As figure 20.2 shows, the expanding and outer Englishes are influencing inner circles of English advertising discourse for the reasons expounded below.

20.10.1 Adaptation

Loveday (1996, p. 144) presents a list of ten different English patterns of word formation equivalents to compounding and clipping in Japanese. Without dwelling further on this point we would like to emphasize that attempts to impose such patterns on native languages together with the tendency for lexico-syntactic and lexico-semantic transfer serve as an important source of innovation and violations which give advertising outside the inner circle its distinct and divergent flavor.

In Japanese advertising, it is not uncommon to find expressions such as the following:

(8)   we grow quality

(9)   interigento yoguruto 'the intelligent yogurt'

(10)   meri bunasu 'the merry bonus'

(11)   **kuizu** ni   kotae-te   **big**gu na   **purezent**o
       quiz   loc.pp answer-imp. big   adj. marker present
       'Let's answer (this) quiz (and) get a big present.'

The English sentence (8), although free from any morphological or phonological adaptation, violates the usual selectional restrictions between the verb and its object argument. The English phrases (9 and 10), which are adapted according to the syllabic structure of Japanese, also show selectional restriction violations between the head nouns and their modifiers. In sentence (11), the English nominal items *quiz* and *present*, and adjectives such as *big*, are subjected to the phonological and syntactic patterns of Japanese.

Consider next an example of a Coca-Cola advertisement in Spanish. The Coca-Cola advertisement in English uses the attention-getter expression *Diet Coke* while this expression is transformed as *Coca-Cola light*. Although some English speakers from the inner circle may wonder about this expression, the use of English is motivated to resolve the structural conflict between Spanish and English. The postnominal adjective is used to satisfy the regular head-initial properties of Spanish and stands in violation of the prenominal adjectival requirement of English. For further details see Bhatia (1992, pp. 210–13).

20.10.2   Double marking and reduplication

Consider the following example from a Russian advertisement.

(12)   children *yaataa*   shoes *i*   *na*-put on- *eli*
                 pl. marker   pl. marker on   past. marker
       'Children put on shoes.'

This example duplicates marking the subject and the object arguments. The Russian plural markers are italicized. Similarly, even the English particle verb construction *put on* undergoes a duplication process by prefixing the italicized Russian equivalent of the English particle *on*.

Korean advertising exemplifies yet another property of English usage which is specific to that region. The colorful usage of the pronoun "my" in Japanese advertising is further extended with a regional flavor in Korea. Expressions such as *MyMy workman* are witnessed frequently in advertising. The duplication of *my* without a space adds the dimension of electronic communication, i.e. no space between words. This usage is catching up in inner-circle English advertising.

20.10.3 Hybridization

Hybridization in compounding is another feature of divergence from advertising in the inner circle. The following examples illustrate this process: haicke-*böeki* 'high tech trade' (high tech [English] + *trade* [Japanese]), america-*sei* 'made in America' (America [English] + *sei* 'made in').

20.10.4 Acronyms and truncation

Consider acronyms such as OL ('office lady,' for a modern Japanese "working girl"), and RP ('retired person'). These are new creations which are highly local to some countries and are not shared by the inner circle. Similarly, Stanlaw (1982, p. 176) points out truncation, or shortening, as a popular device in Japanese English, e.g. *depato* (department store), *terebi* (television).

20.10.5 Archaism

Some terms, such as *girdle*, which originated in the inner circle have become obsolete in their nativized context. These words are no longer in currency in the inner circle and have been replaced by expressions such as *stomach-flattening panties/pants* or *bottom-flattening panties/pants*. However, such expressions as *girdle* have found their way into Asian fashion advertising. A case in point is the Chinese ad from Hong Kong which carries an attention-getting headline, *What is Girdle?*

20.10.6 Analogical patterning

Innovations, such as *walkman*, which originated from the expanding circles (Japan) are now being subjected to analogical patterning. Therefore, one now finds *discman* gaining popularity in the outer and expanding circle. However, analogical change is slow to catch on in the inner circle and its use is quite restricted.

   Features such as the one described above in this section add a distinct flavor to English advertising in the outer and expanding circles.

20.11   Linguistic Accommodation and Advertiser's Perception

From the above discussion, multiple mixing of scripts and languages together with linguistic adaptations represents a linguistic accommodation which in turn leads to global bilingualism. From the spectacular growth of the use of

Table 20.3   Language and domain distribution in Hindi advertising.

Language	Audience	Appeal	Value/aim	Product/discourse domain
English	Male/female	Outgoing	Modern, Western,	Fashion, science
Hindi	Female	Emotional	Utility, pragmatic	Domestic
Sanskrit	Male/female	Deep-rooted cultural	Reliability	Fabrics
Persian	Male	Luxury (royal)	Utility (physical)	Cigarettes, sports, fashion

English in global advertising, one should not conclude that English is a super-language that has conquered all the discourse and structural domains of advertising. The globalization of English does not mean that other languages of the world have been dethroned and English can invade global advertising at will. Bhatia (1992) shows that some domains are still inaccessible to English. Table 20.3 exhibits the domains (product, audience, appeal, and value) carved out by different languages in Indian advertising.

Furthermore, laws regulate the use of English in countries such as France (Martin, 2001); China and Russia regulate the use of English in global advertising. Although government regulation runs counter to linguistic accommodation, even here the examination of ads shows that advertisers bypass laws (e.g. by giving English words in bold and their French translation in fine print) and use English in order to satisfy their creative needs.

It appears that advertisers worldwide either consciously or unconsciously favor bilingualism over monolingualism. This is true of their promotion of local as well as global products. They expect their readers to have some degree of bilingual competence, which is why their concern for intelligibility sometimes takes a back seat to bilingual texting. Take the cases of Japan and the Netherlands. Print advertising in Japan exhibits a strong tendency to mix Japanese with foreign languages, particularly with English. Since the incidence of bilingualism with English is still very low even among the youth, the message of the English text is often incomprehensible. Although consumers often complain about the lack of intelligibility, advertisers are in no mood to yield. Consequently, though English might not be intelligible in some instances, the loss of propositional meaning is not a total loss. It is compensated for by the attention-getting function that lack of intelligibility serves in Japan. This is the predominant trend in Japan – to use English for what we call "cosmetic" reasons, i.e. as an attention-getting device. This adds yet another dimension to the pattern of global bilingualism and English is often considered a "cool" language to attract attention.

As van Elteren (1996, p. 58) rightly points out, globalization should be viewed as the "organization of diversity" rather than the "replication of uniformity," despite the homogenization of English advertising discourse on a global basis. The process of localization of English parallels the process of globalization. The primary carriers of localization are undoubtedly the local languages which have come in contact with English. However, the other notable aspect of localization is the local adaptation of English. This dual role of English may appear paradoxical at first sight, but it is a natural consequence of the globalization of English. The local adaptation of English (discussed in section 20.10), together with its mixing with other languages both inter- and intrasententially, has enabled English to perform both global and local functions in a way which can best be termed *glocalization*. Globalization without localization is a fractional view of the global power of English. Because English has to share the pie of localization with other languages, it is only natural that English has yet to acquire many other socio-psychological features such as deep-rooted cultural traditions, non-Christian religious concepts, local or regional authenticity or appeal, alternative medicine, etc. Consider the domination of French and its appeal in the area of fashion, luxury, and beauty; English has begun to weaken the defenses of French and is gradually making inroads into the territory which was the exclusive domain of French, though French has by no means been dethroned by English. Nevertheless, English is constantly retooling itself to acquire those socio-psychological features and thematic domains which seem distant at the moment. In short, English is still constructing and negotiating these two paradoxical identities.

20.12   Conclusion

From the above discussion, it is self-evident that the negative view of language mixing discussed in section 20.3 is incompatible with the global pattern of advertising. Multiple mixing of languages and script is the hallmark of global advertising. Although the neutral view can account for situations such as that witnessed in Japan, the mixing of English goes beyond the consideration of attention-getting and cosmetic motivation. The positive-systematic view best explains the presence of English in global advertising. In its role as the language of global advertising, not only is English leading to the homogenization of the advertising discourse worldwide, but it is also diversifying itself in a number of ways. Taking into account the two main aspects of global advertising discourse, namely unification and diversification, the role played by English can best be characterized as glocal. The glocalization of English has led to an ever-growing appetite for English in advertising worldwide which has changed and continues to change the quantitative and qualitative patterns of English usage in advertising around the world. This leads us to conclude that language mixing or mixing of English with other languages is motivated by the deeper demands of creativity, which in turn support the positive and systemic view to language mixing and global bilingualism.

ACKNOWLEDGMENTS

This chapter is a revised and expanded version of Bhatia (2001). We are grateful to UniPress and particularly to Professor Edwin Thumboo for their permission to reproduce some plates and discussion from Bhatia (2001).

REFERENCES

Barnet, R. and Cavanagh, J. (1994). *Global Imperial Corporations and the New World Order*. New York: Simon & Schuster.

Bhatia, T. K. (1987). English in advertising: Multiple mixing and media. *World Englishes*, 6(1), 33–48.

Bhatia, T. K. (1992). Discourse functions and pragmatics of mixing: Advertising across cultures. *World Englishes*, 11, 195–215.

Bhatia, T. K. (2000). *Advertising in Rural India: Language, Marketing Communication and Consumption*. Institute for the Study of Languages and Cultures of Asia and Africa, Tokyo University of Foreign Studies. Tokyo: Tokyo Press.

Bhatia, T. K. (2001). Language mixing in global advertising. In E. Thumboo (ed.), *The Three Circles of English*, pp. 195–215. Singapore: UniPress, National University of Singapore.

Bhatia, T. K. and William Ritchie (1996). Bilingual language mixing, universal grammar, and second language acquisition. In William C. Ritchie and Tej K. Bhatia (eds.), *Handbook of Second Language Acquisition*, pp. 627–88. San Diego: Academic Press.

Crystal, D. (1997). *English as a Global Language*. Cambridge, UK: Cambridge University Press.

Friedman, T. (2000). U.S., world face growing challenges of globalization. *The Daily Yomiuri*, March 18, p. 5.

Gerritsen, M., Korzilius, H., van Meurs, F., and Gijsbers, I. (2000). English in

Dutch commercials: Not understood and not appreciated. *Journal of Advertising Research*, July–August, 17–31.

Goodman, S. and D. Graddol (1996). *Redesigning English: New Texts, New Identities*. London: Routledge.

Gumperz, J. J. (1982). Conversational code-switching. In J. J. Gumperz (ed.), *Discourse Strategies*, pp. 233–74. Cambridge, UK: Cambridge University Press.

Heileman, J. (1997). Annals of advertising: All Europeans are not alike. *The New Yorker*, April 28/May 5, pp. 174–181.

Hite, R. E. and Fraser, C. (1988). International advertising strategies. *Journal of Advertising Research*, 28(5), 9–17.

Kachru, B. B. (1985). Standards, codification, and sociolinguistic realism: The English language in the Outer Circle. In R. Quirk and H. G. Widdowson (eds.), *English in the World: Teaching and Learning in Languages and Literatures*, pp. 11–30. Cambridge, UK: Cambridge University Press.

Kachru, B. B. (1992). The second diaspora of English. In R. W. Machan and C. T. Scott (eds.), *English in its Social Contexts: Essays in Historical Sociolinguistics*, pp. 230–52. New York: Oxford University Press.

Kachru, B. B. (1994). World Englishes: Approaches, issues and resources. In

R. W. Machan and C. T. Scott (eds.), *Readings on Second Language Acquisition*. New York: Prentice-Hall.

Kanso, A. (1991). The use of advertising agencies from foreign markets: Decentralized decisions and localized approaches? *International Journal of Advertising*, 10, 129–36.

Kujala, A. and Lehtinen, U. (1989). A new structural method for analyzing linguistic significance in market communications. *International Journal of Advertising*, 8, 119–36.

Loveday, Leo (1996). *Language contact in Japan: a socio-linguistic history*. Oxford: Clarendon Press.

Martin, E. (1998). Code-mixing and imaging of America in France: The genre of advertising. Ph.D. dissertation, University of Illinois, Urbana.

Martin, E. (2001). Mixing English in French advertising. *World Englishes*, 21(3), 375–401.

Meraj, Shaheen. 1993. The use of English in Urdu advertising in Pakistan. In Robert J. Baumgardener (ed.), *The English Language in Pakistan*, pp. 221–52. Karachi: Oxford University Press.

Mueller, B. (1992). Standardization vs. specialization: An examination of westernization in Japanese advertising. *Journal of Advertising Research*, 1, 15–24.

Onkvisit, S. and Shaw, J. (1987). Standardized international advertising: A review and critical evaluation of theoretical and empirical evidence. *Columbia Journal of World Business*, Fall, 43–55.

Ryans, J. and Ratz, D. (1987). Advertising standardization: A re-examination. *International Journal of Advertising*, 6, 145–58.

Stanlaw, J. (1982). English in Japanese communicative strategies. In B. Kachru (ed.), *The Other Tongue: English Across Cultures*, pp. 168–97. Urbana: University of Illinois Press.

Tan, H. H. (2002). A war of words over "Singlish": Singapore's government wants its citizens to speak good English, but they would much rather be "talking cock." *Times ASIA*, 160(3), July 29.

van Elteren, M. (1996). Conceptualizing the impact of US popular culture globally. *Journal of Popular Culture*, 30, 47–81.

FURTHER READING

Technology-assisted learning has progressed from standalone "computer-based training" (CBT) to "distance learning" with the internet (now coined as "e-learning") to "mobile learning" (m-learning) with the introduction of powerful handheld computers that operate in both standalone and web modes. M-learning's key advantage is the tremendous time-and-cost-effectiveness of learning anywhere, anytime without loss of engaging, multimedia interactivity, and feedback. Portable learning platforms better permit learners to fit learning into their busy schedules, as opposed to desktop and site-based learning protocols. Similarly, DVD and internet technology has added a new dimension to language learning and bilingualism. DVD movies support bilingual/multilingual platforms. Advertising discourse is not only an excellent source of pragmatic language input to improve second language proficiency, but also an integral part of democratic communication and values. The internet is posing fresh challenges to understanding bilingualism and increasing richness of language use (in language of the web, email, chat groups, and virtual worlds), which in turn poses new challenges to the typical classroom model of learning a second language. There is a question of death of languages, language rights and minor languages, translations, dissemination of information in Less Commonly Taught Languages or non-Western languages (see Chu, 1999 for discussion of language change, the future of global bilingualism, and human communication in an electronic age).

Crystal, D. (2001). *Language and the Internet*. Cambridge, UK: Cambridge University Press.

Chu, S. W. (1999). Using chopsticks and a fork together: Challenges and strategies of developing a Chinese/English bilingual website. *Technical Communication*, Second Quarter, 206–19.

Dudeney, G. (2000). *The Internet and the Language Classroom: A Practical Guide for Teachers*. Cambridge, UK: Cambridge University Press.

21 What do we Know About Bilingual Education for Majority-Language Students?

FRED GENESEE

21.1 Introduction

In many communities around the world, competence in two, or more, languages is an issue of considerable personal, socio-cultural, economic, and political significance. For some, the issues surrounding bilingualism are viewed as "problems" to be overcome; for others, they are viewed as "challenges" that, once mastered, benefit the individual, the community, and even the nation in which they live. The need to know two or more languages is not new. Historical documents indicate that individuals and whole communities around the world have been compelled to learn other languages for centuries and they have done so for a variety of reasons – language contact, colonization, trade, education through a colonial language (e.g. Latin, Greek), and intermarriage (Lewis, 1976). Notwithstanding historical patterns, changes in the modern world are presenting new incentives for learning additional languages.

- There is growing globalization of business and commerce. During the last 10 to 15 years we have witnessed unprecedented internationalization of industry and white-collar businesses; for example, in the automotive industry, head offices are located in one country (e.g. Japan), manufacture of automobiles takes place in another country (e.g. Brazil), and clients are in a third country (e.g. Canada). Even in North America, a relatively homogeneous linguistic community and trade zone, we are challenged to learn other languages to remain competitive, for example in response to the Spanish-speaking markets in Mexico and the French-speaking market in Quebec. While globalization of the market place often provokes images of English domination, it also increases the demand to do business in local or regional languages (Walraff, 2000).

- A revolution in electronic communications has also created a need for proficiency in multiple languages. The internet makes global communication available and easy, whether it be for personal, professional, commercial, or other reasons. On the one hand, this has created a particular need for proficiency in English as a lingua franca on the internet. On the other hand, as with economic globalization, global communication via the internet has also created the possibility of much greater communication in regional languages. Indeed, domination of the internet by English is giving way to a much stronger presence of regional and local languages as e-commerce takes hold and begins to commit resources to communicating with local and regional markets. In fact, there are presently more internet sites in languages other than English than in English (Global Reach, 2000).
- Voluntary migration of people from country to country is taking place on an unprecedented scale; we have already mentioned economic reasons for this, but there are also political, educational, cultural, and strictly personal reasons.
- At the same time, we are moving into a socio-political era when linguistic domination by "big" languages of "little" languages is becoming more difficult. In particular, indigenous people in a number of regions of the world are organizing to preserve and promote their languages at the same time as they acquire other important national and regional languages, for example Basque in the Basque Country, Mohawk in Canada, and Hawaiian in the US.

Schools have an important role to play in providing the bi- and multilingual skills that are becoming increasingly necessary in the modern world. The educational programs that have been developed to provide such language competence are varied. This chapter focuses on one, namely bilingual education. For the purposes of this chapter, bilingual education is defined with respect to three features: linguistic goals, pedagogical approaches, and levels of schooling. More specifically, bilingual education is defined as education that aims to promote bilingual (or multilingual) competence by using both (or all) languages as media of instruction for significant portions of the academic curriculum. While programs that fit this description exist at the tertiary or post-secondary level (e.g. Burger, Wesche, and Migneron, 1997), this chapter limits itself to programs at the elementary and secondary levels (for students from approximately 5 to 17 years of age). Integrating language and academic instruction is the hallmark of bilingual education (see Genesee, 1987, and Met, 1998, for more detailed explications of this approach). As Met (1998) points out, there currently exist a variety of L2 instructional approaches that integrate language and content instruction, and these can be characterized as falling along a continuum from language-driven to content-driven. In language-driven approaches, content is used simply as a vehicle for teaching target language structures and skills. The primary goal of these programs is language learning. For example, non-academic content, such as holidays or imaginary situations (like life in a family or visiting the supermarket), is often used in foreign language classrooms to support language teaching and learning. At the other end of the continuum are approaches where the content and language are equally important so that mastery of academic objectives is considered as important as the development of proficiency in the target language. Bilingual and immersion education are examples of content-driven approaches.

To clarify the focus of the chapter further, it is useful to provide elaborations of "bilingual competence" and "using both languages for significant portions of the academic curriculum" used in the above definition. *Bilingual competence* is defined as "the ability to use the target languages effectively and appropriately for authentic personal, educational, social, and/or work-related purposes." The criterion for defining *significant portions of the academic curriculum* is "at least 50 percent of the prescribed non-language-related curriculum of studies for one or more years." These should be considered minimal definitions and, while they serve to constrain the programs that were considered for inclusion in this review, they raise a host of questions that cannot be resolved in the limited space of this chapter.

The generic definition of bilingual education that has been adopted here includes programs for students who come to school speaking a majority societal language (e.g. English in Canada, or Japanese in Japan) as well as programs for students who come to school speaking a minority language (e.g. Spanish in the US, or Hungarian in Slovakia). The first type of bilingual education is often referred to as "immersion" after the Canadian French immersion programs (Lambert and Tucker, 1972; see Johnson and Swain, 1997, for a detailed discussion of core features of prototypical immersion). The second type of bilingual education can be found in regions of the world where there are large numbers of immigrants (e.g. the USA, the Netherlands) or speakers of indigenous languages (e.g. New Zealand, Peru). Since the combined literature on both forms of bilingual education is extensive and the issues surrounding each are complex and often very different, both cannot be encompassed in one short chapter. As a result, this chapter focuses on bilingual education for majority-language students; the reader is referred to August and Hakuta (1997), Baker, 2001, Cummins (2000), and Skutnabb-Kangas (2000) for recent and detailed discussions of bilingual education for minority language students.

21.2 Issues in Bilingual Education for Majority-language Students

Bilingual education for majority-language students is varied and complex as each community adopts different programmatic models and pedagogical strategies to suit its unique needs, resources, and goals. A number of useful volumes that describe specific programs are available: see Johnson and Swain (1997) for models of immersion; Cenoz and Genesee (1998) for cases of trilingual education that involve majority-language students; and Christian and

Genesee (2001) for yet other forms of bilingual education for majority (and minority) students. While bilingual education programs in different communities share the general goal of bilingual proficiency along with grade-appropriate L1 development and academic achievement, their specific goals with respect to the L2 differ; the following is one way of characterizing their alternative linguistic goals:

- to promote national policies of bilingualism (e.g. French immersion in Canada);
- to promote national languages in countries with one official language but students who speak a variety of other languages (e.g. Estonian immersion for Russian-speaking students in Estonia);
- to promote proficiency in important regional and/or world languages (e.g. English immersion in Japan);
- to promote proficiency in heritage languages (e.g. Hungarian immersion in Slovakia);
- to promote indigenous languages that are at risk (e.g. Mohawk immersion in Canada);
- to promote foreign language learning for educational enrichment (e.g. French immersion in the US).

The following sections address both theoretical and pedagogical issues concerning bilingual education for majority-language students, since we are dealing, on the one hand, with a fundamental human ability – to learn language – and, on the other hand, with practical educational factors that can influence the implementation and outcomes of bilingual education. The emphasis is on issues that have received some empirical investigation (see Baker, 2000, and Cloud, Genesee and Hamayan, 2000, for practical guides to implementing some forms of bilingual education). Since bilingual education is distinctive in its aim of promoting proficiency in two, or more, languages, much, though not all, of the following discussion focuses on research related to second language (L2) acquisition. There will also be some discussion of first language (L1) development, academic achievement, and other issues, when empirical evidence is available.

A number of caveats are warranted before proceeding. Virtually all bilingual programs reviewed here are based on voluntary participation and, thus, a host of self-selection factors are implicated. As a result, the results reviewed here cannot be generalized to programs where participation is not voluntary, and consideration must be given to a variety of self-selection factors that may be operating if these results are being used to plan or implement a new program. In a related vein, there is a bias to report the results of successful programs and, consequently, the published results cannot be construed as evidence that bilingual education for majority-language students is successful to the same extent in all settings. The success of bilingual education, like general education, depends on the day-to-day quality of instruction (including materials), continuity in program delivery, competence of instructional personnel, class size and composition, etc.

The following topics are considered in this chapter: language development and academic achievement (section 21.3), focus on form or meaning (21.4), age (21.5), time (21.6), students at risk (21.7), language typology (21.8), and multilingual education (21.9). These are considered separately, as single-factor issues. Like many aspects of general education, some of the topics reviewed in this chapter are multidimensional and encompass a host of related factors. Take, for example, the issue of age and L2 acquisition. It implicates, among others: student-related factors, such as motivational and ability differentials that might distinguish younger from older second language learners; and classroom-related factors, such as differences in the composition of classrooms in elementary-versus secondary-level bilingual programs that result from attrition in the case of elementary programs and self-selection in secondary-level programs. When relevant research findings that clarify the role of these additional factors exist, they will be presented; unfortunately, there is little such research. Reference will be made to some of the complexities that these seemingly single-factor issues raise in order to illustrate that careful consideration must be given to a host of factors when educational decisions implicating these issues are made.

21.3 Language Development and Academic Achievement

There has been extensive research on the language development and academic achievement of majority-language students in bilingual education programs since this has been a prominent issue in the minds of theoreticians, educators, policy makers, and parents alike. By far the most extensive body of research with these foci has been conducted in Canada on French immersion programs for English-speaking students in different regions of the country, starting in 1965 with Lambert and Tucker's pioneering evaluation of the St. Lambert French immersion program (Lambert and Tucker, 1972; see also Genesee, 1987, and Swain and Lapkin, 1982). The general findings from the Canadian research have been replicated, for the most part, in other regions of the world where similar programs with majority-language students have been implemented (see Christian and Genesee, 2001, and Johnson and Swain, 1997, for other examples).

Research in diverse settings has consistently shown that students in bilingual programs who speak a dominant societal language acquire significantly more advanced levels of functional proficiency in the L2 than students who receive conventional L2 instruction – that is, instruction that focuses primarily on language learning and is restricted to separate, limited periods of time. Proficiency has been assessed with respect to speaking, listening, reading, and writing, although the specific ways in which these skills have been assessed varies from setting to setting. While it is difficult to make direct statistical comparisons, impressionistically, many researchers have reported that immersion students' comprehension skills (in reading and listening) seem to be more advanced than their production skills (in speaking and writing). There will be more discussion of the quality of students' L2 production skills and factors that influence them in section 21.4.

At the same time, students in bilingual programs who speak a dominant societal language usually develop the same levels of proficiency in all aspects of the L1 as comparable students in programs where the L1 is the exclusive medium of instruction. It should be recalled that these are students who are exposed to the L1 on a daily basis outside school – at home, in the community, in the media, etc. There can be a lag in the development of L1 literacy skills (reading, writing, and spelling) among students in the initial years of bilingual programs in which all academic instruction is presented in the L2 – sometimes referred to as "early total immersion." Parity with control students who have been instructed entirely through the L1 is usually achieved after one year of receiving L1 language arts instruction; for example, at the end of grade 3 in the case of students whose first exposure to instruction in the L1 begins in grade 3. The L1 development of students who begin bilingual education beyond the primary grades of school – in the middle elementary school grades or the initial secondary school grades, usually shows no such lags (Genesee, 1987). Students in the latter programs exhibit age-appropriate L1 skills at all grade levels. In short, reduced exposure to instruction in the L1 as a result of participation in a bilingual program in the elementary or secondary grades does not usually impede the normal L1 development of majority-language students.

With respect to achievement in academic domains, such as mathematics, science, and social studies, evaluations of the progress of majority-language students in bilingual programs indicate that they generally achieve the same levels of competence as comparable students in L1 programs. Parity with L1 controls is often exhibited even when the bilingual students are receiving all academic instruction through the medium of the L2, provided the assessment is conducted in the L2 and modifications are made to take into account that full competence in the L2 has not been acquired. For example, bilingual program students who receive math instruction in French (their L2), but are tested in English (their L1), may exhibit deficiencies in mathematics due to incomplete mastery of the language of testing. Once students receive academic instruction in the L1, these disparities usually disappear. Notwithstanding these qualifications, academic parity with control L1 students is usually exhibited by students in bilingual programs at both the elementary and secondary levels and has been demonstrated using a variety of assessment instruments, including standardized norm-referenced tests, official government tests, and locally devised tests. In sum, instruction in academic subjects through the medium of an L2 does not usually impede acquisition of new academic skills and knowledge in comparison to that acquired by students receiving the same academic instruction through the medium of their L1.

Collectively, these findings make a strong case for the integrated approach to language instruction that defines bilingual education; that is, the use of the L2 to teach significant portions of the school curriculum. Indeed, alternative forms of content-based L2 instruction have proliferated since the first immersion programs were introduced in order to take advantage of this innovative method of L2 instruction (see Met, 1998, for an overview).

21.4 Focus on Form or Meaning

As noted at the outset, a defining characteristic of bilingual education is the use of the target languages to teach prescribed academic subjects. One example of this approach is the well-documented French immersion programs that were introduced in Montreal in the mid-1960s (Genesee, 1987; Lambert and Tucker, 1972). More generally speaking, this approach can be characterized as pedagogy with a "focus on meaning" in contrast to pedagogical approaches which "focus on forms," to use Long's term (Long and Robinson, 1998; see also Lyster, 1994). In the former, students are expected to learn the target language by using it for academic or other authentic communicative purposes; whereas in the latter, mastery of the formal structures and properties (rules) of the language are taught as prerequisites to functional use of the language. The rationale behind integrating language and academic instruction in the first bilingual (immersion) programs was to take advantage of children's natural ability to learn language which occurs during authentic, meaningful, and significant communication with others (Genesee, 1984; see Snow, Met, and Genesee, 1989, for an extended discussion of the rationale of this approach).

The overall effectiveness of an integrated approach has been documented in a number of studies, as noted in the preceding section. Notwithstanding this evidence, there are signs that an exclusive focus on meaning, or language use, is not optimal when it comes to developing students' linguistic competence. For example, research on immersion programs in Canada has revealed that despite participation in immersion programs for many years, immersion students often fail to master important aspects of the target language, such as verb tense, pronouns, and prepositions (Adiv, 1980; Harley and Swain, 1984). In addition, there is evidence that students in bilingual programs with more exposure to the target language do not always outperform students with less exposure (findings that will be discussed later), suggesting that simply extending exposure to and functional use of the target language does not necessarily lead to increased linguistic competence (Genesee, 1987). Genesee (1987) has argued that students in bilingual/immersion programs that emphasize functional use may fail to exhibit continuous growth in both their repertoire of communicative skills and their formal linguistic competence because they are able to get by in school using a limited set of functional and structural skills and they are not compelled by teachers' instructional strategies to extend their linguistic competencies (see also Swain, 1998). Arguably, more systematic language instruction that is linked to students' communicative needs in the classroom along with more explicit focus on the linguistic forms required by classroom communication than has been the case in many bilingual programs to date would advance students' linguistic competence. Some researchers refer to instruction that highlights specific linguistic structures and forms within the context of communicative instruction as instruction with a "focus on form"; this should be distinguished from what Long refers to as "focus on forms" – that is, isolated instruction in linguistic forms. In any case, similar concerns about the linguistic competence of immersion students have been voiced by Day and Shapson (1991), Lyster (1987, 1990), Swain (1985, 1998), and others. Lyster has raised related questions about the role of corrective feedback in promoting linguistic competence in immersion-type bilingual programs (Lyster and Ranta, 1997). These are questions of considerable theoretical and practical significance, even beyond discussions of bilingual education, since they are at the heart of the debate on communicative versus grammar-based approaches to L2 instruction, and they are integral to designing effective L2 pedagogy.

Norris and Ortega (2000) conducted a meta-analysis of studies that have examined alternative types of L2 pedagogy. While bilingual/immersion programs were not treated separately in their analyses, they were part of a broader set of classifications, including instruction that emphasized only or primarily meaning and use of the target language for non-linguistic tasks versus instruction that provided some focus (explicit or implicit) on linguistic forms. Norris and Ortega drew a number of conclusions that are relevant to the present discussion. First, L2 instruction that focused on linguistic forms, either in the context of meaningful communication or otherwise, had significant positive effects on the acquisition of target forms, whether this was assessed by comparing pre- to post-test scores of students or by comparing the scores of students in "treatment conditions" to those in "control conditions" (i.e. in programs with a focus on form(s) versus those in programs with a focus on meaning). Second, instruction with a focus on form was effective in enhancing linguistic competence whether or not there was integration of form and meaning. Third, instruction with an *explicit* focus on form was more effective than instruction with an *implicit* focus on form. Finally, the positive effects of form-focused instruction on acquisition were reliable over time, although there was some tendency for positive effects to diminish as time between instruction and testing increased.

A number of studies included in the Norris and Ortega meta-analysis were, in fact, conducted in bilingual/immersion classrooms and warrant consideration here because of their specific relevance to the present discussion (Day and Shapson, 1991; Harley, 1989; Lyster, 1994). These three Canadian studies examined the effectiveness of instruction on immersion students' acquisition and use of specific linguistic features of French, features that English-speaking students typically have difficulty with: past tense verb forms and grammatical gender (Harley 1989, 1998, respectively), sociolinguistically appropriate use of *tu* and *vous* and other conditional forms to express politeness (Lyster, 1994), and conditional verb forms used to describe hypothetical situations (Day and Shapson, 1991). Instruction in these features was integrated with their use during academic activities. All three studies found that instruction that heightened students' awareness of these forms and gave them opportunities to acquire them had a positive influence on students' competence with these forms. Lyster noted that improvement was more evident in the case of forms that received explicit focus (e.g. the use of *tu/vous*) and less evident in the case of forms that received an implicit or incidental focus (e.g. conditionals as politeness markers). While immediate post-test improvement was noted by all researchers for virtually all forms, long-term improvement (over several months) was evidenced in only some studies, suggesting that it is easier to get short-term than long-term improvement from instruction with a focus on form.

In sum, meta-analysis of the effectiveness of L2 instruction, along with results from individual studies conducted in bilingual/immersion classrooms, has demonstrated the potential benefits of instruction that explicitly teaches forms relevant to students' communicative needs or that draws their attention to linguistic forms by making these forms salient during communicative classroom activities (see also Spada, 1997, for similar conclusions). While these results are encouraging, more investigation in this domain is called for in order to identify techniques that produce clear and reliable long-term effects.

21.5 Age

One of the most controversial issues in the field of L2 acquisition is the question of age. It is widely hypothesized that "younger is better" when it comes to learning a second language (Birdsong, 1999; Genesee, 1978; Harley and Wang, 1997; Long, 1990). This is a theoretical issue of great significance to researchers since it concerns the biological capacity of humans to acquire language effectively and completely at certain stages of development, but not at others. Notwithstanding some compelling arguments (e.g. Long, 1990; Scovel, 1988), empirical evidence in favor of a critical period for L2 acquisition has been equivocal, with some studies claiming evidence for the critical period and others evidence against it (White and Genesee, 1996). The situation is complicated further by the fact that critical period effects may be more significant for L1 than L2 development (Mayberry, 1993). Strictly speaking, findings concerning age and L2 acquisition in non-school settings do not apply readily to school settings since language acquisition in school can be influenced by a host of pedagogical and student factors that are not operative in non-school settings and that have nothing to do with the putative biological predispositions of humans to acquire language (Marinova-Todd, Marshall and Snow, 2000). Thus, it is important to examine the educational research on age and L2 acquisition carefully.

Evaluations of bilingual programs for majority-language students with different starting grades has produced two patterns of results. On the one hand, there is research that shows that, when it comes to learning second languages in school, older students can make impressive progress (see Krashen, Long, and Scarcella, 1979, and Genesee, 1988, for reviews). In support of this conclusion, it has been found by researchers in Canada that students participating in late French immersion programs beginning in secondary school significantly outperform students at the same grade level in core French programs, as one would expect given the considerably difference in L2 exposure enjoyed by the late immersion students (Genesee, 1988; Wesche, Toews-Janzen, and MacFarlane, 1996). As well, evaluations of two-year late immersion programs (i.e. grades 7 and 8) in Montreal have indicated that late immersion students can achieve the same or almost the same levels of L2 proficiency as students in early immersion programs (beginning in kindergarten). Students in the Montreal late immersion programs had had core French instruction throughout elementary school, and thus did not come to late immersion with no exposure to French at all. Despite their elementary school exposure to French, the late immersion students had nevertheless had only half as much total exposure to French as the early immersion students by the end of grade 9, the final grade of the evaluation (Genesee, 1981; see figure 21.1 for schematic representations of early and late immersion programs in Canada). Genesee (1987, p. 56) found that two-year late immersion students outperformed early immersion students on a standardized, norm-referenced test of French when length of exposure to the L2 was equated, again attesting to the learning effectiveness of older students. Evaluations of more conventional L2 programs with different starting-grades have reported similar success for older versus younger learners in school settings (see Burstall, 1974, Fathman, 1975, and Krashen, Long, and Scarcella, 1979, for examples).

On the other hand, other evaluations have reported that students in bilingual programs with an early starting point (i.e. kindergarten or grade 1) achieve significantly higher levels of L2 proficiency than students in programs with a delayed (middle elementary grades) or late (beginning of secondary school) starting point. For example, Genesee (1981) found that early immersion students who started in kindergarten performed significantly better than one-year late immersion students (grade 7) on tests of listening, speaking, reading, and writing. These findings indicate that the advantage of late immersion students in two-year programs is linked to the amount of L2 exposure as well as to the age of exposure. Moreover, in a synopsis of evaluations of early, middle, and late French immersion programs in Canada, Wesche, Toews-Janzen and MacFarlane (1996; p. ii Executive Summary) conclude that "EFI (early French immersion) students consistently outperform MFI (middle French immersion) and LFI (late French immersion) students overall." Genesee's Montreal evaluations of early versus late immersion were not included in this synopsis. Wesche et al. also note that differences between EFI and LFI students tend to diminish as the students approach the end of secondary school, attesting to the rapid progress that late immersion students can make if they stay in the program.

(A) Early total immersion: Time in each language per week.

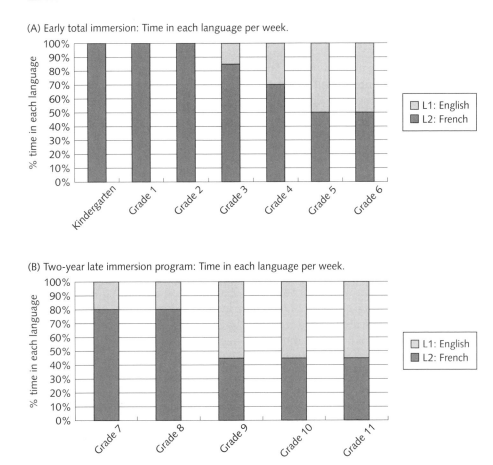

(B) Two-year late immersion program: Time in each language per week.

Figure 21.1 Early and late immersion programs.

The success that has been reported for early-entry bilingual/immersion programs has been attributed to a variety of factors, including: (1) the students' innate or natural language learning ability; (2) their attitudinal openness to new languages and cultures; (3) the opportunity for extended exposure afforded by an early starting grade; and (4) an optimal fit between learning styles of young learners and effective L2 pedagogy. The success that has been reported for students in bilingual programs with a later starting grade can, likewise, be attributed to a variety of factors. First, older students have the benefit of a well-developed L1 and, in particular, fully or well-developed L1 literacy skills that can facilitate acquisition of L2 literacy skills (Cummins, 2000). Parenthetically, the reverse transfer – from L2 to L1 literacy – is probably one explanation for the rapid progress that early immersion students make in L1 literacy development, as discussed earlier. Self-selection may also play an important role in accounting for the success of late L2 learners. Students who voluntarily opt for bilingual education at the secondary level are, arguably, highly self-motivated. There may also be a bias for academically advantaged students to self-select for bilingual education that begins in the late elementary or early secondary grades. The net effect of these selection biases may be to create classrooms in late-entry bilingual/immersion programs that are composed of highly motivated and academically capable students; a combination which in turn can result in a particularly advantageous instructional context.

Notwithstanding the documented success of bilingual programs with a late starting grade, educators and parents are often concerned that students' academic performance will suffer if they begin to receive academic instruction through the medium of a new language in the higher grades. An argument in favor of early introduction of the L2 for purposes of academic instruction is that the academic objectives for primary school students lend themselves well to concrete, experiential, hands-on learning activities. These kinds of activities also lend themselves well to promoting L2 acquisition among young learners. In contrast, teaching academic objectives in the higher grades often calls for the use of sophisticated, advanced language skills, and this can pose challenges for students who are in the beginning stages of L2 acquisition. Research in Canada has shown that achievement in subjects such as mathematics, chemistry, and history is not compromised in late immersion programs (beginning when students are about 11 years of age) if students have had prior L2 instruction during the elementary grades. In contrast, Marsh, Hau, and Kong (2000) report that late immersion students in Hong Kong have academic difficulties. In particular, they found that Chinese-speaking students in late English immersion programs in Hong Kong scored significantly lower in science, history, and geography than students in Chinese-medium programs. The authors of this report do not mention the Canadian results and so offer no explanation for the discrepancy between their findings and those from Canada. A number of factors might explain the discrepancy, including differences between the Hong Kong and Canadian students and/or teachers, the preparation that each student group received during the elementary grades, and typological and orthographic differences between the respective pairs of languages – Chinese and English in comparison to French and English.

In summary, the available evidence concerning age and effectiveness of L2 acquisition in educational settings suggests that bilingual education can be effective with both elementary and secondary level students, provided effective and appropriate pedagogy is implemented. Practically speaking, the question of when to begin bilingual education cannot be answered by theoretical arguments and empirical evidence alone. Socio-cultural and political factors must also be considered. The "best" starting grade for bilingual education can depend on the goals, needs, and resources of the community. In communities such as Quebec, Belgium, and Northern Italy where two or more languages

are commonly used in everyday life, it may be best to begin bilingual education early so that children become accustomed to both (all) languages early on
and, also, so that they can take advantage of language-learning opportunities
that are afforded outside school. In contrast, in communities such as Germany,
Japan, and many communities in the US where monolingualism is the norm
and other languages have no official status and/or are only used in restricted
settings, introduction of bilingual education in higher grades may be sufficient. Indeed, delaying introduction of bilingual education until higher grades
may be "best" in certain communities if parents are concerned about students'
L1 development – members of monolingual communities are often hesitant
about early bilingualism because they fear that it will impact negatively on
students' L1 development. In communities that seek trilingual competence (to
be discussed later), the success of students in bilingual programs with a late
starting grade is a definite advantage because it affords the possibility of introducing a third language after the first two have been established. Early versus
late starting points demand different resources and commitment and these
must also be considered in any discussion of whether it is "better" to start
early or later. For example, to optimize the benefits of early bilingual education,
there must be sufficient personnel, instructional materials, and administrative
resources to extend the program into the secondary grades; otherwise, there is
the risk that gains made in the elementary grades will be lost. Conversely, a
late-entry program requires teachers with certification in particular subject
matter who are also fluent in the target language and qualified to teach their
speciality subject(s) through that language. In short, the notion that there is
"an optimal starting grade" for bilingual education is misguided since what
might be "optimal" in one community may not be in another. (For additional
discussion of age, language acquisition and bilingualism, see chapters 4, 5,
and 12.)

21.6 Time

There has been considerable controversy in the field of bilingual education,
and in L2 education more generally, concerning the link between amount of
L2 exposure and level of L2 achievement. On the one hand, it is often assumed
that there is a direct correlation between the amount of L2 exposure in school
and L2 achievement – the notion of "time on task." Indeed, one of the reasons
schools begin instruction early (be it in second languages, mathematics, or
other subjects) is to provide more time for students to learn. Time is clearly
important for L2 learning, and it is often, though not always, the case that
students learn more when they have more exposure. For example, Canadian
research has shown that students in *total* immersion programs generally acquire
higher levels of proficiency in the L2 than students in *partial* immersion
programs (Genesee, 1987; see also Cenoz, 1998). On the other hand, the link
between time and L2 acquisition is not invariably linear. There appear to be

upper and lower limits to the importance of time. At the lower limits, variations in exposure to a second language in school probably make little difference – 20 versus 30 minutes per day, for example, is probably an unimportant difference, although systematic evidence of the impact of such variation is not available. Likewise, at the upper limits, there may be diminishing returns of extended L2 exposure in bilingual education. Evidence of these limits comes from Canadian research again – Canadian students in two-year late immersion programs (grades 7 and 8) perform as well as or almost as well as early total immersion students despite the fact that the former have significantly less exposure to the L2 (Genesee, 1981). Another case that illustrates this point comes from research in Montreal that compared two groups of students, both in late immersion (Stevens, 1983). In one case, English-speaking students spent 80 percent of their school day immersed in French – all academic subjects, except English language arts, were taught through the medium of French. The other group, in contrast, spent only half as much time – approximately 40 percent of their school day was spent in French – math, science, and language arts were taught in French. Despite the time advantage of the first group, they did not score consistently higher than the second group on a variety of L2 measures.

Intensity of exposure rather than accumulated amount of exposure is also a factor. Lapkin, Swain, Kamin and Hanna (1982) found that a group of grade 8 late immersion students had acquired less L2 proficiency than another group of grade 8 late immersion students who had received more concentrated L2 exposure, but they were more proficient than students in an extended conventional L2 program which, by the time of the evaluation, had amounted to twice as many hours.

Stevens's findings point to the importance of pedagogical considerations. Stevens (1983) attributed the impressive performance of her half-day immersion students to the pedagogical approach of their program. The half-day immersion students participated in an individualized, activity-based program that gave students certain choices about what they would study and how they would meet curricular objectives. Moreover, language use was embedded in interesting and engaging activities. In contrast, the full-day program was characterized by a group-centered approach where all students studied the same topics according to the same timeline. Thus, clearly, time alone is not always the most significant predictor of L2 proficiency – the intensity of exposure and, most importantly, the nature and quality of classroom instruction are very important. The earlier discussion of focus on form(s) versus focus on meaning reinforces the importance of instruction as an important factor in L2 achievement in bilingual education.

21.7   Students at Risk

A practical and ethical concern of educators and parents is whether bilingual education is suitable for students who are otherwise disadvantaged in school owing to home background, cognitive, linguistic, or other factors. The issue behind these concerns is the ability of students who struggle in school to cope with mastery of academic subjects taught through an unfamiliar language. On the one hand, since bilingual programs are usually optional and run counter to the commonsense notion that children should be educated initially through the medium of their L1, it could be considered unethical to admit students who are at risk to bilingual programs if they are not likely to benefit from them or if the bilingual experience is likely to exacerbate their educational difficulties. On the other hand, it could be considered unethical to exclude such students since to do so would, arguably, deprive them of the opportunity to acquire valuable language and cultural skills that would benefit them in their future personal and professional lives. The latter perspective takes on particular relevance in communities where the additional languages are used and, indeed, are necessary for economic success (e.g. French in Quebec). With increased globalization, it could be argued that, indeed, bilingual or even multilingual competence is important for all students.

This section will review extant research on the performance of students with personal or background characteristics that put them at a disadvantage in school. The following learner characteristics, which are generally associated with underachievement in school, have been examined: (1) low academic ability (or intelligence), (2) low socioeconomic background, (3) poor first language ability, and (4) minority ethnic group status (see Genesee, 1992, for more details). It is important to point out that there is a noticeable gap in the extant research – there is no published research on the performance of students with severe sensory-perceptual, cognitive, or socio-affective disorders. This limits our understanding of the suitability of bilingual education for all students considerably and poses real practical difficulties for school authorities who seek to integrate special-needs students in the same classrooms. This is clearly an issue that requires much more investigation.

21.7.1　*Academic ability*

With respect to academic (or intellectual) ability, Genesee (1976, 1987) systematically examined the performance of both elementary and secondary level English-speaking students in French immersion programs in Canada in relation to their intellectual ability. Students were classified as average, below average, or above average based on their scores on a standardized IQ test. Their school performance was assessed with respect to L1 (English) and L2 (French) development and academic achievement. With respect to L1 development and academic achievement, the below-average students in immersion scored at the same level as the below-average students in the L1 program on both L1 and academic achievement measures. In other words, the below-average students in immersion were not further disadvantaged in their L1 development or academic achievement as a result of participation in immersion. In keeping with their at-risk status, the below-average students in both programs scored significantly lower than their average and above-average peers in their respective programs on the same measures. With respect to L2 acquisition, the below-average students in immersion scored significantly higher on all L2 measures than the below-average students in the L1 program who were receiving conventional L2 instruction. In other words, the below-average students were benefiting from immersion in the form of enhanced L2 proficiency.

Comparisons between the elementary and secondary students revealed interesting and differential effects of academic ability on L2 achievement. Specifically, below-average students in both early and late immersion scored lower on measures of French language development related to literacy (reading and writing) than average and above-average students in the same programs; similarly the average students in both program types scored lower than the above-average students. Differential effects of ability were found, however, on measures of speaking and listening. Whereas the late immersion students exhibited the same stratification on measures of speaking and listening as they had demonstrated on the measures of L2 literacy, there were no differences among the ability subgroups in the early immersion program on measures of L2 speaking and listening. In other words, academic ability influenced the development of proficiency in all aspects of L2 acquisition among secondary school students, but had little differential effect on the speaking and listening comprehension skills of immersion students in the elementary school program. Speculatively, acquisition of an L2 when it is integrated with academic instruction is more cognitively demanding at the secondary than at the elementary school level and, as a result, calls on the kinds of cognitive skills that are differentially available to older students. In contrast, acquisition of L2 skills that are integrated with academic instruction at the elementary level calls on the natural language-learning ability that all students possess during their formative years. In any case, these findings argue that early immersion is more egalitarian than late immersion since it appears to be equally effective for students with different levels of general academic ability. Overall, these results indicate that low academic/intellectual ability is no more of a handicap in bilingual education than it is in L1 programs and, to the contrary, low-performing students can experience a net benefit from immersion in the form of bilingual proficiency.

In a related vein, Bruck (1985a, b) examined the role of academic ability in decisions to switch some students out of early immersion. At issue was whether academic ability, or something else, was the primary cause of the students' inability to stay in immersion. More specifically, Bruck compared the academic, familial, and socio-affective characteristics of early immersion students who switched to an L1 program with those of students who remained in the immersion program. She found, as expected, that the students who switched scored lower on a number of achievement measures than most of the students who remained in immersion, but that the academic difficulties of the students who switched were no worse than those of a subgroup of students who remained in immersion despite low academic performance. What distinguished the students who switched from those who remained in the program despite their difficulty was that the former expressed significantly more negative attitudes toward schooling (and immersion in particular) and exhibited more behavioral problems than the latter. Bruck conjectured that it was the behavioral problems that were engendered by academic difficulties that ultimately led to the decision to switch some students out of immersion, in the hope that they would adjust more satisfactorily in an L1 program. In a follow-up investigation, Bruck noted that the students who switched continued to have academic difficulties and to exhibit attitudinal and behavioral problems. Bruck's results suggest that the ability to cope with poor academic performance may be a more serious problem for some immersion students than poor academic performance alone. Her results also support the argument that academic ability alone does not distinguish students who can benefit from bilingual/immersion education and those who cannot. In other words, other things being equal, students with low levels of academic ability should be eligible for bilingual education.

21.7.2 L1 ability

It is generally thought that the level and kind of L1 ability that children acquire prior to coming to school are important predictors of success in school. This follows from the fact that much learning in school is mediated through language, and much of schooling focuses on language learning. Thus, students with well-developed L1 skills, especially those related to literacy, are expected to have a head start. While there is much evidence to support this general prediction (Cummins, 2000), the issue in bilingual programs is whether students with low levels of L1 ability should be excluded from such programs because they will be differentially handicapped in comparison to what they would achieve in an L1 program. Despite the significance of this issue, there is remarkably little systematic investigation of it, one exception being work by Bruck in Montreal. In order to examine this question, Bruck (1978, 1982) identified subgroups of grade 3 immersion and non-immersion students who were "impaired" or "normal" in their L1 development. Classification was based on teachers' judgments, an oral interview, and a battery of diagnostic tests. When Bruck tested the students on literacy and academic achievement measures, she found that the impaired immersion students scored at the same level as similarly impaired students in the L1 program, and both groups scored lower than their normally developing peers in the same programs, as would be expected from the language status of the impaired students. At the same time, the impaired immersion students had developed significantly higher levels of L2 proficiency than both subgroups of non-immersion students (impaired and non-impaired) who were receiving conventional L2 instruction. In sum, and as was found in the case of students with low levels of academic ability, students with low levels of L1 ability demonstrated the same levels of L1 literacy development and academic achievement in immersion as similarly impaired students in L1 programs. At the same time, participation in the immersion program had benefited the impaired students with significantly superior L2 proficiency in comparison to students receiving conventional L2 instruction. While these findings are important and useful, it is essential to examine the progress of students with more specifically defined forms of L1 impairment since, arguably, the operational definitions used by Bruck do not reflect current thinking about language impairment; nor do they capture the full range of language impairment that might cause problems for schoolchildren (Leonard, 1998).

21.7.3   *Socioeconomic status*

Studies in the US and Canada have examined the performance of students from low socioeconomic backgrounds in elementary level bilingual/immersion programs (Bruck, Tucker, and Jakimik, 1975; Cziko, 1975; Holobow, Genesee and Lambert, 1991; Tucker, et al., 1972). It has been found that socioeconomically disadvantaged students usually demonstrate the same level of L1 development in immersion programs as comparable students in L1 programs. At the same time, and as one would predict from their low socioeconomic status, disadvantaged students in immersion usually score significantly lower than their middle-class peers in the same program, as is true for low socioeconomic students in L1 programs. The same pattern has been found for achievement in mathematics and science. Thus, even though the disadvantaged immersion students had received all science instruction in their L2, they scored as well as disadvantaged students who had received academic instruction through the medium of the L1. With respect to L2 development, it has been found that economically disadvantaged immersion students generally perform better than comparable students in conventional L2 programs on all measures of L2 proficiency. Of particular note, they also sometimes perform as well as middle-class immersion students on tests of listening comprehension and speaking, although significantly lower on tests of reading. These patterns are virtually identical to those found for academic ability, a finding that is not altogether surprising given the significant intercorrelation between these learner characteristics.

Caldas and Boudreaux (1999) have similarly reported that socioeconomic disadvantage is not an obstacle to successful performance in immersion programs in the case of English-speaking American students attending French immersion programs in Louisiana. Since these researchers did not have access to information concerning the socioeconomic status of individual students, they compared entire groups of students in immersion classes with high concentrations of poor students (determined by the number of students who participated in a free/reduced lunch program) with that of groups of students in classes with similarly high concentrations of poor students where the L1 was used as the medium of instruction. They found that the immersion students (both white and African American) tended to score higher than non-immersion students in the same school district on standardized state-mandated tests of English and mathematics achievement administered in grades 3, 5 and 7. As the authors themselves point out, the operational definition of socioeconomic status they used calls for caution when generalizing these results to individual students.

21.7.4 Ethnic group status

Yet another risk factor in school is ethnic minority group status. Ethnic minority groups traditionally have disproportionately high rates of failure in North American schools (e.g. Sue and Padilla, 1986), though of course not all students fail. Of interest in this section is the performance of students from ethnic minority groups who speak the societally dominant language – for example, African-American students in French immersion programs in Cincinnati, Ohio (Holobow, Genesee, Lambert, Met, and Gastright, 1987) or Louisiana (Caldas and Boudreaux, 1999). Bilingual programs that have been developed by indigenous language communities in order to revive their heritage languages fall into this category as well – for example, Hawaiian immersion for English-speaking children of Hawaiian descent in the US (Slaughter, 1997) and Mohawk immersion programs for English-speaking children of Mohawk descent in Canada (Jacobs and Cross, 2001; see Christian and Genesee, 2001, for other examples). Although beyond the scope of this chapter, indigenous language immersion programs are of additional interest because of the practical educational challenges they face in creating instructional materials and strategies in indigenous languages that are compatible with the unique cultural traditions of their communities (see Jacobs and Cross, 2001, and Yamauchi and Wilhelm, 2001, for further discussion of these issues). The students in these programs are of interest here because although they come to school speaking English, they are at risk for academic failure because they are members of minority ethnic groups. Moreover, like African Americans, many speak a non-standard variety of the dominant societal language and thus could be said to be learning Standard English as a third language in addition to a heritage language. Research in all of these settings indicates that the ethnic minority students participating in these programs, even those who spoke a non-standard variety of English, demonstrated the same levels of L1 development and academic achievement as comparable students in L1 programs and, in addition, they had developed advanced levels of functional proficiency in the target languages.

21.7.5 Summary

The research reviewed in this section indicates that students who speak a societally dominant language (or a non-standard variety of such a language) and have learner or background characteristics that put them at risk for academic difficulty or failure can achieve the same levels of L1 development and academic achievement in bilingual programs as comparable at-risk students in L1 programs. At-risk students in bilingual education generally perform less well than students in the same program who are not at risk, but their progress is not differentially impeded in comparison to comparable at-risk students in L1 programs. At the same time, research has shown that at-risk students can benefit from bilingual education by acquiring advanced levels of functional L2 proficiency. Practically speaking, the available evidence does not justify arbitrary exclusion of students who are at risk from bilingual programs on the assumption that they are incapable of benefiting from academic instruction through the medium of an L2, or that they will be held back in L1 development as a result of such instruction (see also Sparks et al., 1998, for a similar position with respect to foreign language education). At this time, decisions to exclude individual students or groups of students can only be justified by well-documented difficulties and a sound rationale for why and how these difficulties are likely to be remedied or avoided if they participate in L1 programs. This is not to say that bilingual education is recommended for all at-risk students since, as was pointed out earlier, the effectiveness of bilingual education for students with severe sensory-perceptual, cognitive, or socio-affective problems has not been investigated systematically.

However, even in the case of students with at-risk characteristics that have been examined by researchers, parents and educators should carefully consider the importance of the L2 for the child, his or her family, and his or her future career and personal goals when making decisions about placing individual students in bilingual education. It is much easier to justify placing at-risk students in bilingual programs if there are real benefits to learning two languages, for example if the community is bilingual, or parents or grandparents are bilingual. A further consideration is the availability and effectiveness of intervention options for students with diagnosed difficulties. Placement of a student with a diagnosed difficulty in a bilingual program that lacks relevant services is, other things being equal, probably ill-advised, especially if the student could receive appropriate and effective intervention in the L1 program.

21.8   Language Typology

Bilingual education has come to encompass a variety of languages, including languages that are typologically different. Such programs have already been mentioned in this review: Mohawk-English, Hawaiian-English, and Japanese-English; others are Hebrew-French-English (Genesee and Lambert, 1983), Chinese-English (Johnson, 1997), Estonian-Russian (Asser, Kolk and Küppar, 2001), and Swedish-Finnish (Björkland, 1997). In addition to typological linguistic differences, some of these language combinations entail different types of orthographies – as is the case for Japanese-English and Chinese-English, which entail logographic and alphabetic scripts, respectively, and Hebrew-French-English and Estonian-Russian which entail different alphabetic scripts. Intuitively and pedagogically speaking, typological similarity has important acquisitional and pedagogical implications. The closer the typology and scripts of the two languages, the more transfer is likely to occur (Cenoz, 1998) and, thus, the more acquisition of the two languages will be facilitated. Typological distance might be expected to influence not only the acquisition of literacy skills but also the development of oral communication skills.

Fortunately, evaluations of all of the above programs have been carried out and can be reviewed here. With respect to programs with typologically different languages but the same types of orthography, there is no evidence that typological differences influence student outcomes significantly. More specifically, evaluations of students in Hebrew-French-English immersion in Montreal (Genesee and Lambert, 1983), Hawaiian-English immersion in Hawaii (Slaughter, 1997), Mohawk-English immersion in Montreal (Jacobs and Cross, 2001), Estonian-Russian immersion in Estonia (Asser, Kolk and Küppar, 2001), and Swedish-Finnish immersion in Finland (Björkland, 1997) indicate that the overall pattern of outcomes is the same as in programs with typologically similar languages, such as French-English or Spanish-English, as was summarized earlier. In other words, immersion students demonstrate the same L1 development and academic achievement and, at the same time, acquire advanced levels of functional proficiency in the L2 (and L3 in the case of the Hebrew-French-English program).

When it comes to programs with languages that are both typologically and orthographically different, there is less data. In an evaluation of a English-immersion program for Japanese-speaking students in Japan, Bostwick has reported that the participating students demonstrated the same levels of L1 development and academic achievement as comparable Japanese students following the regular Japanese-medium curriculum within the same school (Bostwick, 2001). The students had also acquired functional proficiency in English. These findings indicate that despite evident differences between written Japanese and English, Japanese students who received only half (or less) of their instruction through the medium of Japanese achieved the same level of proficiency in written forms of Japanese as students whose entire curriculum had been taught through Japanese. Although the immersion students in this school had reduced exposure to academic instruction through Japanese, their Japanese language arts curriculum was the same and had the same amount of time devoted to it as that of students in the regular Japanese-medium stream. Arguably, the reduction in exposure to Japanese in school that English immersion entailed in this case was offset by students' exposure to both written and oral forms of Japanese outside school (and indeed, elsewhere in the school itself).

An even greater concern may arise when the language with the more complex orthography, such as Japanese or Chinese, is not the ambient language in the school and community. Such programs exist – Japanese immersion for

English-speaking students in Oregon, USA (Kanagy, 2001) and Australia (Chapman and Hartley, 1999), and Chinese immersion for English-speaking students in the US (Met, personal communication). However, research in these programs provides no information about the students' level of achievement in the written forms of the target languages. The challenges posed by orthographic differences may extend beyond acquisition of reading and writing to implicate academic achievement, since students with limited literacy skills may also be limited in their ability to assimilate academic skills and knowledge in the higher grades when written language becomes increasingly important as a vehicle for academic development. This is true even in L1 programs, but is likely to be exacerbated in programs that teach in languages such as Japanese whose written forms require extensive practice. Met (personal communication) suggests that whereas distinct academic content can be taught in each language in immersion programs that use cognate languages, it may be necessary in programs that use languages with distinct orthographies to teach those aspects of the academic curriculum that call for advanced literacy skills in the L1 and limit academic instruction in the L2 to content that is not literacy-dependent. There is a need for more research concerning academic achievement and how content can best be taught in immersion programs that use orthographically distinct languages.

21.9 Multilingual Education

Multilingual forms of education have been implemented in communities where more than two languages are used or useful. For example, Scandinavian countries often teach three or more languages in school so that students are able to communicate in other Scandinavian languages and in a world language, such as German or English. Parents in the Basque Country see trilingual education as important in order to foster competence in (1) Basque, the indigenous language, which is at risk, (2) Spanish, the language of broader communication in Spain, and (3) English, a language of economic and scientific communication worldwide (Cenoz, 1998). There are a number of ways in which a third language can be added to the school curriculum (see Cenoz and Genesee, 1998, for examples). In some cases, trilingual education consists of instruction in academic subjects through two languages along with instruction in a third language as a separate subject – for example, for daily 30- to 60-minute sessions. In these cases, the third language is not used to teach academic subjects. In the Basque Country, for example, Spanish and Basque are taught as subjects and are also used for academic instruction during the elementary grades; English, the third language, is taught as a subject beginning in kindergarten, when the students are four years of age (Cenoz, 1998; see Egger and Lardschneider-McLean, 2001, for an example from Italy). English is not used to teach academic subjects at the elementary school level in Basque schools, although there are plans to teach academic subjects through the medium of English at the secondary level. In other cases, all three languages may be used as media of academic instruction, as in prototypical bilingual education programs. For example, in a trilingual program in Montreal, English-speaking students are taught different academic subjects through the medium of French and Hebrew in kindergarten to grade 4; English is introduced as a third language in grade 4 and is used to teach both English language arts and some academic subjects (Genesee, 1998). The European Schools in Luxembourg are trilingual in French, German and Luxemburgish (Hoffmann, 1998; Housen, 2002). Luxemburgish is both taught as a subject and used as a medium of academic instruction from the pre-school years onward. German is introduced as a subject in grade 1 and later used as a medium of academic instruction. Similarly, French is introduced initially as a subject in grade 2 and subsequently used as a medium of instruction. There is considerable programmatic and pedagogical variation among multilingual programs as might be expected from the distinct and complex socio-cultural-political circumstances of the communities in which they are situated. A review such as this cannot begin to do justice to the actual complexities of such programs (see Cenoz and Genesee, 1998, for more detailed descriptions of trilingual programs).

Trilingual education raises a number of interesting and important issues; some are the same as those that have been addressed in the preceding review of bilingual education: How effective are they? Are they effective for students with diverse learner characteristics? Other issues that are particular to trilingual education arise: What is the developmental relationship among the languages? Does the sequencing of languages for literacy or academic instruction matter? What are the limits to acquisition of three languages when there is no or little support for the non-native languages outside school? Unfortunately, there is scant empirical evidence to answer these questions and the extant evidence is highly variable in nature. Programs for which reports have been published appear to be working satisfactorily. Evidence of the effectiveness of the Basque and Canadian trilingual programs comes from assessments of student performance on standardized and school-based tests and includes comparisons with the performance of students in non-trilingual schools in the same communities. Reports of the effectiveness of the European Schools are based on participants' impressions and on the success that program graduates have in gaining admission to tertiary level education (see Cenoz, 1998; Genesee, 1998; and Hoffmann, 1998, and Housen, 2002, for more details). None of the published cases report evidence of interference or impediments to language development as a result of exposure to three languages during the course of elementary education, the level of schooling for such programs. To the contrary, Cenoz and Valencia (1994) provide some evidence that bilingualism favors the acquisition of a third language (see also Bild and Swain, 1989; Swain, Lapkin, Rowen, and Hart, 1991, for specific studies and Cenoz and Genesee, 1998, and Cenoz, Hufeisen and Jessner, 2001, for reviews). The same caveats that apply to the interpretation of evaluations of bilingual education apply here; namely, there is a bias toward reporting successful programs and self-selection factors are operating. The evidence to date concerning trilingual education is encouraging; but we currently lack detailed understanding of the effectiveness of these programs. Clearly, we could benefit from additional research attention to these programs.

21.10   Next Steps and Conclusions

While this review indicates that much has been learned about bilingual education for majority-language students, there is much more that we need to learn. Here are some research questions that need attention:

1   What pedagogical approaches are most effective in promoting acquisition of the L2? In particular, are there particular instructional strategies that enhance students' mastery of the formal features of the L2 (or L3) while maintaining their fluency in the language? What forms of corrective feedback produce significant, long-term gains in student competence?
2   Are there students for whom bilingual education is not effective? In particular, are bilingual programs suitable for students with severe cognitive, perceptuo-motor, or affective disorders?
3   What intervention strategies are effective for students who are at risk in immersion programs? Should services for immersion students with special needs be provided in the target language or can they be provided with good effect in the student's L1 without switching the student to the L1 program?
4   What effect does classroom composition (defined in terms of the distribution of students with average, above-average and below-average academic ability) have on instruction and learning, especially L2 learning?
5   Are there specific instructional strategies that are particularly effective for teaching typologically distinct languages? In a related vein, how can literacy best be taught in languages with orthographically distinct writing systems? Is simultaneous or successive introduction of literacy instruction in two languages with different typologies and/or orthographies preferable?
6   How does the teacher's level of target language proficiency influence instruction and learning?
7   Is there a role for bilingual usage – that is, the use of both languages in the same lessons, in bilingual education? In other words, should the languages always be kept separate and, if not, how can they be used co-extensively to promote language learning?

Notwithstanding gaps in our understanding, research has yielded considerable insights about bilingual education. The following generalizations are compatible with the findings that have been reviewed here:

1 Bilingual education for majority-language students is effective in promoting functional proficiency in a second, and even a third, language at no cost to the participating students' native language development or academic achievement.

2 There is often a positive correlation between amount of exposure to the L2 in bilingual programs and level of L2 proficiency, but not always.

3 Bilingual programs that provide appropriate and continuous instruction can be effective with younger or older students; in other words, advanced levels of functional L2 proficiency can be acquired by students who begin bilingual education in the primary grades and by those who begin in higher grades.

4 Bilingual education is effective for majority-language students with a variety of learner characteristics, even those that put them at risk for poor performance in school.

5 Pedagogy and, in particular, the way the L2 is used and taught is important. More specifically, it appears that L2 acquisition is enhanced when students are given extended opportunities to use the language interactively. It also appears that while functional use of the target languages is generally effective at promoting L2 proficiency, instructional strategies that systematically raise awareness of and create opportunities for students to learn specific linguistic forms that serve their communicative needs and goals can extend L2 learning.

6 Bilingual education in languages with distinct typologies and orthographic conventions can be effective in achieving a school's linguistic and academic objectives, although there may be limits on how far both languages can be used for academic instruction.

These generalizations cannot be taken as universal, invariant truths that pertain to any and all bilingual education programs – present and future. They indicate what can happen when bilingual education is implemented effectively. In any case, the extant findings are reassuring for those interested in bilingual education for majority-language students. (For more discussion of bilingual education, see chapters 15, 23–25, 27, and 28.)

ACKNOWLEDGMENTS

I would like to thank M. Met (National Foreign Language Center, Washington DC), R. Lyster (Education, McGill University) and M. Wesche (Second Language Institute, University of Ottawa) for helpful comments on an earlier version of this chapter. Preparation of this chapter was supported by a grant from the Social Sciences and Humanities Research Council, Ottawa, Canada.

REFERENCES

Adiv, E. (1980). An analysis of second language performance in two types of immersion programs. Ph.D. dissertation, Department of Second Language Education, McGill University, Montreal.

Asser, H., Kolk, P., and Küppar, M. (2001). *Estonian-Language Immersion Programme: Report on Student Achievement and Parental Attitudes for the Academic Year 2000–2001*. Tallinn, Estonia: Estonian Immersion Centre.

August, D. and Hakuta, K. (1997). *Improving Schooling for Language Minority Children: A Research Agenda*. Washington, D.C.: National Academy Press.

Baker, C. (2000). *A Parents' and Teachers' Guide to Bilingualism*. Clevedon, UK: Multilingual Matters.

Baker, C. (2001). *Foundations of Bilingual Education and Bilingualism*. Clevedon, UK: Multilingual Matters.

Bild, E. R. and Swain, M. (1989). Minority language students in a French immersion program: Their French proficiency. *Journal of Multilingual and Multicultural Development*, 10, 255–74.

Birdsong, D. (1999). *Second Language Acquisition and the Critical Period Hypothesis*. Mahwah, NJ: Erlbaum.

Björkland, S. (1997). Immersion in Finland in the 1990s: A state of development and expansion. In K. Johnson and M. Swain (eds.), *Immersion Education: International Perspectives*, pp. 85–102. Cambridge, UK: Cambridge University Press.

Bostwick, M. (2001). English immersion in a Japanese school. In D. Christian and F. Genesee (eds.), *Bilingual Education*, pp. 125–38. Alexandria, VA: TESOL.

Bruck, M. (1978). The suitability of early French immersion programs for the language disabled child. *Canadian Journal of Education*, 3, 51–72.

Bruck, M. (1982). Language disabled children: Performance in an additive bilingual education program. *Applied Psycholinguistics*, 3, 45–60.

Bruck, M. (1985a). Predictors of transfer out of early French immersion programs. *Applied Psycholinguistics*, 6, 39–61.

Bruck, M. (1985b). Consequences of transfer out of early French immersion programs. *Applied Psycholinguistics*, 6, 101–20.

Bruck, M., Tucker, G. R., and Jakimik, J. (1975). Are French immersion programs suitable for working class children? *Word*, 27, 311–41.

Burger, S., Wesche, M., and Migneron, M. (1997). Late, late immersion: Discipline-based second language teaching at the University of Ottawa. In R. K. Johnson and M. Swain (eds.), *Immersion Education: International Perspectives*, pp. 65–84. Cambridge, UK: Cambridge University Press.

Burstall, C. (1974). *Primary French in the Balance*. Windsor, UK: NFER Publishing.

Caldas, S. J. and Boudreaux, N. (1999). Poverty, race, and foreign language immersion: Predictors of math and English language arts performance. *Learning Language*, 5(1), 4–15.

Cenoz, J. (1998). Multilingual education in the Basque Country. In J. Cenoz and F. Genesee (eds.), *Beyond Bilingualism: Multilingualism and Multilingual Education*, pp. 175–91. Clevedon, UK: Multilingual Matters.

Cenoz, J. and Genesee, F. (eds.) (1998). *Beyond Bilingualism: Multilingualism and Multilingual Education*. Clevedon, UK: Multilingual Matters.

Cenoz, J., Hufeisen, B., and Jessner, U. (2001). *Cross-linguistic Influence in Third*

Language Acquisition: Psycholinguistic Perspectives. Clevedon, UK: Multilingual Matters.

Cenoz, J. and Valencia, J. F. (1994). Additive trilingualism: Evidence from the Basque Country. *Applied Psycholinguistics*, 15, 195–201.

Chapman, D. and Hartley, B. (1999). Authentic voices: Insights into a Japanese education practicum. *Japanese-Language Education Around the Globe*, 9, 45–62.

Christian, D. and Genesee, F. (eds.) (2001). *Bilingual Education*. Alexandria, VA: TESOL.

Cloud, N., Genesee, F., and Hamayan, E. (2000). *Dual Language Instruction: A Handbook for Enriched Education*. Portsmouth, NH: Heinle & Heinle.

Cummins, J. (2000). *Language, Power and Pedagogy: Bilingual Children in the Crossfire*. Clevedon, UK: Multilingual Matters.

Cziko, G. (1975). The effects of different French immersion programs on the language and academic skills of children from various socioeconomic backgrounds. MA thesis, Department of Psychology, McGill University, Montreal.

Day, E. and Shapson, S. (1991). Integrating formal and functional approaches to language teaching in French immersion: An experimental study. *Language Learning*, 41, 25–58.

Egger, K. and Lardschneider-McLean, M. (2001). Trilingual schools in the Ladin Valleys of South Tyrol, Italy. In D. Christian and F. Genesee (eds.), *Bilingual Education*, pp. 57–68. Alexandria, VA: TESOL.

Fathman, A. (1975). The relationship between age and second language productive ability. *Language Learning*, 25, 245–53.

Genesee, F. (1976). The role of intelligence in second language learning. *Language Learning*, 26, 267–80.

Genesee, F. (1978). Is there an optimal age for starting second language instruction? *McGill Journal of Education*, 13, 145–54.

Genesee, F. (1981). A comparison of early and late second language learning. *Canadian Journal of Behavioral Science*, 13, 115–27.

Genesee, F. (1984). Historical and theoretical foundations of immersion education. In *Studies of Immersion Education: A Collection for United States Educators*, pp. 32–57. Sacramento, CA: California State Department of Education.

Genesee, F. (1987). *Learning Through Two Languages: Studies of Immersion and Bilingual Education*. Rowley, MA: Newbury House.

Genesee, F. (1988). Neuropsychology and second language acquisition. In L. Beebe (ed.), *Issues in Second Language Acquisition*, pp. 32–57. Rowley, MA: Newbury House.

Genesee, F. (1992). Second/foreign language immersion and at-risk English-speaking children. *Foreign Language Annals*, 25, 199–213.

Genesee, F. (1998). A case study of multilingual education in Canada. In J. Cenoz and F. Genesee, F. (eds.), *Beyond Bilingualism: Multilingualism and Multilingual Education*, pp. 243–58. Clevedon, UK: Multilingual Matters.

Genesee, F. and Lambert, W. E. (1983). Trilingual education for majority language children. *Child Development*, 54, 105–14.

Global Reach (September 30, 2000). www.glreach.com/globstats/ refs.php3.

Harley, B. (1989). Functional grammar in French immersion: A classroom experiment. *Applied Linguistics*, 10, 331–59.

Harley, B. (1998). The role of focus on form in promoting child L2 acquisition. In C. Doughty and J. Williams (eds.), *Focus on Form in*

Classroom Second Language Acquisition, pp. 156–74. Cambridge, UK: Cambridge University Press.

Harley, B. and Swain, M. (1984). An analysis of verb form and function in the speech of French immersion pupils. *Workingpapers in Bilingualism*, 14, 31–46.

Harley, B. and Wang, W. (1997). The critical period hypothesis: Where are we now? In A. M. B deGroot and J. F. Kroll (eds.), *Tutorials in Bilingualism: Psycholinguistic Perspectives*, pp. 19–51. Mahwah, NJ: Lawrence Erlbaum.

Hoffmann, C. (1998). Luxembourg and the European Schools. Genesee, F. (1998). In J. Cenoz and F. Genesee, F. (eds.), *Beyond Bilingualism: Multilingualism and Multilingual Education*, pp. 143–74. Clevedon, UK: Multilingual Matters.

Holobow, N. E., Genesee, F., and Lambert, W. E. (1991). The effectiveness of a foreign language immersion program for children from different ethnic and social class backgrounds: Report 2. *Applied Psycholinguistics*, 12, 179–98.

Holobow, N., Genesee, F., Lambert, W. E., Gastright, J., and Met, M. (1987). Effectiveness of partial French immersion for children from different social class and ethnic backgrounds. *Applied Psycholinguistics*, 8, 137–52.

Housen, A. (2002). Processes and outcomes in the European Schools Model of multilingual education. *Bilingual Research Journal*, 26, 43–62.

Jacobs, K. and Cross, A. (2001). The seventh generation of Kahnawà:ke: Phoenix or Dinosaur. In D. Christian and F. Genesee (eds.), *Bilingual Education*, pp. 109–21. Alexandria, VA: TESOL.

Johnson, R. K. (1997). The Hong Kong education system: Late immersion under stress. In R. K. Johnson and M. Swain (eds.), *Immersion Education: International Perspectives*, pp. 171–89.

Cambridge, UK: Cambridge University Press.

Johnson, R. K. and Swain, M. (1997). *Immersion Education: International Perspectives*. Cambridge, UK: Cambridge University Press.

Kanagy, R. (2001). "Hai, genki desu": Doing fine in Japanese. In D. Christian and F. Genesee (eds.), *Bilingual Education*, pp. 139–50. Alexandria, VA: TESOL.

Krashen, S., Long, M., and Scarcella, R. (1979). Age, rate, and eventual attainment in second language acquisition. *TESOL Quarterly*, 13, 573–82.

Lambert, W. E. and Tucker, G. R. (1972). *The Bilingual Education of Children: The St. Lambert Experiment*. Rowley, MA: Newbury House.

Lapkin, S., Swain, M., Kamin, J., and Hanna, G. (1982). Late immersion in perspective: The Peel study. *The Canadian Modern Language Review*, 39, 182–206.

Leonard, L. B. (1998). *Children with Specific Language Impairment*. Cambridge, MA: Bradford.

Lewis, E. G. (1976). Bilingualism and bilingual education: The ancient world to the Renaissance. In J. Fishman (ed.), *Bilingual Education: An International Sociological Perspective*, pp. 150–200. Rowley, MA: Newbury House.

Long, M. (1990). Maturational constraints on language development. *Studies in Second Language Acquisition*, 12, 251–85.

Long, M. and Robinson, P. (1998). Focus on form: Theory, research, and practice. In C. Doughty and J. Williams (eds.), *Focus on Form in Classroom Second Language Acquisition*, pp. 15–41. Cambridge, UK: Cambridge University Press.

Lyster, R. (1987). Speaking immersion. *The Canadian Modern Language Review*, 43, 84–100.

Lyster, R. (1990). The role of analytic language teaching in French immersion programs. *The Canadian Modern Language Review*, 47, 159–76.

Lyster, R. (1994). The effect of functional-analytic teaching on aspects of French immersion students' sociolinguistic competence. *Applied Linguistics*, 15, 263–87.

Lyster, R. and Ranta, L. (1997). Corrective feedback and learner uptake: Negotiation of form in communicative classrooms. *Studies in Second Language Acquisition*, 19, 37–66.

Marsh, H. W., Hau, K. T., and Kong, C. K. (2000). Late immersion and language of instruction in Hong Kong High Schools: Achievement growth in language and nonlanguage subjects. *Harvard Educational Review*, 70, 302–45.

Marinova-Todd, S. H., Marshall, B., and Snow, C. (2000). Three misconceptions about age and L2 learning. *TESOL Quarterly*, 34, 9–34.

Mayberry, R. (1993). First-language acquisition after childhood differs from second-language acquisition: The case of American Sign Language. *Journal of Speech and Hearing Research*, 36, 1258–70.

Met, M. (1998). Curriculum decision-making in content-based language teaching. In J. Cenoz and F. Genesee (eds.), *Beyond Bilingualism: Multilingualism and Multilingual Education*, pp. 35–63. Clevedon, UK: Multilingual Matters.

Morrison, F. (1981). *Longitudinal and Cross-section Studies of French Proficiency in Ottawa and Carleton Schools*. Ottawa, Ont.: The Ottawa Board of Education.

Norris, J. and Ortega, L. (2000). Effectiveness of L2 instruction: A research synthesis and quantitative meta-analysis. *Language Learning*, 50, 417–528.

Scovel, T. (1988). *A Time to Speak: A Psycholinguistic Inquiry into the Critical Period for Human Speech*. Rowley, MA: Newbury House.

Skutnabb-Kangas, T. (2000). *Linguistic Genocide in Education – or Worldwide Diversity and Human Rights?* Mahwah, NJ: Lawrence Erlbaum.

Slaughter, H. (1997). Indigenous language immersion in Hawai'i: A case study of Kula Kaiapuni Hawai'i. In R. K. Johnson and M. Swain (eds.), *Immersion Education: International Perspectives*, pp. 105–29. Cambridge, UK: Cambridge University Press.

Snow, A., Met, M., and Genesee, F. (1989). A conceptual framework for the integration of language and content in second/foreign language instruction. *TESOL Quarterly*, 23, 201–18.

Spada, N. (1997). Form-focussed instruction and second language acquisition: A review of classroom and laboratory research. *Language Teaching*, 30, 73–87.

Sparks, R. L., Artzer, M., Javorsky, J., Patton, J., Ganschow, L., Miller, K., and Hordubay, D. (1998). Students classified as learning disabled and non-learning disabled: Two comparison studies of native language skill, foreign language aptitude, and foreign language proficiency. *Foreign Language Annals*, 31, 535–50.

Stevens, F. (1983). Activities to promote learning and communication in the second language classroom. *TESOL Quarterly*, 17, 259–72.

Sue, S. and Padilla, A. (1986). Ethnic minority issues in the United States: Challenges for the educational system. In *Beyond Language: Social and Cultural Factors in Schooling Language Minority Students*, pp. 35–72. Los Angeles: Evaluation, Dissemination and Assessment Center, California State University.

Swain, M. (1985). Communicative competence: Some roles of comprehensible input and comprehensible output in its development. In S. M. Gass and

G. G. Madden (eds.), *Input in Second Language Acquisition*, pp. 235–53. Rowley, MA: Newbury House.

Swain, M. (1998). Focus on form through conscious reflection. In C. Doughty and J. Williams (eds.), *Focus on Form in Classroom Second Language Acquisition*, pp. 64–81. Cambridge, UK: Cambridge University Press.

Swain, M. and Lapkin, S. (1982). *Evaluating Bilingual Education: A Canadian Case Study*. Clevedon, UK: Multilingual Matters.

Swain, M., Lapkin, S., Rowen, N., and Hart, D. (1990). The role of mother tongue literacy in third language learning. *Language, Culture and Curriculum*, 3, 65–81.

Tucker, G. R., Lambert, W. E., and d'Anglejan, A. (1972). Are French immersion programs suitable for working class children? A pilot investigation. Unpublished report, Psychology Department, McGill University, Montreal.

Walraff, B. (2000). What global language? *The Atlantic Monthly*, 286 (November), 52–66. Boston, MA: The Atlantic Monthly Group.

Wesche, M., Toews-Janzen, M., and MacFarlane, A. (1996). *Comparative Outcomes and Impacts of Early, Middle and Late Entry French Immersion Options: Review of Recent Research and Annotated Bibliography*. Toronto: OISE/UT Press.

White, L. and Genesee, F. (1996). How native is near-native? The issue of ultimate attainment in adult second language acquisition. *Second Language Research*, 12, 233–65.

Yamauchi, L. and Wilhelm, P. (2001). E Ola Ka Hawai'i I Kona 'Olelo: Hawaiians live in their language. In D. Christian and F. Genesee (eds.), *Bilingual Education*, pp. 83–94. Alexandria, VA: TESOL.

22 The Impact of Bilingualism on Language and Literacy Development

ELLEN BIALYSTOK

22.1 Introduction

Considering the prevalence of bilingualism in the world's population, the number of children who are raised with two languages, and the proportion of students who enter school without speaking the instructional language, the developmental consequences of this experience have been surprisingly ignored. Researchers in language acquisition, education, and cognitive development have essentially developed their models from the simplifying assumption that children have one mind, one conceptual system, and one language. The limitations of this assumption are quickly apparent when one considers the inevitable and prolific interactions between language and thought in virtually every cognitive endeavor, particularly during development. Children's early concepts are learned through their verbal experiences, knowledge is codified in a linguistic form, and communication defines every aspect of development. It is inconceivable that conducting these interactions and learning about the world through two linguistic systems has no effect on the trajectory of development for bilingual children. This chapter explores one aspect of the potential developmental impact of that experience – the development of metalinguistic and literacy skills. An analysis of the way in which bilingualism impacts on non-verbal aspects of cognitive development is explored elsewhere (Bialystok, 2001, forthcoming).

Although it may seem obvious now that linguistic experience impacts on cognition and development, the view is actually recent. The pre-eminent developmental theorist of the twentieth century was undoubtedly Jean Piaget, and for him language was essentially irrelevant. The other great theorist of the twentieth century, Noam Chomsky, marginalized language in a different way. Although Chomsky placed language at the centre of interest for the cognitive sciences, he barricaded it into a module, defined by an innate structure and served by dedicated processes. But it is implausible that language and other cognitive activities could interact in such a way that the type of linguistic knowledge learned by the child could shape broad areas of cognitive development, unless they share the same processes and resources.

These views of language have created theoretical barriers to the examination of the potential impact of bilingualism on development. Research must follow from a context that not only predicts but also interprets the results that might be found. If language and cognition were kept at a protected distance from each other, then the question of bilingual impacts on development would not even arise. Even in the important study that saved bilingualism from the condemned list of experiences that devastate minds, Peal and Lambert (1962) did not expect bilingualism to have an impact beyond language. Their modest hypothesis was that monolinguals and bilinguals would score the same on measures of nonverbal intelligence, but that monolinguals would score *higher* than bilinguals on tests of verbal intelligence. It would have appeared irrationally bold to propose that bilinguals would do better than monolinguals since previous research had always recorded bilingual deficits on verbal tests. (For additional discussion of bilingualism and intelligence, see chapters 1, 5, 15, 17, and 23.)

Another obstruction to this research is the diversity with which the central group is defined: Who are bilingual children? Children become bilingual for many reasons: immigration to a new country, extended family that speaks a traditional language, education in a language other than the language of the home, or temporary residence in another country. These circumstances are often confounded with social and demographic factors that may themselves determine children's level of cognitive achievement. These factors include the education level of the parents, the literacy environment that the child is exposed to, the nature and extent of the child's proficiency in the first (or home) language, the purposes for which the second language is used, the degree and nature of community support for that language, and the extent to which the child identifies with the group which speaks that language. One of these factors, language proficiency, is particularly in need of definition: What level of absolute proficiency in each language or relative proficiency between the languages is sufficient to determine either that a child is bilingual or that there may be cognitive consequences of that bilingualism?

The combination of theoretical and practical barriers to the study of bilingualism creates an almost intractable tangle of variables that intermingle in a seemingly hopeless brew. Bilingualism is a linguistic experience, so it is undoubtedly going to affect linguistic development. How can we imagine what course language acquisition would take for a particular child were that child exposed to one language instead of two, or two languages instead of one? Moreover, we know that social background, parents' education levels, and home literacy environment are massively important in shaping children's language and literacy development. If there is indeed a systematic bias for bilingual children to represent particular configurations of these background factors, then it will be difficult to interpret any group differences in terms of the unique contribution of bilingualism itself to children's development.

Put this way, it is less surprising that few researchers have ventured into the territory of determining how bilingualism may alter the typical course of development. A notable exception to the general dismissal of the significance of bilingualism in children's development is Vygotsky (1962). Although one statement in an entire book is hardly evidence for overwhelming interest in a problem, the statement is distinguished by its uniqueness, especially considering the times in which it was written, and by its connection to Vygotsky's developmental theory. Vygotsky (1962, p. 110) commented about the possible enhancement to linguistic awareness and linguistic flexibility that follows from knowing two language systems: "the child learns to see his language as one particular system among many, to view its phenomena under more general categories, and this leads to awareness of his linguistic operations." The insight is particularly important in the context of Vygotsky's theory in which he attributed a significant role to language, or private speech, as a mechanism for cognitive growth. Further, the general tone of the speculation is similar to that underlying the important work published by Peal and Lambert (1962) in the same year, although Vygotsky's work was completed about 30 years earlier. Peal and Lambert, summarizing their watershed study showing positive advantages of bilingualism on cognition, concluded that the experience of having two ways to describe the world gave the bilingual the basis for understanding that many things could be seen in two ways, leading to a more flexible approach to perception and interpretation. Therefore, both for Vygotsky and for Peal and Lambert, there was a clear prediction that a child learning two languages would be in a different situation from a child learning only one, and that the role of language as an instrument of thought and instruction would make this experience enriching and enhance the child's development.

The present chapter explores the way that bilingualism may alter the manner or rate at which children develop metalinguistic concepts of language and the background skills and early abilities required for reading. To anticipate the conclusion, there is no simple equation and no quick remedy. These are complex skills and children's linguistic experiences influence their development greatly. In some cases, bilingualism on its own is also a crucial factor, in other cases, the specific language that children speak or read determines proficiency, and in others, there is no difference and all children gradually learn these skills in the same way and on the same time course.

22.2 Metalinguistic Concepts

One of the first research areas that claimed consistent advantages for bilingual children over their monolingual peers was the domain of metalinguistic awareness. It is plausible that having two different language systems for examination may make structural patterns more noticeable and hasten the child's attention to the systematic features of language. In an early examination of the role of metalinguistic concepts in children's language acquisition, Clark (1978, p. 36) speculated that "learning two languages at once, for instance, might heighten one's awareness of specific linguistic devices in both." Tunmer and Myhill (1984) went further and postulated metalinguistic awareness as the *mechanism* by which bilingualism exerts its influence on any aspect of cognition. They argued that fully fluent bilingualism increased metalinguistic abilities and those in turn led to higher levels of reading acquisition and academic achievement. Metalinguistic concepts, however, are not monolithic, and there is no reason to expect that bilingualism would affect the subcomponents equally. Therefore, we shall consider the way in which children's awareness of different aspects of language develops and the role that bilingualism might play in promoting that awareness.

22.2.1   Word awareness

Understanding the nature of the relation between words and their meanings consistently emerges as superior in bilingual children. In his famous diary study of his daughter, Leopold (1961) identified the ability to recognize and appreciate this arbitrary basis of meaning in language as a direct benefit of bilingualism. Bilingual children, he suggested, are able to make a distinction between words and their meanings before monolingual children grasp this idea.

Two related insights are required for children to fully appreciate the abstract level of linguistic structure designated by words. The first is that speech can be segmented into meaningful units. Tasks assessing this aspect of word awareness typically ask children to count the number of words in a sentence or define what a word is to demonstrate knowledge of the appropriate boundaries. The second is awareness of how words function to carry their meaning. This aspect, sometimes called lexical or referential arbitrariness, indicates the extent to which children understand the conventional relation by which words convey their designated meanings. The two are related: understanding the *function* of words (referential arbitrariness) is predicated on the ability to *identify* words (segmentation) as relevant units of speech. For this reason, studies often assess both aspects of word awareness so it is difficult to evaluate their development independently. To cite Vygotsky (1962) again, the inseparability of form (boundary) and meaning (reference) in words is at the centre of the kinds of questions in which we are engaged: "The meaning of a word represents such a close amalgam of thought and language that it is hard to tell whether it is a phenomenon of speech or a phenomenon of thought. A word without meaning is an empty sound; meaning, therefore, is a criterion of 'word', its indispensable component" (p. 120). Children's growing awareness of this "amalgam" is an essential ingredient of metalinguistic development.

How do children come to see words as the relevant segmental units of speech? There is nothing in the speech stream that marks word boundaries.

Our notion of "word" is an arbitrary designation that changes across languages, varying from the rather isolating tendencies of English to the famously agglutinating style of German. In Chinese, the notion of word itself makes little sense, as meanings are conveyed through organized strings of morphemes that are represented with characters consisting of different numbers of constituent characters. Studies by Feng et al. (1999) and Hoosain (1992) have demonstrated that adult speakers of Chinese find the task of dividing speech into "words" to be odd and reach little consensus on the boundaries. It may be that for the acquisition of literacy skills, the concept of word is irrelevant unless children are required to learn an alphabetic writing system. Moreover, the various definitions of word for different languages may mean that children who speak two languages would reach different ideas about the segmentational structure of speech into words.

We compared children's knowledge of word boundaries for first-grade children who were monolingual or in immersion programs in which their school language, French, was different from their home language, English (Bialystok, 1986a). These children had been studying French for two years and their reading instruction was in French. We trained them in a procedure to count the number of words in a sentence by listening to the sentence, moving a marker to a new pile for each word, then counting the number of markers. The primary difficulty is in ignoring the meaning of the sentence in order to focus on the individual words; it is as though the sentence meaning makes the words invisible. Therefore, we gave the task in two conditions: one in which the sentences were presented as normal utterances and the second in which the order of (the same) words had been scrambled so that there was no overall meaning. In addition, the sentences varied in the complexity of the constituent words, sometimes containing only simple monosyllabic words, others containing more complex polysyllabic words (e.g. pyjamas), and the most difficult including double morpheme words (e.g. snowmen). All the children performed the same in determining the number of words in the scrambled strings, indicating that their basic knowledge of these units was equivalent. The bilingual children, however, were more successful in isolating the words from meaningful sentences, separating the forms from the meanings, and not being distracted by the overall sentence meaning. In spite of roughly similar knowledge (performance on the scrambled strings), their awareness of that knowledge in terms of the relation between forms and meanings was more developed in the children who had some experience with two languages. By usual standards, these children were not bilingual, but the exposure to another language in school, including literacy instruction in that language, was sufficient to advance their awareness of words and meanings.

Children's understanding of the nature of reference has been examined in several studies. Cummins (1978) administered four metalinguistic tasks to bilinguals and monolinguals and found differences between groups on only some of the tasks, or on some parts of the tasks. For example, one task tested whether a child considered a word to be stable even when the object the word referred to had ceased to exist, such as the continued existence of the word "giraffe" if there were no giraffes left in the world. This task showed a bilingual advantage, especially by the older children. In another task, children were asked whether particular words had the physical properties of the objects they represented, for example, "Is the word *book* made of paper?" Here there were no differences in performance between bilinguals and monolinguals. Cummins concluded that bilinguals had a greater linguistic flexibility but not a greater reasoning ability for problems that extended beyond the domain of language.

A simple test of children's understanding of reference is to adapt Piaget's (1929) sun–moon problem. He asked children if it would be possible to change the names for the sun and moon, and if so, what would be up in the sky at night. The final question was the most difficult: what would the sky look like at night? Although most children could accept the rules of the game sufficiently to say that the names could be changed and that the sun would be up in the sky at night, the majority insisted that the sky would be light. (It would be *dark* – only the names have changed.) Studies using this task have found that bilinguals solve the problem earlier than monolinguals (Bialystok, 1988; Cummins, 1978; Edwards and Christopherson (1988); Eviatar and Ibrahim, 2000).

Feldman and Shen (1971) developed a different means of investigating children's understanding of the nature of reference. They taught groups of monolingual and bilingual children new names for things, where the new names were either the real names for other objects (as in the sun–moon problem) or nonsense words. Both groups of children learned the new names equally well, but only the bilinguals were successful in using the new or nonsense names in sentences. In other words, only the bilinguals accepted that the new names *could* be used arbitrarily in a real linguistic context. Similarly, Ianco-Worrall (1972) asked monolinguals and bilinguals about the viability of changing the names for known objects, and only the bilinguals agreed that names for things could be changed.

Ben-Zeev (1977) developed a creative task to assess children's awareness of the formal properties of words. The task, symbol substitution, assessed children's level of awareness of referential arbitrariness. She said to children, "In this game, the way to say *we* is with *spaghetti*. How would you say, *We are good children?*" Defying all sense, children had to say, "Spaghetti are good children." She found that bilingual children were significantly more reliable in making this substitution than were monolinguals. For some reason, it was easier for them to ignore the meaning and deal with the formal instructions. The monolingual children were more wedded to the familiar meanings of words than were their bilingual peers. The bilingual children were more willing to accept that the meaning of a word is more convention than necessity; more agreement than truth. We are free to break the agreement if we so choose. In a replication, Ricciardelli (1992) reported that fully balanced bilingual children solved this task better than all other children, although the difference just failed to achieve significance.

Results of studies like these do not always favor bilinguals. Ricciardelli (1992) compared the performance of kindergarten and first-grade children who were English monolinguals or Italian-English bilinguals on a battery of cognitive and metalinguistic tasks. In addition, she measured children's proficiency in both languages in order to compare performance in terms of both relative and absolute proficiency levels. This technique is methodologically sound and provided a means of testing important hypotheses but the procedure left relatively small numbers of participants in each cell, making statistical significance particularly difficult to achieve. The word awareness tasks included deciding whether items consisted of one or two words and identifying words in print. There were no group differences for any of these measures of word awareness.

In Ricciardelli's study, the majority of the metalinguistic measures failed to significantly differentiate between the groups (although note the methodological limitation above). Similarly, Rosenblum and Pinker (1983) found no differences between bilinguals and monolinguals in their ability to substitute a nonsense word for an actual word, but there were differences in their explanations. Monolingual children focused on the attributes of objects and explained that the name of an object, such as a table, could be changed to *shig* because it still had four legs. Bilingual children justified their answers in more abstract and general terms, explaining that the name of an object was arbitrary and could be changed under certain conditions.

The majority of studies that have investigated children's understanding of the concept of word, both in the sense of its segmentational definition and its referential arbitrariness, have reported more advanced levels of performance for bilinguals. Awareness of the formal properties of words is a particularly interesting problem because, as Vygotsky pointed out, it is at the level of word that form and meaning are most intricately interwoven. Solving all these problems requires holding form apart from that meaning. This is one of the skills that appear to come more easily to bilingual children.

22.2.2 Syntactic awareness

The need to make a judgment about the grammatical acceptability of a sentence is probably the prototypical metalinguistic task. Although difficult, the tasks have been used successfully with children, and manipulating the instructions or the materials used enables one to isolate specific metalinguistic processes. In addition, comparing performance on standard grammaticality judgment tasks to other metalinguistic tasks leads to a more finely differentiated description of metalinguistic skill.

Galambos and Hakuta (1988) compared monolingual and bilingual children for their ability to solve two kinds of metalinguistic tasks. The first was a standard task in which children were asked to judge and then to correct the syntactic structure of sentences. The second asked children to determine the ambiguity in sentences and then to paraphrase the various interpretations.

The research was conducted longitudinally and showed that bilingual children had a consistent advantage over monolinguals in the syntax task but a bilingual advantage in the ambiguity task was only found in the second testing session, when children were older. These results point to the role of language proficiency and other ability factors in constraining the way in which bilingualism may affect development. The persistent advantage in grammaticality judgment at both ages and the dissociation of that ability from another metalinguistic skill both contribute to a more detailed profile of the metalinguistic impact of bilingualism on these children's development.

A more extensive study based on the same principles was conducted by Galambos and Goldin-Meadow (1990). They presented monolinguals and bilinguals with a range of problems assessing syntactic awareness, including detecting, correcting, and explaining errors. They found that explaining the errors was a qualitatively different skill from noting and correcting them. More importantly, there was a bilingual advantage for noting and correcting errors at all ages tested, but for explaining the errors, there were no consistent group differences. Galambos and Goldin-Meadow (1990) interpreted the developmental progression as moving from a content-based to a structure-based understanding of language, and bilingual children were more advanced than monolinguals in all of these. They note as well the clear division between the explanation tasks and the other two tasks both for their developmental patterns and for their influence from bilingualism. Their conclusion emphasizes that bilingualism alters the rate of development but not its course. Another interpretation, though, is that the skills that underlie the explanation task are different from those involved in the other two and that bilingualism alters only the latter. A possible explanation for this dichotomy is in the distinction between analysis and control, described elsewhere (Bialystok, 2001).

Not all studies report bilingual advantages when the task is to detect grammatical errors in sentences (e.g. Edwards and Christopherson, 1988). A more precise set of tasks is needed to isolate the problems in which bilinguals differ in their solutions from monolinguals. One such manipulation alters the problem by introducing misleading material. This manipulation was first used by de Villiers and de Villiers (1972) and developed into an experimental task to identify differences between judgments made by monolinguals and bilinguals by Bialystok and colleagues (Bialystok, 1986b, 1988; Bialystok and Majumder, 1998; Bialystok and Ryan, 1985). Standard judgment sentences require participants to decide whether or not there are grammatical violations. The extent to which individuals can do this is an indication of their level of grammatical analysis. If the sentence also contains incorrect semantic information, then it becomes more difficult, especially for young children, to ignore these errors and attend only to the well-formedness criteria. Children are trained to make judgments only about whether the sentence is said "the right way" or "the wrong way" and to ignore silly things about the meaning. The sentences they judge are either correct or contain errors in the grammar (*Apples growed on trees.*), or the meaning (*Apples grow on noses.*). The anomalous sentences are difficult because the error in meaning is a compelling magnet for their attention and they are drawn to a conclusion that the sentence is unacceptable. In repeated studies, it has been found that bilingual children are more accurate than monolinguals in judging these anomalous sentences as being said "the right way" but that both groups are the same in detecting the grammatical error in the incorrect sentences (Bialystok, 1986b, 1988; Bialystok and Majumder, 1998; Cromdal, 1999).

Gathercole (1997) used a grammaticality judgment task to determine whether Spanish-English bilingual children could use syntactic cues to distinguish mass nouns (like *water*) from count nouns (like *cups*). She found that older and more fluent bilinguals performed like monolinguals but the younger and weaker bilinguals paid little attention to the syntactic cues. The young bilingual children were not using the formal information as effectively as the monolinguals were, and in this respect, at least, were less developed in a specific metalinguistic function. In another study, Gathercole and Montes (1997) used a more traditional grammaticality judgment task to determine whether Spanish-English bilingual children could make appropriate decisions about sentences containing violations of *that*-trace. They found that monolinguals were better than bilinguals at both judging and correcting the sentences, but that the performance of the bilinguals was significantly influenced by the amount of English input they received at home. (It should be noted that Spanish allows sentences that superficially violate the *that*-trace condition, so this result may be a specific effect of transfer from Spanish rather than a general difference in performance between monolinguals and bilinguals.) This research identifies some areas in which bilinguals do *as well* as monolinguals, but none in which they do better.

Like the research investigating children's concepts of word, this research also shows that there is no uniform advantage for bilingual children. Instead, tasks that maximize a conflict between form and meaning are most likely to be solved better by bilinguals. In judging the grammaticality of sentences, bilinguals sometimes outperform monolinguals, but most of the evidence is that they do not unless there is salient distracting information, such as anomalous meanings, embedded in the sentences. If there is an advantage for bilinguals in solving simple detection problems, it is found only for children who have reasonable competence in both languages, that is, fully balanced bilinguals. In contrast, tasks that are more purely analytic and not based on distracting meanings, such as explaining grammatical errors (Galambos and Goldin-Meadow, 1990) or making complex judgments about *that*-trace (Gathercole and Montes, 1997) are not solved any better by bilinguals. In fact, these tasks appear to be influenced primarily by level of English proficiency. Tasks that tap more directly into knowledge about language, even metalinguistic knowledge, often fail to detect any differences between children in these groups. As with word awareness, the advantage for bilinguals is in understanding how these formal structures can be separated from the meaning inherent in language.

22.2.3   *Phonological awareness*

Of the component abilities of metalinguistic awareness, phonological awareness may be the most significant because of its reliable predictive relation with learning to read in an alphabetic script. Some studies have demonstrated that phonological awareness develops differently for (monolingual) children who speak different languages (e.g. Caravolas and Bruck, 1993), but those studies do not indicate whether children who speak *both* of the languages acquire these concepts differently from monolinguals. Other studies have confirmed that levels of phonological awareness predict levels of reading proficiency in *each* language for bilingual children (e.g. Carlisle, Beeman, Davis and Spharim, 1999; Durgunoğlu (1998); Durgunoğlu, Nagy, and Hancin-Bhatt, 1993; Rickard Liow and Poon, 1998). Some of these studies will be discussed in more detail below. However, given the consensus about the importance of this skill in predicting reading, surprisingly few studies have examined the development of phonological awareness in bilingual children. Those that have are difficult to evaluate because either children were minimally bilingual or sample sizes were very small.

Rubin and Turner (1989) compared the phonological awareness of English-speaking first-grade children who were either in French immersion (giving them a modest command of French) or English programs and found an advantage for the French immersion children. Using a similar population, Bruck and Genesee (1995) compared monolinguals and beginning bilinguals longitudinally from kindergarten to first-grade children on a variety of tasks. The bilingual children were English-speaking children who were attending French school programs (similar to immersion but more intensive). An advantage was found for the children in the French programs on onset–rime segmentation in kindergarten but it disappeared in grade 1. In first grade, there was an advantage for the monolingual children on a phoneme-counting task and a bilingual advantage on a syllable-counting task. The authors proposed different explanations for each of these results. They attributed the bilingual advantage on syllable awareness to the structure of French phonology, which makes the syllable more salient than it is in English. The monolingual advantage on phoneme awareness was ascribed to differences in reading instruction that had provided only the monolingual children with phonological training. The importance of these results is that they demonstrate that factors such as language structure and literacy instruction are ultimately more important than bilingualism in explaining children's level of metalinguistic awareness in this domain.

Using children whose bilingualism was even more limited, Yelland, Pollard, and Mercuri (1993) asked children to judge whether pictured objects had long names or short names. They found an advantage for bilinguals in kindergarten but it disappeared by the end of grade 1. Nonetheless, they also examined some aspects of early reading and found that the grade 1 bilinguals maintained an advantage over monolinguals in word recognition.

A study by Campbell and Sais (1995) offered more rigorous evidence because the children, preschool Italian-English bilinguals, were reasonably competent in both languages. Four tasks were included in the battery. In two of them, children were required to choose a word that did not fit in a set because of either a semantic or a phonological (first sound) mismatch. The semantic detection task is not a measure of phonological awareness, but the two together, which required children to change the criterion for membership in the group, namely from meaning to sound, indicate their access to these structural properties of words. In addition, there was a phoneme deletion task. The bilingual children performed at a higher level than the monolinguals on the phonological tasks but did no better than monolinguals on a letter identification task. These are promising results for bilinguals, although the results must be interpreted cautiously since the sample size was small and language and cognitive differences between the groups were not well controlled. Moreover, the children were only tested in preschool and previous studies showed that these early advantages disappeared in first grade.

We conducted a series of studies to explore the development of phonological awareness in monolingual and bilingual children across a larger range of age and task complexity (Bialystok, Majumder, and Martin, 2003). In the first two studies, children were 5, 6, and 7 years old (corresponding to kindergarten, first grade, and second grade) and were fully bilingual in English and French. The task, called phoneme substitution, was a difficult problem in which children needed to replace the first sound in a target word with the first sound from another word to produce a new word. For example, the word "cat" could be converted to "mat" by substituting the first sound of "mop" into the target word. Children were told, "Take away the first sound from 'cat' and put in the first sound from 'mop.' What is the new word?" (There were also conditions in which the sounds /k/ and /m/ were given to the child, but the results were the same.) The results showed no difference at all between the monolinguals and the bilinguals in their ability to solve this problem.

In the third study, two groups of bilingual children and three different phonological tasks were included to increase the range of assessment. Children were again 5, 6, and 7 years old and were monolingual or bilingual with either Spanish or Chinese as their other language. The three tasks were different in the demands they made on explicit phonological awareness and the involvement of other cognitive components in their solution. First was the sound–meaning task: children were required to select which of two words matched a target for either the sound (rhyme) or meaning (synonym). For example, the experimenter could ask the child, "Which word sounds something like dog – frog or puppy?" This task requires only minimal levels of sound awareness. The second was a segmentation task in which children had to determine the number of phonemes in common words. This task is the purest assessment of phonological awareness because the solution requires explicit attention to the sound structure of words, but the task itself does not invoke many extraneous cognitive processes. Finally, a version of the phoneme substitution task was used to assess children's ability to make computations with the segmented sounds. There were bilingual differences on only one task and for one group – the Spanish-English bilinguals solving the segmentation task. Hence it appears that there is some advantage to bilingual children in learning about the sound structure of spoken language, but it is evident only on relatively simple tasks and apparent only for children whose two languages bear some resemblance to each other. The majority of results from these three studies indicated no advantage for bilingual children. Again, although reliable advantages for bilingual children occur under some circumstances, they are constrained by other factors. Bilingualism itself is insufficient to fundamentally change the path of metalinguistic development.

Muter and Diethelm (2001) corroborate this pattern in a longitudinal study of children between kindergarten and first grade who are either monolingual English or bilingual with a variety of language backgrounds. Children's level of phonological awareness did not depend on whether they were English monolinguals being tested in English, or a speaker of some other first language (usually French), studying and tested in English. They conclude that in the early stages of reading, the effect of literacy instruction interacts with levels of phonological awareness, and the child's language background is less important than this instruction.

A study by Eviatar and Ibrahim (2000) compared two groups of bilingual children with monolinguals but extended the definition of bilingualism in an interesting way. Because written Arabic is substantially different from spoken Arabic, children who learn to read and write Arabic in school are essentially learning a different language. On the basis of this disparity, they classified Arabic speakers in Israel who attended school in Arabic as bilingual. It would be surprising, however, if these children who lived in Israel really had no familiarity with Hebrew. Hence, they may well be bilingual, as the researchers claim, but the reason for their bilingualism may not be the one offered by the researchers. There were three groups in the study – monolingual speakers of Hebrew, bilingual speakers of Hebrew and Russian, and Arabic speakers learning the literate forms in school. Although the bilingual children obtained lower scores than the monolinguals on a vocabulary test, they performed better than the monolinguals on the phonological awareness tasks. These included initial phoneme detection, final phoneme detection, and phoneme-syllable deletion. As in other studies investigating phonological awareness, however, differences found in kindergarten disappeared by first grade.

Phonological awareness appears to be the most challenging aspect of metalinguistic development that children master over these years. Furthermore, because of the relation between the structure of the sound system and the structure of the writing system, children who are learning languages that are written alphabetically have a greater urgency to learn how to isolate the sounds of speech and translate them into written symbols. Some researchers have even argued that phonological awareness is required for learning to read in Chinese, a character-based script, although a less detailed phonological analysis (e.g. syllables but not phonemes) is sufficient (Ho and Bryant, 1997).

The relation between language and orthography is complex. A study by Cheung et al. (2001) compared the phonological awareness of three groups of children who were pre-readers or early readers. The first group spoke Cantonese and read only in characters, the second group spoke Cantonese and read both characters and Pinyin (an alphabetic system for written Chinese) and the third group spoke English. Both language and orthography contributed to the results, rendering the highest scores for phonological awareness to the English-speaking children and the lowest to those who had no exposure to alphabetic writing. In contrast, Huang and Hanley (1994) failed to detect a relation between levels of phonological awareness and early reading ability for Chinese-speaking children, even those who had learned the alphabetic system for written Chinese. These studies examined the effect in different directions, Cheung et al. looking for factors that promoted phonological awareness and Huang and Hanley exploring the effect of phonological awareness on reading. Their results, however, are compatible. There are complex relations between phonological awareness and learning to read that are mediated by the nature of the writing system. Alphabetic reading both requires and promotes phonological awareness.

More so than other aspects of metalinguistic awareness, phonological awareness reflects features of the language, the writing system, and instruction. In the few studies that showed bilingual advantages in phonological awareness that disappeared by first grade, it is plausible to look to literacy instruction as the equalizing force that erased group differences and instilled the same levels of sensitivity to these fledgling readers irrespective of their competence in spoken language. Against these massive effects of instruction and writing system, bilingualism on its own carries little influence in promoting children's awareness of the phonological structure of language.

22.3 Literacy

The question of bilingual influences on development may have some of its greatest impact in the development of early literacy skills by young children. Reading builds out of a set of prerequisite skills, some of which involve the metalinguistic concepts described above. In addition, there are also concepts more specific to literacy that need to be in place before children can become independent readers. These include understanding the discourse structure of stories and mastering the symbolic system that is used to encode that language. Either of these may develop differently for bilingual children and alter the course with which they learn to read. In addition, the profile of skills that are involved in early reading may be different for bilingual children.

22.3.1   *Learning about stories*

Learning how to read is the last step in a long process in which children are immersed in the culture of stories. Written language is a specialized form and does not follow directly from competence with oral speech. In order to understand stories, children need to be familiar with the discourse conventions that bring cohesion and reference to the text. Competence with these literate forms of language develops from experience with story books (Purcell-Gates, 1988), and children's level of mastery of these forms has been identified as the source of the positive relation between preschool children's exposure to storybooks and successful literacy outcomes (Dickinson, De Temple, Hirschler, and Smith, 1992; Snow and Tabors, 1993; Wells, 1985). Therefore, it would be important to determine how bilingualism influences children's access to and mastery of these literate forms.

Studies examining the ability of bilingual children to demonstrate competence in literate forms of discourse in their two languages have typically shown a large transfer of abilities across languages. Consistently with the predictions of Cummins (1979), the uses of language that are defined in terms that have a decontextualized or, as Cummins puts it, academic component, are common across children's languages. In contrast, skills that are based more on interactive or conversational skills develop individually. Hence, research with children's ability to provide formal definitions and picture descriptions (e.g. Davidson, Kline, and Snow, 1986; Snow, Cancino, Gonzalez, and Shriberg, 1989) or understand metaphors (Johnson, 1989, 1991), have shown equivalent levels of skill in each language.

These studies found that across their two languages, children displayed similar skill with formal definitions and with picture descriptions, even though some children were stronger in one language than in the other. However, these studies were carried out in carefully selected schools with bilingual curricula in which decontextualized skills were explicitly taught in each language. Among children in these schools, Snow (1990) found that for bilinguals in grades 2 through 5, the quality of informal definitions was related to home language use, while skill in formal classroom definitions was not.

In subsequent cross-linguistic research, Wu, De Temple, Herman and Snow (1994) found that children's decontextualized skill with oral and written picture descriptions reflected the emphasis of their school curriculum. Some children provided richer picture descriptions in the written mode than in the oral, reflecting their school's emphasis on decontextualized writing over speaking. Wu et al. concluded that second language learners must have direct experience in the target language with the discourse demands of a specific task if they are to carry it out as effectively in the second language as in the native language.

Herman found similar results in a study examining the relation between oral proficiency and the ability to tell a story from a wordless picture book in both languages for bilingual children (Herman, 1996). Kindergarten children who were French-English bilingual and being educated in French were tested on a number of measures. Regression analyses showed that the quality of stories that children were able to tell in French was predicted by children's oral proficiency in French. The quality of their English stories, however, was predicted by both their oral proficiency in English and the extent to which English was used in the home. In other words, for children with the *same* level of English competence, differences in story quality were determined by the amount of English that was available in the home environment. Herman proposed that the difference was that children with more English at home also heard more English stories at home, and it was exposure to English stories specifically, and not just linguistic competence generally, that determined children's success on the story-telling task. Because the children were being educated in French, all the children had ample and equal access to stories in French, so scores on the French story-telling task did not reflect differences in the amount of French available at home.

22.3.2   *Learning about print*

Before children can read independently, they must acquire the concepts that allow them to understand the symbolic system of print and how it conveys meanings. The importance of some of these concepts for learning to read has been investigated for monolingual children by Ferreiro (1983, 1984), and Tolchinsky Landsmann and Karmiloff-Smith (1992). Do bilingual children acquire these concepts differently?

We have used two different tasks to investigate the development of some of these concepts that are prerequisite to literacy in monolingual and bilingual children. In these studies, we have selected prereaders who were 4 or 5 years old and had already mastered many of the formal requirements for reading – they could recite the alphabet, identify letters and their sounds, and print their names. The children in these studies were either monolingual or bilingual, and the bilingual children were learning two languages that either used the same writing system (e.g. English and French) or did not (e.g. English and Chinese). In all cases, the children had experience of hearing stories in both their languages, some preliteracy exposure to the literate forms in preparation for reading, and receptive vocabularies in both languages that were relatively comparable to monolinguals in each language.

The two tasks differ in the detail with which they investigate children's concepts of the symbolic basis of writing systems. The first task, moving word, assesses children's notion of the invariance of print. In any writing system, a written form will always have the same meaning. In the task, a card with a word printed on it is placed under a picture or object that it names and then is moved to be placed under a different picture or object. Children are asked what the word on the card is and must recognize that the word is the same after the card has moved. The second task, word size, explores children's understanding of the principle that relates that written form to a specified meaning. Writing systems differ in how the written form is decoded or interpreted, but they share the feature of having a principled means of retrieving the meaning. In alphabetic systems in which letters make sounds, longer words need more letters. Children are asked to decide about long words and short words when the referent size of those words changes and sometimes conflicts with the word size (e.g. bus-butterfly). This is a more detailed level of understanding – not only do children need to accept the fact that the print carries the meaning as they do in the moving word task, but they also need to understand something about the manner in which that meaning is carried by the print.

In several studies, the consistent results have been that bilingual children invariably outperform monolingual children on the moving word task. Their experience in reading two kinds of story books has presumably alerted them to the importance of the text in those books as the source of the story. Moreover, they are not distracted by the picture and are able to attend to the word and realize that nothing in the word itself has changed. In contrast, the word size task is only solved better by bilingual children who are learning about two different writing systems (Bialystok, 1997; Bialystok, Shenfield, and Codd, 2000; Ricciardelli, 1992). Acquisition of the more detailed knowledge about how the system works requires the contrast of being exposed to two different systems. In both cases, though, one of the crucial prerequisites to literacy is developed earlier in bilingual children, and even greater advantages accrue from experience with different writing systems.

22.3.3   *Reading*

There is an active research enterprise involved in examining children learning to read in a second language. These studies include investigations of minority language children who do not speak the language of school at home (e.g. Hispanic children in the United States) and majority language children who attend school programs in the non-home language (e.g. French immersion in Canada). In both cases, children are learning to read in a language in which they have limited oral proficiency, although the educational outcomes of these two situations are strikingly different. Both cases, too, provide important pieces required to understand the psychological processes of acquiring literacy, the educational outcomes of various school arrangements, and the social consequences of language status. None of these studies, however, directly addresses the role that bilingualism might play in children's initial acquisition of literacy. In the majority of those studies, children are first exposed to the language of schooling and literacy when they enter school, and they begin to learn the language in both its oral and written forms at the same time. While these children do have knowledge of another language, they do not have significant knowledge of two languages, and in that sense, they are not strictly bilingual.

These studies, nonetheless, have implications for the case of bilingual children. Significantly, reading transfers easily across languages and even across writing systems. For example, Geva, Wade-Woolley, and Shany (1997) compared speed and accuracy for first- and second-grade children reading in both English and Hebrew. Unlike in French immersion programs, children receive formal reading instruction in both languages, but the difference in the writing systems prevents children from directly using what they learn about reading in one language to read in the other. Nonetheless, the results indicated that the most decisive variable in children's literacy attainment was individual differences in reading ability irrespective of language. These children are learning literacy skills in a weak language at the same time as they are learning to read in their strong language, and the transfer of skills from the dominant language facilitates literacy in the weaker language. Extrapolating to bilingual children, one might predict that the skill learned for one of the languages would be easily shared by both. It is as though bilingual children need only learn to read in one language and they are effectively literate in all their languages. This, indeed, would be an advantage of bilingualism.

The easy transfer of skills across languages, especially languages that use different writing systems, may not be automatic. Different languages set out different phonological concepts as salient, and different writing systems require different phonological and linguistic concepts. Moreover, different orthographies make the correspondence between written and spoken forms easy (shallow) or hard (deep) to detect. Therefore, predicting what kind of transfer might take place for children's literacy skills requires comparing the languages, the writing systems, and the orthographies.

Rickard Liow and Poon (1998) demonstrated some of these complexities in a study of the spelling ability of bilingual children in Singapore. All the children were attending school in English, but the children's home language was English, Chinese, or Bahasa Indonesia, a language written alphabetically with a regular (shallow) orthography. Children in this last group scored highest on English tests of spelling. Rickard Liow and Poon attribute their success at least in part to the transfer of phonological insights from a phonologically simple language, Bahasa Indonesia, to a more complex system, English.

The facilitating effect of phonological awareness on learning to read may also contribute to the general transferability of reading across languages. Carlisle, Beeman, Davis and Spharim (1999) tested Spanish-English bilingual children in grades 1 to 3 in both languages on vocabulary knowledge, word definition ability, and phonological awareness tasks. The word definition task was modeled on the work by Snow and her colleagues (e.g. Davidson, Kline, and Snow, 1986; Snow, Cancino, Gonzalez, and Shriberg, 1989) and the phonological awareness task was initial phoneme deletion. Regression analyses showed that reading comprehension in English was determined by the vocabulary level and phonological awareness in both languages. There was also a correlation between phonological awareness and vocabulary size in English but not in Spanish; they speculate it may be because of the correspondence between the language of testing and the language of literacy instruction. Phonological awareness, therefore, is necessary for reading in general, not just for learning to read in a particular language. Nonetheless, they found no effect from degree of bilingualism. Similarly, Durgunoğlu, Nagy, and Hancin-Bhatt (1993) and Durgunoğlu (1998) showed that phonological awareness in one language affected reading in the other for Spanish-English bilinguals. These studies emphasize the transferability of general skills across languages for reading, rather than the special contribution of language-specific concepts. Muter and Diethelm (2001) share this view. They used a longitudinal design to examine phonological awareness, letter knowledge, and vocabulary for their ability to predict reading in a group of mixed second language learners. Although the children who were being tested in the first or second language differed in their level of ability in many of these tasks, the regression analysis showed that the pattern of relation between these skills and reading was the same for all the children. They concluded that the same cognitive constructs account for the reading skills of children irrespective of their language background or their oral proficiency.

No matter how much transfer of high-order reading ability crosses over the child's languages, language-specific skills are still necessary. Goswami (1999) provides a summary of the role of the correspondences of phonology and orthography that are unique to each language and enable reading in each. Bilingualism will play a role in learning to read if these language-specific skills transfer across languages. Thus, bilingual children may benefit through transfer or delay through interference when learning to read in one of their languages. Geva and her colleagues (Geva and Siegel, 2000; Geva and Wade-Woolley, 1998) demonstrate the need for both kinds of explanations. Reading depends both on general cognitive and linguistic development making literacy levels equivalent in all the child's languages and on the specific knowledge of the linguistic forms and orthographic principles of individual languages. Factors such as orthographic depth, for example, determine what strategies children will need to use when learning to read the language and the success they will achieve as they acquire these skills. Both sources contribute to children's developing proficiency with written text.

The greater emphasis on general linguistic and cognitive skills relative to language-specific skills found in some studies may reflect the similarity of the languages that were compared. Spanish and English, for example, are written in the same writing system and based on comparable syntactic structures. Different patterns might be found when more disparate languages constitute the two systems of bilingual children.

Huang and Hanley (1994) compared 8-year-old children from three places: Taiwan (monolingual Chinese), Hong Kong (bilingual Chinese-English) and Britain (monolingual English). Three major skills were measured: phonological awareness, visual skills, and reading ability. The results showed that although significant correlations were found between phoneme deletion and reading Chinese in both Chinese samples, regression analyses did not identify phonological awareness as important for learning to read in Chinese. When the effects of IQ and vocabulary skills were taken into account, performance on phonological awareness was no longer significantly related to reading ability in the Chinese samples. Even learning to read Chinese using an alphabetic script (Pinyin) as the children in Taiwan had done did not alter the relation between phonological awareness and learning to read. For the English sample, phonological awareness remained significantly correlated with reading after IQ and vocabulary were controlled. In contrast, performance of visual skills tasks was found to be a powerful predictor for Chinese characters in both the Taiwan and the Hong Kong samples but not important for the British sample learning to read in English. These results point to striking differences in the profile of skills needed to read in different systems, and children who must master both are less likely to enjoy the easy transfer of ability form one language to the other. A similar study by Cheung et al. (2001), described above, investigated factors affecting children's development of phonological awareness and found distinct roles for competence in spoken language and the nature of the writing system. In their studies, children who had been trained with Pinyin were more advanced than those who learned to read Chinese using only the character system, but less advanced than comparable English-speaking children exposed only to an alphabetic script. These studies point to the importance of language-specific factors in learning to read, limiting the general and transferable effects of reading across languages and thereby limiting as well any differences in reading acquisition that may occur for children who are bilingual.

22.4 The Bilingual Connection

If one thing is clear from this summary of some of the studies that have sought evidence for differential metalinguistic and literacy development in bilingual children, it is that bilingualism itself provides an inadequate account of the results. Important roles have been identified for the nature of the language (and presumably the relation between the two languages), the type of writing system, and the demands of the tasks used to assess these measures. Aspects of these skills may be precociously established in bilingual children, but this advantage does not automatically extend to an enhanced awareness of all facets of language structure or to all bilingual children. Explaining how bilingualism affects the development of these skills, therefore, requires identifying the factors that mediate those effects and the conditions under which they occur.

One factor that helps to organize the results is the child's level of language proficiency, especially the balance between proficiency in the two languages that defines the child's bilingualism. The effects of proficiency range from finding bilingual advantages only for fully balanced bilinguals (Bialystok, 1988; Duncan and DeAvila, 1979; Ricciardelli, 1992), or a greater advantage for fully balanced bilinguals (Cromdal, 1999), to disadvantages for partial bilinguals (Gathercole, 1997). This is essentially the pattern predicted by Cummins's (1979) threshold hypothesis, in which he sets out a minimal level of bilingual competence to avoid deficits and a higher level to enjoy advantages. Further, for children who are partially bilingual, there are differences between groups at different levels of second-language proficiency. Hakuta and Diaz (1985) report greater changes in metalinguistic competence in the earlier stages of achieving bilingual proficiency, a result not replicated by Jarvis, Danks, and Merriman (1995) who instead claim, along with the previous studies, that the greater advantages emerge with greater competence. Nonetheless, Hakuta (1987) reported that higher levels of bilingualism predicted performance on a series of nonverbal tasks but not metalinguistic tasks for Hispanic children in American schools. In some cases, the level of proficiency in the language of testing provides an independent prediction of success, irrespective of the level of bilingualism (Galambos and Hakuta, 1988). In the study by Ben-Zeev (1977), a group of Spanish-English bilinguals from a lower socioeconomic and educational family background did not outperform the monolingual controls, although their errors were more sophisticated. Both absolute levels of language proficiency and the relative balance between languages are crucial factors in determining outcomes for bilingual children. Understanding these effects and resolving contradictory findings, however, will require a more detailed description for values on these factors than is usually available in binary classifications. These constraints on proficiency are related to the list of factors that describe the different situations in which children may become bilingual, as discussed in the introduction. It is not only for the sake of classificatory precision that clear criteria for determining who is to be considered bilingual should be stated. It is also necessary to understand children's level of linguistic competence because, at best, the effects of bilingualism are just potential effects. Children who speak two languages poorly, or two languages in the absence of literary experience in at least one of them, may not reap any benefit from their experience. (For more on types of bilinguals, see chapters 1–5 and 7–10.)

A second factor is the necessity of having experiences in each of the languages separately to develop specific skills in those languages. This point was demonstrated by studies that showed that the language of literacy instruction determined levels of phonological awareness (Bialystok, Majumder, and Martin, 2003; Bruck and Genesee, 1995) and exposure to stories promoted the development of knowledge of discourse structure separately for each language (Herman, 1996). Learning two languages has some ability to endow the child with general linguistic concepts that apply to both languages, accelerating the child's understanding of those principles, but other dimensions must be learned individually for each language. In these cases, there is little difference between children who are learning them for one language or for several. Moreover, these relations depend on the specific language pairs. Phonological awareness crosses easily from Spanish to English (e.g. Durgunoğlu, 1998) but not from Chinese to English (e.g. Cheung et al., 2001).

Finally, the difference between cases in which bilingual children perform differently from monolinguals and those in which they do not is determined by the task demands. In the three areas of metalinguistic awareness examined, the general pattern is that tasks that require children to ignore misleading information, such as the meaning of a word or sentence, are solved better by bilinguals. Tasks that assess in a more direct way the child's explicit knowledge of structure, such as defining a word or explaining a grammatical error, are solved the same by both groups. If anything, the advantage of these tasks goes to children who have more formal linguistic knowledge, for example, higher levels of proficiency or larger vocabulary knowledge.

The advantage for bilingual children is that they have a superior ability to ignore misleading information and attend to relevant cues and structures. This difference describes a change in a specific process that is affected by the experience of building up two language systems. To the extent that language can have a broad influence on cognition, this processing can have extensive consequences for intellectual functioning. Those consequences, however, are not expected to appear at the level of complex tasks in which many processes conspire to produce performance. These complex measures include IQ tests, an instrument in which bilingual differences are sometimes sought. But IQ tests involve many processes, and the bilingual advantage in selective attention would probably not emerge as significant. Reading may be another such measure. Integrative assessments of reading ability are probably too complex to reveal such details in processing differences between monolingual and bilingual children.

Reynolds (1991) argued that any description of how bilingualism impacted on cognition needed to be placed in a theoretical framework that connected that impact to a description of cognitive processing. The pattern of results in which bilingual children demonstrate an advantage on tasks that require ignoring misleading information but no advantage on tasks that require understanding detailed linguistic structure is compatible with the analysis-control framework described elsewhere (Bialystok, 2001). In short, the cognitive effect of bilingualism is to enhance the ability to selectively attend to specific features and to ignore or inhibit attention to salient but misleading information. Although arcane in processing terms, the overall effect of such an advantage is vast. All problem solving depends in some measure on this ability. Moreover, bilingual children have been shown to demonstrate this advantage in a wide array of nonverbal domains (Bialystok, in press). Vygotsky (1962) speculated that bilingualism may bring an advantage to children in that they could develop a more explicit representation of language. He was probably correct in thinking that cognition would profit from bilingualism, but likely incorrect in identifying the precise source of that advantage.

Bilingualism is an enriching experience. Sometimes, bilingual children excel in specific tasks that measure their progress in coming to understand the structure of language and in learning how to read but there is little evidence that their *overall* achievement in these skills is significantly different from that of monolinguals. Instead, their advantages make it easier to master these skills by giving them more refined cognitive processes with which to approach them, and the possibility of transferring the effortful learning of these abilities from one language to the other. Most important, though, bilingualism never confers a *disadvantage* on children who are otherwise equally matched to monolinguals, and the benefits and potential benefits weigh in to make bilingualism a rare positive experience for children.

REFERENCES

Ben-Zeev, S. (1977). The influence of bilingualism on cognitive strategy and cognitive development. *Child Development*, 48, 1009–18.

Bialystok, E. (1986a). Children's concept of word. *Journal of Psycholinguistic Research*, 15, 13–32.

Bialystok, E. (1986b). Factors in the growth of linguistic awareness. *Child Development*, 57, 498–510.

Bialystok, E. (1988). Levels of bilingualism and levels of linguistic awareness. *Developmental Psychology*, 24, 560–7.

Bialystok, E. (1997). Effects of bilingualism and biliteracy on children's emerging concepts of print. *Developmental Psychology*, 33, 429–40.

Bialystok, E. (2001). *Bilingualism in Development: Language, Literacy, and Cognition*. New York: Cambridge University Press.

Bialystok, E. (in press). Consequences of bilingualism for cognitive development. Invited chapter for J. R. Kroll and A. de Groot (eds.), *Handbook of Bilingualism: Psycholinguistic Approaches*. Oxford: Oxford University Press.

Bialystok, E. and Majumder, S. (1998). The relationship between bilingualism and the development of cognitive processes in problem-solving. *Applied Psycholinguistics*, 19, 69–85.

Bialystok, E., Majumder, S., and Martin, M. M. (2003). Developing phonological awareness: Is there a bilingual advantage? *Applied Psycholinguistics*, 24, 27–44.

Bialystok, E. and Ryan, E. B. (1985). A metacognitive framework for the development of first and second language skills. In D. L. Forrest-Pressley, G. E. Mackinnon and T. G. Waller (eds.), *Meta-cognition, Cognition, and Human Performance*, pp. 207–52. New York: Academic Press.

Bialystok, E., Shenfield, T., and Codd, J. (2000). Languages, scripts, and the environment: Factors in developing concepts of print. *Developmental Psychology*, 36, 66–76.

Bruck, M. and Genesee, F. (1995). Phonological awareness in young second language learners. *Journal of Child Language*, 22, 307–24.

Campbell, R. and Sais, E. (1995). Accelerated metalinguistic (phonological) awareness in bilingual children. *British Journal of Developmental Psychology*, 13, 61–8.

Caravolas, M. and Bruck, M. (1993). The effect of oral and written language input on children's phonological awareness: A cross-linguistic study. *Journal of Experimental Child Psychology*, 55, 1–30.

Carlisle, J. F., Beeman, M., Davis, L. H., and Spharim, G. (1999). Relationship of metalinguistic capabilities and reading achievement for children who are becoming bilingual. *Applied Psycholinguistics*, 20, 459–78.

Cheung, H., Chen, H-C., Lai, C. Y., Wong, O. C., and Hills, M. (2001). The development of phonological awareness: Effects of spoken language experience and orthography. *Cognition*, 81, 227–41.

Clark, E. V. (1978). Awareness of language: Some evidence from what children say and do. In A. Sinclair, R. J. Jarvella, and W. J. M. Levelt (eds.), *The Child's Conception of Language*. Berlin: Springer-Verlag.

Cromdal, J. (1999). Childhood bilingualism and metalinguistic skills: Analysis and control in young Swedish-English bilinguals. *Applied Psycholinguistics*, 20, 1–20.

Cummins, J. (1978). Bilingualism and the development of metalinguistic awareness. *Journal of Cross-Cultural Psychology*, 9, 131–49.

Cummins, J. (1979). Linguistic interdependence and the educational development of bilingual children. *Review of Educational Research*, 49, 222–51.

Davidson, R. G., Kline, S. B., and Snow, C. E. (1986). Definitions and definite noun phrases: Indicators of children's decontextualized language skills. *Journal of Research in Childhood Education*, 1, 37–47.

De Villiers, J. G. and de Villiers, P. A. (1972). Early judgments of semantic and syntactic acceptability by children. *Journal of Psycholinguistic Research*, 1, 299–310.

Dickinson, D. K., De Temple, J. M., Hirschler, J. A., and Smith, M. (1992). Book reading with preschoolers: Construction of text at home and school. *Reading Research Quarterly*, 7, 323–346.

Duncan, S. E. and DeAvila, E. A. (1979). Bilingualism and cognition: Some recent findings. *NABE Journal*, 4, 15–50.

Durgunoğlu, A. Y. (1998). Acquiring literacy in English and Spanish in the United States. In A. Y. Durgunoğlu and L. Verhoeven (eds.), *Literacy development in a multilingual context: Cross-cultural perspectives*, pp. 135–45. Mahwah, NJ: Erlbaum.

Durgunoğlu, A. Y., Nagy, W. E., and Hancin-Bhatt, B. J. (1993). Cross-language transfer of phonological awareness. *Journal of Educational Psychology*, 85, 453–65.

Edwards, D. and Christopherson, H. (1988). Bilingualism, literacy, and metalinguistic awareness in preschool children. *British Journal of Developmental Psychology*, 6, 235–44.

Eviatar, Z. and Ibrahim, R. (2000). Bilingualism is as bilingual does: Metalinguistic abilities of Arabic-speaking children. *Applied Psycholinguistics*, 21, 451–71.

Feldman, C. and Shen, M. (1971). Some language-related cognitive advantages of bilingual five-year-olds. *The Journal of Genetic Psychology*, 118, 235–44.

Feng, G., Chen, S. Y., Miller, K. F., Shu, H., and Zhang, H. C. (1999). Away with words: Language structure and the development of reading in Chinese and English. Paper presented at the annual meeting of the Psychonomic Society, Los Angeles, November.

Ferreiro, E. (1983). The development of literacy: A complex psychological problem. In F. Coulmas and K. Ehlich (eds.), *Writing in Focus*, pp. 277–90. Berlin: Mouton.

Ferreiro, E. (1984). The underlying logic of literacy development. In H. Goelman, A. Oberg and F. Smith (eds.), *Awakening to Literacy*, pp. 154–73. Exeter, NH: Heinemann Educational Books.

Galambos, S. J. and Goldin-Meadow, S. (1990). The effects of learning two languages on levels of metalinguistic awareness. *Cognition*, 34, 1–56.

Galambos, S. J. and Hakuta, K. (1988).
    Subject-specific and task specific
    characteristics of metalinguistic
    awareness in bilingual children.
    Applied Psycholinguistics, 9, 141–62.
Gathercole, V. C. M. (1997). The
    linguistic mass/count distinction as
    an indicator of referent categorization
    in monolingual and bilingual
    children. *Child Development*, 68,
    832–42.
Gathercole, V. C. M. and Montes, C.
    (1997). *That*-trace effects in Spanish-
    and English-speaking monolinguals
    and bilinguals. In A. T. Pérez-Leroux
    and W. R. Glass (eds.), *Contemporary
    Perspectives on the Acquisition of
    Spanish. Volume 1: Developing Grammar*,
    pp. 75–95. Somerville, MA: Cascadilla
    Press.
Geva, E. and Siegel, L. S. (2000).
    Orthographic and cognitive factors in
    the concurrent development of basic
    reading skills in two languages.
    *Reading and Writing: An
    Interdisciplinary Journal*, 12, 1–30.
Geva, E. and Wade-Woolley, L. (1998).
    Component processes in becoming
    English-Hebrew biliterate. In A. Y.
    Durgunoğlu and L. Verhoeven (eds.),
    *Literacy Development in a Multilingual
    Context: Cross-cultural Perspectives*,
    pp. 85–110. Mahwah, NJ: Erlbaum.
Geva, E., Wade-Woolley, L., and Shany,
    M. (1997). Development of reading
    efficiency in first and second language.
    Scientific Studies of Reading, 1, 119–44.
Goswami, U. (1999). The relationship
    between phonological awareness
    and orthographic representation in
    different orthographies. In M. Harris
    and G. Hatano (eds.), *Learning to Read
    and Write: A Cross-linguistic Perspective*,
    pp. 134–56. Cambridge, UK:
    Cambridge University Press.
Hakuta, K. (1987). Degree of
    bilingualism and cognitive ability in
    mainland Puerto Rican children. *Child
    Development*, 58, 1372–88.

Hakuta, K. and Diaz, R. (1985). The
    relationship between degree of
    bilingualism and cognitive ability:
    A critical discussion and some new
    longitudinal data. In K. E. Nelson
    (ed.), *Children's Language. Volume 5*,
    pp. 319–44. Hillsdale, NJ: Erlbaum.
Herman, J. (1996). "Grenouille, where
    are you?" Crosslinguistic transfer in
    bilingual kindergartners learning to
    read. Unpublished Ph.D. dissertation,
    Harvard University.
Ho, C. S. and Bryant, P. (1997).
    Learning to read Chinese beyond the
    logographic phase. *Reading Research
    Quarterly*, 32, 276–89.
Hoosain, R. (1992). Psychological reality
    of the word in Chinese. In H-C. Chen
    and O. J. L. Tseng (eds.), *Advances in
    Psychology*, pp. 111–30. Volume 90 in
    Language Processing in Chinese, series
    eds. G. E. Stelmach and P. A. Vroon.
    Amsterdam: North-Holland.
Huang, H. S. and Hanley, J. R. (1994).
    Phonological awareness and visual
    skills in learning to read Chinese and
    English. *Cognition*, 54, 73–98.
Ianco-Worrall, A. (1972). Bilingualism
    and cognitive development, *Child
    Development*, 43, 1390–400.
Jarvis, L. H., Danks, J. H., and Merriman,
    W. E. (1995). The effect of bilingualism
    on cognitive ability: A test of the level
    of bilingualism hypothesis. *Applied
    Psycholinguistics*, 16, 293–308.
Johnson, J. (1989). Factors related to
    cross-language transfer and metaphor
    interpretation in bilingual children.
    Applied Psycholinguistics, 10, 157–77.
Johnson, J. (1991). Constructive processes
    in bilingualism and their cognitive
    growth effects. In E. Bialystok (ed.),
    *Language Processing in Bilingual
    Children*, pp. 193–221. Cambridge,
    UK: Cambridge University Press.
Leopold, W. F. (1961). Patterning in
    children's language learning. In
    S. Sapporta (ed.), *Psycholinguistics*.
    New York: Holt, Rinehart & Winston.

Muter, V. and Diethelm, K. (2001). The contribution of phonological skills and letter knowledge to early reading development in a multilingual population. *Language Learning*, 51, 187–219.

Peal, E. and Lambert, W. (1962). The relation of bilingualism to intelligence. *Psychological Monographs*, 76, whole of no. 546, 1–23.

Piaget, J. 1929. *The Child's Conception of the World*. New York: Harcourt, Brace, Jovanovich.

Purcell-Gates, V. (1988). Lexical and syntactic knowledge of written narrative held by well-read-to kindergartners and second graders. *Research in the Teaching of English*, 22, 128–60.

Reynolds, A. G. (1991). The cognitive consequences of bilingualism. In A. G. Reynolds (ed.), *Bilingualism, Multiculturalism, and Second Language Learning: The McGill Conference in Honour of Wallace E. Lambert*, pp. 145–82. Hillsdale, NJ: Erlbaum.

Ricciardelli, L. A. (1992). Bilingualism and cognitive development in relation to threshold theory. *Journal of Psycholinguistic Research*, 21, 301–16.

Rickard Liow, S. J. and Poon, K. K. L. (1998). Phonological awareness in multilingual Chinese children. *Applied Psycholinguistics*, 19, 339–62.

Rosenblum, T. and Pinker, S. A. (1983). Word magic revisited: Monolingual and bilingual children's understanding of the word-object relationship. *Child Development*, 54, 773–80.

Rubin, H. and Turner, A. (1989). Linguistic awareness skills in grade one children in a French immersion setting. *Reading and Writing: An Interdisciplinary Journal*, 1, 73–86.

Snow, C. E. (1990). Rationales for native language instruction: Evidence from research. In A. M. Padilla, H. H. Fairchild, and C. M. Valadez

(eds.), *Bilingual Education: Issues and Strategies*, pp. 60–74. Newbury Park, CA: Sage.

Snow, C. E., Cancino, H., Gonzalez, P., and Shriberg, E. (1989). Giving formal definitions: An oral language correlate of school literacy. In D. Bloome (ed.), *Classrooms and Literacy*, pp. 233–49. Norwood, NJ: Ablex.

Snow, C. and Tabors, P. (1993). Language skills that relate to literacy development. In B. Spodek and O. N. Saracho (eds.), *Yearbook in Early Childhood Education. Volume 4: Language and Literacy in Early Childhood Education*, pp. 1–20. New York: Teachers College Press.

Tolchinsky Landsmann, L. and Karmiloff-Smith, A. (1992). Children's understanding of notations as domains of knowledge versus referential-communicative tools. *Cognitive Development*, 7, 287–300.

Tunmer, W. E. and Myhill, M. E. (1984). Metalinguistic awareness and bilingualism. In W. E. Tunmer, C. Pratt, and M. L. Merriman (eds.), *Metalinguistic Awareness in Children*, pp. 169–87. Berlin: Springer-Verlag.

Vygotsky, L. S. (1962). *Thought and Language*. Cambridge, MA: MIT Press.

Wells, G. (1985). Preschool literacy-related activities and success in school. In D. R. Olson, N. Torrance, and A. Hildyard (eds.), *Literacy, Language and Learning*, pp. 229–55. Cambridge, MA: Cambridge University Press.

Wu, H. S., De Temple, J. M., Herman, J., and Snow, C. E. (1994). L'animal qui fait oink! oink!: Bilingual children's oral and written picture descriptions in English and French under varying conditions. *Discourse Processes*, 18, 141–64.

Yelland, G. W., Pollard, J., and Mercuri, A. (1993). The metalinguistic benefits of limited contact with a second language. *Applied Psycholinguistics*, 14, 423–44.

Part IV   Global Perspectives and Challenges: Case Studies

Introduction

WILLIAM C. RITCHIE

In this day and age, it is important to understand the effects of globalization on the regions of the world from the point of view both of history and of current conditions. The purpose of part IV is to provide such understanding in the form of reviews of the state of bilingualism in each of several major areas of the world. The chapters in part IV examine the state of bilingualism in the Americas, in Europe, in Southern Africa, in East, South, and Central Asia, and finally, in North Africa and the Middle East. These chapters cover many of the issues discussed in more general terms in earlier chapters, including the status of bilingual education, practices of diglossia, code mixing and code switching, the relevance of interference and borrowing to language change, and the varying effects of language maintenance, shift, and endangerment as they bear on the status of bilingualism in many different settings around the world.

The part begins with chapters on the Americas. In chapter 23, "Bilingualism in North America," William Mackey surveys the situation of bilingualism in the United States and Canada with respect to the geography of bilingualism, types and phases of bilingualism within bilingual communities, language maintenance and shift, and, finally, the state of research resources on bilingualism in North America. Anna Maria Escobar's chapter 24, "Bilingualism in Latin America," focuses on the bilingual/sociolinguistic situation in Latin America, including the Caribbean. She treats such issues as bilingual education (which, in Latin America, is concerned primarily with bilingualism between Spanish or Portuguese and the indigenous languages of the area) and government policy toward minority and indigenous languages in general.

Andrée Tabouret-Keller (chapter 25, "Bilingualism in Europe") surveys the increasingly complex multilingual environment of Europe from the settlement of Europe by the Indo-Europeans to the present day, seeing Europe as "a continent of sustained migration." Her chapter examines the effects of immigration as well as those of the relationships among powerful majority languages on one hand and minority or regional languages on the other and the impact of government policies on both. In a second chapter on bilingualism in

Europe, chapter 26, "Turkish as an immigrant language in Europe," Ad Backus takes up a specific case of immigration and its linguistic consequences. Backus provides historical background for the case and then treats issues concerning language choice, the acquisition of majority languages by Turkish speakers (including age differences among learners) and changes in the Turkish of the immigrants. In addition, Backus provides a particularly rich description of code mixing and switching in this population.

In "Bi-/Multilingualism in Southern Africa" (chapter 27), Nkonko Kamwangamalu focuses primarily on government policy regarding the relationship between the indigenous languages of the area and the colonial languages. As in many formerly colonial areas, the conflict is between the promotion of indigenous languages as symbols of liberation from their colonial past and the recognition that the colonial language offers a way out of both isolation from the rest of the world and divisive tribalism at home. Kamwangamalu reviews the policies that have been adopted in Southern Africa to attempt to resolve this conflict.

Three chapters are devoted to bilingualism in Asia. David Li and Sherman Lee (chapter 28, "Bilingualism in East Asia") provide a thorough survey of bilingual issues in China, Hong Kong, Taiwan, and Japan. Topics for each country include historical background, the status of minority languages, diglossia, bilingual education, the influence of European languages, and language maintenance, shift, and endangerment. Tej Bhatia and William Ritchie's chapter (29, "Bilingualism in South Asia") covers the whole of South Asia with a particular focus on India. It emphasizes the fact that there is a historical tradition of linguistic tolerance in India that has given rise to extensive, largely unregulated (natural) multilingualism under which each language has been allowed to find its own domains and functions. A wide range of issues concerning language maintenance and minority languages are addressed, together with an account of a complex pattern of bilingualism present in that region. In chapter 30, "Changing language loyalties in Central Asia," Birgit Schlyter surveys bilingualism in the former Soviet Republics of Central Asia as well as contiguous areas of western China, Mongolia, Pakistan, Iran, India, and Tibet. Her primary focus is on changes in the languages spoken in this area due to Tajik-Uzbek bilingualism and bilingualism of all the languages of the area with Russian.

The final chapter, 31, is "Bilingualism in the Middle East and North Africa: A focus on the Arabic-speaking world" by Judith Rosenhouse and Mira Goral. The authors describe the history of the spread of Arabic after the founding of Islam as well as the present-day diglossia with Modern Standard (Literary) Arabic and Colloquial Arabic, and conventional (non-diglossic) cases of bilingualism of a number of kinds, and educational and political issues. Finally, the authors treat three specific cases of bilingualism involving Arabic – those found in Egypt, Morocco, and Israel.

23 Bilingualism in North America

WILLIAM F. MACKEY

23.1 Introduction

The chapter considers the following topics: borderlands of language and nationality (section 23.2); bilinguals and their communities (23.3); types and phases of bilinguality (23.4); forces of bilingual progression and regression (23.5); effects of bilingualism on the languages (23.6); and research on North American bilingualism (23.7).

To describe bilingualism in North America, one needs answers to four basic questions: (1) Where are the languages? (2) Where are the bilinguals? (3) What sort of bilinguals? and (4) What keeps them bilingual?

23.2 Borderlands of Language and Nationality

Basic to the study of bilingualism in any area are the identification and location of its languages. The area of North America between the Rio Grande and the Arctic Ocean was once the home of hundreds of native languages belonging to about a dozen linguistic families, some as different from one another as Japanese is from English (see figure 23.1). There is evidence that some speakers of these *Amerindian* languages were necessarily bilingual as a result of contacts made in trading, confederacy, intermarriage, and territorial expansion. During and after the sixteenth century, interlingual contacts increased with the arrival of European colonizers, who eventually outnumbered the natives. The result of this European contact was not so much the assimilation of the natives as their annihilation.

23.2.1 Remains of Native America

Unlike the millions of immigrants who followed, the native Amerindian population was decimated by the diseases of Europe, its colonial wars and by intermittent massacres (Spicer, 1962). Within a few generations, their numbers dwindled to a fraction of what they had been, as indeed had been the fate of their cousins to the south where less than a million remained of peoples like the Aztecs and Incas who had numbered more than twenty million (Champagne, 1994). Within a few centuries, most of the North American Indian languages were either dying or dead – with the possible exception of Inuktitut in the Arctic, Cree and Ojibwa in Eastern Canada (Statistics Canada, 1995), Navajo, Hopi, and others in the American Southwest (McMillan, 1988; Mithun, 2001). For their vast domain had fallen under the rule of three European imperial powers – Spain, France, and England – whose languages finally dominated North America and continued to expand within and beyond its national borders (see figures 23.2 and 23.3 for French and Spanish respectively).

23.2.2   National borders

These national borders appear as east–west lines separating the United States from Canada to the north and from Mexico to the south. North–south lines delimit the boundary between the state of Alaska and the Canadian north. None of these lines, however, constitutes a language boundary; they are simply political ones, imposed by the hazards of war and the accommodations of peace. The languages were there before the borders. Amerindian languages have never respected these arbitrary geopolitical segmentations. Nor have the colonial languages themselves, nor indeed the immigrant languages that followed.

23.2.3   Language boundaries

The main language boundaries in North America are not fixed lines: They are more like elastic belts – bilingual borderlands between two unilingual areas. One of them is in the northeast around the French-speaking heartland of Quebec and Acadia, extending well into the New England states and Northern Ontario (Cartwright, 1980). Its permanence depends ultimately on the strength of Canada's French-language institutions. The other bilingual belt is in the southwest, extending from southern California, along the Rio Grande, including parts of the Gulf States. Its survival is assured by the proximity and the mobility of millions of unilingual Spanish speakers to the south.

Within these bilingual belts and beyond – from southern California northward up through the Canadian west coast and Alaska, eastward along the Arctic shorelands and across the sparsely populated Canadian north all the way down the coast of Labrador – one can find bilingual enclaves inhabited by speakers of one or more of the remaining Amerindian languages who also speak the colonial language in which they had been schooled.

Outside these domains, and between the bilingual belts, lies a vast area stretching from the Atlantic to the Pacific and all the way to the Arctic Ocean. This is home to some 300 million speakers of North American English, most of them unilingual.

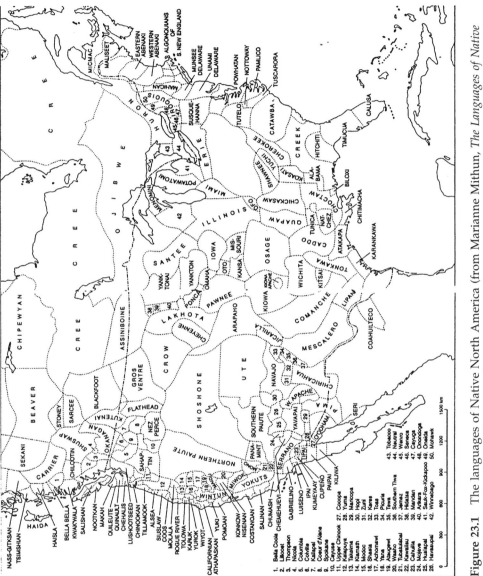

Figure 23.1 The languages of Native North America (from Marianne Mithun, *The Languages of Native North America*, Cambridge University Press, 1999, pp. xx–xxi; reprinted by permission of the publisher).

French North America: Assembling 17 Million People

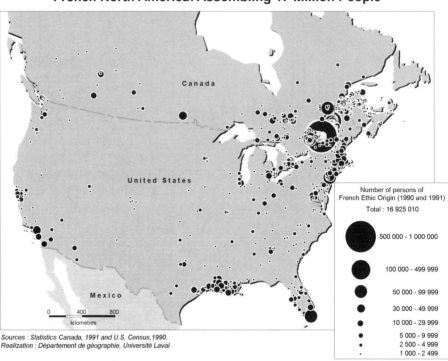

Sources : Statistics Canada, 1991 and U.S. Census,1990.
Realization : Département de géographie, Université Laval

Figure 23.2   French North America (printed with permission of CEFAN, Laval University).

23.2.4   *Population mobility*

These people do not remain fixed in one place; they are in fact the most mobile in the world. Most of them seem to come from someplace else; few die in the same place where they were born (Packard, 1972). They move regularly across state and national borders. Documented annual border crossings are counted in the millions. The number of Americans, for example, in transit during a holiday weekend (like Thanksgiving) can exceed the entire population of Britain, France, or Spain. During the past few decades, the distance between these displacements has increased enormously. So has the range of intercommunication by telephone, e-mail and website visits.

23.2.5   *Linguistic uniformity*

The effect upon the languages of all this mobility and intercommunication has been twofold. Despite the consequent dispersal, it has helped maintain the bilinguality of their bilinguals while accelerating the leveling of social and regional differences in North American English, already reduced to a common

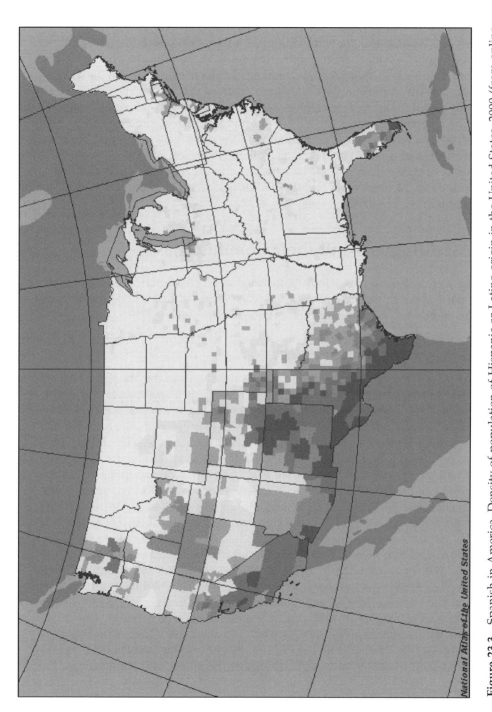

Figure 23.3 Spanish in America. Density of population of Hispanic or Latino origin in the United States, 2000 (from online US National Atlas http://nationalatlas.gov/).

denominator of language and culture by the mass media. Spoken and written throughout the United States and Canada, it is this variety of English which has become the "outside language" of Amerindian bilinguals and the "other tongue" of most immigrants. It is remarkably uniform and free from the pronounced social and regional markers that have characterized the dialects of Europe. Any variations that one does find from the American norm seldom impede comprehension, although they sometimes remain as perceptual markers of social identity (Preston, 1999). Yet, if one listens for them, one can indeed detect speech differences, especially among the older generation and between the ever-dwindling rural populations (Dillard, 1985; Scargill, 1977). These variations have been reasonably well documented in the regional linguistic atlases, in periodicals like *American Speech*, the *Canadian Journal of Linguistics*, and in other specialized journals.

23.3   Bilinguals and their Communities

If one were to take a closer look at the map of North America, one would be surprised at the linguistic variety of its place names. These can be traced back to the languages and language contacts of the first settlers.

23.3.1   *Cartographic evidence*

In the place names of North America we find vestiges of the aboriginal Amerindians: *Canada* ("settlement" in Huron), *Mississippi* ("great river" in Cree), *Massachusetts, Saskatchewan,* and many others. Yet the greatest number of place names of towns reflect the settlements of the first colonists, largely English (*Boston, Halifax, New Hampshire*), but also French and Spanish. The French presence beyond the St. Lawrence Valley, stretching from Hudson's Bay to the Gulf of Mexico is marked by names like *Abbeville, Bordeaux, Beaufort, Calais, Charenton* and many others, some of which reappear in different parts of the continent: *Bourbon* (4 times), *Cleremont* (8), *Laporte* (9), *Macon* (10), and *Paris* (14). Similarly with places baptized by the Spanish colonists: *Florida* (from *Pascua florida* "flowery Easter"), *Los Angeles* (*Santa María de los ángeles* "St. Mary of the Angels"), *Colorado, Nevada, California, San Francisco, Texas,* and many others. The immigrants have also left their mark on the map, with German names like *Hanover, Lunenburg, Braunfels,* and *Berlin* (13 times), and Italian names like *Palermo, Naples,* and *Rome* (10 times). It is true that many of the original names have been replaced by English ones. Dutch *Neuwe Amsterdam* became *New York* when the town was taken over by the Duke of York's regiment. *Berlin* was taken off the map of Ontario during the First World War and replaced with the name of Lord Kitchener of the allied high command.

23.3.2 *Bilingual communities*

In spite of the name changes, descendants of the first settlers remained in their communities and continued practicing their languages and their cultural traditions (Allen and Turner, 1988). Such language-related groupings have a long history in America. Swedish settlements in Eastern Pennsylvania flourished between 1638 and 1655. Along the Hudson River were the Dutch, including the original Yankees, i.e. *Jan* (John) *Kees* (cheese), purportedly an intra-ethnic nickname for the cheese-eating Hollanders. Between 1655 and 1664, they expanded into the Swedish areas and beyond. By 1683 they were in turn outnumbered by German settlers. Thus, after the founding of the Quaker community, the region became a multilingual area inhabited by speakers of Swedish, Dutch, Pennsylvania German, High German, Welsh, and English. Many such communities were later created through successive waves of immigration (Adamic, 1945; Higham, 1992; Kennedy, 1964). Several communities maintained their ancestral tongue and became the objects of study (Barron, 1957; Schermerhorn, 1949). Some of these studies contain sections on bilingualism; others supply information on language use, from which one may deduce the bilinguality of the group (Dallaire and Lachapelle, 1990). For example, one can get an idea of the bilinguality, at different times, of more or less bilingual communities such as the speakers of (alphabetically by language): Amerindian languages (Burnaby and Beaujot, 1986; Christian, 1964; Driver, 1961; Greenberg, 1987; Harrison and Marmen, 1994; Maurais, 1996); Arabic (Elkholy, 1966); Chinese (Liu, 1963); Danish (Ureland, 2001); Dutch (Lucas, 1955; Mulder, 1947; Ureland, 2001; van den Hoonaard, 1991); Finnish (Hoglund, 1960; Ureland, 2001); French (Arsenault, 1989; Benoit, 1935; Butler, 1995; Daigle, 1995; Douaud, 1985; Frémont, 1959; Landry and Allard, 1994; Lapierre and Roy, 1983; Mougeon and Beniak, 1991; Purich, 1988; Tisch, 1959); German (Epp, 1982; Gilbert, 1971; Meynen, 1937; Pochmann and Schultz, 1953; Prokop, 1990; Wood, 1942); Greek (Saloutos, 1964); Greenlandic (Ureland, 2001); Hungarian (Fishman, 1966); Icelandic (Simundsson, 1981); Italian (Musmanno, 1965; Pisani, 1957; Velikonia, 1963); Japanese (La Violette, 1945); Lithuanian (Ureland, 2001); Norwegian (Haugen, 1953; Ureland, 2001); Polish (Wytrwal, 1961); Portuguese (Pap, 1949); Russian (Woodcock and Avakumovic, 1977); Soviet Russian (Andrews, 1999); Serbo-Croatian (Govorchin, 1961); Spanish (Burma, 1955; Grebler, Moore, and Guzman, 1970; McWilliams, 1949; Samora, 1966); Swedish (Nelson, 1943; Ureland, 2001); Syrian (Jabbra and Jabbra, 1984), Ukrainian (Halich, 1937; Lupul, 1982; Young, 1931); Yiddish (Fishman, 1981).

These studies and most others like them have been largely confined to the languages of Europe. They do not include much about the languages of the most recent immigrants from Asia who, at the beginning of this century, topped the list as the most frequent new arrivals from countries whose populations exceed that of all of North America – India, China, and the South Pacific. Most of these new arrivals have headed directly for the big cities.

23.3.3   The urban bilinguals

By the year 2000, the children of the older settlers had migrated in increasing numbers to cities like New York, Toronto, Chicago, Montreal, Vancouver, and Los Angeles. Immigrants have long been attracted to cities with large concentrations of people from their own country now living in bilingual communities where they can be understood (Gans, 1962; Mackey, 2000). Many Poles and Czechs had grouped in Chicago and Detroit, Italians in Montreal and Toronto, Germans and Ukrainians in Philadelphia, Bulgarians and Slovaks in Pittsburgh, Chinese in San Francisco, Los Angeles and Vancouver, Icelanders and Ukrainians in Winnipeg, to name only these (Mackey, 2005a). For two centuries, New York City had provided a home and a living for millions of immigrants from all over the world. They transformed the city into a unique cosmopolitan megalopolis. At the end of the century about a third of its inhabitants had been born abroad, the most recent arrivals coming from Asia and the West Indies (Foner, 2001). This regular influx of immigrants has created conditions for the maintenance of many different languages (García and Fishman, 2002; Glazer and Moynihan, 1970). In Toronto, some 175 languages were spoken in a city, where, at the beginning of this century, some 40 percent of the inhabitants were foreign-born and half the population were from immigrant families.

23.4   Types and Phases of Bilinguality

In addition to the remnants of regional variation in speech and vocabulary, one can often detect in America the foreign accents of first-generation immigrants. Chance encounters with their descendants may reveal that their ancestral tongue, though seldom used, is still remembered. If one were to probe deeply enough, one would find segments of the population who maintain among themselves a language other than that of their workplace. Some would be experiencing their first years of contact with their new language of work (i.e. the *incipient* phase of their bilinguality). Others would be well on their way to mastering English better than had their parents (the *progressive* phase). Others would be functioning equally well in both languages, having integrated them into their daily lives (the *integral* phase). Still others would be well on their way to forgetting the speech of their forebears, in favor of the new and more rewarding language (the *regressive* phase). And finally, one may encounter an increasing number of people with a smattering of their ancestral tongue, its grammar imperfect and its use incidental (the *residual* phase of their bilinguality). In sum, all over North America one finds abundant examples of all these phases (incipient, progressive, integral, regressive and residual) in a large percentage of the population (Mackey, 2005b).

   Although these phases of bilinguality have long been associated with the first, second, third, and succeeding generations of immigrants, in reality each may last from less than a decade to more than a century. They are applicable to any group of people in the process of learning a language or of forgetting one – missionaries, settlers, traders, foreign students and the like.

23.4.1 Incipient bilingualism

The first missionaries, settlers, and fur traders in America, being vastly out-numbered by the surrounding Amerindian populations, had to learn just enough of their languages to do their business. When the number of settlers became dominant, it was the Amerindian population who had to begin practicing a sort of incipient bilingualism (Diebold, 1961). This occurs when only a few have to use the other language and that within only a few domains of activity, demanding a small functional vocabulary used in such a way as to be understood. So used, long enough for a specific purpose, it may rate as a jargon, as did the trade jargons of the fur trade. The early fur traders had to pick up a bit of the language of their trade route. Huron, for example, was used as a trade language along the St. Lawrence River as far as the trading center at Hochelaga (Montreal) where fur traders from the Great Lakes con-gregated. Similarly on the West Coast, at the crossroads of trade at the mouth of the Columbia River, a local language (Chinook) was used in trading over an area ranging from the Oregon Trail through British Columbia all the way to the Alaska Panhandle. In the process, Chinook absorbed elements from other local languages, particularly Nootka and Chehalis, in addition to French and English. The resulting jargon was used bilingually as a trade language through-out the nineteenth century and well into the twentieth. One also finds the effects of incipient bilingualism in the records of the first missionaries. As early as 1633, Paul Le Jeune described the use by French missionaries of a simplified Montagnais with a French flavor. In the West, the Métis had to adapt their speech first to French and then to English (Douaud, 1985; Purich, 1988).

Today, the learning of just enough of another language for a specific pur-pose is also associated with a number of different services, ranging from the military to the medical. During the Second World War, through a specially designed training scheme, the ASTP (Army Specialized Training Program), the US Military trained thousands of soldiers in a number of languages up to a level enabling them to interrogate prisoners. After the war, however, few were motivated to progress any further.

23.4.2 Progressive bilingualism

By contrast, the immigrant family was highly motivated to progress as fast as possible. For the only road up was through literacy and education in English. Progressive bilingualism meant a better and better use of the new language by more and more of their group in an increasing number and variety of situ-ations, with more people, and even among themselves. Progress was acceler-ated, prolonged, or retarded by such influences as the tolerance or interdiction of mixed marriages, the language of schooling, the nucleation or dispersion of the immigrant group. Yet many bilingual communities, both immigrant and Amerindian, were unwilling to progress beyond the point where they would abandon their ethnic tongue.

23.4.3   *Integral bilingualism*

By holding together, some bilingual communities were able to maintain their ancestral tongue for generations (Crawford, 1992). They did so mostly through the strength and permanence of their institutions (family, church, schools, media, commerce and welfare) which functioned in their own language (Fishman, Nahirny, Hofman, Hayden et al., 1966). Other functions, like work, secondary education, politics and civic activities were, of necessity, in the language of the state. This functional repartition of the two languages was integrated into their daily lives (Pendakur, 1990; Statistics Canada, 1993) (see below).

23.4.4   *Regressive bilingualism*

The institutions on which such bilingual practices are based are far from permanent. Unless their communities are replenished by a steady flow of new monolingual speakers to replace their anglicized children, the immigrant tongue is used less and less (Canada, 1993; Veltman, 1983). This stage of regressive bilingualism has been part of the process of the assimilation of ethnic and national minorities, including the French-speaking families outside Quebec (Mougeon and Beniak, 1988). The four most important influences upon such language regression have been urbanization, horizontal and vertical mobility, and mass media. Urbanization shattered the patterns of association, occupation and intergenerational solidarity which had held together the rural immigrant community. Geographical (horizontal) mobility could disperse an ethnic family over a continent. Upward (vertical) mobility into the Anglo middle class often meant the anglicization of immigrant children, often including their family name. Finally, the powerful influence of the mass media made cultural distinctiveness unsustainable.

23.4.5   *Residual bilingualism*

Over several generations, previously isolated rural ethnic communities became more urbanized, dispersed, or otherwise assimilated. The old language became something which almost everyone could do without. Having lost all its utility, it was seldom used and soon forgotten. What remained was a rudimentary grammar and a small vocabulary replete with words from the dominant language (Dorian, 1989). Yet for generations one could still hear snippets of foreign phrases used at times as badges of ethnic identity, typical of the final phase of residual bilingualism. Even as late as 1938 bits of Dutch were identified in the speech of farmers in New York State (Kloss, 1977, p. 188).

23.4.6 Receptive bilingualism

None of these five phases of societal bilingualism supposes an equal competence in both languages. The type of competence may be limited to a comprehension of one of them, and further restricted either to reading or to an understanding of the spoken word. This *receptive* bilingualism has been noted in the first stages of the language development of bilingual American children (Leopold, 1939–49). It has also been noted in the last stages of language survival when the typical third or fourth generation understands the questions in the immigrant language of the grandparents but replies to them in English (Dorian, 1989). This type of language behavior has at times become conventional as a form of intercommunication with neighbors or outsiders whereby each speaks his or her own language while understanding that of the other. It was long ago observed in meetings between Amerindian tribes, even where the languages were mutually unintelligible. It was typical, for example, of Karok-Yurok bilingualism noted in 1877 by a Stephen Powers (quoted in Ferguson and Heath, 1990, p. 175) who observed that "two of them will sit and patter gossip for hours, each speaking his own tongue. A white man listening may understand one but never a word of the other."

23.5 Forces of Bilingual Progression and Regression

The duration of any one of the above five phases and their rates of progression or regression have depended on a number of external factors beyond the control of the bilingual. These have included: continued contact with two monolingual populations, isolation and self-sufficiency, nucleation and language functions, all of which are affected by the relative status of each of the languages in contact.

These mutually modifying dimensions are interrelated and often interdependent. For example, the permanence of Spanish bilingualism in the American Southwest depends on the adjacency of two different monolingual populations. Their numbers have given some of them sufficient political status to have their children schooled in their declining and ill-used home language, thereby providing it with a social function which prolonged its use by maintaining it at a level of bilinguality which would otherwise continue to regress. Spanish bilingualism in the US is assured by a steady stream of Latin American immigrants settling in different parts of the country. Notable is the constant overflow from Mexico whose population has been increasing at a rate twice that of the US. By the end of the twentieth century, there were more than seven million Mexicans living in the US, while half of its 15 million foreign-born immigrants were from Latin America, many of them well-educated professionals from Uruguay, Colombia, Argentina, and Ecuador.

Isolation and self-sufficiency of ethnic and ethno-religious communities in North America had also helped maintain not only their culture, but their language too. This was true for rural French-speaking parishes and also for the rural settlement of Mennonites, Hutterites, Amish, and Doukhobors (Driedger, 2000; Woodcock and Avakumovic, 1977). For example, the model self-sufficient Mennonite village in Steinbeck, Manitoba was equipped with its own printing presses used to publish German textbooks for its own schools (Epp, 1982). Yet in an increasingly mobile and economically dynamic America, it became increasingly difficult to maintain such self-sufficiency and exclusiveness for any length of time, especially since the mid-twentieth century. At that time, half the population was rural; at the end of the century, 80 percent was urban.

The nucleation and size of some of these groups have been such as to favor the maintenance of their binguality. In the democratic regimes of North America a critical concentration can determine the direction of these policies. The concentration of French in Quebec has been crucial to the creation of official bilingualism in Canada. It was also crucial to the use of Spanish as a quasi-official language in parts of the US. Also crucial to the maintenance of bilingualism are the functions of its component languages. For a language without function is without use and unused languages become useless and are forgotten. The more uses a language has the more likely it will be used and remembered. Bilingual communities in America range from those where both languages are used for all purposes to those where the functions are divided, for example between the language of the home, school, and church and the language of work, business and entertainment (Fernándo, 1994). This can be directly observed within an immigrant community. For example, it has been observed that although French was the school language of children of Italian families in Montreal, Italian was the main language of the home and English the main means of communication with other immigrant children. In urban Acadia, French was the language of education and English the language of business (Daigle, 1995; Lapierre and Roy, 1983).

The effects of monolingual contact, isolation, self-sufficiency and language functions on the maintenance of bilingualism in North America have been dependent on the relative demographic, economic, cultural, social, political, and legal status of the languages; that is, on the number of speakers, what their socioeconomic status is, how they live, how they are considered, how they vote and what rights they enjoy. All this can determine who becomes bilingual and to what extent.

23.5.1   *Demographic status*

Number is basic. If there are no speakers, there is no language use. The more there are, the more likely the language will be used. For example, there were so many Germans under Mexican rule in Texas that, when the territory was annexed to the US, they obtained equal political status, since they constituted a third of the population (Kloss, 1977). In Canada, French was the majority language until the end of the eighteenth century. After the British conquest of 1760, there began a long and enduring demographic competition between French and English. The effects of the massive influx of refugees from the American Revolution, coupled with a strong and steady preferential immigration from Britain, placed the French-speaking population into a minority position. Yet its superior rate of fertility somewhat offset the effects of British immigration, so that for almost two centuries it was able to maintain its share of the Canadian population at about a third. That was so, until the time of the Quiet Revolution of the 1970s when its birthrate had fallen below replacement levels (Lachapelle and Henripin, 1982). By the end of the twentieth century its share of the Canadian population was about a quarter, and that of people of English origin had fallen to about a third, while that of people of foreign origin (neither French nor English) had risen to more than a third (Statistics Canada, 1994). While many of the latter had maintained the use of their mother tongue, the majority had acquired English as their usual language (Beaujot and McQuillan, 1982). This placed the monolingual speakers of French in a precarious minority position on the American continent.

If numbers are so important, one wonders why the languages of so many thousands of African slaves did not produce bilingual African communities speaking languages like Hausa and Yoruba, whose speakers in Africa are counted in the millions. It had perhaps to do with the way slaves were captured, regrouped and intermingled to prevent organized mutinies. Some of the slaves did have to understand the orders of slave-masters and chant the hymns of the evangelists. The resulting varieties became pidginized forms of English, some of them – for example, the Gullah dialect of the Sea Islands of Georgia and South Carolina – retaining some African elements. Out of these varieties grew the dialect termed "Black" or "African-American" English by some American linguists (e.g. Dillard, 1975) and "Ebonics" by others (e.g. Smitherman, 2000). These terms are used to refer to a relatively uniform variety used by many African-Americans and some European-Americans as an informal style.

23.5.2 *Economic status*

It is not, therefore, only the number of people who determine the use of a language but also their economic position. This could be seen in their socio-economic profiles (US Department of Labor, 1975). In contrast to the economic status of Mexican *braceros*, that of the elite of Cuban society who had fled to Florida after the Cuban Communist Revolution did much for the entrenchment and duration of Spanish bilingualism. The first wave of Cuban refugees included the cream of Havana's professional and business classes. They did more than pay their way, thus contributing to the ease and rapidity with which their language was accepted in Miami as a medium of instruction in bilingual schools (Beebe and Mackey, 1990). They promoted the creation of

Spanish business firms, Spanish publications, and the enactment of Spanish as an official language of the city. Their new enterprises created more than a hundred thousand new jobs generating some two billion dollars of annual revenue and contributing to the transfer to Miami of more than a hundred international firms. All this also enhanced the social and political status of their language (see subsections 23.5.4 and 23.5.5). Meanwhile, in the agricultural, mining, and service industries, laborers from outside the country had become an indispensable part of the North American economy. Yet, because of their economic status, they became less of an asset to the languages they spoke than to the economy of the people they served.

23.5.3   Cultural status

In North America certain languages have always enjoyed a high cultural status, which enhanced their use among the bilingual population. These have been mostly European languages which were associated in the old world with the liberal arts, science, and diplomacy. At the time of the American Revolution, French was the predominant language of Europe and the exclusive language of diplomacy. Several of the first revolutionaries had spent time in Paris, notably Tom Paine who, during the reign of terror, was jailed by the Jacobins for promoting US-style federalism, against the centralized statism which was finally imposed.

German as the language of science had already begun its rise which continued until the First World War. Yet, the status of German in America owes more to the literacy of a steady stream of German immigrants, which goes as far back as 1608, to the time of the first English settlement in Virginia, and in Nova Scotia to the Scottish settlements of the 1750s. In certain areas, like Philadelphia, the number of Germans was sufficient to support newspapers and periodicals such as the *Philadelphische Zeitung*, started in 1732, and published by Benjamin Franklin. Cincinnati had three German dailies, and there were dozens of weeklies in other parts of Ohio. The state's first legislative document in 1772 (*Statistische Verordnung*) had been published in German. Laws were passed (in 1824) requiring legal notices to be published in German newspapers whose numbers increased sufficiently to warrant the creation of a German press association (*Verein der deutschen Presse*) in 1862.

Other non-English periodicals in America continued to multiply until just before the Great Depression. At that time they numbered about 600 in the US and Canada; almost a quarter were dailies, appearing mostly in German, Polish, Italian, Spanish, Yiddish, French, Czech, and other Slavic languages. After 1930, their numbers went down, as radio took over. By the mid-1950s, there were more than a thousand foreign-language radio programs in the US, broadcasting more than five million hours a week in some two dozen languages. For most of these languages there was a gradual decline in broadcasting starting in the 1960s, as television began to attract most of the listening audiences. Yet their presence remained and their autonomy grew with the proliferation of community radio stations, with their many small audiences, which television networks could not afford to serve. Since US television is about selling audiences to advertisers, the size of the audience must warrant the cost of production. By the end of the century, it became apparent that new technologies could help reduce these costs by adapting and repurposing some of the taped programs which had accumulated in the media libraries. With the fragmentation of television audiences and the phenomenal increase in the number of available viewers it had become relatively profitable to target the larger language minorities who by now had the option of receiving programs via satellite directly from Europe and Asia. So that in the year 2002, in Los Angeles, for example, one could view cable programming in Japanese, Chinese, Russian and Korean. Multinational media conglomerates based outside the United States had taken the lead, notably Sony (Japan), Bertelsmann (Germany), Vivendi (France), News Corp (Australia) and Univision (Latin America). By the year 2000, foreigners also held half of America's national debt and a quarter of its corporate bonds. Television and radio were being used in language promotion as part of the activities of the cultural missions of foreign powers.

Policies of language promotion go back at least to the end of the nineteenth century, with the creation in 1883 of the *Alliance française*, which later founded branches in major American cities. Germany then began supporting chapters of the German Bund in America and continued to do so until the Second World War, after which, branches of the *Goethe Institut* were established. Language promotion included visiting lectures, periodical literature, gifts of books to college libraries, visiting professorships, and academic exchanges arranged with the relevant foreign language departments. Only the standard or literary language was promoted. This was not the same variety as most immigrants used among themselves. For few of the many languages transplanted on American soil during the great waves of immigration had entered in their literary or standard forms. Most nineteenth-century immigrants, many rural and illiterate, had come from the most disadvantaged regions or social strata of European society. The hope of a better life in a classless world attracted millions of these dialect speakers. Their presence did not go unnoticed by the American language-teaching profession. Trained on the literatures of the great languages, their members were keen on transmitting only the "purest" forms of the language to their students. The latter were consequently discouraged from associating with immigrant dialect speakers who in turn were discouraged from electing their home language as a school subject.

Another blow to the cultural status of immigrant bilinguals came with the rise of educational measurement, notably the much publicized Stanford Binet Test (the IQ). Standardized on a few thousand American schoolchildren, it had been used during the First World War to select recruits for the American army. It was widely applied in schools, particularly by educational researchers, who reported in journals of abnormal psychology that low intelligence correlated with bilingualism (Darcy, 1953, 1963). Such research generated a rich literature which concluded that bilingualism was a handicap, to be overcome by accelerating the acculturation of immigrant children, whose parents were likewise discouraged from using their native language at home. In such a climate, bilinguals refrained from flaunting their ethnicity and from using their ethnic language in public. And for good reason. Doing so would have appeared unpatriotic, non-American or anti-social (Haugen, 1972). (For more discussion of bilingualism and intelligence, see chapters 1, 5, 15, 17, and 22.)

The political romanticism that had fired the nationalistic ideologies of Europe came late to America. It arrived in the wake of the thrust toward national unity after the deep and bitter divisions of the Civil War. Subsequently, American nationalism was rekindled whenever the United States got involved in foreign wars. In the First World War, there was a need to raise a large army able to understand orders and willing to fight against countries from which much of the immigrant population had come. The most available indicator, and the most common denominator, was the national language. Indeed, the notion that there was a distinct American language began to gain currency (Mencken, 1919). It responded to the slogan propagated by the US Bureau of Naturalization: "One language, one country and one flag" (Carlson, 1975). It supported the belief that "knowledge of the language led to Americanization and bestowed a higher level of intelligence and loyalty." The textbooks of the time taught that "Unity of speech will bring unity of thought, unity of feeling and unity of patriotism" (Downer, 1924, quoted in Foner, Rumbaut, and Gold, 2000, p. 417). Theodore Roosevelt had preached that language "was the crucible that turns out our people as Americans" (Dyer, 1980). "Our people" did not at that time include "people of color" (Konvitz, 1946).

The linguistic nationalism which prevailed throughout the First World War and during the isolationist period which followed had a profound effect on the cultural status of immigrant bilingualism in America. States which previously had tolerated the use of other languages in their schools formally abolished them. For example, although the use of seven foreign languages had been permitted since 1890 for teaching in Texas schools, a state law was passed in 1919 excluding all of them. The study of foreign languages in school plummeted to an all-time low. Before the First World War, a quarter of America's high-school population studied German; in the post-war period, it fell to less than half a percent. The number of students electing French also fell, from a third to a quarter of the high-school population. Academic bilingualism in the United States continued its long decline throughout the twentieth century. Notwithstanding the large investments of the federal NDEA (the National Defence Education Act, see below), only about one percent of the school and college population had been exposed to a foreign language (Dickhoff, 1965). Except for those who already spoke the language at home, few seemed to have achieved a level of working-language fluency. Although Spanish enrolment did increase, especially among students in the bilingual belt, the numbers for French, Italian, and German continued to decline by as much as a quarter between 1990 and 1995 in favor of the home languages of the new immigrants, especially Chinese and Arabic (Brod and Huber, 1997).

After the Second World War, which had engulfed all quarters of the globe, there developed in America a gradual realization that bilingualism was more of an asset than a liability. This was due not only to wartime experience abroad, but also to a number of nationwide developments which promoted racial tolerance and ethnic diversity in America and national unity in Canada. Notable among these were the civil rights movements and the shock effect of the first satellite launched into space by allegedly inferior Soviet scientists. The effect on the US congress was to pour millions into science and foreign-language teaching under its NDEA programs. At a more basic level, addenda to the anti-poverty legislation promoted the education of children in their home language. At the same time, the counterculture of the rebellious sixties was questioning all the past social stereotypes including those of language, race, culture, and ethnicity.

During this period the phenomenal increase in the range and availability of world travel coupled with the spreading globalization of commerce enabled the forging of relationships between North Americans and people from all over the world. The new generation of immigrants began sending their children abroad for their vacation, or for a year of schooling, among their relatives. Others took increased advantage of the programs of national and local organizations which sent students abroad to live in foreign families. These included exchange programs with Quebec. The proliferation of telephone call-centers used by business, governments, and non-governmental organizations required more and more bilingual people capable of handling calls in different languages. Bilingualism was no longer associated with backwardness in education, especially after the findings of psychologists which seemed to indicate that schooling in two languages was not in itself detrimental to the development of intelligence but might actually enhance it (Genesee, 1987; Lambert and Tucker, 1972). In Canada the promotion of official bilingualism was partly the result of the Quiet Revolution in Quebec, the consequent territorialization of French Canada and the recommendations of the Royal Commission on Bilingualism and Biculturalism leading to the Official Languages Act and the bilingualization of Canada's public service (Laurendeau and Dunton, 1967–70).

23.5.4 Social status

The social status of bilinguals in North America has been provided by their institutions. The natural quasi-biological tendency for people to associate with others who are like them and to be surrounded by kith and kin may explain the creation in the new world of so many ethnolinguistic societies (Mackey, 1985). This ethnolinguistic cohesion of subgroups, like the Italian, Greek, Yiddish, and Hispanic communities, encouraged ethnocentric practices which perpetuated the use of their speech variety within a framework of integral bilingualism and diglossia (Novak, 1977). Contrariwise, it was noticed, early in the last century, that open cultures (largely northern European) quickly acculturated into the English-speaking majority. Their solubility into the great

American melting pot was seen as a positive trait, facilitating the admission of more of their kind to the US according to a new immigration quota system (Glazer and Moynihan, 1970).

In Canada, the selection was even more restrictive; it was simply a policy of British preference, since Canadians were then British subjects (Canadian citizenship dates from 1947). Immigrants were already English-speaking and, by 1870, their numbers had increased the English-to-French ratio to more than two to one. During the following hundred years, ten million more immigrants arrived. This influx, coupled with the assimilation to English of other immigrants, including many French-Canadians living outside the Quebec heartland, upped the ratio to almost four to one. As a counterbalance, early in the last century, a massive recruitment campaign was launched in France. After this was interdicted by French law, French-speaking immigration, which was consequently restricted to Belgium, Switzerland, and Alsace-Lorraine, could not produce the numbers required (Frémont, 1959). Canada, with its vast landmass and rich material resources, required thousands of new workers for its agricultural and extractive sectors and for the construction of roads, canals and railways to bring the resulting products to market. Although most employers were mistrustful of foreigners, Canada was obliged to enlarge its immigration preference policy; it did so by including the countries of northern Europe.

After the Second World War, despite the admission of thousands of European displaced persons, the immigration policy of Canada had to be further broadened. This time, it included immigrants from low-wage countries in southern Europe, the West Indies, and elsewhere to do the sorts of jobs Canadians would no longer accept. Most newcomers, however, ended up in the cities. Within a generation one could count more than a hundred home languages in cities like Toronto, Montreal, and Vancouver.

Meanwhile, the Canadian government was elaborating a new, universal, and non-discriminatory policy, which culminated in the Immigration Act of 1978. Canadian immigration policy had by then evolved from one of the most restrictive to one of the most liberal. Thereby, Canada became a magnet for immigrants from all over the world. Many of these were now "visible" minorities. By the year 2000, about one in three in Toronto and Vancouver were non-white (Driedger, 2000). These new immigrants did not all blend into the mainstream by giving up their language. Nor were they now encouraged to do so. Multiculturalism had become the official policy of the federal government, which promoted both French-English bilingualism and heritage-language maintenance. Existing language-based organizations and ethnic groups were given a helping hand; and they flourished (see below).

From the earliest years, immigrant populations had enjoyed the freedom to create their own societies. Language groups founded their own parochial institutions, including schools where their languages were used as media of instruction. Before the War of Independence there was already a full-fledged German school system in Philadelphia, with some hundred parochial schools. From 1783, the *Deutsche Gesellschaft* of Baltimore encouraged the founding of bilingual schools in Maryland where, by 1875, they accounted for a third of the total. In the New England states one could find an equal number of parochial organizations where French was spoken. Some were supported regularly from Quebec with its hundreds of colleges, some dating back to before the British conquest. In addition, Franco-Americans could count on the support of professional schools, publishers of French textbooks, technology institutes, universities, and other Quebec institutions.

Unlike the early settlers, many of the nineteenth-century immigrants had little or no schooling, especially the peasants from eastern and southern Europe for whom the school represented a new reality. Yet in America they could organize their own schools or have their children attend the parochial schools founded by the older settlers. These included afternoon schools, weekend schools, and all-day bilingual parochial schools. The latter however had eventually to cede to the monopoly of state and provincial education systems which controlled curriculum, student and teacher certification, and teaching methods, all of which excluded bilingual education.

It was not until the 1960s that bilingual education again took hold. In Canada it was part of a movement for national unity. In the US, it was packaged with the "war against poverty," for it was noted that the poorest of the unemployed were those who knew little or no English, without which they could not even acquire a primary education. If this could be provided to them in a language they understood, along with instruction in English, it was argued, they could gradually transfer to mainstream schools and continue their education in English as far as their talents permitted. This was the rationale behind an addendum to the anti-poverty legislation. It was called the Bilingual Education Act of 1968 (Crawford, 1991). As a result, millions of dollars in US federal funding became available for the bilingual education of any underprivileged language minorities that could qualify. The great majority of these were Spanish-speaking, some 40 Amerindian, 10 French, 3 Italian, 3 Filipino, 2 Ilocano (also a Philippine language), 2 Portuguese, and one each for Korean and Chinese children. A notable exception was the pioneers of bilingual education in America, the German communities; they were not poor enough to qualify.

Since education in the US was under state jurisdiction, the bilingual schooling fell under the rules governing public schools. This meant that the teaching had to be done by state-certified teachers, the vast majority of whom had knowledge of no language other than English. In New York City, for example, where some 25 percent of the primary school children were Puerto Rican, less than 4 percent of the teachers knew any Spanish. Even in Los Angeles, where half the Hispanic population never completed primary school, only 5 percent of the teachers were Spanish-speaking. Bilingual programs were far from uniform throughout the country. A few were exceptional, such as the schools founded for the children of the refugees who had fled to Miami after the Communist Revolution in Cuba. Here the teaching was done bilingually to school populations structured so that half were from English-speaking families, half from Cuban families (Beebe and Mackey, 1990). The model approximated the practice of the successful American binational public school in Berlin (Mackey, 1972).

Meanwhile in Canada a certain type of bilingual education was rapidly gaining ground in the context of the crisis of national unity unleashed by the growing popularity of separatist movements in Quebec. This "innovation," whereby children were taught in a language other than that of their home, had long been the only form of schooling available to subjected peoples – from Roman Gaul to colonial Africa. Applied to dominant groups schooled in a minority language it was called "immersion" education. The idea was that the burden of bilingualism, which had hitherto been borne by the French, could be reversed by having the English schooled in French and that some of the perceived injustice could thereby be redressed. Although immersion education, where most if not all the subjects were taught in French, was never compulsory, about a tenth of the English-speaking population opted for it – more in some provinces (20 percent in New Brunswick) than in others (Genesee, 1987). Most of the increase occurred in the 1980s. Attempts were also made to accommodate the Amerindian schools (Kirkness and Bowman, 1992). Also adopted by language minorities, immersion became an instrument for reviving or maintaining a moribund ancestral tongue. Most of the provincially certified teachers outside Quebec and Acadia were unable to teach in any language but English, and even in Quebec and New Brunswick certification for teaching in English schools was in the hands of English-language monolingual school boards. The lack of native French speakers in the school, coupled with the fact that the pupils used French only in class, produced a certain type of bilingual competence quite different from that of students surrounded by classmates who spoke French at home. Despite their shortcomings, most types of bilingual schooling in Canada and the US did contribute to the social status of bilingualism in America. (For more discussion of bilingual education, see chapters 15, 21, 24, 25, 27, and 28.)

23.5.5   *Political status*

Political status is about the power to have laws passed, including those affecting language use. Until the mid-nineteenth century the large German communities in Pennsylvania (some half million voters) supplied most of its state governors. But in the second half of the century the influx of millions of East Europeans changed the political landscape. By 1910 German had disappeared from the schools and by 1940 from the pulpit. For in democracies like the US and Canada political power belongs to the majority of voters. In this context, it is remarkable to note that with the exception of Quebec, no province in Canada nor state in the US has had a majority whose main language was not English (Mackey, 1983). For example, in the American southwest, permanent Spanish settlements dated from 1690; yet of the territory ceded to the US in 1848, no part of it achieved statehood until it had an English-speaking majority. Whereas California was established as a state in 1850 and Nevada in 1864, Arizona and

New Mexico, both of which included large Spanish-speaking populations, were not admitted until 1912. It seems that the Congress was reluctant to create a state where the majority were Spanish-speaking, were likely to maintain a culture based on power and patronage, and might even be inclined to secede from the Union.

A powerful ethnic minority, when given the right to vote, can exert considerable political influence in a democracy with two major contending parties. This has been demonstrated in Florida and in California where at times the Hispanic vote becomes crucial. At the federal level, small regional minorities, if federated and well orchestrated, could exert political influence even to the point of determining the country's foreign policy. When it comes to political status, voting is the name of the game. If most Hispanics in the United States were citizens and most voted in the same way they could represent a powerful political force. Yet less than a third of the eight million Hispanic citizens eligible to vote have actually registered. People have wondered why this is. Coming from a culture that values character and direct personal leadership so highly and from countries with strong centralized regimes, it is not perhaps surprising that Hispanic Americans should harbor some distrust for the abstractions, uncertainties and indirectness of representative government. Yet it is through such representation that any meaningful political status has been won.

Political action has become even more effective at the direct, local level where the bilingual population enjoys a certain territorial dominance. In Miami, for example, there were enough Cuban-American votes to have the city declared a bilingual municipality in 1973; five years later after electing a bilingual Hispanic mayor, Cuban-Americans held a quarter of all the municipal posts.

In Canada, political action in favor of bilingualism has had a long and arduous history, marked with the milestones of small victories. These include: bilingual parliamentary debates (1864), bilingual postage stamps (1934), bilingual currency and the recognition of the "French fact" in America in the 1940s, followed by a ten-year struggle for a bilingual airline, or simply having its name, "Trans-Canada Airlines," changed to "Air Canada." Also at the federal level, the linguistic territoriality of Quebec provided considerable political leverage. It became more marked in 1976 after the election of a separatist Quebec government committed to political, linguistic and cultural autonomy. One of its first pieces of legislation was to make French its official language. French Quebec has been crucial to the Canadian federation. No single Canadian political party has been able to govern nationally without its support.

23.5.6 *Legal and administrative status*

While the US does not have an official language, Canada is officially a bilingual country. The Canadian constitution has always included some language provisions; the US constitution protects no language – not even English, despite demands for its official status (Adams and Brink, 1990). The equality of all citizens before the law does not apply to the languages they speak. The American approach to language has always been more pragmatic than legalistic (Crawford, 2000). Services in other languages may be provided where needed. The principle is not the right of a language to survive but the right of the citizen to know. This is reflected in the US constitution, which guarantees the right of all to a primary education, the responsibility for which devolves upon the states. Should they fail to deliver because of foreign-language incompetence they are in violation of the law and may be taken to court. This was demonstrated in the celebrated *Lau* vs. *Nichols* case, which was won by a Chinese-American citizen (for the complete text, see Appendix E of Andersson and Boyer, 1978).

Since education is conveyed through language, the states may specify which languages may be used in their schools and recognize any language as co-official. More than 20 states have done so at one time or another. So have the Canadian provinces and territories, which also have jurisdiction over education. Manitoba, for example, which was officially bilingual in 1870, enacted a law in 1890 whereby only English would be used in the public schools, while in the US after the purchase of Louisiana from France in 1803, French was permitted in the schools, in the courts, and in official publications until 1870. Ten years later, the new state constitution permitted the operation of bilingual schools in which all subjects could be taught in both English and French. In 1921, all references to French or any other language had disappeared from the constitution as it had from that of all other states during the First World War (see above). After 1930, however, the maintenance of French among the Louisiana survivors of the Acadian diaspora of the 1750s was being supported by distant cousins in the Canadian Maritimes. French was also revived in half a dozen school systems in the 1970s under the provisions of the Bilingual Education Act. These initiatives, however, did not restore the legal status of French, whose presence in the US had had such a long history. It goes back to the founding of New Netherlands in 1614, and particularly New Amsterdam (now New York City) in 1623, which had a strong French (Huguenot) element. By 1656 all official proclamations were being issued in both Dutch and French.

The administrative status of German in America also pre-dates the US Constitution. The Constitutional convention in Philadelphia in 1776 authorized the publication of all its records in both English and German. From 1786 to 1856 a German version of the sessional records appeared annually; it was reprinted, along with official notices, in the German newspapers of the US.

The legal status of Spanish in the US has varied according to the conditions of statehood in the southwest. In general, the existence of Spanish was taken for granted and official services in Spanish were provided as needed. For example, in New Mexico, in the Organic Act of Annexation in 1850 and again in its constitution of 1912 there were provisions for the publication of amendments in both languages in counties with Spanish newspapers. Its Bilingual Multicultural Education Act of 1973 provided for bilingual teaching in the elementary schools of New Mexico although the state itself was not officially bilingual. Puerto Rico, on the other hand, although officially bilingual, remained essentially monolingual Spanish-speaking with an unassimilated English-speaking population. The island was ceded to the US only in 1898 and became an associate state (called a Commonwealth) according to an Organic Act in 1900 which specified that in order to become a member of the House of Delegates one had to be able "to read and write either the Spanish or the English languages." It also provided for the bilingual publication of all the laws.

The legal status of the Amerindian languages, however, has been of little concern, and what was achieved came at a much later date (Frideres, 1988; Havemann, 1999). Of the more than 200 native American languages north of the Rio Grande, few have attained any sort of legal status, save within a number of international conventions against ethnic discrimination. For example, there is the International Covenant of Civil and Political Rights (sec. 27) the United Nations Convention on the Rights of the Child (art. 30), and the Inter-American Charter of Social Guarantees (art. 39). Some principles invoked in these international documents have been incorporated into the laws of Canada and the United States. In the Canada Act of 1982, the second part is devoted to aboriginal rights. In the US the Native American Language Act of 1990 recognized the right to teach in an aboriginal language, empowering the states and the tribes to grant official status to such languages. A few tribes took the lead in establishing their own language policies. For example, the Yaqui nation of Arizona enacted a policy whereby "the Yaqui language is the official language," and "the Spanish language shall be recognized as our second language and the English language as our third language."

In Canada in 1988, the government of the Northwest Territories enacted the Official Languages Ordinance (later inserted into the federal Official Languages Act as article 45, so as not to be modified without federal consent). It included as official languages: Chipewyan, Cree, Dogrib, English, French, Gwich'in, Inuktitut, and Slavey. Similar legislation was enacted in the Eastern Arctic in 1999 for the newly established state of Nunavut; it specified Inuktitut, English, and French as official languages. Further east, Greenland, in its statute of autonomy, obtained from Denmark in 1979, gave the status of "principal language" to Inuit-Inupiaq (Greenlandic) while Danish was permitted for official purposes (art. 9).

23.5.7 *Official bilingualism*

Although the vast majority of the populations of Canada and the US speak one and the same language, Canada, unlike the US, has long been concerned with the official status of its national languages. The distinction in the roles of language policy in national identity was largely expanded during the second half of the twentieth century as Canada struggled toward an accommodation in the relative status of English and French. The end products of ongoing language conflicts within and between Canada and Quebec can be seen in a most comprehensive body of language legislation, founded on hundreds of volumes of research generated by federal and provincial language commissions, consultative groups and research centers. The legislation and the research even became objects of study by legislators from abroad contemplating their own language laws.

The legislation is based on two contradictory principles – the principle of personality and the principle of territoriality (McRae, 1975). The first makes the state accommodate to the language of the individual; the second makes the individual accommodate to the language of the state. It is, in sum, the basic distinction between individual and collective rights. Canada has opted for the first, Quebec for the second. Yet, in practice, the principles themselves had to accommodate to the context in which they had to be applied. At the federal level, it meant that the public service had to serve the Canadian public in the official language of the individual's choosing. Despite its monumental efforts to do so, the federal bureaucracy was unable to bilingualize some quarter million adult monolinguals. Though bound by the law, it proved impossible to provide all services in both languages in thousands of isolated and underpopulated areas where only a few persons, already bilingual by necessity, could elect to be served in the other language. Federal bilingual services were provided only in areas where the numbers warranted it. This territorialization of the principle of personality was provided for in the first Official Languages Act of 1979 whereby, in concert with provincial and municipal governments, a population with a ten percent minority could qualify as a "bilingual district" (McRae, 1989). But the cooperation was not forthcoming except in the already bilingual province of New Brunswick. In practice a complete range of federal bilingual services became available only in the national capital, in large cities and in the federal head offices and websites.

In Quebec it was the principle of territoriality that had to be personalized. Although French was the only state language, there were within the boundaries of Quebec areas with large numbers of monolingual English speakers who had the right to state services. Provisions for these persons appeared in the French Language Charter, which recognized some fifty bilingual municipalities (Caldwell and Waddell, 1982; Legault, 1992). As Quebec's preoccupation with imposing its language became more political, the federal policy of language accommodation evolved imperceptibly from one of protection to one of promotion. The language most in need of support was French, the federal promotion of which did not enthuse the other three-quarters of the Canadian population – neither the Anglos, nor the Amerindian First Nations unwilling to add another "colonial" language to their burden, nor the many descendants of the immigrants unconcerned with the historical underpinnings of the status of French, which goes back to the British conquest of French America. The need to keep some sixty-five thousand French subjects on the English side of the American War of Independence had motivated the entrenchment of French civil and cultural rights in the Quebec Act of 1774 (Lawson, 1989). These rights were reaffirmed and extended when Canada became a confederation by virtue of the British North America Act of 1867. The language rights were later elaborated in the patriated Canadian constitution of 1982. Meanwhile in Quebec there had also been regular legislation in favor of French, passing from a phase of bilingual recognition to the monolingual exclusiveness of the Charter of the French Language (*Charte de la langue française*) and its mass of attendant language regulations and provisions for well-staffed language bureaucracies controlling and promoting the use, enrichment, and standards of the French language in Quebec (Bourhis, 1984, 1994; Quebec, 1977, 1988).

Although it may appear that Canada is a bilingual country, with English and French as dominant languages, in reality it is as linguistically diverse as the US. The desire for cultural recognition from such a large constituency could hardly be ignored by any government (Palmer, 1975; Cummins and Danesi, 1990). As early as the mid-1950s the Canadian government began to realize that its policies of assimilation had not worked. In 1971, it eventually elaborated a policy of "multiculturalism within a bilingual framework," to "support and encourage the various cultures and ethnic groups that give structure and vitality to our society" (Berry, Kalin and Taylor, 1977; Taylor, 1992). Although neither these "heritage languages" nor the native languages of the First Nations were given legal status, they were nevertheless protected, tolerated or promoted by the Canadian government with a watchful eye, a sympathetic ear, and a generous hand (Battiste, 2000; Fettes, 1992).

23.6   Effects of Bilingualism on the Languages

In North America, the dominant colonial languages have been enriched by contact with native and immigrant populations. Their languages have added new concepts and vocabulary to North American English, French, and Spanish (Mencken, 1919 and 1963). For the native and immigrant languages, however, bilingualism has been an instrument of transformation whereby much of their inherited stock of words, morphemes, and concepts has been replaced by those of the dominant language (Bartelt, Jasper, and Hoffer, 1982). The same is partly applicable to Spanish and French in contact with English (Mougeon and Beniak, 1991). The admixture of dialects created new language varieties, especially in urban areas, each developing its own distinct character. A flood of English words and expressions entered into dialectal and non-standard speech varieties used within the bilingual borderlands – into the *joual* of Montreal, the *chiac* of Acadia and into *Tex-Mex* and *Spanglish* (Varo, 1971). Analysis of the urban dialects of spoken American Italian, for example, shows regional differences between New York, Toronto, and Montreal, the latter including loanwords from both English and French, like *sciáuro* < E. *shower*; and *sciomaggio* < F. *chômage* (*unemployment*, as in unemployment insurance).

The absorption of such loanwords was particularly easy for those immigrant European languages which shared the same Indo-European framework and comparable repertoires of cultural concepts. The structure of languages belonging to other linguistic families like those of some Amerindian languages cannot manage these word-for-word borrowings (Mackey, 1953). Indeed, from the outset, there existed an almost unbridgeable gap between the concept categories and the very *Weltanschauung* of the Amerindians and those of their European conquerors, each of whom thought with the notions fashioned for them by their language, history and culture. For example, it was inconceivable to semi-nomadic Amerindians that someone could actually own part of the earth on which all life depended. And it was unacceptable that intruders could claim its ownership simply by discovery, and thereby take away land that did not belong to them by making marks on sheets of paper.

23.7   Research on North American Bilingualism

Writings on North American bilingualism must be distinguished from the numerous writings on bilingualism by North American scholars (see preceding chapters). Most of these writings have been discipline-oriented. They have evolved within the changing paradigms of different disciplines such as linguistics, psychology, sociology, sociolinguistics, psycholinguistics, political science, and human geography (Mackey, 2005a). The few attempts at a multidisciplinary approach have not, however, resulted in the sort of integrated, problem-oriented interdisciplinary synthesis that had been the hope of scholars of bilingualism since its re-definition a half-century ago (Mackey, 1956). While America has become the world's largest producer of writings in the language sciences, it is surprising what a small fraction of this production is devoted to bilingualism in North America. There are several reasons for this.

The first is the lack of reliable, comparable, and usable data. The basic source of these data has been the census. Both Canada and the US make a complete people-count every ten years, Canada at the beginning of the decade (-01) and the US at the end (-00). For example, Canada counted some 30 million inhabitants in 2001, the US some 281 million in 2000. Included in the count are many sorts of people-related data which the government thought it might like to know, as requested by the legislative, judicial, and executive branches and their numerous regulatory agencies including transportation, labor, commerce, immigration, education, citizenship, and others. It is in this context that one may find data on language, including the mother tongues, the ethnic origins, and the usual and home languages of the population. Yet since the definitions of these categories and the methods of gathering language-related data are not the same in the United States as they are in Canada, it is difficult to compile overall North American language-related data. There are also differences in how the two countries have classified their immigrant and Amerindian populations (Nichols, 1998). Second, the US census does not count the language first acquired, but the one "spoken in the home" at the time of the enumeration, from which one may deduce the incidence of bilingualism in the US; but this may range anywhere from incipient to residual bilingualism. In the Canada census, "mother tongue" means "the language first learned as a child and still understood." Third, the consistency of the language data is different in each of the countries. Although Canada has gathered language-related data since 1871, in the US it has been intermittent and inconsistent. For example, in 1940 the US census gathered mother tongue data for only the white population, white and non-white having been census categories; in 1970 data on mother tongue was gathered for the entire population. The same is true for the "usual language." While the US census provides no data on bilingual ability, the Canadian census since 1931 has provided consistent data on the ability to speak English and/or French, in addition to data on ethnic origin and mother tongue. By cross-tabulating these data over time and space it is possible to locate the areas of language retention and language loss (Mackey and Cartwright, 1979).

In both countries it is possible to correlate any available language data with data on country of birth and age, distinguishing between the first (foreign-born) generation, the second (native-born of foreign or mixed parentage), and the third (native-born of native parentage). Since the foreign-born are presumably more competent in their mother tongue than in English, their numbers can be used as an indicator of the incidence of this type of bilingualism. During the inter-census period, however, each country, while testing the validity of its data and methods, turns out a cornucopia of statistics. Yet these inter-census data come from a relatively small population sample of less than fifty thousand households, like those supplied by the monthly population surveys of the US Bureau of the Census. This survey has sometimes included a language supplement which, in conjunction with the complete counts of the immigration service, can provide one with the means to gauge the overall bilinguality of the population. One can estimate, for example, that about one person in eight lives in a household with a language other than English, and that of these, about one in ten actually speaks the foreign tongue, which is the "usual" language of a third of this group.

In addition to the census figures, language-related data may also be obtained from other government agencies responsible for citizenship, immigration, and Indian affairs, and also, in Canada, from the Office of the Commissioner of Official Languages, from Quebec's French-language agencies, especially the *Conseil* and the *Office* (*de la langue française*). One can find demolinguistic data in such surveys as that of Kloss and McConnell (1974–98) and in the descriptive inventories of Amerindian languages (Mithun, 2001). Works on language retention like those of Nahirny, Hofman, Hayden, et al. (1966) can give an idea of the bilinguality of the population. There are also studies of the retention of specific languages (see subsection 23.3.2 above). Most instructive are also the language profiles of the United States (Ferguson and Heath, 1990) and that of Canada (Edwards, 1998). On the ethnicity of the US population, the classic is the atlas of Allen and Turner (1988). A good historical perspective can be obtained from *The American Bilingual Tradition* (Kloss, 1977), and from *The Early Days of Sociolinguistics* (Paulston and Tucker, 1997) which provides a sociolinguistic perspective of the contexts in which bilingualism has been studied. The most comprehensive and at the same time the most succinct guide to research on bilingualism is still Haugen's *Bilingualism in the Americas* (1956) coupled with his later supplements (Haugen, 1973) and his selected articles (Dil, 1972). For Canada there is a research guide in French (Mackey, 1978). Also in French is a vast literature on North American French and language usage in Quebec. A few of these works have been translated into English, for example *French America* (Louder and Waddell, 1992) and *Quebec's Aboriginal Languages* (Maurais, 1996). There also exists a considerable literature on bilingual schooling, notably *Bilingual Schooling in the United States* (Andersson and Boyer, 1978) and in Canada, dozens of research reports on immersion education. One can find articles on bilingualism and bilingual education in North America, intermittently in relevant international periodicals like the *Journal of Multilingual and Multicultural Development*, and also in the journals of three seemingly isolated academic disciplines: modern languages, TESOL (Teaching English to Speakers of Other Languages), and linguistics.

Reference to North American bilingualism can regularly be found in a number of current linguistic bibliographies, notably those of the Modern Language Association of America (MLA) – especially titles published after 1980. Before 1980, titles may be found among the twenty thousand entries of the second edition of the *International Bibliography on Bilingualism* (Mackey, 1982); it includes a voluminous multidimensional index (appended on microfiches).

From all the foregoing information, one must conclude that although North Americans have had a worldwide reputation as English-speaking monolinguals, the incidence of plurilingualism in North America is much greater than first meets the ear. One could hazard an estimate that at least ten to fifteen percent of its 300 million English-speaking inhabitants have some competence in a language other than English – an incidence of bilingualism unlikely to decrease as long as the continent remains a "land of opportunity" that attracts new settlers from all quarters of the globe.

REFERENCES

Adamic, Louis (1945). *A Nation of Nations*. New York: Harper.

Adams, Karen L. and Brink, Daniel F. (eds) (1990). *Perspectives on Official English*. Berlin: Mouton de Gruyter.

Allen, James P. and Turner, Eugene J. (1988). *We the People: An Atlas of America's Ethnic Diversity*, New York: Macmillan.

Andersson, Theodore and Boyer, Mildred (1978). *Bilingual Schooling in the United States*, 2nd edn. Austin, TX: National Educational Laboratory Publishers.

Andrews, David R. (1999). *Sociocultural Perspectives on Language Change in Diaspora*. Amsterdam: John Benjamins.

Arsenault, Georges (1989). *The Island Acadians* (translated by S. Ross). Charlottetown, PE: Ragweed.

Barron, Milton L. (ed.) (1957). *American Minorities*. New York: Knopf.

Bartelt, H. G., Jasper, S. P., and Hoffer, B. L. (eds.) (1982). *Essays in Native American English*. San Antonio, TX: Trinity University.

Battiste, Marie (ed.) (2000). *Reclaiming Indigenous Voice and Vision*. Vancouver: University of British Columbia Press.

Beaujot, R. and McQuillan, K. (1982). *Growth and Dualism: The Demographic Development of Canadian Society*. Toronto: Gage.

Beebe, Von N. and Mackey, William F. (1990). *Bilingual Schooling and the Miami Experience*. Miami, FL: Institute for Interamerican Studies.

Benoit, Josaphat T. (1935). *L'âme franco-américaine* [The Franco-American spirit]. Montreal: A. Lévesque.

Berry, John, Kalin, R., and Taylor, D. (1977). *Multiculturalism and Ethnic Attitudes in Canada*. Ottawa: Supply and Services.

Bourhis, Richard Y. (ed.) (1984). *Conflict and Language Planning in Quebec*. Clevedon, UK: Multilingual Matters.

Bourhis, Richard Y. (ed.) (1994). *French-English Language Issues in Canada* (= *International Journal of the Sociology of Language*, 105–6). Berlin: Mouton de Gruyter.

Brod, Richard and Huber, Bertina J. (1997). Foreign Language Enrolments in United States Institutions of Higher Education: Fall 1995. *ADFL Bulletin*, 28(2), 35–61.

Burma, J. H. (1955). *Spanish Speaking Groups in the United States*. Durham, NC: Duke University Press.

Burnaby, B. and Beaujot, R. (1986). *The Use of Aboriginal Languages in Canada*. Ottawa: Secretary of State.

Butler, G. R. (1995). *Histoire et traditions orales des Franco-Acadiens de Terre-Neuve* [The history and oral traditions of the Franco-Acadians of Newfoundland]. Quebec: Septentrion.

Caldwell, Gary and Waddell, Eric (1982). *The English of Quebec: from Majority to Minority Status*. Quebec:

Institut québécois de recherche sur la culture.

Canada (1993). *Language Retention and Transfer* (= no. 94–319). Ottawa: Statistics Canada.

Carlson, Robert E. (1975). *The Accent for Conformity*. New York: John Wiley.

Cartwright, Donald G. (1980). *Official Language Populations in Canada: Patterns and Contacts*. Montreal: Institute for Research on Public Policy.

Champagne, Duane (ed.) (1994). *Chronology of Native American History*. Detroit, MI: Gale Research.

Christian, Jane M. (1964). *The Navajo: A People in Transition* (= *Southwestern Studies*, 2(3, 4)).

Crawford, James (1991). *Bilingual Education: History, Politics, Theory and Practice*, 2nd edn. Los Angeles: Bilingual Education Services.

Crawford, James (ed.) (1992). *Language Loyalties*. Chicago: University of Chicago Press.

Crawford, James (2000). *At War with Diversity: US Language Policy in an Age of Anxiety*. Clevedon, UK: Multilingual Matters.

Cummins, Jim and Danesi, Marcel (1990). *Heritage Languages: The Development and Denial of Canada's Linguistic Resources*. Toronto: Garamond Press.

Daigle, Jean (ed.) (1995). *Acadians of the Maritimes*. Moncton, NB: Etudes acadiennes, Université de Moncton.

Dallaire, Louise and Lachapelle, R. (1990). *Demolinguistic Profiles of Minority Language Communities*. Ottawa: Secretary of State.

Darcy, Natalie T. (1953, 1963). Bilingualism and the Measurement of Intelligence. *Journal of Genetic Psychology*, 82, 21–57 and 103, 259–82.

Dickhoff, John S. (1965). *NDEA and Modern Foreign Languages*. New York: Modern Language Association.

Diebold, A. R., Sr. (1961). Incipient Bilingualism. *Language*, 37, 97–112.

Dil, Anwar S. (ed.) (1972). *The Ecology of Language* (selected papers of Einar Haugen). Stanford, CA: Stanford University Press.

Dillard, Joey L. (ed.) (1975). *Perspectives on Black English*. Berlin: Mouton de Gruyter.

Dillard, Joey L. (1985). *Toward a Social History of American English*. Berlin: Mouton de Gruyter.

Dorian, Nancy (ed.) (1989). *Investigating Obsolescence*. London: Cambridge University Press.

Douaud, Patrick (1985). *Ethnolinguistic Profile of the Canadian Métis* (= Mercury Series 99). Ottawa: National Museum.

Driedger, Leo (2000). *Mennonites in the Global Village*. Toronto: University of Toronto Press.

Driedger, Leo and Halli, Shiva S. (eds.) (2000). *Race and Racism: Canada's Challenge*. Montreal: McGill-Queen's University Press.

Driver, H. E. (1961). *Indians of North America*, 2nd edn. Chicago: Chicago University Press.

Dyer, Theodore G. (1980). *Theodore Roosevelt and the Idea of Race*. Baton Rouge: Louisiana State University Press.

Edwards, John (ed.) (1998). *Language in Canada*. Cambridge, UK: Cambridge University Press.

Elkholy, Abdo A. (1966). *The Arab Moslems in the United States*. New Haven, CT: College & University Press.

Epp, Frank H. (1982). *Mennonites in Canada, 1920–1940*. Toronto: Macmillan.

Ferguson, Charles and Heath, Shirley Brice (eds.) (1990). *Language in the USA*. Cambridge, UK: Cambridge University Press.

Fernández, Mauro (1994). *Diglossia: A Comprehensive Bibliography: 1960–1990 (and supplements)*. Amsterdam: John Benjamins.

Fettes, Mark (1992). *A Guide to Language Strategies for First Nations Communities*. Ottawa: Assembly of First Nations.

Fishman, Joshua A. (1966). *Hungarian Language Maintenance in the United States*. Bloomington: Indiana University Press.

Fishman, Joshua A. (1968). Sociolinguistic perspectives on the study of bilingualism. *Linguistics*, 39, 21–49.

Fishman, Joshua A. (ed.) (1981). *Never Say Die!* Berlin: Mouton de Gruyter.

Fishman, Joshua A., Nahirny, V. C., Hofman, J. E., Hayden, R. C., and Haugen, E. (1966). *Language Loyalty in the United States*. The Hague: Mouton.

Foner, Nancy (ed.) (2001). *New Immigrants in New York*. New York: Columbia University Press.

Foner, Nancy, Rumbaut, R. G., and Gold, S. J. (eds.) (2000). *Immigration Research for a New Century*. New York: Sage.

Frémont, D. (1959). *Les Français dans l'Ouest canadien* [French (settlers) in the Canadian West]. Winnipeg: Editions La Liberté.

Frideres, J. S. (1988). *Native Peoples in Canada: Contemporary Conflicts*. Scarborough, Ontario: Prentice-Hall.

Gans, H. S. (1962). *The Urban Villagers: Group and Class in the Life of Italian-Americans*, 2nd edn. New York: Free Press.

García, Ofelia and Fishman, Joshua A. (eds) (2002). *The Multilingual Apple: Languages in New York City*, 2nd edn. Berlin: Mouton de Gruyter.

Genesee, Fred (1987). *Learning through Two Languages: Studies of Immersion and Bilingual Education*. Rowley, MA: Newbury House.

Gilbert, Glenn G. (ed.) (1971). *The German Language in America*. Austin: University of Texas Press.

Glazer, Nathan and Moynihan, D. Patrick (1970). *Beyond the Melting Pot*, 2nd edn. Cambridge, MA: MIT Press.

Govorchin, Gerald G. (1961). *Americans from Yugoslavia*. Gainsville, FL: University of Florida Press.

Grebler, Leo, Moore, Joan W., and Guzman, Ralph C. (1970). *The*

Mexican-American People. New York: Free Press/Macmillan.

Greenberg, J. H. (1987). *Language in the Americas*. Stanford, CA: Stanford University Press.

Halich, Wasyl (1937). *Ukrainians in the United States*. Garden City, NY: Doubleday.

Harrison, Brian and Marmen, I. (1994). *Languages in Canada*. Ottawa: Prentice-Hall.

Haugen, Einar (1953). *The Norwegian Language in America: A Study in Bilingual Behavior* 2 vols. Philadelphia: University of Pennsylvania Press.

Haugen, Einar (1956). *Bilingualism in the Americas: A Bibliography and Research Guide* (= Publication of the American Dialect Society, 26). University, AL: University of Alabama Press.

Haugen, Einar (1972). The stigmata of bilingualism. In Anwar S. Dil (ed.), *The Ecology of Language*, pp. 307–24. Stanford, CA: Stanford University Press.

Haugen, Einar (1973). *Bilingualism, Language Contact and Immigrant Languages in the United States* (= Current Trends in Linguistics, 10), pp. 505–92.

Havemann, Paul (1999). *Indigenous Peoples' Rights in Australia, Canada and New Zealand*. Oxford: Oxford University Press.

Higham, John (1992). *Strangers in the Land (1860–1925)*, 2nd edn. New Brunswick, NJ: Rutgers University Press.

Hoglund, A. William (1960). *Finnish Immigrants in America, 1880–1920*. Madison, WI: University of Wisconsin Press.

Jabbra, N. W. and Jabbra, J. (1984). *Voyagers to a Rocky Shore: The Lebanese and Syrians of Nova Scotia*. Halifax, NS: Dalhousie University Institute of Public Affairs.

Kennedy, John F. (1964). *A Nation of Immigrants*. New York: Harper & Row.

Kirkness, Verna S. and Bowman, S. (1992). *First Nations and Schools*. Toronto: Canadian Education Association.

Kloss, Heinz (1977). *The American Bilingual Tradition*. Rowley, MA: Newbury House.

Kloss, Heinz and McConnell, Grant D. (eds) (1974–98). *Linguistic Composition of the Nations of the World. Volume 2: North America* (1978). Quebec: Presses de l'Université Laval.

Konvitz, Milton R. (1946). *The Alien and the Asiatic in American Law*. Ithaca, NY: Cornell University Press.

Lachapelle, Réjean and Henripin, J. (1982). *The Demolinguistic Situation in Canada: Past Trends and Future Prospects*. Montreal: Institute for Research on Public Policy.

Lambert, Wallace E. and Tucker, G. Richard (1972). *The Bilingual Education of Children*. Rowley, MA: Newbury House.

Landry, Rodrigue and Allard, R. (1994). *A Sociolinguistic Profile of New Brunswick Francophones*. Moncton, NB: Centre de recherche en éducation, Université de Moncton.

Lapierre, J. W. and Roy, M. (1983). *Les Acadiens* [The Acadians]. Paris: Presses universitaires de France.

Laurendeau, André and Dunton, Davidson (1967–1970). *Report of the Royal Commission on Bilingualism and Biculturalism*, 6 vols. Ottawa: Queen's Printer.

La Violette, Forrest E. (1945). *Americans of Japanese Ancestry*. Toronto: Canadian Institute of International Affairs.

Lawson, Philip (1989). *The Imperial Challenge: Quebec and Britain in the Age of the American Revolution*. Montreal: McGill-Queen's University Press.

Legault, Josée (1992). *L'invention d'une minorité: les Anglo-Québecois* [Anglo Quebec: The invention of a minority]. Montreal: Boréal.

Leopold, Werner B. (1939–49). *Speech Development of a Bilingual Child*, 4 vols. Chicago: Northwestern University Press.

Liu, Kwang-Ching (1963). *Americans and Chinese: A Historical Essay and Bibliography*. Cambridge, MA: Harvard University Press.

Louder, Dean R. and Waddell, Eric (eds.) (1992). *French America* (translated by Franklin Philip). Baton Rouge: Louisiana State University Press. [*Du continent perdu à l'archipel retrouvé*. Quebec: Presses de l'Université Laval. 1983.]

Lucas, Henry S. (1955). *Netherlands in America*. Ann Arbor: University of Michigan Press.

Lupul, Manoly R. (ed.) (1982). *Heritage and Transition: Essays in the History of Ukrainians in Canada*. Toronto: McClelland & Stewart.

Mackey, William F. (1953). Bilingualism and Linguistic Structure. *Culture*, 14, 143–9.

Mackey, William F. (1956). Toward a re-definition of bilingualism. *Canadian Journal of Linguistic*, 2, 4–11.

Mackey, William F. (1972). *Bilingual Education in a Binational School*. Rowley, MA: Newbury House.

Mackey, William F. (1978). *Le bilinguisme canadien: bibliographie analytique et guide du chercheur* (Canadian bilingualism: A bibliography and research guide) (= Publication B-75). Quebec: Centre international de recherche sur le bilinguisme.

Mackey, William F. (ed.) (1982). *International Bibliography on Bilingualism/Bibliographie internationale sur le bilinguisme*, 2nd edn. Quebec: Presses de l'Université Laval.

Mackey, William F. (1983). US language status policy and the Canadian experience. In Juan Cobarrubias and Joshua A. Fishman (eds.), *Progress in Language Planning: International Perspectives*, pp. 173–206). Berlin: Mouton de Gruyter.

Mackey, William F. (1985). The sociobiology of ethnolinguistic nucleation. *Politics and the Life Sciences*, 4, 1, 10–15.

Mackey, William F. (ed.) (2000). *Espaces urbains et co-existence des langues* [Urban spaces and the coexistence of languages] (= *Terminogramme* 94). Montreal: Publications du Québec.

Mackey, William F. (2005a). Multilingual cities. In Ulrich Ammon, N. Dittmar, and K.J. Mattheier (eds.), *Sociolinguistics: An International Handbook of Language and Society* (article 218). Berlin: Walter de Gruyter.

Mackey, William F. (2005b). Bilingualism and multilingualism. In Ulrich Ammon, N. Dittmar, and K. J. Mattheier (eds.), *Sociolinguistics: An International Handbook of the Science of Language and Society*, 2nd edn (article 145). Berlin: Walter de Gruyter.

Mackey, William F. and Cartwright, Donald G. (1979). Geocoding language loss from census data. In W. F. Mackey and S. Ornstein (eds.), *Sociolinguistic Studies in Language Contact* (= *Trends in Linguistics*, 6), pp. 69–98. The Hague: Mouton.

McMillan, A. D. (1988). *Native Peoples and Cultures of Canada*. Toronto: Douglas and McIntyre.

McRae, Kenneth D. (1975). The principle of personality and the principle of territoriality in multilingual states. *International Journal of the Sociology of Language*, 4, 35–54.

McRae, Kenneth D. (1989). Bilingual language districts in Finland and Canada: Adventures in the transplantation of an institution. *Canadian Public Policy*, 4, 331–51.

McWilliams, Carey (1949). *North from Mexico*. New York: J. B. Lippincott.

Maurais, Jacques (ed.) (1996). *Quebec's Aboriginal Languages*. Clevedon,

UK: Multilingual Matters. [*Les langues autochtones du Québec*. Quebec: Publications du Québec, 1992.]

Mencken, Henry L. (1919). *The American Language* (4th edn. and supplements, 1963). New York: Knopf.

Meynen, Emil (1937). *Bibliography on German Settlements in Colonial North America*. Leipzig: Harrassowitz.

Mithun, Marianne (2001). *The Languages of Native North America*. Cambridge, UK: Cambridge University Press.

Mougeon, Raymond and Beniak, E. (1988). *Le français canadien parlé hors Québec. Aperçu sociolinguistique* [Spoken Canadian French outside Quebec: A sociolinguistic overview]. Quebec: Presses de l'Université Laval.

Mougeon, Raymond and Beniak, E. (1991). *Linguistic Consequences of Language Contact and Restriction: The Case of French in Ontario*. Oxford: Oxford University Press.

Mulder, Arnold (1947). *Americans from Holland*. New York: J. B. Lippincott.

Musmanno, Michael A. (1965). *The Story of Italians in America*. Garden City, NY: Doubleday.

Nelson, Helge (1943). *The Swedes and the Swedish Settlements in North America*, 2 vols. New York: Albert Bonnier.

Nichols, Roger L. (1998). *Indians in the United States and Canada: A Comparative History*. Lincoln, NE: University of Nebraska Press.

Novak, Michael (1977). *The Rise of the Unmeltable Ethnics*. New York: Macmillan.

Packard, Vance (1972). *A Nation of Strangers*. New York: David McKay.

Palmer, Howard (1975). *Immigration and the Rise of Multiculturalism*. Toronto: Copp Clark.

Pap, Leo (1949). *Portuguese American Speech*. New York: King's Crown Press.

Paulston, Christina B. and Tucker, G. Richard (eds.) (1997). *The Early Days of Sociolinguistics*. Dallas, TX: International Linguistics Institute.

Pendakur, Ravi (1990). *Speaking in Tongues: Heritage Language Maintenance and Transfer in Canada*. Ottawa: Multiculturalism and Citizenship.

Pisani, L. F. (1957). *The Italians in the United States: A Social Study and History*. New York: Exposition Press.

Pochmann, Henry A. and Schultz, A. (1953). *Bibliography of German Culture in America to 1940*. Madison: University of Wisconsin Press.

Poplack, Shana (ed.) (2000). *The English History of African American English*. Oxford: Blackwell.

Preston, Denis R. (1999). *Handbook of Perceptual Dialectology*. Amsterdam: John Benjamins.

Prokop, Manfred (1990). *The German Language in Alberta*. Edmonton: University of Alberta Press.

Purich, Donald J. (1988). *The Métis*. Toronto: James Lorimer.

Quebec (1977, 1988). *La Charte de la langue française* [The Charter of the French Language]. Quebec: Editeur officiel du Québec.

Saloutos, Theodore (1964). *The Greeks in the United States*. Cambridge, MA: Harvard University Press.

Samora, Julian (1966). *La Raza: Forgotten Americans*. South Bend, IN: University of Notre Dame Press.

Scargill, M. H. (1977). *A Short History of Canadian English*. Victoria, BC: Sononis Press.

Schermerhorn, Richard A. (1949). *These Our People*. Boston, MA: D. C. Heath.

Simundsson, Elva (1981). *Icelandic Settlers in America*. Winnipeg: Queenston House.

Smitherman, Geneva (2000). *Talkin That Talk: Language, Culture and Education in African American*. New York: Routledge.

Spicer, Edward H. (1962). *Cycles of Conquest: The Impact of Spain, Mexico and the U.S. on the Indians of the*

Southwest, 1533–1960. Tucson: University of Arizona Press.

Statistics Canada (1993). *Language Retention and Transfer*. Ottawa: Industry, Science and Technology.

Statistics Canada (1994). *Languages in Canada*. Scarborough, Ontario: Prentice-Hall.

Statistics Canada (1995). *Profile of Canada's Aboriginal Population* (= no. 94–325). Ottawa: Industry, Science and Technology.

Taylor, Charles (1992). *Multiculturalism: Examining the Politics of Recognition*. Princeton, NJ: Princeton University Press.

Tisch, Joseph LeSage (1959). *Louisiana French*. New Orleans: A. F. Labord.

US Department of Labor (1975). *A Socio-Economic Profile of Puerto Rican New Yorkers*. New York: Bureau of Labor Statistics.

Ureland, P. Sture (ed.) (2001). *Global Eurolinguistics: European Languages in North America*. Tübingen: Max Niemeyer.

Van den Hoonaard, W. C. (1991). *Silent Ethnicity: The Dutch of New Brunswick*. Fredericton, NB: New Ireland Press.

Varo, Carlos (1971). *Consideraciones antropológicas y políticas en torno a la enseñanza del "Spanglish" in Nueva York* [Anthropological and political considerations on the teaching of "Spanglish" in New York]. Rio Piedras, Puerto Rico: Libería internacional.

Velikonia, Joseph (1963). *Italians in the U.S.: A Bibliography* (= Occasional Paper no. 1). Carbondale: Southern Illinois University, Geography Department.

Veltman, Calvin (1983). *Language Shift in the United States*. Berlin: Mouton de Gruyter.

Wood, Ralph C. (ed.) (1942). *The Pennsylvania Germans*. Princeton, NJ: Princeton University Press.

Woodcock, George and Avakumovic, I. (1977). *The Doukhobors*. Toronto: McClelland.

Wytrwal, Joseph A. (1961). *America's Polish Heritage*. Detroit, MI: Endurance Press.

Young, C. H. (1931). *Ukrainian Canadians*. Toronto: Nelson.

Zentella, A. C. (1997). *Growing up Bilingual: Puerto Rican Children in New York*. Oxford: Blackwell.

FURTHER READING

Alba, Richard (1990). *Ethnic Identity*. New Haven, CT: Yale University Press.

Borins, S. F. (1985). *The Language of the Skies: The Bilingual Air Traffic Control Conflict in Canada*. Montreal: McGill-Queen's University Press.

Canada (1992). *Official Languages Act: Annotated Version*. Ottawa: Supply and Services.

Castonguay, Charles (1994). *L'Assimilation linguistique: mesure et evaluation, 1971–1986*. [Language shift: Measurement and evaluation,

1971–1986]. Quebec, Conseil de la langue française.

Commissioner of Official Languages (1970–2001). *Annual Reports*. Ottawa: Office of the Commissioner of Official Languages.

Corbeil, Jean-Claude (1980). *L'aménagement linguistique du Québec* [The language management of Quebec]. Montreal: Guérin.

Dulong, Gaston (1966). *Bibliographie linguistique du Canada français* [Linguistic bibliography of

French Canada]. Paris: Klincksieck.

Edwards, John (1994). *Multilingualism*. London: Routledge.

Fishman, Joshua A., Gertner, M. H., Lowy, E. G., and Milán, W. G. (eds.) (1985). *The Rise and Fall of the Ethnic Revival*. Berlin: Mouton de Gruyter.

Hamers, Josiane and Blanc, Michel (2000). *Bilinguality and Bilingualism*, 2nd edn. Cambridge, UK: Cambridge University Press.

Haugen, Einar (1987). *Blessings of Babel*. Berlin: Mouton de Gruyter.

Huebner, Thom and Davis, K. A. (eds.) (1999). *Sociopolitical Perspectives on Language Policy and Planning in the USA*. Amsterdam: John Benjamins.

Joy, Richard (1972). *Languages in Conflict: The Progress of Bilingualism*. Toronto: University of Toronto Press.

Kelly, Louis G. (ed.) (1969). *Description and Measurement of Bilingualism*. Toronto: University of Toronto Press (for the Canadian Commission for Unesco).

Kymlicka, Will (1995). *Multicultural Citizenship*. Oxford: Clarendon.

Laird, Charlton (1970). *Language in America*. Englewood Cliffs: Prentice-Hall.

Levine, M. V. (1990). *The Reconquest of Montreal*. Philadelphia: Temple University Press.

Li Wei, Dewaele, Jean-Marc, and Housen, Alex (eds.) (2002). *Opportunities and Challenges of Bilingualism*. Berlin: Mouton de Gruyter.

Mackey, William F. (1976). *Bilinguisme et contact des langues* [Bilingualism and language contact]. Paris: Klincksieck.

Maurais, Jacques and Morris, Michael A. (eds.) (2003). *Language in a Globalizing World*. Cambridge: Cambridge University Press.

Philipponneau, Catherine (ed.). (1995). *Vers un aménagement linguistique de l'Acadie* [Toward language management of Acadia]. Moncton, NB: Centre de recherche en linguistique appliquée, Université de Moncton.

Plourde, Michel (2001). *Le français au Québec: 400 ans d'histoire* [French in Quebec: 400 years of history]. Montreal: Fides.

Rebuffot, Jacques (1993). *Le point sur l'immersion*. [Immersion: the state of the art]. Montreal: CFC.

Sheppard, C. A. (1971). *The Law of Languages in Canada*. Ottawa: Information Canada.

Treasury Board (1970–2001). *Official Languages in Federal Institutions*. (Annual Reports.) Ottawa: Supply and Services.

Villa, Daniel (ed.) (2000). *Studies in Language Contact: Spanish in the U.S.* (= *Southwest Journal of Linguistics*, 19(2)). Commerce, TX: A&M University.

Wade, Mason (1968). *The French Canadians*, 2 vols. Toronto: Macmillan.

Wardhaugh, Ronald (1987). *Languages in Competition*. Oxford: Blackwell.

Weinreich, Uriel (1968). *Languages in Contact*. The Hague: Mouton.

24 Bilingualism in Latin America

ANNA MARIA ESCOBAR

24.1 Introduction

Spanish-speaking Latin America consists of 18 countries, Puerto Rico, and the US Southwest (see chapter 23 for this last region). Portuguese-speaking Latin America comprises only Brazil, which, with a population of 174.5 million (2002), is the second-largest country in the Americas after the United States. Latin America is home to eight percent of the world's population (United Nations, 2003).

A history of colonization by Spain and Portugal in the fifteenth and sixteenth centuries unites all of the countries of Latin America. They were settled within the first century of the conquest, which in sociological terms is considered a fairly quick colonization. Because not all of the areas settled were of equal economic importance to the Spanish crown, some less important economic regions were administratively incorporated into larger ones. These initial groupings had consequences for the subsequent histories of the modern countries and for their relationships with each other.

When the Spaniards and the Portuguese came to what is now Latin America, they came into contact with numerous indigenous linguistic communities. Some archaeologists believe that in 1492 approximately 2,000 separate languages were spoken in the Americas (Willey, 1971). Some of these languages became extinct soon after the arrival of the Europeans, as a consequence of the many deaths and displacements that the conquest brought. Among them are Taino, an Arahuacan language spoken in the Caribbean and Venezuela, and Chibcha, a language spoken in what is now Panama and Colombia.

Little is known of the different language families which existed when the Spaniards and Portuguese came, although the languages spoken by the larger and more powerful indigenous groups at the time, such as Náhuatl (in Mesoamerica), Quechua (in the Andean region), Guaraní (in the Paraguayan region), and Mapudungu (in Chile) did become known. These languages were further expanded as lingua francas by the Spanish missionaries, who used them for evangelization purposes and who wrote the first grammars of indigenous languages in the sixteenth and early seventeenth centuries (for example, Quechua in 1560, and Guaraní in 1620).

Although attention to bilingualism in the classroom seems to be a phenomenon of the twentieth century, during the early colonial period various bilingual literacy programs were implemented by the Spanish missionaries as part of the Christianization campaign, and served as examples for other parts of the Spanish colony. These bilingual programs were directed by priests (mostly Jesuits) and maintained until the middle of the eighteenth century, when a Spanish-only policy was instituted by the Spanish crown for all the colony in the New World. The objectives of these programs were twofold: to evangelize in the indigenous language, and to teach Spanish to the indigenous elite who attended the schools.

Independence from Spain and Portugal was obtained by all Latin American countries in the nineteenth century. Differences between the countries are expressed in shared social and linguistic characteristics.

The *Caribbean region* was colonized first. In 1492, Christopher Columbus left the first Spanish settlement in the New World on the northern coast of what is now known as the Dominican Republic. Although the indigenous languages of the Caribbean region became extinct in the early colonization period, from this first period of language contact, many lexical borrowings from indigenous languages remain in Spanish. For example, from the Taino language come *canoa, cacique, maíz, tabaco*. However, many contact linguistic characteristics of Spanish Caribbean dialects are attributed to the influence from African languages (Lipski, 1994), and not to indigenous languages. Spaniards and Portuguese had been bringing African slaves first to Europe, and later to the American continent, since the fifteenth century. Slaves were brought mainly from East Africa, and later from West Africa as well, until the middle of the nineteenth century, when slavery was abolished at approximately the same time in all Latin America. Although Afro-influenced varieties of Spanish can be found in several regions of Latin America, the most pervasive influence is found in the Spanish varieties in the Caribbean and the Atlantic coastal areas (Lipski, 1994).

The first contact with a large indigenous community on the mainland was with the Aztecs, who were in power in what is today *Mexico*. Mexico City, which was founded over the Aztec city of Tenochtitlán, became the most important city of the Spanish colony. Until 1540, Mexico City was the principal destination of newcomers from Spain to the New World, when Lima became the most important destination. During the settlement of Mexico, other Spaniards ventured into what is today the United States (Audience of New Galicia). Although the original Spaniards went as far north as New York in the East, the towns that were founded by the Spaniards were in the western region, which was not occupied by the English or French.

The histories of the countries of *Central America* are intimately linked to that of Mexico. Many of the Spaniards who were not granted lands around Mexico City were given agricultural lands in areas as far away as what are now the countries of Central America. It is not by coincidence, then, that the Central American countries strove to obtain their independence from Spain in the same year as did Mexico, in 1821, in order to secure their new political status.

The modern *Andean countries* were linked even before the Spaniards arrived, because most of the various indigenous communities in the region had been conquered by the Quechua-speaking Incas, and were part of the Inca Empire. This empire extended from part of what is today Colombia down to the Maule River in Chile and the northern part of Argentina. Today, Quechua, the language imposed by the Incas in their conquered lands, is the most widely spoken indigenous language on the American continent, with estimates ranging from 8 to 12 million speakers. Lima, after Mexico City the second most important city in the New World, was founded in 1535 near the coast, where a small Inca town existed. The Andean region has the highest concentration of indigenous populations in the Americas.

Whereas Lima, the capital of the Southern Viceroy, was in the Andean region, the *Southern Cone countries* (Chile, Paraguay, Argentina, and Uruguay) were not only geographically further away and less populated, but the financial benefits of this region to the Spanish crown were considered to be much lower. As a consequence, the historical characteristics of countries in the Southern Cone are different from those of the Andes (see 24.2.3 and 24.2.4).

Contact between Spanish and the indigenous languages began when the Spaniards settled in American territory. However, during colonial times bilingualism was bi-directional, since merchants and priests (who in the early colonial period were present in high numbers) learned the indigenous languages of the region they worked in, and some indigenous elite in turn learned Spanish. By contrast, in modern times bilingualism is mostly unidirectional, from the indigenous language toward Spanish, although different degrees of proficiency in Spanish are evident. Thus, the degree of bilingualism in Spanish varies greatly in the Andean region and Guatemala, whereas in Mexico and Chile, high percentages of Spanish-dominant bilinguals are found.

In modern times, considerable efforts have been made toward the preservation and recording of indigenous languages. Beginning in the middle of the twentieth century, the Summer Institute of Linguistics has done extensive work on indigenous languages (except in Paraguay and Venezuela), and many Latin American countries have created indigenous-language programs. One difficulty in compiling information about the many languages (or even just knowing the actual number of languages) is the fact that several names are given to varieties of the same language. For example, in Mexico, Matlatzinca, Ocuilteco, and Tlahura are three varieties of the same language, and the same is true for Guanano, Anana, Kótedia in Colombia, and Cashibo, Managua, Hagueti in Peru (Grimes, 1988). In 1999, linguists from the State University of Campinas (Brazil) proposed at the Second National Congress of the Brazilian Association of Linguistics that a systematic study of the indigenous languages of Latin America be undertaken in order to promote comparative studies. The project distinguishes the ten linguistic areas differentiated on an archaeological basis by

Willey (1971): Mesoamerica, Caribbean, Intermediate, Peruvian, South Andean, Amazonian, Oriental-Brazilian, Chaco, Pampean, Del Fuego. The project has a website (www.unicamp.br/), a journal (*LIAMES, Revista de Línguas Indígenas Americanas*), and a list-serve.

In the discussion that follows, we divide the countries in Latin America into groups according to historical and linguistic criteria. For each regional grouping, we describe the current sociolinguistic characteristics. The social aspects of their multilingual situations are indicated by data on language policy, bilingual education, urbanization, and illiteracy rates. The linguistic data are limited to numbers of indigenous languages (identifying indigenous languages with more than 500,000 speakers), their areas of concentration, and the general linguistic features of the Spanish of the region.

24.2   Sociolinguistic Characteristics

Although sociolinguists agree that a detailed analysis of the social character-istics of a linguistic community is necessary when studying bilingual and mul-tilingual issues, little in the way of comparative work on the characteristics of the different regions in Latin America has been done. The two primary reasons for this are the sparsity of relevant information found in the census of each country that can be used by language planners and linguists interested in these issues, and the relative isolation of the studies that have been done through the years.

Nevertheless, in recent decades, considerable efforts to collect information on indigenous languages have been made by Latin American linguists. In the early 1960s, a group of Latin American linguists created PILEI (Programa Interamericano de Lingüística y Enseñanza de Idiomas), the Inter-American Program of Linguistics and Teaching of Languages, the main objective of which was to promote research on the different languages spoken in Spanish- and Portuguese-speaking regions in the Americas. Immediately after, ALFAL (Asociación de Lingüística y Filología de América Latina), the Linguistics and Philology Association of Latin America, was founded by the same scholars with the purpose of serving as the platform for researchers to exchange the results of their studies.

At the early meetings of PILEI (which was later absorbed by ALFAL), a consensus was reached to begin with a study describing the standard varieties of all the capitals of Spanish-speaking countries, in order to use it as a bench-mark. This longitudinal study has produced several kinds of materials, includ-ing transcriptions of speakers of the standard varieties of Mexico City, San Juan, Caracas, Bogota, Lima, Santiago, Buenos Aires, and, for comparative pur-poses, Seville and Madrid (Spain). Other varieties of Spanish were also studied, including popular varieties of specific regions, such as Antigua and Mexico City, Bogota, La Paz, Uruguay, the US Southwest, and Seville. Some of these transcriptions are also available on CD-ROM, published by the University of

Las Palmas in the Canary Islands. Independently, other researchers have described varieties of Spanish which have developed in contact situations. The majority of these studies concern varieties of Spanish in contact with Quechua (in the Andean region), with Guaraní (in Paraguay), and with Mayan languages (in Mexico and Guatemala). Only in the 1990s did the study of Spanish in contact with other indigenous languages begin to develop, especially in Mexico.

A later project organized by ALFAL involved the development of materials containing various types of texts representing historical varieties of Spanish of the different Spanish-speaking countries. Although fewer materials are available from this project (see Fontanella de Weinberg, 1993; Rivarola, 2000; Rojas, 1999), at ALFAL meetings (held once every three years), many historical linguistic studies are presented. The latest project involves sociolinguistic studies of several countries, following the methodology the two earlier large projects had established.

While information is available about the linguistic characteristics of various Spanish varieties in Latin America, less is known, in comparative terms, and less has been done, in the areas of language policy and bilingual education. The most comprehensive study of language policy and bilingual education in Latin America is Gleich's (1989) book, which was funded by the Deutsche Gesellschaft für Technische Zusammenarbeit, but now needs to be updated. In the following subsections, Latin American sociolinguistic regions are differentiated with a view to describing their main sociolinguistic characteristics and the types of advances that have been made in the areas of language policy and bilingual education.

Although many European and other world languages (Japanese, Chinese, Hebrew, Arabic) are spoken in the various Latin American countries, when they make reference to bilingual education, the government language policies are directed solely at indigenous languages. For most indigenous languages, estimates of the numbers of speakers are rough approximations. The Ethnologue, published and maintained by the Summer Institute of Linguistics (www.sil.org), provides numbers regarding the indigenous languages spoken in the countries presented below.

24.2.1   Mexico and Central America

The Mexico-Central American region includes Mexico, a large country with close to 100 million inhabitants, and six smaller countries, ranging in population size from Guatemala, with a population of 12.7 million, to Panama, with a population of 2.8 million. Of these countries, Mexico and Guatemala have been very active in bilingual education programs and in studies of the indigenous heritage in their respective countries.

The two indigenous languages with the greatest number of speakers in Mexico are Maya and Náhuatl. According to the 2000 census, indigenous languages are spoken by more than 23 percent of the population in the Southern

Table 24.1 Sociolinguistic characteristics of Mexico and Central America.

	Population (millions)	Indigenous languages[a]	Indigenous languages with more than half a million speakers[a]	Illiteracy (%)[b] Female	Illiteracy (%)[b] Male	Poverty (%)[c]	Urbanization (%)
Mexico (2000)[d]	97.4	56	Náhuatl, Maya	12.8	8.2	32	75
Guatemala (2000)[e]	12.7	24	Maya (20 languages)	42.5	27.1	60	41.5
El Salvador (1999)[f]	6.2	3	—	27	21	48	45
Honduras (1999)[f]	6.3	8	—	31	30	63	43
Nicaragua (1999)[f]	4.9	4	—	37	37		
Costa Rica (2001)[g]	3.8	5		10.4		24	59
Panama (1999)[f]	2.8	8	—	10	9		

[a] For all countries except Mexico and Guatemala, figures are based on data provided by the Ethnologue of the Summer Institute of Linguistics (www.sil.org).

[b] Illiteracy percentages are based on data from the United Nations (www.un.org). The percentages are for urban illiteracy in 1996.

[c] Illiteracy percentages are for urban illiteracy.

[d] Based on information provided by the Instituto Nacional de Estadística, Geografía e Informática (www.inegi.gob.mx) taken from the 2000 census of Mexico, and Francis and Nieto (2000). Urbanization data is based on information of the population living in towns with over 2,500 inhabitants.

[e] Based on information in the Instituto Nacional de Estadística (server.rds.org.ft/~ine/censo) of Guatemala and Prensa Libre (2001).

[f] Based on information in the United Nations Database (www.un.org).

[g] Based on information in the Instituto Nacional de Estadística y Censos (www.inec.go.cr) of Costa Rica for 2001.

Mexican districts of Quintana Roo (23 percent Mayan), Chiapas (25 percent Mayan), Oaxaca (37 percent Otomanguean and Mayan) and Yucatán (37 percent Mayan).

Although Mexico's bilingual programs during the colonial times were the first bilingual literacy experiments in the Western hemisphere, their objective was mainly evangelization. It was in the twentieth century that the Mexican bilingual education programs came to have literacy in two languages as the main objective. Since the Mexican Revolution in 1910, the Mexican government is the institution responsible for educational policy. However, bilingual literacy programs only emerged, albeit briefly, at the end of the 1930s under President Cárdenas's creation of the Autonomous Department of Indigenous Affairs. Although initially the ADIA was interested mainly in agricultural and education matters, in 1947 it was incorporated into the Secretariat of Public Education. It promoted bilingual education at the national level, although with limitations; consequently, it largely failed to reach the main target population, which lived in rural areas.

In 1948, the famous National Institute of Indigenism was created. This institute, a product of the indigenism movement which flourished in Latin America at the time, had had its First Inter-American Congress of Indigenism in 1940 in Mexico, and in the decades to follow similar institutions were created throughout Latin America. Since the 1960s, new bilingual programs have emerged in Mexico, which seek to teach children literacy skills in both their native language and in Spanish. These bilingual programs run until the 5th or 6th grade, after which instruction is in Spanish. In the 1990s, additional bilingual and bicultural programs were established in more distant areas, where the majority of the population were speakers of an indigenous language. Nowadays, the government promotes the development of bilingual literacy materials in Mexico's 56 indigenous languages. It is widely recognized, however, that indigenous languages are being displaced by Spanish because of their oral status, and that they will only survive if a sustainable literary tradition is developed (cf. Salinas Pedraza, 1996). Publications on indigenous languages largely consist of descriptions of the indigenous languages and the creation of literacy materials. Less is also available on varieties of Spanish in contact with indigenous languages.

In Guatemala, it is only since the last constitution of 1985 that the government has recognized and supported the development of all the languages and cultures present inside its territory, ending a transition-to-Spanish policy that had been maintained since colonial times. The new policy entails the publication of materials and the development of bilingual education programs which teach the indigenous language through the 4th grade, with a stated intention of extending it through the 6th grade. However, Richards and Richards (1996) report that since 1985 publications of materials in indigenous languages have increased.

Of a total of 29 modern Maya languages, 20 are spoken in Guatemala. Four languages are spoken by communities of 400 thousand or more: Kaqchikel, Mam, K'iche', and Q'eqchi'; together, speakers of these four languages represent

80 percent of the Maya-speaking population (Richards and Richards, 1996). Speakers of these four languages occupy an extensive territory of Guatemala, concentrated mainly in the departments of San Marcos, Alta Verapaz, El Quiché, and Huehuetenango, that is, the central and west-central regions. Mayan languages in Guatemala use a unified phonemic alphabetic writing system, which was officially adopted in 1987, although Mayan languages had a writing system which combined logographic and phonetic symbols when the Spaniards arrived in the sixteenth century.

Guatemala has been very active in promoting bilingual education at both the governmental and grassroots levels. In 2001, some form of bilingual education was present in half the departments of the country.

El Salvador and Honduras have small indigenous populations, and all speakers are highly bilingual in Spanish. El Salvador's largest indigenous community is the Lenca, with approximately 37,000 speakers. Honduras's largest indigenous community is the Garífuna, with approximately 70,000 speakers.

The largest indigenous population in Nicaragua is the Miskitu, with a population of more than 100,000. The Miskitu language is also used as a lingua franca along the eastern coast of the country. During the Sandinista government, a Spanish-language national literacy program was launched. The reaction to this policy was so pronounced that an indigenous organization called MISURASATA (Miskitu, Sumu, Rama, and Sandinistas in Unity) was formed, and soon succeeded in overturning the policy and forcing the government to allow the development of materials in Miskitu, Sumu, and English, as well as the coordination of a literacy campaign in Miskitu and Sumu in the region (Freeland, 1999).

Costa Rica's largest indigenous community is the Bribri (Chibcha) with approximately 7,500 speakers in 1985 (Lastra, 1992, p. 114). Although the younger generations of the indigenous communities speak Spanish, the government is trying to preserve the indigenous languages of the country. The indigenous population in Panama is also small, with Guaymí (or Ngäbere) being the largest, with approximately 45,000 speakers. Despite the relatively small number of speakers, in 1972 bilingual education was legalized for the indigenous population. In addition, the Kuna and Emberá had their territory legally secured as well (Gleich, 1989).

24.2.2   *Caribbean*

When the Spaniards arrived at the end of the fifteenth and the early sixteenth centuries, most of the indigenous populations in the Caribbean were speakers of Arahuacan languages. Because of the geographical constraints of islands, the numerous diseases they were exposed to, and their weak defense in face of the military confrontations they had with the Spaniards, most indigenous inhabitants of the islands escaped to other areas of the Caribbean or died within the first 100 years of Spanish colonization. As a consequence, the bilingualism we find in the Caribbean region nowadays is not with Amerindian languages,

Table 24.2 Sociolinguistic characteristics of the Caribbean region.

| | Population (millions) | Indigenous languages[a] | Indigenous languages with more than half a million speakers[a] | Illiteracy (%)[b] | | Poverty (%)[c] | Urbanization (%) |
				Female	Male		
Cuba[d]	11.2	0	—	0.2	0.2		75
Puerto Rico[e]	3.8	0	—	7	7		
Dominican Republic[f]	8.6	0	—	21		36	56

[a] Based on data in the Ethnologue of the Summer Institute of Linguistics (www.sil.org).
[b] Illiteracy percentages are based on data from the United Nations (www.un.org). The percentages are for urban illiteracy in 1996.
[c] Numbers for the Dominican Republic are taken from Wodon (2000).
[d] Population and urbanization data for Cuba are found in Oficina Nacional de Estadísticas of Cuba (1999).
[e] Population data provided by the US census (www.census.gov).
[f] Based on data from the Oficina Nacional de Estadística (www.one.do) of the Dominican Republic. Population data are for the year 2000. Data for illiteracy and urbanization are for 1993.

but with other European languages which came later (English in Puerto Rico, French in the Dominican Republic).

Since the sixteenth century, Spanish has been in contact with the African languages spoken by the slaves the Spaniards brought with them. It is generally believed that some African language groups came in greater numbers to certain parts of Latin America. It has been reported that most African slaves who came to Puerto Rico came from the Sudan and spoke Bantu languages. None of these three Caribbean nations today has any speakers of indigenous languages.

Because of Puerto Rico's political status as part of the United States Commonwealth, both English and Spanish are official languages in Puerto Rico. Since the Constitution of 1952, bilingual education in Puerto Rico has promoted the teaching of Spanish, alongside English.

In the Dominican Republic, Haitian Creole is spoken by approximately 2 percent of the total population, mainly in the western region, which borders Haiti.

24.2.3 *Andean region*

The countries included in the Andean region as presented in table 24.3 share economic-political criteria (as do the countries which form the Southern Cone, all members of the economic group called Mercosur; see 24.2.4). In many sociolinguistic studies, however, the Andean region refers to Ecuador, Peru, Bolivia, and, sometimes, because of the concentration of Quechua and Aymara speakers there, the northern part of Argentina. Quechua is the most widely spoken indigenous language in the Americas, as mentioned earlier.

In Venezuela, most of the speakers of indigenous languages are concentrated in the eastern or Amazonian region, which borders Brazil and southeastern Colombia. The largest indigenous communities are the Guajiro, with approximately 100,000 speakers, and the Yanomamö, with approximately 20,000 speakers. Until the late 1980s the government had not given much attention to either indigenous language maintenance or bilingual education (Lastra, 1992, p. 129), although the educational policy does mention respect for the sociocultural value of indigenous populations with the purpose of integrating them into the national society (Gleich, 1989).

The total indigenous population of Colombia is small, although many indigenous languages are represented. Moreover, they are mostly spread throughout the country and there is extensive bilingualism in Spanish. The largest indigenous community is the Colombian Guajiro, with approximately 82,000 speakers. Palenquero, a Spanish-based creole, is spoken southeast of Cartagena in the village of San Basilio de Palenque. This language, derived from a linguistic variety spoken by runaway slaves in the seventeenth century, had 3,000 speakers in 1980 according to the SIL. While the government has officially supported bilingual education since 1978, little has been done to implement bilingual programs.

In Ecuador, communities of indigenous language speakers are found in the highlands, the Amazon basin, and the western tropical regions. Quichua (a

Table 24.3 Sociolinguistic characteristics of the Andean region.

	Population (millions)	Indigenous languages[a]	Indigenous languages with more than half a million speakers[a]	Illiteracy (%)[b] Female	Male	Poverty (%)[c]	Urbanization (%)
Venezuela (2000)[d]	23.5	38	—	9	8	41	
Colombia (1993)[e]	33.1	74	—	10	9	52	
Ecuador (2001)[f]	12.1	22	Quichua	12	8	55	61
Peru (2000)[g]	25.9	83	Quechua, Aymara	17	7	48	72
Bolivia (2000)[h]	8.3	35	Aymara, Quechua	19.6	7.4	66	54

[a] Based on data in the Ethnologue of the Summer Institute of Linguistics (www.sil.org).
[b] Illiteracy data based on information provided by the United Nations (www.un.org). The percentages are for urban illiteracy in 1996.
[c] Numbers for all countries except Peru are taken from Wodon (2000).
[d] Population data based on information provided by the Instituto Nacional de Estadística (ocei.gov.ve/ine/) of Venezuela for the 2001 census. Data on illiteracy and urbanization percentages are taken from the United Nations database (www.un.org).
[e] Based on data from the Departamento Administrativo Nacional de Estadística (www.dane.gov.co) of Colombia for 1993. Data on illiteracy and urbanization percentages are taken from the United Nations database (www.un.org).
[f] Based on data from the 2001 census from the Instituto Nacional de Estadística y Censos (www4.inec.gov.ec) of Ecuador.
[g] Based on data from the Instituto Nacional de Estadística e Informática (www.inei.gob.pe) of Peru for 2000.
[h] Based on data from the Instituto Nacional de Estadística (www.ine.gov.bo) of Bolivia for 2000.

Quechua dialect) is spoken in the highlands. Beginning in the 1960s, ethnic and local political groups emerged to defend their interests, demanding, among other things, education and language policy reform (King, 1996). In 1980, a unified variety of Quichua was agreed upon by representatives of speakers of different varieties, and in the same year, intercultural bilingual education was made official in primary and secondary schools in communities with prominent indigenous populations. The constitution of 1983 acknowledges the pluricultural condition of Ecuador; Spanish is the official language, while all indigenous languages are considered national languages, whose use is guaranteed by the government in areas where their speakers predominate. In 1988, a National Directorate of Bilingual Intercultural Education was established. In 1993, after an experimental project funded by the German government ended, leaving materials and experience behind, the Directorate was renewed.

In the 1980s, ethnic communities organized grassroots movements which have been instrumental in changing policy from the bottom up (Hornberger, 1996). They have led to the development of programs of bilingual education in Ecuador which were not created by foreign institutions and, more importantly, are supported and led by locals. For example, the Shuar (Jíbaro) have bilingual education programs through the radio, and are assisted by local teachers in different parts of the Southeastern region of Ecuador (King, 1996).

Peru's Quechua-speaking population is concentrated in the Andean region, as are its Aymara-speaking communities. The Amazonian region includes many smaller communities of indigenous-language speakers. The situation of Peru is similar to that of Guatemala and Paraguay, in that one indigenous language or language family is spoken by most indigenous-language speakers; thus, Quechua speakers in Peru represent 90 percent of all the indigenous language speakers.

The first programs of bilingual education in Peru were coordinated by the Summer Institute of Linguistics, whose members have worked with Andean and, especially, Amazonian languages since the 1950s, developing materials, training teachers, organizing native literacy and sponsoring workshops (Hornberger, 1994). Bilingual education in Peru started in 1975 with the first National Policy on Bilingual Education, which recognized the need to use indigenous languages in education in areas where they were spoken. This policy served at the time as a model for other regions in Latin America. Although the objective was to promote Spanish as the common language, respect for and the revitalization of indigenous languages were supported. The latest policy, drafted in 1991, reaffirms the need for bilingual education in areas where speakers of an indigenous language are dominant. Bilingual programs derived from these policies have been, however, mainly experimental, and largely funded by foreign institutions. Moreover, these programs reach only 10 percent of the target population (Zúñiga, Sánchez, and Zacharías, 2000). Language planners face many challenges when pursuing bilingual education programs for all indigenous language speakers; they include: the language and dialect diversification that exists in Peru; the lack of precise information about numbers of speakers; the extent of variation in degrees of bilingualism in Spanish; the need for teachers, and, of course, financial limitations. However, parents of the indigenous-language speaking children, and especially teachers, have positive attitudes toward bilingual education. It is seen as a way of acquiring Spanish to better integrate themselves into the national community, while maintaining their cultural identity (Zúñiga, Sánchez, and Zacharías, 2000). The need for bilingual education programs exists in both the Andean and Amazonian regions. In the last decades, however, due to high levels of migration toward the coastal areas, where Spanish monolingualism is the norm, bilingual education programs are also acutely needed there. Concentrations of Quechua language speakers are found mainly in the southern departments of Apurímac, Ayacucho, Cuzco, Huancavelica, and Puno, where the illiteracy rate is also high (higher than 25 percent).

The largest ethnic groups in Bolivia are Quechua (approximately 3 million) and Aymara (approximately 2 million). The total indigenous population in Bolivia is 63 percent, the highest percentage in the Andes, while Ecuador has 30 percent (King, 1996) and Peru had 22 percent in 1983 (Hornberger, 1994). In 1994, the Bolivian government proposed a National Education Reform, which incorporated a bilingual intercultural education program for the whole country. This program had reached one-third of Bolivian schools by 1996 (Hornberger and King, 1996). The commitment of the government and the unification of the varieties of each indigenous language have allowed for the revitalization of the indigenous languages and their use in new domains (Hornberger and King, 1996).

Although national poverty levels in the Andean countries are already high (ranging from 41 percent for Venezuela to 64 percent for Bolivia; Wodon, 2000), the differences between poverty found in urban and rural areas is also striking. Thus, for example, while the poverty in urban areas of Peru is 37 percent, it is 70 percent in rural areas. In Bolivia, while the poverty percentage is 50 percent in urban areas, it is 82 percent in rural areas. Unfortunately, poverty levels are seldom given for urban and rural areas in the census. From a sociolinguistic perspective, however, these figures provide some indication of the services (or lack of services), such as schools, that likely exist in these rural regions where indigenous-language speakers tend to be predominant.

24.2.4   *Southern Cone*

The Southern Cone is defined here in geographic and economic terms, but also, as mentioned earlier, in historical terms. While Paraguay was settled early by the Spaniards, it was mostly abandoned by the Spanish administration and left to the Jesuits, mainly because of the lack of precious metals in the area. The Audience of Charcas, to which Paraguay belonged, included territory that covered Bolivia, Paraguay, Argentina, and Uruguay, with the Bolivian region being the most important because of the silver mines of Potosí. Until they were expelled by the Spanish crown in the eighteenth century, the Jesuits were very active in learning Guaraní and promoting bilingualism in

Table 24.4 Sociolinguistic characteristics of the Southern Cone region.

	Population (millions)	Indigenous languages[a]	Indigenous languages with more than half a million speakers[a]	Illiteracy (%)[b]		Poverty (%)[c]	Urbanization (%)
				Female	Male		
Paraguay (1992)[d]	4.1	19	Guaraní	10		39	50
Uruguay[e]	3.4	0	—	2	3	19	91
Argentina (2000)[f]	36.0	21	Aymara, Quechua	4	4	15	87
Chile (1998)[g]	15.4	6	Mapudungu	5	5	28	86

[a] Based on data in the Ethnologue of the Summer Institute of Linguistics (www.sil.org).
[b] Illiteracy percentages are based on data in the United Nations database (www.un.org). The percentages are for urban illiteracy in 1996.
[c] Poverty percentages for all countries except Chile are based on data provided in Wodon (2000).
[d] Based on data in the Dirección General de Estadística, Encuestas y Censos (www.dgeec.gov.py) of Paraguay, and Gynan (2001) for 1992.
[e] Based on data in the Instituto Nacional de Estadística (ine.gub.uy) of Uruguay for 2002. The urbanization data is for 1996.
[f] Population number taken from the Instituto Demográfico y Censal (www.indec.mecon.ar) of Argentina. Percentages for illiteracy and urbanization are taken from data provided by the United Nations for 1995 (www.un.org).
[g] Based on data from the Instituto Nacional de Estadística (www.ine.cl) of Chile. Since only the total population and urbanization data of the 2002 census are available at this time, their estimated projections for 1998, based on the 1992 census, are presented for illiteracy and poverty percentages.

the region during the early colonial period. Chile, Argentina, and Uruguay, in the twentieth century, are the most Europeanized countries in Latin America.

Languages other than Spanish spoken in Paraguay today are Guaraní, Amazonian languages, and Portuguese. Guaraní was declared an official language of Paraguay along with Spanish in 1992 after the 35-year-long dictatorship of Stroessner. In 1994, 88 percent of the population spoke Guaraní, while only 54 percent spoke Spanish. While some departments are predominantly Guaraní monolingual (San Pedro 81 percent, Caazapá 76 percent, Concepción 69 percent), the capital and its surroundings are mainly bilingual (Asunción 74 percent, Central 79 percent). Sixty-eight percent of rural school-age children are monolingual in Guaraní. Portuguese is strong in some eastern departments (Canindeyú 33 percent, Alto Paraná 17 percent), and in their rural areas it reaches 87 percent of the population. Gynan considers that in view of these numbers, it can only be concluded that the bilingualism situation in Paraguay has been misunderstood and, in fact, the country is not largely bilingual as previously thought (Gynan, 2001). High rates of bilingualism (75 percent) are confined to urban areas, while Guaraní monolingualism reaches 83 percent in rural areas. Spanish monolingualism is mainly found in the capital, Asunción, where it is 20 percent. In the 1990s, a proposal for mother-tongue literacy and bilingual education was implemented. It supports communication in both languages and bilingual education in rural areas. Gynan argues that although Paraguay's language policy is the most progressive in Latin America, the complexity of the country's sociolinguistic reality makes its implementation difficult (2001, p. 163).

Chile was also settled early in the conquest period, but was considered financially productive only in the northern region because of its mines. The southern region was left to the indigenous population, who fiercely resisted the Spanish invasion. Today, the largest indigenous language population is found in the southern region, where Mapudungu is spoken. A small Aymara population also lives in the northern region bordering Bolivia. While the educational policy of Chile respects the indigenous heritage, it promotes integration into national society. Hence, the Mapuche (who are the speakers of Mapudungu) continue fighting for their rights.

Argentina has a large concentration of speakers of Quechua in the northern region which borders Bolivia (approximately 900,000 speakers). Other indigenous-language speakers include Guaraní speakers who live in areas bordering Paraguay (approximately 200,000 speakers), and Mapudungu speakers who live in an area bordering southern Chile (approximately 40,000 speakers). Italian speakers, however, have come in significant numbers since the nineteenth century to Argentina. Chile and Paraguay have also had an important presence of German speakers in the twentieth century. In Argentina, an educational law of 1985 protects the interests of indigenous minorities, but no efforts have been made to create bilingual education programs.

No indigenous languages are reported for Uruguay. Instead, Portuguese-Spanish bilingualism is mainly found in the northeastern region which borders

Brazil, where *Fronteriço*, a contact variety, is also spoken. However, no bilingual education programs exist (Gleich, 1989).

24.3   Bilingualism

Societal bilingualism in Latin America refers to bilingualism between an indigenous language and Spanish (except for Uruguay and that part of Paraguay that combines Spanish and Portuguese, and for Puerto Rico and the US southwest, where Spanish-English bilingualism is found). The sociolinguistic characteristics of bilingualism with indigenous languages in Latin America are defined by the number of languages in the country, the size of the indigenous language populations, their areas of concentration in rural and urban areas (although this last kind of information is not always available), the poverty levels of rural and urban areas, the government's language policy, and the presence of a predominant indigenous language population.

Traditionally, the rural/urban dimension seems to be an important sociolinguistic indicator when describing Latin American countries. High levels of urbanization seem to indicate a predominant shift to Spanish (Chile, Argentina, Uruguay), whereas countries with low levels of urbanization seem to indicate a higher level of maintenance of indigenous languages (Guatemala, Paraguay, Bolivia). However, the survival and maintenance of indigenous languages and the support for bilingual education seem to be highly dependent on other factors, as our overview has suggested. These factors seem to be: the presence of grassroots organizations, the existence of a unified variety of the indigenous language in question, the existence of a unified alphabet for this indigenous language, and governmental support, especially financial support.

The presence of grassroots organizations, that is, the organization of ethnic and local groups, seems to be crucial in the revitalization process of indigenous languages, as has been the case in Nicaragua, and, especially, Ecuador. In Nicaragua, the Miskitu population, although small and concentrated on the eastern coast, has been able to overturn a national policy of Hispanicization, and has been allowed by the government to administer and coordinate its own bilingual education programs; it also receives some financial support from the government. Ecuador is the best example of the importance of grassroots organizations. Ecuadorian grassroots organizations, in existence since the 1980s, have united into the CONAIE (Confederación de Nacionalidades Indígenas del Ecuador; Hornberger, 2000), Confederation of Indigenous Nationalities of Ecuador, and are perhaps the strongest in any Latin American country. Although the Ecuadorian government policy has been supportive since 1981, the main burden is on the grassroots organizations, which are responsible for the bilingual programs. In Guatemala, however, both the grassroots organizations and the government are working closely together to expand bilingual education, which in 2001 reached 50 percent of the population (Prensa Libre, 2001). Bolivia is another example of a country whose government is actively involved in promoting bilingual education: by 1996, two years after the new Bolivian language policy was instituted, programs had already begun at one-third of Bolivian schools (Hornberger and King, 1996).

Although all Latin American countries officially support respect for and maintenance of indigenous languages and cultures as a matter of policy (Gleich, 1989), there is no doubt that the active support of the governments is important. To judge by the reports of researchers in the field, the governments of Guatemala, Ecuador, Bolivia, and Paraguay are participating actively in bilingual education policy; other governments, however, have to date done little, if anything, in the way of actively supporting bilingual education. These examples suggest, then, that official bilingual education policy is not sufficient. What is needed is a government that will take responsibility for understanding literacy as promoting the indigenous language, promulgating indigenous knowledge, and building indigenous identity (Hornberger, 1999). Hence, both players, grassroots organizations and government, are necessary if such programs are to succeed. The presence of grassroots organizations is what has been called language planning from the bottom up (Hornberger, 1996). More research on Latin American grassroots organizations is needed in order for supporters in all countries to learn from each other's successes and failures.

For the purpose of creating bilingual education materials and training the teachers, there seems to be a great need for a unified linguistic variety of the indigenous language, as well as a unified alphabet, although some consider this last requirement to be less crucial. Ecuador (since 1980), Guatemala (since 1987), and Bolivia (since 1994) have been successful in agreeing on a unified linguistic variety and a unified alphabetic system. This allows for greater effectiveness in the creation of materials and the training of teachers. Peru, on the other hand, although it rose as an example to follow in the early 1970s, has not yet been successful in resolving what is called the "3 or 5 vowel" debate with respect to the transcription of Quechua, although an Academy of the Quechua language has been established.

Some researchers also argue that, in addition, the development of a written tradition is essential in promoting the revitalization of indigenous languages (Bernard, 1996). A good example of efforts along these lines is the CELIAC Project (Centro Editorial de Literaturas Indígenas), the Publishing Center of Indigenous Literature, which has been offering publications in indigenous languages in Mexico since the 1970s (Salinas, 1996). Guatemala, Ecuador, and Bolivia have also been producing many publications in indigenous languages, especially in the 1990s. These publications are on all the different aspects of indigenous cultures, including but not limited to language. To this effect, Hornberger (1999) proposes that bilingual education programs should promote multiple literacies, which is defined by the New London Group (1996) as activities beyond reading and writing, expanding to other domains such as visual, audio, poetry, spatial, and behavioral, which are different ways in which societies express their cultures.

The complexity that lies behind the success of bilingual education programs can serve as an indicator of the different directions in which research can go. (For additional discussion of bilingual education, see chapters 15, 21, 23, 25, 27, and 28.)

REFERENCES

Bernard, H. R. (1996). Language preservation and publishing. In N. Hornberger (ed.), *Indigenous Literacies in the Americas: Language Planning from the Bottom Up*, pp. 139–56.

Fontanella de Weinberg, M. B. (1993). *Documentos para la Historia Lingüística de Hispanoamérica siglos XVI a XVIII*. Madrid: Real Academia Española.

Francis, N. and Nieto Andrade, R. (2000). Mexico: The challenge of literacy and multilingualism. *Childhood Education*, 7(6), 374–80.

Freeland, J. (1999). Can the grass roots speak? The literacy campaign in English on Nicaragua's Atlantic coast. *International Journal of Bilingual Education and Bilingualism*, 2(3), 214–32.

Gleich, U. v. (1989). *Educación Primaria Bilingüe Intercultural*. Eschborn: Deutsche Gesellschaft für Technische Zusammenarbeit.

Grimes, B. (1988). *Ethnologue: Languages of the World* and *Ethnologue Index*. Dallas, TX: Summer Institute of Linguistics.

Gynan, S. N. (2001). Paraguayan language policy and the future of Guaraní. *Southwest Journal of Linguistics*, 20(1), 151–65.

Hornberger, N. (1994). Language policy and planning in South America. *American Review of Applied Linguistics*, 14, 220–39.

Hornberger, N. (ed.) (1996). *Indigenous Literacies in the Americas: Language Planning from the Bottom Up*. Berlin and New York: Mouton de Gruyter.

Hornberger, N. (1999). Maintaining and revitalising indigenous languages in Latin America: State planning vs. grassroots initiatives. *International Journal of Bilingual Education and Bilingualism*, 2(3), 159–65.

Hornberger, N. (2000). Bilingual education policy and practice in the Andes. *Anthropology and Education Quarterly*, 31(2), 1–30.

Hornberger, N. and Skilton-Sylvester, E. (2000). Revisiting the continua of biliteracy: International and critical perspectives. *Language and Education*, 14(2), 96–122.

Hornberger, N. and King, K. (1996). Bringing the language forward: School-based initiatives for Quechua language revitalization in Ecuador and Bolivia. In N. Hornberger (ed.), *Indigenous Literacies in the Americas: Language Planning from the Bottom Up*, pp. 299–320.

King, K. A. (1996). Indigenous politics and native language literacies: Recent shifts in bilingual education policy and practice in Ecuador. In N. Hornberger (ed.), *Indigenous Literacies in the Americas: Language Planning from the Bottom Up*, 267–84).

Lastra, Y. (1992). *Sociolingüística para Hispanoamericanos. Una introducción*. Mexico: El Colegio de México.

Lipski, J. M. (1994). *Latin American Spanish*. London and New York: Longman.

New London Group (1996). A pedagogy of multiliteracies: Designing social futures. *Harvard Educational Review*, 66(1), 60–92.

Oficina Nacional de Estadísticas (1999). *Anuario Demográfico de Cuba*. La Habana, Cuba: Centro de Estudios de Población y Desarrollo.

Prensa Libre (2001). *Guatemala Multicultural 11*. Guatemala: Bancafé.

Richards, J. B. and Richards, M. (1996). Mayan language literacy in Guatemala: A socio-historical overview. In N. Hornberger (ed.), *Indigenous Literacies in the Americas: Language Planning from the Bottom Up*, 189–211.

Rivarola, J. L. (2000). *Español andino. Textos de bilingües de los siglos XVI y XVII*. Madrid: Iberoamericana.

Rojas Mayer, E. M. (ed.) (1999). *Estudios sobre la Historia del Español de América*. San Miguel de Tucumán, Argentina: Universidad Nacional de Tucumán.

Sánchez Albornoz, N. (1974). *Population of Latin America: A History*. Berkeley: University of California Press.

Salinas Pedraza, J. (1996). Saving and strengthening indigenous Mexican languages: The CELIAC experience. In N. Hornberger (ed.), *Indigenous Literacies in the Americas: Language Planning from the Bottom Up*, 171–87.

United Nations (2003). World Population Prospects: The 2002 Revision. Highlights. New York: United Nations Population Division (http://www.un.org/popin/data.html#Global percent20Data).

Willey, G. (1971). *An Introduction to American Archeology*. Englewood Cliffs, NJ: Prentice-Hall.

Wodon, Q. with contributions from Ayres, R., Barenstein, M., Hicks, N., Lee, K., Maloney, W., Peeters, P., Siaens, C., and Yitzhaki, S. (2000). *Poverty and Policy in Latin American Countries*. World Bank Technical Paper, report no. WTP 467 (http://www-wds.worldbank.org).

Zúñiga, M., Sánchez, L., and Zacharías, D. (2000). *Demanda y Necesidad de Educación Bilingüe*. Lima: MEP/GTZ/KFW.

CITED WEBSITES

Argentina: Instituto Nacional de Estadística y Censos. http://www.indec.mecon.ar

Bolivia: Instituto Nacional de Estadística. http://www.ine.gov.bo

Chile: Instituto Nacional de Estadísticas. http://www.ine.cl

Colombia: Departamento Administrativo Nacional de Estadística. http://www.dane.gov.co

Costa Rica: Instituto Nacional de Estadística y Censos. http://www.inec.go.cr

Dominican Republic: Oficina Nacional de Estadística. http://www.one.gov.do

Ecuador: Instituto Nacional de Estadística y Censos. http://www.inec.gov.ec

Guatemala: Instituto Nacional de Estadística. http://www.segeplan.gob.gt/ine/

Mexico: Instituto Nacional de Estadística, Geografía e Informática. http://www.inegi.gob.mx

Paraguay: Dirección General de Estadística, Encuestas y Censos. http://www.dgeec.gov.py

Peru: Instituto Nacional de Estadística e Informatica. http://www.inei.gob.pe

Uruguay: Instituto Nacional de Estadística. http://ine.gub.uy

Venezuela: Instituto Nacional de
Estadística. http://www.ine.gov.ve
Summer Institute of Linguistics.
http://www.sil.org/Ethnologue

United Nations. http://www.un.org
United States Census.
http://www.census.gov
World Bank. http://www.worldbank.org

FURTHER READING

Baker, C. and Jones, S. P. (1998).
*Encyclopedia of Bilingualism
and Bilingual Education*.
Clevedon, UK: Multilingual
Matters.
England, N. (1999). *Introducción a la
Lingüística: Idiomas Mayas*. Guatemala:
PLFM Cholsamaj.
Grenoble, L. A. and Whaley, L. (eds.)
(1998). *Endangered Languages: Language
Loss and Community Response*.

Cambridge, UK: Cambridge University
Press.
La Belle, T. J. and White, P. S. (1978).
Education and colonial language
policies in Latin America and the
Caribbean. *International Review of
Education*, 24(3), 243–61.
Hornberger, N. (ed.) (1996). *Indigenous
Literacies in the Americas. Language
Planning from the Bottom Up*. Berlin
and New York: Mouton de Gruyter.

25 Bilingualism in Europe

ANDRÉE TABOURET-KELLER

25.1 Introduction

In Europe, throughout history and throughout individual countries and the Continent as a whole, two or more languages have been in contact. Therefore the term *bilingualism* is taken here in its broadest sense as a cover term for all situations, bilingual and multilingual. It would nevertheless be wrong to pretend that monolingual people are not found in Europe: they are numerous indeed, but they always live in societies and groups where different languages are present in their written and/or oral forms.

The 1999 census of the population of France provides a pertinent example of the intricate picture of multilingual Europe. A large sub-sample (380,000 people, out of a general population of 60 million) were asked what language(s) they had been exposed to during their childhood, had passed on to their own children at the same age, and currently had the opportunity to use on different social occasions (Héran, Filhon, and Deprez, 2002). In spite of the increasing proportion of monolingual francophones (70 percent of the population of France), 6,400 names of languages were registered and about 400 languages were identified according to the repertoire of the Summer Institute of Linguistics. Half of the bilingual instances are linked to the use of immigrant languages, the other half to the use of regional languages. The flow of immigrants coming from various other European countries and other continents, and the existence of regional languages scattered throughout the territory, are the two main factors behind multilingual situations in France as well as the other European countries. A third factor is the youth of the population; in the European Union, eleven countries out of fifteen have a ratio of 30 percent of people under 25 years of age, Italy showing the lowest ratio (26 percent), Ireland the highest (39 percent).

The consequences of migrations, the existence of regional minorities, and the needs of education and communication offer a large frame in which multilingual situations develop and where languages change all the time by coming into contact, staying in contact, or dying out (Weinreich, 1953). In order to be able to sort out the intricate picture of the multilingual Europe we are facing today, we have organized this chapter under three main headings: Europe, a Continent of Sustained Migrations (section 25.2); Europe, a Continent of Linguistically Powerful States and Less Powerful Minorities (25.3); and Recent Trends in Education and Communication in Europe (25.4). The questions to be addressed are the similarities and differences in migration and minority linguistic situations and their social and educational consequences.

The long period of antagonism between East and West after the Second World War still makes it difficult to obtain more than basic information on the linguistic situation in the former USSR and its satellite countries. The more recent turmoil in the Eastern parts of Europe also makes it difficult to get up-to-date views on the linguistic development in the new eastern states. They underwent dramatic changes after the fall of the Berlin Wall between West and East Germany in 1989 and, somewhat later, the disintegration of the Soviet regime itself in 1991 (Paulston and Peckham, 1998). We will therefore take most of our examples from countries which are members of the European Union.

25.1.1   The European Union (EU)

The present EU developed from six countries in 1957 to nine in 1973, ten in 1981, twelve in 1986, and fifteen in 1993, when the former EEC (European Economic Community) became the EU under the Maastricht Treaty (February 7, 1992).

The EU is far from covering the whole of Europe, since the number of European countries varies according to how far you extend Europe towards the east (from the Atlantic Ocean to the Ural Mountains) and at what point in time you set your limit (Barre and Kinkel, 1993); the number is somewhere between forty and fifty countries if you count, for example, Andorra, which was recently admitted to the UN, and the twelve countries that are on the waiting-list for admission to the EU, among them Estonia, Poland, Hungary, and the Czech Republic. The EU includes 304 million people who since January 2002 have shared the same currency, the euro, a means of communication that does away with bilingualism.

No official EU document sets out policies concerning the linguistic needs of immigrants and minorities. The 1977 EEC European Charter for Minority and Regional Languages: The Children of Migrant Workers (EEC, 1977) is restricted to making it possible for children from other EEC countries to be reintegrated in due course into the school system in their country of origin. Despite the numerous recommendations made by international organizations, such as the Council of Europe's Committee on the education of migrants, on the whole these have not been taken up by the member governments in such a way as to effect any substantial changes in policy (Gardner-Chloros, 1997, p. 194). On the other hand, the European Charter for Minority and Regional Languages of Maastricht (EEC, 1992) is restricted by a series of criteria that exclude the migrants' linguistic situations (see subsection 25.3.1).

25.1.2   *Official languages and other languages*

Within the limits of the EU, eleven languages have an official status (Danish, Dutch, English, Finnish, French, German, Greek, Italian, Portuguese, Spanish, Swedish) and a few more have co-official standing (Herreras, 1998). But Europe extends farther than the EU. According to Siguan (1996), twenty-six more official languages can be identified, but if one includes those which benefit from limited official status, their number goes up to fifty.

The typology of European language politics suggested by Siguan (1996) sheds some light on this aspect. Monolingualism can be said to characterize states that constitutionally recognize only one language, such as Portugal or France. But whereas Portugal is practically monolingual, France counts a number of regional or minority languages, from four in its European territory (the Deixonne Law, 1951) to 75 if one includes overseas territories that are part of the French Republic (Cerquiglini, 1999). A second category includes states which protect their minority languages and are tolerant towards them, such as, for example, the United Kingdom towards Welsh, or the Netherlands towards Frisian. Linguistic autonomy characterizes the third group of states which have an official language, but grant language minorities political autonomy and rights to establish their own politics regarding their language, such as Spain (Catalonia, Valencia, Basque, etc.) or Italy (Val d'Aosta, Alto Adige, etc.). Linguistic federalism applies to countries like Belgium or Switzerland, the latter a federate state where each federal entity has its own language and language politics. Institutional plurilingualism can be said to characterize countries which accept two or more languages as official languages and adopt measures to promote them so that they may be spoken all over the country; Luxembourg illustrates this category, also partly Ireland and Finland. The need for bilingualism and the opportunity for it are present all over Europe.

The circumstances that contributed in the past and still contribute today to the existence of heterogeneous linguistic situations in Europe are countless – historical, political, economic, symbolic, psychological – and usually they are interwoven. It would be difficult to avoid schematizing in so short a contribution, but the analysis we propose would lose its interest if it failed to bring to light the complexities of the European bilingual realities.

25.2   Europe, a Continent of Sustained Migrations

Human migration is one of the main factors of language change and therefore of bilingualism. Several examples in Europe, past and present, will illustrate this never-ending process, which results in a great variety of linguistic situations showing various profiles.

25.2.1 Human migrations in the past

25.2.1.1 Indo-European, a long-lasting influence

Linguists have good reasons to agree about a common origin – what they call Indo-European – for a good many European and Asian languages (Martinet, 1986; Walter, 1994). Although the history of the "Indo-European" origin remains a matter of reconstruction and still appears something of a puzzle (Renfrew, 1987), linguistic features, archaeological data, and local names, among other factors, allow one to envisage that vast human migrations, beginning during the first millennium BC, swept from the steppes north of the Black Sea both southwards towards the Indian subcontinent and westwards towards the Danube flatland and from there in several directions. These migrations did not spread into empty lands but met various peoples using non-Indo-European languages; countless geographic names, for example, have pre-Indo-European roots (Rousset, 1988). Nor did they form a united flow. In time, subgroups like, for example, the Celts, Germans, Latins, and Slavs, followed their own itineraries and caused large dialectal continua to emerge, principally, from north to south, the Scandinavian, the West Germanic, the North Slavic, the South Slavic and the West Romance (Chambers and Trudgill, 1980). These areas have kept their linguistic borders up to the present and they contribute to the formation of most of the regional language pockets which we will deal with in section 25.3.

A basic picture of Europe's language complexity in modern times, which makes bilingual communication endlessly necessary, emerges when one lists the languages to which is attributed Indo-European origin. Needless to say, there is no absolute agreement about the language groups and their names, and about the several languages in each of these groups. Our aim in listing them is to illustrate at the very outset of this chapter the density of languages in our part of the world and their great variety. The offer to students by Strasbourg University II, for example, of a choice of twenty-five European languages is a contemporary consequence of this diversity. The seven following language groups are generally ascribed Indo-European origin:

1 *Celtic* (Scots Gaelic, Irish, Manx, Welsh, Cornish, Breton);
2 *Romance* (Portuguese, Spanish, Catalan, Occitan, Galician, French, Italian, Rheto-Roman, Rumanian);
3 *Germanic* (English, Frisian, Dutch, German, Swedish, Danish, Dano-Norwegian, Norwegian, Faroese, Icelandic);
4 *Slavic* (Russian, Ukrainian, Byelorussian, Polish, Slovak);
5 *Baltic* (Lithuanian, Lettish);
6 *Hellenic* (Greek, Tsakonian, Pontic, Cypriot, Cappadocian);
7 *Albanian* with its two dialects, Tosk and Gheg.

The non-territorial languages spoken by various Gypsy groups all over Europe also belong to Indo-European; most of these groups are relatively bilingual in another European language (Williams, 1988); the Yiddishes, no longer first languages today, also form a group of non-territorial languages, having taken in many elements from different languages, most of them of Indo-European origin (Ertel, 1988). Despite the dominance of the Indo-European groups, some non-Indo-European languages persisted in their own territories, where they are still spoken: Basque, Turkish, Hungarian, Estonian, and Finnish.

25.2.1.2 *Latin, a prolific ancestor*

Rome, in the Latin-speaking province of Latium, was already in the fourth century BC an important multilingual trade center between the north (the Etruscan markets) and the south (Greater Greece in the south of Italy). By the third century BC, Italy at large was under Roman domination and one century later its domination was extended towards the East. But before Latin imposed itself on the Mediterranean world, Greek was spoken in Rome, both colloquially among slaves of Greek origin and merchants, and in educated society throughout the third and second centuries BC. Greek culture had such high prestige that in the second century AD measures were taken against its influence.

During the first century BC, the armies of Julius Caesar conquered large parts of Europe; in the second century AD, the period of its widest expansion, the Roman Empire stretched all around the Mediterranean from the Atlantic to the Caspian Sea without interruption. Very gradually the local languages gave way: Iberic, for example, was in use until the end of the first century AD, Gallic in the Po valley until the third century AD (Walter, 1994, p. 112).

But the concept of a unified Latin language would be misleading. Classical Latin, already codified in its written form, coexisted side by side with Latin vernaculars. In its vast colonies, gathering together various populations, the Roman state imposed its administration, ruled by precise laws needing a clear-cut tongue, identical for all. Such were the foundations of Classical Latin as we still know it today. During the first centuries AD, developing Christian faith brought Latin new strength; as the liturgical language of the Catholic Church, Latin fulfilled for centuries a powerful function that it kept until at least Vatican II (1962) at which time it was still used in many European countries for Catholic services.

In the meantime, the vernacular forms of Latin opened up to innovation, followed their own development, differentiating themselves into what gradually became the various Romance languages we know today: Italian, Spanish, Portuguese, French, Rumanian, as well as Catalan, Walloon, Venetian, Sicilian, and many more.

25.2.1.3 *The case of English*

As traveling companions of migration, various forms and degrees of bilingualism developed for centuries in Europe. The case of English offers a pertinent illustration of the threads that are woven into the multilingual fabric of a given language, a multilingual feature common to all European languages.

The dominant use of English, well established today, was preceded in the British Isles by languages of Celtic origin; the process of their replacement by English, starting in the fifth century, still goes on today. During the last ten centuries, English itself has undergone dramatic changes due to contact with the languages of the Vikings (ninth to eleventh century), the Normans (up to the thirteenth century), and the French (until the fifteenth century). Only in the eighteenth century did English become an established language, thanks to codification and standardization under the leadership of men like Dr. Johnson (Akamatsu, 1992, p. 155). New problems emerge today due to recent immigrations of workers, who amount to about 4 percent of the total population of the UK, originating mainly in the Indian subcontinent and in Africa.

Multilingualism, a longstanding phenomenon, not only left linguistic traces in every European language, none of which could be said to be pure, but also brought permanent changes that allowed each of the European languages we know today to have its own form and qualities.

25.2.2 Human migration in the present

Present-day migrants, seeking work, better living conditions, and freedom, also import their languages, but in contrast to the previously mentioned migrations, they have only a minor influence on the local languages and do not produce long-lasting bilingualism; the language of origin is given up in three or four generations and, in any case, deteriorates. This does not prevent migration and its consequences from being of tremendous importance in European society at large. The last two centuries have already been concerned with large worker migrations; in the nineteenth century, these mainly took place from rural areas to towns, whereas in the last century other causes added to the process, first and foremost wars and persecution of populations by totalitarian regimes, secondly technical changes in industrial production which resulted in profound changes in the labor market.

25.2.2.1 Immigration in the European Union

Out of a total population of 371 million people in the EU, 15 million are migrants (4.4 percent of the total population), 5 million originating from within the EU, 10 million from non-EU countries. The main recipient countries are Belgium with an immigrant population of 9 percent of its total, Germany with 7 percent, France with 6.3 percent, and the Netherlands with 4.6 percent. Among the main immigrant groups, 22 percent originate from Turkey, 8 percent from the former Yugoslavia, 20 percent from the other European countries, 15 percent from Asia, and 8 percent from the Americas (Siguan, 1998, p. 10). Immigrants to Germany are for the most part of Turkish and ex-Yugoslavian origin, to France of Maghrebi origin (Algeria and Morocco), and to Great Britain of Irish, South Asian and West Indian origin. Such a multifaceted immigration pattern does not allow for a global view of bilingualism in Europe. Not only do the different immigrant groups behave in specific ways but the host countries also develop specific immigration politics translated into specific linguistic policies.

25.2.2.2   Immigration policies

It would be wrong not to mention the conditions of citizenship when analyzing immigration policies and their consequences for bilingualism in the post-Second World War period. The colonial legacy and the post-war economic boom were significant factors in the overall development of labor migration in Europe. Nevertheless, each country set out its own rules for access to citizenship. In the UK, for example, immigrants from the New Commonwealth had British citizenship and full rights to settle and to work; citizens of former Dutch colonies had similar treatment. But the Federal Republic of Germany did not consider itself a country open to integration of immigrants: foreign workers were *Gastarbeiter* (guest workers) with no permanent status in the country (Gardner-Chloros, 1997, p. 193).

Migration in most European states was, and in some cases still is, associated with long-lasting political ideologies resting on ancient constitutional principles, mainly *jus soli* (citizenship depends on a territorial base) or *jus sanguini* (citizenship depends on blood kinship). The first principle is illustrated by the case of the Swiss Confederation where the language of administration and education is the language of the canton in which one resides, the second by Germany. Here are some details concerning the latter.

25.2.2.3   The example of Germany

For centuries, membership of the German "people" (*Volk*) was defined by blood kinship as well as, but not only, by the use of the language. Social bilingualism was therefore seen as a threat to purity and to the German spirit (*Volksgeist*). Hence the crucial importance of the law adopted recently (March 2002) in the Federal Republic of Germany on "the orientation and the limitation of the immigration flux."

The Federal Republic of Germany has a total population of 82 million people (of whom 27 percent are less than 25 years old) with over 7 million declared foreigners and an additional million illegal immigrants. In such situations, shared by all Western European countries, linguistic questions are generally subjected to political antagonism, the left wing insisting on the economic necessity of immigration, the right on the dangers of an uncontrolled influx. After six hours of severe controversy in the Bundesrat (the law was claimed to violate the Constitution), the law was finally adopted with the following main provisions: in case of need, companies are allowed to call on foreign labor, in particular in information technology, the building trades, manufacturing industries, and the health services, which could not take care of the aging German population without immigrant labor. Immigrants and their families are under obligation to integrate into their host country by pursuing courses on German language and culture; only children under twelve are allowed in as family dependents. Germany, which for centuries was ruled by *jus sanguini*, will now become a country allowing the integration of foreigners, once the complexities of the application of the law are solved.

25.2.2.4 Immigrant languages in France

Despite the 1880 decree according to which "only French shall be used in schools," despite Article 2 introduced in 1992 in the Constitution stating that "French is the language of the Republic," France is not home to only one language, as is shown by the survey mentioned above (section 25.1). In addition to the extreme diversity of the linguistic groups, the main result of the survey shows that from one generation to the next, the French language eventually supplants all immigrants' languages. The longer their stay in France, the more immigrants change over to the use of French within family life. Therefore French monolingualism has been gaining ground for more than a century.

Although each immigrant group behaves linguistically and culturally in a specific way (Vermès, 1988), dominant features emerge. First of all their time of arrival varies. The Italians, for example, started arriving in the nineteenth century (see below), others, like the Poles, in the 1920s, still others, like people from sub-Saharan Africa, arrived mainly after the 1970s. The reasons for their emigration also vary: 100,000 Chinese, for example, arrived between 1916 and 1918 for a limited period as metallurgy workers to replace the French workers who had left to go to the Front during the First World War, but from the 1930s onwards their arrival in small groups was continuous due to poverty and political unrest. On the other hand Armenians were escaping the genocide perpetrated in 1915, whereas Poles and Italians were mainly escaping poverty. Immigrants from Turkey have been arriving mainly since the 1970s, people from the Indo-China Peninsula since 1975, escaping both poverty and extreme political regimes.

The easier and more frequent the visit to the country of origin, the easier the maintenance of the home language: in France, Spanish and Portuguese immigrants are among those who are apt to maintain their bilingualism all the better as both languages can be chosen as first foreign languages within the French secondary school system. The following two examples illustrate the extent of linguistic diversity: within two or three generations, Italian immigrants pass from Italian monolingualism to French monolingualism; sub-Saharan African immigrants who arrive with an experience of multilingualism change over to bilingualism or, less often French monolingualism.

25.2.2.5 Italian immigration into France

Under the Second Empire (1851–1870) 80,000 to 100,000 people migrated from Italy to France. Welcomed in industry, they were severely discriminated against by the local population. A century later, in 1981, they were 630,065 in number, including those with dual nationality. Whereas about 5,000 new Italian immigrants arrived every year, as many left to rejoin their families. Their linguistic situation was dominated by the gap between their everyday vernacular and standard Italian, an ideal language without any vernacular base. In the 1980s, out of the 3 million people of Italian descent and the 500,000 Italian residents, about 2 percent of pupils in colleges were in contact with Italian as a second foreign language (Véglianté, 1988, p. 239). It must be stressed that the French school system is designed to integrate children of foreign origin despite some timid measures to preserve their link with their language of origin (Varro, 2001).

The 1999 survey already mentioned (section 25.1) and an earlier one in 1992 (Héran, 1993) illustrate a permanent feature: the great majority of immigrant parents do not pass on their original language to their children. In the 1992 survey, 16 percent of the population mention a language other than French as their first language but only 5 percent use it with their children. In the Italian case only 7.5 percent of the immigrant children grew up speaking Italian in their families and only 1 percent used (or use) Italian with their own children. In the 1999 survey, 75 percent of the fathers to whom their own fathers spoke Italian in childhood do not use it with their own children.

When children of the second, third, or fourth generation have the opportunity to get in touch with their family in Italy, they use a simplified language that is not without an influence on the Italian language itself, as de Mauro already pointed out in 1963 (III, 2: "Gli effetti dell'emigrazione" [The effects of emigration]). Of course in Italy itself Italian has been undergoing changes, particularly since the end of the Second World War, developing towards a common central Italian in which dialectal differences tend to get neutralized. At present in France, the majority of children of Italian descent are only occasionally in touch with Italian and do not deeply identify with the country of their forebears (Véglianté, 1988).

25.2.2.6   The case of sub-Saharan African immigration in France

Sub-Saharan (referred to hereafter as African) immigration to France started after the First World War but has developed since the end of the 1950s. The restriction on all immigration in 1974 had as a consequence the temporary settlement of immigrants, interrupted by journeys to the country of origin, the arrival of their families, and the birth of new children. According to the 1990 census about 166,000 Africans were living in France; according to the 1999 census, metropolitan France has a sub-Saharan African population of about 380,000, including those who have acquired French citizenship but not the illegal ones. They originate from forty-two countries, the largest number coming from Senegal (over 50,000), followed by Cameroon, Congo, Mali, Ivory Coast, ex-Zaire, Madagascar, and Mauritius (all over 25,000). As a point of comparison, about 1.3 million people originate from Algeria, Morocco, and Tunisia. The main settlements of Africans in France are in the Paris region and along the Seine valley but at present more or less important groups are scattered over all large cities.

With such a very heterogeneous composition – geographically, socially, linguistically – it is obvious that their original linguistic repertoires are also very heterogeneous. Nevertheless, more than half of them have in common the fact that they come from countries where, in addition to several national languages, French is the official language, such as the Republic of Congo (Congo-Brazzaville) and the Democratic Republic of Congo (Congo-Kinshasa), the Ivory Coast, Mali, Senegal, and Togo, or one of two official languages, alongside English, as in Cameroon or Mauritius (La documentation française, 1999–2000). The implication is that they have been in touch with oral and sometimes written French, although literacy is far from general (Chaudenson and Calvet, 2001). Ethnic identities – and not official or national identities – are determinant: they include linguistic and cultural identities and also the social networks of reception and assistance in the country of emigration (lodgings, food and distribution of goods, access to jobs, etc.). In addition to French, Senegal, for example, counts seven large ethnic groups, each of them comprising a more or less large number of subgroups; the Wolof ethnic group represents 40 percent of Senegal's population; Wolof, one of the three national languages, is the vernacular language of 80 percent of Senegal; on the other hand the Democratic Republic of Congo has a dozen ethnic groups with 250 subgroups, four national languages and an unknown number of ethnic languages (see chapter 26 of the present volume).

No wonder the fieldwork picture is always a complex one. Lecomte (2001), in a survey of the linguistic behavior of the African families of 350 schoolchildren in the Rouen region, collected about thirty names given to first languages, spoken in twelve different countries; 17 percent mention French among their first languages. Whereas parents use their original language with each other and with members of their ethnic group, mothers use it more than half of the time (53 percent) with their children and mix it with French in 28 percent of their communications; the proportion for fathers being 40 percent for the ethnic language and 33 percent for the ethnic language and French. When adults have already given up their ethnic language and adopted an African town vehicular before emigration, they are in favor of adopting French in their new urban surroundings, French being also the language of social advancement, hence the African elite language.

Lecomte (2001) has conducted a series of interviews in the same population with women members of an association for the promotion of their autonomy, in particular through learning to write and to drive a car. They were keen to learn to read and write in both their African language and French. Bilingualism, towards which they were at first suspicious, seems at present the solution to fulfill their duty towards their language and their traditions and to emancipate themselves within French society.

No doubt it is impossible either to proceed to an overall appreciation of African mulitilingualism in France or to foresee its development. Nevertheless, several field observations illustrate a shift towards French in the younger generation, for example in the Marseille region in families from Mali (Van den Avenne, 2001). In the same family, the four older children have kept their original language, the four younger ones born in France still understand it but no longer speak it (personal observation).

25.2.3   Transitional remarks on section 25.2

On April 30 2002, a ballot over a general strike issue took place among the workers of the largest steel consortium (IG Metall) in Germany: the results were displayed in eight languages. Contradictory developments are going on at once, from caring for the maintenance of original languages – sometimes linked with a struggle for their recognition as languages of literacy in the country of origin – to caring for the social and cultural integration into the host society, particularly for the younger generations. Such heterogeneous processes go on at different levels – at the linguistic level for instance where code switching might be interpreted as a symptom of either weakness or strength of the immigrant language, and at the social level where mixed couples and their children seek recognition. It is noticeable that in society at large the use of the term "mixed" tends to be an easy metaphor for all sorts of non-standard or unforeseen formations (Varro, 2003). (For an extended discussion of the case of immigrant Turkish in Europe, see chapter 26; for further discussion of code mixing and code switching, see chapters 1–4, 6, 10–14, 26, 28, 29, and 31.)

25.3   Europe, a Continent of Linguistically Powerful States and Less Powerful Minorities

The turmoil caused by the treaty ending the First World War (1914–18) (the setting of new political frontiers all over Europe but also the recognition of the principle of self-determination for all nations) and the turmoil caused afresh by the consequences of the Second World War (1940–45) (the defeat of the Fascist and National Socialist regimes, the reaffirmation of the existence of the large Soviet bloc in the East, and hence the preparation of the "Cold War," and the resetting once more of the political frontiers) gave rise to the complex political, economic, and linguistic conditions that result today in an almost inextricable mosaic of languages.

The development of modern nation-states in Europe involved many rearrangements of their political frontiers, which were constantly set and reset as a result of heritage, wars, and political and economic interests, notwithstanding the realities of the main dialectal areas. As shown in section 25.2, the borders of the very large dialectal areas did not change over centuries, the main result of this centuries-long development being that political frontiers and the borders of dialectal areas do not coincide, causing the development along these borders of more or less long-lasting linguistic pockets. Almost every European frontier can be shown to represent an artificial line whose path is determined by a series of historical coincidences, and which meanders through a continuum of dialects – for instance, German dialects overlapping the French, Belgian, and Italian borders, French overlapping the Belgian, Swiss, and Italian borders, and Catalan as well as Basque dialects overlapping with the French border, among many other examples.

In addition to these trans-frontier linguistic pockets, the Celtic language areas as well as the non-Indo-European language areas like the Basque area form regional language pockets.

As will be shown, the fate of these regional or minority languages is only partly linked with the language policies of the country to which they belong. Within the EU, an opportunity for recognition has opened up for regional and minority languages within the frame of the European Charter, but these new conditions are far from being applied in all European countries, and, when applied, far from being sufficient to counteract increasing monolingualism in the dominant language of the country and from reviving a positive form of bilingualism.

25.3.1 Regional or minority languages in the EU

On March 16 1988, a Resolution on regional or minority languages in Europe was adopted by the EEC (referred to hereafter as Res.). It recognizes the longstanding fact of the existence of more or less vast areas where there are languages in use which are different from the official languages of the state in whose territory they are found (Chambers and Trudgill, 1980). Throughout the nineteenth century the speakers in such territories became more or less bilingual in the state language and the local language. But the spread of education, the increasing weight of administration based on the use of the standard language, and the rapid development of towns with a mixed population speeded up the takeover by the state language.

The definition of the general category of regional or minority languages is based on the following criteria (General Provisions, Art. 1. of the Res.) (Tabouret-Keller, 1992): (1) Regional or minority languages belong to the European cultural heritage; (2) they are traditionally spoken within a region of the state territory; (3) they are different from the language or the languages spoken by the rest of the state's population; (4) they are spoken by nationals of the state; (5) they are spoken by a group numerically smaller than the rest of the state's population, hence the term "linguistic minority." The last criterion gave rise to criticism because in the region where it is spoken a regional language may be the majority language, hence the term "less spoken languages."

25.3.2 Three case studies: French, Breton, and Sorb

The following case studies are chosen because they are very different from one another – success, survival, decline of a regional language – and because each of them represents numerous other cases of the same type, although no two of them could be said to be identical: history, politics, economy, and demography are specific to each. Nevertheless, the trends described here can also be found elsewhere.

25.3.2.1   *A case of unquestioned but questionable success:*
French and the bilingual school system in the Valle
d'Aosta (Italy)

The development in the Valle d'Aosta of an integrated bilingual school system, from infant school to university, is well known in the European regional debate and referred to as a model of a consistent and successful language policy. But more than thirty years after the beginning of its implementation, its success gives rise to questions (Duc, 2001).

The Valle d'Aosta (hereafter the Valley) is located in the north of Italy. The importance of its capital town, Aosta (Augusta Praetoria, founded by Augustus, 27–14 BC), is linked to its geographical location within a large district of mountainous Alpine valleys. Its regional language is a Romance dialect belonging to the Franco-Provençal area (Martinet, 1975, pp. 195–207), called *patois* by its speakers, a term used throughout French-speaking areas with degrading connotations like "rural" or "coarse."

Before 1861 when the Valley became part of the kingdom of Italy, it was a diglossic francophone region: patois was the oral means of everyday communication, French the language of education. After 1861, there was a shift towards the use of Italian, mainly in administration and the economy, but for a long time the schools remained French-speaking. After the period of Fascism (1922–45), during which the use of French and Franco-Provençal was prohibited, the Valley became an autonomous region of the Italian Republic. Article 6 of the Constitution reads "The Republic protects linguistic minorities by appropriate laws" (Carrozza, 1992, p. 217). This allowed the Valley to include in its own legal regional framework Article 38 stating that Italian and French enjoy equal status, and Article 39 stating that "Within the Region, in schools of any level an equal number of hours shall be allocated to the teaching of Italian and to the teaching of French" (Decime, 2000, p. 22). The principle of an equal number of hours for both languages was promptly applied to the teaching of French, but teaching the curriculum in French started only at the beginning of the seventies and took some time to be implemented.

In the Valley, public infant schools for children of three to five years were instituted in 1972. Although attendance is not compulsory, 98 percent of this age group is now enrolled. A text adopted in 1983 stresses that "Education at the infant level shall be distributed in equal time between Italian and French. [. . .] Each of the oral communication systems shall have its own motivations: space and time, specific didactic and teaching material" (Decime, 2000, p. 23). New methods were devised, new orientations introduced such as taking into account "domains of experience," or building on a "methodology for carrying out given schemes."

Towards the beginning of the 1980 the bilingual system was introduced at the primary-school level (six to ten years). Three teachers are in charge of two classes, each teaching one of the following three groups alternatively in Italian or French, for example: (1) Italian, geography, sport; (2) French, history, music; (3) mathematics, sciences, arts. At the beginning of the 1990s the school slogan was "Two languages for one knowledge." Again new methods were devised, and, most important of all, permanent tuition for teachers was organized.

The first level of college (11–13 years) was incorporated into the bilingual scheme around 1990 and the second level (14–18 years) in 1996–7. New programs and methods were designed. The new aim set for the pupil is now to be able to listen, speak, read, and write in the two languages; 20 percent more teachers were trained and English became compulsory for all. This development is still in progress and is surveyed and evaluated with the help of a technical and a consultative committee, the latter made up of principals, teachers, and parents. The complexity of the tasks faced by both teachers and pupils is such that things are still in progress. The most commonly expressed worry is that the bilingual scheme should not be an additional burden for the students who have to acquire knowledge in the various subjects (Decime, 2000, p. 30). Last but not least, the university level was implemented in 1998–9 and was devoted to the training of primary school teachers in specialized courses for secondary school teachers within a bilingual scheme based on the same principle as the other levels of education.

On average, there is a ratio of seven pupils to one teacher for infant and primary schools and for colleges. The Valley is, with South Tyrol, the richest part of Italy, with a regional public per capita expenditure of 12.5 million lire in 1992, whereas in Calabria, one of the poorest regions, the level of per capita public expenditure is 2.4 million lire (Carrozza, 1992). Therefore, for thirty years, the government of the Valley has been able to support generously the efforts of the teaching staff and their requests for permanent pedagogical innovation and also to grant high-level expertise mainly from Switzerland and France.

Without going into the political implications of the adoption of a bilingual scheme not only in the school system but also in the sphere of administration, the main questions under discussion concern the adequacy of this policy in view of the sociolinguistic situation in the Valley. The last census that included information on the linguistic composition of the Aostan population took place in 1922. In 2001, the Fondation Chanoux, a private foundation named after the leader and hero of the anti-Fascist resistance in the Valley, undertook a sociolinguistic investigation: about 7,200 questionnaires were handed out in an overall population of about 120,000 people (Fondation Chanoux). Definitive results are not yet known but I had access to the results concerning the mother tongue: Italian is mentioned by only 63 percent of the sample, Franco-Provençal by only about 35 percent, and French by only 1 percent. In the capital town Aosta, the proportion of people of non-Valdotan origin is 80 percent. Further results will illustrate public opinion about the present linguistic policy in view of the development of the Valley, the benefit of their children, and even the fate of Franco-Provençal.

25.3.2.2   *A struggle for survival: the case of Breton (France)*

Brittany is a large peninsula in the western part of France, with its south coast on the Atlantic and its north coast on the English Channel. Its western part constitutes one of the few remaining Celtic dialectal areas (the others being Ireland, the Isle of Man, Scotland, Wales, and Cornwall). Celtic experienced its greatest expansion in Brittany in the tenth century. During the next eight centuries, its eastern border shifted gradually westwards. In the last century it has remained stable, although its exact locations remain a matter of dispute (Denetz, 1988). It is to this part of Brittany, also called Lower Brittany (Basse Bretagne), that the following text will refer.

The two main contemporary features of Breton, the familiar name of the language, are its gradual loss of use and an active struggle for survival. From early statistics gathered towards the end of the nineteenth century, it appears that Breton was the only language of about 1.3 million people. In the 1890s, 70 percent of the schools in the Western part of Brittany were bilingual and 7 percent monolingual in Breton. 56 percent of the people appearing before a court needed an interpreter (Broudic, 1999b, p. 127). In 1925 Breton was the everyday language of 1.15 million people, and still of about 1 million in 1930, a figure based on the number of people going to church where the service was in Breton; the Breton rural population was strictly of the Catholic faith and known for its large families. The creation of the French public school system (compulsory, free, and secular) in the 1880s did not affect the number of Breton speakers for a very long time.

But between the beginning and the end of the twentieth century the situation shifts from a quasi-monolingualism when more than half the population is still monolingual in Breton and its majority does not use any other language, to a dominant monolingualism in French. From an investigation which was undertaken in 1997 and for which we have a detailed report (Broudic, 1999a), it appears that out of 1,500,000 people in Lower Brittany, 16 percent declared that they spoke the language, 24 percent that they understood it, 11 percent that they read it and 6 percent that they wrote it. But two-thirds of the latter were already over 60 years old, whereas the percentage for the 15- to 19-year-olds was 0.2 percent (Broudic, 1999a). This investigation is to be compared with the results of a survey conducted in 1991, according to which, in the same population, 250,000 declared that they spoke Breton and 650,000 that they understood it (Walter, 1994, p. 96). This decrease is to be compared with the increase in responses in favor of Breton; the question "Do you think Breton should be preserved?" received 76 percent positive answers in 1991 and 88 percent in 1997 (Broudic, 1999a, p. 70).

What happened? The great shift started towards the end of the 1960s when within one or two generations the formerly predominantly rural population became predominantly urban (Le Berre and Le Dû, 1999, p. 74) and local and rural business entered the open market. At the same time a majority of the old Breton-speaking population disappeared and as a consequence the language was no longer passed on within the families; 70 percent of the people of over

60 years of age had Breton-speaking parents, 15 percent only of the 15 to 19 years of age (Broudic, 1999a, p. 62).

Nevertheless, during the last thirty years measures to protect Breton and other regional languages in France have been taken and a steep increase in their symbolic value has been noticeable. In 1951, the Deixonne Law, named after its author, gave a modest place to four regional languages (Breton, Basque, Catalan, and Occitan), but not much was done to foster the application of the law, which gave rise to much criticism (Martel, 1990); seven more regional languages were added later to this list (Tabouret-Keller, 1999, p. 102). These languages were allowed in state schools as optional subjects both for pupils and teachers who in time were able to get tuition in "Regional language and culture." In 1976, a cultural charter was granted to Brittany that led to the foundation of a cultural institute. Parallel schools, Diwan, were opened which used immersion methods; in 1991, 22 Diwan schools enrolled 822 pupils. In addition, 13 bilingual schools were opened, enrolling 545 pupils, of whom 300 were in kindergarten. From 1981 onwards university degrees in Breton from lower to upper level were offered (400 students in 1991). In 1999, about 5,000 pupils out of 600,000 in Lower Brittany in the school district of the Rennes Academy were learning Breton (Le Berre and Le Dû, 1999, p. 77).

Whereas the impact of the regional laws remains slight within the school system, the impact of the symbolic value attributed to the regional language is high. The year 2001 was the European Year of Languages, an occasion for the "Office de la langue bretonne" to organize a Breton Week of which a written account is given in a fat special issue (Louarn, 2001). Every possibility offered by every medium, traditional and recent, is exploited to make a wide public aware of the richness of Breton language and culture and of their potential. Two worrying questions remain: (1) What are the chances for bilingualism to become a sociolinguistic reality outside of schools and of a very small group of militants? (2) Whatever their enthusiasm and their painstaking efforts, will the measures taken by the supporters of the Breton cause, both in public and private areas, be able to guarantee the life and future of the language at a time when neither family nor social life fosters it?

25.3.2.3 *A story of decline: The case of the Sorbs (Germany)*

Lusatia (Lausitz in German), the territory of the Sorbs (also called Wends) with a population of 50,000 to 60,000 speakers (Pech, 2001), is located in Germany eastwards along the Polish border and southwards along the Czech border. The lower-Sorb dialectal group lives north of Cottbus, in Brandenburg, the upper-Sorb group around Bautzen, in Saxony. In the Middle Ages the Sorbs were one of the main groups of Slavic tribes, occupying a much larger territory than today in the same region. After much dispute, Lusatia remained under German rule from the eleventh century onwards. Even after the First World War, when Lusatians claimed to be independent, or at least to have become a part of Czechoslovakia, it remained under German rule.

Sorb, with its two main dialects, belongs to the group of West Slavic languages, distinct from Czech and Slovak on the one hand and from Polish on the other. The decline in the use of the language began as early as the late nineteenth century when Prussia adopted a severe anti-Sorb policy. In lower Lusatia, Sorb children were educated in the German language and had very limited opportunity to use their language in school or in church. In Saxony language policy was more liberal: according to the 1873 School Act, teachers were authorized "to teach the children of the Wendish nation to read Wendish as well as German" (Zwahr, 1966, p. 36). During the short period of the Weimar Republic, from 1919 to 1933, the use of Sorb in schools was given legal status; at that time in Bautzen and Kamenz counties many of the children entered school with a dominant command of Sorb and little or no German.

After the takeover by the National Socialists in 1933, Sorb language instruction was completely discontinued and Sorb publications were removed from teachers' and students' libraries. Hence from 1937 on, the use of Sorb started losing ground, especially among the younger generation.

The end of the Second World War meant new hope, and indeed Sorb policy in the Soviet occupation zone and in the German Democratic Republic resulted in the establishment of minority preservation (Article 11 of the 1949 Constitution). A minority school system was instituted, its practical implementation remaining difficult in Prussian Lusatia. On the other hand, in Saxon Lusatia its results were quite considerable: already in 1950 more than 6,000 pupils participated in or received all language instruction in Sorb. With the implementation of the bilingual school system, the period from 1952 to 1957 was one of expansion of the Sorb language and culture, and Sorb was to become an equally valued means of communication, along with German, in the public and commercial fields, the postal service, the traffic system, trade, the legal system, and State companies, and on farms. By the mid-1950s, over 9,000 students were participating in Sorb language lessons.

After 1957, the subordination of all social activities to the "expansion of socialism," had negative effects on the promotion of Sorb language and culture. But the decrease in the number of students in the Sorb curriculum (from 9,000 to 2,800) resulted from a conjunction of factors: mainly the loss of prestige of Sorb, the burden that was felt by pupils in the local villages called upon to attend Sorb classes, the attempt by various school directors to marginalize Sorb lessons by programming them at inconvenient times (outside bus hours), etc. After 1968, a compromise was found within a new Implementation Order that granted, for example, the right to inform parents about the advantages and disadvantages of Sorb courses. In the early 1970s, about 5,000 students regularly participated in Sorb classes every year.

In a reunified Germany, equal rights for Sorbs to preserve their language and culture are enshrined in law. But immediately after the unification of East and West Germany, the number of students of Sorb dropped to 4,800, rising again to about 5,000 in 2002. Two types of schools are established. Around

Bautzen and Kamenz, there are a small number of Type A schools, involving 1,300 pupils in 2002, the majority of them Sorb-speaking, where besides the teaching of the Sorb language, teaching in Sorb of subjects such as history, geography, and music is offered; elsewhere a much larger number of Type B schools, involving 3,700 pupils in 2002, offer Sorb as an option. Since 1995, the Witaj project, based on the Diwan school example in Brittany, has been tried with "the aim of reconquering the lost language" (Pech, April 2002, personal letter), first in kindergarten classes where the teachers use Sorb, and since 2000 in three primary schools where 12 to 14 hours a week are devoted to teaching in Sorb several subjects, such as mathematics.

25.3.3 Echo from the East

Since the end of perestroika a dominant feature of the linguistic situation in the new eastern republics is their desire to establish freedom of choice for their official and national languages and for the second languages taught in schools – in other words, how to replace the Russian language that over the years of Soviet power had become a dominant medium for development at all social levels. This question also arises in reaction to the unifying identity of "the Soviet people." New political entities are in search of new identities and this search seems to give way to various developments according to the past history and political ambitions of the new leaders. Here are a few examples. In the case of Byelorussia the problem is to differentiate "Byelorussian" from Russian (Fourse, 2000). In the different contexts of the new states emerging after the war in the former Yugoslavia, Croatia also wants to differentiate its language from Serbian and from Serbo-Croatian, in itself a much discussed linguistic entity. In Macedonia heated discussions still continue on the definition of Macedonian as a specific language, for instance different from Bulgarian and as the official language of Macedonia (Sériot, 1997). It is now accepted that Slovak is distinct from Czech, whereas Kachub, no less different from Polish than Slovak is from Czech, is considered a dialect of Polish. The list of specific linguistic problems seems endless and so do the often contradictory solutions adopted. The latest development (June 2002) is the approval of a federal law imposing the Cyrillic alphabet for all official languages in the autonomous republics of the Russian Federation. Time has still to be allowed for situations in turmoil to settle down.

25.3.4 Transitional remarks on section 25.3

No overall picture of the reality and the fate of regional and minority languages can be drafted mainly because the situations are not comparable. The bilingual Catalan–Castilian situation in Spanish Catalonia is a success story but the results of "linguistic normalization" in the Spanish–Basque region are questioned as to the development of the daily use of Basque particularly in towns, although one can observe a sustained progress towards the use of

Basque wherever it can be institutionally implemented. The Irish Republic's institution of Irish Gaelic as its national language at the beginning of the 1920s has had the effect of ensuring that it is taught in all schools, but apart from a small part of the country where the language is still spoken (the *Gaeltacht*), the population has Irish varieties of English as vernacular speech. As we have seen in the case of Sorb, languages spoken by numerically small communities tend to be on the wane; this is also the case with Frisian (Gorter, 1992) or the Finnish Kvens in Norway (Gardner-Chloros, 1997, p. 197). Nevertheless, whatever the differences, it would be difficult not to observe a general trend in favor of the adoption of the dominant languages, usually the official language of the country. (For more on language endangerment, see chapters 15–18, 27, and 28.)

25.4   Recent Trends in Education and Communication in Europe

The main feature in the development of education during the second half of the twentieth century in Europe was the extension of compulsory education from twelve to sixteen years, and the introduction and generalization of foreign language learning into the secondary and recently into the primary level. At the turn of the century, the new media contribute to creating new horizons and new social and individual needs.

The younger generation under 25 years of age – an average of 30 percent of the population in the EU (see section 25.1) – is involved in the new developments in second language learning but we have little means of knowing about their future or the future of the new media. One worrying phenomenon at least affects this generation, i.e. raising the school-leaving age has not resulted in either basic or more extensive knowledge; in France about 8 percent of 20-year-olds are said to be semi-literate (Tabouret-Keller, 1998). An uncomfortable question to be asked is whether there is any point in teaching a second language to people who do not master even their first language. But the most contentious topic concerns the predominance given to English by parents and the general public, and by educational institutions.

25.4.1   *Foreign languages in education in Europe*

A Eurobarometer survey was conducted in all 15 EU member states in December 2000 (*Eurobarometer Report* 54). A sociolinguistic comment is called for right at the outset of discussing the results: the languages are represented by their names and the associated representations are those of the standard language. This is particularly obvious in the answers given to the inevitable question on the mother tongue: for 100 percent of the respondents in Portugal it is Portuguese, for 99 percent in Greece and Italy it is Greek and

Italian respectively. Hence we know nothing about social varieties, or about diglossia.

25.4.2   *Educational bilingualism*

According to the *Eurobarometer* results, 53 percent of Europeans say that they can speak at least one European language in addition to their first language and 26 percent say that they can speak two. 71 percent of Europeans consider that everyone in the EU should be able to speak one European language in addition to their mother tongue and almost the same proportion agrees that this should be English.

The questionnaire makes a difference between "known" and "most often spoken" foreign languages. Whereas English is known by 41 percent of the population, it is most often spoken as a first foreign language by 32 percent, followed by French – known by 19 percent and most often spoken by 9.5 percent. English and French are designated the two most useful languages. A majority (72 percent) tends to believe that knowing foreign languages would be "very" or "fairly" useful and 34 percent of parents say that they want their children to be multilingual. In countries where English is the first foreign language, people tend to state that their knowledge of the language is good (32.5 percent). In Sweden, there are 88 percent who believe so, in Denmark 37 percent even consider it to be very good.

English is the language which is most likely to be selected for travel or with foreign visitors (35 percent), for at least one hour per week (15 percent) and for at least one hour per day (14 percent). Ninety-three percent of the parents of children aged under 20 say it is important that their children learn other European languages, the main reason being that they want them to improve their job opportunities (74 percent).

25.4.3   *The generalization of English as a transnational medium*

Statistics gathered by the European Commission on second languages choice in secondary education in the EU (www.eurydice.org) show that English is chosen as the first foreign language by 88 percent of pupils. In the countries of Middle and Central Europe it is also gaining ground, particularly over Russian, and is chosen by about 65 percent of pupils, except in Rumania where French (75 percent) stands in first place (Truchot, 1999).

This overview confirms the importance given to English by the general public (Truchot, 1997) and sheds some light on the reasons why some people feel other languages should be protected. In the abovementioned Eurobarometer survey a large majority (63 percent) believes that it is necessary to protect their own languages even more as the enlargement of the EU is envisaged. Since 1995, a European Charter for multilingual education (Bressand, 1995) has been circulated and has gained approval from many teachers, educationalists, and politicians. Different countries have developed different language policies: in some countries like Denmark some form of bilingualism is being institutionalized. In the 1970s, in Belgian Flanders English was used to counterbalance French, 20 years later it has completely replaced French, but Flemish Dutch has hardly gained any more room (Nelde, 1993).

On the other hand, many initiatives to foster European languages are being taken at the level of EU institutions like student exchange programs. In most if not all technical high schools, such as the *Ecole centrale de Paris* (ECP), English and one other foreign language are compulsory, the latter to be chosen among seven EU languages and three non-European (Arabic, Chinese, Japanese). Within a double diploma scheme, ECP has established links with 37 universities located in 15 EU countries and, since 2002, with two universities in China. Hence, the choice of the first foreign language being settled (it is English), a new development is taking place in favor of the diversification of the third foreign language.

Nevertheless, the dominance of English as the language of science now seems to be established, although this gives rise to some anxieties (Ammon, 2001; Germain, 2000). European scientific associations, established in a French university, hold their European conferences in English only despite its being the language of only a small minority of participants. Multinational firms generalize the use of English in the working sessions of their boards even when the participants have one or more other languages in common.

25.5   General Conclusions and Open Questions

First of all, some remarks need to be made on the relative value of statistics. According to the latest data circulated by the European office in Brussels, migration of EU citizens within the EU community involves 6 million people, immigration from outside 13 million people, of whom 2.7 million are of Turkish origin and 2.3 million of Northern African origin. Germany, which until now did not apply *jus soli* (see section 25.2) has two-thirds of the Turkish immigrants whereas France, which does apply this principle, has far fewer because Turkish children born in France acquire French citizenship. On the other hand, while Brussels counts 700,000 immigrants from Algeria, the Algerian foreign office, on the occasion of their general election (May 2002), declared that 711,000 Algerian citizens settled in France alone are registered on the official Algerian electoral lists. The main worry of European institutions is not so much the presence of immigrant languages as declining demographic factors due to aging in the European population and the fact that immigrant populations with traditions of high birth rates in their country of origin shift within two generations towards the demographic behavior of their host countries.

The main results of the French survey mentioned at the beginning of this chapter concern the gradual loss of regional languages and of immigrant languages, which implies a parallel loss of bilingualism. Although we have many reasons to differentiate the two cases, we cannot escape the conclusion that currently they share a common fate: after three or four generations, the dominant language of the country is taking over and bi- and multilingualism inside families is coming to an end. The duty to transmit the language to the next generations is being transferred from family and community to public institutions, mainly the school system, with limited success in the case of regional languages, and even less in the case of immigrant languages. Public institutions, mainly educational and administrative bodies, do not have the same commitments as families and communities towards the practical and symbolic duties that sustain community membership.

Several factors in the shaping of linguistic situations intervene, such as constitutions, state politics, educational policies, offers on the job market, and diversity of immigrant waves according to their origin. Our survey illustrates the differences in Europe among at least three types of bilingualism: (1) accompanying political and linguistic colonization (Roman world, ex-USSR), (2) resulting from the integration of linguistic regions within the political frontiers of traditional states using other official languages, and (3) resulting from contemporary labor-related migrations. Whereas the first type may cover centuries-long periods and concern vast populations, the second type, involving much smaller populations, have resulted within the last century in a shift from former regional monolingualism to present state monolingualism, with more or less extended social bilingualisms. The third type is a more or less short-term bilingualism without any noticeable results on the host countries' languages, although the development of press, television and travel facilities may sustain links with the country of origin and, within Europe, transnational family and commercial links as in the case of Turkish emigrants (de Tapia, 2001; see chapter 27 of the present volume). Nevertheless it seems that periods of bilingualism tend to become shorter than they were in past centuries.

Code switching is always present in bilingual situations in Europe but has it any long-term impact on language change (Gardner-Chloros, 1991; see chapter 17)? This is doubtful, as is the impact of mixed language behavior in binational, bilingual families on the language outside of their private circle (Varro, 1995). One may risk the hypothesis that the loss of native languages stresses the need for identities supported by symbolic values.

Bilingual education in Europe from the primary level upwards is on the verge of generalization. There is no doubt that it is necessary for the development of modern management in almost all domains. But the success of bilingual education is far from being achieved in the vast human groups involved in the social changes that stem from this development.

ACKNOWLEDGMENTS

I would like to acknowledge my indebtedness to Dr. Maryvonne Akamatsu for her help with the English version of this chapter, as well as to Dr. Brian Wallis, and to Dr. Pauline Christie for carrying out the final revision of the whole text. I would also like to acknowledge my indebtedness to Dr. Claude Truchot for his help with data on the development of the use of English in Europe and to Dr. Stéphane de Tapia for his insights about the characteristics of Turkish immigration in Europe.

REFERENCES

Akamatsu, M. (1992). Le Royaume-Uni. Les conquêtes de l'anglais [The United Kingdom: The conquests of English]. In J. C. Herreras (ed.), *1992. Situations linguistiques dans les pays de la Communauté européenne.* [1992. Linguistic situations in the states of the European Union], pp. 155–70. Valenciennes: Presses Universitaires de Valenciennes.

Ammon, U. (ed.) (2001). *The Dominance of English as a Language of Science.* Berlin and New York: Mouton De Gruyter.

Barre, R. and Kinkel, K. (eds.) (1993). *Les nouvelles frontières de l'Europe* [The new frontiers of Europe]. Paris: Economica.

Blanchet, Ph., Breton, R., and Schiffman, H. (eds.) (1999). *Les langues régionales de France: un état des lieux à la veille du XXIᵉ siècle/The Regional Languages of France: An Inventory on the Eve of the Twenty-first Century.* Papers of a conference held at rhe University of Pennsylvania, Philadelphia, USA. Leuven: Peeters.

Bressand, J.-M. (ed.) (1995). *La paix par les langues* [Peace through languages]. Besançon: Le monde bilingue.

Broudic, F. (1999a). *Qui parle breton aujourd'hui? Qui le parlera demain?* [Who speaks Breton today? Who will speak it tomorrow?] Brest: Brud Nevez.

Broudic, F. (1999b). Entre histoire et prospective [Past and future]. In C. Clairis, D. Costaouec, and J.-B. Coyos (eds.), *Langues et cultures régionales en France. Etat des lieux, enseignement, politiques,* pp. 125–32. Paris: L'Harmattan.

Carrozza, P. (1992). Situation juridique des minorités en Italie [Legal situation of minorities in Italy]. In H. Giordan (ed.), *Les minorités en Europe. Droits linguistique et droits de l'homme* [Minorities in Europe: Linguistic rights and human rights], pp. 215–32. Paris: Kimé.

Cerquiglini, B. (1999). La Charte européenne des langues régionales ou minoritaires [The European Charter for regional or minority languages]. In C. Clairis, D. Costaouec, and J.-B. Coyos (eds.), *Langues et cultures régionales en France. Etat des lieux, enseignement, politiques* [Regional languages and cultures in France: Current data, education and politics], pp. 107–10. Paris: L'Harmattan.

Chambers, J. K. and Trudgill, P. (1980). *Dialectology.* Cambridge, UK: Cambridge University Press.

Chaudenson, R. and Calvet, L.-J. (2001). *Les langues dans l'espace de la francophonie: de la coexistence au partenariat* [Languages in French-speaking countries: from coexistence to partnership]. Paris: l'Harmattan.

Decime, R. (2000). Une étude de cas: la Vallée d'Aoste. [A case study: The Aosta Valley]. *Le français dans le monde*, special issue: *Actualité de l'enseignement bilingue* [Bilingual education today], January, 22–32.

de Mauro T. ([1963] 1970). *Storia linguistica dell'Italia unita* [History of united Italy]. Bari: Laterza.

Denetz, P. (1988). La langue bretonne. Mémoire de la repression. In G. Vermès (ed.), *Vingt-cinq communautés linguistiques de la France* [Twenty-five linguistic communities in France] (2 vols.), vol. 1, pp. 105–32. Paris: L'Harmattan.

de Tapia, S. (2002). L'offre médiatique en direction des populations turcophones en France: de la presse à la télévision satellitaire [The media offer towards the turcophone population in France: From the press to satellite television]. *Réseaux*, 107 (special issue: *Médias et migrations* [Media and migrations]), 237–62.

Duc, V. (ed.) (2001). *Valle d'Aosta regione d'Europa: l'educazione bi/plurilingue, ponte verso la cittadinanza europea* [The Valley of Aosta, a European region: Bi/plurilingual education, a bridge to European citizenship]. Atti del Convegno: 4 September 2001, Saint-Vincent. Supplement to issue 54 of *L'École Valdotaine*.

EEC (1977). *European Charter for Minority and Regional Languages. The Children of Migrant Workers*. Brussels.

EEC (1992). *European Charter for Minority and Regional Languages of Maastricht*. Brussels.

Ertel, R. (1988). Les langues des sociétés juives – Le yiddish. Entre élection et interdit [The languages of Jewish societies.Yiddish: Between preference and interdiction]. In G. Vermès (ed.), *Vingt-cinq communautés linguistiques de la France* [Twenty-five linguistic

communities in France] (2 vols.), vol. 1 pp. 303–4 and 332–59.

Eurobarometer Report (2001). Europeans and languages. Executive summary, no. 54. http://europa.eu.int/comm/ education/languages/ languagelearning.html.

Fondation Chanoux. http:// www.fondchanoux.org/site/pages/ prestemi.asp.

Fourze, V. (2000). Autour du biélorusse: deux adversaires, un argument [The issue of Byelorussian: Two opponents, one argument]. *Education et sociétés plurilingues* [Education and multilingual societies], 8, 89–96.

Gardner-Chloros, P. (1991). *Language Selection and Switching in Strasbourg*. Oxford: Oxford University Press.

Gardner-Chloros, P. (1997). Vernacular literacy in new minority settings in Europe. In A. Tabouret-Keller, R. Le Page, P. Gardner-Chloros, and G. Varro (eds.), *Vernacular Literacy: A Re-evaluation*, pp. 189–221. Oxford: Clarendon Press.

Germain, P. (2000). Face à la mondialisation. Contribution d'un scientifique [Faced with globalization: A scientist speaks out]. *Education et sociétés plurilingues* [Education and multilingual societies], 9, 7–13.

Gorter, D. (1992). La langue frisonne aux Pays-Bas [Frisian in the Netherlands]. In H. Giordan (ed.), *Les minorités en Europe. Droits linguistiques et droits de l'homme* (Minorities in Europe: Linguistic rights and human rights], pp. 373–93. Paris: Kimé.

Héran, F., Filhon, A., and Deprez, C. (2002). La dynamique des langues en France au XXe siècle [The dynamics of languages in France during the twentieth century]. *Population et sociétés*, 376, 1–4.

Herreras, J. C. (ed.) (1992). *1992. Situations linguistiques dans les pays de la Communauté européenne* [1992. Linguistic situations in the states of the European Union]. Valenciennes: Presses Universitaires de Valenciennes.

Herreras, J. C. (ed.) (1998). *L'enseignement des langues étrangères dans les pays de l'Union Européenne* [The teaching of foreign languages in the countries of the European Union]. Leuven: Peeters.

La documentation française (1999–2000). Etat de la Francophonie dans le monde, données 1999–2000 [The state of French-speaking communities throughout the world: Data from 1999–2000]. Paris: La Documentation française.

Le Berre, Y. and Le Dû, J. (1999). Le *quid pro quo* des langues régionales: sauver la langue ou éduquer l'enfant? [The *quid pro quo* of regional languages: Save the language or educate the child?]. In C. Clairis, D. Costaouec, and J.-B. Coyos (eds.), *Langues et cultures régionales en France. Etat des lieux, enseignement, politiques* [Regional languages and cultures in France: Current data, education and politics], pp. 71–83. Paris: L'Harmattan.

Lecomte, F. (2001). Familles africaines en France: entre volonté d'insertion et attachement au patrimoine langagier d'origine [African families in France: the will to integrate and attachment to linguistic heritage]. *Langage et société* [Language and society], 98, 77–103.

Louarn, N. (ed.) (2001). Bloavezh Europa ar yezhou – Sizhunvezh Breizh [European Year of Languages – Breton week]. *Keleier Ofis ar Brezhoneg*, no. 43. Roazhon: Ofis ar Brezhoneg.

Martel, Ph. (1990). Autour de la loi Deixonne [Comments on the Deixonne Law]. In *Actes de l'Université d'été 1990* [Proceedings of the summer school 1990], 41–57. Nîmes: MARPOC-Institut d'Etudes Occitanes.

Martinet, A. (1975). *Evolution des langues et reconstruction* [Evolution of languages and reconstruction]. Paris: Presses Universitaires de France.

Martinet, A. (1986). *Des steppes aux océans. L'indo-européen et les "Indo-Européens"* [From the steppes to the oceans. Indo-European and the "Indo-Europeans"]. Paris: Payot.

Nelde, P. H. (1993). La Belgique adoptera-t-elle officiellement l'anglais? In M. Cormier and J. Humbley (eds.), L'Europe au rythme de l'anglais [Europe in the rhythm of English]. *Circuit*, 41, 15–26.

Paulston, C. Bratt and Peckham, D. (eds.) (1998). *Linguistic Minorities in Central and Eastern Europe*. Clevedon, UK: Multilingual Matters.

Pech, E. (2001). The Sorbian school system in Germany, 1945–2000. *Education et sociétés plurilingues*, 10, 39–48.

Renfrew, C. (1987). *Archeology and Language: The Puzzle of Indo-European Origins*. London: Cape.

Rousset, P.-L. (1988). *Les Alpes. Leurs noms de lieux. 6000 ans d'histoire? Les appellations d'origine pré-indo-européennes* [The Alps. Their place names. 6000 years of history? Pre-Indo-European terms]. Meylan: Rousset, and Grenoble: Didier and Richard.

Sériot, P. (1997). Le cas du macédonien. Faut-il nommer les langues? [The case of Macedonian: Does a language need to have a name?]. In A. Tabouret-Keller (ed.), *Le nom des langues I. Les enjeux de la nomination des langues* [Names for languages: What is at stake in language-denomination] pp. 167–90. Louvain: Peeters.

Siguan, M. (1996). *L'Europe des langues* [Linguistic Europe]. Sprimont, Belgium: Belgium.

Siguan, M. (1998). *La escuela y los inmigrantes* [The school and the immigrants]. Barcelona: Ediciones Paidos Iberica.

Siguan, M. (2001). *Bilingüismo y lenguas en contacto* [Bilingualism and languages in contact]. Madrid: Allianza Editorial.

Tabouret-Keller, A. (1992). Language contact in focussed situations. In E. H. Jahr (ed.), *Language contact: Theoretical and empirical studies*, pp. 179–94. Berlin and New York: Mouton de Gruyter.

Tabouret-Keller, A. (1998). Lire et écrire: état des lieux et questions pour la psychologie [Reading and writing: The state of the situation and questions for psychology]. *Enfance*, 1, 99–110.

Tabouret-Keller, A. (1999). L'existence incertaine des langues régionales en France [The uncertain existence of regional languages in France]. In *Les langues régionales de France: un état des lieux à la veille du XXIᵉ siècle/The Regional Languages of France: An Inventory on the Eve of the Twenty-first Century*. Papers of a conference held at the University of Pennsylvania, Philadelphia, USA, pp. 95–111. Leuven: Peeters.

Truchot, C. (1997). The spread of English: From France to a more general perspective. *World Englishes*, 16(4) (special issue, *English in Europe*, ed. by M. G. Deneire and M. Goethals, 63–76.

Truchot, C. (1999). Les langues européennes, des territoires nationaux aux espaces globalisés. Observations sur les effets linguistiques de la mondialisation en Europe [European languages, from national territories to globalized spaces: Observations on the linguistic consequences of globalization in Europe]. http://www.uquebec.ca/diverscite.

Truchot, C. (2001). The language of science in France: public debate and language policies. *Contributions to the Sociology of Language*, 84, 319–28 [special issue: U. Ammon (ed.), The dominance of English as a language of science: Effects on other language communities].

Van Den Avenne C. (2001). De l'expérience plurilingue à l'expérience diglossique. Migrants maliens en France [From multilingualism to diglossia. Immigrants Malian in France]. *Cahiers d'études africaines* [African studies papers], 163–4, 619–36.

Varro, G. (1995). *Les couples mixtes et leurs enfants en France et en Allemagne* [Mixed couples and their children in France and Germany]. Paris: Armand Colin.

Varro, G. (2001). Immigrés à l'école. L'argumentation officielle: une analyse sociologique et diachronique [Immigrants in schools. Official argumentation: a sociological and diachronic analysis]. In D. Desmarchelier and M. Doury (eds.) *L'argumentation dans l'espace public contemporain: le cas du débat sur l'immigration* [Argumentation in contemporary public space: the case of the debate over immigration], pp. 129–78. University Lyon II: CNRS, and Fontenay-Saint-Cloud: ENS.

Varro, G. (2003). *Sociologie de la mixité* [Sociology of mixedness]. Paris: Belin.

Véglianté, J. C. (1988). L'italien. Une italophonie honteuse [Ashamed to speak Italian]. In G. Vermès (ed.), *Vingt-cinq communautés linguistiques de la France* [Twenty-five linguistic communities in France] (2 vols.), vol. 2, pp. 234–62. Paris: L'Harmattan.

Vermès, G. (ed.) (1988). *Vingt-cinq communautés linguistiques de la France* [Twenty-five linguistic communities in France] (2 vols.)

Walter, H. (1992). *French Inside Out*. London: Routledge. (First French edition 1988, *Le français dans tous les sens*. Paris: Robert Laffont.)

Walter, H. (1994). *L'aventure des langues en Occident. Leur origine, leur histoire, leur géographie.* [The adventure of languages in the West: Their origin, history, and geography]. Paris: Robert Laffont.

Weinreich, U. (1964 [1953]). *Languages in Contact: Findings and Problems.* The Hague: Mouton. (First edition, New York: Publications of the Linguistic Circle of New York, no. 1.)

Williams, P. (1988). Le jeu "romanès" [The "romanès" play]. In G. Vermès (ed.), *Vingt-cinq communautés linguistiques de la France* [Twenty-five linguistic communities in France] (2 vols.), vol. 2, pp. 234–62. Paris: L'Harmattan.

Zwahr, H. (1966). *Bauernwiderstand und sorbische Volksbewegung in der Oberlausitz (1900–1918)* [Peasants' resistance and people's movements in Upper Lusatia]. Bautzen: Institute for Sorbian Folk Research.

FURTHER READING

Bonnot, J.-F. P. (ed.) (1995). *Paroles régionales. Normes, variétés linguistiques et contexte social.* Strasbourg: Presses universitaires de Strasbourg.

Boutan, P., Martel, Ph., and Roques, G. (eds.) (2001). *Enseigner la région.* Paris: L'Harmattan.

Britain, D. (ed.) (forthcoming). *Language in the British Isles,* 2nd edn. Cambridge, UK: Cambridge University Press.

Price, G. (ed.) (2000). *Encyclopedia of the Languages of Europe.* Oxford: Blackwell.

Price, G. (ed.) (2000). *Languages in Britain and Ireland.* Oxford: Blackwell.

Schnapper, D. (1991). *La France de l'intégration. Sociologie de la nation en 1990.* Paris: Gallimard.

Skutnabb-Kangas, T. and Philipson, R. (1995). *Linguistic Human Rights: Overcoming Linguistic Discrimination.* Berlin and New York: Mouton and De Gruyter.

Szulmajster-Celnikier, A. (1991). *Le yidisch à travers la chanson populaire. Les éléments non-germanique du yidisch.* Leuven: Peeters.

Trudgill, P. (1984). *Languages in the British Isles,* 1st edn. Cambridge, UK: Cambridge University Press.

Vermès, G. and Boutet, J. (eds.) (1987). *France, pays multilingue,* 2 volumes. Paris: L'Harmattan.

26   Turkish as an Immigrant Language in Europe

AD BACKUS

26.1   Introduction

Any first-time visitor to Western Europe is likely to notice a considerable Turkish presence, the modern-day legacy of labor migration in the 1960s and 1970s. The goal of this chapter is to provide a comprehensive overview of the linguistic work that has been done to date on this Turkish diaspora. Language change is the overarching theme of this contribution, since, naturally, any description of Immigrant Turkish tends to focus on what makes it different from Turkish as spoken in Turkey. Section 26.2 provides historical and socio-demographic information on the Turkish immigrant communities in Western Europe. The rest of the text will deal with the effects of contact on the Turkish language, with separate sections on maintenance, acquisition, code switching, and structural change.

26.2   History and Current Situation

The Turkish immigrant community in Western Europe got its start in the 1960s and early 1970s. Encouraged both by the Turkish state, which was battling high unemployment and explosive population growth, and the receiving nations, which had a shortage of workers willing to do undesirable jobs, *Gastarbeiter* (German for "guest workers") from Mediterranean countries, including Turkey, were recruited for factory work in Western European countries and Australia. Officially sanctioned labor migration came to an end with the oil crisis of 1973, after which family reunification, illegal immigration, and marriage have taken over as the main sources of new immigrants.

Apart from small numbers of highly educated political refugees, the early Turkish population in the diaspora consisted mainly of male migrant workers, most of whom came either directly from rural areas in Turkey, especially Central Anatolia, Southwestern Anatolia, and the Black Sea area, or from the *gecekondu* squatter districts that sprung up around the major cities in Western Turkey as a result of an already ongoing process of internal migration (cf. Abadan-Unat, 1985, p. 17; Kıray, 1976). Most had no or only little vocational training. Subsequent migration started to involve more female workers (in, for instance, the textile industry). Saving money was generally the sole purpose of emigration, to be sent home as remittances at regular intervals or to invest in homes or small businesses on return to Turkey. However, such dreams tended to get shattered somewhere along the way (cf. Abadan-Unat, 1976). Though staying for good was not the prevailing long-term plan, family reunification, which got under way in the early 1970s, effectively turned the *migrants* into an *immigrant* community.

In Germany, Turks form the majority among the immigrants, while they share this status with Moroccans in the Low Countries. In other countries, the number and/or the relative importance of the Turks as an ethnic minority varies, but their absolute numbers are impressive in France, Austria, and Switzerland (see table 26.1). Official data regarding numbers of inhabitants with an immigrant background have to be treated cautiously, however, as their reliance on the criteria of "nationality" and/or "country of birth" makes them underestimate the real numbers. On the other hand, statistics given for Turks usually include Kurds and other people who have their roots in Turkey but have a first language other than Turkish (see Extra and Gorter, 2001, p. 8, for these problems and some suggested solutions). It is difficult to say how great the proportion of Kurds is among the immigrants, with estimates sometimes ranging up to 30 percent, a figure which may be correct in some areas. These caveats should be kept in mind when consulting table 26.1. Gogolin and Reich

Table 26.1   Numbers of Turks in various countries, based on figures from Extra and Gorter (2001, p. 14).

Country[a]	Inhabitants with Turkish nationality (beginning of 1994)	Country[b]	Inhabitants with Turkish nationality (year)
Belgium	88,302	Norway (Türker 2000, p. 34)	11,000 (1999)
Denmark	34,685	Austria (www.oestat.gv.at)	134,500 (2000)
Germany	1,918,395	Switzerland (www.statistik.admin.ch)	80,165 (1999)
France	197,712	Australia (Kurtböke, 1998)	27,770 (1991)
The Netherlands	202,618		
Sweden	23,649		
Great Britain	41,000		

[a] The countries of the European Union that have sizable Turkish minorities.
[b] Some other countries.

(2001, p. 197) claim a total of 2.11 million Turks in Germany for 1998, a figure close enough to the 1994 figure given in the table. In the Netherlands and France, on the other hand, the real numbers of Turkish immigrants are estimated at about 300,000 (cf. Akinci and Yağmur, forthcoming; Extra and Gorter, 2001, p. 15).

A second generation is now well established and a third generation is coming of age. In general, relations with the majority population seem to be improving. Turks are, for example, adopting citizenship of the host countries in increasing numbers. The problems of discrimination, alienation, and breakdown of family structure that plagued the first generation have been mitigated for at least part of the immigrant community. Many of the intergenerational problems that are an almost inevitable result of the uprooting associated with labor migration find an eloquent voice in a growing body of migrant literature, often written in the majority languages.

Still, problems abound (cf. Jørgensen, 1998, p. 240). Turkish children and adolescents suffer worrisome, though falling, rates of educational failure, Turks tend to be concentrated in cheap housing districts, and they have minimal clout as a political pressure group. Generally, Western European political and social debates about immigrant minorities center on the notions of "assimilation" and "integration." Fears of a developing economic underclass consisting of ethnically different, and for the most part religiously different, i.e. Islamic, minorities are widespread (cf. Gubbay, 1999). Policy tends to aim at integration of minority populations into the mainstream; the wish that they would just give up their language is often barely disguised, in dry policy documents as well as in stirring political speeches. This assimilationist goal is also what drives many of the initiatives in education, as we will see in the next subsection.

26.2.1   Education

The educational profile of Turkish children is not very good, with relatively few students moving on to forms of higher education. As with immigrant minorities all over the Western world, low levels of proficiency in the majority language are generally claimed to be the reason, with little discussion of the paradoxical fact that most children actually prefer the majority language over Turkish in their everyday language choices (see section 26.4), nor of the "softer" reasons for educational failure, such as marginalization. It has often been observed that, while many Western European governments express great interest in promoting multilingualism among their inhabitants, stimulating children to learn foreign languages such as English, German, and French, the official attitude towards the maintenance of immigrant languages is hostile, as it is commonly viewed as an obstacle to full integration.

Education systems in the various countries generally approach minority children's problems as stemming from a low level of proficiency in the national standard languages. Improving this level of proficiency has always been the primary goal of educational initiatives, including those that involve home language instruction. Recently, a shift in official policy can be discerned, in that cultural, legal, and economic arguments are used to justify the need for home language instruction. However, this second goal, originally heard only in Sweden (which, ironically, is now moving in the opposite direction, cf. Boyd, 2001, p. 187), is not pursued vigorously anywhere.

There is very little European Union legislation on home language instruction, and the ways in which the various countries have tackled the problem vary. In some places, for instance France and some of the German states, responsibility is left to the local Turkish embassies or consulates, with only financial support from the host country. In most countries, minority-language instruction exists to a limited extent, usually as an aid to fostering proficiency in the majority language, certainly in primary education. Home language instruction is a politically sensitive topic, however, since it is sometimes perceived as a barrier to social integration. A side-effect is that Turkish as a subject has a marginalized status, which extends to its teachers. It is often taught extracurricularly, teachers hold a marginal position among the faculty (usually they work at several schools, in order to accumulate enough hours to make a living), specially designed teaching material is only available to a limited degree, grades and credit for the subject often lack the status of "regular" subjects (these last two points are continuously improving, however, with ongoing professionalization of the field), and its very existence is insecure in many places, due to ongoing efforts to get it banned. In Germany, for instance, immigrant language teaching flourishes in some states, but has been abolished in others (see Gogolin and Reich, 2001). In the classroom, Turkish is often relegated to minor or supporting functions, even within bilingual programs (Dirim, 1999; Jørgensen, 1998, p. 242).

Be that as it may, Turkish is available as a school subject, at least theoretically, in most countries where Turks form a substantial minority. Bilingual education is rare, because of the multicultural composition of most urban classrooms. Variation exists between countries primarily as to the extent of home language instruction and the way in which it is fit into the curriculum. In most cases, the class is taught for a few hours per week, more often than not extracurricularly (also see Holmen, Latomaa, Gimbel, Andersen, and Jørgensen, 1995, p. 180). Participation is optional, and it is hard to get a clear idea of how many Turkish children are involved in Turkish classes. While in the Netherlands most of the Turkish children seem to enroll in Turkish classes, the participation rate is only about 53 percent in Sweden (Boyd, 2001, p. 182). Often, children are only eligible if they are classified as "Turkish speakers," as opposed to, for instance, "bilingual" (typically in systems which use home language instruction strictly as an aid to improve proficiency in the majority language).

In secondary education, Turkish, when available as an option, is normally one of the possible "foreign" languages that pupils can choose as part of their examination package. Its status is, therefore, much less marginal than in primary education. In practice, it is virtually only pupils with a Turkish background who choose Turkish.

I wish to end this introduction with a note of caution regarding intra-group variation. In what follows, I will often use terms such as "the Turkish communities" and "Turkish speakers" as if what is reported about particular informants in particular studies holds true for everybody. In an overview article, I feel that is inescapable. Not all Turks are the same, however, and not all Turkish immigrant communities are the same (cf. Jørgensen, 1998, p. 241 on the quite pervasive differences in Danish-Turkish relations between two districts in the same city; also see Pfaff, 1991, p. 125; and Huls 2000 for the considerable differences between two families). There are social, political, cultural, and economic differences between individuals, as in all groups. Some people have dense Turkish networks, some don't. In some neighborhoods, the Turkish community forms the majority; in others, they are few, and hardly visible. Some people use Turkish all the time, others code-switch extensively, yet others prefer the majority language. Some feel maintenance of Turkish is very important, others don't care very much. Some have access to home language instruction; others don't. It is impossible to give the full flavor of this variation here, and this brings the risk of presenting generalizations that are just too broad. Few large-scale surveys have been undertaken except for the most abstract or global of issues, such as language choice. Most studies, instead, are based on a sometimes relatively small pool of informants from a single locale. The next section introduces the most extensive of these.

26.3 Available Data

This overview is mainly meant to be a guide to the various studies undertaken in the past two decades in the various countries involved. While most linguistic studies of Turkish migrants focus on their second language acquisition, large-scale projects with an emphasis on Turkish have been funded at: the Free University of Berlin, on bilingual acquisition in 1- to 8-year-olds (Pfaff, 1991); Copenhagen University, on bilingual development of 5- to 13-year-olds (the "Køge project"; Boyd, Andersson, Berggreen, and Hjulstad Junttila, 1995); Tilburg University in the Netherlands, on both of those topics plus adult code switching and language attrition (Extra and Verhoeven, 1999); and the Institute for the German Language in Mannheim, Germany, on the social networks and linguistic repertoires of bilingual teenagers and twenty-somethings (Kallmeyer and Keim, forthcoming). In many other places, individual researchers have produced research reports, often in the form of MA and Ph.D. theses, and I will attempt to do justice to their efforts throughout this text. So far, there has been no study reviewing all this work (this chapter may be considered a first attempt), but Bayraktaroğlu (1999) and Holmen and Jørgensen (2000) bring together many of the topics to be discussed below. Finally, the work of Lars Johanson must be singled out, in particular because he has integrated the linguistic results of language contact in the diaspora into a wider framework of contact effects with Turkic languages taking center stage (see Johanson,

1992, 1993, 1999a, b; and, for evaluations, Backus, 1996; Boeschoten, 1997; Türker 2000).

   Studies of Immigrant Turkish have focused mostly on first language acquisition, on bilingual language use (code switching) among adolescents, and on language choice. Other aspects of bilingualism, such as language attitudes, dialect mixing, syntactic change, loan translation, phonological change, language attrition, or the psycholinguistic organization of the bilingual mental lexicon, have been studied much less extensively. One overarching question that sometimes comes up explicitly, and is often lurking in the background, is whether a new variety of Turkish has emerged, a variety I will refer to as "Immigrant Turkish."

26.4   Language Choice, Maintenance, and Shift

Most Turkish immigrants are bilingual. Labor immigration tends to lead to rapid language shift, in contrast to some other types of bilingualism, presumably thanks to the generally positive attitudes towards the majority language. Former experience, especially with immigrant languages in the United States, would lead one to expect that the language of such a group does not have a bright future. The case of modern-day migrant workers in Western Europe, however, differs in a number of crucial ways, especially for Turks.

   Various characteristics account for the high degree of language maintenance in this community. First, there are relatively few exogamous marriages. What is more, prospective spouses are generally looked for in Turkey, rather than within the immigrant community. In a French survey of 1997, for instance, it was found that 98 percent of females and 92 percent of males in the Turkish community in France married someone from Turkey (Akinci and Yagmur, forthcoming). Second, maintenance of Turkish is often explicitly recognized as important, as a "commitment," for example because of a possible move back to Turkey. Third, frequent summer-long holidays in Turkey serve to re-establish important Turkish-medium kinship and friendship bonds. Fourth, there is easy access to, and much use of, Turkish media. Though most countries have been providing state-funded Turkish news programs on radio and TV for years (generally averaging between one and three hours a week for television, and a bit more for radio), and the Turkish National Broadcasting Company provides cable companies in Western European countries with its international program, in more recent years many Turks have acquired satellite dishes in order to receive a wider selection of Turkish channels. Written material is widely available as well, especially in Germany, including European issues of Turkish newspapers and homegrown bilingual magazines. Fifth, exposure to standard Turkish in schools is relatively widespread (cf. section 26.2). Sixth, the abundance of Turkish organizations and the density of social networks in general ensure many opportunities for "intra-group" contact, and, hence, for language maintenance. Seventh, the tight link between language and religion ensures that there is one domain, the mosque, for which exclusive use of Turkish is reported in language choice surveys. Finally, language maintenance may sometimes be aided by the negative societal factors of marginalization and physical segregation. Researchers generally shy away from describing ethnic parts of town as "ghettos" (with the exception of the Mannheim group, cf. Keim and Cındark, forthcoming, who emphasize that this is the term their informants use), but that is not to deny that in many urban centers Turks are heavily concentrated in relatively poor areas with cheap housing, such as Kreuzberg in Berlin (30 percent Turks in 1990, with much heavier concentrations in certain neighborhoods, cf. Pfaff, 1994, p. 77). In such areas, Turks encounter relatively few members of the majority culture in their daily lives, limiting the need for the use of the majority language as a lingua franca. One reason for the general reluctance to use terms such as "ghettoization" is that in many of these areas a flourishing microeconomy has developed (not to be confused with an "informal economy"), with Turkish businesses and services, including internet sites. Though many eventually move out of these areas, or wish to do so, growing up in such circumstances obviously facilitates language maintenance.

On a more abstract level, it has been observed that Turks have a relatively high degree of loyalty to their language (Tribalat, 1995, p. 47). In comparative studies of ethnolinguistic vitality, Turkish generally comes out as one of the more vital immigrant languages, for instance in the attitude surveys undertaken by Akinci and Yagmur (forthcoming) in Lyon, France and by Jongenburger and Aarssen (2001) in Utrecht, the Netherlands. Even though many informants in the first study reported using French more than Turkish in their daily lives, they were virtually unanimous in their emphasis on the importance of Turkish as the language of the family, particularly for raising children.

While maintenance may be strong, children do follow the language choice patterns familiar from studies of language shift in bilingual communities, using more Turkish when addressing the parent generation, and more of the majority language among themselves and with friends (Akinci and Yağmur, forthcoming; Boyd, Andersson, Berggreen, and Hjulstad Junttila, 1995). While most data are based on self-reports, the pattern was demonstrated empirically by Huls and Van de Mond (1992, p. 109). They studied language choice in daily interaction in two families, one recently arrived (five years before the fieldwork started), and one which had been in the Netherlands for 15 years. Dutch was used more in the latter family, but the pattern was already in evidence in the first family: children use more Dutch than Turkish, especially among themselves and do not limit themselves to Turkish only when addressing their parents. They conclude: "in both families, the children were 'pushing' the use of Dutch, whereas the parents were 'pushing' the use of Turkish" (p. 109). All this is in contrast to the general public perception, which is that Turks don't want to speak Dutch.

Large-scale surveys generally don't allow for an accurate assessment of the pervasiveness of code switching between, and register variation within, the two languages. For a reliable picture, we need to turn to observations of everyday speech. Such data, discussed in much of the remainder of this chapter, show that the Turkish immigrant communities possess a linguistic repertoire that is much more complex than a simple dichotomy between two languages (see especially subsection 26.6.3). For now, we can conclude that children growing up in the immigrant families get enough exposure to Turkish to acquire it as their first language. The next section looks at language acquisition in the immigration setting in some more detail. (For more on language maintenance and shift, see chapters 14–16, 18, 25, and 28.)

26.5   Acquisition

Studies of bilingual acquisition tend to focus on children growing up in middle-class families in which the parents speak different languages to the child (in Romaine, 1995, pp. 115, 203–5, this is Type 1), rather than where they habitually code-switch (Type 6). Yet, a huge number of children all over the world, many of them in immigrant communities, grow up with exactly the latter kind of input. Section 26.6 goes over the types of code switching encountered in Turkish immigrant communities; for now it is sufficient to note that it occurs and that it is widespread, even within the family. This has ramifications for how language acquisition proceeds.

From the available studies on Turkish in the Western European diaspora, the following general picture of acquisition can be sketched. Children tend to grow up as successive bilinguals, meaning they start off as either Turkish monolinguals or as Turkish-dominant bilinguals (Pfaff, 1999, p. 98). Until age 4, they tend to acquire Turkish in more or less the same way as their monolingual peers in Turkey, a logical outcome of the factors that stimulate language maintenance, discussed in the previous section. From age 4 on, bilingual children start to change the balance of their two languages. There seems to be quite general consensus among researchers that the dominance tips from Turkish towards the majority language after age 8 (see Aarssen, 1996, p. 170; Akinci, Jisa, and Kern 2001; Pfaff, 1999, p. 99), presumably because of a dramatic decrease in Turkish input, as children move into a much more Dutch-, German-, etc. dominated world when they start school. We must beware, of course, of unwarranted generalizations. It is likely to make a world of difference, for instance, whether a child grows up in a solidly Turkish part of town or in an area with relatively few Turks (cf. Pfaff, 1993, p. 126), or whether he or she attends a daycare center, and, if so, whether there are Turkish-speakers among the staff. In general, dominance patterns of individual children correlate with their language use patterns (Pfaff, 1994, p. 87). Subsection 26.5.1 will address early acquisition; subsection 26.5.2 will briefly look at older children.

26.5.1   Early bilingual acquisition

The speech of very young Turkish immigrant children has been studied in the Berlin and Tilburg projects (Pfaff, 1991, 1993, 1994, 1997, 1999; Van der Heijden,

1999; Van der Heijden and Verhoeven, 1994). Four characteristics typify both studies: first, data were mostly audio-recorded in semi-controlled environments. Second, children were recorded in Turkish and in German or Dutch settings (usually with fieldworkers who were, or pretended to be, monolingual). Third, data are longitudinal (sometimes cross-sectional, cf. Pfaff, 1991, p. 101), with age ranges of 1–7 in Berlin and 2–3;6 in Tilburg. Fourth, they generally compare findings with what is known about monolingual acquisition in Turkey (e.g. Aksu-Koç, 1988).

In general, these studies find global similarities to monolingual acquisition of Turkish, except for a few Dutch- or German-dominant children (Pfaff, 1994, p. 81; Van der Heijden and Verhoeven, 1994, pp. 57–64). However, all studies report considerable variation between children, mainly dependent on the degree to which either language is dominant for them, itself presumably dependent on the social and family circumstances. In general, Turkish-dominant children, especially in Berlin, develop like their monolingual peers. Patterns are learned around the same age and, by and large, the same types of acquisition errors occur (Pfaff, 1991, p. 114; 1994, p. 83). The morphosyntactic categories that have been investigated include word order, case marking, plural marking, verbal inflection, person marking, and whether or not overt subject pronouns are used ("pro-drop"). Deviations from monolingual acquisition in the data from German-dominant children and most of the children in the Netherlands shows up not in errors, but in the avoidance of certain structures which monolingual and Turkish-dominant age-mates use fluently. They tend, for instance, to avoid the evidential mood, a category not found in German or Dutch (Pfaff, 1994, p. 85; cf. the contrasting examples in 1a and b). The German-dominant child in (1b) avoids the use of the evidential by construing the event as one which he witnessed himself (by pointing at the picture). This is not incorrect, but the evidential construal in (1a) is the more expected choice.

(1) a. Turkish-dominant child:
         burda da köpek xxx istiyo-muş bunları (Pfaff, 1994, p. 91)
         here and dog xxx want-EVID.3sg these
         "and then here the dog wanted xxx, these"
         ('xxx' = unintelligible speech; EVID = Evidential; 3 = 3rd person;
         sg = singular)
     b. German-dominant child:
         o zaman bu böyle yap-tı, bak! bu bunu yi-cek diye (Pfaff, 1994, p. 91)
         that time this like.this do-PAST.3sg look! this this-ACC eat-FUT.3sg
         because
         "then this did like this, look! because this is going to eat this"
         (PAST = Past tense; ACC = Accusative; FUT = Future tense)

These children also avoid non-finite verb forms, of which Turkish makes liberal use. In addition, Boeschoten (1990), Pfaff (1991), and Van der Heijden (1999, p. 138) conclude that young Turkish-Dutch bilingual children lagged behind monolingual children somewhat in their acquisition of derivational morphology.

Pfaff (1994, p. 82) notes that bilingual children not only acquire the various individual aspects of Turkish, but also the more global norms of language usage. While they initially use Turkish words in their German and German ones in their Turkish, they soon start drifting towards a monolingual variety of German, while their Turkish remains open to code switching. This reflects the immigrant community's norms for the two languages, as we will see in section 26.6. It also presents an interesting twist on what is perhaps the predominant theme in the literature on child bilingualism: the separation of the two languages in the child's mind (cf. the overviews in Bhatia and Ritchie, 1999, Deuchar and Quay 2000, and chapter 4 of the present volume). Recall that most of this literature deals with middle-class children brought up with the one-parent-one-language strategy. Such children are implicitly taught *not* to code-switch. The potential differences from children in immigrant communities have rarely been the subject of investigation, primarily, I believe, because the latter are underrepresented in research on child bilingualism.

Since code switching is prominently present in the input, and is in any case not frowned upon by parents (Pfaff, 1999, p. 109), it is not surprising that its frequency tends to increase in the speech of children in immigrant communities as they get older (cf. Pfaff, 1999, pp. 109, 118; and Boeschoten and Verhoeven, 1987, for 4–7-year-old Turkish children in the Netherlands). Findings for Turkish children generally agree with the results of the few other studies of children in environments where extensive mixing was present in the parental and communal input (cf. McClure, 1981, on Mexican-American children in the US; Moffatt and Milroy, 1992 on Punjabi children in Britain). Children gradually acquire the local norms of communicative competence, including those for language choice.

Backus and Van der Heijden (1998) track the development of code switching in the speech of four young children in the Netherlands, aged 2;0 to 3;6. Most of the Dutch words are nouns or discourse markers; Dutch nouns are, where needed, affixed with Turkish inflection for person, number, and case, and occupy the clausal positions Turkish syntax dictates, as in (2a, b). Dutch discourse markers often pop up in the form of negative or affirmative particles preceding or following a Turkish utterance, as in (2c). While most code switching is very similar to what goes on in adult speech, to be discussed in section 26.6, at least two features are found only in child data. One is the use of Dutch personal and demonstrative pronouns in Turkish clauses, as in (2d). The other is that use of foreign verbs was rare (also see Boeschoten and Verhoeven, 1987), something noted for Turkish-dominant children in Berlin as well (Pfaff, 1991). (The meanings of abbreviations are summarized in the list at the end of the text of the chapter.)

(2)   a.   senin okul-un-da *glijbaan* var mı?
           your school-your-LOC slide there.is Q

"is there a *slide* at your school?"
(LOC = Locative; Q = Question marker)

b. bun-lar *poesje*-nın yemeğ-i.
this-pl pussycat-GEN food-POSS.3sg
"these are the *cat's* food."
(pl = Plural; GEN = Genitive; POSS = Possessive)

c. *nee*: o kapatır.
"*no*, s/he will close (it)."

d. *mij* at he?
me throw.IMP right?
"throw (it) (to) *me*, alright?"
(IMP = Imperative)

If there are structural differences between Immigrant Turkish and its sibling variety in Turkey (see section 26.7), they are not observable in the available data on children's speech, which suggests that these differences have not affected the core grammar. However, there may be more evidence of change in the speech of older children, partly because their more or less completed acquisition process allows the study of the peripheral and more complex elements of syntax, which may be more subject to external influence or imperfect acquisition, and partly because of the shift in dominance patterns, which make such phenomena progressively more likely.

26.5.2 Older children

Relevant data for this age group come from two types of studies. The Berlin and Copenhagen studies are based mainly on spontaneous data (Jørgensen, 1998, p. 243), while in France and especially the Netherlands many studies have made use of language tasks (Aarssen, 1996; Akinci 2001; Boeschoten, 1990; Schaufeli, 1991; Verhoeven, 1988). Overall, the first group of studies interprets its findings in terms of language change (see section 26.7), while the second group, with its basis in school-related tasks and opportunities for cross-group comparison, focuses on proficiency and passive knowledge.

Again, many of the relevant studies have a close link with research in monolingual acquisition, in particular with the influential studies of Dan Slobin and Ayhan Aksu-Koç (see Aksu Koç, 1994). They tend to study the same aspects of Turkish, generally fairly demanding syntactic structures and discourse skills, such as tense and modality, use of pro-drop, clause linkage, and narrative structure. The methodology is similar too, often making use of so-called "Frog Story" or other narratives, in which children tell the researcher what is going on in a picture book. Typically, the experimental group, made up of bilingual children from the immigrant community, is compared to a control group of monolingual children in Turkey of comparable social and regional background (this is necessary because studies of monolingual Turkish acquisition tend to make use of middle-class children in Istanbul, who grow up in a linguistic environment that differs strongly from that of the Anatolian working-class immigrants).

Data show parallel developments in monolingual and bilingual children in some respects, and differences in others. It seems to be the case that the majority of bilingual children initially lag behind monolingual ones (Boeschoten, 1990; Pfaff, 1991; Schaufeli, 1991; Verhoeven and Boeschoten, 1986), then ultimately catch up in school-related aspects of proficiency (i.e. aspects of relatively formal, standard-like language use, cf. Aarssen, 1996, p. 164; Aarts, 1996). In general, the syntactic system seems to be well acquired by age 12. Many of the more complex syntactic structures, as well as much of the lexicon, may be acquired passively, thanks to formal instruction and ever-increasing exposure to Turkish media, but tend to be avoided in actual everyday conversation (Schaufeli, 1994, p. 216). Some studies find, for instance, that bilinguals tend to use conjunctions where monolinguals use synthetic means of clause linkage, and Pfaff (1991, p. 118) notes that bilingual children have trouble with participial structures, relying on discourse markers instead. However, these are often used in colloquial monolingual Turkish as well in place of synthetic clause linkage devices. This illustrates how difficult it is to demonstrate reduced proficiency, or, for that matter, change. It is certainly a desideratum for future research into bilingual development to work out exactly how passive knowledge as demonstrated in linguistic tasks and active knowledge as demonstrated in spontaneous use are to be related, and to what extent children are successful in acquiring Turkish register differentiation.

Whatever changes we may or may not observe in informants' Turkish, one thing in which they undergo a development completely different from their monolingual peers is their increasing proficiency in code switching. Pfaff (1999, p. 100) notes that there are more and more German elements in her informants' Turkish as they grow older. This is most clearly demonstrated by the Danish data (Jørgensen, 1998). While conversations between 7-year-olds are mainly in Turkish, 11-year-olds code-switch a lot, and are able to use code switching for subtle communicative functions. Jørgensen (1998, p. 254) summarizes: "Between the ages of 7 and 12 children develop their linguistic skills tremendously. They acquire literacy, their linguistic awareness increases, and their pragmatic skills become steadily more refined. The same applies to code-switching." Code switching is the subject of the next section. (For additional material on language acquisition and bilingualism, see chapters 4 and 5.)

26.6   Code Switching

Code switching, used here as a cover term for the alternating use of two languages in the same conversation, is probably the best-researched aspect of the Turkish language in its Western European habitat. Given what we know about language choice patterns in the immigrant communities (see section 26.4) and the mixed speech produced by young and older children (section

26.5), it can hardly come as a surprise that code switching is indeed extremely widespread, according to all studies done to date. As is typical of the field, these are generally based on transcribed recordings of spontaneous conversations. Patterns claimed to be absent from the mixed variety are thus simply not attested; they are not necessarily judged ungrammatical. The Mannheim and Køge data are characterized by more elaborate transcripts, reflecting the involved researchers' interest in conversational analysis. Informants tend to be from the second generation (but see subsection 26.6.1).

The rest of this section will deal with intergenerational differences in code-switching patterns (subsection 26.6.1), the general structure of Turkish-based code switching and the specifics of a few selected aspects (26.6.2), and its communicative functions (26.6.3). Throughout, I will use the terms *insertion* and *alternation*. Alternation is the actual "switching" of languages at sentence or clause boundaries, as in (3a), where the first clause is Turkish and the second one Dutch. Insertion, on the other hand, involves the use of single Embedded Language (EL) words in Matrix Language (ML) clauses (see Myers-Scotton, 1997 for these terms). This is illustrated in (3b), where the language of the clause, in structural terms, is Turkish throughout. Insertion is generally studied for its structural characteristics, while alternation tends to be analyzed in terms of pragmatic function.

(3) a. sen de kalkman lazım onlarla *en hoe moet je dan op de rest letten?*
         'you must get up with them as well, *and then how can you keep an eye on the rest?'*
     b. mesela okul-da iki tane kız da bana *verkering* sor-du
         for.instance school-LOC two CLAS girl too me.DAT engagement ask-PAST.3sg
         'For instance, two girls at school have asked me out on a *date'*
         (CLAS = Classifier; DAT = Dative)

26.6.1 Intergenerational variation

Table 26.2 summarizes the empirical results of my own study. Clearly, informants differ not just in their language preferences, which confirm the language choice patterns uncovered in macro- sociolinguistic studies (see section 26.4), they also code-switch in different ways. Generally, first-generation informants speak Turkish with just a few foreign content words thrown in. The dominant speech mode for the intermediate generation (defined as having arrived in the Netherlands when they were between 5 and 12 years old (cf. Mushaben, 1985, for a general, not just linguistic, characterization of this group) was a mix of insertion and alternation, while the second generation engaged in frequent alternation. This pattern of intergenerational variation is likely to be very general, as it is supported by data collected in other places (see Pfaff, 1999, p. 116; Jørgensen, 1998, Kallmeyer and Keim, forthcoming, and Adalar and Tagliamonte, 1998, p. 143; the first two actually show these changes in real

Table 26.2   Distribution of main language choice preferences, main types of code switching, and matrix language in code switching across first, intermediate, and second generations in Turkish-Dutch code-switching data (based on Backus, 1996).

Generation	Preference			Type of CS			ML in CS		
	Turkish	*both*	*Dutch*	*Insertion*	*both*	*Alternation*	*Turkish*	*both*	*Dutch*
First	x			x			x		
Intermediate		x			x		x		
Second			x			x			x

time, as children are shown to go through such stages between the ages 4 and 10). It is very difficult, however, to compare code-switching patterns across studies, not just because the phenomenon is greatly dependent on the dynamics of any particular conversation, but more importantly because, within a linguistic repertoire that is broadly the same all over the diaspora, local communities and subgroups within communities develop separate norms for these varieties and for how and when to use them. I will return to this point, which most likely will dominate the research agenda in the near future, in subsection 26.6.3.

The second-generation informants are the first to mix Turkish words into their Dutch, as a by-product of their shift in language preference. If you speak Dutch all the time, you will have to use Turkish words at times, for instance when talking about Turkish weddings or customs, where first- and intermediate-generation speakers would probably have switched into Turkish completely. The structure of insertional code switching with a Turkish base is discussed in subsection 26.6.2.

26.6.2   Characteristics of insertion

There are at least two levels at which the insertion of EL elements can be described. Most familiar is the description of morphosyntactic *integration*. Semantic and psycholinguistic considerations underlying the *selection* of EL elements are discussed much less often.

Backus (2001) reports on the semantic characteristics of the Dutch words used in the Dutch Turkish data. Most "Dutch" domains are fairly predictable. They are intimately connected with life in the Netherlands, for example education, job hunting, work, and various aspects of social life, such as fashion, sports, and dating (see Necef, 1994, p. 143; Schaufeli, 1992, p. 127). What makes certain domains "typically Dutch" is that speakers have experience with them through Dutch, as is also supported by language choice data (see section 26.4). Since the majority language is used in interactions associated with the semantic field, much of the vocabulary belonging to it has made its way into speakers' idiolects. In addition, bilinguals are keenly aware of subtle meaning differences between translation equivalents (see Weinreich, 1953, p. 59), making, for instance, the use of Dutch *friet* 'French fries' rather than Turkish *pomfrit* almost obligatory in a conversation about fast food in the Netherlands.

There seems to be a fairly clear lexical division in Turkish-based clauses: basic vocabulary (words such as "guy," "eat," "go," "good") is Turkish and a fair amount of specific vocabulary is from the other language, but mainly so if it is in some way linked to non-Turkish contexts.

Morphosyntactically, the immigrant data concur with other data of insertion in Turkic languages, for instance in Balkan, Iranian or Central Asian settings (Csato forthcoming; Eminov, 1997; Johanson, 1992; Kıral, 2001; Menz, 1999; Rudin and Eminov, 1990). Various models have been set up to describe insertion (cf. Johanson, 1993, Myers-Scotton, 1997, and Poplack and Meechan, 1998). Though this is not the place to describe them in detail, it should be pointed out that Turkish data strongly support them (see Backus, 1992, 1996; Türker, 2000), probably because Turkish, being agglutinative, has a wide array of morphological means available for overt integration of foreign elements, making it somewhat of a poster-language for such models. However, in virtually all published work on code switching involving Turkish, the contact language is typologically unrelated (Germanic, Slavic and Iranian languages), which makes it difficult to know whether the strict adherence to matrix-based principles in all these cases is due to the agglutinating character of Turkish, to the typological distance between it and its contact languages, to commonalities in the sociolinguistics of the reported cases, or to a combination of these (cf. Muysken, 2000, pp. 244–9).

Most EL words are taken in as they are, without any *morphological integration* (i.e. without any Turkish derivational morphology). There are three exceptions, though, two minor and one major. Occasionally, the agentive suffix is found on foreign nouns (as in 4a; also see Pfaff, 1999, p. 114, and Türker, 2000, p. 66), and, in Norwegian Turkish, the 3rd person singular possessive morpheme, which Turkish uses to formally mark compound nouns, is regularly affixed to Norwegian compounds, at least in the speech of intermediate-generation immigrants (Türker, 2000, chapter 6), cf. (4b). This, however, is rarely attested elsewhere. Since lexical renewal tends to be achieved through borrowing rather than through new coinages in bilingual settings, language contact may actually be quite damaging for the productivity of, especially, nominal derivational affixes in the matrix language.

(4) a. ordaki *friet*-çi-yi biliyorum
         there fries-AG-ACC know-PROG-1sg
         "I know that *fries* place there"
         (AG = Agentive; PROG = Progressive tense/aspect; 1 = 1st person)
     b. *Velferds-stat*-ı var ya, bu *Velferdsstat*-ı insanlara e: çok imkan veriyor
         de mi? (Türker, 2000, p. 159)

welfare-state-POSS there.is INT this welfare.state-POSS
"This *welfare state*, this *welfare state* provides people with, uhm, a lot
of opportunities, doesn't it?"
(INT = Interjection)

The one major pattern of morphological integration concerns the seemingly
obligatory addition of an auxiliary verb, usually *yap-* ('to do') to EL verbs, so
Dutch *afstuderen* "graduate" is borrowed as *afstuderen yap-*. There is basic agreement among researchers that this is one of the stand-out features of Immigrant
Turkish (Backus, 1996; Pfaff, 2000; Türker, 2000). All Turkish communities in
the Western European diaspora use these bilingual compound verbs, the structure of which is illustrated in (5). A foreign infinitive is followed by the stem of
the auxiliary, which then carries all necessary inflection. The result is a new
Turkish verb that has exactly the same meaning as the foreign infinitive. The
construction is known from many other contact situations (cf. Muysken, 2000,
chapter 7), including virtually all in which a Turkic language is the receiving
language.

(5)   Iki gün önce işte *bioscoop-*a *vrag-en* yap-tı-ydı-m. (Dutch Turkish)
      two day before well cinema-DAT ask-INF do-PAST-PAST-1sg
      "And only two days before, you see, I had *ask*ed her out to the *movies*"
      (INF = Infinitive)

Backus (1996) and Türker (2000) present exhaustive investigations of this
construction in their data. Both overviews show that *yap-* is a very prolific
element. It is used as a pro-form without any complements (e.g. *üç defa
yap-*, 'three time do', i.e. "do [it] three times"), with pronominal objects (*o-nu
yap-* 'it-ACC do', i.e. "do it"), with noun objects (in its presumably basic function as a transitive verb, as in 6a, but also, in combination with abstract nouns,
with decreased transitivity, cf. 6b and c), with verbal noun objects (6d), and, of
course, with the foreign infinitives, as in (5) above. This latter construction is
an innovation, since *yap-* does not combine with native infinitives (cf. 6e).

(6)   a.   kadınlar toplanıyorlar bir araya konuşuyorlar kahve içiyorlar, çay
           içiyorlar, **el iş-i** yap-ıyor- lar (2nd gen.)
           hand work-POSS do-PROG-3pl
           "women get together, talk among themselves, drink coffee, drink tea,
           do some **embroidering**"
      b.   ben artık hayat-ım-da **kına** yap-ma-m. (Şe, 266; 2nd gen.)
           I from.now.on life-my-LOC henna.night do-NEG.AOR-1sg
           "I'll never do **a** *kına* again in my life"
           (NEG = Negative; AOR = Aorist)
      c.   niye, hemen **ayrımcılık mı** yap-ıyo-lar? (O, 165; 1st gen.)
           why immediately discrimination Q do-PROG-3pl
           "why do they immediately **discriminate**?"

Table 26.3 The continuum of constructions involving *yap-* and a complement.

		Semantics	*Syntax*
Transitive construction	complement *yap-*	concrete achievement/creation	direct object transitive verb
Derivational construction	complement	(holistically construed) process	verb stem
	yap-	processualizer	verbalizing derivational marker

     d. biz bir kere böyle **bir konuşma** yap-tı-k Türk-ler-in arasında. (M, 96; 2nd gen.)
         we one time such one discussion do-PAST-1pl Turk-pl-GEN among
         "one time we had **a discussion** like this with Turks"
     e. *o-nu de-mek yap-tı-n mı?
         it-ACC say-INF do-PAST-2sg Q
         "did you say that?"
         (2 = 2nd person)

The bilingual compound verb construction takes its place at the extreme end of a grammaticalization chain that characterizes *yap-* in its full range of uses. This continuum can be characterized in parallel semantic and syntactic terms. The meanings of the nouns and verbal nouns that *yap-* combines with range from very concrete to highly abstract, and *yap-* adjusts its meaning accordingly, from "create, make" to a bleached "do, carry out." The semantic and syntactic characteristics of the two extremes on this continuum, which I call the Transitive Construction and the Derivational Construction, are given in table 26.3; the continuum is illustrated by the four examples in (6a–d).

Because of the increasing concentration of conceptual content in the object noun in these constructions, *yap-* contributes less and less meaning of its own. It basically just provides the temporal profile by carrying the tense and person inflection. Its syntactic status is in dispute, but note that it shares characteristics both with Light Verbs and with derivational (verb-forming) affixes (see Backus, 1996 for discussion). Its status as a derivational marker is supported by the fact that the verb and *yap-* have to be adjacent (7a, b) and by its obligatoriness: no foreign verb can occur without *yap-*. Borrowed verbs have not been attested with any other way of incorporation into the Turkish clause, for example with direct inflection of the foreign stem (7c).

(7) a. *benim-ki-ni *lenen* **mi** yapmak istiyorsun?
         mine-NOM-ACC borrow-INF **Q** do-INF want-PROG-2sg
         (Intended meaning: "Do you want to BORROW mine?")
         (NOM = Nominalizer)

b.   *Şimdi lenen-i yapmak istiyorum.
now borrow-INF-**ACC** do-INF want-PROG-1sg
(Intended meaning: "I want to do the borrowing now"

c.   *Ali bana *kijk*-tı (Ali me.DAT look-PAST.3sg)
'Ali looked at me'

The choice of *yap-* is actually somewhat surprising, because monolingual Turkish tends to use a different verb, *et-* (which also means 'to do') for this function, e.g. with English computer terms (*download et-*). This alternative to *yap-* is sometimes found in contact data, especially in Denmark and Germany. Retention of *et-* seems to be associated with Turkish dominance, as it is mainly found in first-generation immigrants and very young children (Pfaff, 2000). Both groups tend to use *yap-* mostly with foreign nouns (recall from subsections 26.5.1 and 26.6.1 that they don't use many foreign verbs anyway; cf. Backus and Van der Heijden, 2002; Pfaff, 1999, p. 112). Pfaff's data also show decreasing use of *et-* as children get older, certainly in combination with nouns, as in (8). These patterns suggest that the construction with *yap-* arises victorious out of a competition with *et-* and gets established as the community norm, and that its source lies in its productive combination with foreign nouns.

(8)   *Geschenk* et-ti (Pfaff, 2000)
present do-PAST.3sg
"s/he gave a *present*"

Most inserted EL words undergo complete *morphosyntactic integration*. Turkish copulas, possessives, plurals and cases are often found attached to EL nouns or adjectives, see (9). Adalar and Tagliamonte (1998, pp. 145–7) studied the application of vowel harmony systematically and found it to apply categorically, though I have found some variation in its application after Dutch words in which the last vowel was a schwa. Some inserted words require only syntactic integration, i.e. they do not need to be inflected, for instance the German object noun in (9a). The morphosyntactic system seems quite robust: under-marked or *bare forms* are attested only sporadically (Backus, 1996, p. 208; Türker, 2000, p. 68). An example is the missing possessive marker in (9d).

(9)   a.   *Keller*-e gidip de *Hex* yap-mış-lar (Pfaff, 2000)
cellar-DAT go-CONT and spell make-EVID-3pl
"she went to the *cellar* and cast a *spell*"
(CONT = Continuative aspect)

b.   *Skap*-ı doldur-du-k (Norwegian Turkish; Türker, 2000, p. 68)
cupboard-ACC fill-PAST-1pl
"we filled the *cupboard*"

c.   ***eenvoudig*-ti *foto*-yu onlar dört ayda yaptı, ben iki haftada yaptım, anlata
simple-PAST.3sg X-ray-ACC they four month-LOC

biliyorummu
did-3sg
"it was **simple**, they could make an *X-ray* after four months, I did it in two weeks, you see?"

d. Herkes-in orda *køyeseng* var (Norwegian Turkish; Türker, 2000, p. 74)
everybody-GEN there berth exist
"Everybody's *berth* is there"
expected: herkes-in orda *køyeseng*-i var (berth-POSS.3sg)

Insertions are often more complex than just a content word: many are conventional multi-word units, which are likely to have been retrieved as chunks from the lexicon (Wray, 2002; see Backus, forthcoming for the extended argument and an exhaustive analysis of my data). One example is the plural noun, cf. (10), in which the first example illustrates double marking of plurality.

(10) a. *Weisheits-zähn*-ler çık-ınca *rauszieh-en* ed-iyor-lar. (Menz, 1993)
wisdom-teeth-pl come.out-while pull.out-INF do-PROG-3pl
"When the *wisdom teeth* come, they *pull* them *out*"

b. Ben o-nun boy-u-na bak-tı-m vücud-un-a bak-tı-m
I her-GEN length-her-DAT look-PAST-1sg body-her-DAT look-PAST-1sg
***borst-en*-a bak-tı-m, ama ben bir *schat-ten* yap-tı-m. (A)
breast-pl-DAT look-PAST-1sg but I a estimate-INF do-PAST-1sg
'I looked at her length, at her body, at her **breasts**, you know, I *estimate*d [her age]'

c. (. . .) yani *lov-er og regl-er*-e gir-iyor (Türker, 2000, p. 80)
(. . .) I.mean law-pl and regulation-pl-DAT go.into-PROG.3sg
"(. . .) I mean it goes into *laws and regulations*"

Some of these EL plurals are irregular (10a), others just refer to concepts frequently found as plurals (cf. Pfaff, 1997, p. 349), such as Dutch *borsten* 'breasts' in (10b) or the internally complex Norwegian word for "laws and regulations" in (10c). Other cases include compound nouns, Adjective–Noun combinations, prepositional and adverbial phrases, and verb–object collocations; the latter are illustrated in (11). The selection of so many complex units is probably a result of the tendency for insertions to have relatively specific meaning; by virtue of their internal composition and modification, complex units by definition have such relatively specific semantics.

(11) a. kim-e *smoesje verzinnen* yap-tı-n lan (Backus, 1992)
who-DAT excuse make.up.INF do-PAST-2sg INT
'hey man, who did you *make up* an *excuse* for?'

b. *op kamer-s wonen* yap-acağ-ım (Backus, 1992)
on room-pl live.INF do-FUT-1sg
'I'm going to *live on my own*'

Integration of these larger EL elements can occasionally lead to pretty complex patterns of integration. The Dutch PP in (12a) is marked twice for the comitative meaning, with a Dutch preposition and a Turkish postpositional suffix. Even more spectacular, the German adverbial phrase in (12b) starts off with an article that resembles the Turkish 3rd person singular past tense suffix on the immediately preceding finite verb so much that the one syllable -*di* doubles as both. The speaker speaks in a fast style typical of her social network, characterized by many ellipses, here indicated by the double hyphens connecting what would be separate words in a more orthographically oriented transcription (added on the last line).

(12)   a.   Bana birşeyler soruyorlar: "biz bunu fotoğraf çekmek için dört ay
             met de begeleiding-le yaptık
             they asked me a few things: "we worked *with supervision* for four
             months in order to make X-rays"
       b.   o da konuş-ma=die *gan=zeit* ben=d=böyl=ap-tı-m (Keim and Cındark,
             forthcoming)
             he too speak-NEG=PAST.3sg/the whole=time I=too=so=do-PAST-1sg
             "he didn't talk either *the whole time*, and I went like this"
             'orthographic': o da konuş-ma-dı die ganze Zeit, ben de böyle yap-tı-m

26.6.3   *Functions of alternation*

The discourse functions of alternational code switching, the central topic of a flourishing research tradition in Conversational Analysis (cf. Auer, 1998), have been studied extensively in the Køge and Mannheim projects (several contributions to Holmen and Jørgensen, 2000; Jørgensen, 1998; Keim and Cındark, forthcoming). Given the intergenerational trends mentioned in subsection 26.6.1, we can expect alternation to remain the dominant form of language mixing in the immigrant communities.

At least three aspects of alternation have received attention in the literature on Immigrant Turkish. One is the tendency for discourse markers from one language to accompany utterances in the other language (Keim and Cındark forthcoming; cf. 13a), a pattern already in evidence in the speech of young children (see subsection 26.5.1), and found to be a recurrent pattern in language contact around the world (cf. Maschler, 2000). Another is that many cases of alternation involve fixed idioms and constructions from the other language, such as (13b), which are probably selected for the same reasons as the complex lexical units mentioned in the previous subsection (cf. Backus, 2003).

(13)   a.   tam şey-d-ecek-ti weisst du, böyle git-ti böyle gene weisst du (Keim
             and Cındark forthcoming)
             just thing-do-FUT-PAST.3sg know.2sg you such go-PAST.3sg such
             again know.2sg you
             "just wanted to do uh, you know, so, went like this again you know"

   b. kültürle, kültürle dini karıştırıyorlar, *vind ik . . .*
       'they are mixing up culture and religion, *I think*'

The third, and best-known, aspect of alternation is that it often fulfills some kind of pragmatic or communicative function. Often, switches to a minority language are seen to be indexing some kind of group solidarity ("we-code"), and switches to the majority language an appeal to power ("they-code"). A rigid division cannot be maintained in our case, however. In his analyses of conversational functions served by code switching in the speech of children, Jørgensen (1998) clearly shows that switches to Turkish sometimes do relate to the global indexicality of the majority and minority languages, (as in 14a, where the children use Danish when attending to the school task at hand, but switch into Turkish for interpersonal remarks). However, just as often it is not the direction of switching that is important, but the practice of code switching itself. It is the contrast between the languages that the children are exploiting in (14b). If there is a "we-code," it is not Turkish, but Turkish-Danish code switching.

(14) Functions of code switching
   a. Context: children have been carrying out an assigned task which involves cutting out pictures of furniture from a catalogue. This has been done in Danish, but then Mesut's dominating behavior prompts an outburst from Leyla, in Turkish (Jørgensen, 1998, p. 246).
       Mesut: *det har jeg altså klippet den ud nu hvor er spejlet nu?*
               "I have cut it out now, where is the mirror now?"
       Leyla: ni kavat, ih onu kullanmacakta olur kullanmıyacağız ya bu daha güzel
               "you pimp, eh, we don't have to use it, we won't use it, this one is prettier"
   b. Context: 11-year-old boys are carrying out a similar task. Adnan is trying to get a particular point across, in Turkish, but isn't getting any reaction from the others. When he repeats his point, in Danish, he does succeed (Jørgensen, 1998, p. 252)
       Adnan: *nej*, küçük olmayacak ayaklar büyük olacak
               "*no*, they are not going to be small, the legs are going to be big"
       Murat: aha bak, bu ayakkabısı şimdi şurdan da şey gider
               "here, look, this one is the shoe, and from here goes that one"
       Umit: he
               "yes"
       Adnan: *den skal mindst være så stor*
               "it has to be at least this big"
       Erol: *nå jo mand*
               "oh yes, man"

Similar patterns of communicatively motivated, rather than indexicality-related switching, have also been uncovered by the Mannheim research group in four subgroups of young adults, who respond in different ways to their social reality as members of a marginalized minority, mainly depending on the factors gender and future plans. These differences in identity correlate with considerable linguistic differences (Keim and Cındark, forthcoming). Clearly, if there ever has been a time in which it was appropriate to speak of the Turkish immigrant community as a homogeneous group, both socially and linguistically, that time has passed.

Keim and Cındark (forthcoming) emphasize that a particular CS style is just one among many shared features that make up each group's vernacular. Of the four groups, the "Powergirls" (young women between 15 and 22 years of age, who aim to get out of the ghetto through good educational performance, speak a perfect German, a German-influenced Turkish, and, as their preferred in-group variety, a mixed code) have been studied most extensively, and apart from "their" way of CS, their variety or conversational style features frequent interruption and fast speech, frequent use of ellipsis, use of a particular set of discourse markers, a distinct narrative style, certain phonetic and intonational characteristics, and some deviations from standard Turkish syntax, some of which will be discussed in section 26.7. Code-switching patterns themselves are not uniform, which raises an interesting challenge to linguistics as a discipline: is it necessary for a variety to have systematic similarities in structure and lexicon? Some of the girls are more at the German end of the continuum, others more at the Turkish end, and some are in between. All types of code switching illustrated in subsection 26.6.2 occur, as well as frequent alternational code switching, both within turns and at turn boundaries, but to different degrees for different speakers. Yet, despite these formal differences, everybody involved seems to agree that they speak the same variety.

The Mannheim studies make abundantly clear that the bilingual reality of modern-day Turkish immigrant communities is more complex than a simple dichotomy between their two languages can capture. The teenage bilinguals they are studying master a whole range of mixed lects in between the poles of monolingual Turkish and monolingual German, and they master several registers of these languages. In addition, there is a growing body of literature on "crossing" (Rampton, 1995) in German cities, which shows that, on the one hand, urban Turkish teenagers have a broad range of functionally defined German registers, and, on the other hand, non-Turkish teenagers mix Turkish words, discourse markers, greetings, interjections, and terms of address into their discourse, betraying the "covert prestige" of Turkish in multi-ethnic neighborhoods (cf. Auer and Dirim, 2000, forthcoming; Hinnenkamp, 2002). It should be borne in mind that we are dealing with teenagers here, who have notoriously complex linguistic repertoires, tied up in intricate identity-marking mechanisms along with dress, haircut, musical preferences, etc.; in older age groups, the picture may well revert to a simpler menu of options. In any case, studying language use in the immigrant communities will most likely move away from simple language choice and/or code switching research to complex variationist studies, with variation within the immigrant community attracting at least as much attention as the coarser minority–majority dichotomy. (For additional discussion of code mixing and code switching, see chapters 1–4, 6, 10–14, 25, 28, 29, and 31.)

26.7 Language Change

Immigrant languages often show rapid divergence from their ancestral variety, a joint effect of two separate forces. First, *isolation* from the monolingual speech community and the resultant lack of exposure to, especially, non-vernacular speech (Boeschoten, 1994, p. 253), may cause, at least in the absence of a strongly normative standard-oriented ideology, the *loss* of certain features, through either *imperfect acquisition* or *attrition*. Second, *contact* with the majority language causes the *addition* of new features, usually *borrowed* from the other language. Typical for immigration contexts, furthermore, is dialect mixing, but this has largely been ignored in Turkish studies, except by Boeschoten (2000). Studying immigrant languages may be particularly useful in resolving a question raised in the literature on contact-induced change (cf. Thomason, 2001 and chapter 18 of the present volume). In predicting the extent of contact-induced change, both the duration and the intensity of contact are assumed to play a role, but how they interact is not well understood. Turkish immigrant languages are in intense contact with the European languages, but have been so only for a relatively short time.

Though there are many observations about possible changes, the literature on Immigrant Turkish contains no systematic studies of particular grammatical variables and whether they are or are not undergoing change. Relatively few Turkish linguists have studied migrant speech, and non-native researchers have been more likely to study the eye-catching phenomenon of code switching than the more invisible patterns of structural change (this certainly holds for the author).

Once "enough" changes have taken hold, the immigrant varieties can be approached as new dialects of Turkish (Auer, 1998; Backus, 1996; Johanson, 1993; Pfaff, 1994, 2000). However, it is not easy to establish widely agreed criteria for what would constitute solid empirical evidence for established changes, and, by extension, for a new stabilized variety (Johanson, 1999a, p. 251). The evidence we have comes in three kinds. First, there is plenty of *anecdotal evidence* that some change has occurred and is beyond the power of speakers to suppress. Members of the immigrant communities report that they stand out in Turkey because of the way they talk (Akinci and Yağmur, forthcoming; Boeschoten, 2000, p. 152; Keim and Cındark, forthcoming). Second, *code switching* obviously presents some sort of evidence for lexical change. Third, there are direct observations of *deviations from the structure* of the ancestral variety, and these are the focus of this section.

Studies of change generally focus on at least two aspects, on a description of the change itself, and on what may have caused it. As for *descriptive characteristics*, there are various ways in which changes have been classified. I will roughly follow Johanson's (1993, 1999a) model of "selective copies," looking first at loan translations and then at some candidates for more direct borrowing of foreign structure. The *cause* of any change in language is usually hard to pin down. Passionate debates about whether any given change is induced internally or by contact, or both, are largely absent from the literature on Immigrant Turkish (see, however, Boeschoten and Broeder, 1999, pp. 7–8). Interestingly, many investigators observe a close link between lexical and structural borrowing, the former facilitating the latter. Though Pfaff (1994, and 1999, p. 119) concludes that what structural borrowing there is in her child data, is not particularly associated with code switching, Boeschoten (1994, p. 262) maintains that many cases of structural deviation are "basically lexically motivated." What he has in mind are various types of literal translation.

Though the study of Immigrant Turkish contributes valuable data to the study of contact-induced change in general, it needs to be emphasized that it provides a *case study*, in particular one in which the languages in contact exhibit considerable typological distance (see Muysken, 2000, p. 53 for the general impact of this factor).

26.7.1   Loan translations

Loan translation, studied systematically by Türker (2000), has occurred when a combination of morphemes, such as a verb–object collocation, in the majority language is literally translated into Turkish. This is "semantic copying" in Johanson's (1993) framework. Interestingly, examples often involve either borrowed words or cognates. In the former case, part of the combination is translated and part of it borrowed, in what Johanson (1993) calls "mixed copies," cf. (15). In the latter case, this concerns words borrowed into Turkish from a European language at an earlier time in history, cf. (16a, b). Examples of translated combinations without any facilitating cognates exist too, however, cf. (16c–f).

(15) a. *ski* git- ('*ski* go'; Norwegian Turkish, Türker, 2000, p. 178; from Norwegian: *å gå på ski* 'to go on ski', vs. Turkish: *kayak yap-* 'ski do')
      b. *kamer*-lar-da kal- ('live in a rented room'; Dutch Turkish, Boeschoten, 2000, p. 148; from Dutch *op kamers wonen* 'live on rooms')
      c. *college* para-lar-ı ('tuition'; Dutch Turkish, Backus, 1996, from Dutch *college-geld* 'class money'
      d. karn-ın-da *sommerfugl-er* var (stomach-POSS.3sg-LOC butterfly-pl exist; i.e. 'have *butterflies* in one's stomach'; Norwegian Turkish, Türker, 2000, p. 179; from Norwegian *å ha sommerflugler i magen* 'to have butterflies in your stomach' vs. Turkish: *heyecanlan-* 'to be excited')

(16) a. duş al- ('take a shower'; Norwegian Turkish, Türker, 2000, from Norwegian: *å ta en dusj* 'take a shower' vs. Turkish *duş yapmak* 'do shower')

    b. kart oynamak ('play cards'; Dutch Turkish, Schaufeli, 1994, from Dutch *kaart spelen* 'card play' vs. Turkish *kağıt oynamak* 'paper play')

    c. suç ver- ('accuse'; German Turkish; Boeschoten, 2000, p. 148, from German *die Schuld geben* 'the blame give')

    d. yarım sene ('half year'; Norwegian Turkish, Türker, 2000, from Norwegian *et halvt år* 'half a year' vs. Turkish *altı ay* 'six months')

    e. yazma masasi ('writing table'; German Turkish, Boeschoten, 1994, from German *Schreib-tisch* 'writing-table' vs. Turkish *çalışma masası* 'working table')

    f. *hamile-ydi ben-im-le* (pregnant-PAST.3sg me-GEN-with; i.e. 'she was pregnant with me'; Norwegian Turkish, from Norwegian *var gravid med meg* 'was pregnant with me', vs. Turkish *ban-a hamile-ydi* 'me-DAT pregnant-PAST.3sg';

    NB: the loan translation preserves the Norwegian combination of the words 'pregnant' and 'with' (the genitive case marker on the pronoun is forced by the postposition *-le*, which calls for it if it attaches to a pronoun) as well as the foreign word order; cf. Türker, 2000, p. 171).

Loan translation typically involves complex lexical units, while simplex words are normally simply borrowed. However, these may be translated too, which results in what is commonly called "semantic extension." Examples include the replacement of *ders* 'lesson' by *saat* 'hour' in German Turkish, on the basis of the use of *Stunde* 'hour' with this meaning in German (Boeschoten, 1994, p. 255), and the use of *altında* 'under' in the sense of 'among' on the basis of similar figurative use of German *unter* (Johanson, 1993, p. 213).

Mixed copies superficially appear to be single-word code-switches, but they are better understood as insertions of internally complex EL units with one of the elements undergoing relexification with its equivalent Turkish morpheme (compare 15b with 11b above, in which the same Dutch model is used, with all the Dutch morphemes intact). This element tends to be the semantically general or basic one. Consider, for example, the pair in (17). Though Dutch has many verb–object collocations with the verb *hebben* ('to have'), not a single example of the type represented by (17b) occurs in my data. Instead, this semantically basic verb is consistently replaced with its Turkish equivalent (an existential construction), as in (17a).

(17) a. *migraine* var-sa, . . .
       migraine there.is-COND.3sg
       'if she has *migraine*, . . .'

    b. ?*migraine hebb-en* yap-ıyor-sa
       migraine have-INF do-PROG-COND.3sg

While loan translations involving only content elements have little lasting influence on the receiving language beyond the enrichment of the lexicon they instantiate, when functional elements are involved in the translation, more systematic changes may result (Johanson, 1999b). The best-documented case in Immigrant Turkish (Boeschoten, 1994, p. 261) is the extension of the use of the ablative case marker in German Turkish in constructions modeled on German ones with the roughly equivalent preposition *von*, which has ablative, genitive, and partitive uses, cf. (18a), as well as the more idiosyncratic 'about,' cf. (18b).

(18) a. Geri-si de böle *komik Heft*-ler var, on-dan çoğ-u saman ol-uyor
          (Boeschoten, 1994, p. 261)
          rest-POSS too such comic magazine-pl there.is that-ABL most-
          POSS.3sg straw be- PROG.3sg
          "For the rest, there are those *comic strips*; most of them are lousy"
          (Standard Turkish: on-lar-ın çoğ-u 'that-PL-GEN most-POSS.3sg';
          German *da-von* 'that-from'; i.e. 'of those, thereof')
      b. Bazen Atatürk-ten, bazen de sosyal bilgi-ler ed-iyor-uz (Boeschoten,
          1994, p. 256)
          sometimes A-ABL sometimes too social science-pl do-PROG-1pl
          "Sometimes [the lesson is] about Atatürk, and sometimes we do
          social science"
          (Standard Turkish: Atatürk üzerinde 'A about'; German [es handelt]
          von Atatürk; '[it deals] from A.'; i.e. '[it's] about A.')

26.7.2   *Borrowing of structure*

We now turn to cases where the change in question is not linked to specific borrowed words or collocations, but rather to the general structure of phrases and clauses in the contact language. It is such cases where it is particularly hard to prove that the change actually does constitute "structural borrowing," since it is often possible, and sometimes preferable, to interpret the change as either, at least partially, internally motivated, or as an instantiation of language attrition or imperfect acquisition.

As for *phrasal syntax*, aspects of Turkish NP syntax which differ from the majority languages have received some attention and are generally shown to resist change. This holds, for instance, for compound nouns, which are marked formally in Turkish with a possessive marker on the head noun (Türker, 2000, chapter 6, and forthcoming), and for noun phrases that include a numeral, in which Turkish does not allow inflection of the noun with a plural marker. There is some evidence, though not much, of an ongoing change in genitive phrases of the type 'my house.' These may have the possession indicated by a genitive pronoun and/or by an agreeing possessive suffix: *ben-im ev-im* 'I-GEN house-my.' The pronoun is generally optional, but when used, informal Turkish allows the omission of the suffix, resulting in a structure that superficially resembles the Germanic possessive construction: *ben-im ev* 'I-GEN house' (compare *my house*). Some investigators have found increased usage of this construction in Immigrant Turkish (Pfaff, 1991, p. 126; Huls and Van de Mond, 1992, p. 111). However, even here one has to be careful with positing foreign influence, because such structures are quite common in informal Turkish if the possessor is a first person pronoun and the noun is a common one, such as "father" or "house," and many of the examples involve just such contexts.

When *clausal syntax* is studied in the context of Immigrant Turkish, it typically involves clause linkage, word order, or pro-drop. At the most abstract level, Aarssen (1996, p. 165), Huls and Van de Mond (1992, p. 113), and Schaufeli (1993, p. 155) all found that longer residence in the Netherlands tended to correlate with more analytic syntax. Note that, in itself, a change from synthetic to analytic syntax is typical of languages undergoing attrition (Polinsky, 1995) or intense contact with a dominant language that happens to be analytic (Hill and Hill, 1986). On the whole, Turkish is agglutinative, while the languages of Western Europe tend to have relatively little bound morphology. I must reiterate that there are no systematic studies thus far, but on the basis of the available data, we can say that perhaps the most significant change that is ongoing in immigrant varieties of Turkish is the replacement of synthetic means of *clause linkage and subordination* (or at least their decreasing usage), especially of relative clauses, by simple juxtaposition, perhaps with simultaneous occurrence of compensatory devices, such as the development of conjunctions out of discourse markers, and increased usage of existing conjunctions (cf. Aarssen, 1996; Bayraktaroğlu, 1999; Boeschoten, 1990, 1994; El Aissati and Schaufeli, 1999; Haig and Braun, 1999; Huls and Van de Mond, 1992; Schaufeli, 1991; Verhoeven, 1989). As a warning against simplistic contact hypotheses, however, Huls and Van de Mond (1992, p. 111) show that, though immigrant children do not use complex sentence patterns very much, their parents don't either, suggesting that they are not typical of the informal spoken working-class Turkish to begin with (also see El Aissati and Schaufeli, 1999, p. 373 and Akinci, 1999, p. 44).

As for *word order*, it is frequently assumed, but not very often demonstrated, that the immigrant varieties have increased use of SVO order (Keim and Cındark, forthcoming, report this as very frequent in the mixed code of the "Powergirls"). This is presumably a contact-induced change, since Turkish is an SOV language, with SVO only in certain pragmatically motivated contexts (mostly having to do with backgrounding, cf. Erguvanlı-Taylan, 1984), while its contact languages are all SVO. However, even such sweeping syntactic changes may be particularly associated with specific phrases in the other language (Boeschoten, 1999, p. 70; Johanson, 1999b, pp. 45, 52). That is, at some point the end-result is syntactic change, but the change may have been jump-started by full and mixed loan translations of particular phrases. Example (19a) represents a complex calque from German, in which German word order, with a postverbal infinitival object phrase, is preserved. Nevertheless, direct calquing of foreign structure, rather than on the back of specific phrases and idioms, does occur. Example (19b) illustrates that Berlin Turkish children with much exposure to German tend to express themselves in more "German-like" ways than children with little exposure to it (19c); note the overt subject and indirect object pronouns and the choice of verb stem.

(19)   a.   *Lust*-um yok kitap oku-mağ-a. (Boeschoten, 1994)
             inclination-POSS.1sg there.is.not book read-INF-DAT
             'I don't feel like reading books.'
             (German: *'Ich habe keine Lust zum Bücherlesen.'*)
       b.   Peter, sen ban-a top-u ver-ir mi-sin? (Pfaff, 1991, p. 121)
             P. you me-DAT ball-ACC give-AOR Q-2sg
             "Peter, would you give me the ball?"
       c.   Orhan, sarı top-u al-abil-ir mi-yim? (Pfaff, 1991, p. 121)
             O. yellow ball-ACC take-can-AOR Q-1sg
             "Orhan, could I have the yellow ball?"

Since Turkish is a *pro-drop* language, which only uses subject pronouns to express a certain degree of pragmatic contrast (Enç, 1986), and the European languages with which it is in contact are not, researchers have looked for signs of contact-induced change in this area, in the form of increased usage of sub-ject pronouns (along the lines of the contrast between 19b and c). This hypo-thesis has generally not been confirmed, or only weakly (Aarssen, 1996, pp. 119, 163; Özcan et al., 2000; Schaufeli, 1994, p. 216 do not find changes, while Huls and Van de Mond, 1992, p. 111, and Pfaff, 1991, pp. 120–3, do).

In addition, some other types of changes are mentioned here and there, for instance a decrease in use of the evidential mood (cf. section 26.5.1), and the omission of genitive marking on the subjects of embedded clauses. Data on these phenomena are rare, however, so that no conclusions can be drawn. In any case, a list of structural changes in Immigrant Turkish needs to be offset by a probably much bigger list of aspects of the language which prove quite stable (see Johanson, 1992 for principled proposals as to what explains the robustness of certain areas of Turkic grammar; also see Pfaff, 1991, pp. 112–15, 123).

26.7.3   *Phonology*

As is the case for most immigrant languages, phonology has largely been ignored, the sole exception, as far as I know, being Queen (2001). In addi-tion, there are scattered observations in other studies (cf. Boeschoten, 1990; Johanson, 1993, p. 212; Keim and Cındark, forthcoming; Türker, 1998). Queen (2001, p. 73) found that Turkish children in Germany had developed an in-novative intonation pattern in which they used, in *both* languages, a German-derived phrase-final rise pattern to signal one pragmatic distinction (discourse cohesion), and a Turkish-derived one to signal another one (discourse continuation). (For additional discussion of bilingualism and language change and related issues, see chapters 6, 18, and 29–31.)

26.8   Conclusion

This chapter has described the general life course of the Turkish language as an immigrant variety in Western Europe in its first thirty years. Though I have attempted to provide a fair overview, this chapter has necessarily focused on the aspects of immigrant bilingualism that I am myself most familiar with, i.e. code switching and borrowing. Perhaps the most remarkable aspect of this particular case is that, due to improved communications and the maintained contacts with Turkey which modern times allow, language shift is relatively slow. This brings with it that all kinds of contact-induced changes have more time to become permanent features of a maintained heritage language.

Immigrant languages show similarities to and differences from other types of bilingual communities, such as post-colonial and borderland ones. Though the Turkish community is better equipped than most to maintain its heritage language for a long time, the list below, drawn from the present overview, is suggested to give some features that are typical of immigrant communities in general, particularly those resulting from labor migration. Although it is not the purpose of this chapter to give a conclusive picture of what makes immigrant languages special, if there even is a set of circumstances that warrant the category "immigrant languages" as a linguistically relevant one, it is meant to at least contribute to comparative research into types of multilingualism.

1   Low social status, leading to various social problems;
2   low linguistic status, leading to minimal official support for language maintenance;
3   dialect mixing, as migrants come from various parts of the region of origin;
4   a first generation with limited success in second language acquisition;
5   intergenerational variation in use of, and (therefore?) proficiency in, both languages;
6   relatively few constraints on borrowing from the dominant language;
7   an acquisition pattern resulting in successive bilingualism
8   development of a new variety of the heritage language.

Turkish in Western Europe is a relatively well-researched language, having enjoyed a similar degree of attention as South Asian languages in Britain and Spanish in the US. Comparison of these situations would no doubt yield further insight into the effects of various aspects of immigration on the immigrating language.

ABBREVIATIONS

ABL = Ablative; ACC = Accusative;
AG = Agentive; AOR = Aorist; CLAS =
Classifier; COND = Conditional; CONT =
Continuative aspect; DAT = Dative;
EVID = Evidential; FUT = Future tense;
GEN = Genitive; IMP = Imperative;

INF = Infinitive; INT = Interjection;
LOC = Locative; NEG = Negative;
NOM = Nominalizer; PAST = Past
tense; pl = plural; POSS = Possessive;
PROG = Progressive tense/aspect;
Q = Question marker; sg = singular.

REFERENCES

Aarssen, J. (1996). *Relating Events in Two
Languages: Acquisition of Cohesive
Devices by Turkish-Dutch Bilingual
Children at School Age* (Studies in
Multilingualism 2). Tilburg, The
Netherlands: Tilburg University Press.

Aarts, R. (1996). Functional literacy of
Turkish children in Turkey and in
the Netherlands. In L. Johanson, in
cooperation with E. Csato, V. Locke,
A. Menz, and D. Winterling (eds.),
Turkologica, 32: *The Mainz Meeting:
Proceedings of the Seventh International
Conference on Turkish Linguistics,
August 3–6, 1994*, pp. 517–26.
Wiesbaden: Harrassowitz.

Abadan-Unat, N. (1976). Turkish
migration to Europe, 1960–1975. A
balance sheet of achievements and
failures. In N. Abadan-Unat (ed.),
Turkish Workers in Europe 1960–1975,
pp. 1–44. Leiden: Brill.

Abadan-Unat, N. (1985). Identity crisis
of Turkish migrants, first and second
generation. In I. Başgöz and N. Furniss
(eds.), *Indiana University Turkish Studies.
Volume 5: Turkish Workers in Europe.
An Interdisciplinary Study*, pp. 3–22.
Bloomington: Indiana University.

Adalar, N. and Tagliamonte, S. (1998).
Borrowed nouns; bilingual people: The
case of the "Londralı" in Northern
Cyprus. *International Journal of
Bilingualism*, 2(2), 139–59.

Akinci, M.-A. (1999). Turkish spoken by
bilingual children in France: Mother
tongue and weak language? In
Bayraktaroğlu, A. (ed.), *TASG News.
Newsletter of the Turkish Area Study
Group*, 49 (special edition: *Turkish
Language in Diaspora*), 40–6.

Akinci, M.-A. (2001). *LINCOM Studies
in Language Acquisition. Volume 3:
Développement des compétences narratives
des enfants bilingues turc-français en
France âgés de 5 à 10 ans* [Development
of narrative competence of bilingual
Turkish-French children in France
between the ages of 5 and 10].
Munich: LINCOM.

Akinci, M.-A., Jisa, H., and Kern, S.
(2001). Influence of L1 Turkish on L2
French narratives. In L. Verhoeven
and S. Strömqvist (eds.), *Narrative
Development in a Multilingual Context*,
pp. 189–208). Amsterdam: John
Benjamins.

Akinci, M.-A. and K. Yağmur
(forthcoming). Language use and
attitudes of Turkish immigrants
in France and their subjective
ethnolinguistic vitality perceptions.
In A. S. Özsoy (ed.), *Proceedings of
the 10th International Conference on
Turkish Linguistics*. Istanbul: Boğaziçi
University.

Aksu-Koç, A. (1988). *The Acquisition of
Aspect and Modality: The Case of Past*

Reference in Turkish. Cambridge, UK: Cambridge University Press.

Aksu-Koç, A. (1994). Development of linguistic forms: Turkish. In R. A. Berman and D. I. Slobin (eds.), *Relating Events in Narrative: A Crosslinguistic Developmental Study*, pp. 329–85. Hillsdale, NJ: Lawrence Erlbaum.

Auer, P. (ed.) (1998). *Code-switching in Conversation: Language, Interaction and Identity*. London: Routledge.

Auer, P. and Dirim, I. (2000). On the use of Turkish routines by adolescents of non-Turkish descent in Hamburg. In A. Holmen and J. N. Jørgensen (eds.), *Copenhagen Studies in Bilingualism: The Køge Series. Volume 7: Det er Conversation 801, değil mi? Perspectives on the Bilingualism of Turkish Speaking Children and Adolescents in North Western Europe*, pp. 159–94. Copenhagen: The Danish University of Education.

Auer, P. and Dirim, I. (forthcoming). Socio-cultural orientation, youth styles and the spontaneous acquisition of Turkish by non-Turkish adolescents in Germany. In J. Androutsopoulos and A. Georgakopoulou (eds.), *Discourse Constructions of Youth Identities*.

Backus, A. (1992). *Patterns of Language Mixing: A Study in Turkish-Dutch Bilingualism*. Wiesbaden: Otto Harrassowitz.

Backus, A. (1996). *Studies in Multilingualism. Volume 1: Two in One. Bilingual Speech of Turkish Immigrants in the Netherlands*. Tilburg, The Netherlands: Tilburg University Press.

Backus, A. (2001). The role of semantic specificity in insertional codeswitching: Evidence from Dutch Turkish. In R. Jacobson (ed.), *Codeswitching Worldwide II*, pp. 125–54. Berlin: Mouton de Gruyter.

Backus, A. (2003). Units in codeswitching: Evidence for multimorphemic elements in the lexicon. *Linguistics*, 41(1), 83–132.

Backus, A. and Van der Heijden, H. (1998). Life and birth of a bilingual: the mixed code of bilingual children and adults in the Turkish community in the Netherlands. In L. Johanson, in cooperation with E. Csato, V. Locke, A. Menz, and D. Winterling (eds.), *Turkologica, 32: The Mainz Meeting: Proceedings of the Seventh International Conference on Turkish Linguistics, August 3–6, 1994*, pp. 527–51. Wiesbaden: Harrassowitz.

Backus, A. and Van der Heijden, H. (2002). Language mixing by young Turkish children in the Netherlands. *Psychology of Language and Communication*, 6(1), 55–73.

Bayraktaroğlu, A. (1999). Non-standard uses in the mother tongue by the Turkish diaspora adolescents in England. In Bayraktaroğlu, A. (ed.), *TASG News. Newsletter of the Turkish Area Study Group*, 49 (special edition: *Turkish Language in Diaspora*), 28–39.

Bayraktaroğlu, A. (ed.) (1999). *TASG News. Newsletter of the Turkish Area Study Group*, 49 (special edition: *Turkish Language in Diaspora*). London: TASG.

Bhatia, T. and Ritchie, W. (1999). The bilingual child: Some issues and perspectives. In W. Ritchie and T. Bhatia (eds.), *Handbook of Child Language Acquisition*, pp. 569–643. San Diego, CA: Academic Press.

Boeschoten, H. (1990). *Acquisition of Turkish by Immigrant Children*. Wiesbaden: Otto Harrassowitz.

Boeschoten, H. (1994). Second language influence on first language acquisition: Turkish children in Germany. In G. Extra and L. Verhoeven (eds.), *The Cross-linguistic Study of Bilingual Development*, pp. 253–63. Amsterdam: Koninklijke Nederlandse Akademie van Wetenschappen.

Boeschoten, H. (1997). Codeswitching, codemixing and code alternation: What a difference. In R. Jacobson (ed.),

Codeswitching Worldwide, pp. 15–24. Berlin: Mouton de Gruyter.

Boeschoten, H. (1999). Equivalence and levels of analysis. In B. Brendemoen, E. Lanza and E. Ryen (eds.), *Language Encounters in Time and Space*, pp. 63–71. Oslo: Novus.

Boeschoten, H. (2000). Convergence and divergence in migrant Turkish. In K. Mattheier (ed.), *Dialect and Migration in a Changing Europe*, pp. 145–54. Frankfurt: Peter Lang.

Boeschoten, H. and Broeder, P. (1999). Zum Interferenzbegriff in seiner Anwendung auf die Zweisprachigkeit türkischer Immigranten. In L. Johanson and J. Rehbein (eds.), *Türkisch und Deutsch im Vergleich*, pp. 1–21. Wiesbaden: Otto Harrassowitz.

Boeschoten, H. and Verhoeven, L. (1987). Language mixing in children's speech: Dutch language use in Turkish discourse. *Language Learning*, 37, 191–215.

Boyd, S. (2001). Immigrant languages in Sweden. In G. Extra and D. Gorter (eds.), *The Other Languages of Europe: Demographic, Sociolinguistic and Educational Perspectives*, pp. 177–92. Clevedon, UK: Multilingual Matters.

Boyd, S., Andersson, P., Berggreen, H., and Hjulstad Junttila, J. (1995). Minority and majority language use in the family among four immigrant groups in the Nordic region. In W. Fase, K. Jaspaert, and S. Kroon (eds.), *The State of Minority Languages: International Perspectives on Survival and Decline*, pp. 97–111. Lisse: Swets and Zeitlinger.

Csato, Eva Agnes (forthcoming). *Turkologica: Spoken Karaim*. Wiesbaden: Harrassowitz.

Deuchar, M. and Quay, S. (2000). *Bilingual Acquisition: Theoretical Implications of a Case Study*. Oxford: Oxford University Press.

Dirim, I. (1999). *"Var mı lan Marmelade?" – Türkisch-deutscher Sprachkontakt in einer Grundschulklasse* ["Var mı lan Marmelade?" – Turkish-German language contact in an elementary school classroom]. Münster: Waxmann.

El Aissati, A. and Schaufeli, A. (1999). Language maintenance and loss: Evidence from language perception and production. In G. Extra and L. Verhoeven (eds.), *Studies on Language Acquisition. Volume 14: Bilingualism and Migration*, pp. 363–77). Berlin: Mouton de Gruyter.

Eminov, A. (1997). *Turkish and Other Muslim Minorities in Bulgaria*. London and New York: Routledge.

Enç, M. (1986). Topic switching and pronominal subjects in Turkish. In D. Slobin and K. Zimmer (eds.), *Studies in Turkish Linguistics*, pp. 195–208. Amsterdam: John Benjamins.

Erguvanlı-Taylan, E. (1984). *The Function of Word Order in Turkish Grammar*. Berkeley: University of California Press.

Extra, G. and Gorter, D. (2001). Comparative perspectives on regional and immigrant minority languages in multicultural Europe. In G. Extra and D. Gorter (eds.), *The Other Languages of Europe: Demographic, Sociolinguistic and Educational Perspectives*, pp. 1–41. Clevedon, UK: Multilingual Matters.

Extra, G. and Verhoeven, L. (1999). Processes of language change in a migration context: the case of the Netherlands. In G. Extra and L. Verhoeven (eds.), *Studies on Language Acquisition. Volume 14: Bilingualism and Migration*, pp. 29–57. Berlin: Mouton de Gruyter.

Gogolin, I. and Reich, H. (2001). Immigrant languages in federal Germany. In G. Extra and D. Gorter (eds.), *The Other Languages of Europe. Demographic, Sociolinguistic and Educational Perspectives*, pp. 193–214. Clevedon, UK: Multilingual Matters.

Gubbay, J. (1999). The European Union role in the formation, legitimation and implementation of migration policy. In G. Dale and M. Cole (eds.), *The European Union and Migrant Labour*, pp. 43–66. Oxford: Berg.

Haig, G. and Braun, F. (1999). The state of the Turkish language in Germany. In Bayraktaroğlu, A. (ed.), *TASG News. Newsletter of the Turkish Area Study Group*, 49 (special edition: *Turkish Language in Diaspora*), pp. 13–18.

Hill, J. and Hill, K. (1986). *Speaking Mexicano: Dynamics of Syncretic Language in Central Mexico*. Tucson: University of Arizona Press.

Hinnenkamp, V. (2002). "zwei zu bir miydi?" Mischsprachliche Varietäten von Migrantenjugendlichen im Hybriditätsdiskurs ["Zwei zu bir miydi?" Mixed varieties of migrant youths in hybrid discourse]. In V. Hinnenkamp and K. Meng (eds.). *Sprachgrenzen überspringen. Sprachliche Hybridität und polykulturelles Selbstverständnis.* [Crossing language boundaries: Linguistic hybridity and multicultural self-understanding]. Studien zur deutschen Sprache. Forschungen des Instituts für Deutsche Sprache. Tübingen: Narr.

Holmen, A. and Jørgensen, J. N. (eds.) (2000). *Copenhagen Studies in Bilingualism: The Køge Series. Volume 7: Det er Conversation 801, değil mi? Perspectives on the Bilingualism of Turkish speaking Children and Adolescents in North Western Europe.* Copenhagen: The Danish University of Education.

Holmen, A., Latomaa, S., Gimbel, J., Andersen, S. and Jørgensen, J. N. (1995). Parent attitudes to children's L1 maintenance: A cross-sectional study of immigrant groups in the Nordic countries. In W. Fase, K. Jaspaert, and S. Kroon (eds.), *European Studies on Multilingualism. Volume 5: The State of Minority Languages. International*

Perspectives on Survival and Decline, pp. 173–85. Lisse: Swets and Zeitlinger.

Huls, E. (2000). Power in Turkish migrant families. *Discourse and Society*, 11(3), 345–72.

Huls, E. and Van de Mond, A. (1992). Some aspects of language attrition in Turkish families in the Netherlands. In W. Fase, K. Jaspaert, and S. Kroon (eds.), *Studies in Bilingualism. Volume 1: Maintenance and Loss of Minority Languages*, pp. 99–115. Amsterdam: Benjamins.

Johanson, L. (1992). *Strukturelle Faktoren in Türkischen Sprachkontakten* [Structural factors in Turkic language contacts]. Stuttgart: Franz Steiner Verlag.

Johanson, L. (1993). Code-copying in immigrant Turkish. In G. Extra and L. Verhoeven (eds.), *Immigrant Languages in Europe*, pp. 197–221. Clevedon, UK: Multilingual Matters.

Johanson, L. (1999a). Frame-changing code-copying in immigrant varieties. In G. Extra and L. Verhoeven (eds.), *Studies on Language Acquisition. Volume 14: Bilingualism and Migration*, pp. 247–60. Berlin: Mouton de Gruyter.

Johanson, L. (1999b). The dynamics of code-copying in language encounters. In B. Brendemoen, E. Lanza, and E. Ryen (eds.), *Language Encounters in Time and Space*, pp. 37–62. Oslo: Novus.

Jongenburger, W. and Aarssen, J. (2001). Linguistic and cultural exchange and appropriation: A survey study in a multi-ethnic neighbourhood in the Netherlands. *Journal of Multilingual and Multicultural Development*, 22(4), 293–308.

Jørgensen, J. N. (1998). Children's acquisition of code-switching for power wielding. In P. Auer (ed.) *Code-switching in Conversation: Language, Interaction and Identity*, pp. 237–58. London: Routledge.

Kallmeyer, W. and Keim, I. (2003). Linguistic variation and the construction of social identity in a German-Turkish setting: A case study of an immigrant youth-group in Mannheim, Germany. In J. Androutsopoulos and A. Georgapoulou (eds.), *Discourse Constructions of Youth Identities*, pp. 29–46. Amsterdam and Philadelphia: John Benjamins.

Keim, I. and Cındark, I. (forthcoming). Deutsch-türkischer Mischcode in einer Migrantinnengruppe: Form von "Jugendsprache" oder soziolektales Characteristikum? [German-Turkish mixed code in a migrant network: A type of "youth slang" or a sociolectal characteristic?]. In E. Neuland (ed.), *Jugendsprache – Spiegel der Zeit. Tagungsband der internationalen Fachkonferenz in Wuppertal 2001.* [Youth language – Mirror of the times. Proceedings of the international conference in Wuppertal 2001]. Frankfurt.

Kıral, F. (2001). *Das gesprochene Aserbaidschanisch von Iran. Eine Studie zu den syntaktischen Einflüssen des Persischen* [Spoken Azerbaijani in Iran: A study of the syntactic influence of Persian]. Wiesbaden: Harrassowitz Verlag.

Kıray, M. (1976). The family of the immigrant worker. In N. Abadan-Unat (ed.), *Turkish Workers in Europe 1960–1975*, pp. 210–34. Leiden, The Netherlands: Brill.

Kurtböke, Petek (1998). *A Corpus-driven Study of Turkish-English Language Contact in Australia.* Unpublished dissertation, Monash University, Melbourne, Department of Linguistics (available on-line at http://home.vicnet.net.au/~petek/thesis).

McClure, E. (1981). Formal and functional aspects of the code-switched discourse of bilingual children. In R. Durán (ed.), *Latino Language and Communicative Behavior*, pp. 69–94. Norwood, NJ: Ablex.

Maschler, Yael (2000). What can bilingual conversation tell us about discourse markers? Introduction. *International Journal of Bilingualism*, 4(4), 437–45.

Menz, A. (1993). *Studien zum Türkischen der zweiten deutschland-türkischen Generation.* [Studies of the Turkish of second-generation German Turks]. Unpublished MA thesis, Gutenberg University, Mainz, Germany.

Menz, A. (1999). *Turkologica, 41: Gagausische Syntax. Eine Studie zum kontaktinduzierten Sprachwandel* [Gagauz syntax: A study of contact-induced language change]. Wiesbaden: Harrassowitz Verlag.

Moffatt, S. and Milroy, L. (1992). Panjabi/English language alternation in the early school years. *Multilingua*, 11(4), 355–85.

Mushaben, J. M. (1985). A crisis of culture: isolation and integration among Turkish guestworkers in the German Federal Republic. In I. Ba_göz and N. Furniss (eds.), *Indiana University Turkish Studies. Volume 5: Turkish Workers in Europe. An Interdisciplinary Study*, pp. 125–50. Bloomington: Indiana University.

Muysken, P. (2000). *Bilingual Speech: A Typology of Code-mixing.* Cambridge, UK: Cambridge University Press.

Myers-Scotton, C. (1997). *Duelling languages: Grammatical structure in codeswitching* (2nd edn.). Oxford: Clarendon Press.

Necef, M. Ü. (1994). The language of intimacy. In L. Andersen (ed.), *Middle East Studies in Denmark*, pp. 141–58. Odense: Odense University Press.

Özcan, H., Keçik, I., Topbaş, S. and Konrot, A. (2000). A comparative study in pronominal use in the discourse of monolingual Turkish-speaking and bilingual Turkish-Danish speaking children. In A. Holmen and

J. N. Jørgensen (eds.), *Copenhagen Studies in Bilingualism: The Køge Series. Volume 7: Det er Conversation 801, değil mi? Perspectives on the Bilingualism of Turkish speaking Children and Adolescents in North Western Europe*, pp. 121–36. Copenhagen Studies in Bilingualism: The Køge Series, K7. Copenhagen: The Danish University of Education.

Pfaff, C. W. (1991). Turkish in contact with German: Language maintenance and loss among immigrant children in West Berlin. *International Journal of the Sociology of Language*, 90, 97–129.

Pfaff, C. W. (1993). Turkish language development in Germany. In G. Extra and L. Verhoeven (eds.), *Immigrant Languages in Europe*, pp. 119–46. Clevedon, UK: Multilingual Matters.

Pfaff, C. W. (1994). Early bilingual development of Turkish children in Berlin. In G. Extra and L. Verhoeven (eds.), *The Cross-linguistic Study of Bilingual Development*, pp. 75–97. Amsterdam: Koninklijke Nederlandse Akademie van Wetenschappen.

Pfaff, C. W. (1997). Contacts and conflicts: Perspectives from code-switching research. In M. Pütz (ed.), *Language Choices*, pp. 341–60. Amsterdam: Benjamins.

Pfaff, Carol W. (1999). Changing patterns of language mixing in a bilingual child. In G. Extra and L. Verhoeven (eds.), *Studies on Language Acquisition. Voume 14: Bilingualism and Migration*, pp. 97– 121. Berlin: Mouton de Gruyter.

Pfaff, C. W. (2000). Development and use of *et-* and *yap-* by Turkish/German bilingual children. In A. Göksel and C. Kerslake (eds.), *Studies on Turkish and Turkic Languages*, pp. 365–73. Wiesbaden: Harrassowitz Verlag.

Polinsky, M. (1995). Cross-linguistic parallels in language loss. *Southwest Journal of Linguistics*, 14(1/2), 87–123.

Poplack, Shana, and Meechan, Marjorie (1998). Introduction: How languages fit together in codemixing. *International Journal of Bilingualism*, 2(2), 127–38.

Queen, R. (2001). Bilingual intonation patterns: Evidence of language change from Turkish-German bilingual children. *Language in Society*, 30(1), 55–80.

Rampton, B. (1995). *Crossing: Language and Ethnicity among Youths*. London: Longman.

Romaine, S. (1995). *Bilingualism*, 2nd edn. Oxford: Blackwell.

Rudin, C. and Eminov, A. (1990). Bulgarian Turkish: The linguistic effects of recent nationality policy. *Anthropological Linguistics*, 32, 149–62.

Schaufeli, A. (1991). *Turkish in an Immigrant Setting: A Comparative Study of the First Language of Monolingual and Bilingual Turkish Children*. Amsterdam: University of Amsterdam.

Schaufeli, A. (1992). A domain approach to the Turkish vocabulary of bilingual Turkish children in the Netherlands. In W. Fase, K. Jaspaert, and S. Kroon (eds.) *Studies in Bilingualism. Volume 1: Maintenance and Loss of Minority Languages*, pp. 117–35. Amsterdam: Benjamins.

Schaufeli, A. (1993). Turkish language development in the Netherlands. In G. Extra and L. Verhoeven (eds.), *Immigrant Languages in Europe*, pp. 147–57. Clevedon, UK: Multilingual Matters.

Schaufeli, A. (1994). First language text cohesion in a Turkish-Dutch bilingual setting. In G. Extra and L. Verhoeven (eds.), *The Cross-linguistic Study of Bilingual Development*, pp. 199–218. Amsterdam: Koninklijke Nederlandse Akademie van Wetenschappen.

Thomason, S. G. (2001). *Language Contact. An Introduction*. Washington, D.C.: Georgetown University Press.

Tribalat, M. (1995). *Faire France. Une grande enquête sur les immigrés et leurs enfants*. Paris: Éditions la Découverte.

Türker, E. (1998). Turkish as an immigrant language: A descriptive study of second generation immigrant Turkish in Norway. In L. Johanson, in cooperation with E. Csato, V. Locke, A. Menz, and D. Winterling (eds.), *Turkologica, 32: The Mainz Meeting: Proceedings of the Seventh International Conference on Turkish Linguistics, August 3–6, 1994*, pp. 697–704. Wiesbaden: Harrassowitz.

Türker, E. (2000). *Turkish-Norwegian codeswitching: Evidence from intermediate and second generation Turkish immigrants in Norway*. Oslo: Unipub Forlag.

Van der Heijden, H. (1999). Word formation processes in young bilingual children. In G. Extra and L. Verhoeven (eds.), *Studies on Language Acquisition. Volume 14: Bilingualism and Migration*, pp. 123–40. Berlin: Mouton de Gruyter.

Van der Heijden, H. and Verhoeven, L. (1994). Early bilingual development of Turkish children in the Netherlands. In G. Extra and L. Verhoeven (eds.), *The Cross-linguistic Study of Bilingual Development*, pp. 51–73. Amsterdam: Koninklijke Nederlandse Akademie van Wetenschappen.

Verhoeven, L. (1988). Acquisition of discourse cohesion in Turkish. In S. Koç (ed.), *Studies on Turkish Linguistics*, pp. 437–52. Ankara: Middle East Technical University.

Verhoeven, L. (1989). Acquisition of clause linking in Turkish. In A.Van Kemenade and H. Bennis (eds.) *Linguistics in the Netherlands 1989*, pp. 153–62. Dordrecht: Foris.

Verhoeven, L. and Boeschoten, H. (1986). First language acquisition in a second language submersion environment. *Applied Psycholinguistics*, 7, 241–56.

Weinreich, U. (1953). *Languages in Contact*. New York: Linguistic Circle of New York Publication no. 2.

Wray, A. (2002). *Formulaic Language and the Lexicon*. Cambridge, UK: Cambridge University Press.

27 Bi-/Multilingualism in Southern Africa

NKONKO M. KAMWANGAMALU

27.1 Introduction

Southern Africa comprises ten countries,[1] namely Angola, Botswana, Lesotho, Malawi, Mozambique, Namibia, South Africa, Swaziland, Zambia and Zimbabwe. The scramble for Africa, which took place in the nineteenth century, resulted in the division of some of these countries among three colonial powers: Germany, Portugal and Britain. Thus Namibia became a German colony; Mozambique and Angola became Portuguese colonies; and the remaining countries – in addition to South Africa, which had already been under British rule since 1795 – became British colonies. During the colonial era, English was the only official language in all the British colonies in the region, much as was Portuguese in former Portuguese colonies. After the British colonies under consideration became independent states, English retained its status as the sole official language in some of the states, e.g. Malawi, Botswana, Zimbabwe; but it shared this status with one or more selected African languages in other states. For instance, English is a co-official language with Siswati in Swaziland and Sesotho in Lesotho, much as it is with both of these languages in South Africa. English also serves as the official language of Namibia, a country that was never colonized by Britain. It seems that the choice of English in Namibia was based on the status of the language in the Southern African region, coupled with negative attitudes towards Afrikaans, the language of the then apartheid South Africa, which had colonized Namibia after the Germans left the country. Unlike former British colonies, post-independence lusophone Africa has retained its colonial language (Portuguese) as the sole official language of the state. As in most African countries, and ignoring the distinction between language and dialect, the majority of countries in Southern Africa can be

---

1 The list of Southern African countries presented here does not include the Indian Ocean islands of Madagascar, Mauritius, and Reunion, all of which were French colonies.

described as multilingual. It is estimated, for instance, that some 25 languages are spoken in South Africa (Webb, 1995), 20 are spoken in Mozambique (Lopes, 1998), and 14 are spoken in Malawi (Kayambazinthu, 1998), to give just a few examples. Accordingly, it is natural that in Southern Africa bilingualism rather than monolingualism is the norm. Skutnabb-Kangas (1981, p. 81) observes that there are as many definitions of bilingualism as there are scholars investigating it, with every researcher using the kind of definition that best suits their particular area of inquiry. In this chapter the term bilingualism is used to encompass both the individuals who are fluent in two languages only and those whose linguistic repertoire consists of three or more languages. The chapter provides an overview of bilingualism in Southern Africa. In particular, it describes the lives of the indigenous languages vis-à-vis former colonial languages that have currency in the region, namely English and Portuguese, with a focus on issues in language use, language-in-education policy, mother-tongue education, language attitude and language shift.

27.2   Bilingualism, Language Status and Language Use

Following Skutnabb-Kangas (1981), two types of bilingualism can be distinguished in Southern Africa: elite bilingualism and natural bilingualism. Elite bilingualism, also commonly known as institutional bilingualism (Mulamba, 1988), refers to individuals who, in addition to their mother tongue, are highly educated in a foreign language, in this case English or Portuguese. Generally, and since not everyone can afford the cost of an education, in Southern Africa elite bilinguals constitute a minority social class made up of government officials, academics and those in higher positions in business or civil service. In terms of language use, the African mother tongue is generally the language of the home, and is used for interaction with members of one's community. It is also used, especially in former British colonies in the region, as a medium of instruction in the early years of primary education, years during which English is taught as a subject before taking over as a medium of instruction for the remainder of the educational system including secondary and tertiary education. English and Portuguese are also used, each in its respective region, as a means of communication with out-group members. This does not mean that these languages are never used for interaction among in-group members. As we will see later, these languages (and English in particular) are increasingly becoming the medium of communication in "elite" black families. In Southern Africa elite bilinguals also tend to be natural bilinguals in the sense that, in addition to being fluent in a foreign language, they are more often than not also fluent in at least two indigenous languages. The reverse, however, is not always true; that is, a natural bilingual is not necessarily an elite bilingual. Natural bilingualism refers to individuals who are fluent in two or more indigenous languages (including the mother tongue) and use them as a means of communication in everyday life. In the context of Southern Africa these people constitute the majority of the region's population. Apart from the mother tongue, they acquire the other languages as a result of interethnic marriages or of exposure to speech communities that speak different languages.

In terms of language status and depending on a country's colonial history, English is invariably one of the official languages in most former British colonies, whereas Portuguese is the sole official language in the two former Portuguese colonies in the region, Angola and Mozambique. As I have indicated elsewhere (e.g. Kamwangamalu, 1997), in Southern Africa the relationship between former colonial languages such as English and Portuguese and the African languages can be described either from an ideological viewpoint or from the viewpoint of the roles that the two former colonial languages and the African languages play in this part of the world.

From an ideological viewpoint, and except in Namibia and in a few former British colonies as well as in lusophone countries such as Angola and Mozambique, this relationship reflects "pluralism" (Cobarrubias, 1983) – that is, the recognition of more than one language as the official languages of the state. However, such recognition does not necessarily mean that in practice English and the African languages have equal status. Consider, for instance, the role of an official language as described in the literature (e.g. Eastman, 1990; Fasold, 1984; Walker, 1984). Walker (1984, p. 161) defines an official language as one designated by government decree to be the official means of communication of the given state in government, administration, law, education, and general public life. Eastman (1990, p. 71) sees it as one used in the business of government. A true official language, says Fasold (1984, p. 74), fulfills all or some of the functions in (1)–(5), below; to which Fishman (1971, p. 288) would add those in (6) and (7). The official language is used (1) as the language of communication for government officials in carrying out their duties at the national level; (2) for written communication between and internal to government agencies at the national level; (3) for the keeping of government records at the national level; (4) for the original formulation of laws and regulations that concern the nation as a whole; (5) for forms such as tax forms; (6) in the schools; and (7) in the courts.

Language practices in Southern Africa suggest clearly that only English and Portuguese perform, each in its region, the functions listed above. African languages play only a minor role in lower primary education in some former British colonies (e.g. South Africa, Lesotho, Malawi). Therefore, socio-functionally the relationship between English and Portuguese and the African languages can rightly be described as diglossic, with the former as the H(igh) languages, and the latter as the L(ow) languages. One of the characteristics of diglossia, says Ferguson (1959), is that H has more prestige than L and that it has specialized functions and domains of use in the community.

The social status of the African languages vis-à-vis English and Portuguese in Southern Africa attests to this point. English and Portuguese remain status symbols in former British and Portuguese colonies, respectively. For instance, in each of the anglophone countries under consideration English is used as the language of administration, media, education, diplomacy, social mobility, intra-elite and interethnic communication, and international business transactions. Portuguese serves similar functions in lusophone countries. In Mozambique, for instance, and in spite of the country's linguistic diversity, Portuguese is the sole medium of government-controlled national communication, and has also been referred to as the symbol of national unity (Lopes, 1998, pp. 446–7). The African languages of Mozambique, and there are more than twenty of them, do not play any role at all in the business of the state, including education. On the contrary, apart from Portuguese, foreign languages such as French and English are taught as subjects through the national education system, with Portuguese being the exclusive medium of instruction (except in expatriate schools) from first grade onwards. Lopes (1998, p. 454) observes that "since Portuguese is the official language, most parents tend to see it as the means to ensure their children's future, to acquire a profession and to climb socially, as well as a means to link them up with Mozambicans who speak a different language."

27.3   Bilingualism and Language-in-Education Policies

This section will focus on bilingualism in education in former British colonies, for bilingual education is apparently not practiced in former Portuguese colonies in the region.

The majority of African countries became independent states in the early 1960s. At independence one of the problems that the African countries faced was what they would do with former colonial languages, in this case English and Portuguese, which they inherited from the colonial governments. Should these languages be removed and replaced with African languages; and if so at what cost? And what African languages should be chosen as official languages and why? In response to these issues, soon after independence North African countries swiftly made Arabic[2] the medium of instruction. In Southern African, however, not much has changed. Initially the countries in the region called for

---

2   The recognition of Arabic as a medium of instruction did not in any way undermine the status of French in former French colonies in North Africa. In this regard, Bentahila (1988, p. 338) remarks pointedly that French, in contrast to Arabic, is consistently associated with modernity, education, and sophistication, and is perceived as a means of social advancement. It is observed further that in the case of Morocco, for instance, "Moroccans who know French are very conscious of the advantages they gain from [Arabic-French] bilingualism. Although in theory they tend to sympathize with the ideal of Arabization, they are reluctant to abandon the benefits to be derived from a knowledge of French unless convinced that Arabic is practical enough to cope with all their twentieth-century needs" (Bentahila, 1988, p. 342).

the Africanization of education – that is, the replacement of former colonial languages with the indigenous languages as a medium of instruction. This call is evident in the "Language Plan of Action for Africa" proposed by the now defunct Organization of African Unity (OAU), which was recently replaced with a new body, the African Union (AU). In particular, the "Language Action Plan for Africa" has amongst its goals:

1   to liberate the African peoples from undue reliance on utilization of non-indigenous languages as dominant, official languages of the state in favor of the gradual takeover of appropriate and carefully selected indigenous languages in this domain;
2   to ensure that African languages by appropriate legal provision and practical promotions assume their rightful role as the means of official communication in public affairs of each member state in replacement of European languages which have hitherto played this role. (OAU, 1986)

These goals have never been met. On the contrary, all Southern African countries have adopted more or less similar language-in-education policies, policies which, in the main, have put former colonial languages on a pedestal compared with the indigenous languages. And this is despite the fact that each of the countries in the region has its own *linguistic culture*; that is, its own "set of behaviors, assumptions, cultural forms, prejudices, folk belief systems, attitudes, stereotypes, ways of thinking about language, and religio-historical circumstances associated with a particular language" (Schiffman, 1996, p. 5). For various reasons, among them elitism and vested interests, ethnolinguistic rivalries among language groups, financial constraints, and the lack of political will, to name a few, the ruling elite have stuck to the inherited colonial policies, which promote former colonial languages – English or Portuguese – at the expense of the indigenous African languages. This is evident from the multiple functions, as described earlier, that English (or Portuguese) performs in the life of each individual state in Southern Africa. The keeping of former colonial languages as main working languages in the whole administration machinery of African states does not emanate, says Kahombo Mateene (1980, p. 38), from valid reason but rather "from the desire, conscious or unconscious on the part of the minority elite, to keep and protect their short term privileges, inherited from the colonial era."

Where bilingual education is practiced, as is the case in some former British colonies (e.g. Lesotho, Malawi, South Africa), only subtractive rather than additive bilingualism has been the norm. The latter is an enrichment to the person, and the former an aggression which, as Strubell (1996, p. 274) puts it, can easily have negative psychological effects. Subtractive bilingual education, as it is practiced in Southern Africa, is a prelude to English-only education. English-only policies are grounded in the belief that multilingualism is a problem. The argument against multilingualism is often two-pronged. First, there are too many languages but limited resources so the states cannot provide each child with education in their own language. Second, favoring one African language at the expense of the others would entrench tribalism in the country and would entail a reaction from the elite of the neglected languages (Laitin, 1992). Thus, former colonial languages are seen as "neutral" and as the only languages that can unify the people.

In Mozambique, for instance, the choice of Portuguese as the sole official language of the state was aimed at avoiding one of the cardinal sins of multilingualism, namely, tribalism. The late and first president of Mozambique, Samora Machel, explains the choice of Portuguese as the sole official language of the state as follows:

> The need to fight the oppressor called for an intransigent struggle against tribalism and regionalism. It was this necessity for unity that dictated to us that the only common language [Portuguese] – the language which had been used to oppress – should assume a new dimension.   (Machel, 1979, quoted in Lopes, 1998, p. 458)

> The decision to opt for Portuguese as the official language of the People's Republic of Mozambique was a well considered and carefully examined political decision, aimed at achieving one objective – the preservation of national unity and the integrity of the territory.   (Ganhao, 1979, quoted in Lopes, 1998, p. 459)

The same argument about preserving a country's national unity and so avoiding the sins of multilingualism such as tribalism can be found in the language policies of most African states (e.g. de Klerk, 2002; Laitin, 1992). Accordingly, language-in-education policies framed within the multilingualism-as-a-problem paradigm are usually aimed, as Gideon Strauss (1996, p. 6) aptly puts it, at eliminating the source of the problem: "eradicate multilingualism and replace it with monolingualism." One way Southern African countries have attempted to eradicate multilingualism is by theoretically or constitutionally according national status or official status to selected indigenous languages (as is the case for Chichewa, the national language, in Malawi, or for the nine official African languages in South Africa), and at the same time ensuring covertly that these languages do not enjoy significant use in higher domains such as education, parliament, government and administration, and the economy. Consequently, "while the engine of colonialism long ago ran out of steam [in Southern Africa], the momentum of its languages [remains] formidable, and it is against their tyranny that smaller languages fight to survive" (Popham, 1996; quoted in Master, 1998, p. 717). The prominence of former colonial languages such as English and Portuguese in all higher domains has not only rendered the African languages instrumentally valueless, but has also contributed to negative attitudes towards "mother-tongue education" in the African languages. The section that follows looks at this issue of mother-tongue education and its implications for the maintenance of the indigenous African languages spoken in the region.

27.4   Bilingualism and Mother-tongue Education

Mother-tongue education is part of a larger enterprise, language policy and language planning, which Tollefson (1991, p. 16) describes as one mechanism for locating language within social structure so that language determines who has access to political power and economic resources. UNESCO (1953) defines "mother tongue education" as "education which uses as its medium of instruction a person's mother tongue, that is, 'the language which a person has acquired in early years and which normally has become his natural instrument of thought and communication'." The very concept of "mother tongue" has been highly contested, with some arguing that the whole mystique of "mother tongue" should be dropped from the linguist's set of professional myths about language (e.g. Ferguson, 1992, p. xiii).

For Ferguson, the concept of "mother tongue" is vacuous because "much of the world's verbal communication takes place by means of languages that are not the users' 'mother tongue,' but their second, third, or nth language, acquired one way or another and used when appropriate" (Ferguson, 1992, p. xiii). It is worth noting, however, that the concept of "mother tongue" or "mother-tongue education" has been central to language policies of Southern African countries such as South Africa. Here, the whole apartheid system was, in part, built on mother-tongue education. As Barkhuizen and Gough (1996, pp. 453–4) observe, the apartheid system "used promotion of the mother tongue principle, specifically the advancement of the indigenous African languages as subject and medium of instruction, as a central instrument of the policy of divide and rule." Central to the ideology of apartheid was the construction of ethnolinguistic identities, and "mother tongue" was a virtually sacred tool in the construction of these identities (de Klerk, 2002, p. 30). Therefore, it seems to me that the use of concepts such as "mother tongue" or "mother-tongue education" must not be dismissed as essentially vacuous. Rather, these concepts must be contextualized and understood against the background of a country's history or "linguistic culture."

Unlike North Africa, where the entire educational system functions broadly through the medium of a single African language, Arabic, in Southern Africa generally an African child experiences mother-tongue education only in the early years of primary education, after which a world language, in this case English, takes over as instructional medium. The abrupt switch from the mother tongue to a European language as medium of learning, the inadequate linguistic preparation of the pupils in the European language prior to its use as medium of learning, and the pupils' lack of exposure to the European language outside the classroom generally result in high failure rate and drop-outs (Alexander, 1997; Lanham, 1978). These outcomes have made mother-tongue education one of the thorniest issues in Africa since the early 1960s, with some supporting and others opposing it. This issue has been debated both in education and in creative writing. In regard to the latter, the question has been whether the African writer should break with the elite, who defend the use of European languages, and adopt the people as his or her constituency and write in their language. But as Owomoyela (1996, p. 4) observes, in the African context it is not just the colonial tongue which isolates the writers from the people. There is also the question of mass illiteracy even in the local languages. In regard to education, those who support mother-tongue education maintain that effective literacy acquisition and second language proficiency depend on well-developed first language proficiency (see, for instance, Akinnaso, 1993; OAU, 1986; Skutnabb-Kangas, 1988; UNESCO, 1953). Along these lines, Cheik Anta Diop (1990) argues that "the development of our indigenous languages is the prerequisite for a real African Renaissance." His point, which linguists the world over have stressed, is that "one learns better in one's own language because there is incontrovertible agreement between the genius of a language and the mentality of its speakers" (Diop, 1990, p. 35). Moreover, learning in one's own language evidently saves many years that would otherwise have been wasted in knowledge acquisition through a foreign language.

Those who oppose mother-tongue education maintain that research on the merits or otherwise of mother-tongue education is inconclusive, and that for "every research report that indicates that mother-tongue education is effective, there is another one that indicates that it is not" (Fasold, 1984, p. 312). Along these lines, Ricento (2002, p. 7) cautions that "blanket support of mother-tongue education fails to take into account the sociolinguistic complexity of most multilingual settings, as well as the lack of support for such education that might exist (material and nonmaterial); nor does it consider the political agendas attached to mother-tongue education ideologies that might serve the interests of one group at the expense of the aspirations of other groups." Alastair Pennycook (2002, p. 23) gives a similar caution, noting that "whether or not we are promoting mother-tongue education, bilingualism, monolingualism, or multilingualism, we may be reproducing a colonial legacy of language constructs . . . and . . . get stuck between old polarities such as mother-tongue education vs foreign-language education, mother tongues vs global languages; a position that [simply] replicates many of the colonial constructs of the past centuries." While not totally rejecting the concept of mother tongue, Pennycook suggests that it should be understood as a strategically essentialist argument. As such, its strategic use "is useful for mobilization and legislation, but it may also reproduce those fixed categories of identity that many wish simultaneously to avoid" (Pennycook, 2002, p. 24). Tollefson (2002, p. 66) concurs that sociolinguists must be cautious about generalizations regarding the impact of mother-tongue promotion policies; for advocates of mother-tongue use in broad areas of social life tend to use public sympathy for mother-tongue education as part of larger political strategies, as was the case in the former Republic of Yugoslavia during the period 1980–91 or in apartheid South Africa, as pointed out earlier.

Also, the opponents of mother-tongue education have often invoked the apparent curse of multilingualism, which they perceive as a problem. Countries such as South Africa, Malawi, Zambia, Mozambique and Zimbabwe, to list but a few, may use multilingualism as an excuse for not promoting indigenous languages. There are, however, countries in Southern Africa, among them Botswana, Lesotho, and Swaziland, for which the argument that multilingualism is a problem would not hold. These countries can arguably be described as monolingual countries, for an overwhelming majority of the people in each of these countries speak one common indigenous language: Sesotho for Lesotho, Siswati for Swaziland, and Setswana for Botswana. And yet each of these languages plays second fiddle to English, much as do the other indigenous languages in all the multilingual, English-speaking Southern African countries.

Elsewhere (e.g. Kamwangamalu, 2002) I have argued that whatever position one takes on the issue of mother-tongue education, research into language-in-education policies in Africa over the past four decades has shown comprehensively that despite all efforts to make the European languages available to the African masses, the efforts have been resounding failures: the majority remains on the fringe. Language-based division has increased. Economic development has not reached the majority (Alexander, 1997, p. 88). The social distribution of European languages in African communities remains very limited and is restricted to a minority elite group; and the illiteracy rate both in the former colonial language and in the mother tongue among the populace remains high.

Research reports from around the continent bear testimony to these failures. In the Congo (former Zaire), which economico-politically belongs to the block of the Southern African countries under consideration (also known as Southern Africa Development Countries (SADC)), it is reported that only one out of every 25 Zaireans can speak French correctly; and only one out of every 30 Zaireans can write correctly in French (e.g. Rubango, 1986, p. 267). But that was more than a decade ago. It is common knowledge that since then and as a result of mismanagement and civil wars the overall situation in the country has gone from bad to worse. It is not an exaggeration to estimate that today in the Congo only one out of at least every fifty Congolese can write correctly in French.

The situation in lusophone Africa is not any different. Heines (1992, p. 27) notes that less than 10 percent of people are able to function through Portuguese. Similarly, in anglophone Africa research reports indicate that only a thin percentage of between 5 percent and 20 percent can communicate in English (Samuels, 1995, p. 31). In Zambia, for instance, Siachitema (1992, p. 19) and Tripathi (1990, p. 38) report that since independence the number of Zambians competent in the use of English has shrunk. Understandably, the authors do not mention literacy in the mother tongue since, in Zambia, mother-tongue education is practically non-existent. Therefore, since competence in English is a prerequisite for participation in the national political and economic system, the majority of the people, most of whom live in rural areas, have been left out in the cold, on the fringe of privileged political action. In Malawi, it is reported that about 48 percent of the country's population of

8.4 million are illiterate and that the bulk of the population, 89 percent of whom live in rural areas, cannot access information either in print or the electronic media (e.g. Kishindo, 2001).

In South Africa, the 1991 census statistics paint a similar picture. They show that 49 percent of the black youth between 15 and 24 years of age cannot speak, read, or write English (van Zyl Slabbert et al. 1994, p. 109). A recent report by the country's Minister of Education indicates that 12 million South Africans are illiterate and that about 20 million others, mostly schoolchildren, are not fluent readers in any language, including their mother tongue (*Sunday Times* (Johannesburg), April 16, 2000). Ironically, as far as education is concerned, in South Africa the mother tongue appears to be at the crossroads. On the one hand, black South Africans consider English a threat to the maintenance of their indigenous languages, as can be adduced from the following extracts from newspaper articles.

> PROMINENCE OF ENGLISH KILLS AFRICAN LANGUAGES (*Daily News* (Durban), Friday September 24, 1999)
> The New South Africa presides over the death of African languages. Not only are we overseeing the death of African languages, but we are also acting as both executioner and grave-digger. We are truly killing and burying our African languages and the tragedy is that there are very few mourners. For a variety of understandable reasons, African parents are increasingly choosing English as the medium of instruction by sending their children to the more privileged schools in the suburb.

> ENGLISH ONSLAUGHT: INDIGENOUS LANGUAGES UNDER THREAT (*Daily News*, Wednesday December 6, 2000)
> The indigenous languages of South Africa are under tremendous pressure which threatens to literally wipe them off the surface of the linguistic landscape. From the remotest Khoi language of the Kgalakgadi to the pre-eminent Nguni isiZulu tongue in KwaZulu Natal, they all face a common, domineering force – English.

On the other hand, however, against the backdrop of the legacy of apartheid education, black parents who can afford it consciously trade in the mother tongue for English-medium education at all levels of schooling including tertiary education. It is not surprising that, as the University of South Africa reports, the number of undergraduate and graduate students registered for courses in African languages has been declining by half each year since 1996. For instance, in 1997 there were 25,000 undergraduate and 511 graduate students registered for courses in African languages. In 2001 those numbers had dropped to 3,000 undergraduate and 53 graduate students (*Sunday Times*, March 4, 2001).

A commitment to linguistic pluralism (Cobarrubias, 1983) and thus to linguistic democracy means that the use of the mother tongue in education (and other high domains) is, as many linguists have pointed out, a fundamental human right (e.g. Phillipson, 1992; Skutnabb-Kangas, 1988; Tollefson, 1991). Therefore, there is an urgent need for African states to rethink their language-in-education policies, with a view to revitalizing mother-tongue education as a means through which to empower the masses. Like any language planning exercise, revitalizing the indigenous language comes at a price. The success of mother-tongue education will depend on many variables including the availability of human and financial resources, the political will, and people's attitudes which, in turn, are dependent on the pay-off of mother-tongue education vis-à-vis English- or Portuguese-medium education. But as Tollefson (1991) correctly observes, only when the language achieves a full range of functions and no stigma is attached to its use has it arrived.

For African languages "to arrive," the masses need to know what mother-tongue education would do for them in terms of upward social mobility. Would it, for instance, be as rewarding as, say, English- or Portuguese-medium education? African masses would not support or strive to have an education through the medium of the mother tongue, even if such an education were made available, unless it was given a real cachet in the broader political and economic context. Otherwise, the demand for education in the medium of former colonial languages such as English or Portuguese, rather than for bilingual education in either of these languages and the mother tongue, will continue to grow, especially as "humans like to put butter on both sides of their bread – and if possible a little jam as well" (D'Souza, 1996, p. 259).

Until educational resources in the African languages are developed to a higher conceptual level, and only if these languages are perceived to facilitate access to the wider society and economic advancement, the attraction of English or Portuguese as opposed to the African languages will continue to be overwhelming (Luckett, 1992, p. 18). That attraction will overshadow efforts to promote the indigenous languages and will, most likely, contribute to language shift and eventual language death, especially in urban communities. The next section looks at this issue of language shift and language death against the backdrop of the hegemony and spread of English in the region, with a focus on South Africa. (For additional discussion of bilingual education, see chapters 15, 21, 23–25, and 28.)

27.5   Bilingualism, Language Spread and Language Shift

It is a truism to say that English is the most widely spread and spreading language in the world today; it is even being spread by non-English mother tongue interests (see, e.g. Chisanga and Kamwangamalu, 1997; Fishman and Rubal-Lopez, 1992; Kachru, 1986). Elsewhere I have pointed out that two competing theories offer to explain the spread of English (e.g. Kamwangamalu, forthcoming). These include the *Anglo-American conspiracy theory* on the one hand (e.g. Pennycook, 1994; Phillipson, 1992); and the *global grassroots theory* on the other (Ager, 2001; Fishman, Conrad, and Rubal-Lopez, 1996). The former theory suggests that the spread of English has been engineered by powerful

British and American interests even after the removal of direct imperial control through systematic and often semi-secret language-planning policies; policies that are aimed at stymying efforts to develop local languages and that prevent popular participation in public affairs. The latter theory, on the other hand, argues that for mostly economic reasons individuals opt for English rather than alternative languages. Ager (2001, p. 119) concurs with this view, noting that historical factors aside, currently the motivation that individuals and communities demonstrate for English is economic and pragmatic. It is not accident, as Grin (2001, p. 73) remarks pointedly, that even at lower levels of competence a little English is always associated with higher earnings.

The hegemony of English and particularly the intrusion of the language in the family domain has raised concerns about the future of the indigenous African languages. It is feared that such intrusion will gradually result in language shift toward English. Except for South Africa, not much is known about this issue of language shift in most of the Southern African countries considered in this paper; and so research is desperately needed to document the extent to which language shift has taken or is actually taking place in the region.

In this last section of the paper I shall focus on language shift in South Africa, where the concern over this phenomenon has been voiced more loudly than in any other Southern African country. Drawing on previous work (e.g. Kamwangamalu, 2001, and forthcoming), the aim here will be to highlight some of the factors that contribute to language shift in this context. The term language shift refers to "speech communities whose native languages are threatened because their intergenerational continuity is proceeding negatively, with fewer and fewer users (speakers, readers, writers and even understanders) or uses every generation" (Fishman, 1991, p. 1). The opposite of language shift is language maintenance. The literature indicates that many factors are responsible for language maintenance and shift, the most important among them being generation, the numerical strength of a group in relation to other minorities and majorities, language status, socioeconomic value, education, and institutional support/government policies (see Fishman, 1991; Romaine, 1995; Sridhar, 1988).

All these factors obtain in the South African context and contribute in complex ways to language maintenance or shift in the country. For instance, quite a number of scholars maintain that generation is the single most vital factor of language maintenance and shift (Fishman, 1991; Gupta and Yeok, 1995; Sridhar, 1988). It is argued that the ability and desire of parents to transmit the ancestral language to their children (Gupta and Yeok, 1995, p. 302), or the extent to which the language is used among the younger generations (Sridhar, 1988, p. 83), constitute the litmus test for language maintenance and shift.

It is worth noting, however, that individuals' decisions to transmit or not to transmit the ancestral language are often influenced not by generation alone, but also by other factors, such as the status of the ancestral language in the wider society, government's language policy vis-à-vis the ancestral language in question, community support, etc. (Tollefson, 1991). A case in point is the shift from Indian languages to English in the South African Indian community. Prabhakaran (1998, p. 302) describes the shift as a conscious choice that Indian parents made for their children. She explains that parents forced their children to learn English and discouraged them from learning Telugu or any other Indian language, because, first, the social identity associated with English was more desirable than that associated with Indian languages and, second, the government's language policies did not assign the Indian languages any role in the South African society.

As I have observed elsewhere (Kamwangamalu, 2001, 2002), the process of language shift that took place in the South African Indian communities and, before them, in the Khoisan communities is now taking place again, this time in the urban black communities and to some extent in the white, middle-class, Afrikaans-speaking communities. Although neither Afrikaans nor most of the indigenous African languages are in any immediate danger, recent research shows that language shift toward English is clearly taking place at an accelerated rate, and the number of spheres in which languages other than English can be used is rapidly declining (e.g. Reagan, 2001, p. 63). It seems that in these communities English is increasingly becoming the medium of communication in the family, a domain which is traditionally the preserve of the indigenous languages. Domain intrusion, observe Appel and Muysken (1987, pp. 39, 41), is a clear warning sign of language shift. Fasold (1984, p. 213) makes a similar point, that "when a speech community begins to choose a new language in domains formerly reserved for the old one, it may be a sign that language shift is in progress." South Africa's history of language shift appears to be on course to repeat itself. Whether this history can be stopped against the background of the hegemony of English remains to be seen and will depend, in the main, on the communities' attitudes towards their own languages and on the need to preserve the indigenous knowledge the languages embody. (For further discussion of language maintenance and shift, see chapters 14–16, 18, 25, 26, and 28; for more on language endangerment, see chapters 15–18, 25, and 28.)

27.6 Conclusion

The aim of this chapter was to present an overview of bilingualism in Southern Africa. The overview has highlighted issues relating to language status and language use, language-in-education policies, mother-tongue education, the hegemony of English, and language maintenance and shift. I have argued that although colonialism ended a long time ago, its legacy continues to inform policy-makers' decisions on virtually all of the above and related issues. This is evident, for instance, from the language-in-education policies of all Southern African countries. In the main, these policies promote former colonial languages, in this case English and Portuguese, at the expense of the indigenous African languages. One consequence of this state of affairs is that the policies serve only the elite and allow the latter to reproduce themselves. Another consequence of these policies is what Skutnabb-Kangas (2000) has termed *linguistic genocide*, a term she uses to describe the demise of indigenous languages as result of contact with economically and politically more dominant languages, in this case English and Portuguese.

REFERENCES

Ager, Dennis (2001). *Motivation in Language Planning and Language Policy.* Clevedon, UK: Multilingual Matters.

Akinnaso, F. Niyi (1993). Policy and experiment in mother tongue literacy in Nigeria. *International Review of Education*, 39(4), 255–85.

Alexander, Neville (1997). Language policy and planning in the new South Africa. *African Sociological Review* 1(1), 82–98.

Appel, Rene and Muysken, Pieter (1987). *Language Contact and Bilingualism.* London: Edward Arnold.

Barkhuizen, Gary and Gough, David (1996). Language curriculum development in South Africa. *TESOL Quarterly*, 30(3), 453–72.

Bentahila, Abdelali (1988). Aspects of bilingualism in Morocco. In Christina B. Paulston (ed.), *International Handbook of Bilingualism and Bilingual Education*, pp. 229–43. New York: Greenwood.

Chisanga, Teresa and Kamwangamalu, Nkonko M. (1997). Owning the other tongue: The English language in Southern Africa. *Journal of Multilingual and Multicultural Development*, 18(2), 89–99.

Cobarrubias, J. (1983). Ethical issues in status planning. In J. Cobarrubias and J. A. Fishman (eds.), *Progress in Language Planning*. The Hague: Mouton.

de Klerk, Gerda (2002). Mother-tongue education in South Africa: The weight of history. *International Journal of the Sociology of Language*, 154, 29–46.

Diop, Cheik Anta (1990). *Towards the African Renaissance: Essays in African Culture and Development: 1946–1960* (translated from the French by Egbuna P. Modum). London: The Estates of Cheik Anta Diop and Karnak House.

D'Souza, Jean (1996). Creativity and language planning: The case of Indian English and Singapore English. *Language Problems and Language Planning*, 20(3), 244–62.

Eastman, C. M. (1990). Language planning in post-apartheid South Africa. *TESOL Quarterly*, 24, 9–22.

Fasold, Ralph (1984). *The Sociolinguistics of Society.* Chapter 8: Language maintenance and shift, pp. 213–45. Oxford: Blackwell.

Ferguson, Charles A. (1959). Diglossia. *Word*, 15, 325–40.

Ferguson, C. A. (1992). Foreword to the first edition. In B. B. Kachru (ed.), *The Other Tongue: English Across Cultures*, 2nd edn., pp. xiii–xvii. Delhi: Oxford University Press.

Fishman, J. A. (1971). The Sociology of Language. In J. A. Fishman (ed.), *Advances in the Sociology of Language*, vol. 1, pp. 217–404. The Hague: Mouton.

Fishman, Joshua A. (1991). *Reversing Language Shift: Theoretical and Empirical Assistance to Threatened Languages.* Clevedon, UK: Multilingual Matters.

Fishman, Joshua A. (1996). Introduction. In J. Fishman, A. W. Conrad and A. Rubal-Lopez (eds.), *Post-Imperial English: Status Change in Former British and American Colonies, 1940–1990.*

Berlin and New York: Mouton de Gruyter.

Fishman, Joshua A., Conrad, Andrew W., and Rubal-Lopez, Alma (eds.) (1996). *Post-Imperial English: Status Change in Former British and American Colonies, 1940–1990*. Berlin and New York: Mouton de Gruyter.

Fishman, Joshua A. and Rubal-Lopez, A. (1992). Cross-policy analysis of factors affecting English language spread: Predicting three criteria of spread from a large pool of independent variables. *World Englishes*, 11(2–3), 309–30.

Grin, Francois (2001). English as economic value: facts and fallacies. *World Englishes*, 20(1), 65–78.

Gupta, A. and Yeok, Siew Pui (1995). Language shift in a Singapore family. *Journal of Multilingual and Multicultural Development*, 16, 301–14.

Heines, B. (1992). Language policies in Africa. In R. Herbert (ed.), *Language and Society in Africa: The Theory and Practice of Sociolinguistics*, pp. 23–36. Johannesburg: Witwatersrand University Press.

Kachru, Braj B. (1986). *The Alchemy of English: The Spread, Functions and Models of Non-native Englishes*. Oxford: Pergamon.

Kamwangamalu, Nkonko M. (1997). Multilingualism and education policy in post-apartheid South Africa. *Language Problems and Language Planning*, 21(3), 234–53.

Kamwangamalu, Nkonko M. (2001). The Language Situation in South Africa. *Current Issues in Language Planning* 2(4), 361–445.

Kamwangamalu, Nkonko M. (2002). Language policy and mother-tongue education in South Africa: The case for a market oriented approach. In James E. Alatis, Heidi E. Hamilton, and Ai-Hui Tan (eds.), *Georgetown University Round Table on Languages and Linguistics 2000: Linguistics, Language, and the Professions (Education,* *Journalism, Law, Medicine and Technology)*, pp. 119–34. Washington, D.C.: Georgetown University Press.

Kamwangamalu, Nkonko M. (forthcoming 2003). Globalization of English and language maintenance and shift. *International Journal of the Sociology of Language*, 164.

Kayambazinthu, E. (1998). The language planning situation in Malawi. *Journal of Multilingual and Multicultural Development*, 19(5–6), 369–439.

Kishindo, Pascal (2001). Language and law in Malawi: A case for the use of indigenous languages in the legal system. *Language Matters: Studies in the Languages of Southern Africa*, 32, 1–28.

Laitin, D. (1992). *Language Repertoire and State Construction in Africa*. Cambridge, UK: Cambridge University Press.

Lanham, L. W. (1978). An outline history of the languages of Southern Africa. In L. W. Lanham and K. P. Prinsloo (eds.), *Language and Communication Studies in South Africa: Current Issues and Directions in Research and Inquiry*, pp. 13–28. Cape Town: Oxford University Press.

Lopes, A. J. (1998). The language situation in Mozambique. *Journal of Multilingual and Multicultural Development*, 19(5–6), 440–86.

Luckett, Kathy (1992). *National Additive Bilingualism (Report from the Medium of Instruction Sub-group to the Language Policy Research Group)*. Pretoria: National Education Policy Investigation (NEPI).

Master, Peter (1998). Positive and negative aspects of the dominance of English. *TESOL Quarterly*, 32(4), 716–27.

Mateene, Kahombo (1980). Failure in the obligatory use of European languages in Africa and the advantages of a policy of linguistic independence. *OAU/BIL Publications*, 3, 11–42.

Mulamba, Lufuluabo (1988). Some aspects of bilingualism and bilingual education in Zaire. In C. Bratt Paulston (ed.), *International Handbook of Bilingualism and Bilingual Education*, 561–77. New York: Greenwood Press.

OAU (1986). Language Plan of Action for Africa. Council of Ministers, Forty-fourth Ordinary Session, July 1986. Addis Ababa.

Owomoyela, Oyekan (1996). *The African Difference: Discourses on Africanity and the Relativity of Cultures*. New York: Peter Lang.

Pennycook, Alastair (1994). *The Cultural Politics of English as an International Language*. London: Longman.

Pennycook, Alastair (2002). Mother tongues, governmentability, and protectionism. *International Journal of the Sociology of Language*, 154, 11–28.

Phillipson, Robert (1992). *Linguistic Imperialism*. Oxford: Oxford University Press.

Phillipson, Robert (1996). Linguistic imperialism: African perspectives. *ELT Journal*, 50(2), 160–7.

Phillipson, Robert (2001). Global English and local language policies. What Denmark needs! *Language Problems and Language Planning*, 25(1), 1–24.

Prabhakaran, Varija (1998). Multilingualism and language shift in South Africa: The case of Telugu, an Indian language. In N. M. Kamwangamalu (ed.), *Aspects of Multilingualism in Post-apartheid South Africa: A Special Issue of Multilingua*, 17(2–3), 297–319. Berlin: Mouton de Gruyter.

Reagan, Timothy (2001). The promotion of linguistic diversity in multilingual settings: Policy and reality in post-apartheid South Africa. *Language Problems and Language Planning*, 25(1), 51–72.

Ricento, Thomas (2002). Introduction. *Revisiting the Mother-Tongue Question in Language Policy, Planning, and Politics*. Special issue of *International Journal of the Sociology of Language*, 154, 1–9.

Romaine, Suzanne (1995). *Bilingualism*. Oxford: Basil Blackwell.

Rubango, N. ya. (1986). Le Français au Zaïre: Langue "supérieure" et chances de "survie" dans un pays Africain. *Language Problems and Language Planning*, 10, 3, 253–71.

Samuels, J. (1995). Multilingualism in the emerging educational dispensation. *Proceedings of SAALA* (15), 75–84. University of Stellenbosch, South Africa.

Schiffman, Harold F. (1996). *Linguistic Culture and Language Policy*. London: Routledge.

Siatchitema, A. K. (1992). When nationalism conflicts with nationalist goals: Zambia. In N. T. Crawhall (ed.), *Democratically Speaking*. Cape Town: National Language Project.

Skutnabb-Kangas, Tove (1981). *Bilingualism or Not: The Education of Minorities*. Clevedon, UK: Multilingual Matters.

Skutnabb-Kangas, Tove (1988). Multilingualism and education of minority children. In T. Skutnabb-Kangas and J. Cummins (eds.), *Minority Education: From Shame to Struggle*. Clevedon, UK: Multilingual Matters.

Skutnabb-Kangas, Tove (2000). *Linguistic Genocide in Education or Worldwide Diversity and Human Rights?* Mahwah, NJ: Lawrence Erlbaum.

Sridhar, K. K. (1988). Language maintenance and language shift among Asian-Indians: Kannadigas in the New York area. *International Journal of the Sociology of Language*, 69, 73–87.

Strauss, Gideon (1996). The economics of language: diversity and development in an information economy. *The Economics of Language. Language Report* 5(2), 2–27.

Strubell, Miquel (1996). Language planning and bilingual education in Catalonia. *Journal of Multilingual and Multicultural Development*, 17(2–4), 262–75.

Tollefson, James W. (1991). *Planning Language, Planning Inequality*. New York: Longman.

Tollefson, James W. (2002). The language debates: Preparing for war in Yugoslavia, 1980–1991. *International Journal of the Sociology of Language*, 154, 65–82.

Tripathi, P. D. (1990). English in Zambia: The nature and prospects of one of Africa's "new Englishes." *English Today*, 6, 3, 34–8.

UNESCO (1953). *The Use of Vernacular Languages in Education*. Paris: UNESCO.

van Zyl Slabbert, F., Malan, C., Marais, H., Oliver, K., and Riordan, R. (1994). *Youth in the New South Africa: Towards Policy Formation*. Pretoria: HSRC Publishers.

Walker, A. G. H. (1984). Applied sociology of language: Vernacular languages and education. In Peter Trudgill (ed.), *Applied Sociolinguistics*, 159–202. London: Academic Press.

Webb, Vic (1995). Revalorizing the autochthonous languages of Africa. In V. Webb (ed.), *Empowerment through Language: A Survey of the Language Situation in Lesotho and Selected Papers Presented at the 2nd International LICCA Conference*, 97–117. Pretoria: The LICCA Research and Development Program.

28 Bilingualism in East Asia

DAVID C. S. LI AND SHERMAN LEE

28.1 Introduction

The different nations and regions of East Asia covered in this chapter – China, Hong Kong, Taiwan and Japan – represent a range of language situations in terms of the extent of bilingualism and the types of language contact phenomena to be found within their borders.

China is a vast nation characterized above all by ethnic diversity and sociolinguistic complexity. The Han ethnic group, speaking different "dialects" of the "same" Chinese language, make up 92 percent of China's population. There are, in addition, no less than 55 distinct ethnic minority nationalities; most of them speak their own native languages with dialectal variation. In the main, bilingualism with diglossia – more often than not involving the national language Putonghua (Mandarin) – prevails. Ever since the founding of the People's Republic of China (PRC) in 1949, the codification and standardization of the languages, both written and spoken, has been one of the significant aims of the national language policy. In this regard, some modest success has been achieved. Apart from facilitating communication across dialect groups and minority nationalities, the promotion of Putonghua as a national lingua franca has significantly contributed to the enhancement of national unity. To some extent, a non-assimilationist national policy toward the minority nationalities has helped to preserve and promote their indigenous cultures and languages.

Hong Kong, a British colony until 1997, is now a Special Administrative Region of the PRC. During the colonial era, the language situation of Hong Kong could be characterized as diglossic. Since mainly Cantonese was used for intraethnic communication, individual bilingualism between Cantonese and the colonial language was generally limited to those who had received higher education, although more individuals have become bilingual over the past two decades. The return of sovereignty to China has resulted in perceptible changes in the role and status of the different language varieties used in Hong Kong.

Taiwan is clearly an example of bilingualism with diglossia. It has a rich and diverse ethnolinguistic heritage, which is the result of successive waves of immigration and a colonial past. Compared with Hong Kong, individual bilingualism in Taiwan is more widespread largely as a result of the National Language Movement that promoted Mandarin as a High language, while Southern Min, Hakka and the Aboriginal languages remain Low languages. Among the East Asian regions, Hong Kong and Taiwan are two societies in which socio-political events in the last few decades have shaped, and continue to impact on, the territory's language policy.

Japan has traditionally been considered a monolingual and ethnically homogeneous society; indeed many still insist on upholding this view. However, bilingualism has become an increasingly visible issue in recent years as a result of two main factors: a growing movement of ethnic and cultural renewal among minority groups, such as the Ainu; and increasing immigration and internationalization, resulting in an inflow of foreigners from various corners of the world. In addition, an adoration of foreign (in particular North American and Western European) cultures, especially among the younger generations, has helped turn Japan into a nation with growing bilingualism, at least at the individual level.

Key issues pertaining to bilingualism and bilingual education are not the same in different parts of East Asia, and so broad generalizations are difficult to make. There are, nevertheless, at least two discernible commonalities, both being related to the spread of English in the last century. First, through language contact, all major languages of East Asia have been influenced by English at least to some extent, especially in the form of loanwords. Second, English as a second or foreign language is increasingly commodified in East Asia, as shown in sundry "cultural" products promoting English in the domains of education, news media and entertainment. In terms of the demand for English, there is no question that it is seen as a valuable asset, which explains why much effort is put into acquiring it, with varying degrees of success depending essentially on the learner's access to this international language in their lifeworld.

28.2   China

With over 1.26 billion inhabitants within its political boundaries, China is the most populous country in the world: roughly one in five humans is a (Han) Chinese. The Chinese language, in its multifarious dialectal forms, has the largest number of speakers in the world. By default, the term "Chinese" refers to the largest ethnic group, the Han, who make up about 92 percent of the total population in mainland China. The remaining eight percent (about 90 million) is constituted by dozens of more or less distinct ethnic groups – generally referred to as *shaoshu minzu* (official English translation: "minority nationalities") – of which 55 are officially recognized. The distribution of population is very uneven. The overwhelming majority of the population, mainly Han Chinese, live in the plains roughly in the eastern half of the country. Over 90 percent of its border regions, which are very rich in natural resources, are inhabited by minority nationalities whose cultures and economic activities are very different from those of the Han Chinese and among themselves.

There is no shortage of literature detailing the linguistic diversity and socio-linguistic complexity in China (see, e.g. P. Chen, 1996, 1999; Norman, 1988; Ramsey, 1987). These issues are generally described and discussed separately under two sections: the (Han) Chinese language, and the languages of minority nationalities.

28.2.1   *The (Han) Chinese language*

There are broadly speaking seven dialect groups – Mandarin, Wu, Xiang, Gan, Kejia (Hakka), Yue and Min – all of which have distinctive tonal systems. It is widely believed that historically all Chinese dialects evolved from the same stem. The biggest dialect group is Mandarin, which is generally subdivided into four subgroups: Northern Mandarin, Northwestern Mandarin, Southwest-ern Mandarin, and Eastern (Jiang-Huai) Mandarin. Mandarin in its many forms and varieties is spoken by over 70 percent of China's Han population living mainly in areas north of the Yangtze River and in most of the southwest. The vernaculars of the other dialect groups are generally referred to as Southern dialects, of which Cantonese – the vernacular in Guangzhou and the two special administrative regions Hong Kong and Macao – is the most prestigious, which is why more and more mainland Chinese are learning it.

There is considerable variation within each of these major dialects, not only in terms of phonological features, but also in vocabulary and syntax to some extent. From the point of view of intelligibility, the Chinese dialects are more appropriately seen as members of a language family akin to Romance lan-guages. In general, the further one travels away from one's native hometown, the less success one will have communicating in one's own native vernacular. Indeed, depending on the language distance as marked by the speakers' birth-places, intelligibility in some cases may be more problematic than in com-munication between, say, a Spanish and an Italian national, each speaking their native language.

Notwithstanding such inter-dialectal communication barriers, the Han Chi-nese have since antiquity recognized that they share the same ethnolinguistic and cultural heritage. There is a widely shared perception of linguistic and cultural unity among the Han Chinese, which transcends their cross-dialectal variation in speech. Such a perception is generally attributed to a common, logographic writing system or script. Kwan-Terry and Luke (1997), for ex-ample, point out that:

> [T]he Chinese "languages" are called "dialects" because for centuries they have had a special relationship through the writing system, which is by and large

accessible from the different vantage-points of the individual dialects. . . . From the point of view of helping to unite a vast country, there is a certain logic in the use of a logographic script. A non-phonetic script is in fact better suited than a phonetic one in facilitating inter-provincial communication. Precisely because it is non-phonetic, it can have an existence independent of the phonetic systems of the individual dialects. (pp. 276–7, 284)

The Beijing dialect provides the standard for the national language which is officially called Putonghua in China, Guoyu in Taiwan, and Huayu in Singapore. There are some minor differences between these three. The term Putonghua emphasizes spoken Chinese; when reference is made to standard Chinese as both a spoken and a written language, the term "Modern Standard Chinese" is preferred.

For nearly half a century, Putonghua has been promoted as the national lingua franca by the PRC government, especially in the domains of education and the media. Putonghua is now the medium of instruction in most of the schools in urban areas. In response to concerns about disappointing teaching standards, a rigorous assessment scheme was officially piloted in 1994 and subsequently introduced; today teachers and civil servants are required to pass Putonghua examinations as part of their professional qualifications. Thanks to these measures, the number of speakers conversant in the national lingua franca has increased significantly in the past decades. The promotion of Putonghua, however, is in general more difficult in Southern dialect areas, where speakers of non-Mandarin dialects make up about one-third of the entire Han population. This is so largely because standard written Chinese is modeled on Northern Mandarin. Unlike speakers of Mandarin varieties, therefore, the degree to which speakers of Southern dialects are able to write the way they speak is much lower. This helps explain why the rate of achievement is generally higher in the Mandarin-speaking areas.

28.2.2 *Minority nationalities and their languages*

The minority nationalities are found mostly in the border regions to the north, northeast, northwest and southwest, but also in scattered, small enclaves among the Han Chinese. Although only 55 minority nationalities are officially recognized, the total number of distinct language varieties spoken in China ranges from 80 to 100. The size of the minority populations also varies considerably: from over 15.5 million (Zhuang) to only several thousand (Hezhen). Ramsey (1987) and Norman (1988) are two very informative if somewhat dated works on the minority nationalities and their languages in China. A more recent contribution written in English is a special issue of the *International Journal of the Sociology of Language* devoted to the sociolinguistics of China's ethnic minorities (vol. 97, 1992), where a map plus a complete bilingual list of minority nationalities is included (see also *China Statistical Yearbook*, 2001).

The PRC government follows a non-assimilationist national policy of preferential treatment intended to preserve indigenous cultures. Being listed as a minority nationality brings a number of privileges, such as the permission to have more than one child, lower admission requirements for university entrance, and less stringent terms for hiring and promotion (Sautman, 1999). Regarding the promotion of literacy in minority communities, there is the Nationalities Publishing House (*Minzu Chubanshe*) which oversees the publication of newspapers, books and magazines in minority languages, especially those with established written languages. Officially, therefore, the Chinese government is fairly generous toward the well-being of the minority populations; such an enlightened policy, however, was of little help at times of intense political turmoil, for they, their indigenous languages and cultural practices tended to bear the brunt of class struggle and ideological radicalization, making them particularly vulnerable to abuse and humiliation, especially during the decade-long Cultural Revolution (Heberer, 1989). Concrete steps have since been taken to right these wrongs. For example, a special law passed in 1984 reiterated the significance of the autonomy, freedoms, and rights of the minority nationalities.

The most recent census figures concerning minority nationalities date from 1990, showing that only 8.4 percent of the total population are minorities, the rest being Han Chinese (*China Statistical Yearbook*, 2001). All of the minority nationalities speak their own languages except for the Hui and the Manchu, who have adopted Mandarin as their mother tongue, including the writing system. Quite a few minorities speak more than one language. A range of distinct language families are represented: Sino-Tibetan, Altaic, Austral-Asiatic and Indo-European (for a detailed typological classification, see Stites, 1999). Some of them have long-established written languages: Tibetan, Mongolian, Uygur, Zhuang, and Korean; nine written languages have been created since 1949, while many minority nationalities are still without a written language (Postiglione, 1999).

28.2.3   Bilingualism, dialect bilingualism and diglossia

There is general consensus that bilingualism is almost as old as Chinese civilization itself. The systematic survey of regional dialects in the modern era may be traced back to the works of scholars such as Chao Yuen Ren and Li Fang-kuei between the two world wars. The systematic study of bilingualism, on the other hand, is much more recent. Ru Blachford (1997), for example, notes that the word *shuangyu* ('bilingualism') could not be found in major Chinese dictionaries (p. 158). Also lacking is systematic empirical research on code switching between discrete language varieties or dialects, which appears to be fairly common (Pan, 2000; Wu, 2001). Since the late 1980s, a group of sociolinguists and dialectologists headed by Chen Enquan founded the Shenzhen-Hong Kong Linguistic Institute, with a special interest in promoting research on dialectology, (dialect) bilingualism and diglossia. By 1998, five international conferences on these topics had been held, and the proceedings published (see E. Chen, 1999).

Ping Chen (1999) argues that mutual influence as a result of dialects in contact assumes one of three principal patterns: replacement, with strong dialects replacing weaker ones; merging, which is characterized by the leveling of features of dialects in contact; and coexistence, where the dialects in contact exert relatively little influence on each other. In China, Chen points out that there is some evidence of replacement, notably by the two "strong dialects" Northern Mandarin and Cantonese. Of the three patterns of language contact phenomena, coexistence appears to be the most common in China, resulting in bilingualization of their speakers. Further, the "Putonghua Promotion Campaign" during the last few decades has greatly increased the number of Putonghua speakers, leading to a state of diglossia in practically all major dialect areas:

> Modern Chinese society is one which can be characterized by both bilingualism and diglossia. As people become bilingual in Modern Standard Chinese and the local dialect, what were originally geographical dialects have acquired the super-imposed status of so-called social dialects, which are defined in terms of their specific social functions and values within the same community. . . . Bilingualism obtained in vast geographical areas where a lingua franca based upon Mandarin was learned and used for communication with speakers of other dialects, as well as for formal education, legal, and administrative purposes.   (P. Chen, 1999, pp. 50, 53–4)

Ping Chen (1999) further discusses the results of three separate surveys on patterns of language use in parts of three Southern dialect areas (Wu, Cantonese, and Min), and observes that the functional separation of Putonghua and the local dialect in three representative environments – home, school and workplace, and public places – is most marked in the Min dialect area, and least marked in the Cantonese-speaking area. In all of these three dialect areas, however, the local dialect tends to be preferred in the home domain and public places, whereas Putonghua is more often used in school and the workplace. These surveys furnish clear evidence of diglossia, with the local dialect functioning as the L variety and Putonghua the H variety. Ping Chen thus concludes that "diglossia in these Southern dialect areas is evolving into the standard-with-dialect situation" (p. 56).

Further, given that different dialect areas have developed their regional norms vis-à-vis the less prestigious subdialects (e.g. the Min variety spoken in Xiamen is looked upon as the standard by speakers of other Min varieties in Fujian province), it is conceivable that "double-nested diglossia" comparable to that in Swahili-dominant Africa may have evolved (Fasold, 1984), with the regional standard functioning as an L variety (vis-à-vis Putonghua) or as an H variety (vis-à-vis subdialects) depending on context. A similar pattern of sociolinguistic variation may well be found among speakers of minority languages residing in small enclaves among the Han Chinese.

Officially, the purpose of promoting Putonghua to the status of the national lingua franca is not to eliminate dialects and minority languages. Quite the contrary, with the exception of periods of political instability, both dialects and minority languages have enjoyed considerable support from the central government, and this official stance has been reiterated on many public occasions since the late 1970s. Thus, for example, while there is no doubt that Putonghua has taken on the function of *the* H variety in television and radio broadcasting, as well as in films and theatre, targeting audiences throughout the country, one finds at the same time the active use of dialects in semi-official public settings, such as local opera in different regions, which have continued to thrive as regional citizen initiatives. In a similar vein, radio programs in dialects catering for the needs of people who do not understand enough Putonghua have been tacitly tolerated. For example, there exist Cantonese-speaking radio stations in Guangzhou and Shenzhen, although this has reportedly been a matter of concern to the central government, resulting in top-down directives being issued, benignly reminding the regional authorities that Putonghua should be used in public settings and in the mass media (P. Chen, 1999, pp. 57–9). With regard to the development of minority languages, some efforts were made, and with some success, to create romanization-based writing systems for those minority nationalities who did not have an established tradition of a written language.

28.2.4   Bilingual education

To our knowledge, the most informative sources of the state of bilingual education in China are Ru Blachford (1997), J. Lin (1997), and Stites (1999). The rights of the minority nationalities to use, and be educated in, their native languages are protected by the national constitution (Zhou, 1992). At the same time, minority populations are expected to master Chinese. Thus, consistent with the central government's language policy of "dialect bilingualism" among the Han (Erbaugh, 1995), minority nationalities are encouraged to develop bilinguality in Chinese and their native languages. To this end, bilingual education is seen as the principal means. It should be noted that bilingual education in China means only the minority nationalities learning Chinese in addition to their mother tongue (Ru Blachford, 1997). This is so largely because, whereas members of the minority nationalities have to learn the dominant Han language, the Han are under no obligation to learn the languages of minority nationality groups (J. Lin, 1997).

There is general consensus among mainland scholars that mother tongue teaching is the best means for minority education, and it is unwise to push for a Chinese-only policy in minority schools. These premises, however, are observed to different extents in various bilingual education practices, of which there are two main types with minor variations (J. Lin, 1997; Ru Blachford,

1997; there exists a third, called "expedient type," which will not be discussed here for want of space; for details, see Ru Blachford, 1997; Stites, 1999; and Q. Zhou, 1991). The first type approximates the model of "(static) maintenance bilingual education" (Baker, 1996), which aims primarily at developing competence in Chinese in three stages:

Stage I (grades 1 and 2)	using the mother tongue to assist in the teaching and learning of Putonghua;
Stage II (grades 3 and 4)	using both languages when the children begin to understand Putonghua; and
Stage III (grade 5 and beyond)	using Putonghua as the medium of instruction once it becomes clear that the children are able to understand Putonghua; their mother tongue is taught for several hours per week.

A secondary aim of this type of bilingual education practice is to prevent language loss in the children's mother tongue, but little is done to foster its further development. The mother tongue thus serves primarily as a tool to facilitate the transition to learning in Chinese.

The second type of bilingual education practice consists of using the minority language as the medium of instruction throughout primary and secondary education, in some cases up to university, with Putonghua being taught as a school subject. This is especially prevalent in those minority nationalities with established and stable written languages, such as Mongolians, Uygurs, Tibetans, Koreans, and Kazaks. This model is similar to "mainstream education with foreign language teaching" (Baker, 1996), except that in the case of China the heritage language is maintained in the minority group's home ground rather than in an in-migration context such as North America or Australia.

At present, an estimated 70 percent of the minority populations are able to speak their native minority languages. The future of bilingual education, however, is fraught with problems, some of which are related to the quality of teaching, others rooted in the social context in which bilingual education is implemented. The main factors that negatively impact on the quality of bilingual education are a lack of qualified teachers and educationists with the zeal and expertise to develop pedagogically and socio-culturally sound curricula and textbooks. Such a shortage is especially acute in remote, backward, rural areas, which is why it is so difficult to attract qualified teachers. More unfavorable factors, however, are to be found in the inequitable reward mechanisms governing social mobility, as well as the low social status of minority languages. Whereas higher education requires a high level of competence in Chinese, with few exceptions the learning of a minority language receives little support beyond primary education. Learning a minority language, therefore, is often considered a waste of time, which explains why some Zhuang cadres reportedly refused to allow their children to learn the Zhuang language, and preferred that their children acquire Chinese as soon as they could (J. Lin,

1997; Stites, 1999). In addition, bias and discrimination against minority groups continue to prevail among the Han, which is another worrying factor discouraging minority group members from making an effort to maintain their native languages and cultures. Indeed, some minority students are so concerned that they are reluctant to disclose their minority identity in public (J. Lin, 1997).

Ru Blachford (1997) calls for reforms in several minority language policy areas. These include: legislation at the national level to guarantee the effective implementation of bona fide bilingual education practices; adequate and equitable funding of bilingual programs regardless of whether the minority group in question have already developed a written language; and theoretically informed, preferably interdisciplinary, research on sound bilingual education practices. Lin (1997, p. 197) points out that "issues involved in bilingual education are never purely linguistic but are always strongly social and political," which is why no improvement can be expected without reforming language-related reward mechanisms in society.

28.2.5   *Europeanization and lexical borrowing*

Modern Standard Chinese, also known as *Baihua* (literally 'plain speech'), is in fact a mixture of Mandarin (especially "Northern Mandarin") and classical Chinese, plus ingredients from various dialects. At the beginning of the twentieth century, the incipient form of modern Chinese underwent tremendous influence from European languages, notably English, French and Russian, as a result of a dire need to translate western know-how into Chinese. Various men of letters such as Lu Xun modeled their Wu- or Mandarin-based vernacular writing style on the grammars of European languages they admired, resulting in considerable "Europeanization" of the Chinese language, especially at the level of syntax, including induced morphological changes. Y. Tse (1990) makes a distinction between beneficial and adverse Europeanization. In general, those influences which enhance the expressiveness of the Chinese language and yet are in harmony with its major characteristic – terseness with minimal use of redundant grammatical markers – are considered beneficial (e.g. the development of the pronouns *qianzhe* 'the former' and *houzhe* 'the latter'), whereas those which go against these criteria are seen as unwanted, adverse influences (e.g. the overuse of the adverbial marker *di* after the European model of regular adverb formation, as in English *-ly*, French *-ment*, and German *-lich*). Owing to sustained contact with English, the process of Europeanization (or more precisely Englishization) has continued to this day.

At the level of vocabulary, except for a sizeable body of loanwords borrowed from Sanskrit following the spread of Buddhism in imperial China, there were relatively few traces of foreign influence before the modern era (Y. Chen, 2000). The situation changed drastically at the early stage of extensive language contact toward the end of the nineteenth century, when literally hundreds of westernisms in such fields as politics, economics, and technologies plus many other cultural novelties found their way into Chinese. In terms of the preferred method of translation, the initial penchant for direct borrowing through transliteration (e.g. 麥克風, *mai ke feng*, 'microphone'; 煙士披里純, *yan shi pi li chun*, 'inspiration') soon gave way to semantically based renditions such as loan translation (e.g. 話筒, *huatong* 'speech-tube' – 'microphone') or indigenous coinage (e.g. 靈感, *linggan* 'spiritual-feeling' – 'inspiration'). Later on, Japanese became an important source of direct lexical borrowing as the Kanji characters were pronounceable in Chinese. Words like *geming* 'revolution', *wenhua* 'culture' and *shehui* 'society' are a few examples. Today, westernisms, especially in the area of new technologies continue to be translated into Chinese. One interesting development is that a given foreign word may be translated differently across different Chinese societies. Li (2000a: 310), for example, observes that the word *Internet* has been given the translation 互聯網 (*wu6 lyun4 mong5*) in Hong Kong, but rendered as 網際網路 (*wang ji wang lu*) in Taiwan, and 因特網 (*yin te wang*) in Mainland China.

28.2.6   *Language shift and language loss*

The "Putonghua Promotion Campaign" implemented since the 1950s, especially through formal education, has substantially increased the number of Putonghua speakers across the country. One indirect consequence is that some vocabulary items in local dialects and minority languages gradually give way to their corresponding terms in Modern Standard Chinese. A similar trend is found in minority communities, where "[t]he minority languages are continuously influenced by Chinese in that the pronunciations are becoming closer to that of Chinese and large numbers of new words are borrowed from Chinese" (Ru Blachford, 1997, pp. 163ff). Ru Blachford (1997) further notes that advances in various bilingual education programs in minority communities are likely to accelerate the process of language shift or loss, with the numerically small minority groups, those living among Han-dominated communities, and those without their own written languages being the most vulnerable. To some extent, language shift or loss is also taking place in rural Hakka-speaking areas in favor of the "strong dialect," Cantonese (P. Chen, 1999; cf. Lau, 2001). Language death, on the other hand, is virtually a reality with regard to a few ethnic languages, of which Manchu is probably the most often cited example.

28.2.7   *Written Chinese and the anti-illiteracy campaign*

Literacy in Chinese is generally defined as being able to master between 3,000 and 4,000 Chinese characters. This is justified by the fact that some 99 percent of all characters used in modern writings are covered by the most common 3,000 odd characters. In China, however, being literate means officially being "able to recognize some 1,500 Chinese characters, as well as to perform simple calculations on an abacus, write informal notes, keep account books, and read 'easy to understand popular newspapers and journals'" (Woodside, 1992, cited in Kwan-Terry and Luke, 1997, p. 282). Those who are in command of 500 to 1,500 characters are classified as "semi-literate," while an illiterate person is one whose knowledge of (simplified) Chinese characters falls short of 500 (Woodside, 1992, cited in Kwan-Terry and Luke, 1997, p. 282). The problem of illiteracy is further compounded by the "comeback" of traditional written forms, which since the late 1970s have proliferated in public places, especially in shop signs, adverts, and calligraphic works of senior politicians – a social practice which for practical reasons is protected by law throughout the country.

The promotion of literacy has been a high-priority objective of the national language policy since the founding of the PRC. The main focus of language reform since the 1950s – the simplification of Chinese characters generally known as *wenzi gaige* 'script reform' – is aimed primarily at making written Chinese easier to learn for the masses. The list of simplified characters published in 1964 was revised in October, 1986, and has been enforced ever since. Today, the total number of illiterates has been significantly reduced from an estimated 80 percent in 1949, to 6.72 percent in 2000 (*China Statistical Yearbook*, 2001). Since the 1990s, the emphasis of the campaign is to become literate in order to get rich. Kwan-Terry and Luke (1997) point out that the promotion and development of literacy are especially ineffective for three socially disadvantaged groups: women, rural communities and minority communities (pp. 283–8), which is why the promotion of literacy in many parts of China remains a thorny task.

At one time, many believed that the logographic script was in part to blame for the country's woes and the misery of its peoples. During the tumultuous decades prior to the founding of the PRC, the rise of Japan from a backward feudal island kingdom to a modern nation rivaling Russia and other European powers was widely held among Chinese students of Japanese to be attributable at least in part to the adoption of two simple and yet most effective syllabaries, *Hiragana* and *Katakana*, alongside the use of *Kanji* or sinographic characters – effective from the point of view of facilitating mass literacy. It was argued that a similar reform to the Chinese writing system was sorely needed, for it was thought that the logographic script was the main culprit behind the country's sluggish modernization, and that Japan offered a telling example that the 3,500-year-old logographic writing system was after all an obstacle to the goal of promoting mass literacy, and dispensable. In its most radical version, this view held that nothing less than total alphabetization was necessary to rid China of its illiterate citizenry (cf. DeFrancis, 1984). Among ardent supporters of this view were social activists and political leaders such as Lu Xun and Mao Zedong.

There are at least three main reasons why language reform along the lines of total alphabetization did not come to pass (Kwan-Terry and Luke, 1997). First, the Chinese classics and vernacular-based literature to date would in time become worthless following the implementation of total alphabetization, which in effect would amount to a virtual break with the nation's much cherished linguistic and cultural heritage. Second, there are practical difficulties using a romanization system as the national standard, for close to one-third of the entire population – speakers of Southern dialects – do not speak a Mandarin-based variety. To these speakers, literacy has to be learnt strenuously through their vernacular. Toward the goal of literacy development, therefore, alpha-betization is of little help to them – not until they have developed native-like command of Putonghua. Third, despite its shortcomings, the logographic writing system is in fact quite suited to an isolating language like Chinese (cf. Coulmas, 1989). For one thing, owing to the ubiquity of homophones, logographic characters function as effective disambiguators in a way that a romanization system such as Pinyin cannot. For example, it has been pointed out that there are at least 18 distinctive disyllabic words carrying the romanization *shi-shi* (with tonal variations), while no less than 20 are spelt *ji-shi* (Coulmas, 1989). The use of diacritics as in Pinyin may help to some extent, but ambiguity remains nonetheless, making texts written entirely in Pinyin very difficult to parse (Wang, 2000). These are thus three main reasons why "alphabetization is firmly contained in an auxiliary role" (Kwan-Terry and Luke, 1997, pp. 284ff).

Of all the Southern dialects, Cantonese has developed a strong written tradi-tion of its own, a large number of special characters as shown in many types of popular folk literature (Bauer, 1988; Li, 2000b; Snow, 1993). Nevertheless, Cantonese-specific characters tend to be perceived as low in prestige, and their use has been restricted to informal communication purposes, as found in news-paper columns and light-hearted advertising messages in Hong Kong.

28.3   Hong Kong

Hong Kong, an international metropolis situated at the estuary of the Pearl River Delta in South China, is made up of Hong Kong Island, Kowloon Penin-sula, the New Territories and an array of outlying islands, covering a land mass of about 1,098 square kilometers. Home to over 6.7 million people, Hong Kong is among the most densely populated places in the world. It was a British colony for over 150 years until July 1, 1997, when it became a Special Administrative Region (HKSAR) of the People's Republic of China (PRC). Before the PRC government under Deng Xiaoping adopted an open-door policy in the late 1970s, Hong Kong was China's window to the outside world.

Over 95 percent of the population in Hong Kong are ethnic Chinese, who are mainly descendants of migrants or refugees from different parts of the Mainland, especially the adjacent province, Guangdong. They came to settle in the British colony for political and/or economic reasons. Although these early settlers spoke different Chinese varieties, the biggest group had Cantonese as their mother tongue, which explains why Cantonese has always served as the lingua franca among Chinese Hongkongers. Other Chinese varieties include Sze Yap, Mandarin, Hakka, Min (including Taiwanese), Chiuchow and Hoklo, and Shanghainese (for more details, see Bacon-Shone and Bolton, 1998).

After the handover, English remains a co-official language alongside Chinese (spoken Cantonese, standard written Chinese). Putonghua (or Mandarin) is becoming more and more important, although no major language functions have been assigned to it (see below). And, as a correlate of the unprecedented "one country, two systems" socio-political arrangement, printed Chinese in Hong Kong continues to be written in traditional Chinese characters. Dialectal elements, which until recently were banned in Mainland print media, are very common in informal sections of the Hong Kong Chinese press – a clear sign that a distinct "Hong Kong identity" has emerged as a result of decades of separate political and socioeconomic development (Li, 2000b).

Despite the fact that Hong Kong was a British enclave up to mid-1997, in the history of Hong Kong the number of native English-speaking residents has never exceeded five percent. Since colonial times, except for work-related purposes there has been relatively little social interaction between westerners in Hong Kong and the local Chinese communities. This is so partly because both sides have access to various institutions in their preferred language, Cantonese or English (e.g. school, church, radio, television and print media). In short, it is as if the two communities lived in separate "enclosures." In this regard, little has changed since Luke and Richards (1982) made this observation two decades ago.

As English has been the dominant language in the domains of government, business, education, and law, most Hong Kong Chinese have learned at least some English. In terms of language standards, local schools follow British norms, whereas outside of the domain of education, especially in the media, American English is more common. Luke and Richards (1982) observed that the number of Hong Kong Chinese who were bilingual in Cantonese and English was relatively small; hence, in the early 1980s, the kind of Chinese-English bilingualism in Hong Kong approximated Fishman's (1972) model of "diglossia without bilingualism." Considerable change has taken place in the past two decades, however. Both census figures and language surveys yielded similar findings, namely, a significant percentage of Hong Kong Chinese described themselves as competent speakers of English, and had to use at least some English in their workplace, especially in white-collar settings. This is in part a direct consequence of the nine-year compulsory education system since 1978, which means that all children are taught at least some English up to the end of Form 3 (Grade 9, age 14). Sociolinguistically, therefore, post-handover Hong Kong is more appropriately characterized as "diglossia with (increasing) bilingualism."

Apart from ethnic Chinese and westerners, there are a number of minority groups, of which the Filipinos and Indonesians top the list (144,800 and 63,800, respectively, *Hong Kong 2000*). Most of them work as domestic helpers. The Filipinos speak Tagalog, English, and a number of regional varieties of the

Philippines. In their job as domestic helpers, however, they tend to speak some Cantonese as well. This may be observed in the fresh food market, where Filipino domestic helpers and Chinese food vendors would use a mixture of pidgin English and pidgin Cantonese to communicate with each other. As for the Indonesians, there has been little research on their language use patterns.

28.3.1 Cantonese-English code-switching research

Research has shown that Cantonese-English code switching is very common, indeed ubiquitous among educated Chinese Hongkongers. It has been observed that clause-level switching is rare. Instead, English elements of various lengths below the clause level are inserted into the matrix language, Cantonese or written Chinese, hence this practice is also known as "intra-sentential code switching" or "code mixing." Cantonese-English code switching may be regarded as a natural correlate of the fact that Cantonese and English, for historical reasons, have been in contact for more than 150 years. Since the colonial era, English has been the dominant language in the domains of government, business, education, and law. Most schoolchildren start learning ABC from kindergarten. Upon exiting secondary school at the age of 17, a Form 5 school-leaver will have learned English for about 12 years. Given the significance of English in the Hong Kong education system and the intimate relationship between language and culture, it is only natural that English elements of various lengths would be called upon and surface in the middle of Chinese discourses, be it (informal) written Chinese or spoken Cantonese. Li's (1996) study of select Hong Kong Chinese newspapers and magazines in the early 1990s shows that code switching is especially widespread in six domains: computing, business, fashion, food, showbiz, and modern lifestyle (cf. J. So, 1997).

In the literature on code switching worldwide, a general distinction is made between the speaker's concern for three main types of meaning: social, discourse or conversational, and linguistic. In Hong Kong, some scholars argue that Cantonese-English code switching is sociolinguistically motivated, for example, to signal one's status as a member of the English-speaking class in order to achieve some context-specific goal (e.g. hoping to get better treatment in service encounters), or to reflect the speaker's bilingual and bicultural identity (Pennington, 1998b). Others attempt to analyze Cantonese-English code switching from a linguistic or structural perspective (e.g. Chan, 1998; Luke, 1998).

While sociolinguistic motivation cannot be ruled out in context-specific situations, Li and Tse's (2002) experimental study shows that it is not so common in Hong Kong. Among the attested motivations of Cantonese-English code switching in their findings are: availability or specificity of a "translation equivalent" in their L1, a lack of semantic/stylistic congruence, L1 translation already loaded with meaning, the principle of economy, euphemism, and cognitive salience as a result of English-medium education (cf. "concept formation," Gibbons, 1987).

28.3.2   *Language-in-education policy*

There are a number of instructive sources describing the historical background to, and development of, the language policy since the colonial era (see, e.g. Cheng, 2000; Evans, 1996; Johnson, 1994; A. Lin, 1997; Morrison and Lui, 2000). Two of the main educational issues that have been a matter of widespread concern are: (1) the choice of a suitable model of bilingual education, as manifested in the medium of instruction policy, and (2) the proficiency level of the languages: English (spoken and written) and Chinese (written).

In Hong Kong media discourse, there is widespread concern about declining language standards as evidenced in the speech and writing of educated job seekers, university graduates included. This concern is driven largely by a consensus shared by most education experts and the general public, that the well-being and vitality of Hong Kong's knowledge-based economy depends significantly on a well-trained bilingual workforce well-versed in Chinese and English (for a critical appraisal of this position, see A. Lin, 1996). The need for Chinese is obvious given the fact that Hong Kong's sovereignty reverted to China in 1997, and that an overwhelming majority of the local population are ethnic Chinese. As for the need for English, the main argument is that, since Hong Kong's lifeblood is trade and commerce supported by expanding service and hospitality industries such as tourism, a sufficiently high level of communication skills in the international language, English, is crucial for establishing and sustaining solid business links with commercial enterprises and entrepreneurs from other parts of the world, for whom English is the lingua franca. All this explains the Hong Kong government's goals in its language-in-education policy: biliteracy (written Chinese and English) and trilingualism (Cantonese, English, and Putonghua). These goals have constituted the main driving force of a decade-long education reform, triggering heated debates and lively discussions in public discourse in both print and broadcast media.

There is general consensus regarding the significance of Chinese and English for the future of Hong Kong. More controversial is the way in which the goals of biliteracy and trilingualism can most effectively be achieved. As English plays little or no role at all in the lifeworld of most Chinese Hongkongers, the choice of a sound bilingual education model is seen as the most effective means for achieving these goals. Various immersion models have been proposed. In September, 1998, after heated debates in the media among various stakeholders, notably education experts, teachers, principals, and parents, the HKSAR government implemented the mother tongue (Cantonese) education policy at the secondary-school level. As a result, of 411 secondary schools, only 114, which met the government's requirements concerning the teachers' English standards, were allowed to remain English-medium schools; the rest had to switch to Chinese-medium if they had not yet done so. This policy, generally known as the streaming policy, has created a lot of ill-feeling in society. Chinese parents whose children are allocated to Chinese-medium schools are concerned about their children not getting enough exposure to English. Many students, upon being allocated to a Chinese-medium school against their will, feel depressed about being seen as "second best." As for school principals and teachers, their main worry is the school's inability to attract academically competent students, which in turn has implications for the school's public image and overall teaching performance. The effectiveness of mother tongue education is currently being monitored and under review.

To bolster the standards of English, the government implemented a Native English-speaking Teacher (NET) scheme at the secondary-school level in 1998. Every secondary school has been given financial support to hire one NET teacher, who is expected to collaborate with local teachers to motivate students to learn English and to improve the effectiveness of the teaching and learning of English. Preliminary results are encouraging, and so, starting from September 2002, the NET scheme will be extended to primary schools.

Putonghua (Mandarin), which was first introduced into the school curriculum in 1986, is now a compulsory subject in primary school and an optional subject in the Hong Kong Certificate of Education Exam (Grade 11, age 17). It is also the teaching medium in a few subsidized primary and secondary schools. Since standard written Chinese is largely modeled on Putonghua, some scholars argue that one effective means to elevate Hong Kong students' Chinese standards is to use Putonghua as a medium of instruction for teaching subjects in Chinese. While the rationale behind this proposed policy is sound, there are many practical difficulties that may not be easily overcome in the short run, in particular, the availability of teaching materials and well-trained and competent Putonghua teachers. For one thing, research has shown that knowledge of Cantonese may interfere with the learning of Putonghua. It has been pointed out that, if most of the teachers themselves are unfamiliar with using Putonghua, such a policy would be counterproductive. In any case, the merits of adopting Putonghua as a teaching medium have been recognized by government officials, and there are signs that this will be one of the long-term goals in the ongoing education reform.

Such a change, if materialized, would certainly impact negatively on the vitality of Cantonese, the lingua franca of Hong Kong Chinese to date. As Bauer (2000) observes, the scenario of all Hong Kong schoolchildren learning in Putonghua may seem remote, but in a matter of one or two generations' time, there is no telling whether this will become a more and more viable option to the government and society at large, when today's younger generations have grown up, all being competent speakers of Putonghua. Once Cantonese is no longer taught and used as the language for reading written Chinese texts, it is highly probable that many of the functions now assigned to Cantonese will be given over to Putonghua, triggering thereby a language shift, leading possibly to language loss over time (Bauer, 2000). Bauer warns that one needs to look no further than Guangzhou, the capital of Guangdong province, to appreciate the ways in which the adoption of a Putonghua medium-of-instruction policy may affect the vitality of Cantonese.

28.4   Taiwan

Geopolitically, Taiwan designates one major island and several smaller offshore islands of about 35,981 square kilometers, separated from the Chinese mainland by the Taiwan Straits. Today's population is estimated at 22.3 million (Bureau of Statistics, 2001). Taiwan has all the attributes of an independent political entity, in particular, a working democracy characterized by multiparty elections, a free market economy, and a sizeable reserve of foreign currency.

The modern history of Taiwan dates from the beginning of the seventeenth century with the occupation of the island by Dutch (1624–62) and Spanish (1626–42) colonizers, whose purpose was to secure a coastal outpost to facilitate trading activities in the region. The Europeans were subdued by the Chinese Ming general, Zheng Chenggong (alias Koxinga), but his regime was short-lived (1662–83). Under Chinese Qing dynasty rule (1683–1895), Taiwan became a prefecture of Fujian province, then later a separate province of China. In 1895, following China's defeat in the First Sino-Japanese War, Taiwan was ceded to Japan for 50 years until it was "recovered" at the end of World War II by the Chinese Kuomintang (KMT) government headed by Chiang Kai-shek. In the ensuing Chinese civil war, Chiang lost the mainland to the Communists and retreated to Taiwan, establishing a government in exile there in 1949. Taiwan was under martial law for nearly four decades until 1987. The late 1980s saw gradual political liberalization and democratization, which culminated in the peaceful transfer of political power from the KMT to the Democratic Progressive Party (DPP) in 2000 (see further, Hsiau, 2000; S. Huang, 1993, 2000; Tsao 1997, 1999; and J. K. P. Tse, 2000).

28.4.1   Ethnolinguistic groups in Taiwan

Taiwan's population is composed of four main ethnolinguistic groups: Southern Min, Hakka, Mainlanders, and Austro-Polynesian aborigines. In terms of their present ratios, Huang's (1993) estimates, based on the 1990 census, are the most often cited:

Ethnolinguistic group	Southern Min	Hakka	Mainlanders	Aborigines
Population (%)	73.3	12	13	1.7
Native tongue	Southern Min ("Taiwanese")	Hakka	Mandarin and other Chinese	Austronesian languages

The majority of the Taiwanese are descendants of Han Chinese who came to Taiwan in successive waves of migration from the seventeenth century. The first immigrants originated mainly from two cities in Fujian province: Zhangzhou and Quanzhou, and spoke two similar varieties of Southern Min (a variety of Min dialect) as their native tongues. As these people became the dominant ethnolinguistic group in Taiwan, their language variety is often labeled "Taiwanese" (J. K. P. Tse, 2000).

In the eighteenth century, a smaller group of mainland immigrants from Fujian and Guangdong provinces joined the settlement movement. They were mainly speakers of Hakka dialect. The mainlanders who fled to Taiwan with the KMT government in 1949 created a third wave of immigrants. The lingua franca of these people, who originated from various parts of China, was Mandarin.

Aside from the ethnic Chinese, the other major ethnolinguistic group are descendants of the Austro-Polynesian population. According to Tse (2000), Taiwan was predominantly inhabited by native aborigines in the mid-seventeenth century. Today, they are a minority group. These aborigines spoke a number of related but distinct and partially mutually unintelligible Austronesian languages.

28.4.2 Ethnicity and identity

As a correlate of increasing democratization, the notion of ethnicity has become a hotly debated issue. Of the four ethnolinguistic groups, the Southern Min and the Hakka are generally labeled as *ben-sheng-ren* ('indigenous people'). In contrast, the Mainlanders are generally known as *wai-sheng-ren* ('outsiders'). Attributes such as these are indicative of the islanders' deep concern for their identity, which in turn has fueled controversies in public discourse regarding what it means to be "Taiwanese." Liao (2000) presents three such definitions: the traditional definition refers only to the Southern Min people; the second definition includes the Southern Min, Hakka and Austro-Polynesian groups; the third definition includes all four groups. Corresponding to the third definition, "New Taiwanese" (Tsao, 1999; J. K. P. Tse, 2000) was a term coined in the 1990s as part of an attempt to forge a supraethnic Taiwanese identity, but it has been less commonly heard since the DPP came to power in 2000.

28.4.3 Current sociolinguistic situation

28.4.3.1 Diglossia with bilingualism

The official and national language of Taiwan is Mandarin (*Guoyu*). S. Huang (2000) estimates that nearly 90 percent of today's Taiwanese population can speak Mandarin. Many surveys have shown that Mandarin is the lingua franca used in interactions between members of distinct ethnolinguistic groups.

Standard Mandarin in Taiwan is phonologically, lexically and syntactically similar to Putonghua, the national language of Mainland China. This similarity notwithstanding, it has been pointed out that a variety of "Taiwanese-Mandarin," characterized by influences of other local tongues, has evolved (J. K. P. Tse, 2000).

The sheer number of Southern Min speakers explains why it is the second most widely used language variety on the island after Mandarin. According to Liao (2000, p. 167), "the further south one goes, the more one observes a dominance of Southern Min in the mixed code used." This is consonant with van den Berg's (1985, 1988) earlier finding that generally more Mandarin is used in the north, and more Southern Min in the south. Code switching between Mandarin and Southern Min is very common, with the matrix language being either language depending on the speaker (S. Huang, 2000; Liao, 2000). Since High functions tend to be assigned to Mandarin, for those who speak another variety as their native tongue, a diglossic relationship obtains between the two Chinese varieties (Tsao, 1999). Moreover, as Southern Min is so widespread, members of the Hakka and aboriginal communities often find it necessary to learn Southern Min as well, approximating thereby a state of triglossia in these communities (Tse, 2000).

28.4.3.2   Language shift and language death

Surveys carried out in the 1990s provide evidence of language shift toward Mandarin among speakers of the other language varieties. Statistics show that the aboriginal languages are declining at the fastest rate, Hakka close behind and Southern Min less markedly.

The aboriginal population consisted of two main tribes, each of which could be further divided into several subgroups (Tsao, 1997, 1999), namely plain tribes (Ketagalan, Kavaland, Taokas, Pazeh, Papura, Babuza, Hoanya, Siraya, Thao) and mountain tribes (Amis, Paiwan, Puyuma, Saisiyat, Yami, Atayal, Bunun, Rukai, Tsou). The early Chinese migrants tended to settle on flat land areas, which brought them in closer contact with the plain tribes. Over time and through intermarriage, the latter gradually assimilated into the Chinese communities (S. Huang, 1993). In 2000, the indigenous population of Taiwan was made up of 188,784 people of plain tribes ancestry, and 213,668 people of mountain tribes ancestry (Government Information Office, 2001). However, the number of inhabitants who can speak aboriginal languages is very small – in Tsao's (1997) estimate no more than a few hundred Thao speakers in central Taiwan, and 250 Kavaland speakers in the Hualian area of eastern Taiwan. The mountain tribes suffered loss of language and culture to a lesser extent, mainly because contact with the Chinese was less frequent. According to S. Huang (2000), of the 10 Austronesian languages that still exist, four have a better chance of surviving (Paiwan, Amis, Atayal, Bunun), four are moderately endangered (Saisiyat, Yami, Rukai, Tsou), and two are seriously endangered (Puyuma and Thao). Of these, only the last is a plain tribe language. Urbanization, which accompanied political liberalization and democratization, has drastically transformed the lives of many aborigines. Ironically, tourism is one of the most serious threats of deculturation. In a recent feature article appearing in the *South China Morning Post* in Hong Kong, it stated: "the tourist traffic spells doom for the Amis, the largest of Taiwan's 10 aboriginal tribes. To please gawking crowds . . . the tribe will water down or spice up their festivals and other rituals, speeding up the cultural erosion" (Anonymous, January 11, 2002).

Tsao (1999) warns that up to half of the existing aboriginal languages will disappear in a matter of four or five decades if nothing is done to sustain their vitality. It is hoped that recent efforts at preserving and cultivating these languages may go some way to retarding this process of language death.

As a result of the KMT's hegemonic propagation of Mandarin in education and other public domains, the Hakka communities have likewise been undergoing language shift toward Mandarin at an alarming rate. This worrying trend is especially evident among younger generations, who clearly prefer Mandarin to Hakka in their social interactions with others. Shift toward Mandarin is also evident among the Southern Min group, albeit at a much slower rate (Tsao, 1999). Since the Southern Min are the majority group in Taiwan, the effect of the government's past language policy on this group was much less marked.

28.4.4   *Language policy in Taiwan*

28.4.4.1   *National Language Movement: 1940s–1980s*

Mandarin came to prevail in Taiwan as a result of the National Language Movement, a language policy implemented by the KMT regime in 1946 and enforced for almost four decades. In accordance with the KMT's claim of being the sole legitimate government of China, the promotion and spread of Mandarin as a unifying national language was seen as an effective means of cultivating patriotism on the island.

Initially, the main objective of the Movement was to eradicate the influence of Japanese by banning its use in all domains. After 50 years of Japanese rule however, during which Japanese was the High language of many intellectuals and the elite in general, the policy in effect literally rendered these people speechless. Mandarin was strenuously promoted as a school subject and the sole medium of instruction. Gradually, the use of other language varieties was restricted in all public domains – government, media, education, and law.

Language use in the media was rigidly monitored, especially following the passing of the Broadcast Bill (1975–93). As a result, languages other than Mandarin were discouraged in most forms of the media, ranging from news and educational programs to films, songs and other forms of entertainment. Agricultural news was the main exception. After the repeal of Martial Law in 1987, some news broadcasts in Southern Min and Hakka were permitted (S. Huang, 1993).

An equally important concern of the Movement was the implementation of the language-in-education policy. According to Tsao (1999), this policy was driven by two main concerns: (1) nationalism and national unification, and (2) modernization and economic growth. The former naturally favored Mandarin, while the latter explains why English also played a significant role in the language curriculum. Mandarin was taught for at least five hours per week from junior high school. English was taught for five hours per week prior to 1970, later reduced to two or three hours after compulsory education was extended from six to nine years. Community languages other than Mandarin had no official role in the school system at all. To this day, many still have memories of being punished in school for speaking in "dialect" (Hung, 1992).

Only in the mid-1980s, when the political climate gradually became less oppressive, did the use of "dialects" in public begin to be tolerated. By that time, however, the strict enforcement of the Mandarin-only policy had already had its effect, in that clear evidence of language shift toward Mandarin could already be found among the indigenous communities. Given the well-attested impact of the language-in-education policy on language maintenance in multilingual settings worldwide, it comes as no surprise that education level is one of the key social variables to have a direct bearing on the extent of language shift in Taiwan. In a questionnaire survey involving speakers of the community languages, Tsao (1997) found that the higher the speakers' education level, the more frequently Mandarin is used. Moreover, for the aboriginal groups, a higher education level correlated positively with competence in Mandarin, and negatively with competence in their native tongue.

28.4.4.2   Current language policy

28.4.4.2.1   Community languages

Following the lifting of Martial Law and, later, the abolition of the Broadcast Bill, the language policy gradually became more liberal. While Mandarin remains the lingua franca for inter-group social interactions, speakers of the community languages have begun to redefine their indigenous Taiwanese identities (Hsiau, 2000). Despite their relatively small group size, the Hakka are no less assertive than the Southern Min of their indigenous Taiwanese identity, as shown in the Hakka Movement in the late 1980s and their aborted attempt to form a political party in the early 1990s (Hsiau, 2000; Hung, 1992). One consequence of these efforts is the proliferation of books on the history, language, and culture of the three indigenous groups (e.g. Hung, 1992; Liu, 2000; Pu, 1996).

Government support for mother-tongue education and local bilingual education programs is increasingly widespread, as are government efforts to help indigenous groups revive their cultures and languages (Tsao, 1997, 1999). Ilan County in northeastern Taiwan was the first to initiate language courses in Southern Min at elementary and junior high levels from 1990. Others quickly followed suit, and now, elective courses in Southern Min, Hakka and some aboriginal languages are taught in a number of county schools.

Tsao (1997) noted considerable variation in the ways in which community language teaching is delivered, ranging from having it fully integrated into the school curriculum, to treating it as an extracurricular activity. In Wulai, Taipei County, extracurricular Atayal language classes were set up in 1990 in elementary and junior high schools, where the majority of students are of aboriginal descent. Following the amendment of the school curriculum in 2001, it is now compulsory for all primary students to take at least one community language course. Increasingly, various community language teaching materials including textbooks and videos have been published, either by government bureaus or private publishers.

However, the teaching of community languages is also plagued with problems. One obstacle comes from parents who fear that bilingual education may have an adverse effect on students' proficiency levels in standard (written) Chinese. Others believe that knowledge of foreign languages such as English or Japanese is more vital for economic and social advancement. As scholars and advocates of bilingual education try to facilitate the movement toward reviving Taiwan's indigenous languages, it is ironic that the minority speakers themselves are much less enthusiastic. A poignant quote from the ROC yearbook (Government Information Office, 2001) states that "[f]or aborigines who are less well off, economic and social advancement is a much more urgent concern; bilingual education may be a luxury that they feel they cannot afford" (cf. C. M. Huang, 1998).

Other problems in the teaching of community languages include inadequate class time (typically one hour per week), and a lack of funds, trained teachers, and expertise in curriculum design and development. To remedy this situation, the government has provided more support to teachers in the form of handbooks, workshops and teaching materials.

A final problem is codification. A debate is going on regarding the kind of writing system which is most conducive to the teaching and learning of Southern Min and Hakka. Among the alternative models being considered and put to use are Chinese characters, romanization, and a mixture of the two (Hsiau, 2000; S. Huang, 1993; Hung, 1992). More recently, the debate has been extended to the choice of romanization system. The mayor of Taipei, Ma Jing-jeou, himself a member of Kuomintang, is keen on adopting the mainland-based Hanyu Pinyin system for transliterating Mandarin, while a special panel of pro-DPP scholars is in favor of promoting a separate, locally devised "Tongyong Pinyin system," which appears to be capable of transliterating not only Mandarin, but also all the other community languages, including aboriginal languages. Here, it can be seen that the choice is largely politically motivated (Blatt, 2002).

28.4.4.2.2 English and other foreign languages

Of all foreign languages, English is clearly seen as the most important. English classes are now compulsory from elementary Grade 5 onwards, after government plans to extend English teaching to elementary level were implemented in 2001. Some schools have chosen to start teaching it at Grade 4 or even as low as Grade 2. At the tertiary level, most students are required to take at least one year of English at freshman level.

According to Ho (1998), English generally has no place in people's daily lives (except for some in the professional fields) but there is a widely shared perception that a high proficiency in English will facilitate upward and outward mobility. Such expectations have generated a great demand for English. This is partly reflected in the profusion of self-learning English materials, and sundry advertisements promoting various English services ranging from bilingual kindergartens and private language schools to English cram courses. This is not surprising given that a high score in TOEFL or IELTS is a ticket to higher education in North America and other English-speaking areas. Use of English in the media is also increasingly prevalent. English print media in circulation include magazines (e.g. *Time*) and newspapers (e.g. *China Post*, *China News*, *Taiwan News*, *Taipei Times*). English-language radio programs are easily accessible (e.g. International Community Radio Taiwan – 24 hours), and a number of English-language television programs (e.g. CNN and other news programs) can be received via cable. According to S. C. Chen (1996), there are signs that English, especially in the form of code switching, is making inroads into the discourses of various social groups, including youngsters and housewives.

Although English has been the main focus of foreign language education, other foreign languages, including Japanese, French, German, and Spanish are also offered at university level and in some high schools. In view of the need for internationalization, the government is currently promoting a five-year "second foreign language education program" in senior high schools. The second most widely learned foreign language is Japanese. Government statistics (Government Information Office, 2001) reveal that there were 264 Japanese classes offered around Taiwan between September 1999 and July 2000. This compares with 64 French classes, 51 German classes and 11 Spanish classes. The market for Japanese is partly attributed to the large number of second-language speakers of Japanese who live in the territory. According to the Ethnologue (2002), in 1993 there were 10,000 speakers of Japanese in Taiwan, among whom were a few elderly aborigines using Japanese as a second language.

28.4.5   Outlook

Commenting on the intricate language matrix of Taiwan at the turn of the millennium, S. Huang (2000) remarks that local languages are facing competition from two fronts: Mandarin, the official language, and English, the international language. Such a development is likewise the concern of a feature article in *Taipei Journal* entitled "Native dialects go compulsory": "The growing native consciousness in Taiwan presents a paradox by occurring at a time when many other aspects of local society are becoming more internationalized. The challenge now facing society is to respect localization while remaining on the road to globalization" (*Taipei Journal*, February 3, 2000).

28.5 Japan

Situated on the western edge of the Pacific Ocean, the Japanese archipelago comprises four major islands: Hokkaido, Honshu, Shikoku, and Kyushu, and thousands of smaller islands. With a population of nearly 127 million, Japan is currently the world's ninth most populous nation. While at once retaining a large part of their traditional culture of which Shintoism, Buddhism and Confucianism are essential ingredients, the people of contemporary Japan also espouse a modern and western lifestyle. With a strong value on education, Japan boasts a literacy rate of over 99 percent. This, together with a robust work ethic and technological mastery, has helped turn Japan into one of the most advanced and powerful nations in the world.

28.5.1 Ethnolinguistic diversity in a "monolithic" nation: Bilingualism without diglossia

Over 98 percent of the population in Japan are ethnically Japanese. Not surprisingly, Japan has been regarded as an extremely homogeneous society with everyone speaking Japanese, its only national and official language and the medium of instruction throughout the public education system. However, despite the long-held assumption of homogeneity, Japan is in fact home to several communities of diverse ethnic origins.

There exists much regional variation within the Japanese language itself. The biggest differences occur between the Eastern and Western dialects, reflecting the geographical barrier formed by the Japan Alps that run down central Honshu. The largest collection of dialects are the Western dialects found in Honshu's Kansai region, incorporating the cities of Osaka, Kyoto and Kobe. Today's Standard Japanese is based on the Eastern dialect spoken in Tokyo. These Japanese dialects are generally mutually intelligible.

Ethnolinguistic minorities in Japan include indigenous groups as well as migrants. Of the latter, those from Korea and China are the most long-established. Newer immigrants arrived from various Asian and Latin American countries following the economic upturn of the 1980s. By the end of 2000, there were approximately two million foreigners living in Japan, including an estimated 300,000 illegal residents. Korean and Chinese immigrants together comprise over half of the foreign population, while others originate mainly from Brazil, the Philippines, Peru, and the USA (Statistics Bureau, 2002).

Increasing immigration and internationalization, along with a growing trend of revivalist movements among indigenous groups such as the Ainu and Ryukyuans have resulted in a rapid expansion in the number of languages used in Japan. Consequently, issues of biculturalism and bilingualism – both individual and societal – have begun to feature more prominently in public discourse. Besides ethnolinguistic minorities, other types of bilinguals who have attracted attention in emergent Japanese bilingualism research include: (1) Japanese learners of English, (2) *kikokushijo* – children of Japanese expatriates who are repatriated after living overseas for extended periods, and (3) children of international marriages (Yamamoto, 2001). To most Japanese people, the term "bilingual" has positive connotations, and refers to these actual or potential speakers of Japanese and (usually) English; seldom is it used to describe the bilingual experiences of ethnic minority speakers.

28.5.2   Origins of Japan's official language policy

The image of Japan as a monolingual and monocultural society may be traced back to the Meiji period (1868–1912), when the country was reopened to the outside world after two and a half centuries of self-imposed isolation. The promulgation of linguistic and cultural homogeneity was key to the new imperial government's endeavor to create a unified nation. Following the example of technologically advanced nations of the West, the institution of a national language and a system of compulsory education was central to the Meiji government's goals of modernization and industrialization. National language policy measures included the unification of literary and vernacular forms of Japanese, the establishment of a unified standard, and the promotion of the national language (*kokugo*). Attempts to develop a writing system to facilitate modern communication and universal education went hand in hand with efforts to reduce differences between spoken and written Japanese, resulting in reduction in the number of Chinese characters (*kanji*) and simplification of the Japanese syllabic spelling system (*kana*) (Honna, Tajima, and Minamoto, 2000). The *kokugo* became the sole medium of instruction, and was promoted at the expense of dialects and minority languages.

To promote an identity that embraced both cultural uniqueness and uniformity, the Meiji policy toward ethnic minorities was forced assimilation. Assimilation programs, of which language prohibition was an essential component, were initiated against the Koreans and Chinese who came under Japanese colonial rule, and more conspicuously against the Ainu and Ryukyuans, whose cultural practices were also prohibited along with their languages. Moreover, most minorities were required to adopt Japanese family names.

The ideological construct of a monolithic Japanese identity pervaded many aspects of society through successive governments following the Meiji Restoration. Even in the 1990s, the image of racial homogeneity adhered to in official government discourse suffused the media, social policy, and education (Maher, 1997). However, this image has gradually begun to break down in view of the changing sociolinguistic make-up of contemporary Japanese society. Minority groups aside, increasing numbers of Japanese are exposed to cross-cultural experiences through the media, traveling, and living abroad.

Government policy makers are increasingly obliged to acknowledge the reality of the nation's emerging cultural diversity and to find ways to accommodate the needs of Japan's growing bilingual population. In this respect, local authorities are more supportive than the national government, who are slow to depart from tradition (Coulmas and Watanabe, forthcoming).

28.5.3 Japan's principal ethnolinguistic minorities

28.5.3.1 Indigenous groups

28.5.3.1.1 Ainu

Native to northern regions of the country in and around Hokkaido, the Ainu are the minority group with the longest history in Japan (Siddle, 1995, 1997). They maintained their own aboriginal language and culture as a hunting and fishing people until the Meiji era. Estimates of today's Ainu population vary, ranging from 24,000 to 50,000. The difficulty of establishing an authentic figure is attributed to two main factors: the fact that many Ainu routinely deny their ethnicity to avoid discrimination, and the prevalence of mixed marriages between the Ainu and other groups (DeChicchis, 1995). According to the Ainu Association, 88 percent of Ainu marriages today are mixed (Working, 2001). The number of "pure" Ainu is thought to be only about 300 (Honna, Tajima, and Minamoto, 2000).

The number of Ainu native speakers is equally difficult to determine. Current estimates range from 10 to 30 adult speakers, all in their eighties (e.g. Honna, Tajima, and Minamoto, 2000; Miyawaki, 1992). Notwithstanding such a small number of native speakers still alive today, many scholars believe that it is misleading to talk about the decline, let alone the imminent death, of Ainu. This is because strenuous revitalization efforts in recent decades have led to a surge of political and linguistic activity involving Ainu, resulting in a steady increase in the number of second-language learners of Ainu. The language-death point of view is also resented among Ainu communities, who consider it as inaccurate and harmful to the Ainu cause (Anderson and Iwasaki-Goodman, 2001).

Discernible efforts have been made to restore Ainu language and culture since the 1980s. A momentous contribution to the Ainu cause was the declaration on language rights by the United Nations in 1993 (Year of the Indigenous Peoples). Since then, language maintenance efforts have expanded under a new law enacted in 1997 for the promotion of Ainu culture, the first legislation to acknowledge the existence of an ethnic minority in Japan (Noguchi, 2001a). There is currently a spread of Ainu projects throughout Hokkaido communities, ranging from Ainu language classes for adult learners to university courses on Ainu language and history (Honna, Tajima, and Minamoto, 2000). In addition, increasing numbers of publications and audiovisual materials on the Ainu language, music and folklore, as well as a monthly radio broadcast in

Ainu by a local station, bear witness to current Ainu resurgence (Working, 2001).

28.5.3.1.2   Ryukyuan

Currently the largest ethnic minority in Japan, the Ryukyuans are native to what is now the southern prefecture of Okinawa, and the Amami Islands that are part of Kyushu. This region was part of an independent Ryukyu kingdom until it was colonized by Japan in 1609. Today, approximately 1.3 million Ryukyuans live here, while another 300,000 live in other areas of Japan. Okinawa came under US administration after the war in 1945, but was reverted to Japan in 1972. Taira (1997) notes that overt discrimination against Ryukyuans has lessened in post-reversion Japan, but the problem has not totally disappeared. Moreover, there are new problems stemming from the continued presence of huge US military bases in Okinawa.

According to Nakamoto (1988, cited in Osumi, 2001, p. 70), varieties of the Ryukyuan language fall into two main groups: North and South Ryukyu. Each is further subdivided into a number of mutually unintelligible dialects. The Amami and Okinawan dialects belong to the North group. Despite the close genealogical relation between Ryukyuan and Japanese, the two languages are mutually unintelligible (Osumi, 2001). However, regular phonological and tonal correspondences can be found between certain Ryukyuan and Japanese words (Matsumori, 1995).

The Ethnologue (2002) places the number of active Ryukyuan speakers at 900,000, almost all of whom speak Standard Japanese as well. During the last century, most Okinawan communities have shifted from predominant monolingualism in Ryukyuan to the current state of bilingualism without diglossia. Older speakers tend to be balanced bilinguals, whereas speakers aged below 65 can generally understand Ryukyuan but cannot speak it well. Those aged below 35 are mainly Japanese monolinguals. Frequent code switching can be heard in interactions between the older and younger generations (Osumi, 2001).

According to Osumi (2001), there has been a gradual resurgence of ethnic identity among this people since the reversion of Okinawa to Japan. The 1990s in particular saw a strong revival of Okinawan culture. Playing an important role in its popularization are the media. Dialect news programs have been made available through radio broadcasting since the 1970s, and television shows in the 1990s introduced various aspects of Okinawan culture to mainland audiences, ranging from traditional art and craft forms to dance and Okinawan pop music. In addition, a wealth of literature on and in Okinawan, plus local speech contests, drama and plays depicting Okinawan customs, all contribute to its maintenance. Maher (1997) gives some indication of emergent new dialects among the younger generations. Similarly, Osumi (2001) reports that younger Okinawans speak a version of Standard Japanese mixed with elements of Okinawan and a sprinkling of English – a hybrid variety which apparently serves as an expression of a new Okinawan identity.

28.5.3.2   Established immigrant communities

28.5.3.2.1   Koreans

The Korean communities in Japan are largely a legacy of Japanese colonialism. Following the annexation of Korea in 1910, large numbers of Koreans were brought to Japan before and during the Pacific War to satisfy labor shortages (Maher and Kawanishi, 1995). Like other minorities, they were subjected to harsh assimilation policies (Miyawaki, 1992). At the end of the war, while the majority of the estimated 2.3 million Koreans were repatriated, approximately 650,000 remained in Japan (Hanami, 1995).

At the end of 2000, Japan was home to over 635,269 registered Koreans, the largest group of foreigners in the country (Statistics Bureau, 2002). Most are second to fourth generation Koreans. Another 200,000 to 300,000 ethnic Koreans are naturalized Japanese nationals (Cary, 2001, p. 98). As Korean language proficiency among the later generations continues to decline, language maintenance remains a high priority for the Korean communities (Maher, 1997). Maher reports on the use of frequent code switching between the Osaka-Korean dialect and Standard Japanese among later generation Koreans living in Osaka, where the highest concentration of ethnic Koreans in Japan is found. Here, constant signs of the Korean language and culture are seen in the "Koreatown" that houses ethnic shops, banks, community centers, and classrooms for Korean language instruction. The gradual emergence of these distinct Koreatowns in a number of Japanese cities signals a new economic and cultural vitality among this group.

Determined efforts over the decades to increase the vitality of the Korean language are evidenced in the long history of ethnic Korean education in Japan, dating from the immediate post-war period (Cary, 2001). Despite the government crackdown on Korean-medium schools during a revival of the pre-war assimilation program that lasted until 1952, Korean education survived through various channels, such as non-accredited independent schools or extracurricular ethnic classes. Today, the General Federation of Korean Residents in Japan and the Korean Residents Union operate their own highly organized school systems with a bilingual curriculum in Japanese and Korean (Cary, 2001). There are over 200 Korean educational establishments throughout Japan, including kindergartens, primary and secondary schools, and one university, serving altogether over 40,000 students (Maher, 1997). However, the majority of Korean pupils attend Japanese schools, mainly because foreign schools are still not accredited by the government, making their senior high graduates ineligible to take entrance exams for national universities.

Among the conflicts experienced by the Koreans in Japan, the name issue has remained a source of contention (Maher and Kawanishi, 1995). While no longer a legal requirement, many Koreans still use a Japanese-sounding name to avoid discrimination. However, Coulmas and Watanabe (forthcoming) claim that young Koreans, although more assimilated into Japanese society than their parents, are more inclined to use their Korean names since many find it easier nowadays to be more assertive of their ethnic identity.

28.5.3.2.2   Chinese

Chinese communities in Japan today come from linguistically and socially diverse backgrounds as a result of different waves of Chinese settlement (Vasishth, 1997). The total number of registered Chinese nationals in 2000 was 335,575 (Statistics Bureau, 2002). The first major wave of Chinese immigration dates back to the Meiji period. Mainly settling in the urban Tokyo-Yokohama and Kansai regions, Chinese workers established their own communities in these port cities (Miyawaki, 1992). While these original settlers were mainly native speakers of Cantonese, their second- to fourth-generation offspring are Japanese-dominant.

A second group of immigrants originated from Taiwan, which fell under Japanese colonial rule from 1895 to 1945. Like the Koreans, many were brought to Japan as conscripts during the Pacific War. Although they were forced to assimilate into Japanese culture, the majority retained the use of their native tongues at home (Miyawaki, 1992). Many remained in Japan after the war and were joined by newer Taiwanese immigrants who came to start small businesses in established Chinese communities (Maher, 1995).

More recent waves of Chinese immigrants in the 1980s were foreign workers and students. In addition, large numbers of Chinese "war orphans" (*zanryuu koji*) have been repatriated to Japan since the 1970s (Tomozawa, 2001). These were Japanese children separated from their families in China during the Japanese retreat towards the end of the Second World War. At first, these individuals received extensive media coverage when they returned to Japan, but subsequently they have not received much public attention. Language shift from Chinese to Japanese occurs at a rapid rate among these returnees but educational programs to help them maintain their Chinese proficiency are generally lacking.

A small number of private Chinese schools were founded in the Kansai region as early as the 1890s. A primary goal of these schools is to promote bilingualism. Besides learning the Chinese language (Mandarin), fluency in Japanese and English is an important feature of the schools. Despite this, only 1,700 children were enrolled in five schools in 1992, and that number is decreasing year by year (Miyawaki, 1992). Chinese is also offered as a degree subject in over 40 universities throughout Japan, and widely taught as a foreign language through television and radio programs. One suburban radio station in Tokyo broadcasts local events in Chinese alongside Korean and English. The prosperous Chinatowns of Yokohama and the Kansai region also provide cultural and information services for their Chinese communities (Maher, 1995). In addition, local governments in various cities have recently made provisions for interpreting, counseling, and consulting services for speakers of Chinese and other languages (Coulmas and Watanabe, forthcoming).

28.5.4 *Japan's road to internationalisation*

28.5.4.1 *The role of English*

Extensive contact with English began in the mid-nineteenth century when Japan turned away from China toward the powerful countries of Europe and America. Ever since then, Japan has had an ongoing love-hate relationship with English (Kachru, 1997), fluctuating between waves of nationalism and westernization (Ho and Wong, 2000b). English has been the chief medium of communication with the outside world since the Meiji period, and now enjoys prestige as the state's most important foreign language. Literacy and oral proficiency in English is a requirement in an expanding number of fields, including science and technology, commerce and the media. Although English is increasingly learned as a foreign language, its use is not institutionalized. As such, along with other regions in East Asia (China, Korea, and Taiwan), Japan falls into Kachru's Expanding Circle (Kachru, 1997).

Prolonged cultural and linguistic contact between Japan and the West has resulted in a profusion of English loanwords absorbed into Japanese. This process is facilitated by the ease with which the *katakana* spelling system allows foreign words to be incorporated into Japanese vocabulary. According to Honna (1995), foreign words, mainly English-based, constitute 10 percent of the lexicon of a standard Japanese dictionary. English-based loans are particularly widespread in the fields of marketing, engineering, and computing (Loveday, 1996). As these words enter the Japanese language and culture, they undergo a variety of semantic and structural changes. The basic types of borrowing patterns identified by Honna (1995) and Loveday (1996) include the following:

1 simple borrowing (e.g. *bairingaru* 'bilingual');
2 semantic narrowing (e.g. *purojekuto* 'project,' with the narrowed meaning of 'large-scale construction plan');
3 Japanese innovations (e.g. *sukinshippu* 'skinship'; based on an analogy of 'friendship,' it refers to body contact, such as that between parents and children);
4 abbreviations (e.g. *konbi* 'combination');
5 acronyms (e.g. *OL* 'office lady');
6 hybrids (e.g. *gaijin buumu* 'foreigner boom');
7 word play (e.g. *go, go, go* 'five, five, five'; the time that early risers set their alarms for, i.e. 5.55 a.m.).

The creative use of English in the media plays an important role in the spread of Japanese-English code switching. For example, the use of English and other foreign words alongside Japanese is a salient feature of many magazines and commercials, while large-scale code switching is found in Japanese pop music (Loveday, 1996).

28.5.4.2   *English in education*

Foreign language teaching in Japan's public schools usually refers solely to the teaching of English (Honna, Tajima, and Minamoto, 2000). Although not a compulsory subject, English constitutes an important component of the secondary curriculum. Up to 5 hours per week are devoted to English lessons at lower secondary, and 10 at upper secondary level. A good knowledge of English is an indispensable resource for passing the highly demanding entrance examinations for universities, especially high-ranking ones. That students are pragmatically motivated to learn English is reflected in the growing lucrative industry of private cram schools. Educational reform laws after the Second World War stipulated nine years of compulsory schooling (for Japanese nationals) starting at age six, comprising six years of primary and three years of lower secondary education. However, current figures indicate that almost 97 percent of 15-year-olds progress to upper secondary school (Japan Information Network, 2002). This means that most Japanese pupils receive at least six years of English language instruction.

Despite the efforts put into the learning of English, the level of proficiency among Japanese learners of English is not very high. A comparison of TOEFL scores among countries in East Asia reveals that Japan was ranked the third lowest in 1996 (Ho and Wong, 2000b). Moreover, communicative competence in English remains low. Two main explanations have been offered for this. First, the secondary English curriculum is heavily geared toward preparing students for sitting university entrance examinations, which are primarily tests of grammatical knowledge and vocabulary. Hence, oral and communicative competence in English is largely neglected. Second, Japanese students have traditionally embraced a British or American "model" of the English language to the exclusion of other varieties, such as Asian Englishes. Consequently, Japanese learners of English are reluctant to use their non-native English, much less use it as a means of intercultural communication (Honna, 1995; cf. *'eikaiwa'* ideology, Kachru, 1997). However, multi-accented English has become increasingly acceptable in recent years, as can be seen in Yokohama City, where foreign residents from various Asian countries are employed to assist with English teaching in primary schools. The introduction of team-teaching to encourage oral communication began in 1987 with the government-sponsored Japan Exchange and Teaching scheme. By 1995, there were over 4,000 assistant teachers on this scheme, with at least one in every public high school. The majority however, were recruited from the USA and UK (Honna, Tajima, and Minamoto, 2000). The action of Yokohama schools represents a breakthrough in the recognition of English as an international language.

28.5.4.3   *Speakers of English*

Among bilinguals in Japan, *kikokushijo* are relatively privileged in terms of their social background and the institutional support they receive. In the past, the 10,000 or more *kikokushijo* who return to Japan every year (mainly from North

America and Europe) were perceived as a challenge to the education system, because they represented a deviation from the monolingual "norm." This situation has changed considerably since the 1970s. *Kikokushijo* are increasingly viewed as a valuable societal resource (Kanno, 2000a, b) and as "agents of internationalization" (Yashiro, 1995). Currently, school-aged returnees are offered places in schools with special programs to help them reintegrate into the education system. Returnees pursuing higher education also benefit from the special admission procedures that many universities now offer to them. Although Japanese society has become more receptive to *kikokushijo*'s diversity, there is still much that can be done to maintain and advance their bilingual abilities.

International marriages between Japanese and English-speaking (usually American) partners are fewer in number than those between Japanese and Korean or Chinese partners (Yamamoto, 1995). According to Noguchi (2001b), many children of intercultural couples are only passive bilinguals with limited productive ability in the minority language despite the desires of their parents to promote bilingualism in them. One reason for this is the lack of a close-knit community of fellow native speakers who can provide support at the linguistic, cultural, and social levels. Another reason is that the social stigma experienced by those of mixed ethnicity may dampen their desire to speak the minority language (Yamamoto, 1995). Such is the experience of *haafu* ('half,' i.e. mixed) children born to Okinawan/Japanese and American parents in Okinawa (Maher and Yashiro, 1995). A legacy of the region's wartime experience, many of these *haafu* were abandoned as children and cannot speak English.

Children of English-speaking expatriates in Japan are not a conspicuous group. However, several non-accredited English-medium schools in Japan were founded to especially cater for this group, some as early as the mid-nineteenth century. Since the 1970s, these schools have increasingly served pupils from other ethnic backgrounds, including Japanese children. In 1994, there were approximately 8,500 pupils in 27 English-medium schools throughout Japan (Kite, 2001). These students comprise a growing English-Japanese bilingual speech community, whose unique identity is symbolized by the code switching that is commonly heard among fellow students.

28.5.4.4   *English and other foreign languages in the media*

Recent years have seen an increase in the number of newspapers and radio and television programs aimed primarily at non-Japanese audiences. Major English-language newspapers in circulation include the *Japan Times, Mainichi Daily News*, and *Daily Yomiuri*, which are widely available in most urban areas, as are bilingual Japanese-English magazines such as *Nihongo Journal* and the *Hiragana Times*. Radio and television broadcasts of news and information in community and foreign languages have become popular since the early 1990s (Statistics Bureau, 2002). Radio stations such as *InterFM* in Tokyo and *FM-Co-Co-Lo* in Kansai broadcast in languages including English, Chinese, Korean, Portuguese, Spanish, Thai, and Tagalog. The Japan Broadcasting Corporation provides bilingual television news reports in Japanese and English every evening. In addition, foreign-language programs may be received via satellite and cable television.

28.5.5   *Outlook*

From the Meiji period, the Japanese began to characterize themselves as a homogeneous nation. Today, this concept is increasingly controversial. That Japanese society is moving toward a direction of increasing cultural and linguistic diversity is a visible fact. This calls for a national language policy which incorporates goals such as multilingual education and maintenance of minority languages, along with legislation to outlaw racial discrimination. English, despite its unofficial status, remains the only foreign language that enjoys considerable prestige. The past decades have seen increasing efforts to address inequities on the part of the minority communities themselves, supported to some extent by local governments as well as international bodies. In March, 2001, the United Nations Committee on the Elimination of Racial Discrimination issued a report stating that Japan had not taken sufficient steps to address the discriminatory treatment of Koreans and Ainu living in Japan (Working, 2001). It remains to be seen whether the national government will take the necessary action to address these and similar issues faced by other minority groups. (For additional discussion of bilingual education, see chapters 15, 21, 23–5, and 27; for more on code mixing and code switching, see chapters 1–4, 6, 10–14, 25, 26, 29, and 31; for more on language maintenance and shift see chapters 14–16, 18, 25, and 26; for more on language endangerment, see chapters 15–18, 25, and 27.)

ACKNOWLEDGMENT

In the long process of writing up this chapter, we have benefited from the generous and timely help of a number of colleagues and friends: Theresa Chang, Cheng Chinhorn, Li Wei, K. K. Luke, Qin Xiubai, Tim Shi, Tina Tajima, Tsao Feng-fu, Yoko Yamato, and Leah Yeh. Their kind assistance is gratefully acknowledged. We alone are responsible for any inadequacies that remain.

REFERENCES

Anderson, F. E. and Iwasaki-Goodman, M. (2001). Language and culture revitalization in a Hokkaido Ainu community. In M. G. Noguchi and S. Fotos (eds.), pp. 45–67.

Anonymous (2002). Tourism threatens Ami tribe's soul. *South China Morning Post*, Hong Kong, January 11, p. 18.

Bacon-Shone, J. and Bolton, K. (1998). Charting multilingualism: Language censuses and language surveys in Hong Kong. In Martha C. Pennington (ed.), pp. 43–90.

Baker, C. (1996). *Foundations of Bilingual Education and Bilingualism*, 2nd edn. Clevedon, UK: Multilingual Matters.

Bauer, R. S. (1988). Written Cantonese of Hong Kong. *Cahiers de Linguistique Asie Orientale*, 17, 245–93.

Bauer, R. S. (2000). Hong Kong Cantonese and the road ahead. In D. C. S. Li, A. Lin and W. K. Tsang (eds.), *Language and Education in Postcolonial Hong Kong*, pp. 35–58. Hong Kong: Linguistic Society of Hong Kong.

Blatt, J. (with Associated Press). (2002). Tongues twisted over pinyin system. *South China Morning Post*, Hong Kong, July 12, p. 9.

Bureau of Statistics, Taiwan, the Republic of China (2002). www.stat.gov.tw.

Cary, A. B. (2001). Affiliation, not assimilation: Resident Koreans and ethnic education. In M. G. Noguchi and S. Fotos (eds.), pp. 98–132.

Chan, B. H. S. (1998). How does Cantonese-English code-mixing work? In Martha C. Pennington (ed.), pp. 191–216.

Chen, E. (ed.) (1999). *Shuangyu Shuangfangyan yu Xiandai Zhongguo* [Bilingualism, diglossia and modern China]. Beijing: Beijing University of Languages and Culture.

Chen, P. (1996). Modern written Chinese, dialects, and regional identity. *Language Problems and Language Planning*, 20, 223–43.

Chen, P. (1999). *Modern Chinese: History and Sociolinguistics*. Cambridge, UK: Cambridge University Press.

Chen, S. C. (1996). Code-switching as a verbal strategy among Chinese in a campus setting in Taiwan. *World Englishes*, 15, 267–80.

Chen, Y. (2000). *Shehui Yuyanxue* [Sociolinguistics]. Beijing: Commercial Press.

Cheng, N. L. (2000). Hong Kong (Special Administrative Region). In W. K. Ho and R. Y. L. Wong (eds.), pp. 97–111.

China Statistical Yearbook (2001). Beijing: China Statistics Press.

Coulmas, F. (1989). *The Writing Systems of the World*. Oxford: Blackwell.

Coulmas, F. and Watanabe, M. (forthcoming). Japan's nascent multilingualism. In W. Li, J. M. Dewaele, and A. Housen (eds.), *Opportunities and Challenges of Bilingualism*. Berlin: Mouton de Gruyter.

DeChicchis, J. (1995). The current state of the Ainu language. *Journal of Multilingual and Multicultural Development*, 16, 103–24.

DeFrancis, J. (1984). *The Chinese Language: Fact and Fantasy*. Honolulu: University of Hawaii Press.

Erbaugh, M. S. (1995). Southern Chinese dialects as a medium for reconciliation within Greater China. *Language in Society*, 24, 79–94.

Ethnologue: Languages of the world (2002). http://www.ethnologue.com/.

Evans, S. (1996). The context of English language education: The case of Hong Kong. *RELC Journal*, 27, 30–55.

Fasold, R. (1984). *The Sociolinguistics of Society*. Oxford: Blackwell.

Fishman, J. A. (1972). Societal bilingualism: Stable and transitional. Section VI of *The Sociology of Language*, pp. 91–106. Rowley, MA: Newbury House. Also in Joshua Fishman, *Sociolinguistics: A Brief Introduction*, pp. 73–90. Rowley, MA: Newbury House.

Gibbons, J. (1987). *Code-mixing and Code Choice: A Hong Kong Case Study*. Clevedon, UK: Multilingual Matters.

Government Information Office (2001). The Republic of China yearbook – Taiwan. http://www.gio.gov.tw.

Hanami, M. (1995). Minority dynamics in Japan: Towards a society of sharing. In

J. C. Maher and G. Macdonald (eds.), pp. 121–46.

Heberer, T. (1989). *China and its National Minorities: Autonomy or Assimilation?* New York and London: M. E. Sharpe.

Ho, M. C. (1998). Culture studies and motivation in foreign and second language learning in Taiwan. *Language, Culture and Curriculum*, 11, 165–82.

Ho, W. K. and Wong, R. Y. L. (eds.) (2000a). *Language Policies and Language Education: The Impact in East Asian Countries in the Next Decade.* Singapore: Times Academic Press.

Ho, W. K. and Wong, R. Y. L. (2000b). Introduction: Language policies and language education in East Asia. In W. K. Ho and R. Y. L. Wong (eds.), pp. 1–39.

Hong Kong 2000. (2001). Hong Kong: Government Printer.

Honna, N. (1995). English in Japanese society: Language within language. *Journal of Multilingual and Multicultural Development*, 16, 45–62.

Honna, N., Tajima, H. T., and Minamoto, K. (2000). Japan. In W. K. Ho and R. Y. L. Wong (eds.), pp. 139–72.

Hsiau, A. C. (2000). *Contemporary Taiwanese Cultural Nationalism.* London: Routledge.

Huang, C. M. (1998). *Language Education Policies and Practices in Taiwan: From Nationism to Nationalism.* Seattle: University of Washington.

Huang, S. (1993). *Yuyan, Shehui yu Zhuqun Yishi* [Language, society, and ethnicity]. Taipei: The Crane Publishing.

Huang, S. (2000). Language, identity and conflict: A Taiwanese study. *International Journal of the Sociology of Language*, 143, 139–49.

Hung, W. (1992). *Taiwan Yuyan Wenzi* [Language and Writing of Taiwan]. Taipei: Avantgarde Publishing.

Japan Information Network 2002. Retrieved from http://jin.jcic.or.jp/stat/.

Johnson, R. K. (1994). Language policy and planning in Hong Kong. *Annual Review of Applied Linguistics* 14, 177–99.

Kachru, B. B. (1997). Past imperfect: The other side of English in Asia. In L. E. Smith and M. L. Forman (eds.), *World Englishes 2000*, pp. 68–89. Honolulu: College of Languages, Linguistics and Literature, University of Hawaii, with East-West Center.

Kanno, Y. (2000a). Bilingualism and identity: The stories of Japanese returnees. *International Journal of Bilingual Education and Bilingualism*, 3, 1–18.

Kanno, Y. (2000b). Kikokushijo as bicultural. *International Journal of Intercultural Relations*, 24, 361–82.

Kite, Y. (2001). English/Japanese codeswitching among students in an international high school. In M. G. Noguchi and S. Fotos (eds.), pp. 312–28.

Kwan-Terry, A. and Luke, K. K. (1997). Tradition, trial, and error: Standard and vernacular literacy in China, Hong Kong, Singapore, and Malaysia. In A. Tabouret-Keller, R. B. Le Page, P. Gardner-Chloros, and G. Varro (eds.), *Vernacular Literacy: A Re-evaluation*, pp. 271–315. Oxford: Oxford University Press.

Lau, C. F. (2001). *Hakka: Misunderstanding History and Historical Misunderstanding* (in Chinese). Guangzhou: Xueshu Yanjiu Zhazishe.

Li, D. C. S. (1996). *Issues in Bilingualism and Biculturalism: A Hong Kong Case Study.* New York: Peter Lang.

Li, D. C. S. (1999). The functions and status of English in Hong Kong: A post-1997 update. *English World-Wide*, 20, 67–110.

Li, D. C. S. (2000a). Cantonese-English code-switching research in Hong Kong: A Y2K review. *World Englishes*, 19, 305–22.

Li, D. C. S. (2000b). Phonetic borrowing: Key to the vitality of written Cantonese in Hong Kong. *Written Language and Literacy*, 3, 199–233.

Li, D. C. S. (2001). L2 lexis in L1: Reluctance to translate out of concern for referential meaning. *Multilingua*, 20, 1–26.

Li, D. C. S. and Tse, E. C. Y. (2002). One day in the life of a "purist." *International Journal of Bilingualism* 6(2): 147–202.

Liao, C. C. (2000). Changing dominant language use and ethnic equality in Taiwan since 1987. *International Journal of the Sociology of Language*, 143, 165–82.

Lin, A. M. Y. (1996). Bilingualism or linguistic segregation? Symbolic domination, resistance and code switching in Hong Kong schools. *Linguistics and Education*, 8, 49–84.

Lin, A. M. Y. (1997). Bilingual education in Hong Kong. In J. Cummins and D. Corson (eds.), *Encyclopedia of Language and Education. Volume 5: Bilingual Education*, pp. 281–9. Dordrecht: Kluwer.

Lin, J. (1997). Policies and practices of bilingual education for the minorities in China. *Journal of Multilingual and Multicultural Development*, 18, 193–205.

Liu, H. (2000). *Taiwan de Kejiaren* [The Hakka of Taiwan]. Taipei: Chang Min Publishing.

Loveday, L. (1996). *Language Contact in Japan: A Socio-linguistic History*. Oxford: Clarendon Press.

Luke, K. K. (1998). Why two languages might be better than one: Motivations of language mixing in Hong Kong. In Martha C. Pennington (ed.), pp. 145–59.

Luke, K. K. and Richards, J. C. (1982). English in Hong Kong: Functions and status. *English Worldwide*, 3, 47–64.

Maher, J. C. (1995). The Kakyo: Chinese in Japan. *Journal of Multilingual and Multicultural Development*, 16, 125–38.

Maher, J. C. (1997). Linguistic minorities and education in Japan. *Educational Review*, 49, 115–27.

Maher, J. C. and Kawanishi, Y. (1995). On being there: Korean in Japan. *Journal of Multilingual and Multicultural Development*, 16, 87–101.

Maher, J. C. and Macdonald, G. (eds.) (1995)?. *Diversity in Japanese Culture and Language*. London: Kegan Paul.

Maher, J. C. and Yashiro, K. (1995). Multilingual Japan: An introduction. *Journal of Multilingual and Multicultural Development*, 16, 1–17.

Matsumori, A. (1995). Ryukyuan: Past, present, and future. *Journal of Multilingual and Multicultural Development*, 16, 19–44.

Miyawaki, H. (1992). Some problems of linguistic minorities in Japan. In F. Willem, K. Jaspaert, and S. Kroon (eds.), *Maintenance and Loss of Minority Languages*, pp. 357–67. Amsterdam: John Benjamins.

Morrison, K. and Lui, I. (2000). Ideology, linguistic capital and the medium of instruction in Hong Kong. *Journal of Multilingual and Multicultural Development*, 21, 471–86.

Morrow, P. R. (1987). The users and uses of English in Japan. *World Englishes*, 6, 49–62.

Noguchi, M. G. (2001a). Introduction: The crumbling of a myth. In M. G. Noguchi and S. Fotos (eds.), pp. 1–23.

Noguchi, M. G. (2001b). Biliguality and bicultural children in Japan: A pilot survey of factors linked to active English-Japanese bilingualism. In M. G. Noguchi and S. Fotos (eds.), pp. 234–71.

Noguchi, M. G. and Fotos, S. (eds.). *Studies in Japanese Bilingualism*. Clevedon, UK: Multilingual Matters.

Norman, J. (1988). *Chinese*. Cambridge, UK: Cambridge University Press.

Osumi, M. (2001). Language and identity in Okinawa today. In M. G. Noguchi and S. Fotos (eds.), pp. 68–97.

Pan, Y. (2000). Code-Switching and Social Changes in Guangzhou and Hong Kong. *International Journal of the Sociology of Language*, 146, 21–41.

Paulston, C. B. (ed.) (1988). *International Handbook of Bilingualism and Bilingual Education*. New York: Greenwood Press.

Pennington, M. C. (ed.) (1998a). *Language in Hong Kong at Century's End*. Hong Kong: Hong Kong University Press.

Pennington, M. C. (1998b). Introduction: Perspectives on language in Hong Kong at century's end. In Martha C. Pennington (ed.), pp. 3–40.

Postiglione, G. (ed.) (1999). *China's National Minority Education: Culturcide, State, Schooling and Development*. Levittown, NY: Garland.

Pu, Z. C. (1996). *Taiwan Yuanzhumin de Kouchuan Wenxue* [Oral literature of Aborigines in Taiwan]. Taipei: Chang Min Publishing.

Ramsey, S. R. (1987). *The Languages of China*. Princeton, NJ: Princeton University Press.

Ru Blachford, D. (1997). Bilingual education in China. In J. Cummins and D. Corson (eds.), *Encyclopedia of Language and Education. Volume 5: Bilingual Education*, pp. 157–65. Dordrecht: Kluwer.

Sautman, B. (1999). Expanding access to higher education for China's national minorities: Policies of preferential admissions. In G. A. Postiglione (ed.), pp. 173–210.

Siddle, R. (1995). The Ainu: Construction of an image. In J. C. Maher and G. Macdonald (eds.), pp. 73–94.

Siddle, R. (1997). Ainu: Japan's indigenous people. In M. Weiner (ed.), pp. 17–49.

Snow, D. B. (1993). Chinese dialect as written language: the cases of Taiwanese and Cantonese. *Journal of Asian Pacific Communication*, 4, 15–30.

So, D. (1992). Language-based bifurcation of secondary education in Hong Kong: Past, present and future. In K. K. Luke (ed.). *Into the Twenty-first Century: Issues of Language in Education in Hong Kong*, pp. 69–95. Hong Kong: Linguistic Society of Hong Kong.

So, J. (1997). Yingyu dui Xianggang Yuyan Shiyong de Yingxiang [Influence of English on Hong Kong language use]. *Zhongguo Yuwen*, 3, 219–25.

Statistics Bureau and Statistics Center, Ministry of Public Management, Home Affairs, Posts and Telecommunications (ed.) (2002). *Japan Statistical Yearbook 2002*. Japan: http://www.stat.go.jp/english/data/nenkan/index.htm.

Stites, R. (1999). Writing cultural boundaries: National minority language policy, literacy planning, and bilingual education. In G. A. Postiglione (ed.), pp. 95–130.

Taipei Journal (February 3, 2000). Retrieved from Taiwan He@dlines (2000), http://taiwanheadlines.org/20000221/20000215f1.html on February 21, 2000.

Taira, K. (1997). Troubled national identity: The Ryukyuans/Okinawans. In M. Weiner (ed.), pp. 140–77.

Tomozawa, A. (2001). Japan's hidden bilinguals: The language of "war orphans" and their families after repatriation from China. In M. G. Noguchi and S. Fotos (eds.), pp. 133–63.

Tsao, F. F. (1997). *Zhuqun Yuyan Zhengce: Haixia Liang'an de Bijiao* [Ethnic language policy: A comparison of the two sides of the Taiwan Straits]. Taipei: The Crane Publishing.

Tsao, F. F. (1999). The language planning situation in Taiwan. *Journal of Multilingual and Multicultural Development*, 20, 328–75.

Tse, J. K. P. (2000). Language and a rising new identity in Taiwan.

International Journal of the Sociology of Language, 143, 151–64.

Tse, Y. (1990). *Xiandai Hanyu Ouhua Gailun* [An outline of the Europeanization of Modern Chinese]. Hong Kong: Gwong Ming Publishing.

van den Berg, M. E. (1985). *Language Planning and Language Use in Taiwan: A Study of Language Choice Behavior in Public Settings: A Contribution to the Sociology of Language*. Leiden, The Netherlands: Rijks Universiteit te Leiden.

van den Berg, M. E. (1988). Long term accommodation of (ethno)linguistic groups toward a societal language norm. *Language and Communication*, 8, 251–69.

Vasishth, A. (1997). A model minority: The Chinese community in Japan. In M. Weiner (ed.), pp. 108–39.

Wang, R. (2000). Tangshi Songci Gaicheng Pinyin Wenzi? [Converting Tang and Song poetry into Pinyin writing?]. *Ming Pao Monthly*, Hong Kong, September, pp. 48–51.

Weiner, M. (ed.) (1997a). *Japan's Minorities: The Illusion of Homogeneity*. London: Routledge.

Working, R. (2001). Japan's Ainu rebuild their pride. *South China Morning Post*, Hong Kong, August 7, p. 16.

Wu, D. (2001). On Englishization of Chinese morphology (in Chinese). *Contemporary Linguistics*, 3, 81–9.

Yamamoto, M. (1995). Bilingualism in international families. *Journal of Multilingual and Multicultural Development*, 16, 63–86.

Yamamoto, M. (2001). Japanese attitudes towards bilingualism: A survey and its implications. In M. G. Noguchi and S. Fotos (eds.), pp. 24–44.

Yashiro, K. (1995). Japan's returnees. *Journal of Multilingual and Multicultural Development*, 16, 139–64.

Zhou, Q. (1991). Zhongguo Shuangyu Jiaoyu Leixing [Varieties of bilingual education in China]. *Minzu Yuwen*, 3, 65–9.

Zhou, Y. (1992). Bilingualism and bilingual education in China. *International Journal of the Sociology of Language*, 97, 37–45.

29 Bilingualism in South Asia

TEJ K. BHATIA AND WILLIAM C. RITCHIE

29.1 Introduction

This chapter presents a case study of the varied dimensions of bi-/ multilingualism in South Asia (henceforth, SA) with particular attention to India. The chapter argues that bilingualism in SA is shaped primarily by natural forces of networking and communication (e.g. media, trade, multiple identities, etc.) rather than being the result of externally imposed models and government planning. It calls for rethinking socio-cultural diversity in general and linguistic diversity in particular. Although the focus is on India, the generalizations drawn are valid for other countries in SA as well, to varying degrees. In addition to isolating the defining features of bilingualism in India/ SA, the chapter will describe both the contemporary and the historical sources, the processes and the results of bilingualism. An attempt has been made to uncover those dimensions of bilingualism which have been neglected in the sociolinguistics of SA (e.g. bilingualism based in rural vs. urban varieties of speech). For comparative and contrastive purposes, other countries will also receive attention. The term "bilingualism" is used as a cover term for both bilingualism and multilingualism.

South Asia (India, Pakistan, Nepal, Bangladesh, Sri Lanka, Bhutan, and the Maldives) represents an astonishing array of linguistic diversity, with four language families and more than 650 languages as well as numerous geographical, social, ethnic, religious and rural varieties or dialects. The subcontinent competes with Papua New Guinea in terms of the sheer numeric weight of its languages and varieties, a rural–urban dichotomy, and varied social structures. For these reasons, the region is often described as "the linguistic laboratory of the world." Consequently, one finds a complex array of linguistic situations in terms of the extent of bilingualism ranging from diglossic bilingualism to bilingualism based on three of the five highest-ranking languages in the world (Hindi, English, and Bengali) according to the number of speakers. The magnitude and scale of linguistic diversity and parameters of language usage are often beyond the imagination of speakers who are accustomed to Western-style monolingualism.

29.2   A Linguistic Profile of South Asia

29.2.1   South Asia

We begin with a brief overview of the language situation in SA as background for our treatment of bilingualism in India. Approximately one in every four inhabitants of the world (that is, 1.4 billion people) speaks at least one of the SA languages. The four language families (see figure 29.1) to which SA languages belong are Indo-European, Dravidian, Austroasiatic, and Tibeto-Burman. Indo-European, with twelve major and six minor languages, represents the most influential language family both in the number of speakers and in social significance. The major vs. minor language distinction is based on the following criteria: numeric strength, socio-political significance, literary tradition, and regional representation (spatial reach). (Not all criteria need to be met in order for a language to qualify as a major language.) The twelve major Indo-Aryan languages of the Indo-European language family are: Hindi, Assamese, Oriya, Marathi, Konkani, Gujarati (all spoken in India); Urdu, Punjabi, and Sindhi (spoken in both Pakistan and India); Bengali (India and Bangladesh); Nepali (Nepal and India); and Sinhala (Sri Lanka). Hindi and Bengali are

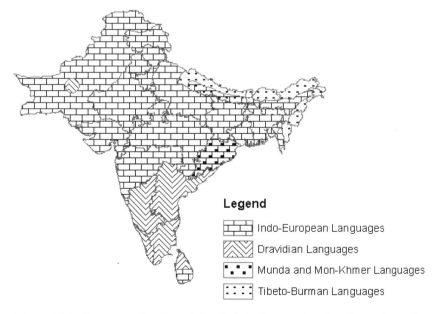

Figure 29.1   Language families of South Asia (international and state boundaries from ESRI World and ArcAtlas datasets).

ranked second and fifth in the world in terms of number of speakers, according to the World Almanac (2002, p. 447). Approximately eighty percent of the population of SA speak languages of the Indo-European stock. Two languages of the Indo-Iranian sub-branch of Indo-European, Pashto and Baluchi, are spoken in the northwestern part of Pakistan. Kashmiri (India and Pakistan) belongs to the Dardic subbranch of Indo-Aryan. The six minor languages are as follows: Khowari (Pakistan), Khohistani (Pakistan), Shina (India, Pakistan), Dogri (India), Bhili (India) and Dhivehi (the Maldives). The Indo-European languages dominate all the countries of the subcontinent. Although the official language of Pakistan is Urdu, it is spoken as a native language by just 8 percent of the population; the majority native language is Punjabi, spoken by approximately 60 percent of the population. With the exception of Brahui (1 percent), a Dravidian language, the remaining 31 percent of the population speak languages of either Indo-Aryan or Indo-Iranian stock. The official languages of other SA countries are also Indo-European: Sinhala (Sri Lanka; spoken by 75 percent of the population); Nepali (Nepal; 90 percent); Bengali (Bangladesh; 90 percent), and Dhivehi (the Maldives).

The second major family is the Dravidian languages, which include four major languages: Tamil, Telugu, Malayalam, and Kannada. These four languages are spoken in South India. Tamil is spoken both in India and in Sri Lanka where 18 percent of the population speaks it. As mentioned above, Brahui is found far to the northwest in Pakistan.

Figure 29.2 Languages of South Asia (international and state boundaries from ESRI World and ArcAtlas datasets).

Two branches of the Austroasiatic language family are found in India: The major members of the Munda subfamily are Santhali, Mundari and Ho, which are spoken in southern Bihar, northeastern Andhra Pradesh and broader areas of West Bengal in India. The Mon-Khmer branch is represented by Khasi which is spoken in Meghalaya state of India.

Tibeto-Burman is represented by many languages, spoken in the subcontinent's northeastern borderlands. While Tibetan or Bhotiya languages are spoken in India (in Laddakh and Sikkim), Bhutan, and Nepal, the major concentration of the Gurung-Tamang group is present in central to eastern Nepal. Newari, for example, belongs to the latter group. Dzongkha, a variety of Tibetan, is the national language of Bhutan. (See figure 29.2 for major languages of South Asia.)

29.2.2   *India*

India is a multilingual country. Twenty four languages are recognized by the Indian constitution. In addition, there are numerous other dialects and languages. The number of vernaculars/dialects reported ranges from 216 to over 1500 (1652 mother tongues self-reported in the 1961 census; 216 mother tongues with more than 10,000 speakers each reported in the 1991 census; see Census of India, 2004).

The linguistic situation and communication networking in India can be represented diagrammatically by a pyramid-type structure, shown in figure 29.3.

29.2.2.1   *Languages and modes of communication*

Hindi and English are the two national and link languages of India. While Hindi is the language of the masses in the north-western and north-central part of India, English is the pan-Indian language of the educated elite. Thus, English and Hindi represent the peak of the pyramid.

As noted earlier Hindi, even without combining with Urdu, has the second-largest number of speakers among the languages in the world and is the lingua franca of India and of the subcontinent. The great Moghul empire in the past, and Hindi films and the mass media in the twentieth century, played a significant role in the spread of Hindi-Urdu, not only in India but also across the subcontinent. Hindi and Urdu are mutually intelligible but are written in different scripts – Hindi is written in the Devanagari script and Urdu in Perso-Arabic script. There is also a difference in literary affiliation – Urdu is associated with Persian and Arabic literary traditions while Hindi is tied to the Sanskrit tradition indigenous to India. In addition, Urdu borrows its technical and learned vocabulary from Persian and Arabic, whereas Hindi borrows the same kinds of terms from Sanskrit.

"Scheduled" languages (henceforth, state languages) are spoken predominantly in their respective states: see table 29.1. Hindi, along with English, is the only state language that is spoken in more than one state. Urdu is the official language of the state of Jammu and Kashmir. However, not all "scheduled" languages are spoken in a particular state. Sindhi is not the official language of any Indian state. Kashmiri is spoken in the state of Jammu and

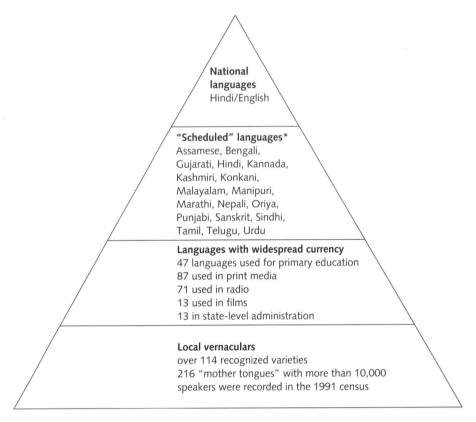

Figure 29.3   The linguistic situation in India. *Bodo, Dogri, Maithili, and Santhali were added in 2003.

Kashmir but the official language of the state is Urdu. Finally, rural dialects (mother tongues or vernaculars) are shown at the base of the pyramid.

As pointed out earlier, Modern Tamil, Telugu, Kannada, and Malayalam are Dravidian languages and are primarily spoken in the South while Indo-Aryan languages, the descendants of the oldest documented Indo-Aryan language, Sanskrit, are primarily spoken in the North. Dravidian languages are the descendants of the proto-Dravidian languages.

Sanskrit is also recognized as an official language of India and is the language of India's cultural and intellectual tradition. English is the language of modern intellectual communication and is the official language of three states and all "union territories"; see B. Kachru (1997) for more details.

29.2.2.2   *Census figures: Discrepancy between the actual and reported situations*

Before continuing with a discussion of the language situation in India, it is worthwhile discussing the source of figures in table 29.1 – the census of 1991.

Table 29.1 Scheduled languages of India.

Name	Language family	State/spoken in	Number of mother-tongue speakers (1991 census: Government of India)
Assamese	Indo-Aryan	Assam	13,079,696
Bengali	Indo-Aryan	Bengal	69,595,738
English[a]	Indo-European; Germanic	Meghalaya, Nagaland, Tripura	178,598
Gujarati	Indo-Aryan	Gujarat	40,673,814
Hindi	Indo-Aryan	*Hindi belt*: Bihar, Chattisgarh, Rajasthan, Haryana, Delhi, Himachal Pradesh, Jarkhand, Madhya Pradesh, Uttar Pradesh,	337,272,114
Kannada	Dravidian	Karnataka	32,753,676
Kashmiri	Indo-Aryan	Jammu and Kashmir[b]	56,690
Konkani	Indo-Aryan	Goa	1,760,607
Malayalam	Dravidian	Kerala	30,377,176
Manipuri	Tibeto-Burman	Manipur	1,270,216
Marathi	Indo-Aryan	Maharashtra	62,481,681
Oriya	Indo-Aryan	Orissa	28,061,313
Punjabi	Indo-Aryan	Punjab	23,378,744
Sanskrit	Indo-Aryan	No state	49,736
Sindhi	Indo-Aryan	Metro areas of western India	2,122,848
Tamil	Dravidian	Tamil	53,006,368
Telugu	Dravidian	Andhra Pradesh	66,017,615
Urdu	Indo-Aryan	Jammu and Kashmir	43,406,932

[a] The number of mother tongue speakers of English decreased in 1991! According to the 1981 census, the mother tongue speakers of English were 202,000.
[b] These figures are not complete as no census was taken in Jammu and Kashmir in 1991.

Because the census asks for self-report of languages, it should be noted that there are a number of problems with these figures (and other census figures regarding language as well). A claimed language may be a language or a non-language – a reflection of regional, religious, caste, social, ethnic, literary, script affiliation, and even occupation. For example, it is not unusual for an ironsmith to report Lohari 'ironsmith' as his mother tongue, or for a villager to report a dialect as simply the name of his village or caste. Alternatively, a language might be a speaker's perception of language/dialect on a language continuum, thus blurring language vs. dialect or language vs. language distinctions (in language contact situations).

One might also come across the following types of discrepancy between the actual linguistic situation and the reported linguistic situation.

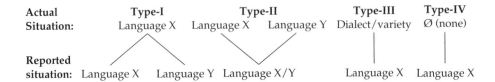

Actual Situation:	Type-I Language X	Type-II Language X	Language Y	Type-III Dialect/variety	Type-IV Ø (none)
Reported situation:	Language X	Language Y	Language X/Y	Language X	Language X

Type-I   Reports of Type-I are witnessed particularly in the reporting of Hindi, Urdu, and Hindustani. A monolingual Hindi or Urdu speaker may report himself as bilingual. If a speech sample is written in the Devanagari script, it will invariably qualify as Hindi while the same sample written in Perso-Arabic script will be reported as a distinct language, "Urdu." If the same sample is written in the Roman script, it will be represented as either Hindi or Urdu. Although Hindi and Urdu are mutually intelligible, the two labels are sensitive to the religion of a speaker. Hindus (and members of other religions except Islam) report their language as Hindi and Muslims report theirs as Urdu; see King, 1994. Mahatma Gandhi preferred the neutral label Hindustani over the religiously sensitive labels Hindi and Urdu. The 1991 census is not strictly a self-reporting phenomenon with reference to Hindi-Urdu-Hindustani. In prior censuses, one was permitted to report Hindustani, but the 1991 census does not accept that choice. Therefore, a Hindustani speaker is asked by the census-taker to choose between Hindi and Urdu.

Type-II   Soon after independence, Hindi and Punjabi were considered as one language, but since the 1961 census they have been classified as two distinct languages.

Type-III   A case in point is that of Konkani-Marathi. Marathi speakers consider Konkani to be a dialect of Marathi while this is not the case for a Konkani speaker in Goa; see Pereira, 1971 for more on this controversy.

Type-IV   Indians tend to express their nonlinguistic affiliation through language. Whereas German speakers with different professional, social, or ethnic background will report their language as German, as mentioned above an ironsmith in a rural Hindi-speaking area will not have any qualms about reporting his mother-tongue as "ironsmith" rather than Hindi.

The label "mother tongue," which is the term used by the census, may also be ambiguous. An individual questioned may interpret this term as referring to his or her cradle language, parent tongue, language ordinarily used, or prestige language only. A prestige language such as English is often over-reported while stigmatized varieties (e.g. immigrant languages such as Saraiki from Pakistan) are under-reported. An illustration of these problems is the fact that almost 50,000 speakers reported Sanskrit as their mother tongue (see table 29.1). It seems extremely unlikely that Sanskrit is the cradle language of any-one. However, its prestige and daily use by some Indians has apparently led them to claim it as their mother tongue. For more details on the issue of interpretation, uses, and misuses of census data, see Khubchandani (1997, pp. 149–63) and Annamalai (2001).

29.3   Sources and Processes of Bilingualism

In this section, we will attempt to describe sources which have initiated lan-guage contact in SA and thus set the stage for processes such as promotion, termination, and revitalization of bilingualism. In order to grasp the complex bilingual situation, language use, and the highly diverse nature of the bilin-gual speech community, their present-day consequences in terms of differen-tial domain allocation of different languages and socio-psychological features, a historical perspective on the language contact situation in SA is imperative.

29.3.1   *The historical roles of Sanskrit, Persian, and English*

Three millennia of language contact have led to the convergence of four lan-guage families in India/SA. Three contact languages have played a particularly important role in the history of SA: Sanskrit, Persian, and English. Each has served as a prime vehicle for language contact and bilingualism both histor-ically and at the present day.

29.3.1.1   *Sanskrit*
As the language of the Hindu scriptures, and of the epic and classical literature, Sanskrit has traditionally constituted the medium of philosophical and tech-nical literature throughout SA. A number of other factors such as past royal patronage and the promotion of Sanskrit education by the Brahmins from the sixth century BC onward have reinforced its prestige (see Bhasham, 1954 for more details). Consequently, Sanskrit has played a leading role not only in the process of Aryanization of Dravidian and other languages, but also in forming the ethos of India and other SA countries to a varying degree.

For example, the effects of borrowings from Sanskrit on the lexical and grammatical systems of Dravidian languages have been profound. Emeneau and Borrow (1962) note the tendency "for all four of the Dravidian literary languages in the South to make literary use of the total Sanskrit lexicon in-discriminately." So massive has the influence been that it is hard to utter more than a few sentences in these languages without using a word borrowed from

Sanskrit. Over a century ago, Western scholars like Pope, Colebrooke, Crey, and Wilkins subscribed to the view that the Dravidian languages were descended from Sanskrit, though Caldwell (1903; 1956 reprint) in his classic work dispelled this misconception. According to Sjoberg and Sjoberg (1956) about 20 percent of the non-cultural part of basic vocabulary in literary Dravidian languages is loaned from Indo-Aryan, mostly from Sanskrit. This proportion peaks to 50–60 percent in some languages due to shared cultural beliefs (e.g. Brahmanic values). This resulted not only in the replacement of content and function words but also had a substantive impact on the phonological, morphological and syntactic structures of the Dravidian languages (Sridhar, 1981). (For more on borrowing, see chapters 1, 2, 6, and 28.)

The Dravidianization of Indo-Aryan languages (Gumperz and Wilson 1971; Pandit 1972) also took place, though the impact of Dravidian languages on Indo-Aryan languages was not nearly as extensive; nevertheless this mutual influence (on lexicon as well as grammar) set the stage for leaky boundaries among the languages of India whether they were genetically related or not.

In addition to this, Sanskrit became a marker of caste identity and, hence, gave rise to diglossic bilingualism through Brahmin speech in Dravidian languages, particularly in Tamil (see Bright, 1960; Bright and Ramanujan, 1964). As a consequence, Sanskrit acquired functional/topical domains such as religion, philosophy, poetics, science, technology, and mathematics in Dravidian as well as Indo-Aryan-speaking areas; Sanskrit thus became the single most important marker of Indian culture – both in the north and in the south.

Sanskrit has played and continues to play a major role in promoting bilingualism and language modernization inside and outside of India (e.g. in South-East Asia) to this day. Today, the All India Radio relays news in Sanskrit and even newspapers are published in the language. Just as terms for technological innovations are created from Latin and Greek for western languages (*television* = Greek *tele-* 'far,' Latin *-vision* 'seeing'), Sanskrit is the source of designative cultural and technical innovations in SA and beyond. Consider, for example, the terms for prime minister (*pradhaan mantrii* = *pradhaan* 'head, principal' + *mantrii* 'minister'), president (*raashTrapati* = *raashTra* 'country' + *pati* 'husband'), radio (*aakaashvaaNii* = *aakaash* 'sky' + *vaaNii* 'voice, speech'), TV (*duurdarshan* = *duur* (Hindi) 'far' + *darshan* 'sight'). The words in parentheses are drawn from Sanskrit unless specified otherwise. For more details of language modernization of Indian languages in the news media (including forms based on Sanskrit), see Krishnamurti and Mukherjee (1984); see Schiffman (1999) on language modernization of South-East Asian languages using Sanskrit.

29.3.1.2   *Persian*

Language contact among Persian, Indo-Aryan, and Dravidian languages (particularly Kannada and Telugu) formally began with the annexation of the Punjab by the Turkish ruler Mahmud Gaznavi (twelfth century) and went through four stages:

1 *Linguistic isolationism (1150–1400)*: The first stage – that of the Moghul Empire – ran for more than two centuries. A study of official documents which were made up of 230 royal decrees and inscriptions from Rajasthan during this period reveals interesting facts and borrowing patterns. During this period, only two words borrowed from Persian (*Muhammad* and *Islam*) appear in the written documents of all Indian/SA languages;

2 *Linguistic accommodation (1400–1600)*: Approximately 20 words related to royal administration and military organization were borrowed into Hindi from Persian (e.g. *fauz* 'army,' *shahanshaah* 'king,' *hukum* 'order');

3 *Linguistic assimilation (1600–1750)*: The third stage of Persian borrowings began from the point where the two cultures began to be amalgamated. In the history of Islamic India, it marks largely the period of greatest harmony between the two cultures and thus the process of linguistic borrowing and assimilation was stimulated. Lexical items related to the military, administration, and culture continued to flow in during this period. Furthermore, linguistic borrowing was extended from the level of lexicon to the morphology and syntax of the Persian language;

4 *Linguistic acculturation (1750–1836)*: During this period Persian attained the administrative, social, and educational domains. Consequently, the place of Sanskrit as a marker of elitism, intellectualization, and power began to shift gradually in favor of Persian, since it was the official court language of the mighty Moghul empire.

Although the influence of Persian extended deep into the Dravidian language areas, it peaked in the north particularly in the Hindi-Urdu and Punjabi belt. The impact of Persian on one SA language – Kashmiri – is best summed up by B. B. Kachru (1997, p. 563):

> The hegemony of Persian lasted over four centuries, resulting in the Persianization of Kashmiri literary and intellectual culture. The ancestral Sanskrit language was reduced to essentially ritualistic roles. The Pandits of Kashmir gradually turned to Persian and used it as a language of access, even to the study of their own Hindu religious and cultural texts such as the Mahabharata, Ramayana, Shivapurana, and the Bhagavad-Gita.

The language contact situation with Persian was different from the Sanskritization of Indian languages. Persian was viewed as an imposed language in much of India; thus, with Moghul patronage, Persian became a marker of Islam. As a consequence, after independence in 1947 when India and Pakistan became independent nations, the influence of Persian continued to regenerate in Pakistan, a Muslim nation, while it reached a state of fossilization in India. In contrast, after independence Sanskrit began to regenerate its original impact in India due to its association with Indian culture (particularly with Hindu religion). Just as extensive Sanskritization played an important role in the separation of Malayalam from Old Tamil (see S. N. Sridhar, 1981), extensive Persianization together with Arabicization led to the separation of Urdu in Pakistan from Hindi-Urdu in India. Similarly, heavy Persianization and

Arabicization of Hindi led Western grammarians like Hadley (1772) and others (Schultz, 1745) to claim that Persian must be the mother language of Hindi. Others thought that the ancestor of Hindi must be a Semitic language, perhaps Arabic or Hebrew (see Bhatia, 1985 on the religious-colonial linguistic models prior to the emergence of the hypothesis of genetic relationships among languages). The concept of Indo-Aryan languages and the genetic hypothesis of languages was still a distant reality of the nineteenth century. As pointed out earlier, Hindi and Urdu in their spoken style are essentially the same language, approximately parallel to British and American English.

Like the effects of Sanskrit, Persianization of Indian languages was not restricted to the lexicon (content and function words); the impact of Persian borrowing on the grammar of Indian languages was also profound. The morphological processes such as reverse *compounding* (*sher-e-panjaab* 'the tiger of Punjab' rather than the unmarked pattern – *panjaab kaa sher* 'Punjab's tiger), inflectional morphology (plural markers), and word compounding with Persian became a part of modern Indo-Aryan languages as is the conjunct verb construction, complementation (with *ki* 'that'), and conjunction with NPs.

Domains such as law and regulation, sports, and business belong to Persian-mixed Hindi to this day in India. Highly Persian-Arabic style is widely employed in the modern-day legal register. Also, newspaper reporting, a business section which includes a price-index report, share market, and reports dealing with economics such as budgetary reporting and so on, incline towards the Persianized style (italicized items below). Consider, for example, the following headlines (Persian-derived words are italicized):

(1) shuru   kii *tezii*   ke baad dillii shair giraa.
     beginning of increase of after Delhi share fell
     'Delhi stock market fell after earlier increase.'

(2) *xarc*   ke *evaz*   men chuuT   dii jaaegii.
     expenditure of exchange in   concession give will-go
     'Concession will be given in exchange of expenditure.'

(3) bajaT   ek *nazar* men
     budget one glance in
     'Budget in one glance.'

(4) aap kii apiil   *xaariz* huii.
     you of appeal reject happened
     'Your appeal was rejected.'

29.3.1.3   English

The latest high-prestige link language to be instituted in SA, English, introduced a new phase of bilingualism and has added greatly to the already mixed character of Indian languages. What is noteworthy is that mixing with

English is an important linguistic feature of SA in general but of India in particular. When the introduction of English to the Indian linguistic landscape opened with the dawn of the British colonial era, English began to develop roots in Indian education. A blueprint for India's educational policy was laid down in Lord Macaulay's *Minute* (February 2, 1835). Macaulay's stated mission for the British Raj of creating "a class of persons, Indian in blood and colour, but English in taste, in opinions, in morals and intellect" introduced English education to India. The primary aim of his educational policies was not to introduce an additive bilingual education (English + Indian languages) in India but to set the stage for subtractive bilingualism (monolingualism in English). The following statement reflects his negative attitude not only toward Indian languages but also toward the languages of southwest Asia – particularly Arabic.

> I have no knowledge of either Sanskrit or Arabic. But I have done what I could to form a correct estimate of their value . . . I am quite ready to take the oriental learning at the valuation of the orientalists themselves. I have never found one amongst them who could deny that a single shelf of a good European library was worth the whole native literature of India and Arabia.

More than one and a half centuries later, English has overcome its status as merely the language of the colonial power, and has become an integral part of the Indian linguistic mosaic. Contrary to the most popular pre-independence consensus, that Hindi would dethrone the English language after independence, English has not only continued to flourish in the educational and official network of India but has also become one of the official languages of the nation and thus continues to enjoy the patronage of the Indian elite. Although the numerical incidence of bilingualism with English is still very low, English has acquired domains such as education, law, government, media, and science and technology, which once belonged to either Sanskrit or Persian. The uses of English, parallel to its predecessor contact languages – Sanskrit and Persian – has led to the Englishization of Indian languages. On the other hand, English has undergone significant changes locally to carry much of the communicative burden of Indian society. The process of nativization of Indian English continues to this day; see Bhatia (1982) and B. B. Kachru (1983).

29.3.2 *Present-day India/SA*

29.3.2.1 *The Hindi-Hindustani-Urdu-Punjabi core/axis*
Turning to the first layer of the pyramid, along with English, Hindi provides a major contact language link within the communicative network. The heart of this link consists in the Hindi-Hindustani-Urdu-Punjabi core/axis. This axis forms a giant speech community with direct links to Bengali in the east, Gujarati and Marathi in the west, and Telugu and Kannada in the south. In contact

with these languages and other regional varieties, Hindi has developed its own regional varieties, for example Mumbai Hindi (Bombay Hindi, Bindi), Kalkatiya Hindi (Calcutta Hindi), Madrasi Hindi (Madras, renamed Chennai), and Dakkani Hindi ("southern Hindi").

29.3.2.2   *Other factors in bilingualism*

In addition to the linguistic sources discussed above, education, the military, migration, literature (particularly devotional literature), religion (pilgrimages), popular and electronic media, and trade are other factors that play an important role in societal bilingualism or multingualism in India.

Education and government policies

The language policies of the government of India are very conducive to the promotion of the language rights of minority languages and the advancement of linguistic diversity and pluralism. This is evident from the facts regarding languages represented in the third tier of the pyramid. The number of languages used in primary education is 47, in the print media 87, in radio and broadcasting 71, 13 in films, and 13 in state-level administration. In addition, the introduction of the Three Language Formula in education is yet another notable feature of national policy. This formula calls for trilingualism or quadrilingualism in education. In addition to the learning of the two national languages – Hindi and English – students are expected to learn a third language beyond their native tongue. For example, in the Hindi-Urdu-Punjabi belt, students are expected to learn one of the four Dravidian languages (Tamil, Telugu, Kannada, and Malayalam). Although the debate concerning the effectiveness of the Three Language Formula is still brewing, the underlying merit of the educational policy in the promotion of multilingualism is hardly questionable and best represents the multilingual character of the nation (see B. B. Kachru, 1997; Krishnamurti, 1998; Schiffman, 1999; and Sridhar, 1996). Similarly, the National Academy of Letters (the Sahitya Akademi) of the Government of India and its regional counterparts promote literary activities at least in the eighteen "scheduled" languages.

Bridging the rural/urban divide: Literature, popular media, and trade

Unchanged for centuries, rural populations constitute the heart of India. According to the 1991 census, for instance, most of the population of India (about 75 percent of the total) lives in more than half a million (627,000) villages and speaks in numerous vernaculars (see the base of the pyramid in figure 29.3). The most obvious linguistic vehicles for reaching rural India are either Hindi or the regional languages and their local vernaculars. The incidence of literacy in English is not significant in rural India. Thanks to literature in the past and popular media at present, the boundaries between rural vernaculars and Hindi have become very fluid. Historically, literature (e.g. the devotional poetry tradition – poets such as Kabir, Tulasi, Surdas and Meera Bai, and others) has played a major role in neutralizing such boundaries and bringing the influence of regional languages (from east to west and south to north; bidirectional) and rural varieties into Hindi. The consequence is a mixed speech which is termed *sadhukari bhasha* (the language of *sadhus* and saints, free from any prescriptive norms). At present the most powerful and vital force for bridging the urban/ rural (and regional) divide is the Hindi film industry and the mass media. These sources of influence offer unique appeal in terms of cinematic techniques, dance, drama, and music, even constitute a viable marketing alternative to Hollywood in the world of entertainment in SA, and in fact in SA- and non-SA-origin communities outside SA. The reach of the Hindi media indeed extends well beyond the one-fourth of the world's population that inhabits SA, reaching members of the Indian diaspora worldwide. Consequently, mutual intelligibility between regional languages and rural varieties of Hindi is growing steadily. At least this is true of spoken Hindi – *caltii* Hindi "colloquial Hindi" or *bazaar* or Dakkini Hindi. Nevertheless, some barriers do remain.

The economic forces of globalization and the emergent trend for seeking out new hot markets (called B2-4B – business to 4-billion, see James, 2001; Prahalad and Hart, 2002) have further weakened the barriers between rural and urban varieties. Those villages and small towns which were once inconsequential dots on the map of India are now receiving the attention of global marketing giants and media planners. Neglected for decades, rural India is no longer perceived by business as an economic basket case. Due to a number of factors such as globalization, economic liberalization, the IT revolution, the Indian diaspora, female power, and improving infrastructure, middle-class rural India today has more disposable income than urban India. Rural marketing is thus gaining new heights. Indian media experts and planners have not only pioneered new media forms (e.g. video vans; see Bhatia, 2000 for details), but also have mastered the art of crafting messages customized to effectively meet their audiences' regional sensibilities and tastes. The array of both conventional and non-conventional media forms together with programming in dozens of major and scores of minor languages of the region adds a new distinct facet to bilingualism which is grounded in local vernaculars (see Bhatia, 2000 for more details).

Marketers are invading Indian villages like the rats in the Pied Piper story. They flock to every *haat* (unregulated periodic rural market), fair, and festival that villagers go to. These events are not only hotspots of business but also of bilingualism. Who knew back in the ninth century, during the period of the philosopher-saint *Shankaracharya*, that the centuries-old tradition of religious pilgrimages to festival centers would become a godsend for marketers in the twentieth century and the new millennium? *Haats* and fairs have traditionally played a key role in promoting inter-rural and rural–urban bilingualism. There has been a continuous, centuries-old tradition in village India of converging on certain locations on certain days and dates to conduct transactions either in monetary or in barter terms. These markets are like the mobile McDonalds and Walmarts of India in terms of their business transactions and earning power. The number of congregating villagers depends upon the nature of the *haat*. Some *haats* – for example, the Sonepur cattle market in Bihar and the Pushkar fair in the state of Rajasthan – can draw millions of visitors, while others are attended by a couple of thousand. Attendance also depends upon the day of the week and the duration of the *haat*. Although the role of rural markets and pilgrimages (see Bhatia, 2000; Masica, 1991) has often been overlooked in the context of the multilingual character of India, its role in promoting pan-Indian multilingualism at the grassroots level can hardly be overestimated.

Another new manifestation of bilingualism is brought about by trade and globalization in the new pattern of rural migration. After the green revolution in the state of Punjab, economic prosperity brought an influx of Hindi-speaking rural labor to Punjab to fill the gaps left by the prosperous Punjabi farmers who moved either to urban or to semi-urban areas. In addition, government employees (military, civil, and excise/taxation) who are posted to regions of India other than their home region often do not retire at home but settle down in the area where they have worked most of the later years of their lives instead.

Before we turn to the question of the present-day result of linguistic contact and change in shaping the pattern of bilingualism in India, let us emphasize that the three historical contact languages together with other sources led to the formation of a network of giant speech communities in the subcontinent. By and large this was achieved by means of subscribing to diverse and multiple models of communication either explicitly or implicitly rather than relying on one monolithic model (e.g. a one-country, one-language, prescriptive model). The forces of prescriptivism have been present ever since the first major language contact among mother-tongue speakers of different languages via Sanskrit; eventually, however, monolithic forces yielded to multicultural and multilingual models. Even imposed languages such as Persian and English have become a natural part of the Indian and subcontinental linguistic landscape. With the emergence of new socially significant languages (e.g. the growing number of scheduled/regional languages), the domains of the languages in contact had to be negotiated and renegotiated both at the political and informal level. In qualitative and quantitative terms, Indian bilingualism was largely nourished naturally rather than by the forces of prescriptivism.

29.4   Salient features of SA bilingualism

From the above discussion, it is clear that linguistic diversity is a hallmark of India. India is often labeled the "Tower of Babel," since it is remarked that India "babbles" chaotically in "hundreds of dialects." Such labels or expressions reflect a lack of understanding of the complex but structured network of linguistic communication and bilingualism in India. The main focus of this section is to highlight the results of prolonged and recent bilingualism in the region.

29.4.1   *Indian bilingualism: A natural phenomenon*

There is no doubt that there are linguistic rivalries and conflicts in India, even language vs. dialect conflict (Kachru and Bhatia, 1978). Centuries of coexistence and an ongoing process of convergence have led to an unmarked pattern of widespread naturalistic linguistic coalescence rather than separation, dominance, and disintegration. Large-scale diffusion of linguistic features across genetic and areal boundaries has resulted in mutually feeding relationships and reciprocity. Although the incidence of "antagonistic bilingualism" of the sort witnessed in Belgium and other parts of the world cannot be ruled out, its incidence is very limited in degree and scope. In short, one of the defining features of SA is long-term stable bilingualism and linguistic accommodation. This situation led Caldwell (1903/1956) to propose implicitly that India/SA is a "linguistic area" – that is, an area in which genetically distinct languages show a remarkable level of similarity and diffusion at the level of grammar. This view has since proven a fertile field of research (Emeneau, 1956, 1969, 1980; Kuiper, 1967; Masica, 1976, 1991; Thomason, 2001, pp. 114–17). The notion has been extended to "South Asia as a sociolinguistic area" which includes consideration not only of formal features but of discourse as well; see Pandit, 1972.

29.4.2   *Language attitudes and linguistic accommodation*

Why has diffusion between genetically distinct languages taken place in India to a degree rarely witnessed in other parts of the world? The answer lies not only in language-internal developments (Shapiro and Schiffman, 1981), but also in linguistic attitudes which are in turn associated with the world-view of Indians since ancient times. Bright (1984, p. 19) characterizes linguistic attitudes in SA as an "accepting attitude, which has brought about the assimilation of features from Dravidian, Indo-Aryan, Islamic, and even Christian and European cultures into a single system, complex, but integrated." Thus, linguistic accommodation is another important feature of Indian bilingualism.

29.4.3   *Stable bilingualism and multiple identities*

Bilingualism is not a borderline phenomenon in India/SA, nor is it restricted to either educated or business communities. Multiple languages and multiple language identities are defining features of Indian and SA bilingualism that reveal the dynamics of language usage and a constant negotiation of identities. For instance, the simple act of a social encounter and associated greetings is likely to begin with the choice of one of three modes of greetings which reveal the religious affiliation of speaker, listener, or both in addition to conveying the social ritual of greetings: *namaste* or *namaskaar* (Hindu), *aadaab* (Muslim), *sat sri akaal* (Sikh), drawn from Sanskrit, Perso-Arabic, and Punjabi, respectively. Not only this, a Hindu speaker may decide to use *raam-raam* and *jai maata dii* to express regional (rural) and ethnic affiliation, respectively within Hinduism. Similar conditions hold true of Muslims and members of other religious and social groups. See Y. Kachru (1997) for communicative meaning and discourse styles in India.

Language identity is stronger than religious identity among the Bengalis in SA. A case in point is Bangladesh and West Bengal in India. Before Bangladesh became an independent nation in 1971, it was a part of Pakistan (referred to as East Pakistan). Although Islamic identity was the main reason that Bangladesh became a part of Pakistan rather than India in 1947, the imposition of Urdu, the national language of Pakistan, over Bengali led to the split of Pakistan and Bangladesh (for more details on the Bengali language movement, see Rahman, 1996, pp. 79–102). However, the Punjabi Muslims' identity with their language is weaker than the Bengalis'. Therefore, although Punjabi speakers form a majority in Pakistan, the imposition of Urdu on Punjabis did not lead to a separatist movement as it did in the former East Pakistan (see Rahman, 1996, pp. 191–209 for the Punjabi language movement in Pakistan). Among the Muslims, Sikhs, and Hindus, Sikhs have the greatest degree of loyalty to Punjabi, comparable to the Bengalis in Bangladesh. Tamil language identity is similar to that of Bengali speakers with Bengali. When Hindi and Sinhala were imposed on Tamil speakers in India and Sri Lanka respectively, there were violent protests in both countries. While these protests reached the point of civil war in Sri Lanka, they subsided in India because of the more open and multilingual policies of the Government of India.

29.4.4   Verbal repertoire

Code mixing and code switching are natural phenomena in the life of a bilingual and are thus all-pervasive in India (see Bhatia and Ritchie, 1996; B. B. Kachru, 1978; Pandharipande, 1990; Singh, 1981; and Sridhar and Sridhar, 1980). Bilingual societies organize their linguistic repertoire differently from monolingual societies. No one language is viewed as suitable for all communicative occasions. For instance, a Punjabi family in Delhi uses Saraiki, Punjabi, Hindi-Urdu and English in conducting daily business inside and outside the home. The domain allocation is shown in table 29.2.

Table 29.2 identifies some of the determinants of language choice which in turn explains why one needs more than one language to meet the communicative needs of an individual in a multilingual society. The language choice is not a random phenomenon. It is determined by a number of factors, such as participant and group identity, language attitudes, social mobility, and the degree of economic power associated with the use of a language. Hindi and English symbolize economic power, social mobility, and wider communicative access to the speakers of other Indian languages. Although Hindi has an immense advantage over English in terms of social reach (i.e. at the level of the

Table 29.2 Code switching and language domains.

Language/variety	Domain
Saraiki	With first-generation parents, brothers, sisters (extended family)
Punjabi	Ethnic family friends; at home with next generation, casual conversations
Hindi	At work; with Indians from other ethnic and linguistic groups
English	At work with boss, in education, administration and other formal domains

masses), economic desirability and access to the Indian/global elite favor English over Hindi (economic power score in the world – Hindi: 131,943; English: 8,226,548; see Navarro, 1997). Although social mobility translates itself into economic benefits (economic power score in India – Hindi 119,190; English 29,880; see Navarro, 1997), Hindi cannot provide as high level global jobs as English is capable of providing. In short, no one language fits all communicative situations; therefore, bilinguals feel compelled to perform a tightrope-balancing act with the languages at their disposal in order to get optimal results.

In addition to constantly shifting between the various languages generally, intra- and intersentential code mixing within a single discourse unit is a way of life. Consider the dialogue (5) below from a Hindi female creative writer. The following exchange takes place between the husband and the wife from a Hindi-speaking area. A dispute flares up between the two regarding male and female roles in correcting the disruptive behavior of their son in school. Tempers heat up when the husband accuses his wife of neglecting her children because of her deep involvement in social and professional activities; his perception is that, as a consequence, she has no time to look after the children:

(5) *English*-Persian-Hindi
    Wife:
    vil yuu shat ap! baRaa mardaanaa ruaab jhaaR rahe ho . . . samajh kayaa rakhaa hai mujhe! gaav-gavaii kii chuii-muii, *baikvarD*, jaahil aurat, ghar kii baandii yaa apne hukam kii gulaam? ghar aur baccon kii jitnii zimmedaarii aurat kii hai, utnii mard kii bhii, bhuul se bhii apne ko tiismaarkhaan samajhne kii zurrat na karnaa. yahaan koii bhii tumhaarii dhaunsa sahnevaalaa nahii baiThaa hai.
    Husband:
    Shat ap! yuu snaab leDii.
    (Wife: *Will you shut up! Why are you shedding off your male egoistic dominant behavior/act? What do you think of me? I am not a submissive, backward, rustic,*

slave, village woman – slave to (your) order. The responsibility of children is as much of men as of women. Don't you ever dare to consider yourself a brave hero. Nobody is going to bear your threats here.
Husband: Shut up! You snob lady.)

Although the matrix language of this example for mixed speech is Hindi, the exchange is loaded with English- and Persian-mixed style. To challenge what she sees as male-chauvinist behavior and to create distancing (We vs. They code), English is used to mark a "they" relationship at the time of the exchange. The concept of slavery is best conveyed by mixing in Persian vocabulary with Hindi because slavery was prevalent during the Moghul empire when Persian was the dominant language (see subsection 29.3.1.2). Although English and Hindi are both capable of conveying the concept of slavery, they are no match for Persian which expresses its miserableness, transactionlessness, medievalness and ruthlessness most effectively. As noted, the italicized words are from English while the underlined words are from Perso-Arabic sources. In addition to overt language shifting, the range of styles available to Hindi speakers within the language is grounded in multilingualism. A wide variety of linguistic and sociolinguistic factors which motivate bilinguals in India to code-switch and code-mix are the following: quotations, addressee specification, interjections, reiteration, message qualification, topic-comment, explanation and a variety of socio-psychological affiliations. (See Bhatia and Ritchie, 1996 and chapters 6, 13, and 14 of the present volume for details on the social and psychological motivation for code switching and code mixing in general.)

The phenomena of code alternation have brought profound changes to the formal grammar of Indian languages. Romaine (1989, p. 143) claims in her examination of the English-based Punjabi complex verb phenomenon that one can find evidence of "covert semantic restructuring." Observe the case of causatives in Hindi. Hindi and other South Asian causatives are derived by the morphological process of suffixation. By adding the suffixes -*aa*- and -*waa*-, the first and the second causative verbs are formed as in: *paR* 'to study/read,' *paRaa* 'to teach' (lit. 'cause to study'), and *paRwaa* 'cause x to cause y to study/read.' We claim that mixing with English has resulted in the introduction of a new class of transitive/causative verbs of a mixed type, i.e. *study karnaa* 'to research (on a topic'; lit. *study* + *karnaa* 'to do study'), *teach karnaa* 'to teach,' *study karwaanaa* 'to guide research,' *teach karwaanaa* 'to guide teaching.' The verb *study karnaa* 'to research' is not just a paraphrase or translational equivalent of Hindi *paR* 'to study/read'; the English-based verb expresses the meaning 'to study a topic from the viewpoint of research' and the causative counterparts, i.e. *study karwaanaa* 'to guide research,' *teach karwaanaa* 'to guide teaching' highlight the "facilitative" (i.e. help the causee to do a particular act) while the Hindi causative marks "compulsive" meanings.

Let us consider an example of semantic restructuring. Before the introduction of English, Hindi had two conjunct verb expressions with the meaning "to travel": *yatraa karnaa* and *safar karnaa*. The former is Sanskrit-based and the latter is Persian-based. The former connotes leisurely travel with religious overtones whereas the latter marks any ordinary travel. The English-based *tour karnaa* has added yet a new semantic dimension which expresses the concept of business travel which is contrary to what the verb *tour* conveys in English.

Semantic restructuring of this sort has syntactic consequences which are often overlooked in the literature on code mixing in South Asia. Consider, for example, the case of the complex verbs, *koshish karnaa*, and *try karnaa* 'to try' which differ from each other in terms of subcategorization restrictions. The former does not take an NP complement (as shown by the ill-formedness of 6b below), whereas the latter (i.e. the English-based complex verb) can (as shown by the grammaticality of 6a). This leads us to conclude that in fact the complex verb *try karnaa* 'to try' is semantically ambiguous, i.e. it expresses the meaning of 'to taste' as well as 'to attempt.' The Hindi equivalent, *koshish karnaa* 'to make an attempt,' expresses the latter meaning and not the former, as shown schematically at (6).

(6) Hindi-*English*
    (a) khaanaa/*food try* kiijiye.
        food   try do-imp
        'Please try (the) food.'
    (b) *khaanaa/*food* koshish kiijiye.
        food   attempt do-imp
        'Please try (the) food.'

For more details on the conjunct verb phenomenon with special reference to its mixed grammar, see Bhatia and Ritchie, 1996, and on the second-language acquisition aspect, see Bhatia and Ritchie, 2001.

Even the phonological and morphological structures of modern Indian languages have been affected by the contact of modern Indian languages with Persian and English. For instance, observe echo-word formation in Hindi. Echo-word formation is a pan-Indian linguistic feature. Indian English is no exception in this regard. For instance, the English word *fit* can render an echo word *fit-vit* 'fit etc.' The echo formation with *v* is an unmarked productive process of standard Indian English. In addition, yet another echo word *fiiT-faaT* 'fit etc.' can be witnessed in the regional varieties of English (e.g. in Bihar by semi-educated politicians). The English stem in this variety has undergone vowel lengthening (sounding like <u>feet</u>) and the echo word follows a marked tendency (starting with *f* instead of *v*). (For more on code mixing and code switching, see chapters 1–4, 6, 10–14, 25, 26, and 31.)

29.4.5 *Diglossic/High–Low pattern*

Diglossia refers to a relatively stable language situation in which two codes/ languages/varieties maintain clear functional separation. Four language situations which show the major characteristics of the diglossic phenomena are Arabic, Swiss German, Greek, and Haitian (French and Creole). One of the important aspects of style shifting is the diglossic distinction between the "low" (L) and "high" (H) varieties (see Ferguson, 1959 for more details). All major languages of India are sensitive to this distinction. Schiffman (1999, p. 435) observes that "diglossia is so deeply rooted in Indian culture that . . . it is an almost inevitable feature of the Indian linguistic scene." In some languages it is so ubiquitous and sharp that it can be equated with hyperdiglossia, as in Tamil and Telugu. While Tamil diglossia is further associated with caste varieties (*brahmin* vs. *non-brahmin*), this is not the case with Telugu. The Sanskritized variety of Tamil is not a feature of an educated variety *per se* but most importantly a marker of the Brahmin caste. Some varying degree of the H–L distinction is found in other Dravidian languages (e.g. Kannada and Malayalam) and Indo-Aryan languages such as Bengali and Sinhala (Gair, 1998). The *saadhubhasha* vs. *calitbhasha* distinction in Bengali is the H and L distinction. The hyperdiglossic pattern of bilingualism is a reminiscent/relic feature of the Indian obsession with linguistic purity/prescriptivism. (For more on diglossia, see chapters 15, 28, and 31.)

29.4.6 *Freedom of choice and language planning*

Linguistic diversity highlights freedom of choice of speech, which is not just a recent, twentieth-century phenomenon in India, but a centuries-old tradition. This attitude has not been seen in many parts of the world. For example, French, Chinese, and some other major languages of the world were imposed on others as part of a movement to eradicate rural and regional language varieties. This in turn also explains why the government's attempts at language standardization either to filter out linguistic variation or to equip Indian languages for new professional domains (e.g. science, technology, higher education, law) often fail to achieve any serious measure of success. Consider the warning labels on cigarettes in Hindi. Although the tobacco and betel-nut (*supaarii*) industries are required by law to display warnings cautioning consumers about the health hazards of their products, the warnings appear in a rather haphazard fashion. The range of variation witnessed is quite remarkable. Observe the following data:

(7) vaidhaanik ishaaraa: tambaakuu aur supaarii khaanaa
　　 legal　　　 hint　　 tobacco　　 and betel nut eating
　　 sehat ke liye haanikaarak hai.
　　 health for　　 harmful　　 is
　　 'Legal Hint: Eating tobacco and betel nut is harmful to health.'

(8) kaanuunii cetaavanii: paan masaalaa cabaanaa svaasthya
　　 legal　　　 warning　 Pan Masala　 chewing health

ke liye haanikaarak ho saktaa hai.
for   harmful   be can   is
'Legal Warning: Chewing Pan Masala can be harmful to your health.'

(9) vaidhaanik cetaavanii: tambaakuu khaanaa svaasthya ke liye
     legal   warning tobacco   eating   health   for
     haanikaarak hai.
     harmful   is
     'Legal Warning: Eating tobacco is harmful for your health.'

(10) "Statutory Warning: Chewing of tobacco is injorious [sic] to health."

The ads for products aimed at rural India carry warnings in either Hindi or English. The spelling mistakes of the English warnings are not even corrected (as exemplified in 10). The key message in (8) is given as a possibility but not a fact. The warning in (7) makes a mockery of the term "warning" and uses the Hindi equivalent for "hint" instead.

29.5 Language Minorities: Language Maintenance and Shift

Home language maintenance is yet another salient feature of Indian bilingualism. Pandit (1977) observed that a "second generation speaker in Europe and America gives up his native language in favor of the dominant language of the region; language shift is the norm and language maintenance an exception. In India language maintenance is the norm and shift an exception." Before Pandit, Emeneau (1962) made a similar observation about Saurashtrian (a variety of Gujarati) in Madurai (Tamil Nadu). According to Emeneau (1962), "In India, immigrant situations often result otherwise than in America. After a period of at least five centuries of migration, Saurashtran still survives as the domestic language of the immigrant silk weavers in Madurai." There are a number of reasons for this language maintenance. Most importantly, linguistic openness, group membership, and language function, together with the lack of negative social/peer-group pressure, enable the second generation to maintain its home language. However, language loyalties and language maintenance of the home language vary across language groups. A Punjabi family in Calcutta tends to shift its home language in favor of Bengali while the reverse is not the case with a Bengali family in Punjab. Secondly, language conflict between two speech communities may also serve as a source of language maintenance and strengthening language loyalties. For instance, Tamil speakers in the Hindi-speaking regions tend to maintain their language in part due to their fierce language rivalry and conflict with Hindi. Although this conflict is gradually subsiding, it continues to this day. (For more on the multiple dimensions of the Hindi-Tamil rivalry and conflict, see Das Gupta, 1970.)

Other factors such as religion, gender and script play important roles in home language or ethnic language maintenance or shift. For example, the non-Muslim Kalasha tribe in Pakistan gave up their language, Kalasha, when they converted to Islam and started using Khowar, the language of Chitrali Muslims, even within the family (Rahman, 1996, p. 225). Women tend to maintain the home language more than men. As a consequence, female speech determines linguistic norms and is thus considered standard (e.g. in the case of Urdu). (See chapter 19 for a general discussion of the role of tradition maintenance for women in traditional societies.) Written proficiency in Punjabi is maintained by Muslims, Sikhs, and Hindus by means of different scripts – Perso-Arabic, Gurmukhi, and Devanagari, respectively.

Although government policies and the social fabric of Indian society promote multilingualism and multiculturalism, it is an uphill battle for minor and tribal language groups to maintain their languages. A minor language is impoverished in terms of its numeric weight, spatial distribution, and functional power. On these three grounds many minor languages become endangered languages. The distinction between majority and minority is instructive as it pertains to India and its census. The dichotomy of majority vs. minority language is a complex and dynamic issue in India. For example, mastery of a minority language like English may carry a high degree of economic power and desirability, so it is not a minor language; it is considered a major language. English may be a minority language in terms of the number of its speakers; however, in terms of economic power and desirability it has more appeal than the most widely spoken language, Hindi. Or a majority language in its own state or region may turn out to be a minority/minor language in another state (see Appendix). The language of the state that has the plurality of speakers turns out to be a minority language when one takes into account the number of other languages spoken in that state. Consider the major vs. minor language distribution as shown in table 29.3.

In states such as Arunachal Pradesh and Nagaland, there is no majority/major language. In short, the majority vs. minority dichotomy is a dynamic rather than static notion in terms of regional appeal and distribution.

There is no doubt though that there are several minor languages in India. These languages are of the Munda and Tibeto-Burman stocks and they run the

Table 29.3 Distribution of major vs. minor languages (based on 1991 census).

State/Union Territory	Largest language (% speakers)	Second-largest language (% speakers)	Third-largest language (% speakers)	Other minority languages (% speakers)
Arunachal Pradesh	Nissi/Daffla (19.9)	Nepali (9.4)	Bengali (8.2)	62.5
Nagaland	Ao (14.0)	Sema (12.6)	Konyak (11.4)	62

risk of becoming extinct. For example, in the Ranchi region of the state of Bihar it is reported that Munda languages (e.g. Kharia) and the Dravidian language Kurux are fading from the urban areas. The urban tribal population seldom show any tendency to preserve their mother tongue. On the contrary, they take special pride in confessing a lack of knowledge of their mother tongue and take pride in associating with the dominant language of the region (i.e. Hindi) while interacting with members of their linguistic group. Some immigrant languages such as Saraiki (also known as Lahanda and Multani) have met a similar fate inside and outside Punjab. Second- and third-generation Saraiki-speaking immigrants from Pakistan feel ashamed to identify themselves as Saraikis (or Multanis), let alone speak Saraiki, because of its negative evaluation. Saraiki speakers are labeled *laRaake* 'quarrelsome.' Their language has shifted in favor of the dominant and prestigious language, Punjabi. Punjabi has, thus, become a marker of larger group identity, i.e. Punjabi subsuming Saraiki.

The Constitution of India provides various measures to safeguard the rights of linguistic, religious and ethnic minorities. In addition to the establishment of the Office of the Commissioner for Linguistic Minorities, the following two articles from the Indian Constitution aim at ensuring the educational rights of such minorities.

> Article 350-A. It should be the endeavour of every state and of every local authority within the state to provide adequate facilities for instruction in the mother tongue in the primary stage of education to children belonging to linguistic minority groups; and the President may issue directions to any State as he considers necessary or proper for securing the provision of such facilities.

> Article 350-B. There shall be a special officer to investigate all matters relating to the safeguards provided for linguistic minorities under this Constitution and report to the President upon those matters at such intervals as the President may direct, and the President shall cause all such reports to be laid before each house of Parliament, and sent to the Governments of the States concerned . . .

In spite of this, linguistic minorities of the Tibeto-Burman and Munda stocks are unable to withstand the linguistic and cultural dominance of majority languages. The newly formed state of Jharkhand is in part aimed at reversing this trend for some Munda languages.

Even majority languages in a bilingual setting may feel threatened by another major language. A case in point is the "English *haTaao* movement" (Abolish English movement) in the Hindi-speaking state of Uttar Pradesh in the 1990s. It is interesting to note that at approximately the same time, another Hindi-speaking state, Bihar, made an apparently reverse move, favoring English compulsorily in its school curriculum. The action of Bihar might appear to be aimed at promoting additive bilingualism; however, underlyingly the two campaigns were motivated by a revolt against the forces of dominance and power of either the elite or of the upper caste (see Aggarwal, 1993) since the promotion of Hindi in Uttar Pradesh was intended to reduce the influence of English (hence of the English-speaking upper class) whereas the promotion of English for all in Bihar was designed to mitigate the influence of a successful English-speaking upper caste there. (For more on language maintenance and shift, see chapters 14–16, 18, 25, 26, and 28; for more on language endangerment, see chapters 15–18, 25, 27, and 28.)

29.6   Conclusion

South Asian bilingualism in general and Indian bilingualism in particular provide an excellent progressive, realistic, contemporary, and multicultural window on the phenomenon of bilingualism. Shaped largely by the natural democratic forces of linguistic accommodation and assimilation, they reveal the complexity of multiple bilingual language choices and use which is conducive to linguistic diversity and additive bilingualism. There is no denial that language rivalry and conflict are natural consequences of bilingualism. However, contrary to the popular conception, language rivalry in India often does not lead to linguistic and national disintegration. On the contrary, it provides an impetus to the forces of national development and anti-discrimination. This chapter reveals that the language use of a bilingual is not strictly a linguistic matter but is also interwoven with complex factors such as multiple identities, a range of affiliations, and emotive factors.

ACKNOWLEDGMENT

We are grateful to Ms. Jennifer L. Smith for her invaluable assistance with the maps produced in this chapter.

REFERENCES

Aggarwal, K. S. (1993). English, Laloo: a Bihari story. *The Independent* (September 32).

Annamalai, E. (2001). *Managing Multilingualism in India: Political and Linguistic Manifestations*. New Delhi: Sage Publications.

Bhasham, A. L. (1954). *The Wonder that was India*. New York: Grove Press.

Bhat, R. M. (1992). Sociolinguistic area and language policies. In E. Dimock, B. Kachru, and Bh. Krishnamurti (eds.), *Dimensions of Sociolinguistics in South Asia*, pp. 47–69. Delhi: Oxford University Press.

Bhatia, T. K. (1982). English and vernaculars of India: Contact and change. *Applied Linguistics*, 3(3), 235–45.

Bhatia, T. K. (1985). Religious-colonial models of language and early Hindi grammars. *Lingua*, 65, 123–34.

Bhatia, T. K. (2000). *Advertising in Rural India: Language, Marketing Communication and Consumerism*. Tokyo: Tokyo Press.

Bhatia, T. K. (2001). Grammatical traditions in contact: The case of India. In H. Kniffka, (ed.), *Indigenous Grammar across Cultures*, pp. 89–115. New York: Peter Lang.

Bhatia, T. K. and Ritchie, W. C. (1996). Bilingual language mixing, universal grammar, and second language acquisition. In W. C. Ritchie and T. K. Bhatia (eds.), *Handbook of Second Language Acquisition*, pp. 627–82. San Diego: Academic Press.

Bhatia, T. K. and Ritchie, W. C. (2001). Language mixing, typology, and second language acquisition. *The Yearbook of South Asian Languages and Linguistics 2001. Tokyo Symposium on South Asian Languages: Contact, Convergence and Typology*, pp. 37–62. London and Delhi: Sage.

Bright, W. (1960). A case study of caste dialect in Mysore. *Indian Linguistics*, 21, 45–50.

Bright, W. (1984). *American Indian Linguistics and Literature*. The Hague: Mouton.

Bright, W. and Ramanujan, A. K. (1964). Sociolinguistic variation and language change. *Proceedings of the Ninth International Congress of Linguistics*. Cambridge, MA: MIT Press.

Caldwell, R. P. A. (1903). *A Comparative Grammar of the Dravidian or South-Indian Family of Languages*. Madras: Oriental Books (1956 edition).

Census of India (2004). *Language Atlas of India 1991*. New Delhi: Government of India.

Das Gupta, J. (1970). *Language Conflict and National Development: Group Politics and National Language Policy in India*. Berkeley: University of California Press.

D'Souza, J. (1992). Dimensions of South Asia as a sociolinguistic area. In E. Dimock, B. Kachru, and Bh. Krishnamurti (eds.), *Dimensions of Sociolinguistics in South Asia*, pp. 15–23. Delhi: Oxford University Press.

Emeneau, M. B. (1956). India as a linguistic area. *Language*, 32(1), 3–16.

Emeneau, M. (1962). Bilingualism and structural borrowings. *Proceedings of the American Philosophical Society*, 106(5), 430–42.

Emeneau, M. B. (1969). Onomatopoeics in the Indian linguistic area. *Language*, 45(2.1), 274–99.

Emeneau, M. B. (1980). India and linguistic areas. In A. N. Dil (ed.), *Language and Linguistic Area: Essays by Murray B. Emeneau*, pp. 126–66. Stanford, CA: Stanford University Press.

Emeneau, M. B. and Borrow, T. (1962). Dravidian borrowings from Indo-Aryan. University of California Papers in Linguistics, 26. Berkeley: University of California.

Ferguson, C. F. (1959). Diglossia. *Word*, 15(2), 325–40.

Gair, J. W. (1998). Sinhala diglossia revisted, or, diglossia dies hard. In B. Lust (ed.) *Studies in South Asian Linguistics: Sinhala and other South Asian Languages*, pp. 224–36. Oxford: Oxford University Press.

Gumperz, J. J. and Wilson, R. (1971). Convergence and creolization: a case from the Indo-Aryan/Dravidian border in India. In D. H. Hymes (ed.), *Pidginization and Creolization of Languages*, pp. 151–67. Cambridge, UK: Cambridge University Press.

Hadley, G. (1772). *Grammatical Remarks on the Practical and Vulgar Dialect of Indostan Language*. Menston, UK: The Scolar Press.

James, D. (2001). B2-4B spells profits. *Marketing News*, November 5 (Lead story).

Kachru, B. B. (1978). Toward structuring code-mixing: An Indian perspective. *International Journal of the Sociology of Language*, 16, 28–46.

Kachru, B. B. (1983). *The Indianization of English: The English Language in India*. Delhi: Oxford University Press.

Kachru, B. B. (1994). English in South Asia. In R. Burchfield (ed.), *The Cambridge History of the English Language*, pp. 497–553. Cambridge, UK: Cambridge University Press.

Kachru, B. B. (1997). Language in Indian society. In S. N. Sridhar and N. K. Mattoo (eds.), *Ananya: A Portrait of India*, pp. 555–85. New York: The Association of Indians in America.

Kachru, Y. (1997). Culture and communication in India. In S. N. Sridhar and N. K. Mattoo (eds.), *Ananya: A Portrait of India*, pp. 645–63. New York: The Association of Indians in America.

Kachru, Y. and Bhatia, T. K. (1978). The emerging "dialect" conflict in Hindi: A case of glottopolitics. *International Journal of the Sociology of Language*, 16, 47–56.

Khubchandani, L. M. (1997). *Revisualizing Boundaries: a Pluralism Ethos*. New Delhi: Sage.

King, C. R. (1994). *One Language, Two Scripts: The Hindi Movement in Nineteenth Century North India*. New Delhi: Oxford University Press.

Krishnamurti, Bh. (1998). Language in school education in India. *Language, Education and Society*, pp. 274–89. New Delhi: Sage.

Krishnamurti, Bh. and A. Mukherjee (eds.) (1984). *Modernization of Indian Languages in News Media*. Hyderabad, India: Department of Linguistics, Osmania University.

Kuiper, F. B. J. (1967). The genesis of linguistic area. *Indo-Iranian Journal*, 10(81)–102.

Masica, C. P. (1976). *Defining a Linguistic Area: South Asia*. Chicago: Chicago University Press.

Masica, C. P. (1991). *The Indo-Aryan languages*. Cambridge, UK: Cambridge University Press.

Navarro, F. A. (1997). Which is the world's most important language? Application of an objective method of assessment to the twelve main world's languages. *Lebende Sprachen*, 1, 5–10.

Pandharipande, R. (1990). Formal and functional constraints on code-mixing. In R. Jacobson (ed.), *Codeswitching as Worldwide Phenomenon*, pp. 33–9. New York: Peter Lang.

Pandit, P. B. (1972). *India as a Sociolinguistic Area*. Poona: University of Poona.

Pandit, P. B. (1977). *Language in a Plural Society*. Delhi: Dev Raj Channa Memorial Committee.

Pereira, J. (1971). *Literary Konhani: A brief history*. Dharwar: Konkani Sahitya Prakashan.

Prahalad, C. K. and Hart, S. L. (2002). *The Fortune at the Bottom of the Pyramid: Strategy and Competition*, issue 26, pp. 1–14 (Reprint No. 02106).

Rahman, T. (1996). *Language and Politics in Pakistan*. Karachi: Oxford University Press.

Ritchie, W. C. and Bhatia, T. K. (eds.) (1996). *Handbook of Second Language Acquisition*. San Diego: Academic Press.

Romaine, S. (1989). *Bilingualism*. Oxford: Basil Blackwell.

Schiffman, H. (1999). South and Southeast Asia. In J. A. Fishman (ed.), *Language and Ethnic Identity*, pp. 431–43. Oxford: Oxford University Press.

Schultz, B. (1745). *Grammatica Hindostanica, collectis in diurtuna inter Hindostanos*. In Johann Heinrich Callenberg (ed.) (1694–1760). Halle S.: In typographia Instituti judaici.

Shapiro, M. and Schiffman, H. F. (1981). *Language and Society in South Asia*. Delhi: Motilal Banarsidass.

Singh, R. (1981). Grammatical constraints on code-switching. *Recherches Linguistiques à Montréal*, 17, 155–63.

Sjoberg, A. and Sjoberg, G. (1956). Problems of glottochronology: Culture as a significant variable in lexical change. *American Anthropologist*, 58(2), 296–300.

Sridhar, K. K. (1996). Language in education: Minorities and multilingualism in India. *International Review of Education*, 42.4, 327–347.

Sridhar, S. N. (1981). Linguistic convergence: Indo-Aryanization of Dravidian languages. *Lingua*, 5, 199–220.

Sridhar, S. N. and Sridhar, K. (1980). The syntax and psycholinguistics of bilingual code-mixing. *Canadian Journal of Psychology*, 34(4), 407–16.

Thomason, S. G. (2001). *Language Contact: An Introduction*. Washington, D.C.: Georgetown University Press.

World Almanac and Book of Facts 2002, The. New York: World Almanac Books.

Appendix: Distribution of Majority vs. Minority Languages (Based on 1991 Census)

State/Union Territory	Largest language (% speakers)	Second-largest language (% speakers)	Third-largest language (% speakers)	Other minority languages (% speakers)
Andhra Pradesh	Telugu (84.8)	Urdu (8.4)	Hindi (2.8)	4.0
Assam	Assamese (57.8)	Bengali (11.3)	Bodo/Boro (5.3)	25.6
Bihar	Hindi (80.9)	Urdu (9.9)	Santhali (2.9)	6.3
Goa	Konkani (51.5)	Marathi (33.4)	Kannada (4.6)	10.5
Gujarat	Gujarati (91.5)	Hindi (2.9)	Sindhi (1.7)	3.9
Haryana	Hindi (91.0)	Punjabi (7.1)	Urdu (1.6)	0.3
Himachal Pradesh	Hindi (88.9)	Punjabi (7.1)	Kinnauri (1.2)	2.8
Karnataka	Kannada (66.2)	Urdu (10.0)	Telugu (7.4)	16.4
Kerala	Malayalam (96.6)	Tamil (2.1)	Kannada (0.3)	1
Madhya Pradesh	Hindi (85.6)	Bhili/Bhilodi (3.3)	Gondi (2.2)	8.9
Maharashtra	Marathi (73.3)	Hindi (7.8)	Urdu (7.3)	11.6
Manipur	Manipuri (60.4)	Thado (5.6)	Tangkhul (5.4)	28.6
Meghalaya	Khasi (49.5)	Garo (30.9)	Bengali (8.1)	11.5
Mizoram	Lusha/Mizo (75.1)	Bengali (8.6)	Lakher (3.3)	13
Orissa	Oriya (82.8)	Hindi (2.4)	Telugu (1.6)	13.2
Punjab	Punjabi (92.2)	Hindi (7.3)	Urdu (0.1)	0.4
Rajasthan	Hindi (89.6)	Bhili/Bhilodi (5.0)	Urdu (2.2)	3.2
Sikkim	Nepali (63.1)	Bhotia (8.0)	Lepcha (7.3)	21.6
Tamil Nadu	Tamil (86.7)	Telugu (7.1)	Kannada (2.2)	4
Tripura	Bengali (68.9)	Tripuri (23.5)	Hindi (1.7)	5.9
Uttar Pradesh	Hindi (90.1)	Urdu (9.0)	Punjabi (0.5)	0.4
West Bengal	Bengali (86.0)	Hindi (6.6)	Urdu (2.1)	5.3
Andaman and Nicobar Islands	Bengali (23.1)	Tamil (19.1)	Hindi (17.6)	40.2
Chandigarh	Hindi (61.1)	Punjabi (34.7)	Tamil (0.8)	3.4
Dadra and Nagar Haveli	Bhili/Bhilodi (55.0)	Gujarati (21.9)	Konkani (12.3)	10.8
Daman and Diu	Gujarati (91.1)	Hindi (3.6)	Marathi (1.2)	4.1
Delhi	Hindi (81.6)	Punjabi (7.9)	Urdu (5.4)	5.1
Lakshadweep	Malayalam (84.5)	Tamil (0.5)	Hindi (0.4)	14.6
Pondicherry	Tamil (89.2)	Malayalam (4.8)	Telugu (4.3)	1.7

30 Changing Language Loyalties in Central Asia

BIRGIT SCHLYTER

30.1 Introduction

Bilingualism in Central Asia is first and foremost to be associated with societal language practice, where proficiency in more than one language is typically presupposed for participants in linguistic interaction. It is a feature of groups, or communities, to such an extent that it may be difficult to distinguish a first or native language from some other language for a particular member of the group. This linguistic complexity is part of a cultural context characterized not only by several languages and different blends of ethnicities but also by a multilayered history of successive religious and political hegemonies. Consequently, Central Asian language identities and cultural identities, as far as common classificatory features are concerned, may seem extraordinarily flexible and fluid, if not indeterminate at times.

As a regional designation, Central Asia may be used and is often used in a wide sense, comprising not only the former Soviet republics of Kazakhstan, Kyrgyzstan, Uzbekistan, Turkmenistan and Tajikistan, but also contiguous territories, such as Outer and Inner Mongolia, Xinjiang, and Afghanistan, as well as parts of Iran, Pakistan, India, and Tibet, all of which have much in common with their northern and western neighbors from a culture-historical point of view. Given this wide delimitation, Central Asia would be of a size comparable to that of the USA, including overseas possessions, i.e. approximately 10 million square kilometers. Although neighboring areas will be referred to in general comments on languages and ethnic distribution and in the final list of recommended literature for further reading, it is the so-called ex-Soviet Central Asia that the present chapter is devoted to. The topics to be discussed are the co-existence of languages and politically caused changes of language loyalty in those parts of the region which for most of the twentieth century were under Soviet jurisdiction and hence were under the firm control of Soviet language ideology. (See figure 30.1.)

Ex-Soviet Central Asia is in a state of fundamental change involving both cultural and linguistic loyalties. Muslim culture was a stronghold not really suppressed under Soviet rule and is for the time being regaining importance as the main religious pattern in the region, counterbalancing the Soviet legacy of atheism embedded in expired communist ideology. At the same time, the former Soviet prestige language, Russian, is challenged by new language policies. This may cause mental turbulence for the individual. Imagine, for example, a person who was brought up in a Muslim Uzbek-speaking family but who had all her school education in Russian and eventually turned into an atheist fluent in Russian, which for the next 25 years was her most used language and, in her own opinion, her "first language." In post-independence Uzbekistan, she finds herself compelled to revert to, perhaps not her childhood faith, but at any event Uzbek as her main language, not only in terms of the spoken dialect she has continued to use occasionally at home, but also in its standard literary form, which she has had no personal training in but which she is now expected to use in writing at work.

(A small number of language examples will appear in the following text, most of which originate from sources using Cyrillic script. The transliteration technique chosen conforms to American standards and will probably not cause any problems in understanding, except perhaps for a less common character, ŭ, employed for rounded mid-vowels, somewhere between [ө] and [Π], in Uzbek and Tajik.)

30.2 The Ethnolinguistic Context

It is important to remember that, because of early mass migrations as well as military campaigns by nomadic warlords and subsequent great-power imperialism, internal sovereign nation-state borders in the Central Asian region were more or less non-existent until late in the nineteenth century and in some areas even much later. As a consequence of this, languages spoken in the region have been geographically and politically confined to a much lesser extent than in many other parts of the world, where bilingualism is mostly to be found along borders. Instead, Central Asian bilingualism is a widespread phenomenon characterizing the region as a whole and shaped by topography and climate rather than by administrative confinements.

With the exception of its southernmost belt, Central Asia has a small number of speakers in proportion to its size. The total population of the ex-Soviet republics, which constitute one-third (*c.* 3.3 million square kilometers) of the wider Central Asian territory, amounts to merely some 55 million. Because of physical conditions, the distribution of people is uneven across this part of the region, where large uninhabitable areas alternate with densely populated fertile soils.

Rural populations still outnumber urban ones in most Central Asian countries and provinces. The exposure to linguistic diversity among this category of

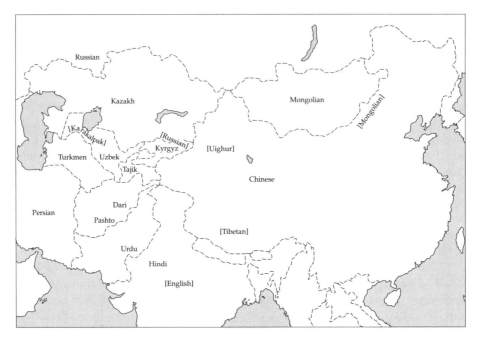

Figure 30.1   Official languages in the Central Asian region.
Within brackets, languages with a special, semi-official, or official status side by side
with the state language of a particular country. For a brief illustrated orientation
about the spread of languages in this part of the world, see Baker and Jones (1998,
pp. 370–84).

people differs fundamentally from linguistic experiences in urban environments.
Urban dwellers are more often than not exposed to bilingual or multilingual
communication in their most immediate neighborhood (apartment house, city
block, work, etc.). Rural communities, by contrast, are as a rule linguistically
homogeneous entities (villages, cooperatives, etc.), where most people live
and work in monolingual groups. Therefore, rural bilingualism at the local
level is in the first place a phenomenon relating to the juxtaposition of different
language communities rather than a feature of intragroup communication. Now,
this is not to say that rural dwellers are generally monolingual as far as language command or language comprehension is concerned. With former Soviet
linguistic and educational politics, habits of bilingual information and communication spread to the Central Asian countryside as well, to an extent that
had not been experienced before. This type of politics has finally been abandoned and new state borders have been drawn, within which new linguistic
codes once again will change the general pattern of public – and perhaps also
private – linguistic interaction for the entire population, whether urban or
rural. (See figure 30.1.)

The main ethnic division in ex-Soviet Central Asia is that between Turkic and Iranian populations. According to figures from the last Soviet census (*Natsional'nyi sostav naseleniia*, Moscow 1989), the proportion is in the region of eight to one in favor of Turkic ethnicities. To the east and south of this region, the proportions are different. In the Chinese province of Xinjiang, where the inhabitants of Turkic ethnicity – mainly Uighur but also Kazakh and Kyrgyz – constitute more than half (*c.* 8.5 million) of the entire population, there is merely a tiny Tajik population in areas along the western border. Mongolia and Tibet have no Iranian populations big enough to be mentioned in official statistical accounts. In Mongolia, which has a very small population (2.5 million), predominantly of Mongol ethnicity, about 10 percent of the inhabitants are Turkic (Kazakh and Tuvinian). In Afghanistan the Iranian population outnumbers the Turkic ethnicities (mostly Uzbeks and Turkmens) six to seven times. Similar proportions can be noted for the Persian-dominated northeastern part of Iran, which borders on Turkmenistan and has a Turkmen minority of about 1 million. Western Pakistan is dominated by Iranians (Pashtuns and Baluchis), more or less to the exclusion of Turkic elements.

30.3   Contact-induced Linguistic Change

Being a region sparsely populated due to physical difficulties and natural severity (mountains, steppes, deserts, etc.), ancient Central Asia was very much a no-man's-land through which travelers and migrating populations passed. Inroads into the region were made from all directions at different times and for different purposes. New waves of people and languages for future settlement came mainly from the east. Trade caravans traveled mostly back and forth in the east-west direction with temporary stops along the Silk Routes. Relations with the north and the south developed out of trade too but turned into foreign hegemonies in the Central Asian region, either politically or from the point of view of religion or languages and scripts (Henze, 1977). Iranian languages and religions were early cultural features in western Central Asia. Buddhism and the Brahmi script spread from the Indian subcontinent. Arab conquerors brought in Islam, which was to provide the dominant cultural pattern henceforth (Gross, 1992), as well as a new prestige language, Arabic, and its alphabet. Russians from the north, finally, seized control of the region enforcing a new political ideology and new linguistic habits (Lewis, 1972).

The long tradition of language contact and bilingualism in Central Asia, which was but a natural corollary of this course of historical events, gives us examples not only of long-term processes where bilingualism developed as a result of seemingly unforced migration and ethnic mixing, but also of planned comprehensive actions where bilingualism was enforced by means of a political program. Turkic-Iranian bilingualism, which will be surveyed below, has been present in Central Asia for several centuries and has to date developed without being directly affected by any language-planning program. In Soviet ideology, language was a prominent factor in the creation of a new political infrastructure in society, and the relationship between languages within one and the same socialist nation was something that had to be consciously managed. What the ultimate goal of Soviet language policy was remains a question to be answered: Was the costly investment program launched in the latter part of the Soviet era, for the purpose of giving Russian the status of "second mother tongue" among citizens with a native language other than Russian, an enterprise for the development of broad-scale societal bilingualism or merely a final desperate attempt to accomplish a complete language shift among these citizens?

New language-planning programs have developed since the disintegration of the Soviet Union. Official languages have been proclaimed for the first time in ex-Soviet Central Asian republics and the symbolic significance of language in post-independence work on state- and nation-building is a new experience for these republics. The introduction of a single official language in settings so much characterized by multilingualism and multiculturalism is a great challenge, demanding linguistic re-identification among many.

30.3.1   *Uzbek-Tajik bilingualism*

The most longstanding and comprehensive type of bilingualism in Central Asia is the one between Uzbek (Turkic) and Tajik (Iranian), stretching from the cities of Bukhara and Samarkand and their surroundings in the Zarafshan Valley through present-day northern Tajikistan to the Ferghana Valley. It is today primarily dialectal bilingualism occurring in speech situations where varieties of both languages may be present simultaneously with speakers having some command of each. It has so far been regarded as a stable bilingualism with little difference in functional status and prestige between the two languages. Code switching from one language to the other is facilitated by the presence of a common Islamic-Arabic stock of concepts and lexical items as well as similarities in sentence structures, which are typically SOV (Subject-Object-Verb; Greenberg, 1963) with the main predicate at the end of the clause or sentence (cf. Uzbek *Muallim shaharga keldi* [teacher town + dat. came] and Tajik *Muallim ba shahr omad* [teacher to town came], 'The teacher came to town,' where *muallim* is a word from Arabic and *shah(a)r* is Iranian).

Another area of Uzbek–Tajik co-existence is northern Afghanistan, although the Iranian idioms practiced by the Tajik population there are not Tajik but the closely related language Dari, and Pashto, the two official languages of Afghanistan. In a historical perspective, interference between languages has occurred in both directions, from Turkic to Iranian and vice versa. The causes can be attributed to both demographic and sociopolitical factors.

Turkic–Iranian co-existence in this region, which was formerly called, among other names, Western Turkestan, dates as far back as the first centuries of the Christian era. Before then this region was populated mainly by people speaking Eastern Iranian languages such as Soghdian, Khwarezmian, Khotan-Saka and Bactrian, at times intruded upon by languages of new invaders, for example

Greek under Alexander the Great and his Hellenic successors. Westward Turkic migration and the subsequent Arabic invasion at the end of the seventh century ended the use of these languages. With the spread of Islam, Arabic and the Western Iranian language New Persian were adopted for high-status administrative and cultural functions, mainly in urban environments. New Persian was later to diffuse into rural and peripheral areas, meeting not only related languages of the Eastern Iranian branch but also various Turkic dialects. Over the next few centuries, the Turkic population grew considerably both in numbers and political importance (Manz, 1992), and a new literary language, Chaghatay, was developed as a high-status Turkic language on a par with Arabic and New Persian. These three languages, under changing conditions, continued to be used side by side as literary languages in Central Asia until the first years of Soviet rule.

The decline of Arabic and eventually also Persian as literary languages in Central Asia was caused by the weakening of cultural ties with their respective homelands. Arabic remained an important religious language but had only a scanty population in Central Asia to support it. The establishment of Shia governance in Iran in the sixteenth century distanced this country from the Sunni environments in Central Asia. By contrast, the number of Turkic-speaking peoples in Central Asia constantly increased, while their literary language Chaghatay gradually replaced Persian in literature and administration.

It must be kept in mind, however, that Arabic and New Persian were for a very long time – even during the centuries of decline – prestigious languages exerting influence in Turkestan, in their capacity as old and highly esteemed languages. Even as late as the time of the Bolshevik takeover in 1917, both languages were part of school curricula in Turkestan, from the first grades of primary school (*maktab*) to the advanced stages of education at Muslim colleges (*madrasa*). Islamic vocabulary was transferred in great abundance into both the vernaculars and Chaghatay. Being the newcomer, and the language least applied as regards several cultural and bureaucratic functions, Chaghatay developed under the direct influence of the other two literary languages. Although most roots of Islamic terminology were Arabic, they were generally transferred through Persian and, consequently, often modified according to Persian phonetics and morphology before entering their Turkic target language. In the long run, Persian had a tremendous impact on the vowel system of Chaghatay and even more so on the most commonly spoken Turkic dialect, Uzbek, disrupting the palatal-velar distinction between vowels, which constitutes the very foundation of Turkic vowel harmony.

Normally, the small intellectual elite in pre-Soviet Turkestan was fully bilingual in Persian and Chaghatay (see Allworth, 1994, pp. 349–433). They read and composed literary texts in both languages, an effect of which was, besides the transfer of lexemes, a morphological as well as syntactic influence by one language upon the other. Most probably due to remaining differences in religio-cultural prestige, the direction of interference went from Iranian to Turkic rather than vice versa.

A syntactic pattern from Persian which is frequently found in Chaghatay texts and which meant a violation against the Turkic SOV pattern of modifier-head order (attribute-noun, possessor-possessed, object-verb, etc.) is the *ezafe*-construction with an ending (-*i* in the examples below) connecting the head noun with a following modifier noun or adjective (*namāz-i shām* [< Pers. prayer evening], 'evening prayer', *ahl-i faẓl* [< Arab. people wisdom], 'learned people', *shahvat-i nafsānī* [< Arab. lust carnal], 'carnal lust'). Another non-SOV Persian syntactic pattern in Chaghatay is a subordinate finite clause following the noun or predicate of the main sentence to which it belongs (examples from Eckmann, 1966, pp. 206–7: *sordum, kim qachan kelgüsi dur* [I-asked, *kim* when his-coming is], 'I asked when he would come', where the subordinate sentence is the direct object of the preceding verb; *dushman cherigi, kim Tash Arıghıda erdi, ol taqı ikki qol bolup* [enemy its-army, *kim* in-T.A. it-was that also two wing divided], 'the enemy's army, which was in Tash Arıghı, also became divided into two wings', where the subordinate clause is an attribute to the preceding head noun). This pattern can be found in still earlier Turkic languages and dialects from the eighth century onwards (Gabain, 1974, pp. 189–92). The subordinating particle *kim* (cf. Uzb. *kim* 'who?'), alternatively *ki*, as in present-day Uzbek (where it is normally added enclitically to the preceding predicate; cf. *bilamanki* [I-know-*ki*] in *Bilamanki, bu tŭghri emas*, 'I know that this is not correct'), is believed to be a loan translation calqued on a Persian *ke*, functioning among other things as an interrogative or relative 'who' (Grönbech, 1936, pp. 54ff, Erguvanlı, 1981).

Interference in the course of spoken-language contacts among mostly illiterate people in a larger range of society, on the other hand, usually went in the opposite direction, from Turkic to Iranian. Thus, besides religious vocabulary and certain learned terms, which somehow had found their way into the dialects, rich quantities of everyday words and expressions from Uzbek are found in Tajik dialects, while Tajik lexemes of this type are less common in Uzbek dialects.

According to Doerfer (1967), the northern Tajik dialects contain more than twelve times as many Uzbek words as the literary Tajik language. Turkic words have entered Tajik at different times, which can be concluded from their phonetic shape and semantic dimension, and mostly from eastern Uzbek dialects spoken in the vicinity of the northern belt of the Tajik language area. Besides the great abundance of terms relating to human beings, physically as well as socially (*kelin*, 'daughter-in-law, young woman', *ota*, 'father', *barmoq*, 'finger', *quloq*, 'ear', *iara*, 'wound', *qishloq*, 'settlement, village', *ti(l)moch*, 'interpreter'), there are words denoting natural phenomena (*iulduz*, 'star', *ilon*, 'snake', *timir*, 'iron') or general concepts, objects and artifacts (*qiliq*, 'act, conduct', *narsa*, 'thing', *iastuq*, 'pillow') as well as describing adjectives (*keksa*, 'old (person)', *qizil*, 'red') and local or temporal expressions (*ŭrta*, 'middle', *iil*, 'year'). Uzbek elements in Tajik verbs are also frequent, especially in the shape of a general Tajik verb, such as *kardan* 'make, do' or *shudan* 'become', preceded by an Uzbek complement (*qŭsh(i) kardan* [< Uzb. *qŭsh* 'pair'; cf. *qŭsh-*, 'add, unite'], 'unite'; *ailanib kardan* [< Uzb. *ailan-* 'turn (about)' + past. gerund *-ib*], 'stroll about') but also in derived verbs (*ichidan* [< Uzb. *ich-* 'drink' + Taj. derivational suffix *-idan*], '(to) drink').

In addition to lexical interference, the impact of Uzbek/Turkic grammar on Tajik dialects is extensive, as regards both morphemes and syntactic structures. Uzbek derivational suffixes, such as *-chi* for *nomina agentis* and *-lik* for denominal abstract nouns denoting state, function or occupation, are frequent and employed as more or less productive suffixes in Tajik (e.g. *pakhtachilik* [< Taj. *pakhta* 'cotton' + Uzb. *-chi* (for 'cotton picker') + Uzb. *-lik*, for the activity of a cotton picker], 'cotton picking/production'). A great many inflexional suffixes have also been borrowed into Tajik dialects from Uzbek, for example, local case suffixes (cf. Taj. *shahr-ga*, 'to the city', with the Uzbek dative ending *-ga* instead of standard Tajik *ba shahr*, with the Tajik preposition *ba*, 'to').

Another convincing example of strong Uzbek influence on Tajik noun phrase structures is the fact that possessive expressions patterned on Turkic genitive constructions are used in certain Tajik dialects (e.g. *dukhtar-a chashmon-ash* [girl-particle (< dir.obj. marker *-ro*) eyes-3.sg.poss.], 'the girl's eyes'; cf. Uzbek *qiz-ning kŭzlar-i* [girl-genitive eyes-3.sg.poss.], 'the girl's eyes'), almost to the exclusion of standard Tajik structures, where in accordance with the Iranian *ezafe* the two noun phrases of the possessive expression are connected in the reversed order (cf. *chashmoni dukhtar* [eyes-marker (*-i*) of *ezafe* girl], 'the eyes of the girl').

30.3.1.1 *The predictability of linguistic interference*

It may seem unproblematic and unprovocative to assert that the influence of one language upon another is to a considerable degree conditioned by its stronger demographic and/or sociopolitical status. The question as to what impact the structural features of languages can have on linguistic interference, on the other hand, has been the object of varying opinions among linguists (cf. surveys and comments in Eliasson and Jahr, 1997; Mühlhäusler, 1985; Romaine, 1995, pp. 23–77; and Thomason, 1986). In contrast to early works on language contact (e.g. Weinreich, 1970, first published in 1953), the general tendency in more recent works (e.g. Edwards, 1995; Thomason and Kaufman, 1988) has been to put still more emphasis on the importance of sociological or sociopolitical factors for contact-induced language change regardless of linguistic structures. In its most unrestricted interpretation this tendency would amount to a claim that, given the right sociopolitical conditions, there is no structural language feature strong enough to prevent linguistic interference (cf. Soper, 1987). Such a categorical statement does not, on the other hand, necessarily imply a complete denial of the capacity of structural features to facilitate or counterbalance linguistic interference, once it has occurred. The instances of Turkic–Iranian language contact referred to above can in fact be a case in point.

From what is known, Turkic languages were originally and have continued to be SOV languages in a very consistent manner, maintaining the order of modifier before head not only on the sentence or verb-phrase levels but also in noun phrases and postpositional phrases. As has already been partly exemplified above (subsection 30.3.1), adjectives and other nominal qualifiers precede their head noun (Uzb. *qara it*, 'black dog'), in genitive constructions the possessor is followed by the possessed (Uzb. *qizning iti*, '(the) girl's dog') and adpositions are not pre- but postposed (Uzb. *it uchun*, 'for the dog'). In this respect, the Turkic language involved in the case of language contact discussed here, Uzbek, is more consistently SOV than its Iranian counterpart, Tajik, which mixes SOV (e.g. sentence word order) and non-SOV parameters (e.g. *ezafe*-constructions; see subsection 30.3.1). The adoption of Turkic SOV-structures in Tajik, such as genitives and postpositional phrases could thus be regarded as a development towards greater typological consistency. By contrast, the emergence of postverbal subordinate sentences in Turkic languages, among others the former Chaghatay literary language (see examples above) and modern Uzbek dialects in northern Afghanistan (Jarring, 1938, and Reichl, 1983) would be an example of less typological consistency. The direction of interference has obviously been determined by sociolinguistic factors, such as language status or size. Now, what could be taken as evidence here for the relevance of structural coherence, or typological consistency, to the further development of linguistic interference is the fact that SOV-consistent Uzbek interference into Tajik has developed into a more or less productive mechanism, whereas subordination patterns violating SOV parameters in Turkic languages have never come close to replacing their originally Turkic, SOV-consistent counterparts but, on the contrary, have in most cases become more restricted and less frequent. (For more on interference, see chapter 6; for more on bilingualism and language change, see chapters 18, 26, 29, and 31.)

30.3.1.2   *Language and geopolitics*
The emphasis on sociopolitical factors in recent works on contact-induced linguistic change may be seen as typical of our age. With the present-day course of events heading towards greater formalization and regulation of intra- as well as interregional relations, political conditions can be expected to become still more crucial and decisive with regard to future language development (see for example articles in Maurais and Morris, 2001). Russian and Soviet colonization and subsequent state- and nation-building have been the primary factors shaping languages and linguistic interaction in present-day Central Asia.

The Soviet division of Turkestan into national republics in the 1920s and 1930s saved the greater part of Iranian dialects spoken in the region from being further dominated and influenced by Turkic dialects, first and foremost Uzbek. Language planners who in those years worked to create a Tajik standard language based on vernacular idioms, continuing the efforts of earlier Turkestani intellectuals (see subsection 30.3.2.1 below), tried to avoid varieties which had been strongly influenced by Turkic dialects. Some Turkic features entered the new Tajik literary language, for example verb serialization, where an infinite participial or gerundive verb carrying the main semantic content is followed by a finite verb which adds aspectual, modal or deictic features to the verb phrase (*khonda nishastan* [read (past ptcl.) sit], 'be reading', *khonda dodan*, [read (past ptcl.) give], 'read (to someone)'; cf. Cejpek, 1956; Rastorgueva, 1963, pp. 84–7; and Soper, 1987), whereas other features extensively used in northern Tajik dialects in areas bordering on Uzbekistan were excluded, for example the Turkic type of possessive constructions exemplified above (see *dukhtara chashmonash* in subsection 30.3.1).

The Iranian influence on the phonetics of many Uzbek dialects, particularly in urban environments, led to a considerable dilemma in the creation of a standard Uzbek language (Fierman, 1991, pp. 69–95). With the loss of vowel harmony, these so-called Iranized Uzbek dialects were regarded by most intellectuals engaged in the issue not to be representative enough of Uzbek as a Turkic language. An attempt was made at a new Latin orthography on the basis of northern Uzbek dialects, which were spoken far from Iranian language areas and in which vowel harmony had been retained. At the same time, Latin orthographies were worked out for Kazakh and Kyrgyz, where vowel harmony was the rule. As for Uzbek, however, the vowel harmonic dialects were marginal and atypical with regard to the branch of Turkic languages to which most Uzbek dialects belong. What was perhaps still more important, these idioms were not the most prestigious dialects of the language. A compromise was reached for a standard language based on a greater variety of dialects. Finally, in 1934, the Uzbek Latin alphabet was revised along the lines of speech habits for prestigious urban Iranized dialects, to the effect that vowel harmony could no longer be reflected in spelling. This orthographic pattern was maintained after the changeover to Cyrillic script in 1940. The most prominent Uzbek dialect was thereafter that of Tashkent, which had been the center of pre-Soviet Russian administration and which had become the capital of the newly established Socialist Republic of Uzbekistan in 1930.

With the emergence of state borders in the late 1980s and early 1990s to replace the former republican borders of the disintegrating Soviet Union, there appeared a still stronger line of demarcation through the Uzbek-Tajik linguistic area, separating varieties of the two languages spoken on one side of the border from those spoken on the other side. In view of the fact that more than one million people on either side of the border are reported to be of the same ethnicity as that of the titular population on the opposite side, Uzbek-Tajik bilingualism can be expected to constitute a prominent linguistic pattern in this region for the foreseeable future. On the other hand, new language policies in the respective states will most certainly change this situation. For Uzbekistan, where language reform is an active political undertaking at present – more so than in Tajikistan – the following comment was given in Schlyter (2001a):

> The conditions for Tajik-Uzbek bilingualism are gradually changing as a result of the requirement that inhabitants of Uzbekistan will have to show some proficiency

in standard Uzbek. At the Tajik departments at the universities of Samarkand and Buchara, for example, Tajik-speaking students studying Tajik are obliged to take a certain amount of standard Uzbek lessons during their university education. For most of these students this Uzbek language variety differs both in form and function from the Uzbek that they have hitherto used side-by-side with their Tajik dialect in their home language community. Consequently, a new status relationship between the two languages will develop for a great number of speakers changing the conditions for the interference of one language into the other and the choice of language for different speech situations. Moreover, although from the Tajik point of view the state-border separation of Tajik language communities from Uzbek ones may provide stronger protection against continued uzbekification on the Tajik side of the border, the new political reality may have a disruptive effect on Tajik speech and writing across this border.   (Schlyter, 2001a, pp. 188f, in its original English version)

30.3.2   *The russification of Central Asia*

The most widely spread type of bilingualism in present-day Central Asia, both in terms of territory and speakers, is that between Russian and other languages in the region. It appears in complex combinations of language varieties typically involving not just two but several varieties at standard as well as substandard language levels. Furthermore, it is not bilingualism characterized by an equilibrium between participating language varieties as far as both language status and language corpus are concerned. For more than a century, Russian in its standard literary form has had a hegemonic status in relation to fellow Central Asian languages, one concrete consequence of which is unidirectional interference from Russian into other languages.

30.3.2.1   *Pre-Soviet Russian penetration of Central Asia*

After centuries of contact through trade as well as diplomatic, religious, and military campaigns, Tsarist Russia finally commenced its political colonization of Turkestan in the 1860s (Allworth, 1994, pp. 131–223, and Soucek, 2001, pp. 177–208). Three small princely states existed in the region at this time: the Khanates of Kokand and Khiva and the Emirate of Bukhara. Tashkent, the main city of Kokand, was seized in 1865, and within the next decade all three states were brought under Russian control either completely (Kokand) or partially (Bukhara and Khiva, which were nominally Russian protectorates till 1920).

Central Asians of the late nineteenth century not only witnessed the beginning of a new political hegemony but also lived in a period of transition from an era characterized by ubiquitously accepted traditional and secluded cultural patterns to a period of intellectual unrest and search for new knowledge and ideals. With the efforts of local reformists ("jadids" < Arabic *jadid*, 'new') who found an opportunity to benefit from closer contacts with Russian culture and erudition, schools operating according to new methods (*usul-i jadid* < Arab. method new) and curricula were opened in Turkestan. The two main classical literary languages used so far by a very small elite of educated persons, Chaghatay and Persian (see subsection 30.3.1 above), were challenged by visions of establishing written standards more closely related to spoken idioms. The first modern newspapers and journals in Turkic vernaculars started to appear around 1870.

Parallel to these innovations, Russian-language schools and publications were introduced in the region, which marked the real starting-point for the diffusion of Russian in Central Asia. The terminological need of the languages used in reformist writing and education very soon brought them under the influence of Russian, which was after all the most modernized language near at hand. Hundreds of loanwords entered the Turkestani literary languages during the decades of Tsarist rule in Central Asia. A list of sociopolitical terms in Uzbek from the period of 1905–17 can be found in Borovkov (1940, pp. 58–103). Besides a great abundance of loanwords mediated through Russian (*eksport, imperializm, inastran* [< Ru. *inostranets*], 'foreigner', *arkestr, burakrat, patrul, partii´, prafessor, pratest/protest, tiramvai/tramvai, firm, kansert,* etc.), the list contains old words which already existed in the language but which had been provided with additional semantic content (e.g. *kochmanchi,* 'nomad', now also with the meaning of 'migrant') and derivations of such words or loanwords for new concepts (e.g. *sailavchi* [< Uzb. choose-*v* (nominalization suffix) -*chi* (agent)], 'voter', *zakunchi* [< Ru. *zakon,* 'law', + Uzb. -*chi* (agent)], 'lawyer') as well as a small number of calques (e.g. *kunlukchi* [< Uzb. *kun,* 'day' + -*luk* (nominalization suffix) + -*chi* (agent)] corresponding to Ru. *podenshchik,* 'day-laborer'). There was no official body regulating the expansion of Uzbek vocabulary in those days, and the lack of consistency in spelling and in the choice of words is apparent (cf. Akiner, 1997). This state of the language caused confusion and was subject to criticism and protest from Turkestani intellectuals. For the Tsarist regime and its representatives, by contrast, these aspects were no matter of immediate concern. Programs for expanded popular education in native tongues were developed. However, Russian was the official language of the Empire and russification was undisguised policy as far as both language (i.e. training in Russian) and religion were concerned (Blank, 1983).

Contacts between Russian and indigenous Turkestani languages amongst larger masses of people were still rather modest. The Russian urban-dwellers in the Tsarist Governorate-General of Turkestan were mostly administrators and bureaucrats living in their own quarters with little or no contact with any locals other than intellectuals. Russian migration to Central Asia for permanent settlement and work was not extensive. Most of the migrants were poor peasants in search of virgin land, who settled in rural areas and were linguistically assimilated to their Turkestani environment to a much greater extent than later Soviet newcomers would be.

The civilizational clash between the Turkestani reformist movement and Tsarist Russian administration became more and more apparent. The reformers strove for modernization within the framework of a cultural pattern that was too non-European, i.e. Muslim, and thus too alien for the Russians to tolerate.

Most of the reformist periodicals and a great many new-method schools were closed and reformists arrested or even killed, despised as they were by both conservative local rulers and the Tsarist regime.

30.3.2.2   *The promotion of Russian as a Soviet all-union language*

The influx of the different types of Russian-mediated terms mentioned and exemplified in the previous section continued after Soviet rule had been established in Central Asia. For the modern strands of life, new concepts and new habits were as a rule articulated by means of Russian loans, often also when there were native words and phrases that could have been used instead.

Even though this was nothing new but rather a further, intensified development of the previous Russian linguistic penetration of Central Asia during the Tsarist colonization of the region, language was, on the other hand, looked upon through new ideological spectacles after the establishment of Soviet power. The principle of equal rights for all comprised the right of access to information and knowledge, and nobody should be discriminated against with regard to his means of obtaining this. Consequently, according to this ideology, all languages were equally important and should not be hierarchized. No all-union state language or otherwise official language was ever proclaimed during the Soviet era.

The political ideals launched by the Bolsheviks concerning the equality of all social and ethnic classes, including languages and enlightenment, drew special attention to the need for improved literacy and paved the way for the development of native languages and the training of locals for political and administrative functions. A special Russian term was coined for the policy of promoting local capacities from among the indigenous nationalities: *korenizatsiia*, the literal meaning of which is 'rooting'. This marked a path towards enforced multilingualism of decisive importance for future language development in Central Asia and elsewhere in the Soviet Union, although new aspects of Soviet language policy would soon materialize to the disadvantage of the idea of linguistic diversity (Lewis, 1972). Dozens of new literary languages were established during the first decade of Soviet rule (Isayev, 1977; Pool, 1992), among others the Central Asian Turkic language Karakalpak in the would-be Autonomous Republic of Karakalpakistan. Of equal significance was the standardization of the other titular languages in Central Asia: Kazakh, Kyrgyz, Uzbek, Turkmen, and Tajik. These were local vernaculars which had just recently been provided with script systems of their own – modified Arabic alphabets. After the delimitation of Turkestan into union republics in the middle of the 1920s, they became so-called national languages in their respective republics with a special status as public, though not official, languages. They were promoted as school-media and publishing in these languages was encouraged. Within the first few years of their becoming national languages they were provided with new Latin alphabets, which event was regarded among other things as being a measure for the modernization or, as it was also put – "internationalization" – of these languages. Another aim was most probably to break with the Muslim past of Central Asia.

During this period, non-native, mostly Russian employees in the Central Asian republics were urged to learn the majority native language used at their place of work. However, due to strong negative attitudes openly demonstrated by Russian workers and the lack of efficient educational opportunities, this policy never showed any good results and seems to have quickly faded into oblivion (cf. Fierman, 1991, pp. 165–92). With a growing suspicion among central authorities that the encouragement of native culture meant too great a risk for "non-socialist" local patriotism, the very idea of *korenizatsiia* came to a dead end already in the first half of the 1930s. In spite of this early interruption, however, the different measures taken during the first decade of Soviet rule, not least in order to raise the level of literacy and the improvement of educational opportunities, helped to strengthen the command and status of native languages in the indigenous population of Central Asia.

One of the greatest Soviet achievements in Central Asia was the rapid growth of literacy rates and the expansion of educational programs. In a few decades after the October Revolution in 1917, literacy in Central Asia was raised from a very low standard of perhaps less than 5 percent to more than 50 percent of the population above 9 years of age (cf. table in Allworth, 1994, p. 376). As independent states in the 1990s all of the five Central Asian republics were reported to have literacy rates at levels higher than 95 percent. All states have 9–11 years of compulsory education, with around 90 percent of the school-age population enrolled (cf. data in *The Europa World Year Book 2001* and later issues). These values can be compared to those for neighboring Afghanistan, where the literacy rate is still far below 40 percent with a greater discrepancy between men and women in this respect. Corresponding figures for Pakistan and Iran are currently around 40 and 70 percent, respectively.

Another interesting detail from the point of view of language development in Central Asia is that ethnic-language maintenance among the titular people of the respective republics scored very high in censuses from the 1920s till the end of the Soviet era (more than 97 percent; cf. figures quoted and commented on in Crisp, 1991; Kirkwood, 1991; and Lewis, 1972, pp. 132–6). The reliability of these data has often been put in question. Nevertheless, although they cannot be interpreted as measures of factual proficiency of the languages concerned, the data do at least imply a positive assessment of one's ethnic language among Central Asians or a belief on the part of these people that command of one's ethnic language is something expected.

30.3.2.2.1 From lingua franca to national language
In the context of all-union Soviet administration and ideology, minority cultures and regional linguistic profiles were counterbalanced not only by the need for a lingua franca but also by ideas about the unity of the Soviet people. Both of these two factors had been matters of concern even during the first phase of Soviet language policy, where emphasis was put on multilingual

development among nationalities in the Union. However, with growing anxiety among communist party leaders and members of the central government in Moscow to obtain uniformity and centralized authority, they became political dogmas opposed to, if not incompatible with, the principle of the equality of all languages.

As a lingua franca for intercommunal communication in all parts of the Union, Russian was the natural choice for two obvious reasons. First, it was by far the largest language, spoken by more than half the population in the newly established Soviet state of the 1920s. By comparison, the speakers of Uzbek, which was the third- or fourth-largest language in the Union throughout the Soviet era, never exceeded 4 percent of the Union's population. Ukrainian remained the second-largest language with an amount of speakers constituting around one-fifth of the total population. The second reason why Russian qualified as an all-union lingua franca more strongly than any other language spoken in the country was the fact that at the beginning of Soviet rule, it was the most modernized language as regards technical, political, and economic terminology.

Language reform actions carried out in the latter part of the 1930s give evidence of the greater demand for general proficiency in Russian among the citizens of the Soviet Union, which was but a natural outcome of this policy. In March 1938 a decree was issued making Russian a compulsory school subject in all of the union republics. The mother tongue was still to be the language of primary school instruction, but Russian should be learnt by all children and was soon expected to be introduced at an early stage in primary education (Kreindler, 1982). In the same time period, in Central Asia, preparations were made for a changeover from the Latin alphabets of barely a decade to Cyrillic script. The new alphabets adopted for Central Asian literary languages contained all or nearly all letters from the Russian alphabet regardless of whether they were motivated by the phonological system of the individual language or not. Furthermore, the spelling of Russian loanwords was standardized by simply making the original Russian-Cyrillic orthography the norm. For example, Russian *komitet*, which as a word borrowed into Uzbek had earlier been written in Arabic script alternatively as *qomitə* or *kamitet* (Borovkov, 1940, pp. 92, 94) and in the Uzbek-Latin script of the 1930s as *qomƅta* (Gabain, 1945; where *ƅ* was used for velar *i*), was now made part of the Uzbek vocabulary in its Russian-Cyrillic spelling, *komitet*. With a growing knowledge of Russian among Central Asians, their pronunciation of Russian loans, sometimes with phonetic and phonotactic qualities unfamiliar to the recipient languages, has typically shown greater adjustment to a pronunciation of Russian loans in the respective languages according to the phonetic rules of Russian.

As for terminology in fields of professional specialization (politics, economy, technical matters, etc.), the principle was all-union conformity (Borovkov, 1934, p. 97; Lewis, 1972, pp. 172–3), which in actual practice meant a continuous, unrestricted influx of Russian vocabulary into other Soviet languages throughout the Soviet era. In post-independence Central Asian languages of the twenty-first century, a great part of this vocabulary will probably be retained (see subsection 30.3.3 below).

With the education reform laws of 1958–9, it was no longer compulsory to choose a native language as medium-of-instruction for a child in its first years of school. Since Russian was the unrivaled prestige language, which one would probably have to choose sooner or later for higher education or for better work possibilities, and also since Russian-medium schools were generally better equipped and better reputed, there was much motivation for parents to choose Russian for their children already in primary school.

Eventually, more emphasis was put on the status of Russian as an all-Soviet language than on its function as an interethnic, inter-republic, etc. lingua franca, and the language was given the epithet "second mother tongue" for people who did not have it as their first language. Already in 1952, the Soviet Turkologist Baskakov wrote: "the attitude of all the peoples of the USSR has changed towards Russian, which is now recognized by all of them as a second native language" (see in English translation Baskakov, 1960, p. 32). This statement was at that time definitely an exaggeration. However, by and by, as communist ideology faded, Russian was increasingly seen as a unifying symbol of Soviet culture. From the famous Stalin slogan about proletarian culture being "national in form, socialist in content" grew an imagined Soviet culture, Russian in form and content.

30.3.2.2.2   The aim of Soviet language policy: bilingualism or language shift?

Had it been carried through in its entirety, the idea of "second mother tongue" would have meant active bilingualism for 75–80 percent or even more of the population in Soviet Central Asia. This goal was never reached, although the idea as such remained part of Soviet political rhetoric till the very last years of the Union's existence.

Now, what mattered was not bilingualism, in fact, but universal knowledge of Russian. This becomes evident from the fact that for persons who already knew Russian but who lived in areas where the predominant or the titular language was not Russian, there was not as strong an urge to become fluent in a second language. The number of Russians in the ex-Soviet Central Asian republics, including Kazakhstan, is still around 8 million, which constitutes 15 percent of the total population in these republics. Their proficiency in local languages has always been very low. For example, less than 5 percent of about 1.3 million Russians living in Uzbekistan know Uzbek. In Kazakhstan, where the share of Russians was the highest in Central Asia in Soviet times (more than 40 percent at its highest), less than 1 percent of the republic's Russian population (in total 4.5 million) know Kazakh. Furthermore, for local non-Russians knowing Russian, there was no concern about proficiency in their own ethnic language. In the first years of independence, about one-third of the ethnic Kazakhs in Kazakhstan were believed to know Russian better than Kazakh, whereas nearly two-thirds of the same ethnic group had claimed fluency in Russian in the last Soviet census of 1989 (cf. figures in Eschment, 1998, and Fierman, 1998).

Soviet language policy could perhaps, at least ideally, be characterized as a long-term strategy aiming ultimately at official monolingualism (cf. Comrie, 1981, pp. 31–7). To talk about language shift for a majority of the population in this connection would not have been appropriate given the ideology of the equality of all languages. Therefore, language change would have to be phrased in another fashion. The following passage from Isayev (1977) is a good illustration of Soviet eloquence in this regard.

> the Russian language has become a means for exchanging experience in communist development, and for giving each nation access to cultural and other achievements of other nations, above all to the revolutionary traditions and rich cultural heritage of the Russian people, to the original versions of the immortal creations of Lenin, to the masterpieces of Russian literature, to the advance of science, and technology. Through Russian the Soviet nations become acquainted with events of world significance. Under such conditions the Russian language is fast becoming another native language, or second mother tongue for the majority of the Soviet peoples. The special role of the Russian language has made it one of the basic sources of further enrichment of national languages.   (Isayev, 1977, p. 300)

The Soviet nationalities and cultures were to be brought closer together within a mental framework of socialist internationalism. Their languages would also be brought together, not by being fused in the true sense of the word but by adopting from Russian the progressive terminology and means of expression constituting this framework. The same thoughts had been articulated in previous decades and continued to be for yet a few more years of Soviet rule (see for example Baskakov, 1960; Borovkov, 1934; and *Hozirgi ŭzbek adabii tili taraqqiiotida rus tilining roli*, 1983).

Russian influence on the indigenous languages of Soviet Central Asia was manifested not only through loanwords but also structurally (phonotactics, word-formation, word order, sentence embeddings etc.) and pragmatically (changes in the meaning of words, new modes of address, etc.). This was often brought about as a result of translation from Russian into the languages in question – a procedure that was explicitly stated to be an effective means for the improvement of these languages as Soviet languages (Borovkov, 1934, *Hozirgi ŭzbek adabii tili taraqqiiotida rus tilining roli*, 1983). There was among other things a great increase in calques on Russian (e.g. Uzb. *qurish maidoni* [construction (< Uzb.) square (< Arab.) + 3.sg.poss.], 'building site'; cf. Ru. *stroitel'naia ploshchadka*), including abbreviations, sometimes in a hybrid bilingual form and sometimes with a word order that was not typical of the particular language (e.g Uzb. *kinoiulduz* ['cinema' (< Ru.) + star], 'film star'; cf. Ru. *kinozvezda, markazkom* [central (abbrev. of Arab. *markazii*) + committee (abbrev. of Ru. *komitet*)], 'central committee'; cf. Ru. *tsentral'nyi komitet*, often abbreviated as *TsK, markaz besh* [center (< Arab.) five], with a non-typical head-modifier order (cf. 30.3.1 and 30.3.1.1 above) calqued on Ru. *Tsentr piat'*, 'Center [no.] 5', alternatively written in its Russian abbreviated form, *Ts-5*, and pronounced as if it were an Uzbek unit as [tsebeʃ]).

Up to the mid-1970s, Soviet rhetoric on language issues included the two terms *sblizhenie*, 'rapprochement', and *sliianie*, 'merging', which had also been used for other aspects of the relationship between nationalities. As far as both language corpus and language function are concerned, these two concepts can be associated in the former case (*sblizhenie*) with closeness between languages through overlapping vocabularies and complementarity in usage, and in the latter (*sliianie*) with the identification and finally replacement of one language by another.

If the aim of Soviet language policy really was *de facto*, and ultimately perhaps even *de jure*, official monolingualism, this could have been accomplished by means of varying combinations of *sblizhenie* and *sliianie*. On the state level, Russian could have been defined as an exclusively supra-nationality, or non-ethnic, official language, regardless of which option had been chosen at lower societal levels, where other languages either had been allowed to co-exist with Russian as public languages of Soviet communities (rapprochement) or had been functionally retarded, losing more and more of their capacity as media of communication (merging).

Such a strategy for language usage made sense, as long as the Soviet Union was an ideologically strong state defined in non-ethnic, supra-nationality terms and in distinction to local, ethnic levels. Lewis (1972) explains this distinction in terms of a dualism between "civic" (state) culture and "group" (personal or local) culture. The Russian language would have had two separate roles: official language at the state level and, at lower intra-state levels, the native language of the largest Soviet ethnic group. With the failure of communist ideology and socialism, Soviet civic culture became void of content and was replaced by nothing but group culture in a Russian disguise, raised from an ethnically pluralistic local level with a low degree of linguistic merging. This policy did not correspond to real-world cultural identities and was doomed to fail.

Russian language teaching was intensified in all of the Soviet Union during its last two decades of existence (Kirkwood, 1991; Kreindler, 1982). The number of school hours devoted to Russian was increased and a change of teaching methods was enforced, the emphasis now being on "communicative competence" and language usage in everyday situations rather than on grammar and translation. It was also expected, as had been announced at a conference on language teaching policy in Tashkent in 1975, that Russian would be introduced in pre-school kindergartens and the very first grade of primary school. A 10-year "model program" was worked out centrally for Russian-language instruction in secondary school with recurring themes, such as family, school, nature, health and sport, city life, the friendship of the peoples of the USSR, science and technology, theater and cinema, our motherland, the moral stature and humanism of the Soviet people, etc. (Kirkwood, 1991). A final major school reform was proposed in 1984 with, among other measures, extended training and retraining programs for Russian-language teachers, supposed to be carried out till the beginning of the 1990s.

Despite these efforts, there have been no strong indications of success as regards either the degree of usage of Russian among Central Asians in rural or urban environments or signs of reorientation in cultural affiliation or ethnic re-identification. Figures quoted in Crisp (1991) for reading and writing in Russian among Kazakhs, from a survey carried out in the early 1980s, are surprisingly low in comparison to the high percentage of Kazakhs claiming command of Russian (see above, this section). This discrepancy of values is most probably due to the fact that, when asked about language proficiency in Soviet censuses, people have in the first place reported on their comprehension of publicly spoken Russian (in radio and television programs, lectures, etc.) and their own ability to give an oral response in Russian in similar situations. (For more on language maintenance and shift, see chapters 14–16, 18, 25, 26, and 28.)

30.3.3   Language renewal processes in ex-Soviet Central Asia

Even though the Russian-language penetration of Central Asia may have been overestimated from the point of view of language usage at all levels of society and in all media of expression, its impact on official and public linguistic communication in Central Asia and its influence on the corpora of indigenous Central Asian languages has been immense, due to the mere fact that this language was for such a long time an unrivaled élite language in the region. Regardless of whether the large rural population has a good command of Russian or not and regardless of how much Central Asians in general use this language in private reading and writing, current post-Soviet language reforms in Central Asia are by necessity conducted in a linguistic context conditioned by Russian-language hegemony created and supported by previous Soviet language policy. The crucial matter of concern – whether explicitly stated or not – is the new status relationship between Russian, on the one hand, and the titular languages of the Central Asian republics, on the other (see for example Dave, 1996; Huskey, 1995; and Schlyter, 1997, 2001a).

The demise of the USSR also meant the demise of concepts such as Soviet language and Soviet people or nation (*sovetskii narod*), once intended to develop into a new cultural identity. After the dissolution of the Union on December 25, 1991, there were no longer any Soviet languages, and in the absence of a Soviet state, Russian lost its role as the supra-ethnic, all-union Soviet language. In Central Asia there were now instead a number of official languages proclaimed already in 1989–90 by the enactment of special state language laws. The recognition of Kazakh, Kyrgyz, Uzbek, Turkmen, and Tajik as official languages had great symbolic value for post-independence work on state- and nation-building in the Central Asian republics. These languages were to be the sole linguistic representatives of the newly born states in all types of official documents and declarations. Thereby they acquired, in addition to their position as ethnic or nationality languages, a new role as supra-ethnic state languages, in like fashion to the former status of Russian as a Soviet language.

The fate of Russian in Central Asia has changed radically. In the state language laws of 1989–90, which were almost exclusively language status laws regulating the public and official use of languages (Carlson, 1994; Schlyter, 2001a), Russian still held a strong position as the prime lingua franca between nationalities (Ru. *iazyk meshnatsional'nogo obshcheniia* 'language of cross-national relations'). What could not be denied, however, was that Russian had been downgraded from its position as an elite and *de facto* state language to more or less the status of a foreign language that not everyone was obliged to learn and that would definitely not be a source to draw upon in future reform work on state languages. This has become still more evident – at least in some of the republics – in activities connected with the implementation of language laws and, not least, in debates and decisions on corpus planning issues, which did not receive much attention in the original state language laws but which have been expected to be dealt with through additional laws and proposals. With the prevailing great proportions of Russians in Kazakhstan (35 percent) and Kyrgyzstan (20 percent), the status of Russian is a particularly sensitive issue in these republics. Through new constitutional provisions and laws in the latter part of the 1990s, the position of Russian has been strengthened and this language has been given the status of official language (*ofitsial'nyi iazyk*), at the same time as Kazakh and Kyrgyz remain the sole state languages (Ru. *gosudarstvennyi iazyk*) of their respective republics.

Present-day language policy in Central Asia is from this point of view an attempt at reversing or mitigating the effects of previous Soviet language policy. Russian interference as a result of translation, which was formerly deemed to be a good technique for rapprochement (*sblizhenie*) between Soviet languages (see 30.3.2.2.2 above), may now be criticized as an impoverishment of one's language. A great many Russian words have been abandoned, and there have at times been strong tendencies among the public to resuscitate an older vocabulary, either Arabic/Persian or elements from one's own language. For new modern-world concepts, particularly in the fields of technology and market economy, Western, mostly English, terminology is often preferred (e.g. *biznes, menezher, lizing*). Responsible linguists, on the other hand, have tried to slow down the pace and formulate general principles for a vocabulary reform. Russian words that are well integrated in the language in question or are intelligible at an international level seem in general to have a good chance to be retained (e.g. *gazeta* 'newspaper', *oblast'* 'province', *aeroport* 'airport'; for Uzbek vocabulary, see Schlyter, 1997, pp. 36–9).

The most comprehensive language corpus planning so far has occurred in Turkmenistan and Uzbekistan, both of which have introduced new Latin alphabets for their respective state languages. The work in Uzbekistan on implementing the 1993 and 1995 script laws, for example, marks a substantial break with the Soviet-Russian legacy. Uzbek schoolchildren no longer learn to read and write in Cyrillic. Neither is Russian a compulsory school subject any longer. For age groups already knowing the current Uzbek Cyrillic alphabet, which is still the most commonly used script in periodicals and books, a gradual transition to Latin script is envisioned. This process is to be completed by September 2005. A Latin alphabet modeled on the Uzbek one has also been introduced for Karakalpak in Karakalpakistan, which is an autonomous republic within the Uzbek state and which has been granted a certain degree of linguistic autonomy (Schlyter, forthcoming). The different versions of Latin alphabets proposed so far in ex-Soviet Central Asia are presented in Schlyter (2001a, pp. 201f). In the remaining republics – Kazakhstan, Kyrgyzstan and Tajikistan – the issue of revising or replacing current alphabets is a matter of concern, too, although no parliamentary laws have been passed yet to this effect.

30.4   Concluding Remarks

Linguistic diversity in Central Asia can be illustrated not only by the enumeration of languages but also by reference to the presence of several different language families, and to multilingual language behavior, where speakers typically alternate between two or more languages in one and the same speech situation. In numerical terms, Turkic languages dominate over other groups, such as Iranian and Slavic languages from among the Indo-European languages, other subgroups of the Altaic languages (Mongolian and Manchu-Tungusic languages), Chinese, etc.

Over the centuries, bilingualism and multiculturalism in this region have developed under continuously changing conditions resulting from both migration and coercive political campaigns. Language contact and interference between languages are thus characteristic phenomena for most parts of the region. With changing political hegemonies, language loyalties have varied considerably over time. In a historical perspective, different shades of diglossia can be identified in terms of status differences between languages as well as between varieties of one and the same language (for present-day Uzbekistan, cf. Schlyter 1997, pp. 17f). For several centuries, up until the early 1900s, when literacy could be noted for just a tiny share of the Central Asian population, the classical languages Persian and Chaghatay were used in the western parts of this region for court literature produced and consumed by a small intellectual élite educated in the traditional Muslim "madrasa" colleges. Another high-status language was Arabic, which was used primarily for religious rituals and scientific texts.

At the same time as Central Asian vernaculars were being attended to for the development of scripts and standard forms, Russian entered the region as a new high-status language towards the end of the nineteenth century. During the era of Soviet rule, this language became the privileged medium of communist ideology and state power, with an immense dominance over other languages of the Union. Proficiency in Russian remains a characteristic feature of generations trained in accordance with Soviet education systems. With the disintegration of the Soviet Union, the position of Russian in Central Asia was irreversibly changed from the status of privileged all-union, "national" language to that of a foreign language, eventually competing with other foreign languages at the international level.

As the titular languages of Central Asian republics are becoming state languages, yet another status hierarchy between languages is developing. Language renewal in this sense of the word means both enhanced proficiency in the state language among citizens and new sociopolitical associations triggered by this language variety. The standardized titular language of each republic, which was formerly sparsely used in public communication, rating only second to the more widely used interethnic Russian language, is now to become the official language of the nation-state and thus of concern to all citizens. This language variety will be on the school curriculum of every child, irrespective of his or her ethnic background and irrespective of what other varieties of either this language or other languages he or she speaks.

It will be a matter of future sociolinguistic research to assess how Central Asian non-official minority languages and non-standard dialects will be affected by the new state-language policies. These policies are now implemented in smaller nation-states with uniform school training in a standard official language – in contrast to the previous situation where the multilingual greater union allowed for more varied linguistic settings in individual republics, at the same time as a centralized all-union language policy was developed on the basis of a *de facto*, though not officially proclaimed, and for most Central Asians superethnic, state language. These aspects have so far been largely neglected. Besides general statements in current Central Asian language debate about the rights of any language to be used and developed, there are very few specific provisions for these languages. Many language minorities have lived in isolated rural communities, such as the small Arab populations, mainly in Uzbekistan (Jastrow, 1997; Schlyter, 2001b), and various minor Iranian populations in Tajikistan. Others are scattered populations, often with a low degree of language maintenance, like the strongly russified ex-Soviet Koreans (Haarmann, 1981; Hur, 1988). In the Soviet era they were largely ignored, if not denied, as ethnicities in their own right. Under present conditions, it is not certain that their situation will change for the better, at least as far as their ethnic languages are concerned. This time, with a state-language policy supervised by a central government present at a much shorter distance than before, these people may become more, rather than less, exposed to all-state political programs, such as language standardization and citizenship education, with consequent negative effects on their ethnic and linguistic identities. (For more on reversing language shift, see chapter 16.)

REFERENCES

Akiner, S. H. (1997). Survey of the lexical influence of Russian on Modern Uzbek (1870–1990). *The Slavonic and East European Review*, 75(1), 1–35.

Allworth, E. (ed.) (1994). *Central Asia: 130 Years of Russian Dominance: A Historical Overview* (3rd edn. of original work, *Central Asia: A Century of Russian Rule*, published in 1967). Durham, NC: Duke University Press.

Baker, C. and Jones, S. P. (1998). *Encyclopedia of Bilingualism and Bilingual Education*. Clevedon, UK: Multilingual Matters.

Baskakov, N. A. (1960). *The Turkic Languages of Central Asia: Problems of Planned Culture Contact* (transl. from Russian). Oxford: The Central Asian Research Centre and St. Antony's College Soviet Affairs Study Group (original work published 1952).

Blank, S. J. (1983). National education, church and state in Tsarist nationality policy: The Il'minskii system. *Canadian–American Slavic Studies*, 17(4), 466–86.

Borovkov, A. K. (1934). Uzbekskii literaturnyi iazyk. *Iazyk i mishlenie*, II, 73–97.

Borovkov, A. K. (1940). *Uzbekskii literaturnyi iazyk v period 1905–1917 gg.* Tashkent: Gosudarstvennoe uchebno-pedagogicheskoe izdatel'stvo UzSSR.

Carlson, Ch. F. (1994). Language reform movements in Central Asia. In I. Baldauf and M. Friederich (eds.), *Bamberger Zentralasienstudien: Konferenzakten ESCAS IV, Bamberg 8.–12. Oktober 1991*, pp. 133–51 (references excluded). Berlin: Klaus Schwarz.

Cejpek, J. (1956). Die verbale Periphrase als ein wichtiges Unterscheidungsmerkmal zwischen Neupersisch und Taǧikisch. *Archiv Orientální*, 24(2), pp. 171–82.

Comrie, B. (1981). *The Languages of the Soviet Union*. Cambridge, UK: Cambridge University Press.

Crisp, S. (1991). Census and sociology: Evaluating the language situation in Soviet Central Asia. In Sh. Akiner (ed.), *Cultural Change and Continuity in Central Asia*, pp. 84–123. London: Kegan Paul.

Dave, B. H. (1996). National revival in Kazakhstan: Language shift and identity change. *Post-Soviet Affairs*, 12(1), pp. 51–72.

Doerfer, G. (1967). *Türkische Lehnwörter im Tadschikischen*. Wiesbaden, Germany: Franz Steiner.

Eckmann, J. (1966). *Chagatay Manual* (Indiana University Publications, Uralic and Altaic Series, 60). Bloomington, IN: Mouton.

Edwards, J. (1995). *Multilingualism*. London: Penguin Books.

Eliasson, S. and Jahr, E. H. (eds.) (1997). *Language and its Ecology: Essays in Memory of Einar Haugen*. Berlin: Mouton de Gruyter.

Erguvanlı, E. (1981). A case of syntactic change: **ki** constructions in Turkish. *Boğaziçi Üniversitesi Dergisi*, vols. 8–9, pp. 111–39.

Eschment, B. (1998). *Hat Kasachstan ein "Russisches Problem"? Revision eines Katastrophenbildes*. Bundesinstitut für ostwissenschaftliche und internationale Studien. Sonderveröffentlichung [Special publication], February.

Fierman, W. (1991). *Language Planning and National Development: The Uzbek Experience*. Berlin: Mouton de Gruyter.

Fierman, W. (1998). Language and identity in Kazakhstan: Formulations in policy documents 1987–97. *Communist and Post-Communist Studies*, 31(2), 171–86.

Gabain, A. von (1945). *Özbekische Grammatik: Mit Bibliographie,*

Lesestücken und Wörterverzeichnis. Leipzig: Otto Harrassowitz.

Gabain, A. von (1974). *Alttürkische Grammatik*, 3rd edn. Wiesbaden, Germany: Otto Harrassowitz.

Greenberg, J. H. (1963). Some universals of grammar with particular reference to the order of meaningful elements. In J. H. Greenberg (ed.), *Universals of Language: Report of a Conference Held at Dobbs Erry, New York, April 13–15, 1961*, pp. 73–113. Cambridge, MA: MIT Press.

Grönbech, K. (1936). *Der türkische Sprachbau*. Copenhagen: Levin and Munksgaard.

Gross, J.-A. (ed.) (1992). *Muslims in Central Asia: Expressions of Identity and Change*. Durham, NC: Duke University Press.

Haarmann, H. (1981). *Aspekte der koreanisch-russischen Zweisprachigkeit: Studien zur Gruppenmehrsprachigkeit der Koreaner in der Sowjetunion*. Hamburg: Helmut Buske.

Henze, P. B. (1977). Politics and alphabets in Inner Asia. In J. A. Fishman (ed.), *Advances in the Creation and Revision of Writing Systems*, pp. 371–420. The Hague: Mouton.

Hozirgi ŭzbek adabii tili taraqqiiotida rus tilining roli [The role of Russian in the development of the present-day Uzbek literary language] (1983). Tashkent: Nizomii nomidagi Toshkent Davlat Pedagogika Instituti.

Hur, S.-Ch. (1988). Aspects of the linguistic assimilation of Soviet Koreans. In *Sullabu hakpo* [Slavic Journal], pp. 123–39. Seoul: Han'guk sullabu hakhoe.

Huskey, E. (1995). The politics of language in Kyrgyzstan. In Fierman, W. (ed.), *Implementing Language Laws: Perestroika and its Legacy in Five Republics*, special issue of *Nationalities Papers*, 23(3), 549–72.

Isayev, M. I. (1977). *National Languages in the USSR: Problems and Solutions* (trans. by Paul Medov). Moscow: Progress.

Jarring, G. (1938). *Uzbek Texts from Afghan Turkestan. With Glossary*. Lunds Universitets Årsskrift, 34(2). Lund, Sweden: C. W. K. Gleerup, and Leipzig, Germany: Otto Harrassowitz.

Jastrow, O. (1997). Wie arabisch ist Uzbekistan-Arabisch? In E. Wardine (ed.), *Built on Solid Rock: Studies in Honour of Professor Ebbe Egede Knudsen on the Occasion of his 65th Birthday April 11th 1997*, pp. 141–53. Oslo: Novus.

Kirkwood, J. M. (1991). Russian language teaching policy in Soviet Central Asia 1958–86. In Sh. Akiner (ed.), *Cultural Change and Continuity in Central Asia*, pp. 124–59. London: Kegan Paul.

Kreindler, I. (1982). The changing status of Russian in the Soviet Union. In I. Kreindler (ed.), *The Changing Status of Russian in the Soviet Union*, International Journal of the Sociology of Language, 33, 7–39.

Lewis, E. G. (1972). *Multilingualism in the Soviet Union: Aspects of Language Policy and its Implementation*. The Hague: Mouton.

Manz, B. F. (1992). The development and meaning of Chaghatay identity. In J.-A. Gross (ed.), *Muslims in Central Asia: Expressions of Identity and Change*, pp. 27–45.

Maurais, J. and Morris, M. A. (eds.) (2001). *Géostratégies des langues* (Terminogramme 99–100). Québec: Les Publications du Québec. (Also published in English by the same editors under the title of *Languages in a Globalising World*. New York: Cambridge University Press, 2003.)

Mühlhäusler, P. (1985). Patterns of contact, mixture, creation and nativization: Their contribution to a general theory of language. In Ch.-J. N. Bailey and R. Harris (eds.), *Developmental Mechanisms of Language*. Oxford: Pergamon Press.

Pool, J. (1992). Soviet language planning: Goals, results, options. In R. Denber (ed.), *The Soviet Nationality Reader: The Disintegration in Context*, pp. 331–52. Boulder, CO: Westview Press.

Rastorgueva, V. S. (1963). *A Short Sketch of Tajik Grammar, International Journal of American Linguistics*, 29(4), part 2; trans. from Russian. Bloomington, IN: Mouton.

Reichl, K. (1983). Syntactic interference in Afghan Uzbek. *Anthropos*, 78, 481–500.

Romaine, S. (1995). *Bilingualism*, 2nd edn. Oxford: Blackwell.

Schlyter, B. N. (1997). *Language Policy in Independent Uzbekistan* (FoCAS Working Paper 1). Stockholm: Forum for Central Asian Studies. (Later published under the title of "New language laws in Uzbekistan," *Language Problems and Language Planning*, 22(2), 1998, pp. 143–81.)

Schlyter, B. N. (2001a). L'évolution sociolinguistique dans les sociétés en mutation de l'Asie centrale. In J. Maurais and M. A. Morris (eds.), *Géostratégies des langues*, pp. 183–212. (Also published in English under the title of "Sociolinguistic changes in transformed Central Asian societies" in *Languages in a Globalising World* (2003); see Maurais and Morris.)

Schlyter, B. N. (2001b). Hos araber i Djejnov [A visit to the Arabs of Zheinov]. *Dragomanen*, 5, 8–13.

Schlyter, B. N. (forthcoming). The Karakalpaks and Other Language Minorities under Central Asian State Rule. In B. N. Schlyter (ed.), *Prospects for Democracy in Central Asia*. Stockholm: Swedish Research Institute in Istanbul.

Soper, J. D. (1987). *Loan Syntax in Turkic and Iranian: The Verb Systems of Tajik, Uzbek, and Qashqay*. Unpublished Ph.D. dissertation, UCLA.

Soucek, S. (2001). *A History of Inner Asia*. Cambridge, UK: Cambridge University Press.

Thomason, S. G. (1986). Contact-induced language change: Possibilities and probabilities. In N. Boretzky, W. Enninger, and Th. Stolz (eds.), *Beiträge zum 2. Essener Kolloquium über "Kreolsprachen und Sprachkontakte" vom 29. und 30. 11. 1985 an der Universität Essen*. Bochum, Germany: Studienverlag Dr. N. Brockmeyer.

Thomason, S. G. and Kaufman, T. (1988). *Language Contact, Creolization, and Genetic Linguistics*. Berkeley: University of California Press.

Weinreich, U. (1970). *Languages in Contact: Findings and Problems* (reprint of 1st edn., 1953). The Hague: Mouton.

FURTHER READING

In the following list of literature suggested for further reading, a wider sphere of Central Asia has been taken into consideration (cf. sections 30.1 and 30.2). Most of the works referred to focus on language development in present-day Central Asia. Besides these, a number of titles have been included for the sake of a culture-historical orientation. For discussions on bilingualism from a general theoretical point of view, the reader is asked to consult the preceding list of references and titles mentioned in other chapters of this book.

Allworth, E. (1964). *Uzbek Literary Politics*. The Hague: Mouton.

Anweiler, O. (1982). Russifizierung durch Unterricht: Fakten und Hypothesen. In I. Kreindler (ed.), *The Changing Status of Russian in the*

Soviet Union, *International Journal of the Sociology of Language*, 33, 41–51.

Baldauf, I. (1993). *Schriftreform und Schriftwechsel bei den muslimischen Russland- und Sowjettürken (1850–1937): Ein Symptom ideengeschichtlicher und kulturpolitischer Entwicklungen.* Budapest: Akadémiai Kiadó.

Bellér-Hann, I. (1991). Script changes in Xinjiang. In Sh. Akiner (ed.), *Cultural Change and Continuity in Central Asia*, pp. 71–83. London: Kegan Paul.

Bennigsen, A. and Lemercier-Quelquejay, Ch. (1964). *La presse et le mouvement national chez les Musulmans de Russie avant 1920.* Paris: Mouton.

Blank, S. (1988). The origins of Soviet language policy 1917–21. *Russian History*, 15(1), 71–92.

Bruun, O. and Odgaard, O. (eds.) (1996). *Mongolia in Transition: Old Patterns, New Challenges.* Richmond, Surrey: Curzon.

Campi, A. J. (1991). The rise of nationalism in the Mongolian People's Republic as reflected in language reform, religion, and the cult of Chingghis Khan. In *Bulletin: The IAMS News Information on Mongol Studies*, The International Association for Mongol Studies, 2(8), 3–15.

Carlisle, D. S. (1994). Soviet Uzbekistan: State and nation in historical perspective. In B. F. Manz (ed.), *Central Asia in Historical Perspective*, pp. 103–26. Boulder, CO: Westview Press.

Dah soli qonuni zabon [Ten years of language law] (1999). Komissiiai tatbiqi qonuni zaboni nazdi hukumati Dzumhurii Todzikiston. Dushanbe: Irfon.

Dave, Bh. (1996). Kazaks struggle to revive their "language of folklore." *Transition*, November 29, 23–5.

Devlet, N. (ed.) (1992). *Milletlerarası Çağdaş Türk Alfabeleri Sempozyumu* [International Symposium on Modern Turkic Alphabets], Marmara

Üniversitesi Yayınları No: 509. Istanbul: Türkiyat Araştırmaları Enstitüsü Yayınları.

Dittmer, K. (1972). *Die indischen Muslims und die Hindi-Urdu-Kontroverse in den United Provinces.* Wiesbaden, Germany: Otto Harrassowitz.

Ercilasun, A. B. (1995). Lâtin Alfabesi Konusunda Gelişmeler [Developments in the question concerning Latin alphabets]. *Türk Dili*, 523(II), 738–79.

Fierman, W. (1995). Independence and the declining priority of language law implementation in Uzbekistan. In Y. Ro'i (ed.), *Muslim Eurasia: Conflicting Legacies*, pp. 205–30.

Fierman, W. (1995). Problems of language law implementation in Uzbekistan. In W. Fierman (ed.), *Implementing Language Laws: Perestroika and its Legacy in Five Republics*, special issue of *Nationalities Papers*, 23(3), pp. 573–95.

Foltz, C. R. (1999). *Religions of the Silk Road: Overland Trade and Cultural Exchange from Antiquity to the Fifteenth Century.* London: Macmillan.

Gabain, A.-M. von (1979). *Einführung in die Zentralasienkunde.* Darmstadt, Germany: Wissenschaftliche Buchgesellschaft.

Gleason, G. (1997). *The Central Asian States: Discovering Independence.* Boulder, CO: Westview Press.

Haarmann, H. (1985). The impact of group bilingualism in the SU. In I. T. Kreindler (ed.), *Sociolinguistic Perspectives on Soviet National Languages: Their Past, Present and Future*, pp. 313–44. Berlin: Mouton de Gruyter.

Haarmann, H. (1995). Multilingualism and ideology: The historical experiment of Soviet language politics. *European Journal of Intercultural Studies*, 5(3), 6–17.

Kho, S. (1987). *Koreans in Soviet Central Asia* (Studia Orientalia, 61). Helsinki: Societas Orientalis Fennica.

Kirkwood, M. (ed.) (1989). *Language Planning in the Soviet Union*. London: Macmillan.

Kreindler, I. T. (1995). Soviet Muslims: Gains and losses as a result of Soviet language planning. In Y. Ro'I, *Muslim Eurasia: Conflicting Legacies*, pp. 187–203.

Krippes, K. A. (1994). Russian loan-words and orthography in the post-Soviet Turkic languages. *General Linguistics*, 34(2), 107–16.

Krippes, K. (1994). Russian code-switching in colloquial Uzbek, Kazakh and Kyrgyz. *General Linguistics*, 34(3–4), 139–44.

Landau, J. M. (1996). Language and ethnopolitics in the ex-Soviet Muslim republics. In Y. Suleiman (ed.), *Language and Identity in the Middle East and North Africa*, pp. 133–52). London: Curzon.

Lenker, M. (1991). The politics of language policy: A case study of Uzbekistan. In A. J. Rieber and A. Z. Rubinstein (eds.), *Perestroika at the Crossroads*, pp. 264–77. New York: M. E. Sharpe.

Lewis, G. (1983). Implementation of language planning in the Soviet Union. In J. Cobarrubias and J. A. Fishman (eds.), *Progress in Language Planning: International Perspectives*, pp. 309–26. The Hague: Mouton.

Lorenz, M. (1967). Postpositionen im Tağikischen, *Mitteilungen des Instituts für Orientforschung*, XIII, 382–93. Berlin: Akademie-Verlag.

Menges, K. (1946–9). Zum Özbekischen von Nord-Afghanistan. *Anthropos*, XLI–XLIV, 673–710.

Olcott, M. B. (1985). The politics of language reform in Kazakhstan. In I. T. Kreindler (ed.), *Sociolinguistic Perspectives on Soviet National Languages: Their Past, Present and Future*, pp. 183–204. Berlin: Mouton de Gruyter.

Oruzbaeva, B. O. (1994). Die kirgizische Sprache als Staatssprache unter neuen Voraussetzungen. In I. Baldauf and M. Friederich (eds.), *Bamberger Zentralasienstudien: Konferenzakten ESCAS IV, Bamberg 8.-12. Oktober 1991*, pp. 165–70. Berlin: Klaus Schwarz.

Pannier, B. (1996). A linguistic dilemma in Kyrgyzstan. *Transition*, November 29, 28–9.

Perry, J. R. (1979). Uzbek influence on Tajik syntax: The converb construction. In *Chicago Linguistic Society: Papers from the Conference on Non-Slavic Languages of the USSR*, pp. 448–61. Chicago: Chicago Linguistics Society.

Qiang, Y. (2000). *Bilingual Education, Cognitive Development and School Achievement: A Study of the Bilingual Programs for Tibetan Children*. Studies in Comparative and International Education, 53. Stockholm: Institute of International Education.

Rahman, T. (2001). The learning of Pashto in North India and Pakistan: An historical account. *Journal of Asian History*, 35(2), 158–87.

Ro'i, Y. (ed.) (1995). *Muslim Eurasia: Conflicting Legacies*. London: Frank Cass.

Rudelson, J. J. (1997). *Oasis Identities: Uyghur Nationalism Along China's Silk Road*, New York: Columbia University Press.

Schlyter, B. N. (2001). Language policies in present-day Central Asia. *MOST Journal on Multicultural Societies*, 3(2), http://www.unesco.org/most/vl3n2schlyter.htm.

Simşir, B. N. (1995). Türkmenistan'da Lâtin Alfabesine Geçiş Hazırlıkları [Preparations in Turkmenistan for a changeover to the Latin Alphabet]. *Türk Dili*, 518, 115–38.

Smith, G., Law, V., Wilson, A., Bohr, A., and Allworth, E. (1998). *Nation-building in the Post-Soviet Borderlands: The Politics of National Identities* (chapters 1, 4, 7, and 9 relate to Central Asia). Cambridge, UK: Cambridge University Press.

31 Bilingualism in the Middle East and North Africa: A Focus on the Arabic-Speaking World

JUDITH ROSENHOUSE AND MIRA GORAL

31.1 Introduction: The Linguistic Situation in the Middle East and North Africa

The region of the Middle East and North Africa is often viewed as one domain because most of its inhabitants speak Arabic (which is at present the sixth world language) or other Afro-Asiatic (particularly, Semitic) languages (see figure 31.1). Underneath this basically uniform language territory, however, there are many linguistic subgroups: various colloquial dialects of Arabic as well as other languages that reflect substrata languages that have survived in the area (e.g. Berber, Eastern Aramaic, Persian) or have been imported to it more recently (e.g. French, Hebrew). The main features of this general picture and the relations between and among these languages are the aspects discussed in this chapter. At present there are about 20 Arabic-speaking states in the area called the Middle East, and one state, Israel, where Hebrew is the official language and Arabic the second official language, spoken by the state's large minority of native speakers of Arabic (see figure 31.2). Arabic dialects are spoken also – as a second language or as the local vernacular in conjunction with the official state language – in several countries in sub-Saharan Africa, Inner Asia, and Southeast Asia. Arabic extends also to Europe, Australia, and America as the mother tongue of the numerous emigrants from the Middle East. The different Islamic ruling systems of the Middle East did not completely efface the local substrata and ad-strata languages over the centuries. Thus, in the North African states many speakers still speak Berber dialects, either monolingually or bilingually, and in the east, other languages, such as Northeastern Neo-Aramaic (in the area of Eastern Turkey or Anatolia, Northern Syria, and Northern Iraq), are used solely or in addition to Arabic (see

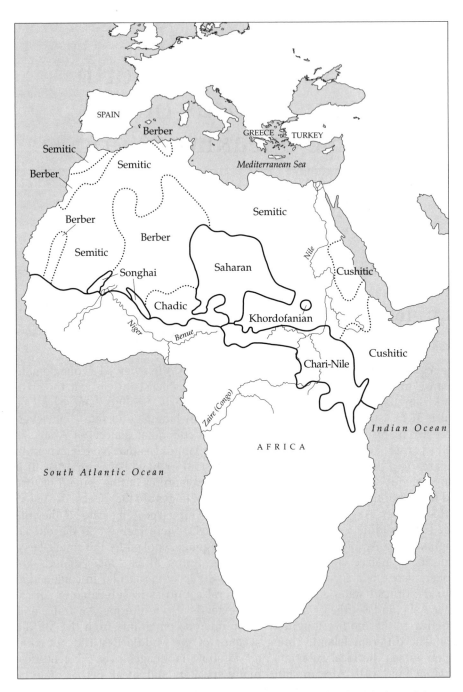

Figure 31.1 Africa, showing the language families of North Africa (adapted from Comrie, Matthews, and Polinsky 1996).

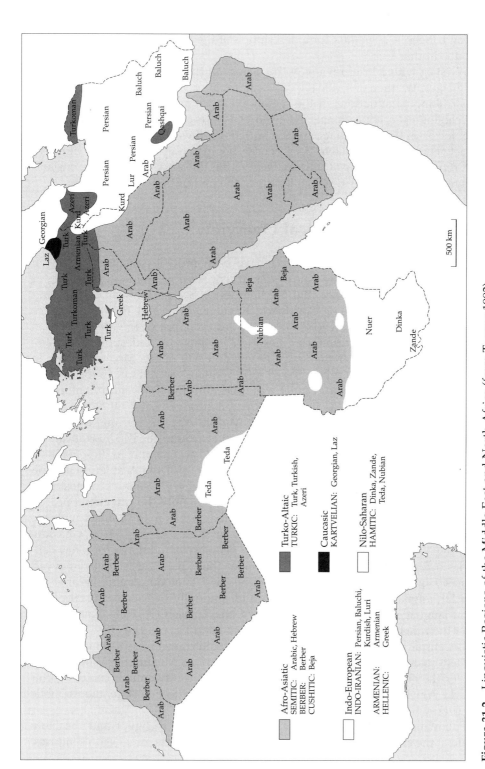

Figure 31.2 Linguistic Regions of the Middle East and North Africa (from Tapper 1992).

below). (See the appendix for a description of the various religious and ethnic groups in this area.)

We start with a brief review of the history of the region and a survey of its languages. We then describe the diglossic situation of the Arabic language and other bilingual situations in the region. Next we address sociolinguistic and psycholinguistic, educational, and political aspects of bilingualism in the region and focus on three language-contact situations, those of Egypt, Morocco, and Israel. These countries have been chosen because they reflect three different but representative cases of bilingualism within this area. Our conclusions and suggestions for further reading appear at the end of the chapter.

31.2   A Brief Historical Overview

The Middle East and North Africa have been much-frequented regions in human history. Even in the time of the ancient Semitic languages, speakers of different languages crossed the Mediterranean Sea and traversed the land around it on horseback or camelback, traveling from east to west and vice versa. The Phoenicians, who lived on the eastern coast of the Mediterranean Sea (roughly where present-day Lebanon is situated) and spoke a Semitic language, left their clear marks in the whole basin of the Mediterranean, in (archeological) material relics as well as in written inscriptions. In the Eastern Mediterranean, Phoenician (Punic) was used until the first century before the Christian era (BC), whereas in North Africa it survived until the fifth century AD. From several centuries BC until the Middle Ages in Europe, the Greek, Roman, and Byzantine empires ruled the lands around the Mediterranean (as well as other regions) and their languages spread accordingly to those territories. The Arabs' new religious movement broke out of the Arabian Peninsula in large waves of people from the middle of the seventh century, almost constantly clashing with the eastern Byzantine Empire until the latter disappeared from the stage. This was not the first time that Arabs made contact with the countries to the north of the Arabian Peninsula: the kingdoms of Hira, Ghassan, and the Nabateans, with Arabic-speaking peoples, were known for a few centuries before the beginning of Islam. Under the expanding Islamic Umayyad dynasty in the seventh to eighth centuries and later on, Arabic became the official language of the whole region and gradually overrode several of the local languages. In the sixteenth century, the Turkish Ottoman Empire took over the rule in the east of the Mediterranean and Egypt (as well as in Eastern and Central Europe), but the west of the Mediterranean basin remained disunited, mainly under the changing rules of various Muslim dynasties (partly under the authority of the Ottoman Empire). In the twentieth century (after World War I) the Ottoman Empire was diminished to one state, the Republic of Turkey.

Following Napoleon Bonaparte's military journey to Egypt and the Holy Land at the end of the eighteenth and the beginning of the nineteenth centuries, much of the area came to be under French influence. In addition to France, Britain, Germany, Italy, and Spain had many interests in North Africa and the major Middle Eastern countries throughout the eighteenth and nineteenth centuries. These economical and cultural interests were expressed both politically and militarily using different means and measures. British rule (protectorate) penetrated the Egyptian area officially in 1882 and extended after World War I to other countries. This period ended in the twentieth century, when the regions formerly under Ottoman rule (provinces or wilayets) and later under British and French Mandates (or protectorates) gradually attained their independence, in the modern sense of the word, often after lengthy struggles (e.g. Egypt 1922, Iraq 1932, Syria 1946, Lebanon 1947, The Hashemite Kingdom of Jordan 1948, Israel 1948, Libya 1951, Tunisia 1956, Morocco 1961, Algeria 1962).

In addition to these major historical events, several internal population migrations that took place in the region laid the foundations of present-day sedentary Arabic dialects. In North Africa there were two main such waves following the Muslims' major invasions of the Middle East in the seventh and eighth centuries. These groups are called the Pre-Hilalian and Hilalian migrations, after the Beni Hilal tribe, whose origin is in Nejd (Saudi Arabia) and who were expelled from Egypt westward in the eleventh century. In the Eastern area, there were similar migrations from the Arabian Peninsula of two (other) main waves of Bedouin tribes in the eleventh-twelfth centuries and in the thirteenth to fourteenth centuries. These movements yielded two main groups (with some subgroups) of Bedouin dialects in the Syro-Mesopotamian and North Arabian deserts: one in the "desert fringe" around the Syrian and north Arabian deserts, the other inside this area, i.e. within northern and central Arabia. The political capital of Islam moved with its religious, historical and cultural development during the centuries from the holiest places, the towns Mecca and Medina in the Arabian Peninsula, to Damascus in the Umayyad Khalifate and then to Baghdad in the Abbasid Khalifate (this city was founded in the middle of the eighth century). However, when the Mongols destroyed Baghdad in 1258, the Abbasid empire was already split into small kingdoms both in the east and in the west. (For example, the Umayyad dynasty in Spain since the end of the eighth century was gradually weakened until the Christians completed the "reconquest" of the Iberian Peninsula in 1492; there were also the Samanis in Persia and Transoxania, the Buwayhis in Western Persia, the Gaznawis in Afghanistan in the ninth to tenth centuries, the Fatimides in North Africa in the tenth century, the Muwahhidin in North Africa from 1147–1269, and later on the Mamluks in Egypt and Syro-Palestine in the thirteenth to sixteenth centuries, and others). Egypt, conquered quite early in the history of Islam (in the seventh century), was also a cultural center over the centuries for travelers who roamed the world from east to west and from north to south and vice versa. Thus Cairo, established near the older town Al-Fustat towards the end of the tenth century and capital of the Fatimides for two centuries, hosts the oldest university in the Islamic world (see figure 31.3).

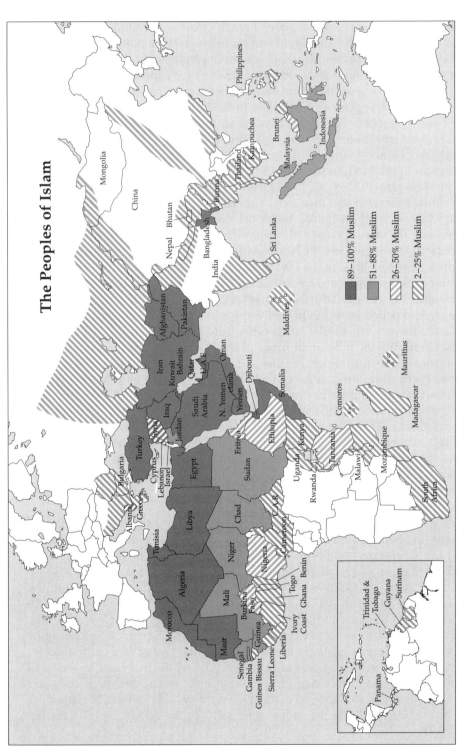

Figure 31.3 The peoples of Islam (from John L. Esposito, *Islam: The Straight Path*, 3rd edn., 1998, Oxford University Press. Used by permission of Oxford University Press, Inc.).

This social and cultural activity inevitably involved many linguistic contacts, sometimes leading to bilingualism. Heath (2002, p. 3), for example, writes that from the end of the seventh century, the Arabs conquered ex-Roman garrisons, such as Volubilis in Morocco, and took the Roman women as their wives or concubines. Their children apparently used a simplified Arabic dialect mixed with Late Latin substratum, which resulted in the first version of Western (Maghrebine) Arabic dialects. Such situations were not limited to North Africa, of course, since the Arab military camps spread out also to the north and east of the Arabian Peninsula. Another activity that attests to the intellectual inter-lingual contacts in the East in that period, mainly during the Abbasid Khalifate (since the eighth century), was a vast translation activity that developed mainly in Baghdad (in "Bait Al-Hikma" 'the house of wisdom'). The establishment of this institute in the first third of the ninth century followed a period of activity of individual translators, usually of Persian or Byzantine origin. Indian, Persian, Greek, Latin, and Egyptian manuscripts of all kinds of sciences and literature were translated there into Arabic, in which, later on, they were further developed. (For historical and literary reviews see, for example, Holes, 1995; Holt, Lambton, and Lewis, 1970; Lewis, 1960, 1973.) These major historical, political and social changes, among others, made their mark on the development and use of Arabic and other languages in the Middle East, creating an intriguing bilingual/multilingual situation in this area.

Today, Arabic is a majority language in the region (in speaker numbers) and the official language in most of the states along the shores of the Mediterranean Sea and in the Arabian Peninsula. In Israel it is a minority language, however, and in the fringe countries its status competes with other local (usually African or Central Asian) languages. An important aspect of bilingualism in the area relates to the feature of prestige or cultural status of Arabic. Due to the Islamic Holy Scriptures and the rest of the Classical Literary Arabic heritage written in it, (literary) Arabic is considered prestigious and the language of culture. In North Africa and Lebanon, however, French has been considered from the nineteenth century the main language of culture, although speakers' attitudes to it are ambivalent.

The history of the Arabic-speaking world has resulted in numerous instances of language contact between substrate languages and Arabic and, in recent centuries, between Arabic and colonial languages. Before we turn to conventional types of bilingualism that have resulted from these situations, we address the situation of diglossia in Arabic, which, we argue, operates for most Arabic speakers as a form of bilingualism.

31.3 Diglossia as Bilingualism

Diglossia refers to a situation of a community (or an individual) having mastery over and use of two forms of a language (or of two languages). Diglossia here denotes the co-existence of colloquial Arabic (CA) and literary Arabic

(LA, or Modern Standard Arabic, MSA). Though diglossia is known also elsewhere, it is associated with the Arabic language in particular (Ferguson, 1959a). This situation was first called "diglossia" by K. Krumbacher in 1902 for Greek, and later by W. Marçais (1930/1961), but Ferguson's paper (1959a), and his comparing Arabic diglossia with similar cases in non-Arabic languages, has made it a general topic of debate (e.g. Fishman, 2002; Hudson, 1999). Ferguson described a "literary" or "high" variety of Arabic, used mainly in specific formal circumstances and contexts, such as reading sacred and secular literature, official written forms, delivering formal lectures and spoken addresses, and written and spoken news bulletins. The modern "high" variety is descended from classical LA, which has evolved to some extent over the ages, and is now also named Modern Standard Arabic (MSA). MSA is practically no one's mother tongue, and good proficiency in MSA requires more than elementary education. In contrast with the high language, there exists a "low" variety, the colloquial language (CA), in its different vernaculars. CA is in fact the speakers' mother tongue, which children learn spontaneously from their caregivers. As such, it is used for the more personal and daily communication needs. The Classical Literary language, called "al-lugha al-fusha:" (the eloquent language) was and still is, however, the ideal of speakers of Arabic, whereas the "low" level (called "al-lugha al-'a:mmiyya," the common language, in Arabic), which is not written, has usually been frowned upon by the literate elite.

This dichotomy in Arabic, with "high" and "low" varieties, existed even before the beginning of Islam. Over the centuries, the structure of Arabic changed, particularly after the first Islamic conquests as Arabic interacted with other languages, but the dichotomy has remained. Theories vary as to the origins of this split; we support the view that claims that LA existed side by side with CA, and that LA was used by the educated elite more or less for communication among members of different dialects (e.g. Blau, 1977; Versteegh, 1984).

The differences between CA and MSA/LA pertain to all the domains of language structure, i.e. phonology, morphology, syntax, semantics and vocabulary, and language use. Moreover, the "high" and "low" varieties are associated with different functions and extra-linguistic circumstances. CA is used on informal occasions, such as spontaneous speech for daily conversations, as well as folkloristic narratives, poetry, etc. For such goals it has different "artistic styles" (see Palva, 1992, for example). Although the colloquial variety is mainly spoken, and is thus in opposition to the "high" variety, it is sometimes used in written form, too, as witnessed in caricatures, plays and literary prose which aim to imitate "real life" dialogs, as well as in personal letters.

It should be noted that the term CA refers to a large number of different mutually unintelligible varieties, often due to geographical distance or social detachment. While many Arabic speakers are able to communicate in more than one of the CA varieties, these varieties may be very different from each other. Indeed, the different CA varieties can be defined on the basis of a number of viewpoints. The first one is geographical, i.e. dividing the dialects into Eastern and Western ones (Barkat, 2000; Fischer and Jastrow, 1980; Kaye and Rosenhouse, 1997). Egypt is the meeting point between these two areas, where features of both dialect types can be found (e.g. Behnstedt and Woidich, 1987; Woidich, 1997). This classification was clearly described already at the beginning of the twentieth century (e.g. Brockelmann, 1908, 1913).

The second major aspect is based on the social division of Bedouins vs. sedentary populations described as early as the fourteenth century by Ibn Khaldoun (1958). The sedentary dialects are also classified into urban and rural dialects. Even at present, often after long periods of living side by side, Bedouin, rural, and urban dialects are distinct in most regions. Interestingly, the native speakers of each dialect distinguish between them and keep up their social affiliations (e.g. Cadora, 1992; Rosenhouse, 1984). This is true despite the fact that in the middle of the twentieth century, Bedouin roaming has been limited almost everywhere and they have often been forced to settle down in certain fixed locations. Due to internal population movements from villages to towns, traditional and new urban dialects have been formed in many of them, bringing about new mixed varieties of dialects (named *urbain* and *citadin* in French, in an attempt to distinguish between the new and traditional dialects).

A third type of classification refers to the different religious communities in the area. Most of the native speakers of Arabic are Muslims, but many others are Christians or Jewish. In addition, there are the Druze and 'Alawis (mainly in Syria and Lebanon) and several other sects that have grown out of Islamic Sunni and Shi'ite sects and their sub-sects. Blanc's book (1964) was a seminal work in this field describing degrees of differentiation among such linguistic groups (see also Piamenta, 2000).

Additional classifications that should be considered include gender, age, and education. Recent literature has demonstrated linguistic differences between male and female speech even within one dialect (Abu Haidar, 1988; Arebi, 1994; Rosenhouse, 1998). As in many other languages, speakers' speech depends also on their age. Basically, the "older" generation preserves the older or more traditional features, whereas the younger speakers, who grow up in educationally, socially, and politically different conditions, present features that are often closer to a major local dialect and/or to MSA. Education, i.e. literacy, tends to modify native speakers' speech habits and the two ends of the scale (High vs. Low Arabic) fill up with numerous variants (e.g. Amara, 1995; Amara and Spolsky, 2001; Spolsky, 1986; Talmoudi, 1984).

Arabic diglossia, however, has proved to be less straightforward than described in Ferguson (1959a), and he himself revised some of his views on it (Ferguson, 1991). In the twentieth century, even less-educated people have increasingly come in contact with MSA. Various lexical elements and several syntactic structures have penetrated their spoken language, and they appear especially when speakers wish to impress listeners. Thus, in the space between the two extremes of the continuum (LA–CA), a "middle language" (which is rather a speech style or register than a full language) has developed informally and spontaneously. Indeed, the linguistic status of Arabic is now viewed rather as a system with a gradually changing scale of features from the most authentic colloquial to the highest literary Arabic. Several models and approaches have been proposed for the description of this situation in the literature (Al-Toma, 1969; Badawi, 1973; Blau, 1977; Cadora, 1992; Diem, 1974; Kaye, 1994; Versteegh, 1984). Among these models, the Arabic term "al-lugha al-wusta" ('the Middle Language') has been used to indicate the increasing mixing of MSA and CA (see Lamrani, 2000; Meiseles, 1979; Mejdell, 2000).

Despite the influence of MSA and CA on each other, they remain two distinct varieties, and educated native speakers of Arabic know both LA and a CA dialect. Fishman (1967) distinguished between diglossia as a sociolinguistic phenomenon and bilingualism, which is a psycholinguistic phenomenon, but this classification is not accepted universally. Fishman also distinguished situations of diglossia with and without bilingualism (see also Fasold, 1984). Al-Falay (1996) defined diglossia as a linguistic behavior using a higher linguistic form (which can be language, dialect, or style) on more formal occasions, and a lower linguistic form for informal communication (Al-Falay, 1996, p. 164). However, he, too, distinguished between diglossia (as defined above) and bilingualism, which is the individual's knowledge of more than one language or dialect or style. It is our view that diglossia (at the individual level) can be considered a basic case of bilingualism. Evidence for this approach can be found not only in aspects of acquisition manner, use, and norms (as described by Al-Falay, 1996), but also of psycholinguistic and linguistic considerations (for further details see Rosenhouse, 1989, 2001). In contrast, native speakers of Arabic usually consider only the "eloquent" Literary Arabic (al-lugha al-fusha:) as "the Arabic language," whereas colloquial or vernacular varieties are considered "not Arabic" or a degraded form of the language. This attitude still prevails throughout the Arabic-speaking countries, and their educational systems emphasize the use of MSA in the classroom not only in reading and writing, but also as an ideal for daily speech. In practice, however, CA (or at least the Middle Language) is used in most spoken interactions as well as in writing, even by adults who are proficient in both CA and LA. Many speakers mix CA and LA, usually unintentionally but also sometimes intentionally, for convenience reasons (e.g. Belnap and Bishop, 2000; Rosenbaum, 2000). Viewing both CA and LA as one system may justify studying bilingualism in this region as reflected in Arabic plus another language (see below), rather than considering such a case as trilingualism or multilingualism (see Edwards, 1994). Indeed, it is likely that diglossia of CA and LA rarely exists without the interference of any other (non-Arabic) language. Such a situation would require literate speakers living in places that are completely isolated from other Arabic dialects and from speakers of foreign languages. This "absolute" situation is not very frequent nowadays, we believe, because mass communication media such as the radio and TV are found now in almost all urban and rural areas and because physical transfer between dialect communities is much easier (and more common) than in the past. (For more on diglossia, see chapters 15 and 28.)

31.4   Conventional Bilingualism

A survey of this region shows that in many of the dialect and language areas in the Middle East, language communities are at least bilingual and often trilingual and multilingual, depending on the specific community. "Conventional" bilingualism in the area includes the following settings: (1) Arabic as the dominant language plus another language, (2) Arabic as a secondary or minority language where another language is dominant, and (3) Arabic as one of many languages of a state (in this case the situation in the state is that of multilingualism rather than bilingualism).

In the first setting, bilingualism of Arabic (MSA and CA) as the main language combined with one of the following languages exists in these communities: Kurdish is used in Iraq and in some parts of Northeastern Syria and Turkey. Eastern Syrian (Neo-Aramaic) is also used in some parts of Turkey, Syria, and Iraq. Berber is used in North Africa (Morocco, Algeria, Tunisia, and Libya). French is used in North Africa (Morocco, Tunisia, and Algeria) and Lebanon.

In the countries that use French as a second language (e.g. Morocco, Algeria, Tunisia and Lebanon), French has the prestige of a "culture language." This status competes with the local colloquial Arabic dialects and with MSA in the literate population. French still holds a very strong position in these countries, although there is a strong movement to "Arabicize" them, especially in Algeria, at the expense of French. Speakers of Arabic in these countries not only study French language, literature and culture at school, but also use it combined with the local colloquial Arabic dialect in abundant code mixing/switching (e.g. Youssi, 2001).

In the second setting, Arabic (MSA and CA) is a secondary language where another language is (or other languages are) official and dominant: This situation is found in Israel, where Hebrew has been the main official language and the language of the majority since the establishment of the state in 1948 and Arabic is also an official language, spoken as a first language by a large minority (see below). Somewhat similarly, Turkish is the official and dominant language in Turkey; however, the use of CA in the Southeastern regions of Turkey is not encouraged and even rather suppressed by the government. This situation is somewhat in contrast with the fact that Muslim Turkey was previously the Muslims' Ottoman Empire, in which the Arabic alphabet was used for writing Turkish until Ata Turk's revolution in the twentieth century.

In the third setting, the fringe area of the Arabic-speaking world, other languages have affected the development of Arabic as well as its present usage. For example, a few centuries ago, Arabic penetrated several more central countries in Africa, such as Mali, Chad, Sudan, and much earlier Ethiopia. In these regions, it has also been influenced by the adjacent African languages. This situation has produced unique Arabic dialects, for example Juba Arabic and Beja Arabic in Southern Sudan (Blanc, 1975; Roth-Lally, 1969; Vanhauve, 2002), or Nigerian Arabic (e.g. Owens, 1993). Africa is known for the widespread multilingualism of its many peoples; Arabic is one of these languages that the Muslims may use. Islands of Arabic dialects (e.g. in Bukhara, Qashqa-Darya, Dushanbe, Balkh and a few other smaller places) also exist in Central Asia (Uzbekistan, Afghanistan, Kazakhstan, Northwestern Iran), which have absorbed the influence of local Central Asian languages such as Tajik, Uzbek, and Turkic (e.g. Chikovani, 2000; Fischer, 1961; Tsereteli, 1941; Vinnikov, 1962). The speakers of Arabic in the Central Asian islands usually use it at home, while speaking the local official language(s), i.e. Uzbeki, Afghani, and/ or Russian (since the regime of the Soviet Union) in public. Because they are Muslims, the men at least are also required to be able to read the Koran.

Maltese also belongs in this category. Though Arabic-based in its linguistic structure, it has absorbed many elements – primarily lexical – from other languages, mainly from the nearby Italian and the ex-rulers' English (who governed it from the beginning of the nineteenth century). Even as a fully independent state (since 1964), Maltese co-exists in Malta with English, which is the second official language of the state. Today, English is more influential than Italian, also due to its present status as the world's lingua franca. Some Maltese schools educate students in English (e.g. British nuns' schools, schools for the higher socioeconomic class) and English is often used for teaching in the higher education institutes. English is also used as the home language in many Maltese families (not only the high socioeconomic classes) who know that English is important (see Ellul, 1978). These groups use, however, a special Maltese-English variety. Thus considering at least part of the Maltese population as bilingual may be justified. Italian is used in Malta more passively. The Maltese people absorb it mainly from numerous Italian radio and television channels, and in addition, many people can still speak it from the period of World War II, when Italy fought there with Germany against Britain and the Allies. The situation in Libya and Ethiopia should also be mentioned. Italian had some influence on the local languages in these countries during some part of the twentieth century (1911–43 in Libya, and a few years of military struggles in Ethiopia in the 1930s). From this episode mainly lexical items have penetrated the local languages, Arabic or Berber in Libya, and Amharic or other African or Semitic languages in Ethiopia.

31.5 Sociolinguistic and Psycholinguistic Aspects

The phenomenon of speakers of different languages who intermingle, have contacts and affect each other linguistically (and culturally) is not new to linguistics. Such contacts lead to various linguistic processes such as koine, leveling, code switching and borrowing (e.g. for Arabic, Bentahila and Davies, 1983; Ferguson, 1959a, b), as well as, in the long run, to the creation of pidgin and creole languages all over the world. Koine, for example, named after the linguistic situation in Ancient Greece, reflects the results of mixtures of speakers of different dialects. It describes the situation in the old Arabian Peninsula, where members of different Arab tribes met for marketing and various cultural purposes (Fück, 1950). This phenomenon, which exists also at present, involves using those linguistic features that are common to interlocutors of several dialects. At the same time, features of leveling may also take place. Leveling refers to speakers' use of avoidance strategies, e.g. not using dialect-specific features that their interlocutors might not understand or avoiding dialect-specific features in order not to be considered "provincial" in using features of a non-prestige dialect. Both Koine and leveling are frequent characteristics of interdialectal speech among speakers of Arabic (e.g. Blanc, 1960; Ferguson, 1959b). (For more on code mixing and code switching, see chapters 1–4, 10–14, 25, 26, 28, and 29.)

Another strategy used in such meetings is "semi-mutual understanding," when speakers use their own dialect without accommodating to their interlocutor(s), relying on common features of the different dialects. These strategies are known also for other languages and are not limited to speakers of Arabic; for Arabic, however, their use can be considered another aspect of the linguistic continuum described above for Literary and Colloquial Arabic.

Other processes that may change the varieties in contact are, for example, interlanguage and language standardization (e.g. Ferguson, 1991; Woidich, 1997). Woidich (1997) discusses dialect contact and inter-dialect forms in Egyptian Arabic. He analyzes the case of the B'eri dialect in Upper Egypt and argues for the role of dialect contact and inter-dialect forms in understanding the characteristics of dialect systems and their features. In addition, speakers may mix the two varieties within the discourse situation as in code switching and borrowing. Koplewitz (1989), for example, studies aspects of code switching and assesses the integration of Hebrew lexemes in spoken Arabic in Israel. He discusses the different criteria for determining integration (morphological adaptation, semantic modification, translatability, frequency of use, awareness of borrowing, and child speech), and shows the different degrees of integration, from code switching of the borrowing type to complete integration of the Hebrew word in the Arabic vocabulary.

These features have been viewed as sociolinguistic or psycholinguistic, depending on the required perspective: in studying the speech of individuals, the psycholinguistic aspect is examined, whereas studying the speech patterns of groups of speakers is the focus of sociolinguistics. Indeed, different linguistic characteristics are addressed in each of these study types (cf., Amara, 1995; Blanc, 1960; Koplewitz, 1989, 1992; Talmoudi, 1984). (For more on bilingualism and language change, see chapters 18, 26, 29, and 30.)

31.6 Educational Aspects

Arabic diglossia has a major effect on the education of native speakers of Arabic (Koplewitz, 1992; Spolsky and Shohamy, 1999; Suleiman, 1999). We recall that the mother tongue of native speakers of Arabic is normally the colloquial dialect of their near environment, i.e. the caretakers' dialects. Only at school (sometimes earlier, in kindergartens) do the children begin studying the literary language, when they learn to read and write. Because MSA is actually a related but different language system, this learning process requires much effort and it takes several years (probably to the end of high school) until the student can be considered proficient in MSA. Frayha (1955) was among the first to refer to the difficulty diglossia places on the Arab student. He tells of his son who complained in the third grade, bursting into tears, that he could not express his thoughts clearly in the literary language and could not answer the questions fluently, although he was a good student and very fluent in CA. In effect, the education system has ignored the fact that LA/ MSA is a different system from CA and therefore almost a completely second language for the student. Even at present, after nearly a century of attention and debates devoted to this subject in the literature, teaching methods do not always differ from those used at the beginning of the twentieth century (Rosenhouse and Shehade, 1986). Students' problems are more severe in places where literacy is still limited (this is usually in rural areas and in certain low socioeconomic populations, which involve fewer of the modernization devices that are used elsewhere to enrich the students' linguistic development).

Furthermore, the Arabic dialects vary in the degree to which they differ from Literary Arabic. Generally, the Eastern dialects are more akin to the MSA (or to Classical LA) than are the Western dialects. This follows from the deeper changes that have taken place in the Western dialects. These include vowel deletion, vowel merging, and different word-stress patterns, decrease of certain morphological distinctions, such as the merging of plural masculine and feminine pronouns and verb inflections to common forms, syntactic structures, such as the analytical construct structures, and many lexical and semantic elements which are not cognate to Eastern lexical elements. Bedouin dialects also have their own peculiarities, which differ between the East and the West (Rosenhouse, 1984) but are somewhat closer to Classical Arabic than most of the sedentary dialects, due to their conservative nature. In general, these linguistic features also differ from their parallels in LA, either Classical or Modern. In those places where school systems are well developed, MSA affects speakers' colloquial dialect, and the resulting "interlanguage," "middle language," or "educated language" further complicates its structure and description. The effect of MSA on colloquial speech has been pointed out in many studies of dialects both in the East and the West of this region. These effects are stronger for relatively young and educated speakers (and often for women more than men) than for older and less educated speakers because the latter tend to retain their traditional speech habits (e.g. Abu Haidar, 1988; Al-Khateeb, 1988; Haeri, 1996; Kaye, 1994; Meiseles, 1979; Sadiqi, 1995; Suleiman, 1985). At the same time, the colloquial dialects affect other features of MSA (Belnap and Bishop, 2000; Meiseles, 1979; Mitchell, 1986; Rosenbaum, 2000; Youssi, 2001). This mutual influence continues to grow, due to the increased use of mass media (TV, radio, journals) almost everywhere. An added difficulty is that within this great variety of dialects, there is no single norm or "standard" pattern which speakers can adopt as their MSA or national dialect.

Educational factors also affect the interaction of Arabic and other languages. In Israel, due to the general structure of the state, native speakers of Arabic study Hebrew as a second language from the third grade on. They may, in addition, have contacts with its speakers before and after the school period, especially if they live in mixed towns or otherwise interact with Hebrew speakers. The knowledge of Hebrew affects especially adult native speakers who work with Hebrew speakers, deal with Israeli official authorities, study at the universities, etc. Thus much code switching and code mixing occur in the speech of many native speakers of Arabic in Israel, which may lead to educational problems (Koplewitz, 1973). A similar situation is found in Morocco, where French is the second language of most Arabic speakers. In spite of the Arabization movement there, with MSA as the state language rather than French (or colloquial Moroccan Arabic), French is still considered the language of high culture. Much literature is published in it, and natives of Morocco not only speak it well but also constantly code-switch with it, mixing it with their colloquial Arabic dialects.

Almost the same degree of bilingual use characterizes the Christian population in Lebanon, which is often educated in schools established as early as two and a half centuries ago by Christian missionaries from France. A recent example of this situation can be found in plays by the Lebanese playwright Yahya Jaber who uses different CA dialects, MSA, French, and English in intentional code switching in his works. El-Tibi's (2002) emphasis on the cultural and international benefits of francophony for the Arabic world as well as the rest of the world is an example of the role of French in Lebanon and North Africa. However, due to nationalistic (political) reasons, the Muslim population in Lebanon and Syria does not seem to have been as affected by French as the Christian population even before the end of the French Mandate rule of these countries in the 1940s.

In spite of the status of French in the region, the Arabic dialect of Cairo is the most prestigious and thus most influential in Egypt, as well as in much of the entire Arabic-speaking world (though it is not a norm anywhere except for Cairo). This is due to Cairo's status as the largest Arabic cultural center of the mass media, the film industry and literature. Consequently, certain features of this dialect affect not only other Egyptian dialects but also dialects of other countries. Literacy in Egypt today still does not encompass all its population, but schooling does reach larger proportions of students than in the past. Thus MSA in Egypt seems to be an important source of linguistic change of its CA – mainly in "modern" fields of the vocabulary and less so in grammar.

French and Turkish were fashionable in the social elite's discourse in Cairo in the nineteenth century. But in the twentieth century, under the British Mandate rule and mainly after World War II, English became a strong source of cultural and linguistic influence and has left its marks on Arabic there. In addition to being studied as a second language, English is used in higher education in several universities or in certain departments in other universities. Thus the main source of conventional bilingualism in Egypt today is, if any, English. A similar situation is found in Jordan and Iraq, which were both under British Mandate rule until they got their independence in the 1930s. Also Saudi Arabia and the other Gulf States have been (and still are) mainly under British and American influence, so that English is now the source of foreign-language influence on their colloquial dialects (Holes, 2000). This influence is expressed mainly in terms of modern vocabulary objects of consumption, work tools, motorcars etc. The North African states (except for Libya) were under French rule as its colonies, and after winning their independence they have been trying to Arabicize themselves. As for Libya, although it was under Italian rule in the first half of the twentieth century, since it got its independence English has been a major source of influence there. However, as its rule is a strict Islamic one since Gadhafi's coming to power, English is not allowed to interfere with the Arabic-oriented education.

A stronghold for MSA in three Arab countries – Egypt, Iraq, and Syria – is the Arabic Language Academy in each of them (following the parallel institution in France). The function of these institutions is language planning, i.e. to research and guard the language as well as innovate or coin new words and terms necessary for communication in modern times. (This is true also for Hebrew in Israel, see, for example, Blau, 1981; Shrayboym-Shivtiel, 1993.) As in certain other countries where language academies exist, here also the linguistic activity is very academic and does not really solve real-life problems. Though the academies publish dictionaries as well as some linguistic journals and their meetings' protocols, these publications largely remain in libraries and not many of their innovations are accepted for daily use. Moreover, the fact that there is an academy in each of three different countries prevents lexical unification of terminology (although attempts towards that have been made) and it is impossible for language users in one country to understand many terms of the others (see Shrayboym-Shivtiel, 1993). As in other languages, then, often the foreign word (nowadays mainly from English) prevails in colloquial speech, and sometimes even in MSA, while the newly coined Arabic expression remains in the shadows or is completely forgotten.

31.7 Political Aspects

Different countries in this region have had to accommodate different languages due to different historical processes and events. "Fringe" areas, where Arabic is used in addition to local languages, include, as mentioned, African countries south of the North African states, Libya and Egypt, and isolated villages in Central Asian countries such as Northwestern Iran, Uzbekistan, Afghanistan, and Pakistan. Because Islam extends these limits in Asia and Africa, and because many Muslim migrants are now living in Europe, the Americas and Australia, it could be argued that bilingual contacts of Arabic exist also beyond the Mediterranean basin. Here, however, we will briefly review only the major forces operating in our region of interest.

The North African states have complex relations with the French language, due to the fact that they used to be French colonies. Education in French is therefore undermined there, especially since the second half of the twentieth century, and more so in Algeria than in Morocco or Tunis. The history of Egypt involves complex relations with France and Britain. Napoleon's cultural delegation opened Egypt to Western culture, as many Egyptian writers have noted. During the second half of the nineteenth century, cultural delegations and individual scholars were sent to France for further education in order to bring back the new skills that were required to modernize Egypt. Thus, the effect of French culture in the nineteenth century was very strong. However, towards the end of the nineteenth century, the British became influential in Egypt and Sudan (cf. the Mahdi's uprising) and supported the king's rule in the first quarter of the twentieth century. The Egyptians' struggle for independence eventually led to the overthrow and expulsion of the king as well as the end of the British rule. Nevertheless, the effect of the English language (rather than French) increased gradually during the twentieth century, and mainly after the end of the "Russian period" of the Egyptian President Nasser in the 1960s, due to growing American influence in the region and the increasing status of English as the world language. In Lebanon and Syria, the effect of French missionaries and education began in the eighteenth century. In fact, this area was in advance of Egypt and the rest of the Middle East with its larger number of schools, the first newspapers, and book publishing. However, due to the bad economic situation many of the Syrian and Lebanese cultural elite migrated to Egypt in the second half of the nineteenth century and enhanced its cultural development.

Politically, after World War I and the defeat of the Ottoman Empire, Syria and Lebanon came under French Mandate rule, whereas Palestine, Jordan and Iraq were under the British Mandate. As in Egypt, the Syrians and Lebanese did not agree to remain under this foreign rule for long, and struggled for their independence, which they achieved in the 1940s. Syria has had its period of support from the USSR (in the 1950s–1960s). This apparently kept English influence away, as in Egypt at the time. Indeed, a number of academicians and social elite from Syria, Egypt, and other Arab states were educated in the USSR or other Eastern European countries, and thus knew Russian. (The present Syrian president, however, had already been educated in England.) Lebanon, in contrast, has kept its relationship with France, probably because of its large Christian population and due to the fact that many Lebanese and Syrians also migrated to France in the twentieth century.

In Iraq, the effect of English on Arabic and on higher education began after Iraq had come under the British Mandate, at the end of World War I. Even at the end of the twentieth century, English was the second language in schools there and foreign affairs were conducted in English rather than in French. Jordan has almost the same attitude to English. It has kept the warm relations with Britain all along, probably due to military and other help it received from the United Kingdom. (For example, British military forces trained the Jordanian Legion, and the king and other members of his family were educated in British institutions.) Thus even now English can be considered the main second (foreign) language in Jordan.

As for Israel, before it was established in 1948, it had been under the British Mandate, since Lord C. O. Wingate at the head of the British army defeated the Ottoman Empire there in 1917. In 1948, native speakers of Arabic who remained in the country (as well as Jewish immigrants from numerous countries) had to adjust to a new official state language, Hebrew. The Jewish population had used Hebrew actively in the country for more than half a century previously and Arabs who had interacted with them had learned it informally. Today, native speakers of Arabic in Israel learn MSA Arabic at their schools, and Arabic dominates their life. But as Hebrew is the dominant language of the country as well as the first official one, they also study Hebrew at school (see below).

In the fringe area of the African territory, in addition to Arabic, mainly Cushitic substratum languages are used. French (in the West African states) and English (in the East African states) were the languages of the colonizing powers of the nineteenth and twentieth centuries and have often therefore remained the prestige languages. In many cases they have been selected to be the local official and cultural languages, because the conflicts of the speakers of the numerous local African languages and dialects prevent the possibility of any of them becoming the state's central language. In the Central Asian region, on the other hand, Russian (of the former USSR) and various Turkic languages are the main linguistic powers with which Arabic has had to contend during the centuries. These influences (or interference sources, from the viewpoint of Arabic speakers) have naturally affected the surviving Arabic dialects in various manners. Some literature describes these Arabic dialects, but much is still unknown about the current linguistic structure of these fringe areas in general and the status of Arabic in them in particular.

31.8   Examples of Bilingualism in the Area: The Cases of Egypt, Morocco, and Israel

In this section we deal in some detail with three locations, each representing a different bilingual situation. The first is Egypt, where bilingualism beyond the Arabic diglossia is limited to borrowing and code mixing. The second is Morocco, where almost all the population is bilingual (in the conventional sense), using Arabic or Berber, and French. The third is Israel, where a large proportion of the Arabic-speaking population speaks Hebrew, the official language, as their second language.

31.8.1 Egypt

As already mentioned, Arabic has been the primary language of Egypt since its Islamic conquest in the eighth century. At that time Greek and Coptic were also in use, but they disappeared within a short time. Coptic is still the prayer language for the Copts in Egypt, but it is not a living language. During the eighteenth to twentieth centuries, in addition to the contacts between Egypt and the Ottoman Empire (until it ceased to exist as an empire), European influence in Egypt was strong, due to economic, cultural and military interests (on both sides). Official missions were sent to study (mainly) in France in the second half of the nineteenth century. These people brought back European culture to Egypt and opened new schools for engineering, agriculture, economics, translation, etc. This sort of activity did not usually leave them speaking French in their daily life in Egypt, however. Among the famous literary writers and cultural leaders of Egypt in the nineteenth and twentieth centuries who studied in France are Al-Tahtawi, Qasim Amin, Muhammad Husain Haykal, Taha Husain, and Tawfiq Al-Hakim. Mostly, however, European literature was quickly translated, literally, into Arabic or modified and adapted to it (mainly when some of their cultural features did not agree with the Arab taste). This new translation movement contributed to the development of MSA from a fossil Classical language of the Middle Ages into a modern, vibrant, and flexible living language. At the beginning of the twentieth century, the Egyptian socio-economic elite used Turkish and French words in their speech and probably code-switched between these two languages. Thus, Egyptian CA now includes many borrowings, mainly from Turkish, French, and English. Other borrowings include words from Persian, dating back to the period of Classical Arabic; from Greek, from even earlier periods; and from Spanish and Italian, from the periods when their peoples were strong and rich seafarers in the Mediterranean basin. Several examples of borrowings are given in table 31.1.

None of these languages, however, has apparently had a long-lasting influence on the Arabic language structure beyond lexical borrowing – except perhaps the present influence of (American) English on Egyptian CA as well as MSA. This influence has been shown even in the written literature from the end of the nineteenth century and much more so in later literary works including plays and novels (e.g. Rosenbaum, 2000, 2000–2002). In such texts, phrases and whole sentences, not only single words, can appear in English, representing code-switching phenomena. One of the roles of the Egyptian Academy of the Arabic language, within the domain of language planning, is to help the development of the language by coining modern terminology based on classical Arabic roots, which will adapt the language to modern communication needs (Madkur, 1967; Shrayboym-Shivtiel, 1993). As in other communities with language academies, the Academy objects (in articles appearing in its journal) to foreign linguistic influence. It cannot stop this borrowing process, however, because the lexical needs – due to the fast cultural developments – are never-ending. Thus both borrowing and code switching exist in Egypt, mainly in Cairo but also in other towns and places where the inhabitants' literacy rate is sufficiently high.

Table 31.1 Examples of lexical borrowings from several languages in Egyptian Arabic (from Mitchell, 1962).

Turkish	Italian	French	English
ha:nim 'Madam'	gawanti 'gloves'	gurna:l 'journal'	ga:s 'petrol'
usta:z 'Sir, Mr.'	garafitta 'tie'	mersi 'thanks'	lubistar 'lobster'
xawa:ga 'Sir, Mr. – non-Arab'	gambari 'prawns'	djaketta < French/English 'jacket'	gine:h 'guinea, 1 pound'
ba:sha 'pacha'	ringa < European: Italian, Spanish . . . 'herring'	?ami:s 'shirt'	shilin 'shilling, 5 pence'
shi:sh kaba:b 'meat grilled on a spit'	rosto 'roast meat'	dira:ma 'drama'	ratl 'pound, rotl'
gumruk 'customs'	lukanda 'hotel'	bufee(h) 'refreshment room'	kabtin 'captain'
kutubxa:na 'library'	sbita:r 'hospital' (or from French)	sintira:l '(tel.) exchange'	wabu:r 'engine' (or from French)
'o:da 'room'	busta 'post, mail'	garso:n 'waiter'	ba:r 'bar' (like pub)
gazma 'shoes'		mayo: 'ladies' bathing suit'	goon 'goal, football'
bo:yagi 'shoe-shiner'			juki 'jockey'
			duktuur 'doctor'

31.8.2 Morocco

The Moroccan population has been classified into three groups. The first comprises speakers of the Pre-Hilalian Northern sedentary Arabic dialects (Moroccan Arabic). In the south of the country there is a mix of Saharan and pre-Saharan Arabic dialects, which are of a later date than the Pre-Hilalian Bedouin dialects and relate to the Ma'qil Bedouins who migrated to Morocco (from the Arabian Peninsula via Egypt) and to the Hassaniya Bedouin (mainly in Mauritania). They are therefore often called Hilalian dialects. The central-type dialects are the "real" Hilalian ones, i.e. dialects originating in the Bedouin tribe Beni Hilal, who wandered to Morocco from the Arabian Peninsula via Egypt, arriving there as early as the eleventh century. These are the Hilalian dialects excluding the Ma'qil; their speakers were Muslims. In addition, there are three Muslim groups of partly nomadic Berbers, classified according to their native languages in three different geographical areas in Morocco. One theory as to the contact between "original Arabs" and Berbers presents the thesis that Moroccan Arabic and Berber form a "linguistic union." Jews make up the third large ethnic group of the population, although many migrated to Israel soon after its establishment in the mid-twentieth century. They are native speakers of Moroccan Judeo-Arabic, which is based on an old (pre-Hilalian) Arabic dialect, and the dialects that were brought over to Morocco with the Jews who were expelled from Spain at the end of the fifteenth century.

France has influenced the region in general since the late eighteenth century and Morocco in particular when it became a French colony; but commercial and cultural contacts with France continued also after Morocco won its independence in 1956. The language of culture, economics, diplomacy, and government in almost all of Morocco continues to be French, and most of the educated speakers (at least) speak it in addition to the local (Arabic or Berber) dialect. It has been claimed that school education assures that students are bilingual in MSA and French (Chami, 1987). The fact that French remained dominant in Morocco but not in Egypt is likely due to the deep involvement of France in its colonization efforts. These included the use of French in the education system as well as enhanced immigration of a large number of French citizens to Morocco. In Egypt, France never really had military holding. (Generally, the British colonization of Egypt and Sudan affected these countries less than France affected North Africa, although both the French and English languages left their linguistic marks on the local vernaculars, as noted above.) Because of these contacts with France, many people emigrated from Morocco to France in the twentieth century and settled there. Many Moroccan immigrants are found also in other European countries, such as the Netherlands, Germany, the Scandinavian countries, and Britain. This large immigrant group is bilingual, using its native dialect and French, or other host languages, and has been subject to many linguistic studies of bilingualism and code switching. In the northern part of Morocco (the Rif) there are still several places (Ceuta, Melila) under Spanish authority, where Spanish, rather than French, continues to be used as the second language. Consequently, because of these longstanding contacts with Spain over the past centuries, words of Spanish origin also abound in certain Moroccan Arabic dialects.

Adult Arabic diglossia (expressed in the use of CA and MSA) is demonstrated very clearly in the use of Arabic in courtrooms, where the participants (litigants, plaintiffs, suspects, witnesses) use the colloquial variety in speaking, but the judge "translates" everything to a "high" formal MSA style in dictating the protocols. Such a process often involves distorting the facts implied in the oral discourse and may lead to miscarriage of justice (Lamrani, 2000, 2002), as also discussed in Morris (1993) for courtroom translation between other languages. Studies of Moroccan dialects also refer to "secret languages" in special social groups, such as Jews who do not want to be understood by Muslim listeners (Chetrit, 1994) or Muslim clergy who do not want to be understood by the lay-people (Berjaoui, 1993), as well as "play speech" (Heath, 1989), which involves changing word forms by inserting various phonemes or syllables in them or by reversing the order of their root consonants.

In recent years, many studies have focused on linguistic and sociolinguistic studies of Arabic and bilingualism in Morocco (e.g. Bos, 1997; Boumans, 1998; Caubet, 1993, 1998; Chetrit, 1980). Code switching and borrowing, two typical features of bilingual situations anywhere in the world, are also found in Morocco, and ample examples and descriptions of the processes involved can be found. The donor languages to CA are mainly Berber, French, Spanish, and Literary Arabic. They also include foreign words that have penetrated French from (American) English. Consider the following examples from Heath (1987): /villa/ 'villa,' /ruppa/ < repas 'meal,' /bubbuya, puppiya/ < poupée, 'doll,' /tran/ < Fr. train, Sp. tren, 'train,' /local/ < Fr. locale, 'premises, site,' /džob/ < 'job,' /džin/ 'pair of jeans,' /kaš/ < 'cash (payment).'

31.8.3 Israel

Arabic in Israel has a status that only partly resembles the case of Arabic in Morocco or other Arabic-speaking countries. The main difference is that the official language in Israel is Hebrew and Arabic is the second official language. This status is expressed in the use of Arabic in, for example, official documents, identity cards, and road signs. It should be noted that since Israel absorbs many Jewish immigrants with numerous mother tongues, many languages are spoken in the state, including local and other Arabic dialects, and thus bilingualism is almost the natural state of every person in the country (see, for example, Spolsky and Shohamy, 1999). We focus here on Arabic, however, because of its position in the whole region and as the topic of this chapter.

Arabic is the mother tongue as well as the language of teaching for the native Arabic-speaking minority, the biggest minority in Israel. Native speakers of Arabic study Hebrew at school from the third grade on and classes include also Jewish history, Hebrew literature, and sections of the Bible (the Old Testament). For most of the Arabic speakers who grow up in the Israeli educational system this means they are biliterate in Hebrew and Modern Standard Arabic. Moreover, Arabic-speakers who speak Hebrew can be quite proficient in Hebrew as they often interact with Hebrew speakers, whether native or not, on informal as well as formal occasions. As in many other countries, many Arab workers from rural areas moved in the twentieth century for employment opportunities to ethnically mixed towns. Bedouins also settled down in certain fixed areas in the north (Galilee) and south (Negev) of the country, acquiring rural life habits, and subsequently some of them moved to work and live in towns. Thus, phenomena of koineization and leveling (Rosenhouse, 1984) as well as mixed language and bilingualism (mainly with Hebrew) have been on the increase (Amara and Spolsky; 1986, Koplewitz, 1989).

In the Arabic sector, students' achievement in Hebrew spans a wide range and many indicators show that, generally, their Hebrew proficiency is not as good as their L1 (e.g. Rosenhouse, Kishon-Rabin, and Shabtay, in preparation; Shehadeh, 1997). Still, there are exceptions and several Arab writers and poets write in Hebrew or translate Arabic literature into Hebrew and vice versa (see Amit-Kochavi, 1999; Snir, 2001). Recent studies of Arab students' attitudes to learning Hebrew as a second language have found that students mainly consider it important for functional goals of communication with Hebrew speakers (Abu Rabia, 1996, 1998). Amara and Mar'i (1999) present four factors that affect the linguistic education of students in the Arabic sector in Israel: (1) diglossia, (2) the political-social environment, (3) teachers' qualifications and their status, and (4) the educational goals, syllabi, and books used in the education system.

In addition to Hebrew, native speakers of Arabic study English as a foreign language at school (from fourth grade on, as a rule). From the beginning of the British Mandate of the country until the establishment of Israel (1918–48), English was the official language of the country (with Arabic and Hebrew). During this period it affected Hebrew and Arabic vocabularies, and some of this borrowed lexicon remains, sometimes with semantic changes (e.g. /ddžinddži/ < ginger, 'red-headed,' /bantšar/ < puncture 'any mishap,' /gi:r/ < 'gear' of a car, /ba:y/ < 'Bye-bye,' /go:l/ 'goal, in football,' /stop/ 'stop!'). Since 1948, it is American English, rather, that has become widespread in Israel and has affected Hebrew and, via Hebrew, Arabic, because of its general status as a world language (see for example Fisherman, 1986).

The contacts between Hebrew and Arabic speakers have led to exchanged borrowing and code switching between them. The Arabic effect on Hebrew is found mostly in its colloquial register, and some of it is due to the Arabic dialects of Jews who came to the country from Middle Eastern and North African countries. Consider, for example, /mala:n/ 'full,' /ahlan/ 'Hi,' /ahbal/ 'foolish,' /walla/ 'by God,' /ahla/ 'the best, great,' /sahte:n/ 'to your health, bon appétit, welcome' /hummus/ 'chickpeas'). In addition, scholars working at the Hebrew Language Academy at the beginning of the twentieth century sometimes used Arab roots and words to coin parallel words in Hebrew. Thus, for example, cf. words such as /qalmar/ 'pencil case' < Arabic /qalam/

'pen'; /'aqlim/ 'climate' < Arabic /'iqli:m/ 'region'; /'adiv/ 'polite, civilized' < Arabic /'adi:b/ 'polite, scholar, civilized'; /avzam/ < Arabic /ibzi:m/ 'buckle'; /ta'arix/ 'date' < Arabic /ta'ri:x/ 'date, history.'

Naturally, Hebrew also affects the local CA, mainly in institutional, cultural, and modern technological vocabulary, but also in more covert borrowings or loan translations (calques) and grammatical elements that have even penetrated the "local" MSA. Some examples are /kupat xolim/ 'sick fund,' /mištara/ 'police,' /beseder/ 'all right,' /mits/ 'juice,' /'uga/ 'cake,' /tik/ 'bag,' /dubi/ 'teddy bear,' /misrad/ 'office,' /ma šlomxa/ 'how are you?' /belefon/ or /pelefon/ 'cell phone,' /šekel/ 'shekel,' the Israeli monetary unit. The large number of these borrowed elements has been the cause of a growing group of speakers, mostly young, beginning to reject the Hebrew borrowings, in an attempt to return to "pure Arabic."

The study of Arabic is also practiced in Hebrew-speaking schools, where it is obligatory for three years (in middle schools) and optional up to matriculation exams (another four years' study). Studies of Hebrew-speakers' attitudes towards learning Arabic have yielded diverging results, due to research methods and educational and extra-linguistic factors (e.g. Ben-Rafael, 2001; Shohamy and Donitsa-Schmidt, 1998). Generally, however, most native speakers of Hebrew do not know Arabic (either CA or MSA) well enough to consider it among their foreign languages.

31.9   Conclusion

In this chapter we have surveyed bilingualism in the Middle East and North Africa. Because the main language of the area is Arabic, and because of its unique diglossic situation, we focused our discussion on this language, its history, its main characteristics and its present status. We have seen that Arabic in this area has three kinds of roles: it can be the official, dominant language of a country; it can be a second official language of a state, where another language is dominant; and it can be one of several languages competing in status in a certain country. These situations have developed due to interacting historical, political, religious, and social factors. Perhaps most characteristic of Arabic-speaking communities is the fact that Arabic is split into colloquial varieties and a relatively uniform literary standard variety in a state of diglossia. Indeed, it has been suggested here that this diglossia can be considered the basic form of bilingualism in this region. However, while every literate native speaker of Arabic experiences diglossia, it has not been considered as bilingualism by native speakers of Arabic. In addition, there are countries in this region where the colloquial varieties are prevalent, MSA is the official language, and yet the prestige language is different (e.g. French in Morocco). Thus, it can be concluded that bilingualism is very much the essence of this region.

In this chapter we focused on the Middle East and North Africa; we have not gone into much detail about fringe countries where Arabic dialects exist, namely, in the sub-Saharan area in Africa and in Central Asian states in the eastern part of this region. These areas are very interesting for further study of bilingualism and multilingualism. As in many other areas where bilingualism is studied, we find in this region inter-language contacts that lead to phenomena such as borrowing, code switching, and language change. The rate and kind of these phenomena depend on the linguistic and social environment of each language. While the traditional aspects of Arabic linguistics have been descriptions of newly discovered dialects and linguistic features, the young study of Arabic bilingualism in the Middle East and North Africa is now becoming an integral part of the sociolinguistic study of this language and this area.

ACKNOWLEDGMENTS

Professor Loraine K. Obler is gratefully thanked for her help with and support of this chapter and for her illuminating comments. We also thank Dr. D. Tsimhoni who has helped with some political and historical references and discussion of the subject, and Professor A. Borg for some references and a discussion of Maltese bilingualism.

Appendix: Some Data on the Main Religions and Population Groups in the Middle East and North Africa

Religions	Countries	Numbers	Notes
Islam: Sunnis, Shi'ites	Bahrain, Egypt, Iran, Iraq, Israel, Jordan, Kuwait, Lebanon, Oman, Qatar, Saudi Arabia, Syria, Turkey, United Arab Emirates, Yemen, Libya, Tunisia, Algeria, Morocco	Population (in millions): Algeria – 32.5; Egypt – 68; Iran 65.6; Iraq – 22.7; Israel – 5.8; Jordan – 5; Lebanon – 3.6; Kuwait – 2; Libya – 5.1; Morocco – 27; Saudi Arabia – 22; Sudan – 29; Syria –16.3; Tunisia – 10; Turkey – 65; Yemen – 17.5	**Sunni majority** in: Bahrain, Egypt, Jordan, Kuwait, Lebanon, Syria, Turkey, UAE., Yemen **Shi'ite majority** in: Iran, Iraq, South Lebanon
Sects derived from **Islam:** Alawite (Nusayris) Druze Ibadi Isma'ilite Kharijis Yezidis	**Alawite:** Syria, Lebanon **Druze:** Syria, Lebanon, Israel **Ibadis** – in Oman **Isma'ilite** Lebanon, Syria, Iraq, Yemen **Kharijis** – in Algeria, Libya, Oman **Yezidis** – in Iraq, Syria, Turkey, Yemen	**Alawite** in: Syria: ~1.5 million **Druze** in: Israel: 80,000; Lebanon: 230,000; Syria: 500,000 **Ibadis:** majority in Oman **Isma'ilites:** in Lebanon, Syria, Iraq, Yemen **Kharijis:** Dominant in Oman. **Yezidis:** <1% in each of these countries	**Alawite** in Syria: ~12% of the population **Druze** in: Israel: 1.5% of the population; Lebanon: 7% of the population **Ibadis:** 58% in Oman **Isma'ilites:** in Yemen: 316,000 **Kharijis:** in Algeria: ~1%; in Libya: ~1.5%; in Oman: ~70%

Religions	Countries	Numbers	Notes
Ethnic **Muslim** groups: Azeris; Baluchis; Berbers; Circassian Kurds; Turkomen; Assyrians	**Azeris** in: Iran; **Baluchis** in: Iran; **Berbers** in Morocco, Algeria, Tunisia, Libya, Egypt; **Circassians** in Israel, Jordan; **Kurds** in Turkey, Iraq, Iran, Syria; **Turkoman**: in Iran; Assyrians: in Iraq	**Azeris:** 15 million; **Baluchis** ~1.3 million; **Berbers** in: Morocco: 80% of population; Algeria: 80%; Tunisia: >60%; Libya: >60%; Egypt: 2%; **Circassians** in Israel: 3,000; in Jordan: fewer; **Kurds:** in Iran: 4.6 million (~10%); in Iraq: 4 million (~23%); in Syria: 1.6 million (~10%); in Turkey ~20%; **Turkoman:** mainly Muslims; (also ~30,000 Christians); in Iran: ~1.5%, in Iraq: 2.5 million (~2%)	2% of population Altogether there are ca. 50 million Berbers in the world
Christianity: Roman Catholic Greek Orthodox (and others)	In Egypt: **Copts** mainly; In Israel: many groups of **Christian** Arabs; In Lebanon: many groups of **Christian** Arabs: small communities; Iraq: Assyrians, Catholics, Armenians, Chaldean, Mandean, Nestorians	Egypt: **Copts:** 6.2 million (~6%); Iran: roughly 200,000, Christian Orthodox (<1%); Iraq: ~3% of the population **Christians** in Israel: 2.5% of the population Jordan: 6% of the population Lebanon: 1.4 million. (30% of the population) Syria: Catholic 300,000 (~10%)	
Ethnic **Christian** groups: Armenians, Turkoman	**Armenians** in: Algeria, Israel, Jordan, Lebanon, Iraq, Egypt, Iran, Libya, Morocco, Saudi Arabia **Turkoman:** Mainly Muslims; also ~30,000 Christians	**Armenians:** Israel, Jordan: small no.; Algeria: 10,000; Egypt: 40,000; Iran: 310,000; Iraq: 50,000; Lebanon: 30,000; Libya: 3,000 Morocco: 7,000; Saudi Arabia: 5,000; Turkey: 300,000;	
Judaism	In Israel: small communities in Iran, Iraq, Syria, Lebanon, Egypt, Morocco, Tunisia Algeria	In Israel: 80% of population	
Baha'i	Iran, Israel	Iran: >300,000 Israel: 650 + ~3,000 pilgrims	Israel is the Baha'i world center, but only its volunteer workers reside there
Zoroastrianism	Iran	<600,000 (<1% of the population)	

Based on Internet sites updated to the period after 1998 including:
http://i-cias.com/e.o/algeria_4.htm (the Encyclopaedia of Orient, and other sections)
http://wgbh/globalconnections/mideast/maps/demotext.html
http://www.library.cornell.edu/coodev/mideast

REFERENCES

Abu Haidar, F. (1988). Male/female linguistic variation in a Baghdadi community. In A. K. Irvine, R. B. Serjeant, and G. Rex Smith (eds.), *A Miscellany of Middle Eastern Articles: In Memoriam Thomas Muir Johnstone 1924–1983*. Harlow, UK: Longman.

Abu Rabia, S. (1996). Druze minority students learning Hebrew in Israel: The relationship of attitudes, cultural background and interest of material to reading comprehension in a second language. *Journal of Multilingual and Multicultural Development*, 17(6), 415–26.

Abu Rabia, S. (1998). The learning of Hebrew by Israeli Arab students in Israel. *Journal of Social Psychology*, 138(3), 331–41.

Al-Falay, I. S. (1996). *Diglossia: Theory and Application*. Riad. (In Arabic.)

Al-Khateeb, M. A. A. (1988). Sociolinguistic change in an expanding urban context: A case study of Irbid City, Jordan. Dissertation, University of Durham, UK.

Al-Toma, S. (1969). *The Problem of Diglossia in Arabic: A Comparative Study of Classical and Iraqi Arabic*. Cambridge, MA: Harvard University Press.

Amara, M. (1995). Hebrew and English lexical reflections of socio-political changes in Palestinian Arabic. *Journal of Multilingual and Multicultural Development*, 15(6), 165–72.

Amara, M. and Mar'i, A. R. (1999). *Issues in Language Education Policy in Arab Schools in Israel*. Surveys on the Arabs in Israel, no. 25. Givat Haviva: The Institute for Peace Research.

Amara, M. and Spolsky, B. (1986). The diffusion and integration of Hebrew and English lexical items in the spoken Arabic of an Israeli village. *Anthropological Linguistics*, 28(1), 43–54.

Amara, M. and Spolsky, B. (2001). The construction of identity in a divided Palestinian village: Sociolinguistic evidence. In: H. Herzog, E. Ben-Rafael and E. Kraus (eds.), *Language and Communication in Israel*, pp. 273–288. Ramat Gan: Israel Sociological Society.

Amit-Kokhavi, H. (1999). Translations of Arabic literature into Hebrew: Their historical and cultural background and their reception by the target culture. Ph.D. dissertation, Tel-Aviv University (in Hebrew).

Arebi, S. (1994). *Women and Words in Saudi-Arabia: The Politics of Literary Discourse*. New York: Columbia University Press.

Badawi, M. (1973). *Levels of Contemporary Arabic in Egypt*. Cairo: Da:r al-Ma'a:rif. (In Arabic.)

Barkat, M. (2000). Determination of reliable acoustic cues for the automatic identification of Arabic dialects. Ph.D. thesis, University of Lyon 2 (in French).

Behnstedt, P. and Woidich, M. (1987). *Die ägyptisch-arabischen Dialekte*, 3 vols. Wiesbaden, Germany: Dr. Ludwig Reichert.

Belnap, R. K. and Bishop, B. (2000). Blurring lines: The spread of 'A:mmiyya into former domains of Fusha:. In A. Youssi, F. Benjelloun, M. Dahbi, and Z. Iraqi-Sinaceur (eds.), *Aspects of the Dialects of Arabic Today: Proceedings of the Fourth Conference of AIDA*, pp. 247–56. Rabat: AMAPATRIL.

Ben-Rafael, E. (2001). A sociological paradigm of bilingualism: English, French, Yiddish and Arabic in Israel. In H. Herzog, E. Ben-Rafael, and E. Kraus (eds.), *Language and Communication in Israel*, pp. 175–205. Ramat Gan: Israel Sociological Society.

Bentahila, A. and Davies, E. E. (1983). The syntax of Arabic-French code switching. *Lingua*, 59, 301–40.

Berjaoui, N. (1993). On the use of a secret language in Morocco. *MAS-GELLAS*, Nouvelle Serie, 5.

Blanc, H. (1960). Style variations in spoken Arabic: A sample of interdialectal educated conversation. In C. A. Ferguson (ed.), *Contribution to Arabic Linguistics*, pp. 81–161. Cambridge, MA: Harvard University Press.

Blanc, H. (1964). *Communal Dialects of Baghdad*. Cambridge, MA: Harvard University Press.

Blanc, H. (1975). Arabic. In T. Sebeok (ed.), *Current Trends in Linguistics*, volume 7, pp. 501–10. The Hague: Mouton.

Blau, J. (1977). The beginnings of the Arabic diglossia: A study of the origins of Neo-Arabic. *Afro-Asiatic Linguistics*, 4: 175–202.

Blau, J. (1981). *The Renaissance of Modern Hebrew and Modern Standard Arabic*. Los Angeles: University of California Press.

Bos, P. (1997). *Development of Bilingualism: A Study of School Age Moroccan Children in the Netherlands*. Tilburg, The Netherlands: Tilburg University Press.

Boumans, L. (1998). *The Syntax of Codeswitching: Analyzing Moroccan Arabic/Dutch Conversations*. Tilburg, The Netherlands: Tilburg University Press.

Brockelmann, G. (1908, 1913). *Grundriss der vergleichenden Grammatik der semitischen Sprachen*, 2 vols. Hildesheim, Germany: Georg Olms.

Cadora, F. (1992). *Bedouin, Rural and Urban Arabic: An Ecolinguistic Study*. Leiden, The Netherlands: Brill.

Caubet, D. (1993). *L'Arabe marocain. Volume 1: Phonologie et morphosyntaxe. Volume 2: Syntaxe et Categories Grammaticales, Texts*. Paris and Louvain: Peeters.

Caubet, D. (1998). Alternance des codes au Maghreb: Pourquoi le français est-il arabisé? In *Plurilinguismes no. 14, Alternance des Langues et Apprentissage en Contextes Plurilingues*, pp. 121–42. Paris: CERPL, Université René Descartes.

Chami, M. (1987). *L'Enseignement en français au Maroc*. Casablanca: Najah.

Chetrit, J. (1980). Niveaux, registres de langue et sociolectes dans les langues judéo-arabes du Maroc. In *Les Relations entre Juifs et Musulmans en Afrique du Nord, XIXe–XX Siècles. Actes du Colloque International de l'Institut d'Histoire des pays d'Outre mer, Abbaye de Senanque, Octobre 1978*, pp. 129–42. Paris: Editions du Centre National de la Recherche Scientifique.

Chetrit, J. (1994). Formes et structures du Mixage Linguistique dans les langues secrètes juives du Maroc. In D. Caubet and M. Vanhove (eds.), *Actes des Premières Journées Internationales de Dialectologie Arabe de Paris*, pp. 519–30. Paris: INALCO.

Chikovani, G. (2000). The verb in the Arabic dialects of Central Asia. In A. Youssi, F. Benjelloun, M. Dahbi, and Z. Iraqi-Sinaceur (eds.), *Aspects of the Dialects of Arabic Today: Proceedings of the Fourth Conference of AIDA*, pp. 179–88. Rabat: AMAPATRIL.

Comrie, B., Matthews, S., and Polinsky, M. (1996). *The Atlas of Languages: The Origin and Development of Language Throughout the World*. New York: Facts on File.

Diem, W. (1974). *Hochsprache und Dialekt im Arabischen*. Wiesbaden, Germany: Kommissionsverlag Franz Steiner.

Edwards, J. (1994). *Multilingualism*. London and New York: Routledge.

Ellul, S. (1978). *A Case Study in Bilingualism: Code-Switching between Parents and their Pre-School Children in Malta*. Cambridge, UK: Huntingdon Publishers.

El-Tibi, Z. R. (ed.) (2002). *La Francophonie et le Dialogue des Cultures*. Beirut: L'Age d'Homme – Dar Al Moualef.

Esposito, J. (1998). *Islam: The Straight Path*. Oxford: Oxford University Press.

Fasold, R. (1984). *The Sociolinguistics of Society*. Oxford: Basil Blackwell.

Ferguson, C. A. (1959a). Diglossia. *Word*, 15, 325–40.

Ferguson, C. A. (1959b). The Arabic Koinè. *Language*, 35, 616–30.

Ferguson, C. A. (1989). Grammatical agreement in Classical Arabic and the modern dialects: A response to Versteegh's pidginization hypothesis. Reprinted in R. K. Belnap and N. Haeri (eds.), *Structuralist Studies in Arabic Linguistics: Charles A. Ferguson's Papers, 1954–1994*, pp. 81–91. Leiden, The Netherlands: Brill.

Ferguson, C. A. (1991). Epilogue: Diglossia revisited. *Southwestern Journal of Linguistics*, 10(1), 214–34.

Fischer, W. (1961). Die Sprache der arabischen Sprachinsel in Uzbekistan. *Der Islam*, 36, 232–63.

Fischer, W. and Jastrow, O. (eds.) (1980). *Handbuch der arabischen Dialekte*. Wiesbaden, Germany: Harrassowitz.

Fisherman, H. (1986). Foreign words in contemporary Hebrew. Ph.D. dissertation, The Hebrew University, Jerusalem (in Hebrew).

Fishman, J. (1967). Bilingualism with and without diglossia; diglossia with and without bilingualism. *Journal of Social Issues*, 23(1), 29–38.

Fishman, J. (ed.) (2002). Diglossia and societal multilingualism. *International Journal of the Sociology of Language*, 157, special issue: *Focus on Diglossia*.

Frayha, A. (1955). *Towards Facilitated Arabic*. Beirut: The American University of Beirut (in Arabic).

Fück, J. (1950). *'Arabiyya*. Berlin: Abhandlungen der sächsischen Akademie der Wissenschaften zu Leipzig, Phil.-Hist. Klasse, 45/1.

Haeri, N. (1996). *The Sociolinguistic Market of Cairo: Gender, Class and*

Education. London and New York: Kegan Paul.

Heath, J. (1987). *Ablaut and Ambiguity: Phonology of a Moroccan Arabic Dialect*. Albany: State University of New York Press.

Heath, J. (1989). *From Code Switching to Borrowing: A Case Study of Moroccan Arabic*. London: Kegan Paul International.

Heath, J. (2002). *Jewish and Muslim Dialects of Moroccan Arabic*. London: Routledge Curzon.

Holes, C. (1995). *Modern Arabic: Structures, Functions and Varieties*. London, New York.

Holes, C. (2000). *Dialect, Culture and Society in Eastern Arabia*. Leiden, The Netherlands: Brill.

Holt, P. M., Lambton, A. K. S., and Lewis, B. (1970). *The Cambridge History of Islam*. Cambridge, UK: Cambridge University Press.

Hudson, A. (1999). Diglossia. In B. Spolsky and R. E. Asher (eds.), *Concise Encyclopedia of Educational Linguistics*, pp. 37–42. Oxford: Elsevier Science.

Hussein, M. (1987). *Atlas of the History of Islam*. Cairo.

Ibn Khaldoun, A. R. (1958). *The Muqaddimah: Prolegomena to History* (trans. by F. Rosenthal). London: Routledge.

Kaye, A. S. (1994). Formal vs. informal in Arabic: Diglossia, triglossia, tetraglossia etc., polyglossia-multiglossia viewed as a continuum. *Zeitschrift für Arabische Linguistik*, 27, 47–66.

Kaye, A. S. and Rosenhouse, J. (1997). Arabic dialects and Maltese. In R. Hetzron (ed.), *The Semitic Languages*, pp. 263–311. London: Routledge.

Koplewitz, I. (1973). Education in the Arab sector: facts and problems. In Ormian A. (ed.), *Education in Israel*, pp. 323–34. Jerusalem: Ministry of Education and Culture.

Koplewitz, I. (1989). The use and integration of Hebrew lexemes in

Israeli spoken Arabic. *Multilingual Matters*, 71: 181–95.

Koplewitz, I. (1992). Arabic in Israel: The sociolinguistic situation of Israel's Arab minority. *International Journal of the Sociology of Language*, 98, 29–66.

Lamrani, F. Z. (2000). Triglossia in the Moroccan criminal courtroom. In A. Youssi, F. Benjelloun, M. Dahbi, and Z. Iraqi-Sinaceur (eds.), *Aspects of the Dialects of Arabic Today: Proceedings of the Fourth Conference of AIDA*, pp. 299–306. Rabat: AMAPATRIL.

Lamrani, F. Z. (2002). Arabic diglossia and court reporting in the Moroccan criminal courtroom. Paper presented at AIDA5, Spain.

Lewis, B. (1960). *The Arabs in History*. New York: Harper and Row.

Lewis, B. (1973). *Islam in History*. London: Alcove Press.

Madkur, I. (1967). The Academy at the service of the Arabic language. *Majallat Majma' Al-Lugha Al-'Arabiyya Bi-l-Qa:hira (Journal of the Language Academy in Cairo)*, 22: 15–24. (In Arabic.)

Marçais, W. (1930). La Diglossie arabe. *L'Enseignement Public*, 97, 401–9; reprinted in *Articles et conférences* (1961) pp. 83–8, Paris: Maisonneuve.

Meiseles, G. (1979). Informal written Arabic. *Israel Oriental Studies*, IX, 272–314.

Mejdell, G. (2000). Features of lugha wusta: Mixed discourse in spoken Arabic in Egypt. In A. Youssi, F. Benjelloun, M. Dahbi, and Z. Iraqi-Sinaceur (eds.), *Aspects of the Dialects of Arabic Today: Proceedings of the Fourth Conference of AIDA*, pp. 317–28. Rabat: AMAPATRIL.

Mitchell, T. F. (1962). *Colloquial Arabic: The Living Language of Egypt*. Teach Yourself Books. London: The English Universities Press.

Mitchell, T. F. (1986). What is educated Arabic? *International Journal of the Sociology of Language*, 61, 7–32.

Morris, R. (1993). Images of the interpreter: A Study of language-switching in the legal process. Unpublished Ph.D. thesis, Department of Law, Lancaster University.

Owens, J. (1993). *A Grammar of Nigerian Arabic*. Wiesbaden, Germany: Harrassowitz.

Palva, H. (1992). *Artistic Colloquial Arabic*. Helsinki: Studia Orientalia, The Finnish Oriental Society, 69.

Piamenta, M. (2000). *Jewish Life in Arabic Language and Jerusalem Arabic in Communal Perspective: A Lexico-Semantic Study*. Leiden, The Netherlands: Brill.

Rosenbaum, G. (2000). Fu Shāmmiyya: Alternating style in Egyptian prose. In M. Mifsud (ed.), *Zeitschrift für arabische Linguistik*, 38, 68–87.

Rosenbaum, G. (2000–2002). "Do you parler 'Arabi?" Mixing colloquial Arabic and European languages in Egyptian literature. *Matériaux Arabes et Sudarabiques*, Nouvelle Série 10, 11–47.

Rosenhouse, J. (1984). *The Bedouin Arabic Dialects. General Problems and a Close Analysis of North Israel Bedouin Dialects*. Wiesbaden, Germany: Otto Harrassowitz.

Rosenhouse, J. (1989). Translation from English into Arabic: Implications for text linguistics. *International Review of Applied Linguistics*, 27(2), 125–36.

Rosenhouse, J. (1998). Women's speech and language variation in Arabic dialects, *Al-'Arabiyya*, 31, 123–52.

Rosenhouse, J. (2001). Colloquial and literary Arabic in Israel: An analysis of a child's texts in colloquial Arabic. In J. Rosenhouse and A. Elad-Bouskila (eds.), *Linguistic and Cultural Studies on Arabic and Hebrew: Essays presented to Moshe Piamenta for his Eightieth Birthday*, pp. 107–34. Wiesbaden, Germany: Harrassowitz.

Rosenhouse, J. and Shehade, K. (1986). Notes on diglossia problems in Arabic: the educational aspects. In I. Idalovichi and N. Ararat (eds.), *Philosophy, Language Arts: Essays in Honor of Alexander Barzel*, pp. 251–72. Haifa: Technion–I.T.T.

Rosenhouse, J., Kishon-Rabin, L., and Shabtay, E. (in preparation). Bilingual speech perception in adverse conditions in Israeli native speakers of Arabic.

Roth-Lally, A. (1969). *Lexique des Parlers Arabes Tchado-Soudanais*. Paris: Edition du Centre National de la Recherche Scientifique.

Sadiqi, F. (1995). The language of women in the city of Fès, Morocco. *International Journal of the Sociology of Language*, 112, 63–79.

Shehadeh, H. (1997). The Hebrew of the Arabs in Israel (in the light of two matriculation examinations, 1970, 1972). In M. Sabour and K. S. Vikør (eds.), *Nordic Research on the Middle East 3: Ethnic Encounter and Culture Change. Papers from the Third Nordic Conference on Middle Eastern Studies, Joensuu, 1995*, pp. 49–71. Bergen: Nordic Society of Middle Eastern Studies.

Shohamy, E. and Donitsa-Schmidt, S. (1998). *Jews vs. Arabs: Language Attitudes and Stereotypes*. Tel-Aviv: The Tami Steinmetz Center for Peace Research.

Shrayboym-Shivtiel, S. (1993). The Arabic Academy of Language in Egypt: Activity and Trends, 1932–1982. Ph.D. Dissertation, Tel-Aviv University.

Snir, R. (2001). Postcards in the morning: Palestinians writing in Hebrew. *Hebrew Studies* (A Journal Devoted to Hebrew language and Literature), 42, 197–224.

Spolsky, B. (1986). *Language and Education in Multilingual Settings*. Clevedon, UK: Multilingual Matters.

Spolsky, B. and Shohamy E. (1999). *The Languages of Israel*. Clevedon, UK: Multilingual Matters.

Suleiman, S. M. (1985). Jordanian Arabic between diglossia and bilingualism: Linguistic analysis. *Pragmatics and Beyond*, 6(8), 1–131.

Suleiman, Y. (1999). Language education policy: Arabic speaking countries. In B. Spolsky and R. E. Asher (eds.), *Concise Encyclopedia of Educational Linguistics*, pp. 106–115. Oxford: Elsevier Science.

Talmoudi, F. (1984). The diglossic situation in North Africa: A study of classical Arabic/dialectal Arabic diglossia with sample text in mixed Arabic. *Acta Orientalia Gothoburgensia*, 8.

Tapper, R. (1992). *Some Minorities in the Middle East*. Occasional Paper 9, London: Centre of Near and Middle Eastern Studies, SOAS, University of London.

Tsereteli, G. V. (1941). K xarakteristike jazyka sredneaziatskix arabov. Trudy vtoroy sessii Assotsiatsii Arabistov, 1937, Moscow–Leningrad.

Vanhauve, C. (2002). Contact de langues et l'alternance bedja-arabe dans l'est du Soudan. Paper presented at AIDA 5, Spain.

Versteegh, K. (1984). *Pidginization and Creolization: The Case of Arabic*. Amsterdam: John Benjamins.

Vinnikov, I. N. (1962). *Slovar' dialecta Buxarskix arabov*, Palestinskij sbornik, 10(73), Moscow-Leningrad.

Woidich, M. (1997). Egyptian Arabic and dialect contact in historical perspective. In A. Afsaruddin and A. H. M. Zahniser (eds.), *Humanism, Culture and Language in the Near East: Studies in Honor of Georg Krotkoff*, pp. 185–97. Winona Lake, IN: Eisenbrauns.

Youssi, A. (2001). Types of multilingualism and multi-dialectalism across the Arabic speaking communities. *Estudios de Dialectologia Norteafricana y Andalusi*, 5, 7–28.

FURTHER READING

Abu-Bakr, R. (in preparation). The influence of one's mother tongue upon examinees taking the matriculation Hebrew examination designed for Arab students, Ph.D. dissertation, Bar-Ilan University, Ramat Gan.

Al-Hajj, M. (1996). *Education among the Arabs in Israel: Control and Social Change*. Jerusalem: Magnes Press, Hebrew University of Jerusalem. (In Hebrew.)

Al-Khatib, M. (2001). Audience design revisited in a diglossic speech community: A case study of three TV programs addressed to three different audiences. *Multilingua*, 20, 393–414.

Ben-Rafael, E. and Brosh, H. (1991). A sociological study of second language diffusion: The obstacles to Arabic teaching in the Israeli school. *Language Problems and Language Planning*, 15(1), 1–23.

Bergman, M. (ed.) (1980). *Aging and the Perception of Speech*. Baltimore, MD: University Park Press.

Blau, J. (1965). *The Emergence and Linguistic Background of Judeo-Arabic: A Study of the Origins of Middle Arabic*. Oxford: Oxford University Press.

Cantineau, J. (1936). Etudes sur quelques parlers de nomades arabes d'Orient. *AIEO*, 2, 1–118.

Cantineau, J. (1937). Etudes sur quelques parlers de nomades arabes d'Orient. *AIEO*, 3, 119–237.

Canut, R. and Caubet, D. (eds.) (2002). *Comment les langues se mélangent*. Paris: L'Harmattan.

Caubet, D. (1996). Ga:les kayexdem, xa:yed kayexdem: Approche sociolinguistique de l'expression de la concomitance en arabe marocain. *Estudios de Dialectologia Norteafricana y Andalusi*, 1, 87–100.

Colon, M. (2002). Line drawing, code switching, and Spanish as second-hand smoke: English-only workplace rules and bilingual employees. *Yale Law and Policy Review*, 20, 227–60.

Eid, M. (1988). Principles for code switching between standard and Egyptian Arabic. *Al-'Arabiyya*, 21, 51–79.

El-Khafaifi, H. (1985). The role of the Cairo Academy in coining Arabic scientific terminology: An historical and linguistic evaluation. Ph.D. dissertation, University of Utah.

Freeman, A. (2000). A working model for diglossia: How can we accommodate the Arab perception that Arabic is a single linguistic system? In A. Youssi, F. Benjelloun, M. Dahbi, and Z. Iraqi-Sinaceur (eds.), *Aspects of the Dialects of Arabic Today: Proceedings of the Fourth Conference of AIDA*, pp. 276–87. Rabat: AMAPATRIL.

Gardner, R. C. and Lambert, W. E. (1972). *Attitudes and Motivation in Second Language Learning*. Rowley, MA: Newbury House.

Guilleminot, C. (2002). L'école publique au Maroc: Un lieu de consolidation ou d'altération de la conscience phonologique? Paper presented at AIDA 5.

Habib-Alla, M. (1991). Arabic education in Israel toward the turn of the millennium. In M. Habiballa and A. Qufti (eds.), *Education and the Arabic Minority in Israel: State of the Art, Problems and Requirements*, pp. 30–5. Haifa: Al-Karma (in Arabic).

Hary, B. (1989). Middle Arabic: Proposals for new terminology. *Al-'Arabiyya*, 22, 19–36.

Henkin, R. (1996). Negev Bedouin vs. sedentary Palestinian narrative styles. *Israel Oriental Studies*, 16, 169–91.

Henkin, R. (1998). Narrative style of Palestinian Bedouin adults and children. *Pragmatics*, 8(1), 47–78.

Holes, C. (1987). *Language Variation and Changing a Modernizing Arab State*. London: Kegan Paul International.

Hudson, A. (2002). Outline of a theory of diglossia. *International Journal of the Sociology of Language*, 157, special issue: *Focus on Diglossia*.

Jabeur, M. (1987). A sociolinguistic study in Tunisia: Rades. Ph.D. dissertation, University of Reading, UK.

Johnstone, T. M. (1967). *Eastern Arabian Dialect Studies*, London: Oxford University Press.

Kinberg, N. and Talmon, R. (1994). Learning of Arabic by Jews and the use of Hebrew among Arabs in Israel. *Indian Journal of Applied Linguistics*, 20(1–2), 37–54.

Kraemer, R. (1990). Social psychological factors related to the study of Arabic among Israeli high school students: A test of Gardner's socio-educational model. *Studies in Second Language Acquisition*, 15(1), 83–106.

Krumbacher, K. (1902). *Das Problem der modernen griechischen Schriftsprachen*. Munich: K. B. Akademie in Kommission des G. Franz'schen Verlags (J. Roth).

Lahlou, M. (1991). A morpho-syntactic study of code switching between Moroccan Arabic and French. Ph.D. dissertation, University of Texas, Austin.

Langone, A. (2002). A study of the Lebanese dialects viewed from the play "Smile, you are Lebanese," by Yahya Jaber. Paper presented at AIDA 5, Spain (in French).

Lenneberg, E. H. (1967). Language in the context of growth and maturation. In E. H. Lenneberg, *Biological Foundations of Language*, pp. 169–81. New York: John Wiley and Sons.

Lévy, S. (1990). Parlers arabes des Juifs du Maroc: Particularités et emprunts – Histoire, Sociolinguistique et géographie dialectale. Ph.D. thesis, Rabat, Université Mohamed V.

Lewis, B. (1964). *The Middle East and the West*. Bloomington: Indiana University Press.

Lewis, B. (1984). *The Jews of Islam*. Princeton, NJ: Princeton University Press.

Maas, U. (2000). L'union linguistique maghreine. In A. Youssi, F. Benjelloun, M. Dahbi, and Z. Iraqui-Sinaceur (eds.), *Aspects of the Dialects of Arabic Today: Proceedings of the Fourth Conference of the AIDA in Honor of Professor David Cohen, Marrakesh, Morocco, 2000*, pp. 211–22. Rabat: AMAPATRIL.

Magiste, E. (1992). Second language learning in elementary and high school students. *European Journal of Cognitive Psychology*, 4(4), 355–65.

Mahi, Z. (2000). Dialects within medical discourse. In: A. Youssi, F. Benjelloun, M. Dahbi, and Z. Iraqi-Sinaceur (eds.), *Aspects of the Dialects of Arabic Today, Proceedings of the Fourth Conference of AIDA*, pp. 307–16. Rabat: AMAPATRIL.

Mahi, Z. (2002). The problem of medical jargon in Moroccan Arabic medical interviews. Paper presented at AIDA 5, Spain.

Meiseles, G. (1975). Ha-'Arvit Ha-Safvutit she-be-Al-Pe: Telchunoteha Ha-'Iqqariyyot be-Dibbur u-vi-Qri'a [Oval Literary Arabic: Its main features in speech and reading]. In Hebrew. Ph.D. thesis, Hebrew University of Jerusalem.

Messaoudi, L. (2000). Le parler ancien de Rabat face à l'urbanisation linguistique. In A. Youssi, F. Benjelloun, M. Dahbi, and Z. Iraqi-Sinaceur (eds.), *Aspects of the Dialects of Arabic Today: Proceedings of the Fourth Conference of AIDA*, pp. 223–33. Rabat: AMAPATRIL.

Messaoudi, L. (2002). Parler citadin, parler urbain. Quelles différences? Paper presented at AIDA 5, Spain.

Nicholson, R. A. (1960). *A Literary History of the Arabs*. (J. J. Rivlin, Hebrew translation.) Jerusalem: Kiryat Sefer. (Original work published in 1930.)

Owens, J. (2000). *Arabic as a Minority Language*. Berlin: Mouton.

Owens, J. and Bani Raslan, Y. (1991). Spoken Arabic and language mixture. *Bulletin d'Etudes Orientales*, 43, 17–31 (Damascus).

Perani, D., Paulesu, E., Galles, N. S., Dupoux, E., Dehaene, S., Bettinardi, V., Cappa, S. F., Fazio, F., and Mehier, J. (1998). The bilingual brain, proficiency and age of acquisition of the second language. *Brain*, 121, 1841–52.

Quane, A. (1995). Vers une culture multilinguistique de l'éducation. Hamburg: Institut de l'Unesco pour l'Education.

Rosenthal, F. (1990). *Science and Medicine in Islam: A Collection of Essays*. Aldershot, UK: Variorum.

Segert, S. (1997). Phoenician and the Eastern Canaanite Languages. In R. Hetzron (ed.), *The Semitic Languages*. London: Routledge.

Simon, R. S., Matter, P., and Bulliet, R. W. (1996). *Encyclopedia of the Modern Middle East*, 4 vols. New York: Simon & Schuster Macmillan.

Spolsky, B. (1989). *Conditions for Second Language Learning*. London: Oxford University Press.

Spolsky, B. and Asher, R. (eds.) (1999). *Concise Encyclopedia of Educational Linguistics*. Kidlington, UK: Elsevier Science.

Stillman, N. (1991). *The Jews of Arab Lands in Modern Times*. Philadelphia and New York: Jewish Publication Society.

Versteegh, K. (1993). Leveling in the Sudan: From Arabic Creole to Arabic dialect. *International Journal of the Sociology of Language*, 99, 65–79.

Weinreich, U. (1953). *Languages in Contact: Problems and Findings*. New York: Linguistic Circle of New York.

Index